THE CAMBRIDGE HANDBOOK OF SURVEILLANCE LAW

Surveillance presents a conundrum: how to ensure safety, stability, and efficiency while respecting privacy and individual liberty. From police officers to corporations to intelligence agencies, surveillance law is tasked with striking this difficult and delicate balance. That challenge is compounded by ever-changing technologies and evolving social norms. Following the revelations of Edward Snowden and a host of private-sector controversies, there is intense interest among policy makers, business leaders, attorneys, academics, students, and the public regarding legal, technological, and policy issues relating to surveillance. This handbook documents and organizes these conversations, drawing together some of the most thoughtful and impactful contributors to contemporary surveillance debates, policies, and practices. Its pages explore surveillance techniques and technologies; their value for law enforcement, national security, and private enterprise; their impacts on citizens and communities; and the many ways societies do – and should – regulate surveillance.

David Gray teaches criminal law, criminal procedure, evidence, international criminal law, and jurisprudence at the University of Maryland's Francis King Carey School of Law. He was voted Professor of the Year in 2012. He has published dozens of articles in leading law reviews, is the author of *The Fourth Amendment in an Age of Surveillance* (Cambridge University Press, 2017), and has submitted amicus briefs in high-profile cases involving surveillance and the Fourth Amendment. Professor Gray is a sought-after speaker and frequently provides expert commentary for national media outlets on questions relating to criminal law and criminal procedure.

Stephen E. Henderson is the Judge Haskell A. Holloman Professor of Law at the University of Oklahoma, where he has received numerous teaching awards and a campus-wide award for Outstanding Research Impact. He served as Reporter for the American Bar Association Criminal Justice Standards on Law Enforcement Access to Third Party Records, and his personal writing has been argued and utilized in resolving contemporary American search and seizure controversies. Professor Henderson obtained a J.D. from Yale Law School and a B.S. in Electrical Engineering from the University of California at Davis (highest honors and College of Engineering Medal).

The Cambridge Handbook of Surveillance Law

Edited by
David Gray
University of Maryland

Stephen E. Henderson
University of Oklahoma

CAMBRIDGE
UNIVERSITY PRESS

CAMBRIDGE
UNIVERSITY PRESS

One Liberty Plaza, 20th Floor, New York, NY 10006, USA

Cambridge University Press is part of the University of Cambridge.

It furthers the University's mission by disseminating knowledge in the pursuit of education, learning, and research at the highest international levels of excellence.

www.cambridge.org
Information on this title: www.cambridge.org/9781107137943
DOI: 10.1017/9781316481127

First published 2017

Printed in the United Kingdom by Clays, St Ives plc

A catalog record for this publication is available from the British Library.

Library of Congress Cataloging-in-Publication Data
Names: Gray, David, editor. | Henderson, Stephen E., editor.
Title: The Cambridge handbook of surveillance law / edited by
David Gray, University of Maryland; Stephen E. Henderson, University of Oklahoma.
Description: New York: Cambridge University Press, 2017. |
Includes bibliographical references and index.
Identifiers: LCCN 2017009648 | ISBN 9781107137943 (hardback)
Subjects: LCSH: Electronic surveillance – Law and legislation – United States. |
Intelligence service – Law and legislation – United States. | Terrorism – Prevention –
Law and legislation – United States. | National security – Law and legislation –
United States. | Computer security – Law and legislation – United States. |
Computer networks – Security measures – United States. | Cyberterrorism –
Prevention – United States. | United States. Privacy and Civil Liberties
Oversight Board. | Privacy, Right of – Government policy – United States.
Classification: LCC KF5399.C36 2017 | DDC 345.73/052–dc23
LC record available at https://lccn.loc.gov/2017009648

ISBN 978-1-107-13794-3 Hardback

For two people I miss and mourn: F. P. Gray, whose fortitude, intellectual curiosity, and unbending independence continue to inspire, and Dan Markel, a true mensch of enormous heart and unflinchingly critical mind.

– DG

For my greatest contribution,
the five I'll leave behind.

– SEH

Contents

Notes on the Contributors

Marc J. Blitz is Alan Joseph Bennett Professor of Law at the Oklahoma City University School of Law. He is a widely published expert on the relationship between surveillance and constitutional protections of thought, expression, and privacy.

Dru Brenner-Beck is Lieutenant Colonel (Retired) of the U.S. Army Judge Advocate General's Corps. Currently, she is a legal consultant on international law matters, is Of Counsel at EosEdge Legal, a Cyber Law Firm, and serves as the President of the National Institute of Military Justice.

Cristina Blasi Casagran is Postdoctoral Researcher at Autonomous University of Barcelona.

Danielle Keats Citron is the Morton and Sophia Macht Professor and Professor of Law at the University of Maryland Francis King Carey School of Law and author of *Hate Crimes in Cyberspace* (2014).

Julie E. Cohen is Mark Claster Mamolen Professor of Law and Technology and a Faculty Director of the Center on Privacy and Technology at Georgetown University Law Center. She is an internationally-recognized expert on privacy and author of *Configuring the Networked Self* (2012).

Geoffrey S. Corn is Professor of Law at South Texas College of Law, and is Lieutenant Colonel (Retired) of the U.S. Army Judge Advocate General's Corps.

Jennifer Daskal is Associate Professor of Law at the American University Washington College of Law. Before entering academia, Professor Daskal was counsel to the Assistant Attorney General for National Security at the Department of Justice and a senior counterterrorism counsel at Human Rights Watch.

Paul De Hert is Full Professor of Law at Vrije Universiteit Brussel, Brussels, where he is currently the chair of "Criminal Law," and "International and European Criminal Law." He is an internationally recognized expert in privacy and technology, human rights, and criminal law.

Lindsay DeFrancesco is an Associate at Reed Smith LLP.

Lothar Determann teaches at Freie Universität Berlin; University of California, Berkeley School of Law; and Hastings College of the Law in San Francisco. He practices technology law as a partner with Baker & McKenzie LLP.

Mihailis E. Diamantis is an Associate Professor at the University of Iowa, College of Law, where he writes about corporate crime and philosophy. He clerked for Judge Alex Kozinski on the Ninth Circuit Court of Appeals and worked on white-collar investigations as an attorney at Debevoise & Plimpton LLP.

Timothy Edgar is Senior Fellow in International and Public Affairs at Watson Institute for International and Public Affairs, Brown University. He served under President Obama from 2009 to 2010 as the first director of privacy and civil liberties for the White House National Security Staff.

Andrew Guthrie Ferguson is Professor of Law at the University of the District of Columbia David A. Clarke School of Law. He is a widely published expert on policing and the Fourth Amendment, including *The Rise of Big Data Policing: Surveillance, Race, and the Future of Law Enforcement* (2017).

Susan Freiwald is Associate Dean and Professor at the University of San Francisco School of Law. She has authored and co-authored amicus briefs in major cases involving electronic surveillance laws and was a major contributor to CalECPA, California's path-breaking privacy law.

Steven I. Friedland is Associate Dean for Innovations in Engaged Learning in Law and Professor of Law and Senior Scholar at the Elon University School of Law, Greensboro, North Carolina. He has served as an Assistant United States Attorney and is an internationally recognized expert on legal education.

Elizabeth Goitein is Co-director of the Liberty and National Security Program at the Brennan Center for Justice at NYU School of Law. Before coming to the Brennan Center, Ms. Goitein served as counsel to US Senator Russell Feingold, as a trial attorney in the Federal Programs Branch of the Civil Division of the Department of Justice, and as a law clerk for the Honorable Michael Daly Hawkins on the U.S. Court of Appeals for the Ninth Circuit.

Mark A. Graber is Regents Professor at the University of Maryland Carey School of Law. An internationally recognized expert on constitutional history, he is author of *A New Introduction to American Constitutionalism* (2013) and *Dred Scott and the Problem of Constitutional Evil* (Cambridge University Press, 2006).

Chris Jay Hoofnagle is Adjunct Full Professor at the University of California, Berkeley School of Information & School of Law. He is author of *Federal Trade Commission Privacy Law and Policy* (Cambridge University Press, 2016).

Margaret Hu is Associate Professor of Law at the Washington and Lee University School of Law. Before entering academia, Professor Hu was an attorney in the Department of Justice where she worked on cases involving national security and civil rights.

Jeffrey Kahn is Professor of Law and Gerald J. Ford Research Fellow at Southern Methodist University Dedman School of Law. He is the author of *Mrs. Shipley's Ghost: The Right to Travel and Terrorist Watchlists* (2013).

Margot E. Kaminski is Associate Professor of Law at the University of Colorado Law School and Director of the Privacy, Cybersecurity, and Drones Initiative at the Silicon Flatirons Center. She is former executive director of Yale's Information Society Project.

Alex Kozinski is a Judge at the United States Court of Appeals for the Ninth Circuit, where he was Chief Judge from 2007 to 2014. He served as Special Counsel to President Ronald Reagan and as a clerk to Chief Justice Warren E. Berger of the United States Supreme Court.

Travis LeBlanc is a Partner at Boies Schiller Flexner LLP, and former Chief of Enforcement for the Federal Communications Commission. He is an Affiliated Scholar at the University of California Hastings College of the Law.

Rachel Levinson-Waldman is Senior Counsel at the Brennan Center for Justice's Liberty and National Security Program where she is actively engaged in research and advocacy on issues relating to surveillance, national security, policing, and civil rights.

Gianclaudio Malgieri is a Ph.D. Researcher in Law at Vrije Universiteit Brussel, where he specializes in information privacy, surveillance, data protection and algorithm regulation, in particular at the intersection with property rights and IP rights.

Alex Marthews is the National Chair of Restore the Fourth.

David Medine is the former Chairman of the Privacy and Civil Liberties Oversight Board. He was an Attorney Fellow for the Securities and Exchange Commission and a Special Counsel at the Consumer Financial Protection Bureau. He has served as a partner at the law firm WilmerHale, a Senior Adviser to the White House National Economic Council, and the Associate Director for Financial Practices at the Federal Trade Commission.

R. Taj Moore is a graduate of Harvard Law School, where he served as an editor of the *Harvard Civil Rights-Civil Liberties Law Review* and of the *Harvard National Security Journal*. He is an attorney and contributor to *Lawfare*.

Esteban Morin is an Attorney Adviser at the Privacy and Civil Liberties Oversight Board. He was an associate in the Washington office of Jenner & Block LLP and a D.C. Bar Associate Fellow in the Appellate Division of the D.C. Public Defender Service. He also served as a law clerk to Judge Carlos Lucero of the U.S. Court of Appeals for the Tenth Circuit.

Dr. Thomas Nolan is Associate Professor and Program Director of Criminology and Criminal Justice Graduate Program at Merrimack College. Professor Nolan has served as a senior policy analyst in the Office of Civil Rights and Civil Liberties at the Department of Homeland Security and is a twenty-seven year veteran of the Boston Police Department.

Paul Ohm is Professor of Law at Georgetown University Law Center, and Faculty Director at the Center on Privacy and Technology where he specializes in information privacy, computer crime law, intellectual property, and criminal procedure. He is a former Senior Policy Advisor to the Federal Trade Commission and Assistant United States Attorney with the Computer Crime and Intellectual Property Section of the Department of Justice.

Faiza Patel is Co-director of the Liberty and National Security Program at the Brennan Center for Justice at NYU School of Law, where she has testified before Congress and authored numerous influential reports. Before joining the Brennan Center, Ms. Patel worked as a senior policy officer at the Organization for the Prohibition of Chemical Weapons in The Hague, and clerked for Judge Sidhwa at the International Criminal Tribunal for the former Yugoslavia.

Stephanie K. Pell is an Assistant Professor and Cyber Ethics Fellow at West Point's Army Cyber Institute and teaches in the Department of English and Philosophy. Professor Pell served as Counsel to the House Judiciary Committee, where she was lead counsel on Electronic Communications Privacy Act reform and PATRIOT Act reauthorization during the 111th Congress. She was also a federal prosecutor for over fourteen years, working as a Senior Counsel to the Deputy Attorney General, and as an Assistant U.S. Attorney in the Southern District of Florida.

Liz Clark Rinehart is an Associate at Venable LLP. She is the author of numerous articles including "Fighting Cybercrime After United States v. Jones" in the *Journal of Criminal Law and Criminology* and "Zoned for Injustice: Moving Beyond Zoning and Market-Based Land Preservation to Address Rural Poverty" in the *Georgetown Journal on Poverty Law & Policy*.

Lawrence Rosenthal is Professor of Law at Chapman University's Dale E. Fowler School of Law. Before entering academia, he prosecuted racketeering and organized crime cases as an Assistant United States Attorney in Chicago, Illinois. He also served as a clerk to Justice John Paul Stevens of the United States Supreme Court.

Mark Rumold is a Senior Staff Attorney at the Electronic Frontier Foundation, where he focuses primarily on privacy, surveillance, government secrecy, and national security issues.

Fritz Schwarz is the Chief Counsel of the Brennan Center for Justice at NYU School of Law. Among other notable services, he previously served as Chief Counsel to the Church Committee and as a litigation partner at Cravath, Swaine & Moore. He is the author of three books including *Democracy in the Dark: The Seduction of Government Secrecy* (2015).

Nicholas P. Silverman is an Associate at Steptoe & Johnson LLP, where he represents clients navigating all stages of criminal investigations, particularly in the healthcare, technology, and government relations fields of white-collar crime.

Christopher Slobogin is the Milton R. Underwood Chair in Law at Vanderbilt University Law School where he directs the school's Criminal Justice Program. He has authored more than one hundred articles, books, and chapters on topics relating to criminal law and procedure, mental health law and evidence, and has served as reporter for three American Bar Association task forces. Among his books is *Privacy at Risk: The New Government Surveillance and the Fourth Amendment* (2007).

Catherine Tucker is the Sloan Distinguished Professor of Management Science and Professor of Marketing at MIT Sloan and Research Associate at NBER.

Stephen I. Vladeck is Professor of Law at the University of Texas School of Law and is a nationally-recognized expert on constitutional law and national security law. He is a senior editor of the *Journal of National Security Law and Policy*, co-editor-in-chief of *Just Security*, and a contributor to *Lawfare*.

Jason M. Weinstein is Partner at Steptoe & Johnson LLP. He was Deputy Assistant Attorney General in the Criminal Division of the Department of Justice and was Assistant U.S. Attorney in the U.S. Attorney's Offices for the Southern District of New York and the District of Maryland.

Dr. Andrew Keane Woods is Assistant Professor of Law at the University of Kentucky College of Law where he writes on cybersecurity and the regulation of technology. He is also a contributor to *Lawfare*.

Introduction

For well-intentioned democracies, surveillance presents a conundrum: how to ensure safety, stability, and efficient markets, while also respecting privacy and individual liberty. Ranging from officers on the street to corporations tracking consumers to intelligence agencies operating overseas – and, increasingly, domestically – surveillance law is tasked with this difficult and delicate balance.

Surveillance law begins in foundational documents such as constitutions, conventions, and charters, including the American Fourth Amendment and Article 8 of the European Convention on Human Rights. It continues in legislative, administrative, judicial, and executive rules that seek to preserve these fundamental rights and interests, securing space for safety, commerce, and privacy by regulating access to, and use of, surveillance means and methods.

In seeking this balance, surveillance law perennially chases a moving target. Techniques and technologies evolve and change, offering criminals and spies new ways to inflict harm, government officials new means to combat those threats, and companies new methods to identify and interact with – or exploit – consumers. These changes have been particularly rapid, dramatic, and far-reaching as of late. Harm travels around the globe at the speed of light with hackers plying their trade to steal industrial secrets and to bring down everything from critical infrastructures to elections to private communications. Sophisticated networks of closed-circuit television systems and widespread tracking of mobile devices make location privacy increasingly rare. Tracking of Internet communications reveals purchasing and entertainment preferences in a granularity heretofore unimaginable – for example, how long a reader lingers on an e-book page or precisely when a viewer discontinues a television series. Data mining of near-ubiquitous information storage teases out inferences that were never meant to be shared, and even secrets that were never consciously known.

While these issues have been simmering for decades – with reporters and activists warning about expanding surveillance capacities and law enforcement agencies claiming that encryption and other privacy technologies cause their surveillance to "go dark" – government surveillance moved to the fore in 2013 with the publication of classified documents leaked by the former US government contractor Edward Snowden. These documents revealed a number of now-notorious surveillance programs of staggering breadth, including the gathering and storing of metadata from Americans' domestic phone calls, the gathering and storing of Internet communications and search histories, and efforts to infiltrate everything from private server networks operated by major Internet companies to mobile devices owned by private individuals. The world became acquainted with the potential reach of a modern national security agency, in this case the American NSA, which describes its own collection posture as "Sniff It All – Know It All – Collect It All – Process It All – Exploit It All – Partner It All."

Private surveillance has also made headlines. In 2012, the *New York Times* revealed that the Target Corporation mined seemingly innocuous data, such as the purchasing of unscented lotions, common vitamin supplements, and cotton balls, in order to identify pregnant customers, to whom it would then send tailored offers and coupons. In one notorious instance, this targeted advertising revealed a teenager's pregnancy to her family, hardly the way one would wish to learn of such a life-altering event. Yet this seems merely a precursor of what is to come. A more recent study found that machine analysis of Facebook "likes" better predicted personality and associated lifestyle choices than did real-world friends. Such commercial data fusion and analysis are of interest in their own right – designed for exploitation by advertisers and employers – but they will also be transferred to or accessed by government agencies.

In short, there is good reason for renewed interest among lawmakers, business leaders, attorneys, academics, and the general public regarding legal and policy issues relating to both public and private surveillance. This handbook documents and organizes these conversations, drawing together some of the most thoughtful and impactful contributors to contemporary surveillance debates, policies, and practices.

The chapters in the first part explore surveillance techniques and technologies – those used by the US National Security Agency in its war on terror (Rachel Levinson-Waldman), those that facilitate the location tracking of individuals historically and in real time (Stephanie K. Pell), those that attempt to "watchlist" dangerous persons (Jeffrey Kahn), those that incidentally collect vast amounts of innocent communications (Jennifer Daskal & Stephen I. Vladeck), those that leverage modern biometrics (Margaret Hu), those that compile information from disparate sources in government fusion centers (Thomas Nolan), those that leverage data mining of merged public-private data sets (Andrew Guthrie Ferguson), and those that rely upon the self-surveillance inherent in the Internet of things (Steven I. Friedland). New technologies have made the problems of surveillance law far more complicated than merely working new wine into old bottles.

The chapters in the second part explore the value of surveillance technologies for law enforcement, national security, and private enterprise – those using traditional and novel techniques in the investigation of "ordinary crime" (Jason M. Weinstein, R. Taj Moore, & Nicholas P. Silverman); those used by the Obama administration in the war on terror (Timothy Edgar); those using video surveillance, including body cameras, for local law enforcement (Marc. J Blitz); those using online tools to detect and deter cyber harassment (Danielle Keats Citron & Liz Clark Rinehart); those applying surveillance to street, financial, and other crimes (Lawrence Rosenthal); those using and cracking encryption to secure and eavesdrop on communications (Geoffrey S. Corn & Dru Brenner-Beck); and those in the private sector responding to the techniques and government demands of surveillance (Lothar Determann). Modern surveillance technologies have a critical role in combating crime and threats to national security; it is not only impossible to put the surveillance genie back in the bottle, it is undesirable from any serious policy perspective.

The chapters in the third part explore the impacts of surveillance – from the rise of the administrative state in the late eighteenth and early nineteenth centuries (Mark A. Graber) to the autocratic surveillance societies of the twentieth century

(Alex Kozinski & Mihailis E. Diamantis); from the chilling of online behaviors (Alex Marthews & Catherine Tucker) to the more general harms of pervasive, networked surveillance (Julie E. Cohen); and the inherent challenges that surveillance provides to intellectual and social freedom (Margot E. Kaminski). Modern technology facilitates broad, indiscriminate, and pervasive surveillance that is fundamentally at odds with human flourishing, which calls for careful surveillance regulation.

The chapters in the fourth part thus address the multivariate ways in which societies regulate surveillance – from the American Church Committee and regulation since (Elizabeth Goitein, Faiza Patel, & Fritz Schwarz) to the European Court of Human Rights and the European Union Court of Justice (Gianclaudio Malgieri & Paul De Hert); from a comprehensive regulatory "toolkit" beyond the familiar warrant structure (Paul Ohm) to a groundbreaking California electronic privacy law (Susan Freiwald); from surveillance in the European Union (Cristina Blasi Casagran) to regulation by specialized executive agencies like the American Privacy and Civil Liberties Oversight Board (David Medine & Esteban Morin). Surveillance regulation can take many forms, including litigating disputes (Mark Rumold), legislating limitations (Christopher Slobogin), improving mutual legal assistance (Andrew Keane Woods), and leveraging administrative agencies (both Chris Jay Hoofnagle and Travis LeBlanc & Lindsay DeFrancesco).

This handbook hardly *solves* the conundrum of surveillance law. We do not foresee that there will ever be a solution in any neat and tidy sense. Each temporary solution needs to balance competing interests that wax and wane, and shift and change, with society and technology. But the chapters comprising this collection expound foundational principles, and anyone interested in being on the right side of these debates – whether a government official, legal practitioner, judge, academic, student, or engaged citizen – will be richly rewarded by considering the material in this handbook.

Part I

Surveillance Techniques and Technologies

1 NSA Surveillance in the War on Terror

Rachel Levinson-Waldman†

On March 12, 2013, Senator Ron Wyden of Oregon asked James Clapper, then-director of national intelligence (DNI), whether the National Security Agency "collect[s] any type of data at all on millions or hundreds of millions of Americans."[1] The question was posed during an open session of the Senate Select Committee on Intelligence, on which Senator Wyden sits. DNI Clapper paused and answered, "No … not wittingly." Three months later, the details of a highly classified program that collected the bulk telephone records of millions of Americans – a program about which Senator Wyden had been issuing cryptic warnings for nearly two years[2] – were published in the *Guardian* newspaper. A month after that, Clapper finally retracted his statement, saying that it was "clearly erroneous."[3]

When Clapper made his statement, Edward Snowden, soon to become the country's most famous whistleblower, was working as an National Security Agency (NSA) contractor with top-secret clearance. However, the regular sharing of raw data with foreign intelligence agencies – often with little oversight or effort to eliminate personally identifiable information found in Americans' private communications – had raised grave concerns for Snowden, and he had already begun questioning the legal and ethical implications of the NSA's secret intelligence operations.[4]

When he heard Clapper's answer, he decided to act. He shared a trove of documents with a set of international reporters, ultimately resulting in the disclosure of a variety of classified surveillance programs, including programs collecting and analyzing the content and metadata of Americans' phone calls and emails, email address books and instant messaging "buddy lists,"[5] and more. These disclosures would reshape both the public's understanding of the post-9/11 legal landscape and the legislative, executive, and judicial

† Senior Counsel, Brennan Center for Justice, Liberty and National Security Program.

1 *Current and Projected National Security Threats to the United States: Hearing Before the S. Select Comm. on Intelligence*, 113th Cong. 66 (2013) (statement of Sen. Wyden, Member, S. Select Comm. on Intelligence).

2 *See, e.g.*, Charlie Savage, *Senators Say Patriot Act Is Being Misinterpreted*, N.Y. Times (May 27, 2011), at A17, http://www.nytimes.com/2011/05/27/us/27patriot.html.

3 Ryan Lizza, *State of Deception*, New Yorker (Dec. 16, 2013), http://www.newyorker.com/magazine/2013/12/16/state-of-deception.

4 James Bamford, *The Most Wanted Man in the World*, Wired (Aug. 22, 2014), https://www.wired.com/2014/08/edward-snowden/.

5 Barton Gellman & Ashkan Soltani, *NSA Collects Millions of E-mail Address Books Globally*, Wash. Post (Oct. 14, 2013), https://www.washingtonpost.com/world/national-security/nsa-collects-millions-of-e-mail-address-books-globally/2013/10/14/8e58b5be-34f9-11e3-80c6-7e6dd8d22d8f_story.html.

appraisal of the legal underpinnings of the surveillance programs. Understanding the magnitude and details of the programs that Snowden ultimately had a hand in revealing – the scope of this chapter – requires rewinding the clock almost twelve years.

I Secret Surveillance: 2001–2008

Less than a month after four planes were flown into the World Trade Center towers in New York City, the Pentagon in Washington, DC, and a field in rural Pennsylvania, President George W. Bush authorized the beginnings of what would become a sweeping mass surveillance program. It would swiftly outgrow even the modest limitations put upon it, ultimately becoming what the inspector general of the Department of Justice would call, in an exhaustive 2009 report, a "permanent surveillance tool."[6]

That top secret program, code-named STELLARWIND (hereinafter, Stellar Wind), involved an "unprecedented collection of information concerning U.S. persons."[7] It was eventually beset by legal and operational problems, some so significant that they prompted threats of mass resignations by top officials at the Department of Justice and FBI that would have eclipsed Nixon's Saturday Night Massacre.

Although no aspects of Stellar Wind remain in precisely the form in which they existed during the years after September 11, 2001, the program laid the foundation for the even more comprehensive surveillance programs that followed. For the last fifteen years, reams of information have been collected about Americans – in the name of fighting terrorism – and crunched using analytical programs looking for insights within the mass of data.

Some of those programs reportedly have been successful at fighting terrorism, though few details are publicly available; others are nearly universally agreed to have contributed little to keeping the nation safe.[8] Some programs have had shifting legal justifications, and some have been seemingly abandoned, only to reemerge under different auspices. And there are pieces that remain obscured behind redactions.

A *STELLARWIND*

1 Background

In the days after the September 11 attacks, U.S. officials scrambled to try to figure out how they had missed the largest attack on American soil since Pearl Harbor. On October 4, 2001, President George W. Bush issued a "highly classified presidential authorization"[9] finding that the September 11 attacks constituted an "extraordinary emergency" and authorizing the NSA to collect warrantlessly three broad categories of signals intelligence: the content of specified "Internet communications" and telephone calls, metadata

6 Offices of the Inspectors Gen. of the Dep't of Def. et al., (U) Annex to the Report on the President's Surveillance Program 396 (2009), https://oig.justice.gov/reports/2015/PSP-09-18-15-vol-III.pdf.

7 *Id.*

8 *See, e.g., id.* at 397, 399; *see also id.* at 401 ("[A]lthough Stellar Wind information had value in some counterterrorism investigations, it generally played a limited role in the FBI's overall counterterrorism efforts.").

9 Privacy & Civil Liberties Oversight Bd., Report on the Surveillance Program Operated Pursuant to Section 702 of the Foreign Intelligence Surveillance Act 16 [hereinafter PCLOB Report on 702] (2014), https://www.pclob.gov/library/702-Report.pdf.

about specified Internet communications, and metadata about specified phone calls.[10] ("Metadata" is data about data – in this case, not the content of the communications, but information *about* those communications, such as when they occurred and who was involved.) The program was referred to both by its code name, Stellar Wind, and by the umbrella term "President's Surveillance Program."

Under Stellar Wind, both content and metadata could be gathered when at least one of the parties to the call or email was outside the United States and was "reasonably believed to be associated with any international terrorist group."[11] In addition, metadata for any Internet communication or phone call could be collected if none of the participants was a US citizen, if at least one person was outside the United States, or if there was "reasonable articulable suspicion to believe the communications related to international terrorism."[12] In other words, if one person *was* inside the United States (but the other was not), or if *all* persons were inside the United States (but they were not U.S. citizens), then metadata about their communications could be gathered, even if their communications had nothing to do with international terrorism.

Once the metadata had been assembled into a database, it could be searched using a phone number or email address (an "identifier") for which there was "reasonable articulable suspicion" (RAS) to believe that the identifier "had been used for communications related to international terrorism."[13] These identifiers were called "seeds" or "selectors." Notably, the determination that a particular seed met the RAS standard occurred inside the NSA, without external oversight.[14]

Absent the emergency declared by President Bush, the data collection – at the very least the collection of content – would have required permission from the Foreign Intelligence Surveillance Court. Instead, as each presidential authorization expired,

10 *See, e.g.*, Charlie Savage & James Risen, *New Leak Suggests Ashcroft Confrontation Was over N.S.A. Program*, N.Y. Times, (June 28, 2013), at A6, http://www.nytimes.com/2013/06/28/us/nsa-report-says-internet-metadata-were-focus-of-visit-to-ashcroft.html. "Internet communications" included emails and Internet phone calls such as Skype (otherwise known as VoIP) that crossed the data links of AT&T, MCI/Verizon, and Sprint. *See, e.g.*, Barton Gellman, *U.S. Surveillance Architecture Includes Collection of Revealing Internet, Phone Metadata*, Wash. Post (June 15, 2013), https://www.washingtonpost.com/investigations/us-surveillance-architecture-includes-collection-of-revealing-internet-phone-metadata/2013/06/15/e9bf004a-d511-11e2-b05f-3ea3f0e7bb5a_story.html. They may have also included "Chat – video, voice, Videos, Photos, Stored data, … File transfers, Video Conferencing, Notifications of target activity – logins, etc., [and] Online Social Networking details." *See* Presentation, Special Source Operations, Nat'l Sec. Agency, Slide 4, (Apr. 2013) http://www.theguardian.com/world/interactive/2013/nov/01/prism-slides-nsa-document. It is not clear which, if any, of these types of communications beyond email and VoIP were also a part of the collection under Stellar Wind.

11 Offices of the Inspectors Gen. of the Dep't of Def. et al., *supra* note 6, at 388. Note that the program is variously described as requiring "reasonable belief" or "probable cause." *See, e.g.*, *id.* at 361. In March 2004, Deputy Attorney General Jack Goldsmith objected to the "any international terrorist group" standard on the grounds that the targeted group was too broad. President Bush then limited the content collection to communications for which at least one person was reasonably believed to be a member of al Qaeda or associated forces. Charlie Savage, Power Wars: Inside Obama's Post-9/11 Presidency, 191–192 (2015).

12 *See* Benjamin Wittes, *The NSA IG Draft Report: An Analysis, a Question, and a Possible Answer*, Lawfare (July 16, 2013, 10:01 PM), https://www.lawfareblog.com/nsa-ig-draft-report-analysis-question-and-possible-answer; Office of the Inspector Gen. of the Nat'l Sec. Agency, ST-09-002 Working Draft (2009), http://www.theguardian.com/world/interactive/2013/jun/27/nsa-inspector-general-report-document-data-collection.

13 Offices of the Inspectors Gen. of the Dep't of Def. et al., *supra* note 6, at 55.

14 *Id.* at 55 (describing process of shift coordinator's review and approval).

White House officials reassessed whether there were facts demonstrating a continued threat of terrorist attacks in the United States.[15] Once the standard was satisfied, the attorney general, with the advice of the Department of Justice's (DOJ) Office of Legal Counsel, signed the authorization attesting that the activities were legal and satisfied the Fourth Amendment's reasonableness requirement.[16] The memos also directed that information about American citizens be minimized, as long as the minimization was "consistent with the object of detecting and preventing terrorism."[17] Once the authorization was in place, the program was renewed for another thirty to sixty days.

As would later be revealed, however, the NSA secretly interpreted its already broad authorization in two ways in order to engage in even more intrusive collection and analysis. First, instead of limiting the categories of metadata to those described in the presidential authorization, it collected phone and email metadata in bulk, to create "a database from which to *acquire* the targeted meta data."[18] The agency then used the RAS standard to determine what searches it could run in the database.[19] It justified this practice on the dubious theory that it did not "acquire" the data until it ran searches, so it could vacuum up huge quantities of information without triggering the language of the presidential authorization.[20]

Second, the NSA crafted a separate "alert" system that operated outside the RAS process for the telephony metadata program. For two years, NSA analysts queried the telephony metadata not only with RAS-approved selectors but also with phone numbers that were simply "of interest" to the analysts.[21] When the selectors produced a hit against the metadata database, the analysts would then look more closely to determine whether the RAS standard was satisfied and contact chaining thus permitted.[22] The existence of this procedure emerged during a briefing with the Department of Justice; because it diverged significantly from the representations the agency had made to the Foreign Intelligence Surveillance Act (FISA) court regarding its compliance with the

15 Office of the Assistant Attorney Gen., Memorandum for the Attorney General Re: Review of the Legality of the STELLAR WIND Program 9 (2004), https://fas.org/irp/agency/doj/olc/stellar.pdf.

16 Offices of the Inspectors Gen. of the Dep't of Def. et al., *supra* note 6, at 389.

17 Office of the Assistant Attorney Gen., *supra* note 15, at 7.

18 Offices of the Inspectors Gen. of the Dep't of Def. et al., *supra* note 6, at 49 (emphasis added).

19 *Id.* at 49. According to the Inspector General's report, because the RAS standard was applied to searches, the NSA only accessed a minuscule fraction of the data it obtained; "By the end of 2006, .001% of the data collected had actually been retrieved from its database for analysis." *Id.* at 50.

20 *See, e.g.*, Office of the Inspector Gen. of the Nat'l Sec. Agency, *supra* note 12, at 38 (observing that the NSA's Office of general counsel and the inspector general accepted the agency's explanation that it "did not actually 'acquire' communications until specific communications were selected. In other words, because the authorization permitted NSA to conduct metadata analysis on selectors that met certain criteria, it implicitly authorized NSA to obtain the bulk data that was needed to conduct the metadata analysis"); *see also* Offices of the Inspectors Gen. of the Dep't of Def. et al., *supra* note 6, at 108 n.123 ("The term 'acquired' was not clarified until the March 11, 2004, Presidential Authorization. That Authorization stated that meta data was 'acquired … when, and only when, the Department of Defense has searched for and retrieved such header/router/addressing-type information, including telecommunications dialing-type data (and not when the Department obtains such header/router/addressing-type information, including telecommunications dialing-type data … for retention).'") (part of final sentence redacted and internal quotation marks omitted).

21 Offices of the Inspectors Gen. of the Dep't of Def. et al., *supra* note 6, at 232–233.

22 *Id.* at 232.

RAS standard, the NSA ultimately shuttered it, and the FISA court imposed additional temporary checks on the agency's authority as described later.[23]

Although the program was originally intended to be a temporary response to the attacks, it soon became clear that the presidential authorizations would be renewed indefinitely.[24] Because a significant fraction of the world's phone calls, and an even more substantial number of the world's Internet communications, go through the United States, the secret presidential authorizations led to a surveillance bonanza for the NSA. As of 2003, more than 37 billion minutes per year of telephone communications – about 20 percent of the total worldwide – either began or ended in the United States.[25] (Another 23 billion minutes traversed the United States without beginning or ending inside the country; the NSA was authorized under a Reagan era presidential order, Executive Order 12333, to capture those calls.)[26] Through relationships with several telecom companies, the NSA could get access to more than 80 percent of those 37 billion minutes' worth of calls.[27] The United States' advantage when it came to Internet communications was even more striking: as of 2002, nearly 99 percent of the world's Internet bandwidth either began or ended in the United States.[28] From October 2001 through January 2007, when the last vestiges of the program were shut down (though reanimated elsewhere under various other authorities, as described later), nearly thirty-eight thousand email addresses and telephone numbers were tasked for content collection under Stellar Wind.[29]

2 Operational Details: Phone and Email Metadata Program

Once the presidential authorizations were in place, they were provided to telecommunications companies, which complied by providing information about their customers' communications.[30] Specifically, the companies – beginning with AT&T, Verizon, and BellSouth – forwarded "call detail records," or routing information that included the phone numbers on either side of a telephone call and the date, time, and length of each call, but not the content of the phone calls.[31] Similarly, the NSA received email metadata revealing the senders and recipients of emails, who was cc'd or bcc'd, and the dates and times those emails were sent (but not the body of the emails or the information in the "subject" or "re" lines).[32]

23 *Id.*; *see infra* section II(A).
24 Office of the Inspector Gen. of the Nat'l Sec. Agency, *supra* note 12, at 11.
25 *Id.* at 27.
26 *Id.*
27 *Id.*
28 *Id.* at 28 ("[D]ata available from 2002 shows that at that time, worldwide international bandwidth was slightly more than 290 Gbps [Gigabits per second]. Of that total, less than 2.5 Gbps was between two regions that did not include the United States.").
29 *Id.* at 15.
30 Lizza, *supra* note 3.
31 Offices of the Inspectors Gen. of the Dep't of Def. et al., *supra* note 6, at 49.
32 *Id.* at 51. It appears that the three main companies that provided their customers' email metadata were AT&T, MCI/Verizon, and Sprint. *See, e.g.*, Office of the Inspector Gen. of the Nat'l Sec. Agency, *supra* note 12; Julia Angwin et al., *AT&T Helped U.S. Spy on Internet on a Vast Scale*, N.Y. Times, Aug. 16, 2015, at A1, http://www.nytimes.com/2015/08/16/us/politics/att-helped-nsa-spy-on-an-array-of-internet-traffic.html?_r=0; Gellman, *supra* note 10.

Once the metadata had been processed into databases, NSA analysts looked for unknown or unexpected links to foreigners by "contact chaining," a process that uncovered "the contacts made by a particular telephone number or e-mail address . . . as well as contacts made by subsequent contacts."[33] NSA analysts tended to go out more tiers with phone numbers than with email addresses because phone calls generally were not made to multiple people at once, unlike spam emails.[34]

Notably, the NSA had requested permission to do contact chaining on Americans' data two years earlier, when alarm bells were ringing about threats from al Qaeda. Under that proposal, Americans' phone numbers would have been "masked," or hidden, unless the NSA received a warrant to uncover them. The Justice Department had refused permission, advising that analyzing Americans' phone records without a warrant was illegal.[35] In the aftermath of September 11, however, Vice President Dick Cheney approached General Michael Hayden, then the head of the NSA, to ask what the NSA could be doing if Hayden was given additional legal authority. Together, they renewed the earlier plan, but without the protections for Americans' information.[36]

3 Legal Reviews

Initially, there was no judicial review and little internal legal review of these authorizations. A month into the program, in early November 2001, then-Deputy Assistant Attorney General John Yoo issued a twenty-one-page memorandum that would come to be roundly criticized for its superficial legal reasoning and failure to represent the basic facts of the program accurately.[37] Although the text of the memo remains almost entirely classified by redaction, Yoo appears to have argued that Article II of the Constitution gives the president an inherent right, which cannot be infringed by Congress or otherwise, to "engage in warrantless searches that protect the national security."[38] Despite the fact that the Foreign Intelligence Surveillance Act expressly limited the president's authority to engage in wiretapping, Yoo asserted that Congress had not acted to restrict the president's authority in this realm.[39] He suggested that intercepting communications crossing into or out of the United States fell under the "border search exception" to the Fourth Amendment.[40] And because few people were read into the program[41] or had access to the legal memo approving it – even the NSA's general counsel was barred from reading it by Vice President Dick Cheney's legal counsel – there was little pressure to

33 Offices of the Inspectors Gen. of the Dep't of Def. et al., *supra* note 6, at 54.

34 *Id.*

35 Lizza, *supra* note 3.

36 Lizza, *supra* note 3.

37 Memorandum from John C. Yoo, Deputy Assistant Attorney Gen. to Attorney Gen. (Nov. 2, 2001), https://www.justice.gov/sites/default/files/olc/legacy/2011/03/25/johnyoo-memo-for-ag.pdf; Offices of the Inspectors Gen. of the Dep't of Def. et al, *supra* note 6, at 10–14.

38 Memorandum from John C. Yoo, Deputy Assistant Attorney Gen. to Attorney Gen., *supra* note 37, at 7.

39 Offices of the Inspectors Gen. of the Dep't of Def. et al., *supra* note 6, at 391.

40 Offices of the Inspectors Gen. of the Dep't of Def. et al., UNCLASSIFIED REPORT ON THE PRESIDENT'S SURVEILLANCE PROGRAM 12 (2009), https://fas.org/irp/eprint/psp.pdf.

41 "The process of being 'read into' a compartmented program generally entails being approved for access to particularly sensitive and restricted information about a classified program, receiving a briefing about the program, and formally acknowledging the briefing, usually by signing a nondisclosure agreement describing restrictions on the handling and use of information concerning the program." *Id.* at 10 n.10.

revisit its legal moorings. The program thus continued in its basic form (albeit with a few tweaks) for two and a half years, until the spring of 2004.

In December 2003 Yoo was replaced by Jack Goldsmith, beginning a four-year-long process of creating new legal analyses – and in some cases new statutes – to justify the three collection programs. When Goldsmith began reviewing the justification for the programs, he concluded that Yoo's legal reasoning was faulty in several respects, as described in more detail in the following, and that Yoo had failed to understand or accurately describe certain factual aspects of the government's surveillance program.[42] The Yoo memos therefore did not even fully cover Stellar Wind – meaning that the White House had been operating a secret mass surveillance program without adequate Office of Legal Counsel review or approval.[43] Goldsmith's attempts to flag the legal problems, and to bring the programs into basic legal compliance, sparked repeated skirmishes between the Department of Justice and the White House.

In March 2004, with the then-current presidential authorization slated to expire on March 11, the conflict came to a head. At Goldsmith's recommendation, Acting Attorney General James Comey (who later became head of the FBI) refused to recertify the program, and Attorney General John Ashcroft refused to overrule him from the hospital bed where he lay with acute appendicitis.[44] On March 11, the day the existing presidential authorization expired, White House Counsel Alberto Gonzales – at the direction of President Bush – certified the continuation of the phone metadata and content collection programs, without approval from the Department of Justice.[45] Two other aspects of Stellar Wind were the subjects of such serious conflict between the DOJ and the White House that one was retroactively authorized and the other temporarily shut down.

The aspect to be retroactively authorized was the NSA's practice, described previously, of collecting far more phone and Internet metadata than was permitted by the authorization, so the agency could later search through its bulk database for the information it was actually authorized to obtain. To "narrow the gap" between what the authorizations allowed and what the NSA was doing in practice, President Bush substantially changed the language of his March 2004 reauthorization and declared it to apply both prospectively and retroactively.[46] Now, in addition to being able to "acquire" metadata when at least one party to the communication was believed to be outside the United States or the message was linked to terrorism, the NSA was also explicitly authorized to "obtain and retain" any telecommunications metadata, including that of wholly domestic communications.[47] Because *collecting* metadata was redefined as "obtaining and retaining" the information, "acquiring" – the activity that was initially sanctioned and regulated by the authorization – was transformed into *querying* the collected metadata for communications involving foreigners abroad or linked to terrorism. In other words, the agency

42 Offices of the Inspectors Gen. of the Dep't of Def. et al., *supra* note 6, at 124.

43 *Id.* Notably, the information identifying the particular program that was not described accurately is redacted from the inspector general's report, though it appears that the problem may have been Yoo's failure to understand that Internet backbone providers do not process or retain email metadata, described *infra* Section I(A)(4). *See, e.g.*, Julian Sanchez, *Reading Goldsmith's STELLARWIND Memo (Part I)*, Just Security (Sept. 10, 2014, 5:05 PM), https://www.justsecurity.org/14789/reading-jack-goldsmiths-stellarwind-memo/.

44 Offices of the Inspectors Gen. of the Dep't of Def. et al., *supra* note 6, at 130–31.

45 Office of the Inspector Gen. of the Nat'l Sec. Agency, *supra* note 12, at 37.

46 Offices of the Inspectors Gen. of the Dep't of Def. et al., *supra* note 6, at 144.

47 *Id.* at 145.

could collect everything, with the limitations entering into effect only when the data was searched. And this new distinction was given retroactive effect, to sanction all the previous overcollection.[48]

The second part of Stellar Wind that came under fire was the Internet metadata program, which had precipitated much of the wrangling between the Department of Justice and the White House. As described later, Goldsmith appears to have concluded that the Internet metadata collection simply was not supported by the existing statutory scheme. The week after President Bush directed his White House counsel to recertify the other two programs on his sole authority, the president rescinded his authorization for the email metadata program, giving the agency "a week to stop collecting it and to block access to its existing database."[49] (This suspension would be short-lived, however, because the bulk of the program would ultimately be reanimated by the Foreign Intelligence Surveillance court under a new interpretation of a provision of FISA, as described later.) On May 6, 2004, Goldsmith submitted a memo to Ashcroft on the legality of the three collection programs, superseding Yoo's earlier memo.[50] Though significant portions of the memorandum are still classified, the memo, along with other sources, demonstrates how Goldsmith tried to shift the content and phone metadata pieces onto firmer ground, and also suggests why the Internet metadata piece provoked a near-crisis.

4 Legal Analysis

Similar to Yoo, Goldsmith took a broad view of the executive's inherent authority to collect foreign intelligence when it came to content collection. Unlike Yoo, however, he grounded it in the Authorization for Use of Military Force (AUMF), the Congressional enactment authorizing the president to go to war against any nations or organizations involved in the September 11 attacks.[51] In Goldsmith's view, because the AUMF authorized war, it also authorized the President to take related steps, including collecting signals intelligence – both content and metadata – about the enemy (even though one end of the communication was likely to be an American in the U.S.). The AUMF thereby took precedence over the otherwise applicable limitations in the Foreign Intelligence Surveillance Act, allowing the content collection program to pass statutory muster.[52]

With respect to metadata collection, however, the landscape was different. The government's bulk collection of metadata under Stellar Wind was explicitly designed to

48 *Id.* at 146; *see also* Charlie Savage, *George W. Bush Made Retroactive N.S.A. 'Fix' after Hospital Room Showdown*, N.Y. Times, Sept. 21, 2015, at A13, http://www.nytimes.com/2015/09/21/us/politics/george-w-bush-made-retroactive-nsa-fix-after-hospital-room-showdown.html.

49 Charlie Savage & James Risen, *New Leak Suggests Ashcroft Confrontation Was over N.S.A. Program*, N.Y. Times, June 28, 2013, at A6, http://www.nytimes.com/2013/06/28/us/nsa-report-says-internet-metadata-were-focus-of-visit-to-ashcroft.html.

50 Office of the Assistant Attorney Gen., *supra* note 15. *See also* Offices of the Inspectors Gen. of the Dep't of Def. et al., *supra* note 6, at 186 (describing memo as "the most comprehensive assessment of the Stellar Wind program drafted by the Office of Legal Counsel"); *id.* at 392 (describing memo as superseding Yoo's earlier opinions).

51 *See* Press Release, Office of the Press Secretary, President Signs Authorization for Use of Military Force Bill, Statement by the President (Sept. 18, 2001), https://georgewbush-whitehouse.archives.gov/news/releases/2001/09/20010918-10.html.

52 *See supra* note 11, regarding the narrowing of content collection so it collected only communications of members of the groups identified in the AUMF.

capture Americans' communications: unlike the content collection piece, it did not focus on the communications of the enemy. The AUMF therefore could not justify the collection of either phone or Internet metadata.

The phone metadata program was nevertheless deemed permissible. Because it involved the collection of existing records from the telecommunications companies, it did not actually constitute "surveillance" under FISA, and it therefore didn't need a statutory workaround. (As described below, it was also not seen as raising any constitutional issues.)

The Internet metadata program presented a graver statutory dilemma, however. It did count as surveillance under FISA, but the AUMF could not rescue it. FISA's definition of "electronic surveillance" includes the "installation or use" of any "device in the United States for monitoring to acquire information,"[53] and this is precisely how the email records were being obtained. Unlike phone companies, email providers do not generate records of email communications for billing purposes; instead, a device that logs email traffic must be installed on a network switch. The installation and use of such a device constitutes electronic surveillance under FISA, which required judicial approval. And because the AUMF only gave the President the authority to surveil "enemies" abroad, not Americans domestically, it could not override the executive's obligations under FISA.[54] Although the relevant part of Goldsmith's memo is redacted, this statutory tension strongly suggests that this is the reason the Internet metadata program was abruptly shut down in mid-2004; there was simply no legal justification for it in its existing form.

The memorandum also evaluated Stellar Wind's consistency with the Fourth Amendment. The closest the Supreme Court has come to addressing the question of constitutional authority for foreign intelligence collection was in the 1972 case *United States v. United States District Court*, commonly known as *Keith*.[55] The Court held in *Keith* that the Fourth Amendment's warrant requirement does apply to investigations of purely *domestic* threats to the nation's security, but reserved the question of whether a warrant was required for the President to exercise his or her *foreign* intelligence surveillance powers.[56] Notwithstanding that silence, the courts of appeals that have endorsed the President's inherent authority to conduct warrantless foreign intelligence surveillance have relied on *Keith* in reaching their decisions.[57]

Following and expanding their lead, the Goldsmith memo concluded that the President has inherent constitutional authority, consistent with the Fourth Amendment, to conduct warrantless searches for foreign intelligence purposes both in wartime and in peacetime, as Commander-in-Chief and as Chief Executive.[58] The memo depicted the arena of foreign intelligence collection as a case of "special needs beyond the normal

53 50 U.S.C. § 1801(f)(4).

54 Julian Sanchez, *Reading Goldsmith's STELLARWIND Memo (Part I)*, Just Security (Sept. 10, 2014, 5:05 PM), https://www.justsecurity.org/14789/reading-jack-goldsmiths-stellarwind-memo/; *see also* Julian Sanchez, *What the Ashcroft "Hospital Showdown" on NSA Spying Was All About*, Ars Technica (July 29, 2013, 9:00 AM), http://arstechnica.com/tech-policy/2013/07/what-the-ashcroft-hospital-showdown-on-nsa-spying-was-all-about/.

55 *United States v. U.S. Dist. Court* (*Keith*), 407 U.S. 297 (1972).

56 *Id.* at 308.

57 Office of the Assistant Attorney Gen., *supra* note 15, at 40.

58 *Id.* at 37.

need for law enforcement," where the Fourth Amendment's reasonableness requirement can be satisfied without a warrant.[59]

The specific surveillance programs were deemed to pass constitutional muster as well. As for the content collection program, the government's interests in preventing attacks during an armed conflict were judged to outweigh the "significant" and "substantial" individual privacy interests in the communications, thus meeting the Fourth Amendment's reasonableness standard[60] – though in light of revelations that Stellar Wind served little discernible purpose in thwarting attacks, a different balance might have been appropriate.[61]

By contrast, the phone and email metadata collection programs were taken not to implicate the Fourth Amendment in the first place, based on a strained interpretation of the 1979 Supreme Court case *Smith v. Maryland*.[62] In *Smith*, the Court held that dialed phone numbers are not protected by the Fourth Amendment because the individual knowingly reveals them to the phone company.[63] The memo reasoned that a person sending an email likewise shares the address information with the service provider to enable delivery of the message. Under *Smith*, the constitutional inquiry would arguably end there.[64] But this analysis presumes too much.

First, when it comes to email metadata, the voluntary dissemination analogy does not hold up to scrutiny. Unlike telephone providers, broadband providers do not collect and store email metadata records as part of their normal business operations; indeed, Goldsmith appeared to have based his statutory objection to the program in large part on this fact, since it meant that FISA surveillance was instead required to acquire the records off the Internet "backbone."[65]

Second, even if it were true that all communications metadata is voluntarily shared with a third party, analogizing the three days of phone call information captured in *Smith* to the vast stores of email and phone data accumulated by the NSA is, in the Supreme Court's recent words, "like saying a ride on horseback is materially indistinguishable from a flight to the moon."[66] Increasingly sophisticated software tools can analyze large sets of aggregated metadata to reveal patterns and relationships that are even more illuminating than information gleaned from content analysis. Aggregated metadata can reveal an individual's social network, typical locations, medical emergencies or chronic

59 *Id.* at 39.

60 *Id.* at 101, 105.

61 *See, e.g.*, Offices of the Inspectors Gen. of the Dep't of Def. et al., *supra* note 6, at 399–401.

62 Office of the Assistant Attorney Gen., *supra* note 15, at 106.

63 *See Smith v. Maryland*, 442 U.S. 735 (1979).

64 Office of the Assistant Attorney Gen., *supra* note 15, at 108. *But see* Stephen E. Henderson, *After United States v. Jones, After the Fourth Amendment Third Party Doctrine*, 14 N.C. J. L. & Tech. 431 (2013) (suggesting that the Supreme Court has a narrower interpretation of *Smith* and the third-party doctrine than most commentators acknowledge).

65 *See also* Julian Sanchez, *Reading Jack Goldsmith's STELLARWIND Memo (Part II)*, Just Security (Sept. 16, 2014, 1:45 PM), https://www.justsecurity.org/14794/reading-jack-goldsmiths-stellarwind-memo-part-ii/; Julian Sanchez, *Reading Jack Goldsmith's STELLARWIND Memo (Part I)*, Just Security (Sept. 10, 2014, 5:05 PM), https://www.justsecurity.org/14789/reading-jack-goldsmiths-stellarwind-memo/; Julian Sanchez, *Are Internet Backbone Pen Registers Constitutional?*, Just Security (Sept. 23, 2013, 7:55 PM), https://www.justsecurity.org/1042/internet-backbone-pen-registers-constitutional/ (collectively, analyzing the email metadata issue and proposing several additional technical reasons why *Smith* is inapposite in this scenario).

66 *Riley v. California*, 134 S.Ct. 2473 (2014).

health problems, political or religious affiliations, sleeping patterns, shopping habits, and business dealings.[67] The ability to put all these pieces of information together yields further inferences about that individual's lifestyle and even their intentions and ambitions.[68]

B *New Legal Authority for the Internet Metadata Program*

Regardless of the constitutional analysis, both the DOJ and the White House had concluded that the bulk Internet metadata program could not be sustained on statutory grounds. In light of President Bush's shutdown of the program, administration lawyers scrambled to find a new legal basis, ultimately settling on a particular provision of the Foreign Intelligence Surveillance Act: the pen register/trap and trace authority. This authority allows the government to apply for a court order to install a device that records metadata about calls made and received on a particular phone line.[69] (This was the device used to capture the phone metadata in *Smith*.) To satisfy FISA, the government's application for the device must show that the call data sought is "relevant to *an ongoing investigation* to protect against international terrorism."[70] If this authority could be applied to entire Internet switches, not just individual phone lines, then bulk email metadata collection could be brought under FISA.

In the late spring or early summer of 2004, Ashcroft's team submitted a memo to the FISA Court proposing this theory.[71] To do so, the DOJ had to thread several needles. First, it had to persuade the court that a massive amount of Americans' email metadata, much of which would have nothing to do with terrorism, was "relevant to an ongoing investigation to protect against international terrorism."[72] Instead of asserting relevance to "*an investigation*," however, the Attorney General argued that the metadata was "relevant to FBI *investigations*" – plural – because the NSA needed to "have the data in bulk" in order to analyze it.[73] This linguistic tweak effectively elided the statute's core requirement, draining the word "relevant" of almost all meaning. Indeed, the DOJ acknowledged that the "vast majority" of the metadata would not be terrorist-related, but asserted that the NSA's need to apply its intelligence tools to the bulk database sufficed.[74] Because terrorists' communications might be *somewhere* in the "billions of bits of data flowing through the United States today," the DOJ took the position that it was reasonable to archive all of it in order to "find the terrorists tomorrow."[75] And because contact chaining was particularly valuable in identifying unknown connections, bulk collection to enable

67 *Ed Felten Explains the Power of Metadata*, TECH POLICY (Nov. 8, 2013), http://www.techpolicy.com/FeltenExplainsThePower-of-Metadata.aspx.

68 Bruce Schneier, *Metadata Equals Surveillance*, SCHNEIER ON SEC. (Sept. 23, 2013), https://www.schneier.com/blog/archives/2013/09/metadata_equals.html.

69 50 U.S.C. § 1842(a)(1); Office of the Inspector Gen. of the Nat'l Sec. Agency, *supra* note 12, at 39.

70 50 U.S.C. § 1842(c)(2) (emphasis added).

71 Memorandum of Law and Fact in Support of Application for Pen Registers and Trap and Trace Devices for Foreign Intelligence Purposes, No. PR/TT (FISA Ct.) [hereinafter Appl. for PR/TT], https://www.documentcloud.org/documents/1376098-application-for-july-2004-prtt-internet-metadata.html (partially redacted) (date fully redacted).

72 *Id.* at 3; *see* 50 U.S.C. § 1842.

73 Appl. for PR/TT, *supra* note 71, at 3–4.

74 *Id.* at 3.

75 *Id.* at 12; *see also id.* at 35 ("[U]nless e-mail meta data is stored at the time of transmittal, it will be lost forever. All of the meta data collected is thus relevant, because it is necessary for the success of the investigative tool.").

contact chaining was necessary.[76] In addition, the DOJ maintained that leads produced by the NSA would "greatly enhance the FBI's ability to 'connect the dots' in existing FBI international terrorism investigations."[77]

Under the government's reading of the statute, the word "relevant" was meant to be a fairly low standard, satisfied as long as it was pertinent in any way to an international terrorism investigation.[78] The DOJ further proposed that the pen/trap statute did not require that the surveillance collect *only* relevant information, and that the appropriate balance was struck here because the government's interest was high (thwarting terrorist attacks) and the privacy interest was low (metadata was not constitutionally protected under the government's reading of *Smith*, and the non-relevant information would never be seen by an NSA analyst).[79]

The DOJ offered some additional limitations on the use of the information: the NSA planned to query the data only when there were "facts giving rise to a reasonable, articulable suspicion" that the email address was associated with certain groups, the identities of which have been redacted.[80] Querying of the data required approval from one of seven managers, and the NSA estimated that less than one query would be conducted per day, with a small fraction of the query results containing U.S. person information.[81] The NSA also guaranteed that certain minimization and oversight mechanisms would be put into place.[82]

The government therefore concluded that "[w]hen the government's need for the meta data collection at issue is balanced against the minimal intrusion on the privacy interest of those innocent users of the Internet whose e-mail meta data would be collected, the balance tips overwhelmingly in favor of the Government."[83] (The government also argued that under a strict reading of the law, the FISA Court had no authority to look beyond the government's bare assertion of relevance.[84])

Ashcroft bolstered the government's argument with examples that primarily serve to undermine its assertions. The application argued, for example, that:

> the bulk collection of meta data is in many respects similar to an investigative response that might be used to deal with the ongoing threat posed by a serial sniper. To identify the sniper, the police may use road blocks to cordon off an area around a shooting and to photograph the license plates of every car leaving the area. Such an approach would undoubtedly gather the license plates of hundreds, if not thousands, of innocent motorists. But the license plate information is not constitutionally protected, and it can provide a vital investigative tool if it is kept and then compared with the license plates of cars present at the next serial shooting.[85]

The disconnect between this scenario and the NSA's actual practice is clear on its face. In the "serial sniper" situation, the police are collecting a relatively small number

76 *Id.* at 12–14.
77 *Id.* at 27.
78 *Id.* at 34.
79 *Id.* at 41, 43–47.
80 *Id.* at 16.
81 *Id.* at 17.
82 *Id.* at 17.
83 *Id.* at 48.
84 *Id.* at 26–34.
85 *Id.* at 48–49.

of license plates, at a discrete time and place, in the immediate aftermath of a specific criminal event. This bears almost no relation to the NSA's collection of information about every single email that an American sends or receives. Even if that collection were limited (which would mark a change from the NSA's previous procedures), and even if the searches within the database were targeted (as the government represented in its application[86]), it would nevertheless represent a far more comprehensive program than the attempt to find a single fleeing criminal.

There was, however, no one to raise these issues to the FISA Court; Foreign Intelligence Surveillance Court (FISC) Judge Colleen Kollar-Kotelly was the only judge read into the program, and the FISC nearly always heard only from the government on an ex parte basis, with no opposing party to challenge the government's theories. Thus, on July 14, 2004, Judge Kollar-Kotelly issued an opinion largely blessing the government's application.[87] While accepting the government's expansive theory of "relevance," the opinion rejected the government's assertion that there was no room for judicial review of its application.[88] It nevertheless concluded that the substantive arguments proffered by the government passed muster, and opined that the court should defer substantially to the executive's judgments in the realm of national security.[89] Based on the government's representations, the decision accepted that the proposed collection, while "enormous," was "necessary" for the NSA's contact chaining, and that the NSA's "analytic tools are likely to generate useful investigative leads" for the FBI and other agencies.[90]

The opinion also accepted without question the government's analogy to *Smith v. Maryland*, finding that the sheer numbers at stake were irrelevant to the Fourth Amendment question.[91] While it acknowledged – unlike the government – that "sophisticated analysis of archived meta data may yield more information about a person's Internet communications than would at first be apparent," it concluded that that worked no independent Fourth Amendment invasion.[92] Significantly, the court relied on *United States v. Calandra*, in which the Supreme Court held that grand jury questions based on illegally obtained evidence do not constitute an independent violation of an individual's Fourth Amendment rights, because the questions are merely a "derivative use of the product of a past unlawful search" and not a new Fourth Amendment wrong.[93] In the FISA court's view, whatever the government extracted from the metadata was simply a derivative use as well.

The analogy is flawed: the government's use of the bulk metadata was arguably more transformative than derivative, because the bulk nature of the data allowed the government to use contact chaining to glean new insights not evident on the face of the data. An adversarial party (or a court-appointed amicus) might have been able to point out the

86 *See, e.g., id.* at 53–54 (describing procedure for searching metadata database).

87 Opinion & Order, No. PR/TT (FISA Ct. July 14, 2004) [hereinafter Op. & Order for PR/TT], https://www.documentcloud.org/documents/1376097-july-14-2004-prtt-internet-metadata-order.html.

88 *Id.* at 26 ("In the Government's view, the Court's exclusive function regarding this certification would be to verify that it contains the words required by [the statute]; the basis for a properly worded certification would be of no judicial concern. The Court has reviewed the Government's arguments and authorities and does not find them persuasive.") (citation omitted).

89 *Id.* at 2–3, 30.

90 *Id.* at 39, 48.

91 *Id.* at 60–63.

92 *Id.* at 65.

93 *Id.* at 65 (citing *United States v. Calandra*, 414 U.S. 338, 354 (1974)).

flaws in this analysis, or pursue and appeal on those grounds, but those options did not exist within the FISA Court.

Finally, the ruling held that as long as the collection was not intentionally targeted at conduct protected by the First Amendment, it was not likely to violate individuals' rights to freedom of speech and association, as long as it comported with the Fourth Amendment.[94] It did, however, put in place some restrictions to safeguard First Amendment rights, including (1) prohibiting the government from premising reasonable suspicion solely on the basis of activities protected by the First Amendment and (2) directing the NSA's Office of General Counsel to review and approve proposed metadata queries "based on seed accounts used by U.S. persons" in order to "ensure appropriate consideration of any First Amendment issues."[95] It also narrowed the datalinks from which the NSA could gather data as well as the number of people permitted access to the information.[96] With this FISC approval and processes in place, the Internet metadata collection program would continue in this form for the next seven years.[97]

Although this approach to collecting email metadata would ultimately be shuttered in 2011, several changes to the program and its legal authority have allowed the NSA to continue gathering Americans' email metadata, as described in more detail below.[98] First, Executive Order 12333 permits the collection of bulk data abroad, even if it contains communications involving Americans. Coupled with a change in the NSA's rules in late 2010 allowing agency analysts to sift through Americans' data captured abroad, this authority helped soften the impact of closing the surveillance program carried out under FISA.[99] In addition, once FISA was amended in 2008, Americans' emails could be collected domestically without a warrant as long as a foreigner was the target of the collection; this statutory change meant that the FISA Court decision no longer needed to form the legal basis for the program.

C *Legal Changes to the Phone Metadata Program*

The year after the Internet metadata program was shut down and then restarted under FISA, the phone metadata program came under fire as well. In late 2005, the *New York Times* disclosed the warrantless surveillance program,[100] prompting one of the participating telephone companies to ask for a court order in place of its voluntary compliance. Administration lawyers got creative again, asking the FISA Court to issue orders to continue the program under a section of the USA PATRIOT Act that had significantly expanded the FBI's authority to use secret orders to get records as part of an investigation.

[94] *Id.* at 66–68.

[95] *Id.* at 83–85 (prohibiting NSA from relying solely on activities protected by the First Amendment).

[96] Office of the Inspector Gen. of the Nat'l Sec. Agency, *supra* note 12, at 39; *see also* Op. & Order for PR/TT, *supra* note 87, at 69 n.50; *id.* at 80–87 (setting out all requirements imposed on installation and use of pen registers for this purpose).

[97] *See, e.g.*, Charlie Savage, *File Says N.S.A. Found Way to Replace Email Program*, N.Y. Times, (Nov. 20, 2015), at A4, http://www.nytimes.com/2015/11/20/us/politics/records-show-email-analysis-continued-after-nsa-program-ended.html (noting that government shut down the program in December 2011 for "operational and resource reasons").

[98] *See id.*

[99] *Id.*

[100] James Risen and Eric Lichtblau, *Bush Lets U.S. Spy on Callers without Courts*, N.Y. Times (Dec. 16, 2005), http://www.nytimes.com/2005/12/16/politics/bush-lets-us-spy-on-callers-without-courts.html.

In the pre-2001 version of FISA, before the passage of the PATRIOT Act, the FBI could obtain a secret order from the FISA Court to get certain business records as part of an investigation. Those orders were limited in scope, however: they could only obtain records from a common carrier (like an airline or bus company), a hotel, a car rental agency, or a storage facility.[101] With the passage in 2001 of Section 215 of the PATRIOT Act, which incorporated and expanded this provision of FISA, the FBI could now request any "tangible things" held by a business; there were no limitations on the type of item.[102] In addition, while pre-PATRIOT Act FISA had required the FBI to show "specific and articulable facts" demonstrating that the person about whom they were seeking records was a foreign power or the agent of a foreign power, Section 215 stripped that constraint; instead, the Bureau only needed to supply a statement that the records were "relevant to an authorized investigation."[103]

Armed with this new authority, and under pressure to shift the phone metadata program onto firmer legal ground, Alberto Gonzales, who was by then Attorney General, secretly proposed to the FISA Court in May 2006 that Section 215 provided the legal authority to order the phone companies to hand over their metadata records to the NSA.[104] The government noted that the FISC had already authorized the NSA to collect email metadata, and indicated that it wanted to use the same "analytic tools" to find "operatives of the enemy." (Although the specific enemy was redacted, it was likely al Qaeda and associated forces.[105]) In particular, the government suggested that carriers' phone records were "tangible things" that the government could lawfully obtain under Section 215.

This proposal raised two immediate issues. First, unlike most business records requests, which aim for records already in the company's possession, these orders sought prospective records – that is, records that the phone companies hadn't yet produced. And there was an even thornier question: how could the phone records of millions of Americans, gathered indiscriminately, be "relevant" to an authorized investigation? The DOJ returned to the argument that it had already made with respect to email records: it needed everything so it could sift through and find the relevant pieces.

The FISA Court agreed. The day after the DOJ submitted its request, Judge Malcolm Howard issued an order requiring phone companies to provide the NSA with their customers' calling records on an ongoing daily basis.[106] The concise order focused entirely

101 *See* Elizabeth B. Bazen, The Foreign Intelligence Surveillance Act: An Overview of the Statutory Framework and Recent Judicial Decisions 10 (2005), http://nsarchive.gwu.edu/NSAEBB/NSAEBB178/surv30.pdf.

102 50 U.S.C. § 1861.

103 50 U.S.C. § 1861(b)(2)(B) (2002).

104 Memorandum of Law in Support of Application for Certain Tangible Things for Investigations to Protect Against International Terrorism, at 15, *In re* Application of the Federal Bureau of Investigation for an Order Requiring the Production of Tangible Things, No. BR 06–05 (FISA Ct. May 23, 2006) [hereinafter Mem. in Appl. for Tangible Things], https://www.dni.gov/files/documents/1118/CLEANED016.%20REDACTED%20BR%2006–05%20Exhibits%20C%20%28Memo%20of%20Law%29%20and%20D-Sealed.pdf.

105 The brief leads by saying that "One of the greatest challenges the United States faces in the ongoing conflict with [– –] is finding operatives of the enemy." *Id.* at 1. Al Qaeda is clearly the name that fits in that redacted space, and while the later redaction is longer, the brief overall is focused on the threat posed by al Qaeda.

106 Order, *In re* Application of the Federal Bureau of Investigation for an Order Requiring the Production of Tangible Things From [redacted], No. BR 06–05 (FISA Ct. May 24, 2006), https://www.aclu.org/files/assets/pub_May%2024%202006%20Order%20from%20FISC.pdf.

on the mechanics of the production, directing the phone companies to provide "call-detail records," or CDRs, to the NSA on a daily basis. The CDRs captured when a call was made, how long it lasted, and the phone numbers on both ends (but not location information), and the FBI and the NSA were required to adhere to minimization procedures governing their management and sharing of Americans' information.

Once the records were in a central database, NSA analysts could use the already established RAS standard, searching the trove with a phone number for which there was reasonable articulable suspicion that the number was associated with terrorism. An NSA official (of whom there were 22 total) had to certify that the RAS standard had been met for the phone number or "seed." Approved numbers did not need to belong to known terrorists; if an enemy operative was apprehended and his cellular phone acquired, for instance, then any number listed in his phone book would meet the RAS requirement.[107] Phone numbers belonging to U.S. citizens could be used as seeds as well, as long as the *sole* justification for their use was not based on First Amendment-protected activities.[108] Once RAS was certified, analysts could contact chain through the database, going "three hops" out from the initial seed number – though in practice, they only used two hops.[109]

The restrictions imposed on the initial searches did not apply to the results they yielded, however. Analysts could query that data, which went into a database called the "corporate store," using a much broader universe of seeds; instead of certifying that the seed met the RAS standard, they needed only to show that it had some foreign intelligence value.[110] Moreover, the corporate store contained not just records of the specific phone calls with the RAS-approved seed or the phone numbers one or two hops out from the seed, but five years' worth of calling records for *every* phone number within the prescribed number of hops.[111] And while queries into the Section 215 database were carefully tracked with audit logs, there was no record of the searches in the corporate store database.[112] As described below, the database may eventually have been used for large-scale data mining on Americans.

The FISC order approving the production of phone metadata records was good for a little under 90 days. As with the Internet metadata transition, the scope of the authority provided by the FISC's order was similar to that authorized under Stellar Wind, with some limitations on the number of people who could access the data and additional oversight and reporting requirements.[113] Judge Howard did not offer any constitutional

107 Mem. in Appl. for Tangible Things, *supra* note 104, at 20.

108 *Id.* at 20.

109 *Section 215 Bulk Telephone Records and the MAINWAY Database*, ELECTROSPACES (Jan. 20, 2016), http://electrospaces.blogspot.com/2016/01/section-215-bulk-telephone-records-and.html.

110 Patrick Toomey, *Raiding the "Corporate Store": The NSA's Unfettered Access to a Vast Pool of Americans' Phone Data*, ACLU (Aug. 2, 2013), https://www.aclu.org/blog/raiding-corporate-store-nsas-unfettered-access-vast-pool-americans-phone-data?redirect=blog/national-security/raiding-corporate-store-nsas-unfettered-access-vast-pool-americans-phone-data; Primary Order, *In re* Application of the Federal Bureau of Investigation for an Order Requiring the Production of Tangible Things from [redacted], No. BR 13–80 (FISA Ct. Apr. 25, 2013), http://www.dni.gov/files/documents/PrimaryOrder_Collection_215.pdf; Privacy & Civil Liberties Oversight Bd., REPORT ON THE TELEPHONE RECORDS PROGRAM CONDUCTED UNDER SECTION 215 OF THE USA PATRIOT ACT AND ON THE OPERATIONS OF THE FOREIGN INTELLIGENCE SURVEILLANCE COURT (2014) [hereinafter PCLOB REPORT ON 215], https://www.pclob.gov/library/215-Report_on_the_Telephone_Records_Program.pdf.

111 *See* Toomey, *supra* note 110.

112 PCLOB REPORT ON 215, *supra* note 110.

113 Office of the Inspector Gen. of the Nat'l Sec. Agency, *supra* note 12, at 40.

or statutory analysis of the program, except for finding that the records were "tangible things" that were "relevant to authorized investigations," and that they could be obtained with a grand jury subpoena, satisfying the requirements of Section 215.

Ultimately, similar orders would be issued approximately every three months for the next nine years, with the exception of periods when significant compliance issues arose. It would not be until August 2013 – seven years after the phone metadata program was "blessed" under the PATRIOT Act – that FISC Judge Claire Eagan would issue an opinion detailing the court's reasoning.[114]

D *Legal and Statutory Changes to the Content Collection Program*

The content collection piece of Stellar Wind was the last to get sustained attention, and this program, too, was transitioned to the FISC, as the DOJ requested that the court issue an order sanctioning the collection of phone calls and emails. (Recall that the content collection program was narrower in scope than the metadata collection programs, since the AUMF authority required that one participant be reasonably believed to be a member of al Qaeda or associated forces.)

At the time of the DOJ request, FISC orders authorized monitoring of specific, identified phone numbers or email addresses – also called "facilities" – that were used by the target. To bring the program under FISC jurisdiction, while maintaining its broad scope, the Department of Justice decided to request an order that would interpret the term "facility" to mean an entire Internet network hub.[115] Under this scheme, the FISC would pre-approve surveillance directed at an entire network switch, but the probable cause determination for specific phone numbers and email addresses selected for content collection would come after the fact.

The FISC agreed with this plan for foreign selectors, but not domestic selectors, and issued multiple orders in the winter and spring of 2007, setting out and clarifying the various requirements for the program.[116] Later that year, Congress passed the

114 *See* Amended Memorandum Opinion, *In re* Application of the Federal Bureau of Investigation for an Order Requiring the Production of Tangible Things, No. BR 13–109 (FISA Ct. Aug. 29, 2013).

115 Office of the Inspector Gen. of the Nat'l Sec. Agency, *supra* note 12, at 41; Order Regarding Preliminary Notice of Compliance Incident, *In re* Production of Tangible Things From [Redacted], No. BR 08–13 (FISA Ct. Jan. 15, 2009), https://www.eff.org/files/filenode/br_08-13_alert_list_order_1-28-09_final_redacted1.ex_-_ocr_0.pdf.

116 Order, *In re* [Redacted], No. [Redacted] (FISA Ct. Jan. 10, 2007), *in* FISA Foreign Large Content Order Documents at 129, *In re* N.Y. *Times Co. v. U.S. Dep't of Justice*, No. 14 Civ. 3948 (VSB) (S.D.N.Y. Dec. 12, 2014), https://www.documentcloud.org/documents/1379006-large-content-fisa-order-documents.html; Order, *In re* [Redacted], No. [Redacted] (FISA Ct. Jan. 10, 2007), *in* FISA Domestic Large Content Order Documents at 149, *In re* N.Y. *Times Co. v. U.S. Dep't of Justice*, No. 14 Civ. 3948 (VSB) (S.D.N.Y. Dec. 12, 2014), https://www.documentcloud.org/documents/1379006-large-content-fisa-order-documents.html; Order and Memorandum Opinion, *In re* [Redacted], No. [Redacted] (FISA Ct. Apr. 3, 2007), *in* FISA Foreign Large Content Order Documents at 129, *In re* N.Y. *Times Co. v. U.S. Dep't of Justice*, No. 14 Civ. 3948 (VSB) (S.D.N.Y. Dec. 12, 2014), https://www.documentcloud.org/documents/1379006-large-content-fisa-order-documents.html; Opinion and Order, *In re* [Redacted], No. [Redacted] (FISA Ct. May 31, 2007), *in* FISA Foreign Large Content Order Documents at 234, *In re N.Y. Times Co. v. U.S. Dep't of Justice*, No. 14 Civ. 3948 (VSB) (S.D.N.Y. Dec. 12, 2014), https://www.documentcloud.org/documents/1379006-large-content-fisa-order-documents.html; *see also* Charlie Savage, *Documents Show N.S.A.'s Wiretap Moves Before Congress's Approval*, N.Y. Times, Jan. 28, 2015, at A13, http://www.nytimes.com/2015/01/28/us/documents-show-nsas-wiretap-moves-before-congresss-approval.html; Office of the Inspector Gen. of the Nat'l Sec. Agency, *supra* note 12, at 41–42.

interim Protect America Act and then in 2008 the FISA Amendments Act (FAA), which enshrined this new "programmatic" surveillance into law.[117] Under Section 702 of the FAA, which is slated for expiration (and potential renewal) in December 2017, communications involving Americans may be collected as long as a "significant purpose" of the surveillance is to gather "foreign intelligence," which is broadly defined to include information that "relates to the conduct of the foreign affairs of the United States."[118] Foreign intelligence need not be the most significant purpose or even the main purpose, however; indeed, the primary purpose could be to gather information for a criminal case. In addition, the FAA removed the requirement that one party to the communication be affiliated with a terrorist organization; instead, one end must be "reasonably believed" to be a non-U.S. person located outside of the United States, and a non-U.S. person must be the intended "target" of the surveillance.[119]

Perhaps more importantly, under Section 702, the government does not need to obtain individualized permission from the FISA Court to intercept the permitted communications, and does not need to identify the specific person or persons who will be monitored.[120] Instead, the NSA may engage in what is called "programmatic" surveillance: the government submits for FISC approval a list of the categories of foreign intelligence that will be subject to collection, and descriptions of its targeting and minimization procedures.[121] The FISC reviews these procedures to ensure that only non-U.S. persons reasonably believed to be outside the U.S. are targeted, and that the acquisition, retention, and dissemination of incidentally acquired information about U.S. persons is properly minimized.[122] Once the court has approved the categories and minimization procedures, the FISC typically has no further oversight role until the program's annual reauthorization.[123] (By contrast, if the government intends to surveil an American, it must get a targeted FISA warrant.)

Communications to, from, or about an American may be retained for up to six years from the start of the surveillance program if they contain foreign intelligence information, among other things, and there is no time limit if the communications are encrypted.[124] While these communications involving Americans are characterized as being "incidentally collected," the legislative history suggests that capture of Americans' communications was a significant purpose of the Statue, if not the most important purpose.[125] And while information identifying Americans generally may not be disclosed

117 Foreign Intelligence Surveillance Act of 1978 Amendments Act of 2008, Pub. L. No. 110–261, 122 Stat. 2435 (2008); *see also* Office of the Inspector Gen. of the Nat'l Sec. Agency, *supra* note 12, at 42.

118 50 U.S.C. §§ 1881a(g)(2)(A)(v), 1801(e)(2)(B).

119 Edward C. Liu, Cong. Research Serv., Reauthorization of the FISA Amendments Act 7 (2012), http://www.fas.org/sgp/crs/intel/R42725.pdf; *see also* 50 U.S.C. § 1881a(a), (b).

120 50 U.S.C. § 1881a(g)(2) (2013).

121 Office of the Dir. of Nat'l Intelligence, *Section 702 of the Foreign Intelligence Surveillance Act*, IC on the Record, https://icontherecord.tumblr.com/topics/section-702 (last visited Aug. 7, 2016).

122 *Id.*

123 *See* 50 U.S.C. § 1881a(i)(1)(A), (l)(3).

124 *See* Eric. H. Holder, Jr., U.S Dep't of Justice, Minimization Procedures Used by the National Security Agency in Connection With Acquisitions of Foreign Intelligence Information Pursuant to Section 702 of the Foreign Intelligence Surveillance Act of 1978, as Amended 3, 8–9 (2011) [hereinafter NSA 702 Minimization Procedures], http://www.dni.gov/files/documents/Minimization%20Procedures%20used%20by%20NSA%20in%20Connection%20with%20FISA%20SECT%20702.pdf.

125 *See, e.g., FISA for the 21st Century: Hearing before the S. Comm. on the Judiciary*, 109th Cong. 9 (2006), http://www.gpo.gov/fdsys/pkg/CHRG-109shrg43453/pdf/CHRG-109shrg43453.pdf (statement of

unless it is necessary to understand foreign intelligence information or assess its importance, data may be kept if it is evidence of a crime and its retention or dissemination is "for law enforcement purposes."[126] This data may be kept indefinitely.[127]

This means that Section 702 surveillance essentially serves as an end run around the otherwise strict Fourth Amendment requirements that protect Americans. Thus, although the FBI would almost always need a warrant to obtain information about an American's possible involvement in a crime, the NSA can warrantlessly obtain communications without even identifying the individual to the FISA Court as long as there is some foreign intelligence purpose to the program of surveillance. The NSA can then hand the raw data over to the FBI for the Bureau's exploitation and indefinite retention. Even if the U.S. person data contains nothing of foreign intelligence value and is not evidence of a crime, the NSA may nevertheless keep the data unless it is determined that it will *never* be of foreign intelligence value – a prohibitively high standard.[128]

Finally, the minimization procedures governing the treatment of the communications collected under Section 702 allow the data to be searched for Americans' information.[129] This practice – often called a "backdoor search" – is another end run around constitutional protections for Americans. The data is collected based on an express certification that the government is targeting foreigners, not Americans – but as soon as it is in the NSA's hands, the NSA, FBI, and CIA may all look through it for the communications of "particular, known Americans," and for the FBI, there need not be any foreign intelligence purpose.[130] (The NSA may not use Americans' identifiers to search through

Michael Hayden, Director, Nat'l Sec. Agency) ("[W]hy should our laws make it more difficult to target the al Qaeda communications that are most important to us – those entering or leaving this country."); *see also* Privacy and Civil Liberties Oversight Bd., Workshop Regarding Surveillance Programs Operated Pursuant to Section 215 of the USA PATRIOT Act and Section 702 of the Foreign Intelligence Surveillance Act 109 (2013), (statement of Steven G. Bradbury, Former Principal Deputy Assistant Att'y Gen., Dep't of Justice Office) ("But it is particularly focused on communications in and out of the United States because ... those are the most important communications you want to know about if you're talking about a foreign terrorist suspect communicating to somebody you don't know inside the United States.").

126 50 U.S.C. § 1801(b).

127 NSA 702 Minimization Procedures, *supra* note 124, at § 6(a); Eric H. Holder, Jr., U.S. Dep't of Justice, Minimization Procedures Used by the Federal Bureau of Investigation in Connection With Acquisitions of Foreign Intelligence Information Pursuant to Section 702 of the Foreign Intelligence Surveillance Act of 1978 § III.G, As Amended § III.G.1.A (2014) [hereinafter FBI 702 Minimization Procedures], https://www.dni.gov/files/documents/ppd-28/2014%20FBI%20702%20Minimization%20Procedures.pdf; Eric H. Holder, Jr., U.S. Dep't of Justice, Minimization Procedures Used by the Central Intelligence Agency in Connection with Acquisitions of Foreign Intelligence Information Pursuant to Section 702 of the Foreign Intelligence Surveillance Act of 1978 §§ 3.A, 7.D, As Amended § 2 (2014) [hereinafter CIA 702 Minimization Procedures], https://www.dni.gov/files/documents/ppd-28/2014%20CIA%20702%20Minimization%20Procedures.pdf.

128 PCLOB Report on 702, *supra* note 9.

129 NSA 702 Minimization Procedures, *supra* note 124, at § 3(b)(5); FBI 702 Minimization Procedures, *supra* note 127, at § III.D; CIA 702 Minimization Procedures, *supra* note 127, at § 4.

130 Robert S. Litt, Gen. Counsel, Office of the Dir. of Nat'l Intelligence, Remarks at the Brookings Institution on Privacy, Technology and National Security: An Overview of Intelligence Collection (July 19, 2013), https://www.dni.gov/index.php/newsroom/speeches-and-interviews/195-speechesinterviews-2013/896-privacy,-technology-and-national-security-an-overview-of-intelligence-collection; *see also* Letter from Deirdre M. Walsh, Dir. of Legislative Affairs, Office of the Dir. of Nat'l Intelligence, to Sen. Ron Wyden (June 27, 2014) [hereinafter ODNI Letter to Wyden], https://www.wyden.senate.gov/download/?id=184d62f9-4f43-42d2-9841-144ba796c3d3&download=1.

the portion of communications collected via "upstream" surveillance, described below.) Indeed, the FBI comingles its Section 702 collection with its "traditional" FISA collection (i.e., that requiring a warrant) and searches everything when it opens a new national security investigation or assessment.[131] A panel convened by President Obama to review the major surveillance programs in the wake of the Snowden disclosures, which panel included a former CIA acting director and former chief counterterrorism advisor to President George W. Bush, concluded that this back door search loophole should be closed, but it remains open as of October 2016.[132]

Several months after the passage of the FAA, the FISA Court held that the warrantless surveillance program established by the statute passed constitutional muster.[133] Because the targets are foreigners, not Americans, and because there must be a foreign intelligence purpose for the surveillance, the program falls under the "foreign intelligence exception" to the warrant requirement.[134] That means that the surveillance need only meet a general "reasonableness" standard, in which the relevant national security interests are weighed against the degree of intrusion into privacy and other Fourth Amendment-protected interests. The FISC concluded that the government has a vital national security interest in conducting foreign intelligence surveillance under Section 702, and that any intrusion on individuals' Fourth Amendment interests was mitigated by the minimization procedures limiting the use and retention of information about Americans.[135]

Thus, while the passage of the FAA marked the final, formal end of Stellar Wind, each of the three programs remained in operation, premised on new legal authority but still functioning largely in secret.

II Compliance and Transparency Issues

A *Phone Metadata Program*

The FISA Court orders and opinions enshrining the metadata programs, as well as the passage of the FAA, were premised on representations that the NSA would follow minimization procedures, limit its collection, and be transparent with the court. Instead, documents disclosed after the Snowden leak reveal that the NSA repeatedly violated its own minimization procedures, disregarded orders from the FISA Court, and misled the court regarding the scope and operation of its surveillance programs.

131 ODNI Letter to Wyden, *supra* note 130.

132 *See* President's Review Grp. on Intelligence & Commc'ns Tech., Liberty and Security in a Changing World (2013) [hereinafter PRG Report], https://www.whitehouse.gov/sites/default/files/docs/2013-12-12_rg_final_report.pdf. The total number of backdoor searches is unknown; in 2015, the NSA and CIA conducted over 4500, but the FBI does not publicly release its statistics. Jenna McLaughlin, *NSA and CIA Double Their Warrantless Searches on Americans in Two Years*, Intercept (May 3, 2016), https://theintercept.com/2016/05/03/nsa-and-cia-double-their-warrantless-searches-on-americans-in-two-years/.

133 Memorandum Opinion, *In re* DNI/AG Certification, No. 702(i)-08–01 (FISA Ct. Sept. 4, 2008), https://www.dni.gov/files/documents/0315/FISC%20Opinion%20September%204%202008.pdf.

134 *See In re* Directives Pursuant to Section 105B of Foreign Intelligence Surveillance Act, 551 F.3d 1004 (FISA Ct. Rev. Aug. 22, 2008) (No. 08–01) [hereinafter *In re* Directives], https://fas.org/irp/agency/doj/fisa/fiscr082208.pdf; 50 U.S.C. § 1805(a)(2).

135 *See* Elizabeth Goitein, *The FBI's Warrantless Surveillance Back Door Just Opened a Little Wider*, Just Security (Apr. 21, 2016), https://www.justsecurity.org/30699/fbis-warrantless-surveillance-door-opened-wider/.

In January 2009, for instance, Department of Justice officials notified the FISC that the NSA had been searching the phone metadata database in ways that were contrary to the court's orders, including the "alert list" described earlier.[136] Shortly after, Judge Reggie Walton issued an order on behalf of the FISC, expressing "exceptional[] concern[] about what appears to be a flagrant violation" of the court's orders, one that was "directly contrary to the sworn attestations of several Executive Branch officials" about how the data was used.[137] In response, the government urged him not to shut the program down, explaining that NSA was terminating the alert-list feature and launching an end-to-end review of both bulk metadata programs to find and fix any problems.[138] Judge Walton was not done with his criticisms, however. In a March 2009 order, he observed that the privacy rules the court had imposed for handling the phone metadata had "been so frequently and systematically violated that it can fairly be said" that the safeguards – a "critical element" for obtaining the FISA Court's legal blessing for the program in the first place – had "never functioned effectively."[139] The FISC's authorization of the phone metadata program had rested on a "misperception," dating from the beginning of the program, of how the agency used the data, "buttressed by repeated inaccurate statements made in the government's submissions, and despite a government-devised and court-mandated oversight regime."[140] He concluded, bitingly:

> The minimization procedures proposed by the government in each successive application and approved and adopted as binding by the orders of the FISC have been so frequently and systemically violated that it can fairly be said that this critical element of the overall [bulk metadata] regime has never functioned effectively.[141]

Judge Walton did not shutter the program, but he ordered the NSA to seek approval from the court for every query unless there was an "imminent threat to human life."[142] In addition, that summer, he ordered the NSA to provide a weekly report of any phone metadata information it shared outside the agency, in light of its previous noncompliance with court orders requiring minimization.[143] Until September 2009, every renewal

136 Ellen Nakashima et al., *Declassified Court Documents Highlight NSA Violations in Data Collection for Surveillance*, Wash. Post (Sept. 10, 2013), https://www.washingtonpost.com/world/national-security/declassified-court-documents-highlight-nsa-violations/2013/09/10/60b5822c-1a4b-11e3-a628-7e6dde8f889d_story.html.

137 Order Regarding Preliminary Notice of Compliance Incident, *In re* Production of Tangible Things from [Redacted], No. BR 08–13 (FISA Ct. Jan. 15, 2009), https://www.eff.org/files/filenode/br_08-13_alert_list_order_1-28-09_final_redacted1.ex_-_ocr_0.pdf.

138 *See* Memorandum of the United States in Response to the Court's Order of January 28, 2009, *In re* Production of Tangible Things from [Redacted], No. BR 08–13 (FISA Ct. Feb. 12, 2009), https://www.documentcloud.org/documents/1348678-fisa-court-feb-12-2009-memorandum-of-us.html; *see also* Jane Chong, *The Latest NSA Documents III: The Government Responds*, Lawfare (Sept. 11, 2013), https://www.lawfareblog.com/latest-nsa-documents-iii-government-responds.

139 *See* Order, *In re* Production of Tangible Things from [Redacted], No. BR 08–13 (FISA Ct. Mar. 2, 2009), https://www.documentcloud.org/documents/1348651-walton-march-2-2009-order-from-fisc.html.

140 *Id.* at 11.

141 *Id.*

142 *Id.* at 18–20.

143 Order, *In re* Application of the Federal Bureau of Investigation for an Order Requiring the Production of Tangible Things from [Redacted], No. BR 09–06 (FISA Ct. June 22, 2009), http://www.dni.gov/files/documents/section/pub_Jun%2022%202009%20Order.pdf.

of the program included the additional minimization and oversight procedures articulated in the March 2009 order.[144]

In June 2009, the NSA finished the end-to-end review of the phone metadata program that it had promised to the FISA Court in an attempt to stave off a shutdown of the program; in August 2009, it shared the results of the review with the FISA Court, accompanied by representations about extra steps it planned to take to mollify the court and bring the program into compliance.[145] Among other things, the review disclosed that a repository of individual metadata one-hop chains had not been audited until February 2009 to ensure queries were supported by reasonable articulable suspicion.[146] The review also revealed other issues related to the RAS standard and sharing of unminimized metadata or query results, both of which the NSA asserted it had remedied by the time of its submission to the court.[147] In September 2009, in response to the government's submission, Judge Walton renewed the government's authority to engage in bulk metadata collection for 90 days and finally lifted the requirement that the NSA get court approval for every individual query.[148] At the same time, the court imposed some additional minimization and oversight procedures, including requiring the NSA to perform "spot checks" on a sampling of call detail records to look for inadvertently collected content; directing DOJ attorneys to periodically review metadata queries; implementing heightened communication protocols between the NSA and DOJ; and requiring both the DOJ and the FISA Court to review and approve any new automated processes for querying metadata.[149]

Almost immediately after these new controls were put into place, however, the NSA again violated them, which the DOJ dutifully reported to the FISA Court. After ordering DOJ lawyers to appear in court and testify about the new compliance incidents – which Judge Walton called "deeply troubl[ing]"[150] – he nevertheless renewed the government's

144 *See* Primary Order, *In re* Application of the Federal Bureau of Investigation for an Order Requiring the Production of Tangible Things from [Redacted], No. BR 09–01 (FISA Ct. Mar. 5, 2009), http://www.dni.gov/files/documents/11714/FISC%20Order,%20BR%2009-01.pdf; Primary Order, *In re* Application of the Federal Bureau of Investigation for an Order Requiring the Production of Tangible Things from [Redacted], No. BR 09–06 (FISA Ct. May 29, 2009), http://www.dni.gov/files/documents/11714/FISC%20Order,%20BR%2009-06.pdf; Primary Order, *In re* Application of the Federal Bureau of Investigation for an Order Requiring the Production of Tangible Things from [Redacted], No. BR 09–09 (FISA Ct. July 9, 2009), http://www.dni.gov/files/documents/0708/BR%2009-09%20Primary%20Order.pdf.

145 *Business Records FISA Team*, Business Records FISA NSA Review (2009) [hereinafter End-to-End Review], http://www.dni.gov/files/documents/section/pub_NSA%20Business%20Records%20FISA%20Review%2020130909.pdf; Report of the United States, *In re* Application of the Federal Bureau of Investigation for an Order Requiring the Production of Tangible Things from [Redacted], No. BR 09–09 (FISA Ct. Aug. 19, 2009), http://www.dni.gov/files/documents/section/pub_August%2019%202009%20Report%20of%20the%20US%20with%20Attachments%2020130910.pdf; *see also* Raffaela Wakeman & Wells Bennett, *The Latest NSA Documents V: the NSA Investigates Its Metadata Compliance Problems, Takes Remedial Steps, and Reports Back to the FISC*, Lawfare (Sept. 12, 2013), https://www.lawfareblog.com/latest-nsa-documents-v-nsa-investigates-its-metadata-compliance-problems-takes-remedial-steps-and.

146 End-to-End Review, *supra* note 145, at 8–9.

147 *Id.* at 11–17.

148 Primary Order, *In re* Application of the Federal Bureau of Investigation for an Order Requiring the Production of Tangible Things from [Redacted], No. BR 09–13 (FISA Ct. Sept. 3, 2009), http://www.dni.gov/files/documents/section/pub_Sep32009PrimaryOrderfromFISC.pdf.

149 *See, e.g.*, Wells Bennett, *The Latest NSA Documents VI: Non-Compliance Redux, With More DOJ*, Lawfare (Sept. 13, 2013), https://www.lawfareblog.com/latest-nsa-documents-vi-non-compliance-redux-more-doj.

150 Order Regarding Further Compliance Incidents, *In re* Application of the Federal Bureau of Investigation for an Order Requiring the Production of Tangible Things from [Redacted], No. BR 09–13, (FISA Ct.

authority to engage in bulk metadata collection for another 90 days, though he ordered the NSA to beef up its reporting to the court and limit the sharing of the metadata query results.[151] The 90-day extensions would continue until the program was ended in 2015 by the USA FREEDOM Act, described below.

B *Email Metadata Program*

The email metadata program was also plagued by compliance issues related to collection, access, and dissemination. In late 2009 or early 2010, the NSA completed an end-to-end review concerning its Internet metadata program that identified several compliance incidents, including eleven "newly identified areas of concern."[152] The NSA's disclosures included querying practices that were not compliant with the RAS process; sharing of unminimized querying results with NSA analysts not authorized to access the Internet communications metadata; and access by the FBI, CIA, and National Counterterrorism Center (NCTC) to a query result database without the necessary determinations that the U.S. person information in the database was related to counterterrorism.[153]

The FISC reviewed these incidents as it weighed the government's request to restart – and expand – the program after it was allowed to lapse for several months due to the complexity involved in resolving the compliance issues.[154] In response, the FISC put in place new training and reporting requirements.[155] The FISC also sharply criticized disclosures of overcollection of Internet communications metadata, including acquisition of data beyond the initial FISC-approved categories, which had occurred continuously since the inception of the program.[156] The FISC observed caustically that in light of the duration of noncompliance and the ostensible supervisory measures in place while it was occurring, "those responsible for conducting oversight at NSA failed to do so."[157]

The FISC ultimately granted approval, in part, for the government's application to restart bulk Internet metadata collection, but not without first castigating the government for its prior handling of the program:

Sept. 25, 2009), http://www.dni.gov/files/documents/section/pub_Sept25 2009 Order Regarding Further Compliance Incidents.pdf.

151 Primary Order, *In re* Application of the Federal Bureau of Investigation for an Order Requiring the Production of Tangible Things from [Redacted], No. BR 09–15 (FISA Ct. Oct. 30, 2009), http://www.dni.gov/files/documents/0708/BR%2009–15%20Primary%20Order.pdf; Supplemental Opinion and Order, *In re* Application of the Federal Bureau of Investigation for an Order Requiring the Production of Tangible Things from [Redacted], No. BR 09–15 (FISA Ct. Nov. 5, 2009), http://www.dni.gov/files/documents/section/pub_Nov 5 2009 Supplemental Opinion and Order.pdf; *see also* Bennett, *supra* note 149.

152 Pen Register/ Trap and Trace Team, Pen Register/Trap and Trace FISA NSA Review (2010), https://www.dni.gov/files/0808/Final%20062.NSA's%20Pen%20RegisterTrap%20and%20Trace%20FISA%20Review%20Report.pdf.

153 Memorandum Opinion [Redacted], No. PR/TT [Redacted], at 15–18 (FISA Ct. [Redacted]), https://www.dni.gov/files/documents/1118/CLEANEDPRTT%202.pdf.

154 Office of the Dir. of Nat'l Intelligence, *DNI Clapper Declassifies Additional Intelligence Community Documents Regarding Collection under Section 501 of the Foreign Intelligence Surveillance Act*, IC On The Record (Nov. 18, 2013), https://icontherecord.tumblr.com/post/67419963949/dni-clapper-declassifies-additional-intelligence.

155 [Redacted], Docket No. PR/TT [Redacted], at 96–97 (FISA Ct. [Redacted]), https://www.dni.gov/files/documents/1118/CLEANEDPRTT%202.pdf.

156 *Id.* at 20.

157 *Id.* at 22.

> The history of material misstatements in prior applications and non-compliance with prior orders gives the Court pause before approving such an expanded collection. The government's poor track record with bulk PR/TT acquisition ... presents threshold concerns about whether implementation will conform with, or exceed, what the government represents and the Court may approve.[158]

C *FISA Amendments Act: Programmatic Collection*

When it comes to the Section 702 program, the biggest surprise may be what is legal. But the revamped content collection program has faced compliance problems as well. As the Snowden documents reveal, the NSA has two main surveillance programs that it carries out under its Section 702 authority. The first is known by its code name, PRISM. Under PRISM, the government compels electronic communications service providers (e.g., Google, Facebook, and Microsoft) to give the NSA any communications sent to and from a specified selector, such as an email address.[159] Copies of this raw data may be shared with the CIA and FBI.[160]

The second (and far more controversial) is called "upstream" surveillance. As the name suggests, this program involves the collection of data – both phone calls and Internet communications – as they transit the telecommunications "backbone," the large fiber-optic cables that carry global communications traffic between networks and data centers managed by service providers. While initial reports suggested that the NSA itself was vacuuming up every communication passing over the backbone, recently disclosed documents indicate that companies operating the Internet instead do searches of transiting emails for the NSA's selectors, and send the selected emails to the surveillance agency for further analysis.[161] (Email surveillance conducted under Executive Order 12333 is much broader: EO 12333 allows for collection of communications outside the United States, as well as emails between foreigners that transit U.S. territory, and can sweep in a much larger mass of emails.)

There are several notable aspects of upstream surveillance. First, it includes not only communications that are to or from a particular foreign intelligence selector, but also communications that are *about* the selector.[162] (Note that emails and phone numbers can be selectors, but names cannot. Thus, an email just discussing Vladimir Putin by name could not be collected under Section 702 authority, but an email containing

158 *Id.* at 72.

159 PCLOB Report on 702, *supra* note 9, at 33–34.

160 *Id.* at 34.

161 See Charlie Savage, *N.S.A. Gets Less Web Data than Believed, Report Suggests*, N.Y. Times, Feb. 17, 2016, at A16, http://www.nytimes.com/2016/02/17/us/report-says-networks-give-nsa-less-data-than-long-suspected.html; Office of the Inspector General of the Nat'l Sec. Agency, Final Report of the Audit on the FISA Amendments Act §702 Detasking Requirements 92 (2010), https://www.documentcloud.org/documents/2712306-Savage-NYT-FOIA-IG-Reports-702-2.html. *But see* Siobhan Gorman & Jennifer Valentino-DeVries, *New Details Show Broader NSA Surveillance Reach*, Wall St. J. (Aug. 20, 2013), http://www.wsj.com/articles/SB10001424127887324108204579022874091732470?mg=id-wsj (reporting that the NSA instead requests blocks of traffic based on certain geographic indicators, and then copies the traffic and keeps communications based on "strong selectors," which could include an email address or a "large block of computer addresses that correspond to an organization it is interested in. In making these decisions, the NSA can look at content of communications as well as information about who is sending the data.").

162 PCLOB Report on 702, *supra* note 9, at 7, 37.

his email address – say, vladimir.putin@email.ru – would be picked up, regardless of whether Putin himself is a participant in the communication.[163]) According to the NSA, this is a function of the way email data traverses cable lines: because emails are broken up into "packets" of data and only reassembled when the email reaches its destination, there is no way to determine at the outset whether a particular selector appears in the "to" or "from" line of an email or in the body of the message instead, and it must thus all be collected to ensure accurate targeting.[164]

Upstream collection also results in a particularly egregious type of overcollection and compliance violation. Because the collection mechanism is imperfect, and because of the way emails are transmitted, upstream surveillance captures email in-boxes with more than one email message, some of which may not contain the designated selector at all and may in fact be between two Americans on American soil.[165] These are called "multiple communications transactions," or MCTs. The NSA employs technical filters to screen out those wholly domestic communications, but with imperfect results; in 2011, after three years of secretly collecting MCTs, the government finally acknowledged to the FISC that tens of thousands of Americans' communications may have been wrongly collected this way.[166] The communications were kept for at least five years and were not handled differently or specially marked, despite the fact that they were unlikely to contain information with foreign intelligence value.[167]

In October 2011, FISC Judge John Bates concluded that the collection of MCTs was problematic on both statutory and constitutional grounds.[168] Describing the privacy intrusion from MCT collection as "substantial," he opined that the government's disclosure "materially and fundamentally alters the statutory and constitutional analysis" that had informed the FISC's previous approvals of Section 702 collection.[169] In light of the earlier compliance issues with Section 215, the court was "troubled that the government's revelations regarding the NSA's acquisition of Internet transactions mark the third instance in less than three years in which the government has disclosed a substantial misrepresentation regarding the scope of a major collection program."[170] In addition,

163 *See, e.g.*, *id.* at 33 ("Because such terms would not identify specific communications facilities, selectors may not be key words (such as 'bomb' or 'attack'), or the names of targeted individuals ('Osama Bin Laden').").

164 *See, e.g.*, Privacy & Civil Liberties Oversight Bd., Recommendations Assessment Report (2016), https://www.pclob.gov/library/Recommendations_Assessment_Report_20160205.pdf (noting that "it is largely unfeasible to limit 'about' collection without also eliminating a substantial portion of upstream's 'to/from' collection"). Notably, the NSA announced in April 2017 that it would be discontinuing "about" collection from upstream surveillance; it maintained that the change would exclude some relevant "to" and "from" communications, but believed the change was nevertheless a "responsible and careful approach." Statement, National Security Agency, NSA Stops Certain Section 702 "Upstream" Activities (Apr. 28, 2017), available at https://www.nsa.gov/news-features/press-room/statements/2017-04-28-702-statement.shtml.

165 PCLOB Report on 702, *supra* note 9, at 7.

166 *Id.* at 38–39; *see also* Memorandum Opinion at 72, [Redacted], No. [Redacted] (FISA Ct. Oct. 3, 2011), https://lawfare.s3-us-west-2.amazonaws.com/staging/s3fs-public/uploads/2013/08/162016974-FISA-court-opinion-with-exemptions.pdf (observing that "each year, NSA's upstream collection likely results in the acquisition of roughly two to ten thousand discrete wholly domestic communications that are neither to, from, nor about a targeted selector, as well as tens of thousands of other communications that are to or from a United States person or a person in the United States but that are neither to, from, nor about a targeted selector").

167 Memorandum Opinion at 59–61, [Redacted], No. [Redacted], (FISA Ct. Oct. 3, 2011), https://lawfare.s3-us-west-2.amazonaws.com/staging/s3fs-public/uploads/2013/08/162016974-FISA-court-opinion-with-exemptions.pdf.

168 *Id.*

169 *Id.* at 16, 72.

170 *Id.* at 16, 17 n.14.

because there was no direct connection to an actual target, the MCT collection violated the Fourth Amendment by failing to comply with its reasonableness standard.[171]

As a remedial measure, the government offered to segregate message streams that might have some purely domestic messages intermingled and put those into a special archive for extra scrutiny and more limited access.[172] The government also reduced its retention period of MCTs to three years from the start of surveillance. The FISC accepted these changes.[173] The following year, the NSA purged all the raw data that had been collected before the creation of these new restrictions, judging that it would be too difficult to sift through the store of data and identify the wholly domestic communications.[174]

III Snowden Disclosures and Subsequent Legal Changes

The next year, in the spring of 2013, Edward Snowden acted on his disillusionment with James Clapper and the surveillance apparatus as a whole, and walked out of the NSA with a cache of documents. The disclosures that began that June are still yielding new information and new insight into past events. One of the first major consequences of the leaks – in addition to the details of previously secret programs being splashed across the front pages – was that the FISC was finally shamed, seven years late, into producing a written legal justification for the phone metadata program.

A *New Court Decisions*

In August 2013, FISC Judge Claire Eagan issued an opinion concluding that the phone metadata program complied with the Fourth Amendment, adopting the government's argument from years earlier that *Smith v. Maryland* blesses the arrangement.[175] The decision ratified the program's compliance with Section 215 of the PATRIOT Act, emphasizing the minimization procedures in place to protect information about U.S. persons.[176] Judge Eagan also embraced the government's approach to relevance, holding that bulk collection was necessary to unearth the connections between "known and unknown international terrorist operatives as part of authorized investigations."[177] In the absence of a statutory definition for "relevant," she held that the standard is met if there are "reasonable grounds to believe that the information sought to be produced has *some bearing* on [the government's] investigations" of terrorist organizations.[178] Finally, Judge Eagan

171 *Id.* at 78–79.

172 *See* Charlie Savage, Power Wars: Inside Obama's Post-9/11 Presidency 572 (2015).

173 Memorandum Opinion (*Bates Opinion & Order Part I*), [Redacted], No. [Redacted] (FISA Ct. Nov. 30, 2011), https://www.dni.gov/files/documents/November%202011%20Bates%20Opinion%20and%20Order%20Part%201.pdf; Memorandum Opinion (*Bates Opinion & Order Part II*), [Redacted], No. [Redacted] (FISA Ct. Nov. 30, 2011), http://www.dni.gov/files/documents/November%202011%20Bates%20Opinion%20and%20Order%20Part%202.pdf.

174 Memorandum Opinion (*Bates Opinion & Order*), [Redacted], No. [Redacted] (FISA Ct. Sept. 2012), https://www.dni.gov/files/documents/September%202012%20Bates%20Opinion%20and%20Order.pdf; *see also* Charlie Savage, Power Wars: Inside Obama's Post-9/11 Presidency 573 (2015).

175 Amended Memorandum Opinion, *In re* Application of the Federal Bureau of Investigation for an Order Requiring the Production of Tangible Things from [Redacted], No. BR 13–109 (FISA Ct. Aug. 29, 2013), http://www.fisc.uscourts.gov/sites/default/files/BR%2013-109%20Order-1.pdf.

176 *Id.* at 11, 23.

177 *Id.* at 18; see also *id.* at 21 (referencing the government's 2006 Memorandum of Law).

178 *Id.* at 19 (emphasis added).

determined that Congress had ratified the FISC's secret understanding of Section 215 by reenacting the statute in May 2011 – despite ample evidence that most members of the House of Representatives were unaware of the court's interpretation.[179]

In October 2013, Judge Mary McLaughlin adopted and expanded on Judge Eagan's analysis.[180] In particular, Judge McLaughlin distinguished the collection of bulk phone metadata from the long-term monitoring of an individual's location, which five Supreme Court justices (in two concurrences) suggested might implicate the Fourth Amendment in a 2012 case called *United States v. Jones*.[181] Judge McLaughlin emphasized that the gathered phone metadata did not include a location element, and observed that the third-party doctrine was still good law, despite a suggestion from Justice Sotomayor in her *Jones* concurrence that it may be time to revisit it.[182] In light of these factors, she granted another 90-day renewal.

Separately, several plaintiffs went to federal court to bring challenges to the bulk phone records program. While several of the opinions held that the program violated the PATRIOT Act and the Fourth Amendment, neither case resulted in closure of the program, largely for procedural reasons.[183] The disputes were ultimately mooted by the passage of the USA FREEDOM Act, described below. (An earlier suit by the ACLU challenging NSA surveillance was dismissed by the Supreme Court in 2013 on the grounds that the plaintiffs could not prove that they had been monitored–this was four months before Snowden's documents revealed the breadth of the programs.[184])

B *Presidential Policy Directive PPD-28*

In addition to these judicial developments, in early 2014 President Obama issued a presidential policy directive announcing several reforms to the government's signals intelligence activities and, in an accompanying speech, called for additional reform measures to be considered by relevant agencies and Congress. Called PPD-28, the order directed the Director of National Intelligence (DNI) to maintain a list of the permissible uses of bulk signals intelligence collection and directed the President's National Security Advisor to review these permissible uses on an annual basis.[185] That list ultimately identified six permissible uses of signals intelligence collected in bulk: detecting and

179 *Id.* at 23–28; *see also Am. Civil Liberties Union v. Clapper*, 785 F.3d 787, 820 (2d Cir. 2015) ("In 2011, briefing papers were also provided to the Intelligence Committees, but only the Senate Committee shared the papers with other members of that body who were not committee members. The House Intelligence Committee did not share the papers at all with non-members, leaving the non-committee Representatives in the dark as to the program.").

180 Memorandum Opinion at 3, *In re* Application of the Federal Bureau of Investigation for an Order Requiring the Production of Tangible Things, No. BR 13–158 (FISA Ct. Oct. 11, 2013), http://www.fisc.uscourts.gov/sites/default/files/BR%2013–158%20Memorandum-1.pdf.

181 *Id.* at 4–6 (citing *United States v. Jones*, 132 S.Ct. 945 (2012)).

182 *Id.* at 5.

183 *Klayman v. Obama*, 957 F. Supp. 2d 1 (D.D.C. 2013), *vacated and remanded*, 800 F.3d 559 (D.C. Cir. 2015); *Am. Civil Liberties Union v. Clapper*, 959 F. Supp. 2d 724 (S.D.N.Y. 2013), *aff'd in part, vacated in part, remanded*, 785 F.3d 787 (2d Cir. 2015).

184 *Clapper*, 785 F.3d.

185 Exec. Office of the President, PRESIDENTIAL POLICY DIRECTIVE/PPD-28 4 (2014) [hereinafter PPD-28], https://www.whitehouse.gov/the-press-office/2014/01/17/presidential-policy-directive-signals-intelligence-activities.

preventing espionage, terrorism, proliferation of weapons of mass destruction, cybersecurity threats, threats to U.S. armed forces, and transnational crime.[186] PPD-28 also calls on the DNI to ensure that all component agencies of the Intelligence Community establish policies and procedures that minimize dissemination and retention of personal information, ensure data security and proper access, and facilitate effective oversight and auditing of agency handling of personal information.[187] Significantly, the directive also requires these safeguards to be applied equally to all individuals regardless of nationality as long as it is "consistent with national security."[188]

President Obama's speech releasing PPD-28 also contained several pledges to a public concerned about the revelations regarding the government's surveillance practices. First, he announced that he was directing the DNI to conduct annual declassification reviews of future FISC opinions and called on Congress to authorize a panel of special advocates to better inform the FISC in significant cases.[189] Next, the President announced he was asking the Attorney General and DNI to institute reforms that would place additional restrictions in the criminal context on the government's ability to retain, search, and use communications between Americans and foreign citizens incidentally collected under Section 702.[190]

Finally, the President mandated two significant changes to the Section 215 program. Specifically, he ordered that collected metadata only be queried up to *two* hops from the original selector instead of three, and he called on the Attorney General and FISC to condition querying on first obtaining a judicial finding that the NSA had met the RAS standard, rather than permitting the NSA to make the determination on its own. The following month, the FISC approved the government's request to modify the most recent bulk collection order to reflect President Obama's ordered changes.[191] The FISC order required that telephony metadata only be queried after a judicial finding that there is a reasonable articulable suspicion that the selection term is associated with an approved international terrorist organization.[192]

C *Privacy and Civil Liberties Oversight Board*

Just a week after the President's address, however, the Section 215 program was pushed onto much shakier legal ground. In late February, the Privacy and Civil Liberties

186 Press Release, Office of the Dir. of Nat'l Intelligence, List of Permissible Uses of Signals Intelligence Collected in Bulk (Feb. 10, 2014), https://www.dni.gov/index.php/newsroom/press-releases/198-press-releases-2014/1014-list-of-permissible-uses-of-signals-intelligence-collected-in-bulk.

187 PPD-28, *supra* note 185, at 5–7.

188 *Id.* at 5.

189 President Barack Obama, Remarks on the Results of Signals Intelligence Review (Jan. 17, 2014), https://www.lawfareblog.com/text-presidents-remarks-nsa-and-surveillance.

190 *Id. See also* Office of the Dir. of Nat'l Intelligence, *Strengthening Privacy and Civil Liberties Protections*, *in* Signals Intelligence Reform 2015 Anniversary Report, IC on the Record, https://icontherecord.tumblr.com/ppd-28/2015/privacy-civil-liberties (describing the new minimization procedures).

191 Office of the Dir. of Nat'l Intelligence, *FISC Approves Government's Request to Modify Telephony Metadata Program*, IC on the Record (Feb. 6, 2014), https://icontherecord.tumblr.com/post/75842023946/fisc-approves-governments-request-to-modify.

192 *Id.*

Oversight Board (PCLOB) – an independent agency established at the recommendation of the 9/11 Commission that is charged with evaluating executive branch counterterrorism initiatives and balancing them against privacy and civil liberties values – released a report that was highly critical of the phone metadata program.[193] In its report, its first on the NSA's surveillance operations, the Board concluded that language of Section 215 did not provide an adequate legal basis to support the bulk telephone records collection program. Because the call records collected by the NSA were not connected to a discrete, authorized, ongoing investigation at the time the government obtained them, the collection did not accord with the statutory language; moreover, bulk records could not be deemed "relevant" to an investigation without redefining the word in a way that was "circular, unlimited in scope, and out of step with precedent."[194] The PCLOB also found that bulk records collection "implicates constitutional concerns under the First and Fourth Amendments," but stopped short of concluding the program was wholly unconstitutional.[195]

In addition, the PCLOB rejected the "reenactment doctrine" theory pressed by the government and accepted by Judge Eagan.[196] Because the doctrine is typically used as an interpretive tool for resolving statutory ambiguity, it had no application to Section 215, given that the bulk collection program was clearly not authorized by the plain words of the statute.[197] The PCLOB was also persuaded that much of Congress was simply unaware of the relevant information.[198]

Ultimately, the PCLOB made several key recommendations, including that the government end the bulk collection program, delete its bulk database, and make only individual requests to the providers as needed. The Board cautioned against requiring providers to keep calling records for a specific length of time, and suggested that the NSA should immediately reduce its own retention period from five years to three.[199]

On July 2, 2014, the PCLOB released its report and recommendations on the Section 702 content collection program.[200] The Board concluded that PRISM collection – issuing targeted requests for information directly to the providers – was authorized by statute.[201] The Board gave its approval to the upstream component of Section 702 collection as well, finding that the statute could reasonably be interpreted to permit collection of communications not just to and from but also about the selector.[202] The report did express concern that the potentially large scope of incidental collection of U.S. persons' communications, and the querying of this collected data for communications involving Americans, "push the program close to the line of constitutional reasonableness under the Fourth Amendment."[203] The Board ultimately concluded that the program did not violate the Constitution, but

193 *About the Board*, Privacy & Civil Liberties Oversight Bd., https://www.pclob.gov/about-us.html (last visited Aug. 7, 2016); PCLOB Report on 215, *supra* note 110.
194 PCLOB Report on 215, *supra* note 110, at 57.
195 *Id.* at 16, 103.
196 *Id.* at 95.
197 *Id.* at 95–96.
198 *Id.* at 96
199 *Id.* at 170.
200 PCLOB Report on 702, *supra* note 9.
201 *Id.* at 81–82.
202 *Id.* at 9, 84–88.
203 *Id.* at 9, 88, 95–97.

warned that the expansion of collection about Americans, or additional uses of that information, could "push the program over the line."[204]

The PCLOB nonetheless made recommendations to improve the Section 702 collections. These include revising the NSA's targeting procedures to better ensure selectors are likely to return valuable foreign intelligence information and updating the FBI's minimization procedures when conducting U.S. person queries of the collected data.[205] The PCLOB also called for additional limits on the FBI's use and dissemination of Section 702 data in connection with criminal investigations unrelated to foreign intelligence matters.[206] (Perhaps ironically, a decision released by the FISC revealed that the FBI did modify its minimization procedures, but perhaps not in the direction the PCLOB envisioned: as explained below, the FBI redefined the term "query" to permit itself to search portions of the Section 702 database for any reason whatsoever.[207]) To reduce the incidental collection of Americans' domestic communications via upstream collection, the PCLOB recommended that the NSA and DOJ periodically assess whether filtering techniques can be improved.[208]

D *President's Review Group*

Another group had also been tasked with reviewing the legality of the Section 215 and Section 702 programs: in August 2013, President Obama announced the creation of a Review Group on Intelligence and Communications Technologies, composed of five experts from across the political spectrum.[209] In December 2013, the Review Group released its final report on the government's foreign intelligence collection activities, making over 40 recommendations, including proposed reforms to both programs.[210]

The Review Group added to the chorus of voices critical of the Section 215 phone metadata program, concluding that the program "was not essential to preventing attacks" and that any vital data could have been obtained using individual business records orders.[211] The report recommended that Congress pass legislation transitioning bulk metadata storage from the government to the providers or a third party, recommendations that were ultimately reflected in the passage of the USA FREEDOM Act in mid-2015.[212] The Review Group also called on Congress to amend Section 215 to narrow the scope of collection.[213]

By contrast, the Review Group described Section 702 as an important and effective tool for preventing terrorist attacks.[214] The report nevertheless recognized that better

204 *Id.* at 97.
205 *Id.* at 134–37.
206 *Id.* at 137.
207 Memorandum Opinion & Order at 3, [Redacted], No. [Redacted], (FISA Ct. Nov. 6, 2015), https://www.dni.gov/files/documents/20151106-702Mem_Opinion_Order_for_Public_Release.pdf.
208 PCLOB Report on 702, *supra* note 9, at 143.
209 *About the Review Group on Intelligence and Communications Technologies*, Office of the Dir. of Nat'l Intelligence, https://www.dni.gov/index.php/intelligence-community/review-group.
210 PRG Report, *supra* note 132.
211 *Id.* at 104.
212 *Id.* at 25.
213 *Id.* at 24.
214 *Id.* at 145.

privacy protections needed to be in place for non-targeted U.S. persons, and that Section 702's use as a tool for gathering evidence against U.S. persons needed to be restricted.[215] To those ends, the Review Group recommended that intercepted communications that include a U.S. person or reveal information about a U.S. person should be purged from government storage unless they are believed to have foreign intelligence value and should be prohibited from being used as evidence in any proceeding against a U.S. person.[216] The report also recommended that the government should only be allowed to search Section 702-acquired data in an effort to identify the communications of a U.S. person when it is necessary to prevent a threat of death or serious bodily harm or the government has obtained a warrant based on probable cause that the individual is planning acts of international terrorism.[217] Notably, as of October 2016, these recommendations have not been enacted.

E *USA FREEDOM Act*

Section 215 was scheduled to sunset on May 31, 2015. A fierce legislative fight over the new scope of the NSA's phone metadata collection authority occupied much of the year leading up to the expiration, until the Senate finally passed the USA FREEDOM Act on June 2, 2015, one day after the program expired.[218] Most significantly, USA FREEDOM ended the government's bulk collection of phone call metadata as of that November, replacing it with a system that keeps the records in the providers' hands and requires the government to get approval from the FISC to ask the providers to conduct searches on the basis of a "specific selection term."[219] A specific selection term is something that "specifically identifies a person, account, address, or personal device," and it must "limit, to the greatest extent reasonably practicable, the scope of tangible things sought."[220] The government must also demonstrate to the FISC that there are reasonable grounds to believe that the call detail records are relevant to an authorized investigation and that there is a reasonable articulable suspicion that the specific selection term is associated with a foreign agent engaged in, or planning acts of, international terrorism.[221]

USA FREEDOM also made a few modest reforms to FISC procedure and prescribed new disclosure requirements. For example, the Act provides for the appointment of amici curiae – or "special advocates" – to assist the FISC when the court believes it is faced with an application that "presents a novel or significant interpretation of the law,"[222] and requires the Director of National Intelligence (DNI) to perform a declassification review of any FISC opinion that "includes a significant construction or interpretation."[223]

215 *Id.* at 150.
216 *Id.* at 28–29.
217 *Id.*
218 H.R. 2048, 114th Cong. § 1 (2015) (enacted); *U.S. Senate Roll Call Votes 114th Congress – 1st Session*, U.S. Sen., http://www.senate.gov/legislative/LIS/roll_call_lists/roll_call_vote_cfm.cfm?congress=114&session=1&vote=00201.
219 Cody Poplin, *NSA Ends Bulk Collection of Telephony Metadata under Section 215*, Lawfare (Nov. 30, 2015), https://www.lawfareblog.com/nsa-ends-bulk-collection-telephony-metadata-under-section-215.
220 USA FREEDOM Act of 2015, Pub. L. No. 114–23 § 107(k)(4)(A)(i), 129 Stat. 268, 274 (2015).
221 USA FREEDOM Act of 2015, Pub. L. No. 114–23 § 101(a)(3)(C), 129 Stat. 268, 270 (2015).
222 USA FREEDOM Act of 2015, Pub. L. No. 114–23 § 401(i)(2)(A), 129 Stat. 268, 279 (2015).
223 USA FREEDOM Act of 2015, Pub. L. No. 114–23 § 402, 129 Stat. 268, 280 (2015).

In April 2016, the Office of the DNI (ODNI) released the first FISC opinion and order, which approved a government application for call detail records under the new standards created by the USA FREEDOM Act.[224] The opinion was mostly unremarkable, with one exception. The government's proposed minimization procedures called for the "prompt destruction" of call detail records that were determined not to contain foreign intelligence information, as required by the USA FREEDOM Act.[225] At the same time, USA FREEDOM requires that the minimization procedures allow, for law enforcement purposes, the retention and dissemination of information that is evidence of a crime. Neither the Act nor the proposed minimization procedures addressed what to do about information that does not contain foreign intelligence (and thus should be promptly destroyed) but is evidence of a crime (and thus may be retained and shared). The FISC ultimately resolved this potential conflict by explaining that "prompt" does not mean "instant"; call detail records containing criminal evidence – but not foreign intelligence – could therefore be retained for a reasonable period of time to permit access by law enforcement agencies before their ultimate destruction.[226]

Also in April 2016, ODNI released a FISC opinion and order, dating from November 2015, regarding the Section 702 programmatic surveillance certifications requested by the government during 2015.[227] The opinion revealed revisions made to the NSA's targeting procedures, a significant change made to the FBI's minimization procedures,[228] and a series of compliance incidents involving the FBI and NSA since the previous year's certification.[229] The FISC's review of these issues included the first appointment of an amicus curiae in accordance with USA FREEDOM's "special advocate" provision.[230]

During the year under review, the NSA had made its targeting procedures more rigorous and less likely to target U.S. persons, in line with a recommendation from the PCLOB. The changes were meant to introduce a more "particularized and fact-based" assessment of the targets' likelihood of communicating foreign intelligence information, and to require written explanations of the assessments to facilitate review and oversight.[231] The FISC approved of these changes as being reasonably designed to prevent

224 Office of the Dir. of Nat'l Intelligence, *Release of Three Opinions Issued by the Foreign Intelligence Surveillance Court*, IC on the Record (Apr. 19, 2016), https://icontherecord.tumblr.com/post/143070924983/release-of-three-opinions-issued-by-the-foreign; *In re* Application of the Federal Bureau of Investigation for Orders Requiring the Production of Call Detail Records, No. [Redacted] (FISA Ct. Dec. 31, 2015), https://www.dni.gov/files/documents/12312015BR_Memo_Opinion_for_Public_Release.pdf.

225 *In re* Application of the Federal Bureau of Investigation for Orders Requiring the Production of Call Detail Records, No. [Redacted], at 21 (FISA Ct. Dec. 31, 2015), https://www.dni.gov/files/documents/12312015BR_Memo_Opinion_for_Public_Release.pdf.

226 *Id.* at 22–23.

227 [Redacted], No. [Redacted], slip op. at 11 (FISA Ct. Nov. 6, 2015), https://www.dni.gov/files/documents/20151106-702Mem_Opinion_Order_for_Public_Release.pdf.

228 Goitein, *supra* note 135; Charlie Savage, *Judge Rejects Challenge to Searches of Emails Gathered without Warrant*, N.Y. Times, Apr. 20, 2016, at A7, http://www.nytimes.com/2016/04/20/world/judge-rejects-challenge-to-searches-of-emails-gathered-without-warrant.html?ref=world.

229 Josh Gerstein, *Court Troubled by Surveillance Excesses at FBI, NSA*, Politico (Apr. 19, 2016), http://www.politico.com/blogs/under-the-radar/2016/04/government-surveillance-fbi-nsa-violations-222162.

230 Jake Laperruque, *Revelations from the Newly Declassified FISC Opinion on Section 702*, Just Security (Apr. 27, 2016), https://www.justsecurity.org/30776/revelations-newly-declassified-fisc-opinion-section-702/.

231 [Redacted], No. [Redacted], slip op. at 11 (FISA Ct. Nov. 6, 2015), https://www.dni.gov/files/documents/20151106-702Mem_Opinion_Order_for_Public_Release.pdf.

U.S. persons from being targeted and consistent with the requirements of the Fourth Amendment.[232]

The more controversial part involved a change to the procedures governing how the FBI queries Section 702 datasets for information about U.S. persons to use in ordinary criminal cases – the "back door" searches described earlier.[233] Unlike the NSA and CIA, the FBI is permitted to use querying terms designed to find evidence of a crime involving U.S. persons – and also unlike the other two agencies, the FBI does not require its personnel to provide written justifications for these queries.[234] (When the FBI does obtain relevant information, the DOJ may not use it in a criminal proceeding without the approval of the Attorney General and a showing that the case has "national security implications" or is a "serious crime."[235] The requirement that the Attorney General give his or her personal approval may end up being the most effective limitation on the use of this information in court.) In the lead-up to the November 2015 opinion, the FBI made another major change, narrowing the circumstances in which a search counts as a "query" in the first place.

Specifically, the FBI narrowed the definition of a query to cover only times when an agent receives *access* to unminimized Section 702-acquired information in response to a search.[236] In other words, under the FBI's current procedures, if an agent runs a search and does not receive any responsive records, the search does not count as a query. If the agent learns that there is responsive information but does not learn what it is, that search also does not count as a query. Moreover, if the agent who ran the search and receives notice of responsive information is not trained to handle it, then he or she can ask a properly trained agent to rerun the same search and decide whether the results reasonably appear to be foreign intelligence information, are necessary to understand foreign intelligence information, or constitute evidence of a crime – somewhat akin to searching a home without a warrant and then asking an authorized agent to redo the search if it appears to have uncovered any relevant evidence.[237] When it is "unclear" whether the results meet any of those standards, the FBI permits untrained agents to access and review the information.[238]

The FISC-appointed amicus had argued that these procedures "go far beyond the purpose for which the Section 702-acquired information is collected in permitting queries that are unrelated to national security,"[239] and "effectively treat Section 702-aquired data like any other database that can be queried for any legitimate law enforcement purpose."[240] She had also proposed that each query should be treated as a "separate action

232 *Id.* at 12.
233 *See, e.g.*, Goitein, *supra* note 135; Laperruque, *supra* note 230.
234 [Redacted], No. [Redacted], slip op. at 26–28 (FISA Ct. Nov. 6, 2015), https://www.dni.gov/files/documents/20151106-702Mem_Opinion_Order_for_Public_Release.pdf.
235 Office of the Dir. of Nat'l Intelligence, *Strengthening Privacy and Civil Liberties Protections*, *in* Signals Intelligence Reform 2015 Anniversary Report, IC on the Record, https://icontherecord.tumblr.com/ppd-28/2015/privacy-civil-liberties.
236 [Redacted], No. [Redacted], slip op. at 28 (FISA Ct. Nov. 6, 2015), https://www.dni.gov/files/documents/20151106-702Mem_Opinion_Order_for_Public_Release.pdf.
237 *Id.* at 29.
238 *Id.*
239 *Id.* at 30.
240 *Id.* at 39.

subject to the Fourth Amendment reasonableness test."[241] The FISC disagreed on both counts, concluding that the procedures met the statutory requirements and were consistent with the Fourth Amendment, and accepting the government's argument that the court should assess the reasonableness of the Section 702 program as a whole.[242]

The court first ruled that each individual query did not count as a "separate Fourth Amendment event;" instead, only the overall program needed to be constitutionally reasonable.[243] Individual queries that violate the Fourth Amendment could thus be sanitized by being a part of the program as a whole. Second, the court excused the fact that the searches would only rarely yield foreign intelligence information, despite the fact that both the Fourth Amendment reasonableness inquiry and the foreign intelligence exception depend upon there being a significant foreign intelligence interest. The court held that the FBI's criminal queries met the constitutional standard because they *could* elicit foreign intelligence information – even though the goal of the queries was to find criminal evidence rather than foreign intelligence.[244]

With respect to the second half of the balancing test, the court pointed to the FBI's use and dissemination restrictions as lessening the intrusion into Fourth Amendment interests, though those procedures do nothing to reduce the intrusion of the search itself.[245] The court also noted that the FBI evidently runs back-door searches on only a portion of the Section 702 database – among other things, the FBI does not have access to communications collected via upstream surveillance.[246] There is, however, no publicly available information on the scope of data available to the FBI.

The FISC also argued that the risk of FBI query results being used in an investigation unrelated to national security may only be a "theoretical" problem, because the FBI rarely gets hits in the Section 702 database – calling into question the argument that the searches may uncover foreign intelligence information and thus meet constitutional standards.[247] Moreover, even if the investigations were related to national security, both the Foreign Intelligence Surveillance Court of Review and Congress have required that foreign intelligence surveillance of American targets occur only where the Americans are foreign powers or their agents.[248] In any event, taking these arguments together, the FISC concluded that the FBI's minimization procedures "strike a reasonable balance between the privacy interests of United States persons, on the one hand, and the government's national security interests, on the other."[249]

Finally, the opinion revealed four compliance issues that had concerned the FISC since the previous year's certification. These issues included non-compliance with minimization procedures for handling privileged attorney-client communications, improperly granted access to unminimized datasets, a failure to purge records obtained through

241 *Id.* at 40.

242 *Id.* at 40–41.

243 *Id.* at 40.

244 *Id.* at 42.

245 *Id.* at 42–43.

246 *Id.* at 43–44.

247 *Id.* at 44. Judge Hogan also ordered the government to report "any instance in which FBI personnel receive and review Section 702-acquired information that the FBI identifies as concerning a United States person in response to a query that is not designed to find and extract foreign intelligence information." *Id.*

248 *In re* Directives, *supra* note 134; 50 U.S.C. § 1805(a)(2).

249 [Redacted], No. [Redacted], slip op. at 44 (FISA Ct. Nov. 6, 2015), https://www.dni.gov/files/documents/20151106-702Mem_Opinion_Order_for_Public_Release.pdf.

unauthorized collection, and a failure to purge records whose authorized retention period had already expired.[250] Regarding the failure to delete unauthorized or time-expired records for more than four years, the court said it was "extremely concerned about the NSA's failure to comply with its minimization procedures,"[251] though "perhaps more disturbing and disappointing ... was the government's failure to convey to the Court explicitly during that time that the NSA was continuing to retain this information."[252] The FISC nevertheless endorsed the program as a whole, and ordered the government to provide "substantive updates" on each of the four compliance issues at a later hearing.[253]

IV Other Collection and Analytics Programs

While the surveillance that occurred until recently under Section 215, and that still continues under Section 702 as of October 2016, has received the most attention, there are a host of other programs that gather and sift through a huge variety of information about both Americans and foreigners, undoubtedly including many that have not been disclosed publicly and may never be revealed. To take one example, the *Washington Post* revealed in late 2013 that an NSA program was "intercept[ing] e-mail address books and 'buddy lists' from instant messaging services as they move across global data links."[254] According to the *Post*, "Online services often transmit those contacts when a user logs on, composes a message, or synchronizes a computer or mobile device with information stored on remote servers."[255] Contact lists can include "telephone numbers, street addresses, and business and family information"; listings of email accounts in the cloud can even include the first few lines of a message.[256] NSA analysts then analyze the data to "search for hidden connections and to map relationships within a much smaller universe of foreign intelligence targets."[257] The volume of collection is high: in a single day, the NSA collected almost 700,000 email address books and 500,000 buddy lists.

The collection – which is premised on Executive Order 12333, the Reagan-era order setting out the guidelines for conducting foreign intelligence surveillance overseas – is not limited to foreign intelligence targets (or anything else). In addition, because the contact lists are collected "'on the fly' as they cross major Internet switches," providers are not involved or notified.[258] U.S. intelligence officials have conceded that although the collection occurs overseas, it is likely to sweep up many Americans' contacts as well, including those of people working or traveling overseas and data that happens to be routed to overseas data centers. Minimization rules should require minimization of information about U.S. persons, but there is insufficient information about precisely how

250 *Id.* at 45–77 (attorney-client communications at 47–52; improper access at 52–55; retention of unauthorized records at 55–60; retention of time-expired records at 60–77).
251 *Id.* at 68.
252 *Id.* at 58.
253 *Id.* at 77, 79.
254 Gellman & Soltani, *supra* note 5.
255 *Id.*
256 *Id.*
257 *Id.*
258 *Id.*

that happens. The sheer scope of the collection has at times overwhelmed the NSA's systems, as analysts have been inundated with spam email threads.[259]

There have also been suggestions that the corporate store of phone metadata has been used for in-depth data mining. The NSA has reportedly used databases of phone call and email logs to "create sophisticated graphs of some Americans' social connections that can identify their associates, their locations at certain times, their traveling companions and other personal information."[260] Although the NSA has indicated that the Section 215 database was not among the stores of data used for analysis, it appears that the corporate store – the database resulting from the Section 215 searches – may have been.[261]

Prior to late 2010, this "large-scale graph analysis" had been conducted only on information about foreigners. Beginning in November of that year, however, the NSA began including Americans' data.[262] The NSA was also searching through vast stores of other information: "material from public, commercial and other sources, including bank codes, insurance information, Facebook profiles, passenger manifests, voter registration rolls and GPS location information, as well as property records and unspecified tax data," along with "location-based services like GPS and TomTom, online social networks, billing records and bank codes for transactions in the United States and overseas."[263] The warrantless data mining was defended on the grounds that because it just involved metadata, only a foreign intelligence justification was required, with no FISA warrant necessary – opening up new opportunities to analyze and exploit Americans' private information.

Conclusion

In the four years since Edward Snowden's disclosures began, it has become de rigueur for intelligence community officials to declare their renewed dedication to transparency. NSA Director Admiral Michael Rogers has called himself a "firm believer" in "public dialogue and transparency."[264] ODNI General Counsel Robert Litt has lauded the office's "commitment to increased transparency," promising to "give the public greater insight into the laws and policies we operate under and how we interpret those authorities."[265] And James Comey, the now former FBI director, asserted during his confirmation

259 *Id.*

260 James Risen & Laura Poitras, *N.S.A. Gathers Data on Social Connections of U.S. Citizens*, N.Y. Times, Sept. 29, 2013, at A1, http://www.nytimes.com/2013/09/29/us/nsa-examines-social-networks-of-us-citizens.html?_r=0.

261 *See also The Corporate Store: Where NSA Goes to Shop Your Content and Your Lifestyle*, emptywheel (Dec. 29, 2014), https://www.emptywheel.net/2014/01/25/the-corporate-store-where-nsa-goes-to-shop-your-content-and-your-lifestyle/.

262 Risen & Poitras, *supra* note 260.

263 *Id.*

264 Admiral Michael Rogers, Address to Intelligence and National Security Alliance (Aug. 13, 2014), http://www.c-span.org/video/?320969-1/discussion-nsa-director-admiral-michael-rogers.

265 Robert S. Litt, Gen. Counsel, Office of the Dir. of Nat'l Intelligence, Keynote Remarks at American University Washington College of Law Freedom of Information Day Celebration (Mar. 18, 2014), https://www.fas.org/sgp/eprint/litt.pdf; Robert S. Litt, Gen. Counsel, Office of the Dir. of Nat'l Intelligence, Remarks on Signals Intelligence Reform at the Brookings Institution (Feb. 10, 2015), https://www.dni.gov/index.php/newsroom/speeches-and-interviews/208-speeches-interviews-2015/1171-odni-general-counsel-robert-litt%E2%80%99s-as-prepared-remarks-on-signals-intelligence-reform-at-the-brookings-institute.

hearing that "[t]ransparency is a key value, especially when it helps the American people understand what the government is doing to try to keep them safe."[266]

These commitments may well be made in good faith. At the same time, the intelligence community agencies have repeatedly violated the promises they have made to the courts, to Congress, and implicitly to the American people, exceeding the lawful boundaries of their surveillance authorities and concealing that information from their overseers. One hopes that the coming years do, indeed, bring greater transparency, insight, and dialogue.

266 Sari Horwitz, *Comey Defends Surveillance Programs but Says He's Open to More Transparency*, Wash. Post (July 9, 2013), https://www.washingtonpost.com/world/national-security/comey-defends-surveillance-programs-but-says-hes-open-to-more-transperancy/2013/07/09/167bf17e-e8a9-11e2-8f22-de4bd2a2bd39_story.html.

2 Location Tracking

Stephanie K. Pell[†]

The use of location data and location tracking technologies by law enforcement agencies is becoming increasingly common as technological developments enable collection of more accurate and precise location data. The law governing law enforcement access to such data and tracking technologies remains, for the most part, unsettled. This chapter explores these technologies, the current state of the law, and many of the vexing questions and issues they raise.

Introduction

"*Location, Location, Location*," the "three things that matter in real estate," are no longer just about property values.[1] Today, *where* you were, *who* was there with you, and exactly *when* you left, especially when all are aggregated over time, can combine to reveal an intimate portrait of your life and self. The collected history of where you have been may disclose what you did, where in the *future* you are likely to go, and what you are likely to do. Moreover, with every bit of personal location data that is stored, we lose the ability to escape our *past* since a permanent record of where we were – and even whom we were with – is available for the asking.

Tracking a suspect's movements or investigating where he might have been are not new methods for law enforcement. Watch a few old episodes of *Law & Order*, for example, and you will encounter a team of police officers working together – in cars and on foot, perhaps even utilizing a helicopter – to follow a suspect in real time and trace, via witness interviews or other means, where he has been in the past. Prior to the advent of the smart phone, this kind of surveillance was very labor intensive, often involving teams of agents working in multiple shifts to piece together a picture of where the suspect has been, follow where he is going, and determine who was with him.

† Assistant Professor & Cyber Ethics Fellow, Army Cyber Institute and Department of English and Philosophy, United States Military Academy at West Point; Non-resident Affiliate Scholar, Stanford Center for Internet and Society. The views expressed are those of the author and do not reflect the position of West Point, the Army or the United States Government. The author would like to thank the editors of this book, David Gray and Stephen E. Henderson, for their helpful comments, along with Matt Blaze and Chris Soghoian for the technical education about location tracking technologies they have generously provided to me, beginning several years ago and continuing to this day.

1 This phrase is often attributed to the British real estate tycoon Lord Harold Samuel. *See* William Safire, *Location, Location, Location*, N.Y. Times Magazine (June 26, 2009), http://www.nytimes.com/2009/06/28/magazine/28FOB-onlanguage-t.html?_r=1.

Tracking technologies and techniques, particularly those integrated into cellular phones, have proven beneficially disruptive to the historically labor-intensive practice of tracking suspects' movements, both prospectively and retrospectively. What once required multiple teams of agents is now available in the form of real-time and historical cell phone location data collected and stored by third party telecommunications companies, which allows law enforcement agents to acquire a full, often very precise, history of a suspect's movements without leaving their desks. Law enforcement can also acquire location data *directly* (that is, without the assistance of a third party provider), through their own use of (1) global positioning system (GPS) tracking devices placed directly on a suspect's car, which communicate with a constellation of global satellites, calculate the vehicle's precise location[2] in relation to those satellites,[3] then transmit these data to a remote government computer; and (2) IMSI[4] catchers, devices that impersonate legitimate cell towers, enabling law enforcement covertly to identify and *locate* nearby cell phones and, in some cases, to intercept the content of calls or text messages those phones send or receive.

These location tracking technologies and techniques have become commonplace investigative tools for federal and state law enforcement agencies, often producing powerful prosecution evidence. The appropriate legal standards governing law enforcement compelled disclosure or direct collection of location data are not, however, settled law, at least with respect to location data produced by cell phones. Moreover, even though the Supreme Court's 2012 decision in *United States v. Jones* likely requires law enforcement to obtain a probable cause warrant before installing a GPS tracking device on a suspect's vehicle in order to follow his movements, the Fourth Amendment doctrine articulated by the *Jones* majority does not translate to the tracking of cell phones – a fact noted by Justice Sonia Sotomayor in her concurring opinion. Indeed, with respect to law enforcement access to cell phone location data, federal and state common and statutory law is still being written.

As courts at various levels grapple with questions of whether or when law enforcement must obtain a warrant to compel disclosure of cell phone location data from a third party, what emerges is a vexing, complicated set of legal and policy questions that present core challenges to the application of the Fourth Amendment in the digital age. Can or will the third party doctrine, which limits constitutional protection of information shared with third parties, continue to be a viable rule in the digital age? What does a voluntary conveyance of information to a third party mean in the digital age? In identifying situations when the third party doctrine does not or should not apply, what factors will influence courts' evaluation of whether there is a reasonable expectation of privacy in location data or in law enforcement's tracking of a suspect's location for short and long periods?

The third party doctrine question was assiduously, if understandably, avoided by the majority's property-based reasoning in *Jones*, leaving it for another day, even as Justice Sotomayor's concurring opinion recognizes a need to reevaluate the third party doctrine in the digital age. That day, at least for the Supreme Court, has not yet come but, as

2 The calculation occurs in measurements of longitude and latitude.

3 The respondent's brief in *United States v. Jones*, 132 S.Ct. 945 (2012), indicates that the GPS calculation occurred in ten-second intervals. *See* Brief for Respondent, *Jones*, 132 S.Ct. 945 (No. 10–1259), at 4.

4 "IMSI" is an acronym for *International Mobile Subscriber Identity* number.

referenced in the conclusion, it may arrive shortly. In the interim, state and federal legislative bodies are free, even encouraged by some justices and judges, to step in and provide the kind of nuanced balancing between privacy and law enforcement interests that is difficult for courts to achieve in the absence of specific legislative direction, wielding only the comparatively blunt instrument of the Fourth Amendment.

For a legislature to regulate, however, it has to be able to see and understand the kind of tracking technologies and practices used by law enforcement, as well as law enforcement's interpretations of how existing statutes may or may not authorize their use. In the law enforcement context, such knowledge often results from court opinions that describe the technologies and practices at issue and the governing state of the law. Here again, the location data discourse is emblematic of critical issues facing policy makers and judges in the digital age: it provides a cautionary tale of the need for greater transparency. While IMSI catcher technology, a technology originally developed for military and intelligence applications, was becoming a routine tool for federal and state law enforcement agencies, courts were unaware that they were approving applications authorizing its use. Through the use of nondisclosure agreements, the Federal Bureau of Investigation (FBI) controlled the disclosure of information about IMSI catcher technology in criminal investigations and prosecutions to such an extent that one state appellate court opined that such secrecy "obstructs the court's ability to make the necessary constitutional appraisal."[5]

This chapter begins with a brief discussion of location tracking technologies and practices used by law enforcement. It then discusses how location tracking issues have been treated by and are developing in the courts and Congress, with a particular focus on the legal and policy issues raised in this Introduction. Finally, the chapter concludes with a brief description of what is now before the Supreme Court.

I Location Tracking Technology

A *GPS Vehicle Tracking Devices*

Perhaps one of the best summary descriptions of GPS vehicle tracking devices can be found in the respondent's brief in the *Jones* case.[6] GPS tracking devices are a prime example of how technology originally developed for military and intelligence use, generally outside the protective scope of Fourth Amendment protection, eventually trickles down to the hands of domestic law enforcement, where it quickly becomes a common and essential investigative technique.

Respondent Jones explains that the Department of Defense, in 1978, launched the Navigational Satellite Timing and Ranging Global Positioning System (GPS) for the U.S. military's use. The system operates through twenty-five government-owned satellites orbiting the Earth, each of which continuously transmits its position. An individual GPS device "listens to the transmissions of the four closest satellites, and, through a process known as trilateration, determines its precise location on earth."[7] GPS devices are thus

5 *State v. Andrews*, 227 Md. App. 350, 376 (2016).

6 *See* Brief for Respondent, *supra* note 3, at 1–3. Respondent Jones draws from and quotes many sources when providing his summary description. Those quotations and internal citations are omitted here, but this description of GPS vehicle tracking technology relies heavily on the description found in Petitioner Jones's brief.

7 *Id.*

able to "produce an accurate, continuous, and three-dimensional digital record of their position and velocity over any period of time – as well as that of any person or object carrying them."[8] These data can be transmitted to a remote computer via a cellphone connection and graphed onto an interactive map. Generally, a GPS tracking device is accurate to within 50 to 100 feet. With the application of additional software, however, law enforcement can identify "the most likely exact longitude, latitude, and address on the mapping system, with accurate positioning to within a few centimeters or even millimeters."[9] Consistent with technological trends in the digital age, GPS technology is rapidly improving.

In the *Jones* case, the FBI attached a GPS tracking device to the undercarriage of Jones's Jeep Grand Cherokee and tracked his movements for four weeks, recording location coordinates every ten seconds.[10] The GPS data were automatically transmitted and stored in a remote FBI computer without the need for real-time monitoring by FBI agents. This GPS vehicle tracking technology, which allows agents to receive precise location information directly at their desks, stands in stark contrast to the old labor-intensive "beeper" technology, which only provided directional location information and required agents physically to follow the signal at a fairly close distance.[11]

B *Cell Phone Tracking*

1 Cell Site Location Information

Unlike conventional "wireline" phones, mobile phones use radio waves to communicate with a carrier's network.[12] Service providers maintain large numbers of radio base stations or "cell sites" spread throughout their coverage areas. These cell sites are generally located on cell towers serving geographic areas of varying sizes, depending upon topography and population concentration. Each base station is responsible for making connections between the regular network and nearby cell phones when they make and receive calls. In order to facilitate continuous coverage, providers keep track of which base station service area or "sector" a cell phone is located in at any given time.

The most basic form of cell phone location data is cell site location information (CSLI), referring to the identity of the tower to which the phone connects and the sector of the particular tower facing the phone. Whenever a user places or receives a call

8 *Id.*
9 *Id.* at 1–2.
10 *Id.*
11 *See, e.g., United States v. Knotts*, 460 U.S. 276 (1983).
12 The description of tracking technologies in this section relies heavily on discussions found in work I have previously coauthored, along with Professor Matt Blaze's congressional testimony: Stephanie K. Pell & Christopher Soghoian, *Can You See Me Now?: Toward Reasonable Standards for Law Enforcement Access to Location Data That Congress Could Enact*, 27 Berkeley Tech. L.J. 117 (2012); Stephanie K. Pell & Christopher Soghoian, *Your Secret StingRay's No Secret Anymore: The Vanishing Government Monopoly over Cell Phone Surveillance and Its Impact on National Security and Consumer Privacy*, 28 Harv. Tech. L.J. 1 (2014); *ECPA Reform and the Revolution in Location Based Technologies and Services: Hearing before the Subcomm. on the Constitution, Civil Rights, and Civil Liberties of the H. Comm. on the Judiciary*, 111th Cong. (2010) (testimony of Professor Matt Blaze); and *Electronic Communications Privacy Act (ECPA)(Part II): Geolocation Privacy and Surveillance: Reform and the Revolution in Location Based Technologies and Services: Hearing before the Subcomm. on Crime, Terrorism, Homeland Sec. and Investigations of the H. Comm. on the Judiciary*, 113th Cong. (2013) (same).

or sends a text message over the cell phone network, the communication is transmitted between the handset and the nearest tower. If the user changes location during the course of a call, the call is handed off to the next closest tower.[13] Moreover, as part of their normal function, mobile phones periodically register and identify themselves to the nearest cell site, which is generally the station with the strongest signal, so that cell providers will know where to direct any incoming calls. This "checking-in" continues even when users are *not* in the process of making or receiving a call. All of these interactions between cell phone and cell towers produce CSLI, much of which subsequently is stored by service providers.

Carriers store CSLI for diagnostic, billing, and other purposes for various periods, according to their particular business needs and practices. Disclosure of these historical data from cell phone providers can be compelled by law enforcement, whether with respect to one or multiple targets, for a single or limited amount of time (a few minutes or hours), or over an extended period (many months). Law enforcement can also request *cell tower dumps* – a full collection of carrier records of every cell phone that registered with a particular tower at a particular time. Cell tower dumps are a useful technique for determining the perpetrators of crimes such as multiple bank robberies, since they allow law enforcement to identify specific phones (and, by implication, phone owners) that were in the vicinity of the crime scenes. Another technique, called a *community of interest* request, involves the disclosure of the location information pertaining to all individuals who were called by or made calls to a particular target. This practice can help law enforcement identify unknown suspects potentially involved in criminal activity of a known target.

Law enforcement can also track a suspect prospectively through the collection of CSLI. Specifically, law enforcement can compel the disclosure of CSLI received by the carrier in real time in the normal course of a phone's communication with various cell sites. At a minimum, cellular providers record the identity of the particular base station (or sector) with which a cellular phone communicates every time it makes or receives a call and whenever it moves from one cellular coverage sector to another. How precisely this information *by itself* enables location of a phone depends on the size of the sector. In relatively unpopulated areas with open terrain, a sector might cover an area miles in diameter. Not surprisingly, phones in smaller sectors can be located with better accuracy than those in larger sectors.

Moreover, "as the density of cellular users grows in a given area, the only way for a carrier to accommodate more customers is to divide the coverage area into smaller and smaller sectors, each served by its own base station."[14] At the same time, users expect their mobile devices to work in any space they inhabit – inside offices and homes, basements and elevators; indoors and out.[15] Accordingly, "the only way to make service more reliable in more places under varying radio conditions is to add base stations that cover dead spots."[16] Adding such base stations further reduces the area of a typical sector's

13 There are circumstances, including natural terrain features such as hills and valleys and weather conditions, where a communication may not be handled by the closest tower. Moreover, if the closest tower is busy, the phone may connect to a different tower.

14 *ECPA Reform and the Revolution in Location Based Technologies and Services: Hearing before the Subcomm. on the Constitution, Civil Rights, and Civil Liberties of the H. Comm. on the Judiciary*, 111th Cong. 24 (2010) (testimony of Professor Matt Blaze).

15 *Id.*

16 *Id.* at 24–25.

coverage. Indeed, in an attempt to fill such gaps in coverage areas, wireless carriers have, over the past several years, distributed to customers hundreds of thousands of microcells, picocells, and femtocells, which connect to the user's broadband Internet connection and provide cellular connectivity to phones within tens or hundreds of meters.[17] These tiny cells are designed to serve very small areas, such as particular floors of buildings or individual offices and homes. Because these devices often broadcast a signal that does not go beyond the walls of a subscriber's home or office, the accuracy of even *single*[18] CSLI can be, in some cases, more accurate than that of GPS, with actual accuracy dependent upon factors such as the density of base stations, whether the target device is connected to a traditional cell site or a femtocell, and the limitations forced upon GPS functionality in urban areas.[19]

Carriers can also monitor their customers more proactively, generating data specifically in response to a court order. In such scenarios, the wireless carrier covertly *pings* a subscriber's phone in order to locate it when a call is not being made. Such pings can reveal the nearest cell site to the subscriber or generate more accurate triangulated data, if requested. Triangulation is a process that occurs on the carrier's network, developed as one response to Federal Communications Commission (FCC) Regulations requiring carriers to be able to locate wireless 911 callers. Multiple towers are used to track the phone's location by measuring the time delay that a signal takes to return to the towers from the phone. Software in the carrier's network then calculates a location position for the phone, typically within fifty meters – and emerging versions of this technology will likely increase accuracy. Some carriers routinely track and record triangulated data, and movement toward this practice is a general trend in the industry. As such, law enforcement agencies can also obtain high-accuracy, triangulated historical data when it is available under a specific company's data collection practices. In addition to carrier-initiated pings, law enforcement agencies can perform "low-tech" pings by calling a target and hanging up before the phone rings, in order to generate cell site data that would then be compelled from and disclosed by carriers.[20]

In summary, as time goes on, service providers are deploying higher-capacity network architectures with the potential to provide more precise information regarding a cell phone user's location. As the coverage area around each traditional cell tower shrinks, and consumers increasingly embrace femtocells in their homes and businesses, single CSLI will become far more accurate – in some cases approaching and even surpassing the precision of GPS. Moreover, as historical CSLI can include microcell-, picocell-, and femtocell-generated data recorded at the beginning and end of a call, the relative precision of historical location data will only increase over time as these technologies are increasingly deployed throughout carrier networks.

17 One of the main differences in these three types of technologies is the range of their coverage area – microcells cover the largest area and are thus relatively more expensive, picocells cover a smaller area, and femtocells cover the smallest area.

18 The term "single CLSI" refers to the location data produced when a phone communicates with a single tower verses the use of data from several towers to triangulate the phone's location.

19 *See* discussion of the limits of GPS functionality in urban areas *infra* p. 50.

20 *See United States v. Forest*, 355 F.3d 942, 947 (6th Cir. 2004) ("In order to reestablish visual contact, a DEA agent dialed Garner's cellular phone (without allowing it to ring) several times that day and used Sprint's computer data to determine which cellular transmission towers were being 'hit' by Garner's phone. This 'cell site data' revealed the general location of Garner").

2 Personal GPS-Enabled Devices

In addition to location data generated by communication with cell sites, mobile phones (and many other personal devices) now include special hardware that enables them to receive signals from the constellation of global positioning satellites discussed earlier. This communication is one-way. Phones receive signals from the satellites but do not transmit anything back to them. Similar to GPS vehicle tracking devices, software on the phone can use these signals to calculate latitude and longitude, often within ten meters of accuracy. Although GPS can be more accurate than other cell phone location technology, there are a few limitations. First, GPS signals are weak high-frequency signals that do not penetrate walls. As a result, GPS often does not work when devices are indoors. Moreover, for the same reason, GPS often does not function well in "urban canyons" because of signal deflection off the sides of tall buildings. Furthermore, the GPS functionality tends to use significant amounts of power, which can lead to shorter battery life. When GPS functionality is available, whether because the user dials 911 or law enforcement agencies compel its use, wireless carriers can determine and prospectively track a device's location. Carriers do not, however, generally have historical GPS data to deliver.

Many smart phones now provide access to GPS functionality through third party "apps" installed on the devices. Accordingly, app developers and location service providers also have access to users' GPS location data. Law enforcement agencies can compel these location service providers to disclose the historical GPS data in their possession, although prospective disclosures are limited to user-initiated "check-ins," as these companies are usually not able to generate their own GPS queries.

C *IMSI Catchers*

Carrier-assisted surveillance is not the only means law enforcement can use to determine a cell phone's location. International Mobile Subscriber Identity (IMSI) catchers impersonate cellular network base stations, thus tricking nearby phones and other mobile devices into identifying themselves by revealing their unique serial numbers, just as they would in registering with genuine base stations in the immediate vicinity. As each phone in the area identifies itself, the IMSI catcher can determine the location from which the signal originated. Moreover, when searching for a particular mobile device somewhere in an urban area, the IMSI catcher sends signals into buildings, calls out to surrounding area devices to identify themselves, and then locates the target device, often with more accuracy than a carrier could provide. These surveillance devices can be carried by hand, installed in a vehicle, or even mounted on a plane or drone.

IMSI catchers, commonly known as "StingRays" according to the Harris Corporation's band name for their version of the technology, are an example of an *active, unmediated* surveillance device. They are active (rather than passive)[21] in the sense that they call out to nearby mobile devices to identify themselves –like a high-tech version of the game Marco Polo. They perform unmediated surveillance because they collect information directly – law enforcement does not have to compel a third party carrier to provide

[21] Earlier versions of this technology were passive in nature; that is, they merely listened to a cell phone communicating with a legitimate tower.

the data. Moreover, they operate covertly and indiscriminately, silently sending signals through the walls of homes, vehicles, purses, and pockets in order to probe and identify the phones and, in the process, often picking up signals of innocent third party phones, particularly when agents using the technology – as is often the case – do not know the location of their target and thus must drive through cities and neighborhoods to locate her phone.

In 2013, the *Wall Street Journal* reported that the United States Marshals Service was using a technology called a DRT box (or "Dirtbox") – a two-foot-square device mounted on a plane that "enables investigators to scoop data from tens of thousands of cell-phones in a single flight, collecting their identifying information and general location."[22] Consistent with the capabilities of IMSI catcher technology, the DRT box identifies itself as having the closest, strongest signal, even when it does not, forcing all the phones that can detect its signal to send it their unique registration information.[23] Presumably, the Marshals Service has found these devices useful for locating fugitives.

The StingRay and other similar devices also have the capacity, if so configured, to intercept data transmitted and received by a target phone, including the content of calls, text messages, numbers dialed, and Web pages visited. These and other interception capabilities are a product of the StingRay's exploitation of a persistent vulnerability in the 2G protocol: telephones operating in 2G cannot authenticate cell towers, which enables rogue towers to impersonate legitimate ones in a cellular network. Although 3G and 4G networks have addressed this vulnerability, these networks can be jammed, forcing nearby phones to communicate using the vulnerable 2G protocol. As long as phones include the capability to communicate using 2G – an essential backward compatibility while 2G service remains widespread in rural areas – the latest smart phones will remain vulnerable to decades-old security flaws.

Moreover, governments friendly to the United States are not the only foreign entities that possess or can acquire IMSI catcher technology. Although originally developed for military and intelligence uses at a cost of six figures per device, IMSI catcher technology is now widely available to local law enforcement agencies and to anyone with the motive and will to obtain it – think, for example, spies, intellectual property thieves, and stalkers – as the technology can be purchased over the Internet from one of many non–United States–based surveillance technology vendors or even built at home by hobbyists. Access to this once prohibitively expensive, rare, unmediated, and essentially undetectable surveillance technology has become globalized and democratized.

II Location Tracking Technology and the Law

Legal standards that govern law enforcement access to location data from third parties, whether historical or prospective, and the use of tracking technologies that enable unmediated surveillance are still developing.[24] But some important questions have been

22 Devlin Bartlett, *Americans' Cell Phones Targeted in Secret U.S. Spy Program*, Wall St. J. (Nov. 13, 2014), http://www.wsj.com/articles/americans-cellphones-targeted-in-secret-u-s-spy-program-1415917533.
23 *Id.*
24 The discussion and analysis in this section rely heavily on work I have previously either authored alone or coauthored: Stephanie K. Pell & Christopher Soghoian, *Can You See Me Now? Toward Reasonable Standards for Law Enforcement Access to Location Data That Congress Could Enact*, 27 Berkeley Tech. L.J. 117 (2012); Stephanie K. Pell, *Jonesing for a Privacy Mandate, Getting a Technology Fix – Doctrine to*

answered. For instance, law enforcement's attachment of a GPS tracking device to a car for the purpose of tracking the vehicle's movements is a search for Fourth Amendment purposes. Other questions, however, such as the Fourth Amendment implications of short- and long-term tracking from historical and prospective location information obtained from third parties or directly via IMSI catchers, have not been considered by the Supreme Court. Federal courts of appeal are weighing in on some these cell phone location issues, along with state courts, one of which has opined on law enforcement use of IMSI catcher technology. Courts are, of course, not the only branch of government with the power to establish and clarify the law in this area. Federal and state legislatures have an important role to play in regulating law enforcement access to location data and use of location tracking technologies. The Electronic Communications Privacy Act (ECPA),[25] a federal statute governing law enforcement access to various kinds of communications data, was written in 1986 and has not been updated since to account for the revolution in mobile devices. The vagaries of this statute when applied to location data and various level courts' attempts to grapple with it, along with many other vexing questions posed by location data, will be explored in this section.

A *Prospective Location Data and the Magistrate's Revolt*

Locating the proper law enforcement access standard for prospective CSLI in the ECPA is, in some respects, like the quest for the Holy Grail, the search for the fountain of youth, or the hunt for a truly comfortable pair of high heels – the desired end may prove forever elusive. This legal mystery remains unsolved primarily for two reasons. First, the ECPA – the primary federal statute governing law enforcement access to wire, oral, and electronic communications and other stored subscriber records and information – does not contain the word "location" or provide any other language that could easily be interpreted as covering law enforcement access to real-time location data from third party providers. Second, Congress, in the Communications Assistance for Law Enforcement Act (CALEA), has only expressed what is *insufficient* for purposes of law enforcement access to prospective location information from a third party provider, but not what is either *necessary* or *sufficient* for such compelled disclosures. Indeed, CALEA merely instructs that "any information that may disclose the physical location of [a telephone service] subscriber" may *not* be acquired "solely pursuant to the authority for pen registers and

Follow, 14 Harv. Tech. L.J. 489 (2013); Stephanie K. Pell & Christopher Soghoian, *Your Secret StingRay's No Secret Anymore: The Vanishing Government Monopoly over Cell Phone Surveillance and Its Impact on National Security and Consumer Privacy*, 28 Harv. Tech. L.J. 1 (2014); Steven M. Bellovin, Matt Blaze, Susan Landau, & Stephanie K. Pell, *It's Too Complicated: How the Internet Upends Katz, Smith and Electronic Surveillance Law*, 30 Harv. Tech. L.J. 1 (2017).

25 Pub. L. No. 99–508, 100 Stat. 1848 (1986) (codified as amended in scattered sections of 18 U.S.C.). This article uses the term "ECPA" to describe the first three titles of the Electronic Communications Privacy Act: Title I ("Interception of Communications and Related Matters"), 100 Stat. at 1848, which amended the Wiretap Act (commonly referring to Title III ("Wiretapping and Electronic Surveillance") of the Omnibus Crime Control and Safe Streets Act of 1968, Pub. L. No. 90–351, tit. III, 82 Stat. 197, 211–25 (codified as amended at 18 U.S.C. §§ 2511–2520 (2010))); Title II ("Stored Wire and Electronic Communications and Transactional Records Access"), commonly referred to as the Stored Communications Act (SCA), Pub. L. No. 99–508, tit. II, 100 Stat. 1848, 1860–1868 (codified as amended at 18 U.S.C. §§ 2701–2712 (2010)); and Title III ("Pen Registers and Trap and Trace Devices"), commonly referred to as the Pen/Trap Devices statute, Pub. L. No. 99–508, tit. III, 100 Stat. 1848, 1868–1873 (codified as amended at 18 U.S.C. §§ 3121–3127 (2010)).

trap and trace devices."[26] Therefore, with respect to a compelled disclosure, if real-time location data cannot be provided to law enforcement "*solely pursuant*" to a court order for a Pen/Trap device, there must be some further requirement. But that requirement, unfortunately, remains undefined in the law.

Lacking clear, affirmative statutory guidance, the Department of Justice (DOJ) has routinely acquired, since at least 2005, certain categories of "less precise" prospective CSLI through the *combination* of two court orders: (1) a Pen/Trap court order pursuant to 18 U.S.C. § 3123; and (2) a "D" Order pursuant to 18 U.S.C. § 2703(d), a section of the ECPA called the Stored Communications Act (SCA) that permits the government to compel the production of noncontent records or information pertaining to a subscriber or customer. When combined, these two orders are known as a "hybrid order."[27] A DOJ manual documents that the rationale behind the "hybrid" use of these two statutes derives from a combination of discrete statutory requisites.[28] First, because "cell-site data is 'dialing, routing, addressing or signaling information,' ... 18 U.S.C. § 3121(a) requires the government to obtain a Pen/Trap order to acquire this type of information."[29] Second, however, because CALEA "precludes the government from relying 'solely' on the authority of the Pen/Trap statute to obtain cell-site data for a cell phone ... [,] some additional authority is required to obtain prospective cell-site information."[30] The DOJ asserts that "Section 2703(d) provides this authority because ... it authorizes the government to use a court order to obtain all non-content information pertaining to a customer or subscriber of an electronic communications service [or a remote computing service]."[31]

The same DOJ manual, published in its third edition in 2009, also provides guidance about the "precision" of the information likely to be obtained from cell site data (exclusive of GPS location technologies). The manual instructs that "cell-site data identifies the antenna tower and, in some cases, the 120-degree face of the tower to which a cell phone is connected, both at the beginning and the end of each call made or received by a cell phone."[32] The manual further explains that "the towers can be up to 10 or more miles apart in rural areas and may be up to a half-mile or more apart even in urban areas."[33] Relying on this description of cell tower technology, the manual concludes, "At best, these data reveal the neighborhood in which a cell phone user is located at the time a call starts and at the time it terminates; it does not provide continuous tracking and is not a virtual map of a cell phone user's movements."[34]

26 47 U.S.C. § 1002(a)(2) (2010).

27 U.S. Dep't of Justice (DOJ), Searching and Seizing Computers and Obtaining Electronic Evidence in Criminal Investigations 160 (3d ed. 2009) [hereinafter DOJ Manual], http://www.justice.gov/criminal/cybercrime/docs/ssmanual2009.pdf.

28 *Id.* at 159–160. Some published decisions also indicate that DOJ prosecutors have, at times, offered the All Writs Act, 28 U.S.C. § 1651 (2010), as a "mechanism for the judiciary to give [the government] the investigative tools that Congress has not." *In re* Application of the U.S. for an Order Authorizing the Use of a Pen Register and a Trap and Trace Device (*In re E.D.N.Y. Application*), 396 F. Supp. 2d 294, 325 (E.D.N.Y. 2005); *see also In re* Application of the U.S. for an Order Authorizing the Installation and Use of a Pen Register (*In re W.D.N.Y. Application*), 415 F. Supp. 2d 211, 219 (W.D.N.Y. 2006). These courts did not endorse this theory.

29 DOJ Manual, *supra* note 27, at 159–160.

30 *Id.* at 160.

31 *Id.*

32 *Id.* at 159.

33 *Id.*

34 *Id.*

This description of the relative precision of CSLI clearly applies only to *single* CSLI (i.e., no multitower, triangulation, or GPS location information). Moreover, it will soon be – if it is not already – outdated with the deployment of microcell, picocell, and femtocell technology that can, in some cases, as previously noted, be more accurate than GPS.

The DOJ manual further advises prosecutors that *in most districts* they may obtain prospective cell site information with the use of hybrid orders, but it also acknowledges that some magistrate judges require a "probable cause" showing before authorizing law enforcement access to any type of prospective CSLI.[35] This split among magistrate judges was characterized by one federal prosecutor as the "Santa Ana Judicial Revolt."[36] Indeed, a growing number of magistrate judges within and across various judicial districts have rejected the government's use of the hybrid theory to obtain any type of prospective cell site information. Some courts have held that, as a matter of statutory construction, the Pen/Trap order and the D order cannot be used to obtain this information, but that Federal Rule of Criminal Procedure 41 provides the necessary authority because "it governs any matter in which the government seeks judicial authorization to engage in certain investigative activities."[37]

Some magistrate and district judges who have accepted hybrid orders and issued published decisions on the question have restricted law enforcement access to limited cell site information yielding only generalized location data. In accepting a government hybrid order, Magistrate Judge Gorenstein from the Southern District of New York specifically noted that

> [the government's request pertained to cell site information] tied only to telephone calls actually made or received by the telephone user … [with] no data provided as to the location of the cell phone when no call is in progress. [And], at any given moment, data is provided only as to a single cell tower with which the cell phone is communicating. Thus, no data is provided that could be "triangulated" to permit the precise location of the cell phone user.[38]

35 *Id.* at 159–160.

36 Email from Tracy Wilkison, U.S. Dep't of Justice, to USACAC-AUSAs Criminal, U.S. Dep't of Justice (July 28, 2008), *in* letter from William G. Stewart, II, Assistant Dir., U.S. Dep't of Justice, to Catherine Crump (Sept. 8, 2008), http://www.aclu.org/pdfs/freespeech/cellfoia_release_074123_20080911.pdf, (informing other prosecutors about changes in office procedures for obtaining GPS and cell site information).

37 *In re E.D.N.Y. Application*, 396 F. Supp. 2d 294, 322 (E.D.N.Y. 2005); *see also In re W.D.N.Y. Application*, 415 F. Supp. 2d 211, 219 (W.D.N.Y. 2005) ("The challenge here is to the *statutory* justification for … [the government's] application. … The Court does not agree with the government that it should impute to Congress the intent to 'converge' the provisions of the Pen Statute, the SCA, and CALEA to create a vehicle for disclosure of prospective cell information on a real time basis on less than probable cause").

38 *In re* Application of the U.S. for an Order for Disclosure of Telecommunications Records and Authorizing the Use of a Pen register and Trap and Trace (*In re S.D.N.Y. Application*), 405 F. Supp. 2d 435, 437–48 (S.D.N.Y. 2005). Judge Gorenstein notes differences between the instant case and three published decisions denying government access to cell site information with a hybrid order insofar as "these cases appear to involve requests for cell site information that go beyond both what has been sought in this case and what has actually been received by the Government pursuant to any cell site application in this District." *Id.* (citing *In re* Application for Pen Register and Trap/Trace Device with Cell Site Location Authority (*In re 2005 S.D. Tex. Application*), 396 F. Supp. 2d 747 (S.D. Tex. 2005); *In re E.D.N.Y. Application*, 396 F. Supp. 2d 294; *In re* Application of the U.S. for an Order Authorizing the Installation and Use of a Pen Register and Caller Identification Sys. on Tel. Numbers [Sealed], 402 F. Supp. 2d 597 (D. Md. 2005)).

Judge Gorenstein further explained that his analysis was based on the "technology that is available to the Government in the District," recognizing that, with respect to future cases, "[he could not] know how ... technology may change."[39] For Judge Gorenstein, then, the current capacity of the cell tower network in question – the court even looked at a map of the location of various cell towers in Lower Manhattan, an area it described as "densely populated by cell towers"[40] – was a factor in authorizing law enforcement access to the cell site data with a hybrid order. If that network's capabilities were to change as a result of an evolution in technology that yielded more precise location information, the court might rule differently in future cases. Indeed, the court's order might be as ephemeral as the capacities of the specific network the opinion seeks to comprehend at a specific moment in time.

Notwithstanding the DOJ's historic view of the relative precision of *single* CSLI and its corresponding position that a warrant is not needed, when seeking to compel "more precise" prospective location data generated by GPS or similar technologies, DOJ's stated policy, at least as of 2011, was to obtain a warrant based on probable cause.[41] As of November 2016, it remains unknown, at least to the general public, whether the DOJ's guidance to prosecutors about seeking a warrant for *single* CSLI has changed. Perhaps as a cautionary response to the concurring opinions in *Jones*, discussed later, the DOJ may choose to advise prosecutors, as a matter of policy, to seek a probable cause warrant for any prospective cell phone tracking, whenever possible.

B *The* Jones *Opinions*

Much of the conversation about contemporary location tracking technologies intersects with the Supreme Court's 2012 decision in *United States v. Jones*. The facts in the *Jones* case involved law enforcement's warrantless tracking of a Jeep Cherokee for thirty days with a GPS device attached to the undercarriage of the vehicle.

The questions presented were:

1 Whether the warrantless use of a GPS tracking device on respondent's vehicle to monitor its movements on public streets violated the Fourth Amendment.
2 Whether the government violated respondent's Fourth Amendment rights by attaching the GPS tracking device to his vehicle without a valid warrant and without his consent.[42]

Prior to the issuance of the decision, it was reasonable to wonder whether the Court's reasoning would have implications for law enforcement cell phone tracking, as well. The oral argument in the *Jones* case certainly had its dramatic moments, especially this

39 *In re S.D.N.Y. Application*, 405 F. Supp. 2d at 450.

40 *Id.* at 437.

41 *The Electronic Communications Privacy Act: Government Perspectives on Protecting Privacy in the Digital Age: Hearing before the S. Comm. on the Judiciary*, 112th Cong. 5 at 7 (2011) (testimony of James A. Baker, Assoc. Deputy Attorney Gen., U.S. Dep't of Justice). In *United States v. Skinner*, 690 F.3d 772 (6th Cir. 2012), however, the DEA appears to have acquired real-time GPS location data without a warrant. The opinion talks about tracking Skinner's phone via real-time GPS and pinging, but, overall, there is not a terribly descriptive or clear explanation of the kind of location data at issue. In any event, the cell phone tracking ended in 2006, well before Associate Deputy Attorney General Baker discussed DOJ's policy with respect to "more precise" prospective location data in 2011.

42 Brief of Respondent, *supra* note 3, at i.

exchange between Chief Justice John Roberts and the government's counsel, Deputy Solicitor General Michael Dreeben:

> **Chief Justice Roberts:** You think there would also not be a search if you put a GPS device on all of our cars, monitored our movements for a month? You think you're entitled to do that under your theory?
>
> **Mr. Dreeben:** The Justices of *this* Court?
>
> **Chief Justice Roberts:** Yes.
>
> [...]
>
> **Mr Dreeben:** Under our theory and under this Court's cases, the Justices of this Court when driving on public roadways have no greater expectation of –
>
> **Chief Justice Roberts:** So, your answer is yes, you could tomorrow decide that you put a GPS device on every one of our cars, follow us for a month; no problem under the Constitution?[43]

Mr. Dreeben's answer, as it unfolded over the course of questioning by the chief justice and several other justices, was essentially reducible to the proposition that when the government is monitoring the movements of any person in public (in this case on the public roadways), there is no constitutional impediment to the use of tracking technologies, including GPS devices. The argument relies on *United States v. Knotts*,[44] a case in which a radio transmitter beeper planted in a five-gallon drum of chloroform emitted signals that assisted the government in physically following an automobile carrying the drum on public streets, where the Court held that "a person traveling in an automobile on public thoroughfares has no reasonable expectation of privacy in his movements from one place to another."[45] The Court applied the standard reasonable expectation of privacy test, which was established in *Katz v. United States*,[46] and decided that, essentially, we do not have a reasonable expectation of privacy in the movements we expose in public.

For anyone in the audience who had read the government's opening brief in *Jones*, Mr. Dreeben's answer to the chief justice's question was not particularly surprising, if palpably uncomfortable – imagine having to argue to the Supreme Court of the United States, on behalf of the entire executive branch, that there is no constitutional impediment to the government's use of GPS devices to track their cars on public thoroughfares! It was a captivating moment, at once both humorous and dramatic: Chief Justice Roberts's hypothetical had threatened the logic of *Knotts* and put Dreeben, temporarily at least, on his heels. The question cut to the core issues before the Court by throwing into high relief law enforcement's unfettered, indiscriminate ability to track any individual's movements in public for days, weeks, even months at a time using a credit card sized GPS device discreetly attached to the undercarriage of a car. If there is little to no check (other than perhaps its better judgment) on the government's covert use of GPS devices to monitor the comings and goings of Supreme Court justices as they drive down public

[43] Transcript of Oral Argument at 9–10, *United States v. Jones*, 132 S. Ct. 945 (2012) (No. 10–1259) (emphasis added), http://www.supremecourt.gov/oral_arguments/argument_transcripts/10–1259.pdf.
[44] 460 U.S. 276 (1980).
[45] *Id.* at 278, 281.
[46] 389 U.S. 347 (1967).

streets, what does that suggest about the lawful scope of the government's ability to track the movements of ordinary citizens?[47]

At a legal symposium on the *Jones* case, Antoine Jones's cocounsel, Walter Dellinger, recounted how he had described such consequences in an interview with Nina Totenberg:

> If the Supreme Court gave a green light to [warrantless GPS tracking, then] any officer can install any GPS device for any reason on anybody's car, even if the officer thinks it would be interesting to know where Supreme Court justices go at night when they leave the courthouse. No one would be immune from having GPS devices installed on their vehicles.[48]

Professor Dellinger went on to relate how that interview had aired the very morning of the *Jones* oral argument, at which Chief Justice Roberts's questioning included the hypothetical – Dellinger's hypothetical – asking the deputy solicitor general whether the government's theory permitted the tracking of Supreme Court justices with GPS devices attached to their cars. Professor Dellinger offered that he knew his client Jones had likely won his case when that question was asked, with "doctrine to follow" – whatever it might be.[49]

Petitioner Jones did, in fact, win, with a unanimous 9–0 ruling in his favor. But the doctrine that followed, at least from the majority opinion, offered little to no guidance to lower courts with respect to whether and under what circumstances warrantless government tracking of a cell phone, with historical or prospective data, would be a violation of the Fourth Amendment. Specifically, the majority opinion offered a property-based rationale – not a reasonable expectation of privacy analysis under *Katz* – in support of the holding that the government's conduct constituted a Fourth Amendment search. Authored by Justice Antonin Scalia, and joined by Chief Justice Roberts, Justices Clarence Thomas, Anthony Kennedy, and Sonia Sotomayor, the majority held that the government's installation of a GPS device on a target's vehicle for the purpose of gathering information constitutes a search.[50] Further defining the offending conduct, the majority explains, "The Government physically occupied private property for the purpose of obtaining information."[51] Consequently, though "trespass alone does not qualify [as a search]," a search does occur when it is "conjoined with … an attempt to find something or to obtain information."[52]

Justice Scalia, while not repudiating the reasonable expectation of privacy test, reasoned that the Fourth Amendment must be interpreted to "assur[e] preservation of that degree of privacy that existed when the Fourth Amendment was adopted."[53] To accomplish a restoration of the status quo by preserving that particular degree of privacy, Justice

47 For an extended argument that these kinds of general threats to the security of the people against unreasonable searches and seizures signal a need for Fourth Amendment regulation, see David Gray, The Fourth Amendment in an Age of Surveillance (2017).

48 Walter Dellinger, Keynote Address at the North Carolina Journal of Law & Technology Symposium: *U.S. v. Jones*: Defining a Search in the 21st Century (Jan. 25, 2013), http://ncjolt.org/multimedia/symposium-videos; *see also* Nina Totenberg, *Do Police Need Warrants for GPS Tracking Devices?* NPR (Nov. 8, 2011), http://m.npr.org/story/142032419.

49 Dellinger, *supra* note 48.

50 *United States v. Jones*, 132 S. Ct. 945, 949 (2012).

51 *Id.*

52 *Id.* at 951 n. 5.

53 *Id.* at 946 (quoting *Kyllo v. United States*, 533 U.S. 27, 34 (2001)).

Scalia "interpreted the Fourth Amendment as protecting against common law trespasses."[54] Accordingly, the government's attachment of the GPS device with the intent to gather information was a common law trespass and, therefore, a Fourth Amendment search. This property-based, trespass rationale neither disturbs the logic of *Knotts*, nor required the majority to apply a *Katz* reasonable expectation of privacy analysis to the facts in the *Jones* case. Indeed, the majority opinion reconciles the two decisions, *Jones* and *Knotts*, by noting that the *Katz* test "*added to*, not *substituted for*, the common law trespassory test," while *Knotts* addressed the *Katz* test only.[55]

The application of this trespass, property-based rationale also allowed the majority to avoid ruling in a way that would have implications for other types of tracking technologies that solely employ the transmission of radio or other electronic signals not enabled by a direct physical trespass, such as tracking a target's cell phone through compelled disclosure of information possessed by a third party. Justice Alito, in his concurrence, which was joined by Justices Ruth Bader Ginsburg, Stephen Breyer, and Elena Kagan, was critical of the majority's approach, questioning the majority's rather tenuous reliance on analogous eighteenth-century situations to address this twenty-first-century surveillance issue. He humorously describes the "very tiny constable" or "gigantic coach" necessary to permit the eighteenth-century version of GPS tracking (that is, the constable hiding in the coach, unbeknownst to the occupants, to monitor its movements).[56]

In contrast to the precomputer age, when significant privacy protections were more practical because the work of surveillance itself required more human labor, new technologies such as GPS-enabled smart phones and GPS tracking devices make long-term tracking much cheaper and easier, thus increasing the government's surveillance powers. In Justice Alito's view, society's expectation has been that law enforcement neither had nor could "secretly monitor and catalogue every single movement of an individual's car" over a long period of time.[57] Thus, under the *Katz* test, long-term monitoring, in this case four weeks of surveillance, was a Fourth Amendment search insofar as it "exceeded pre-GPS societal expectations that such invasive monitoring was" at least "unlikely," if not "impossible."[58]

Justice Sotomayor joined the *Jones* majority opinion, but also wrote a separate concurring opinion. (Although she signaled her broad agreement with Justice Alito's alternative holding, her choice not to join his concurrence preserved a single, clear majority rule.) In that concurrence, she explained that "the majority's opinion reflects an irreducible constitutional minimum: When the Government physically invades personal property to gather information, a search occurs."[59] But her support for the opinion, which (merely) affirms the "constitutional relevance" of the government's physical trespass on private property, did not end her analysis of the privacy interests and expectations at issue with respect to other forms of government surveillance that do not require such physical intrusion.[60] Indeed, she notes that Justice Alito is correct in observing that nontrespassory

54 Orin S. Kerr, *Defending Equilibrium-Adjustment*, 125 HARV. L. REV. F. 84, 88 (2012).
55 *Jones*, 132 S.Ct. at 952.
56 *Jones*, 132 S.Ct. at 958 n.3 (Alito, J., concurring).
57 *Id.* at 964.
58 Kerr, *supra* note 54, at 89.
59 *Jones*, 132 S. Ct at 955 (Sotomayor, J., concurring).
60 *Id.* Indeed, Justice Sotomayor criticizes the Alito concurrence for "discount[ing] altogether the constitutional relevance of the Government's physical intrusion on Jones' Jeep," thereby "erod[ing] that

surveillance techniques will "affect the *Katz* test by shaping the evolution of societal privacy expectations."[61] She therefore agrees that, "at the very least, 'longer term GPS monitoring in investigations of most offenses impinges on expectations of privacy.'"[62]

Having qualified the two other *Jones* opinions as, more or less, addressing constitutional minimums, Justice Sotomayor ventures further to suggest that, in investigations employing "even short term monitoring, some unique attributes of GPS surveillance relevant to the *Katz* analysis will require particular attention."[63] For her, the privacy interests at issue with GPS monitoring include the government's ability to ascertain "a precise, comprehensive record of a person's public movements that reflects a wealth of detail about her familial, political, professional, religious, and sexual associations."[64] She also recognizes that once recorded and stored, depending upon how long the data are customarily retained by the third party in question, the government could mine such information for that person's lifetime or longer. Indeed, depending on time frames of storage, it may become impossible ever to escape one's past. Moreover, she asserts that because government use of GPS monitoring is surreptitious and "cheap" when compared with other traditional methods of surveillance, it evades some of the checks or sources of friction in the system that "constrain abusive law enforcement practices: limited police resources and community hostility."[65]

Justice Sotomayor's succinct analysis of the privacy implications of GPS monitoring, which encompasses location tracking beyond the physical attachment of GPS devices, highlights some of the most significant privacy concerns in the digital age: data mining, the relative strength of access standards, data acquisition practices so cheap and easy they can facilitate abusive police activities, and a limitless flow of third party data law enforcement can use to expose or reconstruct the intimate details of a person's life. Indeed, Justice Sotomayor warns that such cheap, unfettered access to broad swaths of intimate information "may alter the relationship between citizen and government in a way that is inimical to democratic society."[66] For her, then, such technology, which is generating the government's increasingly clear sense of sight with regard to the lives of individuals, facilitates a power shift that is fundamentally inhibitory to open participation in a democratic society.[67]

Notwithstanding Justice Sotomayor's apparent focus on the *Katz* test for purposes of examining and curbing the expanded government power afforded by GPS tracking technologies, she suggests that, "more fundamentally, it may be necessary to reconsider the premise that an individual has no reasonable expectation of privacy in information voluntarily disclosed to third parties."[68] She is referring to the infamous third party doctrine,

longstanding protection for privacy expectations inherent in items of property that people possess or control." *Id.*

61 *Id.*

62 *Id.*

63 *Id.*

64 *Id.*

65 *Id.* at 956 (quoting *Illinois v. Lidster*, 540 U.S. 419, 426 (2004)).

66 *Id.* at 956 (quoting *United States v. Cuevas-Perez*, 640 F.3d 272, 285 (7th Cir. 2011) (Flaum, J., concurring)).

67 For further discussion about the importance of privacy to democracy, see Stephen E. Henderson, *Fourth Amendment Time Machines (and What They Might Say about Police Body Cameras)*, 18 U. Pa. J. Const. L. 933, 954–60 (2016).

68 *Id.* at 957.

a long-standing constitutional principle that, when taken in its strongest expression, suggests that once data is disclosed to a third party, it no longer receives Fourth Amendment protection. Justice Sotomayor notes that in our digital age, "people disclose the phone numbers that they dial or text to their cellular providers; the URLs that they visit and the e-mail addresses with which they correspond to their Internet service providers; and the books, groceries, and medications they purchase to online retailers."[69] Cognizant that the Fourth Amendment provides little to no limit on government acquisition of this information, she is skeptical of Justice Alito's observation that people may find the "tradeoff of privacy for convenience worthwhile" (e.g., we willingly generate more constitutionally nonprotected third party data for the convenience of mobile devices) and that we have come to accept this "diminution of privacy as inevitable."[70] On the contrary, she suggests that this "trade" is not self-conscious and informed in a manner that could support his conclusions.

No other justice joined Justice Sotomayor's concurrence. But her focus on the third party doctrine, which, to date, has not been reconsidered by the Supreme Court in the context of cell phone location tracking or other kinds of communication technologies through which people disclose all kinds of revelatory information to third parties, has become a central point of discussion and disagreement between majority and minority opinions in a line of federal appellate decisions about whether the Fourth Amendment protects government compelled disclosure of historical location data.

C *Historical Location Data, the ECPA, and Federal Appellate Court Opinions*

Unlike the DOJ's creative, if controversial, attempt to compel the production of prospective CSLI by combining different authorities in the ECPA, the DOJ has long taken the position that a D order alone clearly authorizes collection of historical location data. Specifically, the DOJ argues that historical CSLI satisfies each of the three elements necessary to fall within the scope of 18 U.S.C. § 2703.[71] First, a cell phone company is a provider of "electronic communications service" to the public.[72] Second, "cell site information constitutes 'a record of other information pertaining to a subscriber or to a customer of such service.'"[73] Finally, "cell site information is non-content information, as it does not provide the content of any phone conversation the user has had over the

69 *Id.*

70 *Id.*

71 Brief for the United States at 8–9, *In re* The Application of the U.S. for an Order Directing a Provider of Elec. Commc'n Serv. to Disclose Records to the Gov't (*Appeal of In re W.D. Pa. Application*), 620 F.3d 304 (3d Cir. 2010) (No. 08-4227), 2009 WL 3866618.

72 *Id.* at 10. The Wiretap Act and SCA define electronic communication service ("ECS") to mean "any service which provides to users thereof the ability to send or receive wire or electronic communications." 18 U.S.C. §§ 2510(15), 2711(1). Cell phone service providers provide their customers with the ability to send "wire communications," and thus they are providers of electronic communications service. *See* §§ 2510(1), (15). Moreover, the DOJ takes the position that:

> [a] "wire communication" necessarily involves the human voice. *See* § 2510(1) (defining "wire communication") and § 2510 (defining "aural transfer"); S. Rep. No. 541, 99th Cong., 2d Sess. 11 (1986), *reprinted in* 1986 U.S. Code Cong. & Admin. News 3555, 3565 ("cellular communications – whether they are between two cellular telephones or between a cellular telephone and a 'land line' telephone – are included in the definition of 'wire communications' and are covered by the statute").

Id. at 11 n.10.

73 *Id.*

cell phone."[74] Consistent with this statutory analysis, several lower courts have granted government applications to compel historical location data with a D order.[75]

Notably, as is the case when used to compel prospective tracking, a D order does not require a probable cause showing. Rather, law enforcement must provide only "specific and articulable facts that there are reasonable grounds to believe" that the information to be compelled "is relevant and material to an ongoing investigation."[76] The D order standard can be characterized as a "*Terry*-stop" standard, a reference to *Terry v. Ohio*, where the Supreme Court created the reasonable suspicion standard for sidewalk stop-and-frisk encounters.[77] The *Terry* standard is met "when an officer 'point[s] to specific and articulable facts which, taken together with rational inferences from those facts, evince more than an inchoate and unparticularized suspicion or hunch of criminal activity.'"[78]

The first federal appellate court to consider whether a D order authorizes the collection of historical CSLI was the Third Circuit, which held that it "is obtainable under a § 2703(d) order and that such an order does not require the traditional probable cause determination."[79] Specifically, the Third Circuit recognized historical location data as a record concerning an electronic communication service or remote computing service under § 2703(c)(1), and, accordingly, the government was authorized to compel its production with a D order.[80] The Third Circuit also found, however, that magistrate judges have the discretion to deny a government application for a D order, even when the D Order standard has been satisfied, in favor of a probable cause requirement. This determination was based upon the Third Circuit's reading of the D order statutory language as "language of permission rather than mandate."[81] The extent to which a magistrate judge has discretion to deny a D order is unclear, as the opinion merely instructs that the option to require a warrant "be used sparingly," and that judges do not have "arbitrary" discretion such that when requiring a warrant a magistrate judge must "make fact findings and give a full explanation that balances the government's need (not merely desire) for the information with the privacy interests of cell phone users."[82]

Also worth noting is the Third Circuit's statement that "a cell phone customer has not 'voluntarily' shared his location information with a cellular provider in any meaningful way."[83] This pronouncement was a response to the government's argument that *Smith v. Maryland*,[84] the seminal third party doctrine case where the Court held that there is no reasonable expectation of privacy in phone numbers dialed, should control. This

74 *Id.* (citing 18 U.S.C. § 2510(8) and defining the "contents" of communications to include information concerning its "substance, purport, or meaning").

75 *See, e.g., In re* Applications of the U.S. for Orders Pursuant to Title 18, U.S. Code, Section 2703(d), 509 F. Supp. 2d 76, 82 (D. Mass. 2007) (granting the government's application for historical cell site information based on the government's statutory analysis of 18 U.S.C. §§ 2703(c), (d)).

76 18 U.S.C. § 2703(d) (2010).

77 392 U.S. 1, 30 (1968).

78 *United States v. Mason*, 628 F.3d 123, 128 (4th Cir. 2010) (quoting *United States v. Branch*, 537 F.3d 328, 336 (4th Cir. 2008)).

79 *In re* Application of the U.S. for an Order Directing a Provider of Elec. Commc'n Serv. to Disclose Records to the Gov't, 620 F.3d 304, 313 (3d Cir. 2010).

80 *Id.* at 313.

81 *Id.* at 316.

82 *Id.* at 316, 319.

83 *Id.* at 317.

84 442 U.S. 735 (1979).

concept of *voluntary disclosure* – and what it means in the digital age for purposes of the application of the third party doctrine – is of critical importance to other circuit court majority opinions analyzing historical CSLI, as well as a significant point of dispute with the accompanying dissents.

The next federal appellate court to address law enforcement access standards for compelled historical CSLI was the Fifth Circuit,[85] which issued the first federal appellate court opinion directly to address how the Fourth Amendment applies to historical CSLI and a win for the government. The court, however, limited its ruling to the specific kinds of historic CSLI at issue in that case: historical location data created when the user places and terminates a call. Recognizing the changing nature of technology, the court explained that its opinion does not address orders for cell tower dumps, orders for community of interest requests, or orders requesting location information for either the duration of calls or the time when the phone is idle.[86] The Fifth Circuit's ruling also does not address the surreptitious installation of spyware on a target's phone by the government or instances when the government otherwise "hijacks" a phone's GPS, with or without the help of a third party provider.[87]

The Fifth Circuit disagreed with the Third Circuit's interpretation that D order statutory language provides magistrates discretion to require a probable cause showing. In the Fifth Circuit's view, if the government makes a reasonable suspicion showing as expressed by the statute's requirement that the government articulate "specific and articulable facts" that information sought is "relevant and material to an ongoing investigation," then the magistrate judge must grant the D order.[88] For the Fifth Circuit, "the text of the statute shows that Congress does not want magistrate judges second-guessing its calculus."[89]

With respect to the Fourth Amendment question, the Fifth Circuit focused, consistent with a third party doctrine analysis, on *who* is gathering the data – in this case a third party telecommunications provider, not government agents – and analyzed the issue under the Supreme Court's business records cases. In other words, for the Fifth Circuit, the historical CSLI at issue were business records to be analyzed under a traditional third party doctrine analysis, not under GPS tracking precedents that involve the government's *direct* collection of location data. The Fifth Circuit explained that the historical CSLI at issue were clearly business records because the "cell service provider collects and stores historical cell site data for its own business purposes ... the Government does not require service providers to record this information or store it. The providers control what they record and how long these records are retained."[90]

To apply a traditional third party doctrine analysis, however, *Smith v. Maryland* requires that the records in possession of the third party be the result of a *voluntary disclosure* by the user or customer.[91] Unlike the Third Circuit, the Fifth Circuit found that cell phone users understand that providers record their location data when they use their phones, at least to the same extent that, under *Smith v. Maryland*, users of landline

85 *In re* Application of the U.S. for Historical Cell Site Data, 724 F.3d 600 (5th Cir. 2013).
86 *Id.* at 615.
87 *Id.*
88 *Id.* at 607–608.
89 *Id.* at 607 n.8.
90 *Id.* at 611–612.
91 442 U.S. 735, 742–744 (1979).

phones understood they conveyed the numbers they dialed to the phone company.[92] Moreover, the Fifth Circuit characterized this disclosure as *voluntary*: a cell phone user "makes a choice to get a phone, to select a particular service provider, and to make a call, and because he knows that the call conveys cell site information, the provider retains this information, and the provider will turn it over to the police if they have a court order, he voluntarily conveys his cell site data each time he makes a call."[93]

Three other circuits – the Eleventh,[94] Sixth,[95] and Fourth[96] – have also issued opinions holding that the government's compelled disclosure of historical CSLI from a third party provider does not violate a user's Fourth Amendment rights. Like the Fifth Circuit, these courts interpret the third party doctrine to be the controlling precedent, not the concurring opinions in *Jones*, which at best suggested some future rethinking of this rule. These courts also agree with the Fifth Circuit's assertion that a cell phone user voluntary conveys her location information to a provider in the course of making and receiving calls. In his concurring opinion, Eleventh Circuit Judge William Pryor expressed what he believes to be the solution for the user of both a *Smith* wire line phone and the more modern cell phone who does not want to convey information voluntarily: "If a telephone caller does not want to reveal dialed numbers to the telephone company, he has another option: don't place a call. If a cell phone user does not want to reveal his location to a cellular carrier, he also has another option: turn off the cell phone."[97] All three of these majority opinions agree that a straightforward application of the third party doctrine, which is the controlling Supreme Court precedent, compels the conclusion that the government did not violate the Fourth Amendment. Indeed, without a change in the controlling law, they assert that they cannot conclude otherwise.[98]

Dissenting opinions by judges in both the Eleventh and Fourth Circuits challenge this conclusion, particularly with respect to the view that users *voluntary convey* their location data to third party providers. Dissenting Eleventh Circuit Judge Beverly Martin explained that cell phone users "do not affirmatively enter their location to make a call … [and] when a cell phone user receives a call, he hasn't voluntarily exposed anything at all."[99] Moreover, she observed an important distinction between the notice provided to users dialing numbers, as recognized by *Smith*, and creation and conveyance of location data:

92 *In re* Application of the U.S. for Historical Cell Site Data, 724 F.3d at 613.
93 *Id.* at 614.
94 *United States v. Davis*, 785 F.3d 498 (11th Cir. 2015) (en banc).
95 *United States v. Carpenter*, 819 F.3d 880 (6th Cir. 2016). In addition to this historical CSLI case, in *United States v. Skinner*, 690 F.3d 772 (6th Cir. 2012), a Sixth Circuit panel held that the defendant "did not have a reasonable expectation of privacy in the data emanating from his cell phone that showed its location." *Id.* at 775.
96 *United States v. Graham*, 824 F.3d 421(4th Cir. 2016) (en banc).
97 *Davis*, 785 F.3d at 520 (W. Pryor, J., concurring).
98 The Eleventh Circuit majority opinion in *Davis* offers an alternative rationale for why the government's compelled collection of historical CSLI would be reasonable and thus not be a search *even if* the third party doctrine did not apply. For analysis and critique of this alternative rationale, see Orin S. Kerr, *Eleventh Circuit Rules for the Feds on Cell Site Records but Then Overreaches*, Wash. Post (May 5, 2015), https://www.washingtonpost.com/news/volokh-conspiracy/wp/2015/05/05/eleventh-circuit-rules-for-the-feds-on-cell-site-records-but-then-overreaches/.
99 *Davis*, 785 F.3d at 534. (Martin, J., dissenting).

> The *Smith* Court also emphasized that the numbers a person dials appear on the person's telephone bill and referenced the pre-automation process that required the caller to recite phone numbers out loud to a phone operator in order to make a call. Thus, the Court concluded that "telephone users ... typically *know* that they must convey numerical information to the phone company." *Smith*, 442 U.S. at 743, 99 S. Ct. at 2581 [emphasis added]. There is not the same sort of "knowing" disclosure of cell site location data to phone companies because there is no history of cell phone users having to affirmatively disclose their location to an operator in order to make a call. The extent of voluntariness of disclosure by a user is simply lower for cell site location data than for the telephone numbers a person dials. For that reason, I don't think *Smith* controls this case.[100]

Fourth Circuit Judge James Wynn put an even finer point on what "voluntary conveyance" means in the context of third party doctrine Supreme Court precedent. Looking at all of the relevant Supreme Court cases, including *Smith* (defendant dialed phone numbers), *United States v. Miller*[101] (defendant submitted multiple checks and deposit slips), and *United States v. Hoffa*[102] (defendant made statements to an associate disclosing endeavors to bribe [jury] members), Judge Wynn discerned that *voluntary conveyance* meant at least two things: (1) the defendant "knew he was communicating particular information" and (2) the defendant "had acted in some way to submit the particular information he knew."[103] For Judge Wynn, it is crucial in all of these cases that there was an "action" (e.g., "depositing, dialing, speaking"), and "where many pieces of data were compiled into records, like in *Miller* and *Smith*, "there was presumptively a discrete action behind each piece of data."[104] Judge Wynn asserted that Supreme Court precedent has never suggested that the "simple act of signing up for a bank account or a phone line was enough to willingly turn over thousands of pages of personal data."[105] Based upon the interpretation of *voluntary conveyance* as a user's knowledge of a particular piece of information he then actively transmits, Judge Wynn concluded that historical CSLI is not voluntarily conveyed by the cell phone user and, therefore, not subject to the third party doctrine. Specifically, he believes that the cell phone customer neither possesses knowledge of his CSLI nor acts to disclose it to a third party in the same patently active manner found in all relevant Supreme Court precedents.

What it means to convey information voluntarily to a third party and thus trigger application of the third party doctrine has implications beyond the location data space. Indeed, in an IP-based communications environment, users may be completely unaware of when they share data with myriad third parties, some of whom may also be unknown to users.[106] How this question will continue to evolve, or be addressed by the Supreme Court, whether or not in the context of location data, remains to be seen. If the Supreme Court or lower courts determine that the third party doctrine does not apply in a particular circumstance to particular information, then courts will either have to rely on the

100 *Id.* at 534–535.
101 425 U.S. 435, 442 (1976).
102 385 U.S. 293, 302 (1966).
103 *United States v. Graham*, 824 F.3d 421, 443 (4th Cir. 2016) (en banc) (Wynn, J., dissenting).
104 *Id.*
105 *Id.*
106 For a detailed discussion of the concept of voluntary conveyance in the context of an IP-based communications environment, *see* Bellovin et al., *supra* note 24.

Katz reasonable expectation of privacy test or apply different doctrine, existing or new, to determine whether a Fourth Amendment search has occurred.

D *IMSI Catchers*

As previously discussed, IMSI catcher technology permits the covert, direct collection of location data, which I've termed *unmediated surveillance* because production of the data is not compelled from a third party provider and it is difficult, if not impossible, to detect when the surveillance occurs. IMSI catchers silently call out to mobile devices, tricking them into believing they are communicating with legitimate cell towers and forcing them to identify themselves.

In 2011, a decade after the Harris Corporation introduced the StingRay, the FBI's use of the device surfaced during the pretrial stages of a criminal case. The government was prosecuting Daniel David Rigmaiden for his role in a scheme through which he obtained fraudulent tax refunds for hundreds of persons, many of whom were deceased.[107] After a lengthy investigation, federal agents located Rigmaiden, in part by tracking the location of "[a wireless data card] connected to a laptop computer" in his apartment.[108] The government did not know Rigmaiden's actual identity until agents arrested him.[109] Indeed, the government's only solid lead was an Internet Protocol (IP) address associated with the prepaid Verizon data card that Rigmaiden used to transmit fraudulent tax returns to the IRS. To narrow down the location of the data card, the government obtained historical cell-site records from Verizon.[110] Those records indicated that the data card's location was within an approximately one-quarter -square-mile area. Because Verizon did not have the technical capability to provide more precise location information, the government used a StingRay to locate the data card, which led the agents to Rigmaiden's apartment.[111]

Throughout the pretrial discovery and litigation process, prosecutors appear to have made strategic efforts and choices to limit the StingRay's exposure.[112] In response to

107 *United States v. Rigmaiden* (*Rigmaiden I*), 844 F. Supp. 2d 982 (D. Ariz. 2012). The government indicted Rigmaiden in a superseding indictment on seventy-four counts of wire fraud, aggravated identify theft, mail fraud, and conspiracy to commit these offenses. *United States v. Rigmaiden* (*Rigmaiden II*), No. CR 08-814-PHX-DGC, 2013 WL 1932800, at *1 (D. Ariz. May 8, 2013). In April 2014, Rigmaiden pleaded guilty to four felony counts of mail fraud, wire fraud, and conspiracy to commit these offenses. *See* Dennis Wagner, *Tax Scammer Rigmaiden Pleads Guilty, Gets Time Served*, AZCENTRAL (Apr. 8, 2014), http://www.azcentral.com/story/news/politics/2014/04/07/rigmaiden-tax-scammer-pleadsguilty/7448151. He was sentenced to time served, which amounted to the sixty-eight months he spent awaiting trial. *Id.*

108 *Rigmaiden II*, 2013 WL 1932800, at *1.

109 *Id.* at *1–6.

110 *Id.* at *1–4.

111 Investigative Details Report at 7, *Rigmaiden I*, 844 F. Supp. 2d 982 (No. CR 08-814-PHX-DGC), https://ia600707.us.archive.org/33/items/gov.uscourts.azd.396130/gov.uscourts.azd.396130.484.6.pdf (stating in the report, written by U.S. Postal Inspection Services Inspector James L. Wilson, that "on 7/16/08, we were informed that they were able to track a signal and were using a 'Sting[R]ay' to pinpoint the location of the aircard").

112 These strategic choices appear to include conceding, *arguendo*, that its efforts to locate Rigmaiden's data card constituted a Fourth Amendment search and seizure. With the concession, the details about the StingRay and how it was employed in the investigation of Rigmaiden would, presumably, be less or not relevant to Rigmaiden's attempts to litigate various Fourth Amendment–based suppression motions he filed, and thus protect certain details about the technology and its use from disclosure.

certain Rigmaiden discovery requests, for example, the government argued that the technology used to locate the defendant's data card and the manner in which the technology was employed were "sensitive law enforcement information"[113] subject to the qualified privilege recognized in *Roviaro v. United States* and *United States v. Van Horn*.[114] These cases essentially hold that the government can shield information about sensitive investigative techniques when a court determines that such disclosure would not be relevant or helpful to the defense or otherwise "essential to a fair determination of a cause."[115] In an affidavit submitted to support the government's effort to keep details of its technology secret, an investigating agent asserted that disclosure "could result in the FBI's inability to protect the public from terrorism and other criminal activity because, through public disclosures, this technology has been rendered essentially useless for future investigations."[116]

That the federal government sought to protect its use of cell site simulators as a sensitive source and method in the Rigmaiden prosecution – to the extent that it would not even acknowledge the name of the specific equipment it used[117] – is consistent with a much larger effort, affecting state and local law enforcement, to prevent public disclosure of the technology and its capabilities. Notwithstanding these efforts, due in large part to media stories, public records requests, and the advocacy efforts of various civil society groups, law enforcement use of IMSI catcher technology is no longer "secret." The first significant news report appeared in September of 2011, when the *Wall Street Journal* published a story about the surfacing of the StingRay device in the *Rigmaiden* case.[118]

Although there may be valid reasons and appropriate circumstances to protect sensitive sources and methods, the StingRay secrecy effort has involved some government activity that raises significant concerns with respect to the government's candor with courts and its withholding of information that would have been potentially helpful, possibly essential, to defendants' abilities to litigate Fourth Amendment search issues during pretrial motion processes. Such actions included (1) what might be characterized as a purposeful lack of disclosure to magistrate judges when seeking approval to use a cell site simulator in a criminal investigation – specifically, magistrate judges were asked to sign orders unaware that they were authorizing government StingRay use; and (2) strict nondisclosure agreements with state and local law enforcement that, in certain

113 *Rigmaiden I*, 844 F. Supp. 2d at 989.

114 *Id.* at 2 (citing *Roviaro v. United States*, 353 U.S. 53 (1957) and *United States v. Van Horn*, 789 F.2d 1492 (11th Cir. 1986)).

115 *Roviaro*, 353 U.S. at 60–61. With respect to government surveillance equipment, the defendant-target of electronic surveillance is not entitled to learn the location and type of equipment used by the government unless he can show sufficient need for such information. *Van Horn*, 789 F.2d at 1492.

116 Affidavit of Supervisory Special Agent Bradley S. Morrison at 2, *Rigmaiden I*, 844 F. Supp. 2d 982 (No. CR 08-814-PHX-DGC) [hereinafter Morrison Affidavit 2012], http://www.documentcloud.org/documents/1282619-11-10-17-2011-u-s-v-rigmaiden-cr08-814-phx-dgc.html.

117 *Id.* at 1 ("On July 16, 2008, FBI technical personnel used equipment to locate an aircard believe to be used by the defendant in this matter, and that equipment falls within the statutory definition of a pen register/trap and trace device. The actual make and model of the equipment used in any particular operation by the FBI is law enforcement sensitive, and pursuant to FBI policy, cannot be released to the general public").

118 Jennifer Valentino-Devries, *Stingray Phone Tracker Fuels Constitutional Clash*, Wall St. J. (Sept. 22, 2011), http://www.wsj.com/articles/SB10001424053111904194604576583112723197574.

circumstances, prevented state authorities from disclosing information both to courts and to the defense about the use of IMSI catcher technology.

In many cases, if law enforcement did obtain a court order to use a StingRay, it was not by a probable cause warrant but, instead, a Pen Register/Trap and Trace Order ("Pen/Trap Order"), which only requires a law enforcement agent to certify to a court that the information sought is "relevant and material" to an ongoing investigation. In one federal case, *United States v. Lambis*,[119] the DEA obtained a Pen/Trap Order and used an IMSI catcher to locate the defendant inside an apartment building. The federal district court found that this use of the IMSI catcher constituted a Fourth Amendment search. Among other precedents, the court cited *Kyllo v. United States*,[120] a case where the Supreme Court also found that law enforcement's use of a heat sensing device, which was not then in general public use, to explore interior details of a home that were imperceptible to agents without the device's aid constituted a search.

If defendants are unaware that IMSI catcher technology has been used to locate them or otherwise collect information from their mobile devices, then they are unable to raise Fourth Amendment suppression challenges.[121] Such evasions are neither uncommon nor infrequent. In Baltimore, Maryland, for example, the public defender's office is reviewing a log of nineteen hundred cases where StingRays were used to determine whether there are grounds to move to overturn convictions.[122] In other circumstances, prosecutors chose to dismiss cases in lieu of turning over information about StingRays.[123]

The Maryland Special Court of Appeals in *State v. Andrews*,[124] the first appellate court decision to address both constitutional and government disclosure issues involving IMSI catcher technology, had harsh words for the government's use of nondisclosure agreements, suggesting that they undermine courts' abilities to perform their constitutional duties:

> The agreement directs that in the event of a Freedom of Information Act request, or a court order directing disclosure of information regarding Harris Corporation equipment or technology, the FBI must be notified immediately to allow them time to intervene "and potential[ly] compromise." If necessary "the Office of the State's Attorney for Baltimore will, at the request of the FBI, seek dismissal of the case in lieu of using or providing, or allowing others to provide, any information concerning the Harris Corporation wireless collection equipment/technology[.]"
>
> We observe that such an extensive prohibition on disclosure of information to the court – from special order and/or warrant application through appellate review – prevents the court from exercising its fundamental duties under the Constitution. To

119 No. 1:15-cr-00734-WHP (S.D.N.Y. July 12, 2016).

120 533 U.S. 27 (2001).

121 *See, e.g.*, Justin Fenton, *Key Evidence in Murder Case Tossed Due to Stingray Use*, BALT. SUN (Apr. 25, 2016), http://www.baltimoresun.com/news/maryland/crime/bs-md-ci-stingray-murder-evidence-suppressed-20160425-story.html.

122 *See* Sputnik, *2,000 Cases May Be Dismissed over Baltimore PD's Use of Stingrays*, INFOWARS (Aug. 29, 2015), http://www.infowars.com/2000-cases-may-be-dismissed-over-baltimore-pds-secret-use-of-stingrays/.

123 *See, e.g.*, Cyrus Farivar, *Prosecutors Drop Robbery Case to Preserve Stingray Secrecy in St. Louis*, ARS TECHNICA (Apr. 20, 2015), http://arstechnica.com/tech-policy/2015/04/prosecutors-drop-robbery-case-to-preserve-stingray-secrecy-in-st-louis/.

124 *State v. Andrews*, 227 Md. App. 350 (2016). The Maryland attorney general elected not to challenge the *Andrews* decision, which makes it the final rule on the use of IMSI catchers by law enforcement agencies in Maryland.

> undertake the Fourth Amendment analysis and ascertain "the reasonableness in all the circumstances of the particular governmental invasion of a citizen's personal security," it is self-evident that the court must understand why and *how* the search is to be conducted. The reasonableness of a search or seizure depends on a balance between the public interest and the individual's right to personal security free from arbitrary interference by law officers. The analytical framework requires analysis of the functionality of the surveillance device and the range of information potentially revealed by its use. A nondisclosure agreement that prevents law enforcement from providing details sufficient to assure the court that a novel method of conducting a search is a reasonable intrusion made in a proper manner and "justified by the circumstances," obstructs the court's ability to make the necessary constitutional appraisal.
>
> It appears that as a consequence of the nondisclosure agreement, rather than apply for a warrant, prosecutors and police obtained an order under the Maryland pen register statute that failed to provide the necessary information upon which the court could make the constitutional assessments mandated in this case.[125]

In addition to criticizing the operative nondisclosure agreement, the Court of Special Appeals held that the use of IMSI catcher technology – which constituted direct and active interference by law enforcement – to track the defendant in real time violated his reasonable expectation of privacy. Law enforcement must, therefore, obtain a search warrant or an order satisfying the constitutional requisites of a warrant, unless acting under an established exception to the warrant requirement.[126]

Although the constitutional status of IMSI catcher use outside Maryland remains unsettled, the DOJ seems to have adopted a conservative strategic position in light of the challenges. In September 2015, the DOJ issued guidance directing law enforcement components, as a matter of policy, to obtain a search warrant supported by probable cause before they use IMSI catcher technology. The Department of Homeland Security followed suit with its own policy. Both policies require law enforcement agents clearly to inform courts when they are seeking authorization for use of IMSI catcher technology and to delete irrelevant data (i.e., data from innocent parties) quickly once the target is located. There are, however, noted exceptions to the policies, but these exceptions appear to be tailored to situations where exigent circumstances under the Fourth Amendment or other exceptional circumstances exist, such that a warrant would not be required under the law.

What and Which Direction Forward?

Although the Supreme Court definitively held in *Jones* that the attachment of a GPS tracking device to a vehicle with the intent to gain information is a Fourth Amendment search, little else is settled doctrine in the context of law enforcement access to location data and use of tracking technologies. The DOJ, as a matter of policy, is requiring prosecutors and agents to obtain a warrant before using an IMSI catcher to locate or track an individual. As a matter of policy, it also requires law enforcement agents to obtain a warrant when seeking prospectively to track a target, if the location data requested is

125 *Id.* at 375–376 (internal citations omitted).
126 *Id.* at 355.

GPS-generated or collected using a technique that will yield similarly precise data. But what of single cell tower data that, due to deployment of microcell, picocell, and femtocell technologies, can match or even exceed the precision of GPS-generated data? Will the DOJ recognize that even single cell tower data can be as precise as GPS, and that the state of technology will only become more precise? Legislatures would surely need to take such facts into account in writing a statute governing law enforcement collection of cell site data that would not become obsolete in a matter of years or even months, at least if data precision is relevant to their privacy analysis.

These issues and others pertaining to law enforcement access to location data and other types of non-content third party data may finally get their day in court. During the final editing stages of this chapter, the Supreme Court agreed to review a historical location data case, *United States v. Carpenter*, where the Sixth Circuit held that the government's compelled disclosure of 127 days of historical location data from a communications provider, which the court characterized as business records, was not a Fourth Amendment search. How the Supreme Court will approach the various issues, legal and technical, implicated by law enforcement access to historical location data is anyone's guess. How will the amount or precision of the data collected guide the Court's inquiry and analysis? If the Court finds that a search did in fact occur, will it find that a warrantless search is, nevertheless, reasonable under the Fourth Amendment? Ultimately, will the Court provide a new rule that radically alters the third party doctrine?

While Supreme Court guidance about the extent to which the Fourth Amendment regulates law enforcement access to location data is certainly needed, it is important to recognize that federal courts are not the only entities with the power or obligation to consider and resolve these issues. Indeed, Justice Alito, acknowledging that courts applying the Fourth Amendment may not always be the best branch of government to resolve vexing issues of law and technology, writes in his *Jones* concurrence that "in circumstances involving dramatic technological change, the best solutions to privacy concerns may be legislative."[127] Other federal courts, including the Third, Fourth, Fifth, Sixth, and Eleventh circuits, which have considered cases involving law enforcement compelled disclosure of historical CSLI, have said as much, some quoting Alito's concurrence. Since 2010, Congress has held multiple hearings on location data in the context of ECPA reform. Bills have been introduced, but no legislation has passed.

In the short term, movement towards resolution of these and many other unsettled location data questions and issues has developed in state legislatures and state courts. The *Andrews* case from the Maryland Special Court of Appeals is a prime example of state judicial action. Certain state courts, on the basis of an interpretation of the language in their respective state constitutions, are also requiring warrants for the collection of CSLI.[128] Moreover, certain state legislatures are passing laws requiring law enforcement to obtain probable cause warrants before tracking mobile devices,[129] which would include the use of IMSI catcher technology. Indeed, some of the laws directly address law enforcement use of IMSI catcher technology. California, for example, passed a comprehensive digital

127 *United States v. Jones*, 132 S.Ct. 945, 964 (2012) (Alito, J., concurring).

128 *See, e.g., State v. Earls*, 214 N.J. 564, 583, 70 A.3d 630, 641 (2013); *Commonwealth v. Estabrook*, 472 Mass. 852 (2015).

129 Examples include Maine, Maryland, Virginia, Utah, and Vermont.

privacy bill, called "CalECPA," that, with noted exceptions, requires law enforcement to obtain a warrant before compelling records revealing a suspect's geographical location or using IMSI catcher technology.[130] The majority of bills that address CSLI and require law enforcement to obtain a warrant also include appropriate exceptions for emergency services calls, consent from the user/owner of a device (if the device has been reported stolen), and for exigent circumstances that would constitute an existing exception to the Fourth Amendment's warrant requirement.[131] But, in many respects, the absence of further direction from the Supreme Court or action from Congress has left some *Jones*ing for a privacy mandate – we anxiously await the "doctrine to follow."

[130] *See* 2015 Cal. Legis. Serv. Ch. 659 (S.B. 741) (West); *see also* Dave Maass, *Victory in California! Gov. Brown Signs CalECPA, Requiring Police to Get a Warrant before Accessing Your Data*, Electronic Frontier Foundation (Oct. 8, 2015), https://www.eff.org/deeplinks/2015/10/victory-california-gov-brown-signs-calecpa-requiring-police-get-warrant-accessing.

[131] For more information about state legislation regulating both law enforcement access to location data and use of IMSI catcher technology, see *Cell-Site Simulators*, Electronic Frontier Foundation, https://www.eff.org/sls/tech/cell-site-simulators/faq (last visited July 31, 2016).

3 Terrorist Watchlists

Jeffrey Kahn[†]

This chapter assesses the legal history and policy development of the U.S. government's system of terrorist watchlists and the institutions established to create and use them. Watchlisting is in fact an old practice given new meaning by technological change and the societal impact of the September 11, 2001, terrorist attacks. Statutes and judicial precedents from an earlier era on which the first post-9/11 watchlists were built were not made to regulate the expanded uses of the new watchlists and presented few if any constraints on their development. Civil litigation has both revealed the inner workings of terrorist watchlists and spurred some reforms to them. While these reforms have succeeded in adding some due process protections to watchlisting remedies, the underlying premise of the new watchlists, and the hierarchies of citizenship that they produce, have not been subject to much challenge in either the courts or the Congress.

Introduction

"Major Strasser's been shot," police captain Renault tells his men as they rush into the final scene of the film *Casablanca*. "Round up the usual suspects."[1] Renault witnessed the shooting himself, so his order is ironic and subversive. But it also sounds oddly routine; the arriving képis take it in stride. *Of course* they have a go-to list of suspects. Good police work means keeping track of people, especially those whose objectively verifiable criminal record or subjectively assessed character elicits suspicion about their future conduct.

We might call these the first watchlists: quite literally, lists of people worth watching. How else does the cop walking his usual beat "know" his assigned neighborhood save for the list of bad apples he has drawn up in his mind? Thus, "watchlisting" is an idea that has long influenced police practices in the United States and elsewhere, though some now balk as technology grows their size and searchability.[2] In the United States, however, law and tradition have always established a limit, a divide that watchlists could

† Professor of Law and Gerald J. Ford Research Fellow, SMU Dedman School of Law.

1 Casablanca (Warner Bros. 1942).

2 *See, e.g.*, Chicago Police Department Special Order S10-06, July 20, 2015, Targeted Repeat-Offender Apprehension and Prosecution (T.R.A.P.) Program (ordering District Commanders to select up to five individuals each for inclusion on this watchlist, "identified because of their criminal history, propensity for violence, and the [*sic*] involvement in narcotics distribution. The primary goal of T.R.A.P. is focused on enhanced prosecution to detain, convict, and incarcerate these offenders before they commit further crimes of violence").

not cross. The propensity evidence used to watchlist a suspect is generally inadmissible to try the accused in a court of law.[3] Police may wish to "round up the usual suspects," but their conviction depends on admissible evidence of guilt for a particular past act that is publicly presented to a neutral judge and, perhaps, a jury.[4]

Historically, three features marked this boundary – the who, what, and where of this dividing line. Each element established an important check on the state's police power. *Who* decides the individual's fate changes at this divide: executive decision making is now subjected to judicial oversight. The evidence justifying state action – the *what* of watchlists – must satisfy substantial rules of evidence that extend beyond claims of propensity or reasonable suspicion.[5] And *where* that evaluative process occurs is moved from behind closed doors in police stations to courtrooms open to all.

These three features combine both substantive and structural protections for individual liberty. As Justice Frankfurter described the line in rejecting a government list of Communist organizations fashioned by the Attorney General for the Loyalty Review Board of the United States Civil Service Commission:

> Man being what he is cannot safely be trusted with complete immunity from outward responsibility in depriving others of their rights. ... The validity and moral authority of a conclusion largely depend on the mode by which it was reached. Secrecy is not congenial to truth-seeking and self-righteousness gives too slender an assurance of rightness.[6]

The list that resulted from the Attorney General's secret assessment process crossed that line with ruinous consequences for those he listed. "No better instrument has been devised for arriving at truth," Frankfurter argued, "than to give a person in jeopardy of serious loss notice of the case against him and opportunity to meet it. Nor has a better way been found for generating the feeling, so important to a popular government, that justice has been done."[7]

All in all, this dividing line sought to prevent ordinary watchlists from becoming blacklists, which single out individuals "for adverse legal consequences that go beyond the discomfort associated with being the target of a lawfully conducted investigation."[8]

3 *See, e.g.*, Fed. R. Evid. 404 (2016). It must be acknowledged that "in today's criminal justice system, ... the negotiation of a plea bargain, rather than the unfolding of a trial, is almost always the critical point for a defendant." *Missouri v. Frye*, 566 U.S. 133, 144 (2012). Nevertheless, the dividing line remains for those who demand their right to cross it.

4 *Michelson v. United States*, 335 U.S. 469, 475–76 (1948) ("The State may not show defendant's prior trouble with the law, specific criminal acts, or ill name among his neighbors, even though such facts might logically be persuasive that he is by propensity a probable perpetrator of the crime. The inquiry is not rejected because character is irrelevant; on the contrary, it is said to weigh too much with the jury and to so overpersuade them as to prejudge one with a bad general record and deny him a fair opportunity to defend against a particular charge") (internal citations omitted).

5 This would surprise Captain Renault. In the French legal system, the dossier informing the *juge d'instruction* includes propensity and character evidence concerning the accused, based on the theory "*On juge l'homme, pas les faits*" ("One judges the man, not the acts"). Unlike the Anglo-American adversarial tradition, the judiciary are involved in the compilation of the dossier and bear responsibility at various stages for confirming its adherence to procedural rules about its composition.

6 *Joint Anti-Fascist Refugee Committee v. McGrath*, 341 U.S. 123, 171–172 (1951) (Frankfurter, J., concurring) (footnote omitted).

7 *Id.*

8 This distinction, using this nomenclature, was first used in the context of terrorist watchlists by Aaron H. Caplan, *Nonattainder as a Liberty Interest*, 2010 Wisc. L. Rev. 1203, 1206 (2010).

Filtering the executive's lists through the screen of a neutral magistrate reduces the speed and effectiveness of executive action, but this has generally been the preferred check to protect individual liberty. When blacklists have emerged, often in response to national crises, they eventually have been subject to judicial review.[9]

There is something artificial about this divide. By what measure is legal consequence or loss "adverse" or "serious" enough to cross the line? When does an investigation shade into a violation of rights?[10] The state's officers, if they so desire, can make investigation a public spectacle or a secret affair; regardless, the suspect is left to the tender mercies of police and prosecutor, without any judicial intervention. The divide is also based on certain assumptions. Why assume, first of all, that the end goal – the safety of the community – is to be achieved within the rigid confines of the criminal justice system? Why presume the police – local, public, accessible – to be the proper government agents tasked with this goal?

The terrorist attacks in the United States on September 11, 2001, severely challenged these assumptions and this divide. The new watchlists it produced do not pursue the goal of public safety through the criminal justice system. The national security concerns that catalyzed watchlisting tended to complicate public access to the watchlisters themselves. Those complaining that watchlists caused them adverse legal consequences or serious losses – the very nature of any injuries is often disputed – found ordinary avenues to judicial review blocked. At the same time, a technological revolution in communications and data mining fueled the proliferation of these new watchlists as oxygen fuels fire.

It is too early to tell how the changes worked on society by technological revolutions in transportation, communications, and computing have affected this historic divide. Some courts are slowly conforming watchlists to the limits set by our law and past traditions. But other courts have turned away legal challenges and watchlists have generally been upheld in the court of public opinion. The No-Fly List, for example, prevents listed individuals from boarding commercial aircraft. Such watchlists are now an established feature in the country's national security architecture, as natural to a generation of Americans born after 9/11 as submitting to a search at an airport (required by statute only since 1974).[11] Indeed, the very idea of a dividing line has been challenged by national security policy makers and officials on the front line of operations who question whether the world has become too fast, too connected, and too dangerous for checks and balances designed in and for an earlier era.

This chapter evaluates the emergence of these new watchlists, no longer limited to watching. The No-Fly List was the prototype and progenitor for this new model. Its development led to the creation of the much broader based Terrorist Screening Database

9 *McGrath* determined the fate of the Attorney General's list of Communist organizations, *supra* note 6. The rise and fall of passport controls in the 1940s and 1950s, foreshadowing today's No-Fly List, are examined in detail as part of the analysis of today's watchlisting system in Jeffrey Kahn, Mrs. Shipley's Ghost: The Right to Travel and Terrorist Watchlists (2013).

10 Surveillance can also take forms that implicate the Fourth Amendment, in which case the divide between watchlists and arrests becomes harder to define. A neutral magistrate may be involved, but in nonpublic, ex parte ways. Evidentiary requirements may be lower. The complexities of this environment are the reason for this book. But even in this hazier borderland, the same divide must eventually be crossed if the suspect is to become an accused. *Whether* it is crossed is now a more salient question than ever before, and the reason for this chapter.

11 Air Transportation Security Act, Pub. L. No. 93–366, §§ 315(a) & 1111, 88 Stat. 415 (1974).

(TSDB) – the central watchlist from which specialized watchlists are created. It also led to the creation of new offices and agencies to build, stock, and curate the TSDB and other watchlists, most notably the Terrorist Screening Center. The history of this process shows how expectations built by the traditional use of watchlists presented obstacles and opportunities for the parties, lawyers, and policy makers whose first experiences with terrorist watchlists led to the system in place today.

I History

Long before the terrorist attacks of September 11, 2001, there were plenty of watchlists in the United States. For the most part, these were in the possession of local or perhaps regional law enforcement offices, and they were neither computerized nor connected to other departments of government. Few national "databases" (to use an anachronism) existed in this analog era of file cabinets and note cards. The "Official and Confidential" files that FBI Director J. Edgar Hoover kept for more than five decades might come to mind, though at a conservatively estimated seventeen thousand pages in 165 files, it was hardly the largest or most useful collection of its day.[12] At their peak in 1953, the files of Ruth Shipley's passport office in the State Department kept watch on 12 million passport applicants and were housed in 1,250 filing cabinets.[13]

National watchlists came into their own in a computer era that enabled (relatively) speedy processing and distributing of large volumes of information. Post-Watergate, Senator Church's select committee, Vice President Rockefeller's presidential commission, and others uncovered a raft of secret surveillance and intelligence programs that went beyond collecting information. For example, the "Special Services Staff," which operated within the IRS from 1969 to 1973,

> believed its mission included saving the country from subversives, extremists, and anti-establishment organizations and individuals [and] reviewed for audit or collection potential organizations and individuals selected by other agencies, such as the Internal Security Division of the Justice Department and the FBI, on bases having no relation to the likelihood that such organizations or individuals had violated the tax laws.[14]

Using classified documents and top secret clearances, the group reviewed biweekly computer printouts ranging between ten thousand and sixteen thousand names of "officers, members and affiliates of activist, extremist and revolutionary organizations" so designated by the FBI or Justice Department.[15]

More open, and certainly less controversial, were watchlists of a more routine variety. Since 1995, for example, the FBI had maintained a "Violent Gang/Terrorist Organization File" (VGTOF). Federal, state, and local law enforcement could access it in the National Crime Information Center (NCIC) database, which in 2004 contained

12 *A Byte out of History: J. Edgar Hoover's "Official & Confidential" Files*, July 11, 2005, https://www.fbi.gov/news/stories/2005/july/j.-edgar-hoovers-official-confidential-files.

13 Kahn, *supra* note 9, at 154.

14 Supplementary Detailed Staff Reports on Intelligence Activities and the Rights of Americans, Book III, Final Report of the U.S. Senate Select Committee to Study Governmental Operations with respect to Intelligence Activities 881 (Apr. 23, 1976).

15 *Id.* at 880 and 884.

more than 43 million records.[16] (In August 2009, the VGTOF separated into a Gang File and a Known or Suspected Terrorist (KST) File.) The State Department also created a list in 1995 – the Consular Lookout and Support System (CLASS) – that helped vet visa and passport applications. On September 11, 2001, CLASS contained roughly 10 million records on individuals with criminal backgrounds, past visa denials, or other grounds for heightened suspicion.[17] Other agencies tasked with immigration, customs inspection, and intelligence gathering possessed their own lists designed for their specialized purposes. As late as April 2003, the General Accounting Office (GAO) reported that "nine federal agencies, which prior to the establishment of DHS spanned five different cabinet-level departments, currently maintain twelve terrorist and criminal watch lists."[18]

Common features emerge from this history. First, most watchlists had a foreign orientation – consular officers, customs agents, and other officials created lists that reflected their agency mission, which tended to be oriented to foreign threats and concerns at the border. Thus, few paid attention to the effect on the watchlisted themselves, who on the whole lacked legally cognizable interests or political representation. In any event, these were old-fashioned watchlists. Follow-up action – whether an arrest, deportation, visa denial, or asset seizure – was invariably public, traceable to the agency, and subject to judicial review.

Second, information sharing was the exception, not the rule. Interagency rivalries and the desire to protect sources and methods of intelligence created "silos" of information rather than networks for distributing it. The 9/11 Commission called this a Cold War era preoccupation with counterintelligence that was "no longer appropriate." It therefore advised that the "culture of agencies feeling they own the information they gathered at taxpayer expense must be replaced by a culture in which the agencies instead feel they have a duty to the information – to repay the taxpayers' investment by making that information available."[19]

Third, the emergence of computer databases notwithstanding, watchlists tended to produce unwieldy paper documents. One State Department list of particular significance for future watchlists, called "TIPOFF," began its life in 1987 as a shoebox full of index cards.[20] This paper world exacerbated the information-sharing problems agencies experienced with each other. It slowed data transfer to the speed of a fax machine or modem.

The No-Fly List, the first modern terrorist watchlist, followed these patterns. Violent aircraft hijackings and bombings in the 1970s and 1980s led to the creation of a new Federal Aviation Administration (FAA) authority to issue "security directives." The

[16] William J. Krouse, *Terrorist Identification, Screening, and Tracking Under Homeland Security Presidential Directive 6*, CRS Report for Congress (RL32366) 31 (2004).

[17] Thomas R. Eldridge, et al. 9/11 and Terrorist Travel: Staff Report of the National Commission on Terrorist Attacks upon the United States 78 (2004).

[18] U.S. General Accounting Office, Information Technology: Terrorist Watch Lists Should Be Consolidated to Promote Better Integration and Sharing (GAO-03-322) 12 (April 2003).

[19] The 9/11 Commission Report: Final Report of the National Commission on Terrorist Attacks upon the United States 417 (2004).

[20] Krouse, *supra* note 16, at 26.

"do-not-carry" variety were obligatory orders directing commercial airlines not to carry a particular passenger whom the FAA determined to present a "specific and credible threat" to civil aviation (other security directives focused on security infrastructure and other security requirements not targeting specific individuals). Security directives took the form of thermal faxes to airline security officers.

Above the technology that slowed distribution stood a bureaucracy that often slowed it further. Every agency whose intelligence contributed to a security directive had to sign off on its release, prompting natural conflicts over balancing the risk of air piracy with the exposure of sources and methods of intelligence gathering. These impediments reduced the volume and frequency of security directives. On September 11, 2001, a total of three directives prohibited sixteen people from boarding commercial aircraft. None of them was among the attackers.[21]

The 9/11 commissioners were enraged by these statistics. By 2001, the State Department's TIPOFF database (now a part of CLASS) had grown to list more than sixty thousand suspected terrorists who that agency thought should be denied visas. True to their "stovepiped" practices, members of the intelligence community contributed to this database at a miserly rate.[22] And although sharing occurred between some agencies, the FAA was not among them; indeed, one senior FAA official admitted to the 9/11 Commission that he learned of the very existence of TIPOFF the day before his testimony in 2004.[23] The FAA's intelligence office relied on the willingness of other members of the intelligence community to supply it with information and to allow that information to be shared with the airlines. This was classic "stovepiping," or "silo," management of intelligence and the 9/11 commissioners took turns berating the officials who appeared before them for institutionalized hoarding of information.

Notwithstanding their infrequent use, security directives were an important milestone in the history of the new watchlists. Security directives departed from the conventions of the old watchlists in important ways. This system was not linked to the criminal justice system or border protection. Its purposes were not investigatory but were not intended to be punitive either; the purpose was, singularly, aviation security. For the first time, watchlisting results were sent to private actors (airlines) directing them to take concrete action against an individual. They were not only the model but also the legal instrument through which the No-Fly List was created. Michael Jackson, second in command at the Department of Transportation on 9/11 and Deputy Secretary of Homeland Security from 2005 to 2007, recalled:

> It's hard to underestimate the personal sense of responsibility that the senior government leaders felt in trying to do everything that was reasonable and yet doable to prevent another attack. And the watchlist was a core tool in that effort. So it would have been

21 Memorandum from Claudio Manno, Acting Associate Under Secretary for Transportation Security Intelligence, to Associate Under Secretary for Security Regulation and Policy (Oct. 16, 2002).

22 Eldridge, *supra* note 17, at 80 ("In 2001, the CIA provided 1,527 source documents to TIPOFF; the State Department, 2, 013; the INS, 173. The FBI, during this same year, provided 63 documents to TIPOFF – fewer than were obtained from the public media, and about the same number as were provided by the Australian Intelligence Agency (52)").

23 Testimony of Rear Admiral Cathal "Irish" Flynn USN (ret), Associate FAA Administrator for Civil Aviation Security, Seventh Public Hearing of the National Commission on Terrorist Attacks upon the United States, Jan. 27, 2004, at 29.

irresponsible not to develop and actively manage a watchlist of the sort that we ended up with. And there was no disagreement about that, really, amongst the team.[24]

II Creation: Building Institutions

The Aviation and Transportation Security Act, signed by President George W. Bush in November 2001, transferred the FAA's responsibility for aviation security to the new Transportation Security Administration (TSA). That statute instructed the new agency, "in consultation with other appropriate Federal agencies and air carriers," to require airlines

> to use information from government agencies to identify individuals on passenger lists who may be a threat to civil aviation or national security and, if such an individual is identified, notify appropriate law enforcement agencies, prevent the individual from boarding an aircraft, or take other appropriate action with respect to that individual.[25]

This new statute did not grant the TSA the power to create a watchlist. The legal authority for the No-Fly List already existed in the old FAA "do-not-carry" security directives, which were transferred to the new TSA.[26] The new language, read carefully, did not grant any authority to *compose* watchlists at all, merely to "use information from government agencies" – and no particular agency is named. Richard Falkenrath, a special assistant to President Bush who was instrumental in designing this first watchlisting system, recalled:

> It was just accidental that the authority originated in [the TSA's] authorizing statute, I assume, and then some pre-9/11 security directive. It was really grabbed a hold of by the White House, which was driving everything back then – FBI, CIA to a certain extent. And it just became, with every single case that came into the White House post-9/11, and there were lots, we got into the habit of just asking, Is he no-flied? Is he no-flied? Is he no-flied? And the bureaucracy at first would respond, "We don't know," and they couldn't keep track of all these lists.[27]

Although the TSA seemed to possess the list, it was the FBI and other agencies that supplied, and often seemed to control, the content. As one key official at the time put it, this was a continuation of operations begun the day after 9/11:

> At the request of the FBI, the FAA issued SD-108-01-06/EA 129-01-05, which included a list of individuals developed by the FBI as part of the *Pentbom* [*sic*] investigation [PENTTBOM was the codename for the FBI's investigation of the 9/11 attacks]. ... The FBI "controlled," both administratively and operationally, the contents of the list and added or removed names in accordance with the *Pentbom* [*sic*] investigation. The FAA received the list from the FBI and disseminated it to air carriers, without any format or content changes. FAA, in essence, acted as a conduit for the dissemination of their "watchlist."[28]

24 Kahn, *supra* note 9, at 138 (Author's Interview, Mar. 14, 2011, Arlington, Virginia).

25 Pub. L. No. 107–71, § 101(a), 115 Stat. 597 (2001) (codified at 49 U.S.C. § 114(h)(3)(A)–(B)).

26 According to Jackson, who was one of the Bush administration's negotiators for the ATSA bill that established the TSA, "when TSA promulgated the Selectee and the No-Fly List, it was done through security directives." Kahn, *supra* note 9, at 296 n.105.

27 Kahn, *supra* note 9, at 139 (Author's interview, June 8, 2010, New York City).

28 Internal TSA Memorandum on "TSA Watchlists" dated Oct. 16, 2002, from Claudio Manno, *supra* note 21.

This dynamic – the FBI supplying content compiled and distributed by the TSA – rapidly grew the No-Fly List. Growing pains to a name-based watchlist were expected. Similar or even misspelled names caused frustration for passengers denied boarding. News stories abounded of the elderly, toddlers, and even the rich and famous all being subject to the vicissitudes of a No-Fly List that could not distinguish the partial record for "T. Kennedy," possible IRA terrorist, from Ted Kennedy, U.S. Senator.[29]

Another growing pain, however, was bureaucratic: a turf war between the new TSA and the old FBI. Emails between the TSA and FBIHQ, and between FBIHQ and FBI agents throughout the country, reveal growing tensions between these agencies but also the first signs of a twin challenge to the new watchlists: standardization and containment. Emails poured into the TSA from FBI agents throughout the country eager to use the new watchlisting tool to pursue and control suspects. "We've got a guy we want to no-fly," wrote one special agent. "Do you have a copy of the last one we gave you?"[30] The cutting-and-pasting from one request to another was hard to control. Beyond a plaintive TSA request that "you state in the EC [electronic communication] that the FBI believes that the listed individual is a threat to Civil Aviation Security," there was little the TSA could do to verify that the watchlist was used for its intended purpose or based on a consistent quantity and quality of information.[31] The TSA, in turn, could be bureaucratic and unresponsive to FBI agents who demanded updated versions of the list, and who were often left to respond to a public increasingly confused by the new watchlisting regime.

Solutions to these problems of standardization (quality control) and containment (mission control) were sought in the creation of two new institutions. President Bush announced this new direction and the first of these new organizations, the Terrorist Threat Integration Center (TTIC), in his January 2003 State of the Union address to Congress:

> Since September the 11th, our intelligence and law enforcement agencies have worked more closely than ever to track and disrupt the terrorists. The FBI is improving its ability to analyze intelligence and is transforming itself to meet new threats. Tonight I am instructing the leaders of the FBI, the CIA, the Homeland Security, and the Department of Defense to develop a Terrorist Threat Integration Center, to merge and analyze all threat information in a single location. Our Government must have the very best information possible, and we will use it to make sure the right people are in the right places to protect all our citizens.

The president noted both the new orientation of the FBI beyond law enforcement and the need for coordination in the intelligence community to meet national security threats. The TTIC opened in May 2003 at CIA Headquarters in Langley, Virginia, with multiagency staff and funding. (The TTIC would eventually become the National Counterterrorism Center [NCTC], and relocate to a complex called Liberty Crossing in the Washington D.C., suburb of McLean, Virginia.)[32] Its mission is to gather all

[29] Sara Kehaulani Goo, *Sen. Kennedy Flagged by No-Fly List*, WASH. POST, Aug. 20, 2004, at A01; Lizette Alvarez, *Meet Mikey, 8; U.S. Has Him on Watch List*, N.Y. TIMES, Jan. 13, 2010.

[30] Redacted Email dated Feb. 4, 2003 (Bates Stamp B2–130), released in *Gordon v. FBI*, 390 F.Supp.2d 897 (N.D. Cal. 2004).

[31] Redacted Email dated Oct. 11, 2002 (Bates Stamp B2–137), *supra* note 30.

[32] E.O. 13,354, § 5(f), 69 Fed. Reg. 53589 (Aug. 27, 2004). The status of the NCTC was codified a few months later in the Intelligence Reform and Terrorism Prevention Act (IRTPA), Pub. L. No. 108–458, § 1021, 118 Stat. 3638 (2004) (codified at 50 U.S.C. § 3056).

intelligence known to the U.S. government on international terrorism and counterterrorism in one central repository.[33]

In particular, the TTIC/NCTC was tasked to produce reports and analysis but, most importantly, to curate a single, massive database: the Terrorist Identities Datamart Environment (TIDE).[34] The State Department's TIPOFF database – the one that grew from a shoebox to sixty thousand records – was transferred to the TTIC, becoming the seed that started TIDE. To the extent permitted by law, all federal agencies were directed to send to the TTIC "on an ongoing basis all relevant Terrorist Information in their possession, custody, or control, with the exception of Purely Domestic Terrorism Information, which will instead be provided directly to the FBI."[35] According to an August 2014 NCTC "factsheet" on TIDE (the most recent available): "As of December 2013, TIDE contained about 1.1 million persons, most containing multiple minor spelling variations of their names. US persons (including both citizens and legal permanent residents) account for about 25,000 of that total."[36] TIDE was, in the words of one former NCTC director, "the mother of all databases ... if there's a piece of derogatory information on a known or suspected terrorist, it goes in that database."[37]

Roughly contemporaneous with the TTIC's creation, another new organization, the Terrorist Screening Center (TSC), was being developed. The TSC received much less fanfare than the TTIC, and certainly no mention in presidential addresses, but it was the core of the developing watchlist system. The consolidation of the federal government's information was important, but would take time – TIDE did not become operational until May 2005. TIDE also did not resolve continuing problems in the efficient *use* of information, the fundamental feature of the new watchlisting. One problem was interagency coordination, as illustrated by conflicts between the FBI and TSA over the No-Fly List. Another was quality control – a massive database full of inaccurate, partial, or old information could do more harm than good. The TSC was the institutional solution to these problems.

The TSC was authorized by Homeland Security Presidential Directive Six (HSPD-6) on September 16, 2003, as "an organization to consolidate the Government's approach to terrorism screening and provide for the appropriate and lawful use of Terrorist Information in screening processes." The Directive ordered all executive departments and agencies to provide the TTIC with "Terrorist Information."[38] The TTIC, in turn,

33 Intelligence on purely domestic terrorism remained the province of the FBI, a remnant of prohibitions on domestic activity by the CIA that date back to its creation. *See* 50 U.S.C. § 3036(d)(1) (authorizing intelligence collection "through human sources and by other appropriate means, except that the Director of the Central Intelligence Agency shall have no police, subpoena, or law enforcement powers or internal security functions").

34 IRTPA, *supra* note 32, § 1021(d)(6) (codified at 50 U.S.C. § 3056(d)(6)).

35 Memorandum of Understanding on the Integration and Use of Screening Information to Protect Against Terrorism, Sept. 16, 2003 (hereinafter "MOU").

36 https://www.nctc.gov/docs/tidefactsheet_aug12014.pdf. An earlier factsheet provides evidence of the accelerating speed of watchlist expansion: "As of January 2009, TIDE contained more than 564,000 names, but only about 500,000 separate 'identities' because of the use of aliases and name variants. U.S. persons (including both citizens and legal permanent residents) make up less than five percent of the listings."

37 Ronald Kessler, The Terrorist Watch: Inside the Desperate Race to Stop the Next Attack 166 (2007) (quoting Vice Admiral John Scott Redd).

38 This capitalized term is not defined in HSPD-6, a short one-page document. Its accompanying eight-page Memorandum of Understanding, however, defines Terrorist Information as information "about individuals known or appropriately suspected to be or have been involved in activities constituting, in preparation for, in aid of, or related to terrorism."

was directed to provide to the TSC "access to all appropriate information or intelligence in the TTIC's custody, possession, or control that the organization requires to perform its functions." Federal agencies would then use only the filtered products of the TSC to conduct screening. The Congressional Research Service illustrated this relationship in the acronym-rich diagram in Figure 3.1.[39]

The TSC became operational on December 1, 2003. Unlike the NCTC, the TSC has never publicly acknowledged its physical location; its complex in Vienna, Virginia, is known to exist only because the high-pitched buzz of air-conditioning units cooling its array of computers drew a noise complaint before the town council.[40] Administered and funded through the FBI, it was designed, like the TTIC, with a multiagency staff that served all members of what was becoming known as the "Watchlisting Community."[41] This is attested by the signature lines for the Secretary of State, Attorney General, Secretary of Homeland Security, and Director of Central Intelligence that conclude the Memorandum of Understanding accompanying HSPD-6. TSC staff expanded to include personnel borrowed from the Defense Department, Treasury Department, and private contractors.

If the Terrorist Screening Center was the institution designated to consolidate, standardize, and regulate the use of watchlists, the Terrorist Screening Database (TSDB) was the vehicle by which the TSC sought to achieve this mission. In the words of Timothy Healy, the project leader who set up the TSC and would later serve as its director, TSDB was "the bucket that had them all in there."[42] By "them," Healy meant a database from which usable watchlists – such as the No-Fly List – could be derived. A PowerPoint presentation Healy gave to congressional staff (and provided to the author in unclassified form) illustrates this relationship (see Figure 3.2).

Why, one might ask, would "consolidation" mean creating *two* massive databases, TIDE housed at the TTIC/NCTC and the TSDB housed at the TSC? Like an old-fashioned card catalog system, the TSDB kept track of the library of terrorist information housed in the TIDE and in FBI intelligence about domestic terrorism (which by law could not be collected by the CIA). Just as one might ask a librarian for help finding a particular book in the closed stacks of a library, the TSC guided access to the federal government's terrorist information. And by curating the TSDB, the Terrorist Screening Center used the authority given by HSPD-6 to set standards for all agencies submitting biographical and substantive information – known as "derogatory" information in watchlisting nomenclature – into this system.

Interposing the TSC-controlled TSDB between frontline users such as airport screeners or police officers and the NCTC-controlled TIDE served another function. The

39 Krouse, *supra* note 16, at 16.

40 Tom Jackman, *Vienna Tormented by FBI Building's Non-Stop Buzz*, Wash. Post (June 21, 2012). The TSC describes itself simply as "housed in a nondescript building in northern Virginia." *See* Press Release, https://www.fbi.gov/news/stories/2007/august/tsc083107.

41 The TSC director reports through the executive assistant director of the FBI's national security branch to the director of the FBI. Unlike the NCTC, given a statutory foundation by the Intelligence Reform and Terrorism Prevention Act of 2004, the only legal basis for the TSC is HSPD-6. By Fiscal Year 2007, the TSC had secured an $83 million budget and 408 staffed positions. U.S. Department of Justice Office of the Inspector General, Follow-Up Audit of the Terrorist Screening Center (Audit Report 07–41) 1 (September 2007).

42 Kahn, *supra* note 9, at 147 (Author's interview, FBIHQ, Washington D.C., Dec. 4, 2009).

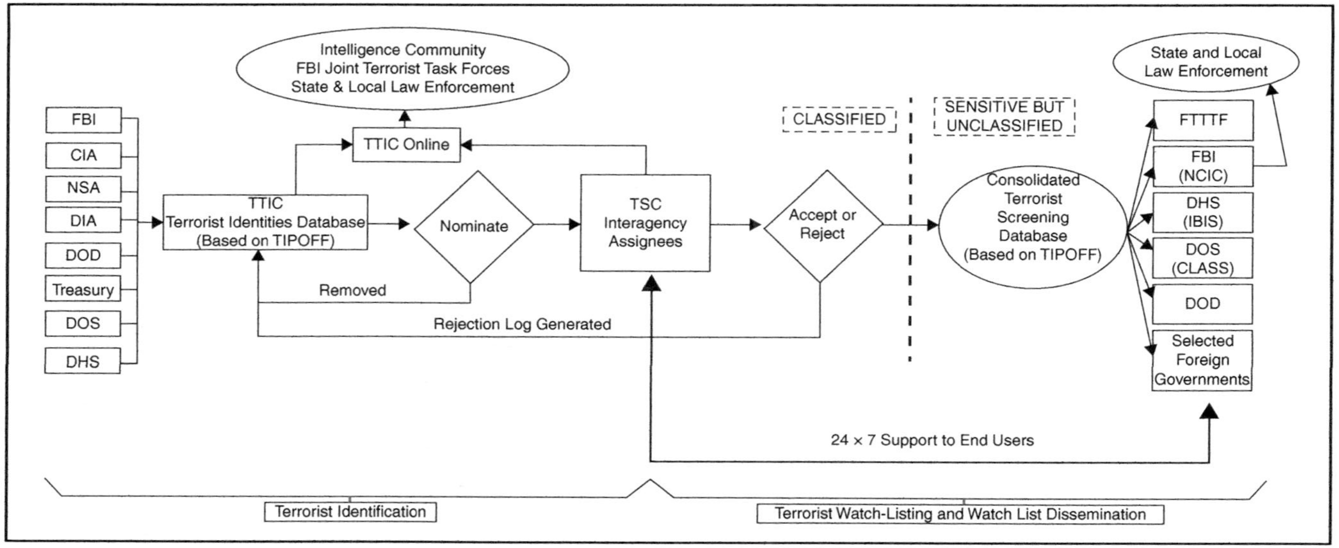

Figure 3.1. Congressional Research Service illustration of the inter-agency watchlisting process.

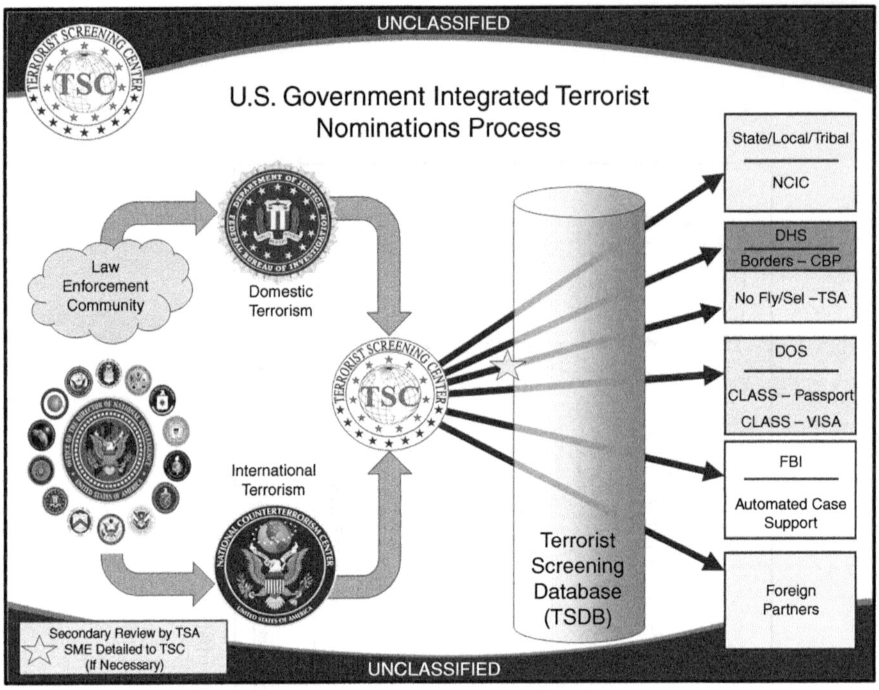

Figure 3.2. TSC PowerPoint Slide Depicting Inter-Agency Watchlisting Process.

TSDB is an unclassified but sensitive watchlist. Its records link to, but do not necessarily reveal, information that is classified either because of its substantive content or because it could reveal sources or methods of intelligence collection. In other words, this "card catalog" provides enough information about the book on the restricted shelves of this closed library to be useful, but no more. Access beyond the card catalog is therefore yet another function of the Terrorist Screening Center, which serves as the liaison between frontline operators and sources of intelligence.

By setting those standards, and constantly evaluating and auditing submissions, the TSC also fulfilled a third, more creative purpose: organizing subsets of the information stored in the TSDB into useful watchlists for recipient agencies (i.e., "downstream" watchlists operated by "customer" agencies). Its multiagency staff includes "subject matter experts" who advise on the particular needs of TSC "customers." Thus, the TSA sends officials to work within the TSC as aides in preparing the No-Fly List. In this way, the watchlists that the TSC constructs are customized to the needs of the downstream agencies that use them.

III Development: Building Watchlists

The NCTC and the TSC changed the way terrorist information is stored and used in the United States. The "stove piping" and "silos" that characterized the pre-9/11 Cold War era were, if not altogether banished, greatly diminished. Now anyone – from the cop walking a neighborhood beat, to the FBI special agent working a case, to the intelligence analyst at a remote foreign outpost – could query a central repository and, through the TSC's 24/7 call center, be connected with the originating source of intelligence about the subject of interest.

But this new system also created new challenges. The greatest of these, on which the success of the entire enterprise depended, was the standard used to decide whether available information warranted including a person in the TSDB (known as "nominating" in the watchlisting nomenclature). This decision determines the size of the TSDB itself and what data are available to compose downstream watchlists. Make the standard too high and the repository would very likely be "too small" in the sense of being incomplete. But make the standard too low and the collections would grow unmanageably large, hiding terrorist needles in watchlisting haystacks. The challenge is made more difficult still by the political pressures riding on either choice. Create a list that generates too many false positives and the public would soon demand public scrutiny in courts or other forums that would create limits the watchlisters were eager to avoid. But create a list that fails to stop successive attacks and its makers would face the wrath of a public angry for the opposite reasons.

The standard of review for successful nomination to the TSDB is the "reasonable suspicion" standard. Although there has been minor variation in its wording, this standard has applied since at least 2009 as a result of a working group convened the previous year in which the TSC legal counsel played an instrumental role.[43] Its most recent public articulation occurred in testimony given in September 2014 by TSC Director Christopher Piehota.[44] But a more detailed and revealing definition is found in the March 2013 Watchlisting Guidance. A leaked copy of this unclassified but "for official use only/sensitive security information" document was published in 2014 by *The Intercept*, a blog operated by the investigative journalist Glenn Greenwald.[45] Its 166-page detailed description of the process, standards, and criteria for watchlisting has largely been accepted as authentic, though it is not officially acknowledged as such by the watchlisting community. In it, the term "reasonable suspicion" is defined as:

> the standard that must be met in order to include an individual in the TSDB, absent an exception provided for in the Watchlisting Guidance. To meet the REASONABLE SUSPICION standard, the NOMINATOR, based on the totality of the circumstances, must rely upon articulable intelligence or information which, taken together with rational inferences from those facts, reasonably warrants a determination that an individual is known or suspected to be or has been knowingly engaged in conduct constituting, in preparation for, in aid of, or related to TERRORISM and/or TERRORIST ACTIVITIES. There must be an objective factual basis for the NOMINATOR to believe that the individual is a KNOWN OR SUSPECTED TERRORIST. Mere guesses or hunches are not enough to constitute a REASONABLE SUSPICION that an individual is a KNOWN OR SUSPECTED TERRORIST. Reporting of suspicious activity alone that does not meet the REASONABLE SUSPICION standard set forth herein is not a sufficient basis to watchlist an individual. The facts, however, given fair consideration, should sensibly lead to the conclusion that an individual is, or has, engaged in TERRORISM and/or TERRORIST ACTIVITIES.[46]

43 Kahn, *supra* note 9, at 158, 303 nn.11–12.

44 *Safeguarding Privacy and Civil Liberties While Keeping Our Skies Safe*: Hearing before the Subcomm. on Transp. Sec. of the Comm. on Homeland Sec., 113th Cong., 14 (2014).

45 Jeremy Scahill & Ryan Devereaux, *Blacklisted: The Secret Government Rulebook for Labeling You a Terrorist*, THE INTERCEPT, July 23, 2014, https://theintercept.com/2014/07/23/blacklisted/.

46 Terms in small caps appear in this fashion throughout the guidance manual, indicating that they are terms defined in appendix I of the manual (this one is at "U"). *See* March 2013 Watchlisting Guidance (hereinafter "Guidance"), page 5 n.1.

The Memorandum of Understanding accompanying HSPD-6 defined "Terrorist Information"; this Watchlisting Guidance builds on that foundation to define "terrorist activities" and "terrorism."[47] As would be expected, these terms are defined to include violent and destructive acts. But they also include "activities that facilitate or support" a range of actions that are not inherently dangerous, their meaning dependent on the actors involved. For example, an innocent commercial exchange, viewed more suspiciously, could be provision of "a safe house, transportation, communications, funds," etc.[48] The terms "known terrorist" and "suspected terrorist" are also defined:

> KNOWN TERRORIST: is an individual whom the U.S. Government knows is engaged, has been engaged, or who intends to engage in TERRORISM and/or TERRORIST ACTIVITY, including an individual (a) who has been charged, arrested, indicted, or convicted for a crime related to TERRORISM by U.S. Government or foreign government authorities; or (b) identified as a terrorist or member of a designated foreign terrorist organization pursuant to statute, Executive Order or international legal obligation pursuant to a United Nations Security Council Resolution.[49]
>
> SUSPECTED TERRORIST: is an individual who is REASONABLY SUSPECTED to be, or has been engaged in conduct constituting, in preparation for, in aid of, or related to TERRORISM and/or TERRORIST ACTIVITIES based on an articulable and REASONABLE SUSPICION.[50]

It is noteworthy that a "known terrorist" is *not* defined as someone formally designated as such; the definition notes these designations as only "including" the universe of possibly known terrorists (indeed, the crime for which the person might be arrested, charged, or convicted need only be "related" to terrorism in unspecified ways). The definition of a "suspected terrorist" is hard to untangle from the standard of reasonable suspicion embedded in the term. As one federal judge put it: "In other words, an American citizen can find himself labeled a suspected terrorist because of a 'reasonable suspicion' based on a 'reasonable suspicion.'"[51]

The March 2013 Watchlisting Guidance provides for numerous exceptions to this standard. For example, the Assistant to the President for Homeland Security and Counterterrorism (or her designee), without any individualized derogatory information, "may direct the TSC and NCTC to place categories of individuals from TIDE or TSDB on the No-Fly List, Selectee List, or into the TSDB for up to 72 hours."[52] An expedited nomination process allows watchlisting over the phone "[i]f exigent circumstances exist (imminent travel and/or threat)," with documentation to follow within three days.[53] As

47 *See* MOU, *supra* note 38. *See* Guidance, §§ 1.14–1.15.
48 Guidance, § 1.15.
49 Guidance, Appendix I at "L". This definition seems to have recently broadened. An affidavit sworn by then–deputy TSC director Piehota filed in federal court on June 3, 2011, refers to the July 2010 Watchlisting Guidance to define a known terrorist "as an individual who has been convicted of, currently charged with, or under indictment for a crime related to terrorism in a U.S. or foreign court of competent jurisdiction." Declaration of Christopher M. Piehota at 6 n.4, *Mohammad v. Holder*, Case No. 1:11-CV-50 (E.D. Va.) (No. 22–1).
50 Guidance, Appendix I at "W."
51 *Mohamed v. Holder*, 995 F. Supp. 2d 520, 531–32 (E.D. Va. 2014).
52 Guidance, § 1.59.2. "To the extent practicable," this order "will be in writing." *Id.* After seventy-two hours, and in thirty-day increments, concurrence must be sought from the Deputies or Principals Committee. *Id.* at § 1.59.3.
53 Guidance, § 1.58.

Table 3.1. TSDB activity, October 1,2008–September 30, 2013

Fiscal year	Nominations	Rejected
2009	227,932	508
2010	250,847	1628
2011	274,470	2776
2012	336,712	4356
2013	468,749	4915

would be expected, non-U.S. persons (especially those outside the United States) are subject to more exceptions than U.S. persons. But even a U.S. person "for whom there is insufficient derogatory information to support entry in TSDB" must be included in TIDE if he or she has "a nexus to terrorism."[54]

Most nominations to the TSDB are successful. This was verified in discovery permitted in recent litigation. In response to an interrogatory, the Justice Department produced the chart in Table 3.1 for TSDB activity between October 1, 2008, and September 30, 2013.[55] Although nominations more than doubled in five years, the percentage of nominations rejected rose from slightly more than 0.2 percent in 2009 to only slightly more than 1 percent in 2013.

Once a name is nominated to the TSDB, it is considered for inclusion in "downstream" watchlists designed for the particular needs of different federal agencies. Thus, the 2013 Watchlisting Guidance provides that an individual may be added to the No-Fly List if the person "represents a threat" of committing various definitions of terrorism found in the U.S. Code to aircraft, the "homeland," or U.S. facilities abroad. A person may also be added to the No-Fly List whose threat of "engaging in or conducting a violent act of terrorism" is judged real although the target is not locatable, so long as the person is "operationally capable" of such action.[56]

How judged? Oddly, the 2013 Watchlisting Guidance makes no reference to any evaluative standard in describing these No-Fly List criteria. Prior to the leak of this manual, high-level individuals familiar with the process struggled in interviews with the author to answer within the confines of an information environment in which the criteria themselves could not be identified. They finally agreed, however, that an analyst "must *at least* have a reasonable suspicion that the criteria were met, but the process of decision making is hard to reduce to the traditional legal standards familiar to lawyers."[57]

54 Guidance, § 3.15.2. How a nexus is found when there is insufficient derogatory information to watchlist in the ordinary fashion is unexplained.

55 Defendants' Objections and Responses to Plaintiff's First Set of Interrogatories, *Mohamed v. Holder*, 1:11-cv-00050-AJT-TRJ (E.D. Va. 2014) (No. 91–3).

56 Guidance, § 4.5. After years of asserting that publication of these criteria would threaten national security, they are now publicly acknowledged by the government. *See Tarhuni v. Lynch*, 129 F. Supp. 3d 1052, 1055 (D. Or. 2015).

57 Kahn, *supra* note 9, at 168–69. The government has since confirmed this conclusion. *See* Declaration of G. Clayton Grigg, Deputy Director for Operations, Terrorist Screening Center, May 28, 2015, *Tarhuni v. Lynch*, No. 3:13-cv-1 (D. Or. Sept. 1, 2015) (No. 105-A). ("Nominations that recommend an individual also be included on either the No Fly or Selectee List are evaluated by the TSC to determine if the derogatory information provided by the nominating agency establishes a reasonable suspicion that the individual

Where did the reasonable suspicion standard originate? An interagency working group developed this standard beginning in 2008.[58] It was modeled on the standard for a police "stop-and-frisk" that the Supreme Court devised in 1968 in *Terry v. Ohio*.[59] The Court held that Police Detective McFadden, though lacking probable cause to arrest John Terry and Richard Chilton, could nevertheless briefly stop, question, and frisk them (the latter for the officer's safety) if McFadden could "point to specific and articulable facts which, taken together with rational inferences from those facts, reasonably warrant that intrusion."[60] Although some in the working group raised concerns about the differences between the law enforcement and intelligence contexts, the group adopted a strikingly similar standard. This was not uncommon. The NSA adopted the same standard for its secret metadata collection program.[61]

But the *Terry* test was designed for the world of the old watchlists, one in which a sharp boundary line divided watching from acting on what was observed. When that limit was reached, the law required a public process in which executive action was assessed by a neutral judge. Indeed, immediately after setting forth the *Terry* reasonable suspicion standard, Chief Justice Warren's very next sentence described the classic boundary against which – and only against which – such an exception to probable cause made sense:

> The scheme of the Fourth Amendment becomes meaningful only when it is assured that at some point the conduct of those charged with enforcing the laws can be subjected to the more detached, neutral scrutiny of a judge who must evaluate the reasonableness of a particular search or seizure in light of the particular circumstances.[62]

Adopted for the new watchlists, the "reasonable suspicion" standard is stripped of this context. The "who, what, and where" of the boundary – which give that boundary meaning – are no longer present. The decisions made by executive officials at the TSC and NCTC (unlike the evaluation of Detective McFadden's judgment by a court) were not intended to be subject to judicial oversight. Nor was there intended to be a second, public forum at which a final determination about the individual's rights would be made under heightened rules of evidence. McFadden stopped Terry because if his suspicions were right, McFadden would arrest Terry, a prosecutor would charge him with a crime, and a judge would oversee his trial. Watchlisting does not proceed past the stop. Loosed of these constraints, imposed as much by the liberty-protecting function of the separation of powers as by the Fourth Amendment, the reasonable suspicion standard that populates

meets additional heightened derogatory criteria that goes above and beyond the criteria required for inclusion in the broader TSDB").

58 A more detailed treatment of its development is found in Kahn, *supra* note 9, at 158, 169–171, & 303 nn.11–12.

59 392 U.S. 1 (1968).

60 *Id.* at 21. Detective McFadden's actions might well have fallen short of the requirements of this test. Cross-examined at one of the criminal trials, he testified: "Some people that don't look right to me, I will watch them. Now, in this case when I looked over they didn't look right to me at the time." John Q. Barrett, *Appendix B State of Ohio v. Richard D. Chilton and State of Ohio v. John W. Terry: The Suppression Hearing and Trial Transcripts*, 72 St. John's L. Rev. 1387, 1456 (1998). Other factual details, as well as the racial undertones and societal context of the case, have come under scrutiny. Lewis R. Katz, *Terry v. Ohio at Thirty-Five: A Revisionist View*, 74 Miss. L. J. 423 (2004).

61 Robert S. Litt, *The Fourth Amendment in the Information Age*, 126 Yale L.J. F. 8, 9 (April 27, 2016).

62 392 *U.S. at 21*.

the TSDB and the No-Fly List gives the false appearance of constraint, as shadows give the illusion of bars on a window.

IV Growth and Use

In the earliest days of watchlisting, closest in time to 9/11, there were few incentives to be underinclusive. In response to a 2005 DOJ Inspector General's audit, the TSC attributed incomplete, inaccurate, or inconsistent information in the TSDB to "the immediate need during the earliest days of the TSC to develop a comprehensive database of potentially high-risk suspects."[63] The first TSC director, Donna Bucella, explained that "to err on the side of caution, individuals with any degree of a terrorism nexus were included" in the TSDB if at all possible.[64] According to Justice Department auditors, Bucella explained that

> one of the benefits of watch listing individuals who pose a lower threat was that their movement could be monitored through the screening process and this could provide useful intelligence information to investigators. In addition, she stated that watch listing lower-threat individuals that have associations with higher-threat level terrorists may lead to uncovering the location of higher watch listed individuals.[65]

Such policies tended to have long tails. Consider, for example, the interconnected nature of the TSDB and the No-Fly List generated from it. From the sixteen names on the FAA "do-not-carry" security directives on September 11, 2001, there were upward of sixty-four thousand "identities" in September 2014 (Table 3.2).[66]

A 2009 DOJ audit found substantially untimely delays in both nominating and removing individuals considered to be "investigative subjects" from the TSDB.[67] Perhaps most disconcerting, the audit found more than sixty thousand nominations for "non-investigative subjects" that had not followed the standard nomination process; internal controls over such nominations were found to be "weak or nonexistent."[68]

63 Follow-Up Audit of the Terrorist Screening Center, *supra* note 41, at 2.

64 U.S. Department of Justice Office of the Inspector General, Review of the Terrorist Screening Center (Audit Report 05–27) 30 (2005).

65 *Id.*

66 These statistics require careful interpretation. Sometimes, officials reveal the number of "records" or "identities" in a database or watchlist. This is not synonymous with the number of unique individuals, which is often much lower because of duplicate records, aliases, and other multipliers in these systems. Thus, the figure of sixty-four thousand identities noted in the text is drawn from testimony provided by TSC Director Piehota. *See Hearing before the Subcomm. on Transp. Sec. of the Comm. on Homeland Sec.*, *supra* note 44 ("The Terrorist Screening Center currently stands at about 800,000 identities. For those identities, for the No-Fly List, we are looking at about 8 percent of the overall population of the TSDB are watchlisted at the No-Fly level; about 3 percent of the overall population of the TSDB is watchlisted at the Selectee level.") The labels in this table are those used in the sources cited for each statistic.

67 Audit Division, Office of the Inspector General, U.S. Dep't of Justice, The Federal Bureau of Investigation's Terrorist Watchlist Nomination Practices 23 & 36 (2009) (finding "78 percent of the FBI terrorist watchlist nominations we reviewed were completed in an untimely manner" and that "the FBI was untimely in its removal of the subjects in 72 percent of the cases we reviewed and when the FBI removed these subjects, it took, on average, 60 days to process the removal requests").

68 *Id.* at 46 ("In total, more than 62,000 watchlist nominations have been made by non-standard FBI nomination processes. We also found almost 24,000 FBI watchlist records that were not sourced to a current terrorism case classification. Many of the records we tested were based on cases that had been closed years ago and should have been removed at that time. These records caused individuals to be screened unnecessarily by frontline screening personnel.").

Table 3.2. Watchlist Expansion Between September 2001 and February 2007

Date	Terrorist screening database (TSDB)	No-Fly List
Sept. 11, 2001		16 people
Nov. 2001		400 people[a]
Dec. 2001		594 people[b]
Dec. 22, 2001 AA Flight 63 Richard Reid ("shoe bomber")		
Apr. 2004	≈ 150,000 records[c]	
July 2004	≈ 225,000 records (≈ 170,000 "unique terrorist identities")[d]	
Feb. 2006	≈ 400,000 records[e]	
July 2006		71,872 records[f]
Start of TSC Review		
Feb. 2007		34,230 records[g]
End of TSC Review		
Apr. 2007	724,442 records[h]	
Sept. 2008	≈ 400,000 "unique individuals"[i]	
Dec. 2008	1,183,447 "known or suspected international and domestic terrorist identity records"[j]	
Sept. 2009		3,403 people[k]
Dec. 25, 2009 NW Flight 253 Umar Farouk Abdulmutallab ("underwear bomber")		
Jan. 2011		10,000 people[l]
Sept. 2011		16,000 individuals[m]
Feb. 2012	≈ 520,000 people[n]	21,000 people[o]
Sept. 2014	800,000 identities[p]	64,000 identities[q]

[a] Internal TSA Memorandum from Claudio Manno, Acting Associate Under Secretary for Transportation Security Intelligence, to Associate Under Secretary for Security Regulation and Policy, Oct. 16, 2002 (ACLU FOIA Release, A1–010).

[b] PowerPoint, TSIS, Dec. 2002 (ACLU FOIA Release, A1–03), *supra* note 30.

[c] Follow-Up Audit of the Terrorist Screening Center, *supra* note 41, at 7.

[d] *Id.*

[e] *Id.*

[f] *Id.* at 31–32.

[g] *Id.* at 31–32.

[h] *Id.* at 7.

[i] U.S. Department of Justice Office of the Inspector General, The Federal Bureau of Investigation's Terrorist Watchlist Nomination Practices (Audit Report 09–25) 1, n.40 (May 2009).

[j] *Id.* at 1.

[k] Author's interview, FBI HQ, Washington D.C., Dec. 4, 2009.

[l] Jamie Tarabay, *The No-Fly List: FBI Says It's Smaller than You Think,* National Public Radio (Jan. 26, 2011).

[m] Hearing before the House Subcommittee on Transportation Security of the Committee on Homeland Security, *supra* note 44 (statement by Congressman Cedric L. Richmond).

[n] Bob Orr, Inside a Secret U.S. Terrorist Screening Center, CBS News, Oct. 1, 2012.

[o] Carol Cratty, 21,000 people now on U.S. No-Fly List, official says, CNN, Feb. 2, 2012 (quoting unnamed official).

[p] Testimony of TSC Director Piehota, *supra* note 44.

[q] *Id.*

The result, as litigation would eventually reveal, was a TSDB and set of downstream watchlists that were sticky: the legacy of once having been watchlisted, even if later removed from one part of the system, tended to linger. In the words of one judge, "Once derogatory information is posted to the TSDB, it can propagate extensively through the government's interlocking complex of databases, like a bad credit report that will never go away."[69]

Whatever its faults, the TSDB had grown into an extraordinarily powerful and useful tool. There was now a watchlist available to every police officer in the United States, expanding the list of bad apples and "usual suspects" far beyond any previous capacity. According to a former TSC director:

> So if you are speeding, you get pulled over, they'll query that name. And if they are encountering a known or suspected terrorist, it will pop up and say call the Terror[ist] Screening Center. So now the officer on the street knows he may be dealing with a known or suspected terrorist.[70]

And even if there is no arrest, or even any indication that the label placed on the individual is the correct one, the police encounter will augment the watchlist record with that person's observed activities, destination, and associates, all entered in the TSDB.[71]

The No-Fly List also came into its own as one of the key counterterrorism tools of the TSA. This was due to two substantial changes in this watchlist from the old security directives from which it emerged. First, the application of the "reasonable suspicion" standard to build the No-Fly List was a departure from the much narrower standard that security directives used "to pass on specific, credible threats and mandatory countermeasures" subject to civil penalties for noncompliance.[72] The "do-not-carry" variety of these security directives were limited to denying boarding to those individuals determined to present "a direct and credible threat to aviation."[73] But when creating the TSA in 2001, Congress expressed interest in the identification of individuals who may be "a threat to civil aviation or national security."[74] The disjunctive "or" was now viewed as authority to use the No-Fly List to prevent air travel by someone who was *not* a threat to civil aviation, but who met the expansive definitions and low standard described above.

Second, control of the watchlist by commercial airlines was significantly reduced. Frustrations in implementing an expanding No-Fly List, and the hazards perceived in a watchlist revealed to persons outside the government, led to the conclusion that watchlist screening – like security checkpoints – should be "an inherently governmental function."[75] This was implemented in 2008 by the "Secure Flight" program, through which

69 *Ibrahim v. DHS*, 62 F. Supp. 3d 909, 928 (N.D. Cal. 2014).

70 Bob Orr, *Inside a Secret U.S. Terrorist Screening Center*, CBS News, Oct. 1, 2012.

71 *Id.*

72 Department of Transportation Selected Aviation Security Initiatives, Appendix H to Report of the President's Commission on Aviation Security and Terrorism 178 (1990).

73 Memorandum for the Record, 9/11 Commission interview with Claudio Manno, Oct. 1, 2003, at 8.

74 *See supra* note 25.

75 DHS Office of the Inspector General, Role of the No Fly and Selectee Lists in Securing Commercial Aviation 4 (2009). The Intelligence Reform and Terrorism Prevention Act, Pub. L. No. 108–458, § 4012(a)(1), 118 Stat. 3638 (2004) (codified at 49 U.S.C. § 44903(j)(2)(C)), transferred the ministerial function of comparing passenger information to watchlists from the airlines to the TSA.

passenger information is sent to the TSA when an airline ticket is purchased for comparison against the relevant watchlists.[76]

Given the power of these watchlists to track and, potentially, affect a wide variety of restrictions on rights, what explains the generally muted public attitude toward them? One answer might reside in the small number of U.S. persons (defined as citizens and permanent residents) who are watch listed. Testifying before Congress in late 2013, TSC Director Piehota estimated that U.S. persons on the No-Fly List were about "0.8 percent of the overall TSDB population," or sixty-four hundred identities.[77] Since so few U.S. citizens find themselves on such watchlists – and so many individuals subject to them lack representation in democratic forums – many are happy to have the costs of security externalized in this fashion.

V Litigation

A key FAA and TSA intelligence official could not recall anyone subject to a pre-9/11 security directive who had contested a denial to board, or even attempted to board a plane, once such an order had been issued. Perhaps because of the long interagency process for sharing intelligence with commercial airlines, such "watchlisted" individuals had stopped flying by that point.[78]

The size and expanded coverage of the No-Fly List, on the other hand, led to litigation both about that watchlist and eventually about the larger TSDB from which it originates. Such lawsuits presented unusual difficulties. Since government officials declined to confirm watchlisting decisions, some plaintiffs had difficulty satisfying standing requirements or found their complaints mooted by agency action on the eve of judicial scrutiny.[79] In their lawsuits, some plaintiffs alleged not only that they were wrongly placed on watchlists, but that they were subsequently approached by FBI agents who offered to restore their ability to travel in exchange for becoming government informants.[80] In other cases, plaintiffs alleged harassment or even torture by the FBI or foreign government agents acting jointly with the FBI, using the No-Fly List as a tool of coercion and control.[81]

If the multiagency design of the watchlisting process was not intended to make litigation more difficult – and there is no available evidence that it was – that was nevertheless a consequence. Authority to curate the TSDB and compose downstream lists lay with the TSC. Operational use of those lists (such as the No-Fly List) resided with "customer" agencies (such as the TSA). Naming a defendant was therefore the first difficulty.

76 Secure Flight Program, 73 Fed. Reg. 64,018 (Oct. 28, 2008) (codified at 49 C.F.R. §§ 1540 & 1560).

77 Testimony of TSC Director Piehota, *supra* note 44.

78 Author's interview with Claudio Manno, FAA HQ, Washington D.C., Mar. 14, 2011.

79 *Scherfen v. U.S. Dep't Homeland Sec'y*, No. 3:CV–08–1554, 2010 WL 456784 (M.D. Pa. Feb. 2, 2010); *Tarhuni v. Lynch*, 129 F. Supp. 3d 1052 (D. Or. 2015); Joint Stipulation Regarding the Effect of Plaintiff's Removal from the No-Fly List, *Fikre v. FBI*, 3:13-cv-00899 (D. Ore. May 27, 2016) (No. 102).

80 *See, e.g.*, Third Amended Complaint, *Latif v. Lynch*, 3:10–750 (D. Or. Jan. 11, 2013); Fifth Amended Complaint, *Fikre v. FBI*, 3:13-cv-00899 (D. Or. Nov. 29, 2015). These and other materials from similar cases may be accessed at the author's Web site, www.watchlistlaw.com.

81 *See, e.g.*, Fourth Amended Complaint, *Mohamed v. Holder*, 1:11-cv-50 (E.D. Va. Mar. 7, 2014).

A lawsuit directed at the TSC alleging that placement on the No-Fly List had injured the plaintiff had to overcome the obstacle that the TSC had not itself prevented the plaintiff from flying. That was the operational decision of the TSA. But a lawsuit directed at the TSA – which put the list into operation by issuing a security directive – faced a problem in obtaining a suitable remedy. A court could not order the TSA to remove a name from the relevant watchlists since that authority rested with the TSC. And courts initially insisted that would-be litigants exhaust their administrative remedies before the TSA (no such process exists at the TSC) prior to seeking judicial remedies against either agency. The administrative appeal process, run by the Department of Homeland Security, is called DHS TRIP (Traveler Redress Inquiry Program). As its name implies, where watchlist related complaints are concerned, it is limited to complaints concerning the No-Fly List and Selectee List, but not the TSDB. In its early form, DHS TRIP generated a "final agency decision" that was often opaque and uninformative, an example of which is provided in an appendix to this chapter, Figure 3.4.

Suing both together presented a separate difficulty. Among the powers and authorities transferred to the TSA upon its creation was a statutory provision dating to the creation of the FAA in 1958 that provided for review of certain agency action only in the U.S. courts of appeals.[82] The government argued, successfully at first, that this provision deprived federal trial courts of jurisdiction to hear such complaints.[83] This also had the effect of preventing pretrial discovery and the submission of evidence by the plaintiff outsideof any administrative record.[84] When such lawsuits occurred, such records would typically be filed under seal. In one early case, a description of the submitted record was docketed, revealing that the record included a number of electronic exchanges between the TSA and the TSC, which had created the list.[85]

Eventually, these impediments started to fall. In August 2008, the Ninth Circuit Court of Appeals was persuaded that the relevant issue in watchlisting cases concerned the *composition* of watchlists, not their implementation at airports. As then Chief Judge Alex Kozinski wrote for the 2–1 majority:

> Our interpretation of section 46110 is consistent not merely with the statutory language but with common sense as well. Just how would an appellate court review the agency's decision to put a particular name on the list? There was no hearing before an administrative law judge; there was no notice-and-comment procedure. For all we know, there is no administrative record of any sort for us to review. So if any court is going to review the government's decision to put Ibrahim's name on the No–Fly List, it makes sense that it be a court with the ability to take evidence.[86]

82 49 U.S.C. § 46110.

83 *Tooley v. Bush*, No. 06–306, 2006 WL 3783142 at *26 (D.D.C. Dec. 21, 2006); *Green v. TSA*, 351 F. Supp. 2d 1119, 1126 (W.D. Wa. 2005).

84 Although that statute provided that when such a petition for review was filed, the agency must then "file with the court a record of any proceeding in which the order was issued," on at least one occasion, the government argued that it was not required to submit an administrative record at all. *Gilmore v. Gonzales*, 435 F.3d 1125, 1133 n.7 (9th Cir. 2006).

85 *Kadirov v. TSA*, No. 10–1185 (D.C. Cir. filed July 12, 2010).

86 *Ibrahim v. DHS*, 538 F.3d 1250, 1256 (9th Cir. 2008).

Since composition was a TSC function, and the TSC was not subject to the jurisdiction-shifting provision of Section 46110, the district courts were open to hear carefully crafted complaints.[87] In 2015, the D.C. Circuit and Sixth Circuit adopted similar positions.[88]

This opened the door for litigation before trial courts that could order discovery and consider evidence outside the record. Attempts to obtain information in the form of interrogatories or document requests, however, were often met with claims of executive privilege based on "sensitive security information" in the record or with assertions of the law enforcement privilege or state secrets privilege.[89]

Only one case has reached the trial stage in federal court. In November 2004, Dr. Rahinah Ibrahim, an accomplished Malaysian architect and academic, was nominated to the No-Fly List by FBI Special Agent Kevin Michael Kelley. Kelley had mistakenly nominated Ibrahim to the No-Fly List by checking the wrong box on a watchlist nomination form, a mistake he acknowledged (and, indeed, seems only to have realized himself) at his deposition: the form was designed to assume nomination to all watchlists save those affirmatively excluded by marking a box.[90] As a result, Ibrahim was arrested and detained when she arrived in a wheelchair at the check-in counter at San Francisco International Airport with her daughter to depart for an academic conference. Further, her student visa was later revoked (as a result of nomination to CLASS) and she has not been permitted to return to the United States despite twenty years as a lawful resident. Although her name was removed from some watchlists, and the government determined in November 2006 that she did not meet the reasonable suspicion standard, her name was repeatedly removed from and then re-added to the TSDB and other watchlists over the next several years.[91]

87 *Id.* at 1255. In so doing, the court also rejected the government's frequently made (and previously successful) argument that TSC composition functions were so "inextricably intertwined" with TSA security orders as to require TSA as an indispensable party, forcing litigation into the courts of appeals. *See, e.g., Latif v. Holder*, No. 10–CV–750, 2011 WL 1667471 (D. Or. 2011), rev'd and remanded, 686 F.3d 1122 (9th Cir. 2012).

88 *Ege v. DHS*, 784 F.3d 791 (D.C. Cir. 2015); *Mokdad v. Lynch*, 804 F.3d 807 (6th Cir. 2015). Following revision to the DHS TRIP that resulted from ongoing litigation in *Latif v. Lynch*, the government took the position that "those conclusions are, in any event, not applicable to the TSA orders generated by the revised redress process. TSA now explicitly makes the final determination and does in fact have the information and the authority to effectuate the relief Plaintiff seeks." *See* Memorandum in Support of Defendants' Motion to Dismiss Plaintiff's 5th Amended Complaint at 5, *Fikre v. FBI*, No. 3:13-cv-00899 (D. Or. Jan. 21, 2016) (No. 90) (internal citation and quotation marks omitted). The government argued that in any such § 46110 review by a court of appeals, "consistent with past practice, classified and privileged portions of the records may be submitted *ex parte* and *in camera* for judicial review in the court of appeals." *Id.*

89 *See, e.g., Ibrahim v. DHS*, 62 F. Supp. 3d 909, 913–914 (N.D. Cal. 2014); Defendants' Opposition to Plaintiff's Motion to Compel at 1, *Tarhuni v. Holder*, 3:13-cv-1 (D. Or. Sept. 16, 2014) (No. 72).

90 *Ibrahim*, 62 F. Supp. 3d at 916. The author served as a testifying expert for the plaintiff in this case.

91 *Id.* at 922–23. Two email exchanges obtained in the course of discovery in this case suggest how the mere fact of being placed on a watchlist, more than the substantive grounds for watchlisting, can drive decision making in other parts of the government. The first email was sent between two officials in the State Department's visa office the day after Dr. Ibrahim's arrest in San Francisco:

> As I mentioned to you, I have a stack of pending revocations that are based on VGTO [the FBI's Violent Gang and Terrorist Organization] entries. These revocations contain virtually no derogatory information. After a *long* and frustrating game of phone tag with INR [the Department of State's Bureau of Intelligence and Research], TSC, and Steve Naugle of the FBI's VGTO office, finally we're going to revoke them.
>
> Per my conversation with Steve, there is no practical way to determine what the basis of the investigation is for these applicants. The only way to do it would be to contact the case agent for each case individually to determine what the basis of the investigation is. Since we don't have the time to do

It was Ibrahim's case that opened the door to the trial courts by removing the jurisdictional impediment of Section 46110. After eight years of litigation, her one-week bench trial – ironically, her U.S. citizen daughter was erroneously prevented by the TSDB from attending and offering testimony[92] – led Judge William Alsup to conclude:

> At long last, the government has conceded that plaintiff poses no threat to air safety or national security and should never have been placed on the no-fly list. She got there by human error within the FBI. This too is conceded. This was no minor human error but an error with palpable impact, leading to the humiliation, cuffing, and incarceration of an innocent and incapacitated air traveler. That it was human error may seem hard to accept – the FBI agent filled out the nomination form in a way exactly opposite from the instructions on the form, a bureaucratic analogy to a surgeon amputating the wrong digit.[93]

Despite these strong words, the court limited its remedy – scrubbing "every single government watchlist and database" – to instances that would be hard to uncover, as this long lawsuit itself demonstrated: "a conceded, proven, undeniable, and serious error by the government – not merely a risk of error."[94]

Therefore, perhaps the case that has had the most significant influence on the No-Fly List is *Latif v. Lynch*. In that case, thirteen U.S. citizen plaintiffs (including several veterans) alleged that the No-Fly List prevented their domestic and international travel. Some of the plaintiffs alleged that FBI agents promised to arrange air travel if they agreed to become government informants.

The long history of this case reads like a staged retreat. In addition to the jurisdictional arguments noted above, the government initially argued that plaintiffs had suffered no injury to their right to travel, a right that the government argued did not include "the most convenient means of travel," by airplane: "counsel's research shows that passenger ships frequently cross the Atlantic."[95] After the Ninth Circuit reversed the trial court's

> that (and, in my experience, case agents don't call you back promptly, if at all), we will accept that the opening of an investigation itself is a prima facie indicator of potential ineligibility under 3(B) [Immigration and Nationality Act, § 212(a)(3)(B)].

Id. at 921 (emphasis in original). The second email was sent a month later between an official at the State Department's visa office and the chief of the consular section of the U.S. Embassy in Malaysia:

> The short version is that [Dr. Ibrahim's] visa was revoked because there is law enforcement interest in her as a potential terrorist. This is sufficient to prudentially revoke a visa but doesn't constitute a finding of ineligibility. The idea is to revoke first and resolve the issues later in the context of a new visa application. ... My guess based on past experience is that she's probably issuable. However, there's no way to be sure without putting her through the interagency process. I'll gin up the revocation.

Id. at 922. As a result, a consular officer wrote the word "terrorist" on the form letter Ibrahim received in December 2009, five years after her initial, erroneous watchlisting. *Id.* at 924–25. After the trial, in December 2013, the court noted and so held that "government counsel has conceded at trial that Dr. Ibrahim is not a threat to our national security. She does not pose (and has not posed) a threat of committing an act of international or domestic terrorism with respect to an aircraft, a threat to airline passenger or civil aviation security, or a threat of domestic terrorism." *Id.* at 915–16.

92 *Id.* at 927.

93 *Id.* at 927–928.

94 *Id.* at 929.

95 Defendants' Motion for Summary Judgment at 24 & 30, *Latif v. Holder*, 3:10-cv-750 (Nov. 17, 2010) (No. 44). The suggestion was answered by one of the plaintiffs, who alleged that his attempt to travel across the Atlantic by cargo freighter was denied by the ship's captain "based on the recommendation of U.S. Customs and Border Protection." 3rd Amended Complaint at ¶ 86, *Latif*, 3:10-cv-750 (No. 83).

dismissal on Section 46110 grounds and remanded the case, Judge Anna Brown of the District Court of Oregon began a long (and still ongoing at the time of this writing) deconstruction of the No-Fly List and its multiagency support structure. The court rejected the argument that international air travel was "a mere convenience in light of the realities of our modern world." "Such an argument," she rightly pointed out, "ignores the numerous reasons an individual may have for wanting or needing to travel overseas quickly such as for the birth of a child, the death of a loved one, a business opportunity, or a religious obligation," all of which were implicated in the plaintiffs' allegations.[96] The court also found the DHS TRIP determination letters to be inadequate, providing neither adequate notice nor a meaningful chance to be heard.[97]

One year later, the court elaborated on this conclusion, finding that the low-threshold reasonable suspicion test, refusal to reveal the fact of or reasons for watchlisting on the No-Fly List, and one-sided nature of an administrative record offered for judicial review all conspired to create a redress process that "contains a high risk of erroneous deprivation" of constitutional rights.[98] Finding that the plaintiffs' right to procedural due process was violated, but unwilling to dictate a suitable process, the court ordered the government to "fashion new procedures that provide Plaintiffs with the requisite due process ... without jeopardizing national security."[99] In the meantime, the court ordered the government to disclose to the plaintiffs their status on the No-Fly List; seven of the thirteen plaintiffs were then informed that they were not on that watchlist.[100]

In spring 2016, Judge Brown upheld in principle the new redress processes that she had compelled the government to devise (while permitting the underlying watchlist to remain operational). In particular, the court held that the No-Fly List could continue to use the reasonable suspicion standard so long as the government provided "(1) a statement of reasons that is sufficient to permit such Plaintiff to respond meaningfully and (2) any material exculpatory or inculpatory information in Defendants' possession that is necessary for such a meaningful response."[101] No live hearing, neutral magistrate, or ability to cross-examine witnesses was necessary in such a process, and even the statement of reasons could be redacted under certain circumstances to protect national security.

On April 21, 2017, the seven-year-old case seemed to come to a close, at least in the District Court.[102] Judge Brown summarized the new DHS TRIP procedures:

> First, DHS TRIP (as noted, in consultation with TSC) would send to the traveler a notification letter that only indicates whether the traveler was on the No-Fly List. If the traveler is on the No-Fly List and requests additional information, the revised procedures

[96] *Latif v. Holder*, 969 F. Supp. 2d 1293, 1303 (D. Or. 2013). This finding established the tangible "plus" necessary for an additional right to be free from false, government-imposed injuries to reputation as suspected terrorists. *Id.* at 1304.

[97] *Id.* at 1307–08.

[98] *Latif v. Holder*, 28 F. Supp. 3d 1134, 1153 (D. Or. 2014).

[99] *Id.* at 1162. The government initially appealed this order to the Ninth Circuit but then moved for voluntary dismissal of its appeal.

[100] *Latif v. Holder*, 2015 WL 1883890 at *1 (D. Or. Apr. 24, 2015).

[101] *Latif v. Lynch*, 2016 WL 1239925, at * 2 (D. Or. Mar. 28, 2016). One of the original plaintiffs, an air force veteran who described a seven-country odyssey by air and land in order to return to his birthplace in New Mexico, died three weeks before this ruling. Notice of the Death of a Party, *Latif v. Lynch*, 3:10-cv-750 (D. Or. Apr. 12, 2016) (No. 324) (noticing death of Steven William Washburn on March 7, 2016). Thus, five plaintiffs remained who contested their status on the No-Fly List.

[102] Latif v. Sessions, 2017 WL 1434648 (D. Or. Apr. 21, 2017).

> call for DHS TRIP (in consultation with the TSC) to send the traveler a second notification letter that identifies the applicable substantive criteria and contains the unclassified summary of the reasons for the traveler's placement on the List. ... [I]f an individual timely responds to the second letter and requests additional review, DHS TRIP forwards the response and any enclosed information to the TSC for consideration. Upon completion of TSC's review of materials submitted to DHS TRIP, the TSC provides a written recommendation to the TSA Administrator as to whether the individual should be removed from or remain on the No-Fly List and the reasons for that recommendation. The information that the TSC provides to the TSA Administrator may be a summary of the information that the TSC relied on to make its determination regarding whether the individual should remain on the No-Fly List and does not necessarily include all underlying documentation. The TSC's recommendation to the TSA Administrator may contain classified and/or law-enforcement sensitive information. In addition, DHS TRIP also provides the traveler's complete DHS TRIP file to the TSA Administrator, including all information submitted by the traveler.[103]

Under the new procedures, the TSA Administrator then issues a final order adopting or rejecting the TSC recommendation concerning retention on the No-Fly List. That order will "state the basis for the decision to the extent possible without compromising national security or law-enforcement interests."[104]

Judge Brown rejected the plaintiffs' arguments that the new process fell short of constitutional requirements.[105] This was all the process the plaintiffs were due, at least with regard to the No-Fly List.[106]

There remained, however, plaintiffs' substantive due process claim.[107] Since the TSA now made the final decision regarding an individual's retention on the No-Fly List, the government argued (as it had begun to argue from the moment it began to revise these procedures) that the court of appeals now had exclusive jurisdiction over this final agency action under the old § 46110. The plaintiffs argued for district court jurisdiction, since the TSC seemed to retain the initial decision to compose the No-Fly List in the first place and was the source of the information that the TSA used to decide any DHS TRIP appeal.[108]

Judge Brown, considering this an issue of first impression, limited the reach of her decision, concluding "in the unique procedural posture of this case that jurisdiction over Plaintiffs' remaining substantive claims explicitly lies in the Ninth Circuit Court

103 *Id.*, at *2, n.2 & *3.

104 *Id.*, at *3.

105 *Id.*, at *4.

106 It is worth emphasizing that the Court focused *only* on the No-Fly List, not the TSDB or other TSC-compiled and controlled watchlists. The plaintiffs sought injunctive relief requiring "the removal of Plaintiffs from any watch list or database that prevents them from flying," which implicated only the No-Fly List. Third Amended Complaint, Latif v. Lynch, 3:10-cv-750 (D. Or. Jan. 11, 2013) (No. 83) at Prayer for Relief, ¶ 2(a).

107 *Id.* at ¶ 145 ("Because Plaintiffs do not present a security threat to commercial aviation, Defendants' actions as described above in including Plaintiffs on a watch list that prevents them from boarding commercial flights to and from the United States, and over U.S. airspace, are arbitrary, lack even a rational relationship to any legitimate government interest, and have unreasonably deprived Plaintiffs of constitutionally protected rights, including their liberty interests in travel, freedom from false stigmatization, and nonattainder.").

108 Latif, 2017 WL 1434648, at *6. *See also supra* note 105.

of Appeals pursuant to § 46110."[109] At the time of this writing, an appeal in this long-running, landmark case seems certain.

Conclusion: The Future of Watchlists

"Electronic databases form the nervous system of contemporary criminal justice operations," Justice Ginsburg observed in 2009. Quoting Justice Stevens's dissent in another database case almost fifteen years earlier, she expressed concern for their reliability:

> Inaccuracies in expansive, interconnected collections of electronic information raise grave concerns for individual liberty. The offense to the dignity of the citizen who is arrested, handcuffed, and searched on a public street simply because some bureaucrat has failed to maintain an accurate computer data base is evocative of the use of general warrants that so outraged the authors of our Bill of Rights.[110]

The dissenting justices' concern for the effect on liberty of inaccurate databases continues to motivate courts, as Judge Alsup's *Ibrahim* opinion and Judge Brown's *Latif* opinions attest. But courts have not been as concerned about the effect on liberty of the increasing use of these databases themselves. The technological innovations that make large, computerized databases integral components of government operations work a qualitative change to traditional modes of state action (investigation, regulation, distribution of benefits/burdens, etc.).[111] "[P]olice and other criminal justice officials are 'trackers' rather than investigators," and "[t]he virtually ubiquitous availability of personal information to law enforcement, coupled with the advent of the investigatory stop, has radically altered the landscape of policing."[112]

Further, many of the new watchlists do not exist in a world in which a criminal trial is the concluding step available to evaluate the merit of state action. As a result, the assumptions that long established a boundary that limited use of the old watchlists via scrutiny by a neutral judge in an open forum are increasingly subject to challenge. Although the No-Fly List is presently the most well-known of the new watchlists, there is no reason its logic must be limited to air travel. And the TSDB is increasingly tapped for new uses, some of which were imagined long ago, as revealed by a PowerPoint slide created by the TSC to brief congressional staff (and provided to the author in unclassified form; see Figure 3.3):

109 2017 WL 1434648, at *7. Noting that the question of TSC's role in disclosing information both to the plaintiffs and to the TSA implicated procedural as well as substantive issues of due process, Judge Brown noted that "this consideration may effectively limit this Court's rationale to the facts of this case. In the ordinary course, judicial review of a DHS TRIP determination will involve both procedural and substantive aspects because the reviewing court must determine both whether the Defendants provided sufficient information to the traveler and whether the TSA Administrator's substantive decision is supported by the record. Because only Plaintiffs' substantive claims remain pending in this case, however, this Court cannot determine whether the hybrid nature of an ordinary judicial review of a DHS TRIP determination would lead to a different result." Id. at *7, n.4.

110 *Herring v. United States*, 555 U.S. 135, 155–56 (2009) (Ginsburg, J., dissenting) (quoting Justice Stevens's dissent in *Arizona v. Evans*, 514 U.S. 1, 23 (1995)) (citations and quotation marks omitted).

111 Margaret Hu, *Big Data Blacklisting*, 67 Florida L. Rev. 1735 (2015).

112 Kathryne M. Young & Joan Petersilia, *Keeping Track: Surveillance, Control, and the expansion of the Carceral State*, 129 Harv. L. Rev. 1318, 1322 & 1330 (2016).

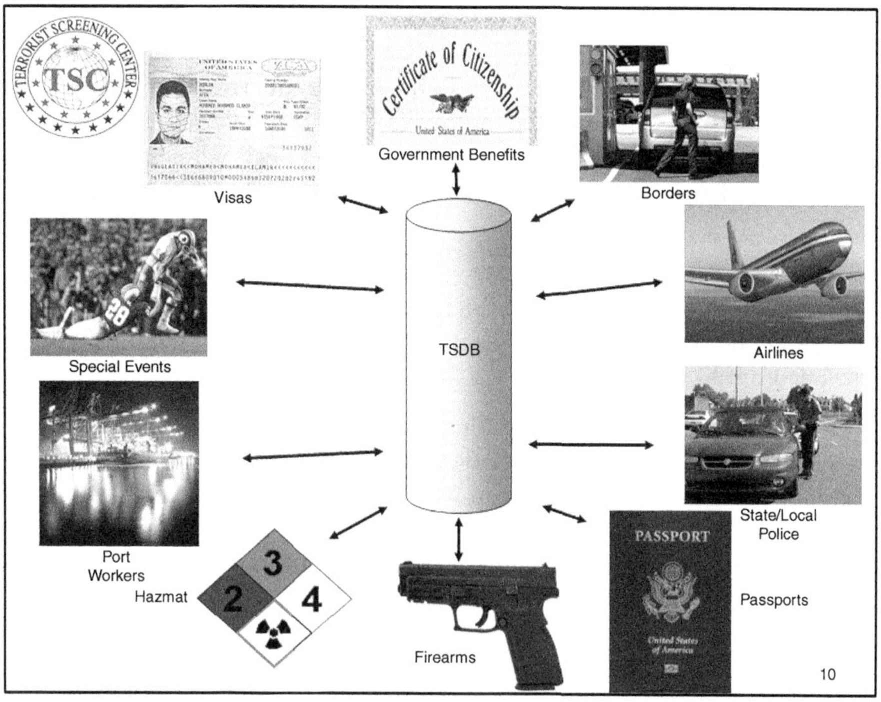

Figure 3.3. TSC PowerPoint Slide *circa* December 2009 on Current and Future Uses of the Terrorist Screening Database (TSDB).

Many future uses of watchlists were envisioned when the slide in Figure 3.3 was created in 2009, from controlling access to sporting events, to patrolling city streets, to vetting government benefits and gun licenses. The politics of gun control in the United States have (so far) limited expansion of watchlists into that last category, although legislation to create a "No-Gun List" has been proposed in the wake of mass shootings.[113] But the argument in favor of expansion has consistently been the same: if a person is "too dangerous to fly," that person is too dangerous for any number of activities that, as the PowerPoint slide at Figure 3.3 shows, are limited only by the imagination.

Indeed, the expansive logic of the new watchlists has led state governments to tap federal watchlists in various ways. New Jersey makes the purchase of weapons contingent on a check of the TSDB, a list never intended to serve this purpose.[114] In West Virginia, a plan by local law enforcement to consult terrorist watchlists before allowing participation

[113] After the mass shooting in June 2016 at a night club in Orlando, Florida, two proposals to use watchlists to restrict firearm transfers were defeated in the Senate. See S.Amdt. 4720 to S.Amdt. 4685 (tabled by voice vote on June 20, 2016), https://www.congress.gov/amendment/114th-congress/senate-amendment/4720, and S.Amdt. 4749 to S.Amdt. 4720 (felled upon tabling of S.Amdt. 4720 on June 20, 2016), https://www.congress.gov/amendment/114th-congress/senate-amendment/4749. A third and more substantial proposal, by Senator Susan Collins (R-ME), received broad bipartisan support; see S.Amdt. 4814, 162 Cong. Rec. S4419-S4420 (daily ed. June 21, 2016), but ultimately not enough. David M. Herszenhorn, *Senate Votes to Keep Gun Proposal Alive, but in Limbo*, N.Y. Times (June 23, 2016). My view of this proposal aligns with the concerns expressed in this chapter. *See* Jeffrey Kahn, *A 'No Buy' List for Guns Is a Bad Idea*, N.Y. Times (July 1, 2016), at A23.

[114] *See* N.J.S.A. 2C:58–3(c)(9) ("No handgun purchase permit or firearms purchaser identification card shall be issued … to any person named on the consolidated Terrorist Watchlist maintained by Terrorist Screening Center administered by the Federal Bureau of Investigation"). This requirement was signed

in an annual "bridge jump" so outraged the libertarian crowd of rappellers and bungee jumpers who make up the bulk of attendees that they decamped to an alternative site in Idaho.[115] In Minnesota, Fox News investigators pursued the logic of the watchlist to its extreme conclusion, asking why someone on the No-Fly List should receive a trucking license from the Minnesota Department of Public Safety. That Minnesotan's lawyer protested the obvious danger of barring an ever-expanding range of lawful activity, noting that his client

> has never been charged with a crime and has sued the government to obtain a fair process to challenge his wrongful inclusion on the No-Fly List. Like many other unemployed Americans, he's trying to obtain credentials for a job so he can build a life for his family, including a baby.[116]

But Fox News investigators picked up on the apparent discrepancy between the federal conclusion that this man was too dangerous to fly and the state view that he was not too dangerous to drive an eighteen-wheeler. Whose "reasonable suspicion" should prevail?

When the Supreme Court created the "reasonable suspicion standard" in its 1968 opinion *Terry v. Ohio*, it included some words of caution about its use:

> Nothing we say today is to be taken as indicating approval of police conduct outside the legitimate investigative sphere. Under our decision, courts still retain their traditional responsibility to guard against police conduct which is over-bearing or harassing, or which trenches upon personal security without the objective evidentiary justification which the Constitution requires. When such conduct is identified, it must be condemned by the judiciary and its fruits must be excluded from evidence in criminal trials.[117]

That might have established a check on the old watchlists, but it does not affect the new watchlists, for which no trial, criminal or otherwise, is contemplated. Indeed, ordinary police are not always even involved. The new watchlists are now so firmly established – but still lacking in legislative and judicial oversight – that younger generations may reach political maturity in a society in which the "new normal" is the idea that access to lawful, everyday activities may be subject to executive control that renders citizenship a characteristic akin to that of first-, second-, and third-class passengers on an airplane or ocean

into law by Governor Chris Christie on August 8, 2013; the bill, A3867 (Linda Stender, primary sponsor) was introduced one month after the shooting at Sandy Hook Elementary School in nearby Newton, Connecticut. *See* Matt Friedman, *Christie Signs 10 Gun Bills, but Leaves Controversial Measures on His Desk*, NJ.Com (Aug. 8, 2013); see also http://www.njleg.state.nj.us/2012/Bills/PL13/114_.PDF. In the wake of the South Carolina AME Church shooting, Senator Charles Schumer (D-NY) issued a press release announcing his support for a similar federal requirement. *See* Senator Charles Schumer, Newsroom Press Release (June 29, 2015), available at: http://www.schumer.senate.gov/newsroom/press-releases/after-south-carolina-tragedy-schumer-launches-new-effort-to-pass-significant-background-check-common-sense-gun-safety-legislation-weak-laws-allow-people-who-shouldnt-obtain-guns-to-get-them-and-use-them-in-massacre-after-massacre-senator-will-invoke-1993-brady-bill-passage-as-model-to-emulate-take-action-americans-are-calling-for-.

115 Erin Beck, *"Other Bridge Day" in Peril Idahoans Don't Want BASE Jumpers There*, Sunday Gazette-Mail (Charleston, WV) (June 7, 2015).

116 Tom Lyden, *Minnesota Terror Suspect Gets a Class A Trucking License*, FOX News 9, Aug. 27, 2015. Amir Meshal is one of the plaintiffs in the *Latif* case.

117 392 U.S. at 15.

liner. Indeed, a June 2016 poll conducted for CNN found that 85 percent of registered voters favored using the TSDB or No-Fly List to restrict gun ownership.[118]

Watchlists developed as a closed system, meaning one in which watchlisting decisions were insulated from outside review. The *Latif* litigation in particular reveals the government interest in preserving that original formulation, notwithstanding a citizen's right to protections like those that established the boundaries for the use of the old watchlists in an earlier time. All the while, society's extraordinary interest in national security hangs over these cases.

This perhaps reveals the wisdom of the framers of the U.S. Constitution in their defense of the separation of powers, for the tendency toward overinclusion has been (understandably) hard to avoid. At their facility in Vienna, Virginia, TSC employees walk past charred artefacts of the World Trade Center that stand as sculptures at the entrance to the facility.[119] Despite sincere efforts to create a culture in the agencies that create and use watchlists that can be trusted to make decisions requiring no external check and balance – and this objective is one repeatedly offered as grounds to exclude watchlisting decisions from judicial review – the record of recent experience suggests that the founding fathers were right to value the separation of powers as a fundamental protection of liberty.

As the former TSC director Timothy Healy explained, "The problem I've got is if I allow that person to get on a plane and something happens, what do I say to those victims that go on the plane?"[120] Or as Captain Renault remarked in *Casablanca*, "Realizing the importance of the case, my men are rounding up twice the usual number of suspects."[121]

118 This percentage was roughly similar across age, gender, race, income, political party, and regional divisions. *See* CNN/ORC International Poll (June 16–19, 2016), available at http://i2.cdn.turner.com/cnn/2016/images/06/20/cnn_orc_poll_june_20.pdf. *See also* Samantha Neal, *Americans Aren't Always as Divided on Gun Control as it Seems*, Huffington Post (June 28, 2016), at http://www.huffingtonpost.com/entry/americans-gun-control-poll-orlando_us_5772b6f1e4b0352fed3e0402.

119 Bob Orr, *Inside a Secret U.S. Terrorist Screening Center*, CBS News, Oct. 1, 2012 ("Throughout the Terrorist Screening Center are placed artifacts from various terrorist attacks including Oklahoma City federal building, the USS Cole bombing, and the World Trade Centers. All sober reminders of how important their work is").

120 Helen Jung, *Case of Tigard Man, Grounded by No-Fly List, Offers Glimpse into Secretive Airport Security Screening*, The Oregonian, Apr. 12, 2012, at A1.

121 Casablanca, *supra* note 1.

Appendix

U.S. Department of Homeland Security

Office of Transportation Security Redress
Arlington, VA 22202

February 8, 2006

[redacted]

Transportation Security Administration

Dear [redacted]

The Transportation Security Administration (TSA) has received your Passenger Identity Verification Form (PIVF) and identity documentation. In response to your request dated, [redacted], we have conducted a review of any applicable records in consultation with other federal agencies, as appropriate. Where it has been determined that a correction to records is warranted, these records have been modified to address any delay or denial of boarding that you may have experienced as a result of the watch list screening process.

TSA cannot ensure that your travel will always be delay free as this redress process does not affect other standard screening procedures in place at the security checkpoint. For example, an individual may be selected by TSA for enhanced screening in order to resolve a walk-through metal detector alarm, because of random selection, or based on certain non-identity based factors reflected in reservation information. Additionally this process may not eliminate the need to go to the ticket counter in order to obtain a boarding pass. For instance, an airline might still require a brief period of time to comply with identity verification requirements prior to issuing a boarding pass.

This letter constitutes TSA's final agency decision, which is reviewable by a United States Court of Appeals under 49 U.S.C. § 46110.

If you have any further questions, please call the TSA Contact Center Office of Transportation Security Redress (OTSR) toll-free at (866) 289-9673 or locally at (571) 227-2900, send an E-mail to TSA-ContactCenter@dhs.gov, or . .i:. to the following address:

Transportation Security Administration
TSA-901
601 South 12th Street
Arlington, VA 22202-4220

Sincerely,

Office of Transportation Security Redress

Figure 3.4. Sample of an early TSA Final Agency Decision.

4 "Incidental" Foreign Intelligence Surveillance and the Fourth Amendment

Jennifer Daskal* & Stephen I. Vladeck†

The United States' foreign intelligence surveillance scheme permits broad-based collection of foreigner data, based largely on the presumption that such foreigners lack Fourth Amendment rights – and that the acquisition of such data is therefore freed from the strictures of the Constitution. For technological reasons, however, such broad-based collection necessarily sweeps in hundreds of millions of U.S.-person communications – those of U.S. citizens and legal permanent residents, and others residing in the United States – which are protected by the Fourth Amendment. This chapter argues for a three-pronged reformulation of Fourth Amendment doctrine to take these interests into account, and thus better serve the interests the Fourth Amendment is meant to protect. First, it calls for a presumptive Fourth Amendment, pursuant to which the Fourth Amendment is generally understood to govern the acquisition of data, regardless of the location or identity of the target. While this does not mean that all such acquisitions are subject to the warrant requirement (we support, with some caveats, the foreign intelligence exception to this requirement), such acquisitions must at least satisfy the Fourth Amendment's reasonableness test. Second, it argues that the Fourth Amendment reasonableness of such large-scale collection of data depends in significant part on the existence and effective implementation of postacquisition limits on the use, retention, and dissemination of incidentally collected U.S.-person data. And, third, it argues that law enforcement querying of that data for U.S.-person information should be understood as a separate Fourth Amendment event that is independently required to meet the applicable constitutional requirements.

Introduction

Section 702 of the Foreign Intelligence Surveillance Act (FISA) Amendments Act of 2008[1] is held out by commentators across the political spectrum as a critically important surveillance tool – one that has helped the nation respond to (and avert) planned

* Associate Professor of Law, American University Washington College of Law.

† Professor of Law, University of Texas School of Law. Our sincere thanks to David Gray and Stephen Henderson for inviting us to contribute to this volume, and for their indefatigable (if not infinite) patience with us thereafter.

1 *See* Foreign Intelligence Surveillance Act of 1978 Amendments Act of 2008 (FISA Amendments Act of 2008), Pub. L. No. 110–261, § 101(a), 122 Stat. 2436, 2438–48 (2008) (codified as amended at 50 U.S.C. § 1881a).

attacks.[2] Yet, it is also controversial. The provision, which was the centerpiece of the 2008 amendments to FISA, authorizes "programmatic" surveillance of noncitizens reasonably believed to be located outside the United States whose communications nevertheless cross through U.S. servers, nodes, or other electronic infrastructure.[3] Even by conservative estimates, the government collects hundreds of millions of communications under Section 702 on an annual basis.[4] Included in that figure are millions of emails and other communications by U.S. persons (defined here as citizens and lawful permanent resident aliens).[5] This occurs despite the fact that Section 702 forbids the direct "targeting" of such communications.[6] Such so-called incidental collection nevertheless occurs when a U.S. person is in communication with foreign targets, or when a U.S. person's communications are bundled with a foreign target's communications, and the government has no way to acquire the targeted communication without also scooping up the nontargeted communications with which it is bundled.[7] As a result, this extremely valuable foreign intelligence surveillance program is predictably collecting large quantities of data about U.S. persons that would *not* be permitted if the U.S. persons whose data is being collected were the direct targets of the surveillance.

Such surveillance has thus far been held to be constitutional because of the intersection of at least three different strands of Fourth Amendment jurisprudence: first, most noncitizens located outside the United States do not enjoy Fourth Amendment protections;[8] second, the incidental collection of the communications of persons protected by the Fourth Amendment generally does not make an otherwise lawful search unlawful;[9] and third, even if the Fourth Amendment might otherwise apply, Section 702

2 *See, e.g.*, Privacy & Civil Liberties Oversight Bd., Report on the Surveillance Program Operated Pursuant to Section 702 of the Foreign Intelligence Surveillance Act 9–10 (2014) [hereinafter PCLOB 702 Report], http://www.pclob.gov/library/702-Report.pdf.

3 *Id.* at 111–113.

4 *See* [Caption Redacted], [Docket No. Redacted], 2011 WL 10945618, at *9, *25 (FISA Ct. Oct. 3, 2011) [hereinafter *October 2011 Bates Opinion*] (referring to the fact that the NSA acquires "more than two hundred fifty million Internet communications each year pursuant to Section 702").

5 Even if only 5 percent of these communications were from U.S. persons, that would add up to more than 12 million U.S.-person communications.

6 *See* 50 U.S.C. §§ 1801(i), 1881a(b) (2012).

7 *See infra* text accompanying note 46. Previously, significant quantities of U.S. person communications were also collected through what was known as "about" collection" – in situations when a U.S. person was communicating "about " a foreign target. As this chapter went to press, however, the NSA announced that it would no longer engage in "about" communications, after concerns were raised by both the FISC and some members of Congress. *See* Nat'l Security Agency, NSA Stops Certain Section 702 "Upstream" Activities (Apr. 28, 2017), https://www.nsa.gov/news-features/press-room/statements/2017-04-28-702-statement.shtml.

8 *See, e.g.*, *United States v. Verdugo-Urquidez*, 494 U.S. 259 (1990). As discussed later, the Supreme Court recently heard arguments in a case that may provide an opportunity for clarifying the scope of *Verdugo-Urquidez*. *See infra* note 22.

9 *See, e.g.*, *In re Directives* [Redacted Text] Pursuant to Section 105B of the Foreign Intelligence Surveillance Act, 551 F.3d 1004, 1015 (FISA Ct. Rev. 2008) [hereinafter *In re Directives*] (concluding that "incidental collections occurring as a result of constitutionally permissible acquisitions do not render those acquisitions unlawful"); *United States v. Bin Laden*, 126 F. Supp. 2d 264, 280 (S.D.N.Y. 2000) ("Incidental interception of a person's conversations during an otherwise lawful surveillance is not violative of the Fourth Amendment"); *see also United States v. Kahn*, 415 U.S. 143, 157–58 (1974).

surveillance falls within a "foreign intelligence surveillance" exception to the Warrant Clause(and the searches are otherwise deemed reasonable).[10]

Section 702 capitalizes upon these threads by authorizing the large-scale collection of Internet communications (including communications to and from U.S. persons) when the government is *targeting* noncitizens abroad, *i.e.*, those who have no constitutional expectation of privacy in such communications. So framed, Section 702 may raise privacy concerns, along with diplomatic and foreign relations hackles, but it seems at least outwardly drawn so as not to implicate the Constitution.

In this chapter, we challenge this understanding, arguing that the scope of incidental collection of U.S. persons' communications pursuant to programmatic foreign intelligence surveillance triggers the Fourth Amendment – not only with respect to how the government *uses* what it incidentally collects, but at the point of acquisition itself. Specifically, we urge three key shifts in doctrine.

First, we argue for the adoption of a *presumptive* Fourth Amendment, pursuant to which Fourth Amendment protections are applied to the acquisition of *all* communications that are anticipated to include a U.S. person's data, regardless of whether the U.S. person is the direct target of the search. To be clear, we are not saying that a warrant is required for all such collection. Rather we support the premise of a foreign intelligence exception (appropriately circumscribed) to the warrant requirement. But we do argue that any such collection, even if it does not require a warrant, must satisfy a reasonableness test to be constitutional.

Second, we argue that an assessment of the postacquisition "use" constraints – namely, retention and dissemination limits – is central to the front-end reasonableness inquiry. This has already been recognized implicitly, if not explicitly, by both Congress and certain courts. The Wiretap Act, for example, requires that law enforcement officials "minimize the interception of communications not otherwise subject to interception" when they conduct Title III wiretaps.[11] In computer search cases, some courts have required specific protocols regarding access, retention, and dissemination of collected data.[12] Section 702 itself requires the executive branch to adopt, and the Foreign Intelligence Surveillance Court (FISC) to approve, so-called minimization procedures, which are

10 *See, e.g.*, *In re Directives*, 551 F.3d at 1012; *United States v. Hasbajrami*, 2016 WL 1029500, at *10–13 (E.D.N.Y. Feb. 18, 2016); *United States v. Mohamud*, No. 3:10-CR-475-KI-1, 2014 WL 2866749, at *16–18 (D. Or. June 24, 2014).

11 18 U.S.C. § 2518(5) (2012).

12 *See, e.g.*, *United States v. Comprehensive Drug Testing, Inc.*, 621 F.3d 1162, 1180 (9th Cir. 2010) (en banc) (Kozinski, J., concurring) (suggesting, albeit as guidance, the use of detailed computer search protocols); *United States v. Bonner*, No. 12–3429, 2013 WL 3829404, at *19 (S.D. Cal. July 23, 2013); *In re Search of 3817 W. West End*, 321 F. Supp. 2d 953, 955 (N.D. Ill. 2004) (requiring use of detailed search protocol); *In re Appeal of Application for Search Warrant*, 71 A.3d 1158 (Vt. 2012) (upholding ex ante requirements that personnel segregated from the investigators review the data and prohibitions on the use of certain search tools). *But see United States v. Burgess*, 576 F.3d 1078, 1094 (10th Cir. 2009) (noting that it would be "folly for a search warrant to attempt to structure the mechanics of the search because imposing such limits would unduly restrict legitimate search objectives"); *United States v. Grimmett*, 439 F.3d 1263, 1270 (10th Cir. 2006) ("[A] computer search 'may be as extensive as reasonably required to locate the items described on the warrant.'") (quoting *United States v. Wuagneux*, 683 F.2d 1343, 1352 (11th Cir. 1982)); *State v. Bizewski*, No. UWYCR110144340, 2013 WL 1849282, at *13 (Conn. Super. Ct. Apr. 10, 2013).

designed, among other things, to limit the retention and dissemination of U.S. person information.[13] A recent Foreign Intelligence Surveillance Court of Review (FISCR) opinion relied on "steps taken by the government to minimize the dissemination of" certain acquired information as a factor in its reasonableness assessment.[14] Other rulings by the FISC have adopted similar analyses.[15] In sum, both Congress and the courts are increasingly recognizing the importance of postacquisition limits on the retention, dissemination, and use of collected data in determining the lawfulness of proposed surveillance programs.[16] In our view, this is the right approach; the existence and robustness of such postacquisition limits are – and should be – an explicit part of the Fourth Amendment assessment into the reasonableness of the collection.[17]

Third, in addition to and independent of the reasonableness assessment, we argue that subsequent law enforcement *queries* of surveillance databases for information about a U.S. person are themselves Fourth Amendment events. The queries themselves must independently satisfy the Fourth Amendment's requirements.[18]

This chapter proceeds in three parts. Part I provides the relevant background – elucidating the current doctrine, the rise of the current foreign intelligence surveillance regime, and the scope of incidental collection that results. Part II explains why, given the scope and anticipated nature of the incidental collection that occurs, Section 702 (as well as the separate collection that takes place pursuant to Executive Order 12333) should be understood to implicate the Fourth Amendment insofar as it inevitably leads to the collection of significant quantities of U.S. persons' communications. Finally, we close in Part III by laying out the shifts in doctrine and policy that we think are needed. With Section 702 due to expire at the end of 2017,[19] our hope is that Congress will take seriously the unique constitutional problems posed by incidental collection in this context as it debates reauthorization – and that the courts will as well.

13 *See* 50 U.S.C. §§ 1801(h), 1881a(e).

14 *See In re Certified Question of Law*, No. 16–01, slip op. at 31 (FISA Ct. Rev. Apr. 14, 2016), https://www.dni.gov/files/icotr/FISCR%20Opinion%2016-01.pdf.

15 *See, e.g.*, *In re Directives*, *supra* note 9, at 1015 (noting that the existence of "effective minimization procedures" supports the reasonableness of governmental surveillance); *October 2011 Bates Opinion*, *supra* note 4, at *27 (noting that both the FISC and FISCR "have recognized that procedures governing retention, use, and dissemination have a bearing on the reasonableness under the Fourth Amendment of a program for collecting foreign intelligence information").

16 *See In re Certified Question of Law*, *supra* note 14, at 7 ("FISC review of targeting and minimization procedures under Section 702 is not limited to the procedures as written; rather, the Court examines how the procedures have been and will be implemented").

17 For a parallel argument made in the context of "Big Data" surveillance programs, see David Gray, The Fourth Amendment in an Age of Surveillance (2017). *See also* Stephen E. Henderson, *Fourth Amendment Time Machines (And What They Might Say about Police Body Cameras)*, 18 U. Pa. J. Const. L. 933, 972 (2016) (emphasizing the importance of "access, use, and dissemination restrictions for our privacy").

18 *See* David Kris, *Trends and Predictions in Foreign Intelligence Surveillance: The FAA and Beyond*, 8 J. Nat'l Sec. L. & Pol'y 377, 399 (2016) (noting the "interesting" but unresolved question as to whether querying should be seen as a "separate Fourth Amendment event" or best seen as part of the "overall Fourth Amendment event described by the FAA").

19 *See* FISA Amendments Act of 2008, Pub. L. No. 110–261, § 403(b)(1), 122 Stat. 2436, 2474 (2008), *amended by* FISA Amendments Act Reauthorization Act of 2012, Pub. L. 112–238, § 2(a)(1), 126 Stat. 1631 (2012).

I The Fourth Amendment, Foreign Intelligence Surveillance, and Incidental Collection

A *The Doctrine*

1 The Fourth Amendment's Territorial Limits

In the 1990 case of *United States v. Verdugo-Urquidez*, Chief Justice William Rehnquist concluded that only citizens and those with substantial voluntary connections to the United States are entitled to Fourth Amendment rights.[20] As Rehnquist put it (writing for himself and Justices White, O'Connor, and Scalia), "'the people' protected by the Fourth Amendment … refers to a class of persons who are part of a national community or who have otherwise developed sufficient connection with this country to be considered part of that community."[21] Whatever its merits, this understanding of the Fourth Amendment's reach appears to be entrenched, at least for the time being.[22] Citizens, persons with sufficient connections to the United States (such as legal permanent residents), and other persons located in the United States are widely understood to be protected by the Fourth Amendment. By contrast, noncitizens located outside the United States who lack sufficient connections to the United States have no constitutional protection from warrantless or otherwise unreasonable searches and seizures carried out by the U.S. government.

This government relies on this doctrine to justify surveillance of noncitizen targets located outside the United States under laxer standards than those required for the targeting of citizens, legal permanent residents, and others residing in the United States.

2 Incidental Collection Permitted

The Supreme Court has long held that only the person whose premises, property, person, or effects have been searched or seized has cognizable Fourth Amendment rights vis-à-vis the government – the so-called personal-rights approach to the Fourth Amendment.[23] Thus, a criminal defendant has no grounds to challenge an illegal search of a third party,

20 494 U.S. 259 (1990).

21 *Id.* at 265. Although Justice Kennedy, providing the fifth vote, joined Rehnquist's opinion in full, his reasoning called into question the core of Rehnquist's logic, *i.e.*, that the term "the people" in the Fourth Amendment restricted its application to U.S. citizens and others with sufficient voluntary connections to the United States. *See id.* at 276 (Kennedy, J., concurring) ("Given the history of our Nation's concern over warrantless and unreasonable searches, explicit recognition of 'the right of the people' to Fourth Amendment protection may be interpreted to underscore the importance of the right, rather than to restrict the category of persons who may assert it.").

22 For a critique of and suggested limits to the ruling, see Jennifer Daskal, *Transnational Seizures: The Constitution and Criminal Procedure Abroad, in* Constitutionalism across Borders in the Struggle Against Terrorism 191 (Federico Fabbrini & Vicki Jackson eds., 2016). In February 2017, the Supreme Court heard arguments in a case in which one of the three questions presented is whether the extraterritorial application of the Fourth Amendment to noncitizens should be resolved on more functional terms, such as those suggested by Justice Kennedy in his *Verdugo-Urquidez* concurrence. As of this writing, the opinion has not yet been handed down. *See Hernandez v. Mesa*, No. 15–118, 2016 WL 5897576 (U.S. Oct. 11, 2016). By way of disclosure, one of us (Vladeck) is co-counsel to the Petitioners in *Hernandez*.

23 *See, e.g., Minnesota v. Carter*, 525 U.S. 83, 88 (1998) ("In order to claim the protection of the Fourth Amendment, a defendant must demonstrate that he *personally* has an expectation of privacy in the place searched, and that his expectation is reasonable") (emphasis added); *id.* (The Fourth Amendment is a personal right that must be invoked by an individual"). For a critique of this view *see* David Gray,

even if that search yields information that is used against the defendant in the criminal proceedings. As the Court put it in *Rakas v. Illinois*:

> A person who is aggrieved by an illegal search and seizure only through the introduction of damaging evidence secured by a search of a third person's premises or property *has not had any of his Fourth Amendment rights infringed*. And since the exclusionary rule is an attempt to effectuate the guarantees of the Fourth Amendment, it is proper to permit only defendants whose Fourth Amendment rights have been violated to benefit from the rule's protection.[24]

This is not just a prudential rule of standing, but reflects an understanding of the Fourth Amendment's limits. If John puts evidence of a crime in his friend Jane's purse, and the police then unlawfully search that purse, only Jane – not John – has suffered a Fourth Amendment injury.

This analysis also carries over to information – not just physical property – voluntarily conveyed to others. The "misplaced trust" doctrine, for example, tells us that individuals do not have a reasonable expectation of privacy in information conveyed to an informant or undercover agent. This is so even if the informant or agent both records and instantaneously transmits the target's conversations to law enforcement officials; after all, the target loses control over the information once it has been transmitted to another. As a plurality of the Supreme Court characterized it, "The law gives no protection to the wrongdoer whose trusted accomplice is or becomes a police agent."[25]

In the context of Section 702 collection, the government relies on the misplaced trust doctrine to argue that

> once a non-U.S. person located outside the United States receives information, the sender loses any cognizable Fourth Amendment rights with respect to that information. That is true even if the sender is a U.S. person protected by the Fourth Amendment, because he assumes the risk that the foreign recipient will give the information to others, leave the information freely accessible to others, or that the U.S. government (or a foreign government) will obtain the information.[26]

Taken to its logical conclusion, this means that all persons lose their reasonable expectation of privacy – and thus any Fourth Amendment protection – in communications transmitted to others. And while the Department of Justice seems to have backed off this extreme position (and separately seems to acknowledge that the use of such shared information can raise Fourth Amendment concerns),[27] the government maintains – as

The Fourth Amendment in an Age of Surveillance (2017) and David Gray, *Dangerous Dicta*, 72 Wash. & Lee L. Rev. 1181 (2015).

24 *Rakas v. Illinois*, 439 U.S. 128, 425 (1978) (emphasis added) (citations omitted); *id.* at 426 (emphasizing that "persons who [are] not parties to unlawfully overheard conversations or who did not own the premises on which such conversations took place [do] not have standing to contest the legality of the surveillance, regardless of whether or not they [are] the 'targets' of the surveillance").

25 *United States v. White*, 401 U.S. 745, 752 (1971); *see also Lewis v. United States*, 385 U.S. 206 (1966); *Hoffa v. United States*, 385 U.S. 293 (1966); *Lopez v. United States*, 373 U.S. 427 (1963).

26 *See* Gov't Unclassified Response to Defendant's Alt. Motion for Suppression of Evidence & a New Trial at 48, *United States v. Mohamud*, No. 3:10-cr-475-KI, 2014 WL 2866749 (D. Or. June 24, 2014). For a thoughtful analysis of the misplaced trust doctrine, *see* Kiel Brennan-Marquez, *Fourth Amendment Fiduciaries*, 84 Fordham L. Rev. 611 (2015).

27 Notably, the above-quoted passage referring to the misplaced trust doctrine was dropped in the appellate brief in the same case, even though much of the rest of the brief tracks the earlier lower court filing. *See* Answering

supported by several courts – that the incidental collection of U.S. (or other protected) persons' communications does not render an otherwise valid search unlawful.[28]

In some isolated cases, courts have nevertheless imposed limits. As Judge John Bates, then presiding judge of the FISC, stated, "There surely are circumstances in which incidental intrusions can be so substantial as to [both trigger the Fourth Amendment and] render a search or seizure unreasonable."[29] Moreover, courts and the government also have recognized that U.S. persons have Fourth Amendment rights with respect to how information collected incidentally is ultimately *used* – hence the focus on minimization.[30] But, in general, the government has been free from the strictures of the Fourth Amendment when it engages in the *acquisition* of non-U.S. persons' data located outside the United States, despite the anticipated incidental collection of U.S. persons' data.[31] To the extent that the Fourth Amendment is triggered, the prevailing assumption is that it is implicated only by what is *done* with a U.S. person's data that has been obtained, not at the point of acquisition itself.

3 Foreign Intelligence Exception

In the context of foreign intelligence collection, this doctrine also intersects with yet another strand of Fourth Amendment jurisprudence: the idea of a foreign intelligence exception to the Fourth Amendment's warrant requirement. Pursuant to this doctrine, searches of foreign powers or agents of foreign powers reasonably believed to be located outside the United States are subject to a "reasonableness" test only, *even* if the direct target of the search is a U.S. person.[32]

B *Foreign Intelligence Surveillance*

1 Section 702 of the FISA Amendments Act

As the now-familiar story goes, the FISA Amendments Act of 2008 (FAA) was a response to a May 2007 ruling by the FISC that prohibited the warrantless targeting of foreigners'

Brief of Plaintiff-Appellee, *United States v. Mohamud*, No. 14–3027 (9th Cir. Dec. 7, 2015); *see also* Robert Litt, *The Fourth Amendment in a Digital Age*, 126 YALE L.J. F. 8 (2016), http://www.yalelawjournal.org/forum/fourth-amendment-information-age (describing it as "significant that the government did not argue in *Jewel* [another case challenging the constitutionality of 702 collection] that the plaintiffs had no reasonable expectation of privacy in the content of the communications even though that content was exposed to a third party").

28 *See, e.g., United States v. Hasbajrami*, 2016 WL 1029500, at *9 (E.D.N.Y. Feb. 18, 2016) ("When surveillance is lawful in the first place – whether it is the domestic surveillance of U.S. persons pursuant to a warrant, or the warrantless surveillance of non-U.S. persons who are abroad – the incidental interception of non-targeted U.S. persons' communications with the targeted persons is also lawful"); *Mohamud*, 2014 WL 2866749, at *16 ("The § 702 acquisition targeting a non-U.S. person overseas is constitutionally permissible, so, under the general rule, the incidental collection of defendant's communications with the extraterritorial target would be lawful"); *In re Directives*, 551 F.3d at 1015; *see also United States v. Kahn*, 415 U.S. 143, 157–58 (1974).

29 *October 2011 Bates Opinion*, *supra* note 4, at *26.

30 *Id.* at *27.

31 There is, however, a statutory prohibition on reverse targeting – targeting a person located outside the United States with the *purpose* of targeting a particular, known person reasonably believed to be in the United States. *See* 50 U.S.C. § 1881a(b)(2) (2012).

32 *See In re Directives*, 551 F.3d at 1012; see also *October 2011 Bates Opinion*, supra note 4, at *24; *Mohamud*, 2014 WL 2866749, at *15–18. The definition of "foreign power" and "agent of a foreign power" can be found at 50 U.S.C. § 1801(a) & (b).

communications transiting through U.S. infrastructure. Whereas prior FISC court judges had approved such searches, Judge Roger Vinson interpreted FISA's requirements of an individualized, court-approved finding of probable cause to apply – regardless of the location or nationality of the target (or the other participants).[33] Claiming that a warrant requirement would kneecap its ability to track and prevent threats, the Bush administration persuaded Congress to enact the temporary Protect America Act of 2007 (PAA),[34] which permitted warrantless foreign surveillance on targets believed to be outside the United States; this included the authority to engage in the warrantless surveillance of U.S.-person targets. In 2008, the PAA was replaced with the (somewhat-more) permanent FAA, the heart of which is Section 702.[35]

While Section 702 does not permit the direct targeting of U.S. persons, it does permit broad-based collection of non-U.S.-person data in ways that lead to *incidental* collection of vast quantities of U.S.-person data. Section 702 gives the government wide latitude to target any non-U.S. person "reasonably believed" to be outside the United States in order to acquire specified categories of foreign intelligence information.[36] There is no probable cause determination, or even a required finding of reasonable articulable suspicion that the target is an agent of a foreign power or in possession of foreign intelligence information. And there is no court review of the specific targeting decisions. Rather, the government applies to the FISC, on an annual basis, for an "authorization" to target, for specified purposes, the communications of noncitizens reasonably believed to be outside the United States.[37] The FISC reviews the authorization application to ensure compliance with the applicable statutory provisions and the Fourth Amendment. In other words, the FISC's job is to oversee the programmatic procedures, not individual applications for, or specific instances of, surveillance. Electronic communication providers are required to assist in these collection efforts; specifically, they must "immediately provide the Government with all information, facilities, or assistance necessary to accomplish the acquisition" that is being sought.[38]

As far as is publicly known, there are two separate foreign intelligence surveillance programs operated under Section 702: what is known as the PRISM program and upstream collection.[39] Pursuant to PRISM, the government sends approved "selectors" (e.g., email addresses) to electronic communication service providers, such as Internet service providers, who then are required to turn over all communications sent over their networks to or from the selector.[40] The PRISM program accounts for approximately 90 percent of communications collected under 702 – yielding upward of 225 million communications each year.[41]

33 *See In re Certified Question of Law*, No. 16–01 (FISA Ct. Rev. Apr. 14, 2016), https://www.dni.gov/files/icotr/FISCR%20Opinion%2016-01.pdf.

34 Protect America Act of 2007 (PAA), Pub. L. No. 110–55, 121 Stat. 552 (formerly codified at 50 U.S.C. §§ 1805a–c), *repealed by* FISA Amendments Act of 2008, Pub. L. No. 110–261, § 403(a), 122 Stat. 2437, 2473–2474.

35 *See supra* note 1.

36 *Id.*

37 50 U.S.C. § 1881a(a).

38 *Id.* § 1881a(h)(1).

39 PCLOB 702 Report, *supra* note 2, at 7.

40 *Id.*

41 *October 2011 Bates Opinion*, *supra* note 4, at *9, *25 (referring to the fact that the NSA acquires "more than two hundred fifty million Internet communications each year pursuant to Section 702," and that

The remaining 10 percent is collected via upstream collection – this time with the aid of the Internet and telecommunications companies that control the fiber optic lines over which Internet communications travel "upstream" of the U.S. Internet service providers.[42] Because of the way the technology operates, such upstream collection yields so-called Internet transactions.[43] Sometimes, such transactions include discrete communications, but oftentimes they include multiple communications bundled together – meaning that totally unrelated communications may be acquired because they are bundled with communications that are to or from the target.[44]

Section 702 thus yields incidental collection of U.S. persons' data in two key ways: (1) when a U.S. person is in direct communication with a targeted non-U.S. person; and (2) when, also as part of upstream collection, the government collects bundled communication transactions that include discrete communications of U.S. persons.[45]

2 Minimization Procedures

To help ameliorate the privacy concerns raised by such collection, Section 702 requires the attorney general, in consultation with the director of national Intelligence, to adopt "minimization procedures."[46] Broadly speaking, they require the attorney general to minimize the acquisition, retention, and dissemination of non–publicly available information concerning nonconsenting U.S. persons "consistent with the need of the United States to obtain, produce, and disseminate foreign intelligence information."[47] Dissemination of non–publicly available, non–foreign intelligence information that identifies a nonconsenting U.S. person is prohibited "unless such person's identity is necessary to understand foreign intelligence information or assess its importance."[48]

Importantly, the requirements include an exception for law enforcement purposes: notwithstanding the otherwise-applicable prohibitions on retention and dissemination of U.S.-person information, information that is "evidence of a crime which has been, is being, or is about to be committed" can be retained and disseminated for law enforcement purposes.[49]

The existence of such "minimization" procedures is hardly unique to FISA. Congress, for example, has prescribed the application of minimization procedures as part of the Wiretap Act, which governs law enforcement's real-time collection of electronic and wire communications.[50] But, as stated previously, the minimization procedures required under the FAA differ from what is required under the Wiretap Act or pursuant to the specific court orders

approximately 91 percent of these communications are acquired directly from Internet Service Providers (ISPs) through the PRISM program); PCLOB 702 Report, *supra* note 2, at 33–34.

42 PCLOB 702 Report, *supra* note 2, at 8.

43 *October 2011 Bates Opinion*, *supra* note 4, at *5; PCLOB 702 Report, *supra* note 2, at 7.

44 PCLOB 702 Report, *supra* note 2, at 39–41; *October 2011 Bates Opinion*, *supra* note 4, at *26.

45 For a more in-depth discussion of the kinds of incidental collection that result from both Section 702 and other surveillance programs, see Jennifer Daskal, *The Un-Territoriality of Data*, 125 Yale L.J. 326, 348–54 (2015).

46 50 U.S.C. § 1881a(e).

47 *See id.* §§ 1881a(e), 1801(h)(1).

48 *Id.* § 1801(h)(2).

49 *Id.* § 1801(h)(3).

50 *See* 18 U.S.C. § 2518(5).

issued in a handful of computer search cases. Wiretap orders and computer search protocols are signed off on and reviewed by a judge. The minimization requirements are tailored to the specific needs of the case. Under the FAA, the FISC signs off on the programmatic *procedures*, but does not review or oversee their application in any individual case. The applicable minimization procedures are thus written, implemented, and overseen on a case-by-case basis exclusively by the executive branch.

3 Executive Order 12333

The executive branch also engages in a range of extraterritorial surveillance activities targeted at non-U.S. persons located outside the United States that are not regulated by Section 702 or any statute, but instead governed by Executive Order 12333. Reports suggest that electronic surveillance pursuant to EO 12333 accounts for an even greater share of electronic surveillance activities than any equivalent surveillance conducted under traditional FISA or the FAA.[51] Of note, collection under EO 12333 reportedly includes "vacuum cleaner" or "bulk" collection, pursuant to which the executive sweeps in all communications that transit a particular cable without using a selector or other search term to limit the scope of the acquired data.[52] Reports suggest that bulk collection has included, among other things, Internet metadata,[53] Web cam chats,[54] cell phone location data,[55] and email address books.[56] Such bulk collection is not deemed to target anyone, thus avoiding the prohibition on targeting U.S. persons. Other collection falls outside the prohibition on targeting U.S. persons on the basis of a largely unreviewable executive branch determination that such collection would not require a warrant if done for law enforcement

51 *See, e.g.*, Alvaro Bedoya, *Executive Order 12333 and the Golden Number*, Just Security (Oct. 9, 2014, 10:14 AM), http://justsecurity.org/16157/executive-order-12333-golden-number/ [http://perma.cc/Q8ZH-NM6G]; John Napier Tye, *Meet Executive Order 12333: The Reagan Rule that lets the NSA Spy on Americans*, Wash. Post, July 18, 2014, http://www.washingtonpost.com/opinions/meet-executive-order-12333-the-reagan-rule-that-lets-the-nsa-spy-on-americans/2014/07/18/93d2ac22-0b93-11e4-b8e5-d0de80767fc2_story.html [http://perma.cc/6DHP-TNES].

52 *See* Presidential Policy Directive – Signals Intelligence Activities § 2 (Jan. 17, 2014) [hereinafter *PPD-28*], http://www.whitehouse.gov/the-press-office/2014/01/17/presidential-policy-directive-signals-intelligence-activities (referencing signals intelligence collected in "bulk" and defining "bulk" collection to mean "the authorized collection of large quantities of signals intelligence data which, due to technical or operational considerations, is acquired without the use of discriminants (e.g., specific identifiers, selection terms, etc.)" for specified purposes).

53 *See* Tye, *supra* note 52.

54 Spencer Ackerman & James Ball, *Optic Nerve: Millions of Yahoo Webcam Images Intercepted by GCHQ*, Guardian (Feb. 28, 2014), http://www.theguardian.com/world/2014/feb/27/gchq-nsa-webcam-images-internet-yahoo/ [http://perma.cc/KN9D-76HM].

55 *See, e.g.*, Barton Gellman & Ashkan Soltani, *NSA Tracking Cellphone Locations Worldwide, Snowden Documents Show*, Wash. Post (Dec. 3, 2013), http://www.washingtonpost.com/world/national-security/nsa-tracking-cellphone-locations-worldwide-snowden-documents-show/2013/12/04/5492873a-5cf2-11e3-bc56-c6ca94801fac_story.html. Though the NSA denies that it is "intentionally collecting bulk cellphone location information about cellphones in the United States," such bulk collection of cell phone location information outside the United States inevitably sweeps in millions of U.S. mobile phone users who travel abroad every year. *Id.*

56 *See* Barton Gellman & Ashkan Soltani, *NSA Collects Millions of E-mail Address Books Globally*, Wash. Post (Oct. 14, 2013), http://www.washingtonpost.com/world/national-security/nsa-collects-millions-of-e-mail-address-books-globally/2013/10/14/8e58b5be-34f9-11e3-80c6-7e6dd8d22d8f_story.html [http://perma.cc/FS9J-2LKY].

purposes in the United States.[57] There is no FISC or other judicial review of such programs, and virtually no statutory limits on how such data can be subsequently used.

II Incidental Collection as a Fourth Amendment Search

There are three separate – but interrelated – reasons why incidental collection should trigger the Fourth Amendment – not just with respect to how the data is ultimately used, but at the point of collection in the first place.

First, and most importantly, in the context of foreign intelligence surveillance under Section 702 and Executive Order 12333, the *scale* of U.S.- person communications being "incidentally" intercepted raises novel Fourth Amendment concerns. As Judge Bates expressed it, "There surely are circumstances in which incidental intrusions can be so substantial as to [both trigger the Fourth Amendment and] render a search or seizure unreasonable."[58] Even by conservative estimates, the government collects millions of communications under Section 702 on an annual basis. Such collection is estimated to include thousands of communications per year in which *both* the sender and all the recipients are among the "people" covered by the Fourth Amendment;[59] it likely yields millions more in which *either* the sender or the recipient is a U.S. person or a person located in the United States.[60] We do not think that Fourth Amendment doctrine ever considered – or can survive – a scenario when incidental collection is on such a massive scale.

Second, the incidental collection doctrine is premised at least in part on the notion that the government "accidentally" intercepts the communication at issue – where it could not reasonably have expected that the surveillance of the target would yield information about a third party wholly unrelated to the target. Whatever the merits of that premise, there are reasons why courts (and the Constitution) should not be as forgiving when the government *knows* that its surveillance will produce information about third parties. As Judge Leonard Sand explained in 2000, it "is significantly more problematic" when the government *anticipates* that lawful surveillance of one target will produce evidence of a nontarget's culpability.[61] Several FISC judges also seem to recognize the need to address anticipated collection of U.S.-person data in evaluating the constitutionality of 702 and related surveillance programs; hence the focus on minimization procedures as an element of assessing Fourth Amendment reasonableness.[62] In fact, in many ways, we are simply seeking to make explicit an understanding of incidental collection and the Fourth Amendment that at least some of the FISC's judges have implicitly adopted.

57 *See* 50 U.S.C. § 1881c(a)(2) (2012) ("No element of the intelligence community may intentionally target, for the purpose of acquiring foreign intelligence information, a United States person reasonably believed to be located outside the United States under circumstances *in which the targeted United States person has a reasonable expectation of privacy and a warrant would be required if the acquisition were conducted inside the United States for law enforcement purposes* [without a FISC-approved order or an Attorney General–issued emergency exception]") (emphasis added).

58 *October 2011 Bates Opinion*, *supra* note 4, at *26.

59 *Id.* at *11.

60 *See supra* notes 4–5.

61 *United States v. Bin Laden*, 126 F. Supp. 3d 264, 281 (S.D.N.Y. 2000).

62 *See, e.g.*, *In re Certified Question of Law*, No. 16–01, slip op. at 37–44 (FISA Ct. Rev. Apr. 14, 2016); *In re Directives*, 551 F.3d at 1015; *October 2011 Bates Opinion*, *supra* note 4, at *27.

Third, the prototypical incidental collection case involves surveillance that is separately covered by the Fourth Amendment. After all, U.S. law enforcement generally lacks jurisdiction to investigate unilaterally outside the U.S. territorial borders; as a result, targets of most searches are either U.S. citizens, legal permanent residents, or people located in the United States. At least someone – even if not the third party implicated by the search – has standing to challenge an illegal search.[63]

Thus, at least in the prototypical case, there is a meaningful judicial check on both the front and back end of the collection. Judges sign off on each aspect of the underlying surveillance – applying the Fourth Amendment's substantive and procedural standards, including individualized judicial review. And in most cases the person whose property is being searched or seized can raise a Fourth Amendment claim, even if the third party whose data is incidentally collected cannot. In contrast, programmatic surveillance under Section 702 or EO 12333 does *not* involve any individualized judicial review. Given that the targets are noncitizens located outside the United States, they have no Fourth Amendment rights to adjudicate on either the front or back end of the surveillance. As a result, the data is being collected pursuant to much *laxer* standards than those that would apply if the U.S. person, whose data is incidentally collected, were the direct target of the search or seizure.

Whether any of these three considerations suffices on its own to demonstrate why incidental collection in the context of foreign intelligence surveillance should trigger Fourth Amendment concerns, they seem to us to support that conclusion when taken together. Foreign intelligence programs yield significant surveillance of U.S. persons on the basis of the much lower standards that apply to the targeting of noncitizens outside the United States. This provides insufficient protection to the very category of persons that the Fourth Amendment is, according to current doctrine, meant to protect.

III Rethinking the Fourth Amendment in Light of Incidental Collection

The rise of the digitalized person, coupled with the scale of foreign intelligence collection, requires a rethinking of Fourth Amendment doctrine. The intermingling of communications, taken together with the scope of contemporary foreign intelligence surveillance, means that the United States is now gathering vast quantities of U.S. persons' communications as it targets non-U.S. persons located outside the United States, but without any of the constraints imposed by the Fourth Amendment. And it is doing so *knowing* that such large-scale incidental collection will occur. As we explain in what follows, this ought to trigger the Fourth Amendment – not just with respect to subsequent questions involving the use of such data, but at the point of collection itself.

In this section, we explore what a reformulated Fourth Amendment doctrine would look like. Specifically, we argue for a presumptive Fourth Amendment that governs the acquisition of data that is anticipated to include U.S. persons' information, regardless of whether a U.S. person is the target of the search. This is justified as a much-needed prophylactic protection for the class of U.S. persons the Fourth Amendment is designed to protect.

We also consider whether and to what extent minimization requirements – in particular limits on retention and dissemination – can independently address Fourth

[63] *See, e.g.*, cases cited *supra* note 12.

Amendment concerns. The U.S. government, after all, acknowledges that U.S. persons are often caught up in foreign intelligence collection, but argues that any privacy concerns are adequately addressed by minimization requirements. We agree that such minimization requirements are essential, and that they need to be evaluated as part of the up-front reasonableness assessment that a presumptive Fourth Amendment requires. But we also think that they have been, in some key respects, insufficient to date.

Finally, we argue that the law enforcement querying of incidentally collected U.S.-person data is itself a Fourth Amendment "event" that must satisfy the applicable constitutional requirements.

A *A Presumptive Fourth Amendment*

In an interconnected, digitalized world, the current myopic focus on the target of the search leaves unprotected the rights of the very "people" the Fourth Amendment is meant to protect. We instead advocate a presumptive Fourth Amendment: one in which the Fourth Amendment is presumed to apply, regardless of the location or identify of the target.[64] Such a presumption could be rebutted if and only if the government establishes that *none* of the parties to the communication or with some kind of ownership interest in a particular document is a U.S. person, *i.e.*, a person protected by the Fourth Amendment.

In practice, this means that bulk collection, wherever it takes place, is subject to Fourth Amendment regulation; communications targeting noncitizens will presumptively be covered by the Fourth Amendment, irrespective of the identity of the particular target; and most foreign intelligence surveillance will also trigger a Fourth Amendment inquiry because it will not be feasible in most cases – at least on the basis of what we know about current technology – to make a showing that none of the parties affected by these programs has Fourth Amendment rights. By contrast, targeted and discrete surveillance, such as programs focusing on North Korean diplomats in North Korea, likely would not trigger the Fourth Amendment – although there may be policy reasons to expand protections across the board, even in those circumstances.[65]

This, of course, is not the same as saying that a warrant is required every time the government searches or seizes electronic communications for foreign intelligence purposes, or that all surveillance necessarily implicates the Fourth Amendment. Both of us are, in fact, persuaded that there should be a foreign intelligence exception to the warrant requirement, although we have concerns about how broadly the exception has been defined – especially insofar as it is being applied even when the collection of foreign intelligence surveillance is not the primary purpose of the search.[66] We also are well aware that there is some surveillance that simply does not trigger the Fourth Amendment,

64 This tracks the approach that one of us has previously recommended. *See* Daskal, *supra* note 46, at 379–87.

65 *See, e.g.*, *PPD-28*, *supra* note 53, § 4(a) (requiring that postacquisition limits on retention and dissemination of data apply "equally to the personal information of all persons, regardless of nationality" to "the maximum extent feasible consistent with the national security").

66 *See, e.g.*, *In re Directives*, 551 F.3d 1004 (FISA Ct. Rev. 2008) (holding that the foreign intelligence surveillance exception to the Warrant Clause requires only that foreign intelligence gathering be a "significant" purpose of the search).

as well as certain categories of surveillance that do not require a warrant, regardless of the application of the foreign intelligence exception.

But we do think that any reasonableness (or warrant) requirement that does apply should be applied consistently to U.S.-person targets and non-U.S.-person targets alike. This in fact was one of the central insights of the 1978 Congress that first enacted FISA. Notably, it required a warrant for *all* covered foreign intelligence surveillance at the time. As the House Intelligence Committee Report explained, such a requirement was imposed "not ... primarily to protect such persons but rather *to protect U.S. citizens* who may be involved with them and to ensure that the safeguards inherent in a judicial warrant cannot be avoided by a determination as to a person's citizenship."[67]

To reiterate, we are not advocating a return to the 1978 surveillance regime – and a warrant requirement for all foreign intelligence surveillance. But we *do* reject the idea that the acquisition of non-U.S.-person data falls outside the Fourth Amendment's scope, especially in situations when it can reasonably be anticipated that such collection will yield U.S. persons' data. Any such collection that falls outside the warrant requirement must still meet the Fourth Amendment's reasonableness requirement. Otherwise, we are providing only nominal protections to the very people who, even under *Verdugo-Urquidez*, the Fourth Amendment is intended to protect.

B *Back End Protections as Part of the Front End Reasonableness Inquiry*

Any surveillance scheme of globally interconnected digitalized communications is going to yield incidental collection of U.S. persons' information. What makes the scheme reasonable – or not – turns in substantial part on how this incidentally collected information is handled (as well as the scope and purpose of the collection itself). Thus, the existence, application, and robustness of these back end protections for incidentally acquired information are essential components of the *front end* constitutional reasonableness inquiry. This is, in fact, what Congress requires as a matter of statutory law as part of the Wiretap Act and FISA Amendments Act, what the executive branch says it does as a matter of policy, what the Ninth Circuit suggested in its computer search protocol cases, and what several FISC judges have already demanded as part of the Fourth Amendment inquiry. Here, we would seek to make these scattershot approaches categorical rules – making the back end protections an essential element of front end reasonableness.

A recent FISC opinion provides an example of some of what we are suggesting. In evaluating a reauthorization certification pursuant to Section 702, Judge Thomas Hogan engaged in a thorough review of CIA, FBI, and NSA minimization procedures, as well as prior compliance incidents.[68] Although we disagree with some of Judge Hogan's ultimate conclusions, we think he engaged in exactly the kind of front end assessments of back end procedures that the Fourth Amendment demands in these cases.

67 H.R. Rep. No. 95–1283, pt. 1, at 26 (1978) (emphasis added).

68 *See In re Certified Question of Law*, No. 16–01 (FISA Ct. Rev. Apr. 14, 2016). Judge Hogan was aided in his review by Amy Jeffress, whom he appointed to act as amica curiae (pursuant to 50 U.S.C. § 1803(i)(2)(B) (2016)) to address the question of whether the minimization procedures met the statutory obligations and were consistent with the Fourth Amendment.

C *Law Enforcement Searches of U.S.-Person Information*

Separate and apart from the required front end inquiry, subsequent law enforcement queries of U.S.-person information should be deemed a search, subject to applicable procedural and substantive protections, and evaluated accordingly. The current rules governing FBI searches of acquired 702 databases fail to provide sufficient protections in this regard. In fact, somewhat ironically given the liberty interests at stake, the rules governing law enforcement searches for U.S. person information are currently *more permissive* than the rules governing intelligence community searches of such data. Under current minimization rules, FBI queries of 702 databases are permitted in order to "find and extract" either "foreign intelligence information" or "evidence of a crime."[69] By comparison, the NSA and CIA are only permitted to query the database using terms "reasonably likely to return foreign intelligence information."[70] The FBI rules thus are more expansive than what is required for the NSA and CIA in two key respects: first, they are not limited by a requirement that the search terms be "reasonably likely" to return the sought-after information; second, they can look for evidence of a crime, in addition to foreign intelligence information.

Moreover, whereas untrained law enforcement personnel are not permitted to access the 702 databases directly, they appear able to ping the database for whatever reason they so choose. If their search term yields a "hit," they can then seek an appropriately trained agent to run an actual query.[71] Both the pings of the database by untrained agents and the official queries can use U.S.-person identifiers or be designed to elicit information about U.S. persons. And whereas both the CIA and NSA are required to document the basis for such requests via a "statement of facts establishing that the use of any [U.S.-person] identifier as a selection term is reasonably designed to return foreign intelligence information as defined in FISA,"[72] no such obligation to document the basis for the query applies to the FBI.[73] Given the Fourth Amendment interests at stake, this is an oversight that, in our opinion, should be corrected.

In a recent FISC opinion, Judge Hogan rejected arguments by one of the FISC's amici curiae, Amy Jeffress, that the FBI queries of the 702 databases should be defined as a "separate action subject to the Fourth Amendment reasonableness test" and were at least in some respects unreasonable. While the court concluded that the querying process was relevant to the *overarching* reasonableness analysis of the program as a whole, it determined that the queries themselves were not separate events that should be independently assessed.

69 *See In re Certified Question of Law*, slip op. at 26–27. The FBI does not receive unminimized information acquired through "upstream collection," but does acquire a "portion" of PRISM collection. *See* PCLOB 702 Report, *supra* note 2, at 7.

70 *See In re Certified Question of Law*, slip op. at 24.

71 Such queries must be approved by both the untrained agent's supervisor and a national security supervisor. *Id.* at 28–29. The untrained agent is generally only permitted to see the results of the query if the information reasonably relates to foreign intelligence information, is necessary to understand foreign intelligence information, or is evidence of a crime. Yet, he or she can review the information if it is "unclear" whether those standards are met so as to help determine whether the information falls into one of those categories. *Id.* at 29. The government claims that the situations in which an untrained agent reviews information prior to a determination that it is foreign intelligence information (FII), relevant to understanding FII, or evidence of a crime are "very rare." *See id.*

72 *Id.* at 25.

73 *Id.* at 39–40 (noting argument that the FBI Minimization Procedures should be amended to require a written justification for each U.S.-person query of the database).

We disagree. The querying process is relevant to the overarching reasonableness analysis *and* is a specific search that should be independently evaluated for Fourth Amendment compliance. This position is supported by, among other cases, the Supreme Court's 2014 decision in *Riley v. California*.[74] In that case, the Supreme Court rejected the claim that law enforcement could engage in the warrantless search of a cell phone seized incident to arrest. Rather, the subsequent search of the cell phone was deemed a separate Fourth Amendment event that will generally require a warrant based upon probable cause.[75]

Congress can and should remedy this situation as part of any reauthorization of Section 702. Specifically, it should consider putting in place standards governing the pinging and querying of the databases for U.S.-person information. Even though the pings do not themselves yield the underlying data, they set in motion the process that does. It thus seems that agents should not be permitted to engage in the standardless pinging of the database for U.S.-person information until they get a positive hit. Rather, agents should be required to demonstrate a reasonable articulable suspicion that the term chosen will yield foreign intelligence information, information necessary to understand foreign intelligence information, or evidence of a crime. Subsequent queries for *metadata* should also be permitted based on a determination that there is a reasonable articulable suspicion that the responsive data is foreign intelligence information, relevant to understanding foreign intelligence information, or evidence of a crime, as approved by a supervisor. The basis for that determination should be documented in writing, so as to ensure transparency and future accountability with respect to such queries.

Queries for *communication content*, however, should only be permitted based on a finding of probable cause as approved by an independent court – either the FISC or an Article III court, depending on the nature of the investigation (*i.e.*, whether the information is being sought for foreign intelligence or ordinary law enforcement purposes). This is, after all, exactly what would be required if the FBI were seeking such information directly from either the target of the investigation or third-party provider that manages the target's data, rather than relying on the fact that it had already been collected pursuant to a separate foreign intelligence collection program. In emergency situations, authorizations can be approved by FBI supervisors, but the FBI should still be required to get post-hoc court approval, as is required with respect to emergency authorization for FISA orders and wiretaps.[76]

Critics are likely to argue that these types of requirements will simply impose additional and inefficient hurdles limiting law enforcement's ability to access potentially critical information. To this concern, we offer three responses: First, we recognize the need sometimes to act quickly and have suggested the application of emergency procedures (properly constrained) to deal with those situations. Second, and more importantly, the U.S. government now acquires millions of U.S. persons' communications every year via warrantless foreign intelligence surveillance programs. If law enforcement sought to access that data directly from either the target of its investigation or the third-party

74 134 S. Ct. 2473 (2014).

75 *Id.* at 2485.

76 *See, e.g.*, 50 U.S.C. § 1811; 18 U.S.C. § 2518(7). We are not the first to suggest a distinction in the standards governing queries of responsive metadata and communications content. *See also* Adam Klein, Michele Fluorney, and Richard Fontaine, Ctr. for a New Am. Security, Surveillance Policy: A Pragmatic Agenda for 2017 and Beyond 6, 36, (2017) (suggesting that the FBI be permitted to query 702 databases for U.S. person information but receive responsive metadata only).

company that holds that data, it would need a warrant based on probable cause. Law enforcement should not be able to make an end-run around this requirement simply because the data is already in the government's possession – pursuant to a collection program that does not require probable cause or anything close. Additional limits are needed to protect against the kind of trawling of databases for U.S. persons' information that arguably runs afoul of the framers' fears of general warrants and raises legitimate concerns about a surveillance state.

Third, while we recognize the requirement of probable cause will be hard to meet, at least initially, in certain situations, responsive metadata can be obtained based on a mere reasonable articulable suspicion that the data contains responsive foreign intelligence information or evidence of a crime. The responsive metadata can in turn provide the relevant information needed to meet the probable cause standard.

In sum, we think that the querying of data collected under Section 702 (and other intelligence databases) for U.S. persons' information triggers the Fourth Amendment; that additional, internal checks on FBI access to these databases are essential, particularly given the incredible power that the FBI holds to affect the liberty interests of U.S. persons; that agents should be required to articulate a reasonable, articulable suspicion that the evidence sought is foreign intelligence information, relevant to understanding foreign intelligence information, or evidence of a crime in order to ping or query the database for responsive metadata; that queries for content should require a finding of probable cause approved by a court; that all such queries should be subject to internal approvals; and that those reasons should be put in writing so as to allow for subsequent review and oversight. Congress should demand each of these requirements as part of any reauthorization of Section 702 – and should consider imposing them on surveillance collected pursuant to Executive Order 12333 as well.

D *Additional Minimization Requirements*

As already stated, we also believe that the applicable use, retention, and dissemination limits should be addressed at the outset as part of the overall reasonableness inquiry. While the question of what *specific* retention, dissemination, and use restrictions ought to apply and how they should be implemented requires a nuanced and particularized assessment on both the programmatic and the individual case level, there are certain common requirements that should aid those assessments. Here, we focus on two: the need for transparency and consistency, and the need for enhanced accountability for and deterrence of error and abuse. We think Congress has erred in failing to require more in these areas. It has a chance to correct these shortcomings in the debate over the renewal of Section 702, currently set to sunset on December 31, 2017.

1 Transparency and Consistency

As the preceding discussion shows, minimization rules vary among agencies. They are often generally classified, although the executive branch has increasingly released unclassified – albeit redacted – versions of such procedures over the last several years. This is critically important. Public disclosure of these rules is needed to allow open and informed debate, particularly given how much is at stake for U.S. persons and their data. In conjunction with Section 702 reauthorization, Congress should require as a matter of statutory law (not just executive branch discretion) the public disclosure of minimization rules from all of the agencies authorized to review and access data collected under Section 702, namely, the NSA, FBI, and CIA. Redactions should be permitted to protect against disclosure of specific programmatic details or technical means by which data is accessed. But there is no good reason to keep secret the substantive and procedural standards for querying, reviewing, retaining, and disseminating the acquired data.

Moreover, Congress should demand consistency, as much as is practically possible, across the different agencies. There will, of course, be a need for variation. It makes sense, for example, that the FBI should be able to access evidence of a crime, whereas the NSA and CIA cannot. But there does not seem to be any good justification for requiring a written justification for U.S.-person inquiries for the NSA and CIA, but not the FBI. Increased consistency will help with training, oversight, and analysis. As already stated, deviations should be permitted, but they ought to be explained and justified.

2 Accountability and Deterrence

The U.S. government does not publicly release the number of "compliance incidents," meaning those situations when executive branch officials fail to comply with the procedural or substantive requirements that either its own procedures or the FISC has imposed on particular collection methods. But there are enough reports of such incidents over enough different stretches of time to infer that even the most substantively robust minimization requirements will not be completely effective; hence, the need to couple meaningful back end protections with reasonable limits on collection itself.

The fact that so many compliance incidents have come to light suggests, in part, that existing internal oversight mechanisms have indeed been effective in many – if not all – cases. But internal oversight, while important, is not sufficient. Not only does it fail to provide any remedies for individuals affected, but it is also potentially subject to capture. The lack of an external check also fuels a *perception* of capture, even if the perception does not reflect reality. This in turn fosters public distrust of the government's actions. Existing oversight requirements thus should be coupled with three additional statutory requirements.

First, the executive branch should be required, by statute rather than merely court or internal executive branch rules, to report all compliance incidents to both the FISC and the intelligence committees and to release unclassified accounts of such incidents whenever it is possible to do so without jeopardizing national security. Whereas reporting of compliance incidents to the FISC is already required pursuant to the FISC's Rules of Procedure,[77] Congress should make this a statutory requirement, not just a matter of internal court rules. It should also consider the imposition of additional penalties for excessive and/or malicious violations of the minimization rules. The intelligence committees, in turn, should push the executive to make the reports public to the maximum

[77] *See* FISC R. 13(b) (2010).

extent possible and to ensure that compliance incidents are not symptomatic of larger flaws in the minimization requirements.

Second, FISC judges should be required to review and analyze prior compliance incidents and the government's responses as part of their consideration of applications for both new and renewed authorizations under Section 702. Judge Hogan took this step in his 2016 opinion reauthorizing a Section 702 certification, but Congress should make such review a statutory requirement of the certification process. In other words, the certification process should be amended to require the executive branch to describe, and the FISC to review, past compliance incidents within the same or related programs, both to provide a means of ensuring that these incidents are accounted for in subsequent minimization procedures, and, where appropriate, to protect against continued acquisition if such compliance problems have not been resolved.

Third, the suppression remedy for use of unlawfully acquired FISA or FISA-derived information should be expanded explicitly to require the suppression of information obtained or used in any manner that violates the applicable minimization requirements.[78] To give this provision meaning, Congress should require the executive branch to provide a criminal defendant's cleared counsel access to the minimization requirements and to information relevant to assessing compliance as part of any non-frivolous motion to suppress.

Conclusion

The 2017 debate over the reauthorization of Section 702 is – or, at least, ought to be – a pivotal moment for the relationship between incidental foreign intelligence surveillance and the Fourth Amendment. As we have argued, we believe both that courts will increasingly conclude that the Fourth Amendment applies to such government searches and that the reasonableness of the surveillance depends in part on how incidentally collected data is handled. Assuming this to be the case, the more Congress does to ensure both the existence of, and the government's compliance with, robust minimization requirements, including appropriate limits on law enforcement access, the more likely it will be that incidental collection under these programs would – and, in our view, *should* – survive a constitutional challenge.

The reforms we propose here are in many ways quite modest. Specifically, the reforms would require individualized suspicion before law enforcement could access information about U.S.-persons contained in intelligence databases; set additional protections with respect to the FBI accessing of U.S. persons communications content; increase consistency across the various agencies' approach to minimization and facilitate oversight and compliance by mandating judicial review of actual practices and imposing a statutory suppression remedy for compliance breaches. Most of the recommended reforms will require little to change in government practice – so long as the executive branch really is honoring the minimization requirements in the ways it has publicly described. The most significant proposed change is a required warrant based on probable

[78] The statute permits suppression if the "the surveillance was not made in conformity with an order of authorization or approval." 50 U.S.C. § 1806(e)(2) (2012). This provision should be amended explicitly to authorize suppression based on the failure to comply with applicable minimization rules.

cause for FBI accessing of U.S. persons' communications content, albeit with emergency exceptions built in. We think this is necessary to ensure that the existence of vast intelligence databases is not used as an end run around the otherwise applicable rules governing law enforcement searches of American's data and thereby protect the values and interests the Fourth Amendment is meant to serve. Not only do these reforms make good policy sense, but we also think that they (or equivalent protections) should be deemed constitutional requirements, necessary in order to satisfy the requirements of the Fourth Amendment.

5 Biometric Surveillance and Big Data Governance

Margaret Hu[†]

This chapter contends that the biometric surveillance systems and precrime rationales fictionally portrayed in Steven Spielberg's film *Minority Report* are now emerging as a governance reality. Biometric surveillance and big data "collect it all" programs are proliferating under preemptive approaches to combatting crime and terrorism. Public and private decisionmaking protocols increasingly depend upon biometric identification technologies – scanned fingerprints and irises, digitalized photos for facial recognition technology, DNA, etc. A biometric identifying anchor – a digitally scanned fingerprint and iris or digital photo, for example – once located in a database, can then be used as a data backbone to support multiple big data tracking and cybersurveillance systems. Biometric-centered data surveillance methods, thus, are often presented as an efficient form of identity screening and as capable of advancing preventive policing goals. As a result, biometric data is evolving into a data surveillance axis. It can tether a person's physical identity to algorithmic-driven biographical and behavioral data screening and analysis. It can also be deployed to assess future risk and to isolate data deemed suspicious. The chapter concludes that without a *Minority Report*–type heuristic, the impact of contemporary biometric surveillance and big data governance cannot be fully understood.

Introduction

Minority Report is set in the year 2054 and revolves around a newly established "Department of Precrime."[1] Based upon a 1956 science fiction short story by Philip K. Dick, *Minority Report* is a 2002 mystery–thriller film directed by Steven Spielberg.[2] The Department of Precrime is a criminal justice agency tasked with identifying and eliminating crimes before they occur. Precrime assessments in *Minority Report* depend upon computer analysis of the images and utterances produced by a trio of psychic "pre-cog[nitive] mutants."[3] In the film, the Department of Precrime has been adopted into a new system of public and private governance that is heavily dependent upon biometric surveillance, or surveillance of the physiological and behavioral characteristics of the populace.

† Associate Professor of Law, Washington and Lee University School of Law.

1 Minority Report (Twentieth Century Fox/Dreamworks Pictures 2002); Philip K. Dick, *The Minority Report*, *in* The Minority Report and Other Classic Stories by Philip K. Dick 71 (2016).

2 *Id.*; Minority Report, *supra* note 1.

3 *Id.*

Although *Minority Report* is born from science fiction, experts note that the biometric surveillance capacities and precrime policy rationales depicted in the film are beginning to emerge as a modern governance reality.[4] In the Spielberg film, biometric-based identification technologies are integrated into day-to-day policing and the modern digital economy. Iris scanners, for example, are used in the film for multiple public and private purposes. Iris identification systems confirm citizen identity, control access to and monitor activities occurring in governmental facilities and on public transportation, target advertising through interactive billboard screens, and personalize retail service.

Once an individual is identified in *Minority Report*, ubiquitous iris scanners appear to access a mass aggregate of stored data. The governmental iris identification system instantaneously allows access to the matched citizen's profile, suggesting an aggregation of biographic and criminal files. The corporate iris identification system appears to allow instant retail recognition of the individual's past purchases and retail history. Interactive billboard screens greet individuals by name and suggest purchases after irises are scanned. The film invites the suggestion that corporate and government databases could be shared.

In what may be viewed as an uncomfortable circumstance of life imitating art, Optic Nerve, a surveillance program revealed by former National Security Agency (NSA) contractor Edward Snowden, references its ambition to imitate the surveillance capacities illustrated in the film *Minority Report*. Optic Nerve, a British Government Communications Headquarters (GCHQ) program, aided by the NSA, collected webcam images from at least 1.8 million Internet subscribers. One Snowden disclosure document states: "'Think Tom Cruise in Minority Report.'"[5] According to one media report describing Optic Nerve, "beyond [collecting images from] webcams and consoles, GCHQ and the NSA looked at building more detailed and accurate facial recognition tools, such as iris recognition cameras."[6]

This chapter contends that *Minority Report*–type biometric surveillance systems and precrime rationales are now embedded in big data governance ambitions. Part I of this chapter will explore how modern governance systems increasingly depend upon biometric identification technologies – scanned fingerprints and irises, digitalized photos for facial recognition technology, DNA, etc. – to "anchor" a person's physical identity to other biographical and behavioral data. This biometric identifying anchor, once located in a database, can then be used to conduct other data tracking activities, such as data mining, database screening, and the implementation of a range of digital watchlisting[7] or

4 Several experts note that governments are increasingly adopting "precrime" or preventive programs that focus on preempting future criminal and terrorist activity. *See, e.g.*, Jude McCulloch & Dean Wilson, PRE-CRIME: PREEMPTION, PRECAUTION AND THE FUTURE (Routledge, 2016); David Cole, *The Difference Prevention Makes: Regulating Preventive Justice*, 19 CRIM. LAW & PHIL. 501 (2014) (characterizing "the post-9/11 full-scale adoption of a paradigm of prevention" as "a sea change"); Jennifer Daskal, *Pre-Crime Restraints: The Explosion of Targeted, Non-Custodial Prevention*, 99 CORNELL L. REV. 327 (2014); Lucia Zedner, *Pre-crime and Post-criminology?*, 11 THEORETICAL CRIMINOLOGY 261–81 (2007).

5 Spencer Ackerman & James Ball, *Optic Nerve: Millions of Yahoo Webcam Images Intercepted by GCHQ*, THE GUARDIAN (Feb. 28, 2014, 5:31AM), https://www.theguardian.com/world/2014/feb/27/gchq-nsa-webcam-images-internet-yahoo.

6 *Id.*

7 *See, e.g.*, Jeffrey Kahn, MRS. SHIPLEY'S GHOST: THE RIGHT TO TRAVEL AND TERRORIST WATCHLISTS (2013); Daskal, *Pre-Crime Restraints*, *supra* note 4; Anil Kalhan, *Immigration Surveillance*, 74 MD. L. REV. 1 (2014); Peter M. Shane, *The Bureaucratic Due Process of Government Watch Lists*, 75 GEO. WASH. L. REV. 804 (2007); Peter J. Spiro, *Expatriating Terrorists*, 82 FORDHAM L. REV. 2169 (2014); Daniel J. Steinbock,

other automated "situational awareness"[8] systems. The rapid adoption of biometric identification and analysis systems has occurred in the years following the terrorist attacks of September 11, 2001, as policymakers have taken a preemptive approach to counterterrorism.[9] As part of this preemptive approach, biometric technologies and other technological advances have been embraced for their potential to prevent crime and terrorism, and to identify better those who may pose a risk to national and homeland security.

Take, for example, the post-9/11 program Total Information Awareness (TIA), a "collect it all"[10] data surveillance program initiated by DARPA (Defense Advanced Research Projects Agency in the U.S. Department of Defense). TIA and similar "collect it all" efforts are premised upon a philosophy of preventive policing – a governing philosophy that supports mass data collection for the purposes of assessing and curtailing future threats.[11] In TIA and multiple other programs that have been tested or adopted since the terrorist attacks of September 11, 2001, experts observe that biometric database screening and analysis have been elevated and are among the preferred methods to track, identify, and establish identity-based inferences as a counterterrorism tool. These post-9/11 biometric identification systems increasingly operate as a surveillance axis: providing pathways by which to achieve other mass surveillance objectives, such as preventive policing goals that mirror the ambitions of the Precrime Department in *Minority Report*. Also as in *Minority Report*, as the private sector captures more and more biometric data, the government–corporate capacity to share biometric data increases as well.

Minority Report, therefore, is particularly resonant of new developments in what has been termed the modern "National Surveillance State,"[12] the focus of the discussion in Part II. In the National Surveillance State, the governing emphases are on the following objectives: ex ante policing;[13] biometric data collection and analysis for identity-based governance;[14] and bureaucratized policymaking that is informed by technological

Designating the Dangerous: From Blacklists to Watch Lists, 30 SEATTLE U. L. REV. 65 (2006); Jeremy Scahill & Ryan Devereaux, *Blacklisted: The Secret Government Rulebook For Labeling You a Terrorist*, THE INTERCEPT (July 23, 2014, 2:45 PM), https://theintercept.com/2014/07/23/blacklisted/.

8 *See, e.g.*, Nestor Ramos, *City Used High-Tech Tracking Software at '13 Boston Calling*, BOS. GLOBE (Sept. 8, 2014), https://www.bostonglobe.com/metro/2014/09/07/boston-watching-city-acknowledges-surveillance-tests-during-festivals/Sz9QVurQ5VnA4a6Btds8xH/story.html ("Situational awareness software analyzes video and provides alerts. … More sophisticated systems can track people in real time as they move through crowds[]"); *see infra* notes 130–142 (discussing situational awareness tracking system at Boston Calling Music Festival).

9 *See, e.g.*, Kelly A. Gates, OUR BIOMETRIC FUTURE: FACIAL RECOGNITION TECHNOLOGY AND THE CULTURE OF SURVEILLANCE (2011); Shoshana Amielle Magnet, WHEN BIOMETRICS FAIL: GENDER, RACE, AND THE TECHNOLOGY OF IDENTITY (2011); Robert O'Harrow Jr., NO PLACE TO HIDE 157–89 (2005); Margaret Hu, *Biometric ID Cybersurveillance*, 88 IND. L. J. 1475 (2013).

10 TIA was not referred to as a "Collect It All" program at the time of its conception. Rather, this phrase is taken from the Snowden disclosures. *See* Glenn Greenwald, NO PLACE TO HIDE: EDWARD SNOWDEN, THE NSA, AND THE U.S. SURVEILLANCE STATE, 97 (2014) (citing NSA slide from Snowden disclosures titled, "New Collection Posture," quoting NSA data collection procedure as "Collect it All"), http://glenngreenwald.net/pdf/NoPlaceToHide-Documents-Compressed.pdf.

11 *See* Nancy Murray, *Profiling in the Age of Total Information Awareness*, 52(2) RACE & CLASS 3, 6 (2010). For sources that discuss precrime programs and policies, see *supra* note 4.

12 *See, e.g.*, Jack M. Balkin, *The Constitution in the National Surveillance State*, 93 MINN. L. REV. 1 (2008); Jack M. Balkin & Sanford Levinson, *The Processes of Constitutional Change: From Partisan Entrenchment to the National Surveillance State*, 75 FORDHAM L. REV. 489 (2006).

13 *See, e.g.*, Balkin, *supra* note 12, at 10–11.

14 *See id.* at 11.

developments.[15] These National Surveillance State objectives are mutually reinforced by an emerging cybersurveillance architecture that is dependent upon rapidly proliferating biometric identification systems.[16]

The simultaneous advent of both big data cybersurveillance governance systems and biometric surveillance simultaneously reflects the symbiotic relationship between the two. Biometric cybersurveillance incentivizes precrime and identity management programs, and big data governance systems. In return, precrime, identity management, and big data governance incentivizes biometric cybersurveillance.[17] In Dick's short story, computers analyze the visions of the precogs. In modern reality, there is no need for the "precog mutants" or the supernatural phenomena portrayed in *Minority Report*. Big data surveillance methods and biometric surveillance systems theoretically support the contention by intelligence experts such as Ira "Gus" Hunt, Central Intelligence Agency (CIA) Chief Technology Officer, that "[i]t is really very nearly within our grasp to be able to compute on all human generated information."[18] Hunt suggests that all digital footprints and data bread crumbs can be collected, stored, and analyzed; and all individuals can be tracked, biometrically and biographically, and assessed for risk.

Because biometric data is considered a data backbone that can support other data surveillance systems motived by preventive policing, Part III will address how biometrics shapes precrime policies and programs. Increasingly, biometric identification and surveillance are methods for risk-based assessment and identity verification. Both the public and private sectors, for example, can utilize biometric screening for employment and immigration authorization.[19] The fusion of biographic and biometric data can be used for the No Fly List and Terrorist Watchlisting,[20] etc. These types of governance assessments, however, fall within the civil law and administrative law structure.[21] After 9/11 as policy initiatives began to focus on preventing crime and terrorism before they occurred, biometric identification and identity assessments emerged as a critical tool in criminal,

15 *See, e.g.*, Balkin & Levinson, *supra* note 12, at 520–21.

16 Experts increasingly describe dataveillance, big data surveillance, and cybersurveillance in architectural terms. *See, e.g.*, Bruce Schneier, Data and Goliath: The Hidden Battles to Collect Your Data and Control Your World, 48 (2015) ("This [digital data collection and analysis] has evolved into a shockingly extensive, robust, and profitable surveillance architecture"); *see also* Greenwald, *supra* note 10; Jeffrey Rosen, The Naked Crowd: Reclaiming Security and Freedom in an Anxious Age (2005); Margaret Hu, *Taxonomy of the Snowden Disclosures*, 72 Wash. & Lee L. Rev. 1679 (2015); Jennifer Stisa Granick, American Spies: Modern Surveillance, Why You Should Care, and What to Do About It (2017).

17 *See, e.g.*, Balkin & Levinson, *supra* note 12, at 520–23 ("The National Surveillance State arose from a number of different features whose effects are mutually reinforcing. The most obvious changes are in how nations conduct war and promote their national security. … Equally important [however] … are new technologies of surveillance, data storage, and computation").

18 Ira "Gus" Hunt, Presentation at Gigaom Structure Data Conference: The CIA's "Grand Challenges" with Big Data (Mar. 20, 2013) [hereinafter Hunt CIA Presentation] (video and transcript available at https://gigaom.com/2013/03/20/even-the-cia-is-struggling-to-deal-with-the-volume-of-real-time-social-data/2/).

19 Employment eligibility database screening systems such as E-Verify are moving toward biometrics through the adoption of the E-Verify photo tool. *See, e.g.*, Hu, *Biometric ID*, supra note 9, at 1490–96, 1511 n.198.

20 The No Fly List and digital watchlisting systems are increasingly biometric-centered. *See, e.g.*, Jeremy Scahill & Ryan Devereaux, *The Secret Government Rulebook*, Intercept (Jul. 23, 2014), https://theintercept.com/2014/07/23/blacklisted/; *see also* Byron Tau, *No Fly List Is Only One of Many U.S. Watchlists*, Wall St. J., (Dec. 8, 2015), http://www.wsj.com/articles/no-fly-list-is-only-one-of-many-u-s-watchlists-1449570602 (explaining that digital watchlisting systems depend upon databases that house biometric and biographic information).

21 *See, e.g.*, Christopher Slobogin, *Policing as Administration*, 165 U. Pa. L. Rev. 91 (2016).

intelligence, and military settings. The discussion that follows, for instance, will show how biometric cybersurveillance can inform targeted killing decisions and drone strikes. Biometric cybersurveillance, therefore, is perceived to augment broader precrime policymaking and decisionmaking.

Minority Report, consequently, presents a timely and important cinematic interpretation of the transformation of government capacities that capitalize upon biometric technologies. Without *Minority Report*, it is much more difficult to understand the following questions: What is biometric surveillance? What is big data governance? How does biometric surveillance differ from other types of surveillance? This chapter attempts to answer these introductory questions by providing an overview of why biometric surveillance is emerging as a core governance tool in a big data world. It contends that bureaucracies will rely more and more on biometric data in the implementation of big data systems to achieve law enforcement and counterterrorism objectives. The chapter concludes that biometric surveillance, especially when combined with big data governing ambitions, threatens constitutionally protected freedoms and liberties in unparalleled ways.

I Overview of Biometric Identification and Verification Technology

Biometrics is generally understood to be "the science of automatic identification or identity verification of individuals using [unique] physiological or behavioral characteristics."[22] Biometric-based identification or identity verification systems can involve the data collection and analysis of "hard biometrics"[23] or what is referred to as "primary biometrics."[24] Hard or primary biometrics is defined as traditional biometric identifiers that are used for identity verification technologies. These automated biometric data systems are understood by the government and industry to serve "secure identification and personal verification solutions." Traditional "hard" or "primary" forms of automated biometric identification and verification technologies may include scanned fingerprints, facial recognition technology (e.g., digital photos and videos), iris scans, and DNA database screening.

Biometric-based identification or identity verification systems can also involve data collection and analysis of "soft biometrics."[25] The distinction between hard and soft biometrics is not a matter of whether the biometric identifier represents an immutable characteristic. Rather, the distinction turns on the biometric identifier's perceived reliability in automated identification matching technologies. Soft biometrics are "anatomical or behavioral characteristic[s] that provide[] some information about the identity of a person, but does not provide sufficient evidence to precisely determine the identity."[26] "Soft" or "secondary" biometric identification systems may include digital analysis or automated determination of age, height, weight, race or ethnicity, color of skin and color of

22 John R. Vacca, Biometric Technologies and Verification Systems 589 (2007).

23 *Id.*

24 *Id.* at 57. Vacca does not define hard or primary biometric data; however, he provides a background on biometric technology and verification system standards. Other scholars have noted the experimental nature of soft or secondary biometric characteristics as a way to supplement hard or primary biometric characteristics; *see, e.g., infra* note 26.

25 *See, e.g.*, Koichiro Niinuma, Unsang Park & Anil. K. Jain, *Soft Biometric Traits for Continuous Use Authentication*, 5 Inst. Elec. Elecs. Eng'r 771, 772 (2010) (defining the characteristics of both "soft" and "hard" biometrics).

26 Encyclopedia of Biometrics 1235 (Stan Z. Li & Anil Kumar Jain, eds., 2009).

hair, scars. birthmarks, and tattoos.[27] Identity verification and analysis can also flow from behavioral characteristics. Behavioral biometric identifiers are "traits that are learned or acquired."[28] Such identifiers may include keystroke patterns and mouse use characteristics, gait analysis, signature analysis, voice ID, and cognitive biometrics, such as neural responses. Virtually any physical or behavioral characteristics can be catalogued and analyzed as a biometric identifier.

Less common biometric identifiers might include skeletal bone scans, brain scans, body odor, and eyebrow shape and ear shape. Other biometric data, such as heart rate, and perspiration and sweat pore analysis, and eye pupil dilation, may or may not be used for identification or identity verification; however, they may be used to infer information about the individual. As evident from the discussion above, biometric identification is difficult to define. Because of the rapidly changing nature of emerging technologies, biometric identifiers are inextricably linked to advances in technology, the development of industry and governmental standards that establish biometric identifier reliability, and changes in corporate and governmental demand that incentivize biometric data collection and the adoption of biometric identification technologies.

The process of biometric identification can be summarized as follows:

> Although an oversimplification, the use of biometric data in identity verification can be described as a four-step process: enrollment, capture, comparison, and decision.[29] Each step is briefly summarized as follows. (1) *Enrollment*: An individual first identifies himself and actually puts his fingerprint down, has a digital photo taken, [or] has his eyes scanned. (2) *Capture for Recognition*: A template for that identity is created to use for future identification purposes. (3) *Comparison*: The individual's later presented biometric data (e.g., fingerprint or iris scan) is cross-referenced with the originally presented or captured biometric data (e.g., enrollment and identity template). And (4) *Decision*: Statistical algorithms are developed to "match" the probability that the initial biometric data can be accurately compared to the currently presented biometric data or to make a determination that the data does not "match."[30]

Utilizing a digitalized biometric ID or biometric database screening technology removes the human element from the matching process, substituting instead the digitalized processes of an automated or semiautomated system. Biometric technology is increasingly considered to be an efficacious policy prescription for a range of complex national security and homeland security matters. This is because biometric data is perceived to be the "gold standard" of identity management systems.

Many identity management systems adopted by the government are moving toward biometric data as a preferred method for identity verification. Biometric data is supposedly scientifically objective and utilize a purportedly neutral analysis of computer driven algorithmic analysis.[31] Big data governance programs now operate to verify identity

27 *Id.*

28 Vacca, *supra* note 22, at 3.

29 *See, e.g.*, Biometric Recognition: Challenges and Opportunities 25–26 (Joseph N. Pato & Lynette I. Millett, eds., 2010) [hereinafter Biometric Recognition]; Vacca, *supra* note 22, at 23–27; *see also* Anil K. Jain, Arun A. Ross, Karthik Nandakumar, Introduction to Biometrics 4–10 (2011).

30 Hu, *Biometric ID*, *supra* note 9, at 1534–35.

31 *See, e.g.*, Simson Garfinkel, Database Nation: The Death of Privacy in the 21st Century 37–67 (2000); Gates, *supra* note 9; Jennifer Lynch, From Fingerprints to DNA: Biometric Data Collection in U.S. Immigrant Communities and Beyond (2012); Magnet, *supra* note 9; Hu, *Biometric ID*, *supra* note 9.

before authorizing the right to work,[32] the right to drive,[33] and the right to vote,[34] in order screen out the potential terrorist and criminal alien or unlawfully present immigrant more effectively.

Once biometric data has been harvested, it must be compiled within a database, which in turn makes identity screening possible. Biometric data that has been harnessed for identity verification and authentication purposes helps to support both what DHS has termed "identity management"[35] goals domestically, and what the U.S. Department of Defense (DoD) has termed "population management"[36] goals internationally. DHS defines identity management as including administrative processes that serve "authentication and authorization" goals through managing technological, facilities, and digital data "access."[37] Identity management serves to mediate "user rights, entitlements, and privileges with the established identity."[38] In the international security context, the U.S. military has employed the term "population management" to describe a wide range of goals considered essential to strategic military objectives. "Population management," for instance, appeared to underscore the justification for the U.S. military's reported objective to obtain biometrics and "contextual data" of "every living person in Afghanistan."[39]

Internationally, governments increasingly acquire biometric identification technologies to facilitate a range of day-to-day governing goals. These include counterterrorism and military or intelligence-related identification, such as fingerprint and facial recognition

32 E-Verify as of yet does not require a biometric data identifier. However, congressional proposals surrounding the extension of the E-Verify program have discussed adding a biometric verification component. *See, e.g.*, Hu, *Biometric ID*, *supra* note 9, at 1485 n. 37–39, 1511 n.198; Lora L. Ries, *B-Verify: Transforming E-Verify into a Biometric Employment Verification System*, 3 ALB. GOV'T L. REV. 271, 274 (2010) (discussing "congressional commitment to E-Verify, including added improvements to the program, while Congress and [DHS] design the next generation of E-Verify, adding biometrics to the program").

33 Similarly, although the REAL ID Act of 2005 does not require the biometric verification of a fingerprint, REAL ID does include technological enhancements and requires digital photos that can be analyzed with facial recognition software. *See* REAL ID Act of 2005, Pub. L. No. 109–13, 119 Stat. 302 (codified as amended in scattered sections of 8 U.S.C.).

34 Help America Vote Act of 2002 (HAVA), which relies upon SSA database screening of Social Security Numbers, does not yet require a biometric data matching component. 42 U.S.C. § 15483(a) (2006) (implementing provision); REAL ID Act of 2005, Pub. L. No. 109–13, § 202(b)–(d), 119 Stat. 302, 312–14 (implementing provisions).); U.S. GOV'T ACCOUNTABILITY OFFICE, GAO-11–146, EMPLOYMENT VERIFICATION: FEDERAL AGENCIES HAVE TAKEN STEPS TO IMPROVE E-VERIFY, BUT SIGNIFICANT CHALLENGES REMAIN (2010), http://www.gao.gov/assets/320/314278.pdf.

35 The U.S. Department of Homeland Security (DHS) offers this definition of identity management: "Identity Management (IdM) is a broad administrative area that deals with identifying and managing individuals within a government, state, local, public, or private sector network or enterprise. In addition, authentication and authorization to access resources such as facilities or, sensitive data within that system are managed by associating user rights, entitlements, and privileges with the established identity." *Identity Management and Data Privacy Technologies Project*, CYBER SEC. RESEARCH & DEV. CTR. (on file with author). For an overview of identity management as a policy concept, see Lucy L. Thomson, *Critical Issues in Identity Management – Challenges for Homeland Security*, 47 JURIMETRICS J. 335 (2007).

36 The 2011 U.S. Army Commander's Guide to Biometrics in Afghanistan specifically offers "a section titled 'Population Management[.]'" *Identity Dominance: The U.S. Military's Biometric War in Afghanistan*, PUBLIC INTELLIGENCE (Apr. 21, 2014), https://publicintelligence.net/identity-dominance/.

37 *Identity Management*, *supra* note 35.

38 *Id.*

39 *Identity Dominance*, *supra* note 36; *see also* Margaret Hu, *Biometric Cyberintelligence and the Posse Comitatus Act*, 66 EMORY L.J. 697 (2017).

technology that utilizes database screening; homeland security, border security, and immigration control identification, such as passport and visa identification systems and border-related surveillance; and criminal identification, such as parole and prison visitor systems. Biometric identification technologies serve civil identification purposes as well. These include drivers' license and voting systems, and benefit-payment systems, such as presenting biometrics as a condition for claiming welfare benefits. Biometrics are also deployed as part of efforts to restrict access to physical locations and informational technology, such as requiring the swiping of biometric IDs before accessing computer and electronic devices and Internet services.

Government-led biometric identification technologies invite surveillance. This is because biometric cybersurveillance encompasses not only identification, but also identity-based assessments. Under such systems, the inquiry expands from simply verification of identity (is this person who he or she claims to be) to include determination of identity (who is this person), as well as intent-related assessments (what is the criminal and terroristic disposition of this person).

Biometric identification can, but does not necessarily involve traditional "surveillance" activities, such as domestic or foreign intelligence gathering. Advances in biometric identification and the pervasiveness of its adoption should be understood to be transforming the nature of cybersurveillance. Big data governance emphasizes the bureaucratization of mass data collection and digitized assessments: data mining and database screening, digital watchlisting, algorithmic intelligence, and risk assessment and predictive analysis. Biometric data is increasingly integrated into these technologies and serves as an anchor point for the execution of cybersurveillance-dependent government programs.

Biometric surveillance can involve capturing, storing, and tracking biometric data; aggregating, databasing, and sharing biometrics; and analyzing biometric identifiers either in combination or standing alone.[40] Biometric surveillance is not a new form of bureaucratized surveillance. Established forms of bureaucratized biometric surveillance include police compilations of photographs to help identify suspects, files consisting of passport photographs compiled for the purposes of identification, and the national fingerprint and DNA databases maintained by the Federal Bureau of Investigation.

Biometric cybersurveillance, however, is new, as are forms of governance that are dependent on big data systems. Biometric cybersurveillance as a form of bureaucratized cybersurveillance, for example, might include a digitalized biometric-based social security card or e-passport. One 2010 comprehensive immigration reform proposal recommended the adoption of a "high-tech" social security card that could be swiped like a credit card.[41] The "high-tech" social security card would replace the numerical-based paper social security card,[42] resulting in a biometric database that can identify both persons and aggregate data, such as locational data (i.e., where and when biometric credentials were presented).

[40] *See, e.g.*, Biometric Information Privacy Act, 740 Ill. Comp. Stat. 14, http://www.ilga.gov/legislation/ilcs/ilcs3.asp?ActID=3004&ChapterID=57.

[41] *See* Charles E. Schumer & Lindsey O. Graham, *The right way to mend immigration*, Wash. Post, (Mar. 19, 2010), http://www.washingtonpost.com/wp-dyn/content/article/2010/03/17/AR2010031703115.html?utm_term=.8f9a895a857b (describing a proposal for a biometric social security card); Hu, *Biometric ID, supra* note 9.

[42] Hu, *Biometric ID, supra* note 9 at 1509 & n.184, 1518.

Developments like these facilitate trends in biometric surveillance and big data governance. As discussed later, precrime rationales can help to explain the long-term surveillance consequences of biometric-based identification systems (e.g., a machine-readable and digitalized biometric-based social security card or passport) that feed into interlocking and comprehensive cybersurveillance systems (e.g., "Total Information Awareness" and "collect it all" systems).

The merger of biometric surveillance with big data governance tools has the potential to exponentially increase governmental cybersurveillance capacities. Government-administered identification systems have the potential to impose compulsory or near-compulsory biometric data collection protocols. Certain government privileges and benefits can be conditioned upon compliance with the government's collection of biometric data. A digitalized biometric-based identification system (e.g., biometric database screening system to establish identity for rights and privileges, such as employment and voting eligibility, or the right to fly and drive) could facilitate the development of a near-universal biometric database, which could effectively serve a variety of governance ambitions.

A universal biometric database could operate as both an identity database and a centralized identity tracking system. It would likely create an unprecedented collection of uniquely identifying information. If this data were combined with, or exchanged for, other collected data in other databases, the possibilities for cross-referenced analysis would compound exponentially. Under such a system, potential inferences of suspicion based upon identity assessment are vastly greater. Because of the predictive nature of big data, identity-based systems of bureaucracy under big data governance can serve precrime goals.

Private applications of biometric verification technologies include restricting technological access, such as fingerprint access to smartphones; restricting physical access, such as the biometric-enhanced security measures of Walt Disney theme park tickets; and membership access restriction, such as submission of biometric requirements for gym or club membership. Behavioral biometric analytics can be used to assess, for instance, product marketability by determining the length and movement of eye gaze, which in turn can be used to assess, adapt, and alter product and product displays in stores. Increasingly, governments also capture or purchase biometric data harvested by the private sector.[43]

Combining biometric databases with multiple public and private databases makes precrime and preterrorism objectives increasingly plausible to policymakers on a theoretical level. *Minority Report*–type governing ambitions that may have been viewed as science fiction are now considered technically possible because of the development of biometric-based identity management systems and other comprehensive cybersurveillance systems that attempt to consolidate 24/7 body tracking with 360° biographical tracking. Instead of *Minority Report*'s psychic "precogs," predictive policing relies on big data tools and algorithms to analyze mass data collection for future risk. Although

[43] *See, e.g.*, Brendan I. Koerner, *Your Relative's DNA Could Turn You into a Suspect*, WIRED, (Oct. 13, 2015, 6:45AM), https://www.wired.com/2015/10/familial-dna-evidence-turns-innocent-people-into-crime-suspects/ (describing the arrest of a man suspected of a hit and run based on DNA evidence located through law enforcement familial DNA searches of Ancestry.com's database).

multiple experts question the validity of precrime programs[44] and interrogate the limits of biometric surveillance,[45] precrime policy rationales increasingly drive the expansion of the adoption of biometric surveillance technologies and other cybersurveillance systems.

Biometric data surveillance, thus, is distinct from other types of data surveillance. Biometric data occupies a place of privilege in emerging cybersurveillance regimes. It is perceived to be a superior data point because it anchors identity-based data points to other data points to facilitate bureaucratized and automated or semiautomated decision-making. Consequently, the collection and analysis of biometric data inform a wide range of public and private services. These services may include border security, including biometric data harvesting and analysis at points of entry; cybersecurity safeguards, including password protection and seeking to identify users, such as Internet users;[46] and attempts to uncover motives and threat-based signifiers in risk assessment protocols, such as precrime indicators.

Biometric data is appealing for security purposes because it appears to be forgery resistant – the data comes from one's own body.[47] Digitalized biometric data is information that provides a unique technological identifier based on an individualized characteristic of one's body.[48] For instance, biometric data can be extracted from digital photographs and voice recordings, and the data can then be processed through facial recognition and voice recognition technologies.[49] Biometric-related surveillance technologies utilized by law enforcement and other government agencies are considered efficacious because they have the potential to accomplish multiple surveillance goals at once (for example, systems that can utilize facial recognition technology and license plate reader systems simultaneously).[50] Other biometric surveillance technologies are sensor network–oriented and are live-streaming sensitive. Emerging "situational awareness" surveillance systems, for example, are able to integrate biometric surveillance

44 *See, e.g.*, Viktor Mayer-Schönberger & Kenneth Cukier, Big Data: A Revolution That Will Transform How We Live, Work, and Think (2013); Cathy O'Neill, Weapons of Math Destruction: How Big Data Increases Inequality and Threatens Democracy (2016); Schneier, *supra* note 16; *see also* Andrew Guthrie Ferguson, *Big Data and Reasonable Suspicion*, 163 U. Pa. L. Rev. 327, 329 n.6 (2015); Alexander Furnas, *Homeland Security's 'Pre-Crime' Screening Will Never Work*, (Apr. 17, 2012), www.theatlantic.com/technology/archive/2012/04/homeland-securitys-pre-crime-screening-will-never-work/255971/.

45 *See, e.g.*, Garfinkel, *supra* note 31; Gates, *supra* note 9; Lynch, *supra* note 31; Magnet, *supra* note 9.

46 *See, e.g.*, Apple Inc., *Use Touch ID on iPhone and iPad*, https://support.apple.com/en-us/HT201371 ("[U]se Touch ID, a fingerprint identity sensor that makes it easy for you to get into your device"); *see also* Bruce Schneier, *Apple Patents Collecting Biometric Information Based on Unauthorized Device Use*, Schneier on Security (Aug. 29, 2016, 6:27 AM), https://www.schneier.com/blog/archives/2016/08/apple_patents_c.html.

47 "The [face and/or finger] prints are unique, but unchangeable.... It's not like a credit card breach and you can change the number," (Paul Bond [partner at Reed Smith, Chicago, IL]) Bond says. "The strength of biometric identifiers is also its weakness." Will Yakowicz, *How Collecting Biometric Information from Employees and Customers Could Get You Sued*, Inc. (Oct. 2016), http://www.inc.com/will-yakowicz/legal-risks-of-biometrics-at-the-office.html.

48 Biometric Recognition, *supra* note 29, at 1–4.

49 *See, e.g.*, *id.*, at 31–34; Vacca, *supra* note 22.

50 Vigilant Solutions, a private contractor that offers its technology to law enforcement, released a mobile app in 2014 that incorporates both license plate reader technology and facial recognition software. *See* Brian Shockley, *Vigilant Solutions Unveils Mobile Companion App at IACP*, Vigilant Solutions (Oct. 23, 2014), https://vigilantsolutions.com/stories-from-the-street/vigilant-mobile-companion-app-iacp ("In addition to the license plate recognition capture and analytic tools, the app also features Vigilant's powerful FaceSearch® facial recognition which analyzes over 350 different vectors of the human face").

technology – such as facial recognition technology – with live streaming social media, and other surveillance.[51] Because biometric identification technologies have advanced in sophistication and multimodal dimensions, they are capable of integrating social media and Internet screening technologies. Consequently, governmental ambitions – including precrime and preterrorism ambitions – increasingly attach to biometric surveillance.

Although biometric data is considered the "gold standard" for identification systems,[52] biometric identity measures are not infallible and may even be less secure.[53] This may seem counterintuitive because automated biometric screening systems are traditionally assumed to be among the most secure, reliable, and technologically advanced methods of identification credentialing. Biometric data, however, earned its reputation as a superior identification data point in a small data context. In a small data world, biometric identification depended upon human judgment and perception, and forensic science.[54]

In a big data world, biometrics are increasingly unstable and prone to fraud. The digitalization of biometric credentialing and screening in fact makes it more vulnerable. In a big data world, algorithms are perceived as superior to human judgment and perception, and supercomputing tools are perceived as superior to small data forensics. Big data biometric credentialing, therefore, is susceptible to digitalized forms of exploitation that weaken its security and reliability: biometric data can be hacked, rigged, spoofed, stolen, or duplicated from digitalized images and data trails left on the Internet. For example, Jan Krissler, a hacker also known as "Starbug," recreated iris scans of world leaders through digitalized photographs and duplicated their fingerprints through high-definition photographs.[55]

II The National Surveillance State and Big Data Governance

At present, biometric verification and identification technologies are not necessarily considered surveillance technologies. As a form of digitalized identification, they are commonly treated by the public and private sectors as largely benign and highly beneficial. Automated biometric database screening is perceived to be a more technologically

51 *See, e.g.*, Chris Faraone, Kenneth Lipp & Jonathan Riley, *Boston Trolling (Part I)*, DIGBOSTON (Oct. 9, 2014), https://digboston.com/boston-trolling-part-i/ (describing a multicomponent surveillance program in Boston involving live video, facial recognition, and social media tracking).

52 *See* Alan Gomez, *Immigrant Tracking May Impede Bill; Partisan Split Developing over Biometric Data on Foreigners Leaving U.S.*, USA TODAY, (May 9, 2013), at A5 ("[Former U.S. Secretary of Homeland Security Michael] Chertoff calls [biometrics] the 'gold standard'").

53 A manufacturing company's fingerprint system that controlled access was hacked, compromising the fingerprint database – and giving the hacker access to add new fingerprints to the system, eliminating any security effects of the biometric program. *See* Madhumita Murgia, *Biometrics Will Replace Passwords, but It's a Bad Idea*, THE TELEGRAPH (May 27, 2016, 12:31 AM), http://www.telegraph.co.uk/technology/2016/05/26/biometrics-will-replace-passwords-but-its-a-bad-idea/.

54 *See, e.g.*, Margaret Hu, *Small Data Surveillance v. Big Data Cybersurveillance*, 42 PEPPERDINE L. REV. 773 (2015).

55 *See* Thomas Fox-Brewster, *Hacking Putin's Eyes: How to Bypass Biometrics the Cheap and Dirty Way with Google Images*, FORBES (Mar. 5, 2015, 8:33AM), http://www.forbes.com/sites/thomasbrewster/2015/03/05/clone-putins-eyes-using-google-images/#61c5deb54f85; Alex Hern, *Hacker Fakes German Minister's Fingerprints Using Photos of Her Hands*, THE GUARDIAN (Dec. 30, 2014), https://www.theguardian.com/technology/2014/dec/30/hacker-fakes-german-ministers-fingerprints-using-photos-of-her-hands.

efficient form of small data verification (e.g., human screening or human-driven protocols that involve the assessment of biometric data or forensic data). In a small data world, biometric verification might have involved comparing a passport photo with the appearance of the person presenting the passport. Yet small data biometric identification is distinct from big data biometric identification, particularly in its surveillance impact. In a big data world, collecting digital photographs may be the first step of the creation of a near-universal photo database that rises to the scale of millions or billions of digitalized facial images.[56] Such big data identification systems also depend upon algorithmic-driven, database-driven facial recognition technology with the potential to enhance surveillance capacities in ways that are difficult to conceptualize without the assistance of science fiction depictions such as *Minority Report*.

Higher-order mass surveillance consequences are part of the problematic nature of biometric credentialing and identification. Like much digital data, biometric data collected for government identification are not limited to their initial collection purpose. In a big data world, biometric identifiers are subject to a broad range of uses: identifying potential suspects or victims in a crowd through real-time analytics, assessing terrorist-related risks and informing tactical decisionmaking, or performing behavioral or genetic research.[57] Beyond secondary uses, biometric data can have tertiary uses, quaternary uses, and so on: populationwide risk assessments that incorporate bureaucratized surveillance in day-to-day governing decisions, policing, and general risk assessments. Biometric data can be infinitely repurposed to serve unlimited big data governance programs. With the support of big data tools, the precrime governance models depicted in *Minority Report* becomes more and more reflected in TIA-type "collect it all" cybersurveillance systems. These systems use biometric data as a surveillance axis both to track and identify individuals and to pinpoint persons, or digital data or devices associated with individuals that may be flagged as suspicious.[58]

From the perspective of a governing body, there is no meaningful distinction between biometric credentialing as a form of reliable identification and behavioral biometric profiling. The end goals are the same: to advance security and precrime through combining credentialing and risk assessment into one integrated protocol. Mission creep – biometric data collected for one purpose and repurposing it for another – is inevitable in a big data world because the biometric cybersurveillance systems are often designed to support mass data integration and analysis, and predictive policing. Biometric surveillance serves a dual purpose as a governing tool to prevent crime and terrorism from occurring in the first place. First, it makes the identity of the population more transparent. Second, it facilitates categorization and assessment of individuals deemed suspect, whether the biometric data examine behavioral characteristics or focus solely on identification.

To understand better how biometric surveillance operates within the broader ecosystem of the National Surveillance State and within the governing philosophy of big

56 *See, e.g.*, James Risen and Laura Poitras, N.S.A. *Collecting Millions of Faces from Web Images*, N.Y. Times (May 31, 2014), http://www.nytimes.com/2014/06/01/us/nsa-collecting-millions-of-faces-from-web-images.html (discussing Snowden disclosures that revealed that NSA collects millions of digital photographs from Internet and social media sources and utilizes facial recognition technology to identify individuals).

57 *See, e.g.*, Troy Duster, Backdoor to Eugenics (2d ed. 2003).

58 *See, e.g.*, Margaret Hu, *Big Data Blacklisting*, 67 Fla. L. Rev. 1735 (2015); Hu, *Small Data Surveillance*, *supra* note 54.

data-driven decisionmaking, it is helpful once again to contrast small data biometric credentialing systems with big data credentialing systems. A paper-based passport photograph, for instance, is a small data biometric-based identification system. In contrast, a digitalized passport system in a big data world can be linked with data from multiple sources such as license plate databases, No Fly Lists, and Terrorist Watchlists. Facial recognition technology that draws upon a passport photo database can be linked to the full range of any digital image of a person: images on social media, the Internet, other photo databases, live streaming video, CCTV surveillance, and hacking into cameras attached to digital devices and laptops. Biometric data collection and storage is increasingly becoming mandatory through either government identification requirements, such as digital photo requirements for passports and driver's licenses, or corporate identification requirements, such as biometric replacement of pass codes on digital devices.

As a result of technological and governance trends, it is increasingly difficult to avoid biometric capture and collection. Opting into biometric surveillance systems is quickly becoming a requirement for social, economic, and political participation in the modern age. Participation in biometric surveillance systems is particularly difficult to resist because of its simultaneously transparent qualities (one cannot generally hide one's biometric data – images of one's face, iris, fingerprints can be digitally captured at any point of public presence) and its compulsory qualities under bureaucratized surveillance traditions (biometric data is often required to establish one's identity). The opt-out difficulty of biometric surveillance is compounded by the fact that biometric data is often supporting much larger big data programs, such as TIA-type risk assessment and identity inference systems.

Consequently, biometric surveillance cannot be understood without understanding big data and how big data developments are changing governance philosophies, such as the adoption of the precrime governance philosophies of *Minority Report*. Big data is predictive and correlative,[59] and can be described as a form of artificial intelligence or machine learning that feeds upon a bottomless pit of digital data to inform its computer-generated conclusions.[60] The National Surveillance State is technologically driven and is, thus, big-data- and cyber-dependent.[61] It fetishizes the automated transparency of identity, purportedly to serve legitimate governance goals.[62]

To understand the National Surveillance State better , both George Orwell's *1984* and *Minority Report* can be informative. Both *1984* and *Minority Report* portray regimes

59 Some scholars have focused particularly on the algorithmic-driven decisionmaking consequences of emerging big data technologies. *See, e.g.*, Frank Pasquale, The Black Box Society (2015); Danielle Keats Citron & Frank A. Pasquale, *The Scored Society: Due Process for Automated Predictions*, 89 Wash. L. Rev. 1 (2014); Neil M. Richards and Jonathan H. King; *Three Paradoxes of Big Data*, 66 Stan. L. Rev. Online 41(2013).

60 Mayer-Schönberger & Cukier, *supra* note 44, at 11–12 ("Though it is described as part of the branch of computer science called artificial intelligence, and more specifically, an area called machine learning, this characterization is misleading. Big data is not trying to 'teach' a computer to 'think' like humans. Instead, it's about applying math to huge quantities of data in order to infer probabilities[]").

61 *See, e.g.*, Balkin, *supra* note 12.

62 *Id.* For a discussion of which documents comprise identity cards and the surveillance consequences of identity documents, see generally Jim Harper, *Identity Crisis: How Identification is Overused and Misunderstood* (2006); Lawrence Lessig, Code Version 2.0 45–54, 68–70 (2006); David Lyon, Identifying Citizens: ID Cards as Surveillance (2009); Playing the Identity Card: Surveillance, Security and Identification in Global Perspective (Colin J. Bennett & David Lyon eds., 2008); Privacy and Technologies of Identity: A Cross-Disciplinary Conversation

reliant on surveillance to control the population and to serve police state ends, whether the means to achieve those ends might be overt or covert. In *1984*, Orwell focuses on how the surveillance state subsumes autonomy, free agency, and human individuality through totalitarianism. In *Minority Report*, the surveillance serves a crime-free, *Brave New World*–like dystopia.

The Snowden disclosures led to multiple references and comparisons to both *1984* and *Minority Report*. Sociologist David Lyon, for example, explained that the Snowden disclosures demonstrated a surveillance digitalization that has shifted surveillance from the past tense "into the future tense."[63] Put differently, in a small data world, surveillance was used to make sense of current or past behavior. In a big data world, surveillance is used to assess future risk and predict future behavior. Criminologist and statistician Richard Berk stated after the Snowden disclosures, "We're not at *Minority Report* yet, but we're getting there."[64]

But what is small data surveillance and what is big data cybersurveillance?[65] Surveillance has been defined in many ways. There is yet no agreed-upon definition of cybersurveillance. The law and technology scholar Lawrence Lessig describes "digital surveillance" as "the process by which some form of human activity is analyzed by a computer according to some specified rule.... The critical feature in each [case of surveillance] is that a computer is sorting data for some follow-up review by some human."[66] The digital media scholar Mark Andrejevic describes a defining characteristic of "big data surveillance" as "the imperative ... to monitor the population as a whole: otherwise it is harder to consistently and reliably discern useful patterns."[67] The computer scientist Roger Clarke is credited with introducing the term "dataveillance,"[68] which he describes as the "systematic use of personal data systems in the investigation or monitoring of the

(Katherine J. Strandburg & Daniela Stan Raicu eds., 2006); Richard Sobel, *The Demeaning of Identity and Personhood in National Identification Systems*, 15 HARV. J.L. & TECH. 319 (2002).

63 Saul Tannenbaum, *Snooping after Snowden: Surveillance, Big Data and Anxiety*, CAMBRIDGE COMMUNITY TELEVISION (Mar. 14, 2014), https://www.cctvcambridge.org/SnoopingAfterSnowden.

64 *Id.*

65 *See e.g.*, Hu, *Small Data Surveillance*, *supra* note 54.

66 *See, e.g.*, Lessig, *supra* note 62, at 209 (describing cybersurveillance or "digital surveillance" as "the process by which some form of human activity is analyzed by a computer according to some specified rule. ... The critical feature in each [case of surveillance] is that a computer is sorting data for some follow-up review by some human.").

67 Mark Andrejevic, *Surveillance in the Big Data Era*, *in* EMERGING PERVASIVE INFORMATION AND COMMUNICATION TECHNOLOGIES (PICT): ETHICAL CHALLENGES, OPPORTUNITIES, AND SAFEGUARDS 56 (Kenneth D. Pimple ed., 2014) ("[I]n the era of 'big data' surveillance, the imperative is to monitor the population as a whole: otherwise it is harder to consistently and reliably discern useful patterns").

> What I am describing is not simply the result of the 9/11 aftermath, although the "war on terror" has contributed tremendously to the further digitizing and globalizing of surveillance.... Today's surveillance is a peculiarly ambiguous process in which digital technologies and personal data are fundamentally implicated and meet in software coding that classifies yet more groups in different ways. Some outcomes are relatively innocuous while others carry both deep dangers for democracy – especially as biometric, location and genomic techniques proliferate – and potential for democratic involvement, ethical critique and alternative practices.

David Lyon, SURVEILLANCE STUDIES: AN OVERVIEW 5 (2007).

68 *See* Roger A. Clarke, *Information Technology and Dataveillance*, 31 COMM. ACM 498, 499 (1988). *See also* Lyon, SURVEILLANCE STUDIES, *supra* note 67, at 16 ("Being much cheaper than direct physical or electronic surveillance [dataveillance] enables the watching of more people or populations, because economic constraints to surveillance are reduced. ... Classically, government bureaucracies have been most interested in gathering such data ").

actions or communications of one or more persons."[69] Lyon elaborates that "dataveillance also automates surveillance."[70]

The ubiquity of modern cybersurveillance in turn is integral to the rise of what is referred to as the National Surveillance State by constitutional law scholars Jack Balkin and Sanford Levinson. The National Surveillance State captures the phenomenon of big data governance. The adoption of a digital data-centered philosophy of governance dependent on the extraction and processing of individuals' biometric and biographical data – or what the privacy scholar Julie Cohen refers to as legal constructs under a biopolitical public domain – assumes that the efficiencies and capacity enhancements of big data and biometric technologies are manifold.[71] As big data has altered the nature of the market into a digital economy in which a person is reduced to a consumer profile of data points subject to corporate surveillance, analysis, and exploitation, so the National Surveillance State can seize upon the citizenry's data trails to regulate and police the big data state.[72]

Biometric surveillance is best understood as a key component of evolving governance practices in the age of big data, the digital economy, the Information Society,[73] and the Internet of Things.[74] Under the National Surveillance State, government by big data means a citizenry whose relationship to its government is increasingly involved. At the same time, that relationship is mediated by the data trails that are collected and monitored by government databases that facilitate the provision of benefits, and the protection and the policing of the citizenry. As our daily data trails are increasingly subject to collection and surveillance by governmental and other watchers, biometrics remains the anchor by which our physical presence and behavioral clues – once digitalized and captured – are converted into data assimilated in the databases that comprehensively collect biographic data.

The cybersurveillance capacities of emerging big data governance systems, such as the No Fly List, are currently in their infancy. At the dawn of the big data revolution, we are only beginning to witness the process of datafication. Datafication mandates the acquisition and collection of increasing amounts of digital data to feed the preexisting cybersurveillance structures or to build new structures, and empowers government

69 Clarke, *supra* note 68, at 499.

70 Lyon, *supra* note 67, at 16.

71 *See, e.g.*, Julie Cohen, *The Biopolitical Public Domain*, GEORGETOWN LAW CTR. (Sept. 28, 2015), http://papers.ssrn.com/sol3/Papers.cfm?abstract_id=2666570.

72 *See, e.g.*, Mayer-Schönberger & Cukier, *supra* note 44, at 157(contending that "the new thinking is that people are the sum of [the data]"). "And because the government knows whom it will want to scrutinize, it collects, stores, or ensures access to information not necessarily to monitor everyone at all times, but so that when someone falls under suspicion, the authorities can immediately investigate rather than having to start gathering the info from scratch." *Id.*

73 *See e.g.*, Nick Moore, *The Information Society*, *in* WORLD INFORMATION REPORT 1997/1998 271 (UNESCO 1997). Moore describes the identifying characteristics of the Information Society as: (1) information as an economic resource and a method to increase organizational efficiencies, (2) information systems that are increasingly integrated into public and private products and decisionmaking, and (3) exponential growth of an information tech sector and the infrastructure necessary to support it. *Id.* at 271–72.

74 *See* Andrew Guthrie Ferguson, *The Internet of Things and the Fourth Amendment of Effects*, 104 CAL. L. REV. 805, 807 (2016) ("Today, with the advent of the 'Internet of Things,' objects in your house, car, office, and smartphone communicate, interact, report, track, and provide vast amounts of data about the activities of their owners"); *see also* Steven I. Friedland, *I Spy: The New Self-Cybersurveillance and the "Internet of Things,"* 72 WASH. & LEE L. REV. 1459 (2015).

actions that are determined by digital data collection and processing protocols, and mass data analyses.[75] Datafication can also be characterized as the government's policy interest in actively developing new forms of stored data and transforming analog data[76] (e.g., paper-based files) into digital data (e.g., centralized databases that are digitally stored and indexed, and electronically searchable).

Various kinds of datafication and new surveillance methods appear to enable the government to engage in a fusion of locational-body surveillance and biographical-behavioral surveillance to infer suspicion. The fusion process facilitates the government's protocols for identity verification and identity management purposes to enable tracking and data analytics (e.g., identifying a potential suspect or terrorist). The 2014 White House report to the president from the President's Council of Advisors on Science and Technology (PCAST), titled *Big Data and Privacy: A Technological Perspective*, is useful to understand the fusion process under big data tools.[77] This report described the fusion process in the private sector consumer context:

> Data fusion occurs when data from different sources are brought into contact and new facts emerge. Individually, each data source may have a specific, limited purpose. Their combination, however, may uncover new meanings. In particular, data fusion can result in the identification of individual people, the creation of profiles of an individual, and the tracking of an individual's activities. More broadly, data analytics discovers patterns and correlations in large corpuses of data, using increasingly powerful statistical algorithms. If those data include personal data, the inferences flowing from data analytics may then be mapped back to inferences, both certain and uncertain, about individuals.[78]

Biometric datafication is the process of transforming individually distinguishing bodily and behavioral characteristics into data – a means of datafying the biological body.[79] Under big data governance, the datafication of the body is conducted through geolocational and biometric data collection, tracking aggregation, storage, and analysis. Surveillance of the body, therefore, can be fused with the surveillance of the biography through big data tools.

The PCAST report recognizes that the government can use fusion in data analytics.[80] This process functions not only to forecast perceived threats from individuals – for example, those perceived to be suspected criminals or terrorists – but increasingly, under programs such as "Social Radar," the fusion process appears to forecast the perceived threats of social and political movements and other "social contagions;"[81] and the perceived threats of mass populations and classes of individuals. Former Chief Scientist of the U.S. Air Force Mark Maybury, has been identified as the primary architect of "Social Radar."[82]

75 *See* Mayer-Schönberger & Cukier, *supra* note 44, at 157.

76 *See* President's Council of Advisors on Sci. & Tech., Exec. Office of the President, Big Data and Privacy: A Technological Perspective, 22 (May 2014) [hereinafter PCAST Report] (explaining information that is "born analog" as coming "from the characteristics of the physical world.").

77 *Id.* at x.

78 *Id.*

79 Mayer-Schönberger & Cukier, *supra* note 44, at 11.

80 PCAST Report, *supra* note 76, at xii.

81 *See, e.g.*, Nafeez Ahmed, *Pentagon preparing for mass civil breakdown*, The Guardian (June 12, 2014, 2:00PM), https://www.theguardian.com/environment/earth-insight/2014/jun/12/pentagon-mass-civil-breakdown.

82 Noah Shachtman, *Air Force's Top Brain Wants a 'Social Radar' to 'See into Hearts and Minds'*, Wired (Jan. 19, 2012), http://www.wired.com/2012/01/social-radar-sees-minds/.

Currently the Vice President and Chief Security Officer of the MITRE Corporation, and Director of the National Cybersecurity Federally Funded Research and Development Center,[83] Maybury has collaborated with the U.S. Department of Defense to construct "a virtual sensor, combining a vast array of technologies and disciplines ... [as] part of a broader Pentagon effort to master the societal and cultural elements of war."[84]

Maybury has presented a "vision document" for Social Radar and has released other documents explaining the program, which includes, "using biometrics, Social Radar will identify individuals. ... Using sociometrics, it will pinpoint groups. [Sociometric datapoints include] Facebook timelines, political polls, spy drone feeds."[85] As of 2012, the Pentagon had more than $125 million in the past three years to "quantify, model – and, eventually, foresee – the human, social, cultural, and behavioral dimensions of conflict."[86] In 2015, MITRE announced that it had licensed its "social analytics technologies" to AtrocityWatch, a "not-for-profit that uses big data to predict and prevent global atrocities."[87] In MITRE's press release that announced the license to AtrocityWatch, Maybury explained that "We are honored to see MITRE's vision and pioneering research in social radar applied to a humanitarian application that has the potential to make the world a better place."[88]

It is important to note that Social Radar appears to trace its philosophical genesis to "Total Information Awareness" (TIA), mentioned earlier. TIA, a project of the U.S. Department of Defense's Defense Advanced Research Projects Agency (DARPA), preceded the Social Radar program in development. Social Radar and multiple other programs that will be discussed later, however, match TIA in the breadth of its comprehensive cybersurveillance ambitions and in the scope of its predictive policing mandate.

TIA was developed after the terrorist attacks of September 11, 2001, and was guided under the newly created "Information Awareness Office" within DARPA.[89] TIA was an effort led by the retired navy vice admiral John M. Poindexter, a former national security adviser to President Reagan.[90] From February 2003 to May 2003, it operated under the name "Total Information Awareness." In May 2003, it was renamed "Terrorism Information Awareness," and operated under this title until it was officially defunded in late 2003.[91] TIA embraced a philosophy of "predictive policing," which "focuses not

83 *Leadership: Dr. Mark T. Maybury*, MITRE, https://www.mitre.org/about/leadership/executive/dr-mark-t-maybury.

84 Shachtman, *supra* note 82.

85 *Id.*, *see also* Mark Maybury, *Social Radar for Smart Power*, MITRE Corp. (2010), https://www.mitre.org/sites/default/files/pdf/10_0745.pdf.

86 Shachtman, *supra* note 82.

87 Press Release, MITRE Corp., Mitre Licenses Social Radar Technology to AtrocityWatch, (May 13, 2015), https://www.mitre.org/news/press-releases/mitre-licenses-social-radar-technology-to-atrocitywatch.

88 *Id.*

89 Poindexter had previously served as deputy national security advisor and national security advisor in the Reagan administration. In the Bush administration, after 9/11, Poindexter served as director of the TIA Information Awareness Office within DARPA. *See* Murray, *supra* note 11, at 5–6 (discussing Pointdexter's history and involvement in TIA).

90 Shane Harris, *Giving In to the Surveillance State*, N.Y. Times (Aug. 22, 2012), http://www.nytimes.com/2012/08/23/opinion/whos-watching-the-nsa-watchers.html ("Mr. Poindexter sketched out a new Pentagon program called Total Information Awareness, that proposed to scan the world's electronic information – including phone calls, e-mails and financial and travel records – looking for transactions associated with terrorist plots.").

91 *See Pentagon's "Terror Information Awareness" Program Will End*, USA Today (Sept. 25, 2003, 7:59AM), http://usatoday30.usatoday.com/news/washington/2003-09-25-pentagon-office_x.htm (explaining that

on collecting evidence about actual wrongdoing but on the broad collection of information about everyday activities with the intention of detecting (and preventing) future behaviour."[92]

TIA faced widespread public protest and was met with congressional concern.[93] Although TIA was officially dismantled by Congress when funding for the program was not included in the Department of Defense Appropriations Act of 2004,[94] nonetheless, experts expressed concern that remnants of the TIA program and its philosophy persisted. Even prior to the NSA Snowden disclosures in June 2013, experts had speculated that the NSA had quietly built a global surveillance apparatus that mirrored TIA.[95] Increased interest in and attention to surveillance architecture over the past decade has revealed multiple government programs that appear to replicate TIA's goals of gathering detailed "digital dossiers" and bulk data to anticipate and prevent future crimes. Other programs attempt to predict "social contagions" through analysis of social media and Internet activity.[96]

TIA aimed to "detect, classify, identify, and track terrorists so that we may understand their plans and act to prevent them from being executed."[97] TIA was also intended to extend beyond the intelligence community; as Poindexter explained, "In the case of counter-terrorism, it is broader to include law enforcement, friendly allies, outside experts, etc."[98] In the *New York Times*, the columnist William Safire described the comprehensiveness of TIA in the following way:

> Every purchase you make with a credit card, every magazine subscription you buy and medical prescription you fill, every Web site you visit and e-mail you send or receive, every academic grade you receive, every bank deposit you make, every trip you book and every event you attend – all these transactions and communications will go into what the Defense Department describes as "a virtual, centralized grand database."
>
> To this computerized dossier on your private life from commercial sources, add every piece of information that government has about you – passport application, driver's license and bridge toll records, judicial and divorce records, complaints from nosy neighbors to the F.B.I., your lifetime paper trail plus the latest hidden camera

initially, the House passed restrictions to T.I.A., but subsequently the Senate "passed a provision in next year's defense appropriation bill killing funding for the TIA program").

92 Murray, *supra* note 11, at 5.

93 *See* Harris, *supra* note 90 ("When T.I.A.'s existence became public, it was denounced as the height of post-9/11 excess and ridiculed for its creepy name.").

94 Murray, *supra* note 11, at 6; Christopher Slobogin, *Government Data Mining and the Fourth Amendment*, 75 U. Chi. L. Rev. 317, 317 n. 4 (citing 10 U.S.C. § 2241 (d)).

95 *See* Harris, *supra* note 90 (explaining that "the legacy of T.I.A. is quietly thriving at the N.S.A." and describing what was then known (pre–Snowden disclosures) about the scope of the National Surveillance State); *see also* Murray, *supra* note 11, at 6 ("But in a secret, classified annex, Congress preserved funding for TIA's component technologies that were transferred to other government agencies, primarily to the National Security Agency").

96 *See* Ahmed, *supra* note 81 ("A US Department of Defense (DoD) research programme is funding universities to model the dynamics, risks and tipping points for large-scale civil unrest across the world, under the supervision of various US military agencies").

97 John Poindexter, Dir., Info. Awareness Office of DARPA, Address at DARPATech 2002 Conference: Overview of the Information Awareness Office (Aug. 2, 2002), http://fas.org/irp/agency/dod/poindexter.html.

98 *Id.*

> surveillance – and you have the supersnoop's dream: a "Total Information Awareness" about every U.S. citizen.[99]

Following the Snowden disclosures, experts have claimed that, rather than cease TIA operations as Congress intended, the program continued in classified form through NSA reincarnation.[100] David J. Farber, referred to as the "Grandfather of the Internet," hypothesized that TIA was not officially terminated but, rather, continued within the NSA, and its existence is now manifested in the programs revealed by Snowden.[101]

It appears that biometric data serves as a type of data backbone in TIA[102] that allows for the creation of multiple identity screening systems to evolve from it, similar to the manner in which the social security and passport number systems have created a numerical data backbone for database screening. The scope of the data collected under cybersurveillance programs – data that encompasses entire populations and subpopulations – requires a means to detect individuals within that population or subpopulation for further investigation. One of TIA's programmatic components includes biometric data collection and analysis. Referred to as "Human Identification at a Distance" under TIA, it is meant to "achieve positive identification of humans using multi-modal biometric technologies."[103] Multimodal biometric data is a combination of biometric identifiers, such as combining facial recognition technology with iris scanning and fingerprint scanning. Multi-modal biometric data purports to serve predictive policing purposes through "authentication [of] biometric data," as described in a DARPA infograph slide.[104] DARPA's TIA slide explicitly lists face, fingerprints, gait, and iris as forms of biometric identity verification and identity determination.

"Collect it all" programs, such as TIA, Social Radar, and the programs revealed in the Snowden disclosures display precrime governing ambitions. These technological capacities allow for cybersurveillance monitoring of entire populations to detect suspicious data profiles. Digital watchlisting. database screening, and other cybersurveillance systems, for example, isolate data, devices, or persons deemed suspicious. Biometric data can be used to pinpoint the specific physical person associated with a suspicious data profile.

III Precrime Policy under Biometric Surveillance and Big Data Governance

In Parts I and II, the discussion focused on how, in a big data world, biometric data can be aggregated with other data as an anchor point. It can be filtered through multiple big data-driven systems, such as database screening systems, digital watchlisting systems, and larger cybersurveillance systems. A wide range of subsequent governmental actions

99 William Safire, *You Are a Suspect*, N.Y. Times (Nov. 14, 2002), http://www.nytimes.com/2002/11/14/opinion/you-are-a-suspect.html?_r=0.

100 John Horgan, *U.S. Never Really Ended Creepy "Total Information Awareness Program,"* Sci. Am. Blog (June 7, 2013), http://blogs.scientificamerican.com/cross-check/2013/06/07/u-s-never-really-ended-creepy-total-information-awareness-program/.

101 *Id.*

102 *See* Poindexter, *supra* note 97 ("Such a system could be used for security systems, for example, or could be used to track potential terrorists").

103 *Id.*

104 Def. Advanced Research Projects Agency, U.S. Dep't of Def., *Total Information Awareness (TIA) System*, TruthMove, http://www.truthmove.org/workspace/photos-content/tia_screenshot.gif (last visited Oct. 26, 2016).

that derive from data analysis can use biometric data as an anchor to a specific individual. This part will focus on how biometric surveillance technologies can inform governmental actions that may run the gamut from detention to death.[105]

The NSA cybersurveillance programs disclosed by Edward Snowden and other media reports suggest that biometric data identifiers,[106] if and when "fully integrated" with other dataveillance systems, provide support for targeted killing technologies.[107] Even before the Snowden disclosures, other media reports indicated that the U.S. military utilized defense contractors to integrate biometric data into targeting technologies.[108] Mass biometric dataveillance technologies that have been integrated into emerging big data cybersurveillance systems could assist in government efforts to identify potential terrorists by "integrat[ing] data from informants' tips, drone footage, and captured phone calls."[109] The "disposition matrix," a database revealed during the Obama administration is one such example. It "is designed to go beyond existing kill lists, mapping plans for the 'disposition' of suspects beyond the reach of American drones."[110] According to the Snowden disclosures, the U.S. drone strike campaign "relies heavily on the NSA's ability to vacuum up enormous quantities of e-mail, phone calls and other fragments."[111] The Snowden disclosures further suggested that data harvesting and data fusion of biometric and biographic information from digital sources – social media and the Internet – appeared to serve intelligence purposes. One NSA goal identified in a Snowden document was to "'compile biographic and biometric information' that can help 'implement precision targeting[.]'"[112] The term "targeting" was not defined in the particular document, but is a term of art that often refers to targeted killing measures, such as drone strikes.

105 Dept. Homeland Security 2008, Privacy Impact Assessment for the Future Attribute Screening Technology (FAST) Project 4 (Department of Homeland Security 2008), http://www.dhs.gov/xlibrary/assets/privacy/privacy_pia_st_fast.pdf [hereinafter Privacy Impact Assessment for FAST (2008)].

106 *See, e.g.*, Risen & Poitras, *supra* note 56.

107 *Id.*; *see also, e.g.*, Barton Gellman and Ashkan Soltani, *NSA Tracking Cellphone Locations Worldwide, Snowden Documents Show*, Wash. Post (Dec. 4, 2013), https://www.washingtonpost.com/world/national-security/nsa-tracking-cellphone-locations-worldwide-snowden-documents-show/2013/12/04/5492873a-5cf2-11e3-bc56-c6ca94801fac_story.html; Greg Miller, Julie Tate & Barton Gellman, *Documents Reveal NSA's Extensive Involvement in Targeted Killing Program*, Wash. Post (Oct. 16, 2013), https://www.washingtonpost.com/world/national-security/documents-reveal-nsas-extensive-involvement-in-targeted-killing-program/2013/10/16/29775278-3674-11e3-8a0e-4e2cf80831fc_story.html ("[A] collection of records in the Snowden trove [] make clear that the drone campaign – often depicted as the CIA's exclusive domain – relies heavily on the NSA's ability to vacuum up enormous quantities of e-mail, phone calls and other fragments of signals intelligence, or SIGINT."); Jeremy Scahill and Glenn Greenwald, *The NSA's Secret Role in the U.S. Assassination Program*, First Look, (Feb. 10, 2014), https://firstlook.org/theintercept/article/2014/02/10/the-nsas-secret-role/ (explaining accuracy limits of what metadata-driven intelligence can yield in identifying appropriate targets for drone strikes).

108 *See, e.g.*, Noah Shachtman, *Army Tracking Plan: Drones That Never Forget a Face*, Wired (Sept. 28, 2011, 6:30 AM), http://www.wired.com/dangerroom/2011/09/drones-never-forget-a-face/; *see also* Hu, *Biometric Cyberintelligence*, *supra* note 39.

109 Shachtman, *supra* note 108.

110 Greg Miller, *Plan for Hunting Terrorists Signals U.S. Intends to Keep Adding Names to Kill Lists*, Wash. Post (Oct. 23, 2012), https://www.washingtonpost.com/world/national-security/plan-for-hunting-terrorists-signals-us-intends-to-keep-adding-names-to-kill-lists/2012/10/23/4789b2ae-18b3-11e2-a55c-39408fbe6a4b_story.html.

111 Miller, Tate & Gellman, *supra* note 107.

112 Risen & Poitras, *supra* note 56. However, the term "targeting" in the defense and intelligence context has been defined as: "'Targeting.' The process of selecting and prioritizing targets and matching the

To provide a more specific example, in a review of combined intelligence documents derived from the Snowden disclosures and WikiLeaks, it was revealed that NSA biometric-based technology was provided to Turkey to inform its tactical decisionmaking against the Kurdistan Worker's Party (PKK). The revelations indicated a close intelligence-related collaboration between American and Turkish intelligence in combating PKK, Kurdish separatists who have been classified as a terrorist organization by the United States and the European Union.[113] A January 2007 NSA document from the Snowden disclosures explained that Turkish intelligence was provided with geolocational data and voice recordings from phone conversations of the PKK. "'Geolocations data and voice cuts from Kurdistan Worker Party communications which were passed to Turkey by NSA yielded actionable intelligence that led to the demise or capture of dozens of PKK members in the past year,'"[114] according to the NSA document.

From 2007 to 2012, it appears that surveillance technology shared by the two nations rapidly evolved to encompass biometric-based analytic technology. In 2007, the two nations had formed a joint effort referred to as the "Combined Intelligence Fusion Cell, a team of American and Turkish specialists working together on projects that included finding targets for possible Turkish airstrikes against suspected PKK members."[115] It appeared that the initial surveillance technology at least from 2007 involved voice recordings taken from phone conversations. However, by 2012, the small data surveillance had moved to big data cybersurveillance that expanded its biometric and big data dimensions, including the use of voice recognition technology. By January 2012, intelligence documents showed that U.S. officials recommended providing Turkey with "access to a state-of-the-art speech recognition system that enabled real-time analysis of intercepted conversations ... [including a] search for keywords and [the ability to] identify the person speaking if a voice sample of that individual has been stored."[116] A real time analytics system like the one in operation in this particular Snowden disclosure requires significant storage and analysis capacity, and voice recognition technology relies upon big data–scale quantities of voice data.[117] Voice biometrics, or "speaker recognition," involves biometric identification based upon an analysis of characteristics of an individual's voice.[118] Each voice is distinct in terms of physical and "manner of speaking" characteristics.[119]

appropriate response to them, considering commander's objectives, operational requirements, capabilities, and limitations." *See* U.S. Dept. of Defense, Office of Counterintelligence, Defense CI & HUMINT Center, Defense Intelligence Agency, Glossary (Unclassified), Terms & Definitions of Interest for DoD Counterintelligence Professionals 167 (May 2, 2011), http://fas.org/irp/eprint/ci-glossary.pdf (last accessed on April 28, 2015).

113 Laura Poitras et al., *How the NSA Helped Turkey Kill Kurdish Rebels*, The Intercept (Aug. 31, 2014, 6:00AM), https://theintercept.com/2014/08/31/nsaturkeyspiegel/ ("Although the PKK is still considered a terrorist organization by the United States and the European Union, its image has been improved radically by its recent success in fighting ISIS in northern Iraq and Syria.").

114 *Id.*

115 *Id.*

116 *Id.*

117 Tim Tuttle, *The Future of Voice-Activated AI Sounds Awesome*, TechCrunch (Mar. 6, 2015), https://techcrunch.com/2015/03/06/the-future-of-voice-activated-ai-sounds-awesome/.

118 Tomi Kinnunen & Haizhou Li, *An Overview of Text-Independent Speaker Recognition: From Features to Supervectors*, 52(1) Speech Comm. 12 (2009).

119 *Id.*

The Snowden disclosures specifically demonstrated how biometrics could inform "precision targeting" by attempting to increase the accuracy of drone strikes.[120] Biometrics are becoming a significant method by which the intelligence community identifies targets and suspicious behavior. One 2010 NSA document explains: "It's not just the traditional communications we're after: It's taking a full-arsenal approach that digitally exploits the clues a target leaves behind in their regular activities on the net to compile biographic and biometric information that can help implement precision targeting."[121] NSA documents indicate that the agency intercepted on a daily basis millions of images including "about 55,000 'facial recognition quality images.'"[122]

The transition from small data surveillance to big data cybersurveillance can once again be seen by witnessing the increasing importance of biometric surveillance to terrorist tracking and targeting. "While once focused on written and oral communications, the N.S.A. now considers facial images, fingerprints and other identifiers just as important to its mission of tracking suspected terrorists and other intelligence targets, the documents show."[123] In other words, in a small data world, the intelligence community focused on collecting and analyzing small data (e.g., "written and oral communications"). In a big data world, biometric data is used as an identifying anchor in order to build other data points around the individual to allow inferences of suspicion. For instance, in a program revealed among the Snowden disclosures, facial recognition technology used to identify an individual from digital photographs taken from the Internet was then combined with an additional "two dozen data points" that included "Transportation Security Administration no-fly list, [the individual's] passport and visa status, known associates or suspected terrorist ties, and comments made about him by informants to American intelligence agencies."[124]

The potential lethality of biometric surveillance, however, is not limited to foreign intelligence application. The U.S. Department of Homeland Security (DHS)'s test pilot program, Future Attribute Screening Technology (FAST), is a biometric-based precrime program intended to detect crime and terrorism before it occurs. Under FAST, physiological and behavioral cues are captured through body and eye movements, eye blink rate and pupil variation, body heat changes, and breathing patterns,[125] voice pitch changes, alterations in vocal rhythm, and changes in intonations of speech.[126] DHS informed test subjects that projected consequences of FAST "can range from none to being temporarily detained to deportation, prison, or death."[127] Even though the FAST program has not been implemented and is only in the test pilot stage, such a program signals big data governance ambitions that rely upon biometrics.

Recent surveillance disclosures highlight the growing capacity of law enforcement to apply biometric surveillance in domestic law enforcement settings. In 2013, it was reported that shortly after the Boston Marathon bombing, the City of Boston collaborated with IBM

120 *See* Risen & Poitras, *supra* note 56.

121 *Id.* The use of the term "targeting" in this 2010 NSA document from the Snowden disclosures does not appear to be defined.

122 *See* Risen & Poitras, *supra* note 56.

123 *Id.*

124 *Id.*

125 Privacy Impact Assessment for FAST (2008), *supra* note 105, at 4.

126 *Id.*

127 *Id.* at 2.

to test an "event monitoring program" that integrated biometric surveillance into video surveillance and social media screening.[128] IBM had been partnered with Boston since March of 2012, when Boston received one of IBM's "Smarter Cities Challenge" grants.[129]

IBM and Boston subsequently collaborated during the 2013 May and September "Boston Calling" Music Festivals in the City Hall Plaza – a citywide concert series that was anticipated to attract large public crowds – to test IBM's Intelligent Operations Center (IOC), which integrated IBM's Smart Surveillance System and Intelligent Video Analytics software.[130] In effect, the Boston Calling concert series provided a setting to capture "a live and detailed birdseye view of concertgoers, pedestrians, and vehicles."[131] The Boston Calling concert event surveillance in the IOC combined real-time social media tracking with existing city cameras "capable of intelligent-video analysis" to "detect traffic congestion and suspicious objects, screen people for possible forensic identification purposes, and conduct real-time video analytics."[132] The surveillance included a "People Search" feature that could identify individuals by skin color, clothing texture, baldness, or glasses.[133] Upon discovery, Boston described the program as "situational awareness software."[134] According to the program's disclosure:

> Situational awareness software analyzes video and provides alerts when something happens. For example, if someone walks into a secure area in view of one of the system's cameras, the software would raise a red flag. More sophisticated systems can track people in real time as they move through crowds – such as following an unauthorized person in the area – without requiring dozens or even hundreds of human analysts to watch video feeds.[135]

Boston insisted that it did not use the program to track individuals by race or other characteristics, and that the searches "were not focused on any individual characteristics of people at all, but rather situations that were deemed a potential threat to public safety [such as] abandoned bags [or] vehicles illegally parked."[136] The Boston Police Department denied that it participated in the surveillance program.[137] IBM asserts that facial capture and facial recognition technology were not used at the event,[138] although the disclosures suggested their application.[139] Situational awareness programs like the one used at the Boston Calling concerts demonstrate that the technological capabilities

128 Reporters disclosed the program after it was alleged that an IBM employee left materials about the tests on an unsecured server. *See* Luke O'Neil, *Beantown's Big Brother: How Boston Police Used Facial Recognition Technology to Spy on Thousands of Music Festival Attendees*, NOISEY (Aug. 13, 2014, 12:00PM), https://noisey.vice.com/en_us/article/beantowns-big-brother.

129 Chris Faraone, Kenneth Lipp & Jonathan Riley, *Boston Trolling (Part II)*, DIGBOSTON (Oct. 9, 2014), https://digboston.com/boston-trolling-part-2/#sthash.fdmnpZxN.dpbs.

130 Faraone, Lipp & Riley, *supra* note 51.

131 *Id.*

132 *Id.*

133 *Id.*

134 Ramos, *supra* note 8.

135 *Id.*

136 *Id.* It is worth noting that Boston spent $650,000 on the short-term license for the test program, but decided not to purchase the software. *Id.*

137 *See supra* notes 130–136 (noting that although photographs from the IOC obtained and published by reporters appeared to show Boston Police Officers present in the IOC during the event).

138 *See* Ramos, *supra* note 8.

139 *See supra* note 51.

for using biometric capture and recognition software in real time are expanding significantly. These programs, however, are highly experimental and the efficacy and accuracy of such systems are still unknown.[140]

In addition to domestic expansion of cybersurveillance systems, the United States appears to be exporting its cybersurveillance technology and philosophy. At least one country, Singapore, appears to have adopted TIA in the form of its Risk Assessment and Horizon Scanning (RAHS) program under the guidance of Admiral Poindexter.[141] Shane Harris, national security correspondent for *Foreign Policy*, reports that "Singapore is testing whether mass surveillance and big data can not only protect national security, but actually engineer a more harmonious society."[142] This goal of using cybersurveillance means to achieve liberalism's ends is an example of how and why big data cybersurveillance is assuming an ideological dimension. Specifically, Harris explains that Singapore has deployed an aggressive national defense program anchored in cybersurveillance that is named Risk Assessment and Horizon Scanning program.[143] RAHS is TIA inspired and is currently at the "forefront of deploying big data in the service of national defense."[144] Harris observes that the U.S. intelligence and defense community has taken note of the Singaporean model of big data cybersurveillance governance.[145] Because RAHS is actually based upon cybersurveillance technologies and policymaking rationales that were born in the United States, this is not surprising.

Importantly, RAHS shows the natural trajectory of big data cybersurveillance that starts its journey as a tool for national security and, within a single decade, is transformed into a governing philosophy. This transformation goes hand in hand with an administrative state that has increasingly facilitated bureaucratized surveillance and bureaucratized cybersurveillance in the years following the 9/11 attacks:[146]

> Ten years after its founding, the RAHS program has evolved beyond anything Poindexter could have imagined. Across Singapore's national ministries and departments today, armies of civil servants use scenario-based planning and big-data analysis from RAHS for a host of applications beyond fending off bombs and bugs. They use it to plan procurement cycles and budgets, make economic forecasts, inform immigration policy, study housing markets, and develop education plans for Singaporean schoolchildren – and they are looking to analyze Facebook posts, Twitter messages, and other social media

140 Approximately two months before Boston Calling, IBM executed a "beta phase" at the 2013 Boston Marathon. *See* Faraone, Lipp & Riley, *supra* note 51. Although Boston Police used surveillance footage to locate the unknown suspects involved in the Marathon bombing, it took an individual identification by a survivor to conclude that the Tsarnaev brothers were the bombers, even though both brothers' faces were in the FBI's database. Tim De Chant, *The Limits of Facial Recognition*, NovaNext (Apr. 26, 2013), http://www.pbs.org/wgbh/nova/next/tech/the-limits-of-facial-recognition/.

141 Shane Harris, *The Social Laboratory*, Foreign Policy (July 29, 2014), http://www.foreignpolicy.com/articles/2014/07/29/the_social_laboratory_singapore_surveillance_state ("After Poindexter left DARPA in 2003, he became a consultant to RAHS, and many American spooks have traveled to Singapore to study the program firsthand.").

142 *Id.*

143 *Id.*

144 *Id.*

145 *Id.* ("Many current and former U.S. officials have come to see Singapore as a model for how they'd build an intelligence apparatus if privacy laws and a long tradition of civil liberties weren't standing in the way").

146 *Id.*

in an attempt to 'gauge the nation's mood' about everything from government social programs to the potential for civil unrest.[147]

Singapore is just the tip of the ideological iceberg. Proponents of big data cybersurveillance assert that the depth and breadth of comprehensive data surveillance allows governments digitally to construct risk assessments of not only known suspects and current threats, but also future threats and potentially unknown future suspects.[148] And from there, of course, big data will allow risk assessments in other contexts, for managing energy resources, predicting social and environmental problems, and understanding and managing public opinion. All of this requires more and more data to construct suspects digitally and to simulate risks of whatever order on a virtual level digitally. "In other words, Singapore has become a laboratory not only for testing how mass surveillance and big-data analysis might prevent terrorism, but for determining whether technology can be used to engineer … society."[149] Which is to say, the national security state is no longer just about security: it is a means of governing in general. It is also important to observe that Singapore has expanded its biometric-based surveillance technologies for national and domestic security purposes: biometric passports,[150] mandatory fingerprint screening at points of entry,[151] and, as recently as 2014, Singapore was considering using iris scanning in its airports.[152]

Meanwhile, identity management programs facilitate – sometimes as a side effect – government surveillance or, increasingly, under big data systems of governance, cybersurveillance. Identity and population management databases across a spectrum of government agencies are becoming interoperable with each other and with other kinds of databases. In addition, the federal government has actively sought access to private databases, and to aggregate public and private data. Beginning in 2008, for example, the U.S. Department of Defense (DoD) launched the "Minerva Research Initiative,"[153] which "partners with universities 'to improve DoD's basic understanding of the social, cultural, behavioral, and political forces that shape regions of the world of strategic importance to the US.'"[154] One aspect of the project involved a study managed by the U.S. Air Force Office of Scientific Research that aimed to study "social movement mobilization and contagions."[155] The project utilizes private social media data[156] to

147 *Id.*

148 *See* Hunt CIA Presentation, *supra* note 18.

149 Harris, *supra* note 141.

150 *See Public Introduction of Singapore Biometric Passport*, Immigration & Checkpoint Authority (Jul. 25, 2006), https://www.ica.gov.sg/news_details.aspx?nid=2952 (discussing the introduction of the "BioPass").

151 *See, e.g.*, Jermyn Chow, *Parliament: Fingerprinting for Every Singapore-bound Traveler at all Land, Air and Sea Checkpoints from June*, Strait Times (Jan. 27, 2016), http://www.straitstimes.com/politics/parliament-fingerprinting-for-every-singapore-bound-traveller-at-all-land-air-and-sea.

152 *See, e.g.*, *Singapore Mulls Iris Scanners for Border Checkpoints*, Planet Biometrics (Sept. 26, 2014), http://www.planetbiometrics.com/article-details/i/2210/desc/singapore-mulls-iris-scanners-for-border-checkpoints/.

153 Ahmed, *supra* note 81.

154 *Id.*

155 *Id.*

156 *See id.* ("'Twitter posts and conversations will be examined 'to identify individuals mobilised in a social contagion and when they become mobilised.'").

examine critical moments in recent social upheavals, such as the Arab Spring and other incidents of mass social unrest.[157]

As presented earlier, TIA – both technologically and philosophically – is reflected in NSA programs such as those revealed by the Snowden disclosures, the U.S. Air Force's Social Radar,[158] the US Department of Defense's Minerva Project, the U.S. Department of Homeland Security's Future Attribute Screening Technology ("FAST") Program, and the recent "situational awareness" surveillance program revealed in Boston. In the years following the terrorist attacks of September 11, 2001, the U.S. Department of Defense for national security and the U.S. Department of Homeland Security and the FBI for domestic security have greatly expanded their own biometric-enabled intelligence programs and biometric surveillance capacities, including biometric databanking. The U.S. Department of Homeland Security's biometric programs include the US-VISIT border security program (digital fingerprint and photo collection of foreign visitors), Apex Air Entry and Exit Re-Engineering Project (AEER)[159] (facial recognition and iris scanning on a test-pilot basis at selected airports), and the Rapid DNA program (portable and rapid DNA testing on a test-pilot basis, currently restricted to kinship verification for immigration purposes).[160]

And, as in *Minority Report*, precrime rationales are now entering the stream of a corporate biometric surveillance environment. The biometric data collection and analysis of the public sphere target potential criminal and terrorist suspects' behaviors, and data trails deemed suspect. The biometric data collection and analysis of the private sphere target potential consumers and economic behaviors deemed potentially relevant to market-driven decisions such as advertising. In *Minority Report*, corporate biometric identification systems provided a method for targeting consumers through interactive billboards. One corporation recently filed a patent to accomplish similar aims through what they refer to as "smart billboards."[161] Smart billboards would target consumers in a similar manner to online advertising[162] through capturing biometric data,[163] vehicle

157 *See id.* ("The project will determine 'the critical mass (tipping point)' of social contagions [sic] by studying their 'digital traces' in the cases of 'the 2011 Egyptian revolution, the 2011 Russian Duma elections, the 2012 Nigerian fuel subsidy crisis and the 2013 Gazi park protests in Turkey.'").

158 *See* Shachtman, *supra* note 82 ("Social Radar ... [will] be more of a virtual sensor, combining a vast array of technologies and disciplines, all employed to take a society's pulse and assess its future health. It's part of a broader Pentagon effort to master the societal and cultural elements of war").

159 *See* DHS Sci. & Tech. Directorate, Apex Air Entry and Exit Re-Engineering (Aug. 11, 2014), https://www.dhs.gov/sites/default/files/publications/Apex%20Air%20Entry%20and%20Exit%20Re-Engineering-AEER-508_0.pdf; *see also* Lorenzo Franceschi-Bicchierai, *U.S. Customs Quietly Launches Facial Recognition Experiment at DC Airport*, Motherboard (Mar. 18, 2015, 12:21PM), http://motherboard.vice.com/read/us-customs-quietly-launches-facial-recognition-experiment-at-dc-airport.

160 *See, e.g.*, Aliya Sternstein, *DHS Delays Rapid DNA Tests Aimed at Stemming Human Trafficking*, Nextgov (Sept. 4, 2015), http://www.nextgov.com/defense/2015/09/dhs-delays-dna-tests-refugee-camps-aimed-stemming-human-trafficking/120356/.

161 Measuring User Engagement with Smart Billboards, U.S. Patent App. No. 14/675,004 (filed Mar. 31, 2015).

162 *Id.* at [0002] (explaining that "while ... billboards represent a step in the direction of the digital age, they lag far behind their online counterparts in a number of respects").

163 *Id.* at [0018] (describing "electronic public advertising" that utilizes "one or more biometric sensors ... (e.g., fingerprint or retinal scanning, facial recognition, etc.)").

data,[164] traffic congestion data,[165] geolocational data through cell towers,[166] drone surveillance data,[167] and other digitalized information.[168]

Some corporate surveillance products are now displacing traditional law enforcement activities. Therefore, corporations are developing ways to monetize corporate data surveillance as both consumer-predictive and precrime products: law enforcement investigative and monitoring techniques can be translated into more accurate consumer monitoring, and consumer monitoring and trend tracking can be exploited for law enforcement investigation. Demonstrating this feedback loop is a recent disclosure regarding a situational awareness product that was deployed by the Baltimore Police Department during the riots in April and May of 2015 after the death of Freddie Gray.[169] Officers received real-time alerts and information posted on social media about the riots that allowed them to formulate responses to ongoing situations – including preventing protestors from reaching protests.[170] In addition, "police officers were even able to run social media photos through facial recognition technology to discover rioters without outstanding warrants and arrest them directly from the crowd."[171] This surveillance revelation provides insight into how law enforcement, homeland security, and the intelligence and military communities increasingly rely upon corporate delegated surveillance to conduct monitoring and biometric analysis.

164 *Id.* at [0023] ("For example, one or more cameras deployed near the digital billboard might capture images or video of vehicles on the highway or street from which the digital billboard is visible, and the camera(s) might communicate directly with the digital billboard via a wired connection or a wireless connection").

165 *Id.* ("In another example, an independently operated traffic sensing system might be deployed near the billboard that senses the speed and/or the congestion of traffic on the nearby highway, the data from which might be acquired by a back end system").

166 *Id.* ("In yet another example, information captured by one or more cell towers deployed and/or under control of telecommunication service providers might be leveraged in a variety of ways to provide information about the context of the digital billboard").

167 *Id.* at [0022] ("For example, a camera or other type of sensor could be tightly integrated with an electronic public advertising display as one of its I/O device or, alternatively, could be deployed and operated independently such as, for example, on an aerial surveillance drone or a satellite that communicates to a back end server").

168 *Id.* at [0024]:

> That is, traffic sensor data, image/video data, audio data, etc., can be used to count or estimate the number of vehicles on the road, from which the size of the audience can be estimated; image/video data can be used to identify the makes and/or models of particular vehicles in the vicinity; mobile device data or image/video data can be used to identify specific individuals in the target audience; vehicle navigation and/or tracking data can be used to identify specific vehicles and/or drivers; light sensors can measure the ambient light; temperature sensors can measure the ambient temperature; etc. And with the increasing instrumentation of ordinary objects such as smart appliance, vehicles, etc. (i.e., the "Internet of Things"), the sources of data and information that may be used to enable the techniques described herein are virtually limitless. That is, any sensors or sensor systems that generate data or collect information in real-time that represent some aspect of the context in which the electronic public advertising display is situated (including the target audience) may be used.

169 *Baltimore County Police Department and Geofeedia Partner to Protect the Public during Freddie Gray Riots*, 1 GEOFEEDIA, https://www.aclunc.org/docs/20161011_geofeedia_baltimore_case_study.pdf (describing how Geofeedia established real time alerts for Baltimore Police during the riots that allowed "social stream information [to] flow directly from [Geofeedia] to the commander in charge").

170 *Id.* at 2 (explaining how Geofeedia monitored protests and alerted Baltimore officers to high school students who "planned to walk out of class and head to the Mondawmin Mall protests" allowing officers to intercept the students before they arrived at a protest).

171 *Id.* at 2.

Yet, many biometric surveillance technologies and cybersurveillance systems are highly experimental. The risk, therefore, is multifold. Initially, biometric identification technologies might be implemented prior to proper testing. Next, these technologies present a substantial risk of abuse – identity verification programs may drift into TIA-type mass surveillance systems to inform a range of predictive inferences. As of yet, there is insufficient oversight to guard against these risks. No federal regulatory body currently exists to establish and oversee comprehensive standards for biometric data and technologies and their uses.[172] Laura Donohue and other legal experts have concluded that neither preexisting statutory frameworks (e.g., surveillance and privacy statutes) nor constitutional frameworks (e.g., current Fourth Amendment privacy jurisprudence) are sufficient to protect against surveillance harms that are implicated by emerging biometric data tracking technologies.[173] In the rush to embrace biometric-based identification systems on a mass scale, insufficient thought has been given to protect individual due process and other rights.[174] Those adversely impacted by an "identity" determination have already and will continue to face difficulty in interrogating the "chain of evidence" relied upon, let alone contest the databases or algorithms from which the conclusions are drawn.[175]

Conclusion

The relationship between biometric surveillance technologies and the precrime program depicted in *Minority Report* is significant. It is easy to dismiss *Minority Report* as a Hollywood fantasy or dystopian parable. This chapter contends that *Minority Report* now serves as an important heuristic. Heuristics and metaphors interpret complex phenomena in accessible ways. Some scholars have suggested that science fiction and dystopian literature can explain modern legal and governance phenomena in a way that the study of relevant law alone cannot.

Currently, biometric surveillance and ubiquitous cybersurveillance systems are largely critiqued and reviewed by the courts and Congress on an individual basis. *Minority Report* is necessary, thus, for its prescient portrayal of precrime governance ambitions. What are the relationships among biometric data, big data surveillance technologies, and the big data governance? Biometric data allow for identity tracking – population

172 Currently, NIST is tasked with overseeing testing of biometric technologies by the federal government but does not set minimally proficient standards. *See* U.S. GEN. ACCT. OFF., GAO-03-174, TECHNOLOGY ASSESSMENT: USING BIOMETRICS FOR BORDER SECURITY 54 (2002) [hereinafter GAO TECHNOLOGY ASSESSMENT], http://www.gao.gov/assets/160/157313.pdf ("Biometric technologies are maturing but are still not widespread or pervasive because of performance issues, including accuracy, the lack of applications-dependent evaluations, their potential susceptibility to deception, the lack of standards, and questions of users' acceptance").

173 *See, e.g.*, Laura Donohue, *Technological Leap, Statutory Gap, and Constitutional Abyss: Remote Biometric Identification Comes of Age*, 97 MINN. L. REV. 407 (2012).

174 BIOMETRIC RECOGNITION, *supra* note 29, at 10–11.

175 Important research has been conducted by scholars in recent years investigating the implications of the mass datafication of forensic evidence through, for example, biometric databases, such as DNA databases. *See, e.g.*, David H. Kaye, *A Fourth Amendment Theory for Arrestee DNA and Other Biometric Databases*, 15 U. PA. J. CONST. L. 1095 (2013); Jennifer L. Mnookin, *The Courts, the NAS, and the Future of Forensic Science*, 75 BROOK. L. REV. 1209 (2010); Erin Murphy, *License, Registration, Cheek Swab: DNA Testing and the Divided Court*, 127 HARV. L. REV. 161 (2013); Andrea Roth, *Safety in Numbers: Deciding When DNA Alone Is Enough to Convict*, 85 N.Y.U. L. REV. 1130 (2010).

identification and indexing – systems that support the "collect it all" protocols of programs such as TIA, Social Radar, and the Snowden disclosures. These "collect it all" programs are not advanced in the name of surveillance per se – but in the name of the prevention of harm. But, nevertheless, the result is more mass surveillance.

As in *Minority Report*, governments are expanding biometric systems to assist with governance functions. Many of these combined biometric surveillance and big data programs rely upon predictive policing models and other algorithmic-driven decision-making programs. Modern criminal justice systems often depend upon two well-settled principles that the concept of precrime challenges: first, that one is presumed innocent until proven guilty, and, second, that punishment both follows and should be proportional to the crime. *Minority Report* illustrates how constitutional rights and procedural justice can be undermined under what appears to be an important governance goal: the prevention of crime and terrorism.

Without a *Minority Report*-like heuristic or metaphor, how core rights and liberties may be impacted by persistent biometric surveillance operating under a big data governance philosophy may be misunderstood. In light of the ubiquity of big data cybersurveillance and biometric dataveillance, and with the advent of precrime programs, constitutional doctrines that protect individual rights and freedoms are becoming strained. Big data cybersurveillance involves mass harms that implicate societywide interests. These injuries are often indirect in nature and involve both tangible and intangible data abuses. Because freedoms and liberties are often protected under doctrines that anticipate direct harms against individuals, constitutional protections under newly emerging surveillance systems must be reconceived.

Constitutional protections that rely upon criminal procedural safeguards to prevent surveillance harms are insufficient, as much of the biometric cybersurveillance architecture and big data governance approaches of the National Surveillance State fall within civil law and administrative law environments, or delegated corporate contexts. Therefore, substantive due process privacy jurisprudence, to take an important example, can and should evolve to redress new forms of surveillance-related harms and deprivations. Without a proportionate constitutional response – such as scaling up substantive due process protections to match the unprecedented scaling up of mass surveillance harms – unrestrained biometric surveillance can render constitutional protections of individual freedom and privacy a nullity.

6 Fusion Centers

Thomas Nolan[†]

Fusion centers are interagency and multijurisdictional organizations that act as liaison resources to law enforcement in the collection, analysis, assessment, and dissemination of intelligence that may be related to a criminal threat or hazard. Fusion centers have raised civil rights and civil liberties concerns in deviating from their original stated mission in combating threats of domestic terrorism to one that has evolved into conventional law enforcement criminal investigations. Fusion centers have generated controversy in the widespread use of covert technologies to collect information on individuals and groups who may be engaging in activities that are protected by the Constitution.

I Institution and Rationale

Originally established in response to the terrorist attacks on the World Trade Center towers and the Pentagon on September 11, 2001, "fusion centers" were intended to "blend relevant law enforcement and intelligence information analysis and coordinate security measures to reduce threats in their communities."[1] H.R.1, the Implementing Recommendations of the 9/11 Commission Act of 2007, directed the secretary of the Department of Homeland Security (DHS) "to establish a State, Local, and Regional Fusion Center Initiative." It further directed "(1) the Under Secretary to assign officers and intelligence analysts from DHS components to such centers; and (2) the Secretary to develop qualifying criteria for a fusion center to participate in assigning DHS officers or intelligence analysts."[2] The act provided funding, personnel, and policy infrastructure for the establishment of fusion centers nationwide.

There are currently fifty-three so-called primary fusion centers that have been established in forty-nine of the fifty states (Wyoming does not have a fusion center), as well as in the District of Columbia, Guam, Puerto Rico, and the U.S. Virgin Islands. These are referred to by DHS as "state and major urban area fusion centers." These primary fusion centers receive the bulk of DHS resources that are allocated to fusion centers and have personnel from the DHS Office of Intelligence and Analysis (I&A) assigned there. DHS I&A is required to provide intelligence officers to each primary (and some recognized)

† Associate Professor and Program Director, Criminology & Criminal Justice Graduate Program, Merrimack College.

1 *DHS Strengthens Intel Sharing at State and Local Fusion Centers*, Department of Homeland Security (2006), https://www.hsdl.org/?view&did=476394.

2 H.R.1 – Implementing Recommendations of the 9/11 Commission Act of 2007, Pub. L. No. 110–53 (2007), https://www.congress.gov/bill/110th-congress/house-bill/1.

fusion centers, and the undersecretary for I&A is the executive agent for federal support to fusion centers.

Additionally, there are twenty-five "recognized fusion centers" that have been established by state and local governments. According to the DHS:

> Primary fusion centers serve as the focal points within the state and local environment for the receipt, analysis, gathering, and sharing of threat-related information and have additional responsibilities related to the coordination of critical operational capabilities across the statewide fusion process with other recognized fusion centers.[3]

Thus, California has six fusion centers (one "primary" and five "recognized"); Texas has seven fusion centers (one "primary" and six "recognized"); Florida, Missouri, Ohio, and Pennsylvania each have three fusion centers; and Massachusetts, Michigan, Wisconsin, Illinois, Virginia, and Nevada each have two fusion centers. There are currently seventy-eight fusion centers in the United States that constitute the National Network of Fusion Centers (NNFC).

According to the General Accounting Office (GAO):

> Recognition as a fusion center within the National Network generally requires that the governor of the state make this formal designation; a state or local governmental agency oversees and manages the center; the center has plans and procedures to function as a focal point for sharing law enforcement, homeland security, public safety, and terrorism information; and the center has achieved requisite baseline capabilities as DHS – on behalf of federal interagency partners – determines through an annual assessment of each fusion center's capabilities. A state or local law enforcement official generally serves as the center director. ... Analyst positions within these centers often make up a substantial portion of the staffing and typically include a combination of state, local, and federal personnel.[4]

Fusion centers operate in what is known as the Federal Information Sharing Environment (ISE). The "environment" is a virtual one that is "designed to facilitate the sharing of terrorism and homeland security information among all relevant entities through the combination of information sharing policies, procedures, and technologies."[5] Participation in the ISE requires the establishment of an agency privacy policy in order to exchange intelligence and other information in the ISE. Fusion centers are also required to have a trained privacy officer.

Fusion centers are "owned" by the state and local governments that have established them, and they are funded in part by federal grant monies, specifically through the Homeland Security Grant Program (HSGP). Fusion centers do not receive funds directly through the HSGP; rather, designated agencies at the state level that are responsible for the allocation of funds received through the HSGP, as well as local or county departments with similar grant disbursement responsibilities, determine the allocation

[3] *Fusion Center Locations and Contact Information*, Department of Homeland Security (2016), http://www.dhs.gov/fusion-center-locations-and-contact-information.

[4] U.S. Gov't Accountability Office, GAO-15–155, Information Sharing: DHS Is AssessingFusion Center Capabilities and Results, but Needs to More Accurately Account for Federal Funding Provided to Centers 6 (Nov. 2014).

[5] *Department of Homeland Security Federal Information Sharing Environment Privacy and Civil Liberties Policy*, Department of Homeland Security 1 (Aug. 31, 2015), https://www.dhs.gov/publication/department-homeland-security-federal-information-sharing-environment-privacy-and-civil.

of funds to the state and major urban area fusion centers. Fusion centers request the funds through the appropriate state or local designated entity, articulating and justifying each request through a process referred to as an "investment justification."[6] For example, in 2010 the General Accounting Office reported that of the fifty-two fusion centers that responded to a budgetary survey conducted by DHS, the federal government funded 61 percent ($62 million) of their operating budgets and states funded 29 percent ($30 million), with 10 percent of fusion center operating budgets being locally funded ($10 million).[7]

According to a 2014 GAO audit, the federal government had assigned 288 personnel to fusion centers in 2013. According to that report, the number of federal personnel assigned to state and major urban area fusion centers had risen to 366, with 116 Department of Justice (DOJ) personnel so assigned along with 241 DHS representatives (9 were from other federal agencies). The GAO further reported that the federal agencies that had deployed personnel to the fusion centers – DHS's Office of Intelligence and Analysis (I&A), the Federal Bureau of Investigation (FBI), Customs and Border Protection (CBP), Immigration and Customs Enforcement (ICE), and the Bureau of Alcohol, Firearms, and Explosives (ATF) – had all provided adequate guidance and support to the fusion centers to ensure that federal personnel were being utilized appropriately and provided with clear direction as to their responsibilities and roles.

II Tradecraft and the Intelligence Community

David Carter has written extensively about intelligence collection at the state, local, and tribal law enforcement (SLTLE) levels and describes two broad classes of intelligence.[8] The first is intelligence as a "discipline, which refers to the set of rules, processes, and lexicon of the intelligence function."[9] He identifies three types of intelligence that SLTLE and fusion center analysts may collect: "1. Law enforcement (or criminal) intelligence, 2. Homeland Security – also known as 'all-hazards' – intelligence, and 3. National Security Intelligence."[10]

The second broad class of intelligence, according to Carter, refers to the "application of intelligence," i.e., the articulation of the particular nexus to a specific criminal activity that the intelligence provides. For example, analysts who receive intelligence regarding activities of outlaw motorcycle gangs (OMGs) must be familiar with the culture, inner workings, symbols, jargon, history, and other relevant characteristics of OMGs generally, and specific OMGs in particular, in order to link the intelligence to criminal activity.

Carter has defined law enforcement intelligence as "the product of an analytic process that provides an integrated perspective to disparate information about crime, crime trends, crime and security threats, and conditions associated with criminality."[11]

6 GAO-15-155, *supra*, note 5, at 10.

7 U.S. Gov't Accountability Office, GAO-10-972, Information Sharing: Federal Agencies Are Helping Fusion Centers Build and Sustain Capabilities and Protect Privacy, but Could Better Measure Results 16 (Sept. 2010), http://www.gao.gov/assets/320/310268.pdf.

8 *Law Enforcement Intelligence: A Guide for State, Local, and Tribal Law Enforcement Agencies* (2d ed. 2009), https://it.ojp.gov/documents/d/e050919201-IntelGuide_web.pdf.

9 *Id.* at 10.

10 *Id.*

11 David L. Carter, *Law Enforcement Intelligence: A Guide for State, Local, and Tribal Law Enforcement Agencies*, 9 (8th ed. 2002), https://fas.org/irp/agency/doj/lei/guide.pdf.

He advises careful distinction between the uses of the terms "information sharing" and "intelligence sharing," as information and intelligence have differing procedural and legal requirements and safeguards (for example, intelligence collection is governed by the provisions of 28 CFR Part 23). "Intelligence" necessarily contains analysis, assessment, estimation, and prediction or "forecasting." "Information," on the other hand, is raw data, such as driver's records; motor vehicle, watercraft, and aircraft registration information; surveillance reports; transcripts of interviews and interrogations; and banking and financial record information – data that must be analyzed and synthesized in order to create an intelligence product.[12]

Homeland security, or "all hazards" intelligence, is, according to Carter, "the collection and analysis of information concerned with noncriminal domestic threats to critical infrastructure, community health, and public safety for the purpose of preventing the threat or mitigating the effects of the threat."[13] This type of intelligence may overlap with law enforcement intelligence when pertaining to criminal activity that may also pose a threat to critical infrastructure or public health, e.g., intelligence related to a biological or chemical attack on the civilian population or intelligence pertaining to the use of explosives to blow up a bridge.

National Security Intelligence (NSI) is not ordinarily within the purview of state and major urban area fusion centers; nonetheless, fusion center personnel need be knowledgeable about what constitutes NSI should they become aware of intelligence or information that may have value to the Intelligence Community (IC).[14] One of the main reasons I&A personnel are assigned to fusion centers is to identify national security intelligence information (Intelligence Information Reports, or IIR) and to ensure it is provided to the intelligence community. Also, fusion center personnel who are working on Organized Crime Drug Enforcement Task Forces with DEA personnel or those working with FBI personnel on Joint Terrorism Task Forces may have access to NSI, since both the DEA and the FBI are members of the IC.[15]

> NSI embodies both policy intelligence and military intelligence. Policy intelligence is concerned with threatening actions and activities of entities hostile to the U.S., while military intelligence focuses on hostile entities, weapons systems, warfare capabilities, and order of battle.[16]

As we shall see in Section III, fusion center analysts and law enforcement personnel assigned to state and major urban area fusion centers should be aware of the potential for constitutional implications in the use of NSI for criminal investigative and criminal intelligence purposes, since the procedural safeguards that protect individuals and

[12] *Id.* at 12.

[13] *Id.* at 14.

[14] The IC consists of seventeen member agencies: Air Force Intelligence, Army Intelligence, Central Intelligence Agency, Coast Guard Intelligence, Defense Intelligence Agency, Department of Energy, Department of Homeland Security, Department of State, Department of the Treasury, Drug Enforcement Administration, Federal Bureau of Investigation, Marine Corps Intelligence, National Geospatial-Intelligence Agency, National Reconnaissance Office, National Security Agency/Central Security Office, Navy Intelligence, and Office of the Director of National Intelligence. The United States Intelligence Community Intelligence Careers, https://www.intelligencecareers.gov/icmembers.html (last visited July 4, 2016).

[15] Carter, *supra* note 12.

[16] *Id.* at 15.

groups as articulated in 28 CFR Part 23, in the Constitution, and in the U.S. Supreme Court and appellate court case law do not necessarily apply to the collection of NSI.

III Governance, Regulation, and Operations

Fusion centers, like other "criminal intelligence systems," are governed and regulated by what is known as 28 CFR Part 23 if they receive funding support under the Omnibus Crime Control and Safe Streets Act of 1968. The CFR is the Code of Federal Regulations, which is a series of fifty titles codifying administrative law promulgated by the executive branch of government. The CFR provides official government policy for dealing with everything from fisheries and wildlife to banking to the collection of criminal intelligence. Fusion center personnel are required to undergo extensive training in the provisions of 28 CFR Part 23, and the regulations contained therein provide the foundation for the collection of criminal intelligence in order to ensure that "all criminal intelligence systems operating through [federal] support ... under the Omnibus Crime Control and Safe Streets Act of 1968 ... are utilized in conformance with the privacy and constitutional rights of individuals."[17]

According to 28 CFR Part 23.3(b), the following definitions apply to the policies contained therein:

(1) *Criminal Intelligence System* or *Intelligence System* means the arrangements, equipment, facilities, and procedures used for the receipt, storage, interagency exchange or dissemination, and analysis of criminal intelligence information;
(2) *Interjurisdictional Intelligence System* means an intelligence system which involves two or more participating agencies representing different governmental units or jurisdictions;
(3) *Criminal Intelligence Information* means data which has been evaluated to determine that it:
    (i) Is relevant to the identification of and the criminal activity engaged in by an individual who or organization which is reasonably suspected of involvement in criminal activity, and
    (ii) Meets criminal intelligence system submission criteria;
(4) *Participating Agency* means an agency of local, county, State, Federal, or other governmental unit which exercises law enforcement or criminal intelligence information through an interjurisdictional intelligence system. A participating agency may be a member or a nonmember of an interjurisdictional intelligence system;
(5) *Intelligence Project* or *Project* means the organizational unit which operates an intelligence system on behalf of and for the benefit of a single agency or the organization which operates an interjurisdictional intelligence system on behalf of a group of participating agencies; and
(6) *Validation of Information* means the procedures governing the periodic review of criminal intelligence information to assure its continuing compliance with system submission criteria established by Regulation or program policy.

[17] Criminal Intelligence Systems Operating Policies, 28 C.F.R. § 23 (2016), https://www.iir.com/28CFR_Program/28CFR_Resources/Executive_Order/.

Thus, 28 CFR Part 23.3 defines criminal intelligence systems and interjurisdictional intelligence systems, what qualifies as criminal intelligence data and an intelligence project, and prescribes which agencies are covered by the policy and what procedures apply to the ongoing review of intelligence data collected. The operating principles governing the collection of intelligence data by criminal intelligence systems are contained in 28 CFR Part 23.20. A partial list of these principles establishes that:

(a) A project shall collect and maintain criminal intelligence information concerning an individual only if there is reasonable suspicion that the individual is involved in criminal conduct or activity and the information is relevant to that criminal conduct or activity.

(b) A project shall not collect or maintain criminal intelligence information about the political, religious or social views, associations, or activities of any individual or any group, association, corporation, business, partnership, or other organization unless such information directly relates to criminal conduct or activity and there is reasonable suspicion that the subject of the information is or may be involved in criminal conduct or activity.

(c) *Reasonable Suspicion* or *Criminal Predicate* is established when information exists which establishes sufficient facts to give a trained law enforcement or criminal investigative agency officer, investigator, or employee a basis to believe that there is a reasonable possibility that an individual or organization is involved in a definable criminal activity or enterprise. In an interjurisdictional intelligence system, the project is responsible for establishing the existence of reasonable suspicion of criminal activity either through examination of supporting information submitted by a participating agency or by delegation of this responsibility to a properly trained participating agency which is subject to routine inspection and audit procedures established by the project.

(d) A project shall not include in any criminal intelligence system information which has been obtained in violation of any applicable Federal, State, or local law or ordinance. In an interjurisdictional intelligence system, the project is responsible for establishing that no information is entered in violation of Federal, State, or local laws, either through examination of supporting information submitted by a participating agency or by delegation of this responsibility to a properly trained participating agency which is subject to routine inspection and audit procedures established by the project.

(e) A project or authorized recipient shall disseminate criminal intelligence information only where there is a need to know and a right to know the information in the performance of a law enforcement activity.

Thus, the operating principles dictate the circumstances under which federally funded criminal intelligence systems are allowed to collect, analyze, store, and disseminate intelligence information on individuals and groups. There must be reasonable suspicion of criminal activity, and the information collected must relate to that activity. Information shall not be collected regarding political, religious, or social beliefs or activities unless those activities are related to criminal activity. Reasonable suspicion and criminal predicate are defined. Information that is obtained illegally cannot be included in any intelligence product or stored in any intelligence database. And the articulations of the "need to know" and "right to know" principles are provided. It should be noted that 28 CFR

Part 23, originally issued in 1980, has not been updated since 1993, with the exception of the release of a 1998 clarification from the Office of Justice Programs regarding identifiable information and the definition of criminal intelligence systems.[18]

IV Privacy

The Homeland Security Act of 2002 called upon the secretary of DHS to appoint a "privacy officer" whose responsibilities include:

> (1) Assuring that the use of technologies sustain, and do not erode, privacy protections relating to the use, collection, and disclosure of personal information; (2) assuring that personal information contained in Privacy Act systems of records is handled in full compliance with fair information practices as set out in the Privacy Act of 1974.[19]

The DHS Privacy Office is responsible for privacy training and compliance with privacy policies in the collection of information and intelligence at fusion centers, for the protection of so-called personally identifiable information (PII), and for ensuring that information is collected in accordance with Fair Information Practice Principles (FIPPs). The DHS defines PII as:

> (A)ny information that permits the identity of an individual to be directly or indirectly inferred, including any information that is linked or linkable to that individual, regardless of whether the individual is a U.S. citizen, legal permanent resident, visitor to the U.S., or employee or contractor to the Department.[20]

PII includes such obvious information as one's name, telephone number, email address, or home address, and fusion centers are required by law to have privacy policies in place that protect PII and place restrictions upon the circumstances under which PII may be collected and stored in fusion center databases.

DHS further identifies "Sensitive Personally Identifiable Information" (SPII) as "Personally Identifiable Information, which if lost, compromised, or disclosed without authorization, could result in substantial harm, embarrassment, inconvenience, or unfairness to an individual."[21] Examples of SPII are one's passport, driver's license, social security, or alien registration number; bank account number; and biometric identifier. Examples of identifiers that, if paired with another identifier, become SPII are one's criminal history, mother's maiden name, date of birth, account passwords, medical information, last four digits of a social security number, and sexual orientation.[22]

Every state and major urban area fusion center has a designated privacy officer whose responsibility it is to ensure compliance with the provisions of the Privacy Act of 1974 as well as other applicable federal laws and regulations relating to privacy in the collection

18 Office of Justice Programs, Policy Clarification (1998), 1–2, https://www.iir.com/Documents/28CFR/1998PolicyClarification_28CFRPart23.pdf.

19 Homeland Security Act of 2002, Pub. L. No. 107–296 (2002), https://www.dhs.gov/xlibrary/assets/hr_5005_enr.pdf; *see also* Privacy Act of 1974, 5 U.S.C. § 552(a) (2009), https://www.gpo.gov/fdsys/pkg/USCODE-2012-title5/pdf/USCODE-2012-title5-partI-chap5-subchapII-sec552a.pdf.

20 *Handbook for Safeguarding Sensitive Personally Identifiable Information*, Department of Homeland Security, 4 (Mar. 2012), https://www.dhs.gov/sites/default/files/publications/Handbook%20for%20Safeguarding%20Sensitive%20PII_0.pdf.

21 *Id.*

22 *Id.*

of PII and SPII. Records collected by a federal government agency on individuals are required under the Privacy Act to be published and available to the public in what is generally referred to as a System of Records Notice, or SORN. The relevant SORN provides the authorization for fusion center personnel operating under federal authority to search federal databases for PII.[23]

In the collection of PII at fusion centers, I&A personnel are required to use the information solely for certain purposes that are approved by the DHS Office of Intelligence and Analysis. They are also required to identify the SORN that authorizes the collection of the PII and to share the PII only if the SORN authorizes such sharing. They must also minimize the PII when sharing, keep a record of agencies and personnel with whom the PII has been shared, and record the justification for the sharing.[24]

V Academic Research

Priscilla Regan, Torin Monahan, and Krista Craven have researched so-called suspicious activity reports (SARs) that are collected, analyzed, classified, and stored on DHS databases in the ISE by fusion center intelligence analysts.[25] Law enforcement has long collected information on "suspicious" activity and persons, but SARs reports have emerged as troublesome and questionable to those concerned with civil rights, civil liberties, and privacy. Additionally, security issues have been raised with the multiple levels of access to SAR information across the spectrum of agencies in the ISE. SARs are reports of activities and behaviors that are believed to be related to terrorist or criminal activities, often generated through the observations of those with little if any training or experience in identifying such activities. Illustrative is DHS's "If you see something, say something" campaign.

Regan, Monahan, and Craven see four privacy concerns with fusion centers' collection, retention, storage, and dissemination of information contained in SARs. First, "these reports are often the result of the reporting person's stereotypes or fears, resulting in racial or ethnic profiling."[26] Second, the individuals (e.g., delivery people, landlords, and neighbors) who are supplying information to authorities may gather that information through access points that are otherwise protected from government intrusion and observation without a search warrant. The third area of privacy concern relates to the storage of PII that may be contained in a SAR database that is searchable by others in the ISE: information such as names, license plate numbers, smart phone data, and credit card numbers that are linked to a particular individual who has been identified as possibly being involved in terrorist or criminal activities "without that person's knowledge or opportunity to challenge the classification or interpretation."[27] Their final privacy concern involves law enforcement and DHS compliance with the provisions of the Fourth Amendment as they pertain to evaluating information that purports to establish the existence of "suspicious activity." In particular, they observe that SARs have "inherent

23 An updated list of DHS and DHS component SORNs is available at https://www.dhs.gov/system-records-notices-sorns.

24 *Handbook for Safeguarding Sensitive Personally Identifiable Information*, *supra* note 20.

25 Priscilla M. Regan et al., *Constructing the Suspicious: Data Production, Circulation, and Interpretation by DHS Fusion Centers*, 47 Administration & Society 740 (Aug. 2015).

26 *Id.* at 749.

27 *Id.* at 750.

limitations" in that they "fundamentally ... remain tips, based on the impressions of individuals – ordinary citizens, service personnel, commercial employees, and law enforcement – who make a judgment that something seems 'suspicious' and are motivated to report the activity."[28] According to these authors, the information aggregation and analysis process generally fails to scrutinize these sources with the constitutional rigor courts would apply when assessing whether information from these sources is sufficient to provide grounds for a finding of reasonable suspicion.

Further, there is the definitional problem of what actually constitutes "suspicious activities." The Congressional Research Service has reported that among the activities that have been labeled as suspicious are the following "suspect actions":

> Uses binoculars or cameras, takes measurements, takes pictures or video footage, draws diagrams or takes notes, pursues specific training or education that indicate suspicious motives (flight training, weapons training, etc.), espouses extremist views.[29]

According to the 2014 National Network of Fusion Centers Final Report, "the percentage of Suspicious Activity Reporting submitted by fusion centers that resulted in the initiation or enhancement of a Federal Bureau of Investigation (FBI) investigation increased from 3.3 percent in 2013 to 5.5 percent in 2014."[30] Critics who call into question the value of the SARs in identifying potential terrorist related activity may be justifiably concerned that the FBI is discounting almost 95 percent of State, Local, Tribal, and Territorial (SLTT) fusion center suspicious activity report submissions as not having any investigatory value. The report offers what is perhaps a weak qualification: "The Nationwide Suspicious Activity Reporting Initiative continues to mature."[31]

Torin Monahan and Neal Palmer analyzed media reports on DHS fusion centers from 2002 to 2008 in order to understand the evolving roles and functions that emerged for the nascent multijurisdictional intelligence gathering agencies in the aftermath of the 9/11 attacks and the War on Terror.[32] Having originally been established to gather intelligence related to potential terrorist activities, most fusion centers had morphed into more traditional law enforcement oriented criminal intelligence gathering entities. This "all crimes and all hazards" model reported on activities that had, at best, a tenuous connection to terrorism.[33]

These authors discovered three major problems plaguing fusion centers – problems that, it will be argued further in this chapter, have remained chronic to the present. The first category of concern, according to Monahan and Palmer, lies in the overall ineffectiveness of fusion centers. Operating expenses for fusion centers are shared between state and local governments and DHS. DHS grants funnel federal funds that are frequently directed at terrorist threats that are not specified or national issues that are unrelated to

[28] *Id.* at 757.

[29] Jerome P. Bjelopera, *Terrorism Information Sharing and the Nationwide Suspicious Activity Report Initiative: Background and Issues for Congress*, Congressional Research Service, 8 (Dec. 28, 2011), https://www.fas.org/sgp/crs/intel/R40901.pdf.

[30] *2014 National Network of Fusion Centers Final Report*, Department of Homeland Security, iv (2015), https://www.archives.gov/isoo/oversight-groups/sltps-pac/national-network-of-fusion-centers-2014.pdf.

[31] *Id.* at v.

[32] Torin Monahan & Neal A. Palmer, *The Emerging Politics of DHS Fusion Centers*, 40 Security Dialogue 617 (Dec. 2009).

[33] *Id.* at 625.

local or state issues in a particular area. "In 2007, for instance, Massachusetts received funding that required the state to develop a plan for responding to improvised explosive devices (IEDs), even though local and state authorities had no existing intelligence pointing to such a threat."[34]

Monahan and Palmer argue that fusion centers could be more effective if states had more say in how allocated funds were used. DHS funding mandates contribute to fusion center ineffectiveness. For example, "on the West Coast, authorities were charged with developing hurricane-evacuation plans in reaction to the muddled government response to Hurricane Katrina on the Gulf Coast, even though states in the West face little danger from hurricanes."[35]

State and local authorities also complain that federal resources are not being directed where they are needed, and thus represent unfunded mandates. For example, "medically related projects, such as mass-casualty response and hospital-patient tracking in the event of an attack, were bypassed in a Virginia grant application to the DHS to the chagrin of hospital representatives."[36]

A second issue of concern regarding fusion centers for Monahan and Palmer is mission creep, which is the extension of the activities of fusion centers in intelligence gathering related to terrorist activities to an "all crimes, all threats, all hazards" model that gathers intelligence related to gangs, drugs, human trafficking, computer fraud, racketeering, and organized crime – all tenuously related to the original mandate in the establishment of fusion centers. The authors observe that

> the way fusion centers are organized also appears to encourage mission creep. Minimal guidelines at the federal level mean that fusion centers develop with different foci and different organizational emplacements. Because police personnel and other employees at fusion centers draw upon their local contexts and perceptions of need, this has led to greater police involvement in counter-terrorism development, as well as to police agencies utilizing counter-terrorism tools against more traditional crimes.[37]

A final issue of concern raised in this research is the one most frequently cited regarding fusion centers and the activities they routinely engage in: widespread, extensive, and ubiquitous surveillance. Surveillance and the pervasive practice, across the spectrum of fusion center tradecraft, of collecting, analyzing, storing, and disseminating untold amounts of information and data on private individuals and groups is of paramount concern to observers and critics. The potential for the violation of the civil rights and civil liberties as well as the privacy of individuals and groups engaging in constitutionally protected activities cannot be overstated.

The embedding of corporate and private security personnel in fusion centers only adds to this concern, particularly when these individuals are not vetted properly or lack requisite government security clearances.[38] Further, Monahan and Palmer emphasize that

> the range of people who now have access to sensitive information, and the expansion of access to people who previously did not have access to files without concurrent ethics

[34] *Id.* at 622.
[35] *Id.*
[36] *Id.*
[37] *Id.* at 626.
[38] *Id.* at 623.

> guidelines, particularly at local and state levels, provides further credence to fears of intelligence abuse and privacy violations.[39]

Priscilla Regan and Torin Monahan (2014) examined the issue of accountability given the multiple layers of jurisdictional authority that exist in fusion centers: federal, state, regional, county, tribal, and local.[40] They sought answers to two primary questions: "What types of information sharing are occurring with – or enabled by – fusion centers?" and "What factors contribute to the information-sharing practices of fusion centers?"[41] These authors point to the uniqueness of each of the fusion centers examined and the lack of governing federal policies regarding staffing, organizational structure, or the responsibilities of the various agencies staffing the fusion centers. Thus, no two are alike. They did find that most of the fusion centers studied were controlled by state or local law enforcement agencies. "Most fusion centers in our study emerged from a law enforcement context, are directed by someone with law enforcement background, are co-located with local law enforcement entities, and focus on local law enforcement activities."[42]

Personnel assigned to fusion centers vary considerably from state to state, although all centers in the study had DHS and FBI personnel assigned. Some fusion centers had CBP, ATF, DEA, and ICE agents assigned to them.

> But the great majority of staff at the fusion centers were from local law enforcement, with other staff from a range of state agencies such as public health, corrections, parole and probation, fire, emergency management, environmental protection, highway, and gaming and fishing.[43]

This organizational model most closely resembles "opportunistic (or dispersed) federalism … where hierarchical notions are de-emphasized and instead the focus is on more flexible collaborations involving many parties with different roles and responsibilities determining goals, priorities, and implementation regimes."[44] Thus, in order to forge a productive and functioning collaboration among federal, state, county, local, and tribal (mostly law enforcement) entities, a "top down," vertical, and hierarchical organizational model was seen as counterproductive to the cooperation, lateral communication, and sharing seen necessary to "fuse" and synthesize intelligence.

What suffered in the trade-off, according to Regan and Monahan, was accountability. Fusion centers have been criticized for having little transparency, public or private oversight, or accountability. They have also been cited for failing to share available information with agencies having a clear operational interest in relevant intelligence. This was made clear in the aftermath of the bombing attack at the Boston Marathon on April 15, 2013, when it was revealed that the FBI had investigated one of the bombers but had failed to share this information with state or local authorities. The Boston Regional Intelligence Center (BRIC), a "recognized" fusion center, and part of the Joint Terrorism

39 *Id.* at 629.

40 Priscilla Regan and Torin Monahan, *Fusion Center Accountability and Intergovernmental Information Sharing*, 44 Publius 475 (2014).

41 *Id.* at 478.

42 *Id.* at 480.

43 *Id.* at 481.

44 *Id.* at 477.

Task Force (JTTF)), prepared a threat assessment of the marathon that revealed no discernible terrorist threat, despite having FBI personnel assigned.

Regan and Monahan conclude that there is little managerial control of fusion centers at the DHS level and little substantive guidance provided to fusion centers nationwide. The attempt by DHS "to strengthen the role of the national government in relation to that of state and local government ... has been unsuccessful" as a result of resistance by state and local government, the complex and nuanced relationships among personnel and the agencies staffing fusion centers, and the history of the interaction among law enforcement agencies at the federal, state, and local levels.[45] The authors call for some measure of "shared professional norms" in order for fusion centers to be successful in the future. Since fusion centers are dominated by local law enforcement, with its long tradition of local control over training, funding, priorities, staffing, and organization, such sharing of professional norms seems unlikely. And without such sharing "the collaborating units that constitute fusion centers will not be able to establish a common means of achieving accountability."[46]

VI Accountability and Performance

A 2012 report from the U.S. Senate Permanent Subcommittee on Investigations found that fusion centers nationwide had largely failed to deliver any useful intelligence relating to terrorist-related activities and that the centers frequently violated civil rights and civil liberties protections in collecting information on individuals and groups. The report also concluded that DHS and the fusion centers resisted congressional oversight and often wasted tax dollars. According to the Senate report, "The Department of Homeland Security estimates that it has spent somewhere between $289 million and $1.4 billion in public funds to support state and local fusion centers since 2003, broad estimates that differ by over $1 billion."[47]

The Senate investigation found that DHS intelligence officers assigned to state and local fusion centers produced intelligence of "uneven quality" that was "oftentimes shoddy, rarely timely, sometimes endangering citizens' civil liberties and Privacy Act protections, occasionally taken from already-published public sources, and more often than not unrelated to terrorism."[48] The investigation also sharply questioned the DHS oversight of expenditures at state and major urban area fusion centers, finding that in five of the fusion centers examined, federal funds were used to purchase dozens of flat screen TVs, two sport utility vehicles, cell phone tracking devices, and other surveillance equipment unrelated to the analytical mission of an intelligence center.[49]

The two-year investigation sought answers to three basic questions regarding the operation of the fusion centers: Did DHS coordinate with the fusion centers to obtain useful intelligence that it then shared with relevant and affected federal, state, and local

45 *Id.* at 494.
46 *Id.*
47 U.S. Senate Permanent Subcommittee on Investigations, Federal Support for and Involvement in State and Local Fusion Centers, 1 (Oct. 3, 2012), https://www.hsgac.senate.gov/subcommittees/investigations/media/investigative-report-criticizes-counterterrorism-reporting-waste-at-state-and-local-intelligence-fusion-centers.
48 *Id.*
49 *Id.*

agencies? Did DHS effectively oversee the distribution of federal funds to the fusion centers? And were the fusion centers effective in collecting timely and accurate intelligence relating to counterterrorism activities? In response to the first question, the subcommittee found that "DHS's involvement with fusion centers appeared not to have yielded timely, useful terrorism-related intelligence for the Federal intelligence community."[50] As to the second issue, the Senate investigation revealed that "DHS did not adequately monitor the amount of funding it directed to support fusion centers."[51] As for the third question posed, the investigation reported that "many centers didn't consider counterterrorism an explicit part of their mission, and Federal officials said some were simply not concerned with doing counterterrorism work."[52]

In response to a request from Congress, the General Accounting Office conducted a performance audit of DHS fusion centers in 2014 and reported the following. In 2010, the fusion centers, in collaboration with DHS and DOJ, established a set of four criteria to evaluate the performance of fusion centers called the "Baseline Capabilities for State and Major Urban Area Fusion Centers." The criteria (or capabilities) were (1) receive (meaning the ability to receive classified and unclassified information from federal partners); (2) analyze (meaning the ability to conduct relevant threat assessment from the intelligence received; (3) disseminate (meaning the ability to disseminate and distribute threat information throughout the jurisdiction to affected agencies); and (4) gather (meaning the ability to receive information locally, conduct threat assessments, and to prepare intelligence products for distribution).

The 2014 audit reported that an assessment conducted in 2013 on the identified baseline capabilities found that "the average overall capability score reported for the National Network was 91.7 out of 100. . . . This score represents an improvement of about 3 points from the 2012 average score of 88.4 and continues an upward trend from the average national score of 76.8 identified in 2011."[53] Thus, the GAO found continued improvement for the four identified baseline capabilities, but raised questions as to the score's applicability to the wide range of other functions performed at fusion centers, particularly since the responsibilities, functions, and duties of fusion centers vary considerably from jurisdiction to jurisdiction. The GAO called for the inclusion of other performance measures in future iterations of the assessment process, particularly as they relate to planning and subsequent outcomes.

What the GAO audit identified as an area of concern was that "FEMA could not reliably report on the amount of federal grants used to support centers, which is needed to help inform future investment decisions."[54] The Federal Emergency Management Agency (FEMA) is the lead DHS component responsible for the distribution of funds through the HSGP to the fusion centers. The audit found that in 2012 numerous states had at least $60 million in grant funds with accounting questions. Congress and many other officials, as well as the media, have called into question the disbursement of funds through the HSGP and state and local sources to the fusion centers.

50 *Id.* at 8.
51 *Id.*
52 *Id.*
53 GAO-15-155, *supra*, note 5, at 11.
54 *Id.*

According to the 2014 National Network of Fusion Centers Final Report, fusion centers received an average score of 96.3 out of 100 in the Fusion Center Performance Program (FCPP), a self-assessment tool that "evaluates fusion centers' achievement of capabilities critical to the fusion process. It also strives to ensure functional consistency across the National Network, regardless of the fusion center size, scope, geography, or mission."[55] The average FCPP score in 2013 was 91.7, and DHS points to this increase as evidence of the increased effectiveness of fusion centers.

The 2014 National Network of Fusion Centers Final Report also described the primary missions of centers as "counterterrorism" and "all-crimes" in 96.2 percent of fusion centers and "all-hazards" in 73.1 percent of fusion centers.[56] Additionally, almost three-quarters of SLTT fusion centers have an "all hazards" mission that includes areas such as fish and wildlife; chemical, biological, nuclear, and radiological threats; critical infrastructure; health care and public health; and tribal, emergency management, and maritime security.[57]

VII Questions about Efficacy, Privacy, and Compliance with Civil Rights and Civil Liberties Protections

Jason Barnosky, writing for the Brookings Institute, described the evolution of fusion centers from their initial stated mission of counterterrorism related intelligence gathering to one in which intelligence pertaining to nonterrorist threats such as criminal activity and natural disasters is collected, analyzed, and disseminated.[58] He observed the value potential for fusion centers' adoption of responsibilities in this area and the nationwide network of fusion centers' ability to channel information directly to the federal government as well as to affected local and regional communities. Barnosky also cited the benefit to state and major urban area fusion centers in having the support of more than three hundred representatives of the DEA, FBI, TSA, and the DHS Office of Intelligence and Analysis assigned to duties at the centers. He did acknowledge that problems with FEMA oversight of federal funds distributed to fusion centers continue to plague fusion centers. Barnosky also agreed with other observers who have criticized the fusion centers for deficiencies in adhering to privacy policies and respecting civil rights and civil liberties protections when collecting information on individuals and groups.

The American Civil Liberties Union (ACLU) filed a lawsuit in July of 2014 in California challenging the SAR program at fusion centers on behalf of five plaintiffs who "were all engaging in innocuous, lawful, and in some cases First Amendment–protected activity, such as photographing sites of aesthetic interest, playing video games, and waiting at a train station."[59] In that case, a federal judge ruled that the federal government

55 *2014 National Network of Fusion Centers Final Report*, *supra* note 30, at iv.

56 By 2016, virtually all of the state, local, tribal, and territorial fusion centers had adopted an "all crimes" mission in addition to their original mandate: counterterrorism.

57 *2014 National Network of Fusion Centers Final Report*, *supra* note 30, at 10.

58 *Fusion Centers: What's Working and What Isn't*, Brookings Institute (Mar. 17, 2015), http://www.brookings.edu/blogs/fixgov/posts/2015/03/17-fusion-centers-barnosky.

59 *Gill v. DOJ – Challenge to Government's Suspicious Activity Reporting Program*, American Civil Liberties Union, 1 (July 11, 2014), https://www.aclu.org/cases/gill-v-doj-challenge-governments-suspicious-activity-reporting-program?redirect=national-security/gill-v-doj-challenge-governments-suspicious-activity-reporting-program.

will have to produce information regarding the SAR program and to defend the practice and its legality in a public court proceeding, something that the ACLU has long sought. Earlier court decisions regarding SARs had largely shielded the government and fusion centers from having to defend the program publicly and from having to disclose information regarding SAR practices, which shroud the program in secrecy. Julia Harumi Mass, writing for the ACLU, notes that because "the government's loose standards define practically anything as suspicious, SARs end up targeting innocent, First Amendment–protected conduct and inviting racial and religious profiling."[60]

Fusion centers have engaged in the collection of information on individuals and groups and have been criticized for having strayed from an "all crimes" and "all hazards" mission to monitoring protests such as "Occupy" events that took place in scores of locations across the United States beginning in 2011. The *New York Times* obtained more than 4000 pages of documents in 2014 through Freedom of Information Act (FOIA) requests and discovered that, in Washington, "officials circulated descriptions of plans in Seattle for an anti-consumerist flash mob to dance to the rock anthem 'Invincible'." The Boston Regional Intelligence Center, one of the most widely recognized centers in the country, issued scores of bulletins listing hundreds of events including a protest of "irresponsible lending practices," a food drive, and multiple "yoga, faith & spirituality" classes.[61]

Fusion center responses to Occupy activities and other public gatherings varied from one location to another, as do many of the intelligence gathering activities across the spectrum of the seventy-eight fusion centers nationwide, resulting in a lack of consistency and uniformity in the gathering of information that critics often cite as evidence of flawed and inconsistent policies and practices. Supporters of local and regional variations in information gathering practices counter, however, that issues and mandates vary considerably across the spectrum of information gathering areas, and that such divergence in practice is solid intelligence gathering tradecraft.

According to the *New York Times*, the Delaware fusion center, in responding to an inquiry regarding its monitoring of Occupy protests, said, "Our fusion center has distanced itself from the movement because of 1st Amendment rights and because we have not seen any criminal activity to date."[62] Meanwhile, in Milwaukee, officials reported that a group intended to sing holiday carols at "an undisclosed location of 'high visibility.'" "In Tennessee, an intelligence analyst sought information about whether groups concerned with animals, war, abortion or the Earth had been involved in protests."[63]

Other critics have questioned the role that the federal government is playing in local law enforcement operations in assigning federal law enforcement personnel and federal intelligence analysts to fusion centers and in providing the majority of funding for what are essentially state and local police department information "fishing" expeditions. Julian Sanchez, in writing for the Cato Institute about fusion centers, found it "absurd" that "the federal government is throwing 'homeland security' funds at institutions that,

60 *This Secret Domestic Surveillance Program Is About to Get Pulled Out of the Shadows*, American Civil Liberties Union, 1 (Feb. 25, 2015), https://www.aclu.org/blog/speakeasy/secret-domestic-surveillance-program-about-get-pulled-out-shadows.

61 Colin Moynihan, *Officials Cast Wide Net in Monitoring Occupy Protests*, N.Y. Times (May 22, 2014), at A12.

62 *Id.*

63 *Id.*

having proven hilariously incapable of making any contribution to counterterror efforts, instead busy themselves trawling Google for information about political rallies."[64]

Critics of fusion centers have also questioned the secrecy surrounding operational practices and policies in the data collection, intelligence analysis, and product dissemination enterprise at fusion centers. Michael German, writing for the Brennan Center for Justice, observed that "the excessive secrecy shrouding intelligence activities means Americans have little public information from which to evaluate whether the intelligence enterprise is worth the investment."[65]

In 2013, the Brennan Center for Justice issued a report on information sharing by law enforcement at the federal, state, and local levels, entitled "National Security and Local Police." The center conducted a study of nineteen fusion centers that were affiliated with sixteen "major police departments" and fourteen Joint Terrorism Task Forces (JTTFs). The report followed the April 15, 2013, terrorist attack at the Boston Marathon and the revelation that the FBI had investigated one of the bombers, Tamerlan Tsarnaev, and may not have shared that information with the local fusion center, the Boston Regional Intelligence Center (BRIC). What the report "found was organized chaos – a sprawling, federally subsidized, and loosely coordinated system designed to share information that is collected according to varying local standards."[66] Finding "serious flaws" that "may jeopardize both our safety and our civil liberties," the Brennan Center discovered an information sharing system plagued by an inability to engage effectively in even basic intelligence collection, analysis, and sharing. The center found that:

1. Information sharing among agencies is governed by inconsistent rules and procedures that encourage gathering useless or inaccurate information. This poorly organized system wastes resources and also risks masking crucial intelligence.
2. As an increasing number of agencies collect and share personal data on federal networks, inaccurate or useless information travels more widely. Independent oversight of fusion centers is virtually non-existent, compounding these risks.
3. Oversight has not kept pace, increasing the likelihood that intelligence operations violate civil liberties and harm critical police-community relations.[67]

The Brennan Center study called for a "fundamental overhaul of the standards for collecting and sharing intelligence and an oversight upgrade."[68] It observed, "We need a consistent, transparent standard for state and local intelligence activities," and "State and local governments should require police to have reasonable suspicion of criminal activity before collecting, maintaining, or disseminating personal information for intelligence purposes. The same rules should apply for data shared on federal networks and databases."[69] In advocating "stronger oversight," the center suggested, "Elected officials

64 *Your Homeland Security Dollars At Work: Tracking 'Occupy,'* Cato Institute, 1 (May 23, 2014), http://www.downsizinggovernment.org/our-homeland-security-dollars-work-tracking-occupy.

65 *The U.S. Intelligence Community Is Bigger Than Ever, but Is It Worth It?*Brennan Center for Justice, 1 (February 6, 2015), http://www.brennancenter.org/analysis/does-1-trillion-national-security-enterprise-actually-make-us-safer.

66 Michael Price, *National Security and Local Police*, New York: Brennan Center for Justice at New York University School of Law, 1 (Dec. 10, 2013), http://www.brennancenter.org/sites/default/files/publications/NationalSecurity_LocalPolice_web.pdf.

67 *Id.*

68 *Id.*

69 *Id.*

should consider establishing an independent police monitor, such as an inspector general. Fusion centers should be subject to regular, independent audits as a condition of future federal funding."[70]

The Electronic Privacy Information Center (EPIC) raised concerns beginning in 2008 regarding privacy issues at fusion centers. EPIC discovered a "Memorandum of Understanding" (MOU) between the Virginia Fusion Center and the Federal Bureau of Investigation that bound the Virginia Fusion Center not to disseminate "FBI information extracted from investigative and intelligence files ... outside the fusion center... or use as a basis for investigative or law enforcement activity by Fusion Center partners without the approval of the FBI Fusion Center representative."[71] The MOU further provided that with respect to any "request(s) for information under the Freedom of Information Act, the Privacy Act, or a Congressional inquiry, such disclosure may only be made after consultation with the FBI."[72]

In a lawsuit filed by EPIC in Virginia, the Virginia court ruled that the Virginia State Police must provide all documents related to the MOU in response to EPIC's Freedom of Information Act (FOIA) request, thus affirming EPIC's contention that fusion centers are required to comply with FOIA requirements.

VIII Threat Assessments: Controversy and Condemnation

Fusion centers have attracted notoriety in the controversial dissemination of intelligence products that describe individuals and groups who are engaging in constitutionally protected activities as potentially dangerous extremists. One particularly noteworthy report prepared and circulated by the Missouri Information and Analysis Center (MIAC) in 2009, entitled "The Modern Militia Movement," described supporters of the presidential candidates Bob Barr, Ron Paul, and Chuck Baldwin – as evidenced by the display of bumper stickers or "political paraphernalia" – as "right-wing extremists."[73] The report also described members of so-called antiabortion groups and those displaying the Gadsden Flag[74] as militants and potential extremists. The report caused much embarrassment for the then–Missouri Governor Jay Nixon as well as the then–Secretary of Homeland Security Janet Napolitano until it was discredited and pulled from MIAC's Web site in March of 2009, having by then been widely circulated.

Similarly, also in 2009, the DHS's Office of Intelligence and Analysis released a threat assessment report through its "Extremism and Radicalization Branch" that categorized "groups and individuals that are dedicated to a single issue, such as opposition to abortion or immigration" as right-wing extremists.[75] The DHS threat assessment also stated

70 *Id.*

71 *Memorandum of Understanding Between the Federal Bureau of Investigation and the Virginia Fusion Center*, Electronic Privacy Information Center (2008), https://epic.org/privacy/virginia_fusion/MOU.pdf.

72 *Id.* at 5.

73 *The Modern Militia Movement*, Missouri Information Analysis Center, 3–7 (2009), http://www.constitution.org/abus/le/miac-strategic-report.pdf.

74 The Gadsden Flag is a symbol of the American Revolution dating to 1775. It depicts a coiled rattlesnake and the words "Don't Tread on Me."

75 *Rightwing Extremism: Current Economic and Political Climate Fueling Resurgence in Radicalization and Recruitment*, Department of Homeland Security, 2 (Apr. 7, 2009), http://fas.org/irp/eprint/rightwing.pdf.

that "the return of military veterans facing significant challenges reintegrating into their communities could lead to the potential emergence of terrorist groups or lone wolf extremists capable of carrying out violent attacks."[76] This report was widely condemned by veterans groups and criticized by political leaders and the media, resulting in a public apology by Secretary Napolitano.

This threat assessment followed an earlier intelligence assessment by DHS's Office of Intelligence and Analysis (through its "Strategic Analysis Group, Homeland Environment and Threat Analysis Division") that described so-called as left-wing extremists those "animal rights and environmental extremists (that) seek to end the perceived abuse and suffering of animals and the degradation of the natural environment perpetrated by humans."[77] The report went on to describe what it labeled "anarchist extremists" as those who "generally embrace a number of radical philosophical components of anticapitalist, antiglobalization, communist, socialist, and other movements,"[78] all otherwise known as political ideologies or beliefs that are protected under the First Amendment. Once again, DHS found itself under the glare of the public spotlight for disseminating controversial intelligence products that it believed might be shielded from public scrutiny through its printed admonition "For Official Use Only."

A 2009 "threat assessment" report compiled by the Virginia Fusion Center (VFC) linked the Muslim American Society and the Council on American Islamic Relations to the Muslim Brotherhood, a suspected Middle East terrorist organization, in its undocumented and unsubstantiated "suspected associations."[79] According to a "tip" received by the VFC, "there are indications the Virginia Commonwealth University chapter of the Muslim Student Association is a front organization for the MB (Muslim Brotherhood) and is possibly involved with terrorism financing and recruitment."[80] The VFC also cited "environmental or animal rights movements" as potential extremist threats, and in particular cited the "Garbage Liberation Front," which the threat assessment reported as engaging in "dumpster diving, squatting and train hopping."[81] The VFC assessment also described the Nation of Islam as posing a potential terrorist threat and linked the religious group to the "New Black Panther Party," which it described as "engaging in organiz[ing] demonstrations across the nation that [call] for black empowerment and civil rights but include inflammatory, racist commentary." According to the report, the group "is actively attempting to recruit college students."[82] Some see this as a training issue for fusion center analysts, one compounded by having intelligence analysts reporting to police commanders who have received little if any training in intelligence tradecraft.

In February of 2016, following the shooting death of LaVoy Finicum by law enforcement officers in Oregon, and after a lengthy occupation of the Malheur Wildlife Refuge in Harney County by Finicum and others, the Utah Statewide Information and Analysis

[76] *Id.*

[77] *Leftwing Extremists Likely to Increase Use of Cyber Attacks over the Coming Decade*, Department of Homeland Security, 8 (Jan. 26, 2009), http://fas.org/irp/eprint/leftwing.pdf.

[78] *Id.*

[79] *2009 Virginia Terrorism Threat Assessment*, Virginia Fusion Center, 41 (2009), http://www.infowars.com/media/vafusioncenterterrorassessment.pdf.

[80] *Id.*

[81] *Id.* at 45.

[82] *Id.* at 49.

Center (SIAC, Utah's fusion center) issued a "situation report" in which it stated that although

> the SIAC assesses no credible threat to law enforcement or to public safety ... caravans of individuals traveling to the funeral services may be comprised of one or more armed extremists. Law enforcement should remain vigilant and aware that confrontation with these potentially volatile persons, may include more than one individual.[83]

The report goes on to cite "visual indicators of these potential extremists and disaffected individuals,"[84] including (once again) the Gadsden Flag, which depicts a coiled snake and the slogan "Don't Tread on Me" as a reference to the American Revolution.

IX "Countering Violent Extremism"

The role of fusion centers in efforts designated as "Countering Violent Extremism" (CVE) has also been called into question and sharply criticized, particularly by organizations such as the Council on American–Islamic Relations (CAIR). Citing the general lack of agreement as to what actually constitutes CVE, CAIR defines it as "the use of non-coercive means to dissuade individuals or groups from mobilizing towards violence and to mitigate recruitment, support, facilitation or engagement in ideologically motivated terrorism by non-state actors in furtherance of political objectives."[85] CAIR's report found "that the current program exclusively targets American Muslims[,] and that claims that the government is targeting all forms of violent extremism are inconsistently supported."

The CAIR report criticized a document generated by the National Counterterrorism Center[86] that offered "a scoring system for measuring an individual's susceptibility to violent extremism." That system includes measures such as "Parent–Child Bonding, Empathic Connection," "Presence of Emotional or Verbal Conflict in Family," and "Talk of Harming Self or Others," all inherently subjective and somewhat common aspects of the human condition and family relationships present in most Americans and their families at some point. Another so-called risk factor for involvement in "violent extremism" contained in the NCTC bulletin (and of concern to CAIR) is "Family Involvement in Community Cultural and Religious Activities," which CAIR views as problematic because "the person filling out the form may subjectively perceive mosque attendance itself as a risk factor."

The CVE mission is a shared mandate among member agencies of the intelligence community (IC), and while DHS fusion centers do not have sole responsibility for collecting intelligence on individuals and groups suspected of potential involvement in violent extremism, CVE does remain part of the core mission of the National Network of Fusion Centers. According to the DHS, "Fusion centers play an important role in countering

83 *SITUATION REPORT (SITREP) Funeral for LaVoy Finicum*, Utah Statewide Information and Analysis Center, 2 (2016), https://d1ai9qtk9p41kl.cloudfront.net/assets/db/14546824645342.pdf.

84 *Id.* at 3.

85 *Brief on Countering Violent Extremism (CVE)*, Council on American-Islamic Relations (2015), http://www.cair.com/government-affairs/13063-brief-on-countering-violent-extremism-cve.html.

86 *Countering Violent Extremism: A Guide for Practitioners and Analysts*, National Counterterrorism Center (May 2014), https://www.documentcloud.org/documents/1657824-cve-guide.html.

violent extremism and protecting local communities from violent crime through their daily operations, including gathering, analyzing, and sharing threat information."[87]

The CAIR report raised several objections and concerns regarding CVE strategies as they pertain to Muslims, mosques, and Muslim organizations, which CAIR contends are the primary targets of CVE initiatives:

1 CAIR believes government-led CVE is not an effective use of public resources;
2 CVE often relies on subjective measures and its efficacy is questionable;
3 CVE is generally driven by news events;
4 The current program exclusively targets American Muslims;
5 Claims that the government is targeting all forms of violent extremism are inconsistently supported at best; and
6 The current CVE initiative undermines our national ideals.

CAIR observed, according to its report, "that a key to diminishing the appeal of extremist inspired violence, which preys on the hopelessness and helplessness and perceived injustices of the disenfranchised, is to empower communities with means of expressing their dissent and criticism in healthy ways."[88]

Conclusion

Writing for the Center for Strategic and International Studies, Rick Nelson and Rob Wise chart the way forward for fusion centers. In their view, the greatest challenges ahead for fusion centers lie in the area of cybersecurity.[89] "The danger posed by cyberattacks extends not only to critical infrastructure systems such as the power grid and water systems but to the nation's economy as well," and it is here, they argue, that fusion centers "represent a valuable means of bringing federal counterterrorism agencies together with the state and local entities who are most likely to observe suspicious terrorism-related activity."[90] They see the need for transparency increasing as more information becomes available on U.S. persons. They argue that "DHS must take steps to ensure that increased controversy over how these centers are employed does not threaten their continued utility."[91] Of critical import, according to Nelson and Wise, is the need for "standardized intelligence training, in order to better equip those on the ground with a better understanding of the intelligence process and equalize some of the disparities between various fusion centers."[92] They also cite the need for increased fusion center engagement with the private sector, since most of the nation's critical infrastructure is held privately.

In order for fusion centers to remain viable for the future, they will need to provide timely, valuable, accurate, actionable, and standardized intelligence that is reflective

87 *The Role of Fusion Centers in Countering Violent Extremism Overview*, Department of Homeland Security (Oct. 2012), https://www.it.ojp.gov/documents/roleoffusioncentersincounteringviolentextremism_compliant.pdf.

88 *Brief on Countering Violent Extremism (CVE)*, *supra* note 86.

89 *Homeland Security at a Crossroads: Evolving DHS to Meet the Next Generation of Threats*, Center for Strategic & International Studies (2013), http://csis.org/publication/homeland-security-crossroads-evolving-dhs-meet-next-generation-threats.

90 *Id.* at 1.

91 *Id.*

92 *Id.*

of uniform professional standards regarding tradecraft. This intelligence must be rigorous in a strict adherence to civil rights and civil liberties protections contained in the Constitution and the Bill of Rights. Finally, intelligence products prepared in fusion centers must posit information on criminal activity that has demonstrable value and clearly apparent, as well as verifiably positive, results and outcomes. Absent these criteria, fusion centers may not successfully confront strident calls for their dissolution.

7 Big Data Surveillance: The Convergence of Big Data and Law Enforcement

Andrew Guthrie Ferguson[†]

"Big data" can be understood as a general term to describe the collection, retention, and analysis of massive amounts of data, allowing for new methods of pattern matching, investigation, and targeted data mining. Surveillance in the law enforcement context means "the systematic monitoring of people or groups, by means of personal data systems, in order to regulate or govern their behavior."[1] Thus, big data surveillance involves the systemic collection and aggregation of numerous discrete data points to create a composite picture of individuals or groups for purposes of monitoring.[2] Whereas big data animates the consumer space to monitor and track potential customers, big data surveillance engages the law enforcement space to monitor and track potential criminals.

In daily practice, private big data companies are suctioning up vast streams of consumer data to target individuals or families for commercial gain. Law enforcement agencies are building information centers to collect, aggregate, and disseminate criminal records data and other forms of biometric data and locational data for investigative advantage. While developing along separate evolutionary paths, these collection and aggregation systems have begun overlapping in practice. Individuals share personal data with private companies. Private companies sell personal data to law enforcement. Law enforcement integrates this information with publicly available data. Databases merge, blend, and share related private–public data. A big data convergence is not far away. Soon many of these discrete data streams will be intertwined into a few quite revealing and perhaps chilling surveillance tools.

The law and regulatory structure governing big data, in contrast, has not seen the same evolution or convergence. The legal and constitutional restrictions on data collection and aggregation remain discrete, disconnected, and limited to particular types of data. Specific laws target specific concerns, but few systemic legal structures exist to police data collection or use. "Big data law" does not exist yet. Small data regulations, not larger protections, remain the only checks on these growing data collection systems.

This chapter examines the risks of big data surveillance as the convergence of private–corporate and public–law enforcement data alters the nature and scope of surveillance capabilities. It seeks to contrast the growth of big data surveillance with the paucity of big

† Professor of Law, University of the District of Columbia David A. Clarke School of Law.

1 Roger Clarke, *Information Technology and Dataveillance*, ROGER CLARKE'S WEB-SITE (1987), http://www.rogerclarke.com/DV/CACM88.html.

2 EXEC. OFFICE OF THE PRESIDENT, BIG DATA: SEIZING OPPORTUNITIES, PRESERVING VALUES 2 (2014), https://www.whitehouse.gov/sites/default/files/docs/big_data_privacy_report_may_1_2014.pdf.

data legal regulations. It also explores the consequences and risks of a police–corporate partnership that emphasizes shared data, shared technology, and a shared mind-set. In tracing the potential convergence of corporate, government, and self-surveillance, this chapter suggests the need for robust big data laws, regulations, and oversight mechanisms.

I The Growth of Big Data Surveillance

Data surveillance is growing in scope and sophistication.[3] Big data involves a capacity to collect, sort, and analyze ever more complex and massive quantities of information.[4] Big data surveillance does not exist as a grand conspiratorial, Orwellian system, although the building blocks may be forming for the future. Currently, discrete technologies are tracking personal data. Consumer technologies now exist for smart televisions to record your conversations at home, smart cars to report your behaviors on the road, and smart personal health monitors to detail the consumption of particular combinations of drugs (legal or illegal).[5] Large government databases now exist with DNA, iris scans, fingerprints, and other biometric information collected for investigative purposes.[6] Law enforcement can identify location data, associational data, and patterns of suspicious actions from direct and indirect personal data we leave behind.[7] The connection of these discrete points of information – aggregated and searchable – presents a potential threat as the web of surveillance information grows without accountability, transparency, or control.

Part I lays out two growth areas of data accumulation, looking at private/corporate collection and then government/law enforcement collection. It provides a brief overview of the types of surveillance being conducted and the extent of legal oversight or controls.

A *Private/Corporate Surveillance*

Private companies now regularly track and study the behaviors of consumers. This private/corporate surveillance has become big business because of the potential insights thought useful to sell goods and services. Companies have developed numerous data streams to try to monitor and predict the needs and desires of consumers. Data-collection companies have grown in scope and power on the basis of the assumption that data can be the fuel of this new economy. Collecting, aggregating, splicing, and selling data have become a multibillion-dollar business.[8] This section briefly describes the different typologies of private/corporate big data surveillance.

3 Omer Tene & Jules Polonetsky, *Big Data for All: Privacy and User Control in the Age of Analytics*, 11 Nw. J. Tech. & Intell. Prop. 239, 240 (2013); James Manyika et. al., Big Data: The Next Frontier for Innovation, Competition, and Productivity, 87 (2011).

4 Viktor Mayer-Schonberger & Kenneth Cukier, Big Data: A Revolution that Will Transform How We Live, Work, and Think, 2 (2013).

5 Andrew Guthrie Ferguson, *The Internet of Things and the Fourth Amendment of Effects*, 104 Calif. L. Rev. 805, 818–23 (2016).

6 Laura K. Donohue, *Technological Leap, Statutory Gap, and Constitutional Abyss: Remote Biometric Identification Comes of Age*, 97 Minn. L. Rev. 407, 461–62 (2012).

7 Andrew Guthrie Ferguson, *Big Data and Predictive Reasonable Suspicion*, 163 U. Pa. L. Rev. 327, 331 (2015).

8 John Furrier, *Big Data Is Big Market and Big Business*, Forbes: Tech (Feb. 17, 2012, 1:26 PM), http://www.forbes.com/sites/siliconangle/2012/02/17/big-data-is-big-market-big-business/#74d05786b353.

1 Types of Private/Corporate Data Surveillance

The goal of this chapter is to provide an overview of the types of big data surveillance technologies in use. The danger of any technology-focused chapter is that new technologies become obsolete quite quickly. This section seeks to set out broad types of corporate surveillance, recognizing that new versions of these consumer technologies will continue to evolve.

Retail Surveillance A headline reporting that "Target Knows You're Pregnant before Your Family Does" makes for great news copy.[9] The story has become the leading example of growing levels of consumer retail surveillance. By studying the purchasing habits of numerous customers, Target could predict life changes with a fair degree of certainty. The secret: Target studied purchases of women who created a baby registry to see the related (and not so related) products chosen by newly pregnant women, and then predicted that other women who bought the same goods together might also be pregnant. Simple clues such as the purchase of vitamin supplements (such as folic acid) and unscented lotion (due to heightened scent sensitivity) provided data points to correlate with early pregnancy. Target is not alone, as companies have joined the data collection effort in order to market particular goods to meet individual consumer needs. All of those loyalty cards from grocery stores, coffee shops, or pharmacies track what you purchase. The reason the store suggested a particular coupon is that it has tracked your past purchases (and those of others like you) to know that people who buy product "X" also buy product "Y." The store also knows your various health needs and illnesses and those of your assorted family members. Some stores combine this personal data with your home address, zip code, and phone number and can determine the type of family size through your purchases. Food, medicine, clothing, and books all reveal insights into the lifestyle of a particular consumer. Consumer surveillance has become so common that most individuals think the proliferation of coupons, specials, and insights about consumer needs is a convenience, not a tracking system. In reality it is both.

Internet Surveillance Consumer tracking also occurs in the virtual world with online retailers.[10] Google and other search engines track each of your search queries, thus gaining a window into your interest in health, politics, travel, news, or favorite activities.[11] Sometimes this information can be quite personal. As Kate Crawford and Jason Schultz have written, "Buying an e-book about breast cancer survival or 'liking' a disease foundation's Facebook page ... can also reveal information about our health."[12] Google's ad revenue depends on this surveillance of interests and needs so it can connect the user with the appropriate advertiser.[13] This personal data is regularly bought, sold, and repurposed

9 Charles Duhigg, *How Companies Learn Your Secrets*, N.Y. Times Magazine (Feb. 16, 2012), http://www.nytimes.com/2012/02/19/magazine/shopping-habits.html?pagewanted=all.

10 Noam Cohen, *It's Tracking Your Every Move and You May Not Even Know*, N.Y. Times (Mar. 26, 2011), https://www.nytimes.com/2011/03/26/business/media/26privacy.html.

11 Robert Epstein, *Google's Gotcha: 15 Ways Google Monitors You*, US News and World Report (May 10, 2013, 12:15 PM), http://www.usnews.com/opinion/articles/2013/05/10/15-ways-google-monitors-you; Andrew William Bagley, *Don't Be Evil: The Fourth Amendment in the Age of Google, National Security and Digital Papers and Effects*, 21 Alb. L.J. Sci. & Tech. 153, 163–64 (2011).

12 Kate Crawford & Jason Schultz, *Big Data and Due Process: Toward a Framework to Redress Predictive Privacy Harms*, 55 B.C. L. Rev. 93, 97 (2014).

13 Epstein, *supra* note 11.

by a whole network of advertisers, ad exchanges, and market researchers.[14] As Thomas Hemnes has described:

> One might think of a person's digital identity by analogy to a pointillist painting. Thousands upon thousands of tiny bits of digital information about an individual, including what we have called basic facts, sensitive facts, and transactional facts, can be assembled to form a picture of the individual: his likes, dislikes, predispositions, resources; and in fact, any facet of his personality that has had contact with the Internet.[15]

Other companies such as Amazon or Walmart literally know what you have purchased over the past few years, what you thought about your purchases, and what others like you have purchased.[16] Amazon Kindle and other e-readers know the books you have bought, whether you finished reading them, and, if not, what page you stopped reading.[17] With linked email and social media platforms, these companies also know your associates, friends, and professional connections. Search browsers know what travel sites you have visited and what airlines you have booked. Google Maps knows your travel plans. Your reservations, tours, and itinerary can be intuited through your search queries. These companies track consumers in order to create marketing profiles for targeted advertising. As Paul Schwartz and Daniel Solove explain:

> Companies generally do not track individuals by name. Instead, they use software to build personal profiles that exclude this item but that contain a wealth of details about each individual. In lieu of a name, these personal profiles are associated with a single alphanumerical code that is placed on an individual's computer to track their activity.... These codes are used to decide which advertisements people see, as well as the kinds of products that are offered to them.[18]

This type of tracking can be valuable to companies who purchase the profiles for Internet marketing or other sales.[19] Be it travel, health, hobbies, or addictions, your search engine knows your plans and concerns probably better than your friends. In fact, these Internet data points can predict future activity. While not definitive, predictions could be made as to where you will be next Friday by examining restaurant reviews, online reservations, mapping queries, and the like. Equally revealing, a pattern of everywhere you searched for the past five years of Fridays can reveal lifestyle habits, associates, and preferences. The Internet has become a wonderfully convenient net of digital surveillance.

Social Media Surveillance The line between Internet searches and social media has blurred as Internet platforms have offered social media connections.[20] Google also knows about your Google+, LinkedIn, and Facebook profiles and related contacts. Other social

14 Omer Tene & Jules Polonetsky, *To Track or "Do Not Track": Advancing Transparency and Individual Control in Online Behavioral Advertising*, 13 Minn. J.L. Sci. & Tech. 281, 282 (2012).

15 Thomas Hemnes, *The Ownership and Exploitation of Personal Identity in the New Media Age*, 12 J. Marshall Rev. Intell. Prop. L. 1, 17 (2012).

16 Marcus Wohlson, *Amazon's Next Big Business Is Selling You*, Wired (Oct. 16, 2012, 11:00 AM), http://www.wired.com/business/2012/10/amazon-next-advertising-giant/.

17 Larry Port, *Disconnect From Tech*, 29 Legal Mgmt., no. 6, Nov.–Dec. 2010, at 46, 49–50.

18 Paul M. Schwartz & Daniel J. Solove, *The PII Problem: Privacy and a New Concept of Personally Identifiable Information*, 86 N.Y.U. L. Rev. 1814, 1854–55 (2011).

19 Julia Angwin, *The Web's New Gold Mine: Your Secrets*, Wall St. J., July 31, 2010, at W1.

20 Chloe Albanisus, *Facebook: Tracking Your Web Activity Even After You Log Out?* PC Magazine (Sept. 26, 2011, 11:59 AM), http://www.pcmag.com/article2/0,2817,2393564,00.asp; Angwin, *supra* note 19.

media programs that share locational data or photographs or require linking to others only expand the scope of information about users.[21] Locations can be targeted,[22] social networks mapped, photographs tagged and linked. Some entities such as Facebook have explicitly partnered with behavioral marketers and data brokers to gain insights about users so as to better target advertisements.[23] Twitter and others have also begun selling personal data to companies seeking to mine it.[24] Newsfeeds, comments, photos, and the daily social network of life, interests, and activities can be reduced to data points for study and commercial advantage. Your life online is a self-generated data source. Aggregated millions of times over, this network of everything you "like" or share becomes a valuable consumer and human data set for companies interested in people like you. While not always appreciated by the user, the creation of social media profiles and spaces to mirror personal interests and connections creates the data that generates value to the companies. Users digitize their lives. Companies sell that user data.

Data Brokers The accumulation of available data has led to the creation of behavioral marketing firms.[25] If you want to market a magazine to parents, you need data that the residents of a home have children. If you want to market age-appropriate toys, you need to know the age of the children. As Julia Angwin wrote in her article *The Web's New Goldmine: Your Secrets*, this information can be disturbingly precise,

> Hidden inside Ashley Hayes-Beaty's computer, a tiny file helps gather personal details about her, all to be put up for sale for a tenth of a penny. The file consists of a single code – 4c812db292272995e5416a323e79bd37 – that secretly identifies her as a 26-year-old female in Nashville, Tenn. The code knows that her favorite movies include 'The Princess Bride,' '50 First Dates' and '10 Things I Hate About You.' It knows she enjoys the 'Sex and the City' series. It knows she browses entertainment news and likes to take quizzes.[26]

"Big data behavioral marketing" has become an influential piece of marketing jargon, justifying financial investment in big data companies.[27] And, the central players in this new economy are data brokers.[28]

21 James Manyika et. al., Big Data: The Next Frontier for Innovation, Competition, and Productivity, 90 (2011).

22 Andrea Peterson, *Your Location History Is Like a Fingerprint: And Cops Can Get It without a Warrant*, Wash. Post (July 31, 2013), https://www.washingtonpost.com/news/the-switch/wp/2013/07/31/your-location-history-is-like-a-fingerprint-and-cops-can-get-it-without-a-warrant/; Manyika, *supra* note 21, at 87; Andrew William Bagley, *Don't Be Evil: The Fourth Amendment in the Age of Google, National Security and Digital Papers and Effects*, 21 Alb. L.J. Sci. & Tech. 153, 163 (2011).

23 Rebecca Greenfield, *Facebook Now Knows What You're Buying at Drug Stores*, Atlantic Wire (Sept. 24, 2012, 11:49 AM), http://www.theatlanticwire.com/technology/2012/09/facebook-tracking-you-drug-store-now-too/57183; Kashmir Hill, *Facebook Joins Forces with Data Brokers to Gain More Intel About Users for Ads*, Forbes (Feb. 27, 2013, 3:11 PM), http://www.forbes.com/sites/kashmirhill/2013/02/27/facebook-joins-forces-with-data-brokers-to-gather-more-intel-about-users-for-ads/.

24 Mitch Lipka, *Your Money: Twitter Is Selling Your Data*, Reuters (Mar. 1, 2012, 11:35 AM), http://www.reuters.com/article/twitter-data-idUSL2E8DTEK420120301.

25 Richard Warner & Robert H. Sloan, *Behavioral Advertising: From One-Sided Chicken to Informational Norms*, 15 Vand. J. Ent. & Tech. L. 49, 58 (2012).

26 Julia Angwin, *The Web's New Gold Mine: Your Secrets*, Wall St. J. (July 31, 2010), at W1.

27 Natasha Singer, *You for Sale: Mapping, and Sharing, the Consumer Genome*, N.Y. Times, (June 16, 2012), http://www.nytimes.com/2012/06/17/technology/acxiom-the-quiet-giant-of-consumer-database-marketing.html; Candice L. Kline, *Security Theater and Database-Driven Information Markets: A Case for an Omnibus U.S. Data Privacy Statute*, 39 U. Tol. L. Rev. 443, 447 (2008).

28 Lois Beckett, *Everything We Know about What Data Brokers Know about You*, ProPublica (June 13, 2014, 1:59 PM), http://www.propublica.org/article/everything-we-know-about-what-data-brokers-know-about-you.

Data brokers mine the gold of consumer surveillance, building massive data warehouses of personal information. In a 2014 report, the Federal Trade Commission (FTC) detailed the extent of the data broker business. The commission studied nine major U.S. data brokers with vast stores of data:

> Of the nine data brokers, one data broker's database has information on 1.4 billion consumer transactions and over 700 billion aggregated data elements; another data broker's database covers one trillion dollars in consumer transactions; and yet another data broker adds three billion new records each month to its databases. Most importantly, data brokers hold a vast array of information on individual consumers. For example, one of the nine data brokers has 3000 data segments for nearly every U.S. consumer.[29]

This information is collected from a variety of public and private sources. Credit reports, employment records, family information, court records, government benefits, address changes, transactional details, etc., are all bought, sold, and traded among companies.[30] Data has become currency with the end goal to understand to whom to market various consumer goods and services.[31] These data points mean that private companies have a wealth of big data about consumer interests, hobbies, reading choices, purchases, and lifestyle preferences.

These data companies segment potential consumers by categories. A lifestyle category of "Rural Everlasting" includes single people older than sixty-six years old who have "low educational attainment and low net worth."[32] Another category is entitled "Married Sophisticates," which includes upper income, childless thirty-something couples.[33] Other categories target individuals with particular health issues. This type of consumer surveillance focuses on consumer needs and selling products, but the data exists for other purposes as well. The data becomes a commodity bought and sold as property owned by the companies. As will be discussed later, this consumer surveillance can provide the building blocks for law enforcement surveillance when the consumer data populates larger government databases.

Sensor Surveillance among Internet of Things "Smart" devices from fitness bands to smart cars, refrigerators, clothing, and medical devices provide another stream of valuable data.[34] Big data companies have recognized that this daily record of personal actions – from steps taken to food eaten – can provide even more insight into a consumer's life. A smart home can tell you when the lights turn on in a particular part of the home, when the television or microwave is used, and even when the homeowner showers. A smart medical device can record the most intimate of personal acts. A smart cup can tell you the amount and type of liquids consumed. All of this data can be filtered into

29 Fed. Trade Comm'n, Data Brokers: A Call for Transparency and Accountability iv (2014), http://www.ftc.gov/system/files/documents/reports/data-brokers-call-transparency-accountability-report-federal-trade-commission-may-2014/140527databrokerreport.pdf).

30 Elspeth A. Brotherton, *Big Brother Gets a Makeover: Behavioral Targeting and the Third-Party Doctrine*, 61 Emory L.J. 555, 563 (2012).

31 Kline, *supra* note 27, at 448.

32 Fed. Trade Comm'n, *supra* note 29, at v.

33 *Id.*

34 Andrew Guthrie Ferguson, *The Internet of Things and the Fourth Amendment of Effects*, 104 Calif. L. Rev. 805, 818–23 (2016).

existing collection mechanisms to create an even more granular understanding of consumer habits and needs. Other chapters in this collection discuss the growth of sensor surveillance among the Internet of Things, but the personal data arising from millions of interconnected objects is going to make big data that much bigger and more valuable. In fact, some analysts see sensor data surpassing consumer or Internet data in terms of quantity and quality. It is one thing, after all, to do a Google search for "the best running routes" or to buy new running shoes on Amazon, but the important health data really is collected from the "smart" device that can tell whether you actually went for a run.

Financial Surveillance One of the most traditional forms of private surveillance involves financial credit rating reports. For years, companies have collected information about personal credit risk. New data collection systems have allowed for even more sophisticated assessments of creditworthiness. In addition to employment, net worth, bill paying, and other traditional indicia of financial responsibility, companies have looked to less traditional clues, such as the rather odd fact that those people who purchase felt pads for under their sofas and furniture tend to be better credit risks (perhaps signifying an extra level of responsibility).[35] The scope of financial surveillance can be observed in any credit report. This type of data has only grown as more financial tracking technologies have been offered to consumers. Whereas before you might know what you spent your money on by balancing a checkbook, today your local bank can provide itemized pie charts and graphs of spending patterns broken down by type of spending, month, and pretty much any other variable. Mobile applications including mobile financial payment services provide another level of locational tracking. This information is also available to banks and financial institutions. The availability of financial data has proved a boon for consumers, but it also allows banks and law enforcement to monitor monetary transfers with much greater ease.

Political Surveillance Big data surveillance has moved into the political arena. Targeted data collection has been a focus of political consultants hired by presidential candidates in national political campaigns.[36] Starting in 2008, with President Barack Obama's get-out-the-vote campaign, political consultants have been hired to map the electorate to the most granular level.[37] Today, both Republicans and Democrats have sophisticated data mapping systems to map each of the households in various swing states.[38] Private groups have replicated the success of the microtargeting approach to support particular candidates.[39] These organizations know individuals' and families' political leanings, community involvements, and interests and use this information to mobilize support

35 Lior Jacob Strahilevitz, *Toward a Positive Theory of Privacy Law*, 126 Harv. L. Rev. 2010, 2021 (2013).
36 Ira S. Rubinstein, *Voter Privacy in the Age of Big Data*, 2014 Wis. L. Rev. 861, 876–83 (2014).
37 Sasha Issenberg, *Obama's White Whale*, Slate (Feb. 15, 2012, 11:28 AM), http://www.slate.com/articles/news_and_politics/victory_lab/2012/02/project_narwhal_how_a_top_secret_obama_campaign_program_could_change_the_2012_race_.html; Terrence McCoy, *The Creepiness Factor: How Obama and Romney Are Getting to Know You*, The Atlantic (Apr. 10, 2012), http://www.theatlantic.com/politics/archive/2012/04/the-creepiness-factor-how-obama-and-romney-aregetting-to-know-you/255499/.
38 Mike Allen & Kenneth P. Vogel, *Inside the Koch Data Mine*, Politico (Dec. 8, 2014, 5:32 AM), http://www.politico.com/story/2014/12/koch-brothers-rnc-113359.html#ixzz3NJNxqsHU.
39 *Id.*

for particular candidates. This type of nanotargeting to potential voters requires detailed digital dossiers about each of the millions of voters in America.[40]

The preceding list of big data consumer surveillance merely scratches the surface of the information available from our digital activities. If you add in information sources such as mobile apps, news articles, and videos, you might have a good sense of what information on a particular subject someone knows (or at least how he or she has been influenced). The accumulation of our digital clues is really a revelation of the influences that shape our worldview. In the context of consumer products these revelations may appear benign, or even a convenient benefit that allows more efficient processing of an otherwise overwhelming amount of information. If we have bought the same deodorant for the past twenty years, it makes sense to target us for a future purchase. If we have a pet, we might need pet food and supplies on a regular basis. If we love music, we might appreciate suggestions for the next "hot" band similar to our favorite musician. Data-driven targeting of our interests and desires adds efficiencies to consumer choice.

The danger, of course, is that this big data surveillance also targets less benign subjects. If we believe that the local government is corrupt, or a local corporation is endangering the environment, revelations of such interest and advocacy could be used to suppress that dissent. Big data can potentially reveal those who are more likely to protest against the government on the basis of reading interests, Internet connections, social media links, or travel patterns. Big data can reveal addiction, depression, or even criminal actions. If you want to target political activists, you can figure out who is Googling directions to protest sites, buying paint for protest banners, or reading "know your rights" books. If you want to target drug dealers, you might want to figure out who is buying tiny Ziploc bags, disposable phones, digital scales, and/or rubber bands in bulk. This type of surveillance through big data consumer technologies raises real privacy concerns. Despite the dangers posed by private surveillance, there are surprisingly few legal restraints on the gathering, aggregation, analysis, and use of *big data* technologies.

2 Legal Restrictions on Private/Corporate Data Surveillance

Private data surveillance quickly grew into a billion-dollar business in part because it remains largely unregulated. In the context of private actors obtaining private information from private citizens, no constitutional barriers exist to collection. In fact, the First Amendment has been used to argue that formal data privacy restrictions could violate the Constitution as an infringement on the commercial free speech rights of companies.[41] Federal legislative action has lagged behind the technology. Most states have not filled in the gaps. This section examines the existing fragmented law surrounding big data surveillance.

The first point to note is that there is no federal law directly targeted to cover private big data consumer surveillance. As the General Accounting Office (GAO) concluded,

40 Thomas B. Edsall, *Let the Nanotargeting Begin*, N.Y. Times (Apr. 15, 2012, 10:39 PM), http://campaignstops.blogs.nytimes.com/2012/04/15/let-the-nanotargeting-begin/; Charles Duhigg, *Campaigns Mine Personal Lives to Get Out Vote*, N.Y. Times (Oct. 13, 2012), http://www.nytimes.com/2012/10/14/us/politics/campaigns-mine-personal-lives-to-get-out-vote.html.

41 *Sorrell v. IMS Health Inc.*, 131 S. Ct. 2653 (2011); Neil M. Richards, *Why Data Privacy Law Is (Mostly) Constitutional*, 56 Wm. & Mary L. Rev. 1501, 1510 (2015).

"No overarching federal privacy law governs the collection and sale of personal information among private-sector companies, including information resellers. Instead, a variety of laws tailored to specific purposes, situations, or entities governs the use, sharing, and protection of personal information."[42] These more tailored laws address particular types of data (financial information, children's data, video rental data, etc.). While these laws and most federal regulations are influenced by the Privacy Act of 1974 and its amendments and have accepted what are known as Fair Information Practices (FIPs), there has been no comprehensive legislative response to the growth of big data.[43]

In the absence of a law directly addressing consumer big data, federal enforcement actions have relied on the Fair Credit Reporting Act (FCRA).[44] The FCRA is a federal law that governs consumer reporting agencies. These consumer reporting agencies traditionally compile reports used "for credit, employment, insurance, housing, or other similar decisions about consumers' eligibility for certain benefits and transactions."[45] The original purpose of the law was to focus on credit reports and address concerns about discrimination and error that could impact financial credit scores. Modern data brokers that collect credit information and employment information and help with consumer or housing eligibility decisions have been deemed to fit under the FCRA law.[46] Other types of consumer data collection companies that specialize in social networks and online resources have also recently faced FCRA regulation.[47]

Although data brokers were not envisioned during the passage of the FCRA, it has become the default law to address data collection in the big data era. Driving this expansion is the Federal Trade Commission (FTC), which in recent years has broadened the reach of the FCRA through a series of targeted enforcement actions.[48] The FTC has brought cases against Internet companies that tracked online behavioral advertising[49] and against mobile applications that collected personal information without appropriate notice.[50] The FTC has also targeted companies that collected personal data from the Internet of Things.[51] Finally, the FTC has brought FCRA complaints against social networking programs designed by Google and Facebook.[52] Notably, these FTC actions have been the primary legal mechanism for policing any big-data-like company.

42 U.S. Gov't Accountability Off., GAO-13–663, Information Resellers: Consumer Privacy Framework Needs to Reflect Changes in Technology and the Marketplace (2013), http://www.gao.gov/assets/660/658151.pdf [http://perma.cc/992Y-6L8L].

43 Richards, *supra* note 41, at 1510.

44 15 U.S.C. §§ 1681–1681x (2014).

45 Fed. Trade Comm'n, Big Data: A Tool for Inclusion or Exclusion? ii (2016), https://www.ftc.gov/system/files/documents/reports/big-data-tool-inclusion-or-exclusion-understanding-issues/160106big-data-rpt.pdf. *See also* 15 U.S.C. §§ 1681–1681x.

46 Fed. Trade Comm'n, *supra note 45, at 13.*

47 *Id.*

48 The role of the FTC in regulating surveillance means, methods, and technologies is discussed at greater length in Chapter 30.

49 Peder Magee, *Privacy and Identity Protection from the Fair Credit Reporting Act to Big Data*, 29 Antitrust 56, Fall 2014, at 56, 58.

50 *Id.*

51 *Id.* at 59.

52 Complaint, *In re Google, Inc.*, Fed. Trade Comm'n (No. C-4336) (2012), http://www.ftc.gov/sites/default/files/documents/cases/2011/03/110330googlebuzzcmpt.pdf.; Complaint, *In re Facebook, Inc.*, Fed. Trade Comm'n (No. C-4365) (2012), http://www.ftc.gov/sites/default/files/documents/cases/2011/11/111129facebookcmpt.pdf.

In addition to FCRA, the FTC has targeted "unfair or deceptive acts or practices in or affecting commerce" using Section 5 of the Federal Trade Commission Act (FTCA).[53] When companies violate their own privacy policies or terms of service, this can be designated as an unfair trade practice.[54] While the reach of the FCRA and FTCA is broadening as a result of FTC enforcement actions, the law does not cover direct use of information derived from a company's own relationship with customers. Similarly, use of data analytics to improve internal policies or strategies does not impact the consumer reporting nature of the law and thus remains outside FTC regulation.[55] As a result of these limitations and the larger absence of comprehensive big data legislation, the FTC itself has called for the development of new federal law to cover these big data problems.[56]

While the consumer data space has not yet benefited from an overarching "big data law," particular types of personal data have protection in certain federal laws designed to protect specific types of data. The Health Insurance Portability and Accountability Act (HIPAA) regulates the privacy of certain medical or health data.[57] The Genetic Information Non-Discrimination Act (GINA) regulates how companies use genetic information for employment and other eligibility requirements.[58] The Children's Online Privacy Protection Act (COPPA) protects against the collection and use of personal information from and about children.[59] The Family Educational Rights and Privacy Act (FERPA) protects the privacy of educational data about schoolchildren.[60] The Computer Matching and Privacy Protection Act of 1988 protects personal information of individuals receiving federal benefits or federal employees.[61] The Driver's Privacy Protection Act (DPPA) governs the dissemination of information obtained by the Department of Motor Vehicles.[62] The Electronic Communications Privacy Act (ECPA) covers protection of email, communications, and stored data.[63] The Video Privacy Protection Act (VPPA) originally protected the privacy of video rentals and has been extended to the world of streaming video.[64] Some of this data is obviously the type of data included (or potentially included) in data brokers' dossiers.

These federal statutes – and state equivalents – form a patchwork of data regulation. But, difficulties arise around enforcement because many of the data and sources are hidden from public view. It could be that a child's personal information was inappropriately vacuumed up to establish a composite consumer picture of a targeted family, but

53 Fed. Trade Comm'n, Big Data: A Tool for Inclusion or Exclusion? 21 (2016), https://www.ftc.gov/system/files/documents/reports/big-data-tool-inclusion-or-exclusion-understanding-issues/160106big-data-rpt.pdf.

54 Sarah Ludington, *Reining in the Data Traders: A Tort for the Misuse of Personal Information*, 66 Md. L. Rev. 140, 142 (2006).

55 Fed. Trade Comm'n, *supra* note 53, at 17.

56 Fed. Trade Comm'n, Data Brokers: A Call for Transparency and Accountability (2014), http://www.ftc.gov/system/files/documents/reports/data-brokers-call-transparency-accountability-report-federal-trade-commission-may-2014/140527databrokerreport.pdf.

57 42 U.S.C. § 1320d–6 (2009).

58 42 U.S.C. §§ 2000ff–2000ff-11 (2008).

59 15 U.S.C. §§ 6501–6506 (1998).

60 20 U.S.C. § 1232g (2012).

61 5 U.S.C. §§ 552a(a)(8)-(13), (e)(12), (o), (p), (q), (r), (u) (2014).

62 18 U.S.C. §§ 2721–2725 (2000).

63 18 U.S.C. §§ 2701 *et seq* (2002).

64 *Yershov v. Gannett Satellite Info*. Network, Inc., 820 F.3d 482 (1st Cir. Apr. 29, 2016), http://media.ca1.uscourts.gov/pdf.opinions/15-1719P-01A.pdf.

disentangling the protected information from the rest of the family's information is quite difficult. Further, the subject of the data collection will remain unaware of the collection, and without government investigation, the wrongful collection will remain unpoliced. Finally, because this data is regularly sold back and forth between companies, it becomes almost impossible to identify the original source of the collection violation or to expunge the information.

As might be evident, the federal laws targeting the national problem of data collection, aggregation, and use remain weak.[65] While the FTC has taken on a leadership role, and certain personal data have been protected by particular legislative enactments, most of those laws predated the big data revolution. The current reality is wide-scale, growing big data collection without commensurate legal regulation.

B *Data-Driven Law Enforcement Surveillance*

Law enforcement has long kept data on persons suspected of involvement in criminal activity. From file systems dating back to the 1880s to modern fusion centers, collecting surveillance data has always been part of policing.[66] In the 1990s, New York City adopted a data-driven approach to police management. The New York Police Department (NYPD) revamped its crime fighting strategy with a renewed focus on crime statistics. Police officers collected data. Police supervisors analyzed data. Police management pushed more data-driven accountability. This focus on data led to a prioritization of policing crime "hot spots" and the aggressive use of stop and frisk tactics. Such police tactics allowed for easy measuring of police contacts in areas deemed to be at a higher risk of crime. As data technology improved, crime analysts went from studying past crime to predicting future crime. Across the country, an interest grew in proactive policing. Companies selling algorithms to forecast criminal activity gave rise to what is now known as "predictive policing." Other companies adapted traditional predictive analytics techniques to fight crime. New technologies to process, aggregate, and use that data have augmented the traditional surveillance capabilities of police. This section looks at the rise of big data surveillance capabilities generated and maintained by law enforcement.

1 Big Data Surveillance by Police

In a chapter about big data surveillance, it is important to differentiate between ordinary policing and big data policing. Both types of law enforcement surveillance seek information useful for investigation, but only big data policing does so primarily though streams of data. The two types of investigation do overlap, but the focus here is on the development of large collections of data.

Mass Surveillance Traditional surveillance involves the visual monitoring of suspects or areas of likely criminal activity. Two forms of data-driven mass surveillance have provided a modern twist on that policing tactic. These technologies allow for vastly more

65 Federal antidiscrimination and equal opportunity laws such as the Equal Credit Opportunity Act (ECOA), Title VII of the Civil Rights Act of 1964, the American with Disabilities Act (ADA), the Age Discrimination in Employment Act (ADEA), and other employment related equality laws might be implicated if big data private data collection were used for discriminatory hiring practices.

66 Wayne A. Logan, *Policing Identity*, 92 B.U. L. Rev. 1561, 1561 (2012).

data to be collected than is possible with any human surveillance team. Further, they do so in a way that allows for relatively inexpensive collection, general secrecy of collection, extensive storage capacity, and the ability to query stored data far into the future.

For example, technologies such as Automated License Plate Readers (ALPRs) are recording the location of all automobiles on a daily basis on roads where they are deployed. These automatic cameras record the license plate number and location of cars on public streets. The data from millions of cars can be stored in searchable databases for potential investigative use.[67] Insights from analysis of this data have been useful for tracking individual suspects (for example, if the same car was at the scene of several burglaries), observing patterns of travel to suspected areas (say, to and from a drug house), and proving (or disproving) witnesses' testimony. Once collected, the data exists as an immense (if not always used) record of car locations.

Second, some large cities are experimenting with integrated video surveillance systems that identify suspects and can be used to study criminal activities or suspicious patterns.[68] For example, the New York City Police Department has partnered with Microsoft to develop a "Domain Awareness System," which links live video streams with crime reports, 911 calls, and other data such as ALPR information into a real time investigative tool.[69] More than three thousand cameras are connected to this system such that police can review a crime and then play back the footage tracing the path of a suspect through the city. Soon additional video cameras, including possibly drone cameras, will augment existing technologies in some cities. In New York City, police can pull up arrest records, map criminal history, and track a person or car through recorded video over the past twenty-four hours.[70] In Los Angeles, networked cameras have facial recognition technology to identify the people on the streets. These developing real time systems exist as an integrated data-driven video surveillance system for a city. The collected digitized information builds on traditional video camera surveillance but allows for longer-term digitized callback and more integrated data features for identification and monitoring.

Data Mining Databases are not new to law enforcement. But the capability to integrate local and national electronic databases into one integrated data set is expanding.[71] The

67 Stephen Rushin, *The Judicial Response to Mass Police Surveillance*, 2011 U. Ill. J.L. Tech. & Pol'y 281, 285–86 (2011).

68 Don Babwin, *Chicago Video Surveillance Gets Smarter*, USA Today (Sept. 27, 2007, 11:25 AM), http://usatoday30.usatoday.com/tech/products/2007-09-27-4171345706_x.htm; Cara Buckley, *Police Plan Web of Surveillance for Downtown*, N.Y. Times (July 9, 2007), at A0; John Del Signore, *NYPD Tightens Surveillance in Subway's "Ring of Steel,"* Gothamist, (Sept. 21, 2010, 9:37 AM) http://gothamist.com/2010/09/21/nypd_ tightens_surveillance_in_subwa.php.

69 Somini Sengupta, *Privacy Fears Grow as Cities Increase Surveillance*, N.Y. Times (Oct. 13, 2013), http://www.nytimes.com/2013/10/14/technology/privacy-fears-as-surveillance-grows-in-cities.html.

70 N.Y.C., *Mayor Bloomberg, Police Commissioner Kelly and Microsoft Unveil New, State-of-the-Art Law Enforcement Technology that Aggregates and Analyzes Existing Public Safety Data in Real Time to Provide a Comprehensive View of Potential Threats and Criminal Activity*, N.Y.C., Office of the Mayor (Aug. 8, 2012), http://www.nyc.gov/portal/site/nycgov/menuitem.c0935b9a57bb4ef3daf2f1c701c789a0/index.jsp?pageID=mayor_press_release&catID=1194&doc_name=http%3A%2F%2Fwww.nyc.gov%2Fhtml%2Fom%2Fhtml%2F2012b%2Fpr291-12.html&cc=unused1978&rc=1194&ndi=1.

71 Eric Lichtblau, *F.B.I.'s Reach into Records Is Set to Grow*, N.Y. Times (Nov. 12, 2003), http://www.nytimes.com/2003/11/12/politics/12RECO.html.

most prominent of these data sets is the National Crime Information Center (NCIC).[72] The NCIC database is made available to federal and state police and includes information about active arrests, offender status, gang membership, prior violence, and other data. As of 2014, the NCIC contained 13 million active records and was accessed by federal, state, and local law enforcement 12 million times a day.[73] Officers can search the NCIC database using computers in their patrol cars. Information from criminal investigations across the country feeds the database, and it continues to grow. Local and state databases also exist and are expanding in size and scope.

Data mining for investigative clues – connecting and aggregating addresses, identifying tattoos and criminal associations, etc. – has proven invaluable to police investigators trying to solve crimes.[74] As aggregation technology develops, this work can be done in real time with centralized command centers tracking associational connections and identifying particular suspects.[75] Whether police are investigating local burglaries or international human trafficking operations, data of past police contacts are available for investigators.[76] Local, state, and federal agents may soon begin merging these data sets into nationally accessible systems.

Intelligence-Led Policing Technology Next generation data mining looks a lot like what is happening in Los Angeles with its intelligence-led policing strategy. Los Angeles Police Department (LAPD) has partnered with the private company Palantir to develop a database that links previously discrete law enforcement data sources.[77] Police can now search arrest records, police contact forms, DMV records, and other sources to identify suspects. The system allows investigators to match partial descriptions, photographs, and other data sources from a single computer. The surveillance data exists in real time and is used to map crime patterns, suspects, and associations between suspects. In addition, Palantir has partnered with the LAPD on "Operation LASER" (Los Angeles Strategic Extraction and Restoration). This program identifies "chronic offenders" for increased police surveillance.[78] Information about these targeted offenders is provided to police for surveillance: "The basic premise is to target with laser-like precision the violent repeat offenders and gang members who commit crimes in the specific target areas.

[72] David M. Bierie, *National Public Registry of Active-Warrants: A Policy Proposal*, FED. PROBATION (June 2015), at 27, 28; Fed. Bureau of Investigation, *NCIC Files*, FED. BUREAU OF INVESTIGATION: NATIONAL CRIME INFORMATION CENTER, https://www.fbi.gov/about-us/cjis/ncic/ncic_files.

[73] Fed. Bureau of Investigation, *supra* note 72.

[74] Fred H. Cate, *Government Data Mining: The Need for a Legal Framework*, 43 HARV. C.R.-C.L. L. REV. 435, 438 (2008); Christopher Slobogin, *Government Data Mining and the Fourth Amendment*, 75 U. CHI. L. REV. 317, 319–20 (2008).

[75] Nate Berg, *Predicting Crime, LAPD-Style: Cutting Edge Data-Driven Analysis Directs Los Angeles Patrol Officers to Likely Future Crime Scenes – but Critics Worry That Decision-Making by Machine Will Bring 'Tyranny of the Algorithm,'* THE GUARDIAN (June 25, 2014, 5:19 AM), http://www.theguardian.com/cities/2014/jun/25/predicting-crime-lapd-los-angeles-police-data-analysis-algorithm-minority-report.

[76] Bernhard Warner, *Google Turns to Big Data to Unmask Human Traffickers*, BLOOMBERG: BUSINESSWEEK (Apr. 10, 2013, 1:46 PM), http://www.bloomberg.com/news/articles/2013-04-10/google-turns-to-big-data-to-unmask-human-traffickers.

[77] *Los Angeles Police Using CIA Software to Track Criminals, Ex-cons*, RT (Nov. 15, 2014, 3:30), http://rt.com/usa/205727-lapd-criminals-data-collection/.

[78] Craig D. Uchida et al., LOS ANGELES, CALIFORNIA SMART POLICING INITIATIVE: REDUCING GUN-RELATED VIOLENCE THROUGH OPERATION LASER 7–10 (2012); Anthony A. Braga et al., SMART APPROACHES FOR REDUCING GUN VIOLENCE 10–11(2014).

The program is analogous to laser surgery, where a trained medical doctor uses modern technology to remove tumors or improve eyesight."[79] This type of targeted surveillance is now possible because of the big data analysis capabilities of these new technologies.

Fusion Centers These state and regional real time surveillance systems are modeled, in part, on the creation of federal fusion centers.[80] The federal government, through the Department of Homeland Security, has set up information sharing entities to coordinate law enforcement activities across the nation. These fusion centers exist to share surveillance data across federal and state lines and among numerous law enforcement agencies.[81] Investigations initiated by fusion centers have focused on fugitive warrants and transnational crimes such as sex trafficking or drug distribution. As discussed in detail in another chapter of this collection, the core of these fusion centers is shared surveillance data including the growing use of criminal justice databases.

Offender Registries Law enforcement also has developed offender registries targeting individuals convicted of sex offenses, gang offenses, gun crimes, or other charges.[82] These registries were designed to maintain surveillance on offenders and monitor the individual's home address, employment, automobile, and even appearance. The databases are digitized and regularly updated with information. Some offenders also are tagged by GPS devices to provide real time locational surveillance monitoring. In addition, the information can be mapped through geospatial technology to observe residences and places of employment for identified offenders.

Social Media Surveillance More informally, police have recognized that certain crimes can be predicted, and others solved, by monitoring social media. Gang rivalries extend to Facebook.[83] Gang hierarchies can be understood by studying social media video communications.[84] Conflict can be monitored via social media channels.[85] Services exist to scrape data from social media sites and outlets in real time looking for keywords or other markers of criminal activity. Prosecutions can be built around comments made on social media (admissions of criminal association or even admission of guilt), so police and prosecutors have focused on increasing surveillance in this social media space.

Social Network Analysis Law enforcement has also adopted social network mapping technologies to find relationships among criminal actors. Researchers in Chicago, New Orleans, Boston, and other major cities have recognized that the majority of violent

79 Uchida, *supra* note 78, at 3.

80 Christopher Slobogin, *Government Data Mining and the Fourth Amendment*, 75 U. Chi. L. Rev. 317, 319–20 (2008); Fred H. Cate, *Government Data Mining: The Need for a Legal Framework*, 43 Harv. C.R.-C.L. L. Rev. 435, 443–44 (2008); Erin Murphy, *Databases, Doctrine & Constitutional Criminal Procedure*, 37 Fordham Urb. L.J. 803, 830 (2010).

81 James B. Perrine et al., *Fusion Centers and the Fourth Amendment: Application of the Exclusionary Rule in the Post-9/11 Age of Information Sharing*, 38 Cap. U. L. Rev. 721, 739 (2010).

82 Joshua D. Wright, *The Constitutional Failure of Gang Databases*, 2 Stan. J. C.R. & C.L. 115, 118 (2005).

83 Ben Austen, *Public Enemies: Social Media Is Fueling Gang Wars in Chicago*, Wired (Sept. 17, 2013, 6:30 AM), http://www.wired.com/underwire/2013/09/gangs-of-social-media/.

84 Joseph Goldstein & David Goodman, *Seeking Clues to Gangs and Crime, Detectives Monitor Internet Rap Videos*, N.Y. Times (Jan. 7, 2014), http://www.nytimes.com/2014/01/08/nyregion/seeking-clues-to-gangs-and-crime-detectives-monitor-internet-rap-videos.html?_r=0.

85 Heather Kelly, *Police Embrace Social Media as Crime Fighting Tool*, CNN (Aug. 30, 2012, 5:23 PM), http://www.cnn.com/2012/08/30/tech/social-media/fighting-crime-social-media.

crime involves only a finite number of interconnected people.[86] These individuals can be mapped in social networks to show family, gang, or other relationships. The violence can also be mapped to show the relational nature – usually retaliatory back and forth – of shootings. Groups identified through this social network analysis can be monitored. In addition, public health–like intervention strategies involving face to face meetings, offers of social services, and additional law enforcement attention have been implemented. For police, this social network mapping has allowed a greater ability to understand the scope and extent of criminal networks in a particular jurisdiction.

Biometrics Law enforcement has rapidly expanded the collection of biometric data about individuals.[87] This biometric information is stored and used for future investigations. The federal DNA database – the Combined DNA Index System (CODIS) – now includes more than 12 million profiles collected by local, state, and federal law enforcement.[88] Fingerprints have also been centralized into a federal database. The Integrated Automated Fingerprint Identification System (IAFIS) allows national access to millions of digitally stored prints.[89] Facial recognition technologies are growing. The FBI has more than 15 million mug shots in a national system being built around facial recognition technology.[90] States have developed their own facial recognition databases.[91] The technology is going mobile with police being able to capture photos and search databases from smart phones on the street. Next Generation Identification (NGI) technologies are also being created to identify individuals through remote biometrics including tattoos or other features.[92] As Laura Donohue describes:

> [The NGI] Interstate Photo System, allows law enforcement to submit still images or video surveillance feeds obtained from any public or private source. The system is designed to store this data and, using [Facial Recognition Technology], to identify individuals, pairing images with biographic information. NGI also uses biographic information to search its Repository for Individuals of Special Concern (RISC).[93]

86 OFFICE OF JUVENILE JUSTICE & DELINQUENCY PREVENTION, U.S. DEP'T OF JUSTICE, PROMISING STRATEGIES TO REDUCE GUN VIOLENCE 26–33 *(1999)*, http://www.cops.usdoj.gov/html/cd_rom/solution_gang_crime/pubs/PromisingStrategiestoReduceGunViolence.pdf.

87 Ellen Nakashima, *FBI Prepares Vast Database of Biometrics*, WASH. POST (Dec. 22, 2007), http://www.washingtonpost.com/wp-dyn/content/article/2007/12/21/AR2007122102544.html; Wayne A. Logan, *Policing Identity*, 92 B.U. L. REV. 1561, 1575 n.91 (2012).

88 *See* Laboratory Services, *CODIS – NDIS Statistics*, Fed. Bureau of Investigation, https://www.fbi.gov/about-us/lab/biometric-analysis/codis/ndis-statistics (last visited July 6, 2016).

89 Erin Murphy, *Databases, Doctrine and Constitutional Criminal Procedure*, 37 FORDHAM URB. L.J. 803, 806–08 (2010); *Integrated Automated Fingerprint Identification System*, FED. BUREAU INVESTIGATION, http://www.fbi.gov/about-us/cjis/fingerprints_biometrics/iafis/iafis (last visited July 6, 2016).

90 Craig Timberg & Ellen Nakashima, *State Photo-ID Databases Become Troves for Police*, WASH. POST (June 16, 2013), https://www.washingtonpost.com/business/technology/state-photo-id-databases-become-troves-for-police/2013/06/16/6f014bd4-ced5-11e2-8845-d970ccb04497_story.html; Sara Reardon, *FBI Launches $1 Billion Face Recognition Project*, NEWSCIENTIST (Sept. 7, 2012), http://www.newscientist.com/article/mg21528804.200-fbi-launches-1-billion-facerecognition-project.html; Ryan Gallagher, *FBI to Give Facial Recognition Software to Law-Enforcement Agencies*, SLATE (Aug. 23, 2012, 5:08 PM), http://www.slate.com/blogs/future_tense/2012/08/23/universal_face_workstation_fbi_to_give_facial_recognition_software_to_law_enforcement_.html.

91 Timberg, *supra* note 90; Sabrina A. Lochner, *Saving Face: Regulating Law Enforcement's Use of Mobile Facial Recognition Technology & Iris Scans*, 55 ARIZ. L. REV. 201, 202 (2013).

92 Nakashima, *supra* note 87.

93 Laura K. Donohue, *Technological Leap, Statutory Gap, and Constitutional Abyss: Remote Biometric Identification Comes of Age*, 97 MINN. L. REV. 407. 412–13 (2012).

The facial recognition databases are being integrated into the larger police intelligence databases and made available to officers on patrol through squad car computers or mobile handheld devices.

Financial Surveillance Finally, police have long monitored financial transactions, banking, and other related areas.[94] Financial data has regularly been flagged for irregular transactions, money laundering, and tax evasion. This type of financial surveillance has only been made easier with more data and more sophisticated analytical search tools.

2 Legal Restrictions on Big Data Surveillance

The rise of big data law enforcement has not been matched by the rise of big data civil liberties protections. This section examines the constitutional and statutory limitations on the collection, use, and sale of government-obtained data. As with the scope of government regulation of private/corporate surveillance, the federal government has not adequately regulated law enforcement access to big data.

Traditional constitutional limitations apply to police whether conducting big data surveillance or regular surveillance. In general, the Fourth Amendment protects the privacy of individuals from government intrusion for areas in which they can claim a reasonable expectation of privacy.[95] Due process protections from the Fifth and Fourteenth Amendments potentially regulate inappropriate collection and use of data, but courts have not been eager to create an enforceable right.[96] Equal protection principles protect individuals from discrimination on the basis of race or gender, and while certainly relevant to algorithmic discrimination in civil rights cases focused on housing, employment, health, and credit, these principles have less application to data collected in police systems.[97]

As an example of how the United States Constitution largely leaves big data surveillance unregulated, data collection from automated license plate readers or surveillance cameras occurs in public and an expectation of privacy under the Fourth Amendment cannot be claimed.[98] Stored data in law enforcement databases involving arrests, convictions, and probation or parole status are generated by law enforcement and, because they are officially created, present no Fourth Amendment issues. Public records are not private under the Fourth Amendment. Even more proactive investigative targeting using large, linked data systems still does not infringe on traditional Fourth Amendment values because the information is all owned (purchased or generated) by law enforcement. Biometric databases certainly implicate personal privacy, but usually the biological material is obtained after an arrest or police contact – a process that has been sanctioned as constitutional by the Supreme Court.[99] Even personal data (Internet searches,

94 Josh Meyer & Greg Miller, *U.S. Secretly Tracks Global Bank Data*, L.A. TIMES, (June 23, 2006), at A1; Eric Lichtblau & James Risen, *Bank Data Sifted in Secret by U.S. to Block Terror*, N.Y. TIMES (June 23, 2006), at A1.

95 *Katz v. United States*, 389 U.S. 347, 357–59 (1967).

96 *Paul v. Davis*, 424 U.S. 693, 712 (1976).

97 Exec. Office of the President, BIG DATA: SEIZING OPPORTUNITIES, PRESERVING VALUES 53 (2014), https://www.whitehouse.gov/sites/default/files/docs/big_data_privacy_report_may_1_2014.pdf.

98 Marc Jonathan Blitz, *Video Surveillance and the Constitution of Public Space: Fitting the Fourth Amendment to a World That Tracks Image and Identity*, 82 TEX. L. REV. 1349, 1354 (2004).

99 *Maryland v. King*, 133 S. Ct. 1958, 1980 (2013).

financial transactions, phone call metadata) held by private companies can be obtained free of constitutional limitations because the Fourth Amendment's "third party doctrine" allows police to obtain data directly from the private third party without running afoul of the Constitution.[100] The third party doctrine allows most information held by a private third party company to be obtained under the theory that if one has shared information with a third party, one loses an expectation of privacy toward others (including the police).[101] While the Supreme Court in *United States v. Jones*[102] left open the possibility of extending Fourth Amendment protection for some aggregated public data collection, as a general matter, the Court has yet to step into the breach, leaving big data surveillance beyond the scope of Fourth Amendment regulation.[103]

Similarly, the Due Process Clause has not been used to regulate police surveillance. Challenges to public surveillance technology, police data collection, and even third party requests have not been cognizable under a due process theory. Although the Supreme Court has been conscious of the dangers of data error[104] and the growth of big data law enforcement systems, it has limited recovery for police data errors under a due process theory.[105] For due process challenges resulting from police data error (for example, the erroneous posting of one's name beside the word "shoplifter") the Supreme Court has required a high bar to demonstrate harm.[106]

The Equal Protection Clause, likewise, has not been used to challenge big data policing. Although data-driven equal protection challenges to the New York City Police Department's stop and frisk practices and systemic challenges to racial profiling have offered some potential remedy for discriminatory surveillance (and policing), these arguments have not yet been used to address more modern surveillance techniques. Concerns over the inherent racial and gender biases in algorithms may change this reality, but currently, equal protection doctrine has not been the preferred constitutional vehicle to challenge big data policing.

The same statutory scheme discussed earlier in the private/corporate context also applies to law enforcement. The list of federal privacy protecting statutes is long and includes the Privacy Act of 1974,[107] the Electronic Communications Privacy Act of 1986 (ECPA),[108] the Stored Communications Act (SCA),[109] the Foreign Intelligence Surveillance Act

100 Stephen E. Henderson, *Beyond the (Current) Fourth Amendment: Protecting Third-Party Information, Third Parties, and the Rest of Us Too*, 34 Pepp. L. Rev. 975, 982–83 (2007).

101 Stephen E. Henderson, *Learning from All Fifty States: How to Apply the Fourth Amendment and Its State Analogs to Protect Third Party Information from Unreasonable Search*, 55 Cath. U. L. Rev. 373, 376–79 (2006).

102 *United States v. Jones*, 132 S. Ct. 945, 948 (2012).

103 Andrew Guthrie Ferguson, *Big Data and Predictive Reasonable Suspicion*, 163 U. Pa. L. Rev. 327, 331 (2015).

104 *Herring v. United States*, 555 U.S. 135 (2009). *See also Menard v. Saxbe*, 498 F.2d 1017 (D.C. Cir. 1974); *Tarlton v. Saxbe*, 507 F.2d 1116 (D.C. Cir. 1974).

105 Wayne A. Logan & Andrew Guthrie Ferguson, *Policing Criminal Justice Data*, 101 Minn. L. Rev. 541, 572-76 (2016).

106 *Paul v. Davis*, 424 U.S. 693, 712 (1976); *Wisconsin v. Constantineau*, 400 U.S. 433, 437 (1971).

107 5 U.S.C. § 552a (1994).

108 Pub. L. No. 99–508, 100 Stat. 1848 (codified as amended in sections of 18 U.S.C.); Communications Assistance for Law Enforcement Act, Pub. L. No. 103–414 at §207(2) (codified as amended at 18 U.S.C. § 2703).

109 18 U.S.C. §§ 2701–2712 (2015).

(FISA),[110] the E-Government Act of 2002,[111] the Financial Privacy Act,[112] the Wiretap Act,[113] the Gramm–Leach–Bliley Act,[114] the Bank Secrecy Act,[115] the Right to Financial Privacy Act,[116] the Fair Credit Reporting Act (FCRA),[117] the Health Insurance Portability and Accountability Act of 1996 (HIPAA),[118] the Genetic Information Non-discrimination Act (GINA),[119] the Children's Online Privacy Protection Act (COPPA),[120] the Family Educational Rights and Privacy Act,[121] the Telephone Records and Privacy Protection Act of 2006,[122] and the Video Privacy Protection Act.[123] However, these statutory protections do not always apply to law enforcement access. In fact, as Professor Erin Murphy has noted, "The United States Code currently contains over twenty separate statutes that restrict both the acquisition and release of covered information.... Yet across this remarkable diversity, there is one feature that all these statutes share in common: each contains a provision exempting law enforcement from its general terms."[124] This means that law enforcement can circumvent statutory restrictions enacted to protect against the collection of personal data.

In addition to there being limited regulation on law enforcement collection of data, there is an equal absence of law protecting how law enforcement can use the data. Once data is appropriately collected, police may use the data as they wish. While some state laws restrict the use of Automated License Plate Readers[125] and biometrics,[126] there is no federal law that covers these technologies. As with the consumer space, a fragmented and confusing system of regulations exists that provides little clear legal protection for individuals concerned about big data surveillance.

II The Convergence of Data Streams

Big data technologies provide new opportunities for enhanced government surveillance. In quite direct ways, the accumulation of data points can help identify potential suspects and improve police investigations. In more indirect ways, new technologies can inspire new approaches – and even new philosophies – to address crime. This section explores the implication of a convergence of private/corporate big data and public/law

110 50 U.S.C. §§ 1801–1885c (2015).
111 44 U.S.C. §§ 101, 3601–3606 (2002).
112 12 U.S.C. §§ 3401–3422 (2010).
113 18 U.S.C. §§ 2510–2522 (2015).
114 15 U.S.C. § 6801–6809 (2015).
115 12 U.S.C. §§ 1951–59 (2014).
116 12 U.S.C. §§ 3401–3422 (2010); 12 U.S.C. § 3407 (1978).
117 15 U.S.C. §§ 1681–1681x (2015).
118 45 C.F.R. 164.512(f)(1)(ii) (2016); 45 C.F.R. 164.512(f)(2) (2016).
119 42 U.S.C. §§ 2000ff to 2000ff-11 (2012).
120 15 U.S.C. §§ 6501–6506 (1998).
121 20 U.S.C. § 1232g (2012).
122 18 U.S.C. § 1039 (2007). *But see* 18 U.S.C. §§ 2703(c)(1)(B), 2703(d) (2009).
123 18 U.S.C. § 2710 (1994).
124 Erin Murphy, *The Politics of Privacy in the Criminal Justice System: Information Disclosure, the Fourth Amendment, and Statutory Law Enforcement Exemptions*, 111 Mich L. Rev. 485, 487 & n.2 (2013).
125 National Conference of State Legislatures, *Automated License Plate Readers State Legislation* (Nov. 13, 2015), http://www.ncsl.org/research/telecommunications-and-information-technology/2014-state-legislation-related-to-automated-license-plate-recognition-information.aspx.
126 Ill. Comp. Stat. 14 / 1 (2008).

enforcement data. While currently innovating on different paths and with different objectives, a convergence of information, technology, and strategies is developing. This convergence necessitates a renewed awareness about privacy interests and the practical risks of big data surveillance.

A *Convergence: Shared Data*

The first point of convergence is that private/corporate interests are sharing data with law enforcement.[127] What was once private–consumer data can quite easily be repurposed as the raw material for law enforcement databases. At the most basic level, law enforcement has simply become another customer for big data information.[128] Cell phone companies sell data about individual suspects to police.[129] Mobile apps sell locational data.[130] Internet service providers sell data analytics to many consumers, including government purchasers. As one commentator has written:

> Your information is for sale, and the government is buying it at alarming rates. The CIA, FBI, Justice Department, Defense Department, and other government agencies are at this very moment turning to a group of companies to provide them information that these companies can gather without the restrictions that bind government intelligence agencies.[131]

The result has been a blending of public and private data sets in the hands of investigative agencies for law enforcement purposes.[132] This outcome presents some concerns. The first is access. Data that law enforcement officers could not obtain on their own can be purchased by a private entity. In this way the data is "laundered," such that otherwise private information can be aggregated into third party (or fourth party) data sets that the government, like any other consumer, can then purchase without restriction.[133]

At a second level, law enforcement can directly collect available information through shared sources. Social media surveillance techniques simply take publicly available information and add it to government databases. Facebook posts, Twitter comments, other social media posts, and shared locational services all reveal information helpful to

127 Chris Jay Hoofnagle, *Big Brother's Little Helpers: How ChoicePoint and Other Commercial Data Brokers Collect and Package Your Data for Law Enforcement*, 29 N.C. J. INT'L L. & COM. REG. 595 (2004).

128 Joshua L. Simmons, Note, *Buying You: The Government's Use of Fourth-Parties to Launder Data about 'The People,'* 2009 COLUM. BUS. L. REV. 950, 951.

129 Bob Sullivan, *Who's Buying Cell Phone Records Online? Cops*, MSNBC (June 20, 2006, 11:59:07 AM), http://www.msnbc.msn.com/id/12534959/; Robert Block, *Requests for Corporate Data Multiply: Businesses Juggle Law-Enforcement Demands for Information About Customers*, SUPPLIERS, WALL ST. J., May 20, 2006, at A4; Heather Kelly, *Police Embrace Social Media as Crime Fighting Tool*, CNN (Aug. 30, 2012, 5:23 PM), http://www.cnn.com/2012/08/30/tech/social-media/fighting-crime-social-media.

130 Andrea Peterson, *Your Location History Is Like a Fingerprint: And Cops Can Get It without a Warrant*, WASH. POST (July 31, 2013), https://www.washingtonpost.com/news/the-switch/wp/2013/07/31/your-location-history-is-like-a-fingerprint-and-cops-can-get-it-without-a-warrant/.

131 Simmons, *supra* note 128, at 951.

132 Fred H. Cate, *Government Data Mining: The Need for a Legal Framework*, 43 HARV. C.R.-C.L. L. REV. 435, 457 (2008); Candice L. Kline, *Security Theater and Database-Driven Information Markets: A Case for an Omnibus U.S. Data Privacy Statute*, 39 U. TOL. L. REV. 443, 448 (2008); Natasha Singer, *You for Sale: Mapping, and Sharing, the Consumer Genome*, N.Y. TIMES (June 16, 2012), http://www.nytimes.com/2012/06/17/technology/acxiom-the-quiet-giant-of-consumer-database-marketing.html.

133 Simmons, *supra* note 128, at 976; Jon D. Michaels, *All the President's Spies: Private-Public Intelligence Partnerships in the War on Terror*, 96 CAL. L. REV. 901, 902 (2008).

law enforcement. Data mining services exist to look for words, images, and photographs that might link suspects to criminal or gang activity. Big data technology companies have partnered with federal government agencies interested in the insights developed in the private data sets.[134] Social media sites such as Facebook have become valuable sources to identify gang members or to link criminal associates across jurisdictions.[135]

At a third level, police can obtain personal data held by private companies using appropriate legal channels (subpoenas, grand juries, official requests). As part of a criminal investigation, police legally can request cell phone record data,[136] financial records,[137] transactional records,[138] Internet search records, and most personal data held by third party companies.[139] These data are regularly used for criminal investigation and monitoring of individuals. Whether as stand-alone information or as part of a larger data set, personal information has become central to many police investigations. Moreover, the data – once obtained – will remain in the government's possession.

The convergence also works the other way. Government – although not necessarily law enforcement – sells personal data to private data companies. The backbone of private data broker databases is court information on individuals made publicly available or sold by state and local governments. Government collection of personal information and its eventual sale to private entities help strengthen the data sets that law enforcement ultimately purchases back for its own use. This convergence of data ultimately unifies the existing police surveillance structure. The convergence puts a vast amount of personal data in the hands of law enforcement. The addition of even a fraction of the available consumer data information to existing law enforcement databases presents a new form of power. We tend to think it permissible to allow law enforcement to have information about past public acts (convictions, arrests, court cases, etc.) but not personal private acts (social media posts, jobs, friendships, etc.). Yet, the line between private and public data has blurred, as all of one's past financial or credit history; past addresses, associates, and employment; and potentially every last social media post could be available with a few quick searches.

This strong convergence of data presents real risks to the quality of big data surveillance. Of course, all data-driven systems risk being infected by data error. It has long been recognized that stand-alone law enforcement information systems such as gang

134 Glenn R. Simpson, *Big Brother-in-Law: If the FBI Hopes to Get the Goods on You, It May Ask Choicepoint: U.S. Agencies' Growing Use of Outside Data Suppliers Raises Privacy Concerns*, Wall St. J. (Apr. 13, 2001), at A1; Pratap Chatterjee, *The Data Hackers*, The Nation (Oct. 8. 2013), https://www.thenation.com/article/data-hackers/.

135 Ben Austen, *Public Enemies: Social Media Is Fueling Gang Wars in Chicago*, Wired (Sept. 17, 2013, 6:30 AM), http://www.wired.com/underwire/2013/09/gangs-of-social-media/.

136 John Kelly, *Cellphone Data Spying: It's Not Just the NSA*, USA Today (Dec. 8, 2013), http://www.usatoday.com/story/news/nation/2013/12/08/cellphone-data-spying-nsa-police/3902809/; Matt Sledge, *Cops Asked for Cell Phone Data More than 1 Million Times Last Year*, Huffington Post (Jan. 25, 2014), http://www.huffingtonpost.com/2013/12/09/cell-phone-data-requests_n_4414059.html.

137 Eric Lichtblau, *F.B.I.'s Reach into Records Is Set to Grow*, N.Y. Times (Nov. 12, 2003), http://www.nytimes.com/2003/11/12/politics/12RECO.html; Josh Meyer & Greg Miller, *U.S. Secretly Tracks Global Bank Data*, L.A. Times, (June 23, 2006), at A1; Eric Lichtblau & James Risen, *Bank Data Sifted in Secret by U.S. to Block Terror*, N.Y. Times, (June 23, 2006), at A1, http://www.nytimes.com/2006/06/23/washington/23intel.html.

138 Christopher Slobogin, *Transactional Surveillance by the Government*, 75 Miss. L.J. 139, 145 (2005).

139 Erin Murphy, *The Politics of Privacy in the Criminal Justice System: Information Disclosure, the Fourth Amendment and Statutory Law Enforcement Exemptions*, 111 Mich. L. Rev. 485, 487 (2013).

databases or arrest warrant systems are filled with errors.[140] Clearly, adding consumer/government data to these systems will only increase the potential for mistakes. This section examines four issues arising from these new big data systems: reliability, bias, volume, and privacy.

The first risk of a shared data convergence is the impurities that can undermine the reliability of big data policing. The errors can be with original collection methods, police interpretation, or human processing error. Both consumer credit ratings and law enforcement arrest records are notoriously inaccurate. Facts, dates, addresses, and even names have been shown to be erroneously recorded. In some contexts, getting the data mostly correct is still beneficial. After all, an incorrect past address may not affect your credit rating. But if that mistaken address links you to a wanted suspect and identifies you as a possible gang member, such an error might have significant negative consequences for individual liberty. Equally damaging, this error undermines the overall reliability and trust in data-driven systems. Most troubling, the interconnected nature of the data streams that are bought and sold means that the error will replicate over many systems. Such replication makes correcting any error quite difficult. While a local police agency could fix the erroneous name in an arrest record, once it is sold, repackaged, and publicized, that wrong name or false arrest may still exist in other data systems.

Beyond factual error, biases may also infect the data. Police data is gathered from police in the real world, and, as has been demonstrated in numerous scholarly, empirical, and anecdotal accounts of policing in America, real world policing reflects racial and class biases.[141] These biases may arise from patterns of police patrol, structural racism, or implicit biases.[142] Whatever the source, these biases can be baked into the data systems. Thus, a data-driven search for the most dangerous individuals in a society might unintentionally skew toward a racially biased result. As has been demonstrated with risk assessment mechanisms, sometimes the data chosen results in disproportionate impact on minority groups.[143] In the big data context, this might result in inaccurate correlations or linkages that replicate existing racial inequities in the world.

A more benign concern involves the sheer volume of data involved. The reality of even a limited big data convergence is that the amount of data available will be too much to be readily useful. The task of synthesizing contacts, arrests, convictions, registries, social media posts, and other forms of surveillance has already proved taxing to law enforcement under limited budgets. For this reason, some law enforcement agencies have been required to outsource collection and analysis. As data streams grow in type, scope, and detail, this pressure will increase. Although such available data may well be useful in specific targeted investigations, and much of the storage will be done by third party providers already collecting the information, the amount of new data may overwhelm some

140 Joshua D. Wright, *The Constitutional Failure of Gang Databases*, 2 Stan. J. C.R. & C.L. 115, 118 (2005).

141 Charles J. Ogletree Jr., The Presumption of Guilt: The Arrest of Henry Louis Gates Jr. and Race, Class, and Crime in America, 129–241 (2010).

142 L. Song Richardson, *Police Efficiency and the Fourth Amendment*, 87 Ind. L.J. 1143, 1147 (2012); Andrew E. Taslitz, *Police Are People Too: Cognitive Obstacles to, and Opportunities for, Police Getting the Individualized Suspicion Judgment Right*, 8 Ohio St. J. Crim. L. 7, 15–16 (2010).

143 Julia Angwin, et al. *Machine Bias: There's A Software Used Across the Country to Predict Future Criminals. And It's Biased Against Blacks*, ProPublica (May 23, 2016), https://www.propublica.org/article/machine-bias-risk-assessments-in-criminal-sentencing.

police departments. At a minimum, the volume of data makes the process of using the data unwieldy and expensive.

Finally, a big data convergence risks undermining the few privacy protections of personal data that currently exist. Under existing constitutional and statutory restrictions, law enforcement is prevented from directly obtaining certain personal information without appropriate legal process. Although, as demonstrated, these protections are not robust and could use enhancement, they do exist. However, the ability to share data, buy data, and essentially launder data undercuts these protections. A world of shared data makes it hard to police privacy, especially if one cannot see how the data was originally obtained. In large aggregated databases filled with commingled government, consumer, social media, and police information, disentangling sources and protecting private information becomes an expensive, time-consuming, and potentially unmanageable task.

B *Convergence: Shared Technology*

The second potential convergence involves shared technology. Police are beginning to partner with big data technology companies to restructure and reinvent their investigative techniques.

Minor innovations involve police departments' adopting technologies to track social media in their communities.[144] Just as marketers look for patterns of consumer sales, police see patterns of criminal activity. By using the technology developed to track social trends, police can monitor crime trends.[145] Gang fights, illegal gatherings, or unsanctioned protests discussed on social media can be quickly disrupted. Some technologies such as "Geofeedia" allow police to search social media sites for keywords in real time and pinpoint the geographic location of those communicating with each other.[146] This technology has been used to identify violent gang members for gang prosecutions and to monitor political protests.[147]

Similarly, the basic idea of developing a usable database system of suspect information builds on the corporate approach to data management.[148] These data systems involve significant investment in money and hardware. Numerous competing companies have developed to support law enforcement in their search for effective data mining tools. Just as Target seeks to predict its potentially pregnant customers, police may seek to predict potentially violent citizens. Public health interventions like those in Chicago involve focused attention on those individuals most at risk of being involved in violence. Instead of folic acid and unscented lotion, police look to precursor events such as being a shooting victim or being arrested with a shooting suspect. Some law enforcement agencies, such as the Bureau of Alcohol, Tobacco, Firearms and Explosives (ATF), have sought to control the technology by developing their own databases, as opposed to being limited

144 Heather Kelly, *Police Embrace Social Media as Crime Fighting Tool*, CNN (Aug. 30, 2012, 5:23 PM), http://www.cnn.com/2012/08/30/tech/social-media/fighting-crime-social-media.

145 Noah Shachtman, *Exclusive: U.S. Spies Buy Stake in Firm That Monitors Blogs, Tweets*, Wired (Oct. 19, 2009, 12:03 PM), http://www.wired.com/dangerroom/2009/10/exclusive-us-spies-buy-stake-in-twitter-blog-monitoring-firm/.

146 Ali Winston, *Oakland Cops Quietly Acquired Social Media Surveillance Tool*, East Bay Express (Apr. 13, 2016), http://www.eastbayexpress.com/oakland/oakland-cops-quietly-acquired-social-media-surveillance-tool/Content?oid=4747526.

147 *Id.*

148 Fred H. Cate, *Government Data Mining: The Need for a Legal Framework*, 43 Harv. C.R.-C.L. L. Rev. 435, 442–43 (2008).

to the use of existing resources.[149] These massive data systems require equally large data support companies and technological assistance.

Major innovations involve wholesale partnerships with information technology companies. Predictive policing technologies owned by Hitachi, IBM, Lexis, and smaller entities such as PredPol, HunchLab, and Risk Terrain Modeling now guide resource allocation decisions in major police departments.[150] Crime data and other information can be collected, analyzed, and then operationalized on the basis of algorithmic guidance from these companies. Some companies including Palantir in Los Angeles and Microsoft in New York City have developed entire command centers to fuse incoming data with real time decision making and investigation. These surveillance systems can no longer be considered merely police tools. They are deep partnerships between technologists and law enforcement. The underlying technological insight is that by studying social networks among criminal groups, and identifying individuals, associations, and connections, data can reveal investigative clues that otherwise would have been missed.[151] This social network approach to law enforcement is directly connected to the technologies invented to study social networks in the consumer space and the technological capacity to find previously unknown insights and linkages.

As new technologies develop, and as law enforcement continues to use them, the opportunities to sell products to police will only increase. Further, as the technologies require more specialized knowledge and maintenance, partnerships involving technologists embedded in police departments or wholesale outsourcing of big data surveillance will continue.

These partnerships create their own risks, most of which fall into one of three categories: control, cost, and correction. First, a growing reliance on technology means a growing reliance on technology companies. Although some larger police departments have data analysts on staff, the type of big data surveillance envisioned in the future will require technical experts. Data must be inputted, organized, analyzed, and corrected. That means that police will need to contract with private companies to do their jobs. This, in turn, could result in a growing dependence on private companies, or a general deference to the technologies. In terms of dependence, this means that private actors, not police, will oversee police allocation decisions, shape investigations, and participate in otherwise secret law enforcement decisions. In terms of deference, if police are not required to understand the technologies (and they may lack the technical competence to do so), the control over policing shifts away from public agencies to private entities. This loss of control matters for a sense of public justice as well as for ordinary democratic accountability. A mayor or city council or community group may wish to fire a failing police chief, but may not be able to fire the private company that controls the technological backbone of their local predictive policing system.

Second, and relatedly, a merging of public police data and private technology means a reliance on particular products. In the current competitive environment with dozens of competing companies vying for contracts, police pick and generally stick with one company. Although police have the ability to change vendors, the reality of sunk costs,

149 Gerry Smith, *ATF Seeks 'Massive' Database For Faster Investigations*, Huffington Post (Apr. 8, 2013, 3:28 PM), http://www.huffingtonpost.com/2013/04/08/atf-database_n_3038271.html.

150 Andrew Guthrie Ferguson, *Policing Predictive Policing*, 94 Wash. U. L. Rev. (forthcoming 2017).

151 Gareth Cook, *Software Helps Police Draw Crime Links*, Boston Globe, (July 17, 2003), at A1.

ongoing contractual obligations, and training requirements means that police usually adopt one technology and remain with it. This might be so even if the technology does not work as well as advertised, might increase in cost, or might be inferior to other products. Once it is built into the system (or practice), many police agencies will simply keep what is familiar so as to avoid the initial costs of restructuring, retraining, and reimagining their data systems. Such a convergence also opens up the question of who owns the data. While obviously the police can claim ownership of the information, can police prevent companies from profiting from this information? What if private companies want to sell the data collected for one police agency to other police departments? What if private companies become bankrupt and want to sell their data to pay off liabilities? When public/police data is no longer collected and controlled by police, these data ownership issues arise.

Finally, shared data governance with proprietary technologies makes fixing errors more difficult. Most of the proprietary systems are not automatically compatible with other systems. This means that it is difficult both to share data and to correct data errors. Automated license plate records have one set of protocols, sex offender registries another, NCIC searches yet another. Adding those together, and integrating social media or financial data, only increases the confusion, redundancy, and difficulty in managing all the data. While a big data convergence should offer a more integrated data control system, it also adds the potential for confusion for analysts interested in correcting error or improving accurate information flow across systems.

C *Convergence: Shared Mind-Set*

The final convergence involves a shared mind-set that this data-driven, technology-assisted approach can improve law enforcement. National law enforcement legends such as Commissioner William Bratton of the New York City Police Department (NYPD), and Chief Charles Beck of the Los Angeles Police Department (LAPD) have embraced smart policing technologies as part of their daily crime fighting mission. More than sixty cities now use predictive policing.[152] Almost all police use federally financed databases to investigate suspects.[153] The federal government has invested millions in studying new surveillance technologies and collecting data about convicted criminals. Increased facial recognition scanners, license plate readers, and biometric databases are only going to grow over time. More integrated surveillance systems can solve crimes if they happen to occur within the area of observation. A news story about Palantir's partnership with the LAPD demonstrates a situation in which a fragment of a license plate and a fragment of a suspect's description are narrowed down to an actual human suspect through a series of quick database queries.[154] That suspect is then linked to his criminal associates, past locations, and possible current location.

[152] Ellen Huet, *Server And Protect: Predictive Policing Firm PredPol Promises To Map Crime Before It Happens*, Forbes (Mar. 2, 2015), http://www.forbes.com/sites/ellenhuet/2015/02/11/predpol-predictive-policing/#782706b8407f.

[153] Fed. Bureau of Investigation, *NCIC Files*, Fed. Bureau of Investigation: National Crime Information Center, https://www.fbi.gov/about-us/cjis/ncic.

[154] Thom Patterson, *Data Surveillance Centers: Crime Fighters or 'Spy Machines'?* CNN (May 26, 2014, 12:56 PM), http://www.cnn.com/2014/05/26/tech/city-of-tomorrow-video-data-surveillance/.

None of these developments would be possible if the fundamental concept of data-driven investigation and data-guided surveillance had not been accepted. Today, the issue is not whether to adopt these technologies but how to afford them. As costs go down, military grade technologies come home from war, and investment ramps up, the ease of adopting big data policing only gets easier. Companies racing to market new surveillance technologies are meeting interested law enforcement buyers. Police chiefs facing reduced manpower budgets have turned to technology as a solution "to do more with less."

This mind-set is not just about technology, but a new philosophy for fighting crime. This data-driven mind-set embraces the underlying insight of big data, namely, that risk, correlations, and connections can be visualized in new ways. For interventions in the community, data-driven policing can assist in identifying areas of future crime. Police patrol resources can be allocated more efficiently. In addition, certain correlations otherwise hidden can be divined from the data. For example, one study directly linked pseudoephedrine sales to the number of meth labs discovered in a community. As reported:

> Using that data, researchers were able to determine how much of the drug was sold in each Kentucky county and compare it with the number of meth busts in local police logs....The researchers found a significant association between pseudoephedrine sales and meth busts: In any given county, an increase in pseudoephedrine sales of 13 grams per 100 people translated to an additional meth lab busted. The results suggest that the computer databases could actually be used to predict where drug busts are most likely to take place.[155]

More attenuated correlations might also begin a move to pure big data policing. As Professor Erin Murphy describes, "The use of databases to generate suspects represents a new kind of investigation altogether – whether based on particular information (e.g., 'who called this number') or upon predefined algorithms (e.g., 'who has traveled to these three countries and bought these two items within a one month period')."[156] Police and prosecutors can add to their existing toolbox the hidden insights of big data, looking for previously unknown patterns, trends, and crime drivers in an area.

As with concerns about shared data and shared technology, a shared mind-set also presents practical risks. For chiefs of police responsible for the daily outcomes of crime rates and human victims, data can become a distraction. Police can end up chasing data points rather than actual criminals. In some early predictive policing cities, patrol officers had to be told to move out of the predicted boxes and continue patrolling other areas because they became too focused on the forecast areas.[157] In New York City, which pioneered the CompStat (COMPuter STATistics) approach to police resource allocation, patrol officers complained of pressure to make arrests just to appease their number crunching superiors.[158] Similar dangers await big data surveillance, as a data-driven focus

155 John Bardin, *Kentucky Study Links Pseudoephedrine Sales, Meth Busts*, L.A. TIMES (Oct. 16, 2012), http://articles.latimes.com/2012/oct/16/news/la-heb-kentucky-counties-pseudophedrine-meth-busts-20121016.

156 Erin Murphy, *Databases, Doctrine, & Constitutional Criminal Procedure*, 37 FORDHAM URB. L.J. 803, 830 (2010).

157 Darwin Bond-Graham & Ali Winston, *All Tomorrow's Crimes: The Future of Policing Looks a Lot like Good Branding*, SFWEEKLY NEWS (Oct. 30, 2013), http://www.sfweekly.com/sanfrancisco/all-tomorrows-crimes-the-future-of-policing-looks-a-lot-like-good-branding/Content?oid=2827968.

158 Jeff Morganteen, *What the CompStat Audit Reveals about the NYPD*, N.Y. WORLD (July 3, 2013), http://www.thenewyorkworld.com/2013/07/03/compstat/.

might generate erroneous investigative correlations or specious linkages. One can imagine resources better served than monitoring all of the growing social media platforms potential criminals might use. Each big data server, service contract, or technological advance costs money, and that money might be at the expense of placing officers in the community or providing direct social services for the community.

At the other end of the spectrum, one might find police leaders who see current big data technologies as doing too little. If a data broker can create a personal, granular, and holistic picture of all the people living in a neighborhood down to the street address, why should police not also have that information? If a big data company can figure out whether someone is a bad credit risk, with a history of substance abuse, domestic violence, and increasing contacts with the law, why should police not also know this information? Both credit agencies and police might make more accurate predictions based on that data. Companies such as Intrado offer services like BEWARE, which provide real-time data – "threat assessments" – to police responding to 911 calls.[159] BEWARE offers this real time information service so that police will know the type of household they are responding to before they knock on the door. The threats were initially color coded and based on commercial big data information about the particular address. Again, for law enforcement interested in social control, violence prevention, and public safety, this type of information – while invasive to privacy – is quite valuable. The Fresno Police Department, which piloted the BEWARE system, received community push back about the color-coded system of threats. But such risk threat programs mirror earlier "threat assessment" programs developed by the Department of Defense in the months after the September 11, 2001, terrorist attacks.[160] Although the early Department of Defense's programs were ended because of public concerns over privacy and liberty, today private companies are using big data technologies to offer similar threat assessment services to local police departments.[161]

As a final risk, police administrators and departments may become captured by the corporate interests themselves. Either because of an honest belief in the product, or because of the substantial financial incentives involved for cities and programs (the NYPD earns a share of the profit from sales of the Domain Awareness System to other localities), police can become marketers for particular companies. Some companies even contractually encourage adopting police departments to market their products to other police departments.[162] Some law enforcement leaders take public roles promoting particular corporate products. Although a shared mind-set may seem unobjectionable since the technology is being implemented as a public–private partnership, police owe a public duty that corporations do not. Big data companies serve the police. But the police serve the public.

159 Justin Jouvenal, *The New Way Police are Surveilling You: Calculating Your Threat Score*, Wash. Post, (Jan. 10, 2016), https://www.washingtonpost.com/local/public-safety/the-new-way-police-are-surveilling-you-calculating-your-threat-score/2016/01/10/e42bccac-8e15-11e5-baf4-bdf37355da0c_story.html.

160 Christopher Slobogin, *Government Data Mining and the Fourth Amendment*, 75 U. Chi. L. Rev. 317, 318 (2008).

161 Candice L. Kline, Comment, *Security Theater and Database-Driven Information Markets: A Case for an Omnibus U.S. Data Privacy Statute*, 39 U. Tol. L. Rev. 443, 451 (2008).

162 Bond-Graham, *supra* note 157.

Conclusion

The data available becomes the data usable if no regulations or limitations are placed on the information. In the context of law enforcement, these regulations may not be immediately forthcoming because the pressures to solve crime and reduce harm – and an abiding faith in police self-regulation – make such restrictions difficult. This chapter has sought to identify the growth of big data surveillance from a consumer/corporate perspective and a public/law enforcement perspective. The chapter also sought to show the growing convergence between the two streams of information in terms of data, technology, and mind-set. The risks identified in this chapter are real, but not insurmountable. Practical changes to improve accountability and transparency can be implemented. Technological changes to increase accuracy and decrease bias can be instituted. Legislative changes to confront the new challenges of big data surveillance adequately can be introduced. As big data grows in power and scope, so must the legal regulations necessary to contain it. Big data surveillance must encourage equally robust regulatory and constitutional surveillance of big data capabilities.

8 The Internet of Things and Self-Surveillance Systems

Steven I. Friedland*

This chapter examines the self-cybersurveillance systems created by the Internet of Things. This new wave of technology, in actuality networks of interconnected devices with radio transmitters that store and communicate information, supports a multitrillion-dollar data-sharing economy. The networks rely on its users to generate data streams that are shared with a variety of private enterprises, especially large technology companies. These companies often transmit the information downstream to government agencies, primarily through government–private industry partnerships. As twentieth-century notions of constitutional and statutory privacy become antiquated in the digital era, twenty-first-century domain-specific regulation is needed to deter excessive, invasive, and abusive information sharing practices to protect users from the evolving Internet of Things.

Introduction

This chapter addresses the legal implications of the Internet of Things – networks of common devices that transmit data to each other through tiny radio sensors. As the title of this chapter suggests, the emerging architectures of the Internet of Things upend traditional notions of surveillance to create a new phenomenon, self-generating mass surveillance systems – in essence, self-cybersurveillance. These self-generating data streams will change the understanding and trajectory of privacy in modern society.

The Internet of Things likely will become fully operational within the next decade. As it evolves, the Internet of Things offers a conduit for merging cyberspace and flesh-and-blood reality. The implications are extensive – "smart" devices will connect to each other in networks through embedded radio transmitters, [1] provide billions of data-collection opportunities, and create what some predict will become a $14 trillion economy[2] affecting every part of our lives.

The quotidian routines of people worldwide will be transformed. For example, when we awaken, there might be smart thermostats installed in our homes that will

* Associate Dean for Innovations in Engaged Learning in Law, Professor of Law and Senior Scholar, Elon University School of Law, Greensboro, North Carolina.

1 *See* Julianne Pepitone, *Google House: Tech Giant Spends Billions to Get Inside Your Home*, CNBC (Jan. 15, 2014, 6:11 AM), http://www.cnbc.com/id/101337483#.

2 *See id.* (stating that Cisco Systems estimates that the Internet of Things could generate $14.4 trillion over the next decade).

automatically set the temperature to reflect activity in the house.[3] A smart meter will track the electricity used in our homes throughout the day, adapting to when and how many people are at home. If we stumble out of bed in the dark of early morning, the lights can adjust so that the light is soft on our eyes; and when people brush their teeth, a smart toothbrush will track the quality of that brushing.[4]

Some prominent features will stand out. The component devices of the Internet of Things will be "smart" – meaning capable of adapting to the circumstances and specific domains to use the data they are collecting to improve efficiencies.[5] The devices will be remotely operable, allowing people to unlock the doors to their home, turn off a kitchen appliance, and check the tire pressure in their cars,[6] all while miles away, perhaps working in their offices or on vacation.[7] Embedded transmitters will gather self-generated information – meaning the information collected will be "bottom-up," initiated in some way by the person who is the subject, instead of "top-down," from the government to an involuntary citizen participant.[8]

Also, the Internet of Things systems generally will not operate as a seamless whole, but rather foster mass self-cybersurveillance differently within specific domains, such as in the home, car, office, and nontangible arenas such as personal health. The domain-specific structure of the Internet of Things is advanced by the purposive nature of the connected devices. For example, the systems in a car generally will concern the safe and efficient operability of the car, as compared to a Fitbit or heart tracker, which are designed to provide particular body metrics for later evaluation.

If the digital age has fundamentally changed mass surveillance, then the Internet of Things is fundamentally changing mass surveillance in the digital age. Individuals use self-surveillance tools executively to manage themselves in ways and orders of magnitude unavailable to previous generations. Industry not only uses these surveillance tools as means to an end, but also treats the data produced as a commodity in commerce. In a sense, the Internet of Things creates a new gold rush of information – determining propensities, habits, and characteristics of users that can lead to greater efficiencies and profits. With a gold rush, though, is a dark side: hacking, ransoms, malware, misuse, and more.

Of critical importance will be who gains access to the growing treasure trove of information from the Internet of Things. Will it be family members, friends, industry, hackers,

3 *See, e.g.*, *Nest Thermostats*, Nest, https://nest.com/thermostat/install-and-explore/ (describing Nest thermostats, which track heat and air conditioning consumption, sense when residents leave their home, and automatically adjust the temperature).

4 *See* Emma Bazilian, *Toothbrush, a Mini Drone and More*, AdWeek (Mar. 11, 2015), http:// www.adweek .com/news-gallery/advertising-branding/week-s-must-haves-smart-toothbrush-phone-charging-bracelet-and-more-163341 (a smart toothbrush "connects to an app on your smartphone to track your brushing habits and provides real-time feedback on how to improve your routine").

5 *See, e.g.*, Steve Lohr, *Homes Try to Reach Smart Switch*, N.Y. Times (Apr. 22, 2015), http://www.nytimes .com/2015/04/23/business/energy-environment/homes-try-to-reach-smart-switch.html (stating a home owner trimmed his electricity bill by 40 percent after installing a smart thermostat).

6 Pepitone, *supra* note 1.

7 As one television commercial noted, we will be able to lock a car remotely, from a cell phone. *See Buick March Madness Event, Remote TV Spot, 'RemoteLink App,'* Ispot, https://www.ispot.tv/ad/A1qT/ buick-march-madness-event-remotelink-app.

8 The Internet of Things creates pathways for data flows that originate, often intentionally, with the subject to be surveilled. In this way, it is considered bottom-up. This information flows to manufacturers of the devices and often to other third parties, either through trade, sale, barter, or hacking.

insurance companies, the public, the government, or all of the above? The information generated by the transmitting devices easily can be shared with application developers, manufacturers, and other third parties. The data trail often is invisible. Unlike a police tail or cameras fixed on buildings, the surveillance from the interconnected devices engages the observed activity or thing silently, like an electric car in motion. The devices can avoid fear of threats precisely because the potential harms from shared information are unseen and often surface far downstream.[9]

The legal issues created by these devices are nuanced, complex, and dynamic, given the ever-advancing nature of interconnected radio-frequency devices. The sharing and dissemination of self-generated data remains largely unregulated. While federal statutes intervene to govern the commercial transmission of data to some extent, and state governments are beginning to tackle regulatory responses, the regulatory response is limited at best. The Fourth Amendment also provides some protection against connected devices' data dissemination, but the courts' continued reliance on cases decided in the latter part of the twentieth century has left this amendment ill-equipped to deal with digital advances.

The main conclusion this chapter draws is that until laws are enacted to afford some protection of self-generated data, particularly for data voluntarily disclosed in a limited fashion, traditional privacy limits will be ineffective. Instead, the most likely short-term protection of privacy should result from the pragmatic concept of interest convergence. This convergence will occur when the interests of consumers and companies align to promote privacy options,[10] especially if privacy becomes an increasingly valued commodity to consumers.

I The Internet of Things

A *What Is the Internet of Things?*

> "The ... first 20 years of the Web have been focused on human beings. The next era is going to be inanimate things."[11]

1 It Is Not What It Says It Is

Rather than simply consisting of *things* connected to the *Internet*, the Internet of Things is something broader and more organic. Although the core component of the Internet of Things consists of a group of devices connected to the Internet through local Internet protocol (IP) addresses,[12] the Internet of Things is more accurately described as a group of devices connected by radio transmitters to a network for a specific purpose. While some of these networks link to the Internet, not all do or need to do so in order to

9 *See, e.g.*, Michael S. Schmidt & Michael D. Shear, *Drones Hover above, Seen but Not Halted*, N.Y. TIMES (Jan. 30, 2015), http://www.nytimes.com/2015/01/30/us/for-super-bowl-and-big-games-drone-flyovers-are-rising-concern.html.

10 Businesses have incentives to protect privacy of customers. Hackers are a threat to their products, and companies that encrypt transmissions and allow for password protection will better protect their standing in the marketplace.

11 Pepitone, *supra* note 1 (quoting Sanjay Sarma, Associate Professor of Engineering, M.I.T.).

12 These addresses are composed of thirty-two bytes expressed as four groups of numbers separated by periods. For example, 356.202.413.100 might be one IP address.

function within their domains. Furthermore, the systems of devices can measure tangible things,such as how many times a heart beats in a minute, or intangibles,such as temperature.

2 What The Internet of Things Really Is: An Amalgamation of Semiindependent Systems of Connected Sensors

A common thread in the Internet of Things is the presence of semiautonomous data-generating sensors. The sensors in the devices generally monitor things with a particular purpose. For example, a smart thermostat monitors temperature, yet it does so not only on the basis of the traditional factor of time, but also using other factors, such as whether people or pets are present. A car might have special sensors for its backup camera to photograph the relevant areas when the car is in reverse, and it also might contain a radar system to determine what objects are nearby. These features are automated to a large extent, allowing devices to operate remotely.

In effect, the term "Internet of Things" is a proxy for a conceptualization of the way devices can communicate and connect with each other to accumulate, sort, and transmit data. Perhaps the most that can be said about pinning down exactly what the Internet of Things comprises is that, as it continues to grow, its definition will evolve.

3 Why Domains Matter

Conceptualizing the Internet of Things as one contiguous whole leads to inaccuracy. The nature and scope of the connected devices often depend on the particular industry, activity, or realm of functionality within which the devices operate, which will be described here as domains. The devices are purposed within the context of the setting and are automated or set to collect and transmit data for a specific reason. That is why there are different types of interconnectivity within the home (such as for appliances and lights), cars (such as for location and brakes), clothing (such as for location and condition), medicine (for heart rate and exercise), unmanned aircraft (drones), businesses, and even cities (for electric grids and security). That is also why the description "Internet of Everything" misses the import of the domain-specific significance within the broad umbrella of the Internet of Things.

B *How Does the Internet of Things Work?*

1 Interconnected Devices

The Internet of Things relies on devices that are able to connect with each other, generally by radio frequency (RF) over networks. These networks include the Internet and Local Area Networks (LANs).[13] Often, the transmitter will connect through a wireless LAN (WLAN) network, or Wi-Fi, which uses 2.4-gigahertz radio frequency. It can communicate through a less powerful connection, though, such as Bluetooth. Ethernet cables also can connect networks. Thus, the networks are essentially an amalgamation of software and devices with transmitters.

[13] These networks use special ways to communicate. The most common one today is the Transmission Control Protocol/Internet Protocol (TCP/IP).

2 Multifunctional Devices

A key to understanding the devices within the Internet of Things is that they are generally multifunctional, such that their form and function can be separated. A smart watch offers the time, but also might provide the temperature and email. A smart car transports its occupants, but also can have systems that collect and transmit data for specific functions, such as automated backup cameras, radar detection, and brake sensors. Smart television sets not only provide programming, but also can be triggered remotely by voice commands.[14]

3 Creating Multiple Levels of Mass Surveillance Systems

The self-generating surveillance systems have differing levels of breadth and depth. Some of the systems are microoriented, such as monitoring how active a person is who wears a biomedical device such as a Fitbit, and some are macrooriented, such as monitoring an area of a city for electricity consumption, traffic patterns, and criminal activity.[15] The microoriented surveillance often becomes a component of larger systems. The heart tracker, for example, joins with blood pressure evaluation, a sleep assessor, and a pedometer to create a better gauge of personal health. A single individual's information, in turn, can be accessed, aggregated – even anonymized – and sorted by health companies or insurers to predict health trends and create more efficiencies in their businesses.

A central feature of these structures is that they are often formed from voluntary self-surveillance facilitated by the Internet of Things. That is, the subjects either initiate surveillance (by, e.g., putting on wearable tech or buying a smart television) or consent to surveillance (through, e.g., html cookies deposited in Web sites). The information then starts flowing by being consensually shared with the application maker or software manufacturer and then often finds its way into the information marketplace. The information stream can then move from within the industry domain to other private domains and the government. While the flow of information is often obscured or hidden, that is not always the case. Some Web sites expressly state they will convey user information. To illustrate, one site declares: "[We] uses cookies to personalize content and ads to make our site easier for you to use. We also do share that information with third parties for ads and analytics."[16] Through such declarations, the information is now free to flow from industry to government.

4 By Domain

Some domains stand out in their Internet of Things development. The domains include the health industry, clothing or wearables, electronic devices, consumer preferences, homes, vehicles, and cities. These domains are discussed in greater detail in the following.

14 *See, e.g., Not in Front of the Telly: Warning Over 'Listening' TV*, BBC (Feb. 9, 2015, 6:20 PM), http://www.bbc.com/news/technology-31296188 ("The policy explains that the TV set will be listening to people in the same room to try to spot when commands or queries are issued via the remote. If your spoken words include personal or other sensitive information, that information will be among the data captured and transmitted to a third party").

15 *See, e.g., Surveillance Society: Wearable Fitness Devices Often Carry Security Risks*, PITT. POST GAZETTE (Aug. 3, 2015), http://www.post-gazette.com/news/surveillance-society/2015/08/03/Surveillance-Society-Wearable-fitness-devices-often-carry-security-risks/stories/201508030023.

16 *See*, TNW, http://thenextweb.com/insider/.

a *Health*

In the digital age, access to health information is readily available to the public through means other than visits to a doctor. For example, cybernetic devices are used to access physiological information and manage one's own biological processes by obtaining data about bodily functions.[17] Perhaps the most common illustration of bioaccess today is the movement tracking monitor, such as the Fitbit. These devices meticulously measure bioactivity, such as steps taken, heart rate, pulse, sleeping proficiency, and other biometric characteristics. The devices record and transmit the biometric data so it can be stored, sorted, and evaluated. In this regard, the devices become a portable medical health technician, one that is on call and able to work seamlessly 24/7. Further, the data can be easily shared with the manufacturers of the devices and other third parties after they are transmitted.[18]

These health-related applications or devices are a major source of self-generating data. While health care self-surveillance would be extremely costly if a health care professional were required to take the time to gather the information, especially at a medical office or hospital, these devices reduce costs substantially. While not every metric can use an automated device as of yet – for example, watching a person sleep all night in a supervised study still occurs at a medical facility – medicine has welcomed remote and patient-generated information.

In addition to leveraging portable private devices used by patients, the medical profession is relying directly on the Internet of Things to increase health care efficiencies. Medical records are now kept electronically and backed up on the Internet cloud, and devices are interconnected in hospitals to promote collaborative care from one department to another, building comprehensive data pools for patients. Private companies are leveraging the national effort to take advantage of the Internet of Things by asking patients to supply information electronically without direct physician or nurse interviews, saving considerable resources.[19] Thus, the Internet of Things is radically transforming health care provider–patient interaction and the efficiencies of data collection.[20]

b *Clothing – Wearable Technology*

The wristwatch is perhaps the most common piece of wearable technology today, but it is far from the only one. There are smart socks, jewelry,[21] shirts, and other clothing as well. Soon, all kinds of wearables will have embedded transmitters, capable of collecting and sending billions of bytes of data. Wearable clothes measure heart rate and breathing and there is a

17 The access to biological information, sometimes called biohacking, offers a systems-based approach for executive self-management. Spencer Michels, *What Is Biohacking and Why Should We Care?* PBS Newshour (Sept. 23, 2014, 2:57 PM), http://www.pbs.org/newshour/updates/biohacking-care/. Thus, people can be viewed as a part of the Internet of Things. *Internet of Things (IoT)*, TechTarget (July 2016), http://internetofthingsagenda.techtarget.com/definition/Internet-of-Things-IoT.

18 *See Fitbit Privacy Policy*, Fitbit, https://www.fitbit.com/legal/privacy.

19 *See 64 Healthcare IoT Startups in Patient Monitoring, Clinical Efficiency, Biometrics, and More*, CB Insights (Mar. 31, 2016), https://www.cbinsights.com/blog/iot-healthcare-market-map-company-list/.

20 To illustrate, Apple's HealthKit works as a data collector from patients without human intermediaries. The information is uploaded to the health care provider through an application. *Health*, Apple, http://www.apple.com/ios/health/.

21 *See, e.g.*, Cuff, http://shop.cuff.io/; Stephanie Ellen Chan, *Smart Jewelry: 5 Gadgets to Keep Notifications at Your Fingertips*, readwrite (Jan. 20, 2014), http://readwrite.com/2014/01/20/5-pieces-of-smart-jewelry-to-keep-notifications-at-your-fingertips/.

sleeve used by baseball players that measures how much force is being placed on elbow ligaments while throwing a ball.[22] Not only do these wearables provide data, but also the data is then readily accessible on devices for download and review. The wearers will purchase these items as part of an intentional effort to create data with a specific purpose.

The wearables will have several functions. Watches, for example, will still provide the time, but also function as monitors, determining how many steps the person is taking in a day to show the level of activity, what kind of breaking news stories are occurring, or what text messages are being sent to the wearer.[23] Jewelry can send emergency alerts, notify the user of calls or texts, and even function as a pedometer.[24] Shirts can track the performance of the athletes who wear them. The nature and scope of the data transmitted are still evolving, but the possibilities are seemingly endless.

c *Traditional Electronic Devices*

Traditional electronic devices provide another Internet of Things arena or domain. These devices include televisions, cell phones, game platforms,[25] MP3 devices, and more. This is especially true for the ubiquitous cellular telephone, which occupies a unique place in the digital era. The cell phone, which gets its name from the cells into which phone companies divide geographic areas from which to select the tower that will provide the best connectivity, is often thought of more as a minicomputer than as a sensor-laden radio transmitter.

Yet, the cell phone serves as a purposed radio transmitter within the Internet of Things in several ways. First, cell phones are constantly tracked by phone companies to determine their locations for proximity to the nearest cell phone towers,[26] maximizing the effectiveness of the transmission. The data, though, can have another function. The cell site location data creates a history of the device, which means we essentially facilitate a self-tracking narrative just by carrying a phone wherever we go.[27] Notably, the phones provide significant and constant locational data even when not in use. This cell site location data applies not only to the phone, but also to other electronic devices, such as tablets using SIM cards to send out radio waves to nearby cell towers on a regular basis.

Cell phones also run a wide variety of applications that permit the transmission of additional types of information. When users play games on a phone, such as Solitaire, Angry Birds, Minecraft, or Words with Friends, the games allow the developers of the applications and third parties, such as advertisers, to acquire information about the players.[28] The nature

22 *See, e.g.* Mike Vorkunov, *Advancing Technology Raises Questions*, USA Today Sports (Sept. 22, 2016), at 10C.; *see also* Blacksocks, www.blacksocks.com.

23 *See, e.g., Fitbit,* Fitbit, http://www.fitbit.com/#i.1r2ovyecs6fal1. The Fitbit can mark steps, sleep time, restfulness, heartbeats, and more. It can be linked to the Internet to store this information. *Id.*

24 *See, e.g.,* Cuff, *supra* note 21.

25 Ashish Mahendra, *How Internet of Things Revolutionize Gaming Industry?* Internet of Things Worms (Nov. 22, 2015), http://iotworm.com/internet-of-things-changes-gaming-industry/. Game platforms include the Xbox360, PlayStation, Wii, GameCube, and more. *Id.*

26 *See* Timothy Menard & Jeff Miller, *GPS Capabilities of the iPhone 4 and iPhone 3G for Vehicle Tracking Using FreeSim Mobile*, Academia.edu, http://www.academia.edu/545842/Comparing_the_GPS_Capabilities_of_the_iPhone_4_and_iPhone_3GS_for_Vehicle_Tracking_using_FreeSim_Mobile. In fact, the cell phone can be tracked almost every seven seconds to ensure it has access to the preferred cell tower for reception purposes.

27 *See* Laura M. Holson, *Privacy Lost: These Phones Can Find You*, N.Y. Times (Oct. 23, 2007), http://www.nytimes.com/2007/10/23/technology/23mobile.html?_r=0.

28 Stephen Braun & Michael Liedtke, *Report: Spies Use Smartphone Apps to Track People*, Yahoo! News (Jan. 27, 2014), http://news.yahoo.com/report-spies-smartphone-apps-track-people-1904 34189.html.

and scope of the information transmitted to the developers, from location, to contacts, to Web sites visited, can be extensive and informative. The dissemination of the information often does not terminate with the developers, but, rather, continues flowing into the information marketplace.

d *Consumer Preferences*

Commercial tracking of present and potential customers offers companies insights and leverage points in the marketplace.[29] While some of this type of tracking is not solely a result of self-surveillance, much of it involves voluntary permission by the surveilled and at least putative knowledge of its occurrence through privacy policies. Many users have at least some understanding that "the price of admission" of accessing a Web site is tracking of the user.

Consumers sometimes are facilitators in the tracking enterprise, even playing a role in determining what ads trackers place. Called "data driven dynamic advertising,"[30] the ads are fitted to user preferences on all kinds of devices. The era of "one size fits all" advertising is receding. For example, Google targets ads to consumers based on user interests and demographics.[31]

Consumers also inadvertently permit corporate tracking. When customers enter a store, the store can track physical movements through cell phones and thereby determine shopping habits, from what floors and departments the customers visit to how long and how often those customers visit.[32] This data provides a treasure trove of information to a company – especially to advertisers – who wish to be responsive to consumer trends. Google Plus, for example, is a social network, but it accesses a plethora of personal information because it aggregates data from all Google services associated with a user's account, including Gmail, Google Maps, and YouTube.[33] This allows Google to track the habits of customers.[34]

The tracking of customers and their cell phones can occur even outside brick and mortar businesses through stationary objects, such as garbage cans[35] and billboards.[36]

29 Elizabeth Dwoskin & Greg Bensinger, *Tracking Technology Sheds Light on Shopper Habits*, WALL ST. J. (Dec. 9, 2013), http://www.wsj.com/articles/SB10001424052702303332904579230401030827722. The tracking of customers often occurs in the retail world and can occur from different vantage points, ranging from physical location to propensities based on inferences drawn from algorithms.

30 *See, e.g.*, *Personalization – Powered by Data*, JIVOX, http://jivox.com/page/personalized-advertising.

31 *See Ad Targeting*, GOOGLE, https://support.google.com/adsense/answer/9713?hl=en.

32 *See* Stephanie Clifford & Quentin Hardy, *Attention Shoppers: Store Is Tracking Your Cell*, N.Y. TIMES (July 14, 2013), http://www.nytimes.com/2013/07/15/business/attention-shopper-stores-are-tracking-your-cell.html?_r=0 (retailers use signals from shoppers' cell phones "to learn information as varied as their sex, how many minutes they spend in the candy aisle and how long they look at merchandise before buying it").

33 Claire Cain Miller, *The Plus in Google Plus? It's Mostly for Google*, N.Y. TIMES (Feb. 14, 2014), http://www.nytimes.com/2014/02/15/technology/the-plus-in-google-plus-its-mostly-for-google.html). Google Plus has 540 million monthly users. *Id.*

34 *Id.*

35 Rachel Savage, *Snooping Garbage Bins in City of London Ordered to Be Disabled*, BLOOMBERG (Aug. 12, 2013), http://www.bloomberg.com/news/articles/2013-08-12/snooping-garbage-bins-in-city-of-london-ordered-to-be-disabled.

36 *See, e.g.*, *Advertising Company Will Use Its Billboards to Track Passing Cellphones*, NPR (Feb. 29, 2016), http://www.npr.org/sections/thetwo-way/2016/02/29/468598100/using-billboards-company-will-collect-personal-information-to-help-advertisers. Smart billboards were introduced to maximize the benefits from outdoor advertising. *Id.*

These tools are part of self-generating data systems because the initiation point is the customer, who is in the possession of a cell phone in public. Smart garbage cans not only welcome waste, but are information collectors as well. The dual functionality can be seen in their price tags – these cans might cost in excess of forty-five thousand dollars.[37] One notable use of such cans occurred during the London Olympics in 2012, when the cans were used to track passing traffic.[38] The Renew Pods, as they were known, were kept operational after the Olympics and continued tracking passersby for several years, with anonymized information collected for use about traffic patterns and potential customers – particularly their shopping habits.[39]

Another notable illustration of cell phone customer tracking outside stores involves the largest supplier of outdoor billboards, Clear Channel Outdoors. It has announced the creation of smart billboards, using a program called Radar.[40] These billboards can track the cell phones of drivers and passengers in their vicinity and then follow up and determine whether these individuals have accessed the site for which a billboard was advertising. While not exactly parallel to the film *Minority Report*,[41] in which a small poster ad specifically targeted the protagonist, John Anderton, to sell him a particular type of beverage, it does create a whole new form of performance tracking.

The tracking of customers is especially prevalent on the Internet, where private companies plant "cookies,"[42] tiny files, on the customers' computers. These cookies act as identification tags, delivered through Web browsers when a computer user visits a Web site. Sometimes, third parties place cookies or tags on the users' computers as well; these are often placed by advertisers who wish to use banners or ads on the visited sites.[43] Internet users can remove cookies or block tracking,[44] but unless users act with intentionality – and understand who the invisible trackers are – they will be subject to multiple cookies and the distribution of information to others.[45] Third parties obtain some of the information from the site owners or through the placement of their own third-party cookies.[46]

Companies have begun using radio frequency identification technology (RFID) to track items from a considerable distance.[47] This technology implants a small radio

37 *See* Savage, *supra* note 36.

38 *Id.*

39 *See id.* (stating that the garbage bins collect data about the shopping habits of people who pass by, so the LCD screens on the bins display targeted ads).

40 *See, e.g.*, *Clear Channel Outdoor America Launches 'RADAR,' – New Data Analytics Solution for Marketers to Plan and Buy out-of-Home Media and Measure Target Audience Segment Outcomes*, Bus. Wire (Feb. 29, 2016), http://www.businesswire.com/news/home/20160229005959/en/Clear-Channel-Outdoor-Americas-Launches-'RADAR'—.

41 *Minority Report*, IMDb (Twentieth Century Fox Film corp. 2002), http://www.imdb.com/title/tt0181689/.

42 *All About Cookies*, Allaboutcookies.org, http://www.allaboutcookies.org/cookies/ ("Cookies are usually small text files, given ID tags that are stored on your computer's browser directory or program data subfolders").

43 *See How Does Third-Party Ad Serving Work?* Allaboutcookies.org, http://www.allaboutcookies.org/ad-serving/ (explaining cookies' role in third-party advertisements on a Web site).

44 The Web site Investis shows users how to block or track cookies in their browsers. *See How to Disable Cookies in Your Browser*, Investis, http://files.investis.com/info/disabling-cookies.html.

45 Max Stul Oppenheimer, *Internet Cookies: When Is Permission Consent?* 85 Neb. L. Rev. 383, 384 (2006).

46 *See id.* at 386 n.15.

47 *See* David R. Hancox, *Using RFID Technology to Enhance Corporate Effectiveness*, Internal Auditor (Apr. 1, 2006), https://iaonline.theiia.org/using-rfid-technology-to-enhance-corporate-effectiveness.

chip in an object so it is subject to monitoring at any time.[48] In 2003, for example, Wal-Mart Stores embedded RFID technology in lipstick containers for sale in its Broken Arrow, Oklahoma, store.[49] These containers could be tracked from seven hundred miles away by researchers, including a video monitor of the consumers handling the products.[50]

e *Homes: Lights, Temperature, and Action*

The smart home will have multiple semiautonomous networks to allow for data accumulation, adjustments, and remote operation. These networks occur with temperature, lighting, appliances, and more, and involve a group of mass self-surveillance systems working in concert.

Start with a smart thermostat, such as the Next brand,[51] which can reveal several data streams all revolving around temperature: whether occupants are currently in the house, how long occupants slept the night before, which rooms are likely occupied, and when. The thermostats are purposed to adjust temperatures automatically in unoccupied areas to save energy.[52] In this regard, the thermostat "learns" about the inhabitants and their propensities at home.[53]

A smart lighting device also adjusts to the circumstances in the home. The lighting device can learn the "household's daily patterns over time and set itself to turn on the lights just before the family starts arriving home in the evening."[54] The lighting mechanism can even learn to adjust the intensity of the light when the occupant gets out of bed at night to soothe the user.[55]

Not only can smart appliances be automated and operated remotely, but overall electric consumption can be tracked, monitored, and assessed. Load monitoring[56] allows devices to be remotely tracked and provides information about varying aspects of usage.[57] Even smart

48 *See id.* (RFID tags were also used by Gillette Corporation, which put hidden tags inside Mach3 razor blade packages).

49 *See* Laura Hildner, *Defusing the Threat of RFID: Protecting Consumer Privacy through Technology-Specific Legislation at the State Level*, 41 Harv. C.R.-C.L.L. Rev. 133, 133 (2006).

50 *Id.* at 134.

51 The company that made the Next Thermostat was purchased by Google for $3.2 billion. Josh Ong, *Google to Acquire Nest Labs for $3.2 Billion*, TNW Blog (Jan. 13, 2014), http://thenextweb.com/google/2014/01/13/google-acquires-nest-3-2-billion/.

52 *See* Kashmir Hill, *When Smart Homes Get Hacked: I Haunted a Complete Stranger's House via the Internet*, Forbes (July 26, 2013, 9:15 AM) http://www.forbes.com/sites/kashmirhill/2014/11/07/how-did-law-enforcement-break-tor/.

53 *Nest Thermostat*, Nest, https://nest.com/ie/thermostat/meet-nest-thermostat/.

54 *See* Sharon O'Malley, *'Internet of Things' Front and Center at Annual Consumer Electronics Show*, CONSTRUCTION DIVE (Jan. 15, 2015), http://www.constructiondive.com/news/internet-of-things-front-and-centerat-annual-consumer-electronics-show/353352/.

55 *Id.*

56 See, e.g., Nonintrusive Appliance Load Monitoring (NALM), which remotely tracks electricity usage. Michael Zeifman & Kurt Roth, *Nonintrusive Appliance Load Monitoring (NAILM): Promise and Practice*, Dep't of Energy (Mar. 1, 2012), http://energy.gov/sites/prod/files/2013/12/f6/nonintrusive_load_monitor.pdf.

57 Mario E. Berges et al., *Enhancing Electricity Audits in Residential Buildings with Nonintrusive Load Monitoring*, 14 J. Indus. Ecology 844 (2010) (stating Nonintrusive Load Monitoring is a technique for deducing the power consumption and operational schedule of individual electricity loads in a building).

washing machines exist.[58] Cloudwash, a prototype, is a connected machine that has interactive capabilities.[59]

There even is a smart home "assistant," as represented by the Amazon Echo. The Echo is a freestanding electronic device that connects to a network through Wi-Fi and can be asked all sorts of questions – about the weather, news, etc. – or tasked with keeping grocery and other lists.[60]

f *Smart Vehicles*

Even before the advent of the self-driving car, vehicles had been driving toward the smart world. Vehicles have a variety of sensor-based systems. They can be started remotely, for example, and have recording devices that accumulate data points about the car's driving history,[61] from "where drivers have been, like physical location recorded at regular intervals, the last location the vehicles were parked, distances and times traveled, and previous destinations entered into navigation systems."[62] Vehicles now have their own "black boxes" containing a device that measures various statistics about the operation of the car.[63] The device tracks miles traveled, speeds, and other pertinent information about the car.[64] This information is obtainable by car manufacturers to track and improve their products.[65] In the near future, cars will not only generate information for drivers and manufacturers, but will engage in direct vehicle-to-vehicle communication, promoting safety (avoiding accidents) and efficiency.[66]

The existing systems have been obscured by the promise of self-driving vehicles, which are simply very smart cars – mass surveillance systems that apply to steering, braking, and strategic maneuvering, such as parking. Some vehicles are already packaging some of these smart features – Tesla automobiles, for example, have automated steering and braking features. The death of a driver using the automated Tesla steering system in May

58 *See, e.g.*, Kyle Vanhemert, *This Brilliant Washing Machine Is a Roadmap for the Internet of Things*, WIRED (Apr. 7, 2014, 6:30 AM), http://www.wired.com/2014/04/this-brilliant-internet-connected-washer-is-a-roadmap-for-the-internet-of-things/ (describing Cloudwash, a prototype washing machine by Berg Co.).

59 *Id.*

60 Amazon has named its voice assistant the Alexa Voice Service. *Amazon Echo*, AMAZON, https://www.amazon.com/gp/product/B00X4WHP5E?tag=googhydr-20&hvadid=88444290302&hvpos=1t1&hvexid=&hvnetw=g&hvrand=10131446964744482445&hvpone=&hvptwo=&hvqmt=e&hvdev=c&ref=pd_sl_5bkerg09re_e_yac_yfmrw4.

61 This information is shared with the manufacturer and third parties. Aaron M. Kessler, *Report Sees Weak Security In Cars' Wireless Systems*, N.Y. TIMES (Feb. 9, 2015), at B4, *available at* http://www.nytimes.com/2015/02/ 09/business/report-sees-weak-security-in-cars-wireless-systems.html?_r=0.

62 *Id.* at B4.

63 Kim Komando, *Your Car's Hidden "Black Box" and How to Keep It Private*, USA TODAY (Dec. 26, 2014, 7:00 AM), http://www.usatoday.com/story/ tech/columnist/ komando/2014/12/26/keep-your-car-black-box-private/20609035/ ("Since the early 2000s, the National Highway Traffic Safety Administration has been collecting black box information to get a better picture of the circumstances surrounding car accidents").

64 Id.

65 *See* David Uris, *Big Brother and a Little Black Box: The Effect of Scientific Evidence on Privacy Rights*, 42 SANTA CLARA L. REV. 995, 1002 (2002) (noting that engineers have utilized the data provided by black boxes to enhance the operation of airbag sensing systems).

66 *See* Kessler, supra note 60, at B4 (noting vehicle-to-vehicle communication is expected to be available in the near future).

of 2016, though, showed that the premise might not be completely ready for the mass consumer marketplace, but remains promising.[67]

g *Cities*

Although smart cities are not as self-generating and bottom-up as other Internet of Things mass surveillance systems, they still are dependent on self-generated data, supplemented by data from companies and municipalities. Cities are under pressure to get smarter. The voluntary appearance of people in public has allowed cities to extend surveillance in all directions. This is particularly true with camera surveillance in the skies, on the ground, and in the seas. What might become a trend, for example, is already in operation in Tijuana, Mexico. A small, desk-sized object circles over the city on a daily basis.[68] The object – a small, unmanned, low-altitude aircraft commonly referred to as a drone – is capable of twenty-minute battery-operated flights. The drone sends live video to screens at the police headquarters. Several drones are being used both day and night in Tijuana for crime interdiction, particularly against burglaries.[69] In Great Britain, multiple cameras appear throughout the country, part of a network of closed-circuit televisions also utilized for crime interdiction.[70] In the United States, "red light cameras" are already installed in many U.S. jurisdictions.[71]

II Privacy

A *Self-Surveillance and Privacy*

> You already have zero privacy – get over it. – Scott McNealy[72]

The different domains of the Internet of Things share a common thread: self-generation of data generally accessible by third parties. By virtue of this sharing, significant pressures are being placed on those wishing to live highly private lives. To live even a pedestrian life off "the grid,"[73] for example, is exponentially more difficult now in the new data-sharing digital age. There are more obstacles to overcome, since government regulation is imposed even on those away from the grid. For example, electricity generation is governed by regulations; individuals cannot simply throw on solar cells on a homemade

67 Bill Vlasic & Neal E. Boudette, *Self-Driving Tesla Was Involved in Fatal Crash, U.S. Says*, N.Y. Times (June 30, 2016), http://www.nytimes.com/2016/07/01/business/self-driving-tesla-fatal-crash-investigation.html?_r=0. In the fall of 2016, Tesla subsequently modified its autopilot system to center more on radar.

68 William M. Welch, *Police Drones Fly at Nation's Doorstep*, USA Today (Jan. 29, 2014), at News 2A. No such mandate to permit low-flying drones exists in the United States.

69 *Id.*

70 Laura K. Donohue, *Anglo-American Privacy and Surveillance*, 96 J. Crim. L. & Criminology 1059, 1185 (2005–2006).

71 *See Speed and Red Light Camera Laws*, Governors Highway Safety Ass'n (Sept. 2016), http://www.ghsa.org/html/stateinfo/laws/auto_enforce.html (noting that thirteen states prohibit red light cameras, twelve states have laws authorizing them, and the rest have no laws on the topic).

72 Jeffrey Rosen, *The Eroded Self*, N.Y. Times Mag. (Apr. 30, 2000), http://www.nytimes.com/library/magazine/home/20000430mag-internetprivacy.html.

73 "Off the grid" generally denotes living away from societal infrastructures such as roads, electricity, and phone. *See generally*, Scott Huler, On the Grid: A Plot of Land, An Average Neighborhood, and the Systems that Make Our World Work (2010).

structure in a remote patch of land and carry on unregulated.[74] Municipalities might find such an unregulated operation "unsafe," and the individual would be at risk of penalties or conviction.[75]

Extensive self-surveillance also would not be readily understood in a predigital era of walls and doors, where most surveillance was by third-party observation.[76] The traditional idea of self-surveillance was narrowly cabined, and almost an oxymoron. In the years preceding the digital age, people would rarely surveil themselves. They might write a diary of the highlights or lowlights of a day or take family pictures for albums or movies but did not generally create purposed, data-rich narratives that could provide around-the-clock details yielding to third parties a vivid picture of their lives. The idea of detailed observation over time, even if initiated by Sherlock Holmes – would be excessively costly and impractical. Consider how difficult would it be to determine, for example, heart rate over time, the exact nutrients one consumed in a week, or what times the lights in a house were turned on and off over a year-long period. Gaps in information likely would abound. The notion of information gaps is understandable, at least before the videotape, electronic medical records, or other transmitting sensors that could track accurately and unobtrusively over time.

When self-surveillance did occur, it generally was private and introspective. People would maintain personal diaries, for example, which could be locked away in a private place, such as a drawer or cabinet. Photos or videos were stored in the home for use with family and sometimes friends, but not generally shared with strangers or the public.

In recent years, the exponential growth of self-surveillance opportunities has caused almost all persons living on the grid to engage in some form of bottom-up surveillance. The growth has provided streams of data heading to third parties – including industry and government. Tracking of physical location paralleled tracking in cyberspace. As one commentator noted, "Now, advertisers are paying a premium to follow people around the Internet, wherever they go, with highly specific marketing messages."[77]

B *The Impact of Invisible Surveillance*

Although the flow of data has been a veritable gold rush for companies and advertisers, it can be pernicious if misused. This is especially true when the tracking is invisible, exposing the data to many intermediaries. A newspaper investigating the number of intermediaries who track people for marketing purposes found that "in between the Internet user and the advertiser, [there were] more than 100 middlemen – tracking companies,

74 See, for example, a Huntsville, Alabama, man who faced his home's being condemned by the city after obtaining his own electricity. WAFF-TV 48, *This Man Fought for His Country, Now He's Facing Arrest for Living Off-Grid on His Own Property* (June 12, 2015), https://www.youtube.com/watch?v=7xL5i3iJpKk.; *see also* Arjun Walia, *Florida Makes Off-Grid Living Illegal*, Collective Evolution (Mar. 9, 2014), http://www.collective-evolution.com/2014/03/09/florida-makes-off-grid-living-illegal-mandates-all-homes-must-be-connected-to-an-electricity-grid/.

75 *Id.*

76 *See, e.g., United States v. Fischer*, 38 F.2d 830, 830 (M.D. Pa. 1930) (considering evidence obtained by law enforcement while they physically observed the defendant from a position directly outside his house).

77 Julia Angwin, *The Web's New Gold Mine: Your Secrets*, Wall St. J., July 31, 2010, at W1.

data brokers and advertising networks – competing to meet the growing demand for data on individual behavior and interests."[78] One cautionary tale is that of Adblock Plus, an ad blocking system currently on more than 100 million devices.[79] It was developed in 2007 to protect Internet users from ads. In 2011, however, the blocker transitioned into a different type of Internet tool. Instead of blocking ads, it "allowed ads it deemed 'acceptable' to be seen, often at a price – a controversial move that has positioned it as a gatekeeper between advertisers and its huge user base."[80]

Thus, an important consequence of invisibility[81] is the diminishment of the experience of surveillance,[82] which can cause feelings of invasion, impropriety, and more.[83] Invisibility is exacerbated by the commoditization and streaming of data produced by the Internet of Things to unobserved third parties far downstream from where the information originated.[84]

Combinatory tracking, using data analytics to create audience profiles, takes invisible data gathering to new heights. For example, the employment of sequential data analytics can be seen in the smart billboards discussed above, which gather the cell phone data of passersby and then follow up to see whether the passersby pursued what was advertised on the billboards.[85] The downstream tracking has made some people uncomfortable, with the concept acknowledged as a bit "creepy."[86] As one commentator noted: "Pass a billboard while driving in the next few months, and there is a good chance the company that owns it will know you were there and what you did afterward."[87]

While some surveillance cameras are visible – "red light" cameras and fixed closed circuit television (CCTV) cameras, for example – there is invisible biometric facial surveillance that people confront throughout the digital day. People trigger this surveillance by accessing common venues, such as Facebook and Instagram, which store and categorize posted photos.[88] A new algorithm can even construct face recognition without having to observe the subject face[89] – advancing the frontier of facial tracking to a new level.

78 *Id.*

79 Sapna Maheshwari, *An Ad Blocker, Created to Protect Users from Ads, Instead Opens the Door*, N.Y. Times (Sept. 19, 2016), at B1.

80 *Id.*

81 Laura K. Donohue, *Anglo-American Privacy and Surveillance*, 96 J. Crim. L. & Criminology 1059, 1185 (2005–2006).

82 *See, e.g.*, M. Ryan Calo, *The Drone as Privacy Catalyst*, 64 Stan. L. Rev. Online 29 (Dec. 2011), https://www.stanfordlawreview.org/online/the-drone-as-privacy-catalyst/.

83 S. J. Azar, *Look Who's Stalking: What It Feels Like to Be Put On Surveillance in London*, Tech Radar (May 2, 2016), http://www.techradar.com/news/home-cinema/look-who-s-stalking-what-it-feels-like-to-be-put-on-surveillance-in-london-1319794.

84 Thorin Kosllowski, *Lots of Health Apps Are Selling Your Data. Here's Why*, Lifehacker (May 9, 2014), http://lifehacker.com/lots-of-health-apps-are-selling-your-data-heres-why-1574001899.

85 Sydney Ember, *See That Billboard? It May See You, Too*, N.Y. Times (Feb. 28, 2016), http://www.nytimes.com/2016/02/29/business/media/see-that-billboard-it-may-see-you-too.html.

86 "Still, Mr. Stevens acknowledged that the company's new offering 'does sound a bit creepy.'" *Id.*

87 *Id.*

88 Bryan Clark, *New Facial Recognition Algorithm Is So Smart It Does Not Need to See Your Face*, The Next Web: Insider (Aug. 2016), http://thenextweb.com/insider/2016/08/08/new-facial-recognition-algorithm-is-so-smart-it-doesnt-need-to-see-your-face/#gref.

89 *Id.*

C *The Constitutional and Statutory Framework for Privacy in an Internet of Things World*

1 The Fourth Amendment

Privacy protected by the Fourth Amendment is still predicated on cases from the latter part of the twentieth century, most notably *Katz v. United States*,[90] a case revolving around a government wiretap of a phone conversation in a telephone booth.[91] That case stands for the proposition that Fourth Amendment "searches" are defined as violations of subjectively manifested and objectively reasonable expectations of privacy.[92] At the time, the case was seen as progressive, promoting rights by untethering the boundaries of the Fourth Amendment from physical spaces, protecting people, not places. The test set forth by Justice Harlan in his *Katz* concurrence had the potential for flexibility and adaptability to new technology. Unfortunately, *Katz*'s promise has yet to be fulfilled, with the Court still reluctant to wade into the ongoing digital revolution and the elasticity of the Internet of Things.

a *The Third-Party Doctrine*

A foundational element of the twentieth-century Supreme Court's interpretation of the Fourth Amendment has become known as the Third-Party Doctrine[93] or Third-Party Records Doctrine. This thread promotes a bright line of all-or-nothing privacy for information disclosed to a third party under the Fourth Amendment and has swallowed up much of the discussion about the nuances and intricacies of consent in a digital world.[94]

The Third-Party Doctrine emerged from several progeny of *Katz*. One important decision, the 1976 case of *United States v. Miller*,[95] addressed the question of whether bank records accessed by the government were private under the Fourth Amendment. The Court concluded there was no expectation of privacy in bank records regarding negotiable instruments intended to be a part of a commercial transaction.[96]

Smith v. Maryland[97] followed in 1979 and, with *Miller*, became the cornerstones of the Third-Party Doctrine. In *Smith*, the Court held that pen registers were not within the privacy protected under the Fourth Amendment.[98] The facts of the case are significant. A person suspected of robbing a woman allegedly was calling the victim and threatening her.[99] The police sought and obtained call records in order to determine who was calling. The records were sought to stop ongoing criminal activity, and, further, the police had reason to believe the phone calls were from a person directly involved in the prior robbery.[100]

90 389 U.S. 347 (1967).
91 *Id.* at 348.
92 *Id.* at 362 (Harlan, J., concurring).
93 John Villasenor, *What You Need to Know about the Third-Party Doctrine*, The Atlantic (Dec. 30, 2013).
94 Orin Kerr & Greg Nojeim, *The Data Question: Should the Third-Party Records Doctrine Be Revisited?* A.B.A. J. (Aug. 1, 2012, 9:20 A.M.), http://www.abajournal.com/magazine/article/the_data_question_should_the_third-party_records_doctrine_be_revisited/.
95 425 U.S. 435 (1976).
96 *See id.* at 440.
97 442 U.S. 735 (1979).
98 *Id.* at 751.
99 *Id.* at 737.
100 *Id.* at 737-38.

Smith and *Miller* have been used to justify many forms of bulk data collection, including phone metadata,[101] and the cases appear to legitimize collection of much of the data that flows through the Internet of Things as well. The facts of *Smith*, however, are far removed from justifying bulk data collection, which is a dragnet wholesale appropriation of information, without any prior reasonable expectation of criminality in the data. This wholesale collection is arguably not consonant with the Fourth Amendment's vertical or retail approach to permissible data collection, building on reasonable government action. In essence, the steady stream of information automatically collected from a network of devices is likely far greater than that which occurs from any single pen register focused on specific criminality. This difference reflects not just a change in a matter of degree, but rather a fundamental shift in the nature of police activity – sifting data to find a crime, instead of obtaining evidence to solve a crime.

Although the United States Supreme Court has taken an all-or-nothing approach to voluntarily disclosed information pursuant to *Smith* and *Miller*, the flood of data produced by the Internet of Things and the Internet in general were undoubtedly unforeseen. Today, it makes more sense to some observers to view privacy as relative, supported by gradations, rather than as all or nothing.[102] As one commentator observed:

> The idea that information exposed to others is no longer private has been oversold. Millions of Americans expect all sorts of things exposed to third parties to remain private under state law. And as technology advances and the information we give to ISPs and telcos becomes more and more revealing, even federal courts are beginning to rethink whether *Smith* is the absolute rule the government claims it should be. … On its 35th birthday, *Smith's* vitality is on the decline, and that's a good thing.[103]

b *Due Process*

The due process clause only applies to government conduct, not private companies, limiting its applicability. Also, it will most likely apply, if at all, to the ways governments use Internet of Things data streams, not at the point governments gather the data. If the government uses information to deprive persons of property or liberty interests, the clause can be triggered. For example, if the data causes deprivations of government benefits or increased criminal sentences, the clause might apply. Due process challenges could be made to policing as well. If Internet of Things information is used by the police to calibrate a citizen's threat level in a police–citizen interaction, for example, or if the government misused collected data to spy on spouses or others, a due process argument could be advanced if the use of such information deprived the citizen of liberty without appropriate process. While such arguments are possible, the odds are against their success. It is difficult to attack what you cannot see, given the state of invisibility of the information acquisition and transmission. Also, it might be difficult to explain and understand the algorithms that are challenged.

101 Joseph D. Mornin, *NSA Metadata Collection and the Fourth Amendment*, 29 Berkeley Tech. L.J. 985, 987 (2014) (explaining that the government relies on *Smith* to defend the constitutionality of its bulk data collection).

102 *Smith v. Maryland*, 442 U.S. 735, 748 (1979) (Marshall, J., dissenting).

103 Hanni Fakoury, *Smith v. Maryland Turns 35, But Its Health Is Declining*, Electronic Frontier Found. (June 24, 2014), https://www.eff.org/deep links/2014/06/smith-v-maryland-turns-35-its-healths-declining.

c *Equal Protection*

Equal protection under the law is another constitutional limit, but it also only applies to government conduct, not private entities, and suffers from many of the same limitations as due process. Invisible data accumulation is difficult to evaluate or challenge on the basis of alleged bias against suspect groups. Further, even if government algorithms sort data in ways leading to discriminatory impacts, there generally must be intentional discrimination by the government against suspect classifications for the government conduct to be actionable under equal protection principles. Disparate impact from facially neutral laws is generally insufficient to make out an actionable claim.[104] Yet, facial neutrality could hide valid equal protection claims. Algorithms may appear to sort information neutrally, but developers could incorporate implicit or express biases buried deeply within the software.

2 Statutes

There are few federal statutes that directly impact the self-generation of Internet of Things data. Some of the general statutes are briefly described in the following.

a *The Fair Credit Reporting Act*

While there is no regulation directly monitoring the Internet of Things and the transmission of sensor data through its networks, the Fair Credit Reporting Act (FCRA)[105] governs how credit reporting agencies operate to ensure that their reporting is fair and accurate.[106] The act also regulates information suppliers and has been used to oversee some of the conduct of data brokers.[107] These data brokers get some information originating in the Internet of Things data streams. The FCRA has been used by the Federal Trade Commission to enforce data collection in consumer arenas implicating credit information, as well as social networks and other online companies, such as those using targeted marketing.

b *The USA FREEDOM Act of 2015*

The USA FREEDOM Act[108] was adopted in 2015 as a substitute for some of the provisions of the expiring USA PATRIOT Act. The act was perhaps a reaction in part to the revelations by Edward Snowden about the extensiveness of some of the covert government surveillance programs.[109] The act refined the federal government's powers over obtaining business records, pen registers, and devices for gathering information for purposes involving foreign intelligence, counterterrorism, and crime interdiction.[110] While

104 *See Washington v. Davis*, 426 U.S. 229 (1976); *see also* Richard A. Primus, *Equal Protection and Disparate Impact: Round Three*, 117 U. Harv. L. Rev. 493 (2003).

105 15 U.S.C. § 1681 (2012).

106 *Id.*

107 *Id.*

108 The Act Originally was an acronym, Uniting and Strengthening America by Fulfilling Rights and Ensuring Effective Discipline over Monitoring Act of 2015, Pub. L. No. 114–23, 129 Stat. 268 (2015).

109 *See generally* Paul Rosenzweig, *The Cybersecurity Act of 2015*, Lawfare (Dec. 16, 2015), https://www.lawfareblog.com/cybersecurity-act-2015.

110 Preamble, H.R. 2048, 114th Cong. (2015).

the act did not directly concern the Internet of Things, some of the data governed by the act emanates from sensor-based networks. In particular, the act reigned in collection of phone call records involving metadata and importantly prohibited the bulk or dragnet collection of some data.[111]

c *Cybersecurity Information Sharing Act of 2015*

This act regulates private information shared with the government, including some produced by the Internet of Things.[112] If the information to be shared is not directly related to a cyber threat and the private entity knows that to be the case at the time of sharing, that information is not to be disclosed to the government. If the private entity complies with the statute, liability protection will occur.[113]

d *The Wiretap Act*

The Wiretap Act regulates the interception and disclosure of wire, oral, or electronic communications.[114] The law prohibits the intentional interception or disclosure of the contents of these communications. This act, though, generally does not restrict the transfer of Internet of Things information, if only because the generator of such information generally agrees to its interception or disclosure.

III Legal Issues Relating to Self-Surveillance from the Internet of Things

A *Emerging Threats: Lack of Protection, Hacking, and Profiling*

Threats revolving around the Internet of Things involve increased opportunities for hacking, profiling, and more.[115] These threats are discussed in the following section.

1 A Predicate: Lack of Privacy Protection

The lack of privacy legal protection afforded to data shared by the Internet of Things has led to a heavily trafficked and highly commoditized marketplace in self-generated information. Although much of this information trafficking is in and of itself benign, it also can be readily abused during its aggregation, sorting, and marketplace transfers – especially if a subsequent possessor targets groups and improperly profiles others invisibly. In essence, self-surveillance can be as dangerous as other-surveillance, if not more because of the regular generation of important and often sensitive biological, financial, or other personal information. Self-surveillance, especially when used to profile people, can form a mosaic of intrusions in a manner similar to that described by Justices Samuel Alito and Sonia Sotomayor in their concurrences in the GPS tracking device case, *United States*

111 *See* USA FREEDOM Act of 2015, *supra* note 109 at § 201.
112 S. 754, 114th Cong. (2015).
113 *Id.* at § 106.
114 18 U.S.C. § 119.
115 *See* Katherine Noyes, *"Sometimes I'm Terrified" of the Internet of Things, Says the Father of the Internet*, PC World (Aug. 25, 2015, 6:18 AM), http://www.pcworld.com/article/2975738/internet-of-things/vint-cerf-sometimes-im-terrified-by-the-iot.html.

v. Jones.[116] Under the "mosaic theory," a privacy violation does not require a physical trespass and can even occur in public after an unreasonable amount of time.

a *Surveillance and Power*

Significantly, surveillance is an expression of power yielding valuable and often personal information. This power, as it gathers exceedingly personal data, gives rise to fears of its abuse, especially if its deployment is concentrated in the largest cyber companies or in the government. These abuses are particularly dangerous if they occur in secret, away from the checks and balances provided under the Constitution. As Neil Richards and Jonathan King have observed about possible power abuses, "We cannot have a system, or even the appearance of a system, where surveillance is secret, or where decisions are made about individuals by a Kafkaesque system of opaque and unreviewable decision makers."[117] By recognizing the imbalances caused by data aggregation and sorting, government regulation is needed to prevent the eventual misuse of that data as they flow to the government with or without the intent to harm others.

Perhaps one of the most significant current surveillance power issues is the ease with which the data can be obtained by governments and criminals, who can use the information improperly to their advantage. Criminals can steal identities and credit cards, hold computers for ransom, and stalk victims. Government agents can use imitation cell towers (e.g., Stingrays), weak encryption, and partnerships with private companies to obtain information. Police, for example, in multiple jurisdictions have used Stingrays to spy on cell phones in the local area and refused to account for it or explain why.[118]

i **Government Access to Data: Public–Private Partnerships**

Tracking today often originates from the efforts of private technology or retail companies, combined with our own efforts to self-surveil every aspect of our lives. With these collaborative sources, governmental power to collect, store, and analyze data can seem almost incidental. Yet, a critical point of government access to self-generated data occurs through public–private partnerships, whereby the government intentionally aligns with companies to obtain data. Some partnering has included industry's agreeing to weak encryption of software products that the government could easily break,[119] such as including back doors in software programs.[120]

116 132 S. Ct. 945, 956 (2012) (Sotomayor, J., concurring); *id.* at 961 (Alito, J., concurring). Writing for the majority, Justice Scalia found that the installation of a tracking device on a car was a trespass and search within the meaning of the Fourth Amendment. *Id.* at 952.

117 . Neil M. Richards & Jonathan H. King, *Three Paradoxes of Big Data*, 66 Stan. L. Rev. Online 41, 43 (2013) ("Big data will create winners and losers, and it is likely to benefit the institutions that wield its tools over the individuals being mined, analyzed, and sorted. … Individuals succumb to denial while governments and corporations get away with what they can by default, until they are left reeling from scandal after shock of disclosure"). *Id.* at 45.

118 *See, e.g.*, Ryan Sabalow, *Indiana State Police Tracking Cellphones, But Won't Say How or Why – Law Enforcement Using Methods From NSA Playbook*, Indianapolis Star (Dec. 9, 2013), http://www.indystar.com/story/news/2013/12/08/indiana-state-police-tracking-cellphones-but-wont-say-how-or-why/3908333/ (The article states that the police paid $373, 955 for the Stingray).

119 *See id.* ("The F.B.I., the intelligence agencies and David Cameron, the British prime minister, have all tried to stop Google, Apple and other companies from using encryption technology").

120 With the technology companies holding a key to unlocking their own software, the government could more easily obtain a key as well.

The deep relationship between government and private business began to surface after the Snowden revelations, but government–industry partnerships can be seen as far back as the Cold War.[121] Some of the partnering appeared to be based on "mutual interest."[122] In recent years, these relationships quietly proliferated:

> Thousands of technology, finance and manufacturing companies are working closely with U.S. national security agencies, providing sensitive information and in return receiving benefits that include access to classified intelligence. ... These programs, whose participants are known as trusted partners, extend far beyond what was revealed by Edward Snowden.[123]

Government agencies have used data collected and stored by the telecommunications companies,[124] as well as makers of hardware and software, banks, Internet security providers, and satellite telecommunications companies. The information gathered may be used not just to defend the nation but also to help infiltrate the computers of its adversaries.

While the relationships between government and private companies were symbiotic ones in prior years, many companies are now expressing hesitation to enter into a relationship for various reasons. Some companies realize that government requests for information were "an intrusion into the privacy of their customers and a risk to their businesses."[125] This theme of privacy as a valuable commodity continues today.

ii The Doctrine of Consent

Another major problem associated with the lack of regulation of Internet of Things data involves consent to disseminate the data. Consent figures prominently in assessing many of the legal implications of data transfers from the Internet of Things. Numerous issues revolve around consent – whether mere acquiescence suffices to meet the consent standard, what exactly is its scope, and does consent to disclose to one source mean consent to disclose to all?

aa One Illustration: College and Professional Athletes Many college sports teams now have deals with apparel companies for millions of dollars.[126] These deals will become transformative when the players begin to wear smart apparel, allowing the collection and evaluation of biometric data.[127] Wearable technology just might be the next frontier for

121 *See, e.g., Swiss Cryptography Firm Helped NSA during Cold War*, SWISSINFO.CH (July 30, 2015), http://www.swissinfo.ch/eng/society/codebreaker_swiss-cryptography-firm-helped-nsa-during-cold-war/41576576.

122 *See* David Sanger & Nicole Perlroth, *Obama Heads to Security Talks amid Tensions*, N.Y. TIMES (Feb. 13, 2014), http://www.nytimes.com/2015/02/13/business/obama-heads-to-security-talks-amid-tensions.html ("The long history of quiet cooperation between Washington and America's top technology companies – first to win the Cold War, then to combat terrorism – was founded on the assumption of mutual interest").

123 Mike Riley, *US Agencies Said to Swap Data with Thousands of Firms*, BLOOMBERG TECH. (June 15, 2013), https://www.bloomberg.com/news/articles/2013-06-14/u-s-agencies-said-to-swap-data-with-thousands-of-firms.

124 *See* Sanger & Perlroth, *supra* note 123 (stating that intelligence agencies buy information about flaws in widely used hardware and software and do not reveal the flaws to manufacturers).

125 See Sanger & Perlroth, *supra* note 123 at A3.

126 Marc Tracy, *With Wearable Tech Deals, New Player Data Is Up for Grabs*, N.Y. TIMES, Sept. 9, 2016, at SP1.

127 *Id.*

athletes' rights in big-time college sports.[128] At the University of Michigan, which has a contract for wearable technology, this issue is already emerging.[129] The wearable clothing incorporates different sensors that can collect an array of data, such as data related to speed, distance, vertical leap, height, maximum time aloft, shot attempts, length of ball possession, heart rate, and running routes.[130]

When student-athletes wearing smart apparel start transmitting data to third parties, a significant question involves the security and privacy protection the young athletes will have. Once the information is released, it will be next to impossible to restore it to a "forgotten" status. While the contract at the University of Michigan apparently states that the data collection will be anonymous and comply with all of the applicable laws, how difficult would it be to deanonymize the data, hack them, or do both? The dilemma of who owns self-generated information is an especially thorny one in this context and is not readily resolved by existing legal structures.

This dilemma also will arise at other levels of sport. Major League Baseball approved wearable technology during games in 2016.[131] For example, players can wear the Zephyr Bioharness to track their breathing and heart rate, as well as the Motus sleeve, which has a chip in it that tracks arm angles and the forces placed on the ligaments in the elbow by throwing.[132] The privacy issues created by these emerging self-surveilling sports technologies have become sufficiently important to earn a spot on the agenda in talks between the players' association and Major League Baseball.[133]

Smart sports apparel offers athletes potential advantages, the extra edge that athletes seek. But the unresolved privacy issues from even consensual use raise alarms and suggest caution until the issues can be sorted out.

The pliability and varying contexts of consent arise outside the world of smart sports apparel as well as in it. As a general matter, consent can vary, ranging from express approval to implicit acknowledgment, such as downloading content from a site or clicking a link on a site that leads to another site. In these situations, we generally provide consent to the site's rules by making use of it. Without greater regulation and protection, our acquiescence to tracking by third parties will have no limit and can easily replace thoughtful and knowing behavior, particularly if reading consent agreements online could take tens of minutes or even hours.

The acquiescence of using a Web site often bleeds into the acquiescence to being tracked. We do not see these trackers, what they gather, and what they do with the fruits of their efforts. Instead, we know they are out there somewhere, but do not see the dangers. As a commentator noted:

> It's no secret that we're monitored continuously on the Internet. Some of the company names you know, such as Google and Facebook. Others hide in the background as you

128 *Id.*

129 *Id.* The University of Tennessee signed a similar contract with Nike.

130 *Id.*

131 *See* Vorkunov, *supra* note 22; *see, e.g.*, the Zephyr Bioharness, measuring heart rate and breathing, and the Motus sleeve, measuring arm angles and force on ligaments and the elbow.

132 *Id.*

133 "[H]ow to handle emerging technology is part of the [collective bargaining] talks. 'It's a very hot topic with the union,' Cole, the Pirates' union rep, told USA TODAY Sports." *Id.*

move about the Internet. There are browser plugins that show you who is tracking you. One *Atlantic* editor found 105 companies tracking him during one 36-hour period.[134]

Industry privacy agreements are long and technical, often more of a consumer irritant than a form of welcome privacy protection. For customers who want access to a site, accepting the terms and rules of the host usually stands as a prerequisite.[135] For consumers to access common services, they often must comply with extensive user agreements that generally involve allowing company access to information that can be transferred to third parties without consumers' truly understanding how the information transfer system works.[136] Consent does not indicate an understanding of how much information is gathered and disseminated. With a "beacon," for example, a sophisticated software package that can track everything people are typing on their computers when they are on a Web site, revealing interests from movies to food, the amount of data obtained can be staggering.[137] While information is often aggregated, to find trends for groups, it also can be isolated, even distinguishing a particular person.[138]

Web companies are happy to trade or sell information directly in a distinct market of their own.[139] Consumers often trust companies not to distribute information, but generally have no idea about what information is collected or distributed, or to whom.[140] Large companies have long privacy policies with fine print, and likely do not expect users to read the agreements in their entirety before agreeing to them.[141] Indeed, the users can agree with the company's policy just by checking a box, without any apparent incentive for or interest in reading a legal document.

b *Eliding Constitutional Checks and Balances*

Our constitutional system is based on the separation of powers, dividing power horizontally among the three branches of government, and vertically between two sovereigns, the federal government and the state governments. Rather than merely separating power, it was devised by the framers to be interdependent, requiring two branches, for example,

134 Bruce Schneier, *Do You Want the Government Buying Your Data from Corporations?* THE ATLANTIC (Apr. 30, 2013), http://www.theatlantic.com/ technology/archive/2013/04/do-you-want-the-government-buying-your-data-from-corporations/275431/.

135 *See, e.g., Customer Agreement*, AMAZON, http://aws.amazon.com/ agreement/ ("This AWS Customer Agreement ... contains the terms and conditions that govern your access to and use of the Service Offerings.").

136 "Hidden inside Ashley Hayes-Beaty's computer, a tiny file helps gather personal details about her, all to be put up for sale for a tenth of a penny." Angwin, *supra* note 76, at W1. "The file consists of a single code – 4c812db292272995e5416a323e79bd37 – that secretly identifies her as a 26-year-old female in Nashville, Tenn." Angwin, *supra* note 76, at W1.

137 Angwin, *supra* note 76, at W1.

138 *Id.*

139 *Id.* ("Consumer tracking is the foundation of an online advertising economy that racked up $23 billion in ad spending last year.").

140 *See* Viktor Koen, *Getting to Know You*, ECONOMIST (Sept. 13, 2014), http://www.economist.com/news/special-report/21615871-everything-people-do-online-avidly-followed-advertisers-and-third-party.

141 *See* Drew Guarini, *Hold Your Gasp, Facebook Is Under Fire for Its Privacy Policy Again*, HUFF. POST (Sept. 5, 2013), http://www.huffington post.com/2013/09/05/facebook-privacy-ftc_n_3873764.html (highlighting a policy that states that if the user is underage and agrees to the terms, it means "at least one of [the] parents or legal guardians have also agreed to the terms of the selection on the [child's] behalf" despite the fact that most parents are unaware of the privacy changes).

to execute the appointments clause requirements. Secret surveillance by the government, especially with data from the Internet of Things that was not supposed to end up in government storage for use in perpetuity, has a way of avoiding the checks on power through its secrecy and longevity. Secrecy can lead to aggrandizements in power. For example, in reaction to the tragedy of 9/11, General Michael Hayden, the former director of the Central Intelligence Agency and the National Security Agency, stated, "What I viewed as reasonableness on the night of September 10th, [2001], I viewed in a very different light on the afternoon of September 11th at the National Security Agency and I actually started to do different things. And I didn't need to ask another, 'May I' from Congress or anyone else. It was within my charter."[142]

Although secrecy in government surveillance is intended as a means to an end, it can become an end in itself, breeding further intrusiveness into privacy and other rights. It diminishes the deep structure of the Constitution's separation of powers, which ensures accountability through interdependence and effective oversight. If transparent disputes between branches occur, most can be resolved within the accepted process of the judicial system. Even if the judicial system plays a role, it will become less effective without a check by the public, especially data stored for years or decades.

2 Hacking

While consent is a prevalent method for obtaining access to data streams, involuntary access through hacking is also a major concern. One example is the group "Fancy Bear,"[143] a Russian cyberespionage organization that has apparently breached the cyber records of governments, nonprofit organizations, and corporations.[144] For example, the group is believed to be responsible for hacking the World Anti-Doping Agency's athlete database and revealing the records of three famous American athletes, Simone Biles, Serena Williams, and Venus Williams, to show they were apparently using medical exemptions to take banned drugs during the Rio Olympics.[145]

Hacking has become big business and hackers are not averse to accessing Internet of Things domains. In fact, as domains increase their reliance on the Internet of Things, more hacking is likely. For example, one private company advertises the ability to help someone spy on iPhone users, their location, texts, and voice messages, at a price.[146] In the past year, hackers were able to disable a car, hack the Wi-Fi of a connected Barbie doll, disable medical devices, and even interfere with the operability of a smart gun.[147] The hack of a car while it was in operation at seventy miles per hour on a highway was an experiment set up by the driver. The two hackers first remotely changed the radio station

142 General Michael Haydon (ret.), *Keynote Address at the Washington & Lee Cybersurveillance Law Symposium*, YouTube (Jan. 23, 2015), https://www.youtube.com/watch?v=VUEuWiXMkBA.

143 Rebecca Ruiz, *Vengeful Russian Hackers Leak Medical Files of Top U.S. Athletes*, N.Y. Times, Sept. 14, 2016, at 1.

144 *Id.* at 1.

145 *Id.* at 1.

146 N. Perlroth, *Phone Spying Is Made Easy, but Not Cheap*, N.Y. Times, Sept. 3, 2016, at 1 (describing how one company, the NSO Group, offers such access for $650,000 and a $500,000 setup fee).

147 Andy Greenberg & Kim Zetter, *How the Internet of Things Got Hacked*, Wired (Dec. 28, 2015), https://www.wired.com/2015/12/2015-the-year-the-internet-of-things-got-hacked/.

and turned on the air-conditioning. The hackers then took control of the car's driving system and disabled it.[148]

This chilling account of a vehicle hacking technique, subject to use in tens of thousands of situations, makes the prospect of government regulatory avoidance as unappealing as the hackers made the Jeep Cherokee after they disabled it. The silver lining in these accounts is that increased public awareness makes future regulatory action more likely.

3 Policing and Profiling

The digital era has greatly impacted police investigative techniques,[149] particularly profiling. Physical profiling is permitted to some degree under the Fourth Amendment, at least in the form of pretextual stops. Its excessive use without reasonable suspicion, however, particularly against minorities, has been the subject of high-profile lawsuits, such as the one settled in New York City,[150] where police stopped many more persons than *Terry v. Ohio*[151] permitted.

Yet profiling and policing overall will expand greatly in the digital era, particularly with the development of the Internet of Things. "Today's police have to follow hunches, cultivate informants, [and] subpoena ATM camera footage. ... Tomorrow's police ... might sit in an office or vehicle as their metal agents methodically search for interesting behavior to record and relay."[152]

a *Threat Scores*

Another illustration of how the Internet of Things can provide information to the police from the ground up involves the use of threat scores to assess police-citizen situations initiated by 911 calls.[153] One vivid example is the implementation of a software program called "Beware." The Fresno police department is using the program to evaluate its response to various situations, from terrorism to domestic violence calls. In one actual case, after a 911 call was made in Fresno, the police dispatch operator in a situation involving a man who had threatened his ex-girlfriend consulted the program, which "scoured billions of data points, including arrest reports, property records, commercial databases, deep Web searches and the man's social-media postings. It calculated his threat level as the highest of three color-coded scores: a bright red warning."[154] It turns out that the man had a gun, warranting the score. But there are more questions than

148 *Id.*

149 One illustration of the new technology is the Range-R, a stud-finder-like device that effectively permits an operator on the outside of a home or building to detect whether someone is in the home and where that person is. This "motion detector" has been used by police domestically before entering the home of private individuals. *See* Laura Sullivan, *New Tools Let Police See Inside Peoples' Homes*, NPR (Jan. 21, 2015, 10:18 PM), http://www.npr.org/blogs/thetwo-way/2015/01/21/378851217/new-tools-let-police-see-inside-peoples-homes.

150 *See Floyd v. City of New York*, 959 F. Supp. 2d 540 (2013).

151 392 U.S. 1 (1968).

152 Calo, *supra* note 83, at 32.

153 Justin Jouvenal, *The New Way Police Are Surveilling You: Calculating Your Threat 'Score,'* Wash. Post (Jan. 10, 2016), https://www.washingtonpost.com/local/public-safety/the-new-way-police-are-surveilling-you-calculating-your-threat-score/2016/01/10/e42bccac-8e15-11e5-baf4-bdf37355da0c_story.html.

154 *Id.*

answers about such a calculation. Where does crime interdiction end and privacy of citizens begin? How much information about citizens should the police be able to use in their investigations?

b *Phone Videos*

The flip side of the threat score is the opportunity for citizens to record events digitally and immediately post the recordings online. This has shed light on police–citizen interactions in a way not previously possible. One poignant illustration was a 2016 video made by a passenger in a car after her boyfriend, who was driving, was shot by a police officer during a traffic stop.[155]

B *Opportunities*

Given that it is unlikely that comprehensive legislation will account for the evolution of the Internet of Things, the best recourse for privacy protection might find its locus in a pragmatism in which the interests of otherwise unaligned groups converge. The prospect of interest convergence might be the best immediate solution to reining in the untrammeled information trafficking produced by the Internet of Things.

1 Interest Convergence of Companies and Consumers

Especially over the past several years, companies increasingly have found that public disclosure of government requests for information could be bad for business.[156] This idea emerged from the standoff between Apple and the government over the hacking of an iPhone belonging to one of the San Bernardino terrorists.[157] Apple's refusal to comply with the magistrate judge's demand[158] might have been motivated by company interest, but it coincided with user privacy. Many users supported Apple's refusal to attempt to hack its own product.[159]

Interest convergence can raise awareness and support for privacy through alignment. One by-product might be to pressure legislatures to create company and government accountability for how information from the Internet of Things can be utilized as a commodity in an appropriate manner. Improving the Internet of Things infrastructures by requiring encryption[160] likely will require at least pragmatism – and, ideally, legislation will follow.

155 *See, e.g., Woman Streams Graphic Video of Boyfriend Shot by Police*, CNN.com (July 7, 2016), http://www.cnn.com/videos/us/2016/07/07/graphic-video-minnesota-police-shooting-philando-castile-ryan-young-pkg-nd.cnn. The man died from his wounds.

156 Sanger & Perlroth, *supra* note 123.

157 On December 2, 2015, Syed Farook and his wife, Tashfeen Malik, attacked coworkers at a holiday gathering, killing fourteen. In a shoot-out with the police, both were killed. The federal government wanted to determine whether the Islamic State, known as ISIS, was involved in any way, but was apparently blocked by Mr. Farook's locked iPhone.

158 Mike Levine, Jack Date, & Jack Cloherty, *DOJ Escalates Battle With Apple over San Bernardino Shooter's Phone*, ABC News (Feb. 19, 2016), www.abcnew.go.com/US/doh-escalates-battle-apple-san-bernardino.

159 Mike Isaac, *Why Apple Is Putting Up a Fight over Privacy with the F.B.I.*, N.Y. Times, Feb. 18, 2016, at B4.

160 *See* J.D. Meier et al., *Threats and Countermeasures*, Microsoft (June 2003), https://msdn.microsoft.com/en-us/library/ff648641.aspx.

If this interest convergence continues, there also could be greater scrutiny of the substance and narrative of consent – what exactly does a user consent to disseminate when collecting self-generated surveillance data? What type of consent should suffice? Do password-protected or encrypted data presumptively indicate a greater interest in privacy? In addition, more companies likely will produce transparency reports and fewer people will rely on watchdog groups[161] to keep score about how well companies perform in protecting consumers' privacy.[162]

2 Interest Convergence II: Citizens and Hackers

Although hackers violate the law every time they hack and enter another's domain without permission and should be punished for doing so, sometimes the hacks reveal how important governmental and company transparency can be related to privacy matters. This transparency aligns with citizen interests. Disclosures about the reach of government (and private) programs offer the opportunity for dialogue about government and private company practices, and about excesses and improprieties. The impact of hacks can sometimes move to the surface unlawful systemic activity by the government or large technology companies, checking the growth and perpetuation of such illicit practices.

Conclusion

This chapter has examined the complex and dynamic implications of the Internet of Things, particularly as it creates mass self-surveillance systems. The development of the Internet of Things, involving interconnected multifunctional devices that can learn and spy on us as they learn, has numerous implications for self-cybersurveillance issues. In a very real sense, the Internet of Things creates a data-sharing economy, one that feeds numerous private companies, but also government agencies, especially through government–private industry partnerships. As twentieth-century notions of privacy recede and become antiquated, domain-specific regulation is needed to deter excessive, invasive, and abusive information sharing practices. Just as housing codes ensure livability for occupants, there should be similar "livability" codes for the Internet of Things so that the transmission of data is safe and meets evolving privacy guidelines.

161 *See Who Has Your Back? Protecting Your Data From Government Requests*, ELECTRONIC FRONTIER FOUND., https://www.eff.org/who-has-your-back-2014 (providing a review of major companies based on their privacy policies).

162 Much like ingredients posted on food packages, there also could be legislative requirements for posting notices about how companies deal with privacy issues, and not just the government.

Part II

Surveillance Applications

9 Balancing Privacy and Public Safety in the Post-Snowden Era

Jason M. Weinstein,[†] R. Taj Moore,[‡] & Nicholas P. Silverman[1]

Over the past year or two, the United States has been engaged in a national conversation about privacy in the digital age. That conversation actually began in the courts several years ago, with judges beginning to raise questions about the privacy issues presented when law enforcement applies "old school" investigative authorities to "new school" technology. But the nature and volume of the discussion increased after former National Security Agency (NSA) contractor Edward Snowden leaked classified information about NSA surveillance programs. In the wake of those leaks, criminal law enforcement agencies – who had nothing to do with the types of collection activities that were the subject of the Snowden leaks – increasingly found themselves on the defense in the courts, in Congress, and with service providers.

For law enforcement, this discussion could not be more urgent. Because criminals of all types use cell phones, mobile devices, and Internet-based means of communication, electronic evidence is critical to prosecuting cases involving violent crime, drug trafficking, kidnapping, computer hacking, sexual exploitation of children, organized crime, gangs, white-collar offenses, and espionage. And this type of evidence is critical to efforts to prevent, detect, and investigate acts of terrorism. From emails and text messages to cell tower and GPS location information to social media message platforms to data stored on devices and in the cloud, evidence from the online world is increasingly critical to investigating and prosecuting all types of crimes in the "real world."

† Partner, Steptoe & Johnson LLP. Before joining Steptoe, Mr. Weinstein served as a Deputy Assistant Attorney General in the Criminal Division of the Department of Justice where he supervised the Computer Crime and Intellectual Property Section, the Organized Crime and Gang Section, and the Human Rights and Special Prosecutions Section. Prior to joining the Criminal Division, he served for nearly 10 years as an assistant US attorney in the US Attorney's Offices for the Southern District of New York and the District of Maryland, where he investigated and litigated all aspects of criminal cases involving financial fraud, racketeering, public corruption, cybercrime, national security, narcotics, money laundering, immigration offenses, and violent crime. At Steptoe, Mr. Weinstein advises clients in a variety of matters relating to white collar defense, government investigations, cyber security, and financial technologies. The views expressed in this chapter are Mr. Weinstein's alone and do not represent the views of Steptoe, his clients, or the Department of Justice.

‡ Contributor, *Lawfare*. Mr. Moore previously worked in the International Group at Steptoe & Johnson LLP. Before law school, Mr. Moore was a Scoville Fellow at the Stimson Center. He is a graduate of Harvard Law School and Brown University.

1 Associate, Steptoe & Johnson LLP. Mr. Silverman's practice focuses on matters relating to white collar defense and government investigations. Before joining Steptoe, Mr. Silverman attended Reed College and Georgetown University Law Center.

At its core, this conversation is about the tension between privacy and public safety – between digital security and physical security – and the trade-offs between them that we have to make as a society. It is a serious issue that demands respectful and thoughtful consideration by privacy groups, public safety officers, and everyone in between. And it is a conversation we all need to join, because the outcome will affect all of us.

In this chapter, we review various types of electronic evidence-gathering techniques and how law enforcement has increasingly faced challenges to its authority to use them, and we examine the impact of the Snowden leaks in the courts and on the relationships between law enforcement and providers. We also discuss the prospects for a legislative solution to some of these issues.

I Digital Evidence-Gathering Techniques under Attack

One of the ironies of this debate about privacy and public safety is that it was partially ignited by the Snowden leaks about the NSA's bulk collection and surveillance activities, when what the NSA was doing had nothing to do with the way criminal law enforcement authorities operate. In the criminal context, law enforcement authorities have to obtain court authorization – based on individualized suspicion – in advance and meet stringent evidentiary standards.

In the courts, we have seen growing challenges both to the investigative techniques law enforcement uses as "building blocks" to get to the level of probable cause, and to its ability to execute search warrants once it does reach that standard. To be clear, probable cause is the standard that criminal investigators must meet to utilize the most intrusive law enforcement techniques, such as wiretaps, search warrants, and use of precision location data from cell phones. But the reality is that law enforcement agents do not begin their investigations with probable cause; they have to build up to probable cause using other, less intrusive techniques. And in the wake of Snowden's leaks, judges are increasingly questioning or restricting the use of time-honored techniques for gathering evidence and building up to probable cause, such as analyzing cell tower records. So it is harder than ever to get to probable cause, and increasingly concerning for law enforcement agents not to be able to execute warrants when they do satisfy that level of proof.

A *Search Warrants for Computers and Email Accounts*

Law enforcement agents have been executing search warrants for computers for almost as long as there have been personal computers. But as digital devices have become more a part of the fabric of our daily lives, and as the volume of personal information stored on them has increased, courts have grown more and more uncomfortable with the use of search warrant authority in the digital context. Some judges take the view that searches of digital devices present serious privacy challenges because of the sheer volume and nature of personal information they contain. These judges have sought to impose protocols in an attempt to constrain the way law enforcement officers execute such searches. Other judges treat digital searches as the functional equivalent of physical searches of file cabinets. For these judges, the privacy issues involved in searches of electronic devices are not unique, and so such judges seek to follow the same rules that apply in the case of searches of physical locations.

The first illustration of the new approach to digital searches was *United States v. Comprehensive Drug Testing, Inc.* (*CDT*).[2] The *CDT* majority, in *dicta*, instructed magistrate judges in the Ninth Circuit to impose search protocols as a condition for approving future applications for search warrants for computers. The court required that these protocols include, among other things:

- government agreement to waive reliance on the "plain view" doctrine;
- the use of an independent third party or specialized personnel to segregate and redact all nonresponsive information;
- a disclosure in applications and subpoenas detailing the actual risks of destruction of information specific to the case at hand, rather than mere allusion to general risks of deletion upon unauthorized entry;
- a search procedure designed to uncover only responsive information; and
- a requirement that the government destroy or return all nonresponsive data and file a return as soon as practicable detailing what has been kept.

The Ninth Circuit later made its proposed search protocols advisory, rather than mandatory, issuing a *per curiam* opinion in the underlying case and relegating the search protocols to a concurrence.[3] But the case has resulted in confusion within the Ninth Circuit among law enforcement officers, defense lawyers, and magistrate judges over what rules govern digital searches, as well as a split with other circuits over the question of search protocols. The vast majority of other circuits have rejected the use of either *ex ante* search protocols or requirements that the government forgo reliance on plain view as a condition of approving search warrants for computers.[4] Several of these other circuits have acknowledged that officers executing search warrants for computers are permitted to open and review every file where evidence of the crime under investigation might reasonably be found, recognizing that file names and extensions can be manipulated, enabling a criminal to conceal illegal materials by labeling them something mundane and misleading.[5]

The debate over the scope of searches of computers later evolved to include questions about the scope of search warrants for email accounts, with a similar split emerging among courts over whether special rules are needed to limit the scope of such searches. Typically, when agents serve a search warrant on an email provider as part of a criminal investigation, the provider does not screen the emails for relevance. On the contrary,

[2] 473 F.3d 915 (9th Cir. 2006), *withdrawn and superseded by* 513 F.3d 1085 (9th Cir. 2008), *on reh'g en banc*, 579 F.3d 989 (9th Cir. 2009) (en banc), *reh'g by entire Ninth Circuit denied*, 621 F.3d 1162 (9th Cir. 2010) (en banc) (per curiam).

[3] United States v. Comprehensive Drug Testing, Inc., 621 F.3d 1162, 1178–80 (9th Cir. 2010) (en banc) (Kozinski, J., concurring).

[4] *See* United States v. Richards, 659 F.3d 527, 538, 542 (6th Cir. 2011); United States v. Stabile, 633 F.3d 219, 237–38, 240–41 (3d Cir. 2011) (16 ECLR 268, 2/23/11); United States v. Mann, 592 F.3d 779, 785 (7th Cir. 2010) (15 ECLR 240, 2/17/10); United States v. Williams, 592 F.3d 511, 522 (4th Cir. 2010); United States v. Burgess, 576 F.3d 1078, 1094 (10th Cir. 2009); United States v. Cartier, 543 F.3d 442, 447–48 (8th Cir. 2008); United States v. Khanani, 502 F.3d 1281, 1290–91 (11th Cir. 2007); United States v. Upham, 168 F.3d 532, 535 (1st Cir. 1999) (4 ECLR 183, 2/24/99).

[5] *See, e.g.*, *Williams*, 592 F.3d at 522; *Upham*, 168 F.3d at 535. *But see* United States v. Galpin, 720 F.3d 436, 451–52 (2d Cir. 2013) (18 ECLR 2174, 7/17/13) (holding that searches of computers must be targeted at evidence of the crime covered by the warrant and suggesting that to the extent that officers' subjective intent is to seek information outside the scope of the warrant, plain view would be unavailable).

the provider sends a copy of all of the emails in the account to the agents, who then review them for responsiveness to the warrant. But a growing number of federal magistrate judges have refused to approve searches of email accounts in the absence of protocols requiring that an independent third party or separate group of agents – or even the email provider itself – screen out nonresponsive material before turning over evidence to investigators.

In August 2013, a federal district judge in Kansas became one of the first, if not the first, federal judges to reject a search warrant application for an email account on the basis of the possible scope of the search. The court rejected five applications for warrants that would have required Google, GoDaddy, Verizon, Yahoo!, and Skype to disclose, among other things, the contents of all emails, instant messages, and chat logs associated with the target accounts as part of an investigation into the theft of computer equipment.[6] The court took issue with the warrants for two reasons: first, the warrants sought all content, regardless of whether that content was relevant to the criminal activity law enforcement was investigating; second, the warrants included no filtering procedures by which relevant evidence would be culled from either irrelevant or privileged material.[7] In the court's view, the government was essentially requesting a "virtual carte blanche" to review the entire email account of the target, observing that "the breadth of the information sought by the government's search warrant ... is best analogized to a warrant asking the post office to provide copies of all mail ever sent by or delivered to a certain address so that the government can open and read all the mail to find out whether it [contains evidence]."[8]

The court held that the government had not been sufficiently particular in its description of the scope of the material to be collected, declaring that warrants for Internet communications must contain articulated limits or boundaries.[9] Unlike the Ninth Circuit in *CDT*, the court did not announce any specific search protocols and left the manner of limiting searches up to the government. The court did express approval of the following methods for limiting searches: asking the provider to disclose only content that contains certain key words or that was sent to or from certain parties, appointing a special master with authority to hire an independent vendor to use computerized search techniques, or setting up a "filter group" or "taint team" within the investigating agency.[10]

In what has been referred to as the "Magistrates' Revolt"[11] – an effort by magistrates across the country to push back against law enforcement's access to electronic information – a magistrate judge in the District of Columbia went further, rejecting numerous search warrant applications for electronic evidence, all on essentially the same grounds: the failure to adopt search protocols to prevent the government from seizing or searching emails or other data outside the scope of the warrants, and the failure to

6 *In re* Search Warrants for Info. Associated with Target Email Accounts/Skype Accounts, No. 13-MJ-8163-JPO, 2013 WL 4647554 (D. Kan. Aug. 27, 2013).

7 *Id.* at *8.

8 *Id.* at *8, 9.

9 *Id.*

10 *Id.* at *10.

11 Ann E. Marimow & Craig Timberg, *Low-Level Federal Judges Balking at Law Enforcement Requests for Electronic Evidence*, Wash. Post, Apr. 24, 2014, http://www.washingtonpost.com/local/crime/low-level-federal-judges-balking-at-law-enforcement-requests-for-electronic-evidence/2014/04/24/eec81748-c01b-11e3-b195-dd0c1174052c_story.html.

provide any timetable for when, if ever, the government intended to return the devices.[12] The judge had previously instructed the government to include strict protocols in its applications, specifically: the application of key word searches, the use of an independent special master to conduct initial screening, or the implementation of a taint team. When the government failed to incorporate his protocols, the judge rejected eleven search warrant applications in a two-month period.[13]

Federal judges in at least three other courts have taken a decidedly different view. Each approved the issuance of, or denied motions to suppress evidence from, warrants that required providers to turn over all emails sent to or from target accounts, even in the absence of search protocols or other indications from the government about how the searches would be conducted or what would be done with nonresponsive emails after the search.[14] As one judge observed, searches of electronic communications create "'practical difficulties' that require a flexible approach to the application of the particularity requirement."[15]

Notably, these issues were first raised not in response to defense motions during adversary proceedings, but rather by judges *sua sponte*, during the inherently *ex parte* process of seeking a search warrant, clearly reflecting a growing concern on the part of these judges about the volume and nature of the personal information available to law enforcement in the digital age.

B *Searches of Cell Phones Incident to Arrest*

In *Riley v. California*, the Supreme Court unanimously held that law enforcement officers generally must obtain a warrant before searching the contents of a cell phone seized from an arrestee, rejecting the argument that such searches qualify for the "search incident to arrest" exception to the warrant requirement.[16] In doing so, the Court clearly indicated its view that digital devices are different from physical items that can be searched incident to arrest because of the greater privacy concerns modern cellular phones present.

Under the "search incident to arrest" doctrine, police are generally permitted to search, without a warrant, an arrestee's person and the area within her immediate control, including some physical containers. The doctrine recognizes that an arrestee has a diminished expectation of privacy once she is in police custody and is based on the need to protect officer safety and prevent the destruction of evidence.

The doctrine has been used to search cell phones seized from arrestees for as long as arrestees have been carrying cell phones. But that all changed with *Riley*. The Supreme Court found that the rationale for the doctrine did not apply to cell phones. First, the

12 *See, e.g., In re* Search of Apple iPhone, IMEI 013888003738427, 31 F. Supp. 3d 159, 168–69 (D.D.C. 2014); *In re* Search of Black iPhone 4, 27 F. Supp. 3d 74 (D.D.C. 2014); *In re* Search of Info. Associated with Facebook Account Identified by the Username Aaron.Alexis that is Stored at Premises Controlled by Facebook, Inc., 21 F. Supp. 3d 1, 9–11 (D.D.C. 2013).

13 *See, e.g., supra* note 11; *In re* Search of ODYS LOOX Plus Tablet, 28 F. Supp. 3d 40 (D.D.C. 2014).

14 *See* United States v. Ayache, No. 3:13-cr-153, 2014 WL 923340 (M.D. Tenn. Mar. 10, 2014); United States v. Deppish, 994 F. Supp. 2d 1211 (D. Kan. 2014); United States v. Taylor, 764 F. Supp. 2d 230 (D. Me. 2011).

15 *Ayache*, 2014 WL 923340, at *2.

16 134 S. Ct. 2473 (2014).

digital data on a phone cannot be used as a weapon.[17] While the data could indirectly protect officers by, for example, alerting them that accomplices were en route, the government had not offered evidence to show that this was a real problem and, in any event, other case-specific exceptions, such as that for exigent circumstances, could be used to justify a warrantless search if officer safety were at risk.[18]

The Court also found that a warrantless search of a phone is not generally necessary to prevent the destruction of evidence. Although a cell phone can be remotely wiped, that risk could be addressed by placing the phone in a "Faraday bag" – a bag made of aluminum foil that can block radio waves – or by turning the phone off or removing its battery.[19]

But most importantly, the Court determined that even if a suspect has a diminished privacy interest post arrest, "modern cell phones, as a category, implicate privacy concerns far beyond those implicated by the search" of physical containers.[20] The Court observed that phones are essentially "minicomputers" that can also be used as, among other things, cameras, video players, rolodexes, maps, calendars, and diaries.[21] In addition, because cell phones have "immense storage capacity," enough to hold "millions of pages of text, thousands of pictures, or hundreds of videos," a search of a phone can far exceed the scope of any search of a physical container.[22] Indeed, the Court recognized that even one type of information typically stored on a phone – such as browsing history, photographs, or location data – can reveal a great deal of private information about a person's life.[23] As the Court noted, "A person might carry in his pocket a slip of paper reminding him to call Mr. Jones; he would not carry a record of all his communications with Mr. Jones for the past several months, as would routinely be kept on a phone."[24] Moreover, a search of a cell phone might allow the police to search data not stored on the device at all, but somewhere in the cloud.[25]

The *Riley* case has had and will continue to have a profound and direct impact on law enforcement, making what was a routine practice slower and more cumbersome, and creating an increased risk that important evidence will be lost or encrypted before a warrant can be obtained. But the impact of *Riley* on law enforcement goes beyond the need to get warrants where none were previously required. Indeed, the Court's recognition that existing Fourth Amendment doctrines do not squarely apply to digital devices or evidence – that is, that digital evidence is just different – could signal even more dramatic legal changes and challenges for law enforcement in the years to come.

Only time will tell how *Riley* will impact the case law on the scope of digital searches. We have already seen at least one post-*Riley* case in which a magistrate judge rejected a search warrant for a seized cell phone in part on the basis of a failure to satisfy the particularity requirement of the Fourth Amendment. The judge in that case relied extensively on the *Riley* Court's discussion of the vast amount of private data contained on cell phones and the differences between searches of cell phones and searches of

17 *Id.* at 2485.
18 *Id.* at 2485–86.
19 *Id.* at 2487.
20 *Id.* at 2488–89.
21 *Id.* at 2489.
22 *Id.*
23 *Id.* at 2490.
24 *Id.* at 2489.
25 *Id.* at 2491.

physical items.[26] But just three weeks later, a judge in the Southern District of New York seemed to push in the opposite direction, granting a warrant to search an entire Gmail account, and noting that as with searches of paper files, "ample case authority sanctions some perusal, generally fairly brief, of … documents (seized during an otherwise valid search) … in order for the police to perceive the relevance of the documents to crime."[27] The court declined to impose a search protocol in advance, observing that the Supreme Court has specifically said that "nothing in the language of the Constitution or in th[e] Court's decisions suggests that … search warrants … must include a specification of the precise manner in which they are to be executed."[28] Moreover, the court found that imposing such restrictions *ex ante* would be a bad practice because "there is no way … to know in advance how a criminal may label or code his computer files" or emails,[29] and because the government might need to examine "seemingly innocuous" emails as new information is obtained during the investigation.[30] Future cases will tell us whether *Riley*'s observations about the difference between digital devices and physical containers will lead to new restrictions on the scope or methodology of electronic searches.

C *Use of Cell Tower Records*

Cell phone location information can be divided into two broad categories: cell tower information and precision-location information, often referred to as "GPS." Cell tower information – the records made by a cellular network provider indicating which cell tower serves a user's phone when that user places or receives a call or text message – can also be divided into two categories – "historical" and "prospective."

It is clear that, when seeking precision-location information for a suspect's cell phone, federal law enforcement must obtain a warrant based on probable cause. But the standards for obtaining cell tower information have been much less clear and have been the subject of an extended debate in the courts.

Since the middle of the last decade, there has been a split among magistrates over the standards for obtaining prospective cell tower records. To some magistrates, this is a question of statutory interpretation – whether the combination of the Stored Communications Act and the Pen/Trap Statute provides clear authority for the government to obtain these records. For others, it is a question of constitutional law – whether users have a reasonable expectation of privacy in the records. But whatever the rationale, the result is that some courts require an order based on "specific and articulable facts showing that there are reasonable grounds to believe that the … information sought [is] relevant and material to an ongoing criminal investigation," while other courts require a warrant based on probable cause.[31]

26 *See In re* Search of Cellular Tels. Within Evidence Facility Drug Enf't Admin., Kan. City Dist. Office, Case No. 14-MJ-8017-DJW, 2014 WL 7793690 (D. Kan. Dec. 30, 2014); *see also* State v. Henderson, 854 N.W.2d 616 (Neb. 2014) (relying on *Riley* and holding that the scope of a warrant to search a cell phone was overly broad because of vast amounts of personal information stored on the phone).

27 *In re* Warrant for All Content & Other Info. Associated with the Email Account xxxxxxxx@gmail.com Maintained at Premises Controlled by Google, Inc., 33 F. Supp. 3d 386, 391 (S.D.N.Y. 2014) (quoting United States v. Mannino, 635 F.2d 110, 115 (2d Cir. 1980)).

28 *Id.* at 396 (quoting United States v. Grubbs, 547 U.S. 90, 97–98 (2006)).

29 *Id.* at 400 (quoting United States v. Bowen, 689 F. Supp. 2d 675, 681 (S.D.N.Y. 2010)).

30 *Id.* at 395.

31 *See* 18 U.S.C. §§ 2703(d), 3122–24. *Compare* United States v. White, 62 F. Supp. 3d 614, 622 (E.D. Mich. 2014) (requiring probable cause to track real-time location data for four weeks), *In re* Orders

Until recently, it had been well settled that to obtain historical cell tower records, law enforcement officers were not required to show probable cause but rather were required to obtain a court order based on a showing of "specific and articulable facts" under 18 U.S.C. § 2703(d) (a "2703(d) order").[32] For years, courts largely adopted the view that no warrant was required because under the "third-party doctrine" articulated by the Supreme Court in *United States v. Miller*[33] and *Smith v. Maryland*,[34] a person lacks a reasonable expectation of privacy in information voluntarily conveyed to a third party,[35] or because the user had no reasonable expectation of privacy regarding his location while in a public place.[36] But in recent years defendants have increasingly challenged, and courts have increasingly questioned, whether a warrant should be required for historical records as well.

The initial result was a circuit split. The Fifth Circuit,[37] Sixth Circuit,[38] and the *en banc* Eleventh Circuit (which reversed a panel decision imposing a warrant

Authorizing the Installation & Use of Pen Registers & Caller Identification Devices on Tel. Nos. [Sealed] & [Sealed], 416 F. Supp. 2d 390 (D. Md. 2006) (requiring probable cause to obtain prospective cell-site information), *In re* Order Authorizing the Monitoring of Geolocation & Cell Site Data, Nos. 06–0186, 187, 188, 2006 WL 6217584, at *4 (D.D.C. Aug. 25, 2006) (agreeing with the "majority rule" that Criminal Rule 41 governs the request for prospective cell-site location information and requires probable cause), *In re* Pen Register & Trap/Trace Device with Cell Site Location Auth., 396 F. Supp. 747, 764 (S.D. Tex. 2005), *and* Tracey v. State, 152 So. 3d 504, 526 (Fla. 2014) (holding that a person has a reasonable expectation of privacy in his cell-site location data in the context of real-time tracking), *with In re* Order Authorizing the Use of Two Pen Register & Trap & Trace Devices, 632 F. Supp. 2d 202, 205 (E.D.N.Y. 2008) (holding that the government may obtain prospective cell-site information without a showing of probable cause), *In re* Order for Prospective Cell Site Location Info. on a Certain Cellular Tel., 460 F. Supp. 2d 448, 459–62 (S.D.N.Y. 2006) (holding that 18 U.S.C. § 2703(c), (d) permits a court to order the disclosure of prospective cell-site information without a showing of probable cause), *and In re* Order (1) Authorizing the Installation & Use of Pen Register & Trap & Trace Device, & (2) Authorizing Release of Subscriber and Other Info., 433 F. Supp. 2d 804, 806 (S.D. Tex. 2006) (holding that 18 U.S.C. § 2703(d) permits a court to order the disclosure of prospective cell-site information without a showing of probable cause).

32 18 U.S.C. § 2703(d) (2012).

33 425 U.S. 435 (1976).

34 442 U.S. 735 (1979).

35 *In re* Historical Cell Site Data, 724 F.3d 600, 611–15 (5th Cir. 2013); *accord* United States v. Moreno–Nevarez, No. 13-CR-0841-BEN, 2013 WL 5631017, at *2 (S.D. Cal. Oct. 2, 2013); United States v. Graham, 846 F. Supp. 2d 384, 404 (D. Md. 2012); United States v. Benford, No. 2:09-CR-86, 2010 WL 1266507, at *2–3 (N.D. Ind. Mar. 26, 2010); *In re* Orders Pursuant To 18 U.S.C. § 2703(d), 509 F. Supp. 2d 76, 81 (D. Mass. 2007).

36 *See, e.g.*, United States v. Skinner, 690 F.3d 772 (6th Cir. 2012); United States v. Navas, 640 F. Supp. 2d 256 (S.D.N.Y. 2009), *rev'd in part on other grounds*, 597 F.3d 492 (2d Cir. 2010); *In re* Order, 411 F. Supp. 2d 678 (W.D. La. 2006). *Compare* United States v. Knotts, 460 U.S. 276 (1983) (holding that using a beeper to monitor a person's location on public roads is not a search), *with* United States v. Karo, 468 U.S. 705 (1984) (holding that using a beeper to monitor a person's location inside a private residence is a search). The problem with this argument is that tracking cell-site location data will inevitably lead to tracking a person in both public and private places. *See* United States v. White, 62 F. Supp. 3d 614, 622 (E.D. Mich. 2014) (requiring probable cause because the cell-site location data include private spaces and a four-week period justified an expectation of privacy).

37 *In re* Historical Cell Site Data, 724 F.3d 600, 611–15 (5th Cir. 2013) (holding that there is no expectation of privacy in geolocation data and therefore probable cause is not required).

38 United States v. Carpenter, 819 F.3d 880, 890 (6th Cir.) (holding that law enforcement access to historical cell-site data is not a search under the Fourth Amendment, and thus does not require a warrant), *petition for cert. granted*, No. 16-402 (June 5, 2017).

requirement)[39] held that no warrant was required, while the Third Circuit permitted judges to require probable cause[40] and a district judge in the Ninth Circuit found that the Fourth Amendment demanded it.[41]

In *United States v. Graham*, a panel of the Fourth Circuit sided with the panel of the Eleventh (whose decision had been withdrawn and replaced by the *en banc* decision), holding that a warrant was required for historical records,[42] but the *en banc* Fourth Circuit later decided as the Eleventh did, holding that there was no reasonable expectation of privacy in that data. In *Graham*, the government used 221 days' worth of cell-site information, obtained using a 2703(d) order, to establish the locations of two defendants over the course of a series of robberies. The panel decision, in a 2–1 vote, held that the defendants had a reasonable expectation of privacy in their cell-site location information and that the government therefore should have obtained a warrant. Writing for the panel majority, Judge Andre Davis found that locational tracking of an individual and his or her property continuously over an extended period constitutes a search. Judge Davis also rejected the government's reliance on the third-party doctrine, which he found inapplicable because cell-site information is passively generated, not voluntarily "conveyed" to third-party service providers.

On rehearing, however, the Fourth Circuit *en banc* disagreed, and reversed by a 12–3 vote. The court found that the third-party doctrine does apply to historical cell-site information, explaining that when a person uses a cell phone, he expects, at a minimum, that the service provider will route incoming and outgoing calls and text messages: "A cell phone user voluntarily enters an arrangement with his service provider in which he knows that he must maintain proximity to the provider's cell towers in order for his phone to function."[43] For the phone service to work, the cell phone owner is "permitting – indeed, requesting – his service provider to establish a connection between his phone and a nearby cell tower."[44] Thus, the information is voluntarily conveyed to the service provider.

In its *en banc Graham* opinion, the Fourth Circuit emphasized that controlling Supreme Court precedent mandated its decision. The *en banc* majority acknowledged that the "Supreme Court may in the future limit, or even eliminate, the third-party

39 United States v. Davis, 785 F.3d 498, 512–13 (11th Cir.) (*en banc*) (relying on third-party doctrine to reverse an Eleventh Circuit panel's probable cause requirement for historical cell-site location data), *cert. denied*, 136 S. Ct. 479 (2015).

40 *In re* Order Directing a Provider of Elec. Commc'n Serv. to Disclose Records to the Gov't, 620 F.3d 304 (3d Cir. 2010) (holding that while § 2703(d) does not require probable cause, a magistrate judge may require probable cause to avoid violating a person's reasonable expectation of privacy).

41 United States v. Cooper, No. 13–cr–00693–SI–1, 2015 WL 881578, at *6–8 (N.D. Cal. Mar. 2, 2015) (holding that a person has a reasonable expectation of privacy in historical cell-site location data, even for calls made in public, collecting state cases holding the same).

42 United States v. Graham, 796 F.3d 332, 348 (4th Cir. 2015) (observing that "much like long-term GPS monitoring, long-term location information disclosed in cell phone records can reveal both a comprehensive view and specific details of the individual's daily life" and holding that "the government invades a reasonable expectation of privacy when it relies upon technology not in general use to discover the movements of an individual over an extended period of time. Cell phone tracking through inspection of CSLI is one such technology"), *aff'd on other grounds*, 824 F.3d 421 (4th Cir.) (en banc), *petitions for cert. filed*, Nos. 16-6308 (Sept. 26, 2016), 16-6694 (Oct. 27, 2016).

43 United States v. Graham, 824 F.3d 421, 430 (4th Cir.) (en banc), *petitions for cert. filed*, Nos. 16-6308 (Sept. 26, 2016), 16-6694 (Oct. 27, 2016).

44 *Id.*

doctrine,"[45] but the Supreme Court seemed uninterested in taking up the issue. Even when the split with the Fourth Circuit had existed, the Court denied without comment the defendant's petition for *certiorari* in the Eleventh Circuit case. After this chapter was written, however, the Supreme Court granted certiorari in *United States v. Carpenter*, which will bring the issue of cell-site location information before the Court in 2017.

D *Cell-Site Simulators*

Over the past several years, judges and defense lawyers have begun to question the use of cell-site simulators,[46] which have been in use to some degree since at least the 1990s.[47] In substance, a cell-site simulator mimics a wireless carrier's cell tower; wireless devices within simulator range communicate and attempt to connect to the simulator as they would any nearby tower, and the simulator then records and stores the location and electronic identifying information of each such wireless device. Legally, these devices have historically been considered to qualify as pen registers/trap and trace devices under the Pen/Trap Statute[48] because they capture "dialing, routing, addressing, or signaling information" from a mobile device. Accordingly, federal prosecutors have generally sought Pen/Trap orders – requiring only that the government certify that the information likely to be obtained is relevant to an ongoing criminal investigation – to authorize the use of these devices.

But in recent years, there has been an onslaught of criticism over the manner in which these devices have been used and the legal standards law enforcement should have to satisfy to use them in the first place. In 2012, for example, a magistrate judge in the Southern District of Texas held that a cell-site simulator is equivalent to a mobile tracking device, and therefore requires probable cause under the Mobile Tracking Device statute, 18 U.S.C. § 3117.[49]

At the same time, media reports indicate that in many local police departments, these devices have either been used without judicial authorization or based on court orders obtained without disclosing to the judge the true nature of the device.[50] In some cases, defense lawyers have challenged evidence obtained from these devices only to have local authorities refuse to provide information about their use, justifying refusal on nondisclosure agreements between local police and the FBI.[51]

45 *Id.* at 425.

46 Other common terms for a cell-site simulator are International Mobile Subscriber Identity (IMSI) catcher, digital analyzer, StingRay, and Triggerfish.

47 *See, e.g., In re* Order Authorizing the Use of a Cellular Tel. Dig. Analyzer, 885 F. Supp. 197, 198 (C.D. Cal. 1995); Stephanie K. Pell & Christopher Soghoian, *A Lot More than a Pen Register, and Less than a Wiretap: What the StingRay Teaches Us about How Congress Should Approach the Reform of Law Enforcement Surveillance Authorities*, 16 Yale J. L. & Tech. 134, 142 (2014).

48 18 U.S.C. § 3127(3), (4).

49 *In re* Order Authorizing the Installation & Use of a Pen Register & Trap & Trace Device, 890 F. Supp. 2d 747, 752 (S.D. Tex. 2012).

50 Kim Zetter, *Florida Cops' Secret Weapon: Warrantless Cellphone Tracking*, Wired, Mar. 3, 2014, 9:00 AM, http://www.wired.com/2014/03/stingray/ (Florida police have used StingRays over 200 times without judicial permission).

51 *See* Linda Lye, *In Court: Uncovering Stingrays, A Troubling New Location Tracking Device*, ACLU, (Oct. 22, 2012, 12:42 PM), https://www.aclu.org/blog/free-future/court-uncovering-stingrays-troubling-new-location-tracking-device?redirect=blog/national-security-technology-and-liberty/court-uncovering-stingrays-troubling-new-location (stating that *United States v. Rigmaiden*, 844 F. Supp. 2d 982 (D. Ariz.

Some state courts appear to be joining the chorus. In March 2016, the Court of Special Appeals of Maryland held that "the use of a cell site simulator requires a valid search warrant, or an order satisfying the constitutional requisites of a warrant, unless an established exception to the warrant requirement applies." The court made clear that "people have a reasonable expectation that their cell phones will not be used as real-time tracking devices by law enforcement."[52]

In the wake of press coverage of potential abuses by local law enforcement, Congress has demanded more information from the Justice Department about the use of the technology, and federal law enforcement agencies have adopted updated policies regarding the use of these devices and clarifying that the legal standard for using them is probable cause.[53]

II The Snowden Effect

In the aftermath of the Snowden leaks, criminal law enforcement agencies have found themselves on the defensive in courtrooms, in boardrooms, and in the halls of Congress.

A *Changing Attitudes on the Bench*

It is clear that there was judicial anxiety about the privacy implications of evidence gathering in the digital age well before Edward Snowden became a household name. But it is also clear that this anxiety only intensified after Snowden leaked classified documents in June 2013, revealing that the NSA was collecting bulk records regarding Americans' telephone calls from U.S. telecommunications providers pursuant to Section 215 of the USA PATRIOT Act as well as the content of and other data regarding Internet communications involving targets believed to be overseas from nine major Internet providers under Section 702 of the FISA Amendments Act.[54]

In the wake of these disclosures, there was an explosion in coverage of digital privacy issues in the mainstream media. It became difficult to avoid articles about Section 215, the FISA Amendments Act, and the PRISM program. It soon became virtually impossible to escape coverage of the Snowden leaks and the dramatic revelations about the extent to which the NSA was collecting data regarding Americans. Judges read the papers and watch television as the rest of us do, so it stands to reason they followed the coverage too.

2012), represented the "first case in the country to address the constitutional implications of [cell site simulators]"). In *Rigmaiden*, the court denied the defendant's motion for discovery holding that the information was protected by a qualified law enforcement privilege. 844 F. Supp. 2d at 1002. The court then denied the defendant's motion to suppress evidence obtained using the cell-site simulator. United States v. Rigmaiden, No. CR 08-814-PHX-DGC, 2013 WL 1932800 (D. Ariz. May 8, 2013) (noting that defendant had been placed "at no disadvantage by the government's withholding of sensitive law enforcement information").

52 State v. Andrews, 134 A.3d 324, 327 (Md. Ct. Spec. App. 2016).

53 Office of Pub. Aff., Justice Department Announces Enhanced Policy for Use of Cell-Site Simulators: Increased Privacy Protections and Higher Legal Standards to Be Required (2015), https://www.justice.gov/opa/pr/justice-department-announces-enhanced-policy-use-cell-site-simulators.

54 *See, e.g.*, Glenn Greenwald, *NSA Collecting Phone Records of Millions of Verizon Customers Daily*, Guardian (London), June 5, 2013; Glenn Greenwald & Ewen MacAskill, *NSA Prism Program Taps in to User Data of Apple, Google and Others*, Guardian (London), June 6, 2013.

But judges' interest in these issues was not merely academic. Judges' phone records were among those collected by the NSA, just like those of the rest of us. Judges also use laptops, and have tablets, and carry smart phones, as the rest of us do. As the Supreme Court observed in *Riley v. California*, 90 percent of American adults own a cell phone, and many of them "keep on their person a digital record of nearly every aspect of their lives – from the mundane to the intimate."[55] As judges at all levels become adopters of technology, it is only natural that they, like ordinary citizens, would become more aware of and concerned about the potential privacy invasions that result from surveillance, search, and seizure in the digital era. As a Florida judge declared during a hearing about the use of cell phone location information, "What right does law enforcement have to hide behind the rules and to listen in and take people's information like the NSA? … Inhibiting law enforcement's rights are second to protecting mine!"[56] Although certainly colorful, this judge's comments may actually reflect a broader sentiment among members of the bench that digital privacy issues are important not just for the constitutional implications but for their practical impact on all of our, and their, lives.

The post-Snowden media coverage ultimately turned from the intelligence community's collection practices to reporting on evidence-collection techniques used by law enforcement, with major newspapers reporting on techniques such as cell phone location tracking.[57] These reports helped fuel concerns among privacy groups and the public about perceived government abuses of privacy – often without making distinctions among different parts of "the government."[58]

Despite this conflation, the NSA's bulk collection and surveillance activities that were the subject of Snowden's leaks have nothing to do with the way criminal law enforcement authorities operate. In the criminal context, law enforcement authorities have to obtain court authorization in advance, based on individualized suspicion, and meeting

55 134 S. Ct. 2473, 2490 (2014).

56 Ellen Nakashima, *Secrecy Around Police Surveillance Equipment Proves a Case's Undoing*, Wash. Post (Feb. 22, 2015).

57 *See, e.g.*, Ellen Nakashima, *FBI Clarifies Rules on Secretive Cellphone-Tracking Devices*, Wash. Post (May 14, 2015), http://www.washingtonpost.com/world/national-security/fbi-clarifies-rules-on-secretive-cellphone-tracking-devices/2015/05/14/655b4696-f914-11e4-a13c-193b1241d51a_story.html; Tom Jackman, *Experts Say Law Enforcement's Use of Cellphone Records Can Be Inaccurate*, Wash. Post (June 27, 2014), http://www.washingtonpost.com/local/experts-say-law-enforcements-use-of-cellphone-records-can-be-inaccurate/2014/06/27/028be93c-faf3-11e3-932c-0a55b81f48ce_story.html; Matt Richtel, *A Police Gadget Tracks Phones? Shhh! It's Secret*, N.Y. Times (Mar. 15, 2015), http://www.nytimes.com/2015/03/16/business/a-police-gadget-tracks-phones-shhh-its-secret.html; Devlin Barrett, *CIA Aided Program to Spy on U.S. Cellphones*, Wall St. J. (Mar. 10, 2015, 7:79 PM), http://www.wsj.com/articles/cia-gave-justice-department-secret-phone-scanning-technology-1426009924?KEYWORDS=cellphone+signals; Devlin Barrett, *Americans' Cellphones Targeted in Secret U.S. Spy Program*, Wall St. J. (Nov. 13, 2014, 8:22 PM), http://www.wsj.com/articles/americans-cellphones-targeted-in-secret-u-s-spy-program-1415917533?KEYWORDS=devlin%20barrett%20cellphone%20Marshals.

58 *See, e.g.*, David E. Sanger & Brian X. Chen, *Signaling Post-Snowden Era, New iPhone Locks Out N.S.A.*, N.Y. Times (Sept. 26, 2014), http://www.nytimes.com/2014/09/27/technology/iphone-locks-out-the-nsa-signaling-a-post-snowden-era-.html?_r=0 ("At Apple and Google, company executives say the United States government brought these changes on itself. The revelations by the former N.S.A. contractor Edward J. Snowden not only killed recent efforts to expand the law, but also made nations around the world suspicious that every piece of American hardware and software – from phones to servers made by Cisco Systems – have 'back doors' for American intelligence and law enforcement.").

stringent evidentiary standards – precisely what the NSA was criticized for failing to do. As FBI Director James Comey observed:

> In the wake of the Snowden disclosures, the prevailing view is that the government is sweeping up all of our communications. That is not true. And unfortunately, the idea that the government has access to all communications at all times has extended – unfairly – to the investigations of law enforcement agencies that obtain individual warrants, approved by judges, to intercept the communications of suspected criminals.[59]

Nevertheless, there can be little doubt that Snowden's leaks made an already difficult environment for law enforcement even more challenging.

The growing unease among judges with digital privacy issues has implications for the future of the third-party doctrine. Will the government continue to be able to rely on the doctrine to obtain digital data disclosed to a third party with a subpoena or court order, much as it does with bank, credit card, and other third-party records? Or will digital data be treated differently? The answer to these questions, which will play out in courtrooms – and possibly the Supreme Court – in the coming years, will have a profound impact on both public safety and privacy.

B *Push Back from Providers – the "New Normal"*

In addition to increased judicial skepticism regarding electronic evidence-gathering techniques, law enforcement has encountered a more challenging relationship with telephone and Internet providers, including many with whom law enforcement had historically enjoyed a cooperative relationship. Whether providers were motivated by anger at the reputational damage suffered as a result of the Snowden leaks, anxiety about customer reactions to perceived privacy abuses, or concern about competitive difficulties in privacy-conscious European markets – or some combination of all of these – providers have taken steps, both private and public, to distance themselves from law enforcement as never before.

In the immediate aftermath of the Snowden leaks, providers whose user information was collected as part of the PRISM program, such as Apple, Google, Facebook, Skype, AOL, and Microsoft, faced immediate criticism from users and quickly took steps to distance themselves from the NSA and PRISM. Apple released a statement in which it claimed it "first heard of the government's 'Prism' program when news organizations asked us about it on June 6. We do not provide any government agency with direct access to our servers, and any government agency requesting customer content must get a court order."[60] Facebook's CEO Mark Zuckerberg similarly denied participating in a program to give the U.S. government direct access to its servers or receiving a request or order seeking data in bulk and said that it would fight any such order aggressively.[61] But as the controversy over PRISM grew, and as competitors abroad used PRISM to competitive advantage, U.S. providers began distancing themselves from the government more

59 James B. Comey, Director, FBI, Going Dark: Are Technology, Privacy, and Public Safety on a Collision Course? (Oct. 16, 2014), http://www.fbi.gov/news/speeches/going-dark-are-technology-privacy-and-public-safety-on-a-collision-course.

60 *Apple's Commitment to Customer Privacy* (June 16, 2013), https://www.apple.com/apples-commitment-to-customer-privacy/.

61 Mark Zuckerberg, Facebook (June 4, 2013), https://www.facebook.com/zuck/posts/10100828955847631.

generally – including from criminal law enforcement agencies, which had nothing to do with PRISM.

Providers' desire to be seen as protective of privacy and to avoid being perceived as closely aligned with the U.S. government has manifested itself in a number of ways. For instance, some providers aggressively challenged restrictions on what information they could put in their periodic transparency reports about U.S. government surveillance requests, resulting in litigation brought by Twitter and a coalition of tech companies.[62]

Providers also made operational or policy changes reflecting their proprivacy, antisurveillance positions. For example, Apple and Google made encryption the default setting on their cell phones, with the providers unable to assist law enforcement in breaking that encryption even pursuant to a search warrant.[63] Microsoft challenged the Justice Department's efforts to use search warrants to obtain data stored overseas. And more generally, providers have been less likely to cooperate voluntarily and more likely to challenge law enforcement than at any time in recent memory.

1 Apple and Google Encryption Policies

As of May 2014, Apple, in response to a search warrant, was able to access and turn over data stored on an iPhone including "SMS messages, pictures and videos, contacts, audio recordings, and your phone's call history."[64] In October 2014, Apple announced default security upgrades for iPhones and iPads that now prevent the company from accessing data kept on those devices without a user's passcode.[65] Apple also posted a message on its Web site in which it detailed the ways in which it protects customer data in the face of government information requests.[66] Apple stated that "for all devices running iOS 8.0 and later versions, Apple will not perform iOS data extractions in response to government search warrants because the files to be extracted are protected by an encryption key that is tied to the user's passcode, which Apple does not possess."[67] In the statement, Apple further stated that "in its latest 'Who Has Your Back?' report, the Electronic Frontier Foundation awarded Apple 6 out of 6 stars for our commitment to standing with our customers when the government seeks access to their data." Google gave users the

62 Mike Isaac, *Twitter Reports a Surge in Government Data Requests*, N.Y. Times Bits (Feb. 9, 2015, 10:00 AM), http://bits.blogs.nytimes.com/2015/02/09/twitter-reports-surge-in-government-data-requests/?_r=0; Ben Lee, *Taking the Fight for #Transparency to Court*, Twitter (Oct. 7, 2014, 5:19 PM), https://blog.twitter.com/2014/taking-the-fight-for-transparency-to-court; Craig Timberg & Adam Goldman, *U.S. to Allow Companies to Disclose More Details on Government Requests for Data*, Wash. Post (Jan. 27, 2014), http://www.washingtonpost.com/business/technology/us-to-allow-companies-to-disclose-more-details-on-government-requests-for-data/2014/01/27/3cc96226-8796-11e3-a5bd-844629433ba3_story.html.

63 Kevin Poulsen, *Apple's iPhone Encryption Is a Godsend, Even if Cops Hate It*, Wired (Oct. 8, 2014), https://www.wired.com/2014/10/golden-key/.

64 Andrew Cunningham, *New Guidelines Outline What iphone Data Apple Can Give to Police*, Ars Technica (May, 8, 2014, 1:25 PM), http://arstechnica.com/apple/2014/05/08/new-guidelines-outline-what-iphone-data-apple-can-give-to-police/.

65 Trevor Timm, *Your iPhone Is Now Encrypted. The FBI Says It'll Help Kidnappers. Who Do You Believe?*, The Guardian (Sept. 30, 2014, 7:15 PM), http://www.theguardian.com/commentisfree/2014/sep/30/iphone-6-encrypted-phone-data-default.

66 *Government Information Requests*, http://www.apple.com/privacy/government-information-requests/ (last visited Aug. 13, 2016).

67 *Id.*

ability to encrypt data on Android devices such that it remains outside the reach of law enforcement, even in the face of a valid search warrant.[68]

These policy changes raised significant concerns in law enforcement agencies. Leslie Caldwell, assistant attorney general for the Criminal Division, expressed concern about a "zone of lawlessness" created if law enforcement were unable to access information on seized phones despite lawful court orders.[69] FBI Director Comey questioned why companies would "market something expressly to allow people to place themselves beyond the law."[70] He later observed that "there's no doubt that all of us should care passionately about privacy, but we should also care passionately about protecting innocent people."[71] Other Justice Department officials expressed similar concerns that the new systems would "make it harder, if not impossible, to solve some cases," with one observing that the companies had promised their customers "the equivalent of a house that can't be searched, or a car trunk that could never be opened."[72]

Local officials echoed those concerns as well. In an op-ed in the *Washington Post*, Cyrus Vance Jr., the district attorney for Manhattan, argued that Apple and Google's encryption of smart phones posed a threat to public safety and national security.[73] He wrote that "when threats to the common public safety arise, we ask Congress to do everything within its constitutional authority to address them. The provision of cloaking tools to murderers, sex offenders, identity thieves and terrorists constitutes such a threat. Absent remedial action by the companies, Congress should act appropriately."[74]

Google CEO Eric Schmidt brushed aside law enforcement's concerns, stating that "there are many ways law enforcement can get to data."[75] Apple CEO Tim Cook echoed that sentiment: "Look, if law enforcement wants something, they should go to the user and get it. It's not for me to do that."[76] U.S. officials have observed that this dispute marks "a new low in relations between Silicon Valley and Washington since former National Security Agency contractor Edward Snowden began leaking state secrets last spring."[77]

68 *A Sweet Lollipop, with a Kevlar Wrapping: New Security Features in Android 5.0.*, ANDROID OFFICIAL BLOG (Oct. 28, 2014), http://officialandroid.blogspot.co.uk/2014/10/a-sweet-lollipop-with-kevlar-wrapping.html.

69 Julian Hattem, *DOJ Fears Tech 'Zone of Lawlessness'*, THE HILL (Jan. 27, 2015, 10:09 AM), http://thehill.com/policy/technology/230840-doj-fears-tech-zone-of-lawlessles.

70 Brian Naylor, *Apply Says iOS Encryption Protects Privacy; FBI Raises Crime Fears*, NAT'L PUB. RADIO (Oct. 8, 2014, 5:17 PM), http://www.npr.org/sections/alltechconsidered/2014/10/08/354598527/apple-says-ios-encryption-protects-privacy-fbi-raises-crime-fears.

71 Ellen Nakashima, *Tech Giants Don't Want Obama to Give Police Access to Encrypted Phone Data*, WASH. POST (May 19, 2015), http://www.washingtonpost.com/world/national-security/tech-giants-urge-obama-to-resist-backdoors-into-encrypted-communications/2015/05/18/11781b4a-fd69-11e4-833c-a2de05b6b2a4_story.html.

72 Delvin Barrett & Danny Yadron, *New Level of Smartphone Encryption Alarms Law Enforcement*, WALL ST. J. (Sept. 22, 2014, 7:42 PM), http://online.wsj.com/articles/new-level-of-smartphone-encryption-alarms-law-enforcement-1411420341.

73 Cyrus R. Vance Jr., *Apple and Google Threaten Public Safety with Default Smartphone Encryption*, WASH. POST (Sept. 26, 2014), http://www.washingtonpost.com/opinions/apple-and-google-threaten-public-safety-with-default-smartphone-encryption/2014/09/25/43af9bf0-44ab-11e4-b437-1a7368204804_story.html.

74 *Id.*

75 Danny Yadron, *Google's Schmidt Fires Back over Encryption*, WALL ST. J. (Oct. 8, 2014, 7:49 PM), http://www.wsj.com/articles/googles-schmidt-says-encrypted-phones-wont-thwart-police-1412812180.

76 Devlin Barrett, Danny Yadron, & Daisuke Wakabayashi, *Apple and Others Encrypt Phones, Fueling Government Standoff*, WALL ST. J. (Nov. 18, 2014, 10:30 PM), http://www.wsj.com/articles/apple-and-others-encrypt-phones-fueling-government-standoff-1416367801.

77 *Id.*

The issue came to a head in 2015, when the Justice Department sought an order pursuant to the All Writs Act requiring Apple to unlock an iPhone so that agents could execute a lawful warrant to search that phone. In October 2015, a magistrate judge in the Eastern District of New York indicated that he was unwilling to issue such an order, instead giving Apple an opportunity to submit a reply brief in the case.[78] The judge suggested that he was unconvinced, although admittedly unsure, that the All Writs Act could be used to compel tech companies to unlock phones if the process would be overly burdensome.[79] Ultimately, the government dropped the case once it secured a way to access the phone without Apple's assistance.[80] Nonetheless, the judge's resistance to granting the order is consistent with growing judicial discomfort with the impact on privacy of electronic evidence-gathering techniques, and the case reflects providers' growing willingness to oppose lawful government requests in the name of user privacy.

A similar battle played out in the investigation of the December 2015 domestic terrorist attack in San Bernardino, California.[81] In February 2016, a California magistrate judge ordered Apple to provide "reasonable technical assistance" to the FBI in order to unlock an iPhone belonging to one of the attackers so the phone could be searched pursuant to a valid search warrant.[82] Apple refused to comply with the order, asserting that compliance would mean compromising customer security and creating a backdoor for law enforcement to access individual cell phone content, setting a dangerous precedent. Later in February, after Apple received the court order, Apple CEO Tim Cook published an open letter to customers about why it would not comply with the order, mentioning the potential threat to customer security and expressing concern that the order would force Apple to develop a method to hack its own customers' devices.[83] Apple also took the position that if it obeyed the FBI requests and court orders, it then would have to do the same for other countries, including China.[84] Several leaders of other technology companies expressed support for Apple's stance.[85] Some industry leaders, though, thought Apple was creating an "unnecessarily high-stakes battle" with the government, especially given that many tech companies, including Apple, previously had complied with similar court orders.[86]

78 *In re* Order Requiring Apple, Inc. to Assist in the Execution of a Search Warrant Issued by this Court, 1:15-mc-01902-JO, 2015 WL 5920207 (E.D.N.Y. Oct. 9, 2015).

79 *Id.* at *6–7.

80 Christie Smythe, *Second U.S. Bid to Force Apple to Unlock Phone Ends in a Whimper*, BLOOMBERG (Apr. 22, 2016), http://www.bloomberg.com/news/articles/2016-04-23/u-s-drops-appeal-seeking-apple-help-in-brooklyn-iphone-case-incgxa37.

81 Christopher Goffard, *They Met Online, Built a Life in San Bernardino – and Silently Planned a Massacre*, L.A. TIMES (Dec. 5, 2015), http://graphics.latimes.com/san-bernardino-syed-farook-tashfeen-malik/.

82 Eric Lichtblau, *Judge Tells Apple to Help Unlock iPhone Used by San Bernardino Gunman*, N.Y. TIMES (Feb. 16 2016), http://www.nytimes.com/2016/02/17/us/judge-tells-apple-to-help-unlock-san-bernardino-gunmans-iphone.html.

83 http://www.apple.com/customer-letter/.

84 Katie Benner & Paul Mozur, *Apple Sees Value in Its Stand to Protect Security*, N.Y. TIMES (Feb. 20, 2016), http://www.nytimes.com/2016/02/21/technology/apple-sees-value-in-privacy-vow.html.

85 Nick Wingfield & Mike Isaac, *Apple Letter on iPhone Security Draws Muted Tech Industry Response*, N.Y. TIMES (Feb. 18, 2016), http://www.nytimes.com/2016/02/19/technology/tech-reactions-on-apple-highlight-issues-with-government-requests.html; Mark Scott, *Mark Zuckerberg Backs Apple in Its Refusal to Unlock iPhone*, N.Y. TIMES (Feb. 22, 2016), http://www.nytimes.com/2016/02/23/technology/mark-zuckerberg-backs-apple-in-its-refusal-to-unlock-iphone.html.

86 Wingfield & Isaac, *supra* note 86; Mark Scott, *Mark Zuckerberg Backs Apple in Its Refusal to Unlock iPhone*, N.Y. TIMES (Feb. 22, 2016), http://www.nytimes.com/2016/02/23/technology/mark-zuckerberg-backs-apple-in-its-refusal-to-unlock-iphone.html.

Ultimately, the FBI indicated that it no longer needed Apple's assistance, relying on a third-party solution to unlock the phone.[87] But the FBI made clear that the method it used to unlock the San Bernardino iPhone would not be effective for newer versions of the phone, so the issue will likely arise again.[88] Nevertheless, the San Bernardino case illustrates the degree to which, post Snowden, providers who previously would have complied with lawful court orders to search users' devices or obtain users' information are now determined to oppose them in the name of protecting user privacy.

2 Jurisdictional Challenges to Search Warrants

Apple is not the only provider mounting new challenges to established techniques for gathering digital evidence. On December 4, 2013, a magistrate judge in the Southern District of New York granted the government's application for a warrant for the search and seizure of information "associated with a specified web-based e-mail account that is 'stored at premises owned, maintained, controlled, or operated by Microsoft Corporation.'" That warrant required Microsoft to disclose, among other things, the content of all emails stored in the target account and account identifying information.[89] Microsoft provided the noncontent data it had stored on United States-based servers but refused to provide the emails' contents, which were located on servers at a data center in Ireland.[90] Microsoft moved to quash the warrant under the theory that the Stored Communications Act only authorizes warrants to be issued pursuant to the Federal Rules of Criminal Procedure, which do not allow for extraterritorial enforcement.[91] Apple, Cisco, and Verizon filed *amicus* briefs in support of Microsoft's position.[92]

In its response, the government argued that electronic records controlled by a party are reachable by compulsory process no matter where the records are stored and that warrants issued pursuant to the Stored Communications Act were fundamentally different from those authorizing law enforcement to enter physical premises and seize evidence.[93] Microsoft responded that such an argument rewrites the statute and ignores the Fourth Amendment. Microsoft also argued that enforcing the warrant would "authorize the Government (including state and local governments) to violate the territorial integrity

87 Katie Benner & Matt Apuzzo, *U.S. Says It May Not Need Apple's Help to Unlock iPhone*, N.Y. Times (Mar. 21, 2016), http://www.nytimes.com/2016/03/22/technology/apple-fbi-hearing-unlock-iphone.html.

88 *FBI Director Says Unlocking Method Won't Work on Newer iPhones*, Reuters (Apr. 8, 2016), http://www.reuters.com/article/us-apple-encryption-fbi-idUSKCN0X4266.

89 *In re* Warrant to Search a Certain E-Mail Account Controlled & Maintained by Microsoft Corp., 829 F.3d 197, 200 (2d Cir. 2016).

90 *Id.*; *see also* David Howard, *One Step on the Road to Challenging Search Warrant Jurisdiction*, Microsoft Blog (Apr. 25, 2014), http://blogs.microsoft.com/on-the-issues/2014/04/25/one-step-on-the-path-to-challenging-search-warrant-jurisdiction/ (noting that the U.S. government should not have the power to search email content located abroad).

91 Microsoft's Objections to the Magistrate's Order Denying Microsoft's Motion to Vacate in Part a Search Warrant Seeking Customer Information Located Outside the United States, *In re* Warrant to Search Certain E-Mail Account Controlled & Maintained by Microsoft Corp., No. 13-MAG-2814 (S.D.N.Y. June 6, 2014).

92 The authors' law firm represented Verizon in connection with the filing of this brief, although the authors were not involved in that representation.

93 Government's Memorandum of Law in Opposition to Microsoft's Motion to Vacate Email Account Warrant, *In re* Warrant to Search Certain E-Mail Account Controlled & Maintained by Microsoft Corp., No. 13-MAG-2814 (S.D.N.Y. Apr. 20, 2014).

of sovereign nations and circumvent the commitments made by the United States in mutual legal assistance treaties expressly designed to facilitate cross-border criminal investigations." Microsoft complained that if the government's position were adopted, it would have a "significant negative impact on Microsoft's business, and the competitiveness of US cloud providers in general." However, the government maintained that Microsoft's position would serve "as a dangerous impediment to the ability of law enforcement to gather evidence of criminal activity." The magistrate judge ruled in the government's favor, and when Microsoft refused to produce the documents at issue, the company agreed to be held in contempt of court pending its appeal to the Second Circuit, which ultimately ruled in Microsoft's favor. The Second Circuit found that the Stored Communications Act does not authorize courts to issue and enforce against United States-based service providers warrants for the seizure of customer e-mail content that is stored exclusively on foreign servers.[94] The case was remanded to the district court, with instructions to "quash the warrant insofar as it directs Microsoft to collect, import, and produce" user content stored outside of the United States.[95]

As one Microsoft official characterized it, Snowden's revelations had "certainly put a premium on demonstrating to people that we are fighting."[96] Significantly, this is the kind of issue about which there would have been no fight prior to Snowden. Previously, the only litigated issue was whether the United States had jurisdiction over the served company, not where the data was stored. The outcome of this litigation will have a tremendous effect either way – either it will dramatically change the way law enforcement collects evidence even from U.S. providers, or it will profoundly affect the ability of providers to compete in overseas markets. Meanwhile, Microsoft has opened up a new front in its battle with the Justice Department, filing suit in April 2016 seeking to invalidate "gag orders" that prevent Microsoft from alerting its customers that their data has been seized as part of a criminal investigation.[97]

3 Less Cooperation and More Confrontation

Providers' public demonstrations of opposition to law enforcement have been matched by private efforts to distance themselves from the government. Anecdotally, law enforcement officials have observed that their relationships with providers are fundamentally different post Snowden. Relationships that were friendly are now more arm's length, and relationships that were already arm's length are more distant. For instance, providers are more likely to require warrants or court orders where subpoenas previously would have

[94] *In re* Warrant to Search a Certain E-Mail Account Controlled & Maintained by Microsoft Corp., 829 F.3d 197, 222 (2d Cir. 2016).

[95] *Id.*; Joe Mullen, *Microsoft Agrees to Contempt Order So E-Mail Privacy Case Can Be Appealed*, ARS TECHNICA (Sept., 9, 2014, 6:00 PM), http://arstechnica.com/tech-policy/2014/09/microsoft-agrees-to-contempt-order-so-e-mail-privacy-case-can-be-appealed/.

[96] Ellen Nakashima, *Microsoft Fights U.S. Search Warrant for Customer E-Mails Held in Overseas Server*, WASH. POST (June 10, 2014), http://www.washingtonpost.com/world/national-security/microsoft-fights-us-search-warrant-for-customer-e-mails-held-in-overseas-server/2014/06/10/6b8416ae-f0a7-11e3-914c-1fbd0614e2d4_story.html.

[97] Ellen Nakashima, *Microsoft Sues over Law Banning Tech Firms from Telling Customers about Data Requests*, WASH. POST (Apr. 14, 2016), https://www.washingtonpost.com/world/national-security/microsoft-sues-to-block-law-banning-tech-firms-from-telling-customers-about-search-warrants/2016/04/14/6f8c36e4-01dc-11e6-9d36-33d198ea26c5_story.html.

sufficed, and they are less likely to agree not to disclose government requests to users without a court order directing them not to do so.[98]

C *The Changing Politics of Privacy*

Post Snowden, the politics of privacy have shifted, turning traditional supporters into skeptics and traditional skeptics into outspoken critics. As a result, the Justice Department has faced increasing resistance to efforts to maintain, let alone address gaps in, its ability to gather electronic evidence.

In the two years since Snowden's leaks, many members of Congress who were once reliably pro-law enforcement and pro-national security have expressed increasing concern about government abuse of authority and surveillance overreach. Dissent has been heard from liberals and conservatives alike and has endangered the passage of new legislation proposed by the Department of Justice. Members of Congress have also become vocal in questioning perceived overreaching by local law enforcement, asking new questions about StingRays, tracking devices, and cell-site simulators.

Since at least 2009, the FBI has made it a priority to pass legislation that would address the "Going Dark" problem – law enforcement's decreasing ability to execute court-authorized wiretaps to intercept modern forms of communication because providers lack the technical ability to comply.

This "Going Dark" issue arises in the context of, among other things, chat services, instant messaging, FaceTime, photo-sharing services, peer-to-peer Internet calls, social media channels, and chat features on gaming sites. But most recently, the public discourse on "Going Dark" has focused on the increasing use of encryption to protect both communications and mobile devices. Law enforcement officials have warned that the increasing use of unbreakable encryption is compromising their ability to fight crime and to detect and prevent acts of terror. Privacy advocates and some technologists have decried what they perceive as efforts to give the government a "backdoor" into their systems and warned that any such effort will weaken cybersecurity.

While the Communications Assistance for Law Enforcement Act (CALEA) requires telecommunication carriers and broadband providers to build interception capabilities into their networks for court-ordered surveillance, that law does not apply to providers of newer forms of communication. As a result, in many cases law enforcement is unable to execute a lawfully obtained wiretap order for a suspect's communications because the provider lacks the technical capability to implement it – the core issue in the San Bernardino iPhone case. The FBI and DOJ worked for years on a legislative proposal to address this issue. As has been publicly reported, the basic idea was to provide an economic incentive for providers not covered by CALEA to develop their own solutions, rather than have a government-imposed solution. Even pre Snowden, that proposal was an uphill battle politically, with privacy groups lining up to characterize the proposal as an expansion of authorities, when the proposal was actually about enhancing law enforcement's ability to execute its existing authorities. In any event, post Snowden, what

[98] Craig Timberg, *Apple, Facebook, Other Defy Authorities, Increasingly Notify Users of Secret Data Demands after Snowden Revelations*, Wash. Post (May 1, 2014), https://www.washingtonpost.com/business/technology/apple-facebook-others-defy-authorities-increasingly-notify-users-of-secret-data-demands-after-snowden-revelations/2014/05/01/b41539c6-cfd1-11e3-b812-0c92213941f4_story.html.

was politically sensitive has become political plutonium.[99] The White House has now disavowed attempts to seek a legislative solution, instead relying on engagement with industry.

However, there are some signs that the pendulum may be swinging back the other way. In the wake of the San Bernardino case, members of the Senate Select Committee on Intelligence introduced legislation to require tech companies to provide the government with unencrypted data in response to a court order or to provide technical assistance to the government in obtaining unencrypted data, while House Homeland Security Committee Chair Michael McCaul and Senator Mark Warner introduced a bill to create a national commission to study the issue.[100]

In addition, there is broad support from both privacy groups and the technology industry for Congress to pass bipartisan legislation to modernize and reform the Electronic Communications Privacy Act (ECPA). Although there are multiple iterations of the proposal, all would require the government to seek a warrant based on probable cause in order to obtain stored emails, eliminating ECPA's current distinctions based on how old the emails are and whether they were opened. Many of those proposals would also require a warrant to obtain any cell phone location information – including both prospective and historical cell tower information. DOJ has said that it does not oppose a "warrant for all content" rule with limited exceptions,[101] but its ability to push back against other aspects of these bills with which it disagrees is almost certainly more limited post Snowden. In June 2016, an ECPA reform bill requiring a warrant for all stored emails passed the House, but it then stalled in the Senate.[102]

Conclusion

The debate over public safety and privacy in the digital age, both before and after the San Bernardino case, has tended to present the issue as black and white and has not done justice to its complexity or its importance to our society. But there are certain baseline principles on which both sides of the debate should be able to agree.

First, there is a trade-off between privacy and public safety. We cannot have a perfect version of either one without some compromise of the other. These are the types of choices we make in a democracy, but we should make no mistake that we are making a choice, and it is naïve to suggest otherwise.

99 Ellen Nakashima, *Proliferation of New Online Communications Services Poses Hurdles for Law Enforcement*, Wash. Post (July 26, 2014), http://www.washingtonpost.com/world/national-security/proliferation-of-new-online-communications-services-poses-hurdles-for-law-enforcement/2014/07/25/645b13aa-0d21-11e4-b8e5-d0de80767fc2_story.html.

100 Cory Bennett, *Senate Intel Panel Releases Official Encryption Bill Draft*, The Hill (Apr. 13, 2016, 2:39 PM), http://thehill.com/policy/cybersecurity/276181-senate-intel-panel-releases-official-encryption-bill-draft; Erin Kelly, *Bipartisan Encryption Bill Seeks to End Feud between FBI, Tech Industry*, USA Today (Feb. 26, 2016, 9:27 AM), http://www.usatoday.com/story/news/2016/02/24/bipartisan-encryption-bill-seeks-end-feud-between-fbi-tech-industry/80849930/.

101 *See ECPA Part 1: Lawful Access to Stored Content: Hearing before the S. Comm. on Crime, Terrorism, Homeland Security, and Investigations*, 113th Cong. (2013) (statement of Acting Assistant Att'y Gen. Elana Tyrangiel).

102 Dustin Volz, *Email Privacy Bill Unanimously Passes U.S. House*, Reuters (Apr. 27, 2016, 4:56 PM), http://www.reuters.com/article/us-usa-congress-email-idUSKCN0XO1J7.

Second, this is the rare issue where everyone gets to be at least a little bit right. Privacy advocates and providers are right that user information should be protected, that encryption is a valuable service that customers are increasingly demanding, and that, all things being equal, there are fewer risks if encryption does not include a mechanism for government access. Providers are also right that the misperception in other parts of the world, cultivated by overseas competitors, that the U.S. government has easy access to user information harms the ability of United States-based providers to compete overseas. Ironically, in many of the countries where U.S. providers are trying to compete, the local government has fewer restrictions on government access to data, with little or no judicial oversight over the issuance of wiretap orders. And post Snowden, while the United States has reined in surveillance programs, some of those foreign countries have become even more aggressive, not less, about government access to data. But somehow the facts have failed to get in the way of foreign competitors' good story.

Meanwhile, law enforcement officials are correct that there are public safety consequences when agents are unable to execute lawfully obtained, court-authorized search warrants based on probable cause because providers lack the technical ability – whether because of encryption or otherwise – to assist in the execution of those warrants. The extent of the impact of encryption or other "Going Dark"-type problems is not always easy to quantify. In the course of conducting time-sensitive investigations, prosecutors and agents do not tend to track the number of times they had to change investigative techniques, or when an investigation just fell apart, because a warrant could not be executed. But the reality is that without the ability to carry out wiretap orders or search phones pursuant to a warrant, there are investigations that will suffer, if not collapse altogether. Sometimes law enforcement can try to get the information they need through other means, but many times it cannot. That is true for violent crime and terrorism cases, but it is also true for investigations of other types of crimes, including identity theft, hacking, and other crimes that impact privacy. Reasonable people can debate the magnitude of those public safety consequences or disagree about how they should be weighed against the impact on privacy, but there should be no doubt that the public safety consequences are real.

Third, one can support both sides at the same time. Just because you support strong encryption does not mean that you do not also support public safety, and vice versa. Providers are good corporate citizens who care about protecting public safety. And law enforcement officials care about privacy and about doing their jobs in a way that protects privacy. Prosecutors and agents are citizens too. But more than that, they have taken an oath to protect the Constitution, and they face professional and personal consequences for violating that oath. And if they obtain evidence in a way that violates the Constitution, they face significant consequences – not the least of which is that they risk suppression of evidence and letting criminals go free.

So as a nation, we are drawing lines between two values that we can all agree are both extremely important. But to do so, we need to engage in a truly informed, reasoned debate that is fair to both sides and that reflects the importance of this issue in our society.

10 Obama's Mixed Legacy on Cybersecurity, Surveillance, and Surveillance Reform

Timothy Edgar[†]

The jury is still out on whether Barack Obama or Edward Snowden will be remembered as having had a greater impact on cybersecurity during the past eight years. Obama inherited Bush era National Security Agency (NSA) surveillance that had been institutionalized through review by the Foreign Intelligence Surveillance Court. In 2013, Obama embraced surveillance reforms to ensure transparency and privacy protection after the Snowden leaks forced his hand. NSA's aggressive overseas collection remains largely unregulated. Policy makers have done little to address the impact of those operations on the security and stability of the Internet. On cybersecurity, surveillance, and surveillance reform, there is much more to do.

Introduction

Barack Obama's two terms of office included significant achievements, and much unfinished business in coping with the consequences of pervasive cyber insecurity and in starting a global conversation on surveillance and surveillance reform. While the world is still grappling with how to preserve the values of digital openness and privacy in an era of insecurity, the challenges faced by the Obama administration – Edward Snowden chief among them – will shape the direction of the Internet for decades.

Within a few months of taking office, Obama made history by becoming the first American president to devote an entire speech to the subject of cybersecurity. In the East Room of the White House in May 2009, Obama laid out his administration's plan for securing computer networks against malicious attacks, based on a recently completed policy review. I had the honor and good fortune to participate in that review.

Obama's advisers were mindful that his focus on cybersecurity should not be misconstrued as support for government monitoring of the Internet. "Let me also be clear about what we will not do," Obama said. "Our pursuit of cybersecurity will not – I repeat, will not include – monitoring private sector networks or Internet traffic."

Obama was determined to avoid the battles over surveillance and privacy that had confronted his predecessor, George W. Bush, when it became known that President Bush had authorized the NSA to engage in surveillance activities inside the United States in

[†] Senior Fellow, Watson Institute for International and Public Affairs, Brown University. Mr. Edgar served in the Office of the Director of National Intelligence from 2006 to 2010 and under President Obama from 2009 to 2010 as the first director of privacy and civil liberties for the White House National Security Staff. He is the author of BEYOND SNOWDEN: PRIVACY, MASS SURVEILLANCE AND THE STRUGGLE TO REFORM THE NSA (2017).

violation of federal law. "We will preserve and protect the personal privacy and civil liberties that we cherish as Americans," Obama proclaimed.[1]

Inside the intelligence community, Obama's promise about not "monitoring private sector networks or Internet traffic" raised a few eyebrows. The NSA and other agencies had numerous ways, under a variety of legal theories, to monitor Internet communications to discover intelligence about cyber threats. Some of these surveillance operations involved aggressive efforts to take advantage of cyber vulnerabilities. What did the president mean by his disclaimer?

I NSA Surveillance before Obama

In 2009, civil libertarians, human rights activists and the technology community saw the Obama presidency as offering hope for a new approach to issues of privacy, surveillance, and cybersecurity. By 2013, some were marching in demonstrations against Obama's mass surveillance policies. From Berlin to San Francisco, they carried signs saying "Thank you, Edward Snowden," seeing Obama as a grave disappointment.

Polls show that more Americans believe Snowden's leaks served the public interest than harmed the public interest, although the margin is slim. An overwhelming majority of the global public view surveillance by the United States government as unacceptable.[2] In April 2015, activists erected a bust of Snowden in a public park in Brooklyn. The short-lived tribute – it was removed the same day – was meant to honor Snowden's courage in telling the world about the National Security Agency's programs of mass surveillance.[3]

On the other hand, within the NSA and other intelligence agencies there is little sympathy for Edward Snowden's decision to leak classified information. For most, the issue is straightforward: Snowden betrayed his country's most valuable secrets. If you argue that Snowden is a whistle-blower, then you are apt to get an earful about the myriad threats the nation and the world face today, along with a lecture about the complex rules and multiple oversight mechanisms that prevent intelligence agencies from abusing their advanced surveillance capabilities.

NSA surveillance operations are conducted in accordance with federal laws, executive orders, and internal regulations, policies, and directives. The rules are primarily intended to protect the privacy and civil liberties of Americans. By far, the most important dividing line for the NSA is the definition of "electronic surveillance" in the Foreign Intelligence Surveillance Act of 1978, or FISA.[4] If the NSA's direct target is an American or anyone else inside the United States, or if the NSA collects from a switch or a server on U.S. soil, it must get an order from the Foreign Intelligence Surveillance Court (FISC), whose eleven members are drawn from ranks of the sitting federal district court judges.

1 *Remarks by the President on Securing Our Nation's Cyber Infrastructure*, The White House: Off. of the Press Secretary (May 29, 2009, 11:08 AM), https://obamawhitehouse.archives.gov/video/President-Obama-on-Cybersecurity#transcript.

2 *Global Opinions of U.S. Surveillance*, Pew Research Center (July 14, 2014), http://www.pewglobal.org/2014/07/14/nsa-opinion/; *NSA Coverage Wins Pulitzer, but Americans Remain Divided on Snowden Leaks*, Pew Research Center (Apr. 15, 2014), http://www.pewresearch.org/fact-tank/2014/04/15/nsa-coverage-wins-pulitzer-but-americans-remain-divided-on-snowden-leaks/.

3 Julian Hattem, *Artists Secretly Install Snowden Monument*, The Hill (Apr. 6, 2015), http://thehill.com/policy/technology/237977-artists-secretly-install-snowden-monument-in-nyc.

4 § 101(f), 50 U.S.C. § 1801(f).

The bulk of the NSA's mass surveillance programs do not fit this definition of electronic surveillance. Its collection of satellite communications and essentially all of its collection overseas, whether directly or through friendly intelligence services, are governed only by an order signed by Ronald Reagan – Executive Order 12333. E.O. 12333 requires rules to protect the privacy of "United States persons" – American citizens and permanent residents, along with U.S. corporations and organizations composed substantially of U.S. persons. However, unlike collection under FISA, the rules for U.S. persons are administered entirely within the executive branch.

The rules are a legacy of congressional investigations of intelligence activities during the 1970s. The most significant was the Senate committee chaired by Frank Church of Idaho. As it concerned electronic surveillance, Church's investigation focused primarily on FBI wiretapping and two NSA programs, SHAMROCK and MINARET, which clearly involved spying on Americans. (Among the NSA's targets in the MINARET program was Senator Church himself; however, he never learned this.)[5] The Church Committee took for granted that much of what the NSA did – surveillance focused on foreign persons outside the United States – was legitimate.

Church was most concerned that the NSA's surveillance capabilities should not be used for domestic surveillance. In a dramatic televised interview in 1975, Church explained, "The United States government has perfected a technological capability that enables us to monitor the messages that go through the air." He accepted that these NSA surveillance capabilities were "necessary and important to the United States as we look abroad at enemies or potential enemies." But he warned that this "capability at any time could be turned around on the American people, and no American would have any privacy left, such is the capability to monitor everything – telephone conversations, telegrams, it doesn't matter. There would be no place to hide."[6]

When Glenn Greenwald quotes Church at the beginning of *No Place to Hide* – his account of his role in the Snowden revelations – he edits out entirely Church's acknowledgment of the necessity of NSA surveillance "as we look abroad at enemies or potential enemies."[7] Congress chose its words carefully when it wrote FISA's definition of electronic surveillance. While Congress did not authorize the NSA's global capabilities for warrantless surveillance of foreigners, it consciously decided to leave those capabilities unregulated. Even as it adopted rules to prevent the NSA from spying on Americans,

5 *See* 3 Church Committee, Supplementary Detailed Staff Reports on Intelligence Activities and the Rights of Americans, *in* Final Report of the Senate Select Committee to Study Governmental Operations with Respect to Intelligence Activities, S. Rep. No. 94–755, at 271–372 (1976) (warrantless FBI electronic surveillance and microphone surveillance); *see also id.* at 733–84 (NSA programs affecting Americans, including SHAMROCK and MINARET). The fact that Frank Church was a target of MINARET was not publicly known until 2013. It was a startling revelation, although it received little attention because it occurred during an avalanche of stories about more contemporary NSA spying. *See* Matthew M. Aid & William Burr, *"Disreputable If Not Downright Illegal": The National Security Agency versus Martin Luther King, Muhammad Ali, Art Buchwald, Frank Church, et al.*, The National Security Archive Electronic Briefing Book No. 441 (Sept. 25, 2013), http://nsarchive.gwu.edu/NSAEBB/NSAEBB441/.

6 Church's comments were made in an August 17, 1975, interview on NBC's "Meet the Press." They were replayed for a roundtable discussion about surveillance on that show a few months after the Snowden revelations began. *See MTP Roundtable: Looking for Patterns in an Era of "Big Data"* (Meet the Press broadcast Aug. 4, 2013), http://www.nbcnews.com/video/meet-the-press/52669293#52669293.

7 Glenn Greenwald, No Place to Hide: Edward Snowden, the NSA, and the U.S. Surveillance State (2014) (the quotation appears in the front matter before the table of contents).

Congress chose "to exempt from the procedures of the bill certain signals intelligence activities of the National Security Agency."[8] To accomplish this goal, FISA contains a complex, four-part definition of the activities Congress intended the new FISA court to review. This definition, in line with the communications technologies of the late 1970s, adopts a looser standard for interception of signals from the air, which mostly carried long-haul communications, than for signals traveling by wire.

From 1978 to 2001, the NSA's warrantless surveillance scrupulously avoided running afoul of this definition, even when it meant forgoing available intelligence from foreign targets whose data traveled on switches, servers, and other equipment inside the United States. Technology and society changed dramatically, but FISA's definition of electronic surveillance was not significantly amended. While the NSA continued to collect signals from the air, by the end of the millennium most of the world's communications, both telephone and Internet, were traveling as digital packets – usually by fiber-optic undersea cable rather than by satellite signal.[9]

By the time George W. Bush took office, many communications of foreign persons outside the United States were transiting the international gateways inside the United States that sit along the Internet backbone. Servers maintained by companies inside the United States also stored email accounts belonging to foreign persons residing overseas, even for Internet services that were not obviously American. The Justice Department began to obtain communications of foreign terrorists using a FISA court order – a procedure designed to govern surveillance inside the United States. Although the targets were not American citizens or residents located inside the United States, the orders had to meet a variety of detailed legal safeguards, including probable cause that the target was a foreign power or an agent of a foreign power – protections that seemed to make little sense as applied to foreign citizens located outside the United States, and therefore apparently outside the protections of the Fourth Amendment.[10]

Shortly after the terrorist attacks of September 11, 2001, Bush asked his national security team whether the government was doing everything it could to prevent another terrorist attack. Michael Hayden, a four-star Air Force general who had been named as director of the NSA in the Clinton administration, said his agency was not. Hayden explained how the NSA was constrained by FISA and by its own rules against domestic surveillance from following foreign terrorists – or their data – as they crossed into the United States.[11]

8 S. REP. NO. 95–604–Part 1, at 34, *as reprinted in* 4 U.S. CONG. & ADM. NEWS '78–30, at 3935.

9 The only amendment to section 101(f) of FISA, 50 U.S.C. § 1801(f), passed during this period was a minor amendment to (f)(2) in the Patriot Act to harmonize the treatment of computer trespassers under FISA with their treatment under criminal wiretap laws. *See* 50 U.S.C. § 1801 note. For an excellent discussion of the overall issue, see Charlie Savage, POWER WARS: INSIDE OBAMA'S POST-9/11 PRESIDENCY 170–77 (2015).

10 *See United States v. Verdugo-Urquidez*, 494 U.S. 259 (1990). For a discussion of the government's use of FISA orders based on probable cause to obtain the communications of foreigners outside the United States, *see* Privacy & Civil Liberties Oversight Board, *Report on the Surveillance Program Operated Pursuant to Section 702 of the Foreign Intelligence Surveillance Act*, July 2, 2014, 16–20, https://www.pclob.gov/library/702-Report.pdf.

11 The story of STELLARWIND has been told many times. The best single account may be in Savage's POWER WARS, *supra* note 9, at 162–223. The public's understanding of the program has been greatly aided by the government's post-Snowden transparency drive, including the release of previously classified reports by the inspectors general of five agencies on the program. *See "The Department of Justice Release Inspectors*

The moment was a golden opportunity for Vice President Dick Cheney to advance his agenda of enhancing executive powers, which he believed had been improperly eroded by the intelligence reforms of the 1970s. As President Ford's chief of staff, Dick Cheney had opposed the creation of the Foreign Intelligence Surveillance Court, arguing that the president's decisions to engage in intelligence surveillance to protect the country were never a proper subject for second-guessing by the courts. Now, he and his counsel, David Addington, argued that FISA was impeding the president's ability to engage in surveillance of the enemy in time of war, in violation of Article II of the Constitution.

At the time, Congress was considering a number of amendments to FISA and other changes to surveillance law that would become the USA PATRIOT Act. Nevertheless, Bush did not ask Hayden to produce a wish list of additional amendments to address his concerns. Instead, he ordered the NSA to ignore FISA, citing his authority as commander in chief in the newly declared war on terrorism. In early October (less than a month after 9/11), the NSA was engaged in a massive program of collecting data about domestic communications and eavesdropping on communications without the court orders required by federal law. Instead, the president's program relied on periodic authorizations by the attorney general, which were issued to cooperating telecommunications providers.

Code named STELLAR WIND, the program permitted the NSA to collect international communications from major telecommunications companies. Under the program, the NSA could listen to telephone calls or collect the content of Internet communications (such as email) as long as one party to the communication was a suspected operative of al Qaeda. The target could be foreign or domestic, although most were foreign. For communications metadata, which include telephone numbers; date, time, and length of call; email addresses; and other routing information, there was a very different rule. The NSA collected metadata in bulk – i.e., it vacuumed up everything for further analysis.

Among lawyers in the NSA, the FBI, and the Justice Department, the new program raised doubts. By 2004, those doubts provoked a crisis. The new head of the Justice Department's Office of Legal Counsel, Jack Goldsmith, reviewed some of the more outlandish claims of executive power that had been made after 9/11, including the decision to approve waterboarding of terrorist detainees. Goldsmith decided he could not sign off on the legality of all aspects of STELLARWIND. On the basis of Goldsmith's advice, the Justice Department refused to approve the next reauthorization.

James Comey, who would become the FBI director under Obama, was then serving as deputy attorney general. Comey made clear to White House officials that he would not acquiesce to pressure to reverse the Justice Department's decision. At the time, the attorney general, John Ashcroft, was in the hospital recovering from surgery. Ashcroft had relinquished his authority temporarily to his deputy. Nevertheless, Bush sought to strong-arm Ashcroft into overruling his deputy, going so far as to dispatch his counsel, Alberto Gonzales, to Ashcroft's hospital room. Ashcroft told Gonzales to get lost.

For the next three years, lawyers at the NSA, the Justice Department, and the newly created Office of the Director of National Intelligence labored to assign the activities

General Reports Concerning Collection Activities Authorized by President George W. Bush after the Attacks of September 11, 2001," IC ON THE RECORD (official government transparency site) (Apr. 25, 2015), https://icontherecord.tumblr.com/post/117330907753/the-department-of-justice-releases-inspectors.

that had been part of STELLARWIND under the authority of the Foreign Intelligence Surveillance Court. In 2004 and 2006, the surveillance court secretly approved orders for bulk collection of Internet metadata and telephone records, accepting an exceedingly aggressive interpretation of the Patriot Act. In January 2007, a FISC judge signed off on a similarly strained argument permitting the NSA to collect content as well, with a single blanket order.

In April, another judge of the surveillance court reviewed the government's creative lawyering on the content issue, disagreed with the government's argument, and refused to allow collection inside the United States against Al Qaeda targets outside the United States unless the government obtained individual court orders. The Justice Department was able to obtain approval for only a fraction of the foreign targets. Michael McConnell, Bush's second director of national intelligence and a previous director of the NSA – informed Congress of a dangerous intelligence gap. In August, despite the protests of civil libertarians, Congress enacted the Protect America Act – a temporary law giving the NSA authority to resume collection with a blanket order from the surveillance court.

After January 2007, the NSA's surveillance activities inside the United States were again conducted entirely under the authority of the court. Instead of resuming STELLARWIND when the surveillance court balked, the intelligence community went to Congress for an amendment to FISA. Bush's claims of unilateral executive power to engage in warrantless wiretapping were now mainly a matter for legal academics and historians to debate. Cheney's attempt to undo one of the Church Committee's singular achievements – subjecting intelligence surveillance inside the United States to rules set by Congress and review by the federal courts – had ultimately proved a failure. However, the surveillance continued. Indeed, it was now on a firmer legal basis. It had the approval of all three branches of government.

II President Obama

From his post in Geneva in the summer of 2008, Edward Snowden, then a CIA computer specialist disillusioned by the NSA's warrantless wiretapping program and other counterterrorism policies, decided it was not yet time to become a whistle-blower. It appeared likely that a young idealistic senator from Illinois, Barack Obama, would become the next American president. "I think even Obama's critics were impressed and optimistic about the values that he represented," Snowden later said in an interview with James Bamford, the author of several books about the NSA. "He said we're not going to sacrifice our rights. We're not going to change who we are just to catch some small percentage more terrorists."[12]

Many Americans shared Snowden's optimism about the chance for a fresh start in the "war on terrorism." Privacy and civil liberties activists had some reason to hope for a sharp break with the Bush approach. During the campaign, Obama had faulted Bush for excessive claims of executive power, denouncing the NSA's program of warrantless surveillance. He promised that, if elected, he would ask his legal team to review NSA

[12] James Bamford, *The Most Wanted Man in the World*, Wired (June 13, 2014), http://www.wired.com/2014/08/edward-snowden/#ch-1.

programs and would reverse executive orders that he believed were excessive "with the stroke of a pen."[13]

Careful observers noticed nuances in Obama's language that were lost on much of the general public. In remarks on the campaign trail, Obama did not echo his supporters' harsh criticisms of the Patriot Act. Instead, Obama reproached Bush for authorizing surveillance by claiming unilateral executive authority, instead of asking Congress for approval. Charlie Savage, a Pulitzer Prize–winning national security reporter, explains that Obama consistently advocated a rule of law critique rather than a civil liberties critique of the Bush approach to national security. Obama saw the "war on terror" – as it was understood by Bush, Cheney, and their national security lawyers – as a threat to the separation of powers among the executive, legislative, and judicial branches. Obama did not voice nearly as strong an opinion on whether Bush's surveillance policies violated individual rights.[14]

During the summer of 2008, then-Senator Obama made a significant choice that made the rule of law critique less relevant. The previous year, Obama had voted against the temporary law that allowed the NSA to resume its domestic collection of content about foreign targets without individual court orders. However, as the law was about to expire, Obama voted for the FISA Amendments Act, which kept the program going and granted retroactive legal immunity to telecommunications providers who had cooperated with the NSA's warrantless surveillance. Obama's decision created a headache for his campaign. There was a torrent of criticism for his vote on his Web site, "my.barackobama.com," an innovative platform intended to make his followers feel part of a movement. Obama responded with a thoughtful post, explaining that, while he believed the FISA Amendments Act was far from perfect, new safeguards for the NSA made it an improvement over the temporary law it replaced.[15]

Shortly after Obama took office, he was briefed on the NSA programs by Ben Powell, the outgoing general counsel and chief lawyer for the intelligence community, and Matt Olsen, who led the Justice Department office that appears before the FISA court. Powell's goal was to ensure the NSA programs would survive the presidential transition. Obama was joined by his new White House counsel, Greg Craig, and his new attorney general, Eric Holder.

Powell and Olson explained that the FISA court was now regularly issuing classified orders for four types of data: call detail records, Internet metadata, telephone calls, and Internet content. They also had some bad news. They had recently informed Judge Reggie Walton that the NSA had bungled its handling of the metadata program – one of the NSA's automated systems was querying program data using selectors that had not been approved as required under the court's orders. "I want my lawyers to look into this," Obama responded, indicating Craig and Holder.[16]

Despite the compliance problems, Obama decided to continue the NSA programs without substantial change and turned his attention to a broader privacy agenda. The major items were strengthening consumer privacy and addressing the growing problem

13 CNN, 2008: *Obama Vows to Reverse Bush Laws*, YOUTUBE (Mar. 31, 2008), https://www.youtube.com/watch?v=AzgNf9iZ2Bo.

14 SAVAGE, *supra* note 9, at 50–55.

15 Barack Obama, *My Position on FISA*, HUFFINGTON POST (July 11, 2008, 5:12 AM), http://www.huffingtonpost.com/barack-obama/my-position-on-fisa_b_110789.html.

16 Ryan Lizza, *State of Deception: Why Won't the President Rein in the Intelligence Community?*, THE NEW YORKER, Dec. 16, 2013.

of cybersecurity, which posed its own complex and difficult privacy issues. Obama announced an ambitious plan to strengthen security for government and critical infrastructure networks.[17]

In Obama's cybersecurity address, he also announced that he would appoint a privacy and civil liberties official to the White House National Security Staff, serving its new Cybersecurity Directorate: "To ensure that policies keep faith with our fundamental values, this office will also include an official with a portfolio specifically dedicated to safeguarding the privacy and civil liberties of the American people."[18]

I was chosen to fill that position. Obama's decision to create my position reflected how important privacy issues had become in national security policy. While the National Security Council had long employed a small staff to address human rights issues, I became the first privacy and civil liberties official to serve on the National Security Council (NSC) staff.

III Director of Privacy and Civil Liberties

At the White House, my primary job was to review Obama's cybersecurity agenda. To do so, I put together an interagency committee of privacy and civil liberties officers from the Department of Homeland Security, the Office of the Director of National Intelligence, the Department of Justice, and many other departments and agencies. We used our meetings not only to discuss cybersecurity initiatives, but also to exchange information about our common challenges in protecting privacy and civil liberties in agencies better known for spying and surveillance.

Our job was made more difficult by Obama's delay in setting up the Privacy and Civil Liberties Oversight Board – an independent board recommended by the 9/11 commission. The first such privacy board was short lived, lasting from 2006 to 2008 as a body attached to the Executive Office of the President. Amid questions about its independence, Congress restructured the board as an independent agency. As Obama took office, the White House spent years wrangling over what the new board should look like. Obama did not manage to nominate its full membership until December 2011, and it took until May 2013 for all members to be confirmed, allowing the board to begin work.

In the meantime, our committee of privacy bureaucrats took up the slack. Although most meetings were in the Eisenhower building, for our first I chose the White House Situation Room, hoping to inspire a sense of seriousness and purpose. The NSA did not yet have a full-time privacy and civil liberties official. It was represented by John DeLong, a lawyer with a degree in mathematics who had just been named head of its new compliance office. With the increasingly complex rules the NSA was facing as a result of court oversight, the idea was to treat compliance as a function as critical as any other aspect of the NSA's mission.

And that idea was well warranted. By 2014, DeLong estimated that "about 300 people" within the NSA were focused on "core compliance activities," such as audits, spot checks, and training.[19] One recurring problem was "roamers" – foreign targets who

17 *Supra* note 1.

18 *Id.*

19 Gregory J. Millman, *Compliance in Government: Q&A with John DeLong of the NSA*, Wall St. Journal: Risk & Compliance Journal (Jan. 23, 2014, 12:26 PM), http://blogs.wsj.com/riskandcompliance/2014/01/23/compliance-in-government-qa-with-john-delong-of-the-nsa/.

moved inside the United States, where continued monitoring required a warrant based on probable cause. In the popular imagination, an intelligence analyst can determine a target's location within seconds, and with complete accuracy. In fact, the NSA's system is far from foolproof. Every six months, a detailed accounting of "compliance incidents" is provided to Congress and the FISA court. One unconfirmed document provided to the Washington Post was said to be internal NSA report that tracked compliance incidents, including roamers, resulting in an embarrassing front-page headline about the NSA's repeated violations of privacy rules.[20]

Court review had focused new attention on the NSA's imperfections, and the serious consequences of seemingly small mistakes. Roamers are not a problem unique to collection authorized by the FISA court. The NSA mistakenly picks up phones inside the United States from its overseas and satellite collection as well. Nonetheless, the NSA's typical "compliance incident rate" – the compliance incidents during the reporting period as a percentage of the number of selectors tasked – was impressive, at less than 0.5 percent.[21] It spoke well of the NSA's rules-based culture and DeLong's leadership. Given the gigantic volume of NSA's collection, however, a small percentage still means a large number of mistakes.

At meetings of our White House privacy committee, DeLong asked the kind of perceptive questions one might expect of a mathematician. There seemed to be a lot of resources devoted to compliance with privacy rules, but were we really getting more privacy? How could we measure that? As a result of the FISA court's attention, domestic collection of data had been put under a microscope. Yet the NSA's foreign collection still consumed most of its resources and generated most of the data. Fewer resources and even less high-level attention were focused on these programs.

In retrospect, we were all missing the big picture. The focus on the domestic collection programs that had started after 9/11 distracted us from other programs whose impact on privacy would make them as controversial, or even more controversial, when press articles that said they were based on the Snowden leaks appeared in 2013 – targeting foreign leaders and aid organizations, mass surveillance of the communications of foreign nations, and pervasive efforts to undermine Internet security.

If we failed to see the privacy impact of much of what the NSA did, however, this was in part a product of the law's myopia. The FISA court does not review the NSA's overseas activities unless the agency intentionally targets a U.S. person. Executive Order 12333, which does, authorizes "all means" to collect "intelligence information." The NSA and other agencies are charged with finding a vast array of information about foreign governments, organizations, international terrorists, and other "foreign persons," not only for countering terrorism and other security threats, but for broad "foreign affairs" purposes, so long as they comply with rules designed to protect the privacy of U.S. persons.

NSA analysts enjoy a great deal of freedom. Although Edward Snowden certainly did not have "the authority," as he later claimed, to target the email account of the president of the United States, or of any U.S. person, without a court order, software

20 Barton Gellman, *NSA Broke Privacy Rules Thousands of Times Per Year, Audit Finds*, Wash. Post, Aug. 15, 2013.

21 Semiannual Assessment of Compliance with Procedures and Guidelines Issued Pursuant to Section 702 of the Foreign Intelligence Surveillance Act: Reporting Period June 1, 2012-November 30, 2012, at 7, 23 (2013), https://www.aclu.org/files/assets/semiannual_assessment_of_compliance_with_procedures_and_guidelines_issued_pursuant_to_sect_702_of_fisa.pdf.

tools give analysts broad desktop access to an array of signals intelligence databases. The NSA's inspector general found a dozen compliance incidents in the decade prior to 2013 involving NSA analysts targeting ex-spouses and romantic partners, none of whom were U.S. persons, or otherwise using the system for personal reasons.[22]

During my time in government, there was no law, executive order, or policy designed to protect the privacy of foreigners. Because I was an official charged with protecting "privacy and civil liberties," it was taken for granted that my concerns should be the impact of intelligence programs on U.S. persons. In the absence of the kind of intentional abuse uncovered by the NSA inspector general, surveillance of foreigners is fair game as long as an analyst has a valid intelligence purpose.

In retrospect, the biggest blind spot for our privacy committee concerned how the NSA's methods of breaking into global communications were affecting the security of the Internet in a way that could not help but diminish everyone's privacy. Of course, the NSA was founded as a spy agency precisely to read protected foreign communications. If the NSA's capabilities are directed to a valid end – obtaining foreign intelligence – and if rules to protect U.S. person information are followed, then "all means" are authorized. The NSA also has another mission: protecting the security of U.S. military and national security systems. Indeed, we hoped to leverage the NSA's expertise to protect other government agencies and privately owned critical infrastructure from foreign cyber attacks. A single-minded focus by the NSA on "enabling" signals intelligence by undermining Internet security would frustrate this goal.

Although the National Institute of Standards and Technology (NIST) – an agency of the Department of Commerce – has the lead on technical standards development when it comes to cryptography, by law the NSA also participates. Randomness is a key element in designing a secure crypto system. At a leading conference of cryptographers in 2007, Dan Shumow and Niels Ferguson of Microsoft pointed out a weakness in one of four random-number generators NIST had recommended in 2006. There was speculation about an NSA "backdoor." In 2013, the issue resurfaced in the press. "Trust has been violated," remarked Matt Green, a leading cryptographer at Johns Hopkins University.[23] Deeply embarrassed, NIST withdrew its recommendation.

IV The Snowden Revelations

In June 2013, the Obama administration was rocked by an extraordinary series of revelations about NSA surveillance based on leaks from the former NSA contractor Edward Snowden. The administration's agenda for securing computer networks belonging to government agencies and critical infrastructure sectors was knocked off balance by the need to address the resulting crisis in confidence.

The new mood was captured in a parody of the famous "Hope" poster by the artist Shepard Fairey, which features a thoughtful Obama shaded in red, white, and blue. The new poster outfitted Obama with eavesdropper's headphones. The new slogan riffed on Obama's campaign slogan, reading, "Yes, we scan." In an interview in May 2015, Fairey

22 Letter from NSA Office of the Inspector General to Senator Charles E. Grassley (Sept. 11, 2013), http://icontherecord.tumblr.com/post/62457835497/nsa-inspector-generals-letter-to-senator-charles.

23 Matthew Green, "*On the* NSA," Cryptography Engineering (Sept. 6, 2013), https://blog.cryptographyengineering.com/2013/09/06/on-nsa/.

said he supported the parody because Obama had not lived up to the image he had created. "I mean, drones and domestic spying are the last things I would have thought" Obama would support, Fairey said.[24]

The Obama administration's initial response strategy drew from the playbook its predecessors had successfully used to ward off the Bush era NSA controversies. Officials defended the NSA's programs by claiming they had successfully thwarted dozens of terrorist attacks. They pointed to the U.S. person rules and the oversight of the surveillance court. They denounced Snowden for betraying government secrets. The strategy fell flat. According to a leading opinion poll, more Americans viewed Edward Snowden as a whistle-blower than a traitor. They did not trust the NSA's assurances that their data was protected by privacy rules and were skeptical of its success stories.[25]

The backlash surprised intelligence officials who had been accustomed, ever since the attacks of 9/11, to receiving the benefit of the doubt when it came to programs they said were needed to fight terrorism. Within weeks, two members of Congress from Michigan – Justin Amash, a Tea Party Republican, and John Conyers, a liberal Democrat – teamed up to push for a vote to end funding for the NSA's bulk collection of telephone records. In the face of dire warnings from the NSA director, it was defeated, but the vote was a squeaker: 205–217, with more than one hundred Democrats joining almost as many Republicans to vote against the Obama administration.[26]

Before a crowd of tens of thousands in Berlin back in the summer of 2008, candidate Obama had argued for "allies who will listen to each other, who will learn from each other [and] who will, above all, trust each other."[27] Germans were not happy when they read stories in the German press saying the NSA had been listening to telephone calls of their popular chief executive, Chancellor Angela Merkel. "This is not done," she said sternly, as if scolding a naughty child. The German magazine *Der Spiegel* published many additional stories about the NSA. Germany's position as an Internet hub between Europe and the Middle East makes the data that transits German territory of immense intelligence value.

Stung by the criticism, Obama apologized to Merkel. "We're not leaving it to Jim Clapper anymore," said one official, referring to the director of national intelligence. Not everyone thought the new approach was such a good idea. Obama was looking for "immaculate collection," Clapper complained.[28]

24 Matt Patches, *Shepard Fairey on the Future of Political Art and Whether Obama Lived Up to His "Hope" Poster*, Esquire (May 28, 2015), http://www.esquire.com/news-politics/interviews/a35288/shepard-fairey-street-art-obama-hope-poster/; Andres Jauregui, *Yes We Scan: Shepard Fairey Likes Obama NSA Parodies, "Pleased" with Subversive Symbolism*, Huffington Post, (June 23, 2013), http://www.huffingtonpost.com/2013/06/28/yes-we-scan-shepard-fairey-obama-nsa_n_3517213.html.

25 *Snowden Is a Whistle-Blower, Americans Say in Poll*, NPR (July 10, 2013), http://www.npr.org/sections/thetwo-way/2013/07/10/200878660/snowden-is-a-whistle-blower-americans-say-in-poll.

26 *See* Cong. Rec. H5028 (daily ed., July 24, 2013).

27 Jonathan Freedland, *US Elections: Obama Wows Berlin Crowd with Historic Speech*, The Guardian (July 24, 2008), http://www.theguardian.com/global/2008/jul/24/barackobama.uselections2008.

28 Adam Entous & Danny Yadron, *Some Senior U.S. Officials Not Comfortable with Obama's Curbs on NSA Spying on Leaders*, Wall St. Journal (Dec. 30, 2015), http://www.wsj.com/articles/some-senior-u-s-officials-not-comfortable-with-obamas-curbs-on-nsa-spying-on-leaders-145150680; David E. Sanger, *Obama Panel Said to Urge N.S.A. Curbs*, N.Y. Times (Dec. 12, 2013), http://www.nytimes.com/2013/12/13/world/americas/obama-panel-said-to-urge-nsa-curbs.html.

The Brazilian president Dilma Rousseff was equally furious when she read stories saying that the NSA had monitored her communications, along with those of many ordinary Brazilians. Brazil, like Germany, is host to important communications links innervating the whole of South America. In 2014, Brazil organized an international conference on Internet governance. It raised awkward questions about U.S. dominance of the Internet's physical, economic, and technical infrastructure.[29]

Edward Snowden did not limit his leaks to information about spying on allies. In March 2014, the *New York Times* published a detailed front-page exposé of what were said to be operations against Huawei Technologies and other Chinese targets.[30] In 2012, Huawei Technologies became the largest manufacturer of telecommunications equipment in the world. Huawei's ties to the Chinese government – its founder, Ren Zhengfei, was an engineer in the People's Liberation Army (PLA) – has long raised alarm bells in the national security establishment. The risk that China might use Huawei to facilitate its cyber exploits was a major national security concern.

The story was a godsend to Beijing. The reports of spying on Huawei and other Chinese companies put the Justice Department in an exquisitely awkward position just as it was getting ready to take legal action against Chinese economic espionage. In May, prosecutors indicted five Chinese PLA members for hacking into U.S. companies. The Justice Department argued that the Chinese spying was different. The PLA hackers were stealing trade secrets to give them to Chinese companies, while the NSA collects foreign intelligence for policy makers. Although true, it was a lawyerly point, unlikely to convince the global public.

V The Fallout: Increased Transparency

"It's gut wrenching for me to see so much of this so casually exposed," explained James Clapper in an interview in 2014, describing his reaction to the Snowden revelations. While he could "almost accept" Snowden's actions if they were limited to the NSA's domestic collection of data, "what he did, what he took, what he has exposed, goes way, way, way beyond the so-called domestic surveillance programs."[31]

Clapper became infamous days after the Snowden revelations began. At a congressional hearing in March 2013, only a few months earlier, Clapper had publicly denied that the NSA "wittingly" gathered records belonging to "millions or tens of millions of Americans." Clapper contended that his answer, given under oath, was "the least untruthful" statement he was able to give while preserving the secrecy of the NSA's bulk collection programs.[32] Rand Paul, the Republican senator and 2016 presidential

[29] *See* Harold Trinkunas & Ian Wallace, Converging on the Future of Global internet Governance: The United States and Brazil (Brookings 2015).

[30] David E. Sanger & Nicole Perlroth, *N.S.A. Breached Chinese Servers Seen as Security Threat*, N.Y. Times (Mar. 22, 2014), http://www.nytimes.com/2014/03/23/world/asia/nsa-breached-chinese-servers-seen-as-spy-peril.html.

[31] Eli Lake, *Spy Chief James Clapper: We Can't Stop Another Snowden*, The Daily Beast (Feb. 23, 2014, 8:00 PM), http://www.thedailybeast.com/articles/2014/02/23/spy-chief-we-can-t-stop-another-snowden.html.

[32] Glenn Kessler, *Clapper's 'Least Untruthful' Statement to the Senate*, Wash. Post, June 12, 2013, https://www.washingtonpost.com/blogs/fact-checker/post/james-clappers-least-untruthful-statement-to-the-senate/2013/06/11/e50677a8-d2d8-11e2-a73e-826d299ff459_blog.html.

candidate, later quipped that Clapper and Snowden should share a jail cell, where they could talk about liberty and security.

With the public on Snowden's side, Obama ordered Clapper to reveal more about the NSA to put the revelations in context. Clapper embraced his new role as truth teller with the zeal of a convert. He launched "IC on the Record" to provide authorized dumps of declassified documents. The site is hosted on Tumblr, a social media site popular mainly with teens and young adults who create their own sites, or "Tumblrs." Most Tumblrs discuss celebrities and popular culture; Clapper's hosts thousands of pages of once-secret surveillance court opinions and internal NSA documents.

By the fall of 2013, one transparency advocate, Steven Aftergood, marveled, "Already we've seen a more extensive disclosure of classified information about current intelligence programs than we've seen for at least 40 years, and maybe ever." By March 2014, the Intelligence Community's new Tumblr had resulted in the authorized disclosure of more than twice as many documents as Snowden had leaked.[33] At least some credit should therefore go to the man civil libertarians learned to hate: James Clapper. In the fall of 2013, I organized a forum at Brown University, inviting Aftergood, along with other advocates, reporters, and government officials, to explore the NSA's new "big transparency." My old boss Alex Joel tried to put into words just how unsettling the changes were. "The intelligence community is not designed and built for transparency," he wryly observed. "Our culture is around finding our adversaries' secrets and keeping our own secrets secret."

Transparency was not the only culture shift Clapper had to manage. He also had to contend with a new sensitivity about the impact of NSA programs on people around the world. Since the Church Committee reforms of the 1970s, U.S. intelligence agencies had dismissed accusations of unchecked surveillance by pointing to the rules designed to protect the privacy of U.S. persons. That defense did nothing for some of Obama's strongest supporters – top executives in Silicon Valley. If anything, the constant talk about protecting U.S. persons was counterproductive because it implied that no one else's privacy mattered. American technology companies were facing a real danger from foreign competitors who promoted themselves as not being in bed with the NSA. Estimates of lost business ranged from $35 billion to $180 billion.[34]

By the end of 2013, there were rising expectations that the NSA would make reforms beyond increased transparency to address the concerns of American allies and the technology industry. Obama appointed my old White House colleagues Peter Swire and Cass Sunstein to a five-member "review group" to make recommendations on surveillance reform. The review group's mandate overlapped with that of the Privacy and Civil Liberties Oversight Board, which had finally begun operation in May. Creation of the review group puzzled many, including me, who had been pushing for years to empower

[33] Steven Aftergood, *ODNI Rethinks Secrecy and Openness in Intelligence*, FED'N OF AM. SCIENTISTS: SECRECY NEWS (Mar. 20, 2014), https://fas.org/blogs/secrecy/2014/03/litt-transparency/; Carrie Johnson, *Snowden's Leaks Lead to More Disclosure From Feds* (NPR Morning Edition broadcast Oct. 11, 2013, 4:00 AM), http://www.npr.org/2013/10/11/231899987/snowdens-leaks-lead-to-more-disclosure-from-feds.

[34] Dominic Rushe & Paul Lewis, *Tech Firms Push Back against White House Efforts to Divert NSA Meeting*, THE GUARDIAN (Dec. 17, 2013), http://www.theguardian.com/world/2013/dec/17/tech-firms-obama-meeting-nsa-surveillance; Claire Cain Miller, *Revelations of N.S.A. Spying Cost U.S. Tech Companies*, N.Y. TIMES (Mar. 21, 2014), http://www.nytimes.com/2014/03/22/business/fallout-from-snowden-hurting-bottom-line-of-tech-companies.html.

the privacy board, but the White House was impatient to show progress on surveillance reform. The privacy board had been slow to organize, and its members had made clear that they were planning to take a step-by-step approach to their review of the NSA. In December 2013, the review group released a comprehensive report, touching on privacy, foreign relations, and cybersecurity. The report devoted an entire chapter to protecting the privacy of non-U.S. persons.[35]

In January 2016, Obama issued new rules on signals intelligence. Presidential Policy Directive (PPD) 28 extended the mechanisms for protecting "U.S. person" information to protect information belonging to anyone, anywhere in the world.[36] While the substance of the rules is relatively modest, the concept was revolutionary. Retention and minimization limits that once applied only to U.S. persons now apply to all personal information. PPD 28 limited bulk collection of signals intelligence to six specific national security threats: espionage, international terrorism, proliferation of weapons of mass destruction, cybersecurity threats, threats to U.S. or allied military forces, or transnational crime. Signals intelligence cannot be used to disadvantage anyone, anywhere in the world, on the basis of race, gender, sexual orientation, or religion. The rules now explicitly prohibit such misuse of intelligence information – for example, by blackmailing a foreign leader who is gay.

VI A Final Step (for Now): The USA Freedom Act

For Michael Hayden, surveillance reform had gone far enough – quite possibly too far. In late 2014, the former CIA and NSA director was up in arms about a surveillance reform bill on the Senate floor. That bill proposed to end the NSA's bulk collection of telephone records and create an independent advocate in the FISA court. The legislation was a result of a year and a half of painstaking negotiations by the intelligence community, technology companies, and privacy and civil liberties groups. Together with the former attorney general Michael Mukasey, Hayden blasted the bill. The result, Hayden and Mukasey said, was "exquisitely crafted to hobble the gathering of electronic intelligence."[37]

The reform bill's main sponsors were Senator Patrick Leahy of Vermont and Representative James Sensenbrenner of Wisconsin. In 2001, Leahy and Sensenbrenner had been the main sponsors of the USA PATRIOT Act, whose extravagantly Orwellian name is an acronym for the "Uniting and Strengthening America by Providing Appropriate Tools Required to Intercept and Obstruct Terrorism Act." The Snowden revelations convinced Leahy and Sensenbrenner that the Patriot Act needed reform. They gave their new bill an acronym that leaned in favor of civil liberties: the "Uniting and Strengthening America by Fulfilling Rights and Ending Eavesdropping, Dragnet-Collection and Online Monitoring Act," or USA FREEDOM Act.

35 Richard A Clarke et al., LIBERTY AND SECURITY IN A CHANGING WORLD: REPORT AND RECOMMENDATIONS OF THE PRESIDENT'S REVIEW GROUP ON INTELLIGENCE AND COMMUNICATIONS TECHNOLOGIES (Dec. 12, 2013), http://www.whitehouse.gov/sites/default/files/docs/2013-12-12_rg_final_report.pdf.

36 *Presidential Policy Directive – Signals Intelligence Activities (Presidential Policy Directive 28/PPD-28)*: THE WHITE HOUSE: OFF. OF THE PRESS SECRETARY (Jan. 17, 2014), https://obamawhitehouse.archives.gov/the-press-office/2014/01/17/presidential-policy-directive-signals-intelligence-activities.

37 Michael V. Hayden & Michael B. Mukasey, *NSA Reform That Only ISIS Could Love*, WALL ST. JOURNAL (Nov. 17, 2014, 7:00 PM), http://www.wsj.com/articles/michael-v-hayden-and-michael-b-mukasey-nsa-reform-that-only-isis-could-love-1416268847.

The Freedom Act replaced bulk collection with a new system under which telephone records remain with the companies, but are subject to rapid queries by NSA analysts pursuant to FISC orders. NSA analysts must use a "specific selection term" to retrieve data. Much of the debate over the bill concerned the breadth of this definition. The Freedom Act also requires the FISA court to issue declassified versions of significant opinions, including opinions that interpret a "specific selection term." The Freedom Act also provides a "special advocate" to the FISA Court, a cleared independent lawyer who can be assigned to challenge the government's positions in *ex parte* proceedings.

The Freedom Act became law on June 2, 2015.[38] The short-term effect was not to end bulk collection, but to restart it. The Patriot Act provision that the Bush administration had used to persuade the FISA court to authorize bulk collection had expired the day before, and the NSA had shuttered the program. Under the Freedom Act, the NSA had a six-month grace period to transition to a new system. Bulk collection was on shaky ground in any event. The Privacy and Civil Liberties Oversight Board had recommended ending the program, finding it had not contributed unique intelligence in any terrorism investigations.[39] Although the FISA court continued to embrace bulk collection, civil liberties groups had challenged the theory in other federal courts. In May 2015, a federal appeals court rejected bulk collection.[40] A surveillance reform bill that the former NSA director Michael Hayden said "only ISIS could love" had become the agency's best bet to preserve its domestic access to telephone records.

Before anyone had ever heard of Edward Snowden, many inside the intelligence community understood that its rules for protecting privacy and civil liberties, designed in the 1970s to prevent "spying on Americans," had become inadequate to the digital age. Today, our personal lives are both digital and global. Our electronic communications cross international boundaries. A system of rules that neglects these realities allows for mass surveillance.

The most important thing for Congress to do is to broaden the conversation. The continuing fallout over Edward Snowden shows that global surveillance has touched a nerve in an interconnected world.[41] A narrow focus on whether surveillance programs involve domestic or foreign collection would be a missed opportunity for civil liberties, privacy, and human rights. In the Internet age, it is no longer desirable or even possible to protect the privacy of Americans while leaving the rules for most global surveillance programs entirely to the executive branch. We should continue to draw the NSA's global surveillance out of the shadows and under a legal framework that is designed for this century. Now is the time to both build on Obama's accomplishments and to learn from his mistakes by thinking big about cybersecurity, surveillance, and surveillance reform.

38 The version that become law softened the title a bit, while preserving the acronym: Uniting and Strengthening America by Fulfilling Rights and Ensuring Effective Discipline over Monitoring Act of 2015 (USA FREEDOM Act), Pub. L. No. 114–23, (June 23, 2015), 129 Stat. 268.

39 Privacy & Civil Liberties Oversight Board, *Report on the Telephone Records Program Conducted under Section 215 of the USA PATRIOT Act and on the Operations of the Foreign Intelligence Surveillance Court*, Jan. 23, 2014, 11, https://www.pclob.gov/events/2014/january23.html.

40 *American Civil Liberties Union v. Clapper*, 785 F.3d 787 (2d Cir. 2015).

41 *See* Amos Toh, Faiza Patel & Elizabeth Goitein, Overseas Surveillance in an Interconnected World (Brennan Ctr. for Just. 2016), https://www.brennancenter.org/publication/overseas-surveillance-interconnected-world.

11 Local Law Enforcement Video Surveillance: Rules, Technology, and Legal Implications

Marc J. Blitz[†]

Emerging video surveillance technology is changing the way police combat crime and the threat of terrorism. Many cities in the United States and elsewhere are installing large-scale closed circuit television (CCTV) camera systems to monitor and record individuals' actions in public streets. Law enforcement's hope is that it will be able to find – in such an extensive video record of public life – previously unavailable evidence crucial for investigating a crime, and perhaps stop unfolding criminal activity. Police departments are also now turning video cameras on themselves: Faced with many high-profile complaints about unjustified use of force, police departments are requiring officers to don "body-worn cameras" to record their interactions with the public. The hope is that officers can be accountable for abuses but can also be exonerated when confronted with false allegations.

While offering benefits in safety and accountability, these technological developments raise interesting legal and policy questions about what measures courts, legislators, and administrators should take to assure that powerful forms of video surveillance do not undermine individuals' privacy. This chapter briefly reviews both law enforcement use of such video surveillance technology and the still-evolving legal framework that governs it. It reviews the Fourth Amendment case law that courts have generated regarding when public video surveillance (or similar forms of surveillance in public) might constitute a Fourth Amendment "search" of the kind government can only conduct with a warrant based on probable cause and surveys some of the legislative, administrative, and policy proposals that city governments and police departments have adopted to govern CCTV surveillance systems and body-worn camera programs. It also looks at why such permanent and ongoing video surveillance may require courts to rethink old legal rules and assumptions, adopted in the many cases when only one or two video cameras have been temporarily installed by police to gather evidence in a specific investigation focused on a specific target.

Introduction

The U.S. Constitution, said the Supreme Court in 1948, places "obstacles in the way of a too permeating police surveillance."[1] One interesting question that has long occupied the Court is whether the technological sophistication of a police investigation might

† Alan Joseph Bennett Professor of Law, Oklahoma City University School of Law.

1 *United States v. Di Re*, 332 U.S. 581, 595 (1948).

itself make it "too permeating." Might it be the case, for example, that even if police are left free by the Constitution to watch a person walk through the streets, this does not mean they are similarly free to photograph or video-record him, or use a zoom lens to capture small details in such images? Or that, even if police are free to tail and observe a driver on a public roadway, this does not mean they are free to track him over days or weeks with a radio transmitter or Global Positioning Satellite (GPS) device?

In the 1980s, the Court's answer to such questions was generally that whether a police technique constituted a "search" did not depend on whether it was high-tech or low-tech. What mattered was rather whether the police were making their observation in public, where they had a right to be even without a warrant, or in a private space, where a warrant would typically be required. If, for example, police do not need a warrant to tail and watch a driver on a public road, they should not – said the Court – need a warrant to "augment[t] their sensory faculties" as they do so, with a radio transmitter that tracks the car they can already see.[2] If, the Court said in another case, police do not need a warrant to look out of a plane window to view an open and visible patch of ground below,[3] they also do not need a warrant when they make the same observation but their "human vision is enhanced somewhat" with the aid of a high-powered camera.[4]

In short, the constitutional ground rules governing police surveillance did not depend on the technology police used. They rather depended on whether what police observed was visible from a public place, or some other place from which police could permissibly make observations without a warrant. This was true for the radio transmitters the police used to engage in location tracking in the 1980s. The Court emphasized in *United States v. Knotts* that "a person traveling in an automobile on public thoroughfares, has no reasonable expectation of privacy in his movements" and can thus raise no Fourth Amendment objection when police use technology to track those movements.[5] Police do need a warrant, by contrast, to monitor in the home, as the Court made clear in *United States v. Karo*.[6] The same was true of aerial observation: It is permissible, said the Court in *California v. Ciraolo*, for a law enforcement officer to fly over a person's backyard in an airplane and view – or, the Court later made clear, photograph with a high-powered camera – space he can see "from a public vantage point where he has a right to be and which renders the activities clearly visible."[7]

In recent years, however, the Supreme Court and some lower courts have shown more openness to the possibility that technological enhancement of a certain kind can change its constitutional status. In *United States v. Jones*, for example, Justice Alito wrote – in a concurring opinion joined by three other justices, and endorsed in large part by a fourth – that there is a constitutionally significant difference between old-fashioned

2 *United States v. Knotts*, 460 U.S. 276, 282 (1983).

3 The Supreme Court held, in *California v. Ciraolo*, 476 U.S. 207 (1986), that such aerial observation does not count as a Fourth Amendment search.

4 *Dow Chem. Co. v. United States*, 476 U.S. 227, 238 (1986).

5 *Knotts*, 460 U.S. at 281.

6 *United States v. Karo*, 468 U.S. 705, 714 (1984) (holding that warrantless "monitoring of a beeper in a private residence, a location not open to visual surveillance" violates the Fourth Amendment).

7 *Ciraolo*, 476 U.S. at 213. I have presented a longer description of this type of judicial analysis in Marc Jonathan Blitz, *Video Surveillance and the Constitution of Public Space: Fitting the Fourth Amendment to a World That Tracks Image and Identity*, 82 Tex. L. Rev. 1349, 1375–76 (2004) (describing how courts have acted "as though [] novel and far-reaching technological developments are not really novel at all – but rather more effective and cost-efficient variants of long-accepted methods of police work").

police monitoring of a person and GPS tracking. With only cars and personnel, constant monitoring of a suspect over a period of a week would likely require "a large team of agents, multiple vehicles, and perhaps aerial assistance."[8] By contrast, wrote Alito, GPS tracking dramatically lowers the costs and burdens of such tracking and allows police to use it far more frequently.[9] In *Riley v. California*, the Court likewise rejected the argument that police search of a smart phone found on a person is "materially indistinguishable" from a search of a "zipper bag" or an "address book." "That is like saying," wrote the Court, that "a ride on horseback is materially indistinguishable from a flight to the moon. Both are ways of getting from point A to point B, but little else justifies lumping them together. Modern cell phones, as a category, implicate privacy concerns far beyond those implicated by the search of a cigarette pack, a wallet, or a purse."[10] And in *Klayman v. Obama*, Judge Leon likewise noted that there are times when a sophisticated phone tracking system like that used by the NSA "become[s] so thoroughly unlike" previous, more primitive incarnations of such technology (such as a pen register) that old Fourth Amendment rules no longer apply.[11]

Moreover, even where the old Fourth Amendment rules *do* apply, emerging technology may nonetheless merit new legislative or administrative rules: Even if the Constitution does not restrict video surveillance with zoom-lens-equipped cameras, for example, other laws or departmental rules perhaps should. It is thus worth taking a closer look at some of the ways emerging technology is transforming modern policing and briefly considering what constitutional or other legal difference such transformations might make. This chapter focuses on changes in the way police are using powerful forms of video surveillance. City dwellers increasingly live under the gaze of powerful cameras, many operated by government, and others operated by private actors. In London, New York, and Chicago, for example, law enforcement has erected vast networks of CCTV cameras to watch over streets, helping police both thwart crime and collect evidence for solving crimes that have already occurred. Cameras can also be mounted on aerial vehicles such as drones, where they might capture images they cannot capture from the ground. And police officers have turned cameras not only on sites they wish to monitor for criminal

8 *United States v. Jones*, 132 S. Ct. 945, 963–64 (2012) (Alito, J., concurring).

9 *Id.*

10 *Riley v. California*, 134 S. Ct. 2473, 2488 (2014).

11 *Klayman v. Obama*, 957 F. Supp. 2d 1, 31 (D.D.C. 2013), vacated and remanded, 800 F.3d 559 (D.C. Cir. 2015). Fourth Amendment scholarship has likewise argued that certain technological shifts in how police make a certain kind of observation, even in public settings, might require different Fourth Amendment analysis. *See, e.g.*, David C. Gray & Danielle Keats Citron, *A Technology-Centered Approach to Quantitative Privacy*, 98 Minn. L. Rev. 62, 71–83 (2013) (arguing that technology should be subject to greater Fourth Amendment constraints when it "has the capacity to facilitate broad and indiscriminate surveillance"); Marc Jonathan Blitz, James Grimsley, Stephen E. Henderson, & Joseph Thai, *Regulating Drones under the First and Fourth Amendments*, 57 Wm. & Mary L. Rev. 49, 71 (2015) ("use of technology as a force multiplier can be a difference in kind, not merely in degree"); Stephen E. Henderson, *Nothing New under the Sun? A Technologically Rational Doctrine of Fourth Amendment Search*, 56 Mercer L. Rev. 507, 510 (2005) (observing that Fourth Amendment doctrine "crafted in light of one developing technology, the telephone networks" might have to be reconfigured to "accommodate[] the amazing but intrusive technologies of the twenty-first century"); Blitz, *supra* note 7, 1443–48 (2004) (arguing that emerging technologies of public surveillance may merit different Fourth Amendment analysis when they change the "architecture" of public space in ways prior technologies did not); Christopher Slobogin, *Public Privacy: Camera Surveillance of Public Places and the Right to Anonymity*, 72 Miss. L.J. 213, 296–97, 313–14 (2002) (describing how technological changes, including the rise of CCTV camera systems, can transform focused surveillance into dragnet surveillance).

activity, but also on their own actions: They have mounted "dash cams" on their vehicles and (more recently) donned "body-worn" cameras on their uniforms, both to gather accurate records of the challenges they confront and to deter officers from abusing their power (and to hold them accountable for such abuse when it occurs).

I Investigation-Specific Video Surveillance

The most prominent news coverage and public debate about the use of video surveillance by law enforcement have dealt with large-scale deployment of CCTV or other cameras – networks of cameras that watch over public streets, for example, or plans for requiring body-worn cameras for all of a department's officers. However, law enforcement also uses, and has long used, video surveillance in a more modest way: to gather evidence in a specific investigation.

Consider, for example, the way that police used video surveillance in the drug investigation at issue in *United States v. Jackson*, a criminal case decided by the United States Court of Appeals for the Tenth Circuit.[12] FBI and local police were conducting a drug investigation in Elk City, Oklahoma, and they decided to see whether they could video-record drug transactions outside the two homes they suspected were at the center of a crack cocaine distribution ring. The FBI installed a camera on the top of a telephone pole overlooking each of these homes. Each camera could "zoom in close enough to read a license plate," but "neither had the capacity to record sound, and neither could view the inside of the houses."[13] These FBI-operated cameras were not permanent features of the environment. They were installed temporarily at specific locations that police and the FBI had come to believe were linked to the illegal drug distribution they were investigating.

They were, in other words, technological supplements to a stakeout, where a stakeout is a measure police take to monitor a place secretly looking for evidence of criminal activity, generally by surreptitiously posting one or more officers nearby. As noted in a recent article in *Police: The Law Enforcement Magazine*, stakeouts have long been – and often still are – "low tech" affairs, involving only an officer or officers to watch the target, a "pair of binoculars, a car or van, and a steady supply of bad coffee."[14] However, they are increasingly supplemented with cameras or other types of recording devices because technology can "make the process easier" by, for example, capturing evidence even when an officer is not on-site or is not focused on it.[15] Cameras can also make a stakeout "more likely to yield good results," because video evidence is often more informative – and harder for a defendant to refute in court – than a verbal recollection of what an officer saw.[16] Indeed, in investigations like that in *Jackson*, video surveillance not only supplements the observations of an officer or officers stationed near the site – it replaces those observations. It is only the installed camera that remains on site, while the

12 213 F.3d 1269 (10th Cir. 2000).

13 *Id.* at 1276.

14 Tim Dees, *Surveillance Technology: An End to Stakeouts?* POLICE: THE LAW ENFORCEMENT MAG. (2010), http://www.policemag.com/channel/technology/articles/2010/12/surveillance-technology-an-end-to-stakeouts.aspx.

15 *Id.*

16 *Id.*

officers who use it to observe or record suspected criminal activity do so from a remote location or retrieve and review the camera's footage at a later time.

A *Court Rulings*

The cases that have so far shaped United States law on video surveillance virtually all involve use of cameras in police stakeouts – or as replacements for them. This is true of the Fourth Amendment precedents on video surveillance in the 1980s and 1990s: They almost all deal with cases when police set up a camera or cameras in order to capture evidence for a specific investigation.

In 1984, for example, the Seventh Circuit decided a case in which the FBI surreptitiously installed television cameras in a Chicago apartment it suspected was being used as a safe house by a Puerto Rican separatist group.[17] It then observed residents of the apartment assembling bombs and videotaped them as they did so. The Seventh Circuit found that even in a private residence such video surveillance could count as a permissible police search under the Fourth Amendment, and did in this instance given that "the benefits to the public safety" from thwarting such bomb making were "great," and "the costs to personal privacy" were "modest" given that the safe house was not a place for the privacies of life, but rather was "dedicated exclusively to illicit business."[18] Still, Judge Posner wrote in this case, given the immense threat that television surveillance posed to privacy, it could be permissible in a house or other private environment only where police could first obtain a warrant, and they could do so only after making a showing akin to that which Congress demanded for law enforcement wiretaps under its 1968 Wiretap Act: Namely, to obtain the warrant police must demonstrate (1) that other methods, less intrusive than video surveillance, have failed or are futile; (2) that they can describe for a magistrate the specific nonverbal conduct to be watched or recorded (in this case, the bomb assembly); (3) that they will minimize the time of the recording so it is no longer than is necessary to achieve their objectives; and (4) that they will also take steps to avoid, to the greatest extent possible, video-recording conduct unrelated to the criminal conduct specified in the warrant.[19] Other federal circuits have applied very similar requirements to police decisions to install cameras in homes or other settings where individuals have a reasonable expectation of privacy.[20]

By contrast, where police utilized cameras in an investigation but aimed those cameras at a street, a front yard, or some other area visible to the public, courts have typically held that such video surveillance is *not* a Fourth Amendment search and, thus, is something police are free to do without a warrant and, in fact, without any showing of reasonable suspicion. In other words, the courts have relied in the cases on the same dichotomy between private and public space the Supreme Court established for location tracking in *Knotts* and *Karo*.

17 *United States v. Torres*, 751 F.2d 875, 875–77 (7th Cir. 1984).
18 *Id.* at 883.
19 *Id.* at 883–84.
20 *United States v. Williams*, 124 F.3d 411, 416 (3d Cir. 1997); *United States v. Falls*, 34 F.3d 674, 680 (8th Cir. 1994); *United States v. Koyomejian*, 970 F.2d 536, 542 (9th Cir. 1992), opinion corrected (July 16, 1992); *United States v. Mesa-Rincon*, 911 F.2d 1433, 1438 (10th Cir. 1990), holding modified by *United States v. Castillo-Garcia*, 117 F.3d 1179 (10th Cir. 1997); *United States v. Cuevas-Sanchez*, 821 F.2d 248, 252 (5th Cir. 1987); *United States v. Biasucci*, 786 F.2d 504, 510 (2d Cir. 1986).

For example, in *United States v. Jackson* itself, the Tenth Circuit Court of Appeals found that the FBI did not need to meet any Fourth Amendment threshold to video-record the defendants' front yards: "The use of video equipment and cameras to record activity visible to the naked eye," said the Court, "does not ordinarily violate the Fourth Amendment."[21] Numerous other courts have reached similar conclusions when video cameras were aimed at outside areas. In *State v. Holden*, for example, a Utah court found that police did not require a warrant or need to show reasonable suspicion of any kind when – in response to a tip from Holden's neighbor that Holden may be selling drugs – they obtained the neighbor's consent to install a video camera and record Holden's front yard. Police were "merely record[ing] on tape what was open to public view."[22] In *United States v. Gonzalez*, the Ninth Circuit Court of Appeals held that the Fourth Amendment does not place any hurdles in the way of police conducting a drug investigation who wish to record an individual in a "public mailroom": The Fourth Amendment is not "akin to J. K. Rowling's Invisibility Cloak," allowing individuals "to create at will a shield impenetrable to law enforcement view even in the most public places."[23] Although police need a warrant to install a camera in a house, private office, or other private space, there is "no objectively reasonable expectation of privacy that would preclude video surveillance of activities already visible to the public."[24] In *United States v. Vankesteren*, the Fourth Circuit likewise concluded that the Virginia Department of Game did not engage in a Fourth Amendment search when it used video surveillance to confirm its suspicion that the defendant was trapping and killing protected wildlife on the open fields enclosed in his property: While the "idea of a video camera constantly recording activities on one's property is undoubtedly unsettling to some," said the Court, that does not make it a Fourth Amendment search, let alone an unreasonable one.[25] Anyone, it said, could have walked onto the defendant's property and observed his bird traps, and "that the agents chose to use a more resource-efficient surveillance method does not change [the] Fourth Amendment analysis."[26]

In fact, even after the concurring justices in *Jones* explained why technologically enhanced observation in public, such as with long-term GPS tracking, may sometimes be a Fourth Amendment search, courts have generally continued to classify use of video surveillance in particular investigations as a nonsearch, as long as it is aimed at public places, areas visible from a public vantage point, or other settings where the targeted individual has no reasonable expectation of privacy. In the 2015 case of *United States v. Wells*, for example, the Tenth Circuit reiterated that "video surveillance will not run afoul of the Fourth Amendment if the individual whose actions are being recorded has no reasonable expectation of privacy at the time of the surveillance."[27]

To be sure, one unpublished Sixth Circuit decision did raise doubts about the impact that the *Jones* concurrences may have on video surveillance. In *United States v. Anderson-Bagshaw*, the government sought to collect evidence to use against a disability benefits recipient it suspected was fraudulently misrepresenting her physical abilities.[28] She said

[21] 213 F.3d 269, 280 (10th Cir. 2000).
[22] 964 P.2d 318 (Utah 1998).
[23] 328 F.3d 543, 548 (9th Cir. 2003).
[24] *Id.*
[25] *United States v. Vankesteren*, 553 F.3d 286, 291 (4th Cir. 2009).
[26] *Id.*
[27] 739 F.3d 511, 518 (10th Cir.), cert. denied, 135 S. Ct. 73 (2014).
[28] 509 Fed. Appx. 396, 398 (6th Cir. 2012).

her pain was all-consuming and that she had no ability to tend the alpacas in her backyard "alpaca farm" that she and her husband maintained as part of their business.[29] But a government-installed camera on a pole overlooking the backyard revealed her working there during a twenty-four-day observation period, in which an agent could view the camera images over the Internet and use a pan, tilt, or zoom function to aim the camera or magnify the image.[30]

The Sixth Circuit stressed that the defendant's activities in her backyard were as visible from the street as they were from the camera. But it nonetheless "confess[ed] some misgivings about a rule that would allow the government to conduct long-term video surveillance of a person's backyard without a warrant."[31] "Few people," it noted, "would expect that the government can constantly film their backyard for over three weeks using a secret camera that can pan and zoom and stream a live image to government agents."[32] However, it ultimately decided that since admitting the warrantless video evidence would at most be "harmless error," there was no need to decide whether such evidence was collected in violation of the Fourth Amendment.

But another Sixth Circuit decision soon after, *United States v. Houston*, returned to the more familiar Fourth Amendment rule, under which video surveillance conducted from public places is not a search when it is aimed at what is already visible there. In *Houston*, law enforcement (more specifically, the Bureau of Alcohol, Tobacco, Firearms and Explosives, ATF) once again used a pole-mounted camera with pan, tilt, and zoom functionality to watch – over an Internet connection – a felon it suspected was storing weapons he was not allowed to have.[33] The Sixth Circuit downplayed its prior decision in *Anderson-Bagshaw* as "an unpublished opinion, in which we did not rule on the issue." Rather than treating the ten-week pole camera surveillance as akin to the long-term GPS monitoring that five justices had classified as a Fourth Amendment search in *United States v. Jones*, it instead cited the Supreme Court's language in the *Knotts* case on radio transmitting (that individuals may "augment [] the sensory faculties") and held that when law enforcement chooses to mount a camera on a utility pole instead of stationing "an agent disguised as a construction worker," it is just as free to use this high-tech, "more efficient" method of observation without a warrant.[34]

II CCTV Public Surveillance Systems – Permanent Video Surveillance

A *CCTV Systems in London, New York, Chicago, and Washington, D.C.*

When police use a video camera to record footage for a particular investigation, they necessarily make a choice about which individual or location to record. By contrast, large CCTV camera networks emerging in many cities are not limited in this way: They continuously record all activities in the public space they cover. The massive CCTV network that London raised over itself in the 1990s, and that it has continued to build since that time, provides an example. In the wake of IRA terrorist attacks in London's financial

29 *Id.* at 400.
30 *Id.* at 401.
31 *Id.* at 405.
32 *Id.*
33 813 F.3d 282, 285–86 (6th Cir. 2016).
34 *Id.* at 288–89.

district in 1993 and 1994, the British government installed CCTV cameras overlooking every entrance to the city's center.[35] Each camera in this so-called ring of steel was designed to video-record the license plate number and vehicle of every driver entering the city.[36] These cameras were integrated with private cameras in office buildings and banks.[37] And numerous other CCTV systems have been erected in other shopping districts and neighborhoods. The London subway system – the Tube – has had video monitoring since 1961, and in the 1990s it began installing thousands of more sophisticated cameras with the goal of covering all 250 stations in its system.[38] CCTV cameras also watch over Heathrow Airport, virtually all major sports stadiums, and key tourist attractions such as the British Museum, the London Zoo, the Tower Bridge, and Westminster Abbey.[39] One account in 1999 estimated that "in a single day a citizen of London could be expected to be filmed by over 300 cameras in over thirty separate CCTV systems."[40]

London was not the only British city to cover itself with CCTV cameras in the 1990s. According to Michael McCahill and Clive Norris, it was a coastal town, Bournemouth, that in 1985 became the first town in Great Britain to make "permanent surveillance of public space and all those who ventured into it a reality."[41] Prior to that time, CCTV systems had been used primarily by private retail centers and in malls. In the wake of the 1993 and 1994 London terrorist attacks, however, and under pressure to address a significant crime wave, London and other British cities rapidly expanded installation of public video surveillance systems. In a 2001 *New York Times* article on cameras in Great Britain, Jeffrey Rosen reported that "by 1998, 440 city centers were wired" with surveillance camera systems.[42]

American cities have also increased their use of CCTV camera systems. As in Great Britain, even before the large-scale expansion of public video surveillance, private business had already made significant use of CCTV surveillance to protect against theft, or increase safety on their premises. And there were early experiments in police or other government use of CCTV surveillance. In 1968, Olean, New York, installed video cameras on its main business district in order to deter and capture evidence of crime.[43] In 1973, police likewise installed cameras in Times Square in New York City.[44] The footage from these cameras was often too grainy to be useful. Mt. Vernon, New York, police experimented in 1971 with a prototype of a more powerful, remotely operated camera

35 Michael McCahill & Clive Norris, *Working Paper No. 6, CCTV in London* 6, Urban Eye (2002), http://www.urbaneye.net/results/ue_ wp6.pdf; Jeffrey Rosen, *A Watchful State: A Cautionary Tale for a New Age of Surveillance,* N.Y. Times Mag., Oct. 7, 2001, http://www.nytimes.com/2001/10/07/magazine/07SURVEILLANCE.html?pagewanted=all.

36 McCahill & Norris, *supra* note 35, at 6.

37 *Id.* at 6.

38 *Id.* at 7–8.

39 *Id.*

40 *Id.* at 6 (citing Clive Norris & Gary Armstrong, The Maximum Surveillance Society: The Rise of CCTV 42 (Oxford 1999)).

41 McCahill & Norris, *supra* note 35, at 3.

42 Rosen, *supra* note 35.

43 *See* John Ebert, *Nation's First Video Surveillance Cameras Were Installed in Olean,* Olean Times Herald, Oct. 5, 2008, oleantimesherald.com/news/nation-s-first-surveillance-camera-were-installed-in-olean/article_fa09f59d-4ce3-558d-b713-1aa287a57de.html.

44 *See* Quentin Burrows, *Scowl Because You're on Candid Camera: Privacy and Video Surveillance,* 31 Val. U. L. Rev. 1079, 1103 (1997).

with the capacity to pan, tilt, rotate, and zoom. But this too had significant limitations at the time, because the storage tapes were expensive and had to be reused frequently.[45]

In the 1990s, as camera technology became more powerful and cheaper, police again began installing cameras in public spaces, although not nearly on the same scale as Great Britain at the time. American cities' interest in large-scale CCTV networks intensified after the September 11 attacks on the World Trade Centers. Camera systems were installed in Washington, D.C.; New York; Chicago; and many other major cities. Two of the most extensive and sophisticated CCTV networks are those in New York and Chicago.

New York City had numerous surveillance cameras over public streets even before September 11, 2001. In 1998, the New York Civil Liberties Union (NYCLU) counted 2,397 cameras "visible from the street-level" in Manhattan.[46] And the city had also placed video surveillance cameras in housing projects throughout the city as part of its "Video Interactive Patrol Enhancement Response" (or "VIPER") system.

In 2007, the New York City Police Department (NYPD) announced the Lower Manhattan Security Initiative (or LMSI).[47] The LMSI's goal was to install and link three thousand cameras, all feeding footage over fiber-optic cables to a central command center. The LMSI was soon supplemented by the Mid-Town Security Initiative (or MMSI).[48] In 2011, the camera network generated by these programs was reported to include feeds from more than 1,850 cameras.[49] And in 2012, the New York City Mayor's Office announced that "NYPD has begun to expand camera coverage to the boroughs outside of Manhattan."[50] The camera footage drawn by the system includes not only cameras set up and operated by NYPD, but also cameras maintained by private businesses. And the LMSI and MMSI draw not only video feeds, but also feeds on one hundred license plate readers that capture images and generate records of license plate tag numbers.[51]

Also in 2012, the NYPD partnered with Microsoft to build what it called a "Domain Awareness System," which Mayor Michael Bloomberg's office described as "a sophisticated law enforcement technology solution that aggregates and analyzes existing public safety data streams in real time, providing NYPD investigators and analysts with a

45 Jeremy Brown, *Pan, Tilt, Zoom: Regulating the Use of Public Video Surveillance in Public Places*, 23 Berkeley Tech. L.J. 755, 756–57 (2008).

46 *See* Loren Siegel, Robert A. Perry, & Margaret Hunt Gram, Who's Watching: Video Camera Surveillance in New York City and the Need for Public Oversight 2 (N.Y. Civil Liberties Union 2006) ("A 1998 study conducted by the NYCLU identified 2,397 video surveillance cameras visible from street level in Manhattan").

47 *See* Olivia J. Greer, Note, *No Cause of Action: Video Surveillance in New York City*, 18 Mich. Telecomm. & Tech. L. Rev. 589, 590–91 (2012); Cara Buckley, *New York Plans Surveillance Veil for Downtown Manhattan*, N.Y. Times, Jul. 9. 2007, http://www.nytimes.com/2007/07/09/nyregion/09ring.html?_r=0.

48 Greer, *supra* note 47, at 590–91.

49 *See* Larry Greenemeier, *The Apple of Its Eye: Security and Surveillance Pervades Post-9/11 New York City*, Sci. Am., Sep. 9, 2011, http://www.scientificamerican.com/article/post-911-nyc-video-surveillance/.

50 Press Release, Mayor Bloomberg, Police Commissioner Kelly and Microsoft Unveil New, State-of-the-Art Law Enforcement Technology That Aggregates and Analyzes Existing Public Safety Data in Real Time to Provide a Comprehensive View of Potential Threats and Criminal Activity (Aug. 8, 2012) [hereinafter Press Release, Mayor Bloomberg], http://www.nyc.gov/cgi-bin/misc/pfprinter.cgi?action=print&sitename=OM&p=1467070824000.

51 Laura Mathews, *NYPD and Microsoft Partner on "Domain Awareness System" to Fight Crime and Make a Profit*, Int'l Bus. Times (Aug. 9 2012), http://www.ibtimes.com/nypd-microsoft-partner-domain-awareness-system-fight-crime-make-profit-742575.

comprehensive view of potential threats and criminal activity."[52] The system retrieves, aggregates, and displays on a dashboard information retrieved not only from video cameras and license plate readers, but also from environmental sensors that can, for example, detect possible chemical or radiological threats, and from numerous police databases.[53] The system also analyzes the images it receives and, for example, will call analysts' attention to "suspicious packages and vehicles" and allows them to conduct searches for specific images in the video feeds.[54] New York City announced that, together with Microsoft, it would license the Domain Awareness System technology to other municipalities, and that New York would receive 30 percent of the profits generated from such licensing.[55]

Chicago's video surveillance is even more extensive than that of New York City. In fact, the former Department of Homeland Security secretary Michael Chertoff has described it as the "most extensive and integrated" video surveillance system in the United States.[56] A 2009 *Wall Street Journal* article reported that the police had set up fifteen hundred cameras over streets, and then linked them to a fiber-optic network that also pulls footage from many other government- and privately run cameras.[57] The fiber-optic network, dubbed "Operation Virtual Shield," then, like New York's system, feeds footage to a central command center.[58] Video feeds can also be viewed by police at local precinct offices and on computers in some police vehicles.[59] The 911 operators can also activate, and view footage from, any camera located within 150 feet of the source of a 911 call.[60]

Chicago is continuing to expand the system. In 2013, it was reportedly operating more than twenty thousand surveillance cameras, including police-operated cameras in downtown Chicago and other neighborhoods, and cameras operated by the Chicago Transit Authority and city school system.[61] And a 2011 report on Chicago's camera system by the ACLU of Illinois noted that, in addition to the government-operated cameras, Chicago's public video surveillance included cameras operated by the Chicago Park District and numerous cameras at O'Hare and Midway Airports.[62]

The cameras, which the Chicago Police Department calls "Police Operated Devices" or "PODs,"[63] are technologically sophisticated: Operators can remotely pan

52 *See* Press Release, Mayor Bloomberg, *supra* note 50.
53 *Id.*
54 *Id.*
55 *Id.*
56 Don Babwin, *Cameras Make Chicago Most Closely Watched U.S. City*, Assoc. Press, Apr. 6, 2010.
57 William M. Bulkely, *Chicago's Camera Network Is Everywhere*, Wall Street J., Nov. 17, 2009, http://www.wsj.com/articles/SB10001424052748704538404574539910412824756.
58 *Id.*
59 *Id.*
60 *Id.*
61 *See* Ted Cox, *Number of Chicago Security Cameras 'Frightening', ACLU Says*, dnainfo, May 9, 2013, https://www.dnainfo.com/chicago/20130509/chicago/rahm-boosts-number-of-security-cameras-frightening-number-aclu; *Chicago Police Start Using Facial-Recognition Software to Arrest Suspects*, RT News, Jul. 15, 2013, http://on.rt.com/yta41d (referring to "the city's 24,000 surveillance cameras"); Michael Tobin, *Security Camera Surge in Chicago Sparks Concerns of 'Massive Surveillance System'*, Fox News Politics, May 12, 2014, http://www.foxnews.com/politics/2014/05/12/security-camera-surge-in-chicago-sparks-concerns-massive-surveillance-system.html (stating that "at last count, there were an estimated 24,000 cameras in place").
62 ACLU of Illinois, *Chicago's Video Surveillance Cameras: A Pervasive and Unregulated Threat to Our Privacy*, Feb. 2011 [hereinafter ACLU of Illinois], http://www.aclu-il.org/wp-content/uploads/2012/06/Surveillance-Camera-Report1.pdf Report1.pdf?docID=3261.
63 *See* Jennifer Helsby, *Police Surveillance in Chicago*, https://redshiftzero.github.io/policesurveillance/.

and tilt the cameras and can zoom in on details, allowing operators, for example, to read license plates. One operation center staff member stated that the cameras can "zoom in up to 32 times optically, and up to 184 times digitally."[64] And like the Domain Awareness System created by NYPD and Microsoft, Chicago's system has the capacity to analyze images obtained through the video feed quickly. Chicago partnered with IBM both to deploy fiber-optic and wireless infrastructure for carrying the information gained from the surveillance system, and then to "to add analytics that provide license plate recognition, trending projections and intelligent search capabilities to the existing infrastructure."[65] Its computers have facial recognition software that can compare faces in recorded video footage to records of faces in a database of mug shots from police bookings. In 2014, Chicago police used this face recognition technology to identify the perpetrator of a pair of armed robberies on the Chicago subway system (he was later also identified by witnesses).[66] And in 2016, they used it again to identify and apprehend a bank robber.[67] Like New York's system, it has the power to alert officials to certain types of activities. When Chicago announced the system in 2004, the *New York Times* reported that its "sophisticated new computer programs will immediately alert the police whenever anyone viewed by any of the cameras placed at buildings and other structures considered terrorist targets wanders aimlessly in circles, lingers outside a public building, pulls a car onto the shoulder of a highway, or leaves a package and walks away from it."[68]

Washington, D.C., is another metropolitan area that has installed CCTV cameras to protect against terrorism and other criminal activity. As the nation's capital, and one of the metropolitan areas targeted on September 11, D.C. has as much reason as any city to be vigilant about a possible terrorist attack. But its existing CCTV system is not as extensive as those in New York and Chicago. The Metropolitan Police Department of D.C. (MPD) has built a network of nineteen CCTV cameras downtown, "focus[ed] on public spaces around the National Mall, the US Capitol, the White House, Union Station and other critical installations, as well as major arteries and highways that pass through downtown DC."[69] However, the system is not, the MPD stresses, a "round-the-clock monitoring operation" but is rather activated only during major celebrations or other events, large protests, or "during periods of heightened alert for terrorism."[70] This system was deployed in 2001, shortly after the September 11 attacks. In 2006, after being authorized to do so by the D.C. Council's

64 Erin Moriarty, *Surveillance Cameras and the Right to Privacy*, CBS News, Aug. 13, 2010, http://www.cbsnews.com/news/surveillance-cameras-and-the-right-to-privacy/.

65 *The City of Chicago's OEMC and IBM Launch Advanced Video Surveillance System*, IBM Newsroom, Sep. 27, 2007, https://www-03.ibm.com/press/us/en/pressrelease/22385.wss.

66 Rebecca Borison, *Chicago Police Caught a Robber with Facial Recognition Technology, and He's off to Prison for 22 Years*, Bus. Insider, Jun. 9, 2014, http://www.businessinsider.com/chicago-robber-caught-by-facial-recognition-2014-6.

67 Kelly Bauer, *Facial Recognition Software Used to Bust Rush Street Bank Robber*, Feds Say, dnainfo, Jun. 10, 2016, https://www.dnainfo.com/chicago/20160610/gold-coast/facial-recognition-software-used-bust-rush-street-bank-robber-feds-say.

68 Steven Kinzer, *Chicago Moving to "Smart" Surveillance Cameras*, N.Y. Times (Sep. 21, 2004), at A18, http://www.nytimes.com/2004/09/21/us/chicago-moving-to-smart-surveillance-cameras.html.

69 *See* Metro. Police Dep't, CCTV – Systems Operations and Capabilities, http://mpdc.dc.gov/node/214462.

70 *Id.*

Emergency Crime Prevention and Emergency Amendment Act of 2007, the MPD also added additional networks of CCTV cameras to specific neighborhoods principally in order to deter and investigate criminal activity other than terrorism.[71] It now operates more than 120 such neighborhood cameras and posts the location of each camera on its Web site.[72] The chief of police is responsible for choosing each camera location but is required to take into account recommendations from Advisory Neighborhood Commissions, the crime control needs of public housing areas, and data about how frequently a particular location generates calls for police service.[73] In contrast to the MPD's nineteen downtown cameras, which are only activated on as-needed basis, and then only record footage when the chief of police authorizes such recording, the neighborhood cameras record footage continuously – footage that is then reviewed by police only when necessary to "solve crimes if criminal activity is reported in areas where the cameras are situated."[74] The MPD, however, has requested authority to view these video feeds in real time, arguing that such authority would better help them to respond to criminal activity.[75]

Many other American cities have installed CCTV systems with some of the same capacities as those of New York, Chicago, or Washington, D.C. A 2009 report prepared for the California Research Bureau, for example, stated that "a growing number of local law enforcement departments across California are employing fixed video surveillance ... of public space."[76] Citing data collected by the ACLU, it noted that thirty-seven California cities have "some sort of public video surveillance program in place" and that eighteen of those "have 'significant' surveillance programs for public streets and plazas."[77] It also listed other American cities outside the state (besides New York and Chicago) that have employed public video surveillance systems: Pittsburgh, New Orleans, St. Paul, Madison, Baltimore, and Philadelphia.[78] The Department of Homeland Security has provided grants to many cities to help with installing such CCTV systems[79] and was reported to be "main source of funding" for New York's Domain Awareness System[80] and for the expansion of Chicago's CCTV system in 2011.[81]

71 *See* Metro. Police Dep't, CCTV – NEIGHBORHOOD CAMERAS, http://mpdc.dc.gov/node/214482; Use of Closed Circuit Television (CCTV) to Fight Crime in Neighborhood Cameras, MPDC Fact Sheet, Mar. 2011, http://mpdc.dc.gov/sites/default/files/dc/sites/mpdc/publication/attachments/CCTV_neighborhood_FAQ.pdf.

72 Metro. Police Dep't, CCTV – NEIGHBORHOOD CAMERAS, *supra* note 71.

73 Use of Closed Circuit Television (CCTV) to Fight Crime in Neighborhood Cameras, *supra* note 71.

74 *Id.*

75 *DC Police Want Real Time Monitoring for Hundreds of Surveillance Cams* (RTNEWS, Jul. 9, 2013), http://on.rt.com/168vta.

76 Aundreia Cameron, Elke Kolodinski, Heather May, & Nicholas Williams, *Measuring the Effects of Surveillance on Crime in Los Angeles*, California Research Bureau (May 5, 2008) at 4.

77 *Id.* at 7.

78 *Id.* at 6.

79 Timothy Zick, *Clouds, Cameras and Computers: The First Amendment and Networked Public Places*, 59 FLA. L. REV. 1, 17 (2007) ("As Department of Homeland Security grant money continues to flow to communities across the country, CCTV systems will likely become more and more prevalent, and potentially more intrusive, in public areas").

80 *See* Greenemeier, *supra* note 49.

81 *See Chicago Expands Surveillance Camera Network*, HUFFINGTON POST, Aug. 15, 2011, http://www.huffingtonpost.com/2011/06/15/chicago-expands-surveilla_n_877681.html.

B *Constitutional and Policy Implications*

Are permanent CCTV camera systems subject to the same Fourth Amendment rules that courts have applied to use of video surveillance in, or as a substitute for, police stakeouts? This is not a question that judges appear to have squarely addressed. But one might well argue that some of the same reasons that led Justice Alito to conclude that long-term GPS monitoring was a search when use of an old-fashioned location radio transmitter was not might also lead courts to conclude that permanent (and massive) CCTV monitoring constitutes a search even if targeted video surveillance most often does not. Permanent CCTV systems may lower costs and burdens of ongoing video surveillance to a far greater extent than use of similar video surveillance technology in a specific investigation.

In *Illinois v. Lidster*, Justice Breyer noted that "practical considerations," such as "limited police resources," can constrain proliferation of police highway checkpoints.[82] And, as noted previously, Justice Alito made a similar point in his concurring opinion in *United States v. Jones*, stating that "traditional surveillance" of a person "for any extended period of time" has, for much of the twentieth century, been "difficult and costly" and thus reserved for "usually important investigations" that can justify their expense and effort.[83]

Similar considerations might constrain police use of video surveillance to engage in long-term monitoring of a particular home's front yard. If, as one analysis wrote of police spending in 2001, "about 95 percent of a typical law enforcement agency's budget is dedicated to personnel," and much of what remains is "spent on basic equipment such as cars, radios, and side arms," then use of video cameras or other advanced technology will likely be limited.[84] Police would not own enough cameras to place a camera for days over everyone's backyard, and then monitor what each captures. To be sure, even use of a single camera can dramatically decrease a police department's monitoring costs: When the Sixth Circuit, in *United States v. Houston*, justified the ATF's ten-week-long video surveillance of the suspect's property, it did so in part on the ground that "the ATF theoretically could have staffed an agent disguised as a construction worker to sit atop the pole or perhaps dressed an agent in camouflage to observe the farm from the ground level for ten weeks."[85] But it may be that the ability to use a small Internet–connected camera to record what would otherwise require a dedicated agent is precisely the kind of transformation that Justice Alito worried might free law enforcement to engage in new kinds of round-the-clock observation, even when it has little basis to think its target is involved in criminal activity.

In any event, once a large-scale CCTV camera system covers a city, the costs of targeting a particular individual might become even lower for law enforcement. If, as in London, a CCTV camera system can already capture a city dweller an average of three hundred times a day,[86] then police will not have to make special efforts to create footage of such

82 *Illinois v. Lidster*, 540 U.S. 419, 426 (2004).

83 *United States v. Jones*, 132 S. Ct. 945, 963–64 (2012) (Alito, J., concurring).

84 William Schwabe, *Needs and Prospects for Crime Fighting Technology* (RAND 1999), Executive Summary. This point was also illustrated in episodes of the HBO show *The Wire*, which depicts a Baltimore police officer's frantic, days-long attempt to retrieve a stolen video surveillance camera before his superior finds out the costly camera has disappeared. *See The Wire*, Season 4, Episodes 7–8, 10, 12 (2006).

85 *United States v. Houston*, 813 F.3d 282, 288–89 (6th Cir. 2016).

86 *See* McCahill & Norris, *supra* note 35, at 6 (citing Clive Norris & G. Armstrong, The Maximum Surveillance Society: The Rise of CCTV (Oxford 1999), at 42).

an individual, since an always-on CCTV system will do so routinely.[87] As a consequence, just as GPS technology has transformed what used to be a burdensome task limited by costs and practical barriers into a surveillance measure that can be used freely unless limited by law, so CCTV video surveillance may do the same for pervasive video monitoring of individuals.

Of course, tracking of an individual will still be burdensome unless CCTV systems are supplemented with software that can lower the burden of searching through hours of footage, from thousands of cameras, in order to find specific individuals or vehicles. For example, while, CCTV played a crucial role in identifying the bombers who struck the London subway system in 2005, such identification could take place only after police "scoured thousands of hours of CCTV footage."[88] However, modern computer search methods might address this problem: As one article points out, New York's Domain Awareness System, for example, is designed to locate individuals wearing a certain color of clothing quickly or "spot a vehicle that's just been put on a watch list" or "flag a bag that's been left unattended too long."[89] And where CCTV systems use face recognition, as Chicago's does, they may be able to take advantage of a computer "algorithm that can recognise faces in images from many different angles, which could mean even more powerful search engines for CCTV systems in the future."[90]

C *Statutory and Administrative Restrictions*

Of course, it is not only the Constitution that can constrain emerging and powerful forms of video surveillance. But neither Congress nor states have extensively regulated police use of video surveillance. Silent video surveillance is still not regulated by the electronic surveillance framework Congress created in the Wiretap Act in 1968, amended in the Electronic Communications Privacy Act in 1986. A 2010 push to add video surveillance to this framework did not succeed.[91] So, as the Tenth Circuit pointed out in 2014, "No federal statute applies to video surveillance and recording. Instead, such surveillance is governed by the strictures of the Fourth Amendment."[92] States have also left the kind of surveillance conducted through CCTV generally free of video surveillance–specific

87 This feature of CCTV camera recording thus makes them a part of what Stephen Henderson describes as a "dramatic technosocial change" wherein technology "for the first time" gives authorities the ability "to feasibly record and store most all behavior – both online and off," Stephen E. Henderson, *Fourth Amendment Time Machines (and What They Might Tell Us about Police Body-Cameras)*, 18 U. Pa. J. Const. L. 933, 971 (2016). This requires careful thinking about the legal framework that should govern "investigatory time machines" that allow law enforcement to view (or otherwise obtain detailed records) of events that have been routinely preserved for later possible examination. *Id.* at 953–54.

88 Will Knight, *CCTV Footage Shows London Suicide Bombers*, New Scientist Live (Jul. 13, 2005), https://www.newscientist.com/article/dn7669-cctv-footage-shows-london-suicide-bombers/.

89 Jeff Rossen & Tracy Connor, *NYC Has 'Smart' Camera Network to Thwart Terror Attacks* (Apr. 25, 2013), http://usnews.nbcnews.com/_news/2013/04/25/17916487-nyc-has-smart-camera-network-to-thwart-terror-attacks?lite.

90 Mary-Ann Runson, *Face Recognition Algorithm Breakthrough Can Spot Even Partially Hidden Faces*, Int'l Bus. Times, Feb. 19, 2015, http://www.ibtimes.co.uk/face-recognition-algorithm-breakthrough-can-spot-even-partially-hidden-faces-cctv-1488698.

91 *See* Gabrielle E. Bensur, *Cover Your Webcam: ECPA's Lack of Protection against Software That Could Be Watching You*, 100 Cornell L. Rev. 1191, 1209 (2015).

92 See *United States v. Wells*, 739 F.3d 511, 518 n.16 (2014) (citing *United States v. Larios*, 593 F.3d 82, 90 (1st Cir. 2010) and *United States v. Mesa–Rincon*, 911 F.2d 1433, 1437 (10th Cir. 1990)).

legislation. Those video surveillance limits that do exist tend to protect individuals from video surveillance in certain situations where there is a reasonable expectation of privacy, with an exemption for lawful investigations by police or other law enforcement entities.[93]

State legislatures have been very active in raising safeguards against a newer, less frequently used type of video surveillance: namely, law enforcement video surveillance using unmanned aerial systems, more commonly known as "drones."[94] In past years, the Federal Aviation Administration's (FAA's) stringent rules on use of drones have placed strict limits on when law enforcement can use them.[95] Now that the FAA is loosening these restrictions, police drone use might increase. However, states have not waited to enact legislation placing limits on when drone-mounted cameras may video-record individuals' homes or backyards, or even some activities in public places. These laws do address a significant type of government video surveillance that may be common in the future. But they do not address the more commonly used present-day law enforcement video surveillance I have been discussing in this chapter.

To date, the constraints that have existed in the United States have largely consisted of administrative guidelines adopted by police departments. The Washington, D.C., Metropolitan Police Department posts guidelines on its Web site and notes that in addition to promulgating its own guidelines, it is also bound by rules enacted by the D.C. Council in 2002.[96] As a result, it claims, "the District's CCTV system is the most tightly regulated of its kind in the nation."[97]

Moreover, a number of organizations concerned about the privacy implications of these cameras – including the American Bar Association, the Constitution Project, and the ACLU and its local affiliates – have made recommendations for how these administrative guidelines and rules, or legislative limits, can be improved. Some of these have gone so far as to question whether CCTV systems like those of New York, Chicago, and D.C. are worthwhile at all. The ACLU, for example, has stated that while it has "no objection to cameras at specific, high-profile public places that are potential terrorist targets, such as the U.S. Capitol, the impulse to blanket our public spaces and streets with video surveillance is a bad idea."[98] It has cited sociological evidence questioning whether CCTV systems deter or otherwise reduce crime and notes that they are susceptible to police abuse and cause chilling effects on speech.[99] Other organizations' recommendations have focused more on emphasizing the need for transparency, democratic accountability, and – in some circumstances – judicial oversight of camera operations,

93 *See, e.g.*, Ariz Rev. Stat. § 13–3019 (2001) (making surreptitious photography or video surveillance unlawful in restrooms, bathrooms, bedrooms, and certain other private settings or circumstances, but specifying it does not apply in settings where individuals lack a reasonable expectation of privacy and does not apply to "surveillance by law enforcement during a lawful investigation").

94 *See* Marc Jonathan Blitz, James Grimsley, Stephen E. Henderson, & Joseph Thai, *Regulating Drones under the First and Fourth Amendments*, 57 Wm. & Mary L. Rev. 49, 64, 84 (2015).

95 *See* Unmanned Aerial Systems (UAS) Guidebook in Development, 7 Community Policing Dispatch, Issue 8, August 2014 ("Currently, police agencies wanting to use a UAS must submit a Certificate of Authorization (COA) application to the FAA.").

96 24 Dist. of Columbia Mun. Reg. § 2500, et seq.

97 *See* Metro. Police Dep't, CCTV – Policies and Procedures, http://mpdc.dc.gov/node/214522.

98 *What's Wrong with Public Video Surveillance*, ACLU, https://www.aclu.org/whats-wrong-public-video-surveillance.

99 *Id.*

or some form of administrative oversight that provides effective safeguards against abuses of CCTV systems including unnecessary invasion of privacy.[100]

1 What Can Be Recorded or Viewed

Existing guidelines and regulations tend to focus on a few topics. First, some of them place limits on what locations or activities can be observed or recorded by the police. As noted earlier, D.C.'s rules allow use of its nineteen downtown cameras "only during major events or emergencies" and then only "upon authorization of the Chief of Police or his designee."[101] Its neighborhood crime cameras, by contrast, record routinely.[102]

Both the New York and D.C. camera guidelines limit the police to observing only public locations or activities "where there is no reasonable expectation of privacy."[103] D.C.'s rules also commit the police department to refrain from "target[ing] or track[ing] individuals arbitrarily or based on race, gender, ethnicity, sexual orientation, disability or other classifications protected by law,"[104] and New York's Domain Awareness System privacy guidelines include a similar antidiscrimination provision.[105] Both the D.C. and New York guidelines also limit the extent to which police can target First Amendment activities. D.C.'s guidelines, for example, require police to refrain from "focus[ing] on hand bills, flyers or other materials distributed or carried pursuant to the First Amendment."[106] New York's guidelines bar police from targeting or monitoring individuals on the basis of their "political affiliation or beliefs."[107]

Chicago's publicly released guidelines are less comprehensive, but have similar provisions. The Chicago superintendent of police released a "general order" in February 2012 providing "guiding principles" for all police use of surveillance technology.[108] This was followed a day later by a "special order" dealing with the "Police Observation Device (POD)" program.[109]

100 *See, e.g.*, ABA Standards for Criminal Justice on Electronic Surveillance, Section B: Technological Assisted Physical Surveillance (3d ed. 1999), Standard 2.9.1(f) on "Accountability and Control" (video surveillance must be subject to "a politically accountable law enforcement official or the relevant politically accountable governmental authority"); Guidelines for Public Video Surveillance, The Constitution Project, at 9, 27–28 (discussing importance of accountability, and requiring a warrant for tracking with video surveillance technology).

101 *Id.*

102 Use of Closed Circuit Television (CCTV) to Fight Crime in Neighborhood Cameras, MPDC Fact Sheet (Mar. 2011), http://mpdc.dc.gov/sites/default/files/dc/sites/mpdc/publication/attachments/CCTV_neighborhood_FAQ.pdf.

103 Metro. Police Dep't, CCTV – Policies and Procedures, *supra* note 97; 24 Dist. of Columbia Mun. Reg. § 2501.5.

104 *See* Metro. Police Dep't, CCTV – Policies and Procedures, *supra* note 97; 24 Dist. of Columbia Mun. Reg. § 2501.4.

105 *See Public Security Privacy Guidelines*, III-Policy-C-Operation, http://www.nyc.gov/html/nypd/downloads/pdf/crime_prevention/public_security_privacy_guidelines.pdf.

106 *See* Metro. Police Dep't, CCTV – Policies and Procedures, *supra* note 97; 24 Dist. of Columbia Mun. Reg. § 2501.3.

107 *See Public Security Privacy Guidelines*, *supra* note 105, III-Policy-C-Operation.

108 *See* Chicago Police Dep't, Video Surveillance Technology, General Order G03–05, Feb. 22, 2012 [hereinafter Chicago Police Dep't, Video Surveillance], http://directives.chicagopolice.org/lt2015/data/a7a57bf0-12f50ce3-69712-f50c-e4837157be0c4aa5.html?ownapi=1.

109 *See* Chicago Police Dep't, Police Operation Device Program, Special Order S02-04-01 [hereinafter Chicago Police Dep't, Police Operation Device Program] http://directives.chicagopolice.org/lt2015/data/a7a57b33-129f0be8-b5912-9f0e-c6e29b6b3727a6d2.html?ownapi=1.

Like the New York and D.C. guidelines, the Chicago guiding principles limit police to "only monitor[ing] public areas and public activities where no legally protected reasonable expectation of privacy exists (e.g., street, sidewalk, park)."[110] They also contain an antidiscrimination provision similar to those of the D.C. and New York guidelines.[111] And they insist that police use video surveillance in a way that "conform[s] to all laws applicable to the use of video surveillance technology, including viewing and recording images consistent with the First and Fourth Amendment"[112] and mandate that police department members "will receive training concerning the First Amendment, the Fourth Amendment, [and] consent-to-search issues," together with the training they receive in camera operation.[113]

More generally, all three guidelines limit the use of the cameras to law enforcement purposes. D.C. and New York limit the use of cameras to "legitimate law enforcement objectives." New York's policies also list a set of counterterrorism-related purposes for the Domain Awareness System.[114] Chicago's guiding principles similarly list a set of safety-related objectives that video surveillance can be used to achieve (including "enhance[ing] public safety and security in public areas" and "observ[ing] preschedule public events") and add that "all information and recorded images obtained through the use of video surveillance technology will be used strictly for law enforcement purposes."[115]

2 Access and Storage

D.C. and New York City's guidelines include provisions intended to assure that, once captured, video footage is kept securely, accessed only for good reasons, and deleted when law enforcement no longer requires it. The New York Domain Awareness System policies state that video footage will generally be retained for thirty days, metadata and license plate reader data for five years, and environmental data – for example, about levels of radiation – for an indefinite period.[116] They also specify that all such data not deleted in accordance with the guidelines will be reviewed after they have been held for five years and deleted if they are without continuing "law enforcement and public safety value."[117]

D.C. provisions state that "video recordings [from neighborhood cameras] will be indexed and maintained by the MPDC for a maximum of 10 business days," unless they "contain evidence of criminal activity or an occurrence that may subject the MPDC to civil liability," in which case "the recordings will be maintained until final disposition of the case."[118] They also state that recordings might be retained longer for "training purposes."[119] They also require that, if the MPD will retain recordings longer than ten days, it must specify the "purpose of the retention, the nature of the recording, and length of

110 *Id.* at II. General Guidelines, B-3.
111 *Id.* at II. General Guidelines, B-4.
112 *Id.* at II. General Guidelines, B-2.
113 *Id.* at II. General Guidelines, A.
114 *See Public Security Privacy Guidelines*, *supra* note 105, III-Policy-B-Objectives.
115 Chicago Police Dep't, Video Surveillance, *supra* note 108.
116 *See Public Security Privacy Guidelines*, *supra* note 105, III-Policy-G Safeguarding and Protecting Stored Data.
117 *Id.*
118 24 Dist. of Columbia Mun. Reg. § 2505.5–2505.6.
119 *Id.* § 2505.6.

time for the retention," and, for video to be used for training, provide "a description of the recording's unique suitability for the training purpose."[120] Moreover, it is the responsibility of the chief of police to "provide, in writing, any decision to retain any recording beyond ten (10) calendar days."[121]

With regard to access, the New York guidelines use both administrative and technological safeguards to prevent unauthorized access to, or misuse of, video data. Access is monitored in part by "guards who will keep access logs and locked facilities requiring badges or access cards for entry."[122] The guidelines also state that "digital watermarking or an equivalent technique will be used to create an immutable audit log of where and when data is accessed."[123] As a general matter, the video footage generated by police-operated cameras is available only to police officials and to "authorized invited guests," but representatives of other entities that supply the police with feeds from private cameras may also access information in such private video feeds.[124]

D.C. guidelines include less detail about how the police will handle storage and access. However, they do state that all recording shall be indexed and that the police shall keep a catalog of all recordings kept beyond ten days, including the "purpose of the retention, the nature of the recording, and length of time for the retention."[125] Chicago's principles say far less about retention: Chicago's special order on PODs states that "all images captured by the fixed remote-surveillance PODS will be recorded over after a 72-hour period for non-wireless and after 15 days for wireless cameras," unless there are "retrievals" made within that time frame.[126]

3 What Technological Enhancement Can Be Used (and Other Gaps in Guidelines)

Existing CCTV guidelines differ from those proposed by the Constitution Project and those of some ACLU chapters as to whether and when camera operators can use advanced technologies to enhance images – for example, by using pan and tilt functions, or zooming in on a particular person or car. None of the guidelines prevents use of panning and tilting the camera, or magnifying images of interest. Nor do they require that camera operators receive authorization or have any kind of reasonable suspicion to enhance their view technologically in this way. This puts them at odds with the stance of the ACLU of Illinois, which argues that video surveillance rules in Chicago should "require individualized reasonable suspicion either of criminal activity or of a threat to public safety, before a camera operator uses the [pan-tilt-zoom] function to magnify the image of a particular person, or anything in his possession."[127] The guidelines of New York City, Chicago, and D.C. also all leave out a similar type of requirement proposed by the Constitution Project, namely, that "law enforcement" be required to "obtain a warrant

[120] *Id.* § 2505.8.
[121] *Id.* § 2505.7.
[122] *See Public Security Privacy Guidelines*, *supra* note 105, III-Policy-G Safeguarding and Protecting Stored Data.
[123] *Id.*
[124] *Id.*
[125] 24 Dist. of Columbia Mun. Reg.§ 2505.8.
[126] Chicago Police Dep't, Police Operation Device Program, *supra* note 109.
[127] ACLU of Illinois, *supra* note 62, at 4.

prior to using a public video surveillance system to track or identify an individual."[128] The D.C. rules do state that their downtown cameras, for monitoring events, are "used primarily to monitor wide areas of public space, not the individuals within that space."[129]

Both the ACLU of Illinois and the Constitution Project also recommend that police be required either to have reasonable suspicion or to obtain a warrant before using facial recognition technology to identify individuals. The D.C. and New York policies make clear that their systems do not use such facial recognition technology.[130] But Chicago's camera system, as noted earlier, has been supplemented with facial recognition analysis, and Chicago's guiding principles place no limits on use of such facial recognition technology (except those that apply to video surveillance more generally, such as rules that bar discrimination based on race or other prohibited categories).

More generally, the guidelines fall short of what the advisory proposals recommend in a number of ways and some critics have argued that they provide far too little in the way of protection. Olivia Greer points out that New York City's Domain Awareness System Guidelines specifically state that "nothing in these Guidelines is intended to create any private rights, privileges, benefits or causes of action in law or equity," and the guidelines "are not legally enforceable" against the police.[131] She also notes that NYPD "has attempted to avoid making background information about that policy available to the public at large," undermining the transparency of the system.[132] Adam Schwartz likewise argues that there has been little transparency concerning the capabilities and uses of Chicago's CCTV system.[133] More generally, neither New York nor Chicago goes as far as D.C.'s rules and procedures do in identifying the location of each neighborhood camera and mandating that the department consult neighborhood authorities about placement.[134] Nor do New York or Chicago's rules have the legal force of D.C.'s, which are embodied in official city regulations.[135]

III Body-Worn Cameras (and Dash Cameras)

The same qualities that lead police to embrace video surveillance systems to detect and deter crime have led citizens and many police officials to call for its use to detect and deter police misconduct. In fact, since 2014, news reports have been filled with stories about police departments adopting "body-worn cameras," which officers are required to wear on their uniforms to record any use of force they engage in and other interactions with citizens that might give rise to allegations of police wrongdoing.[136] Police

128 Guidelines for Public Video Surveillance, The Constitution Project xii, 28.

129 *See* Metro. Police Dep't, CCTV – Systems Operations and Capabilities,), http://mpdc.dc.gov/node/214462.

130 *See id.* ("The CCTV system does not use face-recognition or any other biometric technology.").

131 Olivia Greer, Note, *No Cause of Action: Video Surveillance in New York City*, 18 Mich. Telecomm. & Tech. L. Rev. 589, 599–600 (2012).

132 *Id.*

133 Adam Schwartz, *Chicago's Video Surveillance System: A Pervasive and Poorly Regulated Threat to our Privacy*, 11 Nw. J. Tech. & Intell. Prop. 47 (2013).

134 *See* text accompanying note 73 *supra*.

135 *See* text accompanying note 96 *supra*.

136 *See, e.g.*, Drew Harwell, *The Body-Worn Camera Industry Is 'Feeling Phenomenal' after Ferguson*, Wash. Post, Dec. 3, 2014, http://www.washingtonpost.com/blogs/wonkblog/wp/2014/12/03/the-body-worncamera-industry-is-feeling-phenomenal-after-ferguson/; Cory Siemazko, *Body Cameras Win*

department after police department has adopted a body-worn camera program. Indeed, a recent survey reported that 95 percent of large police departments now either have such a program in place or plan to adopt one.[137]

The most important impetus for this movement was a series of high-profile incidents in which African Americans died in encounters with police: the killing of Eric Garner, in Staten Island, New York, in July 2014; of Michael Brown in Ferguson, Missouri, in August 2014; of Laquan McDonald in Chicago, Illinois, in October 2014; of Walter Scott, in North Charleston, South Carolina, in April 2015; and of Freddie Gray in Baltimore, Maryland, in April 2015. In the wake of these incidents, many citizens and political figures called for major steps in police reform, with one common element of such reform being the mandatory adoption of body-worn cameras. Indeed, President Obama lent his own support to such initiatives, proposing a "Body Worn Camera Partnership" program that would direct $75 million to increasing use of such cameras by local police departments.[138]

The technology was already in use by many police departments and under study by many police organizations: Oakland, California, had begun requiring use of body-worn cameras in 2010.[139] Police departments in Rialto, California, and Mesa, Arizona, conducted pilot programs in 2012 to test the effectiveness of body-worn cameras in what have become two of the most influential and significant studies of this kind.[140] The Phoenix, Arizona, Police Department likewise studied body-worn cameras' impact in 2013.[141] And New York City had already begun preparing to enact a body-worn camera program after being ordered to do so by Judge Schira Scheindlin in a decision finding New York's stop-and-frisk practices to be illegal.[142] This program was expanded in 2016 from a small pilot program to one that includes one thousand cameras.[143]

Converts among Police Officers on the Beat, NBC News, May 8, 2016, http://www.nbcnews.com/news/crime-courts/body-cameras-win-converts-among-police-officers-beat-n566311.

137 *See* Mike Miciag, *Survey: Almost All Police Departments Plan to Use Body Cameras*, Governing The States and Localities, Jan. 26, 2016, http://www.governing.com/topics/public-justice-safety/gov-police-body-camera-survey.html.

138 *See* Andrea Peterson, *President Obama Wants to Spend $75 Million to Buy Police Bodycams*, Wash. Post, Dec. 1, 2014, http://www.washingtonpost.com/blogs/the-switch/wp/2014/12/01/president-obama-wants-to-spend- 75-million-to-buy-police-bodycams/.

139 Matier & Ross, *Police Body Cameras Don't Catch People at Their Finest Hour*, San Fran. Chron., May 3, 2015, http://www.sfchronicle.com/bayarea/article/Police-body-cameras-don-t-catch-folks-at-their-6239647.php.

140 Police Foundation, *Self-Awareness to Being Watched and Socially Desirable Behavior: A Field Experiment on the Effect of Body-Worn Cameras on Police Use of Force* (2013) (describing the results of a large-field experiment in Rialto, California), available at https://www.policefoundation.org/publication/self-awareness-to-being-watched-and-socially-desirable-behavior-a-field-experiment-on-the-effect-of-body-worn-cameras-on-police-use-of-force/; Lee Rankin, *End of Program Evaluation and Recommendations: On-Officer Body Camera System* (Mesa Police Dep't, 2013) (describing results of Mesa, Arizona, on-body camera study); *see also* Implementing a Body-Worn Camera Program: Recommendations and Lessons Learned, Police Exec. Research Forum (2014) [hereinafter Implementing a Body-Worn Camera Program], http://ric-zai-inc.com/Publications/cops-p296-pub.pdf

141 *See* Charles Katz, et. al., *Evaluating the Impact of Officer-Worn Body Cameras in the Phoenix Police Department*, ASU Ctr. for Violence Prevention & Community Safety (2014), https://publicservice.asu.edu/sites/default/files/ppd_spi_feb_20_2015_final.pdf.

142 *See* Pervaiz Shallwani, *NYPD Prepares to Expand Body Camera Use*, Wall Street J. (Mar. 2, 2016), http://www.wsj.com/articles/nypd-wrapping-up-body-camera-pilot-program-1456916402.

143 *Id.*

Many police and civil liberties organizations were already discussing the benefits, and the concerns, generated by body-worn cameras: The Police Executive Research Forum (PERF) convened a major conference on the subject in 2013 and gathered data that became the basis of a substantial 2014 report reviewing body-worn cameras' use by police and proposing recommended guidelines.[144] The ACLU had likewise published an analysis of body-worn cameras in 2013[145] (issuing a revised version in 2015),[146] which called for greater adoption of such cameras and proposed guidelines for limiting the threats to privacy and for assuring fair and effective use of such cameras.

Moreover, body-worn cameras are not themselves the first use of cameras to capture evidence of police interactions systematically: In the 1980s and 1990s, police departments began mounting cameras – dashboard cameras, or "dashcams" – on police cars.[147] One important driver for this was police departments' desire to capture evidence better in drunk driving stops.[148] Dashcams were also valuable for documenting narcotics interdictions.[149] And in 1999, in response to allegations of racial profiling by police, the Department of Justice's Office of Community-Oriented Policing launched an "In-Car Camera Initiative Program" to provide funds for greater adoption and use of dashcams.[150] In part because dashcams had been adopted before the current push for widespread adoption of body-worn cameras, they have provided evidence in more high-profile incidents: In 2014, for example, dashcam footage from 2012 led to the exoneration of a New Jersey man, Marcus Jeter, who had been charged with resisting arrest and assaulting a police officer.[151] While an initial dashcam from one of the police cars failed to capture the full event, a second dashcam showed Jeter cooperating with police even as one of the arresting officers accused him of resisting and of trying to take the officer's gun.[152]

A *Body-Worn Camera Technology*

As is true for CCTV systems and other police uses of cameras, advances in technology allow police to capture evidence that would have been difficult or impossible to capture before. First, the miniaturization of powerful cameras allows police to video-record events unfolding in front of them that would once have required heavier equipment. Devices such as Taser's Axon camera or VieVu's PR camera (the two industry leaders) are small enough to be clipped to the middle of an officer's uniform or headgear. For example, the body-worn cameras used by the Rialto, California, Police Department weighed

144 *See* Implementing a Body-Worn Camera Program, *supra* note 140.

145 Jay Stanley, *Police Body-Mounted Cameras: With Right Policies in Place, a Win for All*, ACLU (Oct. 9, 2013), https://www.aclu.org/files/assets/police_body-mounted_cameras.pdf.

146 *Id.* I have valuated these proposals, and added suggestions of my own, in Marc Jonathan Blitz, *Police Body-Worn Cameras: Evidentiary Benefits and Privacy Threats*, Am. Consti. Soc. (2015), https://www.acslaw.org/sites/default/files/Blitz_-_On-Body_Cameras_-_Issue_Brief.pdf.

147 Daniel N. Rosenblatt, Eugene R. Cromartie, & John Firman, *The Impact of Video Evidence on Modern Policing: Research and Best Practices for the IACP Study on In-Car Cameras*, U.S. Dept. of Justice, Office of Community Oriented Policing Services, at 5.

148 *Id.*

149 *Id.*

150 *Id.*

151 *See* Sasha Goldstein, *Police Dash Cam Video Exonerates New Jersey Man, Indicts Cops*, N.Y. Daily News (Feb. 25, 2014, 8:14 PM), http://www.nydailynews.com/news/crime/police-dash-cam-video-exonerates-nj-man-implicates-cops-article-1.1701763.

152 *Id.*

only four ounces.[153] And the Phoenix Police Department set a maximum weight of five ounces and sought to assure that the camera's size and design would allow the officer "to change the placement of the device to several locations, including the ear, shoulder and lapel."[154] Also important is the amount of time a camera can record without a battery replacement: Some of Taser's cameras have a battery run time of twelve hours, Phoenix's Police Department mandated a battery life of at least eight hours, and a set of Department of Homeland Security (DHS) Guidelines on Body-Worn Cameras recommended a battery that could assure three hours of continuous recording.[155] The camera's memory also needs to have a significant storage capacity: The DHS and Phoenix Department guidelines, respectively, mandated three and four hours of storage.[156]

Another essential part of the technological infrastructure for body camera surveillance is the data capacity for police departments to store the footage that their officers record. A department may not know, until days or weeks after footage is recording, whether it will be needed to investigate a citizen complaint or in future litigation. As a consequence, police departments have generally adopted guidelines calling for body-worn camera footage to be routinely stored for a set length of time. Most recommendations – for example, those of PERF and those of the ACLU – generally agree that in order to protect privacy, police generally should not keep video footage longer than necessary to deal with a possible complaint. PERF suggests that departments routinely keep such video for sixty to ninety days.[157] Some departments may keep the video for longer periods: New York's pilot body-worn camera program, for example, retains video for one year, unless it is archived (as it is automatically, for example, it if "captures an arrest").[158] Regardless of the specific storage time a department sets, however, it will need storage capacity to keep the video in a form in which police can access and review video when necessary, and possibly share the video in response to state open records law requests, or when video must be submitted as evidence at trial. Departments will thus need to keep digital video stored in a computer server operated by the police department itself, or on "the cloud," that is, in servers operated by a third party vendor. In either case, PERF stresses in its recommendations, police will have to assure that the storage system has capacities that allow the agency to safeguard the integrity of the video and the privacy of those depicted in it. One such capacity, for example, is a "built-in back up" system. Another is technology that creates a "built-in audit trail," for example, showing "who access[ed] video data, when, and for what purpose."[159]

Another, more controversial aspect of technological design has been how much an officer can control what is recorded. The ACLU has strongly advocated limiting, to the greatest extent possible, officers' discretion to turn off recording: Body-camera programs, it has stressed, "must be designed to ensure that police cannot 'edit on the fly' – i.e.,

153 Tod Newcombe, *For the Record: Understanding the Technology behind Body-Worn Cameras, Digital Communities*, Sep. 8. 2015, http://www.govtech.com/dc/articles/For-the-Record-Understanding-the-Technology-Behind-Body-Worn-Cameras.html.

154 *Id.*

155 *Id.*

156 *Id.*

157 Implementing a Body-Worn Camera Program, *supra* note 140, at 17.

158 Mark G. Peters & Philip K. Eure, Body-Worn Cameras in NYC: An Assessment of NYC's Pilot Program and Recommendations to Promote Accountability (2015).; The Constitution Project, Guidelines for Public Video Surveillance Report – Body Camera Program 34 (2015).

159 Peters & Eure, *supra* note 158, at 16/The Constitution Project, *supra* note 158, at 16.

choose which encounters to record with limitless discretion."[160] Initially calling for almost continuous recording, it has since modified its position so as to permit officers to allow for greater privacy in certain circumstances (for example, when interviewing an informant or witness who desires confidentiality). The ACLU has thus stressed the desirability of "some form of effective automated trigger ... that would allow for minimization of recording while capturing any fraught encounters – based, for example, on detection of raised voices, types of movement, etc." or, in the absence of such technology, "tightly effective means of limiting officers' ability to choose which encounters to record."[161] Some technologies already constrain alteration of recorded data. The PERF report notes that "some body-worn camera systems are sold with technological safeguards that make it impossible for an officer to access the data prior to downloading."[162] Alex Mateescu, Alex Rosenblat, and danah boyd note that "the AXON Body by TASER International forbids users from deleting a video on the camera and marks the video with a security hash, which verifies that the video hasn't been tampered with."[163]

B *Body-Worn Camera Policies and Procedures*

Body-worn camera programs are far newer than the CCTV camera networks that American cities – emulating London – began to build in the first years of the twenty-first century. But many of the issues that police departments confront in generating body-worn camera program rules are similar: What locations or subjects should be recorded, or protected against being recorded? How long should video be stored before it is deleted, and how should it be protected from unauthorized access while it is kept? How should police handle requests from the media and other third parties to see the videos?

One important resource for department guidelines are the model rules by organizations such as the International Association of Chiefs of Police (IACP)[164] and recommendations of PERF,[165] the Constitution Project,[166] the ACLU,[167] and the Leadership Task Force on Civil and Human Rights.[168] Almost all of these groups agree on key questions about how long videos should be retained. IACP's model rules state simply that video should be retained "no longer than useful for purposes of training or for use in an investigation or prosecution." The PERF report is more specific, recommending that departments retain

160 Stanley, *supra* note 145, at 2–3. Henderson, *supra* note 87, at 969–70, has likewise argued that "to be most effective, that video must record all police–citizen interaction – lest officers only turn it on when it serves their purposes – and be tamper-resistant."

161 Stanley, *supra* note 145, at 4.

162 Implementing a Body-Worn Camera Program, *supra* note 140, at 16.

163 Alexandra Mateescu, et al., *Police-Worn Body-Worn Cameras* 6 (Data & Soc. Research Grp, Working Paper Feb. 2015).

164 *See* Int'l Ass'n of Chiefs of Police, *Body-Worn Cameras Model Policy 1* (2014) [hereinafter Int'l Ass'n of Chiefs of Police], http://www.aele.org/iacp-bwc-mp.pdf.

165 *See generally* Implementing a Body-Worn Camera Program, *supra* note 140, at 17.

166 *See* The Constitution Project, The Use of Body-Worn Cameras by Law Enforcement 5 (2015), http://www.constitutionproject.org/wp-content/uploads/2015/02/TCP-The-Use-of-Police-Body-Worn-Cameras.pdf.

167 *See generally* Stanley, *supra* note 145.

168 *See* The Leadership Conference on Civil and Human Rights, Civil Rights, Privacy, and Media Rights Groups Release Principles for Law Enforcement Body Worn Cameras [hereinafter The Leadership Conference on Civil and Human Rights], May 15, 2015, http://www.civilrights.org/press/2015/body-camera-principles.html.

video for only sixty to ninety days.[169] The Constitution Project likewise recommends that "policies should clearly state the length of time data is to be retained," and – echoing PERF – notes that "most existing policies retain such footage between 60–90 days."[170] The ACLU likewise argues that, unless a confrontation has been captured on a video, it should be kept only weeks, not years.[171] As already noted, New York City's pilot program mandates that video be kept for one year, and the New York Police Department inspector general has recommended extending this period to eighteen months, so that it can "capture the entirety of the [Civilian Complaint Review Board] and NYPD's 18-month statute of limitations on filing administrative charges and specifications and the three-year statute of limitations on filing federal civil rights claims."[172]

1 Access and Storage

Existing recommendations also agree on the need for strong protections against unauthorized access, deletion, or alteration of the videos. In its summary of its model rules, IACP states that "officers should never erase or in any manner alter recordings. The agency must maintain strict managerial control over all devices and recorded content so that it can ensure the integrity of recordings made by officers."[173] Failing to secure recordings in this way "can risk the credibility of the program and threaten its continuation as a source of credible information and evidence."[174] PERF similarly stresses that "policies should include specific measures to prevent data tampering, deleting, and copying" and recommends "using data storage systems with built-in audit trails" and assuring that video footage is transferred quickly (and under careful supervision) from each officer to the department, and "downloaded [to the storage system] by the end of each shift in which the camera was used."[175] The Constitution Project similarly offers recommendations for assuring that "the chain of custody" for camera data is "preserved and recorded" and "method of storage" is kept "safe from data tampering or unauthorized access," and for establishing "effective audit systems in place and clear policies on who may access the data and when."[176]

The inspector general for the New York City Police Department, in reviewing and making recommendations on the local order governing the body-worn camera pilot program, also emphasizes the importance of "establishing parameters in which supervisors and ["Integrity Control Officers within a precinct," designated to review footage for possible problems] are authorized to access [body-worn camera] recordings for review purposes."[177] Such parameters, it notes, can "allay officers' concerns that [body-worn camera] footage reviews may be arbitrarily or maliciously conducted."[178]

169 Implementing a Body-Worn Camera Program, *supra* note 140, at 17.
170 The Constitution Project, *supra* note 166, at 4.
171 Stanley, *supra* note 145, at 6.
172 Peters & Eure, *supra* note 158, at vi, 35–36.
173 Int'l Ass'n of Chiefs of Police, *supra* note 164, at 5.
174 *Id.*
175 Implementing a Body-Worn Camera Program, *supra* note 140.
176 The Constitution Project, *supra* note 166, at 4.
177 Peters & Eure, *supra* note 158, at v, 25.
178 *Id.*

2 Discretion to Record (or Not Record)

With respect to where and what body-cameras may record, model rules and recommendations resemble CCTV rules in either expressly ruling out or at least giving police officers authority to avoid recording of certain private places or activities. The IACP model rules, for example, generally bar recording in "any location where individuals have a reasonable expectation of privacy, such as a restroom or locker room."[179] They do the same with respect to "encounters with undercover officers or confidential informants," personal conversations with other police officers, and "breaks and other personal activities."[180] They also emphasize that officers must have "discretion to discontinue recording in sensitive situations as long as they record the reason for deactivating the recording. For instance, when talking to a sexual assault victim, or on the scene of a particularly violent crime or accident scene."[181] The Constitution Project and PERF offer similar recommendations[182] and, despite its emphasis on the need to limit officer discretion, the ACLU endorses protecting privacy in such circumstances.[183] New York City's rules for its pilot body-worn camera program list many of the same circumstances as unsuitable for recording.[184]

There is one worry, however, that is far more prominent for body cameras than for CCTV cameras, and that is the concern that a police officer may turn the camera off when he wishes to hide the kind of footage that assures accountability for abuse or mistakes. The ACLU, for example, reported that in Albuquerque required cameras had "been used sporadically," with police often turning them off when they did not wish to be recorded.[185] As a consequence, recommended rules often require not only that cameras be turned off in certain situations, but that they be turned on and kept on in others. PERF notes that a common approach among jurisdictions that have adopted body-worn cameras "is to require officers activate their cameras when responding to calls for service and during law-enforcement related encounters and activities, such as traffic stops, arrests, searches, interrogations, and pursuits."[186] The Constitution Project likewise states recording "should begin either (1) during every interaction with the public, or (2) when responding to law enforcement-related calls for service, meaning calls for service, traffic stops, arrests, searches, interrogations, and pursuits."[187] Moreover, it says, when there is doubt about whether an incident should be recorded, "the default should be to record the encounter."[188] As noted, the ACLU largely agrees – favoring a program that would assure accountability and integrity by recording as much police activity as possible – but agreeing that officers probably have to be left with discretion to turn cameras off to protect privacy and should therefore instead be under rules that are as clear as possible

179 Int'l Ass'n of Chiefs of Police, *supra* note 164, at III.D.
180 *Id.*
181 *Id.*
182 Implementing a Body-Worn Camera Program, *supra* note 140, at 11–12; The Constitution Project, *supra* note 166, at 5, 9.
183 Stanley, *supra* note 145, at 3–4.
184 Peters & Eure, *supra* note 158, at 10–11.
185 *See* Jay Stanley, *Police Body-worn cameras: The Lessons of Albuquerque*, ACLU (Mar. 24, 2015), https://www.aclu.org/blog/police-body-cameras-lessons-albuquerque.
186 Implementing a Body-Worn Camera Program, *supra* note 140, at 13.
187 The Constitution Project, *supra* note 166, at 2.
188 *Id.*

about when recording is mandatory. Ultimately, it agrees that the key prompt for activation of recording should be "a call for service or at the initiation of any other law enforcement or investigative encounter between a police officer and a member of the public."[189] The PERF report also notes that "most [police departments using body worn cameras] require officers to articulate in writing their reasons for not activating the camera or to say on camera why they are turning the camera off."[190]

3 Police Access to Body-Worn Camera Videos prior to Making Statements or Drafting Written Reports

In addition to these issues, there are two others that have generated more controversy in the discussion of body-worn cameras than in discussion of CCTV or other programs. One stems from one of the central purposes of body-worn camera footage, which is to evaluate, and hold accountable, the police officer who records such footage when use of force has occurred, or where she has interacted with a citizen in some other way that includes possibility of police misconduct. Long before body-worn cameras were created, police were responsible for documenting these encounters in a police report or statement. And body cameras do not spare them this responsibility: Officers must still write police reports and make statements about such events. As the IACP model rules note, camera "recordings are not a replacement for written reports."[191]

One question that naturally arises, then, is whether an officer providing such an account should have the opportunity first to review footage of the incident. PERF notes that most departments favor allowing police to use the footage as a source of evidence for the report: "The majority of police executives consulted by PERF," it states, "are in favor of allowing officers to review body-worn camera footage prior to making a statement about an incident in which they were involved. They believe that this approach provides the best evidence of what actually took place."[192] And PERF notes that it agrees with this position. IACP notes that video enhances the accuracy of written reports. But it also takes a more agnostic position when it states that "the question of whether an officer should be allowed to review recordings before writing a report, especially following an officer-involved shooting or accident, is a matter that should be examined closely by administrators."[193] The League of Civil and Human Rights, by contrast, is more worried about this circumstance: it urges police departments to "preserve the independent evidentiary value of officer reports by prohibiting officers from viewing footage before filing their reports."[194] "Footage of an event presents a partial – and sometimes misleading – perspective of how events unfolded," it writes, and "pre-report viewing could cause an officer to conform the report to what the video appears to show, rather than what the officer actually saw."[195] Along similar lines, the New York City Police Department inspector general similarly recommends that, at least where an officer is "a subject or a witness in an internal or external investigation," he or she "should be

189 Stanley, *supra* note 145, at 4.
190 Implementing a Body-Worn Camera Program, *supra* note 140, at 13.
191 Int'l Ass'n of Chiefs of Police, *supra* note 164, at III.C.10.
192 Implementing a Body-Worn Camera Program, *supra* note 140, at 29.
193 Int'l Ass'n of Chiefs of Police, *supra* note 164, at III.C.10.
194 The Leadership Conference on Civil and Human Rights, *supra* note 168.
195 *Id.*

restricted from viewing footage of an incident ... until after the officer has provided an official statement."[196] It likewise recommends that "NYPD should not permit individual members of the public to view footage prior to providing an official statement for an investigation in any circumstance."[197]

4 Public Access to Body-Worn Camera Videos

Another significant controversy concerns when journalists or others should be able to obtain access to video recorded by police. On the one hand, state open records laws often require disclosure of such data – and if the purpose of the video is to hold police accountable for wrongdoing, there are circumstances when that may not happen without media access. The video showing how Laquan McDonald was killed in a police shooting, for example, did not lead police or Chicago authorities to reject the officer's claim that the shooting was in self-defense until journalists succeeded in obtaining the footage.[198] The League of Civil and Human Rights insists that "footage that captures police use of force should be made available to the public and press upon request." On the other hand, the release of some body-worn camera footage may threaten victims' privacy. One discussion of this issue notes that police videos have sometimes ended up on YouTube.[199] As Jay Stanley of the ACLU observes:

> Police body cameras mean that many instances of entirely innocent behavior (on the part of both officers and the public) will be recorded. Perhaps most troubling is that some recordings will be made inside people's homes, whenever police enter – including in instances of consensual entry (e.g., responding to a burglary call, voluntarily participating in an investigation) and such things as domestic violence calls. In the case of dashcams, we have also seen video of particular incidents released for no important public reason, and instead serving only to embarrass individuals. Examples have included DUI stops of celebrities and ordinary individuals whose troubled and/or intoxicated behavior has been widely circulated and now immortalized online. The potential for such merely embarrassing and titillating releases of video is significantly increased by body cams.[200]

Perhaps with such examples in mind, a few states have amended state open records laws so as to allow police to withhold footage from body-worn camera incidents. Of course, if such amendments prevent the public – or worse, the family of a police shooting victim (or the subject of a police encounter herself) – from reviewing a use-of-force incident, then they may undermine the body-worn camera program's role in promoting accountability and trust. To resolve this tension, the Constitution Project proposed a compromise whereby information from a video should be redacted when the public and media do not need to see it, and "unredacted ... recordings" should be released to the public only with "the consent of the subject of the recording."[201]

196 Peters & Eure, *supra* note 158 at vi, 43.
197 *Id.*
198 *See* Wayne Drash, *The Killing of Laquan Mcdonald: The Dashcam Video vs. Police Accounts*, CNN, Dec. 19, 2015, http://www.cnn.com/2015/12/17/us/laquan-mcdonald-video-records-comparison/.
199 The Leadership Conference on Civil and Human Rights, *supra* note 168.
200 Stanley, *supra* note 145, at 5.
201 *See* The Constitution Project, *supra* note 166, at 10.

Conclusion

Constitutional protections are far from the only safeguards against "a too permeating police surveillance." We are also protected against pervasive state surveillance by the physical and social world itself: We are shielded from police surveillance not only by laws, but also by walls that block monitoring by law enforcement or great distances that make such monitoring difficult. Even when we are in public, and easily amenable to observation, the demands and costs of police surveillance often require police to make choices about whom they watch and when.

One of the central legal challenges of the late twentieth and early twenty-first centuries is that emerging surveillance technologies are allowing police to lower the costs of round-the-clock surveillance dramatically and to circumvent the walls, or overcome the distances, that can provide individuals with refuge from it. As Justice Alito noted in *Jones*, Global Positional Satellite (or GPS) technology "make[s] long-term monitoring relatively easy and cheap."[202] Similarly, the technological developments that allow police to install thousands of powerful cameras, remotely control them over the Internet, zoom in on details of interest, and then analyze the camera images with powerful computer analysis, make it far easier for police to subject great stretches of public space to long-term video surveillance.

The answer to this situation is not simply to deny police access to technological tools that improve their anticrime and antiterrorism efforts. As the Seventh Circuit has said in a recent case concerning GPS technology, the Fourth Amendment's proscription against "unreasonable search and seizure" cannot plausibly be read as condemning police to use primitive or outmoded technology: It "cannot sensibly be read to mean that police shall be no more efficient in the twenty-first century than they were in the eighteenth."[203] Nor, as the Sixth Circuit has stated, can the Fourth Amendment sensibly be read to mean that technological developments should "one-sidedly give criminals the upper hand. The law cannot be that modern technological advances are off-limits to law enforcement when criminals may use them freely."[204] Rather than outright bans, where the nature of the world no longer protects us against more powerful forms of police surveillance, legal limits can and should still do so, assuring that police observe us only for good and sufficient reasons. These limits may not take the form of Fourth Amendment or constitutional protection – under current law, they generally do not. But administrative rules and guidelines, such as many implemented by law enforcement departments – and others recommended by police groups, civil liberties organizations, and think tanks – can play an important role in assuring that as law enforcement departments take advantage of novel video surveillance to fight crime and terrorism and protect against abuse of power by the police itself, they do so in a way that respects the privacy and individual rights of citizens, including police officers themselves.

202 *United States v. Jones*, 132 S. Ct. 945, 963–64 (2012) (Alito, J., concurring).
203 *United States v. Garcia*, 474 F.3d 994, 998 (7th Cir. 2007).
204 *United States v. Houston*, 813 F.3d 282, 290 (6th Cir. 2016).

12 The Surveillance Implications of Efforts to Combat Cyber Harassment

Danielle Keats Citron & Liz Clark Rinehart[†]

The Internet can be used for great and lofty ends – to connect with the world, conduct research, forge relationships, engage in public discourse, and create culture. But, like any technology, it can be abused. Sometimes, its misuse wreaks havoc on people's lives. Consider the phenomenon of cyber harassment. Harassers harness networked tools to terrorize, defame, invade privacy, and silence individuals. Victims cannot escape abuse appearing in their email inboxes, text messages, blog comments, Twitter feeds, and searches of their names. Cyber harassment deprives victims of life's crucial opportunities – to obtain and keep employment, to acquire an education without fear of physical harm, and to participate freely in discourse and public life both on- and off-line.

Surveillance law has a key role to play in combating cyber harassment – a role that we explore in this chapter. Using surveillance technology, law enforcement and victims can investigate online abuse and identify cyber harassers. Improved investigation can, in turn, increase the number of successful prosecutions. It can also increase deterrence, because cyber harassers no longer feel shielded by online anonymity. Harnessing the power of surveillance for cyber harassment investigations could help change the experience of networked life for hundreds of thousands of users.

Surveillance of cyber harassers, however, is still surveillance. And any surveillance entails a risk of societal and individual harm from the potential of government overreach. Although combating cyber harassment is an important goal, respecting constitutional and statutory commitments is equally important. Ultimately, we need to strike the appropriate balance between the potential government intrusion of surveillance and the very real harms inflicted on cyber harassment victims. This chapter is an introduction into that challenge.

The chapter begins with a brief explanation of cyber harassment and how the law currently addresses the problem. It explores both legal constraints on surveillance and law enforcement's current use of surveillance to combat cyber harassment. The chapter then examines how investigations of cyber harassment can benefit from techniques used in

[†] Danielle Keats Citron is the Morton and Sophia Macht Professor and Professor of Law at the University of Maryland Francis King Carey School of Law and author of HATE CRIMES IN CYBERSPACE (Harvard University Press 2014). Liz Clark Rinehart is a 2015 graduate of the University of Maryland School of Law and author of *Zoned for Injustice: Moving beyond Zoning and Market-Based Land Preservation to Address Rural Poverty*, 23 GEO. J. ON POVERTY L. & POL'Y 61 (2015), Clapper v. Amnesty International USA: *Allowing the FISA Amendments Act of 2008 to Turn "Incidentally" into "Certainly,"* 73 MD. L. REV. 1018 (2014), and *Fighting Cybercrime after* United States v. Jones, 103 J. CRIM. L. & CRIMINOLOGY 745 (2013) (with David Gray & Danielle Keats Citron).

investigations of other cybercrimes. Finally, it considers potential abuses of surveillance techniques in cyber harassment investigations, and why these pitfalls must be avoided.

I Understanding the Nature of Cyber Harassment

Before exploring how surveillance can combat cyber harassment, it is important to define the offense. Cyber harassment involves a repeated "course of conduct" targeted at a specific person. The conduct is designed to, and does, inflict substantial emotional distress on the person who is the target of the conduct.[1] A subset of cyber harassment is cyber stalking, a "course of conduct" causing a reasonable person to fear for his or her safety. For simplicity's sake, this chapter will use the term "cyber harassment" to refer to both harassment and stalking.

Cyber harassment often involves a perfect storm of abuse. The crucial features of cyber harassment are that the interaction is repeated, is targeted at a specific individual, and often comprises speech that itself enjoys little to no constitutional protection.[2] Cyber harassment is much more than a one-time unpleasant exchange or bothersome email. Some victims experience significant fear of physical harm. Others lose their jobs or have difficulty finding work. They struggle with emotional distress and are driven off-line.

A common component of cyber harassment is threats. Harassers threaten physical violence in emails or texts sent to victims, or in social media posts. Some threaten graphic violence in certain and clear terms. Other threats are subtler, implying that the harasser knows where the victim lives and that others can easily hurt him or her. Harassers also terrorize victims by posting doctored images that show their victims being harmed; they impersonate victims and suggest their interest in sex, leading to additional harassment and, in some cases, sexual assaults.

Cyber harassment also commonly involves defamation. Harassers post reputation-damaging lies about victims. These lies may claim that the victims have stigmatizing illnesses or are unfit to be employed or raise their children. Harassers manipulate search engines to ensure that the falsehoods appear prominently in searches of victims' names.

Many harassers go beyond threats and lies. Harassers routinely invade victims' sexual privacy by posting their nude images without their consent. The phenomenon of nonconsensual posting of nude images has been inaptly called revenge porn. But nothing about the posting involves pornography, and the posting may not necessarily be motivated by revenge. Once posted, these images are difficult, if not impossible, for victims to remove.

In addition to posting private photos, harassers may disclose sensitive personal information such as social security numbers. They may obtain such private information by hacking into victims' accounts. Sometimes, harassers use sensitive data and private photos to extort victims, in addition to causing them significant distress.

1 Danielle Citron, *Defining Cyber Harassment*, FORBES, www.forbes.com/sites/daniellecitron/2014/10/23/defining-online-harassment/#750360ea4360.

2 Cyber harassment typically involves true threats, defamation of private individuals, invasions of sexual privacy involving the nonconsensual posting of nude photos or videos, and intentional infliction of emotional distress of private persons involving purely private matters. *See* Danielle Keats Citron, HATE CRIMES IN CYBERSPACE (2014).

In other cases, harassers use technology to silence victims. For instance, they engage in distributed denial-of-service attacks to shut down victims' Web sites. They file false reports claiming that victims' social media profiles violate platforms' terms of service. These attacks wear down victims until many simply lack the will to continue rebuilding their online presence. So they leave social media and other online services behind. Some victims are forced to change jobs, sell homes, and move cities to escape their tormentors.

For example,[3] a blogger who wrote about body acceptance and personal issues became the target of a vengeful mob for no apparent reason. The harassers created numerous Web sites calling her a "stupid, ugly fat whore" and accused her of having "untreated herpes." They released her personal information, such as her phone number and email address. A fake Twitter account appeared in her name, claiming she fantasized about rape. The harassers created posts accusing her of being unfit for employment. The posts were so prevalent that they occupied the vast majority of first-page results when her name was searched. She was forced to include a note in her resume to explain the results.

II The Victims of Cyber Harassment

Cyber harassment victims have diverse backgrounds, but some people are much more likely to be targeted for cyber harassment than others. The statistics are sadly predictable and demonstrate parallels between victims of cyber harassment and victims of hate crimes, and discrimination more generally. For example, people of color are targeted disproportionately. A recent study found that more than half of all African American and Hispanic Internet users had been harassed.[4] Women are more frequently targeted with the type of sustained and pervasive abuse and threatening behavior that constitute cyber harassment. Indeed, younger women face a far greater risk of cyber gender harassment than their older counterparts. Cyber harassment is so common among young women, in fact, that it has become part of a sad rite of passage confronting victims with the visceral realities of lingering misogyny in a patriarchal society. Not surprisingly, women are disproportionately the targets of nonconsensual disclosure of nude images. When protected characteristics intersect, the risks are greater still. At least one study found that women of color are the most likely to be harassed online,[5] and this data has been reaffirmed by anecdotal accounts.

Gender and sexuality frequently play a critical role in cyber harassment, in identifying both who is at risk for cyber harassment and what types of topics are likely to trigger harassment. Women are targeted for speaking about gender inequity in technology, sexually taboo topics, or, perhaps ironically, cyber harassment. LGBTQ individuals are also targeted, often for speaking out about how they are mistreated and discriminated against for their sexual preferences.

Just as gender, race, and sexuality are predictors of who is harassed, so too do gender, race, and sexuality permeate the harassment. Thus, the harassment typically involves

3 *See generally*, Citron, *supra* note 2, at 1.

4 Pew Research Center, Online Harassment 15 (Oct. 22, 2014), www.pewinternet.org/files/2014/10/PI_OnlineHarassment_72815.pdf.

5 Bradford W. Reyns, Being Pursued Online: Extent and Nature of Cyberstalking Victimization from a Lifestyle/Routine Activities Perspective (May 7, 2010) (unpublished Ph.D. dissertation, University of Cincinnati), http://cech.uc.edu/content/dam/cech/programs/criminaljustice/docs/phd_dissertations/2011-2010/Reyns%20Bradford%20W.pdf.

threats of rape or anal rape in the case of men. The defamation often involves accusations that victims have sexually transmitted diseases or are prostitutes. The privacy invasions often involve the posting of nude images, which for women are especially embarrassing because of gender stereotypes and social attitudes. The very core of individuals' identity and self-worth is demeaned and stigmatized.[6] It punishes them for daring to speak, work, and engage via networked tools that should be, and have rightly been, fiercely defended as crucial to our civil rights and our civil liberties.

III The Harms of Cyber Harassment

The Internet pervades most people's lives. It is a requirement of most employment. Many people make their living via networked platforms, from journalists and business consultants to video entertainers and media critics. It is this centrality that harassers exploit to deprive victims of life's crucial opportunities, and it is this pervasiveness that makes cyber harassment so difficult to avoid.

The harms of cyber harassment can potentially touch every aspect of victims' lives. Cyber harassment victims lose their jobs or have difficulty finding employment because online searches of their names prominently feature the abuse. They feel compelled to change their names because their online reputations have been so thoroughly damaged. They may spend hundreds or thousands of dollars attempting to remove harassing content from the Internet, but these efforts may inevitably prove fruitless. They suffer from depression, posttraumatic stress disorder, and anxiety. They engage in self-injurious behavior. Tragically, some commit suicide. In other cases, the cyber harassment is a precursor to telephone harassment, physical attacks, and even murder.[7]

For example, in 2009, a woman was bound, blindfolded, and raped by a stranger who thought he was responding to the woman's ad on Craigslist. In reality, the woman's ex-boyfriend had posted the ad and provided those who responded with the woman's address.[8] In another incident involving impersonation, a woman's ex-husband posted Craigslist ads in the woman's name. In the ads, he purported to offer sexual encounters with her and her children. More than fifty men appeared at her house, some even attempting to break in. The woman was forced to pull her children out of their school, find new employment, and move to another state.

Although governmental and private surveillance can be avoided with technical strategies to mask identity, cyber harassment – often a form of unwanted private

6 In this sense, cyber harassment of women, people of color, and LGBTQ individuals is different from the type of cyber harassment typically experienced by white, heterosexual males, who are not targeted with attacks on their identity.

7 United States v. Matusiewicz, No. CR 13-83, 2015 WL 9305641, at *1 (D. Del. Dec. 21, 2015) (quoting 18 U.S.C. § 2261(b)(1)). The Matusiewiczes and their son, David, and daughter, Amy Gonzalez, engaged in a pattern of cyber harassment, kidnapping, and surveillance against the son's ex-wife, Christine Belford, who had obtained full custody of their children. "In 2013, David Matusiewicz, Lenore Matusiewicz, and David's father, Thomas Matusiewicz, travelled to Delaware for a family court hearing. At the Delaware New Castle County Courthouse, Thomas Matusiewicz shot and killed Christine Belford and her companion on February 11, 2013 and took his own life." *Id.* The surviving Matusiewiczes and Gonzalez were all found guilty of cyberstalking and sentenced to life in prison. Jessica Masulli Reyes, *Matusiewicz Siblings Sentenced to Life in Prison*, Delaware Online (Feb. 18, 2016), www.delawareonline.com/story/news/crime/2016/02/18/david-matusiewicz-amy-gonzalez-sentencing/80518104/.

8 Citron, *supra* note 2, at 6.

surveillance – is frequently immune to such efforts. Victims cannot realistically hide from their attackers. Nor should they have to take these or more extreme measures in order to avoid harassment. Turning off the computer is not a sustainable solution for victims, and avoiding social media is impossible if victims are to work, socialize, and express themselves online.[9] Even if individuals turn off their computers or go off-line, cyber harassment is still available for employers, friends, and clients to see.

IV Law's Role in Combating Cyber Harassment

Despite the fact that cyber harassment exacts great costs from individuals, groups, and society, many reject efforts to regulate it. The abuse is dismissed as pranks; victims are told to ignore it.[10] This kind of reactionary and defensive response overlooks the fact that online harassment chills victims' ability to engage in life's crucial opportunities, including the ability to speak freely. It minimizes the extent of the harm and falsely assumes that cyberspace is some "other" place that can be avoided. It conspicuously ignores the parallels to similar concerns about digital surveillance. Finally, these misconceptions of cyber harassment discourage victims from reporting, despite the fact that criminal law can and in fact does proscribe much of the abuse.[11]

Until far too recently, the burden of prosecuting cyber harassers fell to the victim. Law enforcement was not trained in what constituted cyber harassment or what laws could be used to prosecute cyber harassment. As a result, victims were told that they had no recourse or that their only recourse was to pursue civil remedies. These obstacles and the limited assistance from law enforcement, coupled with the existing embarrassment and fear from the harassment, discouraged victims from reporting it. As prosecutions and awareness about the harms of cyber harassment increase, this legacy may diminish, but resistance to reporting continues to be an obstacle to combating cyber harassment. It is an obstacle surveillance technology could address by making it easier to collect evidence and strengthen the government's case. More successful prosecutions empower victims to report and deter would-be harassers.

Despite what victims may be told, in reality, many state and federal criminal laws proscribe cyber harassment, and the law continues to develop. There are state laws criminalizing cyber harassment, cyber stalking, threats, video voyeurism, invasions of sexual privacy, identify theft, and extortion.[12] Federal criminal law prohibits cyber stalking, cyber harassment, threats, and extortion. Although the level of effectiveness and dedication varies, law enforcement agencies at the state and federal levels have begun to recognize and respond to the dangers of cyber harassment. In this regard, state attorneys general have played a crucial role in the evolution of cyber harassment prosecutions and policy changes. California Attorney General Kamala Harris has made remarkable

[9] Even online activities that would not presumably be social are often connected to social media. For example, the online music application Spotify will log users into Facebook if the user initially registered with a Facebook account, even if the user had temporarily suspended the Facebook account.

[10] *See* Citron, *supra* note 2, at 79.

[11] Although the potential for civil actions does exist in theory, often sounding in copyright or tort, it is rarely pursued in practice because civil litigation is expensive and time-consuming. And in the end, harassers may have little to no assets, making them virtually liability-proof.

[12] For an updated list, *see United States Laws*, WORKING TO HALT ONLINE ABUSE, http://www.haltabuse.org/resources/laws/ (last visited June 12, 2016).

strides against purveyors of revenge porn, through both legislative proposals and outreach with major Internet corporations. She has prosecuted those who extorted money from revenge porn victims. This led the Federal Trade Commission to bring its own enforcement against a revenge porn site operator.[13] Given this recent momentum, the next step for combating cyber harassment is to analyze continually how best to investigate and deter cyber harassment in response to changing technology and changing harassment behaviors.

V Constitutional and Statutory Protections Limiting Detection and Surveillance of Perpetrators

Some form of governmental surveillance and tracking will be necessary for the investigation and prosecution of harassers. Showing that a defendant engaged in a harassing "course of conduct" requires evidence that harassing posts, emails, and texts occurred over a period of time. Surveillance may also be necessary to identify the person responsible for the abuse. For instance, both the Internet Protocol (IP) addresses connected to the harassment and proof linking the defendant to those IP addresses have to be obtained. Real-time monitoring of a harasser's online behavior or electronic communications may be important for the government to make its case, but, as we shall discuss, such intrusive surveillance requires much more justification and even a warrant.[14] This part explores the constitutional and statutory constraints on the government's ability to conduct such surveillance.

The key constitutional protection from overreaching government surveillance is the Fourth Amendment and its prohibition against unreasonable searches and seizures. The Supreme Court has come to recognize technology's role in threats to Fourth Amendment protections. When Justice Potter Stewart concluded that the government violated the Fourth Amendment by eavesdropping on Charles Katz as he used a pay phone, he emphasized "the vital role that the public telephone has come to play in private communication."[15] The Court held that in a world of changing technology, the critical issue is not whether government agents physically intruded into an individual's physical space, but whether they violated the individual's "reasonable expectation of privacy."

No doubt the Internet, cell phones, and social media interactions have overtaken the telephone's role in personal communications and expression. If the government wants to monitor, investigate, and prosecute cyber harassment, whether or not the communication or conduct enjoys Fourth Amendment protection will affect how the government will accomplish its task.

The Fourth Amendment has been understood to recognize two exceptions crucial to the investigation of cyber harassment: the public observation doctrine and the third-party doctrine. Under the public observation doctrine, information voluntarily exposed to the public

13 Danielle Keats Citron, *The Privacy Policymaking of State Attorneys General*, 92 Notre Dame L. Rev. 747, 775 (2016).

14 *See, e.g.*, *Guidelines for Law Enforcement*, Twitter, https://support.twitter.com/articles/41949 (explaining that Twitter retains IP logs "for a brief period of time"); *Guide for Law Enforcement*, Snapchat, https://www.snapchat.com/static_files/lawenforcement.pdf?version=20150604 (explaining that Snapchat, a photo sharing app, does not keep the content of users' "snaps" for more than thirty days and that most snaps are deleted once they are opened).

15 United States v. Katz, 389 U.S. 347, 352 (1967).

enjoys no Fourth Amendment protection. Therefore, the government can freely search, without a warrant, information shared publicly. If an individual posts on a social network that he is going to rape and beat a particular individual, law enforcement can use the post as evidence without obtaining a warrant, just as if the defendant had posted the same information on a sign in a public square.[16]

The third-party doctrine holds that information revealed to another person or entity is, for Fourth Amendment purposes, no longer private. If a third party with whom the information was shared reveals that information to a government agency or law enforcement, the Fourth Amendment is not implicated; that is the risk the original speaker took when sharing the information. For example, if an individual sends threatening messages to another person and the person turns the messages over to law enforcement, then the original sender cannot claim that his Fourth Amendment rights were violated. The Fourth Amendment only concerns governmental intrusions. Most cyber harassment is voluntarily disclosed to at least one person (the victim) and sent through a third party (the Internet service provider) to yet another third party (a hosted platform). The government could ask any of these actors to reveal the information without any risk that the government would violate the Fourth Amendment rights of the original sender – though there may be statutory restrictions on such sharing. With so many private actors receiving voluntarily disclosed information, cyber harassment is an excellent example of the power of the third-party doctrine.

As mentioned previously, the Fourth Amendment only constrains the activities of government actors and those acting under the orders of the government. This means that the searches of private actors cannot violate the Fourth Amendment, assuming they are acting independently of the government.[17] While other laws, discussed in this chapter, may limit a third party's ability to collect information not voluntarily disclosed, private searches do not implicate the Fourth Amendment, and the findings of those searches can be turned over to the government if the government can replicate the search to verify the evidence. Of course, the mere existence of a private search does not give the government free reign; the government is limited to the extent of the private search.[18] This means that if, for example, a private investigator finds a vaguely titled document and sends it to law enforcement, law enforcement can legally have possession of the document. But because the private search did not involve opening the document, the government cannot rely on the private search doctrine to open the document.[19] This would exceed the scope of the private search. To open the document, the government would most likely need a warrant based on probable cause. Despite these limitations, the private search doctrine can be a powerful tool. Victims of cyber harassment can perform their own surveillance of their harassers. Online activist groups can scour forums for abusive posts. Perhaps most common, significant others who suspect partners of abusive or exploitative behavior can search household computers. Of course, as with private investigations in the physical world, such private searches run the risk of violating the privacy of their

16 This hypothetical puts to the side evidentiary requirements such as authentication.

17 United States v. Jacobsen, 466 U.S. 109, 114–15 (1984).

18 Walter v. United States, 447 U.S. 649, 657 (1980).

19 *See* United States v. Lichtenberger, 786 F.3d 478 (6th Cir. 2015). This example uses the more conservative approach of the Sixth Circuit. Other circuits have adopted a more liberal approach based on whether the officers were "virtually" or "substantially certain" of the contents. *See, e.g.*, Rann v. Atchison, 689 F.3d 832, 837–38 (7th Cir. 2012).

targets, and may even become a form of cyber harassment. Used within proper restraints, however, private searches can be helpful.

The public observation doctrine, the third-party doctrine, and the private search doctrine together make a wealth of information available to law enforcement without implicating the Fourth Amendment. Posts shared on social networks, texts sent to victims, and comments on blogs may enjoy no constitutional protection from government searches. This eases the government's burden because cyber harassment victims may not know the identity of their harassers. Crafting a warrant with the required specificity would be difficult when, as in many cyber harassment cases, the abuse is posted under pseudonyms or anonymously. Law enforcement can gather valuable information about cyber harassment without having to obtain a warrant.

What about the constitutional implications of monitoring a defendant's real-time conversations to obtain evidence about cyber harassment? In *Berger v. New York*,[20] the Court made clear that "the fantastic advances in the field of electronic communication constitute a great danger to the privacy of the individual."[21] The Court held that wiretapping statutes needed to include special privacy protections for governmental monitoring to pass constitutional muster because the indiscriminate nature of electronic surveillance devices was reminiscent of the reviled general warrant.

In the shadow of *Berger*, Congress passed the Wiretap Act in 1968, which was amended and expanded by the Electronic Communications Privacy Act of 1986. The Wiretap Act laid out a regime of protections "to compensate for the uniquely intrusive aspects of electronic surveillance."[22] Law enforcement has to meet stringent warrant requirements to intercept telephone calls over the wires. These warrants are often called "super warrants" because they have stricter requirements than typical probable cause warrants. Law enforcement can obtain wiretap orders only on a showing of special need, a predicate felony offense, and high-level Justice Department or state approval. Wiretap orders have to be narrowly tailored and time limited. Officers have to minimize the interception of innocent conversations. Such minimization is essential to satisfy the Fourth Amendment's particularity requirement; it makes up for the fact that law enforcement has access to all of the target's communications, including those unconnected to the crime under investigation.[23] Internet services such as Skype and Google's video chat Hangouts, both of which transmit voice, as well as email and other text chat services, are covered under the act.

Under current law, law enforcement's ability to obtain electronic communications is a complicated question. The answer depends on where the communications are, whether they are opened, and how old they are. Intercepting an email in transit requires a super warrant under the Wiretap Act.[24] Once emails are received, the law becomes less arduous. Title II of the ECPA, the Stored Communications Act (SCA), requires a warrant to obtain unopened emails that are less than 180 days old and located on a remote server. Once an unopened email is more than 180 days old, the standard under the SCA is less

20 388 U.S. 41 (1967).
21 *Id.* at 62.
22 James X. Dempsey, *Communications Privacy in the Digital Age: Revitalizing the Federal Wiretap Laws to Enhance Privacy*, 8 Alb. L.J. Sci. & Tech. 65, 71 (1997).
23 Danielle Keats Citron, *Spying, Inc.*, 72 Wash. & Lee L. Rev. 1243, 1262–63 (2015).
24 18 U.S.C. § 2516 (2014).

stringent, requiring only a subpoena.[25] Since a 2010 Sixth Circuit court case found that provision unconstitutional,[26] most federal agencies have switched to using warrants, but the provision remains.[27] Opened emails stored on a remote server can potentially be obtained with a subpoena, but major email service providers such as Google, and several jurisdictions, often ask for warrants.[28] Of course, if the emails have been downloaded to a user's computer and are no longer on the email provider's server, law enforcement needs a warrant to retrieve them from that computer.

The ECPA has been criticized for being unnecessarily complex and for failing to provide needed protection in the face of changing technology. California's recently adopted Electronic Communications Privacy Act (CalECPA), S.B. 178, sought to fill in the gaps left by the ECPA, at least for state law enforcement. Under CalECPA, state law enforcement must obtain a warrant for all electronic communications, no matter how long they are stored. CalECPA requires a probable cause warrant for all digital content, location information, metadata, and access to devices such as cell phones. Government entities must obtain a warrant, subject to limited exceptions, before they may compel the disclosure of electronic communication information from service providers or obtain such information directly from electronic devices.[29] In practice, the law simplifies the more complicated elements of the federal ECPA: whether information is stored and for how long, or whether it is communication or device information, no longer dictates whether a warrant is required. Obtaining the information requires at least a probable cause warrant,[30] absent consent. Warrants must be particularized and require that extraneous information not related to the investigation be sealed absent a court order. The law also expanded standing to challenge any action under the law. Targets and service providers can petition for information to be destroyed, a magistrate to be appointed, or the court to rescind the order. Finally, the law requires the government to notify the targets of any surveillance, unless the government obtains a court order to delay notification. Failure to abide by the terms of the law would allow a defendant to suppress the information obtained.

25 18 U.S.C. § 2703(a). State law enforcement is governed by state wiretapping laws.

26 United States v. Warshak, 631 F.3d 266 (6th Cir. 2010).

27 The proposed Email Privacy Act would require a warrant, but it remains to be seen whether federal agencies will succeed in convincing the bill's drafter to include language allowing them easier access to email content in emergencies and in civil cases when agencies do not need to meet the probable cause standard required for a warrant, Mario Trujillo, *Judiciary chairman wants warrant exception in email privacy bill*, The Hill, http://thehill.com/policy/technology/261616-house-chairman-endorses-exceptions-in-email-privacy-bill.

28 *See, e.g.*, Theofel v. Farey-Jones, 359 F.3d 1066, 1071–72 (9th Cir. 2004); *Transparency Report*, GOOGLE, https://www.google.com/transparencyreport/userdatarequests/legalprocess/ ("On its face, ECPA seems to allow a government agency to compel a communications provider to disclose the content of certain types of emails and other content with a subpoena or an ECPA court order (described below). But Google requires an ECPA search warrant for contents of Gmail and other services based on the Fourth Amendment to the U.S. Constitution, which prohibits unreasonable search and seizure."). This issue is far from settled, however, as some courts have found open emails on a server are not "electronic storage" as envisioned by the SCA and so obtaining them does not require a warrant. *See, e.g.*, United States v. Weaver, 636 F. Supp. 2d 769, 769–70 (C.D. Ill. 2009).

29 *Letter in Support of CalECPA* (Sept. 12, 2015), https://www.aclunc.org/sites/default/files/SB178ScholarsSupport.pdf.

30 The law permits obtaining information through a wiretap order as well, which, as in the federal statutory framework, requires a higher standard than a warrant. *See* Cal. Penal Code 629.52 PC.

CalECPA received the support of major Internet intermediaries including Google, Facebook, Twitter, and Microsoft, as well as the support of legal and privacy rights organizations, such as the American Civil Liberties Union of California and the Electronic Frontier Foundation.[31] Of course, the law can only curtail the surveillance of California law enforcement. While other states have passed laws requiring warrants for certain kinds of digital information, CalECPA remains the only law that comprehensively requires warrants for both electronic communication information and device identification information. What this means for investigating cyber harassment is that law enforcement in California will need to perform more of their investigation before obtaining information covered by CalECPA, in order to develop probable cause for a warrant. This higher standard could delay or even stymie prosecution, although as discussed later, there are still many techniques available that CalECPA does not reach. Whether CalECPA will, in practice, strike a proper balance between privacy and investigation is not yet clear.

VI Investigation Using Data Analysis

Up to this point, we have seen how the Fourth Amendment fails to extend to certain electronic information and how laws help fill in the gaps, while still providing a way for law enforcement to investigate cybercrimes. These concepts examined traditional investigations, in which law enforcement, alerted to a potential crime, typically reviewed information on a small scale such as individual emails or Web sites. But what if law enforcement used technologies aggregating data or engaged in long-term surveillance of a suspect, collecting large amounts of information that could then be analyzed? Would that change the analysis? This question is not as hypothetical as it may seem. Already law enforcement has employed such techniques to investigate other crimes. Because of the nature of cyber harassment, having the ability to scan large amounts of data over time could help address the difficulty of identifying harassers and provide general deterrence.

This type of data aggregative investigation stretches the limits of traditional Fourth Amendment doctrine. One proposed way of conceptualizing how the Fourth Amendment could adapt is the mosaic theory. A mosaic theory of the Fourth Amendment, embraced by five concurring justices in *United States v. Jones*, contends that law enforcement's ability, using ever-improving technology, to collect and analyze massive amounts of data about individuals should trigger Fourth Amendment protections.[32] As Laura Donohue explains in her book *The Future of Foreign Intelligence*, a "shadow majority" in *Jones* "indicated unease with the intrusiveness of modern technology, endorsing a mosaic theory of privacy."[33] Five concurring justices suggested that long-term monitoring of a defendant's activities impinges on expectations of privacy. Building upon those concurrences in *Jones*, David Gray and one of us (Citron) argue that surveillance technologies that "facilitate broad and indiscriminate surveillance" of individuals implicate the Fourth Amendment.[34] When exactly Fourth Amendment protections should be triggered has not been resolved by the courts, but adopting a mosaic or quantitative theory of privacy might provide for more protection against government surveillance, including

31 The privacy scholar Susan Freiwald was instrumental to the passage of CalECPA.

32 David Gray & Danielle Keats Citron, *The Right to Qualitative Privacy*, 98 Minn. L. Rev. 62, 72 (2013).

33 Laura Donohue, The Future of Foreign Intelligence 126 (2016).

34 Gray & Citron, *supra* note 32, at 72.

technologies that continuously and indiscriminately collect individuals' online activities. The trade-off would be that investigating cybercrimes such as cyber harassment might be more difficult.

As we will discuss in Section VII, the chief tools law enforcement uses to investigate cyber harassment do not typically require massive or continuous data collection. Much of the evidence of cyber harassment is found in public posts and individual messages, all of which are easily obtained by a single officer or team. Collecting this evidence does not require analytical software or even extensive surveillance because at base, the officer can simply review what the victim has seen. Such investigative techniques would not implicate a quantitative theory of the Fourth Amendment. These theories are still worth discussing, even hypothetically, because in drafting solutions to the problems cyber harassment poses, we must not lose sight of the privacy concerns inherent in all cyber investigations. As cyber harassment is taken more seriously as a threat, it is only natural that law enforcement will look for more effective investigation techniques. Data aggregation and long-term surveillance have been effective in combating child exploitation and fraud.[35] Their potential to combat cyber harassment is virtually untapped. At the same time, serious disagreements exist about the ideal balance between extensive surveillance and privacy. Cyber harassment investigations that employ these technologies would not be immune to these concerns. If, therefore, in an overzealous attempt to combat cyber harassment, law enforcement continuously and indiscriminately tracked everything people (including harassers) did, a quantitative theory of the Fourth Amendment would offer greater protection against such intrusive surveillance than is currently available.

To be clear, the solution to cyber harassment cannot be indiscriminant surveillance, the harms of which are well documented.[36] Individuals living under the threat of surveillance experience anxiety and tend to self-censor. These are familiar feelings to victims of cyber harassment. This is not a coincidence. Indeed, cyber harassers often use surveillance because it has the power to cause such harm and invoke such fear.[37] Cyber harassers can watch the victim's posts on social media. They can use programs to hack into the victims' accounts and steal personal information or photos. They can use tracking technology to record the victims' activity online. The prospect of a government actor such as law enforcement using pervasive surveillance to combat cyber harassment is a scenario in which the cure is akin to the disease. Such a proposal would be met with significant backlash, particularly from those who have not been targeted but would still be subject to the intrusion. It also fails to restore to cyber harassment victims the privacy that has been violated; it merely substitutes a (presumably) benevolent actor for a malevolent one. A reasonable balance must be struck between the compelling need to investigate, deter, and prevent cyber harassment and the need to protect the privacy of all Internet users, including victims of cyber harassment.

[35] *See generally*, David Gray, Danielle Keats Citron & Liz Clark Rinehart, *Fighting Cybercrime after* United States v. Jones, 103 J. of Crim. Law & Criminology 745, 765 (2013).

[36] Gray & Citron, *supra* note 32, at 73; Danielle Keats Citron & David Gray, *Addressing the Harm of Total Surveillance*, 126 Harv. L. Rev. F. 262 (2013), http://harvardlawreview.org/2013/06/addressing-the-harm-of-total-surveillance-a-reply-to-professor-neil-richards/.

[37] Nat'l Inst. of Justice, *Intimate Partner Stalking Tactics*, http://www.nij.gov/topics/crime/intimate-partner-violence/stalking/pages/tactics.aspx#cyber.

VII Implications for Cyber-Harassment Investigations

Throughout Section VI, we have hinted at how cyber harassment investigations, including surveillance, would interact with constitutional and statutory law protecting privacy. In this part, we dive deeper into that interaction by examining in greater detail how law enforcement investigates cyber harassment. When law enforcement initiates an investigation in a cyber harassment matter, it is likely because the victim has complained or because the abuse is implicated in a separate investigation. Cyber harassment investigations do not typically follow the type of dragnet and mass surveillance procedures used in other online crime investigations, such as for child exploitation and terrorism. This need not be the case, and there may be distinct advantages to this approach, as will be discussed later, but it is the current reality.

Even when law enforcement is investigating an individual case of cyber harassment, surveillance is an invaluable tool. Although law enforcement has any number of the resources and laws previously discussed at its disposal, the most common surveillance technique is a variation on the oldest: personal surveillance. An investigating officer will create a social media account and watch the activity of the alleged perpetrator. The officer can also monitor the victim's account. Because this information is publicly shared, there is no need for a warrant or subpoena. The officer can take screen shots of the activity,[38] can log the activity for analysis, and may even interact with the perpetrator. People share remarkably personal information on the Internet, which is often enough to identify them even if they attempt to remain anonymous.

Take, for example, *United States v. Elonis.*[39] Anthony Elonis posted on Facebook under the pseudonym "Tone Dougie." Although he was using a pseudonym, his identity was obvious: he posted pictures of himself. His posts included violent rap lyrics in which he threatened to kill his ex-wife, coworkers, a federal agent, and elementary school children. Some posts included disclaimers that the lyrics were "therapeutic" or an exercise of his constitutional right to freedom of speech. Others made no attempt to mask the threats: in one post Elonis stated, "If I only knew then what I know now.... I would have smothered your ass with a pillow. Dumped your body in the back seat. Dropped you off in Toad Creek and made it look like a rape and murder." In another post, Elonis responded to a post by his wife's sister by suggesting that his son dress up as "Matricide" for Halloween and have his wife's "head on a stick" as part of the costume.[40] Despite the occasional claim of creative license, the subjects of his posts found them frightening, and his employer fired him after the head of security saw one of his posts. Elonis's employer also contacted local law enforcement and the FBI. The FBI agent set up a fake Facebook account and began "monitor[ing] [Elonis's] online activity." An agent event visited Elonis at his home, after which he posted the following lyrics:

38 *See, e.g.*, State v. Bishop, 774 S.E.2d 337, 340 (N.C. Ct. App. 2015) *review allowed, writ allowed, appeal dismissed*, 775 S.E.2d 834 (N.C. 2015) and *appeal dismissed, review allowed*, 775 S.E.2d 843 (N.C. 2015). The Court in *Bishop* explained: "Detective Sykes began an investigation and used undercover Facebook profiles to search for posts and comments in which Dillion was mentioned. Detective Sykes testified '[w]henever [he] found anything that appeared to have been ... cyber-bullying [he] took a screen shot of it.'"

39 135 S. Ct. 2001 (2015).

40 Brief of the United States, Elonis v. United States of America, 2014 WL 4895283 (U.S.), 4 (U.S. 2014).

You know your s***'s ridiculous
when you have the FBI knockin' at yo' door
Little Agent lady stood so close
Took all the strength I had not to turn the b**** ghost
Pull my knife, flick my wrist, and slit her throat
Leave her bleedin' from her jugular in the arms of her
partner
[laughter][41]

Notably, the agent did not need a warrant or any other authority to obtain this information. Elonis provided it freely and openly to the public.[42] The case illustrates the importance of social media to cyber harassment investigations. No permission or court order is required to view publicly available posts. Victims can assist law enforcement by producing screen shots of harassing material, thereby preserving evidence.

Law enforcement is increasingly using social media to identify perpetrators and develop an accurate picture of the participants in online crimes. A recent study of law enforcement's use of social media revealed that almost 80 percent of law enforcement responders planned to use social media more in the coming year.[43] Almost 70 percent felt "social media monitoring is a valuable process in anticipating crimes."[44] It is important to recognize the scope of surveillance that can occur on social media. Law enforcement can target an individual for surveillance on the basis of suspicion of a specific crime, such as the cyber harassment of an individual victim or victims. Law enforcement can also target specific groups, such as a Facebook hate group, for surveillance based on that group's propensity to engage in harassing behavior.

Although surveillance of social media is an increasingly popular way to deter and investigate crimes, "few agencies have adopted formal training, policies or have dedicated staff in place."[45] For social media to be an effective tool against cyber harassment, law enforcement must have the training and resources to use them properly. If officers do not follow proper procedure when using social media, then they are less likely to use the information effectively and more likely to make mistakes that render the evidence inadmissible. Because so much cyber harassment occurs on social media sites, lack of training and proper procedure for social media investigations is likely to undermine cyber harassment prosecutions.

Of course, many, if not most, harassers make some attempt to conceal their identities, including on social media. In these cases, identifying the harassers is a requisite step to

41 *Elonis*, 135 S. Ct. at 2006.

42 The Supreme Court reversed Elonis's conviction under the federal terroristic threats statute, 18 U.S.C. 875(c), on statutory grounds. The trial court did not task the jury to find that the defendant had an intent to threaten or knew that his comments would be understood as threatening because the statute did not require such proof. The Court held that when Congress is silent as to the mens rea requirement, courts should not read into the statute a mens rea requirement of negligence, as the trial court had. *Id.* at 2010–11. Currently, Senator Diane Feinstein is working on a bill that would amend the federal threats statute to require a showing of recklessness as to the nature of the threat. Some of Elonis's posts, however, such as the one suggesting his son use his wife's severed head as a Halloween costume, could easily be prosecuted under the current intent or knowledge standard if the government chose to do so on remand.

43 LexisNexis, Social Media Use in Law Enforcement 2 (2014), http://www.lexisnexis.com/risk/downloads/whitepaper/2014-social-media-use-in-law-enforcement.pdf.

44 *Id.*

45 *Id.*

prosecution. Often the information obtained is a form of metadata – noncontent data such as login times, location, and other data about data, which can be used to determine a poster's real name.[46] Under the SCA, law enforcement can track IP and media access control (MAC) addresses and obtain information about users' identities from Internet service providers (ISPs).[47] Law enforcement officers seeking subscriber information will need to provide only the date and time the IP address was in use.[48] Law enforcement only needs to issue subpoenas to obtain information essential to tracing the identity of harassers.[49] Except in California state prosecutions, law enforcement does not need to obtain a warrant because individuals lack a societally recognized expectation of privacy in information entrusted to third parties such as social media platforms. Information obtained from preliminary orders then can be used to obtain a warrant for areas that enjoy more protection under the Fourth Amendment, such as the home, or to obtain a warrant for real-time communication under the Wiretap Act.

Law enforcement can also track cookies to determine a harasser's identity. Cookies are bits of text that sites use to remember information about users. Cookies are frequently stored on an individual's computer, but some cookies, known as tracking cookies, can report activity back to Web sites, which may store and analyze the information. At their most benign, cookies allow sites to remember a user's login information, and online ad providers use cookies to tailor ads to the user's interests. Although some sites ask users to consent to the use of cookies, most sites do not warn users about cookies in their privacy policies. Similarly, hash values are unique markers used to identify image files. These markers can be used to track images and the computers associated with them by employing search technology that scans areas of the Web and monitors Web traffic. Cookies and other data stored by third parties are useful in tracking browsing history, particularly data stored by third parties, which can be accessed without needing to access the user's computer. This data can be used to create a profile that allows law enforcement to track a user's online activity, like following cookie crumbs.

Consider a hypothetical scenario. On the basis of interviews, law enforcement pinpoints the time that a suspected harasser visited a site. An officer uses a subpoena to obtain a list of IP addresses using the site at that time. Law enforcement then looks for patterns and trends of users to figure out the IP address of the suspected harasser. Once a suspect's IP address is identified, law enforcement accesses the Whois database to identify the ISP, and then subpoena account information from that ISP.

What if harassers use technologies to mask their IP addresses? Or, if they are less technologically advanced, what if a harasser accesses the Internet from a cafe or library to make it difficult to trace their posts? For example, Tor is a service that funnels online data transfer through a series of servers to maintain anonymity.[50] In order to follow the more circuitous rail left by Tor users, law enforcement can locate a relay point, such as

46 Adapted from *Merriam-Webster* definition of "Metadata."

47 18 U.S.C. § 2703 (c)(1) & (2).

48 Comcast Cable, Law Enforcement Handbook 6 (2015), http://www.comcast.com/~/Media/403EEED5AE6F46118DDBC5F8BC436030.ashx.

49 *See, e.g.*, United States v. Allen, No. 13-CR-22, 2014 WL 6810626, at *3 (W.D.N.Y. Dec. 2, 2014) (explaining that investigating officers "conducted witness interviews of the minor females, analyzed information received pursuant to subpoenas issued and ultimately, made a determination that James Allen, a resident of New Baltimore, Michigan was involved in the matter").

50 Tor, *Tor: Overview*, https://www.torproject.org/about/overview.html.en.

a volunteer server host, and, with a warrant, search the relay point computer. Somewhat more troubling to privacy advocates, law enforcement can also upload malware to Tor, which can allow them to track user activity using IP addresses, or confiscate a particular host server and run it themselves, documenting IP addresses that access the server.[51]

For public networks, law enforcement could attempt to identify the MAC address of the computer used by the harasser. MAC addresses are visible on the user's network, so law enforcement would need to locate the network and employ a device to observe the network undetected if the network is private. For public networks, law enforcement would need to join the network without identifying themselves as law enforcement.[52] At one time, MAC addresses were relatively permanent and unique identifiers. In 2014, however, Apple announced that it would implement dynamic, randomized MAC addresses in its mobile devices. This was in response to concerns that government and marketers were tracking individuals using their MAC addresses.[53] Although this development makes it more difficult to investigate and conduct surveillance on a potentially harassing user, Apple's adoption of MAC randomization is legitimizing a concept already in existence in the form of hacks used to spoof or change MAC and IP addresses. MAC randomization also requires that the user turn on certain settings, so, as with hacks, it requires a level of sophistication not all harassers will possess.

As can be deduced, the existence of so many types of data in a cyber harassment investigation means that there is the potential for another type of surveillance, which involves analyzing the data on a large scale and in the aggregate to discover digital footprints such as IP addresses, profiles, and other forms of background data. This type of surveillance is often invoked in child exploitation cases, where law enforcement may spoof known Web sites that deal in illegal activity. As users go to the Web sites to view or trade images, law enforcement can record their IP addresses using network investigative technology (NIT). This happened most recently when the FBI seized control of a "Playpen," a Web site featuring extremely graphic sexual violence against children, that at its peak had more than 200,000 members and 11,000 unique visitors a week.[54] Using one warrant, the FBI obtained permission to install a hacking software on computers that visited the site. The software would report back with the IP address, MAC address, Host Name, and other information that allowed investigators to identify the machine and eventually bring charges if warranted. All told, the software identified 1,300 users.

As one might expect, the Playpen case was extremely troubling to privacy advocates. In fact, many courts have ruled the Playpen searches illegal,[55] although at least one

51 *Justice Department to Judge: Tor Users Have No Expectation of Privacy*, MOTHERBOARD (Feb. 6, 2016), http://motherboard.vice.com/en_uk/read/justice-department-to-judge-tor-users-have-no-expectation-of-privacy-playpen.

52 U.S. Dept. of Justice, INVESTIGATIONS INVOLVING THE INTERNET AND COMPUTER NETWORKS 34 (2007), https://www.ncjrs.gov/pdffiles1/nij/210798.pdf ("Monitoring may reveal the investigator's identity, thus compromising the investigation. Use of an undercover computer and Internet Service Provider (ISP) account or other covert methods should be considered.").

53 Aaron Mamiit, *Apple Implements Random MAC Address on iOS 8. Goodbye, Marketers*, TECH TIMES (June 12, 2014), http://www.techtimes.com/articles/8233/20140612/apple-implements-random-mac-address-on-ios-8-goodbye-marketers.htm.

54 Joseph Cox, *The FBI's 'Unprecedented' Hacking Campaign Targeted over a Thousand Computers*, MOTHERBOARD (Jan. 5, 2016), http://motherboard.vice.com/read/the-fbis-unprecedented-hacking-campaign-targeted-over-a-thousand-computers.

55 *See, e.g.*, United States v. Levin, Crim. No. 15-10271 (D. Mass. April 20, 2016).

court has held that the officers acted in good faith and therefore did not suppress the evidence.[56] As the Playpen case illustrates, at some point, the level of surveillance can go too far – if it is indiscriminate rather than a focused investigation of suspected criminals and if it extends beyond the jurisdiction of the court issuing the warrant.

The Playpen case represents an illustrative extreme. But used appropriately, these types of digital surveillance techniques could be adapted to investigating cyber harassment. This would be particularly useful in cases when the victim, for whatever reason, cannot assist in the investigation or when cyber harassment was a prelude to kidnapping or murder. It is therefore worth exploring how an appropriately constrained investigation would look.

Law enforcement could, theoretically, identify for increased surveillance locations or sites that primarily host cyber harassment or revenge porn. This identification could be from citizen reports, other investigations, or simple searches. Within this narrow universe, law enforcement could use software to screen public posts for specific terms or phrases and log the usage of the terms. It is even possible that the software would be able to adapt and learn from usage patterns.[57] Of course, the screening terms would need to be sufficiently narrow to avoid chilling freedom of expression. Once the publicly available data is collected, it could be analyzed to identify trends or areas where law enforcement should narrow their scope even further. Eventually, the scope could become narrow enough for more traditional, human surveillance techniques.[58] Imagine if a program scanning a Web site found threats posted anonymously. Law enforcement could use the data collected from those sites, analyzed on the basis of usage patterns and location markers, to narrow down the universe of suspects and potentially identify the poster. A similar technique could be used to track harassing, nonconsensually posted images using hash values. Because this data is shared publicly, law enforcement does not need a subpoena or warrant to track it or analyze it.

Consider the mobile app Yik Yak, which allowed users to post anonymously to others within a small geographical radius. On college campuses, Yik Yak was used to post death threats and bomb threats.[59] The app made no attempt to hide users' identities beyond allowing them to post anonymously. In fact, Yik Yak engaged in the type of data collection one should expect from a free social media app – extensive and long lasting.[60] Yik Yak shared the data with third parties and aggregated it for analysis. And, yet, users frequently posted to Yik Yak as if they were untraceable. This type of misplaced confidence resulted in prosecution of several users for making threats.[61]

The Yik Yak prosecution is a prime example of the current state of cyber harassment investigation as well as the potential for more sophisticated methods. If a harasser

56 United States v. Werdene, Crim No. 15-434 (E.D. Pa May 18, 2016).

57 *See* Frank Pasquale, The Black Box Society 20–22 (2015).

58 David Gray et al., *supra* note 35, at 798.

59 Jonathan Mahler, *Who Spewed That Abuse? Anonymous Yik Yak App Isn't Telling*, N.Y. Times (March 8, 2015), http://www.nytimes.com/2015/03/09/technology/popular-yik-yak-app-confers-anonymity-and-delivers-abuse.html?_r=1. Notably, Yik Yak experienced a significant decline in popularity after requiring users to adopt usernames rather than post anonymously. Maya Kosoff, *Anonymous Gossip App Yik Yak is in Trouble*, Vanity Fair (April 7, 2016), http://www.vanityfair.com/news/2016/04/anonymous-gossip-app-yik-yak-is-in-trouble.

60 Yik Yak, *Yik Yak Privacy Policy* (March 7, 2016), https://www.yikyak.com/privacy/.

61 Kate Knibbs, *Asshole Gets Busted Because Yik Yak's Not Really Anonymous*, Gizmodo (Nov. 11, 2015), http://gizmodo.com/asshole-gets-busted-because-yik-yaks-not-really-anonymo-1741931009.

assumes erroneously that activity on a social media app like Yik Yak is anonymous, law enforcement is well equipped to subpoena the company running the app for the harasser's identity. If the harasser takes additional steps to mask his identity, the app collects enough additional information about its users for law enforcement to analyze and identify the harasser. This is the next step of surveillance. Under both scenarios, the app has likely also collected locational information, which makes it easier for law enforcement to identify and ultimately locate the poster.

Conclusion

As we have seen, cyber harassment presents a complicated question of how to protect competing rights online. Attempts to address and curtail the prevalence of cyber harassment through laws and regulation have been met with impassioned pleas to consider the implications for free speech. Law enforcement's tracking of online abusers can raise the same free speech apprehensions, but also the specter of significant government intrusion into individuals' private online lives. These are valid concerns. But they must be balanced against the harms cyber abusers are inflicting upon their victims, because the ability for victims to abandon their Internet lives is not – and should not be – considered an acceptable solution. Victims of cyber harassment have the same right to speak and enjoy their privacy as anyone else. Complete resolution of the tensions between these rights continues to elude policy makers, but progress has been made.

A key to further progress may be to look at how the appropriate balance has been struck in other cyber investigations, such as for child exploitation. Analogizing cyber harassment to other cybercrimes will require acknowledging and accepting that the harms of cyber harassment are real and deserve to tip the scale at least slightly to allow for some level of controlled government intrusion. Where the scale settles will depend on the severity of the harms, but it can no longer depend solely on the limits of technology, which are ever-evolving, or the limits of law enforcement resources and training, which are improving. Government should not indiscriminately watch, record, and track citizens' every on- and off-line activity. But it can and should employ surveillance techniques to investigate cyber harassment cases. There is tremendous potential for narrowly tailored surveillance to make significant and important improvements in combating cyber harassment by increasing the likelihood of successful prosecutions. As it has in the past, the law can and must ensure that a reasonable balance is struck between the harm of cyber harassment and the harm of surveillance.

13 The Case for Surveillance

Lawrence Rosenthal[†]

It is easy to condemn surveillance. Its benefits are often uncertain, yet it necessarily imposes a cost by compromising the privacy of those who become the objects of official scrutiny. The case against surveillance as the enemy of privacy is easy to make, and many have done so.[1] And, given this cost of surveillance, many legal scholars have argued that it should be prohibited unless there is adequate predication to justify the contemplated intrusion on privacy.[2] It is much more difficult to find within legal scholarship a case for surveillance, at least absent what is regarded as sufficient predication. Yet, there is such a case to be made.

One might start the case for surveillance with a thought experiment. Consider a legal regime in which the government was forbidden to acquire information about individuals' activities otherwise concealed from public view until it had surmounted an individualized threshold standard of predication, such as reasonable suspicion or probable cause.[3] The problem should be immediately apparent. If an investigation can begin only after surmounting such a threshold, then unless the authorities somehow blunder onto sufficient evidence of predication, they will be stymied. Especially for the type of crimes that are committed covertly, and are unlikely to be uncovered absent proactive investigation, a universal requirement of predication could cripple law enforcement.

An inquiry into a world without unpredicated surveillance, however, need not be conducted as a thought experiment. In fact, a regime along those lines represented the

† Professor of Law, Chapman University, Dale E. Fowler School of Law. The author is grateful to Sherry Leysen and the staff of Chapman University's Rinker Law Library for highly capable research assistance.

1 *See, e.g.*, Daniel J. Solove, Nothing to Hide: The False Tradeoff between Privacy and Security (2011); Neil M. Richards, *The Dangers of Surveillance*, 126 Harv. L. Rev. 1934 (2013).

2 *See, e.g.*, Christopher Slobogin, Privacy at Risk: The New Government Surveillance and the Fourth Amendment 151–64 (2007); Gerald D. Ashdown, *The Fourth Amendment and the 'Legitimate Expectation of Privacy'*, 34 Vand. L. Rev. 1289, 1313–17 (1981); Sherry F. Colb, *What Is a Search? Two Conceptual Flaws in Fourth Amendment Doctrine and Some Hints of a Remedy*, 55 Stan. L. Rev. 119, 126–59 (2002); Lewis R. Katz, *In Search of a Fourth Amendment for the Twenty-First Century*, 65 Ind. L.J. 549, 565–69 (1990); Arnold H. Loewy, *The Fourth Amendment as a Device for Protecting the Innocent*, 81 Mich. L. Rev. 1229, 1254–56 (1983); Daniel J. Solove, *Fourth Amendment Pragmatism*, 51 B.C. L. Rev. 1511, 1536–38 (2010); Scott E. Sundby, *Everyman's Fourth Amendment: Privacy or Mutual Trust between Citizens and Government?* 94 Colum. L. Rev. 1751, 1757–58 (1994).

3 I will use the term "surveillance" in this fashion; I refer to it as embracing any effort by the government to learn about information about the activities of others without their consent. Surveillance, in other words, occurs when the government functions as "the intruding eye" or "the uninvited ear." *Katz v. United States*, 389 U.S. 347, 352 (1967).

predominant approach to policing for many decades. Part I considers the defects of that regime, and in so doing, makes the case for surveillance. Part II then questions whether all activities that are concealed from public view can appropriately be considered private when, in fact, a great deal of nonpublic activity is thought properly subject to regulation. Part II makes a case for surveillance by considering the so-called binary search, which discloses no more than the presence of contraband or other evidence of wrongdoing. Part III then considers the case for surveillance when it comes to the crimes that are most likely to be committed covertly – white-collar offenses generally committed by the wealthy. A regime that raises the barriers to surveillance, in all likelihood, would make it even more difficult to identify these offenses, and thereby produce a criminal justice system even more heavily skewed toward the punishment of the poor and disadvantaged than our current system.

I Lessons of History: Policing and Public Surveillance from the Founding to Today

Until relatively recently, the duties of public officials did not include endeavoring to identify and apprehend lawbreakers; that was an entirely private affair. In England, until roughly the time of the American Revolution, the only thing resembling a modern police officer was a constable, an official charged with executing warrants but who also had authority to appoint beadles responsible for clearing the streets of beggars and vagrants by day and keeping the community safe at night.[4] This system emerged in the colonies and remained in place in the framing era, with the duties of law enforcement officials largely confined to the execution of warrants, and the remaining law enforcement duties of constables, sheriffs, and their employees consisted of responding to breaches of the peace.[5] Thus, in his framing era treatise, St. George Tucker described the duties of constables as limited to keeping the peace, and the duties of sheriffs as limited to apprehending those who had breached the peace, hearing minor civil cases, and executing process.[6] As one scholar summarized framing era law enforcement:

> The formal agencies of control, the justices of the peace, sheriffs, constables, and watchmen, were all derived from the English, pre-urban past. Their effectiveness in Massachusetts depended upon the same conditions, which made the town meeting workable. Through the eighteenth century[,] the use of legal force was ordinarily a direct response to the demands of private citizens for help. The victim of robbery or assault called a watchman, if available, and afterward applied to a justice for a warrant and a constable to make or aid in the arrest. The business of detection was largely a private matter, with initiative encouraged through a system of rewards and fines paid to

4 *See* Elaine A. Reynolds, Before the Bobbies: The Night Watch and Police Reform in Metropolitan London, 1720–1830, 7–44 (1998).

5 *See, e.g.*, Lawrence M. Friedman, Crime and Punishment in American History 28–29, 68 (1993); Thomas Y. Davies, *The Fictional Character of Law-and-Order Originalism: A Case Study of the Distortion and Evasion of Framing-Era Arrest Doctrine in* Atwater v. Lago Vista, 37 Wake Forest L. Rev. 239, 419–32 (2002).

6 Blackstone's Commentaries: With Notes of Reference to the Constitution and Laws of the Federal Government of the United States and of the Commonwealth of Virginia 343–45, 355–56 (St. George Tucker ed., 1803).

> informers. Neither state nor town made any provision for the identification or pursuit of the unknown offender, except through the coroner's inquest.[7]

Thus, as George Thomas put it, what framing era officers "did not do was investigate crime."[8] Even their authority to make arrests absent judicial authorization was sharply limited. For misdemeanor offenses, a warrantless arrest was considered justifiable only if the offense occurred in the presence of the person making the arrest and the arrestee was in fact guilty, meaning that the acquittal of the arrestee exposed the individual making the arrest to liability for trespass.[9] For felonies, a warrantless arrest was justified only if a felony had in fact been committed and there was "probable cause of suspicion" to believe that the arrestee had committed the offense.[10]

Beyond their limited authority, framing era law enforcement officials had to be wary of undertaking search and seizure because of the threat of tort liability. Framing era officers acting without a warrant faced personal liability in tort if they undertook search and seizure under circumstances later deemed inadequate.[11] Officers executing a valid warrant, in contrast, were immune from liability,[12] although there is evidence that they faced liability for seeking a warrant that did not produce contraband or evidence of a crime.[13]

The framing era regime accordingly kept official surveillance at a minimum. It included no law enforcement officials responsible for undertaking surveillance and gathering evidence of wrongdoing. At most, officials responded to an overt breach of the peace, but made little effort to uncover evidence of wrongdoing, much less prevent crime. An approach to law enforcement that so enfeebled the law enforcement function, however, proved deeply problematic as the nation grew.[14] As Carol Steiker observed, "The colonial institutions of the constabulary and the watch were extremely ineffectual in combatting any serious threats to public security."[15] Thus, in the nineteenth century, large cities began establishing police forces in response to growing urban lawlessness and instability.[16] These newly established police forces, however, were far from perfect.

7 Roger Lane, Policing the City: Boston 1822–1885 6–7 (1967). For a similar description of framing era policing in New York City, *see* James F. Richardson, The New York Police: Colonial Times to 1901 3–22 (1970).

8 George C. Thomas III, *Stumbling toward History: The Framers' Search and Seizure World*, 43 Tex. Tech L. Rev. 199, 201 (2010) (footnote omitted).

9 *See* Davies, *supra* note 5, at 323–24.

10 *See* Thomas Y. Davies, *Recovering the Original Fourth Amendment*, 98 Mich. L. Rev. 547, 621–22, 624–25, 631–33 (1999).

11 *See, e.g.*, Akhil Reed Amar, The Constitution and Criminal Procedure: First Principles, 11–17, 20–21 (1997); William J. Cuddihy, The Fourth Amendment: Origins and Original Meaning, 602–1791 593–96, 760–61 (2009); Davies, *supra* note 10, at 621–22, 624–25, 665–66; Thomas, *supra* note 8, at 225–28.

12 *See, e.g.*, Amar, *supra* note 11, at 12–13, 15–16; Fabio Arcila, Jr., *The Framers' Search Power: The Misunderstood Statutory History of Suspicion and Probable Cause*, 50 B.C. L. Rev. 362, 373–74 (2009); Roger Roots, *The Orginalist Case for the Fourth Amendment Exclusionary Rule*, 45 Gonz. L. Rev. 1, 8 n.39 (2009–10).

13 *See* Thomas Y. Davies, *Can You Handle the Truth? The Framers Preserved Common Law Search and Arrest Rules in Recent, Destructive Myth*, 43 Tex. Tech L. Rev. 51, 91–93 (2010).

14 *See, e.g.*, Friedman, *supra* note 5, at 27–28, 68; Donald A. Dripps, *Responding to the Challenges of Contextual Change and Legal Dynamism in Interpreting the Fourth Amendment*, 81 Miss. L.J. 1085, 1097–1101 (2011).

15 Carol S. Steiker, *Second Thoughts about First Principles*, 107 Harv. L. Rev. 820, 831–32 (1997).

16 *See, e.g.*, Friedman, *supra* note 5, at 68–71; David R. Johnson, Policing the Urban Underworld: The Impact of Crime on the Development of the American Police, 1800–1887, at 12–40 (1979); Thomas

Because the spoils system was a central feature of local politics, most positions on the police forces were awarded on the basis of patronage and other political considerations.[17]

Patronage was not the only attraction that policing had for politicians. As Robert Fogelson has observed, the rapidly rising immigrant populations of the late nineteenth and early twentieth centuries introduced values that were often quite different from those reflected in the frequently puritanical American legal codes. By controlling law enforcement, politicians could exploit the increasing clash of cultures between traditional elites and newer immigrant populations, currying favor with one side or another:

> Those who controlled the police had the opportunity to implement a policy about vice consistent with the prevailing life-style and underlying morality of their constituents. As the moral and cultural conflict between the natives and the ethnics intensified, many politicians found this opportunity a heavy burden, but not one that they dared turn over to anyone else.[18]

This system created ample opportunities for corruption, not only among politicians willing to overlook unlawful activities, but among the police as well. Officers generally walked a beat, and because supervisors lacked radios or other means of establishing a reliable command-and-control system, officers on patrol exercised enormous discretion.[19] In this environment, brutality and corruption flourished.[20] This state of affairs, however, eventually produced a backlash – a powerful reform movement that, in fits and starts, transformed the character of urban policing, creating a new model that came to be regarded as the "conventional" approach.[21]

The reform movement had two central objectives. The first was to remove patronage from policing by creating civil service systems in which police would be hired and promoted using "merit-based" procedures – often administered by commissions insulated from political influence.[22] The second was an emphasis on centralized command and control. Patrol officers were assigned to conduct motorized patrol throughout an assigned beat, responding speedily to orders from dispatchers directing them to the scene of a reported crime or breach of the peace, with detectives and other specialized personnel later assigned to engage in retrospective investigation of offenses when necessary.[23]

A. Repetto, THE BLUE PARADE 2–23 (1978); James F. Richardson, URBAN POLICE IN THE UNITED STATES 6–15, 19–32 (1974); Samuel Walker, POPULAR JUSTICE: A HISTORY OF AMERICAN CRIMINAL JUSTICE 49–51 (1st ed. 1980).

17 *See, e.g.*, Robert M. Fogelson, BIG-CITY POLICE 3–31 (1977); Samuel Walker, A CRITICAL HISTORY OF POLICE REFORM: THE EMERGENCE OF PROFESSIONALISM 8–12 (1977); George L. Kelling & Mark H. Moore, *From Political to Reform in Community: The Evolving Strategy of Police*, *in* COMMUNITY POLICING: RHETORIC OR REALITY, 3, 8–9 (Jack R. Greene & Stephen D. Mastrofski eds., 1988); Albert J. Reiss, Jr., *Police Organization in the Twentieth Century*, *in* MODERN POLICING 51, 67–70 (Michael Tonry & Norval J. Morris eds., 1992) [hereinafter MODERN POLICING].

18 Fogelson, *supra* note 17, at 21. Fogelson added that many of the vice laws enacted in the so-called Progressive Era around the turn of the century can be viewed as an effort by traditional elites to regulate what they regarded as dangerous signs of disorder and cultural conflict among immigrant populations. *See id.* at 20–21.

19 *See, e.g.*, Walker, *supra* note 17, at 13–14; Reiss, *supra* note 17, at 59–61.

20 *See, e.g.*, Fogelson, *supra* note 17, at 22–35, 148–49; Walker, *supra* note 17, at 15–18; Kelling & Moore, *supra* note 17, at 8–9; Reiss, *supra* note 17, at 79–82.

21 *See, e.g.*, Fogelson, *supra* note 17, at 58–60; Walker, *supra* note 17, at 56–68; Reiss, *supra* note 17, at 70–71.

22 *See, e.g.*, Fogelson, *supra* note 17, at 58–60; Walker, *supra* note 17, at 39, 74, 168; Reiss, *supra* note 17, at 57, 70–72.

23 *See, e.g.*, George L. Kelling & Catherine M. Coles, FIXING BROKEN WINDOWS: RESTORING ORDER AND REDUCING CRIME IN OUR COMMUNITIES 13–14 (1996); Walker, *supra* note 17, at 136–37; Kelling &

In this way, the reform movement fought the evils of discretionary justice in a classic way – it sought to bureaucratize policing by creating an effective hierarchy that was able to control a large workforce by routinizing organizational behavior.[24]

In an era in which political machines controlled virtually every aspect of urban governance, the success of the reform movement was remarkable: "In all but a handful of cities, [the reformers] weakened the position of the ward leaders, undermined the influence of the precinct captains, severed the connections between them, and thereby destroyed the territorial basis of decentralization that had heretofore been an integral feature of the American police."[25] Indeed, as George Kelling and Mark Moore observed:

> So persuasive was the argument of reformers to remove political influences from policing that police departments became one of the most autonomous public organizations in urban government. Under such circumstances, policing a city became a legal and technical matter to be left to the discretion of professional police executives, under guidance of law. Political influence of every kind came to be seen as a failure of police leadership and as corruption in policing.[26]

Yet the rise of professionalism in policing was unable to stem a dramatic spike in violent crime occurring in the late 1980s and early 1990s. The violent victimization rate in the mid-1980s was approximately 40 per 1,000 population age twelve or older; it then rose until reaching a peak of 52.2 in 1993, and from there it fell steadily, reaching 25.9 by 2001, a decline of 50.4 percent from its peak and by far the lowest rate since the survey had begun in 1973.[27] After that, the violent victimization rate continued dropping, albeit less steeply, reaching 20.1 in 2014.[28] By 2008, the overall violent victimization rate was 63 percent below its peak.[29] Similarly, the homicide victimization rate rose from 7.9 per 100,000 population in 1984 to a peak of 9.8 in 1991, but had declined to 4.8 by 2010.[30]

These aggregate statistics, however, tell only part of the story. The spike and subsequent decline in violent crime in recent decades were not uniform – they were disproportionately experienced by urban minority youth, and they were largely the product of trends in handgun-related crime.

The crime spike involved urban handgun crime. During this period, homicide rates were essentially flat in cities with populations below 250,000, and the rise and subsequent fall in homicide occurred in cities with populations exceeding 1,000,000.[31] And

Moore, *supra* note 17, at 13–14; Mark Harrison Moore, *Problem-Solving and Community Policing, in* Modern Policing, *supra* note 17, at 99, 108–11; Reiss, *supra* note 17, at 58–61.

24 *See, e.g.*, Herman Goldstein, Problem-Oriented Policing, 6–7(1998); Reiss, *supra* note 17, at 57–58; 70–72.

25 Fogelson, *supra* note 17, at 226.

26 Kelling & Moore, *supra* note 17, at 11 (citation omitted).

27 Callie Rennison, U.S. Dep't of Just., Criminal Victimization 2001: Changes 2000–01 with Trends 1993–2001, at 11–12 (Sept. 2002).

28 Jennifer L. Truman & Lynn Langdon, U.S. Department of Justice, Criminal Victimization 2013, at 1, fig.1 (rev. Sept. 29, 2015).

29 Michael R. Rand, U.S. Dep't of Just., Criminal Victimization 2008, at 2 (Sept. 2009).

30 Alexia Cooper & Erica L. Smith, U.S. Dep't of Just., Homicide Trends in the United States, 1980–2008, at 2 (Nov. 2011).

31 *See James Alan Fox, Jack Levin & Kenna Quinet*, The Will to Kill: Making Sense of Senseless Murder 44–45, fig.3.2 (rev. 2008).

virtually the entire spike in homicide during this period was a consequence of increases in handgun-related killings.[32]

The concentration of the crime spike in cities suggests that urban crime poses special challenges for law enforcement policy and practice. Even in urban areas, however, crime is not randomly distributed. It was Clifford Shaw who first demonstrated that crime is in large part a function of geography. Analyzing Chicago crime data in the first decades of the twentieth century, he showed that crime rates were much higher in certain neighborhoods than others, and that these neighborhood crime rates are remarkably stable over time.[33] In the intervening decades, it has come to be well understood that crime tends to cluster in discrete geographic areas and is relatively stable within those areas.[34]

There are a variety of likely explanations for this phenomenon. Empirical evidence, for example, consistently demonstrates that crime rates, especially for violent crime, are particularly high in areas of concentrated poverty.[35] Moreover, it has become a fairly widespread view among urban sociologists that communities experiencing concentrated poverty suffer from an isolation effect, in which the absence of middle-class role models promotes a culture that rejects middle-class values, including norms of law-abidingness.[36] Urban sociologists also frequently argue that communities experiencing concentrated poverty tend to lack mechanisms of social control – social arrangements by which norms of law-abidingness are inculcated and enforced.[37] The sociologists Robert Sampson, Stephen Roudenbush, and Felton Earls have used the concept of "collective efficacy" to make this point. In a particularly influential paper, they demonstrated that rates of violent crime in communities are highly related to indicia of collective efficacy: that is, community residents' sense that the community as a whole effectively endeavors to prevent crime.[38] But whatever the explanation for the relationship between community and

32 *See* Committee to Improve Resources Information & Data on Firearms, National Resources Council, FIREARMS AND VIOLENCE: A CRITICAL REVIEW 61 (Charles F. Wellford, John V. Pepper & Carol V. Petrie eds., 2005) [hereinafter FIREARMS AND VIOLENCE].

33 *See* Clifford R. Shaw et al., DELINQUENCY AREAS: A STUDY OF THE GEOGRAPHIC DISTRIBUTION OF SCHOOL TRUANTS 198–206 (1929). For an explication of the import of the work of Shaw and his colleagues, *see* Robert J. Bursik & Harold J. Gramsick, NEIGHBORHOODS AND CRIME: THE DIMENSIONS OF EFFECTIVE COMMUNITY CONTROL 29–45 (1993).

34 *See, e.g.*, David Weisburd, Elizabeth R. Groff & Sue-Ming Yang, THE CRIMINOLOGY OF PLACE: STREET SEGMENTS AND OUR UNDERSTANDING OF THE CRIME PROBLEM, 50–53 (2012); John E. Eck, *Preventing Crime at Places, in* PREVENTING CRIME: WHAT WORKS, WHAT DOESN'T, WHAT'S PROMISING: A REPORT TO THE UNITED STATES CONGRESS 7–1 (Lawrence W. Sherman et al. eds., 1987); Lawrence W. Sherman, *Hot Spots of Crime and Criminal Careers of Places, in* CRIME AND PLACE 35, 36–39 (John E. Eck & David Weisburd eds., 1995) [hereinafter CRIME AND PLACE].

35 For useful surveys of research on the relationship of poverty and crime, see, for example, Elliot Currie, CRIME AND PUNISHMENT IN AMERICA 120–47 (1998), and Gary LaFree, LOSING LEGITIMACY: STREET CRIME AND THE DECLINE OF SOCIAL INSTITUTIONS IN AMERICA 117–34 (1998).

36 *See, e.g.*, James F. Short JR., POVERTY, ETHNICITY, AND VIOLENT CRIME, 55–74 (1997); William Julius Wilson, THE TRULY DISADVANTAGED: THE INNER CITY, THE UNDERCLASS, AND PUBLIC POLICY 7–9, 46–62 (1987); Lauren J. Krivo & Ruth D. Peterson, *Extremely Disadvantaged Neighborhoods and Urban Crime*, 75 SOC. FORCES 619 (1997); Edward S. Shihadeh & Nicole Flynn, *Segregation and Crime: The Effect of Black Social Isolation on the Rates of Black Urban Violence*, 74 SOC. FORCES 1325 (1996).

37 *See, e.g.*, Bursik & Grasmick, *supra* note 33, at 15–18, 34–35; John Hagan, CRIME AND DISREPUTE 67–99 (1994); Dan A. Lewis & Greta Salem, FEAR OF CRIME: INCIVILITY AND THE PRODUCTION OF A SOCIAL PROBLEM, 11–22 (1986); Francis T. Cullen, *Social Support as an Organizing Concept for Criminology: Presidential Address to the Academy of Criminal Justice Sciences*, 11 JUST. Q. 527 (1994).

38 *See* Robert J. Sampson, Stephen W. Roudenbush & Felton Earls, *Neighborhoods and Violent Crime: A Multilevel Study of Collective Efficacy*, 277 SCI. 918 (1997).

crime, there is no doubt that it exists. Research consistently discloses much higher crime rates in communities that display various indicia of instability.[39]

The geographic "lumpiness" of crime, however, is not solely a function of community. Even within what are considered high-crime communities, crime tends to cluster in discrete places.[40] This phenomenon is explained by the "routine activities" approach to criminology, which analyzes crime the way that other routine activities are analyzed to determine how they come to be performed as they are. The advocates of the routine activities approach posit that crime rates will be highest where three factors intersect: motivated offenders, desirable targets, and a lack of guardians, such as parents, friends, neighbors, private security guards, or police, who occupy space in a manner that deters crime.[41]

All of this should cast considerable doubt on the efficacy of largely reactive policing. Areas in which motivated offenders, desirable targets, and a lack of guardians intersect are not randomly distributed, and it is those locations where "guardianship" is most needed Indeed, the defects in reactive policing became apparent during the crime spike of the late 1980s and early 1990s.

There is something approaching a consensus among criminologists that the crime spike of the 1980s and 1990s was a function of the introduction of crack cocaine into major cities.[42] A number of studies have demonstrated that lagged increases in violent crime followed the introduction of crack to an urban area.[43] Although there are fewer studies that reliably measure the proportion of violent crime that is drug related, what is probably the best study of this issue – a sampling of homicides in New York City during an eight-month period in 1988 – found that 52.7 percent of homicides were drug related. Of those, 60 percent involved crack, and 74 percent were classified as "systemic" or involving "the normally aggressive patterns of interaction within the systems of drug use

39 The literature is reviewed in Ronald C. Kramer, *Poverty, Inequality, and Youth Violence*, 567 Annals Am. Acad. Pol. & Soc. Sci. 123 (2000).

40 *See, e.g.*, Weisburd, Groff & Yang, *supra* note 34, at 9–14; Ralph B. Taylor, *Crime and Small-Scale Places: What We Know, What We Can Prevent, and What Else We Need to Know*, *in* Crime and Place: Plenary Papers of the 1997 Conference on Criminal Justice Research and Evaluation, 3–9 (U.S. Dep't of Just. 1998); Lawrence W. Sherman et al., *Hot Spots of Predatory Crime: Routine Activities and the Criminology of Place*, 27 Criminology 27 (1989).

41 *See, e.g.*, Bursik & Grasmick, *supra* note 33, at 62–72; Michael R. Gottfredson & Travis Hirschi, A General Theory of Crime 22–44 (1990); Weisburd, Groff & Yang, *supra* note 34, at 6–9, 90–118; John E. Eck & David Weisburd, *Crime Places in Crime Theory*, in Crime and Place, *supra* note 34, at 1, 7–18; Lawrence E. Cohen & Marcus Felson, *Social Change and Crime Rate Trends: A Routine Activities Approach*, 44 Am. Soc. Rev. 588 (1979).

42 *See, e.g.*, Alfred Blumstein & Jacqueline Cohen, Diffusion Processes in Homicide, 6–9 (Nat'l Crim. Just. Ref. Serv. July 17, 1999); Fox, Levin & Quinet, *supra* note 31, at 87–88; Benjamin Pearson-Nelson, Understanding Homicide Trends: The Social Context of a Homicide Epidemic, 37–41 (2008); Alfred Blumstein & Joel Wallman, *The Crime Drop and Beyond*, 2006 Ann. Rev. Soc. Sci. 125, 131 (2006); Philip J. Cook & John H. Laub, *After the Epidemic: Recent Trends in Youth Violence in the United States*, *in* Crime & Justice: A Review of Research 1, 21–31 (Michael Tonry ed., 2002).

43 *See, e.g.*, Eric Baumer, et al., *The Influence of Crack Cocaine on Robbery, Burglary, and Homicide Rates: A Cross-City, Longitudinal Analysis*, 35 J. Res. Crime & Delinq. 316, 328–30 (1998); Daniel Cork, *Examining Space–Time Interaction in City-Level Homicide Data: Crack Markets and the Diffusion of Guns among Youth*, 15 J. Quantitative Criminology 379, 403–04 (1999); Jeff Grogger & Michael Willis, *The Emergence of Crack Cocaine and the Rise of Urban Crime Rates*, 82 Rev. Econ. & Stats. 519, 525–28 (2000); Steven F. Messner, et al., *Locating the Vanguard in Rising and Falling Homicide Rates across U.S. Cities*, 43 Criminology 661, 677–87 (2005); Graham Ousey & Matthew R. Lee, *Examining the Conditional Nature of the Illicit Drug Market–Homicide Relationship: A Partial Test of Contingent Causation*, 40 Criminology 73, 94–98 (2002).

and distribution" as opposed to homicides that were a function of the pharmacological effects of drugs or the economic compulsion to commit crimes to finance drug use.[44]

One organization particularly well suited to the violent competition that accompanied the emergence of crack during the crime rise period is the criminal street gang.[45] Indeed, one consistent observation in the scholarly literature about gangs is their heavy involvement in drug distribution.[46] Surveys of youth gang members reflect the involvement of gang youth in drug trafficking at much higher rates than other youth.[47] To similar effect, ethnographic research on gang crime reports that gangs endeavor to organize drug

44 Paul J. Goldstein, et al., *Crack and Homicide in New York City, 1988: A Conceptually Based Event Analysis*, 16 CONTEMP. DRUG PROBS. 651, 655–56, 681–82 (1989).

45 Among criminologists, the definition of a "gang" is a matter of some controversy. *See, e.g.*, Randall G. Shelden, Sharon K. Tracy & William B. Brown, YOUTH GANGS IN AMERICAN SOCIETY, 17–21 (2d ed. 2001); Richard A. Ball & G. David Curry, *The Logic of Definition in Criminology: Purposes and Methods for Defining "Gangs,"* 33 CRIMINOLOGY 225 (1995); Finn-Aage Esbensen et al., *Youth Gangs and Definitional Issues: When Is a Gang a Gang, and Why Does It Matter?* 47 CRIME & DELINQ. 105, 106 (2001). The definition offered by Ball and Curry is particularly useful for present purposes because its stresses structural features:

> The gang is a spontaneous, semisecret, interstitial, integrated, but mutable social system whose members share common interests and that functions with relatively little regard for legality but regulates interaction among its members and features a leadership structure with processes of organizational maintenance and membership services and adaptive mechanisms for dealing with other significant social systems in its environment.

Supra, at 240.

46 *See, e.g.*, James C. Howell & Scott H. Decker, U.S. DEPARTMENT OF JUSTICE, THE YOUTH GANGS, DRUGS, AND VIOLENCE CONNECTION, 2–5, 7 (Jan. 1999); C. Ronald Huff, U.S. Department of Justice, COMPARING THE CRIMINAL BEHAVIOR OF YOUTH GANGS AND AT-RISK YOUTHS, 4, 7 (Oct. 1998); Herbert C. Covey, Scott Menard & Robert J. Franzese, JUVENILE GANGS 51–54 (2d ed. 1997); Scott H. Decker & Barrick Van Winkle, LIFE IN THE GANG: FAMILY, FRIENDS, AND VIOLENCE 153–71 (1996); Martin Sanchez Jankowski, ISLANDS IN THE STREET: GANGS AND AMERICAN URBAN SOCIETY 120–21 (1991); Joan W. Moore, HOMEBOYS: GANGS, DRUGS, AND PRISON IN THE BARRIOS OF LOS ANGELES 75–93 (1978); Felix M. Padilla, THE GANG AS AN AMERICAN ENTERPRISE 97–117, 129–51 (1993); Carl S. Taylor, DANGEROUS SOCIETY 92, 97, 99 (1990); Brenda C. Coughlin & Sudhir Alladi Venkatesh, *The Urban Street Gang after 1970*, 2003 ANN. REV. SOC. 41, 43–45 (2003); Finn-Aage Esbensen & David Huizinga, *Gangs, Drugs, and Delinquency in a Survey of Urban Youth*, 31 CRIMINOLOGY 565, 573–75 (1993); Jeffrey Fagan, *The Social Organization of Drug Use and Drug Dealing among Urban Gangs*, 27 CRIMINOLOGY 633, 635, 648–51 (1989); Ronald Glick, *Survival, Income, and Status: Drug Dealing in the Chicago Puerto Rican Community*, *in* DRUGS IN HISPANIC COMMUNITIES 77–101 (Ronald Glick & Joan Moore eds., 1990); Tom Mieczkowski, *Geeking Up and Throwing Down: Heroin Street Life in Detroit*, 24 CRIMINOLOGY 645, 648–49 (1986). To be sure, there is ample evidence that less structured and organized gangs are less effective drug sellers. *See, e.g.*, Malcolm W. Klein, THE AMERICAN STREET GANG: ITS NATURE, PREVALENCE, AND CONTROL, 40–42, 126–29 (1995). Still, there is widespread agreement that better organized gangs have become adept at drug trafficking. *See, e.g.*, Arlen Egley Jr., et al., U.S. DEPARTMENT OF JUSTICE, NATIONAL YOUTH GANG SURVEY 1999–2001, at 33–34 (July 2006); Scott H. Decker, *Youth Gangs and Violent Behavior, in* THE CAMBRIDGE HANDBOOK OF VIOLENT BEHAVIOR AND AGGRESSION 388, 392–93 (Daniel J. Flannery et al. eds., 2007) [hereinafter CAMBRIDGE HANDBOOK OF VIOLENT BEHAVIOR]; Finn-Aage Esbensen, et al., *Initiation of Drug Use, Drug Sales, and Violent Offending Among a Sample of Gang and Nongang Youth, in* GANGS IN AMERICA III 37, 39–40 (C. Ronald Huff ed., 2002); Malcolm W. Klein, *Street Gang Cycles, in* CRIME 217, 219–21, 227 (James Q. Wilson & Joan Petersilia eds., 1998) [hereinafter "CRIME"]; Malcolm W. Klein & Cheryl Lee Maxson, *Gangs and Crack Cocaine Trafficking, in* DRUGS AND CRIME: EVALUATING PUBLIC POLICY OPTIONS 42, 47–52 (Doris Layton McKenzie & Craig D. Uchida eds., 1994) [hereinafter DRUGS AND CRIME].

47 *See, e.g.*, Decker & Van Winkle, *supra* note 46, at 159–60; Terence P. Thornberry et al., GANGS AND DELINQUENCY IN DEVELOPMENTAL PERSPECTIVE 110–15 (2003); C. Ronald Huff, *Comparing the Criminal Behavior of Youth Gangs and At-Risk Youth, in* AMERICAN YOUTH GANGS AT THE MILLENNIUM, 78, 81–82, n.3 (Finn-Aage Esbensen, Stephen F. Tibbets & Larry Gaines eds., 2004) [hereinafter GANGS AT THE MILLENNIUM].

markets to maximize the economic benefits of drug dealing while using the threat of violence to suppress competition.[48] The ethnographic studies also find that drug-dealing gangs endeavor to establish monopolies in identifiable turf in order to enhance their profitability.[49] The desire of gangs to maximize their profitability in impoverished communities is understandable. After all, another observation frequently encountered in the ethnographic literature is that the lure of money is often central to the appeal of gangs in the inner city.[50]

The need to control identifiable turf in order to limit competition, as well as the prevalence of open-air markets, necessitates the use of violence and intimidation tactics.[51] Gangs could hardly run open-air drug markets or obtain effective control over a neighborhood unless they were able thus to cow law-abiding community residents, making it unlikely that they would complain to the police or testify in court.[52] Violent intimidation is also necessary to suppress competition.[53] Unsurprisingly, the literature confirms the prevalence of gang intimidation as a means of inhibiting community cooperation with the authorities.[54]

In light of the challenges to law enforcement posed by the prevalence of drug-related violence, it should be apparent that a purely reactive form of policing reflected in the conventional model – in which officers on patrol are dispatched in response to calls for service – will likely prove inadequate to the task. When criminals are able to intimidate the law-abiding, they will fear calling the authorities for assistance and cooperating with them after a crime has occurred. Thus, it should be unsurprising that the conventional approach to policing was unable to prevent the crime spike of the late 1980s and the early 1990s. The question then becomes what produced the subsequent crime decline?

48 *See, e.g.*, Decker & Van Winkle, *supra* note 46, at 163–64; Jankowski, *supra* note 46, at 126–29; PADILLA, *supra* note 46, at 129–66; Irving A. Spergel, THE YOUTH GANG PROBLEM: A COMMUNITY APPROACH, 47–49 (1995); Ansley Hamid, *The Political Economy of Crack-Related Violence*, 17 CONTEMP. DRUG PROBS. 31, 61–63 (1990); Jerome H. Skolnick et al., *The Social Structure of Street Drug Dealing*, 9 AM. J. POLICE 1, 16–17 (1990).

49 *See, e.g.*, Padilla, *supra* note 46, at 137–41; Taylor, *supra* note 46, at 6; Jacqueline Cohen et al., *The Role of Drug Markets and Gangs in Local Homicide Rates*, 2 HOMICIDE STUDS. 241, 246–47 (1998); Paul J. Goldstein et al., *Crack and Homicide in New York City: A Case Study in the Epidemiology of Violence*, *in* CRACK IN AMERICA: DEMON DRUGS AND SOCIAL JUSTICE 113, 118–24 (Craig Reinarman & Harry G. Levine eds., 1997); John M. Hagedorn, *Neighborhoods, Markets, and Gang Drug Organizations*, 31 J. RES. CRIME & DELINQ. 264, 289–91 (1994).

50 *See, e.g.*, G. David Curry & Scott H. Decker, CONFRONTING GANGS: CRIME AND COMMUNITY, 62–63, 137–40 (2d ed. 2003); Jankowski, *supra* note 46, at 40–42; Joan W. Moore, GOING DOWN TO THE BARRIO: HOMEBOYS AND HOMEGIRLS IN CHANGE, 42–44 (1991); Padilla, *supra* note 46, at 101–03; Spergel, *supra* note 48, at 94; Mercer L. Sullivan, "GETTING PAID": YOUTH CRIME AND WORK IN THE INNER CITY 117, 222–50 (1989); Taylor, *supra* note 46, at 5–6, 10–12, 61, 99–102; Jeffrey Fagan, *The Political Economy of Drug Dealing among Urban Gangs*, *in* DRUGS AND THE COMMUNITY: INVOLVING COMMUNITY RESIDENTS IN COMBATING THE ILLEGAL SALE OF DRUGS, 19, 27–45 (Robert C. Davis et al. eds., 1993); Joan W. Moore, *Understanding Youth Street Gangs: Economic Restructuring and the Urban Underclass*, *in* CROSS CULTURAL PERSPECTIVES ON YOUTH AND VIOLENCE 65, 71–72 (Meredith W. Watts ed., 1998).

51 *See, e.g.*, Decker & Van Winkle, *supra* note 46, at 163–64.

52 *See, e.g.*, Al Valdez, GANGS: A GUIDE TO UNDERSTANDING STREET GANGS 19–20 (1997).

53 *See, e.g.*, Jankowski, *supra* note 46, at 126–31.

54 *See, e.g.*, Valdez, *supra* note 52, at 19–20; Bruce D. Johnson et al., *Drug Abuse in the Inner City: Impact on Hard-Drug Users and the Community*, *in* 13 CRIME & JUSTICE: A REVIEW OF RESEARCH 35–37 (Michael Tonry & James Q. Wilson eds., 1990).

Perhaps the most logical explanation for a decline in drug-related crime is that the demand for illegal drugs – crack in particular – declined, reducing the incentives for violent competition to control crack markets. But there is little evidence to support this supposition. Although it is difficult to measure the demand for cocaine, the available statistics suggest no dramatic reduction during the crime drop era.[55] Cocaine-related emergency room admissions, for example, actually rose from 1994 to 2001, as did the proportion of emergency room admissions that involved crack.[56] Federal seizures of cocaine remained roughly constant from 1989 through 2002.[57] Trends in the price of crack were also not noticeably different during the crime rise and crime decline periods.[58]

One might also look to a demographic explanation for the crime decline – perhaps there was a fall in the size of the high-crime urban population cohort. But demographic studies have consistently found that there was no change in the size of the high-crime cohort that explains the rise, and then even larger decline, in rates of violent crime.[59]

A particular demographic claim has been advanced by John Donahue and Steven Levitt, who argue that as much as half of the crime decline was a function of the legalization of abortion, which reduced numbers of disproportionately at-risk youth in postlegalization cohorts.[60] There have been a number of challenges to the methodology and evidence supporting this thesis.[61] I will not enter this methodological debate here, except to note that some basic questions of timing seem to undermine this thesis. The Supreme Court held prohibitions on abortion unconstitutional in 1973.[62] The abortion thesis accordingly suggests that crime rates should have already been falling for some time by 1993, when all teenagers had been born after legalization. Instead, as we have seen, violent crime peaked in 1993, casting considerable doubt on the abortion thesis. Moreover, critics of this thesis argue that there is no apparent demographic explanation for the magnitude of the crime decline even when abortion rates are considered.[63]

55 *See* Craig Reinarman & Harry G. Levine, *The Crack Attack: Politics and Media in the Crack Scare, in* Crack in America: Demon Drugs and Social Justice, 20, 29–31 figs. 2.1–2.3 (Craig Reinarman & Harry G. Levine eds., 1997).

56 *See* Substance Abuse & Mental Health Services Administration, Office of Applied Studies, Department of Health & Human Services, Emergency Department Trends from the Drug Abuse Warning Network: Final Estimates 1994–2001, at 50, 53 fig.3 (Aug. 2002).

57 *See* Bureau of Just. Stats., U.S. Dep't of Just., Sourcebook of Criminal Justice Statistics: 2003, at 390 tbl.4.36 (Aug. 2004).

58 *See* Office of National Drug Control Pol'y, Exec. Office of the President, The Price and Purity of Illicit Drugs: 1981 through the Second Quarter of 2003, at 9–10, 29 fig.10 (Nov. 2004).

59 *See, e.g.*, Franklin E. Zimring, The Great American Crime Decline 56–60 (2007); Alfred Blumstein & Richard Rosenfeld, *Explaining Recent Trends in U.S. Homicide Rates*, 88 J. Crim. L. & Criminology 1175, 1187–91 (1998); Blumstein & Wallman, *supra* note 42, at 140; Cook & Laub, *supra* note 42, at 22–25; Stephen D. Levitt, *Understanding Why Crime Fell in the 1990s: Four Factors That Explain the Crime Drop and Six That Do Not*, 18 J. Econ. Persp. 163, 171–72 (2004).

60 *See* John J. Donahue III & Steven D. Levitt, *The Impact of Legalized Abortion on Crime*, 116 Q. J. Econ. 379, 407–15 (2001).

61 *See, e.g.*, Blumstein & Wallman, *supra* note 42, at 141–42; Cook & Laub, *supra* note 42, at 22–25.

62 *See Roe v. Wade*, 410 U.S. 113 (1973).

63 For powerful attacks on the abortion thesis along these lines, *see* Cook & Laub, *supra* note 42, at 22–25; Theodore Joyce, *Did Legalized Abortion Lower Crime?* 39 J. Hum. Res. 1, 1–2, 25 (2004); Gary L. Shoesmith, *Four Factors That Explain Both the Rise and Fall of US Crime, 1970–2003*, 42 Applied Econ. 2957, 2969–70 (2010).

For present purposes, most important is Donahue and Levitt's observation that crime declined sooner in the states that legalized abortion prior to 1973 than it did elsewhere.[64] If the thesis about abortion were true, by now the disparity between crime rates in early legalization and other states should have diminished, if not disappeared. As we will see, this prediction has not been borne out in New York City, where the crime decline has been particularly dramatic. Abortion may have played some role in the crime decline, but the New York data suggests that its role was limited, at least in that city. Indeed, Donahue and Levitt agree with this last point; they concede that abortion had less effect in New York than in most jurisdictions, noting that because New York abortion rates are unusually high, they may well have reached a point of diminishing returns in terms of crime reduction in that state.[65] The effects of abortion rates on crime, at best, seem to be limited.

Another demographic explanation for the crime decline focuses on increases in rates of incarceration, which incapacitates potential offenders and offers the possibility of general deterrence.[66] While increased incarceration probably had some effect on crime rates, sorting out its effects is a perilous business. For one thing, as we have seen, both the crime rise and ensuing decline occurred among youthful offenders, and incarceration rates are lower for youth.[67] For another, incarceration may have crime-generating effects. For example, one study in New York City found that high rates of incarceration in high-crime communities adversely affect the economic prospects of offenders and their families, and therefore destabilize communities and ultimately contribute to increased crime rates.[68] Indeed, in inner-city communities already plagued by social instability, high rates of incarceration may exacerbate social disorganization with criminogenic effects.[69] Moreover, in the inner city, where demand for drugs is high and many residents likely believe that alternative sources of legitimate income are limited, the incentive to deal in drugs may be so great that the calculus of potential offenders is likely to be only marginally affected by an increase in drug prosecutions or sentences.[70] Whatever the reason,

64 *See* Donahue & Levitt, *supra* note 60, at 395–99.

65 *See id.* at 405–06.

66 *See, e.g.*, Levitt, *supra* note 59, at 178–79 (arguing that incarceration explains one-third of the crime drop); William Spelman, *The Limited Importance of Prison Expansion*, *in* THE CRIME DROP IN AMERICA 97, 123–25 (Alfred Blumstein & Joel Wallman eds., 2d ed. 2006) [hereinafter CRIME DROP IN AMERICA] (estimating that incarceration explains one-quarter of the crime drop). For a metaanalysis of studies of incarceration effects that afford it moderate significance in determining crime rates, *see* Travis C. Pratt & Francis T. Cullen, *Assessing Macro-Level Predictors and Theories of Crime: A Meta-Analysis*, *in* CRIME AND JUSTICE: A REVIEW OF RESEARCH 373, 416–17 (Michael Tonry ed., 2005).

67 *See* Cook & Laub, *supra* note 42, at 29–30.

68 *See* Jeffrey Fagan, Valerie West & Jan Holland, *Reciprocal Effects of Crime and Incarceration in New York City Neighborhoods*, 30 FORDHAM URB. L.J. 1551, 1588–95 (2003).

69 *See* Jeffrey Fagan & Tracey L. Meares, *Punishment, Deterrence, and Social Control: The Paradox of Punishment in Minority Communities*, 6 OHIO ST. CRIM. L.J. 173 (2008).

70 *See* Jeffrey A. Fagan, *Do Criminal Sanctions Deter Drug Crimes? in* DRUGS AND CRIME, *supra* note 46, at 188, 204–07. The same may be true of efforts to target the unlawful use of firearms in connection with drug trafficking through the use of felony prosecutions. *See* Steven Raphael & Jens Ludwig, *Prison Enhancement: The Case of Project Exile*, *in* EVALUATING GUN POLICY: EFFECTS ON CRIME AND VIOLENCE, 251, 274–77 (Jens Ludwig & Philip J. Cook eds., 2003) [hereinafter EVALUATING GUN POLICY]. One study of an effort to target gun offenders for federal felony prosecutions in Richmond known as "Project Exile" found no statistically significant results. *See id.*; *accord* Jens Ludwig, *Better Gun Enforcement, Less Crime*, 4 CRIMINOLOGY & PUB. POL'Y 677, 691–98 (2005). A more recent study using a different methodology did find statistically significant crime reductions following the Richmond program. *See* Richard Rosenfeld, Robert Fornango & Eric Baumer, *Did* Ceasefire, Compstat, *and* Exile *Reduce Homicide?* 4

the evidence of a relation between incarceration rates and the crime drop is wanting. As proof of this point, studies show that between 1975 and 2000, even as incarceration rates increased dramatically, there was no statistically significant relationship between incarceration and homicide rates.[71]

Without satisfactory evidence supporting a demographic explanation for the crime drop, one might turn to economics. We have seen that violent crime concentrates in areas of economic disadvantage; it could follow that an improving economy drove rates of violent crime down in the 1990s. But again, the statistical evidence offers little support for this thesis – there is no relationship between local economic conditions and crime rates.[72] Nor does the national economy provide an explanation – inflation-adjusted wages were essentially flat from the mid-1980s to 1996, so economic explanations for the dramatic movements in violent crime rates during that period are unpromising.[73]

John Lott and David Mustard have suggested yet another possibility: arguing that reductions in crime rates are produced by laws authorizing the carrying of concealed firearms, which are said to enhance the likelihood that an intended victim will be able to provide armed resistance.[74] The study's methodology, however, has been subject to fierce criticism.[75] In any event, Lott and Mustard studied the period from 1979 to 1992, prior to the crime decline.[76] Ian Ayres and John Donohue then extended the analysis forward seven years and found no relationship between concealed carry laws and crime reductions.[77] The debate has continued with more recent studies reaching divergent conclusions.[78] Lott himself makes no effort, however, to establish that any significant portion of the crime drop since the early 1990s resulted from concealed carry laws.[79]

CRIMINOLOGY & PUB. POL'Y 419, 436–38 (2005). Still, Richmond's homicide rate remained significantly higher than the average rate for cities with a population of 175,000 or more. *See id.* at 428–32, fig.1. The same study found no statistically significant effects of Boston's effort to generate deterrence by direct communication with gang youth about the consequences of firearms possession and use. *See id.* at 434–35.

71 *See* Zimring, *supra* note 59, at 50–52.

72 *See* Richard B. Freeman, *Does the Booming Economy Help Explain the Fall in Crime? in* PERSPECTIVES ON CRIME AND JUSTICE: 1999–2000 LECTURE SERIES 23, 40–41 (2001) [hereinafter PERSPECTIVES ON CRIME AND JUSTICE]; Levitt, *supra* note 59, at 170–71.

73 *See* Zimring, *supra* note 59, at 66–67.

74 *See* John R. Lott, Jr. & David B. Mustard, *Crime, Deterrence, and Right-to-Carry Concealed Handguns*, 26 J. LEGAL. STUD. 1, 65–66 (1997).

75 *See, e.g.*, David Hemenway, PRIVATE GUNS PUBLIC HEALTH 100–04 (2004); Mark V. Tushnet, OUT OF RANGE: WHY THE CONSTITUTION CAN'T END THE BATTLE OVER GUNS, 85–95 (2007).

76 *See* Blumstein & Wallman, *supra* note 42, at 134–35.

77 *See* Ian Ayres & John J. Donohue III, *Shooting Down the "More Guns, Less Crime" Hypothesis*, 55 STAN. L. REV. 1193, 1296 (2003). This finding has since been replicated. *See* FIREARMS AND VIOLENCE, *supra* note 32, at 125–51.

78 *Compare, e.g.*, John R. Lott, JR., MORE GUNS, LESS CRIME: UNDERSTANDING CRIME AND GUN CONTROL LAWS 170–336 (University of Chicago Press 3d ed. 2010) (finding crime reductions in an analysis updated through 2005), *and* Carlisle E. Moody & Thomas B. Marvell, *The Debate on Shall-Issue Laws*, 5 ECON J. WATCH 269, 291 (2008) (finding crime reductions as well); *with* Ian Ayres & John J. Donohue III, *Yet Another Refutation of the More Guns, Less Crime Hypothesis: With Some Help from Moody and Marvell*, 6 ECON J. WATCH 35, 55–56 (2009) (disputing crime reductions).

79 *See* Lott, *supra* note 78, at 253–305. A similar claim – although not linked to declining crime rates – is that firearms are used for defensive purposes at very high rates. *See, e.g.*, Gary Kleck & Marc Gertz, *Armed Resistance to Crime: The Prevalence and Nature of Self-Defense with a Gun*, 86 J. CRIM. L. & CRIMINOLOGY 150, 179–81 (1995). More recent work has cast great doubt on this claim. *See, e.g.*, Philip J. Cook & Jens Ludwig, U.S. Department of Justice, GUNS IN AMERICA: NATIONAL SURVEY ON PRIVATE OWNERSHIP AND USE OF FIREARMS, 8–11 (May 1997); HEMENWAY, *supra* note 75, at 66–69, 239–40.

A more promising explanation for the crime decline involves the effect of policing. There is considerable evidence of a statistical relationship between increases in the number of police and subsequent decreases in violent crime.[80] But this explanation is, at best, incomplete.

There are a great many studies regarding the effect of increased numbers of police or frequency of patrol, and their results are mixed.[81] Indeed, more frequent patrols, unaccompanied by changes in police tactics, are likely to have limited efficacy because, as Mark Moore has observed, "Police on patrol cannot see enough to intervene very often in the life of the community."[82] Indeed, at the city level, the relationship between numbers of police and crime breaks down – there is little relationship between the size of a city's police force and the magnitude or duration of the crime spike.[83] Nor does it stand to reason that increased policing alone is likely to reduce crime regardless of the tactics employed. Officers who merely drive through a neighborhood on patrol are unlikely to be very effective at disrupting drug or gang activity – a gang or drug dealer with a modicum of sophistication need only post a lookout who can warn his confederates to cease any overt criminality as the squad car drives past. It seems likely that the tactics police use must be at least as important as the number of officers.

In fact, the 1990s saw alterations in the tactics employed by a great many urban police departments that moved from more passive and reactive patrol to proactive efforts at intensive and aggressive patrol of specific high-crime areas.[84] Particularly impressive crime reductions were experienced in New York City, which, between 1991 and 2009, experienced the broadest crime declines of any major American city.[85] In 1991, the size of New York's police force began to increase, and subsequently, after the appointment by Mayor Rudolph Giuliani of William Bratton as commissioner in 1994, the department placed greater emphasis on aggressive stop-and-frisk tactics for misdemeanor arrests for drug and public order offenses, adopted a system of statistical analysis labeled "CompStat" that focused enforcement efforts on statistical "hot spots" of criminal activity, and imposed greater managerial accountability.[86] A number of studies have concluded

80 *See* Steven D. Levitt, *Using Electoral Cycles in Police Hiring to Estimate the Effect of Police on Crime*, 87 Am. Econ. Rev. 270, 286 (1997); Steven D. Levitt, *Using Electoral Cycles in Police Hiring to Estimate the Effects of Police on Crime: Reply*, 92 Am. Econ. Rev. 1244, 1244–46 (2002); Thomas B. Marvell & Carlisle E. Moody, *Specification Problems, Police Levels, and Crime Rates*, 34 Criminology 609, 630–40 (1996).

81 *See* Committee to Review Resources on Police Policy and Practices, National Resources Council, Fairness and Effectiveness in Policing: The Evidence 224–25 (Wesley Skogan & Kathleen Frydl eds., 2004) [hereinafter Fairness and Effectiveness in Policing]; John E. Conklin, Why Crime Rates Fell, 60–63 (2003); John E. Eck & Edward R. Maguire, *Have Changes in Policing Reduced Violent Crime? An Assessment of the Evidence*, *in* The Crime Drop in America, *supra* note 66, at 207, 209–17; Lawrence W. Sherman & John E. Eck, *Policing for Crime Prevention*, *in* Evidence-Based Crime Prevention 295, 306–07 (Lawrence W. Sherman et al. eds., rev. 2006) [hereinafter Evidence-Based Crime Prevention].

82 Moore, *supra* note 25, at 112.

83 *See, e.g.*, Pearson-Nelson, *supra* note 42, at 152–54; Graham C. Ousey & Matthew R. Lee, *Homicide Trends and Illicit Drug Markets: Exploring Differences Across Time*, 24 Just. Q. 48, 73 (2007); Pratt & Cullen, *supra* note 66, at 425–26. *See also* Shoesmith, *supra* note 63, at 2971–72 (finding crime declines relate to arrest rates rather than size of police force).

84 *See, e.g.*, Eck & Maguire, *supra* note 81, at 228–45; Debra Livingston, *Police Discretion and the Quality of Life in Public Places: Courts, Communities, and the New Policing*, 97 Colum. L. Rev. 551, 572–84 (1997).

85 Franklin E. Zimring, The City That Became Safe: New York's Lessons for Urban Crime and Its Control 3–27 (2012).

86 *See id.* at 108–21.

that this alteration in policing tactics deserves substantial credit for New York's crime decline.[87]

Few national studies have endeavored to examine the effect of changing police tactics on crime rates. There are indeed many difficulties in conducting such an analysis – efforts to determine what tactics are most prevalent in each city and when they became prevalent are fraught with peril. Even so, the leading effort to conduct such a study found that the introduction of CompStat tactics in major cities was the only law enforcement tactic that had a demonstrable relationship to subsequent reductions in crime.[88] Beyond that, an impressive number of studies throughout the nation have found that aggressive policing at hot spots reduces crime.[89]

To be sure, stop-and-frisk is not always warranted. In March 2013, for example, the New York Police Department issued a new directive requiring officers to provide a detailed narrative justifying stops, which officers interpreted as an indication that their stops would be scrutinized and potentially sanctioned, leading to a dramatic decline in the rate of stops, while increasing the rate at which weapons were recovered during stops.[90] There is indeed reason to believe that prior to March 2014, New York was engaged in overenforcement; the number of investigative stops by police officers in New York rose from 314,000 in 2004 to a high of 686,000 in 2011.[91] It may well have been the case that New York's success caused it to push stop-and-frisk tactics well beyond the point of diminishing returns. In such a case, depolicing may be just what the doctor ordered. The critical point, of course, is that it is only when aggressive patrol is targeted at hot spots at which additional guardianship is necessary that it is likely to prove efficacious.

The success of CompStat and hot spot policing suggests the case for surveillance. Aggressive patrol targeting criminogenic hot spots is a mechanism for adding guardianship at locations where motivated offenders and vulnerable victims intersect. An enhanced police presence in these locations increases the risks of engaging in criminal activities and is therefore likely to produce crime declines.

The same point can be made when nonhuman guardianship is added in the form of surveillance cameras. The most comprehensive study of a large surveillance network in

87 *See, e.g.*, *id.* at 131–44; David Weisburd, Cody Telep & Brian Lawton, *Could Innovations in Policing Have Contributed to the New York City Crime Drop Even in a Period of Declining Police Strength?: The Case of Stop, Question and Frisk as a Hot Spots Policing Strategy*, 31 Justice Q. 129, 136–46 (2014).

88 *See* Olivia Roeder, Lauren-Brook Eisen & Julia Bowling, Brennan Center for Justice, What Caused the Crime Decline? 73–79 (2014).

89 *See* Fairness and Effectiveness in Policing, *supra* note 81, at 235–40; Firearms and Violence, *supra* note 32, at 230–35; Anthony A. Braga, Andrew V. Papchristous & David M. Hureau, *The Effects of Hot Spots Policing on Crime: An Updated Systematic Review and Meta-Analysis*, 41 Justice Q. 633, 643–60 (2014); Blumstein & Wallman, *supra* note 42, at 136–37; Daniel S. Nagin, *Criminal Deterrence Research at the Outset of the Twenty-First Century*, *in* Crime and Justice: A Review of Research 1, 29–33 (Michael Tonry ed., 1998); Lawrence W. Sherman, *Reducing Gun Violence: What Works, What Doesn't, What's Promising*, *in* Perspectives on Crime and Justice, *supra* note 72, at 69, 78–79; Lawrence W. Sherman, *The Police*, *in* Crime, *supra* note 47, at 327, 328–34; Lawrence W. Sherman & John E. Eck, *Policing for Crime Prevention*, *in* Evidence-Based Crime Prevention, *supra* note 81, at 295, 308–10; Cody Telep & David Weisburd, *What Is Known about the Effectiveness of Police Practices in Reducing Crime and Disorder?*, 15 Police Q. 331, 333–36 (2012).

90 *See* Jonathan Mummolo, *Can New Procedures Improve the Quality of Policing? The Case of "Stop, Frisk, and Question" in New York City*, 3–4, 16–20 (Feb. 18, 2016) (unpublished manuscript), http://papers.ssrn .com/ sol3/papers.cfm? abstract_id=2739222.

91 *Floyd v. City of New York*, 959 F. Supp. 2d 540, 573 (S.D.N.Y. 2013).

a major city to date found that Chicago's network of more than one thousand cameras produced significant crime reductions when cameras were placed in high-crime areas, but little effect in other areas.[92]

Embedded within this narrative, in other words, is the case for surveillance. Official surveillance can add guardianship where it is most needed. It is warranted, however, only at those locations at which additional guardianship is needed. Surveillance is accordingly required both to identify locations where additional guardianship is required and then to supply that guardianship. At the same time, the case for surveillance is not dependent on individualized predication. If the government cannot engage in surveillance absent individualized predication, then it cannot offer surveillance as a form of guardianship at criminogenic hot spots prophylactically. Indeed, if the government cannot surveil hot spots until after it receives information that amounts to reasonable suspicion that an individual is about to commit a crime, its subsequent efforts to provide such guardianship are likely to occur too late. Guardianship works prophylactically, and accordingly requires that surveillance be in place before a likely offender arrives on the scene.

Thus, the case for surveillance is reflected in both the failure of the framing era approach to law enforcement and the conventional model of policing. Both were primarily reactive in that law enforcement resources were deployed only after a crime had been committed and reported to the police. The entirely reactive framing era model proved grossly inadequate to the needs of an urbanizing nation and was largely abandoned in urban America by the dawn of the twentieth century. Yet, in an effort to professionalize policing, a largely reactive approach to motorized patrol replaced it, offering only a marginal improvement. If police arrive on the scene only by responding to a request for assistance, they are likely to be too late. Even worse, such a system creates an incentive for wrongdoers to intimidate those who might summon the authorities – an approach often taken by criminal street gangs. Reactive policing thus has little capacity to provide guardianship where it is most needed. Surveillance is instead required in order to determine how police resources are best deployed, and then to ensure that those resources can prevent rather than respond to crime. The history of policing, in short, reflects the growing awareness of the centrality of surveillance to effective law enforcement.

II Binary Searches of Private Areas

The preceding discussion might make a case for official surveillance of activities conducted in public – for example, monitoring that is not regarded as a "search" within the meaning of the Fourth Amendment's prohibition on unreasonable search and seizure because it involves scrutiny only of that which is "knowingly exposed to the public."[93] The government may offer guardianship to those in public places without waiting for evidence that unlawful activity is under way. This case, however, stops well short of justifying surveillance in other contexts. Surveillance of activities conducted out of public view, whether involving scrutiny of financial transactions or Internet searches, surely requires some additional justification.

92 *See* Rajiv Shah & Jeremy Braithwaite, *Spread Too Thin: Analyzing the Effectiveness of the Chicago Camera Network on Crime*, 14 Pol. Practice & Res. 415 (2013).

93 Katz, 389 U.S. at 351.

At the same time, a casual assumption that the government has little justification for scrutinizing what are commonly regarded as private activities is difficult to justify. In fact, not everything that occurs behind closed doors is properly regarded as private.

Consider what some have labeled a "binary" search, in which an investigative technique discloses no more than probable cause to believe a particular location hidden from public contains contraband.[94] A classic example is the use of a reliable narcotics detection dog, which can be characterized as a binary search – binary because it reveals no more than whether there is probable cause to believe that an otherwise concealed area contains contraband.[95] The binary search, however, is not limited to such pedestrian contexts. For example, a search program might one day be developed that could be used to search the hard drive of every computer connected to the Internet and identify the presence of digital contraband, such as an illegally modified program or child pornography.[96] It is far from easy to explain why this form of surveillance should be regarded as problematic. A binary search compromises no liberty or privacy interest in possessing lawful items, and otherwise results in no intrusion, physical or otherwise, on privacy. With respect to the innocent, a binary search tells investigators nothing about what is in a home or other location otherwise concealed from public view; instead, they learn only what is not present. Moreover, the target of the technique will be entirely unaware it occurred. Thus, it is hard to understand how such an investigative technique compromises the privacy interests of persons, houses, papers, or effects to any meaningful extent – except for the interest in possessing contraband. Therefore, an argument against official surveillance through binary search techniques must identify some coherent social good served by regulating official scrutiny that discloses no more than the presence or absence of contraband. There is, to be sure, a pragmatic argument for protecting the guilty to deter unjustified intrusions on the security of the innocent.[97] That consideration, however, has little force for binary search techniques that disclose nothing about the innocent.

Justice Brennan once endeavored to make a libertarian case against the binary search. Deregulation of binary search techniques, he contended in *United States v. Jacobsen*, would mean that

94 *See, e.g.*, David A. Harris, *Superman's X-Ray Vision and the Fourth Amendment: The New Gun Detection Technology*, 69 TEMP. L. REV. 1, 36–37 (1996); Renée McDonald Hutchins, *Tied Up in* Knotts? *GPS Technology and the Fourth Amendment*, 55 UCLA L. REV. 409, 440–42 (2007); Ric Simmons, *The Two Unanswered Questions of* Illinois v. Caballes: *How to Make the Word Safe for Binary Searches*, 80 TUL. L. REV. 411, 413, 424–27 (2005).

95 *See* Simmons, *supra* note 94, at 415–17, The Supreme Court has held that if a bona fide organization has certified a dog as reliable, or the dog has recently completed a training program that assessed its proficiency, "a court can presume (subject to any conflicting evidence offered) that the dog's alert provides probable cause to search." *Florida v. Harris*, 133 S. Ct. 1050, 1057 (2013).

96 A search program along these lines was first hypothesized in Michael Adler, Note, *Cyberspace, General Searches, and Digital Contraband: The Fourth Amendment and the Net-Wide Search*, 105 YALE L.J. 1093, 1097–1100 (1996). For a helpful elaboration on how such a program could be used to search computers connected to the Internet for contraband, *see* Richard P. Salgado, *Fourth Amendment Search and the Power of the Hash*, 119 HARV. L. REV. 38 (2005).

97 *See, e.g.*, *Minnesota v. Carter*, 525 U.S. 83, 110 (1998) (Ginsburg, J., dissenting); *United States v. Sharpe*, 470 U.S. 675, 719 (1985) (Brennan, J., dissenting); *Rawlings v. Kentucky*, 448 U.S. 98, 120–21 (1980) (Marshall, J., dissenting); *United States v. Rabinowitz*, 339 U.S. 56, 82 (1950) (Frankfurter, J., dissenting); *Brinegar v. United States*, 338 U.S. 160, 181 (1949) (Jackson, J., dissenting).

> if a device were developed that could detect, from the outside of a building, the presence of cocaine inside, there would be no constitutional obstacle to the police cruising through a residential neighborhood and using the device to identify all homes in which the drug is present.... Under the interpretation of the Fourth Amendment first suggested in *Place* and first applied in this case, these surveillance techniques would not constitute searches and therefore could be freely pursued whenever and wherever law enforcement officers desire. Hence, at some point in the future, if the Court stands by the theory it has adopted today, search warrants, probable cause, and even "reasonable suspicion" may very well become notions of the past.[98]

Some of this argument is surely overstated. Treating a binary search as constitutionally unregulated does not render the standard of probable cause or the warrant requirement obsolete as long as a judicial official must determine whether the binary search has produced probable cause and issue a warrant prior to a physical entry. Moreover, if a warrant is obtained on the basis of an alert from a drug sniffing dog or technology with similar binary search capabilities, then judicial review of the sufficiency of the evidence of probable cause will occur prior to any physical search and seizure, eliminating the pragmatic concern that those engaged in law enforcement will be too quick to conclude that probable cause is present.

Still, aside from the unsupportable claim that an unregulated binary search renders the probable cause and warrant requirements superfluous, it is worth considering whether the Fourth Amendment ought to prevent the government from learning where contraband is concealed – and where it is not – at least absent a warrant issued on probable cause. Even if binary search techniques involve little intrusion on the interest of the innocent in secluding the home from official scrutiny, one might argue for imposing some limitation on the government's investigative powers.

It is not very difficult to envision an argument for protecting the security of the home when it comes to a binary search – even though it discloses no more than the presence or absence of contraband. The argument might begin by observing that, within one's home or similarly "private" zone, on the libertarian account, the individual is sovereign, and accordingly beyond the government's reach, at least absent a warrant issued on probable cause. The point even has constitutional resonance: the Fourth Amendment grants a right to be "secure" against unreasonable search and seizure; presumably the right to be secure against official scrutiny is of Fourth Amendment concern.[99] This objection gains force, it could be argued, when a binary search discloses information about the home, the location in which privacy and autonomy interests are generally thought to be at their greatest.[100]

98 *United States v. Jacobsen*, 466 U.S. 109, 138 (1984) (Brennan, J., dissenting).

99 For helpful discussions of the manner in which the Fourth Amendment's guarantee of security against unreasonable search and seizure illuminates its meaning, *see* Thomas K. Clancy, *What Does the Fourth Amendment Protect: Property, Privacy, or Security?* 33 Wake Forest L. Rev. 307, 350–66 (1998); Jed Rubenfeld, *The End of Privacy*, 61 Stan. L. Rev. 101, 119–31, 138–51 (2008).

100 *See, e.g.*, Lewis R. Katz & Aaron D. Golembiewski, *Curbing the Dog: Extending the Protection of the Fourth Amendment to Police Drug Dogs*, 85 Neb. L. Rev. 735, 775–78 (2007); Leslie A. Lunney, *Has the Fourth Amendment Gone to the Dogs? Unreasonable Expansion of the Canine Sniff Doctrine to Include Sniffs of the Home*, 88 Or. L. Rev. 829, 887–89 (2009); Renee Swanson, Comment, *Are We Safe at Home from the Prying Dog Sniff?* 11 Loy. J. Pub. Int. L. 131, 150–53 (2009); Mark E. Smith, Comment, *Going to the Dogs: Evaluating the Proper Standard for Narcotic Detector Dog Searches of Private Residences*, 46 HOUS. L. REV. 103, 132–36 (2009).

On this point, the Court majority's response to Justice Brennan in *Jacobsen* is instructive, holding that the use of a field test for the presence of cocaine was not a "search" within the meaning of the Fourth Amendment because

> Congress has decided – and there is no question about its power to do so – to treat the interest in "privately" possessing cocaine as illegitimate; thus governmental conduct that can reveal whether a substance is cocaine, and no other arguably "private" fact, compromises no legitimate privacy interest.[101]

This observation presents a serious concern with the libertarian challenge to the binary search. If, as a matter of substantive law, there is no right to possess cocaine in one's home, it should follow that there is no cognizable privacy interest that society is obligated to treat as legitimate in secreting cocaine within one's home – as long as the government uses binary search methods that do not compromise any legitimate security interest in the privacy of the home.

Consider *Gonzales v. Raich*,[102] in which the Court, echoing its earlier observation in *Jacobsen*, held that Congress can prohibit even the wholly intrastate manufacture and possession of marijuana as an incident of its authority to regulate interstate commerce because these intrastate activities necessarily affect interstate markets:

> One need not have a degree in economics to understand why a nationwide exemption for the vast quantity of marijuana (or other drugs) locally cultivated for personal use (which presumably would include use by friends, neighbors, and family members) may have a substantial impact on the interstate market for this extraordinarily popular substance.[103]

It follows that Congress may legitimately concern itself with the possession and use of controlled substances even when they are secreted within an individual's home: to the extent that limitations on the government's ability to undertake surveillance circumscribe its ability to locate contraband stored within homes, this will inevitably increase the demand, and hence the price, for such contraband, stimulating its production, distribution, use, and attendant social harms. In this respect, the individual is not "sovereign" over the contents of his own residence – not when it comes to contraband. Accordingly, a libertarian conception that circumscribes surveillance premised on identifying the limits of governmental authority has difficulty treating contraband within the home as beyond the legitimate ambit of official scrutiny, at least as long as substantive law permits the government to proscribe even the purely "private" possession of such contraband.

The point is also illustrated by the hypothesized computer worm that could search for images of unlawful child pornography on any computer connected to the Internet. In *Osborne v. Ohio*,[104] the Supreme Court rejected an argument that the criminalization of the private possession of child pornography in one's home infringed a constitutional "right to receive information in the privacy of [one's] home,"[105] concluding instead that the prohibition was an appropriate measure to reduce the economic incentive to exploit children sexually in order to supply the market for child pornography.[106] Thus, in terms

101 Jacobsen, 466 U.S. at 123 (footnote omitted).
102 545 U.S. 1 (2005).
103 *Id.* at 28. To similar effect, *see id.* at 39–41 (Scalia, J., concurring in the judgment).
104 495 U.S. 103 (1990).
105 *Id.* at 108.
106 *Id.* at 108–11.

of child pornography, as a matter of substantive law, the Court has rejected libertarianism on the ground that the mere existence of child pornography creates a tangible harm to children that justifies treating it as contraband.

If *Osborne* is a sound statement of the legitimate sweep of governmental authority, then it becomes difficult to understand why an investigative technique that does no more than enforce the government's substantive entitlement to prohibit even the "private" possession of child pornography can be branded as a somehow illegitimate form of surveillance. After *Osborne*, the possession of child pornography is not properly regarded as "private" as a matter of substantive constitutional law. The government is entitled to make even the entirely "private" possession of such material its affair because of what is regarded as the harmful effect that such material has on third parties outside the privacy of the home. To be sure, a libertarian might argue that there is some cognizable liberty interest in permitting people to indulge their taste for child pornography as long as they do so in the privacy of their homes, but that was precisely the libertarian argument of the dissenters that failed to carry the day in *Osborne*.[107] Thus, once libertarians lose their argument for protection of the purely "private" possession of child pornography as a matter of substantive law, there is little justification to recognize a cognizable liberty interest in secreting child pornography in one's home (or elsewhere).

So it goes with a binary search for any item, the private possession of which is forbidden under substantive law; there is no tenable way to stretch the people's right to be secure from "unreasonable" search and seizure into a right to violate valid laws without fear of official scrutiny.[108] Surveillance that does no more than identify lawbreaking compromises no interest that the government is obligated to treat as legitimately private.

III False Positives and Nonbinary Searches of Private Areas

To the preceding, one might object that binary search techniques represent an unfair case because they assume away any risk of error. Practically, systems of surveillance will scrutinize not only the activities of lawbreakers, but also the activities of the innocent. But this argument elides important complexities that justify surveillance even in the face of the risk that the privacy of the innocent will be compromised.

It is hard to make the case that we can tolerate no risk of error when it comes to surveillance. The Fourth Amendment, for example, authorizes the issuance of warrants authorizing search and seizure on probable cause, even though probable cause requires only a "fair probability,"[109] which is "a standard well short of absolute certainty."[110] If we

107 *Id.* at 139–45 (Brennan, J., dissenting).

108 To be sure, when substantive law recognizes a right to possess contraband privately, even binary search techniques compromise a legitimate privacy interest. Thus, in *Stanley v. Georgia*, 394 U.S. 557 (1969), the Court held that the First Amendment protects the private possession of obscene materials that may not lawfully be distributed in public. *See id.* at 564–68. Yet, this is a narrow exception to the general rule; in *Stanley*, the Court stressed that its holding "in no way infringes on the power of the State or Federal Governments to make possession of other items, such as narcotics, firearms, or stolen goods a crime.… No First Amendment rights are involved in most statutes making mere possession criminal." *Id.* at 568 n.11.

109 *E.g.*, *Saffold Unified Sch. Dist. v. Redding*, 557 U.S. 364, 371 (2009); *United States v. Grubbs*, 547 U.S. 90, 95–96 (2006); United States v. Sokolow, 490 U.S. 1, 7 (1989); *New York v. P.J. Video, Inc.*, 475 U.S. 868, 876–77 (1986); *Illinois v. Gates*, 462 U.S. 213, 238 (1983).

110 *County of Los Angeles v. Rentelle*, 550 U.S. 609, 615 (2007) (per curiam).

assume that a binary search technique provides a sufficiently reliable indication of criminality to amount to probable cause,[111] whatever error rate may inhere in such a binary search technique is one that the Fourth Amendment regards as acceptable. After all, the standard of probable cause itself tolerates a degree of error.[112]

The case for surveillance, however, is not confined to binary -search techniques that reliably generate evidence of probable cause. As we have seen, if all surveillance were forbidden absent a threshold of predication such as probable cause, then the government's ability to obtain sufficient evidence to surmount the threshold would be radically circumscribed. Such a regime would have serious consequences for law enforcement. We have already considered one example of the benefits of surveillance in the absence of individualized predication – surveillance of public places in order to increase the risks associated with lawbreaking in those places, explored in Part I. Not all crimes, however, take place in public. Indeed, it is generally more sophisticated lawbreaking that is most likely to be undetected if surveillance requires individualized predication, or is limited to public places.

Consider the Supreme Court's holding in *United States v. Miller*,[113] that a subpoena calling for the production of a bank depositor's financial records infringed no reasonable expectation of privacy of the depositor because the depositor "can assert neither ownership nor possession" over the records,[114] and because the records contained only information that the depositor had voluntarily disclosed to the bank and that federal law requires to be maintained.[115] *Miller* has been subject to fierce criticism from those who regard it as insufficiently protective of privacy interests.[116] Yet consider a regime in

111 The binary search technique most frequently litigated to date involves the use of narcotics detection dogs, and the Supreme Court unanimously held that if a bona fide organization has certified a dog as reliable, or the dog has recently completed a training program that assessed its proficiency, "a court can presume (subject to any conflicting evidence offered) that the dog's alert provides probable cause to search." *Florida v. Harris*, 133 S. Ct. 1050, 1057 (2013).

112 One could argue pragmatically that binary search techniques are problematic because of the potential for their arbitrary or discriminatory use. *See, e.g.*, Amanda M. Basch, Note, *Sniffing Out the Problems: A Casenote Study of the Analysis and Effects of the Supreme Court's Decision in* Illinois v. Caballes, 25 St. Louis U. Pub. Int. L. Rev. 417, 441–42 (2006); Brett Geiger, Comment, People v. Caballes: *An Analysis of* Caballes, *The History of Sniff Jurisprudence, and Its Future Impact*, 26 N. Ill. L. Rev. 595, 615–16 (2006). If this is a problem, however, it is one for all of Fourth Amendment jurisprudence. The Court has held that the alleged discriminatory motive of an investigator is irrelevant to the reasonableness inquiry under the Fourth Amendment. *See Whren v. United States*, 517 U.S. 806, 813 (1996). Although allegedly discriminatory enforcement decisions are subject to challenge under the Equal Protection Clause, the demanding standard governing such claims requires proof of that a similarly situated individual was treated differently. *See United States v. Armstrong*, 517 U.S. 456, 465–68 (1996). If the risk of arbitrary and discriminatory enforcement is thought to be sufficiently great to require doctrinal innovation, surely the last place to begin is the binary search, which constitutes the investigative technique that is are less invasive likely to compromise the interests of the innocent than techniques that currently receive fairly little constitutional scrutiny.

113 425 U.S. 435 (1976).

114 *Id.* at 440.

115 *Id.* at 442–43.

116 *See, e.g.*, Gerald G. Ashdown, *The Fourth Amendment and the "Legitimate Expectation of Privacy"*, 34 Vand. L. Rev. 1289, 1313–14 (1981); Susan W. Brenner & Leo L. Clark, *Fourth Amendment Protection for Shared Privacy Rights in Stored Transactional Data*, 14 J.L. & Pol'y 211, 240–65 (2006); Susan Freiwald, *First Principles of Communications Privacy*, 2007 Stan. Tech. L. Rev. 3, 38–49 (2007); Stephen E. Henderson, *Beyond the (Current) Fourth Amendment: Protecting Third-Party Information, Third Parties, and the Rest of Us Too*, 34 Pepp. L. Rev. 975, 985–88 (2007); Katz, *supra* note 2, at 570–71.

which the government could not obtain financial records unless it had already acquired substantial evidence of wrongdoing. In such a regime, individuals would have far greater ability to conceal ill-gotten gains from the government. Those engaged in cash businesses, for example, could easily underreport their income without much fear that cash deposits into their bank accounts would be discovered by the government. Those who had profited from investments could decide to omit those profits from their tax returns, again without much fear that bank records disclosing these profits would be obtained by the government. In a regime in which the government is permitted to regulate a wide variety of financial activity, circumscribing the government's ability to undertake surveillance of financial activity will similarly circumscribe the efficacy of any regulatory regime. As the late William Stuntz once observed, a regime that sharply circumscribes the government's ability to scrutinize financial and other regulated activity is difficult to square with emergence of a regulatory state in which the zone of what was thought to be private activity beyond the reach of the regulatory government radically shrank.[117] If government regulation is to be effective, the government must be afforded adequate capacity to undertake surveillance of regulated activity.

Indeed, even *Miller* results in what may be inadequate financial surveillance, since it upholds a regime that permits scrutiny of financial records only after an investigation has begun and a subpoena has issued. *Miller* offers the government no good vehicle for obtaining the kind of information that would enable it to determine where it should target its subpoenas. A good example of the need for some additional form of surveillance of financial transactions is provided by the cash transaction report. In an effort to facilitate identification of those who are endeavoring to deposit the proceeds of illicit transactions in financial institutions, Congress has required that cash transactions involving at least ten thousand dollars be reported to the Internal Revenue Service.[118] Another is the Securities and Exchange Commission's use of risk-based analytics to scrutinize large databases concerning financial transactions in order to identify suspicious transactions that merit closer scrutiny.[119] More generally, data mining can be used to identify individuals likely to be engaged in unlawful activity or transactions likely to reflect unlawful activity.[120] Without surveillance of this character, which calls to the government's attention potential investigative targets, the government has little ability to target investigative resources efficiently and effectively at those who are able to commit crimes in a covert fashion, out of public view.[121]

117 *See* William J. Stuntz, *Privacy's Problem and the Law of Criminal Procedure*, 93 Mich. L. Rev. 1016, 1031–34 (1995).

118 For a helpful discussion of the rationale for and scope of this reporting requirement, *see* Patricia T. Morgan, *Money Laundering, the Internal Revenue Service, and Enforcement Priorities*, 43 Fla. L. Rev. 939, 953–68 (1991).

119 *See* Rachel E. Barkow, *The New Policing of Business Crime*, 37 Seattle U.L. Rev. 435, 451–52 (2014).

120 For a helpful discussion of data mining techniques and their application to law enforcement, see, for example, Liane Colonna, *A Taxonomy and Classification of Data Mining*, 16 SMU Sci. & Tech. L. Rev. 309, 358–66 (2013).

121 This point discloses the inadequacy of efforts to permit investigators to obtain otherwise private information absent individualized suspicion of wrongdoing only when a completed crime comes to the attention of law enforcement, at which point information can be gathered if directed toward identification of the offender. For a proposal along these lines, *see* Jane Bambauer, *Other People's Papers*, 94 Tex. L. Rev. 205, 233–38 (2015). This approach offers investigators no tools to determine when a covert crime has been committed that might not otherwise have come to their attention, such as tax evasion or money laundering.

A regime that sharply circumscribes official surveillance of activity not in public view has dramatic implications not only for the efficacy of regulation, but for equity in the criminal justice system. Although racial minorities are incarcerated for drug-related offenses at disproportionate rates relative to their representation in the population, this may well reflect the fact that they are disproportionately found at inner-city open-air drug markets that are particularly vulnerable to police surveillance and enforcement.[122] To the extent that the law increases the difficulty of undertaking surveillance of nonpublic activities, law enforcement will focus its resources on activities occurring in public, which are likely to involve offenses committed by relatively poor and disadvantaged populations who lack the resources to commit crimes in sophisticated and covert fashion.[123]

Conclusion

Liberty and order are often thought to be in considerable tension, and this inquiry into surveillance reflects that tension. History suggests that some measure of official surveillance is essential to maintain order in a complex society; this explains the failure of the framing era regime in which surveillance was held to a minimum, as well as the failure of reactive policing. In a society that permits regulation of activities conducted out of public view, moreover, some measure of surveillance is essential if regulation becomes ineffective whenever violators acquire the means to conduct regulated activities away from the view of others.

When surveillance is circumscribed, liberty is enhanced. Liberty, however, can be used for good or ill. When surveillance is circumscribed, the risks of engaging in unlawful behavior decline, and we can expect the incidence of crime to increase. Beyond that, when surveillance is limited to activities not regarded as private, such as activities occurring in public places, then those who have the resources and sophistication to commit crimes in a particularly covert fashion will run the least risk of detection. This final point suggests that not only the values of liberty and order are implicated by decisions about the extent to which official surveillance is to be permitted: equality is implicated as well. A criminal justice system that is able to detect lawbreaking by the rich and poor alike is a system that requires substantial leeway to engage in surveillance.

122 *See, e.g.*, Michael Tonry, Malign Neglect: Race, Crime, and Punishment in America, 105–16 (1995); R. Richard Banks, *Beyond Profiling: Race, Policing, and the Drug War*, 56 Stan. L. Rev. 571, 583–84 (2006); William J. Stuntz, *Race, Class, and Drugs*, 98 Colum. L. Rev. 1795, 1819–24 (1998).

123 *Cf.* William J. Stuntz, *The Distribution of Fourth Amendment Privacy*, 67 Geo. Wash. L. Rev. 1265 (1999) (arguing that greater protection for privacy is likely to encourage criminal enforcement targeting the poor).

14 "Going Dark": Encryption, Privacy, Liberty, and Security in the "Golden Age of Surveillance"

Geoffrey S. Corn* & Dru Brenner-Beck**

This chapter explores the complexities of the current "going dark" debate surrounding encryption, focusing on both constitutional and other public policy implications. Encryption offers citizens a way to remain confident that their private data and communications are secure from unauthorized, outside intrusions. However, the type of encryption associated with the notion of "going dark" also has a cost. Encryption has substantially complicated, and sometimes entirely prevented, government and law enforcement access to information, even when authorized by law. Central to the going dark debate is a clash of interests – the advancement of individual liberty, privacy, and security on one side and the preservation of government interests related to public and national security on the other. If and how Fourth Amendment considerations should influence the regulation of this technology is Section I of this chapter. This section ultimately concludes that although the Fourth Amendment cannot be read as imposing a prohibition against going dark encryption, such restrictions would be consistent with the amendment, and may be perceived as advancing a balance between privacy and public security – a balance some believe is consistent with the Fourth Amendment. This leads one of the coauthors to advocate legal restrictions on going dark encryption that ensure reasonable and lawful government access to private data. The chapter then considers numerous technical and practical considerations that should inform any public policy reaction to what the government asserts is a major source of societal risk. This evaluation leads to the conclusion by the other coauthor that robust user-controlled encryption is the best solution to the host of individual and national security risks that exist in the modern digital age, benefits that far outweigh those reaped from mandatory governmental access. For this coauthor, the marketplace of technological innovation should be left unfettered

* Professor of Law, South Texas College of Law; Lieutenant Colonel (Retired), U.S. Army Judge Advocate General's Corps. Prior to joining the faculty at South Texas, Professor Corn served in a variety of military assignments, including as the Army's Senior Law of War Advisor, Supervisory Defense Counsel for the Western United States, Chief of International Law for U.S. Army Europe, and Tactical Intelligence Officer in Panama. We both thank the outstanding support provided to us by Jennifer Whittington, Houston Texas College of Law Class of 2016, and Emily Arnold, Houston College of Law Class of 2017.

** Lieutenant Colonel (Retired), U.S. Army Judge Advocate General's Corps. Formerly served as Deputy Legal Counsel, U.S. Army's Office of the Inspector General and Chief, Military and Civil Law, U.S. Army Europe. Prior to serving as a JAG, Colonel Brenner-Beck was a tactical and signals intelligence officer. After retirement, she served as a law clerk to the Honorable Carlos F. Lucero, U.S. Court of Appeals for the Tenth Circuit. Currently, she is a legal consultant on international law matters, is Of Counsel at EosEdge Legal, a Cyber Law Firm, and serves as the President of the National Institute of Military Justice.

by government efforts to restrict such capabilities. Thus, the chapter illustrates a range of legal and policy questions and considerations central to this ongoing debate.

> I don't want a back door ... I want a front door. And I want the front door to have multiple locks. Big locks.
>
> – Adm. Michael S. Rogers, director of the NSA[1]

> Experience should teach us to be most on our guard to protect liberty when the Government's purposes are beneficent. Men born to freedom are naturally alert to repel invasion of their liberty by evil-minded rulers. The greatest dangers to liberty lurk in insidious encroachment by men of zeal, well-meaning but without understanding.
>
> – Louis Brandeis, justice of the U.S. Supreme Court[2]

Introduction

Although encryption has existed for millennia, its modern incarnation arose within the military and intelligence communities during World War II and the ensuing Cold War.[3] Originally the purview of national security agencies, the rapid development of global telecommunications, personal computing, the Internet, and smart phones in the past thirty years has pushed encryption into the daily lives of millions of people around the world, changing the nature of encryption itself. No longer confined to high-tech communications systems controlled exclusively by government agencies, today encryption programs, applications, and services are ubiquitous and are embedded within services and devices available for both commercial and individual use.

Unlike earlier embedded encryption provided by a telecommunications company, newer forms of encryption are not susceptible to governmental access because the encryption keys are solely controlled by the user, and not retained by cell phone manufacturers, distributors, or service providers. As a result of this technological development, governmental access to digital communications information pursuant to lawful authorization is made more difficult and may become impossible – a phenomenon described as "going dark."[4] In response to this development, Federal Bureau of Investigation (FBI) Director James B. Comey, representing the law enforcement community, proposed a legislative mandate requiring continued government access to encrypted data and communications through the use of back/front doors into the encryption system.[5] In response,

1 Ellen Nakashima & Barton Gellman, *As Encryption Spreads, U.S. Grapples with Clash between Privacy, Security*, Wash. Post (Apr. 10, 2015), https://www.washingtonpost.com/world/national-security/as-encryption-spreads-us-worries-about-access-to-data-for-investigations/2015/04/10/7c1c7518-d401-11e4-a62f-ee745911a4ff_story.html (discussing the different interests in the debate over data privacy).

2 *Olmstead v. United States*, 277 U.S. 438, 479 (1928) (Brandeis, J., dissenting).

3 Encryption is the process of encoding data so that only those with authorized access can read it. A basic tenet of cryptography is that the security of the crypto system should rely upon the secrecy of the key and not the secrecy of the system's encryption algorithm. *See* Susan Landau, Surveillance or Security?: The Risks Posed by New Wiretapping Technologies 43 (2013).

4 *See* Brian Naylor, *Apple Says iOS Encryption Protects Privacy; FBI Raises Crime Fears*, Nat'l Pub. Radio (Oct. 8, 2014, 5:17 PM), http://www.npr.org/blogs/alltechconsidered/2014/10/08/354598527/apple-says-ios-encryption-protects-privacy-fbi-raises-crime-fears (discussing concerns about Apple's policy on data encryption).

5 *See* James B. Comey, Dir., FBI, Remarks at Brookings Institution: Going Dark: Are Technology, Privacy, and Public Safety on a Collision Course? (Oct. 16, 2014), http://www.fbi.gov/news/speeches/going-dark-are-technology-privacy-and-public-safety-on-a-collision-course (explaining the challenge of maintaining

proponents of this encryption evolution question whether such a mandate is even technologically feasible, and if it is, whether it comports with the Fourth Amendment's protection of the people's "right to be secure in their persons, houses, papers, and effects." In response, proponents for legislatively mandated front door access to encrypted data respond that such a law would be "reasonable" and consistent with maintaining the equilibrium between public security and privacy that has long existed under the Fourth Amendment. They argue that although the Fourth Amendment may not mandate such access, it certainly does not prohibit Congress from requiring it.

As recent events indicate, user-controlled encryption implicates vital legal and public policy questions, among these whether encryption goes too far in favoring privacy and individual security over public security, and if so, whether it should be legislatively restricted or prohibited. Is user-controlled encryption really a debate over the question of security versus security – that of the individual versus that of the nation as a whole; and is "national security" actually dependent on the security of "the people" themselves? Clearly encryption promotes individual security and privacy and the digital trust upon which products and markets depend, but at what cost?[6] Although it is difficult to quantify the individual privacy and security interests at stake, there can be no doubt that the widespread adoption of end point and end-to end (E2E) encryption will protect increasingly voluminous amounts of private communications and data; and because of this, encryption simultaneously represents a real and significant impediment to lawful government access to potentially vital information necessary to protect the nation as a whole. Building access to user-generated keys for the government – by requiring a second decryption master key, a secret trapdoor, or access to user-generated keys – may facilitate government surveillance efforts, but it also exacts a price, one that many consider to be substantial. No matter what mechanisms are put in place to protect these encryption keys, or to limit the government's access to them, the very existence of another "door" or "special government magic key" increases the risk of unauthorized or illicit access.[7] Indeed, the entire rationale for embedding mobile devices with end point encryption (and E2EE) is based on consumer demand for maximum data and privacy protection

national security because of emerging technologies). "The FBI has a sworn duty to keep every American safe from crime and terrorism, and technology has become the tool of choice for some very dangerous people." *Id.* The terms "front door," "backdoor," "exceptional access," and "mandated access" all refer to the concept of a building weaknesses into the encryption system, through the creation of a key escrow system, trusted third party encryption, or deliberate engineering of government access to encryption keys, all of which create inherent insecurities in the system. Those using the term "front doors" argue that the vulnerability would be accessed only with proper authorization in a transparent system authorized by law. Regardless of the term used, the creation of third party access for the government creates weaknesses that can be exploited by others. *See id.*; Harold Abelson et al., *Keys Under the Doormat: Mandating Insecurity by Requiring Government Access to All Data and Communications*, 1 J. CyberSecurity 69, 70 (2015); The Chertoff Group, The Ground Truth about Encryption and the Consequences of Extraordinary Access 5–6 (2016), https://chertoffgroup.com/cms-assets/documents/238024–282765.groundtruth.pdf; Jeffrey Vagle & Matt Blaze, *Security "Front Doors" vs. "Back Doors": A Distinction without a Difference*, Just Security (Oct. 17, 2014), https://www.justsecurity.org/16503/security-front-doors-vs-back-doors-distinction-difference/.

6 *See* Comey, *supra* note 5 (explaining that the increased use of data encryption has resulted in increased crime); Andy Greenberg, *Over 80 Percent of Dark-Web Visits Relate to Pedophilia, Study Finds*, Wired (Dec. 30, 2014), http://www.wired.com/2014/12/80-percent-dark-web-visits-relate-pedophilia-study-finds/ (explaining that a great deal of anonymous Internet traffic is directed at pedophilia-related Web sites).

7 *See* The Chertoff Group, *supra* note 5, at 5–6; Vagle & Blaze, *supra* note 5.

and security. Furthermore, largely in response to exposure of classified government surveillance programs that require communications providers to cooperate with the government, E2EE and end point encryption is seen as an important check on the risk of abusive government surveillance tactics that erode individual privacy and liberty.[8]

The ongoing debate over encryption is indicative of broader upheavals in legal and public policy as technology unravels previous consensus over the appropriate measures necessary to preserve and balance individual security, privacy, and freedom and public security (including both law enforcement and national security interests). Prior consensus unravels as questions arise as to whether existing checks and balances function in light of new technological realities. In the midst of the turmoil produced by this intersection of "old" law and "new" technology, existing legal rules provide the foundation upon which to construct policy responses to these challenges – a foundation that, it is hoped, ensures advancement of individual liberty, privacy, and security interests and governmental interests related to public and national security.[9]

In order to explore the legal and policy considerations central to this ongoing debate, this chapter will first consider whether statutorily mandated front door access to encrypted data runs afoul of the Fourth Amendment, concluding that such legislation would not violate the Fourth Amendment and may in some ways be consistent with the balance between privacy and public security reflected in much of the contemporary Fourth Amendment jurisprudence. Next, this chapter will consider a range of legal and policy considerations implicated by any such legislative effort. Ultimately, the chapter's authors reach divergent conclusions on the wisdom of imposing a statutory mandate that ensures government access to encryption keys when lawfully authorized. For one author, such a mandate strikes a necessary and logical balance between the competing privacy and security interests at stake, a balance consistent with the notion of reasonableness central to Fourth Amendment jurisprudence. For the other author, the policy considerations involved in such a mandate indicate that, on balance, the benefits of allowing user-controlled encryption with no front/back door access available for governmental exploitation far outweigh the very real costs associated with "going dark." For this author, because of its dramatic effects on the people's right to be secure, legislation mandating government access would ultimately be "unreasonable" under the Fourth Amendment.

I The Technology and the Resulting Debate

Prior to the 1970s, encryption required the separate exchange of a private key between two parties (private key encryption), which allowed the use of an algorithm with this shared key both to decrypt and to encrypt messages (symmetric encryption).[10] This

[8] *See* Joshua Kopstein, *The FBI Wants Apple to Make a Defective Phone*, Al Jazeera (Oct. 24, 2014), http://america.aljazeera.com/opinions/2014/10/fbi-surveillanceappleprivacyencryption.html (discussing the wishes of law enforcement agencies for companies to sell phones with less protected data).

[9] We will use the term "collective security," "public security," or "national security" to reflect the interests of traditional national security and intelligence agencies and law enforcement.

[10] The Chertoff Group, *supra* note 5, at 3 (private key encryption is based on encryption keys shared privately by two parties, involving three separate components – the "plaintext," the "algorithm," and the "key." The algorithm is the general system of encryption or the rules for transforming a plaintext into a cipher text or encrypted text. The key is the specific set of instructions used to apply the algorithm to the message. With private key encryption only someone with both the algorithm and the key can decrypt the cipher text, and it is symmetric, meaning the same key is used both to encrypt and to decrypt messages).

method required the parties to know each other and securely exchange encryption keys and algorithms prior to any communication. With private key encryption the information was only as secure as the private key that was exchanged. The development of public key encryption in 1976 dramatically changed the field. In "public key encryption," the system depends on a pair of interrelated encryption keys, one public and one private, that are developed from the multiplication of two "impossibly large prime numbers" and complex one-way mathematical functions.[11] The resulting public key is widely disseminated and can be used to encrypt messages sent to the holder of the associated private key, who then uses the private key to decrypt the message (asymmetric encryption).[12] Thus the ability to associate a public and private key allowed individuals who did not know each other or who did not have an existing secure communication channel to encrypt information on the basis of publication of a public key. Because "properly implemented public key encryption is essentially undecryptable" with current technology, the question of who holds the decryption key and governmental access to it are at the forefront of the new (and the old) encryption debates.[13]

Currently, if the encryption of data is carried out by a cloud service provider, such as has been done by Google or Dropbox, for example, the data is encrypted by the service provider when uploaded to cloud storage and the encryption key is retained by the service provider. Access via user identification and password allows seamless and quick decryption by the user, but the encryption key remains with the service provider, not the user. Alternatively, with end point encryption, the user holds the encryption key and encrypts data with a program on his computer or smartphone. As a result, the data is encrypted before it is stored on a computer or phone, sent via phone or Internet, or uploaded to the cloud, and can only be decrypted if the key is provided by the user. In 2010, Google changed the default to be end point encryption for its Gmail service, and Apple did the same for its iPhones in 2014.[14] Government access to these user-held encryption keys

[11] One-way mathematical functions are those that are much more difficult to compute in one direction than in the reverse. An analogy is the ease of mixing two colors together to obtain a third color, compared to the difficulty of breaking down the resulting color into the two original colors. In public key encryption, the results of the multiplication of two impossibly large prime numbers are manipulated using modular arithmetic, with the result published as a public key. Because of the difficulty of the one-way mathematical function only the holder of the related private key can decrypt a message encrypted with the related public key. *See* The Chertoff Group, *supra* note 5, at 5; Art of the Problem, *Public Key Cryptography – Diffie-Hellman Key Exchange (full version)*, YouTube (July 30, 2012), https://www.youtube.com/watch?v=YEBfamv-_do&feature=youtu.be (explaining public key encryption using color analogies); Landau, *supra* note 3, at 46; Stephen Levy, Crypto: How the Code Rebels Beat the Government Saving Privacy in the Digital Age 66–106 (2002).

[12] The Chertoff Group, *supra* note 5, at 4. The development of the RSA cryptographic algorithm, a public key technology at the core of many commercial encryption systems, also allowed the authentication of users through the use of digital signatures created by public key systems by reversing this process in which the sender encrypts the message with his private key, and the recipient decrypts it with the public key associated with the person purporting to send the message.

[13] *Id.* Similar debates, called the crypto wars, during the 1990s between government agencies that wanted to limit nongovernmental use of strong encryption technology and technology companies desiring to sell and export strong encryption programs were ultimately resolved in favor of encryption. *See* Levy, *supra* note 11, at 187–260.

[14] Google changed the defaults for its email in January 2010, and Apple in 2014. *See* Landau, *supra* note 3, at 47; Cyrus Farivar, *Apple Expands Data Encryption under Ios8, Making Handover to Cops Moot*, Ars Technica (Sept. 18, 2014), http://arstechnica.com/apple/2014/09/apple-expands-data-encryption-under-ios-8-making-handover-to-cops-moot/; Alex Hern, *Apple Defies FBI and Offers Encryption by Default on*

is the focus of the recent going dark debate.[15] Finally, end-to-end encryption (E2EE) encrypts messages that are in transit, such as done by Skype, PGP (Pretty Good Privacy), ProtonMail, or messaging applications such as Telegram, Signal, WhatsApp, or Google's End-to-End Allo and Duo applications, with the encryption keys similarly held only by the end point user's computers or smart phones.[16] Although they were originally seen as difficult to use, businesses have focused on providing seamless E2EE email and messaging, and ProtonMail announced in March 2016 that it had applications available for iOS and Android,[17] making its use likely to expand. Because encryption keys under E2EE systems are also held by the user, they raise the same concerns over the loss of legitimate government access as end point encryption. This chapter will use the term "encryption" to refer to encryption with user-controlled keys, as in end point and E2E encryption systems, and the term "data" to refer to both data and the communications themselves.

Embedding mobile devices and computers with encryption to provide data protection and security is not controversial. Few would dispute the benefits of allowing consumers to avail themselves of technological features enabling them essentially to lock the door to the data stored on their mobile devices and computers and protect the confidentiality and security of their digital communications, particularly given the increasing incidence of computer crime and identity theft.[18] Increasingly, mobile device manufacturers and providers embed devices with end point encryption and E2EE in order to provide consumers with strong security and an impenetrable zone of privacy. Unlike earlier encryption capability embedded in cell phones or supplied by service providers, this type of encryption is not susceptible to "front door" access through the use of encryption keys retained by the cell phone manufacturer and distributor or service provider and available to government agents pursuant to lawful authorization.[19]

This trend is accelerating, and oftentimes these services and products are provided by companies that are not controlled by U.S. law.[20] The uncontroversial effort to protect

New Operating System, The Guardian (Oct. 17, 2014), https://www.theguardian.com/technology/2014/oct/17/apple-defies-fbi-encryption-mac-osx.

15 These settings have been available on iPhones for years, but the change to making them default settings has increased their use, raising the concern of law enforcement and national security agencies.

16 *See* Andy Greenberg, *Hacker Lexicon What Is End-To-End Encryption?* Wired (Nov. 25, 2014), https://www.wired.com/2014/11/hacker-lexicon-end-to-end-encryption/ ("Only the endpoint computers hold the cryptographic keys, and the company's server acts as an illiterate messenger, passing along messages that it can't itself decipher"). Google is also implementing E2EE with its Allo and Duo (message and video calling applications). Allo will allow encrypted communications in its incognito mode by using the Signal encryption system, although encryption is not yet the default. Duo will also use E2EE for its video calls. This trend follows the addition of E2EE offered by Facebook's FaceTime, and Apple's iMessage through use of WhatsApp. Viber also provides E2EE encryption for its messaging services. *See* Andy Greenberg, *With Allo and Duo, Google Finally Encrypts Conversations End-to-End*, Wired (May 18, 2016), https://www.wired.com/2016/05/allo-duo-google-finally-encrypts-conversations-end-end/; Brian Barnett, *700 Million People Just Got Encryption that Congress Cannot Touch*, Wired (Apr. 20, 2016), https://www.wired.com/2016/04/viber-encrytpion/.

17 *Announcement ProtonMail Has Launched Worldwide!*, ProtonMail Blog (Mar. 17, 2016), https://protonmail.com/blog/protonmail-launch-worldwide/. ProtonMail also enables the creation of self-destructing emails and as a Swiss company is protected by that country's privacy laws.

18 Alex Hern, *Mark Zuckerberg Hacked on Twitter and Pinterest*, The Guardian (June 6, 2016), https://www.theguardian.com/technology/2016/jun/06/mark-zuckerberg-hacked-on-twitter-and-pinterest.

19 *See* Naylor, *supra* note 4 (discussing concerns about Apple's policy on data encryption).

20 A 2016 survey of encryption products available worldwide identified 865 hardware or software products incorporating encryption from fifty-five different countries, including 546 encryption products from outside the United States. *See* Bruce Schneier et al., A Worldwide Survey of Encryption Products (version

data and communications becomes controversial, however, when encryption renders digital data and communications inaccessible to court-ordered government surveillance efforts, either because the encryption keys are held only by the user or because the provider is not responsive to U.S. legal service.

Government officials have decried the type of total encryption enabled by user-controlled encryption keys – a problem characterized as going dark – for several decades.[21] However, the late-2015 high-profile confrontation between Apple and the U.S. government over access to data stored on an iPhone used by the San Bernardino killer[22] moved the debate over this issue again to the forefront of public policy and national security discourse. Other nations are also confronting these issues.[23] User-controlled encryption provides citizens with a high degree of confidence that the massive amount of private data capable of being retained on a mobile device or computer will be beyond the reach of unauthorized intrusions, and that communications will be private and secure. However, this type of encryption entails a cost: preventing – or at least substantially complicating – government surveillance or access to information even when authorized by law.

As the San Bernardino debate highlights, this unqualified encryption capability is increasingly viewed by democratic governments as a dangerous evolution of publicly

1.0 2016), https://www.schneier.com/academic/paperfiles/worldwide-survey-of-encryption-products.pdf. These products will therefore be available regardless of U.S. societal/legal decisions. Because of these technical realities, policy makers will have to evaluate whether mandated government access is functionally achievable, particularly for those technologically astute foes who take care to hide their criminal or malicious activities using robust end point or E2EE encryption. Nonetheless, U.S. decisions will influence other nations.

21 The debate over the availability of public crypto actually extends back to the mid-1970s and 1980s with the advent of public cryptology and the beginnings of the commercialization of encryption, followed by the crypto-wars of the 1990s. These earlier crypto-wars resulted in a national policy determination that "on balance, the advantages of more widespread use of cryptography outweigh the disadvantages." *See* Whitfield Diffie & Susan Landau, Privacy on the Line, The Politics of Wiretapping and Encryption 218–48, 243 (MIT Press 2d ed. 2010) (quoting National Research Council Report, Cryptography's Role in Securing the Information Society (1996)); *see also* Levy, *supra* note 11 (an excellent discussion of the history of the development of public cryptography and government opposition to it). The 1990s "crypto-wars" involved the attempt by U.S. government agencies to control the export of strong commercial encryption and the resistance of commercial developers to that effort. *See supra* note 13.

22 Because the San Bernardino shooter had disabled the automatic cloud backup on his iPhone, the alternative of accessing cloud backup was not available.

23 Opposition to a proposed Swiss law, the Nachrichtendienstgesetz (NDG)/Loi sur le rensiegnement (LRens), by privacy oriented groups in Switzerland resulted in a referendum effort to overturn the law. The vote was to take place in September 2016. *See* Andy Yen, *Impact of Swiss Surveillance Laws on Secure Email*, ProtonMail (Dec. 16, 2015), https://protonmail.com/blog/swiss-surveillance-law/; EDRI, *Swiss Civil Society Struggles Against Digital Surveillance Laws*, EDRi (June 15, 2016), https://edri.org/swiss-civil-society-struggles-digital-surveillance-laws/. Agence France-Presse, *Switzerland votes in favor of greater surveillance*, The Guardian, (Sep. 25, 2016), https://www.theguardian.com/world/2016/sep/25/switzerland-votes-in-favour-of-greater-surveillance. (Over 65% of Swiss voters vote to approve government surveillance law; highlighting a shift in public attitudes after recent terrorist attacks in Brussels, Nice, and Paris.) *See also* Tom Whitehead, *Internet Firms to Be Banned from Offering Unbreakable Encryption Under New Laws*, Telegraph (Nov. 2, 2015), http://www.telegraph.co.uk/news/uknews/terrorism-in-the-uk/11970391/Internet-firms-to-be-banned-from-offering-out-of-reach-communications-under-new-laws.html (UK bills to prohibit certain encryption); Amar Toor, *France's Sweeping Surveillance Law Goes into Effect*, The Verge (July 25, 2015), http://www.theverge.com/2015/7/24/9030851/france-surveillance-law-charlie-hebdo-constitutional-court (France); Matt Zuvela, *German Court: Anti-Terror Laws Partially Unconstitutional*, Deutsche Welle (Apr. 20, 2016), http://www.dw.com/en/german-court-anti-terror-laws-partially-unconstitutional/a-19200199 (Germany).

available technology.[24] Many in government view the pervasive use of cell devices and electronic communications (to include computers networked to the Internet) equipped with this type of encryption as creating an unacceptable obstacle to the lawful searches and surveillance necessary to protect the public from criminal and national security threats.[25] But even within governments, there seems to be growing disagreement on the cost/benefit equation related to public encryption. For example, in early 2016, National Security Agency (NSA) Director Admiral Michael Rogers stated that "encryption is foundational to the future," recommending that the debate focus instead on how to meet the needs of both security and privacy.[26] Two former NSA directors, Michael Hayden and John Michael ("Mike") McConnell, have also supported end-to-end encryption with no "backdoors" as "good for America."[27]

This encryption debate –over the legality and legitimacy of enabling consumers to go dark and the propriety of prohibiting or restricting access to such technological capabilities – exemplifies and exacerbates the frictions existing among individual liberty, privacy, and security, and collective national security and law enforcement, frictions that are quite complex.[28] Indeed, the public and judicial dispute between Apple and the government over access to the San Bernardino iPhone captured national and international attention for good reason. Arrayed on both sides of this dispute were forces committed to the deeply held values implicated by a government demand for access to private data and communications and a manufacturer's refusal to facilitate that access. On one side were those committed to the essential role encryption plays in digital security, a function

24 *See* The President's News Conference with Prime Minister David Cameron of the United Kingdom, 2015 Daily Comp. Pres. Doc. 1 (Jan. 16, 2015) (discussing the potential dangers of data encryption); Comey, *supra* note 5 ("The FBI has a sworn duty to keep every American safe from crime and terrorism, and technology has become the tool of choice for some very dangerous people").

25 *See* Comey, *supra* note 5 (noting the ability to evade law enforcement as data encryption becomes more common).

26 *See* Jenna McLaughlin, *NSA Chief Stakes Out Pro-Encryption Position, in Contrast to the FBI*, The Intercept (Jan. 21, 2016), https://theintercept.com/2016/01/21/nsa-chief-stakes-out-pro-encryption-position-in-contrast-to-fbi/.

27 *Id.* Some argue that there is no such thing as total or complete encryption; that the going dark characterization is a government exaggeration. Skeptics point to the San Bernardino outcome as evidence of the invalidity of the entire notion of "complete" or "absolute" encryption; that the government will always find "backdoor" access to encrypted data. However, it is invalid to ignore the reality that even when "backdoor" penetration of encrypted data is used as a work-around to user-controlled encryption, "front door" systemic access would be more efficient and effective for law enforcement. Certainly, this is the FBI's view. Long before the San Bernardino disagreement between Apple and the U.S. government, FBI Director James Comey raised concerns about the problem of going dark. In his October 16, 2014, speech at the Brookings Institute, he challenged both the wisdom and the legal validity of end point encryption, anticipating the rapid expansion of encryption technologies that are now commonly available within the United States and globally, in both the public and private sectors. *See supra* note 5.

28 *See Global Encryption Software Market 2019–Incidence of Data Breaches Drives Growth*, PR Newswire (Mar. 18, 2015), http://www.prnewswire.com/news-releases/global-encryption-software-market-2019–incidence-of-data-breaches-drives-growth-296759501.html (explaining that recent data breaches have motivated organizations to encrypt data). Nonetheless, the inability of the government to access certain encrypted information is not new; prosecutors and investigators in the first World Trade Center bombing were not able to break certain encrypted files on Ramzi Yousef's computer, and the original government attempts to mandate the Clipper chip were an attempt to maintain governmental access in the face of burgeoning commercial strong encryption. *See* Simon Reeve, The New Jackals: Ramzi Yousef, Osama Bin Laden and the Future of Terrorism 248 (1999) (citing 25 July 1996 testimony of FBI Director Louis Freeh to Senate Commerce Committee).

promoted by the government itself.[29] On the other are those legitimately concerned for public safety and national security, who fear encryption systems that create zones of information and communications immune from legitimate government access.

II Competing Interests and the Fourth Amendment

The myriad technological and public policy considerations associated with the going dark debate are of little legal significance if the Fourth Amendment's protection against unreasonable searches and seizures prohibits restricting individual access to and use of this technology. This would place legislative or other efforts to limit or restrict user-controlled and E2E encryption beyond the reach of government. It is therefore important to consider, at the outset, the relationship between this technology and established Fourth Amendment principles.

In many ways, the going dark debate exemplifies the inherent friction between protection of individual privacy, security, and liberty and efficient government investigatory efforts that protect national security and law enforcement interests – efforts that must accord with the requirements of the Fourth Amendment. This friction is inherent in the reasonableness requirement at the amendment's core. Contemporary Fourth Amendment jurisprudence consistently reinforces the importance of protecting the citizen from *unreasonable* searches and seizures, creating not an absolute right to be secure, but one qualified by reasonable governmental intrusions. Thus, this jurisprudence routinely reflects the Court's effort to strike a rational balance between the people's interest in the security of their persons, houses, papers, and effects and the government's interest in efficient law enforcement, so long as those efforts are assessed as *reasonable*. In the context of the encryption debate, this leads to an important but unresolved question: is the notion of a zone of privacy and security effectively immune from government surveillance, even when legally authorized, consistent with the Fourth Amendment? Or is that notion inconsistent with the equilibrium between privacy and security to which this jurisprudence seems to point?[30]

There is nothing remarkable in the notion that the government may, so long as it complies with the Fourth Amendment, penetrate any zone of privacy or security. This is merely a reflection of the contemporary notion of Fourth Amendment reasonableness, which is not that privacy must be protected against all government intrusion, but that all government intrusions into interests protected by the Fourth Amendment must be reasonable. Indeed, reasonableness is the fulcrum for assessing the equilibrium between privacy and security, characterized by the Supreme Court as the "touchstone" of the

29 *See* Kara Swisher, *Obama: The Re/Code Interview*, Re/Code (Feb. 15, 2015), http://recode.net/2015/02/15/white-house-red-chair-obama-meets-swisher/ ("There's no scenario in which we don't want really strong encryption"); Mindy McDowell, *Security Tip (ST04-019): Understanding Encryption*, US-CERT (Jan. 13, 2010, rev. Oct. 1, 2016), https://www.us-cert.gov/ncas/tips/ST04-019 (explaining how data encryption works); *see also, e.g.*, Darrell Foxworth, *Smartphone Users Should Be Aware of Malware Targeting Mobile Devices and the Safety Measures to Help Avoid Compromise*, Fed. Bureau of Investigation (Oct. 22, 2012), http://www.fbi.gov/sandiego/press-releases/2012/smartphone-users-should-be-aware-of-malware-targeting-mobile-devices-and-the-safety-measures-to-help-avoid-compromise (providing advice on how to protect your smartphone from hackers).

30 *See* Orin Kerr, *An Equilibrium-Adjustment Theory of the Fourth Amendment*, 125 Harv. L. Rev. 476 (2011).

Fourth Amendment. Evolving encryption technology impacts this equilibrium because it may (and in the view of some already has) frustrate, or perhaps even prevent, the government from effectively utilizing legally authorized surveillance to reach encrypted data. If it is true that encryption technology impacts the balance between individual privacy and security and public security, does it go too far in favor the former interest? This certainly seems to be the view of a number of high-level government officials in the United States and abroad. Of course, this leads to other complicated but vital questions: May the government constitutionally restrict development and/or use of such encryption? And should it?

The Fourth Amendment and its associated jurisprudence will almost certainly not provide a dispositive answer to this question. Instead, as will be explained later in this chapter, addressing this question implicates a range of interests necessitating the type of policy assessment best suited to the legislative process. Indeed, a central premise of this chapter is that this question must not be left to the courts to address on an ad hoc basis, with hyperbolic dramas such as the Apple litigation playing out in courts all across the country. Nonetheless, it is almost equally certain that Fourth Amendment considerations will and should influence any effort to address encryption through the legislative process. Legislative attempts to reconcile individual liberty, security, and privacy with the societal interests in law enforcement and national security will necessarily implicate reasonableness balancing, a core precept of the Fourth Amendment.

A *The Central Role of Balance in Fourth Amendment Application*

The Supreme Court has consistently emphasized that when assessing the reasonableness of government surveillance, it is necessary to acknowledge the government's interest in effective law enforcement.[31] For example, in *Schneckloth v. Bustamonte*,[32] the Court addressed the validity of consent obtained without providing notice of a right to refuse the officer's request.[33] The Court endorsed a totality of the circumstances test for assessing the validity of consent, rejecting the Ninth Circuit's more restrictive ruling that consent is invalid unless an individual is notified of his right to decline the consent request.[34] The Court's opinion emphasized the importance of consent, not in abstract terms, but in direct connection with the function of law enforcement – solving crimes:

> In situations where the police have some evidence of illicit activity, but lack probable cause to arrest or search, a search authorized by a valid consent may be the only means of obtaining important and reliable evidence.... A search pursuant to consent may result in considerably less inconvenience for the subject of the search, and, properly conducted, is a constitutionally permissible and wholly legitimate aspect of effective police activity.[35]

31 *See Schneckloth v. Bustamonte*, 412 U.S. 218, 225 (1973) (discussing the need for police questioning); *see also Smith v. Maryland*, 442 U.S. 735, 735 (1979) (noting that the expectation of privacy must be weighed against the government action).

32 412 U.S. 218 (1973).

33 *See id.* at 223 (discussing voluntariness in responding to questions by law enforcement).

34 *See id.* at 225–30 (noting that officers are not required to inform individuals of the right to decline consent).

35 *Id.* at 227–28.

Later in the opinion the Court noted that "the community has a real interest in encouraging consent, for the resulting search may yield necessary evidence for the solution and prosecution of crime."[36] Of course, consent is not implicated by the question raised in this chapter – whether user-controlled end point/E2E encryption should be prohibited. Nonetheless, the Court's recognition of the important societal interest in facilitating effective investigations that is served by its more liberal rule on the requirements for constitutionally valid consent is also applicable to the debate on the legality and wisdom of end point or E2EE encryption.

Perhaps most importantly, *Bustamante* reflects the principle that overly restrictive standards that frustrate legitimate law enforcement surveillance efforts conflict with the Fourth Amendment's core objective: balance between the competing interests of individual liberty and public security. As the Court noted when it explained its preference for an assessment of consent based on the totality of the circumstances:

> The problem of reconciling the recognized legitimacy of consent searches with the requirement that they be free from any aspect of official coercion cannot be resolved by any infallible touchstone. To approve such searches without the most careful scrutiny would sanction the possibility of official coercion; to place artificial restrictions upon such searches would jeopardize their basic validity. Just as was true with confessions, the requirement of a "voluntary" consent reflects a ***fair accommodation*** of the constitutional requirements involved.[37]

Using encryption to prevent government surveillance of data is, of course, the antithesis of consent, as it is an effort to prevent any access, to include governmental access, to private information. However, it is understandable why government officials might consider impenetrable encryption that prevents legally authorized government surveillance an "artificial restriction" on lawful government law enforcement and security efforts.[38] In *Bustamante*, the Court rejected a heightened "informed" consent test because it concluded, inter alia, that it would impose an unjustifiable barrier against "the only means of obtaining important and reliable evidence." In other words, the requirement that consent be fully "informed" could not be justified even if it might enhance the protection of privacy and security, in part because this requirement would frustrate government efforts to investigate and solve crime. Impenetrable encryption raises similar considerations, albeit in a quite different context. As a result, it may be appropriate to consider the extent to which encryption technology may frustrate legally authorized law enforcement investigations when assessing the propriety of imposing restrictions on user-controlled encryption.

Admittedly, prohibiting user-controlled encryption will force individuals to assume increased risk of unauthorized access to their data and communications – from government entities abusing their authority and from malevolent actors lurking in cyberspace. This is in fact a significant argument against government efforts to impose limits on access to such encryption (explored in greater depth later in this chapter).[39] Some, including my coauthor, believe the nature of this risk tips the policy balance in favor of unrestricted public access to user-controlled encryption, even if such encryption

36 *Id.* at 243.
37 *Id.* at 229 (emphasis added).
38 *See id.* (discussing the dangers of placing unnecessary restrictions on police searches).
39 *See* Kopstein, *supra* note 8 (discussing the benefits of data encryption).

effectively prevents government efforts to surveil data/communications, even when such surveillance is authorized pursuant to the Fourth Amendment.

This may ultimately be the outcome of legislative consideration of the many interests at stake in this debate. However, Fourth Amendment jurisprudence, and the effort reflected in that jurisprudence to strike a rational balance between privacy and security, and between governmental interests and individual liberties, should inform legislative efforts to address this issue, including the baseline premise that *all* lawful government access to zones of privacy produces some risk of unlawful or unjustified intrusion. That such risks result from *lawfully authorized* government surveillance techniques is not inherently inconsistent with the Fourth Amendment. Instead, the Fourth Amendment's fundamental touchstone of reasonableness compels a careful assessment of the consequences of unrestricted public access to user-controlled encryption to *both* liberty *and* public security interests.

Ultimately, the validity of unrestricted public access to user-controlled encryption should not turn exclusively on whether prohibiting such encryption creates a risk of unlawful government access to information. Instead, the more appropriate questions are, first, whether the risks it creates are consistent with the inherent balance of interests embedded in the Fourth Amendment; and, second, whether the benefit of facilitating access outweighs the costs inherent in those risks. In making this assessment, however, the risks should be assessed broadly, as in any complex societal question. If, as suggested previously, erecting an impenetrable barrier to government access to data/communications represents a distortion of the Fourth Amendment's core logic, the second question becomes decisive.

Risk of unauthorized access to private data should be a significant consideration in this debate, but so should technological and legislative measures that mitigate this risk. Indeed, in his dissenting opinion in *Smith v. Maryland*,[40] challenging the logic of what is today known as the "third party doctrine," Justice Marshall argued that the risk of exposure of privacy imposed on citizens is a better touchstone for assessing whether a given activity falls within the scope of the Fourth Amendment. In *Smith*, the Court laid the foundation for almost all arguments in support of government collection of communications metadata, a premise that is under increasing pressure given the breadth and depth of private and sensitive content exposed in modern telecommunications systems. The *Smith* Court held that individuals cannot claim a reasonable expectation of privacy in the numbers dialed from a private telephone in their own homes, because the numbers are divulged to the third party phone company.[41] Accordingly, government access to those numbers through the telephone company did not qualify as a search within the meaning of the Fourth Amendment.[42]

Justice Marshall rejected this conclusion. In his view, it is invalid to reject the reasonableness of a privacy expectation simply because information is exposed to a third party.[43] Instead, Justice Marshall asserted that normal daily function in a free society necessitated

40 *See Smith v. Maryland*, 422 U.S. 735, 735 (1979) (weighing the risk of government interference).

41 *See id.* at 745–46 (explaining that privacy expectations should be lower because the information has already been given to a third party).

42 *See id.* (discussing the fact that government access to that information does not unreasonably interfere with privacy expectations).

43 *See id.* at 748–50 (Marshall, J., dissenting) (arguing against the third-party doctrine in the majority opinion).

its citizens to divulge certain information to third parties – in this case, phone numbers.[44] Thus, for Justice Marshall, the notion that an individual somehow forfeits an expectation of privacy, and the accordant protections of the Fourth Amendment, whenever information is disclosed to a third party, conflicted with the logic of the amendment.[45] Instead, he argued that the more logical test was not "whether privacy expectations are legitimate [based] on the risks an individual can be presumed to accept when imparting information to third parties, but on the risks he should be forced to assume in a free and open society."[46] Justice Marshall's skepticism of the "third party doctrine" seems to be gaining new momentum as courts struggle to adapt Fourth Amendment principles to the digital era. Judges across the United States, from magistrates to the Supreme Court, are becoming increasingly persuaded that the dynamics of this balance have shifted as a result of these "superstorage" containers, such as computers and smart phones.[47]

Two recent Supreme Court decisions highlight the challenge of reconciling a digitized and highly interconnected society with established Fourth Amendment principles: *United States v. Jones*[48] and *Riley v. California*.[49] As Justice Sonia Sotomayor noted in her *Jones* concurrence, what is an objectively reasonable expectation of privacy should not turn exclusively on the fact that an individual exposes the information to the public or a third party. Instead, the more important inquiry should focus on whether the collection of that information is so extensive as to "alter the relationship between citizen and government in a way that is inimical to democratic society."[50] Thus, Justice Sotomayor seems to be echoing Justice Marshall's view when she argues that "it may be necessary to reconsider the premise that an individual has no reasonable expectation of privacy in information voluntarily disclosed to third parties."[51]

This theme continued in *Riley*, when the Supreme Court considered whether a warrantless search of a cellular telephone incident to arrest was reasonable within the meaning of the Fourth Amendment.[52] The Court rejected extension of the almost automatic search incident to lawful arrest authority to the contents of a cell phone. The Court based this rejection entirely on the massive amount of information, and the accordant privacy interest, that can be accessed by exploring the contents of the modern smart phone.[53] Thus, Chief Justice John Roberts concluded, such devices are quantitatively

44 *See id.* (noting that calling a phone number should not kill any expectation of privacy).

45 *See id.* (disagreeing with the third party doctrine that the Court adopted).

46 *Id.* at 750.

47 See Stephen E. Henderson, *After* United States v. Jones, *After the Fourth Amendment Third Party Doctrine*, 14 N.C. J.L. & Tech. 431 (2013) (illustrating the trend away from the third party doctrine in Fourth Amendment jurisprudence since *United States v. Jones*).

48 132 S. Ct. 945, 946 (2012) (introducing the difficulty in applying existing doctrine to emerging technologies).

49 134 S. Ct. 2473, 2482 (2014) (discussing the reasonableness of searching information stored in a cell phone without a warrant).

50 *Jones*, 132 S. Ct. at 956 (citing *United States v. Cuevas–Perez*, 640 F.3d 272, 285 (7th Cir. 2011)).

51 *Id.* at 957 ("I would not assume that all information voluntarily disclosed to some member of the public for a limited purpose is, for that reason alone, disentitled to Fourth Amendment protection" (citing *Smith v. Maryland*, 442 U.S. 735, 749 (1979) (Marshall, J., dissenting) ("Privacy is not a discrete commodity, possessed absolutely or not at all. Those who disclose certain facts to a bank or phone company for a limited business purpose need not assume that this information will be released to other persons for other purposes"))).

52 *See Riley*, 134 S. Ct. at 2480 (questioning the constitutionality of warrantless cell phone searches).

53 *See id.* at 2489 (considering the storage capability of current technology).

and "qualitatively different"[54] from other physical containers subject to search incident to lawful arrest.

Any statutory restriction on or prohibition of end point and E2EE encryption will, to some extent, increase the risk of unlawful government access. But, as noted, this risk is inherent in all government surveillance capabilities. But is this a risk that members of a free society *should* accept as a necessary cost to protecting the broader societal interest in facilitating lawful investigatory activities? Certainly, allowing the continued development and use of end point/E2EE encryption protects individuals from unreasonable government searches. However, this protection is not limited to unreasonable searches, but extends to *any* search. Thus, end point encryption may frustrate *legitimate* governmental and societal interest in discovering crime and protecting national security not as the result of unauthorized government access to data, but from lawfully authorized access. Of course, there are many actions taken by individuals that frustrate lawful government surveillance efforts. But technology that makes it not only difficult to engage in lawful surveillance, but also near-impossible, creates consequences flowing from access to such technology that may very well justify subjecting citizens to the risks inherent in ensuring government agents are able to access data lawfully.

The preceding conceptualization of the risks attendant to prohibiting user-controlled encryption is too narrow, in the view of one author. If the aperture is widened to account for other risks of unauthorized intrusion facilitated by limited encryption – to include those posed by criminal hackers, foreign governments, and other nefarious third parties – the calculation of the risks that a citizen is expected to accept in a free society becomes far more complicated. And, when other societal interests, including the value of privacy and robust self-expression in democratic self-government discussed later, are included in the public policy equation, the justification for prohibiting or limiting user-controlled encryption may not ultimately balance in the government's favor.

[54] *Id.* at 2490. Some courts and scholars pushed this argument further, asserting that even searches conducted pursuant to warrants should be strictly constrained in their scope when applied to digital devices because of the enormous amounts of data those devices can store. *See, e.g., United States v. Comprehensive Drug Testing, Inc.*, 579 F.3d 989, 994 (9th Cir. 2009), *opinion revised and superseded*, 621 F.3d 1162 (9th Cir. 2010) (discussing the need to protect privacy interests); *see also In re Search of Apple iPhone*, 31 F. Supp. 3d 159, 160 (D.D.C. 2014) (denying a search warrant to search an iPhone); *In re Search of Black iPhone*, 27 F. Supp. 3d 74, 78 (D.D.C. 2014) (discussing the risk of the government gaining access to too much private information); *In re Search of Odys Loox Plus Tablet*, 28 F. Supp. 3d 40, 44–46 (D.D.C. 2014) (discussing issues that arise from a search warrant request's lack of clarity in how law enforcement will search the cell phone); *In re The Search of Premises Known As: A Nextel Cellular Telephone*, No. 14–MJ–8005–DJW, 2014 WL 2898262, at *3–7 (D. Kan. June 26, 2014) (denying a search warrant because the application failed to meet the particularity requirement). Those arguing that digital searches are so different as to require entirely new protocols to control searches seem to believe that the framers of the Constitution could never have imagined allowing searches of containers that could hold so much personal information. Yet that is exactly what they contemplated when they made abundantly clear that the government should have the authority to search homes – the most sacrosanct of all protected areas. One could argue that the "quantitative and qualitative" difference of modern electronic devices is that they compile much more information than would ever have occurred in the eighteenth century. While this is true, we should also recall that polymaths such as George Washington, Thomas Jefferson, and James Madison were notoriously meticulous in documenting and storing their thoughts, communications, and even business records in their homes. Nonetheless, prominent founders developed and used robust encryption systems to protect their public and personal communications. *See infra* at note 68.

B *The Unusual Notion of Impenetrable Privacy*

Ultimately, opposition to unfettered encryption reflects a deep-seated concern that allowing the proliferation of such seemingly beneficial technology may distort the balance between privacy and security at the core of the Fourth Amendment. A desire to preserve that balance may, in the view of some, point to a fundamentally different approach: the preservation of "front door" access with a carefully constructed mechanism to guard that front door against unlawful entry. At least from a Fourth Amendment perspective, enabling government agents to access zones of privacy, when lawfully authorized, is unremarkable. Indeed, not even the most carefully guarded zone of privacy – the home – is immune from such access.

Balancing the competing interests of collective societal security and individual liberty is central to the Fourth Amendment touchstone of reasonableness. The notion that the Fourth Amendment provides an individual right to an impenetrable zone of privacy is therefore inconsistent with the text and judicial interpretation of the amendment. Instead, balance remains the operative concept: protection against *unreasonable* search and seizure inherently acknowledged that the people can be subjected to *reasonable* searches and seizures. In short, the amendment never imposed an absolute restraint on government surveillance, even when directed against the interests protected by the amendment's text (persons, homes, papers, and effects). Instead, the people were provided an absolute right to be secure against *unreasonable* government intrusions into those places and things protected by the Fourth Amendment.

What is protected by the Fourth Amendment has been an evolving concept. The amendment expressly addresses "persons, houses, papers, and effects," textual interests unquestionably protected against unreasonable search and seizure. However, since the seminal Supreme Court decision in *Katz v. United States*,[55] the amendment's protections extend to anything over which an individual may assert a "reasonable expectation of privacy." The Court's most recent jurisprudence addressing the scope of the amendment's protection resurrected the dormant "trespass" doctrine, holding that any physical intrusion on a textually protected interest qualifies as a search within the meaning of the amendment, regardless of reasonable expectation of privacy. However, as the Court noted in its two decisions resurrecting this trespass doctrine, the reasonable expectation of privacy test was not replaced by this trespass doctrine, but is instead properly understood as a supplement to the protection against an investigatory trespass against a textually protected interest. Thus, a search within the meaning of the Fourth Amendment occurs whenever government agents engage in a physical trespass against a person, home, paper, or effect for the purpose of gathering information, *or* when they intrude on any other reasonable expectation of privacy.

The collective impact of Fourth Amendment jurisprudence results in a broad range of protected interests. However, among these interests none is considered more protected than the home. As the Supreme Court noted in *Silverman v. United States*, "At the very core of the Fourth Amendment stands the right of a man to retreat into his own home and there be free from unreasonable governmental intrusion."[56] Indeed, the "physical entry of the home is the chief evil against which the wording of the Fourth Amendment

[55] 389 U.S. 347 (1967).
[56] 365 U.S. 505, 511 (1961).

is directed."[57] Accordingly, for purposes of Fourth Amendment protection, as the Court noted in *Florida v. Jardines*, "when it comes to the Fourth Amendment, the home is first among equals."[58] This is an important point of analytical departure for assessing whether user-controlled encryption comports with the balance of interests inherent in the Fourth Amendment. If the home is considered one of the most protected zones of privacy, yet is still subject to lawful investigatory intrusion, it raises a simple question: why would statutory restrictions on access to private encryption run afoul of the Fourth Amendment if data storage devices are accorded no greater protection than the home itself?

In *Kyllo v. United States*, the Supreme Court explained that the heightened Fourth Amendment protected status afforded to the home results from two primary considerations. First, since inception of the nation, the home has provided a sanctuary for the citizen, where she can retreat into her maximum zone of privacy. Second, surveillance into the home poses a genuine risk of exposing the most intimate and private activities engaged in by the citizen. Thus, it was not merely the historical status of the home that necessitated treating it as "first among equals" for purposes of Fourth Amendment protection, but also the nature of information at risk of exposure by government surveillance. According to the Court:

> In the home, our cases show, *all* details are intimate details, because the entire area is held safe from prying government eyes. Thus, in [*United States v.*] *Karo*, the only thing detected was a can of ether in the home; and in *Arizona v. Hicks*, the only thing detected by a physical search that went beyond what officers lawfully present could observe in "plain view" was the registration number of a phonograph turntable. These were intimate details because they were details of the home, just as was the detail of how warm – or even how relatively warm – Kyllo was heating his residence.[59]

In short, with the very narrow exception of the sanctity of the human body from physical penetration (which itself is not per se incompatible with the Fourth Amendment), protection of the home from government intrusion is among the most carefully guarded Fourth Amendment interests, even when the intrusion is limited in scope, duration, or investigatory objective.[60]

Ultimately, it would be overbroad to suggest that either the Fourth Amendment or its interpretive jurisprudence points to a constitutional right to utilize encryption that effectively prevents even lawfully authorized government access to data. As with access to the home, so long as such access is legally authorized and reasonably executed, it complies with the Fourth Amendment. In short, like almost all other interests protected by the Fourth Amendment, surveillance of private communications and data is consistent with the Fourth Amendment so long as it is reasonable. Exploration of the various

57 *United States v. United States District Court*, 407 U.S. 297, 313 (1972).

58 *Florida v. Jardines*, 569 U.S. 1, 8 (2013).

59 *Kyllo v. United States*, 533 U.S. 27, 37–38 (2001) (internal citations omitted).

60 Protecting the individual from physical bodily intrusion is arguably the only interest considered more significant than the sanctity of the home. However, the Court has not interpreted the Fourth Amendment as imposing a per se prohibition against such investigatory procedures, even when the government seeks to recover evidence by subjecting an individual to a nonconsensual physical intrusion, to include surgery. Instead, the reasonableness of such procedures is assessed on a case-by-case basis, balancing the government's need for the evidence (and availability of alternatives) with the degree of physical intrusion and mortal risk imposed upon the suspect. Thus, even when assessing the reasonableness of a surgical intrusion of a suspect, there appear to be no absolutes. See *Winston v. Lee*, 470 U.S. 753 (1985).

justifications that render intrusion into the home reasonable is beyond the scope of this discussion. What is significant, however, is the analogy between the *qualified* protection of the home and other privacy interests, and how this analogy undermines any assertion that the Fourth Amendment provides a *right* to utilize end-to-end encryption in order to ensure *unqualified* privacy of data stored on a mobile device.

The Supreme Court's periodic emphasis that the home is afforded special or heightened protection by the Fourth Amendment suggests that while protection of private data may be *as* important as protection of the home, it is not *more* important. Protection of the privacy interests associated with electronic data and communications is, of course, nonetheless substantial, perhaps justifying Fourth Amendment protection at least as strong as that provided to the home. Indeed, protection of personal security and privacy in any form is a central objective of the Fourth Amendment, a point emphasized by Justice Louis Brandeis in his dissent in *Olmstead v. United States*:

> It is not the breaking of his doors, and the rummaging of his drawers, that constitutes the essence of the offence; but it is the invasion of his indefeasible right of personal security, personal liberty and private property, where that right has never been forfeited by his conviction of some public offence – it is the invasion of this sacred right which underlies and constitutes the essence of [the history that lies behind the Fourth and Fifth Amendments].... The protection guaranteed by the Amendments is much broader in scope. The makers of our Constitution undertook to secure conditions favorable to the pursuit of happiness. They recognized the significance of man's spiritual nature, of his feelings, and of his intellect. They knew that only a part of the pain, pleasure and satisfactions of life are to be found in material things. They sought to protect Americans in their beliefs, their thoughts, their emotions and their sensations. They conferred, as against the Government, the right to be let alone – the most comprehensive of rights, and the right most valued by civilized men.[61]

It is therefore unsurprising that today many question the assumption that the home should be more carefully protected than the often intimate communications and data passing through and stored on modern digital devices. Massive volumes of information on a person's thoughts, beliefs, activities, or concerns may be accessed by exploring the contents of a mobile device or computer, and this digital information can encompass the intimate activities traditionally protected within the sanctity of the home. In the modern information age, this data can include intimate communications such as sexting and dating application communications, sexually explicit photographs, personal writings, family photographs, messages, emails, health care records; communications with priests, health care providers, attorneys; searches for information on gender or other identity, religious exploration, or other intimate activities. While this should not render this data immune from government inquiry if appropriately cabined within the law, it should be recognized that data at rest or in transit and other digital communications often reveal a person's innermost thoughts, opinions, beliefs, emotions, and intimate activities and can even reflect the process of thought formation itself.[62] Nonetheless, at least to date, there is little jurisprudential support for the conclusion that the privacy interests in data should be, at least in terms of Fourth Amendment considerations, elevated to a status *above* that

61 *Olmstead v. United States*, 277 U.S. 438, 475, 478 (1928) (Brandeis, J., dissenting).
62 *See infra* at section III.D., and note 96.

of the home – a status that would point to a Fourth Amendment *right* to utilize end point encryption.

In contrast, analogizing protection of private data to protection of the home is instructive, for it bolsters the conclusion that as for the home, there is no Fourth Amendment right to absolute immunity from lawful government surveillance efforts of private data. It should therefore be within the range of legitimate government authority to adopt laws that ensure the viability of such surveillance activities by managing the consequences of encryption. Indeed, government agents may lawfully intrude into the home when such intrusions are reasonable within the meaning of the Fourth Amendment. These lawful intrusions need not always be permissive; when the occupant of a home is unwilling to submit to assertions of lawful intrusion authority, and when there is a reasonable basis to believe providing the occupant the opportunity to do so will create an exigency, police may forcibly enter the home.

It is, of course, difficult to imagine a situation when police, armed with lawful search and/or seizure authority, encounter a truly impenetrable home. Because of this, society has never seriously encountered the question of whether rendering the home completely immune from even lawful government investigatory access would comport with the Fourth Amendment. This is, however, the precise question raised by the development of end point encryption: would a statutory restriction on access to technology creating an impenetrable zone of information privacy violate the Fourth Amendment? Or, does the *qualified* restriction on the government's authority to intrude upon a Fourth Amendment interest imply an expectation that the government should be permitted to adopt laws that ensure access to zones of privacy so long as that access is consistent with the Fourth Amendment?

At least where the home is concerned, the answer to this question seems to be "yes." While the Supreme Court has never encountered the "impenetrable home" problem, it has indicated that the government has a right to access the home when doing so is justified consistent with the Fourth Amendment. In *Payton v. New York*, the Court struck down a New York statute that authorized warrantless home entry to effect a felony arrest based on probable cause. The Court once again emphasized the maximum protection afforded the home by the Fourth Amendment. However, the Court also noted that once armed with a search *or arrest* warrant, police are authorized to enter the home to satisfy the warrant's objective:

> It is true that an arrest warrant requirement may afford less protection than a search warrant requirement, but it will suffice to interpose the magistrate's determination of probable cause between the zealous officer and the citizen. If there is sufficient evidence of a citizen's participation in a felony to persuade a judicial officer that his arrest is justified, it is constitutionally reasonable to require him to open his doors to the officers of the law. Thus, for Fourth Amendment purposes, an arrest warrant founded on probable cause implicitly carries with it the limited authority to enter a dwelling in which the suspect lives when there is reason to believe the suspect is within.[63]

Erecting an impenetrable barrier to home entry would obviously frustrate this lawful government authority. Prohibiting analogous barriers to lawful access to private data therefore seems consistent with the core logic of *Payton*. Ultimately, the Court's

63 *Payton v. New York*, 445 U.S. 573, 602 (1980).

treatment of the home in Fourth Amendment jurisprudence points to what appears to be an important premise: the amendment requires a rational balance between privacy protection and legitimate government investigatory interests. This is, however, only the starting point in the encryption debate; the end point must be based on a much wider array of public policy considerations.[64]

III Interests beyond the Constitution

A *Encryption as a Societal Good*

As recognized by the former deputy secretary of defense William J. Lynn III, "The Internet was designed to be collaborative and rapidly expandable and to have low barriers to technological innovation; security and identity management were lower priorities."[65] Because it is a fully open packet-switching network with smart endpoint hosts (computers), security issues are inherent to the Internet because the security of the majority of end point computers is generally poor with machines unpatched and open to attack.[66] These insecurities can be used to attack the network infrastructure itself or the integrity and privacy of communications and data passing over it.[67] "Absent encryption, all networked communications are fundamentally insecure."[68] These weaknesses are shared by cellular telephone networks that rely upon radio waves to transmit voice and SMS messages between the cell tower and the phone. Although modern "digital cellular systems are encrypted in the 'air interface' between the handset and the cell tower," the equipment to decode a digital signal is readily available, and the standard commercial encryption, "which varies with the type of network, is not considered very secure."[69]

Asymmetric public key encryption, in its various uses, can thus provide four vital services that mitigate security risks that exist in both computer and cellular networks: (1) confidentiality, (2) authentication, (3) verification or integrity, and (4) nonrepudiation. First and most familiar, encryption can ensure confidentiality by protecting communications against eavesdropping. Second, encryption – usually through the use of digital signatures – authenticates, or establishes the identity of, a remote user or system.[70] Third, encryption can provide assurance that the communication has not been viewed or altered while in transit or in storage, referred to as verification or integrity. Finally, nonrepudiation is a rigorous form of authentication, usually used to establish identity for legal purposes.

64 But does government access under the Fourth Amendment assure success at finding what is sought, or understanding what is found? A self-destructing safe is not illegal, nor notes kept in a secret code known only to the homeowner.

65 William J. Lynn III, *Defending a New Domain: The Pentagon's Cyberstrategy*, Foreign Affairs (Sept./Oct. 2010), https://www.foreignaffairs.com/articles/united-states/2010-09-01/defending-new-domain.

66 Landau, *supra* note 3, at 37–64.

67 *Id.* at 56 ("Security issues are inherent in any fully open packet-switching network with smart hosts").

68 ACLU, Submission to the Special Rapporteur on the Promotion and Protection of the Right to Freedom of Opinion and Expression 8 (Feb. 10, 2015), http://www.ohchr.org/Documents/Issues/Opinion/Communications/ACLU.pdf [hereinafter *ACLU Submission to Special Rapporteur*].

69 *Id.* at 178.

70 *See* Jeff Tyson, *How Encryption Works*, HowStuffWorks.com (Apr. 6, 2001), http://computer.howstuffworks.com/encryption.htm; Panayotis Vryonis, *Public-Key Cryptography for Non-Geeks*, Vrypan (Aug. 28, 2013), https://blog.vrypan.net/2013/08/28/public-key-cryptography-for-non-geeks/.

As important as the technical advantages offered by encryption is the public's commonsense understanding of its ability to restore some of the privacy and security lost in the modern information age, an understanding well expressed by a panel of the Ninth Circuit Court of Appeals in *Bernstein v. United States*:

> We note that the government's efforts to regulate and control the spread of knowledge relating to encryption may implicate more than the First Amendment rights of cryptographers. In this increasingly electronic age, we are all required in our everyday lives to rely on modern technology to communicate with one another. This reliance on electronic communication, however, has brought with it a dramatic diminution in our ability to communicate privately. Cellular phones are subject to monitoring, email is easily intercepted, and transactions over the Internet are often less than secure. Something as commonplace as furnishing our credit card number, social security number, or bank account number puts each of us at risk. Moreover, when we employ electronic methods of communication, we often leave electronic "fingerprints" behind, fingerprints that can be traced back to us. Whether we are surveilled by our government, by criminals, or by our neighbors, it is fair to say that never has our ability to shield our affairs from prying eyes been at such a low ebb. The availability and use of secure encryption may offer an opportunity to reclaim some portion of the privacy we have lost. Government efforts to control encryption thus may well implicate not only the First Amendment rights of cryptographers intent on pushing the boundaries of their science, but also the constitutional rights of each of us as potential recipients of encryption's bounty. Viewed from this perspective, the government's efforts to retard progress in cryptography may implicate the Fourth Amendment, as well as the right to speak anonymously, the right against compelled speech, and the right to informational privacy.[71]

It is this broad definition of the public interest that remains relevant in formulating a modern-day national cybersecurity policy that specifically includes strong encryption.

B *Economic Benefit from Encryption*

In addition to the legitimate interests of law enforcement and intelligence agencies, a broader aperture evaluating encryption (and its limits) must include both its contribution to the economic vitality of the nation, as well as the harms to that same vitality in its absence. The post-2000 development and commercialization of public key encryption that occurred after the resolution of the first crypto wars[72] in favor of strong pubic key encryption led to the explosion of Internet commerce in the early twenty-first century.[73] As a result, by 2011 e-commerce revenue worldwide generated $8 trillion per year and accounted for approximately 6 percent of GDP in mature nations. In the United States alone by 2014 the Internet earned more than $966 billion, generating 6 percent of the

71 *Bernstein v. United States*, 176 F.3d 1132, 1145–46 (9th Cir. 1999) (internal citations omitted), *en banc rev. granted and opinion withdrawn*, 192 F.3d 1308 (9th Cir. 1999); John A. Fraser, III, *The Use of Encrypted, Coded and Secret Communications Is an "Ancient Liberty" Protected by the U.S. Constitution*, 2 Va. J.L. & Tech. art. no. 2 (1997) (describing extensive use of unbreakable ciphers and codes in both public and private correspondence by prominent founders such as John Adams, George Washington, James Madison, James Lovell, James Monroe, John Jay, Benjamin Harrison, Edmund Randolph, William Lee, and Benjamin Franklin, among others).

72 *See supra* note 13.

73 *See* Levy, *supra* note 11, at 310–11.

U.S. economy.[74] The Internet is a critical element of GDP growth, a catalyst for net job creation, and a generator of consumer surplus – all public goods.[75] Strong public key encryption was *the* mechanism that allowed the secure financial transactions necessary to support e-commerce on the inherently insecure Internet.[76] Because of its adoption, in 2011 the United States captured more than 30 percent of global Internet revenues and more than 40 percent of net income,[77] something unlikely to have occurred without the security offered by strong public key encryption systems.[78]

C *Losses from the Lack of Encryption*

Any calculation of national security interests related to encryption must account for the losses caused by delays in implementing strong encryption in both the public and private sectors. Many critics attribute these losses to U.S. government resistance to approving the commercial availability of strong encryption during the 1990s.[79] These delays affect both the public[80] and private sectors, which in the United States and other Western nations protect sensitive personal and financial information and sensitive national security information, and control a significant amount of critical infrastructure. The increasing number of data breaches was hardly news in 2016, and given the asymmetrical nature of the cyber threat, individual hackers, groups of determined computer programmers, or foreign state actors can easily locate and exploit vulnerabilities in computer and communications networks.

A few examples illustrate the magnitude of the cyber security risk. Recent "garden variety" criminal hacks of financial and credit card records, such as those against T. J. Maxx, Target, Heartland Payment Systems, and Anthem, compromised almost 200 million credit card records. These ongoing, pervasive attacks certainly argue for the right of individuals to exercise self-defense through the use of encryption to protect their online activity, particularly as wireless payment solutions are becoming ubiquitous. As for intrusions directly affecting national security, in 2008 the U.S. military experienced a significant compromise of its classified computer networks initiated by a single flash drive corrupted with malware, resulting in "the most significant breach of U.S. military

74 Matthieu Pélissié du Rausas et al., McKinsey Global Institute Report, Internet Matters: The Net's Sweeping Impact on Growth, Jobs, and Prosperity, 1 (May 2011), http://www.mckinsey.com/industries/high-tech/our-insights/internet-matters [hereinafter MGI Report]; Tom Risen, Study: The U.S. Internet Is Worth $966 Billion, U.S. News & World Rep. (Dec. 11, 2015), http://www.usnews.com/news/blogs/data-mine/2015/12/11/the-internet-is-6-percent-of-the-us-economy-study-says.

75 MGI Report, supra note 74, at 2–3.

76 See generally Levy, supra note 11 (because computational power accelerated during this same time frame, from 1996 to 2011, encryption systems had to become ever stronger in order to remain secure and unbreakable); U.S. House of Representatives, Homeland Security Committee, Majority Staff Report, Going Dark, Going Forward, A Primer on the Encryption Debate 3 (June 2016), https://homeland.house.gov/wp-content/uploads/2016/07/Staff-Report-Going-Dark-Going-Forward.pdf [hereinafter Going Dark Primer].

77 MGI Report, supra note 74, at 4.

78 Levy, supra note 11, at 301–11.

79 Id. at 226–68;

80 Diffie & Landau, supra note 21, at 256 (because of government decisions adopting commercial off-the-shelf procurement policies weaknesses in commercial computers and cell phones affects government users as well).

computers ever."[81] In June 2015, the United States Office of Personnel Management (OPM) disclosed that the Chinese government had breached the security clearance databases and systems involving the personal information of millions of current and former government employees, contractors, and journalists going back to 1985.[82]

Although seemingly large in scale and acknowledged as a cyber-intelligence coup by Director of National Intelligence James Clapper,[83] this breach pales in comparison to the breach and posting online of what appeared to be the personal information of all (49 million) Turkish citizens.[84] Because of the difficulties of attribution and the amorphous nature of the threats in cyberspace, national leaders have concluded that "deterrence will necessarily be based *more on denying any benefit to attackers* than on imposing costs through retaliation."[85] There can be no doubt that encrypting data in databases and in transit provides a powerful means to deny hackers, of whatever motivation, the benefits of their breach. Had the OPM security clearance databases been strongly encrypted, for example, their attack would have resulted in theft of data that were unreadable and therefore unusable to the thief.

National security threats in the United States and other Western nations are not limited to military targets. In the United States as in most Western nations, critical infrastructure is owned and operated by the private sector, making national security depend not only on governmental cyber defenses but also on cyber defense more broadly applied. Securing these critical entities means allowing them to secure their communications. Sophisticated intrusions into networks that control critical civilian infrastructure, such as power grids, transportation networks, dams, and financial systems, can cause massive physical damage resulting in economic disruption.[86] Many of the supervisory control and data acquisition system (SCADA) networks that control sensitive utilities were built prior to the current threat environment and are thus having to add security against cyber threats retroactively, again a function that can be met with various software programs using strong encryption. Clearly, the threats posed by the insecurity of these systems can be taken advantage of by criminals who may use them to extort money, or by hostile

81 Lynn, supra note 65 ("The Pentagon's operation to counter this attack, known as Operation Buckshot Yankee, marked a turning point in U.S. cyberdefense strategy." Thousands of files have also been taken from U.S. networks and those of U.S. allies and industry partners, to include weapons blueprints, operational plans, and surveillance data).

82 See Michael Adams, Why the OPM Hack Is Far Worse Than You Imagine, LawFare (Mar. 11, 2016), https://www.lawfareblog.com/why-opm-hack-far-worse-you-imagine; Ellen Nakashima, Chinese Hack of Federal Personnel Files Included Security-Clearance Database, Wash. Post (June 12, 2015), https://www.washingtonpost.com/world/national-security/chinese-hack-of-government-network-compromises-security-clearance-files/2015/06/12/9f91f146-1135-11e5-9726-49d6fa26a8c6_story.html; Lisa Rein, The Chinese Didn't Just Hack Federal Employees. Journalists Were Swept up in the Massive Breach, too, Wash. Post (Dec. 14, 2015), https://www.washingtonpost.com/news/federal-eye/wp/2015/12/14/the-chinese-didnt-just-hack-federal-employees-journalists-were-swept-up-in-the-massive-breach-too/.

83 Colin Clark, DNI Clapper IDs China as 'The Leading Suspect' in OPM Hacks; Russia 'More Subtle,' Breaking Defense (June 25, 2015), http://breakingdefense.com/2015/06/clapper-ids-china-as-the-leading-suspect-in-opm-hacks-russia-more-subtle/.

84 Paul Rosenzweig, The Largest PII Hack Ever – or So It Seems, LawFare (Apr. 5, 2016), https://www.lawfareblog.com/largest-pii-hack-ever-or-so-it-seems.

85 Lynn, supra note 65.

86 Id.

nation states or terrorists. We have already seen hostile takeovers of electrical grids and other dangerous industrial controls causing damage in the physical world.[87]

Even more critical for the long-term national security of the United States are its economic vitality and creativity. The threats posed by cyber espionage, either by criminals or by hostile nation states, have resulted in what General Keith Alexander, the former director of the National Security Agency, has referred to as "the greatest transfer of wealth in history."[88] Annual thefts of intellectual property amount to more than $250 billion,[89] or as the former deputy secretary of defense William Lynn III has stated, the *annual* theft of intellectual property from U.S. business, university, and government networks exceeds that contained in the Library of Congress.[90] Unsecured systems and networks – or those with inadequate or weakened security – create opportunities for cyber espionage, or its less exotic incarnation, cyber crime, which is estimated to cost the U.S. economy another $114 billion annually.[91]

D *Encryption's Contribution to Democratic Processes and to Freedom of Opinion and Expression*

In addition to the economic aspects of our national security that must be considered when evaluating a national encryption policy, the consequences of any particular choice on our system of government must also be evaluated. The ability to communicate privately or anonymously has important implications for self-government in democratic societies. These issues are particularly important for a nation such as the United States that depends both on institutional checks and balances and on the trust of the people. President Obama's handpicked panel chosen to review intelligence and communications technologies noted that "excessive surveillance and unjustified secrecy can threaten civil liberties, public trust, and the *core processes of democratic self-government*."[92] Although recognizing that one of the government's most fundamental responsibilities is to "counteract[] threats that come from those who seek to do the nation and its citizens

87 Daniel Wagner, The Growing Threat of Cyber-Attacks on Critical Infrastructure, The Huffington Post (May 24, 2016), http://www.huffingtonpost.com/daniel-wagner/the-growing-threat-of-cyb_b_10114374.html (describing Dec. 2015 cyber-attack seizing control of, and shutting down the power system grid in western Ukraine); Susan Landau, What David Cameron Doesn't Get, LawFare (Jan. 20, 2016), https://www.lawfareblog.com/what-david-cameron-doesnt-get (describing German government report of cyber seizure of steel mill control systems resulting in inability to shut down blast furnaces and massive damage); Issue Summary: Cyber Security, U.S. Government Accountability Office, http://www.gao.gov/key_issues/cybersecurity/issue_summary#t=0 (last visited Oct. 13, 2016) (identifying significant challenges remaining to enhance the protection of cyber-reliant critical infrastructures); Cheryl Pellerin, Cybercom Chief Details U.S. Cyber Threats, Trends, DoD News (Nov. 21, 2014), http://www.defense.gov/News-Article-View/Article/603696; Katherine Brockelhurst, DHS Confirms U.S. Public Utility's Control System Was Hacked, The State of Security (May 21, 2014), http://www.tripwire.com/state-of-security/incident-detection/dhs-confirms-u-s-public-utilitys-control-system-was-hacked/.

88 Josh Rogin, NSA Chief: Cybercrime Constitutes the "Greatest Transfer of Wealth in History," Foreign Policy (July 9, 2012), http://foreignpolicy.com/2012/07/09/nsa-chief-cybercrime-constitutes-the-greatest-transfer-of-wealth-in-history/.

89 Id.

90 Lynn, supra note 65.

91 Rogin, supra note 88.

92 Richard A. Clarke et al., Liberty and Security in a Changing World, Report and Recommendations of the President's Review Group on Intelligence and Communications Technologies, 12 (Dec. 12, 2013), https://www.whitehouse.gov/sites/default/files/docs/2013-12-12_rg_final_report.pdf (emphasis added).

harm,"[93] this panel also recognized the equally important task of ensuring that the people remained secure in their privacy, a protection they noted was both ensured by the Fourth Amendment and consistent with traditional physical security. For the panel:

> in a free society, one that is genuinely committed to self-government, people are secure in the sense they need not fear that their conversations and activities are being watched, monitored, interrogated, or scrutinized. Citizens are free from this kind of fear. In unfree societies, by contrast, there is no right to be let alone, and people struggle to organize their lives to avoid the government's probing eye. The resulting unfreedom jeopardizes all at once, individual liberty, self-government, economic growth, and basic ideals of citizenship.[94]

The panel recognized that government surveillance can undermine public trust, destroying the very security it seeks to secure, and it can often be misused if not subject to strict control.[95] More critically for democratic self-government, fears of mass surveillance pose direct threats to liberty. The panel continued:

> Liberty includes a range of values, such as freedom of speech, freedom of religion, and freedom of association, that go well beyond privacy. If people are fearful that their conversations are being monitored, expressions of doubt about, or opposition to current policies or leaders may be chilled and the democratic process itself may be compromised.[96]

Critically, an open and secure Internet (and cellular telephone system) protects the free expression of opinions and ideas, a necessary component of self-government and accountability. In addition to enhancing the ability to communicate ideas freely without fear of government repression, encryption provides confidential avenues of complaint and communication for whistle-blowers, journalists, or other government officials, which contribute to government accountability and democratic processes.[97]

The freedoms of opinion, expression, association, and religion encompassed within the First Amendment, and of privacy within the Fourth, however, also seek to provide something more fundamental: the *pursuit of happiness* sought by our founders, a pursuit that encompasses the emotional, the intellectual, the spiritual in each person.[98] This pursuit also requires a zone of privacy that in the modern digital age depends upon encryption and anonymity, a conclusion similarly recognized by the United Nations Special Rapporteur on Encryption, Anonymity and the Freedom of Expression.[99] In its

93 Id. at 43.
94 Id., at 44.
95 Id. at 46–47.
96 Id. at 47.
97 Id. at 1; see also Henry Porter, Privacy from State Snooping Defines a True Democracy, The Guardian (Apr. 3, 2012), https://www.theguardian.com/commentisfree/2012/apr/03/privacy-state-snooping-true-democracy; see, e.g., Securedrop.org (journalist).
98 See Olmstead, 277 U.S. 438, 478 (1928).
99 Report of the Special Rapporteur (A/HRC/29/32) on Encryption, Anonymity, and the Freedom of Expression 8 (May 22, 2015) [hereinafter U.N. Encryption Report] (recognizing the importance of encryption and anonymity to the fundamental human rights of privacy and freedom of opinion and expression). In the digital age, the mechanisms of both forming and holding opinions and beliefs are inextricably tied to digital interaction on the Internet and with other electronic communications. The processes of searches, queries, saving, and drafting as opinions are formed all provide insight into an individual's thinking, no longer an "abstract concept limited to what may be in one's mind." Id. In fact, Chinese keyboards are interactive to the extent that they can act as keystroke monitors, allowing surveillance that "could eventually be conducted in real time" and can even with the development of

conclusion, President Obama's advisory panel recommended that the U.S. government "not in any way subvert, weaken, or make vulnerable generally available commercial [encryption] software."[100]

The rights of freedom of expression, opinion, and redress, so essential in the United States, are also recognized in human rights treaties that the United States is party to, and that we champion internationally. Recognition of the intrinsic tie between online activities and fundamental human rights is not novel and has been part of U.S. foreign policy for some time. The United States recognizes that "the same rights that people have offline must also be protected online, in particular, freedom of expression.... [The United States] has long worked to promote accessibility, security, privacy and freedom of expression online."[101] The importance of encryption and anonymity[102] tools in protecting fundamental civil liberties motivated the United States to contribute to the development of Tor, an online anonymizing tool, and powerful end-to-end encryption. These tools provide secure communications that can be used by dissidents, human rights defenders, and civil society organizations seeking to challenge oppressive or corrupt regimes and have been provided by the U.S. State Department to foreign activists in the past.[103] Because of the threats posed to modern telecommunications systems (the Internet and cellular phone systems) due to criminal hackers, foreign government threats, and mass surveillance by one's own government or its allies, "individuals and civil society organizations, both in the U.S. and abroad, require real options to protect themselves in digital space."[104] Although U.S. legal and policy decisions are unlikely to influence foreign government encryption policies, they will impact the ability of the United States to leverage "soft power" in support of expressive freedoms, which "is most effective when it is wielded without overt hypocrisy."[105] Furthermore, U.S. efforts to limit encryption and anonymizing programs may encourage other governments – some with dubious human rights track records – to implement their own measures to limit anonymity and chill dissent.[106]

forensic techniques identify individual users. Tom Mullaney, The Hidden Vulnerabilities in Chinese Information Technology, Foreign Affairs (June 5, 2016), https://www.foreignaffairs.com/articles/china/2016-06-05/how-spy-600-million-people. Encryption (and anonymity) protects the privacy of this thought formation and refinement process.

100 Clarke et al., supra note 92, at 36.

101 Letter from Pamela K. Hamamoto, The Permanent Representative of the United States of America to the United Nations and Other International Organizations in Geneva, to David Kaye, Special Rapporteur on the Promotion of the Right to Freedom of Opinion and Expression (Feb. 27, 2015), http://www.ohchr.org/Documents/Issues/Opinion/Communications/States/USA.pdf [hereinafter U.S. Letter to U.N. Rapporteur].

102 Anonymity is the condition of avoiding identification and "may liberate a user to explore and impart ideas and opinions more than she would using her actual identity." Online users can remain anonymous or use pseudonyms to hide their identities, but without anonymizing tools their identities can be ascertained. U.N. Encryption Report, supra note 96, at 5.

103 See The Chertoff Group, supra note 5, at 14; see also ACLU Submission, supra note 68, at 10; U.S. Letter to U.N. Rapporteur, supra note 101, at 1 ("Encryption, as well as tools that assist with anonymity, are especially important in sensitive contexts where attribution could have negative political, social or personal consequences or have the privacy interests in the information are strong").

104 Id.

105 The Chertoff Group, supra note 5, at 14.

106 Governments with less robust legal protections for privacy are already moving to require data to be stored within their territorial borders. See Reuters, Iran Orders Social Media Sites to Store Data inside Country (May 29, 2016), http://www.reuters.com/article/internet-iran-idusl8n18q0in.

E *"The Modern Four Horsemen of the Apocalypse: Drug Dealers, Kidnappers, Child Pornographers, and Terrorists"*

The legitimate needs of law enforcement and intelligence agencies to conduct surveillance to protect the nation and its citizens from those who would do them harm are without dispute,[107] and the "ability to wiretap under legal authorization [remains] an important tool for law enforcement and national security."[108] FBI Director Comey is only the latest in the long line of law enforcement officials to make the case forcefully for the necessity of law enforcement access to modern telecommunications systems in order to protect the country from criminals and terrorists. In November 2014 he condemned the decision by Apple to make user-controlled encryption the default on its new operating system. Similar condemnation arose from Manhattan District Attorney Cyrus Vance, who asserted that the default encryption changes by Apple and Google (for its Android phones) had resulted in an inability to access seventy-four iPhones.[109] Both officials argued for the legislation of mandatory access to encrypted data on cell phones and computers through a ban on user-controlled encryption.

Interestingly, these public statements were made after the Obama administration decided not to pursue legislation requiring mandatory access because of the risks such a requirement created,[110] and after the panel reviewing intelligence and communications technologies specifically recommended against weakening commercially available encryption to accomplish such mandatory access.[111] This same panel also recommended that any government surveillance decision should not be based on intuitions or anecdotes, but instead on a careful analysis of evidence, to include an assessment of the anticipated consequences, benefits, and costs where available, and the "full range of relevant risks."[112] This commitment to quantitative, evidence based analysis goes back to 1981, is required by several executive orders, and should include "retrospective analysis" to explore "what policies have actually achieved, or failed to achieve, in the real world."[113]

107 Levy, supra note 11, at 300 (caricaturization of the U.S. government's position circa 1996); see also National Research Council, Cryptography's Role in Securing the Information Society § 3.2 (May 30, 1996).

108 Landau, supra note 3, at 247.

109 Andy Greenberg, Manhattan DA: iPhone Crypto Locked Out Cops 74 Times, Wired (July 8, 2015), https://www.wired.com/2015/07/manhattan-da-iphone-crypto-foiled-cops-74-times/ (comparing the figure to the 100,000 cases handled by the Manhattan DA office annually). Vance later updated this figure to 175. See Alyssa Newcomb, New York DA Says He Can't Access 175 iPhones from Criminal Cases Due to Encryption, ABC News (Feb. 18, 2016), http://abcnews.go.com/Technology/york-da-access-175-iphones-criminal-cases-due/story?id=37029693; see also Report of the Manhattan District Attorney's Office on Smartphone Encryption and Public Safety (Nov. 2015), http://manhattanda.org/sites/default/files/11.18.15%20Report%20on%20Smartphone%20Encryption%20and%20Public%20Safety.pdf.

110 See Nicole Perlroth & David E. Sanger, Obama Won't Seek Door to Encrypted User Data, N.Y. Times (Oct. 10, 2015), http://www.nytimes.com/2015/10/11/us/politics/obama-wont-seek-access-to-encrypted-user-data.html (Obama administration concluding that it is not possible to give American law enforcement and intelligence agencies access to encrypted data on iPhones and other digital devices without also creating an opening that China, Russia, and cybercriminals and terrorists could exploit).

111 Clarke et al., supra note 92, at 22 ("The US Government should take additional steps to promote security, by (1) fully supporting and not undermining efforts to create encryption standards; (2) making clear that it will not in any way subvert, undermine, weaken or make vulnerable generally available commercial encryption; and (3) supporting efforts to encourage the greater use of encryption technology for data in transit, at rest, in the cloud, and in storage").

112 Id. at 16, 50–51; Diffie & Landau, supra note 21, at 207; see also Landau, supra note 3, at 105.

113 Clarke et al., supra note 92, at 50.

Statistical evidence on law enforcement reliance on wiretaps and the detrimental effect of encryption on that ability is provided, to a limited extent, in the annual *Wiretap Report*. In this report, the Administrative Office of the Federal Courts publishes a list of all wiretap orders issued under Title III and associated state statutes.[114] Although the statistics do present difficulties – they do not distinguish wiretaps from bugs and likely involve some underreporting – they at least provide some quantitative evidence to assess government policy proposals in this area. More critical is that the *Report* does not tell whether (or not) a wiretap played a significant role in obtaining a conviction. Only an analysis of the court transcripts can do that, and some studies question whether the available statistics establish the usefulness of wiretap evidence in obtaining convictions in all cases.[115]

Despite law enforcement assertions that wiretaps are critical to their success, the actual numbers of wiretaps are quite low, with the majority issued for "portable device" or cell phones.[116] Historical evidence shows that the initial main focus for wiretapping was in gambling cases, shifting in 1997 to drugs cases, which remain the vast majority of offenses for which wiretaps are used – currently at 89 percent of wiretaps in 2014.[117] Terrorism is not listed as an independent offense in the law enforcement data.[118] Although wiretapping's use in kidnapping cases is often cited in public testimony to oppose strong public encryption, the statistics do not support this assertion. Although important to law enforcement in corruption or conspiracy cases or where victims would have difficulty testifying,[119] the overall number of wiretap-involved cases (3,554 intercepts installed in 2014, with 3,554 arrests, and 553 convictions that year)[120] pales against the 75,836 convictions in the federal system alone in 2014.[121]

114 Diffie & Landau, supra note 21, at 207.

115 Landau, supra note 3, at 104–05 ("The lack of hard evidence of the efficacy of wiretaps has been a concern since at least the passage of Title III; A 1972 Schwartz study of four-and-a-half years' of Title III wiretaps found that the assumption that the arrests and convictions that are reported are a result of the installations involved is not adequately dispelled by the Administrative Office [of the U.S. Courts]").

116 In 2014, 3554 wiretap intercepts were authorized (1,279 federal and 2,275 state), down from 2013 figures of 3,576 (1,476 federal and 2,100 state); 96 percent of these were for a "portable device" or cell phone. Drug offenses constituted 89 and 87 percent of the wiretaps, respectively. U.S. Courts, The Wiretap Report 2014, at tbl. Wire 7 (Dec. 31, 2014), http://www.uscourts.gov/statistics-reports/wiretap-report-2014. In 2015, the number of wiretaps increased 17 percent to 4,148 (1,403 federal, 2,745 state) wiretaps authorized. See U.S. Courts, The Wiretap Report 2015, at tbl. Wire 7 (Dec. 31, 2015), http://www.uscourts.gov/statistics/table/wire-7/wiretap/2015/12/31.

117 Landau, supra note 3, at 106; see also The Wiretap Report 2014, supra note 116, at tbl.7. In 2015, 79 percent of wiretaps were authorized for drug cases. See The Wiretap Report 2015, supra note 116, at tbl. Wire 7.

118 The Wiretap Report 2014, supra note 116, at tbl. 7 (Terrorism is not listed as an independent offense in the law enforcement data. Depending on the investigation specifics, terrorism might be included in the Homicide/Assault category; the next most prevalent major offense category constituted only 3.8 percent in 2014 (5 percent in 2015); the Arson/explosives/weapons category at 0.28 percent (0.5 percent in 2015); or the other/unspecified category at 3.4 percent in 2014 (8.9 percent in 2015)). See id. (for 2015 data).

119 Landau, supra note 3, at 104.

120 See The Wiretap Report 2014, supra note 116, at tbl.9 for arrest and conviction rates from 2004 through 2014 (these statistics include both federal and state and are on a calendar year basis; because the arrest and conviction numbers can lag after the year an intercept is installed it is difficult to make direct comparisons as there is a lag on their efficacy because of the delay, but the overall gross comparison against just the federal sentencing numbers remains relevant to reflect the (un) importance of wiretaps in gross criminal cases). See id. at tbl. 6 (Types of Surveillance Used, Arrests, and Convictions for Intercepts Installed.

121 See U.S. Sentencing Commission, Overview of Federal Criminal Cases, Fiscal Year 2014 (Aug. 2015), http://www.ussc.gov/sites/default/files/pdf/research-and-publications/research-publications/2015/FY14_Overview_Federal_Criminal_Cases.pdf (for the total number of federal criminal cases in which the offender was sentenced in FY 2014).

According to the *Report*, which pursuant to a 2000 amendment includes data on encryption-related problems encountered in wiretapping investigations,[122] encryption posed little challenge to law enforcement in criminal cases. In 2014, only twenty-two state wiretaps encountered encryption (down from forty-one in 2013), and in only two of cases were the officials unable to decrypt the plaintext. Of the three federal wiretaps that were encrypted in 2014, two could not be decrypted.[123] In 2015, the numbers fell further, with only seven state and six federal wiretaps encountering encryption, and seven and four ultimately being unbreakable.[124] Although Manhattan District Attorney Vance updated his claim to be unable to access 175 cell phones because of encryption, this claim too is small in comparison with the overall one hundred thousand cases handled annually by his office.[125] Data pertaining to the impact of encryption on national security–related surveillance are insufficient to support any meaningful conclusions.[126]

F *Other Effective Law Enforcement Methods – Assessment of the Risks*

It is equally important that any assessment of encryption control consider already available alternatives to mandated investigatory access to encrypted data. In most cases, data uploaded to the cloud are not affected by recent default encryption changes and remain encrypted, if at all, by the service provider. In such cases, this data is efficiently accessible to law enforcement with appropriate authorization.[127]

Law enforcement also retains many effective traditional investigative practices, not involving communications or data monitoring or access. These include analysis of open source information such as social media activity, use of informants, or development of relationships with local communities to identify at-risk members.[128] Traffic analysis, location data, and end point compromise are available even if the information itself

122 The Wiretap Report 2014, supra note 116, at 215.

123 Id. at Summary and Analysis of Reports by Judges (Additionally, officials were able to decipher four of the five encrypted wiretaps that were reported from prior years for the first time in 2014).

124 The Wiretap Report 2015, supra note 116 (In 2015 state officials encountered encryption in only seven, and was unable to break all seven; federal wiretaps encountered encryption in six cases, four of which were unbreakable, with one case from the prior year reported, which was also unbreakable).

125 See generally supra note 109.

126 As for intelligence- and counterterrorism-related surveillance, the Foreign Intelligence Surveillance Court issued 749 orders authorizing electronic surveillance (not including pen registers or trap and trace) in the final six months of 2015. There is no statutory requirement to capture the effect of encryption on this effort, leaving policy makers (and the American public) ill-informed on its effect on national security investigation intercepts. Although these FISA authorizations are not traditional Fourth Amendment warrants, being oriented toward foreign intelligence targets, the gross numbers authorized under FISA for electronic surveillance are not large. Report of the Director of the Administrative Office of the U.S. Courts on Activities of the Foreign Intelligence Surveillance Courts for 2015 (covering Jun. 8, 2015 to Dec. 30, 2015) (including 80 orders issued under 50 U.S.C. § 1805; 749 under both 50 U.S.C. §§ 1805, 1824; and 45 under 50 U.S.C. § 1881c. The number issued under 50 U.S.C. § 1881a is classified).

127 See The Chertoff Group, supra note 5, at 18 (synchronicity across devices usually results in data in cloud storage being encrypted with the service provider's encryption, not the user's, and although this can be defeated by turning off cloud backup or encrypting data prior to backing it up to the cloud, the lack of efficiency makes this less likely); Berkman Center for Internet and Society at Harvard University, Don't Panic, Making Progress on the "Going Dark" Debate (Feb. 1, 2016), https://cyber.law.harvard.edu/pubrelease/dont-panic/Dont_Panic_Making_Progress_on_Going_Dark_Debate.pdf [hereinafter Don't Panic] (centralized data services and ubiquitous connectivity provide business and personal motives working against encryption because it interferes with ease of use).

128 See, e.g., The Chertoff Group, supra note 5, at 9.

is encrypted. Traffic analysis, or the study of the patterns of communication, a form of metadata, has long been a component of signals intelligence and includes "the study of who is talking to whom, when, and for how long."[129] Analysis of Call Detail Records (CDRs) is the primary mechanism used by law enforcement and intelligence agencies for similar purposes, to determine communities of interest around a particular known phone number. Studying calling records to identify "unnatural communications patterns appears to offer great benefit to law enforcement at relatively low cost." Knowing only eight friends on a social network can enable the mapping of that social network, and research has shown that that if only 8 percent of the email traffic data of nodes in a network were surveilled, "investigators could determine the communications 'circle' of forty-five percent of the users, while if the traffic of twenty-eight percent of the users were known, then investigators could determine the behavior of fully ninety-five percent of the users."[130] The analysis of such communications patterns has been useful in identifying friends of terrorist suspects and can provide useful leads to follow[131]

Another alternative investigative tool is access to location data. This data is provided by cellular telephones or other digital devices or by pen registers and is obviously valuable to investigators. Indeed, the value of such data was emphasized by Justice Sonia Sotomayor in her *United States v. Jones* concurrence.[132] This data has been used by the U.S. Marshalls Service to reduce its average investigation time to apprehend fugitives from forty-two to two days.[133] Past location information can be sought through a court order for CDR information, prospective information by seeking a pen register order, and at least one court has held that a warrant is required to access real-time location data.[134]

Finally, legally authorized spyware or keystroke loggers surreptitiously placed on computers or cellular phones, or in known locations of targets, have been used with effect by law enforcement since 2005.[135] Given the known statistics on the use of wiretaps in law enforcement, alternate methods, and the fact that encryption will remain available to foreign states, terrorists, and criminals, the going dark debate may offer a timely opportunity for a much broader qualitative reassessment of "what various enforcement means have actually achieved, or failed to achieve, in the real world."[136]

129 Landau, supra note 3, at 134–36 (It can disclose the chain of command, where and when activity is likely to occur, the existence of personal relationships, organization within a corporation, even whether a merger discussion is ongoing in civilian life).

130 Id. at 138.

131 Id.

132 Jones, 132 S. Ct. 945, 954 (2012).

133 Landau, supra note 3, at 100.

134 See e.g. Spencer S. Hsu, A Maryland Court Is the First to Require a Warrant for Covert Cellphone Tracking, Wash. Post (Mar. 31, 2016), https://www.washingtonpost.com/world/national-security/a-maryland-court-is-the-first-to-require-a-warrant-for-covert-cellphone-tracking/2016/03/31/472d9b0a-f74d-11e5-8b23-538270a1ca31_story.html (Maryland Court of Special Appeals ruled that Fourth Amendment required warrant and probable cause for cell phone real time location data). See also In re *Application of US from an Order Authorizing Disclosure of Location Information of a Specified Wireless Telephone*, 849 F. Supp. 2d 526, 559 (D. Md. 2011); contra *United States v. Graham*, 796 F.3d 332 (4th Cir.) reh'g en banc granted, 624 F. App'x 75 (4th Cir. 2015), and adhered to in part on reh'g en banc, No, 12-4659 2016 WL 3068018 (4th Cir. May 31, 2016); *Unites States v. Skinner*, 690 F.3d 722 (6th Cir. 2012).

135 Landau, supra note 3, at 133.

136 Clarke et al., supra note 92, at 50.

G *Futility*

The availability of alternative investigative tools has not been viewed by law enforcement and intelligence officials as an adequate substitute for access to encrypted data. These officials assert a continuing need to prevent terrorist and violent criminal access to user-controlled encryption that can prevent lawful interception and access to their communications.[137] With the changes in default encryption by telecommunications companies, and the growing number of encryption products and services available overseas, these concerns are likely to increase. After the Snowden revelations were made public, encrypted traffic on the Internet in North America increased from 2.9 percent in peak hours to 3.8 percent.[138] In Europe, encrypted traffic went from 1.47 percent to 6.10 percent, and in Latin America, from 1.8 percent to 10.37 percent.[139] The assertions by District Attorney Vance in mid-2015 certainly support the claim that the default encryption changes – or going dark – will lead to an increasing number of circumstances when law enforcement will be unable to access evidence, even when lawfully authorized.[140] This, however, already may be an unavoidable aspect of contemporary government investigations.

If the proverbial genie is out of the bottle, the value of restrictions on encryption may be substantially undermined. And this may in fact be the case. For example, an early 2016 study "identified 865 hardware or software products incorporating encryption from 55 different countries," including 546 products from outside the United States.[141] This trend is accelerating, as many users of the Internet and cellular phones legitimately see increasing threats in the digital world and are providing a lucrative marketplace for developers.

These new encryption products are produced both as proprietary and as free open-source projects and are downloadable from the Internet, making the control of their dissemination very difficult.[142] Many are designed to exist on multiple servers and across multiple

137 Paul Rosenzweig, The IC Thinks Harvard Is Wrong about Encryption, LawFare (May 8, 2016), https://www.lawfareblog.com/ic-thinks-harvard-wrong-about-encryption; see also The Chertoff Group, supra note 5, at 8–9 (summarizing recent incidences when encryption may have interfered with law enforcement terrorism investigation).

138 Klint Finley, Encrypted Web Traffic More than Doubles after NSA Revelations, Wired (May 16, 2014), http://www.wired.com/2014/05/sandvine-report/.

139 Id.

140 See Report of the Manhattan District Attorney's Office on Smartphone Encryption and Public Safety, supra note 109; but see Andy Greenberg, Manhattan DA: IPhone Crypto Locked Out Cops 74 Times, Wired (July 8, 2015), https://www.wired.com/2015/07/manhattan-da-iphone-crypto-foiled-cops-74-times/ (No statistics, however, exist to capture objectively encryption's effect on law enforcement's inability to investigate their cases or ultimately obtain convictions).

141 Schneier et al., supra note 20, at 2. The sophistication of foreign-designed or -developed encryption products or services is not new – it has been an ongoing process since the resolution of the first crypto-wars in 1999 when the United States government relaxed its export prohibitions on strong encryption programs. In fact, "both recent NIST encryption standards – AES and SHA-3 – were designed outside of the US, and the submissions for those standards were overwhelmingly non-US." Id. at 5; see also Levy, supra note 11, at 310 (noting that the competition for AES – the Advanced Encryption Standard – was decided in 2001 in an open competition with more than half of the contenders from outside the United States).

142 Additionally, advocates of key escrow systems have not clarified how such a system will be administered in the highly mobile global economy: will computers and cell phones be required to install a government-mandated program at each border as a condition of entry implementing each nation's deencryption ability? See, e.g., Abelson et al., supra note 5, at 71, 74–75.

countries, making their control increasingly difficult. Additionally, several countries with strong encryption industries have publicly disavowed backdoors (or front doors) in encryption products, and many foreign (and now U.S.) companies have manufactured their products to be technically inaccessible to subpoenas or other legal process, at least process served on any but the owner of the device or data, viewing "technology, specifically end-to-end encryption, [a]s the best possible defense for privacy."[143] In at least one of these countries, the democratic process itself is at work to overturn what is perceived as a repressive surveillance law.[144] In other words, Apple's change of its default settings can be seen as simply a response to a global marketplace that has already implemented these changes in response to consumer demands for self-defense against the myriad threats in cyberspace.[145] Thus, U.S. consumers will have user-controlled end point and E2E encryption available to them regardless of any U.S. law implemented to mandate a key escrow or other government access system. Given the ubiquitous nature of encryption products and services, criminalization, while possible, is not a practical solution.

Furthermore, sophisticated terrorist organizations are well aware of the intelligence and intercept capabilities of Western governments. ISIS, for example, has banned the use of any Apple device or any device using GPS services.[146] Modern terrorists have used the "Snowden-approved" Signal messaging app to communicate, as well as Telegram, "a Russian-designed, Berlin-based secure messenger app." And there are other alternative forms of communications that avoid government monitoring, such as "the dark web," steganography (imbedding communication in pictures), and in-game chat messaging features available on Sony PlayStation and Microsoft XBOX platforms, to name just a few.[147]

None of this suggests that limiting encryption will necessarily be futile, or that mandated government access to data will produce no positive law enforcement/intelligence outcome. But it would be naïve to ignore the reality that such a mandate might only have a marginal impact against the most dangerous threats. It is therefore incumbent upon policy makers carefully to assess the ultimate payoff of such a mandate, an assessment that should account for the inherent limitations on mandated data access.

143 Schneier et al., supra note 20, at 5 (Germany and the Netherlands with 113 and 20 products have denounced backdoors); ProtonMail has publicly announced that its email is end-to-end encrypted so that even if forced to hand over the data by new Swiss surveillance laws, only the owner of the emails will have the power to decrypt them, additionally arguing that, "there is a distinction between handing over the data we already have (which is end-to-end encrypted), and being forced to actively hack users"). See Andy Yen, Impact of Swiss Surveillance Laws on Secure Email, ProtonMail (Dec. 16, 2015), https://protonmail.com/blog/swiss-surveillance-law/.

144 See id.; see also Swiss Surveillance Laws Headed for Nationwide Referendum!, ProtonMail (Jan. 14, 2016), https://protonmail.com/blog/swiss-surveillance-law-referendum/ (describing successful national effort to submit unpopular Swiss surveillance laws to national referendum).

145 See ACLU Submission, supra note 68, at 10–14 ("Strong encryption is our first line of defense against [the threat of cyberattacks]"). Conceptualizing encryption as a "self-defensive" weapon is not as far-fetched as it may seem; the U.S. government in the 1990s regulated the export of strong encryption under the International Traffic in Arms Regulations, which required State Department permission for export. See Levy, supra note 11, at 106–57.

146 The Islamic State (known as #ISIS) Bans Its Soldiers from Using iPhone, iPad, and GPS Phones and Devices, ArabCrunch EN (Dec. 21, 2014), http://arabcrunch.com/2014/12/the-islamic-state-known-as-isis-bans-its-soldiers-from-using-iphone-ipad-and-gps-phones-and-devices.html.

147 See Leonid Bershidsky, A BackDoor to Encryption Won't Stop Terrorists, BloombergView (Nov. 18, 2015), https://www.bloomberg.com/view/articles/2015-11-18/a-back-door-to-encryption-won-t-stop-terrorists; The Chertoff Group, supra note 5, at 10–11.

IV Front Door Access and the "Split Key" Mechanism – a Reasonable Risk Mitigation Measure?

Both Manhattan District Attorney Vance and FBI Director Comey have called for a "front door access" to encrypted traffic in the United States, or as an alternative for telecommunications companies to revert to the prior systems where the companies maintained the encryption keys rather than the user. This chapter will now consider the split key encryption proposal and criticisms of that proposal.

Critics on both ends of the encryption debate – those who warn of the specter of going dark and those who see total encryption as a benefit – each raise legitimate concerns. On one end of the spectrum, some advocates for privacy rights emphasize the risk that government collusion with cell device manufacturers will make access to encryption keys too easy, leading to inevitable abuse.[148] On the other end of the spectrum, advocates for public and national security emphasize the dangers of user-controlled encryption and how that danger necessitates government access to encryption keys.[149] Still others view the issue as far more nuanced than the extremes suggest.

There is, however, a response to this problem that seeks to strike a balance between the two extremes: a "split key" approach. Under this approach, to protect the government's interest in lawful access to encrypted data, manufacturers would be required, by statute, to preserve encryption keys for the devices and services they produce and distribute in the United States. To mitigate the risk of unlawful government access as the result of collusion with manufacturers or the abuse of the manufacturers themselves, these keys would be "split" and retained by two (or more) distinct entities: the manufacturer and a privacy rights organization.

The advantages of this "split key" approach are obvious. Unlike with going dark, or user-controlled encryption, the government's interest in efficient lawful access to encrypted data would be preserved. By splitting control of the encryption key between two entities – one of which would be susceptible to neither government pressure nor profit motives, but instead devoted to protecting the privacy interests of the public – the risk of unlawful government access would be substantially reduced. Of course, this exacts a cost: increased risk of unauthorized access. But this is the unavoidable consequence of the reality that any effort to find a middle ground cannot fully satisfy all concerns.

Such an approach is obviously contrary to the objectives of some privacy advocates, most notably those who have launched a series of retorts intent on snuffing out the development of mechanisms to preserve efficient lawful access to cell data.[150] These advocates, including one of this chapter's coauthors, are unpersuaded that the benefits of such a middle ground outweigh the costs to privacy protection and technological

148 See Mike Masnick, Everybody Knows FBI Director James Comey Is Wrong about Encryption, Even the FBI, TechDirt (Oct. 20, 2014, 10:22 AM), https://www.techdirt.com/articles/20141019/07115528878/everybody-knows-fbi-director-james-comey-is-wrong-about-encryption-even-fbi.shtml (discussing the current state of data encryption).

149 See Eric Chabrow, Obama Sees Need for Encryption Backdoor, Bank Info Security (Jan. 16, 2015), http://www.bankinfosecurity.com/cameron-obama-a-7809/op-1 (explaining a few of the different approaches to allowing government access of encrypted information).

150 See With Liberty to Monitor All, Human Rights Watch (July 28, 2014), http://www.hrw.org/node/127362/section/2 (providing a summary of a 120-page report that "documents how government surveillance and secrecy are undermining press freedom, the public's right to information, and the right to counsel, all human rights essential to a healthy democracy").

innovation.[151] These opponents frame efforts to preserve such access as a call for the creation of "backdoors" that can be exploited by the U.S. and any other government.[152] They argue that the creation of backdoors will introduce unacceptable vulnerabilities in products and systems[153] and point to examples where, in the past, such vulnerabilities have been exploited by hackers.[154]

To be clear, this "split key" proposal is not a subterfuge method of creating backdoor access to data. Unlike a backdoor, which generally refers to an undisclosed vulnerability in an application or device, a front door is a well-documented and clear mechanism for both encrypting and decrypting data, whether it be data in motion (communications) or at rest (stored data). To be secure, encryption should be subject to rigorous testing. Thus, its presence should be open to the public and available for attack, both in laboratories and in the real world. This is the only real way to evaluate the trustworthiness of encryption, with vulnerabilities being corrected as they are discovered, to strengthen the protocol and its implementation constantly. Essentially, a front door is the digital equivalent of a big, ingeniously engineered lock on the only entrance to an otherwise secure building. It is a lock that has been tested by every available lock picker and found to be secure, with any identified weaknesses being constantly fixed. Such a lock is always superior to a secret entrance in the rear of a building.

Any requirement to ensure lawful access to encrypted data raises another critical question: Who should have access to the key, and under what circumstances? One could imagine leaving the key to such a lock in the hands of the manufacturer, the police, or even locked inside another container with a similar lock. All of these scenarios carry different, but arguably manageable, risks. They are also just as available in the digital world as the real world – in fact more so, as encryption likely is stronger than the most ingenious physical lock ever created.

Implementing a split key approach would necessitate a statutory mandate to create, split, and retain encryption keys. Imposition of such a mandate would be based

151 See id. (opposing any changes that would make data less secure).

152 See id. (same).

153 Some have argued that the creation of additional encryption keys will be an attractive target for hackers no matter where they are stored. While that is true, it must be acknowledged that hackers, as do all logical actors, recognize that a chain is only as strong as its weakest link. Thus, hackers generally seek the path of least resistance to achieve their goals. It would generally be much easier for a hacker to compromise a user's device through a Trojan or to obtain his credentials through social engineering than it would be to hack into two or more well-protected systems. Moreover, despite modern society's obsession with connectivity, nothing requires a database maintaining encryption keys to be connected to the Internet. Thus, such a database could be immensely more secure than encryption keys or passwords found on users' devices.

154 See Benjamin Wittes, The LawFare Podcast, Episode #98: Chris Soghoian Responds to FBI Director James Comey, LawFare (Nov. 1, 2014), http://www.lawfareblog.com/lawfare-podcast-episode-98-chris-soghoian-responds-fbi-director-james-comey (discussing potential problems with weak data security). The Athens Affair, cited by Soghoian in this podcast, is probably the most frequently referenced example of the danger of creating "back doors" in communications networks. It is, however, a poor example that speaks more to the need for solid network security than it does to the creation of back doors. For an explanation of how Vodafone's failure to purchase and install Ericsson's Intercept Management System allowed this hack to occur, see Vassilis Prevelakis & Diomidis Spinellis, The Athens Affair: How Some Extremely Smart Hackers Pulled Off the Most Audacious Cell-Network Break-in Ever, IEEE Spectrum (June 29, 2007), http://spectrum.ieee.org/telecom/security/the-athens-affair (discussing a major hack of cell phone data in Greece).

on federal authority to regulate interstate commerce and communications.[155] A closely related example of such a mandate can be found in the Communications Assistance for Law Enforcement Act (CALEA).[156] While this statute is focused on another aspect of communication access, it is an example of imposing obligations on telecommunication providers to advance legitimate government investigatory interests, as noted by Congressional Research Service:

> CALEA is intended to preserve the ability of law enforcement officials to conduct electronic surveillance effectively and efficiently, despite the deployment of new digital technologies and wireless services by the telecommunications industry. CALEA requires telecommunications carriers to modify their equipment, facilities, and services to ensure that they are able to comply with authorized electronic surveillance.

The same report also emphasizes that CALEA was never designed to expand law enforcement surveillance authority, but instead was intended

> only to ensure that after law enforcement obtains the appropriate legal authority, carriers will have the necessary capabilities and sufficient capacity to assist law enforcement in conducting digital electronic surveillance regardless of the specific telecommunications systems or services deployed.[157]

Accordingly, CALEA requires telecommunication providers to establish the capability to respond expeditiously to government surveillance orders, including the requirement to "consult with telecommunications equipment manufacturers to develop equipment necessary to comply with the capability and capacity requirements identified by the FBI."[158]

But CALEA also offers the type of safeguards a split key decryption requirement would incorporate. First, it requires telecommunications carriers "to ensure that any interception of communications or access to call-identifying information that is conducted within their premises can only be done with a court order."[159] Second, it provides for a certain degree of execution oversight in that it also requires the affirmative intervention of an individual officer or employee of the carrier acting in accordance with regulations prescribed by the Federal Communications Commission.[160]

As CALEA does, the split key proposal reflects a compromise between public security and individual privacy, facilitating lawful access to data while mitigating the risk of unlawful access or investigatory overreach.

V On the Other Hand, We've Been down This Road Before

It is important to note that the proposal of key escrowing or split key escrowing is not new – it was the core of the Clipper chip proposal in the 1990s, an idea that was

155 See notes 153–57 and accompanying text (analogizing to the Communications Assistance for Law Enforcement Act as a basis for authority to mandate a split key approach to data encryption).
156 47 U.S.C. §§ 1001–1010 (2012).
157 Patricia Maloney Figliola, Cong. Research Serv., RL30677, Digital Surveillance: The Communications Assistance for Law Enforcement Act 2 (2007), http://fas.org/sgp/crs/intel/RL30 677.pdf.
158 Id. at 3.
159 Id.
160 Id.

ultimately rejected by U.S. business and governmental interests, and by our partners in the Organization of Economic Co-operation and Development because of the technical difficulties of building key escrow systems at scale, their enormous expense, the governance issues, and the risk.[161] In examining the renewed proposals for escrowed (split key or not) key systems made by Director Comey and others, critical experts have concluded that "the damage that could be caused by law enforcement exceptional access requirements would be even greater today than it would have been 20 years ago."[162] First, and most critically, building in exceptional access would increase system complexity, and as determined by neutral experts, although theoretically feasible, introduce so many new potential points of attack (increasing the attack surface of the cryptographic system) that it would significantly decrease the overall level of security.

> The reason [for this] lies in how modern-day asymmetric cryptographic solutions are constructed. Best practices for secure devices dictate that cryptographic keys are generated in specialized hardware devices that protect each key, ... which are specifically designed to ensure that the private keys they generate never leave the cryptomodule; the sensitivity of these keys is believed to be so important that any path allowing the keys to be exported from the cryptomodule would erode the security model of the system.[163]

Thus, moving from such a secure nonexportable key system to a key escrow system would require developing a way to export a copy of each key solely for key escrow purposes, transporting the escrowed key to the escrowed location(s) without compromise or intercept; creating secure storage with billions of other keys without compromise; and developing a system to manage access to those keys only when lawfully authorized.[164] These engineering challenges were formidable in the 1990s, but the scale and scope of the systems now dependent on strong encryption[165] and a society dependent on "far-flung digital networks," both of which are subject to daily attacks by sophisticated malevolent actors, have significantly increased these already formidable challenges. Two recent examples of the "difficulties that scale and system integration pose in building

161 See Abelson et al., supra note 5, at 70. Clipper involved the Escrowed Encryption Standard (EES), which consisted of NSA's new classified encryption algorithm (Skipjack), implemented by an 80-bit key split into two components, "each of which was to be stored at a secure facility operated by an executive branch federal agency." The EES was "unofficially known as 'Clipper,' after the tamper-resistant chip implementing the 80-bit encryption algorithm." See Landau, supra note 3, at 114–15; see also Diffie & Landau, supra note 21, at 234–35, 245–46 (describing rejection of key escrow systems by the Organization for Economic Cooperation and Development in 1996); Sean Gallagher, What the Government Should've Learned about Backdoors from the Clipper Chip," Ars Technica (Dec. 14, 2015), http://arstechnica.com/information-technology/2015/12/what-the-government-shouldve-learned-about-backdoors-from-the-clipper-chip/.

162 Abelson et al., supra note 5, at 69.

163 The Chertoff Group, supra note 5, at 6 (explaining that the Federal Personal Identity Verification system used by all federal employees to authenticate into federal computer systems does not permit exportation of such keys and is a best practice followed by both government and business). There are other methods for generating secure keys, but the crypto-module approach is considered a best practice. The challenges in a key escrow system remain.

164 Id. at 6. The management of law enforcement access credentials alone is a formidable task that creates significant security risks, not to mention global diplomatic implications. See Abelson et al., supra note 5, at 70, 74.

165 Think e-commerce, the power grid, Internet banking, the financial industry, critical infrastructure, military and civilian command and control networks, to name just a few.

large software systems" pointed to by critics of key escrow systems are the poorly executed Healthcare.gov initiative and the FBI Trilogy program, a five-year, $170-million effort to build an electronic case management program that was ultimately abandoned as unworkable.[166]

Additionally, engineering failures in encryption systems that were specifically designed to accomplish law enforcement's exceptional access are not unprecedented. These include the ability to spoof the Clipper "system so that communications were encrypted without the government having access to the keys," and flaws in wiretapping technologies that allowed criminals to deceive and manipulate the law enforcement equipment directed against them.[167] These flaws allowed the exploitation by unknown outsiders of vulnerabilities installed in communications architectures, including, for example, the ten-month monitoring of the cell phones of more than one hundred Greek government officials in 2004–2005 by still-unknown parties who took advantage of the intercept features on an Ericsson CALEA-compliant telephone switch; major security holes discovered in Cisco wiretapping architecture for IP networks that allowed unauthorized parties to receive intercepted communications easily; and the wiretapping of more than six thousand people by insiders at Telecom Italia between 1996 and 2006 that monitored "business, financial, and political leaders, judges, and journalists."[168] Finally, in 2015, it was disclosed that a major breach of the Juniper computer network company, believed to have been the work of a foreign government, allowed spying on encrypted communications of U.S. government and private companies worldwide for three years. The breach was described by a U.S. official as "stealing a master key to get into any government building."[169]

Not only must modern systems and computer engineers confront the significant challenges in engineering a secure system; they must also contend with the security of hardware that has become increasingly insecure. "The risk of compromise in the manufacturing process," when malfunctions can be inserted into software or written onto computer chips, "is perhaps the least understood cyberthreat."[170] When the NSA examined telephone switches built to comply with government-mandated access for wiretapping, it discovered security problems with *all* the switches submitted for testing.[171]

Finally, although the majority of government officials act in good faith, there is more than hypothetical potential for official misuse of monitoring and interception

166 Abelson et al., supra note 5, at 75; see also Levy, supra note 11, at 257–59 (describing Bell Lab scientist who discovered fatal flaw in Clipper's law enforcement access field implementation, which could be counterfeited, resulting in "unbreakable" encryption with no key transmitted to law enforcement).

167 Landau, supra note 3, at 196.

168 Id.; Abelson et al., supra note 5, at 75.

169 The Chertoff Group, supra note 5, at 12–13; see also Evan Perez & Shimon Prokupecz, Newly Discovered Hack Has U.S. Fearing Foreign Infiltration, CNN (Dec. 19, 2015), http://edition.cnn.com/2015/12/18/politics/juniper-networks-us-government-security-hack/ (major breach allowed spying on encrypted communications of U.S. government and private companies for three years, described by U.S. official as "stealing a master key to get into any government building.").

170 Lynn, supra note 65; see also Jeffrey Smith, Counterfeit Chips Plague Pentagon Weapon Systems, Center for Public Integrity (Nov. 7, 2011), https://www.publicintegrity.org/2011/11/07/7323/counterfeit-chips-plague-pentagon-weapons-systems; Dawn Lim, Counterfeit Chips Plague U.S. Missile Defense, Wired (Nov. 8, 2011), https://www.wired.com/2011/11/counterfeit-missile-defense/ (describing nightmare scenario of "Trojan horse" parts being embedded in parts).

171 Abelson et al., supra note 5, at 73.

capabilities given documented instances of such misuse after September 11.[172] The history of U.S. surveillance activities is replete with instances of misuse of those authorities, often against political enemies or those with unpopular political views.[173] Title III wiretaps involve numerous safeguards and protections against such government abuse, including strong judicial oversight. Given the likely operational necessity for government access to escrowed keys, discussed later, such procedural and judicial protections are less likely, and, given the covert nature of the access, abuse is less likely to be disclosed.

In addition to the complexities of a key escrow system that contravene technological best practices for cryptographic security,[174] law enforcement demands during the Clipper chip debates included a requirement for immediate access to escrowed keys around the clock, making "it impossible to employ the full range of safeguards that could ameliorate some of the risks inherent in commercial key recovery systems."[175] The potential operational demands for law enforcement's rapid covert access to encrypted data would introduce still more complexities and security risks and would limit the technological safeguards available to mitigate the risk. Implementation of such a system would also be extremely expensive – both in its creation, in the reengineering of the cryptographic systems contained within computers and cell phones, and in the costs of managing and implementing such an escrow system. There should be some discussion of who would bear such a cost – the government, the user, the private civil liberty organization?

It is also important to consider the risk that might flow from the concentration of the escrowed keys. This would create a lucrative target for hostile governments, hackers, and other criminal third parties – or heighten the threat posed by insiders – and would result in a catastrophic loss if a breach occurred. Far less valuable troves of data have been the subject of concerted efforts of hackers and foreign adversaries. The Chinese hack of the OPM security clearance database, discussed previously, caused significant damage to national security due to the concentration of valuable data in a single institution. In May 2016, hackers breached servers at the Democratic National Committee Headquarters and obtained documents containing research into the opposing candidate.[176] In 2009, Chinese hackers breached Google servers and gained access to a sensitive database with several years of information about U.S. government surveillance

172 Changes implemented after the attacks of September 11 have led to public disclosures of blatant violations of surveillance and monitoring authorities, to include the FBI's misuse of exigent letters to obtain call data records without following the procedures established by law and the use of "sneak peeks" by FBI agents to review phone company records with no legal process in place; see Landau, supra note 3, at 192–94, as well as the establishment of secure room at AT&T's San Francisco switching facility by the NSA in which high-speed screening of fiber-optic inter-ISP traffic was occurring. Id. at 176–77.

173 Diffie & Landau, supra note 21, at 156–71 (describing history of misuse of government surveillance in the United States, often based on First Amendment activities of dissidents or on prohibited discrimination).

174 Id. at 6 (and would likely require reengineering of most current PCs, laptops, and mobile devices).

175 Hal Abelson, Ross Anderson, Steven M. Bellovin, Josh A. Benaloh, Matt Blaze, Whitfield Diffie, John Gilmore, Peter G. Neumann, Ronald L. Rivest, Jeffrey I. Schiller, Bruce Schneier, The Risks of Key Recovery, Key Escrow, & Trusted Third Party Encryption 5 (1998), http://www.crypto.com/papers/escrowrisks98.pdf.

176 Dan Goodwin, Lone Wolf Claims Responsibility for DNC Hack, Dumps Purported Trump Smear File, Ars Technica (June 15, 2016), http://arstechnica.com/security/2016/06/lone-wolf-claims-responsibility-for-dnc-hack-dumps-purported-trump-smear-file/ (contrasting claim of lone wolf hacker with earlier claims of two Russian intelligence-affiliated adversaries).

targets.[177] In 2011, hackers – believed to be state sponsored – breached RSA Security LLC and stole SecurID seed keys used to generate other encryption keys for hardware used by sensitive Department of Defense contractors, showing that any encryption key repository will be a significant target of attack.[178]

Ultimately, requiring key escrowing may produce adverse consequences for ongoing encryption best practices and future innovations. These include the use of *forward secrecy* and the developing trend toward ephemeral communications. Any impediment to such innovation should be carefully considered in order to avoid stifling development of even more effective data and communications protection. For example, forward secrecy generates private keys that are discarded for each session, limiting the damage from any particular breach;[179] a mandatory key escrow system would necessarily change that, preserving keys that would otherwise be discarded. For these reasons, some argue that "all known methods of achieving third-party escrow are incompatible with forward secrecy."[180] Key escrow would also impose impediments on the use of transient identities and strong location privacy.

Congress and other policy makers must carefully consider the significant risk that mandating governmental access through a key escrow system would also adversely affect the other critical functions of encryption beyond ensuring confidentiality – those of authentication and verification/integrity. Authenticated encryption – "ensuring that the entity at the other end of the communication is who you expect, and that the message has not been modified since being sent"[181] – depends on the protection of the private key.

177 Ellen Nakashima, Chinese Hackers Who Breached Google Gained Access to Sensitive Data, U.S. Officials Say, Wash. Post (May 20, 2013), https://www.washingtonpost.com/world/national-security/chinese-hackers-who-breached-google-gained-access-to-sensitive-data-us-officials-say/2013/05/20/51330428-be34-11e2-89c9-3be8095fe767_story.html.

178 The Chertoff Group, supra note 5, at 12.

179 Abelson et al., supra note 5, at 74 ("With forward secrecy, a new key is negotiated with each transaction, and long-term keys are used only for authentication. The transaction (or session) keys are discarded after each transaction – ... an attacker ... who breaches a network and gains access to keys can only decrypt data from the time of the breach until the breach is discovered and rectified; historic data remains safe. In addition, since session keys are destroyed immediately after the completion of each transaction, an attacker must interject itself into the process of each transaction in real time to obtain the keys and compromise the data." Escrowing of any private key creates a long-term vulnerability – i.e., all information ever encrypted using a person's/organization's related public key can then be decrypted if the escrowed private key is compromised).

180 Abelson et al., supra note 5, at 74. Requiring key escrowing also goes against the trend against ephemeral messaging and limiting data retention. Id. (discussing trends toward chat rather than email, transient messaging such as Snapchat, and the practices of many companies to remove emails after an established period). Many of these practices also echo new claims for a "right to be forgotten," as seen in recent European cases against Google and Facebook. See, e.g., EU Court Backs 'Right to Be Forgotten' in Google Case, BBC News (May 13, 2014), http://www.bbc.com/news/world-europe-27388289; Jeffrey Toobin, The Solace of Oblivion, The New Yorker (Sept. 29, 2014), http://www.newyorker.com/magazine/2014/09/29/solace-oblivion; Jeffrey Rosen, The Right to Be Forgotten, 64 Stan. L. Rev. Online 88 (2012), http://www.stanfordlawreview.org/sites/default/files/online/topics/64-SLRO-88.pdf.

181 Abelson et al., supra note 5, at 74; see also Landau, supra note 3, at 46 (Digital signatures "use public-key cryptography to provide authentication in a digital environment. To sign, Alice encrypts a cryptographically created shorter version of her message with her private key and appends this signature to her communication. When Bob receives the message, he uses Alice's public key to decrypt her message-dependent signature. Because only Alice has the [private] key to enable signing this cryptographically shortened form of the message, only Alice was able to have signed the message. Thus Alice cannot successfully later deny that the signature is hers; this is called the property of non-repudiation. By comparing

If the private key is disclosed (via key escrow) to a third party, the message recipient is no longer provided with the assurance of the message's integrity. The third party can not only read the message, but also forge traffic and make it appear to be from the original sender because he has access to the private key.[182]

User trust is essential to innovation on the Internet. Built-in government controls undermine that trust, particularly in the area of authentication and integrity. The prime minister of Estonia, who has digitized much of its government, has remarked that more than two-thirds of Estonian citizens vote online. "How" he asked, "will they trust the results of the election if they know that the government has a backdoor into the technology used to collect the citizen's votes?"[183]

Will built-in government controls fundamentally undermine the user trust that many believe is essential to Internet innovation? No one can answer this question with certainty, but those responsible for striking the balance between security and privacy must certainly consider it. As with the many other public policy concerns addressed in this chapter, these considerations may tip the balance in favor of allowing end-to-end encryption, even if that encryption imposes certain risks in the realm of public security.

Conclusion

The risks related to going dark are real. Encryption technologies are making it increasingly easy for individual users to prevent even lawful government access to potentially vital information related to crimes or other national security threats. When the president of the United States,[184] the prime minister of the United Kingdom,[185] and the director of the FBI[186] all publicly express deep concerns about how this phenomenon will endanger their respective nations, this risk should not be ignored or minimized.

This evolution of individual access to increasingly robust encryption represents a fundamental shift in the traditional balance between government surveillance authority and individual liberty. And "balance" is the operative word. The protections provided by the Fourth Amendment against unreasonable searches and seizures must be carefully protected. Ideally, that protection will produce equilibrium between societal interests

the decrypted signature with his own computation of the cyptographically shortened version of the message, Bob can discover whether any alterations have been made to the message in transit, thus ensuring the message's integrity").

182 Abelson et al., supra note 5, at 74 (This undermines the entire structure supporting the trust and legality of digital signatures. Additionally, "the same cryptographic keys used to protect confidentiality of data in systems are also used in many cases to protect and control the systems themselves… [thus] a key escrowed for the purposes of allowing access to data flowing through these systems could also allow the holder of the escrowed key to access administrative functions for that system"); The Chertoff Group, supra note 5, at 16 (additionally, "most Infrastructure-as-a-Service (IaaS) and Software-as-a-Service (SaaS) cloud offerings are administered remotely, while the security of the control traffic for these systems is managed through cryptographic keys using standard protocols like SSL/TLS").

183 Daniel J. Weitzner, The Encryption Debate Enters Phase Two, LawFare Blog (Mar. 16, 2016), https://www.lawfareblog.com/encryption-debate-enters-phase-two.

184 Nakashima & Gellman, supra note 1.

185 James Ball, Cameron Wants to Ban Encryption – He Can Say Goodbye to Digital Britain, The Guardian (Jan. 13, 2015), http://www.theguardian.com/ commentisfree/2015/jan/13/cameron-ban-encryption-digital-britain-online-shopping-banking-messaging-terror (discussing David Cameron's views on data encryption).

186 Comey, supra note 5.

advanced by government surveillance efforts and the privacy and individual security interests at stake – a balance that is perceived by the public as advancing, and not undermining, individual liberties.

The difficulty of achieving consensus on user-controlled encryption is not due to a disagreement about the threats facing the nation or the individual. The dangers posed by the ability of criminals and terrorists to use encryption to plan, organize, and execute plots that harm our people and our nation are significant and clear. The need expressed by the FBI and law enforcement to preserve their access to those communications is understandable. But just as clear are the dangers posed by leaving our citizens, our industries, our government, our military, the producers of our intellectual property, and those operating our critical infrastructure exposed to the criminals, foreign governments, and terrorist hackers who stalk the Internet and cyberspace and target all of us. Our desires for a means of self-defense, and our expectation of national defense, are also understandable.

The real disagreements arise in the varying assessments of the solutions to these threats and the attendant risks perceived in each choice. Indeed, the two coauthors of this chapter arrive at very different conclusions about the wisdom of government-mandated limits on user controlled encryption. For one author, the notion of unlimited access to end-to-end encryption unjustifiably compromises legitimate government authority and ability to intercept and monitor cellphone and computer communications. This belief unsurprisingly leads him to conclude that requiring mandatory access to encrypted communications and data through a key escrow system is not only logical, but consistent with the Fourth Amendment's balance between individual privacy and legitimate government investigatory efforts. For those who share this view, the warrant and probable cause requirements of the Fourth Amendment, coupled with split key implementation, provide the oversight necessary to protect individuals from unauthorized government intrusion on their privacy. As noted earlier, there is no question that such an approach will inevitably increase the risk of both unlawful government access to data and access by nefarious private actors. But such risk is inherent in almost all privacy interests protected by the Fourth Amendment. Accordingly, for this author, the decisive question is not whether a split key statutory mandate increases risk to individual privacy, but instead whether that is a risk that members of our society should accept in the interests of collective security. By treating private data analogously to the privacy interests protected by the sanctity of the home, the balance tips in favor not of an impenetrable zone of privacy, but instead of a carefully protected zone subject to lawful government access.

But others, to include the second author of this chapter, assess robust user-controlled encryption as the best solution to the host of individual and national security risks that exist in the modern digital age, including the risks posed by cyber criminals and terrorists. For her, and other proponents of user-controlled end-to-end encryption, proposals for mandated access to encrypted data and communications build unjustified and unnecessary weaknesses into the security that encryption provides to us all – governments, individuals, private industry, critical infrastructure, military, and journalists. As a result, she views the benefits of mandated access as far outweighed by its costs, particularly in light of the quantitative data on historic wiretapping and the alternatives available to law enforcement and national security entities. Although law enforcement and intelligence agencies have become accustomed to expansive access to digital communications and data in this "golden age of surveillance,"[187] it may be that the "pendulum of security has begun to swing back to the more long-term norm of comparatively stronger protection of confidential information."[188] For one of the authors, such a reassessment and rebalancing of the interests of citizens and the government is overdue. The technological foreclosure of methods of investigation the government has become accustomed to will require law enforcement and national security organizations to restore the more traditional balance between the government and the citizen, a balance that can be effectively controlled by court supervision and effective governmental oversight.

Trust serves many functions in our society. It is necessary in the social compact between the government and the governed. If innovation and commerce are to thrive in cyberspace, trust in the secure confidential communications upon which these economic benefits depend must be protected. Trust is particularly relevant in evaluating the competing claims for access to our private conversations, thoughts, deliberations, amorous activities, political activism, search for identity, private health information, and financial information, all exposed through our use of computers and cellular smart phones in the modern digital age. The sophisticated threats faced by any modern user of the Internet or cell phone are real and growing, and encryption remains perhaps the only weapon available for self-defense. The looming threats to critical infrastructure posed by insecurities in cyberspace only reinforce the need for a strong defense.

It is certainly true that terrorism and crime pose real and substantial threats, and that surveillance is often a vital tool to protect the nation from these threats. But the public must believe in the government's commitment to respect civil liberties. It is simply impossible to ignore the reality that recent default setting changes by Apple and Google and other Internet and cellular phone service providers reflect a profound lack of trust in the government's commitment to respect citizen privacy, as consumers embrace the conclusion that "encryption algorithms offer protection through mathematical law which always holds true, no matter how many laws the US Congress passes."[189] Consumer appetite for encryption may also reflect a belief that our governmental institutions are insufficient or unwilling to provide the oversight of American national security agencies

[187] See Don't Panic, supra note 127.

[188] The Chertoff Group, supra note 5, at 19 ("For the last 10 to 15 years law enforcement has enjoyed uniquely expansive access to digital data, [reflecting] a relatively unique moment in time when individuals (citizens and criminals alike) have taken to using the digital domain for the creation and storage of confidential information without giving significant consideration to the security of that information. Before this era, physical security and the discontinuous nature of the kinetic domain had made practical access to stored information comparatively difficult for the government. The digital transition has, briefly, created a golden age of easy lawful access to data.... It is ... no surprise that the pendulum of security has begun to swing back to the more long-term norm of comparatively stronger protection of confidential information. The commercial spread of strong encryption products is but one aspect of that trend and, like most technological developments, ... almost impossible to resist"); see also Fraser, supra note 70 (prior to the twentieth century those wishing to maintain the privacy and security of their communications only had to walk into a field away from eavesdroppers; many of our framers routinely used ciphers and codes to protect their official and private communications, often employing ciphers so strong no government could break them); see also ACLU Submission to Special Rapporteur, supra note 68, at 15 n.68 ("In the century following the invention of the telegraph in 1844, forty-four new commercial ciphers were patented by Americans for both commercial and private users").

[189] Swiss Surveillance Laws Headed for Nationwide Referendum!, supra note 144.

that is necessary to preserve civil liberties and democratic processes.[190] Indeed, despite the many rational recommendations to enhance transparency made by the Presidential Review Group on Intelligence and Communications Technologies discussed earlier[191] – a panel that recognized the corrosive effect mass surveillance can have on the democratic process and our system of government – neither the president nor Congress adopted any meaningful changes.

In situations such as this, involving the complex interplay of conflicting legitimate interests, democracies entrust the resolution of intractable policy dilemmas to legislatures, which are subject to democratic processes established to ensure that all viewpoints are considered and respected. A core defect in the current debate over going dark, however, is that that debate is "being framed by both sides as a deep conflict between freedom and security; between the civil rights of users to maintain their privacy, and the legitimate needs of law enforcement and national security."[192] It may be that, but it is also a conflict between security on the individual and societal levels, interests not necessarily in conflict, but dependent in many ways. And, it remains a debate about the best way to "secure the blessings of Liberty to ourselves and our Posterity" in the face of the sophisticated and rising cyberthreats that menace each of us, our economy, and our nation. That perhaps is the real reason for the vitriol. Reasonable people will differ in their evaluations of the threat and the various proposed solutions,[193] as do the two authors of this chapter, but it is hoped that ground exists for our representatives to forge a consensus to restore the oversight, transparency, and accountability over our institutions that most of us would agree are essential whatever solution is chosen – oversight that our founders considered necessary in the Fourth Amendment itself. Failure to do so will only reinforce the choice of many to "escape to technology" as the solution.[194]

190 Yochai Benkler, We Cannot Trust Our Government, So We Must Trust the Technology, The Guardian (Feb. 22, 2016), https://www.theguardian.com/us-news/2016/feb/22/snowden-government-trust-encryption-apple-fbi (arguing that it is instead, "a conflict about legitimacy … about confidence in the oversight of an American [law enforcement and] national security establishment").

191 Clarke et al., supra note 92.

192 Benkler, supra note 190 (rejecting this premise and arguing that the "fundamental problem is the breakdown of trust in institutions and organizations. In particular, the loss of confidence in oversight of the American national security establishment"); but see Going Dark Primer, supra note 76, at 6 ("Technology, such as encryption, protects our data and our infrastructure, and helps to ensure the privacy of our citizens; yet it is also exploited by bad actors, including drug traffickers, child predators, and terrorists, to facilitate criminal activities, and threaten our national security. Thus, what we are really dealing with is not so much a question of "privacy versus security," but a question of "security versus security").

193 Dave Aitel, Enhancing National Cybersecurity Requires Surrendering the Crypto War, LawFare (May 27, 2016), https://www.lawfareblog.com/enhancing-national-cybersecurity-requires-surrendering-crypto-war (arguing that the government must surrender in the crypto-wars and no longer hinder strong information security standards; that reconciliation with the technology community is the first step in ensuring constructive public–private partnerships necessary for real national cybersecurity).

194 Id.

15 Business Responses to Surveillance

Lothar Determann†

Companies have different perspectives and responses regarding surveillance, the "continuous observation of a place, person, group, or ongoing activity in order to gather information."[1] Some companies sell surveillance cameras, software, and services to government agencies, businesses, and consumers. Some sell defensive equipment or insurance against unwanted surveillance and cyber-threats.[2] Most companies are targets of surveillance by competitors, government entities, and criminals. Most companies also conduct surveillance on market trends, competitors, their own employees, and visitors of their premises. Many companies get caught in the crossfire of security and privacy interests concerning surveillance – some more, some less, depending on their particular business focus.

In Section I of this chapter, I identify key questions that all companies should consider regarding surveillance. In Sections II–VI, I provide an overview regarding conflicting needs and requirements that companies should consider as they find their individual responses to surveillance. Finally, I conclude with a summary of common business responses to surveillance.

I Key Questions Regarding Surveillance for Businesses

A *Embrace or Oppose Surveillance*

As threshold questions, every company has to ask whether a particular form of surveillance is necessary, beneficial, or harmful to its business; whether such surveillance is legally required, permissible, or unlawful; and whether the risks of embracing or opposing surveillance outweigh the respective benefits. Most companies will find different answers to these questions for different business lines, operational scenarios, and jurisdictions. Some forms of surveillance can be required in one country and prohibited in another. Companies have to differentiate – no one size fits all.

For example, a company that sells smart phones, cloud storage solutions, or communication services for anonymous speech will tend to view government surveillance as

† Lothar Determann teaches computer, Internet, and data privacy law at Freie Universität Berlin; University of California, Berkeley School of Law; and Hastings College of the Law, San Francisco; and practices technology law as a partner with Baker & McKenzie LLP. He is admitted in California and Germany. Opinions expressed here are those of the author only, not his firm's, clients', or others'.

1 Surveillance, www.dictionary.com/browse/surveillance. The English term "surveillance" originates from the French verb *surveill* and Latin *vigilāre*, to watch. *Id.*

2 For example, antivirus software, firewall technology, and cyber-insurance.

a threat to its business and oppose government surveillance as much as possible. If the products are vulnerable to third party surveillance, enterprise customers and consumers may shun the products because of privacy and security concerns. But, the same customers may expect a high degree of security on retail Web sites and e-commerce marketplaces that must be subject to a certain level of private and government surveillance to protect against fraud. Also, an operator of a social network for sharing of data may focus on keeping sexual predators and shady businesses off its platform and find it necessary or beneficial to conduct surveillance on Web site users, call center employees, and logistics providers to detect, prevent, and investigate crimes and threats. Businesses that are plagued by fraud and safety concerns tend to feel a need to maintain good relations with law enforcement agencies to protect and serve their customers. Such companies may embrace government surveillance to some extent. They may want to position themselves legally to be able to cooperate with law enforcement as much as possible. Such companies may want to provide tips proactively and release user data on request.

But even a company that generally seeks good relations with law enforcement agencies in most countries may want to keep a distance from governments in countries that pursue agendas considered incompatible with public policy in the company's home jurisdiction or key markets. For example, an operator of a marketplace for used books may do its best to cooperate with law enforcement agencies in the United States and Europe to protect sellers and buyers from fraud, yet refuse to cooperate with governments in China or Russia that censor political speech and compel companies to release information on dissidents. As another example, a number of United States–based technology companies have recently publicized their efforts to oppose government surveillance by openly resisting data access requests, refusing to cooperate with law enforcement agencies, challenging warrants and court orders, publishing transparency reports about government surveillance, lobbying for legislative change, engaging in technological obstruction via end-to-end encryption or immediate data deletion, and transferring custody over customer data to companies in other jurisdictions for the declared purpose of avoiding government requests in their home jurisdiction.[3] Technology companies in the United States consciously pursue such agendas as a result of perceived global market pressures and opportunities, even risking the ill will of federal and state authorities. But such choices would be much harder or impossible to make for companies that depend on government procurement, are subject to heavy regulation, or are headquartered in jurisdictions governed by totalitarian regimes.

Separately, as an employer, every company has to find the right country-specific balance between protecting employee privacy and workers' rights. on the one hand, and, on the other hand, detecting and preventing employee misconduct. Therefore, companies have to find jurisdiction- and sector-specific responses to the question whether and where they embrace or oppose surveillance.

[3] *See, e.g.*, John Herzfeld, *New York Judge Orders Twitter to Produce Wall Street Protester's Postings within Days*, 11 PVLR 1413 (2012); ELEC. FRONTIER FOUND., WHO HAS YOUR BACK? PROTECTING YOUR DATA FROM GOVERNMENT REQUESTS (2015), www.eff.org/who-has-your-back-government-data-requests-2015; Mark Hamblett, *Microsoft Prevails on Appeal in Dodging Warrant for Foreign Emails*, RECORDER (July 14, 2016); *Deutsche Telekom to Act as Data Trustee for Microsoft Cloud in Germany*, DEUTSCHE TELEKOM AG (Nov. 11, 2015), www.telekom.com/media/company/293260; GOOGLE TRANSPARENCY REPORTS, www.google.com/transparencyreport/; *ECPA Reform: Why Now?* DIGITAL DUE PROCESS (2010), http://digitaldueprocess.org/.

B *Possess Data or Not*

Companies must be thoughtful about data collection and retention. Whatever data they collect and retain can be a valuable asset, a source of liability, or an attractive target for criminals, private litigants, government surveillants, and others. Companies have a margin between data collection requirements and prohibitions and between minimum and maximum data retention requirements. Companies have to decide carefully what data they must, may, or must not collect and how long they must, may, and should keep data.

C *Where to Keep the Data*

A company that depends on good government relations in one jurisdiction and needs to resist government requests in certain other countries has to take this into account when it plans data center locations. Companies have traditionally focused on operational, tax, connectivity, and energy price considerations when selecting locations for data centers, but they increasingly keep an eye on privacy laws and public perception regarding government surveillance.

Not all countries give companies a legal choice in this respect. China, Germany, Indonesia, and Russia have started to enact broad data residency requirements to secure access to personal data on their respective territories.[4] To avoid compliance obligations and enforcement exposure, some multinationals have to consider refraining from doing business in jurisdictions that are particularly hostile to individual privacy or civil rights.

D *Encrypt, Possibly End-to-End*

Companies that want to oppose government surveillance and data access requests have another option besides not collecting data in the first place, quickly deleting data, or storing data offshore: they can offer end-to-end encryption to their customers with a setup where the company itself does not have the key. Even companies that do not care to offer end-to-end encryption and that retain keys for themselves have to ask whether they must, should, or can encrypt data to prevent unauthorized access and resulting liabilities and harms.

E *What to Tell Data Subjects*

Companies that want to engage in surveillance and cooperate with government surveillance and data access requests can negate or qualify privacy expectations in notices to customers, employees, site visitors, and other data subjects. In some cases, companies seek consent, *e.g.*, to monitor calls for quality assurance or analyze emails for placement of advertisements. But companies must consider that if they seek consent from users for their own surveillance (*e.g.*, to analyze email content for marketing purposes), then they may lose arguments to oppose surveillance by government agencies on privacy grounds. Companies that want to preserve the ability to oppose governments regarding data access

[4] Lothar Determann, Data Residency Rules Cutting Into Clouds: Impact and Options for Global Businesses and IT Architectures, Bloomberg BNA Data Privacy & Security Law Report (16 PVLR 496 - 04/03/2017); Lothar Determann & Michaela Weigl, *Data Residency Requirements Creeping into German Law*, Bloomberg BNA: Privacy & Sec. Law Report, 15 PVLR 529 (2016); Lothar Determann, Edward Bekeschenko, Vadim Perevalov & Inna Wood, *Keep Russian Data in Russia and Out of Clouds?* 32 Computer & Internet Law. 6, 1 (2015).

requests on privacy grounds should consider refraining from monitoring content themselves and from seeking consent or issuing broad notices regarding monitoring, which could negate data subject privacy claims. All companies need to craft their privacy policies, notices, and protocols carefully.[5]

F *Prepare for Government Data Access Requests*

Larger organizations need to provide employees with training and written protocols to prepare for surveillance cooperation requests, dawn raids, subpoenas, visits by process servers, and other forms of data access requests. Receptionists need a short checklist how to react when government officials demand access to premises. IT professionals need more detailed guidance on how to select and operate security and surveillance technologies. In-house legal counsel must be briefed on international attorney–client privilege rules and how to handle surveillance matters that span across jurisdictions. At the same time, companies need to plan and manage proactively which employees have access to what types of data.

II Companies Caught in the Middle: Lay of the Lands Internationally

All around the world, companies can be compelled to endure surveillance, searches, or seizures, or actively to provide information to governments for surveillance operations and other investigations.[6] At the same time, companies are prohibited from unlawfully intruding into individual privacy. Companies face significant restrictions regarding the sharing of personal data, including sharing with government agencies. When a government agency demands data about customers or other individuals, a company can get caught in the middle between obligations to respect individual privacy rights and obligations to respond to requests from governments. If the company refuses to provide data despite an enforceable government request, the government can apply sanctions and ultimately force. If the company provides data voluntarily or pursuant to an unlawful or unenforceable government request, the company can be liable to the data subject or sanctioned by a data protection authority. Companies cannot assume that every government agency will accept legal views taken by an agency of the same government; data protection authorities may well take the position that police surveillance or information requests from the same country's government are illegal and that companies are obligated to resist such illegal requests. Therefore, companies have to be prepared to determine quickly whether and when they can, must, or may share data with a particular government agency and on the basis of what process.

For a high-level overview regarding surveillance laws and regulations around the world, consider Baker & McKenzie's global surveillance law survey[7] and the following maps:

5 For practical tips on drafting privacy-related documentation, see Lothar Determann, California Privacy Law – Practical Guide and Commentary, Chapter 3–5 (2nd Ed. 2017), and Lothar Determann, Determann's Field Guide to Privacy Law, Chapter 3 (2d ed. 2015).

6 *See* Paul Schwartz, *Systematic Government Access to Private-Sector Data in Germany*, 2 Int'l Data Privacy L. 289 (2012); Ian Walden, Law Enforcement Access to Data in Clouds (2014); Ian Brown, *Government Access to Private-Sector Data in the United Kingdom*, 2 Int'l Data Privacy L. 230 (2012); *see also* Fred H. Cate, James X. Dempsey & Ira S. Rubinstein, *Systematic Government Access to Private-Sector Data*, 2 Int'l Data Privacy L. 195 (2012).

7 An interactive survey with comparison options between selected jurisdictions is publicly available at http://globalitc.bakermckenzie.com/surveillance/.

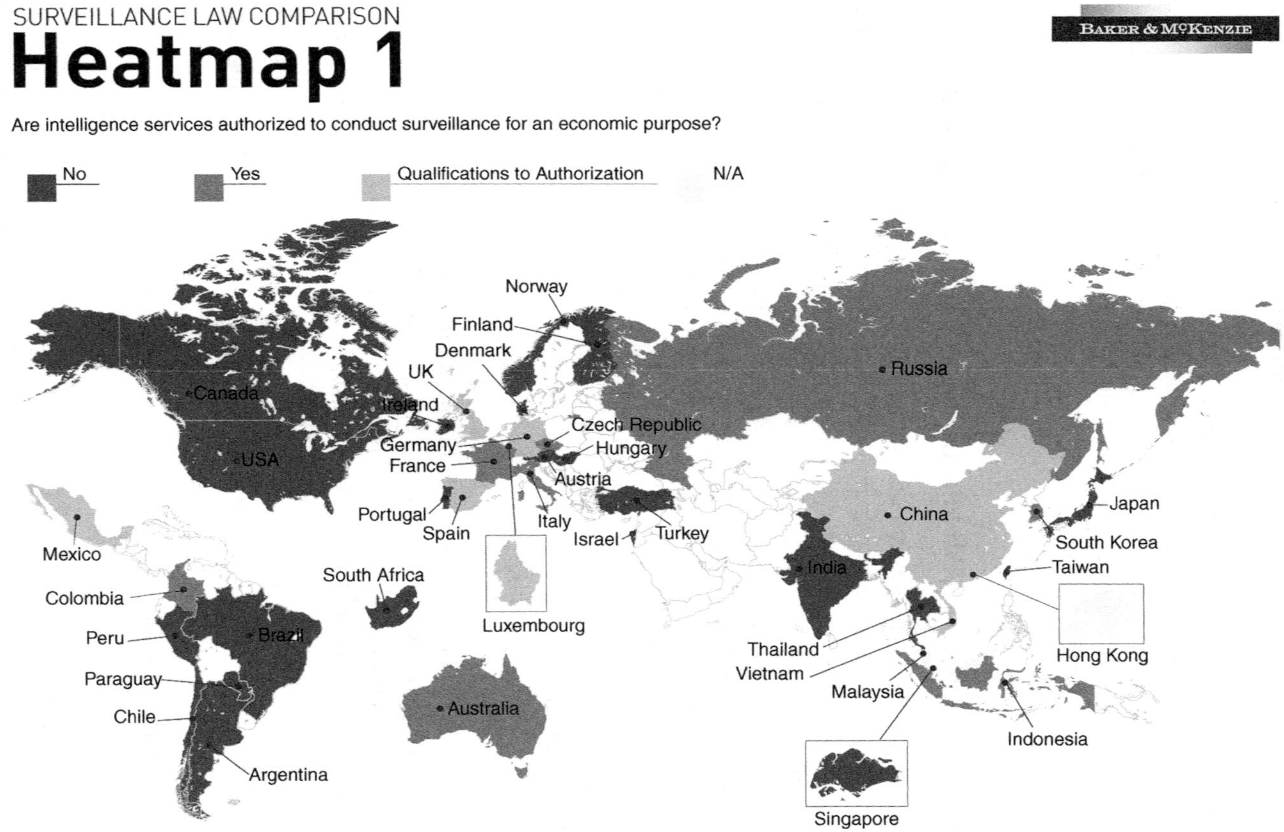

Figure 15.1. Map 1.

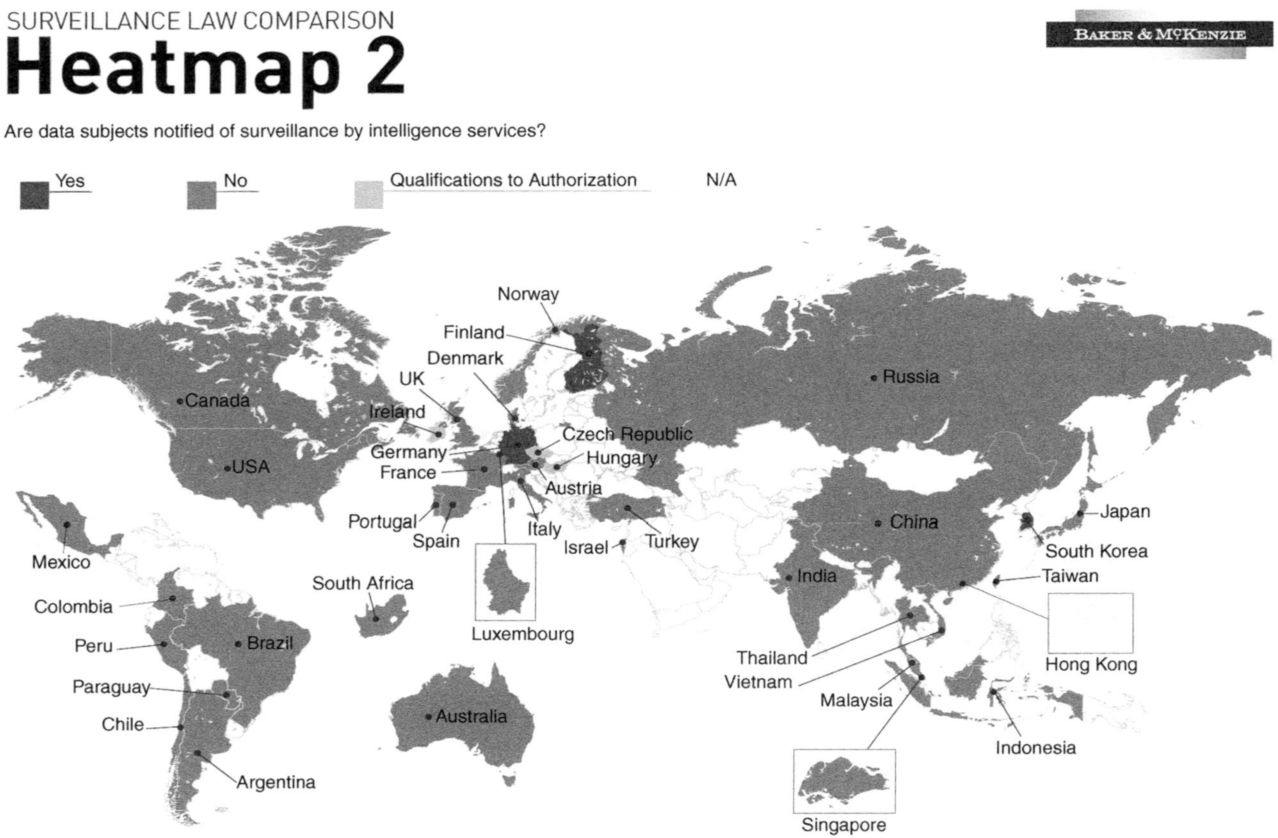

Figure 15.2. Map 2.

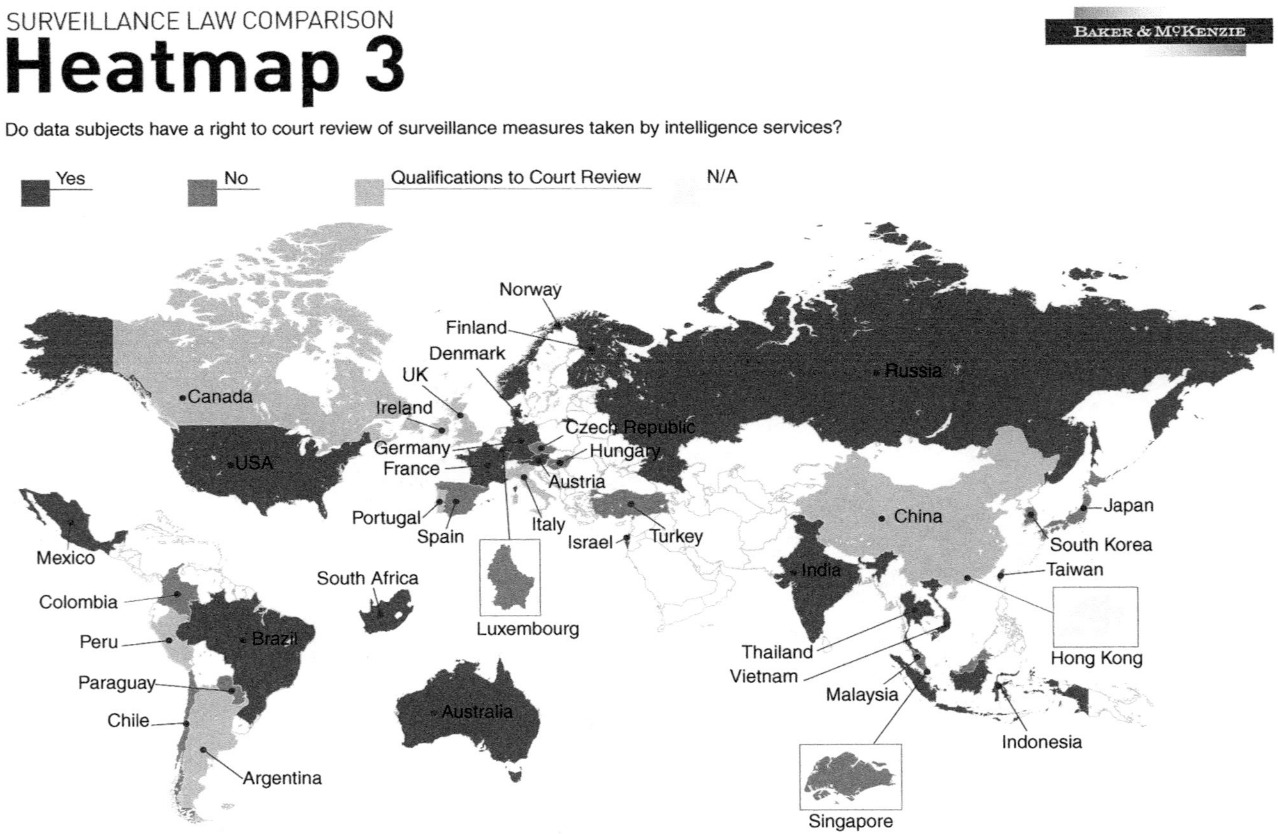

Figure 15.3. Map 3.

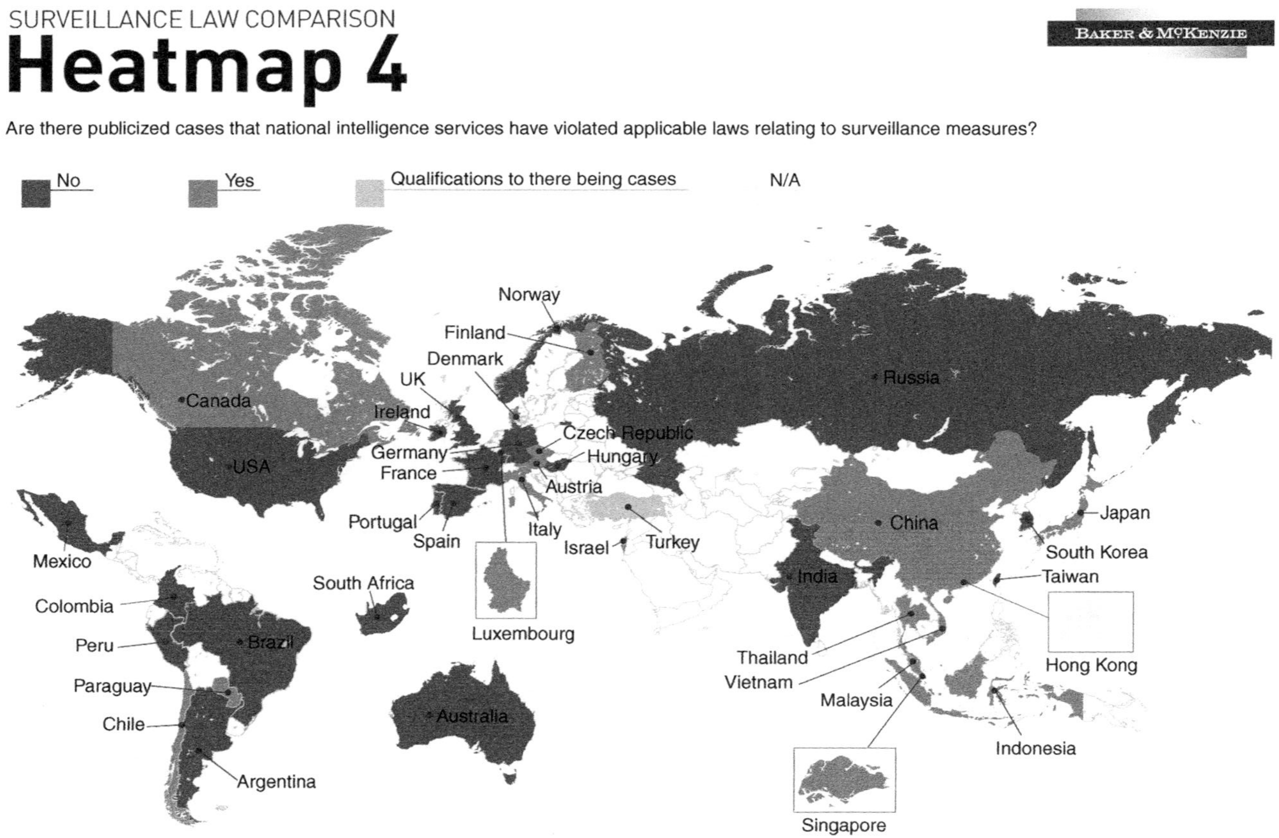

Figure 15.4. Map 4.

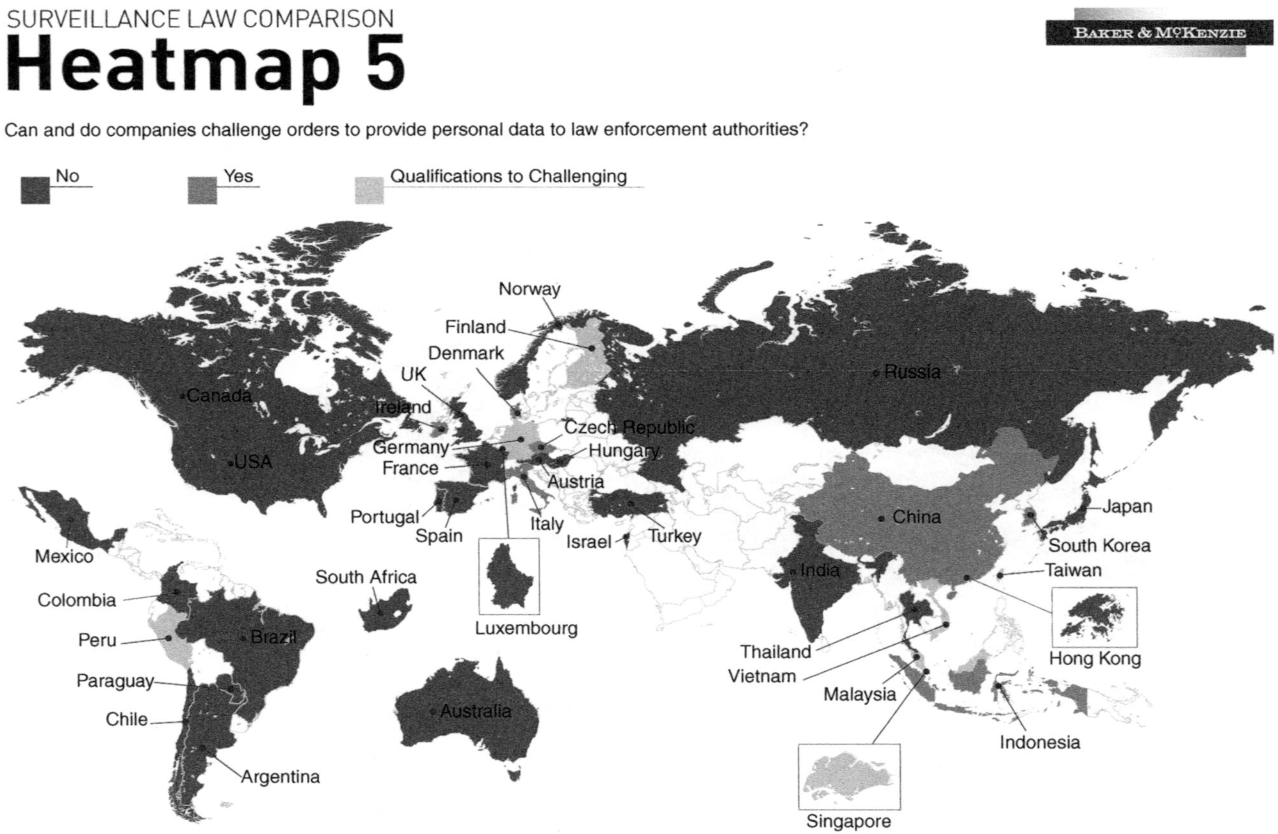

Figure 15.5. Map 5.

As the graphics illustrate, companies are confronted with government surveillance for law enforcement and national security purposes around the world. Surveillance laws and actual practices vary much less between nations than public outrage and political finger-pointing after Snowden's revelations might have suggested. A number of countries – not including the United States – have also tasked their intelligence agencies with economic agendas. Multinational businesses have to be particularly concerned about economic espionage as well as the fact that national governments not only demand cooperation with their own surveillance operations but also prohibit cooperation with foreign governments' surveillance and data access requests.[8]

III Companies Caught in the Middle: Government Requests for Data and Privacy Rights

A *Privacy Rights in the United States*

Individuals are particularly affected in their data privacy interests when they are under investigation by government agencies, subject to civil or criminal charges, on trial, in prison, and released from prison. Individuals find privacy protections in the United States Constitution (particularly the First, Fourth, Fifth, and Fourteenth Amendments), respective state constitutions, and various federal and state statutes. It would be impossible to do justice to these diverse laws here, but a very brief overview will be given.

The Fourth Amendment of the United States Constitution provides that "the right of the people to be secure in their persons, houses, papers, and effects, against unreasonable searches and seizures, shall not be violated, and no warrants shall issue, but upon probable cause, supported by oath or affirmation, and particularly describing the place to be searched, and the persons or things to be seized." The Fourth Amendment applies only against state actors, *i.e.*, government officials.[9] When government officials violate the Fourth Amendment to gather evidence, a defendant can request that unlawfully collected evidence be suppressed, *i.e.*, that prosecutors not use that evidence or evidence derived from it to convict the defendant. Several exceptions that focus on the culpability of the government agents involved and the deterrence value of excluding evidence have significantly limited the suppression remedy's availability, however.[10] Government officials are largely immune from liability for common law privacy torts and under many statutes. Individuals can seek damages and injunctions under 42 U.S.C. § 1983 if state officials violate their constitutional rights, but there are constitutional immunity provisions as well.[11]

Precisely when a government intrusion into personal privacy constitutes an unreasonable search or seizure under the Fourth Amendment has been subject to much controversy. The text explicitly proscribes unreasonable intrusions into the security of homes, people, and tangible property ("papers and effects").[12] But, with emerging technologies

8 For more on this concern, see Section VI of this chapter.

9 *See United States v. Jacobsen*, 466 U.S. 109, 113–14 (1984).

10 *See Davis v. United States*, 131 S. Ct. 2419, 2428–29 (2011).

11 *See, e.g., Doe v. Borough of Barrington*, 729 F. Supp. 376 (D.N.J. 1990).

12 *See United States v. Jones*, 132 S. Ct. 945, 949 (2012); *Olmstead v. United States*, 277 U.S. 438, 465 (1928); *United States v. White*, 401 U.S. 745, 748 (1971).

and changing social habits, individuals have found their intangible communications and activities at risk of unreasonable government investigation, such as by wiretapping and location tracking, through video surveillance and eavesdropping of private places and conversations, and by access to their emails. When considering these practices, courts have from time to time ruled against the government surveillance.[13] In cases when defendants had entrusted their personal data with third parties, however, the government has often been able to avoid Fourth Amendment scrutiny under the "third party doctrine," the proposition that people have no reasonable expectation of privacy in information they expose to others, including service providers.[14]

To grant individuals additional privacy protections, legislatures have enacted statutory electronic communications privacy laws. Such statutes can apply to both state actors and private individuals, and offer different remedies depending on how and by whom their rights are violated. Some statutes provide a suppression remedy on their own, and constitutional suppression remedies can be available for statutory violations that are simultaneously unconstitutional. Even when a court finds a statutory law unconstitutional for insufficiently protecting an individual's Fourth Amendment rights to the privacy in his communications, however, the constitutional suppression remedy may be denied to the defendant as a result of one of the good faith exceptions to suppression.[15]

Generally, United States citizens and people in United States territory are protected against unreasonable searches and seizures. Nonresident aliens outside the United States territory may not be protected against privacy intrusions by U.S. government officials,[16] but Congress has afforded additional protections to citizens of friendly countries in recent

[13] *See, e.g., Riley v. California*, 134 S. Ct. 2473 (2014) (holding that the police generally may not, without a warrant, search digital information on a cell phone seized from an individual who has been arrested); *Kyllo v. United States*, 533 U.S. 27 (2001) (holding that use of thermal imaging to measure heat emanating from a home constitutes search for purposes of the Fourth Amendment); *United States v. Jones*, 132 S. Ct. 945 (2012) (holding that attachment of a GPS tracking device to a vehicle, and subsequent use of that device to monitor a vehicle's movements on public streets, was a search within the meaning of the Fourth Amendment); *Katz v. United States*, 88 S. Ct. 507 (1967) (holding that use of electronic eavesdropping equipment to record a defendant's telephone conversations in a public telephone booth constituted a search for purposes of the Fourth Amendment).

[14] *See United States v. Miller*, 425 U.S. 435, 442–44 (1976) (finding no Fourth Amendment interest in bank records stored with a bank in the ordinary course of its business); *Smith v. Maryland*, 442 U.S. 735, 745–46 (1979) (holding that the defendant had no reasonable expectation of privacy in the phone numbers he dialed because he voluntarily and knowingly conveyed them to the phone company, a third party); *see also In re:* § 2703(d) Order, 787 F. Supp. 2d 430, 439–40 (E.D. Va. 2011) (finding no Fourth Amendment protection in IP addresses associated with users' Twitter accounts at specified dates and times); Hanni Fakhoury, Smith v. Maryland *Turns 35 But Its Health Is Declining*, Elec. Frontier Found. (June 24, 2014), www.eff.org/deeplinks/2014/06/smith-v-maryland-turns-35-its-healths-declining; *cf.* Stephen E. Henderson, *After* United States v. Jones, *After the Fourth Amendment Third Party Doctrine*, 14 N.C. J. L. & Tech. 431 (2013) (chronicling instances in which the Court has not followed the doctrine).

[15] *See United States v. Warshak*, 631 F.3d 266, 288–92 (6th Cir. 2010) (holding the Stored Communications Act unconstitutional to the extent it permitted government investigators to obtain Warshak's stored email without first obtaining a warrant based on probable cause, but finding the statute's unconstitutionality insufficiently clear at the time of the investigation to justify suppression of the email evidence).

[16] *See United States v. Verdugo-Urquidez*, 110 S. Ct. 1056 (1990), *and* Mark Andrew Marionneaux, *International Scope of Fourth Amendment Protections:* United States v. Verdugo-Urquidez, 52 La. L. Rev. 455 (1991); Leonard X. Rosenberg, *Fourth Amendment – Search and Seizure of Property Abroad: Erosion of the Rights of Aliens*, 81 J. Crim. L. & Criminology 779 (1990–1991); Steven H. Theisen, *Evidence Seized in Foreign Searches: When Does the Fourth Amendment Exclusionary Rule Apply?* 25 Wm. & Mary L. Rev. 161 (1983).

legislation.[17] The rights guaranteed by the United States Constitution extend to "all 'persons' and guard against any encroachment on those rights by federal or state authority."[18] In a case involving police searches of cell phones incident to arrest, the Supreme Court noted that the Fourth Amendment's requirement is "simple – get a warrant."[19] Although this is true for some circumstances, some searches and seizures can survive constitutional scrutiny without a warrant and some can violate the Fourth Amendment even with a warrant.[20]

B *Companies Compelled to Provide Personal Data in the United States*

When courts or law enforcement authorities demand personal data from companies, *e.g.*, email and online services providers, companies are caught in the middle between the government's law enforcement interests and individuals' privacy interests. If a company wants to protect its customers' privacy, it must challenge the subpoena, court order, or warrant. This takes effort and resources and can be difficult because the company is not directly affected in its own rights and may not be allowed to represent its customers' privacy interests in court. Also, by resisting requests for information, a company risks causing tension with the government and potentially being charged with contempt.[21] But if a company releases user data too readily, it will be publicly criticized and can be sued by its own customers.[22]

Increasingly, companies are challenging government subpoenas in the interest of protecting customer privacy.[23] In a case involving government agents' not securing a warrant prior to obtaining the contents of a defendant's emails, the Sixth Circuit Court of Appeals held that "a subscriber enjoys a reasonable expectation of privacy in the contents of emails 'that are stored with, or sent or received through, a commercial ISP.' … The government may not compel a commercial ISP to turn over the contents of a subscriber's emails without first obtaining a warrant based on probable cause."[24] If companies release personal data without a legal obligation to do so, they themselves can become subject to liability for privacy violations.

17 *See* Lothar Determann & Teresa Michaud, *U.S. Privacy Redress and Remedies for EU Data Subjects*, Bloomberg BNA: Privacy & Sec. Law Report, 14 PVLR 206 (2015).

18 *Bridges v. Wixon*, 326 U.S. 135, 161 (1945) (Murphy, J., concurring).

19 *Riley v. California*, 134 S. Ct. 2473, 2495 (2014).

20 *See* Dan Solove & Paul Schwartz, Information Privacy Law 257 (5th ed. 2014).

21 *See* Hanni Fakhoury, *UPDATE: New York Judge Tries to Silence Twitter in Its Ongoing Battle to Protect User Privacy*, Elec. Frontier Found. (Sept. 14, 2012), www.eff.org/deeplinks/2012/09/ny-judge-tries-silence-twitter.

22 *See, e.g.*, *Sams v. Yahoo! Inc.*, 713 F.3d 1175 (9th Cir. 2011) (class action alleging Yahoo! violated the Stored Communications Act when it disclosed noncontent subscriber information to the government pursuant to allegedly invalid subpoenas); *Freedman v. America Online, Inc.*, 325 F. Supp. 2d 638 (E.D. Va. 2004) (action by a subscriber against America Online under the Electronic Communications Privacy Act on the ground that the ISP wrongfully disclosed the plaintiff's subscriber information to a Connecticut law enforcement officer in response to a warrant application that had not been signed by a judge); *see also* Elec. Frontier Found., *supra* note 3.

23 *See, e.g.*, *In re* U.S. for an Order Pursuant to 18 U.S.C. Section 2703(D), 707 F.3d 283 (4th Cir. 2013); *Gonzalez v. Google*, 234 F.R.D. 674 (N.D. Cal. 2006); *In re* Warrant to Search Certain E-mail Account Controlled and Maintained by Microsoft Corp., 15 F. Supp. 3d 466 (S.D.N.Y. 2014).

24 *Warshak*, 631 F.3d at 288.

Under the federal All Writs Act of 1789, law enforcement authorities can request courts to "issue all writs necessary or appropriate in aid of their respective jurisdictions and agreeable to the usages and principles of law" in support of valid warrants against persons or companies reasonably close to investigations so long as the cooperation is not unreasonably burdensome.[25] The FBI referred to the All Writs Act when it tried to compel a manufacturer of smart phones to help circumvent data security measures to access personal data on phones that were relevant to investigations against terrorists and an alleged drug dealer.[26] Also, the FBI deploys various hacking tools for its investigations and pushes for relaxed jurisdictional restraints on courts to issue warrants against defendants whose whereabouts are unknown.[27]

All U.S. government entities have to comply with the Fourth Amendment and federal statutes protecting individual privacy, including the Electronic Communications Privacy Act (ECPA). Companies operating within a particular state are subject to additional restrictions. For example, California government entities also have to comply with the California Constitution as well as various California statutes, including the California Electronic Communications Privacy Act (CalECPA").[28] In comparison to the federal ECPA, CalECPA provides broader and more robust protections for individuals, companies, and other entities when California government entities seek to gather electronic communications information,[29] including "any information about an electronic communication or the use of an electronic communication service."[30] This includes both content and metadata, and CalECPA explicitly protects data commonly sought by law enforcement, including user geolocation data and IP addresses. Government entities may compel disclosure of data protected by CalECPA from service providers only pursuant to (1) a search warrant, wiretap order, or order for electronic reader records; or (2) a subpoena issued in accordance with existing state law, provided that the purpose is for investigating or prosecuting a criminal offense, and as long as the subpoena is not prohibited by other state or federal regulations.[31] Also, government entities must provide detailed notice to targets of investigations with a copy of the warrant or a written statement setting forth facts giving rise to the investigation.[32] CalECPA also requires government entities

25 28 U.S.C. § 1651 (1911) (based on parts of Judiciary Act of 1789).

26 *See In re* Order Requiring Previous Apple, Inc. to Assist in the Execution of a Search Warrant, No. 15-mc-1902 (E.D.N.Y 2015 (withdrawal of application on April 22, 2016); Christie Smythe, *U.S.-Apple Brooklyn Encryption Battle Ends in Whimper*, Bloomberg BNA: Privacy & Sec. Law Report, 15 PVLR 903 (April 23, 2016); *In re* Search of Apple iPhone Seized during Execution of Search Warrant on Black Lexus IS300, No. 16-cm-0010 (C.D. Cal. Feb. 19, 2016) (status report and motion to withdraw filed March 28, 2016); Edvard Pettersson, Alex Webb & Chris Strohm, *U.S. Drops Apple Case after Getting into Terrorist's iPhone*, Bloomberg BNA: Privacy & Sec. Law Report, 15 PVLR 691 (March 28, 2016).

27 Chris Strohm, *Supreme Court Rule Expands FBI Computer Search Power*, Bloomberg BNA: Privacy & Sec. Law Report, 15 PVLR 906 (April 28, 2016).

28 *See* Cal. Penal Code §§ 1546–1546.4.

29 Susan Freiwald, *How CalECPA Improves on Its Federal Namesake*, Concurring Opinions (Oct. 16, 2015), http://concurringopinions.com/archives/2015/10/how-calecpa-improves-on-its-federal-namesake.html; Susan Freiwald, *It's Time to Look to California for Robust Privacy Reform – CalECPA*, Am. Constitution Soc'y: Blog for Law and Policy (Sept. 8, 2015), www.acslaw.org/acsblog/it's-time-to-look-to-calirfornia-for-robust-privacy-reform–calecpa.

30 Cal. Penal Code §1546(d).

31 Cal. Penal Code § 1546.1(b).

32 Cal. Penal Code § 1546.2(a).

to destroy information within ninety days, subject to specific exceptions, for example, for child pornography.[33] Furthermore, CalECPA provides an alternative suppression remedy available to targets, service providers, and others involved in the investigation "to order the destruction of any information obtained in violation of [CalECPA], or the California Constitution, or the United States Constitution."[34] CalECPA does not prohibit companies from voluntarily disclosing information to government entities where otherwise permitted by applicable law and provides liability privileges to companies that are compelled to disclose information pursuant to CalECPA.

C *Data Protection, Retention, and Residency Requirements*

Some companies have been resisting requests from governments for personal data on the basis of claims that the data is hosted offshore and that they are not permitted to produce the data because of restrictions applicable in the jurisdiction where they host such data.[35] Some governments have responded with laws requiring companies to keep data locally for easy government access. Governments can compel companies much more easily if the companies have a presence – and ideally the data at issue – on the country's territory, because national enforcement powers end at national borders. Legislatures have taken a number of steps to prevent data from leaving their territories or at least keep a copy locally. The purposes and effects of international data transfer restrictions, data retention requirements, and data residency laws are quite different.[36]

Data transfer restrictions protect individual privacy of personal data, limiting companies' ability to transfer personal data from one jurisdiction to another. More and more countries have followed the European example and enacted restrictions on international transfers of personal data, including Russia in 2006.

Record retention and residency laws, on the other hand, secure government access to personal data and records, including for tax authorities, regulators, law enforcement, and intelligence agencies.[37] Most countries, including the United States, require companies to maintain certain records for accounting audit and tax purposes, and such record retention laws are relatively uncontroversial from a data privacy perspective. But, European data protection authorities have opposed and challenged European communications data retention requirements as hostile to data privacy. A number of national courts in the EU and ultimately the European Court of Justice have invalidated communication data

33 Cal. Penal Code § 1546.1(g).

34 Cal. Penal Code § 1546.4(c); *see also* Susan Freiwald, *How CalECPA Improves on Its Federal Namesake*, Concurring Opinions (Oct. 16, 2015), http://concurringopinions.com/archives/2015/10/how-calecpa-improves-on-its-federal-namesake.html.

35 *See, e.g.*, *Microsoft Corp. v. United States* (In re Warrant to Search a Certain E-Mail Account Controlled & Maintained by Microsoft Corp.), 829 F.3d 197 (2d Cir. 2016); Daniel R. Stoller, *No Microsoft Ireland Emails for Feds, 2nd Cir. Rules*, Bloomberg BNA: Data Privacy & Sec. Report, 15 PVLR 1465 (2016).

36 Lothar Determann, *Data Privacy in the Cloud: A Dozen Myths and Facts*, 28 Computer & Internet Law. 11, 1, 4 (2011); *see id.* at "myth 6."

37 See examples discussed in Promoting Economic Growth through Smart Global Information Technology Policy: The Growing Threat of Local Data Server Requirements (2012), http://businessroundtable.org/sites/default/files/Global_IT_Policy_Paper_final.pdf; Stuart Lauchlan, *Secret Plans to Rip Up Data Sovereignty Rules, but Does Data Center Location Matter Any More?* Diginomica (July 2, 2014).

retention laws.[38] Yet Germany introduced even more restrictive data residency rules on a national basis in 2016.[39] The United States has not followed suit and (so far) has not enacted data residency or retention laws for communications data.

IV Companies Caught in the Middle: Individual Privacy and Safety Interests

In terms of conflicts of interest, companies are caught in the middle not only between governments and citizens, but also between conflicting privacy and safety interests of individuals. Social media companies that allow anonymous use and protect privacy against government surveillance have been sued by victims of terrorism on the basis that the social media companies should have prevented certain uses of the platform,[40] which would require more surveillance and cooperation with governments than the social media companies cared for. More broadly, companies that fall victim to hackers and cybercriminals are sued by users whose personal data is compromised.

Under U.S. laws, companies can make choices and emphasize either privacy or safety on their platforms to appeal to relevant customer preferences and interests. Internet companies in particular can opt against user surveillance and rely on liability privileges for online service providers, including under section 230 of the Communications Decency Act and section 512 of the Digital Millennium Copyright Act.[41] In other jurisdictions, companies find it much more difficult to navigate conflicts. Germany, for example, makes it particularly hard for companies to navigate conflicting rights and requirements. Germany offers far less generous liability privileges for online service providers[42] and aggressively enforces a statutory requirement that online service providers must allow anonymous usage, even though some providers prefer that users must identify themselves to reduce the risk of fraudulent and offensive content.[43] Germany also imposes strict limitations on tracking and monitoring of browsing behavior.[44] But German courts hold even private Wi-Fi network operators strictly liable for copyright violations

38 *Digital Rights Ireland Ltd. v. Minister for Commc'ns, Marine & Natural Res.*, No. C-293/12 (E.C.J. Apr. 8, 2014), http://curia.europa.eu/juris/liste.jsf?num=C-293/12#; Stephen Gardner, *ECJ Invalidates EU Data Retention Directive; Member State Laws Now Open to Challenge*, 13 PVLR 660 (2014).

39 Lothar Determann & Michaela Weigl, *supra* note 4.

40 *See* Ben Hancock, *Twitter Fends Off Suit over ISIS Attack*, Recorder, Aug. 10, 2016.

41 Congress enacted these two statutes in the 1990s to protect Internet service providers from contributory liability for user-generated content to address concerns that providers would otherwise excessively curb free speech and information on the Internet; these protections continue to be very important for companies; see, for example, Online Intermediaries *Promoting Innovation, Defending Critical Online Policies: Michael Beckerman, President and CEO, the Internet Association*, 20 ECLR 1729 (2015).

42 Lothar Determann, *The New German Internet Law*, 22 Hastings Int'l & Comp. L. Rev. 113 (1998); Lothar Determann, *Case Update – German CompuServe Director Acquitted*, 23 Hastings Int'l & Comp. L. Rev. 109 (1999).

43 *See Facebook Inc. v. ULD, VG Schleswig*, Nos. Az. 8 B 61/12 & Az. 8 B 60/12 (Feb. 14, 2013), www.datenschutzzentrum.de/facebook/Facebook-Ireland-vs-ULD-Beschluss.pdf; Jabeen Bhatti, *German DPA Orders to Facebook Quashed*, 12 PVLR 332 (2016).

44 *See Tracking – Nutzerverfolgung im Internet*, www.datenschutzzentrum.de/tracking/; Damian Clifford, *EU Data Protection Law and Targeted Advertising: Consent and the Cookie Monster – Tracking the Crumbs of Online User Behaviour*, 5 J. Intell. Prop., Info. Tech. & E-Commerce L. 194 (2014), www.jipitec.eu/issues/jipitec-5-3-2014/4095; Lara O'Reilly, *The Online Advertising Industry Is About to Be Severely Disrupted – 'It's the Amputation of a Significant Revenue Stream,'* Bus. Insider (Dec. 16, 2015), www.businessinsider.com/how-the-new-eu-data-laws-will-affect-the-online-advertising-industry-2015–12.

committed via their networks.[45] The German government expects companies to prevent "hate speech," a nebulous reference to unpopular political opinions.[46] Additionally, Germany enacted a data residency and retention requirement for telecommunications metadata,[47] despite its general claim to offer residents particularly high data protection standards and its extreme outrage regarding the accessing of telecommunications metadata by intelligence agencies in Germany and the United States revealed by Edward Snowden in 2013.[48] In such challenging environments, companies find much more limited operating margins and little room for business choices and positions.

Organizations that amass data for surveillance purposes are particularly exposed to data security breaches and resulting liability. The National Security Agency (NSA) set one example when it let an employee of a contractor walk out with a host of highly sensitive data. Since then, security and intelligence services have suffered various other breaches.

Private sector organizations are, of course, not immune from to similar liabilities. Legislatures are starting to hold companies engaged in surveillance responsible for resulting security and privacy risks. For example, California passed a data security law effective January 1, 2016, for operators and users of automated license plate recognition (ALPR) systems.[49] Any company, government agency, or person must comply with the new California law if it uses or operates an ALPR system, *i.e.*, a searchable computerized database resulting from the operation of one or more cameras combined with computer algorithms to reach and convert images of registration plates and the characters they contain into computer-readable data. The statute does not specify any geographic limitations on its applicability. Thus, persons acting outside California may theoretically be held responsible under the California law if and to the extent they capture California license plate information and harm California residents. Companies or persons who operate or use ALPR systems must maintain certain prescribed security procedures and practices and publish details in a privacy policy that must contain certain specified information and be published on the company or person's Web site, if any.[50]

45 *See* BGH judgment, 12.5.2010 – I ZR 121/08; *German Court Says You Must Secure Your Wi-Fi Or You May Get Fined*, TECHDIRT (2010), www.techdirt.com/articles/20100512/1116409394.shtml; *New Law in Germany Will Further Reduce Liability of Wi-Fi Providers for Copyright Infringement by Users* (May 12, 2016), www.out-law.com/en/articles/2016/may/new-law-in-germany-will-further-reduce-liability-of-wi-fi-providers-for-copyright-infringement-by-users/.

46 *German Justice Minister Tells Facebook to Curb Hate Speech*, DEUTSCHE WELLE (July 17, 2016), www.dw.com/en/german-justice-minister-tells-facebook-to-curb-hate-speech/a-19406616.

47 Lothar Determann & Michaela Weigl, *supra* note 4.

48 Anthony Faiola, *Germans, Still Outraged by NSA Spying, Learn Their Country May Have Helped*, WASH. POST (May 1, 2015), www.washingtonpost.com/world/europe/nsa-scandal-rekindles-in-germany-with-an-ironic-twist/2015/04/30/030ec9e0-ee7e-11e4-8050-839e9234b303_story.html.

49 CAL. CIV. CODE §§ 1798.90.5, 1798.29 & 1798.82.

50 CAL. CIV. CODE §§ 1798.90.51 & 1798.90.53. The usage and privacy policy shall, at a minimum, include all of the following: (1) The authorized purposes for using the ALPR system and collecting ALPR information. (2) A description of the job title or other designation of the employees and independent contractors who are authorized to use or access the ALPR system, or to collect ALPR information. (3) The training requirements necessary for those authorized employees and independent contractors. (4) A description of how the ALPR system will be monitored to ensure the security of the information and compliance with applicable privacy laws. (5) The purposes of, process for, and restrictions on, the sale, sharing, or transfer of ALPR information to other persons. (6) The title of the official custodian, or owner, of the ALPR

An operator of an ALPR system must keep access logs and require users to comply with usage limitations set forth in the California ALPR law and the operator's privacy policy.[51] Operators and users of ALPR information must notify data subjects of data security breaches.[52] Government agencies may not sell, share, or transfer ALPR information, except to other government agencies and as otherwise permitted by law and the government agency's ALPR privacy policy. Government entities that operate or intend to operate an ALPR system must provide an opportunity for public comment at regularly scheduled public meetings before implementing the program. A private sector company can sell, share, or transfer ALPR information in compliance with the company's ALPR privacy policy.

Individuals harmed by a violation of the California ALPR law may bring a civil action against persons who knowingly caused the harm, including harm by data security breaches.[53] Courts may award actual damages (but not less than liquidated damages in the amount of twenty-five hundred dollars); punitive damages, upon proof of willful or reckless disregard of the law; reasonable attorneys' fees and other litigation costs; and preliminary and equitable relief.

V Companies Caught in the Middle: Compliance Requirements and Employee Privacy

Companies have to ensure that their employees comply with applicable laws, protect the company's assets, and refrain from harassing coworkers and others. To pursue these objectives, companies resort to various forms of workforce surveillance, including email monitoring, data loss prevention tools, and security cameras. In the United States, employers are particularly exposed to liability for employee misconduct and relatively free to deploy any surveillance technologies that they deem necessary, so long as they issue appropriate privacy notices to their employees.[54] In Europe, on the other hand, employees are protected by general data protection laws, and employers are largely prohibited from engaging in continuous surveillance of employees.[55] Companies have to respond by developing region- or country-specific protocols for internal investigations and differentiate regarding the deployment of surveillance technologies.[56]

system responsible for implementing this section. (7) A description of the reasonable measures that will be used to ensure the accuracy of ALPR information and correct data errors. (8) The length of time ALPR information will be retained, and the process the ALPR operator will utilize to determine if and when to destroy retained ALPR information.

51 Cal. Civ. Code § 1798.90.52.

52 Cal. Civ. Code §§ 1798.29 & 1798.82.

53 Cal. Civ. Code § 1798.90.54(a) (expressly refers to "harmed by a violation … including … unauthorized access or use of ALPR information or a breach of security of an ALPR system" whereas general data security breach laws (Cal. Civ. Code §§ 1798.29 & 1798.82) do not provide for specific sanctions or remedies for the breach itself (only for failure to notify the breach).

54 Lothar Determann & Robert Sprague, *Intrusive Monitoring: Employee Privacy Expectations Are Reasonable in Europe, Destroyed in the United States*, 26 Berkeley Tech. L.J. 979 (2011).

55 Lothar Determann, *When No Really Means No: Consent Requirements for Workplace Monitoring*, 3 World Data Protection Rep. 22 (2003).

56 Lothar Determann & Lars Brauer, *Employee Monitoring Technologies and Data Privacy – No One-Size-Fits-All Globally*, 9 IAPP Privacy Advisor 1 (2009).

VI Companies Caught in the Middle: Between Governments

Companies have to cope not only with conflicting interests within countries, but also with conflicts of laws across national borders. National governments conduct, require, or permit surveillance for national security purposes abroad and at the same time prohibit any foreign surveillance and domestic cooperation with foreign governments as high treason. Companies can easily be caught in the middle between conflicting laws and policy objectives, in war and peace.[57]

After the terror attacks on the United States of September 11, 2001, the U.S. government required airlines to cooperate with surveillance measures at U.S. borders while European governments prohibited airlines from cooperating with U.S. surveillance. Picturing a pilot flying a passenger jet over the Atlantic and faced with exactly opposite requirements at the departure and arrival airport illustrates the situation of companies caught in the middle with particular intensity.[58]

Since Edward Snowden revealed details about government surveillance in 2013, politicians around the world have been publicly condemning foreign espionage while secretly refining their own surveillance programs.[59] Governments have been sending spies to foreign territories for centuries. Surveillance has become an accepted practice as a matter of customary public international law.[60] Most countries conduct foreign intelligence programs and spy on each other. At the same time, most countries have national laws against espionage, treason, and other acts affecting national security that prohibit foreign surveillance against them. International law does not prohibit countries from spying abroad or from punishing spies at home.[61]

Just as the act of sending a spy is typically permissible under the sending nation's domestic laws and illegal under the spied-upon country's domestic laws, intercepting foreign communications and accessing foreign computers for surveillance purposes are usually strictly prohibited under the spied-upon country's domestic laws.[62] Every country's international surveillance programs regularly violate other countries' domestic laws. This tends to be not much of a practical problem for governments because they can claim immunity from the jurisdiction of other countries. But, the conflicts can become life-threatening for individual spies who are caught abroad and multinational businesses that become entangled in disputes between nations regarding international surveillance.

Recently, for example, various national and European Union (EU) institutions took out their discontent with international surveillance by the NSA on multinational businesses in the United States and in Europe. On October 6, 2015, the Court of Justice of

57 Lothar Determann & Karl-Theodor zu Guttenberg, *On War and Peace in Cyberspace: Security, Privacy, Jurisdiction*, 41 Hastings Const. L.Q. 1 (2014).

58 *See* Lothar Determann, *Conflicting Data Laws: Airlines Are Damned if They Do, Don't*, 8 Cyberspace Law. 6 (2003).

59 *Supra* note 57.

60 Chesterman, Simon Chesterman, *The Spy Who Came in from the Cold War: Intelligence & International Law*, 27 Mich. J. Int'l L. 1071, 1078 (2006). *But see, e.g.*, Ingrid Delupis, *Foreign Warships & Immunity for Espionage*, 78 Am. J. Int'l L. 53, 67 (1984).

61 John Radsan, *The Unresolved Equation of Espionage & International Law*, 28 Mich. J. Int'l L. 595, 601 (2007).

62 For example, unauthorized access to computers on U.S. territory is punishable by severe prison terms under the U.S. Computer Fraud & Abuse Act. Lothar Determann, *Internet Freedom & Computer Abuse*, 35 Hastings Comm. & Ent. L.J. 429 (2013).

the European Union invalidated the 2000 Commission decision on the adequacy of the Safe Harbor Program, which many companies in the European Union and the United States had come to rely on; overnight this destroyed companies' ability to exchange personal data lawfully.[63] The EU court did not express any concerns regarding misconduct by any companies and cited only concerns regarding government surveillance in the United States. Yet, companies – not government agencies or civil servants – took the brunt of the consequences and adverse effects of the judgment because they had to rearrange their compliance programs, renegotiate contracts, revisit vendor selection, and otherwise deal with the ensuing disruption of transatlantic business relations.[64]

Additionally, a number of countries have enacted specific "blocking statutes" that prohibit individuals and businesses from responding to data access requests from foreign governments.[65] Within a multinational group of companies, one subsidiary may be pressured by a government to release data that another subsidiary is prohibited from providing.

In Summary: Business Responses to Surveillance

All companies have to conduct, endure, oppose, and embrace surveillance to some extent. They have to analyze their obligations, rights, and operating margins carefully according to jurisdiction, business segment, and data use scenario.

Most companies are caught between conflicting expectations and legal requirements. Some businesses have to conduct or embrace surveillance more than others because their shareholders, customers, regulators, or employees demand safety, security, or compliance, or because they are headquartered in a particular area. Other businesses must go out of their way to resist and oppose government surveillance to appeal to their customers and prospective customers.

All businesses need to find responses to the key questions raised in this chapter and consider the conflicting demands on their organizations discussed here. Most companies have to develop differentiated responses for different departments, jurisdictions, and business lines.

All companies have to implement data security measures to protect themselves, their employees, their customers, and their business partners from unlawful surveillance by governments and cybercriminals. Effective data security measures may, again, require surveillance. All companies should prepare themselves for government requests for access to data, whether in the form of dawn raids or more civil approaches.

63 *Maximilian Schrems v. Data Protection Commissioner*, No. C-362/14 (Oct. 6, 2015), http://eur-lex.europa.eu/legal-content/EN/TXT/HTML/?uri=CELEX:62014CJ0362&from=EN; Lothar Determann, *U.S. Privacy Safe Harbor – More Myths and Facts,* Bloomberg BNA: Privacy & Sec. Law Report, 14 PVLR 2017 (2015); Lothar Determann, **Adequacy of data protection in the USA: myths and facts**, International Data Privacy Law 2016; doi: 10.1093/idpl/ipw011; US-Datenschutzrecht – Dichtung und Wahrheit, NvWZ 2016, 561.

64 See for more details, Lothar Determann, Brian Hengesbaugh & Michaela Weigl, *EU-U.S. Privacy Shield v. Other EU Data Transfer Compliance Options*, Bloomberg BNA: Data Prot. Report, 15 PVLR 1726, 9/5/16 (2016).

65 See, for example, Art. 271 Swiss Penal Code and Art. 48 of EU Regulation 2016/679 on the protection of natural persons with regard to the processing of personal data and on the free movement of such data (GDPR), http://eur-lex.europa.eu/legal-content/EN/TXT/HTML/?uri=CELEX:32016R0679&from=EN.

If and where companies want to position themselves to conduct or cooperate with surveillance, they have to deploy appropriate systems to collect and retain relevant data, store data in jurisdictions where they wish to cooperate with governments, and warn data subjects in privacy notices to reduce the risk of conflicting privacy expectations and claims.

If and where companies want to bolster their abilities to oppose surveillance and government requests for access to data, they have to keep data and company representatives offshore as much as possible; apply strong encryption, possibly end-to-end (so the company with custody cannot provide access); impose other factual limitations on ability to access data (including transferring data custody to foreign companies that are not subject to a government's jurisdiction); and promise data subjects strong privacy rights in contracts and privacy policies that can be cited in legal proceedings to justify opposition against government surveillance.

Part III

Impacts of Surveillance

16 Seeing, Seizing, and Searching Like a State: Constitutional Developments from the Seventeenth Century to the End of the Nineteenth Century

Mark A. Graber[†]

Controversies over what constitutes an unconstitutional search are driven by expansions in state capacity to see. Sometimes, these expansions are technology. New devices permit government officials to see what they could not previously see. During the eighteenth and nineteenth centuries, these expansions were institutional. The rise of the British administrative state that employed numerous persons to enforce excise taxes in both Great Britain and the United States inspired the attacks on general warrants that were eventually codified by the Fourth Amendment. State judges responded to the creation of police departments in Jacksonian America by loosening common law rules that hindered official investigation of ordinary crimes. When Congress during the late nineteenth century established administrative agencies in the United States and charged those agencies with investigating business crimes, opponents wielded the Fourth Amendment and other constitutional provisions when they attempted to prevent those institutions from learning about business affairs and business crimes.

Introduction

Conventional constitutional histories of rights against unlawful searches and seizures are marked by remarkable discontinuities. Commentary on the search and seizure controversies at one time and place often have little if any relationship to commentary on the search and seizure controversies at other times and places. Eighteenth-century Englishmen complain about searches of known political dissidents. Eighteenth-century Americans complain about searches of suspected smugglers. Persons suspected of ordinary criminal offenses during the mid-nineteenth century complain about the powers and practices of newly established police departments. Businesspersons in the United States during the last third of the nineteenth century complain about federal power to investigate commercial activity. "Wets" and their supporters during the early twentieth century complain about new state powers to implement prohibition, while the other suspected criminals complain about state use of such new technologies as wiretapping (police, in turn, complained about how criminals were making use of such new technologies as automobiles to frustrate law enforcement). African Americans and other minorities during the mid-twentieth century complain about how racial prejudice infects the search and seizure process. Contemporary Americans complain about how twenty-first-century

† Regents Professor, University of Maryland Carey School of Law.

technologies such as Global Positioning System– (GPS-) enabled devices allow police to aggregate information that was previously only available in discrete form and by traditional and costly means such as tailing and human surveillance.

These discontinuities in the concerns that generate controversies over state power to investigate criminal behavior play havoc with interpreting the Fourth Amendment's promise that "the right of the people to be secure in their persons, houses, papers, and effects, against unreasonable searches and seizures, shall not be violated." Supreme Court justices note problems with applying language ratified in 1791 to technologies that were not even dreamed of during the late eighteenth century. Justice Samuel Alito in *United States v. Jones* suggested that the eighteenth-century analogy to a GPS device "would have required either a gigantic coach, a very tiny constable, or both, not to mention a constable with incredible fortitude and patience."[1] Commentators point to difficulties applying the Fourth Amendment to institutions that postdate the Bill of Rights. For example, Wesley MacNeil Oliver observes that Fourth Amendment norms in the eighteenth century have little relation to modern realities because "professional police departments did not exist in the eighteenth century, and Framing Era constables did not investigate crimes."[2]

This essay suggests that constitutional controversies over searches and seizures at different times and places are united by concerns with changes in what James Scott and others describe as "state capacity to see."[3] The constitutional rules for investigating crimes and suspected criminals have historically developed in response to changes in governmental capacity to investigate crimes and suspected criminals. Technological developments increase state capacity to see. Government officials who have access to airplanes see more evidence of crime and criminal behavior (and citizen behavior more generally) than government officials limited to walking the earth when ferreting out crime. A customs office staffed by one hundred investigators can see more smuggling than a customs office staffed by ten investigators.

Much historical writing on the evolution of constitutional powers of search and seizure suffers from a cramped understanding of what increases state capacity to see. A substantial literature exists on how technological changes have influenced the course of Fourth Amendment law.[4] Legal historians elaborate on how political departments established during the mid-nineteenth century influence the constitutional law of search and seizure.[5] What commentators too often miss is that new institutions such as police departments and new technologies such as wiretapping spawn constitutional developments for the same reason. Both affect state capacity to see. Throughout Anglo-American history, whenever states acquire by any means the power to see more, the resulting debates

1 *United States v. Jones*, 132 S. Ct. 945, 958 n.3 (2012) (Alito, J., dissenting).

2 Wesley MacNeil Oliver, *The Neglected History of Criminal Procedure, 1850–1940*, 62 Rutgers L. Rev. 447, 447–48 (2010); *see* Thomas Y. Davies, *Recovering the Original Fourth Amendment*, 98 Mich. L. Rev. 547, 620–22 (1999); William J. Stuntz, The Collapse of American Criminal Justice (2011).

3 *See* James C. Scott, Seeing Like a State: How Certain Schemes to Improve the Human Condition Have Failed (1998).

4 *See, e.g.*, David Gray, The Fourth Amendment in an Age of Surveillance (2017); David Gray and Danielle Keats Citron, *The Right to Quantitative Privacy*, 98 Minn. L. Rev. 62 (2013); Orin S. Kerr, *The Fourth Amendment and New Technologies: Constitutional Myths and the Case for Caution*, 102 Mich. L. Rev. 801 (2004).

5 *See, e.g.*, Oliver, *supra* note 2.

between state officials who wish to see more and those who wish their behavior to remain unseen alter the path of the constitutional rules governing search and seizure

The following pages have two purposes. The first is to survey constitutional developments in the law of search and seizure during the eighteenth and nineteenth centuries. The second is to suggest how focusing on changes in state capacity to see explains the course and salience of search and seizure issues both in the period studied and throughout American constitutional development. This chapter makes no attempt to elaborate the original meaning of federal and state constitutional prohibitions on certain searches and seizures or even to survey the enormous literature on what that meaning might be. This reticence is partly based on a historical sensibility that regards the search for original meanings as distorting what was a dynamic process. Different Englishmen and Americans at different times and in different places had different reactions to the changes in state capacity to see that fostered controversies over state power to search and seize. As important, this essay seeks to highlight the connections between what people were fighting over during the eighteenth and nineteenth centuries when they fought over state capacity to see. How we understand the consequences of those fights is for the present to decide.

Part I briefly considers search and seizure in Stuart England, when the British state had a limited capacity to see. In this political universe, sporadic controversies over official investigations broke out, but sustained controversies over official investigations did not occur because government officials lacked the capacity to investigate ordinary crime or to enforce revenue laws strictly. Part II details how the rise of the British administrative state placed search and seizure issues in the foreground of English constitutional concerns. Members of the English Country Party, when seeking to cabin the discretion of administrative officials with dramatically increased capacities to enforce revenue laws and crack down on official dissent, condemned general warrants as inconsistent with long-standing constitutional practice. Part III focus on how American revolutionaries adopted and deepened the English Country Party's critique of the emerging British administrative state. Americans who found themselves subject to increased customs searches as a consequence of the increased British administrative presence in the colonies condemned as unconstitutional writs of assistance and began to develop a consensus that constitutional warrants had to specify the places to be searched and the items to be sought. Part IV discusses how constitutional rights against certain official searches and seizures were adjusted with the rise of police departments during the mid-nineteenth century. American elites who had previously been determined to prevent customs officials from seeing revenue crimes now sought to take the blinders off newly established police departments when officers investigated ordinary crimes. Part V discusses how the Supreme Court of the United States during the late nineteenth century revitalized eighteenth-century concerns as newly established state and federal bureaucracies sought to regulate and investigate American business activity. The result was a bifurcated constitutional law of search and seizure, which put significant limits on state capacity to see some crimes and activities, but far fewer limits on state capacity to see others. The conclusion highlights the interaction between increased state capacities for crimes that elites prefer to remain hidden and increased state capacities to detect crimes that elites prefer the state see and punish.

State capacity to see is hardly the only driver of the constitutional law of search and seizure. Fourth Amendment law has historically been concerned with what state officials are seeing as well as their capacities for investigation. Constitutional disputes arise over whether the state should see personal papers or evidence of drinking as well as whether states should take a closer look at some people on the basis of certain characteristics. William Stuntz and others have pointed out that the constitutional law at every time and place also depends on whether crucial decision makers want the state to see what the state has gained the capacity to see.[6] Government officials wanted to exercise state capacity to see ordinary crimes. Hence, constitutional rights have tended to shrink when those state capacities are at issue. Government officials have been ambivalent about prohibition and related crimes. Hence, constitutional rights have tended to fluctuate when state capacities to see drinking and other alleged victimless crimes are at issue. Americans more often oppose searching for evidence of political beliefs. Hence, personal papers and related documents have a special status under Fourth Amendment law.

State capacity is best conceptualized as the internal driver of Fourth Amendment law. The Fourth Amendment and related state constitutional provisions set out the conditions under which states may investigate. Changes in state capacity to see, thus, directly influence the values underlying the Fourth Amendment. What the state sees with these capacities are best conceptualized as external drivers because the text of the Fourth Amendment provides no reasons for investigating some crimes more rigorously than others. An excellent literature exists on the external drivers of the Fourth Amendment during the eighteenth and nineteenth centuries.[7] The later emphasis on state capacity to see provides an important supplement on the internal drivers of the Fourth Amendment and related constitutional practices then and now.

I In the Beginning: The Seventeenth Century

Seventeenth-century Englishmen were great constitutional complainers.[8] They complained about the royal prerogative. They complained about taxation without representation. They complained about royal suspensions of habeas corpus. They complained that their free speech rights were being violated and that they were being compelled to testify against themselves. Some complained that the government was not tolerating their religious practices while others complained that the government was too tolerant of dissenting religions. By the end of the seventeenth century, complaints were heard that loyal subjects were being denied their right to bear arms and that some persons accused of crime had been denied rights to hire an attorney.

These vociferous complaints rarely included assertions of rights against unlawful searches and seizures.[9] The great documents of the English Civil War and Glorious Revolution do not catalog illegal searches or rail against general warrants. Parliament spent little if any time constraining royal power to search and seize. Legal provisions authorizing official investigations were not controversial. Englishmen complained about the hated Game Law of 1672, but those complaints hardly ever included attacks on the

6 *See, e.g.*, William J. Stuntz, *The Substantive Origins of Criminal Procedure*, 105 Yale L.J. 393 (1995).

7 *See* sources cited *supra* note 3; Stuntz, *supra* note 2.

8 The complaints and documents discussed in this and the following two paragraphs can be found in Mark A. Graber & Howard Gillman, The Complete American Constitutionalism. Volume One: Introduction and the Colonial Era (2015).

9 For this and the information in the next paragraph, see William J. Cuddihy, The Fourth Amendment: Origins and Original Meaning, 602–1791, at 433 (2009).

language authorizing justices of the peace to search private residences. No influential common law case decided during the seventeenth century asked justices to consider at great length the constitutional powers royal or parliamentary authorities had to search or seize.

Colonial Americans, who were also constitutional complainers, limited their complaints to those of their brethren in England. Such colonial documents as the Massachusetts Body of Liberties and the Pennsylvania Charter of Liberties catalog numerous rights and privileges of colonial Americans, but do not discuss general warrants or freedom from unreasonable searches. Both list rights of persons suspected of criminal offenses; none consider the investigatory process. As in England, no sustained constitutional controversy broke out in the colonies during the seventeenth century over state power to see, search, or seize.

Controversies over official searches and seizures did sporadically occur in both seventeenth-century England and seventeenth-century colonial America; these controversies were noted by legal commentators, but they did not substantially affect constitutional thinking about state power to investigate unlawful behavior. William Cuddihy details at great length how Tudor and Stuart officials searched, with and without general warrants, persons suspected of religious and political unorthodoxy.[10] Parliament passed resolutions condemning the searches that took place in the events leading up to the English Civil War. Sir Edward Coke condemned general warrants in his *Institutes on the Law of England*.[11] Nevertheless, these events, resolutions, and writings were not part of any broader movement aggressively to challenge official power to search and seize. Coke and other treatise writers aside, the complaints that arose during the seventeenth century were more often implicitly based on the notion that royal authorities were searching the wrong persons rather than that royal authorities lacked general authority to conduct searches of that nature.[12]

The relative dearth of complaints about illegal or unconstitutional searches and seizures was rooted in the undeveloped seventeenth-century English state. Charles II and other Stuarts did not have "swarms of Officers" to carry out their commands. This lack of an English bureaucracy was reflected in the nature of the measures Parliament found most oppressive. Ship-money required communities to supply the king with ships or money for ships, in part because the king had little capacity to assess individual wealth. Duties were collected at the border or not at all. The Stuarts had almost no capacity to investigate personal homes for smuggled goods. The English presence in colonial communities during the seventeenth century ranged from minimal to nonexistent.

The means by which the hated Game Law authorized investigations into contraband weapons both illustrates the intrusive searches English law permitted during the seventeenth century and explains why those intrusive searches did not generate sustained political controversies over constitutional authority to search and seize. "The act of 1671," Chester Kirby notes, "authorized every lord of a manor to appoint a gamekeeper who should have the power to confiscate all paraphernalia of sport, such as guns, dogs, or nets found in the possession of unqualified persons. For this purpose he was to search the houses of suspected persons and thus he acted somewhat as a government official."[13] No

10 *Id.*
11 Edward Coke, The Fourth Part of the Institutes of the Laws of England 176 (London, E. & R. Brooke, 1797).
12 *See* Cuddihy, *supra* note 9, at 134.
13 Chester Kirby, *The English Game System*, 38 Am. Hist. Rev. 240, 241–42 (1933).

member of the royal court conducted investigations under the Game Act. The measure was enforced by a local justice of the peace, a minor local noble who might or might not have an interest in carrying out royal policies. The gamekeepers who actually conducted the searches were typically employees of the nobility. While "the gamekeeper served largely as a police officer, following suspicious characters about the manor in order to discover them poaching, watching snares in order to take the poacher who came for his booty, patrolling the fields at night,"[14] royal authorities standing alone had almost no capacity to learn about game law violations or punish them. Chester Kirby notes, "The government supplied justices of the peace, laws, and the framework of justice; but much, in the form of gamekeepers and prosecutions, assisted by the game associations, was left to the activity of those interested."[15] The end result of a state that was forced by lack of manpower to farm criminal investigation out to local elites was that the only persons in Great Britain with the capacity to raise constitutional challenges to the investigatory provisions of the Game Act were the persons who had the practical power to conduct investigations under the Game Act.

The most significant common law cases on search and seizure decided during the first half of the eighteenth century reflected continued limitations on the capacity of the English state to see. In both *Rex v. Dr. Purnell*[16] and *Regina v. Robert Mead,*[17] state prosecutors sought court orders mandating that criminal defendants produce certain documents. The justices refused in each instance, ruling that persons had a right not to produce documents that incriminated them. What is interesting for present purposes is how the nascent English state sought to see evidence of illegal behavior. English officials, lacking substantial bureaucratic assistance, asked the defendants to produce the documents in courts, rather than searching for and seizing those documents themselves. Significantly, perhaps, one defendant conceded that such a search was lawful. Defense counsel in *Dr. Purnell* conceded, "But suppose the Crown, has a right to visit the university, that is a reason for this Court not to interpose, because there would be another plain method of proceeding."[18] The defect lay in the requirement that the defendant produce incriminating documents. "The rule could not be granted," Chief Justice Lee ruled, "because it was a criminal proceeding, and that the motion was to make the defendants furnish evidence against themselves."[19] Had the English state the capacity to conduct a search, the English state might have seen the incriminating documents in *Purnell*.

II Seeing, Searching, and Seizure in the New English State

Eighteenth-century Englishmen made fewer constitutional complaints than their seventeenth-century ancestors, but those complaints more often emphasized allegedly

14 *Id.* at 246.
15 *Id.* at 256.
16 (1748) 1 Wil. 239 (KB).
17 (1703) 2 Ld. Raym. 927 (KB).
18 *Dr. Purnell*, 1 Wil. at 239.
19 *Id.* at 242; *see Mead*, 2 Ld. Raym. at 927 (moving to require the production of books because "they are perfectly of a private nature, and it would be to make a man produce evidence against himself in a criminal prosecution").

unconstitutional searches and seizures. Parliament debated with greater vigor royal power to search private residences. William Pitt proffered the most eloquent descriptions of the rights persons enjoyed against promiscuous investigations when, objecting to the search provisions of the bill authorizing a cider tax, he declared,

> The poorest man may, in his cottage, bid defiance to all the force of the Crown. It may be frail; its roof may shake, the wind may blow through it: the storm may enter; the rain may enter; but the King of England may not enter; all his force dares not cross the threshold of the ruined tenement.[20]

The foundational cases of contemporary Fourth Amendment law, *Entick v. Carrington*[21] and *Wilkes v. Wood*,[22] were handed down during the 1760s.

The resulting constitutional protections against certain searches and seizures coincide with the rise of the administrative state in Great Britain. Protests against unconstitutional searches increased dramatically in Great Britain when a government armed with more employees had more capacity to see, search, and seize. William Pitt, John Wilkes, and the other elites who led fights against promiscuous searches were associated with what was known as the country interest, the interest that simultaneously fought against the rise of the administrative state in Great Britain. Their criticisms of general warrants were a part of their more general criticisms of the administrative state and rooted in the same principles. Just as Englishmen expressed concern that the administrative state increased executive discretion, so they complained that general warrants increased the discretion of the dramatically increased number of civil servants employed by the administrative state.

The British administrative state matured in the eighteenth century.[23] Responding to various foreign policy crises, Great Britain developed an administration capable of organizing the military and collecting revenue far more efficiently than had previously been the case. The number of employees in the executive branch of the government increased geometrically. Best estimates suggest that the number of civil servants in Great Britain increased tenfold from 1650 until 1720 and then continued to increase substantially in the following years. These increases were particularly dramatic in the state department and the customs office, the institutions responsible for ferreting out political dissent and collecting revenue.

Much of this growth was dedicated to improving state capacity to see. John Brewer's study of the growth of the English state during the eighteenth century observes:

> Information was also needed to ensure that government policy proved effective. Was a tax producing its expected yield? Had high duties succeeded in their goal of excluding the goods of foreign competitors? How effective was the campaign against smuggling? Such inquiries led senior officials to accumulate information not only about the activities of the state's subjects but also about the action of its employees.[24]

20 1 Henry Brougham, The Critical and Miscellaneous Writings of Henry Lord Brougham, 264 (Philadelphia, Lea & Blanchard 1841).
21 (1765) 19 Howell's State Trials 1029 (CP).
22 (1763) 19 Howell's State Trials 1153 (CP).
23 This paragraph and the next borrow heavily from John Brewer, The Sinew of Power: War, Money and the English State, 1688–1783 (1988).
24 *Id.* at 222.

In order to gain this information, new officials in state and customs spent their time seeing, searching, and seizing. Brewer points out:

> The premises on which a candlemaker worked, the tools that he used, the time that he worked, the way in which he transported and sold his goods – all of these were supervised by the excise branch of the revenue service. It was difficult to evade these regulations. For chandlers, like soapmakers, could not legally ply their trade without first being inspected by the officer who kept their vats, moulds and utensils under lock and key.[25]

When state searches and seizures increased, so did protests against state searches and seizures. "The intellectual switchboard that signaled the grievousness of particular categories of searches and seizures," William Cuddihy notes, "was most sensitive to sudden surges of unaccustomed activity."[26] Businessmen, many complained, "can never properly call either their Time or their Goods their own, being always exposed to the Molestation of these petty Tyrants, to the neglect and interruption of their business."[27]

The protests against the bureaucratization of English politics were led by elites associated with the "Country Party" or "country interest," a loose group of intellectuals and politicians who claimed that the proliferation of executive positions was corrupting the English Constitution.[28] Such aristocrats as Henry St. John Bolingbroke, Thomas Gordon, John Trenchard, and John Wilkes raised several related criticisms of the new administrative state. First, old money did not appreciate being supervised by members of the lower middle classes. Second, members of the Country Party claimed that through appointment and patronage power the executive department of the national government was aggrandizing power. Third, Bolingbroke and others insisted that the discretion fostered in these new executive officials produced arbitrary government in violation of rule of law principles.

The British complaints against increased searches and seizures echoed these complaints against the new British administrative state. General warrants were unconstitutional because they allowed a lowly governmental employee to determine whom to search, where to search, and what to seek. Both American and British elites objected to being searched by their social inferiors.[29] Both American and British elites objected to arbitrary government. Blackstone complained that "the rigour and arbitrary proceedings of the excise laws seems hardly compatible with the temper of a free nation" in light of those measures giving "the officers a power of entering and searching the houses of such as deal in exciseable commodities at any hour of the day, and, in many cases, of the night likewise."[30] An important line of protest maintained that state officials were normally not allowed to enter houses, even when a warrant specified the house to be entered and the items to be sought. The *London Evening Post* stated, "Every Englishman has the satisfaction of seeing that his house is his castle, and is not liable to be searched, nor his papers pried into, by the malignant curiosity of King's messengers."[31] *The Monitor* captured these complaints when asserting, "To search and ransack houses, shops, offices

25 *Id.* at 214–15.
26 Cuddihy, *supra* note 9, at 373.
27 Brewer, *supra* note 23, at 215.
28 This paragraph relies heavily on Caroline Robbins, The Eighteenth-Century Commonwealthman (1959).
29 Cuddihy, *supra* note 9, at 292.
30 1 William Blackstone, Commentaries on the Laws of England, 318 (London, S. Sweet, 18th ed. 1829).
31 Cuddihy, *supra* note 9, at 460.

and studies, to empower men, Lowlif'd ignorant to enter, and to act at discretion, and to overhaul of the most private nature, in the house of him devoted to the passion, resentment, or groundless suspicion of a courtier" Violated basic English liberties.[32]

Wilkes v. Wood, *Entick v. Carrington*, and the other Wilkesite cases were direct consequences of the new English administrative state. They resulted from searches done by government officials. Civil servants ransacked the homes of John Wilkes and John Entick. This was in sharp contrast to such previous cases as *Rex v. Parnell*, when a government lacking manpower demanded that persons suspected of political heresies take the offending papers into court. The searches were notorious in part because they occurred while Parliament was engaged in a bitter debate over the search and seizure provisions in the Cider Tax of 1763. That measure permitted excise authorities to search at will anyone who made cider for personal use, a category that included a very high percentage of ordinary citizens. "Because the percentages of such households in the 'cyder counties' west of London was huge," Cuddihy notes, "everyone in those families was henceforth vulnerable to promiscuous searches."[33] *The North Britain 43*, which Wilkes edited, bitterly attacked the cider tax and the procedures for implementing the cider tax. The text began:

> I am not surprised at the general alarm, which has spread not only through the capital, but likewise through the whole kingdom, from a well grounded terror of the fatal consequences so justly to be apprehended from the new tax on *cyder*. This *odious* and *partial* tax is likewise to be enforced in the most *odious* and *partial* manner possible.... By the mode of the tax on *cyder*, not only possessed dealers in that commodity, but many new orders of men become subject to the laws of *excise*, and an insolent *exciseman*, under the influence, perhaps by the order of an insolent minister, may force his way into the house of any private gentleman, or farmer or freeholder, who has been guilty of voting contrary to a ministerial mandate.[34]

Wilkes and *Entick* articulated what began to be regarded as the traditional English rights against general warrants and unreasonable searches, even as that tradition largely began with *Wilkes* and *Entick*. *Wilkes* bluntly condemned general warrants. The opinion for the court declared:

> The defendants claimed a right, under precedents, to force persons' houses, break open escrutores, seize their papers, &c. upon a general warrant, where no inventory is made of the things taken away, and where no offenders' names are specified in the warrant, and therefore a discretionary power given to messengers to search wherever their suspicions may chance to fall. If such a power is truly invested in a Secretary of State, and he can delegate this power, it certainly may affect the person and property of every man in this kingdom, and is totally subversive of the liberty of the subject.[35]

Entick spelled out the conditions necessary for a specific warrant.

> There must be a full charge upon oath of a theft committed. The owner must swear that the goods are lodged in such place. He must attend at the execution of the warrant to shew them to the officer, who must see that they answer the description. And, lastly, the

32 *Id.* at 461.
33 *Id.* at 465.
34 1 The North Briton 249 (Dublin, James Williams 1766).
35 *Wilkes*, 19 Howell's State Trials at 1167.

> owner must abide the event at his peril; for if the goods are not found, he is a trespasser; and the officer being an innocent person, will be always a ready and convenient witness against him.[36]

The broad language in the Wilkesite decisions did contain two implicit limitations. First, the cases involved searches for the papers of political dissenters. *Entick*, in particular, had the potential to be converted into a free speech case or be restricted to personal papers (as opposed to stolen goods or contraband). Second, the Wilkesite decisions concerned the legality of executive searches and did not directly concern the constitutionality of parliamentary legislation authorizing general warrants. Parliamentary legislation passed in the wake of *Wilkes* and *Entick* did not fully abandon general warrants.[37] English courts, accepting parliamentary supremacy, did not challenge such measures.

Crucial features of the Wilkesite decisions nevertheless practically guaranteed that the rulings would transcend those narrow limitations. *Wilkes* spoke of general warrants, making no reference to the particular context in which that general warrant was issued. Given the close relationship between the arguments in the Wilkesite cases and the arguments in Parliament against the cider tax, no one in Britain would have interpreted the language of *Wilkes* and *Entick* (which spoke of limits on searches for stolen property) as confined to officials searching suspected political dissenters. Wilkes made the same constitutional arguments in court that Pitt and others made in Parliament because these English opponents of the administrative state believed that bureaucratic discretion granted by the general warrant was unconstitutional, even as they recognized legislative supremacy over constitutional interpretation. Parliament might have the final say on the constitutional status of administrative searches, but Wilkes, Pitt, and others insisted that a Parliament committed to long-standing constitutional values would curb bureaucratic discretion by insisting that official searches occur only after a warrant had been issued describing with some particularity the places to be searched and the items to be sought.

III Seeing, Searching, and Seizing in the Eighteenth-Century American Antistate

Americans inherited these constitutional complaints against searching and seizing from their English brethren. James Otis was complaining about general warrants when he called on English courts to declare parliamentary enactments unconstitutional.[38] Samuel Adams repeated the inherited status, privacy, and arbitrariness attacks on general warrants when drafting a resolution condemning such practices for a Boston town meeting. He declared:

> Our houses and even our bedchambers, are exposed to be ransacked, our boxes chests & trunks broke open ravaged and plundered by wretches, whom no prudent man would venture to employ even as menial servants; whenever they are pleased to say they suspect there are in the house wares &c. for which the dutys have not been paid. Flagrant instances of the wanton exercise of this power, have frequently happened in this and other sea port Towns. By this we are cut off from that domestick security which renders the lives of the most unhappy in some measure agreable. Those Officers may under

36 *Entick*, 19 Howell's State Trials at 1067.
37 *See* Cuddihy, *supra* note 9, at 475.
38 M. H. Smith, The Writs of Assistance Case 331–86 (1978).

> colour of law and the cloak of a general warrant, break thro' the sacred rights of the Domicil, ransack mens houses, destroy their securities, carry off their property, and with little danger to themselves commit the most horred murders.[39]

Every American state constitution that included some rights included provisions prohibiting general warrants or unreasonable searches. The 1776 Constitution of Virginia states, "That general warrants, whereby any officer or messenger may be commanded to search suspected places without evidence of a fact committed, or to seize any person or persons not named, or whose offense is not particularly described and supported by evidence, are grievous and oppressive and ought not be granted." The Fourth Amendment to the Constitution of the United States declares, "The right of the people to be secure in their persons, houses, papers, and effects, against unreasonable searches and seizures, shall not be violated, and no Warrants shall issue but upon probable cause, supported by Oath or affirmation, and particularly describing the place to be searched and the persons or things to be seized."

Increased public complaints about official searches coincided with dramatic increases in the British state's capacity to see what was happening in the American colonies.[40] Cuddihy points out that for much of colonial American history, protests against state investigations were dampened by state incapacity to investigate.

> Although searches and seizures under colonial law were overwhelming general, local police officers were incapable of enforcing the law with enough severity to excite widespread protests. The largest cities in eighteenth-century America, such as Boston, New York, Albany, and Philadelphia, could count no more than six to sixteen constables, while Hartford, Providence, and other sizable towns averaged constabularies of half that size. Most areas had even fewer enforcers of the law.[41]

Matters changed sharply during the mid-eighteenth century when Great Britain decided to tax the American colonies. These excises were accompanied by the same state apparatus that efficiently collected taxes in England. As excise searches became routine in many colonies, protests against the main instrument justifying those searches also became routine. "The causes of the general warrant's loss of legitimacy in England were also present in America by 1760," Cuddihy details, "massive enactment and enforcement of general searches and seizures."[42] Massachusetts led the fight against general warrants because the English made their best administrative efforts to implement excise laws in that state. The events that led to *Paxton's Case* began when Governor Shirley of Massachusetts dramatically increased state capacity to halt smuggling. Other colonies, which had been slow to condemn general warrants, joined Massachusetts once British capacity to see smuggling and related crimes increased in their jurisdiction.

The Declaration of Independence condemned the practices used to enforce the hated excise taxes. Jefferson excoriated King George III for "erect[ing] a multitude of New Offices, and sen[ding] hither swarms of Officers to harass our people and eat out their substance." While the phrasing may seem obscure to the twenty-first-century mind, eighteenth-century colonists understood that general warrants were the instrument

39 A Report of the Record Commissioners of the City of Boston Containing the Boston Town Records, 1770 Through 1777, at 100–01 (Boston, Rockwell & Churchill 1887).

40 This paragraph relies even more heavily on Cuddihy, *supra* note 9, than the rest of this part.

41 *Id.* at 249.

42 *Id.* at 252.

"swarms of Officers" used "to harass our people." In the United Kingdom and in the nascent United States, problems of search and seizure were intimately related to the "swarms of Officers" English and Americans were experiencing as part of the new and expanded British administrative state.

Americans adopted the commonwealth critique of the constitutional developments associated with the rise of the administrative state in Great Britain. Bernard Bailyn documents how the most important influence on American revolutionaries were the Country Party dissenters in England.[43] From persons like Trenchard and Gordon, Samuel Adams and other American revolutionaries learned how the English Constitution was being corrupted by patronage and placeholders. As did their counterparts in Great Britain. Americans believed that the strict separation of powers that formerly characterized Great Britain was being destroyed by ministerial prerogative. As did their counterparts in Great Britain, Americans believed that government by administrators was arbitrary government inconsistent with the constitutional principles of rule by law. General warrants and excise searches were intimate parts of this conspiracy against republican government that Americans eventually concluded justified separation from Great Britain. Bailyn notes, "Unconstitutional taxing, the invasion of placemen, the weakening of the judiciary, plural officeholding, Wilkes, standing armies – these were major evidences of a deliberate assault of power upon liberty. Lesser testimonies were also accumulating at the same time: small episodes in themselves, they took on a large significance in the context in which they were received. Writs of assistance in support of customs officials were working their expected evil."[44]

American revolutionaries followed their British brethren when criticizing the discretionary powers that general warrants vested in the increasing number of ordinary officials enforcing English laws in the colonies. James Otis complained that the general writ was "a power that places the liberty of every man in the hands of every petty officer," which allowed officers "to enter our houses when they please," an instrument of "arbitrary power."[45] Mercy Warren regarded general writs as "a detestable instrument of arbitrary power" that led to "capricious house searches by insolent officers of the new central government."[46] Virginians asserted that it was "unconstitutional to lodge such a Writ in the hands of the officer which gave him unlimited power to act under it according to his own arbitrary Discretion."[47] Patrick Henry observed how general warrants permitted government officials to see, search, and seize "in the most arbitrary manner, without any evidence or reason." "Everything the most sacred may be searched," he informed the Virginia Ratification Convention, "and ransacked by the strong arm of power."[48]

Americans by the time the Constitution was ratified placed increased emphasis on restricting what the state could see as well as curbing state discretionary power to see. As

43 This paragraph relies heavily on Bernard Bailyn, The Ideological Origins of the American Revolution (1967).

44 *Id.* at 117.

45 Smith, *supra* note 38, at 342.

46 "A Columbian Patriot," Observations on the New Constitution, and on the Federal and State Conventions (1788), *reprinted in* Pamphlets on the Constitution of the United States, 13 (Brooklyn, NY, Paul Leicester Ford ed., 1888).

47 Davies, *supra* note 2, at 581.

48 3 The Debates in the Several State Conventions on the Adoption of the Federal Constitution 588 (Washington, DC, Jonathan Elliot ed., 1836) [hereinafter Elliot's Debates].

did the British, Americans thought houses were special. Cuddihy declares, "That houses were castles was the most recurrent theme" of attacks on writs of assistance and commentaries on proposed constitutional amendments to restrict official searches.[49] "This [general writ of assistance] is against the fundamental Principles of Law," James Otis thundered. "The Privilege of House. A Man, who is quiet, is as secure in his House, as a Prince in his Castle, not with standing all his Debts, and civil Processes of any kind."[50] Another countryman observed, "You subject yourselves to see the doors of your houses them impenetrable Castles of freemen, fly open before the magic wand of the excisemen."[51] Americans during the 1780s spoke of specific matters persons had a right not to expose to the state. Luther Martin told Marylanders that general warrants procured to implement excise taxes enabled government officials to "examine into your private concerns."[52] An anti-Federalist complained that excise searches enabled "our bed chambers ... to be searched by the brutal tools of power."[53]

This concern with the discretionary power of officials not directly accountable to the people inspired the constitutional bans on general warrants in state constitutions and the Constitution of the United States. Not content with banning the general warrant, the American framers went beyond English practice in at least one and probably two ways. The Constitution of the United States and most state constitutions mandate the specific warrant as the constitutional alternative to the general warrant. The Fourth Amendment requires all warrants to "describe[e] the place to be searched, and the persons or things to be seized." This specificity requirement was not adopted in Great Britain until later.[54] The Fourth Amendment prohibits "unreasonable searches and seizures" in addition to mandating specific warrants. This language, which first appeared in the 1780 Constitution of Massachusetts, suggests constitutional limitations other than specific warrants on state capacity to see, search, and seize.

Much debate exists over the relationship between the provision in the Fourth Amendment prohibiting unreasonable searches and the provision mandating specific warrants. Thomas Davies maintains that these two provisions have identical scope. The framers, in his view, thought reasonable searches were those authorized by a specific warrant or those warrantless searches that satisfied the narrow conditions established by the common law.[55] Akhil Amar claims that the two provisions in the Fourth Amendment express a broad hostility to all warrants, general or specific. While specific warrants were tolerated in narrow instances, he believes that the Fourth Amendment reflected a desire among the framers to have most official searches examined by a jury for reasonableness.[56] William Cuddihy suggests that "reasonable" in the Fourth Amendment had specific content. The framers, in his view, intended to prohibit general warrants and, as "unreasonable," such practices as nocturnal searches and unannounced house

49 Cuddihy, *supra* note 9, at 766.

50 Smith, *supra* note 38, at 339.

51 "Cato Uticensis," Va. Indep. Chron. (Oct. 17, 1787), *reprinted in* 5 The Complete Anti-Federalist, 124 (Herbert J. Storing ed., 1981).

52 4 Elliot's Debates, *supra* note 48, at 30.

53 "A Son of Liberty," N.Y. J., Nov. 8, 1787, *reprinted in* 13 The Documentary History of the Ratification of the Constitution, 481 (John P. Kaminski & Gaspare J. Saladino eds., 1981).

54 *See* Cuddihy, *supra* note 9, at 602.

55 Davies, *supra* note 2.

56 Akhil Reed Amar, The Constitution and Criminal Procedure: First Principles (1997).

searches.[57] David Gray contends that the reasonableness clause sets limits on the authority of state agents to conduct searches and seizures using means and methods that, if left to the discretion of state agents, would threaten the security of the people in ways similar to the threats posed by general warrants.[58] On his view, the warrant clause provides an example of the kinds of remedial restraints of search and seizure powers that the framers regarded as effective and enforceable.[59]

These very different interpretations of the Fourth Amendment are united by shared recognition that Americans in the framing era were determined to curb state capacity to see, search, and seize. Davies and Cuddihy maintain that the Constitution provided two legal safeguards against unlimited bureaucratic discretion. Government investigators could not search whomever for whatever at any time or place they pleased. Their warrants had to specify who was being searched for what goods and where. Judicial officials rather than the executive minions determined whether the evidence warranted a specific warrant. Amar maintains that the Fourth Amendment provided a political safeguard against unlimited bureaucratic discretion. By disfavoring warrants, he maintains, the Constitution enabled juries rather than state employees to have the final say over whether government had constitutionally exercised the power to see, search, and seize. Gray contends that the Fourth Amendment imposes a duty on courts and the political branches to enforce remedial measures capable of securing subjects from threats of unlimited, discretionary, and therefore unreasonable search and seizure. State capacity to see, search, and seize was severely constrained by the Fourth Amendment, all agree, even as they dispute the substance of that constraint and how that constraint was to be implemented.

IV The Police State and the Nineteenth Century

The middle nineteenth century witnessed the establishment of a new institution that dramatically increased state capacity to see.[60] By the Civil War most major urban areas had professional police departments, whose employees were given substantial powers to investigate crimes. When exercising these investigatory powers, police officers exercised discretion quite similar to that exercised by the hated customs inspectors of the eighteenth century. The difference was that Americans, or at least Americans exercising constitutional authority, favored police discretion when police were investigating ordinary crimes. The result was that important constitutional restrictions on discretionary authority during searches and seizures were relaxed. When, however, elites felt less comfortable with increased official discretion, as was the case with searches implementing prohibition laws, constitutional rights against searches and seizures were enforced more strictly.

Neither state capacity to see nor the constitutional rules governing search and seizure changed dramatically during the first years after the Constitution of the United States was ratified. Neither the national government nor the states employed many persons who were charged with the responsibility for investigating and prosecuting ordinary

57 Cuddihy, *supra* note 9, at 748–49

58 Gray, *supra* note 4. David Gray, *Fourth Amendment Remedies as Rights: The Warrant Requirement*, 96 B.U. L. Rev. 425 (2016).

59 *Id.*

60 This section borrows heavily from Davies, *supra* note 2, and Oliver, *supra* note 2.

crimes. This lack of state capacity helps explain why few cases arose under the Fourth Amendment and similar provisions in state constitutions. Significantly, perhaps, *United States v. Burr*, the first crime of the century case in American history, raised constitutional questions about the right to an impartial trial, the right to confront witnesses, the right to self-incrimination, and the right to compulsory process, but not the right against search and seizure, partly because the federal government lacked the capacity to have agents investigate Burr's activities.[61]

Justice Joseph Story's opinion in *United States v. The La Jeune Eugenie* (1822)[62] set out the rules for search and seizure without a warrant when the Fourth Amendment was framed and during the first third of the nineteenth century. That case concerned the search of a ship thought to be engaged in the illegal international slave trade. Story began by pointing out that the warrantless search of *La Jeune Eugenie* was a common law trespass. He stated, "In such a case you do not acquire a right of search which justifies your encroachment upon the private concerns of a foreign ship."[63] Nevertheless, because state officials had the right to seize contraband, the trespass would be excused if the search was successful. "Having a right to seize for breach of your own laws," Story wrote, "you may seize at your peril; and if the case turns out to be innocent, you are responsible for damages, if guilty, you are justified by the event."[64] That the searcher was a captain in the navy of the United States had no special constitutional status. State capacity to see was conditioned on the state's demonstrating, either before or after the search took place, that the state would discover or had discovered evidence of crime.

State constitutional law similarly treated governing officials operating without a warrant no differently than private citizens. The leading state constitutional case, *Mayo v. Wilson* (1817),[65] arose when James Wilson and Simeon Dodge made a warrantless arrest of Solomon Mayo, whom they witnessed traveling with commercial goods on Sunday in violation of state laws. Although Wilson and Dodge were constables in the town of Francestown, New Hampshire, the Supreme Court of New Hampshire refused to give their actions any special status under state constitutional law. Rather, the opinion discussed the "cases where the law warrants a private person to arrest and imprison another."[66] As was the case in *La Jeune Eugenie*, both private persons and constables arrested at their peril when they did not witness the crime. Chief Justice William Merchant Richardson declared, "He who arrests upon suspicion must take care that his cause of suspicion be such, as will bear the test, for otherwise he may be punishable for false imprisonment."[67]

The middle third of the nineteenth century witnessed the rise of professional police forces and the related constitutional adjustments that enabled professional police forces to function. Most Americans living in the Jacksonian era, at least most Americans who were constitutional decision makers, wanted to increase state capacity to see, at least state capacity to see ordinary crimes. Constitutional rules were adjusted to enable police to exercise more discretion in the absence of a warrant than could constables at common

61 *See* Peter Charles Hoffer, The Treason Trials of Aaron Burr (2008).
62 26 F. Cas. 832 (D. Mass. 1822) (No. 15,551).
63 *Id.* at 843.
64 *Id.*
65 1 N.H. 53 (1817).
66 *Id.* at 56.
67 *Id.*

law. Eager to ferret out crime, Americans also embraced the line of English common law decisions that permitted illegally seized evidence to be used in a criminal proceeding rather than an alternative line of common law decisions that might have analogized those goods as the products of coerced confessions. When, however, Americans were less enthusiastic about state capacity to see, they became less enthusiastic about state searches and seizures. Cases involving state capacity to see people selling intoxicating liquors in violation of prohibition laws often differed from the line of cases involving police efforts to investigate "ordinary" crimes.

Rohan v. Sawin (1850)[68] became the leading case for permitting substantial police discretion under constitutional rules for search and seizure. The case arose when Charles Sawin, a member of the Boston police force, arrested Edward Rohan for knowingly receiving stolen goods. After Rohan was released by a city magistrate, he sued Sawin on the grounds that Sawin neither had a warrant for the arrest nor witnessed the actual crime. These were traditional justifications for a legal arrest under the common law. A lower state court found for Rohan, but that decision was reversed by the Supreme Judicial Court of Massachusetts. In sharp contrast to *Mayo v. Wilson*, Justice Charles Dewey distinguished searches and arrests done by private persons and those done by government employees. The traditional common law rules, in his view, governed only arrests by private persons. "The right appertaining to private individuals to arrest without a warrant," Dewey stated, "is confined to cases of the actual guilt of the party arrested; and the arrest can only be justified by proving such guilt."[69] The fight against ordinary crime required that police officers be given more discretion. Dewey wrote, "The public safety, and the due apprehension of criminals, charged with heinous offenses, imperiously requires that such arrests should be made without warrant by officers of the law."[70] For this reason, Dewey and other justices in the mid-nineteenth century began to permit police officers to arrest without a warrant when they had reason to believe a crime had been committed, even if they did not personally witness that crime. "But as to constables, and other peace-officers, acting officially," he maintained, "the law clothes them with greater authority, and they are held justified, if they act, in making the arrest, upon probable and reasonable cause for believing the party guilty of a felony."[71]

The beginning of professional police forces provided the occasion for Americans to reject the exclusionary rule in circumstances when police unconstitutionally or illegally seized evidence. The seminal case was *Commonwealth v. Dana* (1841),[72] although the actual discussion of the exclusionary rule was *dicta*. Elisha Dana was arrested after a police officer with a warrant found illegal lottery tickets in his office. The main issue in the case was whether the state constitution permitted the state legislature to authorize magistrates to issue search warrants for lottery tickets with a warrant. On this matter, the court and past law were clear. Judge Samuel Wilde stated, "The legislature were not deprived of the power to authorize search warrants for probable cause, supported by oath or affirmation, and for the punishment or suppression of any violation of law."[73] Wilde

68 59 Mass. (5 Cush.) 281 (1850).
69 *Id.* at 285.
70 *Id.*
71 *Id.*
72 43 Mass (2 Met.) 329 (1841).
73 *Id.* at 336.

then noted that the legality of the search was not a necessary condition for legally admitting the discovered evidence at trial:

> Admitting that the lottery tickets and materials were illegally seized, still this is no legal objection to the admission of them in evidence. If the search warrant were illegal, or if the officer serving the warrant exceeded his authority, the party on whose complaint the warrant issued, or the officer, would be responsible for the wrong done; but this is no good reason for excluding the papers seized as evidence, if they were pertinent to the issue, as they unquestionably were. When papers are offered in evidence, the court can take no notice how they were obtained, whether lawfully or unlawfully; nor would they form a collateral issue to determine that question.[74]

No state court before the Civil War questioned whether prosecutors could admit unconstitutionally seized evidence during criminal trials.

The Supreme Judicial Court of Massachusetts was largely following long-standing common law practice in *Dana*, but under different circumstances a different strand of the common law might have inspired a different result. English courts admitted as evidence fruits of unconstitutional or illegal searches. In *The King v. Jane Warwickshall*,[75] the seminal common law case on self-incrimination, the justices declared evidence obtained because of a confession admissible even when the confession was not admissible as illegally obtained.[76] This practice was rooted in the legal fiction that government officials were behaving as government officials only when acting consistently with their legal obligations. Victims of unconstitutional searches could not blame the government for that illegal conduct because by definition police officers who conducted illegal searches were not acting within their scope of duties. Police officers who conducted illegal searches, by comparison, could not claim any immunity as government officials when sued for trespass by victims of their unconstitutional actions because they were by definition not acting as government officials when conducting the illegal search. But that also meant that the victims of the search could not blame the government for that illegal conduct because, again by definition, police officers who conducted illegal searches were not acting within their scope of duties. Still, justices less enthralled with new police departments and the discretionary powers of police might have found common law support for an exclusionary rule in *Dana*. Coerced confessions had historically been excluded from criminal trials without inquiry into whether the government official who secured that confession had acted within the scope of his or her duties. Justices less sympathetic to state power in the late nineteenth century would analogize extracting information from a person by an illegal search to extracting information from a person by a coerced confession. Jacksonian officials who wanted police discretion to search for evidence of ordinary crimes, however, were not as inclined to be creative in limiting the use of illegally seized evidence as they were when expanding the scope of police discretion.

Americans were less enthusiastic about government power to see when state officials sought to learn whether citizens were violating prohibition laws. Although state courts did not declare temperance laws unconstitutional per se, they asserted limited state power to search and seize in ways that made prohibition measures difficult to enforce. *Fisher*

74 *Id.* at 337.
75 (1783) 168 Eng. Rep. 234 (KB).
76 *See* Davies, *supra* note 2, at 660–67.

v. McGirr (1854)[77] was the most prominent instance in which state judges employed state constitutional provisions on search and seizure to frustrate state restrictions on alcohol. Patrick McGirr, a local police officer, entered the home of Theodore Fisher and seized a large quality of intoxicating beverages pursuant to a warrant supported by a Massachusetts law that required judges to issue a warrant when "any three persons … make complaint, under oath or affirmation, that they have reason to believe … that spirituous or intoxicating liquors are kept or deposited and intended for sale, by any person not authorized … in any building or place, in said city or town."[78] Chief Justice Lemuel Shaw insisted that this statute unconstitutionally authorized general warrants. His opinion condemned the statute for not requiring investigators to specify what person was keeping the intoxicating liquors and not requiring magistrates issuing the warrants to declare that they believed the complainants. Shaw acknowledged that in numerous instances his ruling would make the law impossible to enforce because frequently "neither the complainants nor the magistrate can know, before search, who is the owner, or has the custody, or intends to sale, and therefore cannot name him."[79] Nevertheless, rather than emphasize "the due apprehension of criminals" as the Supreme Judicial Court of Massachusetts did in *Rohan*, the same justices in *Fisher* insisted that constitutional rules trumped official discretion. "If these modes of accomplishing a laudable purpose, and of carrying into effect a good and wholesome law," Shaw concluded, "cannot be pursued without a violation of the constitution, they cannot be pursued at all, and other means must be devised, not open to such objection."[80]

V Administration Comes to the United States

The capacity of governmental officials in the United States to see increased dramatically during the late nineteenth century and that increased capacity influenced the constitutional rules for search and seizure. A "new administrative state,"[81] or "Yankee leviathan,"[82] developed during and after the Civil War. Congress created new administrative agencies and gave those agencies the legal powers, staffing, and resources necessary to investigate and regulate business affairs. Many prominent justices responded by imposing constitutional limitations on what those bureaucracies could regulate and what those bureaucrats could see. Police forces, which enjoyed broad powers to investigate ordinary crimes, were left untouched by this reaction to increased state capacity to see business crimes. As in previous years and previous centuries, what new institutions could constitutionally see depended on what American elites wanted new institutions to see.

The American administrative state dates from the last third of the nineteenth century. During the decades after the Civil War, the governing Republican Party became convinced that national commercial life needed far greater regulation than had been the case. This need for regulation required national institutions with far greater capacity to

77 67 Mass. (1 Gray) 1 (1854).
78 *Id.* at 22.
79 *Id.* at 20.
80 *Id.*
81 Stephen Skowronek, Building a New American State: The Expansion of National Administrative Capacities, 1877–1920 (1982).
82 Richard Franklin Bensel, Yankee Leviathan: The Origins of Central State Authority in America, 1859–1877 (1991).

see than had been the case during the Jacksonian era. As Ken Kersch and others note, legibility was central to regulation.[83] Congress and state legislatures had to know how business enterprises were operating when passing proper regulations. Federal and state governments needed greater investigatory powers to determine whether regulations were being obeyed.

The United States Reports subtly document the increased presence of the new administrative state during the late nineteenth century and cotemporaneous limitations on the federal capacity to investigate ordinary crimes. The Supreme Court after the Civil War adjudicated numerous claims that new administrative agencies were conducting investigations that violated constitutional rights or limits on national constitutional powers. By comparison, persons reading all Supreme Court opinions handed down from 1865 until 1900 might conclude that no federal officer even arguably violated the rights of a person suspected of such criminal offenses as murder, robbery, and assault. Supreme Court opinions referred to "the fourth amendment" only three times outside the administrative and congressional investigatory context. Two references to the Fourth Amendment were in cases raising questions about the powers of other expanding federal bureaucracies. *Ex parte Jackson*[84] forbade Congress to mandate that post officers open ordinary mail. *Fong Yue Ting v. United States* (1893)[85] declared that certain immigration laws required immigration officials to violate Fourth Amendment rights. The only Supreme Court opinion to mention the Fourth Amendment in the context of ordinary crime was *Miller v. Texas* (1894),[86] which held that state police officials were not bound by the Fourth Amendment.

Americans opposed to the new administrative state challenged on constitutional grounds almost every characteristic of what they perceived to be an intrusive bureaucratic regime. Many litigants and supportive judges maintained that the due process clauses of the Constitution of the United States and various state constitutions imposed substantive limitations on official power to regulate business activity.[87] Litigators challenged congressional capacity to delegate powers to new regulatory agencies and insisted that the powers delegated be construed narrowly.[88] These litigation movements also included challenges to new state powers to see. In some instances, the Supreme Court ruled that various constitutional amendments limited congressional capacity to investigate business crimes. In other cases, the Supreme Court limited judicial capacity to compel businesspersons to take allegedly incriminating documents into court.

The first constitutional challenges to the new administrative state were to congressional capacity to see.[89] During the Civil War, Congress conducted several investigations into alleged corrupt practices. Those investigations proliferated after the Civil War. What was once a discrete phenomenon became an ongoing practice during the last third of the nineteenth century that was often assigned to permanent institutions such

[83] *See* Ken I. Kersch, Constructing Civil Liberties: Discontinuities in the Development of American Constitutional Law 29–66 (2004).
[84] 96 U.S. 727 (1877).
[85] 149 U.S. 698 (1893).
[86] 153 U.S. 535 (1894).
[87] *See* Howard Gillman, The Constitution Besieged: The Rise and Demise of Lochner Era Police Powers Jurisprudence (1993).
[88] *See* Skowronek, *supra* note 80.
[89] This paragraph relies heavily on Kersch, *supra* note 82.

as the Interstate Commerce Commission. Persons hauled before Congress and these commissions often insisted that their rights against self-incrimination were violated and, if they were requested to take materials, that their rights against unreasonable searches were violated. They claimed no difference existed between having a constable rummage through their house or place of business and being ordered to do the search themselves and supply possibly incriminating material for government officials to inspect.

The Supreme Court curbed these new state powers to investigate in two cases. *Kilbourn v. Thompson* (1880)[90] unanimously held that Congress had no general power to conduct investigations. Congress could investigate only when exercising an enumerated power, and investigating criminal behavior was not within the enumerated powers of Congress. The congressional attempt to investigate pooling among railroads, the unanimous court concluded, "assumed a power which could only be properly exercised by another branch of the government, because it was in its nature clearly judicial."[91] *Counselman v. Hitchcock* (1892)[92] limited national power to investigate matters within the enumerated powers of Congress. The issue in that case was whether the Interstate Commerce Commission (ICC) when administering concededly constitutional laws passed under the interstate commerce clause could compel a person to testify as to possible criminal activity. The Supreme Court unanimously ruled that administrative efforts to compel such testimony were unconstitutional. *Counselman* made no distinction between compelling a person to testify and compelling a person to reveal potentially incriminating documents to an administrative agency. Justice Samuel Blatchford's opinion stated, "The witness is protected from being compelled to disclose the circumstances of his offense, the sources from which, or the means by which, evidence of its commission, or of his connection with it, may be obtained, or made effectual for his conviction, without using his answers as direct admissions against him."[93]

Interstate Commerce Commission v. Brimson (1894)[94] considerably muddied the waters surrounding national power to investigate. The issue was whether the ICC could order William Brimson to testify about whether the railroad lines he managed were owned by the Illinois Steel Company in violation of federal antitrust law and compel him to provide to the commission various documents identifying the persons owning stock in those rail lines. Federal law provided the ICC with authority to compel the production of various documents, in particular, the "power to require, by subpoena, the attendance and testimony of witnesses and production of all books, papers, tariffs, contracts, agreements, and documents, relating to any matter under investigation."[95] Brimson and the other railroad officials claimed Congress had no power to pass such a law. Justice John Harlan in a 5–3 opinion had little difficulty disposing of this issue in favor of federal power, but his comments on individual rights raised questions about whether the power to see he acknowledged with one hand was removed by the other.

Harlan's analysis of the national power question began from the premise that Congress had the power to investigate and that these investigations could be delegated to other

90 103 U.S. 168 (1880).
91 *Id.* at 192.
92 142 U.S. 547 (1892).
93 *Id.* at 585.
94 154 U.S. 447 (1894).
95 *Id.* at 461.

national bodies. He declared, "Undoubtedly, congress may confer upon a nonjudicial body authority to obtain information necessary for legitimate government purposes."[96] Harlan found that the ICC was serving a legitimate government purpose by investigating compliance with constitutional federal laws on interstate commerce. "The prohibition of unjust charges, discriminations, or preferences, by carriers engaged in interstate commerce, in respect to property or persons transported from one state to another, is a proper regulation of interstate commerce," he wrote.[97] Thus, Congress acted constitutionally when "empowering the [ICC] to inquire into the management of the business of carriers subject to the provisions of the act, and to investigate the whole subject of interstate commerce as conducted by such carriers, and, in that way, to obtain full and accurate information of all matters involved in the enforcement of the act of congress."[98] Requiring businesspersons to produce their books and other documents was simply an incident of this broader regulatory power. Harlan stated:

> An adjudication that congress could not establish an administrative body with authority to investigate the subject of interstate commerce, and with the power to call witnesses before it, and to require the production of books, documents, and papers related to that subject, would go far towards defeating the object for which the people of the United States placed commerce among the states under national control.[99]

Kilbourn was dubiously distinguished because Congress in that case was "making inquiry into the private affairs of the citizen."[100]

Having demonstrated that Congress had the power to compel persons to testify and produce papers, Harlan proceeded to insist in *dicta* that the citizen might have a constitutional right to refuse. Responding to claims that federal law was "in derogation of those fundamental guaranties of personal rights that are recognized by the constitution as inhering in the freedom of the citizen," he noted that a person subpoenaed by the ICC had the right "to contend before that court that he was protected by the constitution from making answer to the questions propounded to him, or that he was not legally bound to produce the books, papers, etc. ordered to be produced."[101] Harlan then quoted a federal law, passed after *Counselman v. Hitchcock* and the ICC order in *Brimson*, which gave persons testifying before the commission immunity from subsequent prosecution. Rather than clarify further the limits on administrative power to learn about illegal business activities, Harlan simply noted that Brimson had challenged only federal power under the commerce clause to investigate his activities and had not claimed that he had an independent constitutional right not to have the administrative state pry into the details of his business affairs.

Boyd v. United States (1886)[102] provided strong precedential support for businesspersons resisting federal efforts to see the details of their business affairs. The case arose when the federal government claimed fraud in the construction of a federal building. Following federal law, the local federal attorney insisted that E. A. Boyd provide the

96 *Id.* at 469.
97 *Id.* at 472.
98 *Id.* at 473.
99 *Id.* at 474.
100 *Id.* at 478.
101 *Id.* at 479.
102 116 U.S, 616 (1886).

government with invoices for the glass he had previously imported, with the threat that the glass would be forfeited if the invoices were not forthcoming. The Supreme Court unanimously declared unconstitutional the federal statute empowering federal attorneys to obtain potentially incriminating documents. When doing so, the justices forged a connection between the Fourth and Fifth Amendments that had previously appeared nowhere in constitutional law and imposed sharp limits on federal efforts to learn whether businesses were violating federal law.

Justice Joseph Bradley's opinion implicitly distinguished for constitutional purposes business crimes from other criminal violations. His analysis interpreted past practice as granting papers a unique status under the Fourth Amendment. Bradley asked whether "a search and seizure, or … a compulsory production of a man's private papers, to be used in evidence against him" is "an 'unreasonable search and seizure.'"[103] He interpreted *Entick v. Carrington* as answering this question. In Bradley's view, *Entick* stood for the proposition that the state should not be able to learn about a person's private papers by any means. "Breaking into a house and opening boxes and drawers are circumstances of aggravation," he insisted, "but any forcible and compulsory extortion of a man's own testimony, or of his private papers to be used as evidence to convict him of crime, or to forfeit his goods, is within the condemnation of that judgement."

Whether business papers enjoyed this special constitutional status was not clear when *Boyd* was decided. Bradley without any analysis treated business papers as enjoying the same constitutional protection as political papers. *Entick*, which concerned political papers, did not discuss the legal status of searches for other papers. Moreover, *Entick*, as noted previously, made clear that the rule of that case applied to all official investigations. *Boyd* implied that different rules might apply to searches that discovered stolen goods and searches that uncovered incriminating papers.

Bradley pointed to "the intimate connection between" the Fourth and Fifth Amendments when explaining why administrative agencies could not use unconstitutionally obtained business papers when prosecuting business crimes. *Boyd* held that searches or seizures conducted for gaining evidence to be produced at trial were the constitutional equivalent of obtaining coerced confessions. The "searches and seizures condemned in the fourth amendment," Bradley wrote, "are almost always made for the purpose of compelling a man to give evidence against himself." That goal, he continued, "is condemned in the fifth amendment." This "intimate connection" between constitutional prohibitions against unreasonable searches and against self-incrimination prevented government officials from searching for Boyd's incriminating papers as an alternative to demanding Boyd produce the papers in court. Bradley concluded, "We have been unable to perceive that the seizure of a man's private books and papers to be used in evidence against him is substantially different from compelling him to be a witness against himself."[104]

The logic of Bradley's opinion in *Boyd* could have been, but was not, employed to curtail police behavior. When nineteenth-century police officers were searching for weapons or contraband, they were searching for "evidence to be produced at trial." As such, the relevant provisions in state constitutions on searches and investigations might have been interpreted as prohibiting prosecutors from using unconstitutionally obtained

103 *Id.* at 622.
104 *Id.* at 633.

evidence at criminal trials. Nevertheless, state courts during the last third of the nineteenth century did not connect constitutional bans on unreasonable searches with constitutional bans on coerced confessions. "Ordinary" criminals were routinely convicted on evidence obtained in violation of state constitutional provisions prohibiting unreasonable searches. "Courts in the administration of the criminal law," the Supreme Court of Illinois declared in *Gindrat v. People* (1891),[105] "are not accustomed to be over-sensitive in regard to the sources from which evidence comes, and will avail themselves of all evidence that is competent and pertinent." Persons who violated prohibition laws lost their immunity to the exclusionary rule. This issue arose in *State v. McCann* (1873),[106] an appeal from a conviction for violating state laws against possessing intoxicating beverages intended for sale. "It is objected that the seizure was illegal, the officer having proceeded to search without any warrant," the Supreme Judicial Court of Maine observed.[107] That objection was dispatched in a sentence. Chief Justice Appleton's unanimous opinion stated, "Suppose it was so, that is no defense for the defendant's violation of law. If the sheriff has violated any law he is responsible for such violation, but that will not constitute any justification or excuse for the defendant."[108]

Counselman/Boyd and *Gindrat/McCann* created a sharp divide in the constitutional law of search and seizure at the dawn of the twentieth century. That divide simultaneously distinguished between federal and state capacity to see and government capacity to see business and "ordinary" crimes. During the late nineteenth century, the Supreme Court of the United States imposed sharper curbs on administrative investigations than state courts imposed on police investigations. Given the different subjects of federal and state investigations, this instance of constitutional federalism had the effect of making business crimes harder to see than street crimes. Federal courts reacted to increased state power to see business crimes by setting sharp limits on the authority of such new administrative agencies as the Interstate Commerce Commission. State courts, by comparison, reacted to increased state power to see ordinary crimes by adopting or maintaining the pre–Civil War broad powers of police departments, which during the late nineteenth century were often granted even more resources and manpower to ferret out theft and related offenses.

Conclusion

Far greater continuities mark the history of search and seizure than has commonly been thought to be the case. Controversies over what constitutes an unconstitutional search are driven by expansions in state capacity to see. Sometimes, these expansions are technology. New devices permit government officials to see what they could not previously see. During the eighteenth and nineteenth centuries, these expansions were institutional. A government official in 1890 could see, for the most part, only what a government official in 1750 could see. The difference was that far more government officials were charged with seeing. Government saw more in 1890 than in 1750 because government employed more people who were authorized to investigate, search, seize, and see.

105 27 N.E. 1085, 1087 (Ill. 1891).
106 61 Me. 116 (1873).
107 *Id.* at 117.
108 *Id.*

Every sustained controversy that arose during the eighteenth and nineteenth centuries over government power to search and seize was sparked by the rise of new government institutions with new capacities to see. The rise of the British administrative state that employed numerous persons to enforce excise taxes in both Great Britain and the United States inspired the attacks on general warrants that were eventually codified by the Fourth Amendment. State judges responded to the creation of police departments in Jacksonian America by loosening common law rules that hindered official investigation of ordinary crimes. When Congress during the late nineteenth century established administrative agencies in the United States and charged those agencies with investigating business crimes, opponents wielded the Fourth Amendment and other constitutional provisions when attempting to prevent those institutions from learning about business affairs and business crimes.

Some commentaries may have missed the continuities between eighteenth- and nineteenth-century debates over government searches and seizures by adopting too narrow a definition of crime. Commentaries on the Fourth Amendment commonly observe that contemporary law enforcement investigatory practices did not develop until police departments were established in the nineteenth century.[109] This observation is true with respect to such crimes as murder and robbery, but false with respect to such crimes as smuggling and tax evasion. The British administrative state during the eighteenth century devoted considerable resources to investigating and ferreting out smuggling and tax evasion. The scholarly failure to recognize the similarities between eighteenth-century excisemen and nineteenth-century police officers is rooted, one suspects, in an implicit assumption that smuggling and tax evasion are somehow not ordinary crimes.

Tax evasion and robbery have distinctive Fourth Amendment histories because constitutional decision makers have historically been more interested in seeing some crimes rather than others. Americans celebrated constitutional bans on general warrants during the eighteenth century because a people who cried, "No Taxation without Representation" were unsurprisingly as hostile to the primary means by which government officials investigated efforts to evade what Americans thought were unconstitutional excise laws. American elites during the nineteenth century approved the exercise of discretionary search and seizure powers by police officers because they supported police efforts to uncover evidence of robbery, murder, and other related crimes. The same elites who rejected the exclusionary rule when police departments found evidence of stolen goods enthusiastically insisted on exclusion when administrative agencies seeking to learn about business crimes sought to compel persons to turn over business records.

Constitutional criminal procedure in general and search and seizure in particular are, as William Stuntz correctly observed, as much about the substance of the underlying criminal law as about procedural regularity.[110] State capacity expanded during the eighteenth and nineteenth centuries because important state actors wanted to have greater capacity to regulate certain behaviors. The government of Great Britain sought to improve revenue collection by gaining greater capacity to see violations of customs law. Jacksonians sought to stamp out crime by establishing police departments with greater capacity to see evidence of robberies and murders. Resistance to these greater capacities to see arose from those who had an interest in preventing the state from learning about

109 *See* sources cited *supra* note 3.
110 *See supra* note 7.

certain activities. Eighteenth-century Americans did not want government agents to see the rum they smuggled from the West Indies. Nineteenth-century railroad magnates did not want the state to inspect their books.

These connections between procedure and substance highlight how constitutional protections against searches and seizures are not constitutional islands cut off from the rest of constitutional developments in the United States and Great Britain. The rise of the administrative state in Great Britain was a major cause of the American Revolution. Americans objected to all the incidents of that state, the need for increased revenues, the increase in bureaucratic discretion, and the frequency of administrative searches. *Boyd* and other cases limiting federal power to see business activity were politically connected to *Lochner v. New York*[111] and other cases limiting federal and state power to regulate business activity. How Americans react to the new technologies of the twentieth-first century, this history suggests, will depend both on procedural concerns with how much those new technologies permit government to see and substantive concerns about the rights of people to keep those behaviors hidden from prying government eyes.

[111] 198 U.S. 45 (1905).

17 An Eerie Feeling of Déjà Vu: From Soviet Snitches to Angry Birds

Judge Alex Kozinski[†] & Mihailis E. Diamantis[‡]

The U.S. government knows a lot about us. Literally, from the moment we're born to the moment we die, it tags and monitors us. We provide some of that information on the forms we file for licenses, taxes, and major life events. Much of the rest the government collects, without our help, using security cameras, body scanners, license plate readers, and the like. But the data the government gathers itself is a small drop in the ocean of information we constantly generate.[1] Every time we open a bank account, use a credit card, email a friend, upload a video, browse the Internet, make a phone call, create and store a digital file, or go anywhere with a cell phone in our pocket, we shed reams of very personal information. Even while sleeping, most of us generate data that someone's interested in, if only as evidence of inactivity.

To collect and analyze this sort of information, governments need to outsource to private parties. The traditional way to do this, and the old favorite of totalitarian regimes like the Soviet Union, is to recruit the citizenry. Get them to spy on each other and report back. That method is clumsy, but effective to an extent. The slicker, modern approach used in the United States (and almost everywhere else now) relies on the private sector – the corporations that collect our data in the ordinary course of business. This includes just about every corporation that interacts with individual customers, and many more besides, from banks, cell phone companies, and Internet service providers, to loan collectors and straight-up data collectors watching on the sidelines. These corporations meticulously record every transaction we have with them, and many transactions we don't. For a price, it's all transferable to the government – or anyone else willing to pay – with the click of a button: no need for dark alleys and hushed voices.

These two approaches raise overlapping concerns. We expose our most vulnerable and intimate details to the private parties we love and trust, the neighbors and corporations we interact with on a daily basis. Through these private interactions, we develop those idiosyncratic personal identities that are the lifeblood of American individualism,

† Judge, United States Court of Appeals for the Ninth Circuit.

‡ Associate Professor, University of Iowa, College of Law.

1 Some put this number currently at three to ten data points per second. Theresa M. Payton & Theodore Claypoole, Privacy in the Age of Big Data: Recognizing Threats, Defending Your Rights, and Protecting Your Family 12 (2014). Everyone expects that number to mushroom in the coming years.

the engines of our innovation, and the seeds of our social progress.[2] The privacy of that space is crucial; if the secrets revealed in it are openly available to those with the power to punish us, it disappears. Censorship, even if self-imposed, is the enemy of the free.

How can we protect this private space in America today? We live in a world where we generate and record literally two and a half quintillion bytes of data every day.[3] We have no choice but to trust almost all of this data to the private third parties who transmit and store it. And these third parties have strong financial and legal incentives to turn much of it over to the government. This is not the first time a society has had to deal with omnipresent private informants. The experiences of regimes like the Soviet Union hold lessons for the rise of private surveillance today.

I Soviet Snitches

Policing is largely about negotiating information asymmetries. The targets and the people around them are always going to know more about themselves, whether before they're suspected of anything, while they're being investigated, or during any trial. The asymmetry becomes more of an obstacle as a government tries to police more people and wider swaths of their lives. It could seem downright insurmountable to a totalitarian regime like the Soviet Union.

To cope, the Soviets recruited an army of private informants – and how! The number of private informants working for them peaked at around 20 million during World War II.[4] With a population of just less than 200 million, that means one in ten Soviets was in the business of ratting out his neighbors. Soviet-influenced East Germany trailed slightly, with one informant for every sixty-six citizens.[5] But with surveillance files on nearly a quarter of the population, East German officials were still very thorough.[6] The information these citizens relayed was crucial to the success of the Soviet and East German secret services.[7] Still, from a vantage where a 16-gigabyte thumb drive capable of holding nearly 11 million pages of text sells for less than ten dollars, it's hard to imagine just how much pencil sharpening this required. No one accused the Soviets of being halfhearted.

True to its egalitarian roots, the Soviet Union recruited informants in all social strata, from peasants to soldiers to clergy. That, after all, was the best way to get information *on* all social strata. Informants were divided into *osvedomiteli*, ordinary people who reported information in the course of their regular lives, and the *rezidenty*, to whom they reported. For the information network to penetrate into the most secret nooks of people's lives, instinctive protectionism toward friends and family had to be overcome. If their legends are to be believed, the Soviets succeeded. The best-known story told of a thirteen-year-old peasant named Pavel Morozov, who caught whiff that his father was secretly assisting

2 Sygmunt Bauman & David Lyon, Liquid Surveillance 28 (2013) ("Privacy is the realm that is meant to be one's own domain, the territory of one's undivided sovereignty, inside which one has the comprehensive and indivisible power to decide 'what and who I am'").

3 Matthew Wall, *Big Data: Are You Ready for Blast-Off?*, BBC News (Mar. 4, 2014), http://www.bbc.com/news/business-26383058.

4 Robert W. Stephan, Stalin's Secret War: Soviet Counter-Intelligence Against the Nazis 61 (2003).

5 John O. Koehler, Stasi: The Untold Story of the East German Police (1999).

6 Gary Bruce, The Firm: The Inside Story of the Stasi 11 (2010).

7 James Heinzen, *Informers and the State under Late Stalinism: Informant Networks and Crimes against "Socialist Property," 1940–53*, 8 Kritika: Explorations in Russian & Eurasian Hist 789, 790 (2007).

other peasants outside the normal Soviet channels. As a true Soviet, Pavel dutifully reported this to authorities, and his father was executed soon after.

How do you get people to snitch, even on their most intimate associates? Instilling a sense of patriotic duty helps. Pavel's family didn't much appreciate his patriotism and killed him shortly after his father's trial. But Pavel's spirit would live on in a martyr's tale commemorated in hundreds of children's books. Still, as the family's response suggests, patriotism can only go so far. A bit of government-led blackmail can help drum up enthusiastic informants and was a common recruitment tactic. Once officials received reports against one person, they could offer lenience for reports on others in an ever-widening information Ponzi scheme. The Soviets didn't get all of their information from true patriots or through coercion. Just to be sure they covered all their bases, they also offered cold, hard cash in return for good information. As discussed further below, this mix of voluntary and involuntary informants is an important parallel to the way private surveillance works today.

What was the effect of this surveillance in the Soviet Union? In the United States, we might say something measured like "Awareness that the Government may be watching chills associational and expressive freedoms."[8] But this doesn't even begin to describe the dangers. Lavrenti Beria, the head of Stalin's secret police, famously proclaimed, "Show me the man, and I'll show you the crime." With that kind of power, you can wrap freedom in a bag and deep-freeze it.

II Angry Birds

The U.S. government must also cope with information asymmetries between enforcement authorities and their targets. The events of September 11, 2001, prompted a frenzied effort to close the information gap. In this, the U.S. government had an advantage the Soviets did not: modern commerce, and its extremely sophisticated, ready-made information-gathering infrastructure. Long before 2001, private corporations logged just about everything they could find out about us. Every step we took, whether we liked it or not, was recorded, sorted, packaged, and sold to advertisers. The government just had to sign up as one more customer of the data brokers. And with each passing year, the sort of information these corporations can get their hands on becomes more detailed and more personal. Eat your heart out, Lavrenti Beria.

Here's a typical business model for accessing customer data: Angry Birds is a great game. And better yet, it's free. How can Rovio, the developer of Angry Birds, be worth more than $1 billion if it gives away free software? It turns out it's much more profitable to watch you playing a free app than to try to sell it to you. And Angry Birds does watch you. Want to install the cool new take on the game, Angry Birds Transformers? At the time of writing, you must give the app and its developers access to your identity, the files and photos on your phone, control over your camera, and information about your calls and Wi-Fi connections. Earlier versions of the game, like so many other free apps, tracked your location, even while you weren't playing. All of this data allows Angry Birds to feed you tailored advertising that marketers will pay a high premium to secure. That's how Rovio pays its pricey coders to give us a streamlined experience without touching our wallets, while still turning an enviable profit.

8 *United States v. Jones*, 132 S. Ct. 945, 956 (2012) (Sotomayor, J., concurring).

It's not only apps that do this. Almost anything you do that puts you in touch with a service provider produces a stream of information that is advertising gold. Some points of contact are obvious, as when we memorialize our personal data on social network sites like Facebook. In these cases, what may not be obvious is just how *much* of that data is collected and stored. When Austrian law student Max Schrems used European Union laws to force Facebook to give him a copy of the data they had on him, they sent him a 1,200-page PDF.

Other points of contact are less apparent, at least to the uninitiated. There are more than one hundred different companies that track just about every move you make on the Internet. You may never have heard of any of them, but they know you very well. They track you without disturbing your surfing experience and without even telling you. They do this by installing bits of data called "cookies" behind the scenes onto your computers. These cookies identify you and store information about your browsing history. On the basis of your Internet trail, when you visit a Web page, the advertising space is auctioned in real time to, for example, a pharma company that manufactures sleep aids; you might see their ad if the cookies on your system indicate you recently searched Wikipedia for information about insomnia. Some of this tracking data publicly purports to keep your identity hidden; others, such as code used by most popular sites, can track you directly back to your social networking profiles.

Your phone, and not just the apps on it, is like your personal homing beacon. Mobile phone carrier networks log your GPS data, tracking you throughout your day within a few meter radius. Even if you turn off GPS location tracking, cell companies can and do track you through the cell phone towers your phone automatically connects to. And even if you have no cell connection, companies track you using your phone's Wi-Fi and Bluetooth signals by planting devices on streets and in stores specifically for that purpose. Carrier networks sell the location data they gather to companies such as Sense Networks, which crunch it to create very specific user profiles. Advertisers then buy these profiles for targeted marketing.

Scrapping your cell phone and computer won't let you cut a hole in the corporate dragnet. Anytime you use a credit card, store membership card, bank account, etc., you produce data that private corporations collect and monetize. Even just driving your car, there's a good chance your location is being logged by any number of companies that mount license plate scanners on vehicles in their fleet. These companies got started with a mind to help lenders track down cars with defaulted loans, but now they track any car that comes within range. In the near-future, face scanners will supplement plate scanners and will biometrically log drivers, passengers, and pedestrians.

This frighteningly precise information is just the tip of the iceberg of customer data private corporations can, do, and will gather. But it's more than enough to show why Google CEO Eric Schmidt could, with a straight face, say, "We know where you are. We know where you've been. We can more or less know what you're thinking about."[9] Acxiom, one of the largest big data brokers, claims to have fifteen hundred data points on each of more than 700 million people. Those data points give them enough insight into your psychological makeup to fit you into hundreds of refined consumer categories, estimating, for example, how likely you are to pay cash for a new Korean vehicle.

[9] Derek Thompson, *Google's CEO: 'The Laws Are Written by Lobbyists'*, ATLANTIC (Oct. 1, 2010), http://www.theatlantic.com/technology/archive/2010/10/googles-ceo-the-laws-are-written-by-lobbyists/63908.

It's private corporations collecting all this data. What's that got to do with the U.S. government? A lot, it turns out. Just as Soviet citizens could secure financial and political benefits by informing on their neighbors, it can be very profitable for American companies to sell customer data to the government. By one estimate, intelligence contracts with the U.S. government are worth $56 billion a year. With this kind of money on the table, it's unsurprising that the likes of Acxiom have worked hard to cultivate relationships with law enforcement. License plate scanners and cell companies, too, regularly send their information to police. And, yes, even Angry Birds has drawn the attention of U.S. intelligence organizations as a potential source of information.[10]

Dollar amounts aren't always publicly available, but those that are show just how lucrative sales to the government can be. AT&T, for example, charges the government twenty-five dollars per day to track a phone, and Sprint charges thirty dollars. At this price, the data sells for much more than the cell service of the customers they're tracking. But it's still a good deal for police, who send cell companies millions of data requests each year. The number of requests is so overwhelming that some cell service providers have set up automated Web interfaces for processing requests.

What the U.S. government can't get from private corporations with a financial carrot, it gets from them with an enforcement stick. They don't use Soviet-style blackmail tactics, but they have just as effective tricks available to them. As discussed in more detail later, the stick is backed up by a broad subpoena power federal officials can use to force corporations' hands. When the government exercises that power, it means business. In one instance, the National Security Agency threatened Yahoo with fines of $250,000 per day if it refused to turn over user data; that figure was set to double every week.

Despite some high-profile clashes between the government and private data brokers – like the one with Yahoo and the more recent one between the Department of Justice and Apple over encrypted user data on iPhones – the relationship between the two is generally cozy. As one leading commentator observes, "Corporate and government surveillance interests have converged."[11] Before Edward Snowden showed the public just how much information the government was collecting, tech companies by and large provided customer data to the government on request.[12] Now, in a bid to win back customer confidence, companies sometimes put up at least a pretense of resistance.

Today, as much as ever, private data broker and government interests are aligned along many dimensions. Commercially: Data brokers make good money when the government buys data that would cost much more to acquire itself. Logistically: Data corporations and the government rely on each other for amassing as much data as possible. Corporations have no choice but to get some of that information from the government, such as voter registration records or driver's license information. Government agencies have no choice but to buy this data back from the corporations once it's analyzed and supplemented with corporate databases. Professionally: Even if we don't know details, we do know there are secret meetings between top tech company CEOs and government intelligence agencies. These sorts of personal connections help build the well-documented

10 Jordan Robertson, *Leaked Docs: NSA Uses 'Candy Crush,' 'Angry Birds' To Spy*, SF Gate (Jan. 29, 2014), http://www.sfgate.com/technology/article/Leaked-docs-NSA-uses-Candy-Crush-Angry-5186801.php.

11 Bruce Schneier, Data and Goliath: The Hidden Battles to Collect Your Data and Control Your World 25 (2015).

12 Robert Scheer, They Know Everything About You 19 (2015).

revolving door between the private and public intelligence professions, as personnel move freely between the two.

III Consent, a Vanishing Privilege

One obvious difference between a Soviet neighbor fingering you to the government and Angry Birds doing the same is consent. The Soviet neighbor will peep in your window regardless. Angry Birds gains access to your information only after you click "I Agree." But this formalistic consent ritual amounts to true consent only for a wealthy and sophisticated few. The vast majority of users either don't know what they're "consenting" to, or don't really have a choice. Even for the rich and knowledgeable, withholding consent isn't always an option.

What do you "agree" to when you allow Angry Birds access to your location data and all your photos and files? Chances are high you don't have a clue. This is intentional. The privacy terms you formally agree to are usually available through some hyperlink, but you've got at least a couple of hurdles preventing you from reading them. These documents are long, sometimes dozens of pages, and seem longer still when reading them on a four-inch screen. Even if you're a fast reader, the value of the time it would take to go through the document line by line probably exceeds the value of the app. This even assumes you're capable of understanding what you read. The privacy agreements are written by lawyers and techies, for lawyers and techies, usually with no effort to make them penetrable to the vast majority of users. When the implications of such agreements are made apparent, as when the press let users know that Angry Birds was tracking their location and selling the data, users are shocked.

Suppose you are a lawyer with the extraordinary patience to read a privacy agreement. You may understand what you've agreed to formally. But unless you know a good deal about big data science, you probably have no idea what you've *really* agreed to. The app developers, and whomever else they sell your data to, will know the information you've allowed them to collect, but also everything they can infer from aggregating all that information. Those inferences are the most valuable part.

Suppose you agree to let Angry Birds collect anonymous location data. You may think you'll just appear in some database as a random number with a series of times and coordinates. False. There is no such thing as "anonymous" location data; this data *identifies you*. At MIT, researchers were able to identify by name 95 percent of Americans in a database from just four date/location points. Even if you agree to something much less voyeuristic than location tracking, such as providing your zip code, date of birth, and gender (some of the most common lines to register for any Web site), there's an 87 percent chance this data picks you out uniquely. The margin of error closes dramatically once brokers aggregate this data with that from other sources, and can triangulate among them all. Aggregation of different databases also exponentially increases the inferences data brokers can draw. Even if data brokers only have metadata, they can infer everything else if they aggregate enough of it. As former NSA general counsel Stewart Baker put it, "Metadata absolutely tells you everything about somebody's life. [With] enough metadata you don't really need the content."[13] Data brokers with Angry Birds' location data

[13] Alan Rusbridger, *The Snowden Leaks and the Public*, N.Y. Rev. of Books (Nov. 21, 2013), http://www.nybooks.com/articles/archives/2013/nov/21/snowden-leaks-and-public.

can do much the same thing. If they can put you and a colleague in the vicinity of an out-of-town motel a couple of times, they probably know about your tryst. Did you agree to let them know *that?*

If you are sophisticated enough to understand – *really* understand – a privacy policy and its implications, you may have some options. Free apps that recoup their expenses by collecting and selling your data sometimes have paid versions that are less invasive. Other developers may make for-pay equivalents. Moving beyond apps, you can also register for subscription-based privacy-protective email services (such as Riseup) and cloud storage (such as SpiderOak) and software that masks your location and identity when you surf the Web. The cost of everything you'll need can add up. Julie Angwin, a former *Wall Street Journal* reporter, documented her various efforts to minimize the data private corporations could collect about her.[14] It wasn't cheap. And she had a persistent sense that rather than disappearing, she was raising red flags as a tin-foil-wrapped conspiracy nut.

Because of these costs, only a resourceful few actually have some option besides clicking "I Agree." Judge Kozinski may be prepared to pay up to twenty-four hundred dollars a year to protect his privacy, but, as he well knows, not everyone is so fortunate.[15] "Poor people are entitled to privacy, even if they can't afford all the gadgets of the wealthy for ensuring it."[16] This issue came to a head a few years ago over government use of tracking technology. In 2012, the Supreme Court decided that the government can't put a GPS device on your car without getting a warrant first.[17] But in the lead-up to that decision, the law, at least in the Ninth Circuit, was developing in a way that would have placed the poor – and even many middle class – at a distinct disadvantage. In *United States v. Pineda-Moreno*,[18] a Ninth Circuit panel concluded that a person has no reasonable expectation of privacy if he or she parks in an open driveway. Accordingly, without a fence and a gate, the government can attach GPS devices to a car anytime, warrant be damned. As Judge Kozinski pointed out in dissent, that's exactly the way you might expect federal appellate judges who live in gated communities and make more than $200,000 a year to think about the problem. But "the Constitution doesn't prefer the rich over the poor,"[19] and it should protect you equally, whether or not you can afford gates and guards and walls.

The worse off you are, the more invasive corporate surveillance becomes and the fewer options you have to prevent it. Consider single mothers on welfare. The state already has them picked out as surveillance targets to monitor the appropriateness of continued welfare support. For them, the state recruits all available resources, private and otherwise, in a panoptic machine what would make even seasoned criminals cower. "In their pursuit of food, healthcare, and shelter for their families, they are watched, analyzed, assessed, monitored, checked, and reevaluated in an ongoing process involving supercomputers, caseworkers, fraud control agents, grocers, and neighbors."[20] If the Constitution really

14 Julia Angwin, Dragnet Nation: A Quest for Privacy, Security, and Freedom in a World of Relentless Surveillance (2014).

15 Matt Sledge, *Alex Kozinski, Federal Judge, Would Pay $2,400 a Year, Max, for Privacy*, Huffington Post (Mar. 4, 3013), http://www.huffingtonpost.com/2013/03/04/alex-kozinski-privacy_n_2807608.html.

16 *United States v. Pineda-Moreno*, 617 F.3d 1120, 1123 (2010) (Kozinski, C. J., dissenting from denial of rehearing en banc).

17 *United States v. Jones*, 132 S. Ct. 945 (2012); *see also Grady v. North Carolina*, 135 S. Ct. 1368 (2015).

18 *United States v. Pineda-Moreno*, 591 F.3d 1212 (2010), *cert. granted, vacated* 132 S. Ct. 1533 (2012).

19 *Pineda-Moreno*, 617 F.3d at 1123.

20 John Gilliom, Overseers of the Poor: Surveillance, Resistance, and the Limits of Privacy vii-viii (2001).

does not distinguish between wealthy and poor, shouldn't it protect welfare recipients as much as anyone else?

Even the super rich don't always have consent as an option. Setting aside apps that steal personal data without notice, such as Brightest Flashlight, some services just need your data to function. Google Maps can't give you directions without knowing where you are. Social networking sites only work if you reveal something about yourself. Your cell phone needs to know where you are to connect to the nearest cell towers, and because the FCC requires cell companies to be able to locate you for 9-1-1 emergency response.

Even for several services that don't require personal data, escaping the corporate dragnet is well-nigh impossible. Driving an older car with no navigation system shouldn't require anyone to know your whereabouts, but there's no way to avoid the companies that scan your license plates. Taking steps to protect your privacy is often ineffective. Suppose you invest in a privacy-sensitive email client. The provider may encrypt everything you've saved in its databases and promise to collect no information about you. But it cannot make promises on behalf of the email clients your friends and colleagues use. Google, for example, can and probably does scoop up any messages you send to anyone with a Gmail account, regardless of which service you use. With that, Google can fashion your marketing profile.

The bottom line is that, even with all the money in the world, the best chance you have of avoiding the corporate dragnets is to become a cash-carrying, libertarian luddite, in other words, Ron Swanson.[21] For most of us, Soviet citizens had about as much choice.

IV Laws Limiting Corporate Informants (or, the Lack of Them)

There's very little to stop corporations from turning your data over to the government. The law, as it currently stands, certainly isn't getting in the way. To get its hands on the sort of data corporations have, the Fourth Amendment would usually require the government to get a warrant, backed up with "reasonably trustworthy information" that the data will turn up evidence of crime.[22] But there's a rule-swallowing exception – the third-party doctrine – "A person has no legitimate expectation of privacy in information he voluntarily turns over to third parties."[23] Under this doctrine, any information you reveal to a third party doesn't get Fourth Amendment protection; the government can just take it.

The implications of the third-party doctrine in the modern age are tremendous. Every email we send, every website we visit, every file we store in the cloud, every phone call we make utilizes the software and hardware of third parties: servers, satellites, cell towers, etc. It's far from clear that we "voluntarily" expose all this data to these third parties in any conventional sense of the term. But the legal sense is not always the common sense. The Supreme Court has applied the doctrine to banking and phone call records,[24] so

21 *Parks and Recreation: Gryzzlbox* (NBC television broadcast Jan. 27, 2015) ("We need to talk.... This is a flying robot I just shot out of the sky after it delivered a package to my house.... The package was addressed to my son – who is four years old, and does not own a Gryzll [data mining company] doodad. Somehow the robots looked at Diane's computer and learned something about my child and then brought him a box of presents, so I destroyed the robot").

22 *Brinegar v. United States*, 338 U.S. 160, 175–76 (1949).

23 *Smith v. Maryland*, 442 U.S. 735, 743–44 (1979).

24 *See Smith v. Maryland*, 442 U.S. 735 (1979) (phone records); *United States v. Miller*, 425 U.S. 435 (1976) (bank records).

there's a natural extension to email, search engines, and cloud servers.[25] As a result, the vast majority of government information requests to companies such as cell phone carriers don't need a warrant; a subpoena with no judicial review will often suffice. These give your data very little protection.[26]

The statutory framework that developed post 9/11 has exacerbated the situation. Shortly after the attacks, Congress passed the USA PATRIOT Act, which amended the Foreign Intelligence Surveillance Act by weakening restrictions on domestic surveillance by the government. The text now seems to permit domestic surveillance so long as foreign intelligence gathering is a "significant purpose"; previously, it had to be "*the* purpose."[27] Section 505 of the PATRIOT Act, as interpreted by the National Security Agency (NSA), allows the NSA to send "national security letters" to corporations, complete with gag orders, demanding the records, files, emails, etc., of their customers. Such requests typically require no warrant and receive no judicial review. Only one in every five thousand or so does require a warrant. The secretive Foreign Intelligence Surveillance Court (FISC) reviews these warrants and overwhelmingly approves them, rejecting just .03 percent.[28] This is hardly surprising, given that the warrant applications are *ex parte* and rarely see the light of day through, for example, a criminal trial.

In addition to issuing subpoenas for information about specific individuals, the government enlists corporations in mass domestic surveillance programs. In 2002, Department of Defense Admiral John Poindexter set about developing the Total Information Awareness (TIA) program. Its purpose was plain from its name – to know *everything*. More specifically, it sought to do this with help from the companies that transmit our electronic communications. In the words of one *New York Times* correspondent, TIA was "determined to break down the wall between commercial snooping and secret government intrusion."[29] But even the name was too evocative of Big Brother for most members of Congress. TIA was formally defunded. Behind the scenes, though, it was broken into several separate programs and continued under different names using black budgets. Today the program is thriving through the data gathering and mining operations of the NSA. Edward Snowden drew attention to some of these programs, such as PRISM

25 One court has held that the third-party doctrine would not necessarily compromise Fourth Amendment protections of the content of emails when the government tries to compel an Internet service provider to turn them over. *See United States v. Warshak*, 631 F.3d 266 (2010). But between metadata and material ISPs may turn over voluntarily, there's not much need for the content anyway.

26 Daniel J. Solove, Nothing to Hide 93 (2001). There are some statutory protections for email and phone records, *see e.g.* Stored Communications Act, 18 U.S.C. § 2702 (2012), but these are changeable and do not provide the level of security ensured by the Fourth Amendment. Stephen J. Schulhofer, More Essential than Ever, 128 (2012). For example, under the Stored Communications Act, the government can obtain record and content information (more than six months old) from electronic service providers by clearing a "reasonable grounds" bar. Stored Communications Act § 1703(d). The Fourth Amendment's probable cause requirement is more demanding.

27 USA PATRIOT Act, Pub. L. No. 107–56, § 218, 115 Stat. 272 (2001) (amending Foreign Intelligence Surveillance Act of 1978, 50 U.S.C. §§ 1804(a(7)(B), 1823(a)(7)(B)) (emphasis added). *But see* In re Sealed Case, 310 F.3d 717, 735–36 (FISA Ct. Rev. 2002)

28 Colin Schultz, *The FISA Court Has Only Denied an NSA Request Once in the Past 5 Years*, Smithsonian (May 1, 2014), http://www.smithsonianmag.com/smart-news/fisa-court-has-only-denied-nsa-request-once-past-5-years-180951313/?no-ist; Erika Eichelberger, *FISA Court Has Rejected .03 Percent of all Government Surveillance Requests*, Mother Jones (June 10, 2013), http://www.motherjones.com/mojo/2013/06/fisa-court-nsa-spying-opinion-reject-request.

29 William Safire, *You Are a Suspect*, N.Y. Times (Nov. 12, 2002), http://www.nytimes.com/2002/11/14/opinion/14SAFI.html.

(which collects Internet data) and MAINWAY (which collects phone call data). Some of these programs were approved using the processes, such as they are, set in place by FISA; others were not. As to the other ways the NSA accesses the data corporations collect on us – we don't know what we don't know.

V A Change Is Warranted

You don't need to be a privacy nut or an anarcholibertarian to see that there's a problem here. Nor do you need to have lived in a totalitarian surveillance state, surrounded by private informants, to see the frightening potential of the corporate–government intelligence alliance. It's no coincidence that the United States is the only country in the West without fundamental data protection laws.[30] Europe, which has firsthand experience with surveillance states using private informants, is well ahead of the curve in giving consumers enhanced control over their data.[31] People like Professor Orin Kerr, who say the current regime in the United States just levels the playing field between the government and sophisticated criminals, must be wrong.[32] The concern is not about how surveillance affects criminals, but about how it affects the rest of us.[33] Reflecting on the problems with private informants in totalitarian regimes can help frame the search for a solution that could work in the United States.

The problem in the Soviet Union was not that private parties knew what you were doing. Ordinary social interaction is impossible without revealing personal information to others. Pavel Morozov couldn't have had a meaningful relationship with his father had the two not shared important facets of their private lives. The trouble begins when the government strongly incentivizes private associates to snitch on each other. In that environment, the sort of interpersonal confidences needed for individual autonomy disappear.

Similarly, there's nothing inherently troubling about private corporations collecting data on us. Scholarly calls to impose hard limits on what data corporations can collect or how long they can store it are misplaced.[34] We like our free apps and lower-cost cell phone service, and these are only possible when data sales and advertising can help cover the developers' overhead. Not all of us can afford to pay out-of-pocket for the suite of social, entertainment, and productivity software we have on our phones. For those of us with limited disposable income, data collection gives us more options, not fewer; we can trade our data, which we have, in place of money, which we may not. Although studies show two-thirds of Americans say they don't like being tracked by corporations online, everyone likes the free apps such tracking supports. No one likes spending money either, but everyone likes what he gets in return.

30 Schneier, *supra* note 12, at 200; Pauton & Claypoole, *supra* note 2, at 232 ("How did the impulse to treat privacy as a human right arise in Europe, and not in the United States? … Much of Europe is not more than a generation or two from fascist or communist dictatorships, in which the government strove to know all the secrets of its citizens").

31 *See, e.g.*, Commission Regulation (EU) 2016/679 of Apr. 27, 2016, On the Protection of Natural Persons with Regard to the Processing of Personal Data and on the Free Movement of Such Data, and Repealing Directive 95/46/EC, 2016 O.J. (L 119) 1.

32 Orin S. Kerr, *The Case for the Third Party Doctrine*, 107 Mich. L. Rev. 561 (2009).

33 *See* David Gray, The Fourth Amendment in an Age of Surveillance (2017).

34 One such call comes from Pauton & Claypoole, *supra* note 22, at 234–36.

Of course, there should be *some* limits on data collection. Norms of consent should govern to the extent possible. That will require corporations to be more forthcoming about what data is collected and how it is used. Shorter, simpler, and more transparent privacy policies would go a long way toward helping customers understand what "I Agree" really means. Many American companies are already complying with such transparency requirements in order to do business in Europe. The Department of Commerce runs a program that registers companies as Safe Harbor Compliant, meaning, in part, that they follow Europe's more stringent data transparency laws. Bringing the same norms to bear in the American market shouldn't be very troublesome. While there may also be uses that should be disallowed even with customer consent (Facebook's confessed manipulation of customer emotions comes to mind),[35] freedom of contract should be the strong default.

As with individual informants, corporate data collection begins to raise serious problems when government access to that data enters the picture. The worst corporations can usually do on their own with our data is lure us into purchasing products we may not need; they can't throw us into jail; that's the sole prerogative of the government. The possibility that the information we expose to corporations may make its way into government hands has uniquely chilling effects. In the words of Chief Justice Warren Burger, "When an intelligence officer looks over every nonconformist's shoulder in the library, or walks invisibly by his side in a picket line, or infiltrates his club, the America once extolled as the voice of liberty heard around the world no longer is cast in the image which Jefferson and Madison designed, but more in the Russian image."[36] Ditto for nonconformists' email accounts, phone calls, and electronic files.

We need to balance corporate interests in data collection, government interests in law enforcement, and individual interests in privacy. Thinking through how to strike the right balance, we need to reflect on the ways government induces private parties to turn over our data. The Soviet Union recruited its informants with both carrots and sticks, and the same is true of how the U.S. government gets information about us from corporations. Let's talk about the sticks first. As discussed, the government has easy access to customer information under the PATRIOT Act and FISA. And it *should* have some sort of access. That's how it keeps us safe from terrorists and other criminals. But the level of access should be balanced against Fourth Amendment civil liberties with an eye to what actually works.

One thing that doesn't work: dragnet style surveillance à la PRISM and MAINWAY. There is little to no evidence of its effectiveness. From a mathematical standpoint, the problem is one of data overload. Dragnet systems pull in a ton of information. Advanced searching algorithms can help to an extent and may work well for mundane criminal activity. But the sort of criminals the dragnets are meant to catch, such as terrorists, don't fit into well-defined profiles. Algorithms that try to pick out potential criminals on the basis of profiles are unworkable since they overwhelm the system with false positive results.[37] In 2014, the Privacy and Civil Liberties Oversight Board, appointed by President

35 Vindo Goel, *Facebook Tinkers with Users' Emotions in Newsfeed Experiment, Stirring Outcry*, N.Y. Times (June 29, 2014), http://www.nytimes.com/2014/06/30/technology/facebook-tinkers-with-users-emotions-in-news-feed-experiment-stirring-outcry.html.

36 *Laird v. Tatum*, 408 U.S. 1 (1972).

37 Schneier, *supra* note 12, at 136–40.

Obama, found no evidence that mass surveillance of telephone calls ever made a significant security contribution. "We have not identified," the Board wrote, "a single instance involving a threat to the United States in which the telephone records program made a concrete difference in the outcome of a counterterrorism investigation."[38]

If dragnet surveillance is out, that leaves us with targeted surveillance, as when the NSA asks a cell carrier to provide location data on a single customer. Under current law, a subpoena will do the trick. But here's something curious: If the government were to get the same information using costlier old-school techniques, such as tailing or GPS locators, the Fourth Amendment would require it to get a warrant. This makes no sense. Why should the government have to go to a judge for a warrant to follow someone on foot at a cost of $275/hour but just present a subpoena to get cell-tracking data for one-thousandth the price?

We may be in one of those transitional points when the law has to catch up to technology and common sense. In the early part of the twentieth century, wiretapping was the new technology. In 1928, the Supreme Court first considered whether police wiretapping counted as a "search" and so whether the Fourth Amendment applied to it. The Court decided it did not, since wiretapping doesn't involve any sort of physical intrusion: "There was no entry of the houses or offices of the defendants."[39] Justice Brandeis, in dissent, saw the danger of the precedent, but was unable to persuade his colleagues:

> The progress of science in furnishing the Government with means of espionage is not likely to stop with wire-tapping. Ways may someday be developed by which the government, without removing papers from secret drawers, can reproduce them in court, and by which it will be enabled to expose to a jury the most intimate occurrences of the home.... Can it be that the Constitution affords no protection against such invasions of individual security?[40]

It was forty more years before the implications of the ruling became fully apparent to a majority of the Court. In 1967, the Supreme Court reversed course. In doing so, it developed a more refined understanding of the Fourth Amendment: It protects "reasonable expectations of privacy" rather than just physical boundaries.[41]

Today, the conceptual sticking point is not privacy as it relates to physical intrusions, but privacy as it relates to third parties. Under current law, there can be no reasonable expectation of privacy, and so no Fourth Amendment protections, for information one person reveals to another. That may make enough sense if you're speaking loudly to the guy seated beside you on a crowded subway. Then you truly have forfeited your privacy. But there's an obvious difference when you're speaking in your own home, and the "third party" is a cell company algorithm logging the call. Hopefully it won't take us forty years to catch on. At least one member of the Supreme Court, Justice Sotomayor, is already hot on the trail.[42]

38 Privacy & Civil Liberties Oversight Bd., *Report on the Telephone Records Program Conducted under Section 215 of the USA PATRIOT Act and on the Operations of the Foreign Intelligence Surveillance Court* (Jan. 23, 2014), https://fas.org/irp/offdocs/pclob-215.pdf.

39 *Olmstead v. United States*, 277 U.S. 438, 464 (1928).

40 *Id.* at 474 (Brandeis, J., dissenting).

41 *Katz v. United States*, 389 U.S. 347 (1967).

42 *United States v. Jones*, 132 S. Ct. 945, 957 (2012) (Sotomayor, J., concurring) ("It may be necessary to reconsider the premise that an individual has no reasonable expectation of privacy in information voluntarily disclosed to third parties. This approach is ill suited to the digital age, in which people reveal a

Some scholars, such as Stephen J. Schulhofer, have proposed alternative conceptions of privacy that might do the trick. He argues that privacy is not really about keeping information secret from third parties. Information we share with our spouses, friends, and doctors is private, even if it's no longer totally secret. Schulhofer suggests that privacy is about having control over our information rather than keeping it secret.[43] Though he needs to do some line drawing (if you tell everyone except your spouse about an affair, have you still kept it private?), Schulhofer may be headed in the right direction. He argues that, at least with respect to corporations that provide services for which customers have no realistic alternative, the government should need a warrant to force corporations to turn over customer data.

Perhaps because he didn't have in mind the fuller history of using private informants, Schulhofer's proposal doesn't go far enough. Not all informants in the Soviet Union were compelled to talk. Many willingly pointed fingers at neighbors, sometimes out of a sense of duty; but surely just as often they did it to collect financial rewards. As documented earlier, the same happens in the United States; providing information to the government can be very lucrative for corporations.

Now let's talk about the carrots the government offers private informants. How do we limit corporations from voluntarily revealing to the government what they know about us, often for profit? Laws directly barring corporations could bump up against complications with the First Amendment freedom of speech.[44] Some commentators have suggested that intervention may not be necessary. Perhaps free market forces will take care of matters as consumers become more interested in the privacy of their data. There is some evidence that these forces are pushing a few corporations to get serious about privacy. Several large tech companies have announced, for example, that they will violate the gag orders attached to national security letters and tell customers when the government requests their data.[45] Google, among others, has also started publishing bulk statistics on data requests it receives.

But protecting consumer data is too important to leave to the whims of market forces. However warm and fuzzy Google or Apple may make us feel when it promises to tell us about national security letters or to protect our encrypted data, they are still for-profit corporations. Warm and fuzzy isn't their modus operandi; profit is. The winds of increased market share may tell one day in favor of privacy, and another against it. We should not forget that the same Google that will tell us today whether the government is poking

great deal of information about themselves to third parties in the course of carrying out mundane tasks" [internal citations omitted]).

43 Schulhofer, *supra* note 27, at 8–9; *see also* Stephen E. Henderson, *Expectations of Privacy in Social Media*, 31 Miss. C.L. Rev. 227, 229–33 (2012) (offering a similar definition of "privacy," which became the benchmark for the American Bar Association's Criminal Justice Standards on Law Enforcement Access to Third Party Records).

44 Though no corporations have, so far as we know, raised such First Amendment objections yet.

45 Craig Timberg, *Apple, Facebook, Others Defy Authorities, Increasingly Notify Users of Secret Data Demands after Snowden Revelations*, Wash. Post (May 1, 2014), https://www.washingtonpost.com/business/technology/apple-facebook-others-defy-authorities-increasingly-notify-users-of-secret-data-demands-after-snowden-revelations/2014/05/01/b41539c6-cfd1-11e3-b812-0c92213941f4_story.html. The Electronic Frontier Foundation has ranked companies on how often they notify users about such demands. Marcia Hoffman et al., *2012: When the Government Comes Knocking, Who Has Your Back?*, EFF (May 31, 2012), https://www.eff.org/files/who-has-your-back-2012_0_0.pdf.

around about us was arguing in favor of the third-party doctrine in court yesterday.[46] And the day before that had a CEO who would proclaim, "If you have something that you don't want anyone to know, maybe you shouldn't be doing it in the first place."[47] Even if you do trust Google to do right by you, can you trust hundreds of other companies, such as Acxiom, who collect your data behind the scenes and have little interest in your goodwill?

VI Corporate Instruments of State

If we can't directly prevent corporations from turning over our data, and we can't trust them to limit themselves, we need some way to place restrictions on the other party in the transaction: the government. The Fourth Amendment was designed to rein in the government anyway, not corporations. The usual way the Fourth Amendment limits the government is by forcing it to get a warrant before searching us. To get a warrant, it has to persuade a judge that there's a good chance the search will turn up some evidence of crime. Something like a warrant requirement might do the trick here too. But there's a snag: Under current doctrine, the government could only possibly need a warrant if it is *compelling* a corporation to turn over data. What we're talking about now is how to restrict corporations from *voluntarily* (usually in exchange for cash) turning over our information.

There's conceptual space for requiring the government to get a warrant before it even *requests* customer data from corporations. Then the government would have to convince a judge that there's some likelihood the request will turn up evidence of crime before it can send the request. The practical effect of this would be that the government would have to get a warrant before a corporation could voluntarily provide our data. Without a warrant, the government could not make a request for data. And without a request, the corporation wouldn't know what to send. This would make the government's legal burden for getting, e.g., location data on a customer from a cooperative cell phone company just as high as getting authorization to put a GPS tracker on the same customer's car.

But is there legal space for a warrant requirement for data requests? The executive branch could voluntarily abide by the requirement, or a similar sort of restriction. After all, the executive branch has the power to establish internal norms governing investigations. But we shouldn't hold out for that to happen anytime soon. Snowden's revelations in 2013 showed just how data hungry the executive branch is.

Passing new laws might be another approach to getting the warrant requirement for data requests. We've been talking about "the government" as though it were a unitary entity. In fact, there are three branches, and they don't always see eye to eye. A privacy-friendly Congress might try to pass some statutory limits on data requests. But doing so would be risky. All of the three branches have constitutionally designated domains,

46 Paul Calahan, *Google: Gmail Users Can't Expect Privacy When Sending Emails*, INDEPENDENT (Aug. 14, 2013), http://www.independent.co.uk/life-style/gadgets-and-tech/news/google-gmail-users-can-t-expect-privacy-when-sending-emails-8762280.html ("Just as a sender of a letter to a business colleague cannot be surprised that the recipient's assistant opens the letter, people who use Web-based email today cannot be surprised if their emails are processed by the recipient [email] provider in the course of delivery").

47 *Google CEO on Privacy (VIDEO): 'If You Have Something You Don't Want Anyone to Know, Maybe You Shouldn't Be Doing It'*, HUFFINGTON POST (Mar. 18, 2010), http://www.huffingtonpost.com/2009/12/07/google-ceo-on-privacy-if_n_383105.html.

and they're not supposed to overstep their bounds. It's the executive branch that has the authority and discretion to direct investigations. If Congress tried to meddle, it might find itself butting heads with an executive branch keen to guard its turf.

No branch of government can violate the Constitution, even when exercising one of its constitutionally designated powers. So if there's little hope of the executive restricting itself, and separation of powers or political problems with Congress trying to do it, constitutional limits on the executive branch might do the trick. Congress wouldn't have to get involved, just as it didn't when the Supreme Court found that the Constitution requires the executive branch to get a warrant before attaching GPS trackers. The only problem is that the current understanding of the Fourth Amendment, and the third-party doctrine in particular, cuts against a warrant requirement for data requests.

Or does it? The third-party doctrine is not absolute. It doesn't treat all third parties alike. Some differences are irrelevant for purposes of the Fourth Amendment. For example, it's probably beside the point how much information the third party collects. Corporations collect much more information than natural persons, but the third-party doctrine applies regardless of how sophisticated the third party is at persuading you to open up. But some differences are extremely relevant, such as whether or not the third party is really an "instrument of state."[48] When a third party is acting at the direction or encouragement of the government in collecting information or investigating possible crime, the third party is considered an instrument of the state. Since instruments of state are basically operating as agents of the government, the third-party doctrine doesn't apply – there are still effectively just two parties, the government and the target of the investigation. So the protections of the Fourth Amendment remain in full force.

Admittedly, the typical instruments of state recognized by the Supreme Court don't look much like huge corporate data mongers. Mostly they're just ordinary individuals, like airline employees who open a customer's luggage looking for drugs. But there's no reason that corporations couldn't also be considered instruments of state.[49] Indeed, in light of the tight public–private intelligence partnership discussed previously, there may be very good reasons a lot of them should be. Courts consider two factors when determining whether someone is an instrument of state: 1) the degree of government involvement, knowledge, or acquiescence, and 2) the intent of the party conducting the search.[50] As with any multifactor, balancing test, most scenarios fall in a "gray" area and need individualized consideration.

The argument for treating data-gathering corporations as instruments of the state is stronger in some cases than in others. Consider cell phone companies collecting location data. The government's level of involvement, knowledge, and acquiescence in collecting that data is extremely high. As mentioned, a government agency, the FCC, even requires cell phone companies to track customers. As to the intent of the cell companies,

48 *Coolidge v. New Hampshire*, 403 U.S. 443, 487 (1971).

49 David Gray and Danielle Citron take a first step in this direction, but limit their discussion to the most sweeping corporate data collectors. David Gray & Danielle Citron, *The Right to Quantitative Privacy*, 98 Minn. L. Rev. 62, 133–43 (2013). It is important that a corporation can qualify as an agent of the state whether it collects "limited" or "broad and indiscriminate" information. *Cf. id.* at 143. Corporate and government entities can cheaply aggregate limited information to end up with the equivalent of broad and indiscriminate information.

50 *United Sates v. Walther*, 652 F.2d 788 (9th Cir. 1981).

part of their motive is surely commercial profit from selling the location data to marketers. But another substantial motive must be complying with FCC regulations and, at the same time, profiting from selling location data to the government. Both factors tell pretty strongly in favor of treating cell phone companies as instruments of state when they collect customer location data. So there's a good argument that the third-party doctrine shouldn't apply in such a case, and some sort of warrant requirement should intermediate the government's access to that data.

The argument may be not be quite as strong with information such as email metadata or Kindle reading habits. These are different from cell phone location data in that there is no government mandate that corporations collect the data and no immediate revenue stream (that we know of) from the government to the corporation for that information. But even if government agencies aren't directly involved in gathering the customer data, they certainly know about it and acquiesce to it. As to the second factor, third party intent, the overriding incentive corporations have for collecting the data is, without a doubt, commercial. But the wheels of commerce travel far, and we know government agencies are one of the downstream purchasers (if not sometimes a direct purchaser) of this data. At a minimum, part of the revenue stream the corporations enjoy from collecting this sort of data is due to government sales. Corporations collecting this sort of data are in the gray area for identifying instruments of state. As a consequence, so are possible Fourth Amendment protections under this analysis.

Corporate instruments of state differ in another respect from typical instruments of state – they'd collect our information even without government prompting. We can't just tell them to stop without sacrificing all the social benefits that result from collecting and marketing this data. We also can't just tell them never to talk to the government, since there are cases when the government has a legitimate interest in consumer data. What's needed is for corporations to be more sophisticated in how they segregate and share data they collect. Corporations should implement internal controls to ensure that customer data is never shared with the government, unless it is subject to a legitimate request. Other downstream entities to which the corporation sells data would need to implement the same controls. This may sound like a tall order. But it should be a walk in the park compared to the complex data management that already goes into complying with laws that protect customer health and financial information.

The analogy to customer health data protections raises another provocative possibility – giving consumers private remedies against corporations that improperly turn their data over to the government. While the Health Insurance Portability and Accountability Act,[51] which protects health data, provides no private right of action, some state laws do. Perhaps something similar could be done to enable consumers to protect their privacy interests against corporations that are too cozy with the government.[52] Giving corporations some skin in the game and empowering a citizenry of private enforcers will surely help the government stay within Fourth Amendment bounds when requesting data.

[51] Pub. L. No. 104–91, 110 Stat. 1936 (1996).

[52] Kiel Brennan-Marquez has one interesting proposal about how to do this that involves treating corporate data collectors as "information fiduciaries." Kiel Brennan-Marquez, *Fourth Amendment Fiduciaries*, 84 Fordham L. Rev. 611 (2015).

Conclusion

The United States is not a totalitarian state. The Soviet Union was, in large part because it had the capacity, if not to monitor all aspects of everyone's life, to raise an omnipresent fear of being monitored through its use of private informants. But it's not for nothing that William Binney, a former NSA official, could gesture with a single hand and say, "We [Americans] are, like, that far from a turnkey totalitarian state."[53] The infrastructure for a potential surveillance state is in place, and it is largely in private hands. If this worries us (and it should), we need to think about the unique complications, legal and philosophical, that private informants raise. The third-party doctrine, which currently gives the government easy access to any information that passes through the private infrastructure, is dangerously outdated. We have suggested one possible way to rein it in, by treating many corporations with access to customer data as instruments of state. Maybe it works. If not, we sure hope someone else figures out something sensible.[54] Nothing short of the freedoms that define us as Americans, not to mention the next free-play release of Angry Birds, are at stake.

53 James Bamford, *The NSA Is Building the Country's Biggest Spy Center (Watch What You Say)*, Wired (Mar. 15, 2012), https://www.wired.com/2012/03/ff_nsadatacenter/.

54 The Electronic Privacy Information Center (EPIC) has made substantial inroads into this many-headed problem for more than twenty years from legal, political, and technical fronts. To read about some of its cutting-edge, interdisciplinary work in the area, see Privacy in the Modern Age: The Search for Solutions (Marc Rotenberg et al. eds., 2015).

18 The Impact of Online Surveillance on Behavior

Alex Marthews[†] & Catherine Tucker[‡]

Mass digital surveillance differs from older, analog, and more overt forms of physical surveillance. Nonetheless, empirical research after the Snowden revelations shows that it still has a meaningful chilling effect on online behavior, including Google searches, use of Wikipedia, and expression of controversial opinions. In the courts, these studies may help plaintiffs challenging mass surveillance programs in both the United States and the European Union to demonstrate standing. In the executive and legislative branches, the studies enable the discussion to move on from the question of whether a chilling effect exists from surveillance, to the question of what, if anything, to do about it.

I How Online Surveillance May Affect Behavior Differently from Offline Surveillance

A common trope in surveillance debates claims that subjects of digital surveillance are less affected than subjects of more traditional direct surveillance. A driver might panic and hit the gas at the sight of a police cruiser parked along the side of the road, but the same driver might not much care about or respond to the kinds of mass surveillance programs revealed by the Snowden documents. This skepticism stems mainly from an accurate perception that overt, individualized analog surveillance conveys a stronger signal of interest by the government in a particular citizen's activities than does mass digital surveillance, which by definition is general rather than particular.[1]

Conventional surveillance prior to the broad adoption of the Internet tended to involve intense physical surveillance of individuals by other individuals. This is costly and labor-intensive; even states such as the former East Germany, which employed both overt and covert physical surveillance on a grand scale, were only able to keep dossiers on a little more than one-third of their people.[2] Physical surveillance, the cultivation of informants,

† Alex Marthews is the National Chair of Restore the Fourth, rt4chair@protonmail.com.

‡ Catherine Tucker is the Sloan Distinguished Professor of Management Science and Professor of Marketing at MIT Sloan, cetucker@mit.edu, and Research Associate at NBER.

1 For the purposes of this discussion, we consider collection of data to be "mass surveillance" if it is not particularized to a particular investigatory target and his or her direct associates in a criminal enterprise, rather than adopting the perspective of the U.S. government and others that collection of data is not "mass" so long as it involves the use of some selector prior to collection.

2 Joel D. Cameron, *Stasi*, Encyclopedia Britannica (Apr. 14, 2015), http://www.britannica.com/topic/Stasi.

and infiltration of dissident groups by undercover police officers continue,[3] have in some respects expanded,[4] and are still highly controversial. But the digital superstructure of surveillance has become, since the advent of the Internet, both much more pervasive than offline surveillance and much more understandable using empirical methods than it was before.

In the area of communications surveillance, analog methods tended to require a physical tap on individual phones or the physical reading of individual envelopes and letters, so, in practice, it was also knowably harder and more expensive on a per-individual basis than mass digital surveillance is today. Surveillance agencies and the political leaders who defend them are often at pains to stress this difference,[5] arguing that mere collection of communications metadata on all citizens does not really constitute surveillance until an individual human agent looks at the results of a query on a particular person or pattern of behavior, as happens in a small percentage of the overall data points collected.[6]

Digital surveillance's impact on a given individual may on average be smaller than the impact of analog surveillance on a given person physically followed, because it is more diffuse and inherently covert in nature. However, it also offers important advantages to researchers interested in the effects of surveillance on individuals. To an extent, if mass digital surveillance is so relatively unobtrusive that it is possible to be surveilled and be only marginally aware of it day to day, then empirically measuring the effect of such systems on behavior could provide a lower bound for the effects of surveillance in general. Furthermore, the high trackability of online behavior allows us to determine the impact of surveillance most clearly in the context of online behavior, using information on search terms used and Web sites visited to demonstrate empirically the existence of a chilling effect on citizens' free expression and association online.

II Chilling Effects and Legal Approaches to Measuring Impacts of Surveillance

It is this technological change – this digitization of the streams of our thoughts and actions – that leads to surveillance's being not only more prevalent in the abstract but more realistically litigatable in the particular. Professor Frederick Schauer argued in 1978 that the chilling effects of his day were "likely unprovable" and so argued for a conceptual rule whereby the courts would err in favor of the freedom of speech of "overcautious" speakers that would not require individualized proof of actions not taken or thoughts not expressed.[7] Professor Vincent Blasi went further in 1987, condemning

3 Gilbert Ramsay et al., *Report: Impacts of Surveillance on Contemporary British Activism*, OpenDemocracyUK (May 24, 2016), https://www.opendemocracy.net/uk/gilbert-ramsay/report-impacts-of-surveillance-on-contemporary-british-activism.

4 *Terror Probes Have FBI's Informant Numbers Soaring*, NPR (Aug. 21, 2011, 5:10 PM), http://www.npr.org/2011/08/21/139836377/the-surge-in-fbi-informants.

5 Herbert Lin, *Having a Conversation about Bulk Surveillance*, 59 Comm. of the ACM 2, 40 (2016).

6 Perhaps the best available estimate is from internal documents showing data processing of MI5's "Preston" program, which indicate that perhaps 3 percent of the information gathered is viewed by a human agent, and a much smaller percentage than that is synthesized into meaningful "end product." Ryan Gallagher, *Facing Data Deluge, Secret U.K. Spying Report Warned of Intelligence Failure*, Intercept (June 7, 2016, 4:38 AM), https://theintercept.com/2016/06/07/mi5-gchq-digint-surveillance-data-deluge/.

7 Frederick Schauer, *Fear, Risk and the First Amendment: Unraveling the Chilling Effect*," 685 B.U. L. Rev. 730–31 (1978).

even the idea of chilling effects of surveillance as being based on "crude behavioral speculation."[8]

American courts in the predigital era generally, though not without controversy, adhered to this view that chilling effects were speculative. In *Laird v. Tatum*, the 1972 U.S. Supreme Court dismissed, by a 5–4 vote, the claims of the director of an advocacy group for conscientious objectors that he was subject to army surveillance in his political activities, opining that "allegations of a subjective 'chill' are not an adequate substitute for a claim of specific present objective harm or a threat of specific future harm."[9] Citing *Laird*, in 2013 in *Clapper v. Amnesty International*, another divided 5–4 Court likewise condemned the idea that the respondents could "manufacture standing merely by inflicting harm on themselves based on their fears of hypothetical future harm that is not certainly impending."[10] Both Courts thus dismissed the cases on standing grounds.

The privacy expert Daniel Solove (2007) accurately characterizes the conundrum faced by courts in such cases:

> Determining the existence of a chilling effect is complicated by the difficulty of defining and identifying deterrence. It is hard to measure the deterrence caused by a chilling effect because it is impossible to determine with certainty what people would have said or done in the absence of the government activity. Often, the primary evidence will be a person's own assertions that she was chilled, but merely accepting such assertions at face value would allow anyone claiming a chilling effect to establish one. At the same time, demanding empirical evidence of deterrence is impractical because it will often be impossible to produce.[11]

III The Snowden Revelations

On June 6, 2013, new information emerged about U.S. government surveillance practices based on top-secret documents leaked by the National Security Agency (NSA) contractor and systems administrator Edward Snowden. These contained revelations about the PRISM program (now termed "downstream"), which was a code name for a mass electronic surveillance data mining program managed by the NSA. The NSA's slides disclosed partnerships of a kind with nine major tech companies, including

8 Vincent Blasi, *Pathological Perspective and the First Amendment*, 85 Colum. L. Rev. 449, 482 (1985).

9 408 U.S. 1, 13–14 (1972).

10 133 S.Ct. 1138, 1151 (2013). The *Clapper* Court relied on assertions by Solicitor-General David Verrilli that if data derived from mass surveillance were used against a defendant in court, that defendant would be notified of that fact and would be able to challenge the basis of that surveillance. Reply Brief for the Petitioners at 15, *Clapper v. Amnesty Int'l*, 133 S.Ct. 1138 (2013) (No. 11–1025), http://www.americanbar.org/content/dam/aba/publications/supreme_court_preview/briefs/11-1025_pet_reply.authcheckdam.pdf. The Court then used the absence of such notices as evidence that mass surveillance was not sufficiently prevalent for the claim of standing to be credible, not realizing – as Verrilli found out shortly afterward – that it was not in fact true that the government did notify defendants of the use of surveillance-derived data. Adam Liptak, *A Secret Surveillance Program Proves Challengeable in Theory Only*, N.Y. Times (July 15, 2013), http://www.nytimes.com/2013/07/16/us/double-secret-surveillance.html?_r=0.

11 Daniel J. Solove, *First Amendment as Criminal Procedure*, 82 N.Y.U. L. Rev 112, 155 (2007).

Microsoft, Google, Yahoo!, AOL, and Skype, through which the NSA was able to obtain real-time data content.[12] In the intervening months and years, many further disclosures from the same set of leaked documents have refined and expanded our understanding of how these programs work. In our study "Government Surveillance and Internet Search Behavior,"[13] we studied the impact of the revelations as a whole on people using Google search, therefore beginning at the point of initial disclosure on June 6. Later disclosures suggest that the NSA slides may have overstated the official nature of its partnerships with the companies named; arguments continue over the extent to which PRISM collection is voluntary or involuntary. However, NSA internal documents attest that PRISM constituted a very large proportion – 91 percent, as of mid-2011[14] – of the signals intelligence data gathered by the NSA. Later disclosures relating to other programs such as TEMPORA or tools such as XKEYSCORE could also, for highly informed users, have further affected their search behavior. However, our study considers the impact on search behavior among the general public after the publicization of the general fact of government mass surveillance, rather than the unpublicized operation of the programs themselves, so the distinctions among these programs, while substantial, will not be material for our analysis.

The Snowden revelations provoked controversy, both from domestic privacy activists and from international governments who were concerned about the privacy of their own citizens given the worldwide reach of the data collection. The U.S. government emphasized in its initial response that the "authority [under which the program falls] was created by the Congress and has been widely known and publicly discussed."[15] But it was not generally understood prior to June 2013 that the authority in question, Section 702 of the FISA Amendments Act, authorized consumer data held by such companies, including data on individuals' search behavior, to be made available to the U.S. government on a mass rather than an individualized basis. Various efforts are under way in Congress to reform this authority, in advance of its next sunset date in December 2017.

It was immediately apparent when the Snowden revelations began that they were different in kind from previous surveillance-related revelations, such as those of William Binney[16] or Russell Tice.[17] Unlike these previous whistle-blowers, Edward Snowden took away with him internal documents of unquestionable authenticity that attested to the existence of surveillance programs that were near-universal in scope. Consequently, his evidence was more likely to push courts to recognize the plausibility of surveillance

[12] Earlier that morning, the "Verizon scandal" had disclosed to the public that phone companies, including Verizon Wireless, had been ordered by a secret court continually to disclose the metadata associated with all calls – location, caller, caller identification, and call duration.

[13] Alex Marthews & Catherine Tucker, GOVERNMENT SURVEILLANCE AND INTERNET SEARCH BEHAVIOR (2017), http://papers.ssrn.com/sol3/papers.cfm?abstract_id=2412564.

[14] John W. Rollins & Edward C. Liu, NSA SURVEILLANCE LEAKS: BACKGROUND AND ISSUES FOR CONGRESS 4 (2013).

[15] Director of National Intelligence, FACTS ON THE COLLECTION OF INTELLIGENCE PURSUANT TO SECTION 702 OF THE FOREIGN INTELLIGENCE SURVEILLANCE ACT, 1 (2013), https://www.dni.gov/files/documents/Facts%20on%20the%20Collection%20of%20Intelligence%20Pursuant%20to%20Section%20702.pdf.

[16] *See* Newton Lee, COUNTERTERRORISM AND CYBERSECURITY 153 (2013).

[17] *See EXCLUSIVE: National Security Agency Whistleblower Warns Domestic Spying Program Is Sign the U.S. Is Decaying into a "Police State,"* Democracy Now! (Jan. 3, 2006), http://www.democracynow.org/2006/1/3/exclusive_national_security_agency_whistleblower_warns.

litigants' standing claims – namely, that mass surveillance could produce individual claims that were cognizable as "injury in fact." Four years after the initial Snowden revelations, the legal effects were mixed, but they are still far-reaching. In the European Union, Max Schrems was able to bring a case before the European Court of Justice that invalidated the Safe Harbor agreement under which U.S. and EU firms share data.[18] Schrems expressly relied on the Snowden revelation of the PRISM program to allege injury to his privacy rights under Article 8 of the European Convention on Human Rights. In the U.S. Second Circuit Court of Appeals, the Snowden revelations led to a decision that a mass metadata surveillance program conducted under USA PATRIOT Act Section 215 was not in fact authorized by that statute as it then read.[19] A modified form of the program was shortly afterward authorized by the USA FREEDOM Act of 2015.[20] In *Klayman v. Obama*, plaintiffs were awarded standing to challenge surveillance of their communications in part on the basis of information contained in the Snowden documents, but the passage of the USA FREEDOM Act mooted their challenge for prospective relief from the surveillance under the 215 program – a risk that reformers and legal scholars were well aware of prior to its passage –[21] in that the surveillance conducted after that act passed now differed materially from the program described in the Snowden files. In *Wikimedia Foundation v. NSA*, the plaintiffs alleged that the NSA's "upstream" collection of all Americans' international communications, including emails, Web-browsing content, and search engine queries, violated the First and Fourth Amendments of the U.S. Constitution; the U.S. District Court for the District of Maryland dismissed the suit for lack of standing, 22 but in May 2017, the Fourth Circuit Court of Appeals revived the suit with respect to Wikimedia Foundation only, accepting their probabilistic reasoning that it was inconceivable that no Wikipedia page had been intercepted.[22] What these cases show is that courts may still, even after Snowden, be institutionally reluctant to award standing to individual plaintiffs when the ramifications of actually shutting down aspects of government mass surveillance programs become apparent.[23]

18 Case C-362/14, Schrems v Data Protection Comm'r, (Oct. 6, 2015), http://curia.europa.eu/juris/document/document.jsf?docid=169195&doclang=EN.

19 Am. *Civil Liberties Union v. Clapper*, 785 F.3d 787, 829 (2d Cir. 2015).

20 Pub. L. No. 114–23, 129 Stat. 268.

21 *See* Steven Nelson, *Freedom Act's Advance Threatens NSA Court Cases: Obama's Signature Could Spare the Government a Courtroom Reckoning, Legal Experts Say*, US News & World Report (Nov. 14, 2014), http://www.usnews.com/news/articles/2014/11/14/freedom-acts-advance-threatens-nsa-court-cases. The USA FREEDOM Act contained some elements of reform, some of modernization, and some of expansion, rendering analysis of its effects especially vexed. However, it is critical to observe that the Section 215 mass metadata program represented a very small proportion of overall U.S. government surveillance. More than 90 percent of data gathered are estimated to be gathered under the PRISM program, which is the one whose effects on user search behavior we analyze and which is authorized under a different U.S. law, Section 702 of the FISA Amendments Act of 2008. Pub. L. No. 110–261, 122 Stat. 2436, § 702.

22 *Wikimedia Found. v. Nat'l Sec. Agency*, 143 F. Supp. 3d 344 (D. Md. 2015), documents at https://www.aclu.org/legal-document/wikimedia-v-nsa-d-md-opinion. *Wikimedia Foundation et al. v National Security Agency et al.*, 4th U.S. Circuit Court of Appeals, No. 15–2560.

23 *Id.* at 351 (quoting *Clapper v. Amnesty Int'l*, 133 S.Ct. 1139, 1157 (2013) ("Importantly, the standing inquiry is 'especially rigorous when reaching the merits of the dispute would force [a court] to decide whether an action taken by one of the other two branches of the Federal Government was unconstitutional,' particularly 'in the fields of intelligence gathering and foreign affairs'").

Paradoxically, we can see that the very breadth and scale of government mass surveillance programs act to insulate them. It is relatively easier to overrule the government on the surveillance of a particular individual, as would have been authorized by the Foreign Intelligence Surveillance Court in the 1970s and 1980s, because one individual can only inflict a relatively small amount of harm. However, shutting down a whole surveillance program, even on the grounds of a constitutional violation, begins to look like judicial activism, and courts would on the whole still prefer to see legislators act to rein in the abuses than to leave it up to them.[24] This may then be compounded further by a chilling effect among legislators. The apparatus of congressional oversight of surveillance programs limits specific knowledge of secret surveillance programs to the members, and sometimes only to the chair and ranking member, of the Senate and House Intelligence Committees, forcing ordinary lawmakers to defer to the expertise of lawmakers who may themselves be chosen by leadership for their sympathy to intelligence community concerns. More worryingly, if the allegations of Russell Tice were true, and are still operative, that the NSA specifically targets for surveillance lawmakers, political candidates, and judges who might have authority to regulate its activities or budget,[25] legislators may feel directly chilled from acting to regulate intelligence agencies by the potential for their own careers to be damaged by the disclosure of embarrassing secrets. The questions of what political surveillance is conducted in the United States, and especially the extent to which NSA data may properly be exploited by White House staff, have resurfaced vividly with the allegation made in March 2017 by President Trump that his campaign was "wiretapped" by his predecessor, and the upcoming sunset in December 2017 of the FISA Amendment Act authorities under which both `downstream' (=PRISM) and `upstream' collection is conducted.

Given this legal and political landscape in the United States, it would be exceptionally useful to both courts and policy makers if researchers were able to document empirically some of the actual effects of surveillance on individuals' behavior. It was immediately clear to us as researchers that the Snowden revelations represented the kind of exogenous

24 *See United States v. Jones*, 132 S.Ct. 945, 964 (2012) (Alito, J., concurring) ("In circumstances involving dramatic technological change, the best solution to privacy concerns may be legislative. A legislative body is well situated to gauge changing public attitudes, to draw detailed lines, and to balance privacy and public safety in a comprehensive way") (internal citation omitted).

25 "Okay. They [the NSA] ... went after members of Congress, both Senate and the House, especially on the intelligence committees and on the armed services committees and ... judicial. But they went after other ones, too. They went after ... heaps of lawyers and law firms. They went after judges. One of the judges [Samuel Alito] is now sitting on the Supreme Court that I had his wiretap information in my hand. Two are former FISA court judges. They went after State Department officials. They went after people in ... the White House – their own people. They went after antiwar groups. They went after U.S.... companies that that do ... business around the world. They went after U.S. banking firms and financial firms that do international business. They went after NGOs ... like the Red Cross that that go overseas and do humanitarian work. They went after a few antiwar civil rights groups. So, you know, don't tell me that there's no abuse, because I've had this stuff in my hand and looked at it. And in some cases, I literally was involved in the technology that was going after this stuff. And you know, when I said to [former MSNBC show host Keith] Olbermann, I said, my particular thing is high tech and you know, what's going on is the other thing, which is the dragnet. The dragnet is what Mark Klein is talking about, the terrestrial dragnet. Well my specialty is outer space. I deal with satellites, and everything that goes in and out of space. I did my spying via space. So that's how I found out about this." *NSA Whistleblower: NSA Spying on – and Blackmailing – Top Government Officials and Military Officers*, Fox Nation (June 20, 2013), http://nation.foxnews.com/2013/06/20/nsa-whistleblower-nsa-spying-%E2%80%93-and-blackmailing-%E2%80%93-top-government-officials-and-military.

shock that could be used to gain a much more precise understanding of the effects of knowledge or fear of surveillance on behavior than had been possible for decades.[26] The Snowden revelations began at a defined point, were very broadly reported across the world, and related only to the topic of surveillance. Thus, unlike for the Watergate scandal of the 1970s or the fall of the German Democratic Republic in 1989, reactions to the Snowden revelations could plausibly be attributed to shock specifically from surveillance, as opposed to shock from a spectrum of abusive governmental behavior including surveillance. Such a "clean" shock is unlikely to occur again in the near future. It therefore presented, and continues to present, a uniquely rich research opportunity.

Within the first six months after the Snowden revelations began to break, it appeared that the only information becoming available regarding any potential chilling effects was survey based. Opinion polling on the topic in June 2013 by the Pew Internet & American Life Project did not at that stage focus on changes in behavior.[27] A contemporaneous PEN America survey focused on the effects on writers in particular, with 28 percent of writers reporting "curtailed social media activities" in response to the Snowden revelations, 24 percent reporting that they "deliberately avoided certain topics in phone or email conversations," and 16 percent reporting that they "avoided writing or speaking about a particular topic."[28] Of course, the survey approach – while quick relative to well-constructed empirical work – suffers from significant limitations. Writers may have been subject to substantial social desirability bias,[29] feeling that they *ought* to say that they responded in some meaningful way to knowledge that their writings were under more government scrutiny than they had supposed, even if they in fact had not responded. There was no indication that methods to reduce social desirability bias were employed in this study. Castro reports the results of a Cloud Security Alliance survey conducted in June and July of 2013 of its members, who are industry practitioners, companies, and other cloud computing stakeholders, about their reactions to the NSA leaks.[30] For non-U.S. residents, 10 percent of respondents indicated that they had canceled a project with a United States–based cloud computing provider and 56 percent said that they would be less likely to use a United States–based cloud computing service.[31] For U.S. residents, slightly more than one-third (36 percent) indicated that the NSA leaks made it more difficult for them to do business outside the United States.[32] The 10 percent reporting actual

26 This, of course, evokes the famous prison proposed by Jeremy Bentham in Panopticon, or, the Inspection-house:

> The more constantly the persons to be inspected are under the eye of the persons who should inspect them, the more perfectly will the purpose of the establishment have been attained. Ideal perfection, if that were the object, would require that each person should actually be in that predicament, during every instant of time. This being impossible, the next thing to be wished for is, that, at every instant, seeing reason to believe as much, and not being able to satisfy himself to the contrary, he should *conceive* himself to be so.

Jeremy Bentham, Panopticon; or, the Inspection House, 3 (1791) (emphasis in original).

27 Pew Research Center, Few See Adequate Limits on NSA Surveillance Program (2013), http://www.people-press.org/2013/07/26/few-see-adequate-limits-on-nsa-surveillance-program/.

28 Pen American Center, Chilling Effects: NSA Surveillance Drives U.S. Writers to Self-Censor 3 (2013), https://pen.org/sites/default/files/Chilling%20Effects_PEN%20American.pdf.

29 Robert J. Fisher, *Social Desirability Bias and the Validity of Indirect Questioning*, 20 J. Consumer Research 303 (1993).

30 Daniel Castro, How Much Will PRISM Cost the U.S. Cloud Computing Industry? (2013), http://www2.itif.org/2013-cloud-computing-costs.pdf.

31 *Id.* at 3.

32 *Id.*

contract cancellation provides stronger evidence of an economic chill than the 56 percent thinking that they might have to not use, or cancel a project with, a U.S. provider in the future; but no follow-up was conducted with either group to establish what contracts were canceled or whether decisions not to use U.S. providers were in fact made.

We do not suggest that it is entirely meaningless that writers and cloud security professionals reported that they had made changes at this level or were thinking of doing so. Stating publicly that you intend to behave in line with a societal expectation both attests to the existence of that societal expectation and may itself act to shape behavior via formation of a stronger social norm. Not finding evidence of a behavioral change in the short term therefore would not necessarily exclude the possibility that this longer-term process would work slowly outward from intent to action.

IV How Did the Snowden Revelations Affect Search?

We believe that the strongest and best evidence of the effect of a sharp increase in knowledge of surveillance is empirical measurement of actual behavioral changes that can reasonably be said to have been caused by a particular shock.[33] Fortunately for our purposes, Google makes publicly available Google Trends, a data source covering all search terms entered by individual users across the world. Google Trends has been used in other studies to predict economic and health behaviors.[34] It does not provide raw search volumes or individually identifiable data, but instead is an index of a particular search term's popularity in a given region relative to other regions.

What follows is a summary of the paper that we wrote on this topic using Google Trends data.[35] Readers who are interested in more technical details about the exact empirical methodology can consult the full paper.

We confronted the question of how people perceived the likelihood of their searches' triggering interest from the U.S. government in the following fashion. We required some external source of search terms of potential interest to the U.S. government. Fortunately, such a list does exist in the public domain; it is provided for the use of analysts working in

[33] As a further note on longer-term norm formation and economic effects, now that four years have passed, we can see the longer-term formation of a stronger social norm in the technology industry in favor of end-to-end encrypted products and more aggressive discarding of data, which is surely strongly influenced by the Snowden revelations, though not in ways that are easily measured using empirical techniques. Indeed, if technology companies were to adopt stronger data practices, and their sales were to rise as a result, we might be in the strange position of effectively arguing that mass surveillance, by giving rise to the Snowden revelations and thereby to stronger data practices and higher sales for such companies, had provided economic benefits. Equally, if sales by United States- or UK-based firms were to suffer, because they were perceived as being insecure, and sales of firms based in other countries were to rise, because they were perceived as being more secure, we cannot argue that this means that mass surveillance is economically damaging in a general sense, but only insofar as it inflicts reputational costs disproportionately on companies wittingly or unwittingly participating in mass surveillance systems, and thereby potentially disproportionately on particular countries rather than others. That assessment, however, would obscure the high level of variation in data security practices within countries, and even within firms in the case of firms with multiple products.

[34] Hyunyoung Choi & Hal Varian, *Predict the Present with Google Trends*, 88 Econ. Rec. 2 (2012); Herman Anthony Carneiro & Eleftherios Mylonakis, *Google Trends: A Web-Based Tool for Real-Time Surveillance of Disease Outbreaks*, 49 Clinical Infectious Diseases 1157 (2009).

[35] Alex Marthews & Catherine Tucker, Government Surveillance and Internet Search Behavior (2015), http://papers.ssrn.com/sol3/papers.cfm?abstract_id=2412564.

the Media Monitoring Capability section of the National Operations Center, an agency under the Department of Homeland Security (Table A.1).[36] The list was made public in 2012 and continued to be used and reproduced within the Department of Homeland Security (DHS) up to the time of the Snowden revelations.[37] As far as we are aware, it remains in effect today, though we cannot be certain that no changes have been made. It is therefore the most relevant publicly available document for assessing the kinds of search terms that the U.S. government might be interested in collecting under PRISM or under its other programs aimed at gathering Google search data, even though it is focused on surveillance of social media Web sites rather than search engines. As far as we are aware, neither the DHS nor any other surveillance agency has revealed or has had leaked its list of search terms that would raise flags for searches on Google itself.[38] Later, we use independent raters on Mechanical Turk to evaluate whether users perceive particular search terms as likely to get you in trouble with the U.S. government.

Second, we used a crowdsourced list of embarrassing search terms (Table A.2). Our overall aim in establishing a reasonable list of "embarrassing" terms was to find terms that would not implicate national security issues of interest to DHS, or duplicate any term found in that list, but which would instead cause embarrassment for most people if third parties found out about those searches.[39] We were also seeking a list that had a broad range of terms, rather than simply being sexual in nature. We crowdsourced a group of participants who were part of the local technology community. The participants were young (twenties and thirties), well educated, and balanced equally between men and women. The list is the result of that process. Examples of terms included in this list are "white power," "erectile dysfunction," and "My Little Pony."

We also needed a list of neutral search terms to use as a control. We also wanted to obtain a list of more "neutral" search terms to use as a quasi-control (Table A3), that were plausibly treated less intensively by the revelations about PRISM. To find a more neutral set of search terms, we turned to the nature of Google as a search engine. Users across the world use Google to search for local services and businesses. This type of search behavior provides a reasonable baseline measure of usage of search engines. To obtain words to capture this behavior, we first obtained a list of the most common local businesses in the US based on the North American Industry Classification System. We associated this list

36 Department of Homeland Security, Analyst's Desktop Binder 20–23 (2011), https://epic.org/foia/epic-v-dhs-media-monitoring/Analyst-Desktop-Binder-REDACTED.pdf.

37 Department of Homeland Security, Analyst's Desktop Binder, 18–21 (2013), https://assets.documentcloud.org/documents/1086613/dhs-noc-mmc-analyst-desktop-foia-1340-redacted.pdf.

38 The list itself is in some ways not what people might expect. It includes, for example, the terms "agriculture" and "cloud," perhaps out of concerns over terrorism directed at the food supply. But it is hard to see how the mention of "agriculture" in a social medium posting is in itself suspicious. The list also reads as if it was constructed with an analyst's idea of what was relevant, rather than constructing a plausible idea of what potential attackers might write in a social media post. For example, someone involved with organized crime is, we suspect, very unlikely to use the term "organized crime" in a posting on social media.

39 We may not be able to assume safely that, either in the view of the intelligence agencies or in the minds of citizens, there is a bright-line distinction between politically and personally sensitive terms. Intelligence agencies have shown themselves willing to use personally embarrassing but not prosecutable information about surveillance targets to shape their behavior. Leaked documents that form part of the current scandal, for example, show the NSA recommending using the online pornography viewing habits of "radicalizers" to discredit them. Also, the strong similarity of ratings of political and personal sensitivity in our study suggests that citizens may not accurately distinguish the two in their minds, instead thinking of government surveillance as being similar in many ways to a parent looking over their shoulder.

with search terms that would plausibly capture these businesses, namely: Gym, restaurant, nursing home, thrift store, butcher, gardener, beauty salon, cleaners, childcare, arcade, movies and weather.

Using these three lists, we were able to analyze how close the relationship is between what Google users *perceive* to be searches that cause them to be recognized by the U.S. government and search terms that might actually result in their being flagged in some way by the algorithms developed by U.S. surveillance agencies. It is not clear, for example, why using the search term "agriculture" might be perceived by an average Google search user as more likely to call him or her to the attention of the U.S. government than the term "gardener," but the first term is on the DHS list and the second is from the list of neutral businesses. Legally, in order to demonstrate standing to bring a claim against the U.S. government for its conduct of mass surveillance, it might be necessary to show that a specific search was likely to trigger actual U.S. government interest, whereas in order for a chilling effect to exist it is only necessary for a searcher to believe that it would.

In the survey, we asked participants to rate each term by how likely it is that it would "embarrass" them or "get them into trouble" with their family, their close friends, or the U.S. government. We also asked them to rate how privacy sensitive they considered the term, how much they would like to keep the search secret, and how likely they would be to try to delete their search history after using this term. We asked all these ratings on a 5-point Likert scale, where 1 reflects the least sensitive and 5 reflects the most sensitive rating. As might be expected, the terms on the DHS list are most likely to be rated as "getting you in trouble with the government," at a mean value of 1.62 out of 5. The search terms from the "embarrassing" list were rated the most likely to embarrass the user with his or her family or close friends, at mean values of between 2.2 and 2.3 out of 5 in terms of whether they would embarrass the user if his or her close friends or family knew about them and whether the user would want to keep the search secret or delete their search history, but at a lower sensitivity value of 1.59 in terms of whether the search would get them into trouble with the government. The neutral terms were in general rated the least embarrassing, with mean sensitivity values ranging between 1 and 1.22 out of 5 on all measures. As our list of search terms is in no sense random, we then performed further validation to ensure that the search terms did represent politically and personally sensitive topics.[40]

Overall, across the 41 countries we studied, we found that the Google Trends search index fell for "high government trouble" search terms by roughly 4 percent after the Snowden revelations. It was surprising to us to find any difference in the search terms traffic, because there had been significant doubts expressed as to whether any macro-level effect on search behavior would be observable as a result of shocks such as the Snowden revelations. In countries other than the United States, there was a smaller, but still significant, decline for search terms that raters thought would give them an above-average

[40] Even for search terms that people might think plausibly signify some sort of malevolent intent, such as "anthrax" and "pipe bomb," the vast majority of the site traffic resulting from that search was to innocent destinations such as the Centers for Disease Control and Wikipedia. This may throw into question the utility of governmental efforts to flag Internet traffic unconnected to any predicate or suspicion that an individual is involved in criminal behavior; the evident risk is that government agencies will be snowed under with false positive findings deriving from innocent searches and mentions on social media, and will therefore inevitably miss "needles" that they might be more able to find by gathering less "hay."

likelihood of getting in trouble with a friend. We used a battery of robustness checks to validate the results, including controlling for news coverage and using different time windows as a falsification check.

This was, for us, an unexpected result. We began this study with considerable skepticism about whether the surveillance revelations were capable of affecting search traffic at such a macrolevel in the countries concerned. It seemed very possible that we would see no empirically demonstrable effect, and would then be drawing on the political science literature on low-information voters and political apathy as a guide for why search behavior was not affected.[41]

A natural concern is whether other factors could plausibly have shifted user behavior in early June relating to these specific keywords. However, the keywords cover a large variety of topics, so another news story relating to a small portion of them, such as an extreme weather event (for the DHS search terms) or the holiday season (for the list of neutral business terms) is unlikely to have shifted behavior for the whole list. Similarly, if we are looking at user behavior across the world, it is less likely that a smaller story could affect user behavior in the same way as the Snowden leaks. The only plausible shifters would be Google-specific, i.e., whether there was an internal change in the way the search engine operated at the time that would have a coherent and similar effect on search behavior in multiple countries. We are not aware of any such change.

We used Google in our study because Google represents such a large share of the worldwide search market, at around 70 percent during this period. An effect on search activities that was not perceptible on Google would therefore leave most Internet users unaffected. Our work addresses the question of whether more privacy-conscious users simply shifted their searches away from Google and to more secure search engines, such as SafeSearch or DuckDuckGo. Take-up of these services indeed boomed after the surveillance revelations, but from such a small base that adoption of secure search engines can only represent a small proportion – at most, around 10 percent – of the effect that we identified. At any rate, this noticeable shift away from Google to search engines perceived as more secure from government surveillance in the wake of the Snowden revelations necessarily bolsters, rather than undermines, the broader finding that there is a measurable chilling effect of surveillance.

V How Did the Snowden Revelations Affect Nonsearch Online Behavior?

Building on this work, and using the same DHS list and a very similar methodology, Jon Penney found a comparable chilling effect on traffic to Wikipedia pages dealing with topics relating to terrorism, which provides evidence that the effect we observed may extend beyond the large, though limited, universe of Google search results.[42] Other

41 *See* Ilya Somin, *Deliberative Democracy and Political Ignorance*, 22 Geo. Mason U. Critical Rev. 253 (2010) http://papers.ssrn.com/sol3/papers.cfm?abstract_id=1694650.

42 Jon Penney, *Chilling Effects: Online Surveillance and Wikipedia Use*, Berkeley Tech. L. J. Vol. 31, No. 1, p. 117, 2016, http://papers.ssrn.com/sol3/papers.cfm?abstract_id=2769645. Soren Preibusch, *Privacy Behaviors after Snowden*, 58 Comm. of the ACM 48 (2015), authored by a researcher employed by Microsoft, attempts to disprove the effect we found, but tried to do so using search results from Bing, a Microsoft-created search engine with a low market penetration. The article did not address the potential for selection bias (that users of such a minor-league search engine might systematically differ from search engine users in general in their tastes for privacy or their online behavior). For example, Bing users may use Bing only because it is set as the default search engine, and may have a lower level of education or of

academics are investigating the same topic with respect to Twitter, but no papers have yet been published relating to that platform. Investigations examining the effect on social media posts on platforms such as Facebook and Instagram are problematic because these platforms allow users control over their privacy settings, which themselves are not necessarily exogenous to the surveillance revelations. Thus, data for those platforms are simultaneously harder to collect and more ambiguous when collected.

VI Other Methods of Studying the Effect of Surveillance on Behavior

Although this particular empirical technique has proved to be an adaptable way to examine the effects of mass surveillance programs, that does not mean that there are no other interesting ways to get at this difficult problem. In the communications literature, for example, Elizabeth Stoycheff sets up a lab experiment that primes social media users through their terms of service agreements to expect that their social media usage will be surveilled.[43] She then finds that those who are so primed, and hold what they perceive to be opinions that are distant from mainstream opinion regarding U.S. airstrikes on ISIS in Iraq, are particularly likely to be deterred from posting their opinions. There is also a substantial surveillance studies literature using sociological methods to hypothesize the effects on society of mass government and commercial surveillance, but not to our knowledge focusing on the empirical quantification of such effects, so we do not consider it in this chapter.

Conclusion

It has become possible, primarily as a result of the exogenous shock of the Snowden revelations and the increased scholarly attention devoted to this problem, to analyze more precisely the chilling effect of surveillance on people's behavior, and, with limitations, to quantify the extent to which people's actual behavior is altered in response to knowing more about the scale and nature of surveillance. This has important ramifications in the legal sphere for ongoing litigation relating to privacy violations, especially in the area of being able to demonstrate a legally cognizable injury that would enable courts to confer standing to bring suit. In the policy sphere, it enables the discussion to move on from the question of whether a chilling effect exists, to the question of what, if anything, to do about the chilling effect that exists.

technical literacy, which in turn may affect how much they adopted more sophisticated search techniques to avoid surveillance. Second, despite asserting that he was performing a "longitudinal" study, his work appears to be based on snapshots of overall Bing traffic at different points in time, which is not longitudinal. Third, he appears to have misinterpreted our study as being based on "survey data," leading him to overstate the originality of his own work.

43 Elizabeth Stoycheff, *Examining Facebook's Spiral of Silence Effects in the Wake of NSA Internet Monitoring*, 93 J. Mass Comm. Q. 296 (2016).

Appendix

Table A.1. Random One-Third Sample of DHS Search Terms

agent	1.1
agriculture	1.05
air marshal	1.74
alcohol tobacco and firearms	2
anthrax	2.76
antiviral	1.65
assassination	2.44
authorities	1.35
avian	1.24
bacteria	1.15
biological	1.25
border patrol	1.37
breach	1.63
burn	1.63
center for disease control	1.6
central intelligence agency	1.55
chemical	2.1
chemical agent	2.21
chemical burn	1.85
chemical spill	1.89
cloud	1.05
coast guard	1.3
contamination	1.7
cops	1.39
crash	1.22
customs and border protection	1.65
deaths	1.25
department of homeland security	1.55
dirty bomb	3.74
disaster assistance	1.37
disaster management	1
disaster medical assistance team	1.18
dndo	1.84
domestic security	2.15
drill	1.06
drug administration	1.79
drug enforcement agency	1.85
ebola	1.17
emergency landing	1.42
emergency management	1.76
emergency response	1.4
epidemic	1.68
evacuation	1.35

(continued)

Table A.1 (continued)

explosion	2.2
explosion explosive	3.15
exposure	1.5
federal aviation administration	1.1
federal bureau of investigation	1.63
first responder	1
flu	1.58
food poisoning	1.6
foot and mouth	1.45
fusion center	1.75
gangs	1.56
gas	1.55
h1n1	1.44
h5n1	1.6
hazardous	1.61
hazmat	1.35
homeland defense	1.42
homeland security	1.75
hostage	2.06
human to animal	2.2
human to human	1.45
immigration customs enforcement	1.47
incident	1.47
infection	1.6
influenza	1.2
infrastructure security	1.75
law enforcement	1.3
leak	1.4
listeria	1.47
lockdown	1.7
looting	2.11
militia	1.89
mitigation	1.45
mutation	1.58
national guard	1.37
national laboratory	1.45
national preparedness	1.6
national security	1.79
nerve agent	3.21
north korea	1.75
nuclear	2.1
nuclear facility	2.42
nuclear threat	2.17
organized crime	2.32
outbreak	1.6
pandemic	1.42
pipe bomb	4

plague	1.68
plume	1.11
police	1.2
pork	1.16
powder white	2.3
prevention	1.15
public health	1.3
quarantine	2.15
radiation	1.85
radioactive	2.05
recall	1.39
recovery	1.3
red cross	1.2
resistant	1.5
response	1.1
ricin	2.6
riot	1.6
salmonella	1.26
sarin	2.89
screening	1.3
secret service	1.89
secure border initiative	1.55
security	1.21
shooting	1.9
shots fired	2.11
sick	1.1
small pox	1.79
spillover	1.11
standoff	1.47
state of emergency	1.4
strain	1.39
swat	1.55
swine	1.25
symptoms	1
tamiflu	1.5
task force	1.15
threat	1.7
toxic	1.44
transportation security administration	1.35
tuberculosis	1.2
united nations	1.2
u.s. citizenship and immigration services	1.5
vaccine	1.2
virus	1.4
wave	1.05
world health organization	1.22
Mean	**1.62**

Table A.2. Embarrassing Search Terms

abortion	2.3
accutane	1.26
acne	1.1
adultery	2.26
agenda 21	1.47
aids	1.63
alcoholics anonymous	2.11
alien abduction	1.4
animal rights	1.16
anonymous	1.18
atheism	1.45
bail bonds	1.55
bankruptcy	2
bittorrent	1.37
black panthers	1.6
body odor	1.63
breathalyzer	1.65
casinos	1.21
celebrity news	1.11
chemtrails	1.78
coming out	2.05
communism	1.37
conspiracy	1.37
cop block	1.35
cutting	2.75
debt consolidation	1.79
depression	2
divorce lawyer	1.65
drones	1.42
eating disorder	2
erectile dysfunction	2
escorts	2.6
feminism	1.11
filesharing	1.45
fireworks	1.2
food not bombs	1.45
gay rights	1.47
gender reassignment	2.11
ghosts	1.25
gulf of tonkin	1.32
guns	2.05
herpes	1.89
hitler	1.85
hoarding	1.45
honey boo boo	1.33

incontinence	1.45
islam	1.25
keystone	1.16
kkk	2.11
larp	1.74
liposuction	1.26
lolcats	1.16
lonely	1.68
lost cause	1.26
marijuana legalization	1.5
marx	1.42
my little pony	1.5
nickelback	1.85
nose job	1.6
occupy	1.7
online dating	2
pest control	1.17
peta	1.2
police brutality	1.25
polyamory	1.8
porn	1.95
pregnant	1.7
protest	1.61
psychics	1.65
revolution	1.4
sexual addiction	2.45
shrink	1.65
socialism	1.22
sovereign citizen	1.21
sperm donation	2.06
strip club	2.26
suicide	2.68
tampons	1.85
tax avoidance	1.9
therapist	1.45
thrush	1.17
torrent	1.28
transhumanism	1.47
turner diaries	1.74
tuskegee	1.16
unions	1.28
vaccines and autism	1.33
vegan	1.3
viagra	2.16
warts	1.55

(continued)

Table A.2 (continued)

weed	2.11
weight loss	1.5
white power	3.05
white pride	2.47
wicca	1.8
witchcraft	1.84
world of warcraft	1.35
Mean	**1.64**

Table A.3. Google Search Terms

arcade	1
beautysalon	1.22
butcher	1.22
childcare	1
cleaners	1
gardener	1
gym	1
movies	1
nursing home	1
restaurant	1
thrift store	1
Weather	1
Mean	**1.04**

19 Surveillance versus Privacy: Effects and Implications

Julie E. Cohen[†]

The ongoing transition from industrialism to informationalism has prompted repeated predictions of the death of privacy. Digital information networks and the granularity of the information they collect and transmit seem inconsistent with the preservation of older, analog conceptions of private information and private space. Digital information networks, however, are designed with particular purposes in mind. To decode and evaluate the rhetoric of doomed privacy, one must understand the purposes that current patterns of development are thought to serve. That inquiry requires consideration of the theory and practice of surveillance. This chapter takes up that project, exploring the nature of surveillance, its effects on self-development, and the societal implications of those effects.

Introduction

The ongoing transition from industrialism to informationalism has prompted repeated predictions of the death of privacy.[1] Some reasons that appear to justify such predictions are technological. Digital information networks and the granularity of the information they collect and transmit seem inconsistent with the preservation of older, analog conceptions of private information and private space. Other reasons are cultural and linguistic. To speak of privacy in terms of preservation, as narratives of inexorable technical and economic progress seem to force us to do, is to position the idea of privacy itself as old-fashioned and retrograde.

There is more here than meets the eye, however. Digital information networks are developed with particular purposes in mind. To decode and evaluate the rhetoric of doomed privacy and its accompanying narratives about the power of innovation in information processing markets, one must understand the purposes that current patterns of development are thought to serve. That inquiry requires consideration of factors that are political, economic, and epistemological. This chapter takes up that project.

Part I sketches provisional definitions of "surveillance" and "privacy," with particular attention to the relationship between surveillance and economic and technological development. Part II explores the effects on self-development of emerging practices of

[†] Mark Claster Mamolen Professor of Law and Technology, Georgetown University Law Center.

[1] On the emergence of informationalism as a mode of economic development and its articulation within capitalist modes of production, *see* James R. Beniger, The Control Revolution: Technological and Economic Origins of the Information Society (1986); 1 Manuel Castells, The Information Age: The Rise of the Network Society 14–18 (1996); Dan Schiller, How to Think About Information 3–35 (2007).

governance organized around pervasive, networked surveillance. Part III considers the societal implications of those effects.

I Defining Terms

In this chapter, I will focus principally on the understandings of surveillance and privacy that have developed at the intersection of surveillance studies and law. That project requires acknowledging and accounting for important methodological differences that have complicated efforts at interdisciplinary dialogue.[2] Law owes allegiance principally to liberal theory and surveillance studies principally to critical theory, two traditions with radically different approaches to the topics of power and subjectivity. Yet the misalignments between law and surveillance studies also have created the potential for productive confrontation.

Consider first surveillance. Legal scholars have been inclined to consider surveillance simply as a collection of techniques that together constitute (potential) subjects of regulation. By contrast, scholars in surveillance studies consider surveillance – defined generically as attention that is purposeful, routine, systematic, and focused[3] – to be a mode of social control. From the latter perspective, although the reasons offered to justify surveillance often characterize surveillant attention as passive or reactive – for example, directed toward preventing crime or responding to the preferences revealed by consumer behavior – surveillant attention is productive, and it is important to pay attention to what it produces.

Understanding surveillance as a mode of social control suggests two important lines of inquiry for law. The first concerns the political and ideological preconditions for surveillance. Drawing on a cluster of allied disciplines – including sociology, geography, organization studies, cultural studies, and media and information studies – scholars in surveillance studies have documented the ways that surveillance tools and techniques pervade modern organizational practice. Governments, businesses, and other organizations worldwide have invested in the development of surveillance infrastructures and practices for a wide variety of reasons. That work makes plain that a wide range of contemporary societies are surveillance societies. While totalitarian governments may view surveillance as holding out the promise of more complete control, democratic and capitalist systems have valued surveillance for reasons more closely connected to its purported efficiency and rationality: "Surveillance may be viewed as progress towards efficient administration, in Max Weber's view, a benefit for the development of Western capitalism and the modern nation-state."[4]

2 For more detailed development of the points about method made in this section, *see* Julie E. Cohen, *Studying Law Studying Surveillance*, 13 SURVEILLANCE & SOC'Y 91 (2015).

3 Kirstie Ball, et al., SURVEILLANCE STUDIES NETWORK: A REPORT ON THE SURVEILLANCE SOCIETY 8 (David Murakami Wood ed., 2006) [hereinafter Report on the Surveillance Society].

4 *Id.* at 1 (citing H.H. Gerth & C. Wright Mills, FROM MAX WEBER: ESSAYS IN SOCIOLOGY [1964]). The linkage between surveillance and public administration has deep roots in both English and Continental European political traditions. *See* Jeremy Bentham, PANOPTICON OR THE INSPECTION-HOUSE: CONTAINING THE IDEA OF A NEW PRINCIPLE OF CONSTRUCTION APPLICABLE TO ANY SORT OF ESTABLISHMENT, IN WHICH PERSONS OF ANY DESCRIPTION ARE TO BE KEPT UNDER INSPECTION; AND IN PARTICULAR TO PENITENTIARY-HOUSES, PRISONS, HOUSES OF INDUSTRY, WORK-HOUSES, LAZARETTOS, MANUFACTORIES, HOSPITALS, MAD-HOUSES, AND SCHOOLS WITH A PLAN OF MANAGEMENT ADAPTED TO THE PRINCIPLE (1787); Michel Foucault, DISCIPLINE AND PUNISH: THE BIRTH OF THE PRISON (1975); Michel Foucault, MADNESS AND CIVILIZATION: A HISTORY OF INSANITY IN THE AGE OF REASON (1961).

The second important line of inquiry concerns the relationship between surveillance and economic development. Understood as a mode of social control, surveillance has meshed especially well with developed economies' ongoing shift from industrialism to informationalism. Networked information and communication technologies enable the intensification of surveillant attention, providing the material conditions for it to become continuous, pervasively distributed, and persistent. Those capabilities in turn enable modulation: a set of processes in which the quality and content of surveillant attention can be modified continually according to each subject's behavior, sometimes in response to inputs from the subject but according to logics that ultimately are outside the subject's control.[5] Via the turn to modulation, surveillance has emerged as a distinct modality of profit generation, or what Shoshana Zuboff has called surveillance capitalism.[6] In the contemporary information economy, private-sector firms use flows of information about consumer behavior to identify and target high-value consumers and to extract surplus from all consumers. Government also is an important secondary beneficiary of commercial surveillance practices and techniques, routinely accessing and using flows of behavioral and communications data for its own purposes.

Situating surveillance within its ideological and economic contexts makes plain that it is more than a mode of social control. It is a mode of governance, one deeply enmeshed with both Western philosophical commitments to rationality and the rise of informational capitalism as a model of political economy. Its institutional forms should be matters of deep concern to legal scholars.

Accounts of privacy, by contrast, originate predominantly within law. Indeed, scholars in surveillance studies have been inclined to dismiss privacy as essentially an artifact of liberal philosophy and political theory.[7] There is more than a grain of truth to that charge. Privacy theory in the liberal tradition has been resistant to the reality of social shaping, insisting that the subject of privacy protection is the autonomous self and then drawing on idealized conceptions of autonomy to derive the appropriate contours of privacy protection.[8] There are also important mismatches between privacy and liberal theory, however. Efforts to theorize privacy have struggled to overcome two related problems.[9] First, characterizing privacy as a right seems to violate the core methodological commitments of liberal political theory, which prize most highly those definitions of rights that are susceptible to formal, quasi-scientific derivation from core principles. So, for example, many privacy theorists working in the liberal tradition have tended to think that the key to success lies in locating privacy's essence in one or another overarching principle (such as liberty or inaccessibility or control), but have been frustrated to find

5 *See* Greg Elmer, PROFILING MACHINES: MAPPING THE PERSONAL INFORMATION ECONOMY 41–50 (2004); William Bogard, *Simulation and Post-Panopticism*, in ROUTLEDGE HANDBOOK OF SURVEILLANCE STUDIES 30, 32–33 (Kirstie Ball, Kevin Haggerty, & David Lyon eds., 2012). For a more detailed typology of the ways that networked information technologies facilitate surveillance, *see* Christian Fuchs et al., *Introduction: Internet and Surveillance*, in INTERNET AND SURVEILLANCE: THE CHALLENGES OF WEB 2.0 AND SOCIAL MEDIA 1, 16–19 (Christian Fuchs, et al. eds., 2012).

6 Shoshana Zuboff, *Big Other: Surveillance Capitalism and the Prospects of an Information Civilization*, 30 J. INFO. TECH. 75 (2015).

7 *See, e.g.*, David Lyon, SURVEILLANCE SOCIETY: MONITORING EVERYDAY LIFE (2001).

8 *See, e.g.*, Jeffrey Rosen, THE UNWANTED GAZE: THE DESTRUCTION OF PRIVACY IN AMERICA 166 (2000) ("I'm free to think whatever I like even if the state or the phone company knows what I read").

9 For more detailed discussion, *see* Julie E. Cohen, CONFIGURING THE NETWORKED SELF: CODE, LAW, AND THE PLAY OF EVERYDAY PRACTICE 107–20 (2012).

that such definitions inevitably prove both over- and underinclusive when measured against the types of privacy expectations held by real people.[10] The difficulty of defining privacy in terms of traditional liberal first principles has led some critics to conclude that privacy is simply a good to be traded off against other goods, most notably security and convenience. That characterization, though, fails to account for the collective and synergistic nature of privacy benefits.[11]

More recently, legal scholarship on privacy has developed both an account of privacy that is less reductive and an account of privacy's subject – the self – that accords more closely with the reality of social shaping. Pathbreaking works by Helen Nissenbaum and Daniel Solove acknowledge and explore the heterogeneity and variability of privacy expectations.[12] Nissenbaum in particular links privacy with the integrity – and hence sometimes the necessary separation – of the different contexts in which personal information may be accessible to others. My own work and that of Valerie Steeves relate privacy both positively and normatively to emergent subjectivity.[13]

Understood through the lenses of contextual integrity and emergent subjectivity, privacy fulfills an essential function that the view from surveillance studies (and sometimes also from law) risks overlooking. Privacy is not an abstract right or a static good to be traded off against other possible goods; nor is it a conceptual and historical anachronism. It is both a structural condition and a related entitlement. The condition of privacy is dynamic and is best described as breathing room for socially situated subjects to engage in the processes of boundary management through which they define and redefine themselves as subjects.[14] Rights to privacy are rights to the sociotechnical conditions that make the condition of privacy possible. To say that individuals (or communities) have – or should have – rights to privacy is to make a normative statement about the importance of preserving the breathing room necessary for self-articulation.

When surveillance and privacy are defined as I have done here, it becomes evident that the two terms denote modes of ordering that are to a very great extent orthogonal to one another, and that the two modes of ordering often will enter into conflict both practically and politically. That insight in turn suggests new criteria for interrogating the effects of surveillance, and especially those of the pervasive, networked surveillance that the rise of informationalism has enabled.

II Effects of Heightened Surveillance on Self-Development

The emergence of pervasive, networked surveillance has important implications for self-development because it radically extends the reach and enhances the power of social

10 For a good discussion of the under- and overinclusiveness of reductive conceptions of privacy, *see* Daniel J. Solove, Understanding Privacy 14–38 (2008). A magisterial exploration of privacy's conflicts with principles of liberty is Anita Allen, Unpopular Privacy (2011).

11 Priscilla M. Regan, *Privacy and the Common Good; Revisited*, in Social Dimensions of Privacy; Interdisiplinary Perspectives 50 (2015).

12 Helen Nissenbaum, Privacy in Context: Technology, Policy, and the Integrity of Social Life (2009); Solove, *supra* note 10.

13 Cohen, Configuring the Networked Self, *supra* note 9, at 127–52; Julie E. Cohen, *What Privacy Is For*, 126 Harv. L. Rev. 1904 (2013); Valerie Steeves, *Reclaiming the Social Value of Privacy*, in Lessons from the Identity Trail: Anonymity, Privacy, and Identity in a Networked Society 191 (Ian Kerr, et al. eds., 2009).

14 Cohen, Configuring the Networked Self, *supra* note 9, at 148–52.

shaping.[15] Subjectivity – and hence selfhood – exists in the gap between the reality of social shaping and the experience of autonomous selfhood. It is real in the only way that counts; we experience ourselves as having identities that are more or less fixed. But it is also malleable and emergent and embodied, and if we are honest that too accords with experience. Subjectivity evolves as individuals and communities engage in practices of mutually constituting self-definition that are both culturally embedded and open ended. Surveillance alters those processes by undermining their open-endedness.

Processes of self-development do not conform to the idealized theoretical models preferred by liberal legal theorists, which revolve around the purposive exercise of expressive or market liberty; nor do they automatically produce that caricature, the dominated, postmodernist subject. The everyday practice of situated subjects is messy, heterogeneous, and tactical. People are born into networks of relationships, practices, and beliefs, and over time they encounter and experiment with others, engaging in a diverse and ad hoc mix of behaviors that defies neat theoretical simplification. Situated subjects exercise a deliberate, playful agency that is (sometimes) enormously creative. People find ways to push back against the institutional, cultural, and material constraints that they encounter in their everyday lives, often drawing on the resources available within their territorial and cultural networks to craft new strategies. They also exploit the unexpected encounters and juxtapositions that everyday life supplies.

Surveillance presses against the play of subjectivity and self-development in ways both metaphorical and literal, seeking to strip away the breathing room that emergent subjectivity requires. Subjectivity emerges within the interstices of social shaping; control over the processes of self-development exists more fully to the extent that the interstices are larger and the linkages less complete. Emergent subjectivity can evolve in ways that produce a robust sense of agency, supportive and resilient networks of relational and communal ties, and critical independence of mind. But other results are also possible, depending on the nature of the constraints that are in place and on how tightly they bind.

Some effects of surveillance are informational and epistemological. The information collected from and about people is used to constitute individuals and communities as transparent objects of others' knowledge. Foundational texts for the study of those processes include Michel Foucault's landmark study of the emergence of modern techniques of social discipline that are statistical in nature and Gilles Deleuze's work on networked processes of social control.[16] Work in surveillance studies builds upon those texts and others to elaborate the operation of modern surveillance societies and the processes of surveillance capitalism.[17] As that work explains, even surveillance ostensibly directed only toward measuring and documenting individual attributes also helps to produce the framework within which those attributes are located and rendered intelligible. It both creates and reinforces the categories and classifications that it presents as observed truths. Such processes, moreover, do not require official coercion for their effects to take hold;

15 This section is adapted from Cohen, Configuring the Networked Self, *supra* note 9, at 127–52, and Cohen, *What Privacy Is For*, *supra* note 13, at 1906–11.

16 Foucault, Discipline and Punish *supra* note 4; Gilles Deleuze, Negotiations 1972–1990 (Martin Joughin trans., 1995).

17 For useful overviews, *see* Kirstie Ball, Kevin D. Haggerty & David Lyon, eds., Routledge Handbook of Surveillance Studies (2012); Lyon, *supra* note 7; Report on the Surveillance Society, *supra* note 3; Kirstie Ball, *Elements of Surveillance: A New Framework and Future Directions*, 5 Info. Comm'n & Soc'y 639 (2009).

nor do they depend on a centralized authority to administer them. Instead, they are most powerful when they are most widely dispersed among the civil and market institutions that govern everyday life.

Other effects of surveillance are spatial. Surveillance reorders the spaces of everyday life in ways that channel embodied behavior and foreclose unexpected behavior. Processes of boundary management operate along dimensions that are spatial and material as well as informational.[18] When, surveillance inculcates norms of pervasive, continual observation and tracking, those norms shape both behavior and sense of identity. The awareness of surveillance fosters a kind of passivity – a ceding of power over space. As the geographer Hille Koskela puts it, visual surveillance constitutes space as a "container" for passive objects.[19] It instills an expectation of being surveilled and (contrary to the conventional legal wisdom about reasonable expectations and the contours of privacy) that reasonable expectation is precisely the problem: it normalizes the disciplinary effects of surveillance, making them more difficult to contest.

Surveillance also alters the affective dimension of everyday spaces. Koskela observes that "to be under surveillance is an ambivalent emotional event," because "a surveillance camera ... can at the same time represent safety and danger."[20] This point contrasts usefully with U.S. privacy theorists' comparatively single-minded focus on the "chilling effect" of surveillance.[21] One may feel safer from crime in spaces subject to surveillance, but also more vulnerable to other unpredictable actions, including actions by those in authority. The spaces constituted by and for pervasive, continual observation are characterized by a condition of exposure, and exposure is a design principle that can be deployed to constrain and channel the behavior of surveilled subjects and populations.

Networked information and communication technologies intensify both the informational and spatial effects of surveillance. Self-development requires access to information, and it requires access to the various communities in which individual subjects claim (or might wish to explore) membership and the physical spaces where those communities are located. In an increasingly networked information society, all of those kinds of access increasingly are mediated by information platforms that use complex algorithms to offer or withhold content and to structure the presentation of content according to what is known or inferred about the searcher. Algorithmic mediation by mobile operating systems also structures experienced space, suggesting routes and offering or withholding suggestions about goods and services available along the way.

The configurations and affordances of networked information and communication technologies lend surveillance in postindustrial, digitally networked societies both extraordinary resilience and powerful normative force. Surveillance functionality enabled by digital sensors, networks, and databases has become deeply embedded within market and political institutions, resulting in a set of heterogeneous but interconnected data flows that are extraordinarily robust and impervious to disruption. Of critical importance to those arrangements, processes of data harvesting operate upon their subjects not

18 For more detailed discussion of privacy's spatial aspects, *see* Cohen, Configuring the Networked Self, *supra* note 9, at 120–25, 138–43.

19 Hille Koskela, *The Gaze without Eyes: Video Surveillance and the Changing Nature of Urban Space*, 24 Progress Hum. Geog. 243, 250 (2000).

20 *Id.* at 257.

21 *See, e.g.*, Neil M. Richards, *The Dangers of Surveillance*, 126 Harv. L. Rev. 1934 (2012).

only by the "normalized soul training" of Foucauldian theory, but also by seduction.[22] They promise a cornucopia of benefits and pleasures, including convenience, price discounts, enhanced services, entertainment, and social status. The surveillance society is not (necessarily) the grim dystopia that privacy advocates have assumed – and that privacy skeptics argue has failed to materialize. In return for its benefits and pleasures, however, the surveillance society demands full enrollment.

Additionally, the information platforms on which people increasingly rely – to connect and to further their own self-presentation – are designed to encourage and reward practices of self-exposure and peer exposure.[23] Although some may deplore the conduct exposed to public view, it is hard to look away. From nude selfies and #fail videos to leaks, hacks, and data breaches, the scandal and titillation that can result from practices of mediated exposure via information networks have become the morality plays of contemporary networked life. They operate as both spectacle and discipline, and through them surveillance becomes an exercise of distributed moral and political power.

Human beings, of course, are not only passive bodies, and may understand and interact with surveillant attention in varying ways. As explained previously, the everyday practice of situated subjects is complex and playful. People may take steps to obfuscate their own data trails or evade surveillant attention, and they also may pursue different forms of transparency and exposure for their own reasons. Sometimes, such practices of self-exposure can operate as resistance to narratives imposed by others.[24] Similarly, some consumers may be knowing and only partially compliant participants in their own seduction.

At the same time, however, pervasive, networked surveillance changes the consequences of selective self-exposure in unpredictable and often disorienting ways. As millions of subscribers to social-networking sites continue to learn, the ability to control the terms of self-exposure in networked space is largely illusory. Body images intended to assert feminist self-ownership are remixed as pornography. Revelations intended for particular social networks are accessed with relative ease by employers, police, and other authority figures.[25] Many employers now routinely search the Internet for information about prospective hires, and public authorities also seek to harness the distributed power of peer surveillance for their own purposes – for example, by requesting the identification of people photographed at protest rallies. Psychologists have long recognized that loss of control over personal space and its associated space-making mechanisms produces sensations of physical and emotional distress.[26] Similarly, when words and images voluntarily shared in one context reappear unexpectedly in another, the resulting sense of unwanted exposure and loss of control can be highly disturbing.

Ultimately, surveillant attention seeks to eliminate surprises. Surveillance directed toward informational transparency seeks to systematize, predict, and channel individual

[22] Kevin Haggerty & Richard V. Ericson, *The Surveillant Assemblage*, 51 Brit. J. Sociol. 605, 614–15 (2000); *see also* Mark Andrejevic, iSpy: Surveillance and Power in the Interactive Era (2007).

[23] *See* Kirstie S. Ball, *Exposure: Exploring the Subject of Surveillance*, 12 Info. Comm'n & Soc'y 639 (2009).

[24] *See, e.g.*, John McGrath, Loving Big Brother: Performance, Privacy, and Surveillance Space (2004); Hille Koskela, *Webcams, TV Shows, and Mobile Phones: Empowering Exhibitionism*, 2 Surveillance & Soc'y 199 (2004).

[25] *See* Jane Bailey & Ian Kerr, *Seizing Control? The Experience Capture Experiments of Ringley and Mann*, 9 Ethics Info. Tech. 129 (2007).

[26] *See* Irving Altman, The Environment and Social Behavior: Privacy, Personal Space, Territory, Crowding 156–61 (1975).

behavior. Toward that end, it works to make its subjects more amenable to observation, prediction, and suggestion. In so doing, however, it imposes its own logics, presumptions, and biases. Surveillance directed toward exposure seeks to prevent unsystematized, unpredictable differences from emerging. Toward that end, it works to instill expectations of continual observation. In so doing, however, it alters the capacity of places to function as contexts within which identity is developed and performed. As reliance on digital tools and platforms deepens, pervasive data harvesting and exposure become not only ordinary and expected but also desirable. If the right to privacy is to consist of anything more than post hoc ratification of whatever residual degree of privacy currently comports with the socially, politically, and institutionally constructed reasonable expectations that ordinary people have, it needs to take account of these interlinked, mutually reinforcing effects.

III Implications of Surveillance for Society

Why, though, should the law care about the ways that surveillance reshapes self-development? In particular, if pervasive, networked surveillance is a logical outgrowth of the ongoing shift from industrialism to informationalism, perhaps it is inevitable that privacy should gradually disappear. Put differently, perhaps privacy is an artifact not of liberal political thought, but rather of the system of industrial-era political economy with which liberalism was linked – a historical contingency rather than a necessary good, much less something to be claimed as a right.

For believers in deontological morality, it may be sufficient rebuttal to say that respect for individual dignity requires protection for privacy even at some cost to "innovation"; for others, however, it may be necessary to say more. This section develops three interrelated arguments about the social importance of privacy, each of which flows from the effects of pervasive, networked surveillance on self-development. The social implications of pervasive, networked surveillance extend across the domains of the state, civil society, and the market. In each domain, they are far too profound to write off as simply the aftereffects of progress.

A *Surveillance and Citizenship*

One obvious effect of the collision between surveillance and privacy is political.[27] Over the past several decades, scholars in a variety of fields have noted the seeming decline of liberal democracy and the ascendancy of new models of ostensibly democratic politics that blend populist and authoritarian elements.[28] Networked surveillance infrastructures fuel those developments in two interrelated ways. Citizens who are subject to pervasive, networked surveillance and modulation by powerful commercial and political interests increasingly lack the capacity to practice active, critical citizenship. Additionally, because the mechanisms of such surveillance and modulation typically are both secret

27 Portions of the discussion in this section are adapted from Cohen, *What Privacy Is For*, *supra* note 13 at 1912–18.

28 *See, e.g.*, Wendy Brown, *Neo-Liberalism and the End of Liberal Democracy*, 7 Theory & Event 1 (2003); David Harvey, *Neoliberalism as Creative Destruction*, 610 Annals Am. Acad. Pol. & Soc. Sci. 22 (2007); Thomas Lemke, *"The Birth of Bio-Politics": Michel Foucault's Lecture at the Collège de France on Neo-Liberal Governmentality*, 30 Econ. & Soc'y 190 (2001); Mark Tushnet. *Authoritarian Constitutionalism*, 100 Cornell L. Rev. 391 (2015).

and technologically opaque, they threaten to destroy the accountability on which the rule-of-law ideal depends.

Just as breathing space within the interstices of social control is foundational to the development of critical independence of mind, so it is foundational to the practice of informed and reflective citizenship. Critical citizenship requires habits of mind, of discourse, and of self-restraint that must be learned. Those are the very same habits that support a mature, critical subjectivity, and they require privacy to form. In systematically eradicating the breathing space necessary for self-development, pervasive, networked surveillance denies both critical subjectivity and critical citizenship the opportunity to flourish.

The pervasive spread of profit-driven patterning and modulation into areas such as search, social networking, and current events coverage infuses information access and social interaction with an instrumental, market-oriented sensibility. The modulated society is the consummate social and intellectual rheostat, continually adjusting the information environment to each individual's perceived or inferred comfort level. The unrelenting drive to fulfill revealed preferences, however, is antithetical to the practice of critical citizenship. Liberal democratic citizenship requires a certain amount of *dis*comfort – enough to motivate citizens to pursue improvements in the realization of political and social ideals. The modulated citizenry lacks the wherewithal and perhaps even the desire to practice that sort of citizenship.

Pervasive, networked surveillance also exploits the contemporary condition of information abundance to alter the character of political discourse more directly. Citizens who have Internet access experience "an unimaginably unmanageable flow of mediated information."[29] New platform-based information businesses offer ways of cutting through the clutter, but the resiting of power over information flow within platforms, databases, and algorithms means that meaning is easily – and inevitably – manipulated. The same techniques of mediation that present themselves as solutions to information abundance locate surveillance and modulation at the core of contemporary processes of information access and exchange.

One consequence of the pervasive intermediation of information flows is an electorate that is both increasingly divided and increasingly manipulable. Political candidates, political action committees, and other entities seeking to influence elections and shape public policy increasingly rely on algorithmic mediation of information flows to engage in microtargeting of information and political appeals to receptive audiences. For-profit content publishers exploit demographic and political correlations as well. Online audiences, for their part, cluster around information outlets that align with their political views, and also rely more and more heavily on news feeds curated by like-minded friends.[30] A wealth of social science research, however, shows that more homogeneous groups can more easily develop beliefs and perceptions of reality that are resistant to

29 Mark Andrejevic, Infoglut: How Too Much Information Is Changing the Way We Think and Know 2–3 (2013).

30 *See* Alex Thompson, *Journalists and Trump Voters Live in Separate Media Bubbles*, VICE News, Dec. 8 2016, https://news.vice.com/story/journalists-and-trump-voters-live-in-separate-online-bubbles-mit-analysis-shows; Julia Carrie Wong, Sam Levin, & Olivia Solon, *Bursting the Facebook Bubble: We Asked Voters on the Left and Right to Swap Feeds*, The Guardian, Nov. 16, 2016, https://www.theguardian.com/us-news/2016/nov/16/facebook-bias-bubble-us-election-conservative-liberal-news-feed.

external challenge.[31] Ideological and cultural homogeneity produces complacency, reinforces existing biases, and inculcates resistance to contradictory facts, leading to polarization of wider debates on issues of public importance.

Recent developments bear out these predictions about the polarization of public discourse and of political culture more broadly. As in-group "filter bubbles" have become more pronounced, crossing cultural and ideological lines has become more difficult.[32] Both the recent "Brexit" vote in the United Kingdom and the selection of Donald Trump as the President of the United States have focused attention on the nativist fears and resentments of an angry, largely white, and newly cohesive economic underclass. Although the filter bubble effect did not produce the economic stratification that has become so pronounced in both countries, it contributed to the growth and entrenchment of sharply divergent narratives about the linkages among trade, immigration, and economic prosperity, and to the sense of surprise expressed by wealthier and more cosmopolitan voters who had been insulated from the concerns of their less fortunate neighbors by their own media bubbles.[33]

Additionally, the opacity that surrounds pervasive, networked surveillance raises the prospect of secret, unaccountable exercises of power – of government not by laws but rather by powerful corporate entities. Within contemporary systems of pervasive, networked surveillance, both the data and the analytics are maintained as proprietary trade secrets that function as sources of comparative advantage.[34] There is mounting evidence that techniques for mediating and modulating information flows can be used to alter user behavior. Facebook has publicly acknowledged conducting experiments on how personalization of the content in news feeds can affect users' moods and other experiments reminding users to go to the polls and vote, and Google's chief economist has characterized Google's user base as subjects for experimentation.[35] No laws currently require information businesses to disclose the details of such experiments; nor do information businesses consider themselves bound by ethical guidelines similar to those that constrain human subject experimentation in other contexts.

Liberal democracy has always been an ideal to be pursued and approximated, and a polity's ability to approximate liberal democracy has both institutional and material preconditions. For example, in the generations following the framing of the U.S. Constitution, those who sought to build a functioning liberal democracy had to contend with the gulf between liberalism's aspirations to egalitarianism and the concentration of political power in an entitled minority of landed white males, many of whom also owned slaves. In the generations to come, those who seek to maintain a functioning liberal

[31] For good summaries, *see* Danielle Keats Citron, Hate Crimes in Cyberspace 56–72 (2015); Cass Sunstein, *Believing False Rumors*, in The Offensive Internet 91–106 (Martha C. Nussbaum & Saul Levmore eds., 2010).

[32] *See* Eli Pariser, The Filter Bubble: What the Internet Is Hiding from You (2011); *see also* Andrejevic, Infoglut, *supra* note 29. For an example of the way that group affiliation shapes online communication styles, *see* Karolina Sylwester & Matthew Purver, *Twitter Language Use Reflects Psychological Differences between Democrats and Republicans*, 10 PLoS ONE 9: e0137422 (2015).

[33] *See* Thompson, *supra* note 30; Wong, Levin, & Solon, *supra* note 30; Katharine Viner, *How Technology Disrupted the Truth*, The Guardian, July 12, 2016, https://www.theguardian.com/media/2016/jul/12/how-technology-disrupted-the-truth.

[34] *See generally* Frank Pasquale, The Black Box Society (2015).

[35] *See* James Grimmelmann, *The Law and Ethics of Experiments on Social Media Users*, 13 Colo. Tech. L.J. 219 (2015); Hal R. Varian, *Beyond Big Data*, 49 Bus. Econ. 27 (2014).

democracy will need to contend with the gulf between liberalism's aspirations to self-government by an informed and vigilant citizenry and the relatively blunted capacities of a modulated citizenry. They will also need to contend with all of the ways that opaque, algorithmic mediation of information and communication flows jeopardizes commitments to open, democratically accountable processes of public decision making. The liberal democratic society will cease to be a realistic aspiration unless serious attention is given to the conditions that produce both active, engaged citizens and transparent, accountable governance institutions.

B *Surveillance and Civil Society*

What I have said about the effects of surveillance on the practice of citizenship also holds true for the relationship between surveillance and civil society more generally. Privacy fosters interpersonal dynamics that strengthen the social fabric. Pervasive, networked surveillance weakens the foundations of civil society, replacing diverse, ideologically porous communities with more rigid hierarchies and divisions that foster intolerance and incivility.

The privacy embedded in social practices of boundary management by situated subjects preserves room for the development of a critical, playful subjectivity that is always-already intersubjective – informed by the values of families, confidants, communities, and cultures. Put differently, privacy and community are two halves of a cohesive and durable whole. Privacy shelters emerging subjectivity by preventing the seamless imposition of patterns predetermined by others, and it shelters the processes of communication and interchange that can enable new relationships and patterns to form – sometimes in ways that cross or challenge preexisting boundaries.

The processes of social sorting and segmentation that result from pervasive commercial surveillance eliminate the diversity and serendipity required to build robust communal ties. As processes of commercial and government surveillance construct and reify population cohorts based on difference, they create and entrench distinctions and hierarchies among surveilled populations. Many such hierarchies revolve around socioeconomic status, and often play out in ways that also reflect and reinforce racial privilege and racial division. Scholars in surveillance studies have documented the use of surveillance techniques within modern social welfare states to control underprivileged, often minority populations.[36] As discussed in more detail later, similar techniques of economic and racial segmentation play an increasingly prominent role in today's information-intensive, mediated markets. Additionally, the filter bubble effect described in the previous section feeds the emergence of polarized and seemingly irreconcilable worldviews. The consequences of these practices reverberate throughout civil society. They minimize connection and commonality and magnify intergroup resentments and suspicions.

The affordances of networked information technologies also facilitate new kinds of incivility that both feed on and reinforce polarization. Networked information technologies

[36] *See* John Gilliom, Overseers of the Poor: Surveillance, Resistance, and the Limits of Privacy (2001); Oscar H. Gandy Jr., *Data Mining, Surveillance, and Discrimination in the Post-9/11 Environment*, in The New Politics of Surveillance and Visibility 363 (Kevin D. Haggerty & Richard V. Ericson eds., 2006); Michele E. Gilman, *The Class Differential in Privacy Law*, 77 Bklyn. L. Rev. 1389 (2012); Torin Monahan, ed., Surveillance and Security: Technological Politics and Power in Everyday Life (2006).

are widely and justly celebrated for lowering the costs of connecting affinity groups, facilitating distributed processes of information production, and organizing collective action. In networked spaces populated by likeminded, similarly situated individuals, however, affinity groups can become echo chambers. Crowd-based judgments about relevance can create information cascades that lend sensationalized, defamatory, and hurtful online material extraordinary staying power. Affordances for collective action can prompt the rapid formation of angry, vengeful mobs, eager to shame real or apparent transgressors. In particular, women and members of racial, sexual, and religious minorities often become targets of mob-based harassment.[37]

In brief, choices about privacy are constitutive not simply of civil society, as some privacy theorists have argued, but of a particular type of civil society that prizes particular types of communities, relationships, and subjects.[38] In this respect, protection for privacy functions as a sort of social Rorschach test: It exemplifies a culture's normative, collective commitments regarding both the scope of movement – both literal and metaphorical – accorded to its members and the robustness of the resulting social fabric. Pervasive, networked surveillance undermines those commitments.

C *Surveillance and Markets*

Third and finally, pervasive, networked surveillance distorts the operation of markets for consumer products and services.[39] In capitalist societies and in liberal political theory more generally, markets play an important governance role. At least according to theory, markets are supposed to be both equality-promoting and self-correcting. Under conditions of pervasive, networked surveillance, they are neither.

Recall from Part I that commercial surveillance practices are first and foremost mechanisms for consumer surplus extraction. At the most general level, modulation of surveillant attention operationalizes a system for identifying (or inferring) consumers' interests and predicting what consumers would be willing to pay to satisfy those interests. For more complex goods that entail ongoing allocation of risk, predictive analytics assist providers in determining what terms to be willing to offer. The purpose of commercial surveillance, in other words, is to identify and systematize consumers as sources of both profit and potential loss.

In general, critiques of those practices by legal scholars and policy makers have followed the paths suggested by liberal anxieties about autonomy and paternalism. Those anxieties suggest certain types of objections to commercial surveillance and modulation of consumer behavior, which in previous work I have called the diminished autonomy and invidious discrimination objections, respectively.[40] We might not want to respect people's preferences to disclose certain kinds of personal information in exchange for

37 *See* Citron, Hate Crimes in Cyberspace, *supra* note 31; Whitney Phillips, This Is Why We Can't Have Nice Things: Mapping the Relationship between Online Trolling and Popular Culture (2015); *see also* Martha C. Nussbaum, *Objectification and Internet Misogyny*, in The Offensive Internet 68 (Martha C. Nussbaum & Saul Levmore eds., 2010).

38 *See* Ferdinand Schoeman, Privacy and Social Freedom (1992); Robert C. Post, *The Social Foundations of Privacy: Community and Self in the Common Law Tort*, 77 Cal. L. Rev. 957 (1989).

39 Portions of this section are adapted from Julie E. Cohen, *Irrational Privacy?* 10 J. Telecomm. & High Tech. L. 241 (2012).

40 *See id*. at 245–46.

perceived market benefits if the people in question lack the capacity for informed choice. Similarly, we might not want to respect the preferences of consumer-facing businesses to condition the provision of goods or services on particular disclosures, or to respect the preferences of employers to hire only certain kinds of people, if the preferences simply reflect bias and are harmful to society. More generally, as Ryan Calo points out, we might simply conclude that certain kinds of information are both irrelevant and too distracting; in such cases, privacy facilitates the transaction-specific trust that enables markets to form, scale up, and persist.[41] These objections seem to dictate limited interventions aimed at narrow sets of particularly egregious practices,[42] but they do not disturb the background presumption of autonomy, which suggests that we ought to let consumers and prospective employees make their own choices most of the time. Nor do they disturb the equally fundamental background presumption that ordinarily, in markets characterized by freely flowing information, consumers' choices will operate to discipline the conduct of businesses and employers.

The impact of pervasive, networked surveillance on markets is even more profound than the conventional critiques recognize, however. We have already seen some of the ways that data harvesting, modulation of surveillant attention, and mediation of information flows alter the character of political discourse and rupture the fabric of civil society. Those activities also alter the operation of markets. Conventional wisdom about markets has long held that better information about both goods and participants can only improve the functioning of the market mechanism – that freely flowing information will produce the most frictionless and responsive markets, and that the most frictionless markets will produce the fairest distribution of benefits and penalties. But the conventional wisdom is wrong. The increased variety and granularity of the information collected via pervasive, networked surveillance profoundly disrupt the governance function of markets.

The contemporary condition of information abundance creates new asymmetries and inequalities that revolve around access to data and capacity for data processing.[43] Put simply, well-resourced entities that can capture, store, and process data on a massive scale enjoy enormous marketplace advantages when transacting with ordinary consumers. For ordinary people, the increasing amounts of information associated with even basic consumer products can be bewildering.[44] In markets for information-related goods and services, consumer awareness is easy to manipulate more directly, either by tailoring promotions and disclosures to consumers with particular profiles or by versioning the goods or services in ways that embed material nonprice terms within price discrimination frameworks.[45] Reliance on search tools provided by other participants in the data

41 Ryan Calo, *Privacy and Markets: A Love Story*, 91 NOTRE DAME L. REV. 649 (2016); *see also* William McGeveran, *The Law of Friction*, 2013 U. CHI. LEGAL F. 15 (2013).

42 For examples of proposed approaches based on limited interventions of this sort, *see* the White House, *Consumer Data Privacy in a Networked World: A Framework for Protecting Privacy and Innovation in the Global Digital Economy*, Feb. 2012, https://www.whitehouse.gov/sites/default/files/privacy-final.pdf; Executive Office of the President, *Big Data and Differential Pricing*, Feb. 2015, https://www.whitehouse.gov/sites/default/files/docs/Big_Data_Report_Nonembargo_v2.pdf.

43 *See generally* Andrejevic, INFOGLUT, *supra* note 29, at 15–18; *see also* Calo, *supra* note 41, at 671–73.

44 For example, on the informationalization of food, *see* Lisa Heinzerling, *The Varieties and Limits of Transparency in U.S. Food Law*, 70 FOOD & DRUG L. J. 11 (2015).

45 *See* Andrew D. Gershoff, Ran Kivetz & Anat Keinan, *Consumer Response to Versioning: How Brands' Production Methods Affect Perceptions of Unfairness*, 39 J. CONSUMER RES. 382 (2012); Hal R. Varian,

harvesting economy to help consumers sort through the barrage of offers and promotions may actually make matters worse.

At the same time, information abundance and mediated access also raise fundamental challenges for the various legal institutions that regulate information markets. For example, consumer protection regulators typically seek both to require disclosure of material information and to prevent marketing practices that are deceptive or that prey upon vulnerable populations, but both strategies become much more difficult when market participants can cheaply and easily use other information channels to route around regulatory roadblocks.[46]

As a result, modulated markets are anything but equalizing. To the contrary, pervasive, networked surveillance is rapidly producing a system characterized by preferential treatment for the wealthy and the maximum extraction of consumer surplus from everyone else.[47] For favored consumers, privileges may include price discounts, enhanced products and services, more convenient access to resources, and heightened social status.[48] For less favored consumers, the consequences of commercial profiling are quite different, and may include reduced access or limited functionality, a constricted universe of employment opportunities, and disadvantageous or abusive credit terms.[49]

Finally, under conditions of pervasive, networked surveillance, market processes also lose the capacity for self-correction. Modulated markets work to alienate consumers from their own data as an economic resource, and from their own preferences and reservation prices as potentially equalizing factors in market transactions. But consumers who lack control over those items of information cannot use that control to discipline producers in any of the traditional ways. Neither exit nor voice is feasible when one's counterpart already knows exactly how far it can go.[50] Modulated markets strip away opportunities for bargaining and arbitrage, reshaping demand to match supply. For the same reasons, modulated markets are far more difficult for would-be competitors to disrupt.

In short, although advocates for the information industries characterize practices of data harvesting and modulation as market-facilitating, the changes now under way as a result of pervasive, networked surveillance are altering consumer markets beyond recognition. Choices about privacy therefore are also constitutive of markets as markets, and are essential to preserving the marketplace mechanism in the form that Anglo-American political culture purports to value.

Versioning Information Goods, in INTERNET PUBLISHING AND BEYOND: THE ECONOMICS OF DIGITAL INFORMATION AND INTELLECTUAL PROPERTY 190 (Brian Kahin & Hal R. Varian eds., 2000); Lauren Willis, *Performance-Based Consumer Regulation*, 82 U. CHI. L. REV. 1309, 1321–26 (2015) (summarizing research on consumer manipulation).

46 *See* Julie E. Cohen, *The Regulatory State in the Information Age*, 17 THEOR. INQ. L. 369, 385–87 (2016).

47 The classic study of marketplace sorting is Oscar H. Gandy, JR., THE PANOPTIC SORT: A POLITICAL ECONOMY OF PERSONAL INFORMATION (1993).

48 For a detailed exploration of these processes, *see* Andrejevic, iSpy, *supra* note 22.

49 *See* Solon Barocas & Andrew Selbst, *Big Data's Disparate Impact*, 104 CAL. L. REV. 671 (2016); Seeta Gangadharan, *Digital Inclusion and Data Profiling*, FIRST MONDAY, May 19, 2012; Mary Madden, Michele Gilman, Karen Levy & Alice Marwick, *The Class Differential in Privacy Vulnerability* (Working Paper 2016).

50 *See generally* Albert O. Hirschman, EXIT, VOICE, AND LOYALTY: RESPONSES TO DECLINE IN FIRMS, ORGANIZATIONS, AND STATES (1970).

Conclusion

Both "privacy" and "surveillance" refer to complex sets of processes and sociotechnical conditions. That complexity too often masks an essential reality: the processes and conditions that produce privacy or surveillance are contingent and chosen, not natural and inevitable. Making those choices requires attention to both benefits and costs. While surveillance may produce efficiency benefits, loss of privacy implicates both individual interests in self-development and collective interests in individual and social well-being. Privacy is an indispensable structural feature of liberal democratic political systems, of a flourishing civil society, and of functioning markets. Legally enforceable rights to privacy function – or should – to set limits on surveillance in ways that preserve the breathing room for boundary management on which the condition of privacy depends.

20 Intellectual and Social Freedom

Margot E. Kaminski[†]

Surveillance threatens intellectual and social freedom. Both courts and legislators have recognized these threats. While this chapter focuses on United States law and legal literature, the notions of intellectual freedom and social freedom are global. This chapter offers an overview of the sources of United States legal protections for intellectual and social freedom in the face of surveillance, charts their development over time, notes their limitations, and briefly discusses recent trends and ongoing disputes.

I Intellectual and Social Freedom: An Overview

Intellectual freedom consists of the freedom to form ideas and make up one's own mind.[1]

Intellectual freedom is broader than, and sometimes understood to be the foundation of, freedom of speech. It includes the ability not just to speak freely, but to gather information, make decisions about what ideas to ingest, and think. You cannot speak freely if you have no idea of what you want to say. The freedom to explore ideas is thus a necessary precursor to freedom of expression.[2]

Intellectual freedom is also necessary for effective democratic self-governance. Intellectual freedom is central to the decision-making process of citizens in the idealized democratic state. If the idealized democratic state consists of individuals making

† Associate Professor, University of Colorado Law School.

1 Legal scholars have written at great length about the connections between privacy and intellectual and social freedoms. This footnote offers references to these scholars for further reading. *See* Marc Jonathan Blitz, *Constitutional Safeguards for Silent Experiments in Living: Libraries, the Right to Read, and a First Amendment Theory for an Unaccompanied Right to Receive Information*, 74 UMKC L. Rev. 799, 799–809 (2006); Julie E. Cohen, *A Right to Read Anonymously: A Closer Look at "Copyright Management" in Cyberspace*, 28 Conn. L. Rev. 981, 981–83 (1996); A. Michael Froomkin, *Anonymity and Its Enmities*, 1995 J. Online L. art. 4, ¶¶ 44–46 (1995), http://groups.csail.mit.edu/mac/classes/6.805/articles/anonymity/froomkin.html; A. Michael Froomkin, *Flood Control on the Information Ocean: Living with Anonymity, Digital Cash, and Distributed Databases*, 15 J.L. & Com. 395 (1996); Seth F. Kreimer, *Sunlight, Secrets, and Scarlet Letters: The Tension between Privacy and Disclosure in Constitutional Law*, 140 U. Pa. L. Rev. 1, 12, 69–71 (1991); Lyrissa Barnett Lidsky, *Silencing John Doe: Defamation and Discourse in Cyberspace*, 48 Duke L. J. 855 (2000); Lyrissa Barnett Lidsky, *Anonymity in Cyberspace: What Can We Learn from John Doe?*, 50 B.C. L. Rev. 1373, 1378 (2009); Neil M. Richards, *Intellectual Privacy*, 87 Tex. L. Rev. 387, 387–93 (2008); Lee Tien, *Who's Afraid of Anonymous Speech? McIntyre and the Internet*, 75 Or. L. Rev. 117, 128–31 (1996). Neil Richards has also written a book on the subject. Neil M. Richards, Intellectual Privacy: Rethinking Civil Liberties in the Digital Age (2015).

2 *See, e.g.*, Seana Valentine Shiffrin, *A Thinker-Based Approach to Freedom of Speech*, 27 Const. Comment. 283 (2011).

informed and autonomous political choices, intellectual freedom is necessary for that process. Citizens need the freedom to read op-eds and articles, watch the news, and ruminate in private to arrive at political choices that best represent their interests. Absent intellectual freedom, political freedom would be threatened.

Intellectual freedom is essential to self-creation. Individuals form and develop their selfhood by consuming ideas and defining their identities in conjunction with or in opposition to those ideas. If one believes in the autonomous, liberal self, then intellectual freedom is a core component of that self's autonomy. If one believes that selfhood is a more complicated behavioral proposition, intellectual freedom is still crucial to identity formation and to preserving space for play in selfhood.[3]

Social freedom as discussed in this chapter is closely related to intellectual freedom. Individuals form social identities by associating and affiliating with groups. Individual identity is in constant play with social identity. Social freedom allows individuals to associate with and organize into groups, enabling information flows and identity formation, and providing strength in numbers. Like intellectual freedom, social freedom is necessary for both self-governance and the formation of individual identity.

Surveillance threatens both intellectual freedom and social freedom. Social science suggests that individuals are less likely to communicate freely about deviant ideas if they know that somebody is watching. A classic study suggesting this effect was conducted by Gregory White and Philip Zimbardo in the late 1970s.[4] The researchers told their student subjects that they were being videotaped, and half the subjects were told that the videotape would be given to the police and FBI for training purposes. The researchers then asked the subjects to give a talk on marijuana possession and legalization. Only a subset of each group was videotaped; the others were told that the video camera was broken and no tape would be shared with the police and FBI. The results were striking. While 73 percent of students who were not surveilled advocated marijuana legalization, only 44 percent of those in the surveilled group did.[5] The researchers concluded that not only were those under surveillance less likely to advocate legalization or reduction in penalties, but the mere threat of surveillance "exerts a powerful influence over behavior, beliefs, and feelings, whether or not that threat is realized."[6]

Other studies support this idea that surveillance leads individuals to conform to group norms. Several researchers have found that people conform to more accepted behavior when a surveillance cue – such as an image of watching eyes – is present. In one study, a picture of eyes above a collection box caused people to contribute nearly three times as much money to pay for office coffee and tea.[7] In another, littering in a cafeteria dropped by half when researchers placed posters with eyes on the walls.[8] In a third study,

[3] Julie Cohen, Configuring the Networked Self: Law, Code, and the Play of Everyday Practice, 16–20 (2012).

[4] Gregory L. White & Philip G. Zimbardo, *The Effects of Threat of Surveillance and Actual Surveillance on Expressed Opinions toward Marijuana*, 111 J. Soc. Psychol. 49, 59 (1980).

[5] Of the students 67 percent were marijuana users. *Id.* at 58.

[6] *Id.* at 59.

[7] Melissa Bateson, Daniel Nettle & Gilbert Roberts, *Cues of Being Watched Enhance Cooperation in a Real-World Setting*, 2 Biology Letters 412, 412 (2006).

[8] Max Ernest-Jones, Daniel Nettle & Melissa Bateson, *Effects of Eye Images on Everyday Cooperative Behavior: A Field Experiment*, 32 Evolution & Hum. Behav. 172, 174–75 (2011).

researchers observed a 60 percent drop in bicycle thefts when placing eyes above a bicycle rack with the words "Cycle Thieves, We Are Watching You."[9]

Surveillance leads individuals to avoid not just deviant communication and deviant behavior, but deviant information gathering. A 2015 cross-national study suggests that after the 2013 revelations of NSA surveillance, Google's users were less likely to use both search terms they believed might get them in trouble with the United States government and search terms rated as personally sensitive.[10] Similarly, a 2016 study found that traffic to Wikipedia articles on controversial topics decreased after the Snowden leaks.[11] In both studies, surveillance led to a chill in intellectual inquiry, particularly in topics that subjects believed were controversial.

A more humorous – and less scientific – illustration of this phenomenon is a *Saturday Night Live* skit from 2012.[12] The skit spoofed an advertisement for an Amazon Kindle e-book reader. It suggested that what Mother wanted for Mother's Day was a Kindle, so that nobody would know she was reading *Fifty Shades of Grey*, a kinky romance novel. If Mother had privacy, she would read risqué books. If not, she would lose her freedom to read the substance of her choice. Of course, the Kindle e-reader is far less private in practice than a print book, since Amazon knows exactly what its readers are reading, including what they reread and where they linger.[13]

Librarians have historically embraced the notion that surveillance of readers impinges upon intellectual freedom. In 1939, the American Library Association (ALA) adopted its Code of Ethics, which includes a statement that "it is the librarian's obligation to treat as confidential any private information obtained through contact with library patrons."[14] The ALA reiterated this commitment to confidentiality in its 1975 Statement on Professional Ethics, during a period of heightened conflict with government officials over surveillance of patron records.[15] In the 1970s, IRS agents requested circulation records from public libraries; the ALA responded by condemning the requests as unconstitutional invasions of privacy.[16] In the early 1970s, the Federal Bureau of Investigation (FBI) targeted academic libraries for surveillance of Vietnam War protestors.[17] In response, the

9 Daniel Nettle, Kenneth Nott & Melissa Bateson, *"Cycle Thieves, We Are Watching You": Impact of a Simple Signage Intervention against Bicycle Theft*, 7 PLOS ONE, Dec. 2012, at 1–2, http://www.plosone.org/article/info%3Adoi%2F10.1371%2Fjournal.pone.0051738.

10 Alex Marthews & Catherine Tucker, *The Impact of Online Surveillance On Behavior*, *in* THE CAMBRIDGE HANDBOOK OF SURVEILLANCE LAW (David Gray & Stephen Henderson, eds., 2017); Alex Marthews & Catherine Tucker, Government Surveillance and Internet Search Behavior (Apr. 29, 2015) (unpublished manuscript), http://ssrn.com/abstract=2412564.

11 Jonathon W. Penney, *Chilling Effects: Online Surveillance and Wikipedia Use*, 31 BERKELEY TECH. L.J. 117 (2016), http://papers.ssrn.com/sol3/papers.cfm?abstract_id=2769645.

12 *Saturday Night Live: Amazon Mother's Day Ad* (NBC television broadcast May 5, 2012), http://www.nbc.com/saturday-night-live/video/amazon-mothers-day-ad/ n13488.

13 *See* Alexandra Alter, *Your E-Book Is Reading You*, WALL ST. J. (July 19, 2012), http://online.wsj.com/news/articles/SB10001424052702304870304577490950051438304.

14 Office of Intellectual Freedom, Am. Library Ass'n, INTELLECTUAL FREEDOM MANUAL 191, 257 (7th ed. 2006) [hereinafter INTELLECTUAL FREEDOM MANUAL].

15 *Statement on Professional Ethics, 1975*, AM. LIBRARY ASS'N (Aug. 26, 1979),http://www.ala.org/advocacy/proethics/history/index3.

16 Herbert N. Foerstel, SURVEILLANCE IN THE STACKS: THE FBI'S LIBRARY AWARENESS PROGRAM 4–6 (1991) (recounting confrontations between FBI agents and librarians regarding the Library Awareness Program).

17 INTELLECTUAL FREEDOM MANUAL, *supra* note 14, at 297.

ALA passed a resolution condemning government spying, and resolving that librarians should not voluntarily hand over patron records to the government.[18] From 1973 to 1976 and again beginning in 1985, the FBI ran a Library Awareness Program through which it sought out reader records, against the strong opposition of librarians.[19] In response to government surveillance attempts, librarians successfully lobbied for library privacy laws in states around the country.[20] Librarians failed, however, to stop the adoption of Section 215 of the USA PATRIOT Act in 2001, which permits the government to request "any tangible things (including books, records, papers, documents, and other items," including "library circulation records" (with the latter language adopted explicitly in 2006).[21]

Surveillance threatens not just intellectual but social freedom because it can threaten the formation of minority groups and political engagement. Surveillance has been asserted as a mechanism of social control, to prevent political and intellectual minorities from gathering, accumulating membership, or asserting social presence and power. In East Germany, the Stasi kept files on nearly 6 million of its approximately 16 million citizens, to squelch dissent.[22] In the United States, the FBI repeatedly and famously targeted and spied on political subversives, including Martin Luther King Jr., as part of a broader effort to isolate politically active government critics.[23] These systemic approaches to surveillance were aimed not just at information gathering, but at asserting control over the formation of ideas and social groups.

The U.S. government's interest in obtaining information about the formation of ideas and social groups extends into the present. In 1997, the Drug Enforcement Administration (DEA) sought the identities of Arizona residents who purchased a book on how to grow marijuana.[24] In 1998, Kenneth Starr subpoenaed Monica Lewinsky's book purchase records.[25] In 2006, the U.S. attorney subpoenaed Amazon for the used book purchase records of more than twenty-four thousand people.[26] The Internal Revenue Service recently asked nonprofits for reading lists. In response, members of the Tea Party,

[18] Foerstel, *supra* note 16, at 9.

[19] *Id.* at 14, 54–71 (recounting confrontations between FBI agents and librarians regarding the Library Awareness Program).

[20] *State Privacy Laws Regarding Library Records*, Am. Library Ass'n,http://www.ala.org/advocacy/privacy-confidentiality/privacy/stateprivacy; *see also* Anne Klinefelter, *Library Standards for Privacy: A Model for the Digital World?* 11 N.C. J.L. & Tech. 553 app. (2010); BJ Ard, *Confidentiality and the Problem of Third Parties: Protecting Reader Privacy in the Age of Intermediaries*, 16 Yale J.L. & Tech. 1 (2013)

[21] USA PATRIOT Act of 2001, Pub. L. No. 107–56, 115 Stat. 272; USA PATRIOT Act Additional Reauthorizing Amendments Act of 2006, Pub. L. No. 109–178, 120 Stat. 278.

[22] Andrew Curry, *Piercing Together the Dark Legacy of East Germany's Secret Police*, Wired (Jan. 18, 2008), http://www.wired.com/2008/01/ff-stasi/ (noting that the agency indexed 5.6 million names in its central card catalog, which "helped the Stasi quell dissent").

[23] David J. Garrow, The FBI and Martin Luther King, Jr. (1980).

[24] Henry K. Lee, *Dope on Pot Book Buyers Sought: DEA Subpoenas Publisher for List of Manual Purchasers*, S.F. Chron., Oct. 29, 1997, at A19, http://www.sfgate. com/news/article/Dope-on-Pot-Book-Sought-DEA-Subpoenas-2824507.php.

[25] *See In re* Grand Jury Subpoena to Kramerbooks & Afterwords Inc., 26 Med. L. Rptr. 1599, 1599 (D.D.C. 1998).

[26] Sealed Order at 1, *In re* Grand Jury Subpoena to Amazon.com, No. 07-GJ-04 (W.D. Wis. Aug. 7, 2006), http://dig.csail.mit.edu/2007/12/In-re-grand-jury-sub poena-amazon.PDF; Ryan J. Foley, *U.S. Withdraws Subpoena Seeking Identity of 24,000 Amazon Customers Sought as Witnesses*, Assoc. Press (Nov. 27, 2007), https://www.highbeam.com/doc/1A1-D8T66MU81.html.

a conservative American political movement, sent in the Constitution.[27] In New York City, the police for at least fourteen years monitored and mapped Muslim communities and their social and religious institutions, without any suspicion of wrongdoing, before agreeing to a settlement in January 2016 (the revised settlement was approved in March 2017).[28] And in 2016, lawmakers were attempting to advance legislation that would allow the FBI to obtain Internet browsing information without a warrant, using far less protective national security letters.[29] FBI Director James Comey described this as the bureau's top legislative priority for the year.[30]

Surveillance asserts control over intellectual and social freedom by taking advantage of human propensities for both conformity and fear. Surveillance threatens intellectual and social freedom when a person fears that there will be retaliation for membership in a particular group, or identification with particular ideas. Surveillance also threatens intellectual and social freedom by exploiting human inclinations toward conformity with group norms.[31] It is not the case that people change their habits and minds only when threatened with physical violence or economic repercussions. People also change their minds and behavior when they think somebody is watching them, and that their behavior deviates from group norms. Observing a phenomenon called the "spiral of silence," researchers have shown that individuals are less likely to speak up if they believe they are in the minority.[32] Surveillance thus threatens social and intellectual freedom not only because individuals may choose to dissociate from ideas and groups out of fear of retaliation, but because individuals will often eschew minority viewpoints and affiliations if they believe they are being watched.

Since 2013, leaks by Edward Snowden and others have revealed the extent of the U.S. government's national security surveillance apparatus, which includes surveillance of reading and viewing material. One program, XKEYSCORE, was described in leaked documents as a tool to collect "nearly everything a user does on the Internet."[33] While it remains unclear what exactly the government does with this material, leaked documents suggest that the NSA monitored the pornography viewing habits of individuals

[27] Abby D. Phillip, *IRS Asks for Reading List, Tea Party Group Sends Constitution*, ABC News (May 14, 2013), http://abcnews.go.com/blogs/politics/2013/05/irs-asks-for-read ing-list-tea-party-group-sends-constitution/.

[28] *Factsheet: The NYPD Muslim Surveillance Program*, Am. Civil Liberties Union, https://www.aclu.org/factsheet-nypd-muslim-surveillance-program (last visited Sept. 17, 2016); *Raza v. City of New York – Legal Challenge to NYPD Muslim Surveillance Program*, Am. Civil Liberties Union (Jan. 7, 2016), https://www.aclu.org/cases/raza-v-city-new-york-legal-challenge-nypd-muslim-surveillance-program.

[29] Ellen Nakashima, *FBI Wants Access to Internet Browser History without a Warrant in Terrorism and Spy Cases*, Wash. Post (June 6, 2016), https://www.washingtonpost.com/world/national-security/fbi-wants-access-to-internet-browser-history-without-a-warrant-in-terrorism-and-spy-cases/2016/06/06/2d257328-2c0d-11e6-9de3-6e6e7a14000c_story.html.

[30] *Id.*

[31] Margot E. Kaminski & Shane Witnov, *The Conforming Effect: First Amendment Implications of Surveillance, Beyond Chilling Speech*, 49 U. Rich. L. Rev. 465 (2014). A similar observation that the subjects of studies will change their behavior as a result of knowledge that they are being studied is referred to in the literature as the "Hawthorne effect." *See, e.g.*, Rob McCarney et al., *The Hawthorne Effect: A Randomized, Controlled Trial*, 7 BioMed Cent. Med. Res. Methodology 30 (2007), https://www.ncbi.nlm.nih.gov/pmc/articles/PMC1936999/.

[32] Keith N. Hampton et al., Pew Research Ctr., Social Media and the Spiral of Silence 8, 3 (2014), http://www.pewinternet.org/files/2014/08/PI_Social-networks -and-debate_082614.pdf.

[33] Glenn Greenwald, *XKeyscore: NSA Tool Collects "Nearly Everything a User Does on the Internet,"* Guardian (July 31, 2013), http://www.theguardian.com/world/2013/jul/31/ nsa-top-secret-program-online-data.

as a means of potentially harming their reputations.[34] Another leaked document shows that government attention can be triggered by "searching the web for suspicious stuff."[35]

Disturbingly, the U.S. government appears to have targeted journalists for surveillance. In 2013, the Justice Department obtained two months of phone records for the Associated Press. This practice disclosed information about news-gathering operations that likely revealed the identity of sources, and relationships between news-gatherers.[36] While the U.S. Supreme Court has observed that journalists are not more deserving of constitutional protections than ordinary citizens,[37] targeting news gathering implicates the intellectual freedom of all citizens who rely on a free and critical press.[38] Moreover, even generalized surveillance has implications for a free press. A 2013 PEN America study of more than five hundred writers indicated that, since the Snowden leaks, 28 percent had curtailed social media activities while 24 percent had avoided certain topics in both phone and email conversations.[39]

The extent of national security surveillance has troubling implications for intellectual and social freedom not only in the United States but around the world. In the famous 2015 *Schrems* decision, the Court of Justice of the European Union invalidated the EU–U.S. Safe Harbor framework for transnational data transfers against the backdrop of U.S. national security surveillance.[40] Also in 2015, the Grand Chamber of the European Court of Human Rights unanimously held that secret interception of mobile phone communications violated Article 8 of the Convention for the Protection of Human Rights and Fundamental Freedoms, finding unacceptable "a system … which enables the secret service and the police to intercept directly the communications of each and every citizen without requiring them to show an interception authorisation."[41] Advocates in the United Kingdom have asked the European Court of Human Rights to release information about intelligence sharing between governments across borders, and challenged the UK government's mass surveillance regime.[42]

In 2015 the UN Human Rights Council established a new UN special rapporteur on "The Right to Privacy in the Digital Age," who delivered his first report in March

[34] *See* Glenn Greenwald, Ryan Gallagher & Ryan Grim, *Top-Secret Document Reveals NSA Spied on Porn Habits as Part of Plan to Discredit "Radicalizers,"* HUFFINGTON POST (Nov. 26, 2013), http://www.huffingtonpost.com/2013/11/26/nsa-porn-muslims_n_43 46128.html.

[35] NSA, *XKeyscore, PowerPoint Presentation*, Feb. 25, 2008, slide 15, *in XKeyscore Presentation from 2008*, GUARDIAN (July 31, 2013), http://www.theguardian.com/world/interactive/2013/jul/31/nsa-xkeyscore-program-full-presentation.

[36] Erik Wemple, *AP: Government Subpoenaed Journalists' Phone Records*, WASH. POST (May 13, 2013), https://www.washingtonpost.com/blogs/erik-wemple/wp/2013/05/13/ap-government-subpoenaed-journalists-phone-records/.

[37] *See Branzburg v. Hayes*, 408 U.S. 665, 682, 690–91 (1972).

[38] *See* Sonja West, *Press Exceptionalism*, 127 HARV. L. REV. 2434 (2014); Barry McDonald, *The First Amendment and the Free Flow of Information: Towards a Realistic Right to Gather Information in the Information Age*, 65 OHIO ST. L.J. 249 (2004).

[39] THE FDR GRP. & PEN AM. CTR., CHILLING EFFECTS: NSA SURVEILLANCE DRIVES U.S. WRITERS TO SELF-CENSOR 3–4 (Nov. 12, 2013) [hereinafter THE FDR GROUP], http://www.pen.org/sites/default/files/Chilling%20Effects_PEN%20American.pdf.

[40] *Schrems v. Data Protection Comm'r*, No. C-362/14 (H. Ct. of Ireland Oct. 6, 2015), http://curia.europa.eu/juris/documents.jsf?num=C-362/14.

[41] *Zakharov v. Russia*, No. 47143/06 (Eur. Ct. H.R. Dec. 4, 2015).

[42] *Privacy International v. United Kingdom*, PRIVACY INTERNATIONAL, https://privacyinternational.org/node/83; *Privacy International v. Secretary of State for the Foreign and Commonwealth Office et al.*, PRIVACY INTERNATIONAL, https://privacyinternational.org/node/66.

2016.[43] The special rapporteur affirmed that "there exists world-wide … a considerable legal framework which can be useful to the protection and promotion of privacy," including Article 12 of the Universal Declaration of Human Rights and Article 17 of the International Covenant on Civil and Political Rights.[44] He noted, however, that countries still struggle to define exactly what privacy is.[45]

As discussed previously, mass government surveillance appears to have affected both free speech and intellectual inquiries. Surveillance can change behavior, and when that behavior is intellectual inquiry, the consequences for a free society, and a free world, are troubling. Courts, lawmakers, and advocates are only beginning to react.

II Sources of Legal Protection for Intellectual and Social Freedom

The rest of this chapter discusses how intellectual and social freedom are protected in the United States. In the United States, aspects of both social and intellectual freedom are protected by the First Amendment to the Constitution, which protects the related freedoms of religion, speech, the press, association, and assembly. Courts have also protected intellectual and social freedom under the Fourth Amendment, which protects against unreasonable government searches and seizures. Both state and federal legislators, moreover, have enshrined protections for intellectual and social freedom in enacted laws. This section provides an introduction to the legal landscape on intellectual and social freedom and surveillance in the United States, starting with the First Amendment.

A *The First Amendment*

The First Amendment protects freedom of religion, speech, the press, assembly, and association.[46] The First Amendment's protections of freedom of speech have been justified under several theories, sometimes competing but often complementary. First, the First Amendment protects speech in order to facilitate the "marketplace of ideas," wherein individuals can shop among competing ideas in a search for overarching truth.[47] Second, the First Amendment protects speech in order to enable democratic self-governance, so that informed citizens can make decisions reflective of their political and social views.[48] Third, the First Amendment protects speech as an aspect of protecting individual autonomy.[49] There are other theories of the First Amendment, but these three – the

43 Nicholas Seidler, *UNHRC Creates New UN Special Rapporteur on "The Right to Privacy in the Digital Age,"* Internet Soc'y (Mar. 26, 2015), https://www.internetsociety.org/blog/public-policy/2015/03/unhrc-creates-new-un-special-rapporteur-%E2%80%9C-right-privacy-digital-age%E2%80%9D; Joseph A. Cannataci, Report of the Special Rapporteur on the right to privacy (2016), http://www.ohchr.org/Documents/Issues/Privacy/A-HRC-31–64.doc.

44 Statement by Mr. Joseph A. Cannataci, Special Rapporteur on the Right to Privacy (2016), http://www.ohchr.org/Documents/Issues/Privacy/SRonprivacy_Statement_HRC_9March2016.pdf.

45 *Id.*

46 Although freedom of religion can be understood as both an intellectual and social freedom, Establishment Clause jurisprudence represents a body of law unto itself that is beyond the scope of this chapter.

47 *See Abrams v. United States*, 250 U.S. 616, 630 (1919) (Holmes, J., dissenting).

48 *See* Alexander Meiklejohn, Political Freedom: The Constitutional Powers of the People, 27 (Galaxy Books 1965) (1948).

49 *See* Martin H. Redish, *The Value of Free Speech*, 130 U. Pa. L. Rev. 591, 593 (1982); C. Edwin Baker, *Scope of the First Amendment Freedom of Speech*, 25 UCLA L. Rev. 964, 966 (1978).

marketplace of ideas, democratic self-governance, and autonomy – are most frequently referenced by both courts and the legal literature.[50]

All three of these theories also justify the protection of a broader array of intellectual and social freedoms. If we seek to enable a robust marketplace of ideas, there must be some protection for freedom in information gathering, information consumption, decision making, and group association that helps spread ideas. If we protect speech as central to democratic self-governance, we must similarly afford at least some protection to the mechanisms by which political information is gathered, used, and spread. And if we protect speech as part of protecting individual autonomy, nothing is more central to individual autonomy than the ability to make up one's own identity and mind. For these reasons, some suggest that freedom of thought is central to First Amendment protection.[51] Freedom of speech follows from intellectual freedom, not the other way around.[52]

The Supreme Court has recognized First Amendment protection for both intellectual and social freedom. The Court has also recognized that privacy can be necessary to protect these freedoms.[53] Although direct First Amendment protection for privacy has significant limitations, discussed below, the Court has repeatedly recognized the connection between privacy and intellectual and social freedom.

The Court connected privacy protections to intellectual and social freedom in a series of cases assessing the constitutionality of registration requirements and the divulging of group membership lists. As early as 1945, the Supreme Court recognized in *Thomas v. Collins* that requiring an individual to register with the government before making a public speech impinged on both freedom of speech and freedom of assembly.[54] The appellant in *Thomas* was a union president, and vice president of the CIO, the parent organization of multiple local unions. He planned to give an address to a Texas union meeting, and was served a restraining order when he failed to comply with registration requirements. He addressed the meeting regardless, and was arrested for violating the temporary restraining order. The Court reasoned that it is "in our tradition to allow the widest room for discussion … particularly when this right [to free speech] is exercised in conjunction with peaceable assembly."[55] While suggesting that registration requirements could be permissible where the state has a valid interest in preventing a non-speech harm,[56] the Court explained that "if the exercise of the rights of free speech and

50 Robert C. Post, Citizens Divided: Campaign Finance Reform and the Constitution 8, 41 (2014); Jack M. Balkin, *Digital Speech and Democratic Culture: A Theory of Freedom of Expression for the Information Society*, 79 N.Y.U. L. Rev. 1, 3–4 (2004) (proposing that "the purpose of freedom of speech … is to promote a democratic culture" that "allows ordinary people to participate freely in the spread of ideas and in the creation of meanings that, in turn, help constitute them as persons").

51 Shiffrin, *supra* note 2; Jed Rubenfeld, *The Freedom of Imagination: Copyright's Constitutionality*, 112 Yale L.J. 1, 37 (2002).

52 *But see* Lawrence Byard Solum, *Freedom of Communicative Action: A Theory of the First Amendment Freedom of Speech*, 83 Nw. U. L. Rev. 54 (1989) (suggesting that the First Amendment is centrally concerned with a communicative moment).

53 *See* Neil M. Richards, *Intellectual Privacy*, 87 Tex. L. Rev. 387 (2008).

54 *Thomas v. Collins*, 323 U.S. 516, 539 (1945) (stating that "a requirement of registration in order to make a public speech would seem generally incompatible with an exercise of the rights of free speech and free assembly").

55 *Id.* at 530.

56 *Id.* at 540 ("Once the speaker goes further, however, and engages in conduct which amounts to more than the right of free discussion comprehends, as when he undertakes the collection of funds or securing subscriptions, he enters a realm where a reasonable registration or identification requirement may be

free assembly cannot be made a crime, we do not think this can be accomplished by the device of requiring previous registration as a condition for exercising them."[57] The Court was concerned with the registration requirement primarily because it acted as a prior restraint – preventing speech before it could be made – and a pretextual enforcement mechanism, allowing the government to pursue speakers for violating a registration requirement in lieu of pursuing them for their actual speech. In this *Thomas* decision, the Court was not yet explicitly concerned with privacy. Nonetheless, invalidating the registration requirement laid the groundwork for later cases.

In 1958, during the height of the civil rights movement in the United States, the Court more explicitly addressed the connection between intellectual and social freedom and privacy in *NAACP v. Alabama*.[58] The Court considered whether the state of Alabama could require the National Association for the Advancement of Colored People (NAACP) to turn over its membership lists. The Court found that freedom of association – or social freedom – required the protection of NAACP members' privacy. The NAACP had shown that identifying its rank-and-file members would expose them to serious reprisals, such as the loss of jobs and physical threats.[59] The Court found that this fear of reprisal created a deterrent effect on the right of association, which the state's purported interests did not outweigh.[60] Violating the privacy of NAACP members in their association with the NAACP, in other words, threatened their intellectual and social freedom.

NAACP v. Alabama is often cited for explicitly linking social freedom – that is, freedom of group association – with privacy protections. The Court explained that the "inviolability of privacy in group association may in many circumstances be indispensable to preservation of freedom of association, particularly where a group espouses dissident beliefs."[61] However, because the Court explicitly found a threat of reprisal, it was possible that the case would ultimately stand for the principle that privacy should be protected only when groups can show the possibility of economic or physical harm. Similarly, in the 1960 case *Bates v. Little Rock*, the Court again referenced the "substantial uncontroverted evidence that public identification of persons in the community as members of the [NAACP] had been followed by harassment and threats of bodily harm."[62] In *Bates*, the Court found that the government, an Arkansas municipality, had failed to show a compelling enough reason to obtain the names of members of a local branch of the NAACP.[63]

That same year, however, the Court found an identification requirement unconstitutional without requiring any allegation or showing of actual reprisals triggered by government registration or identification requirements. In 1960, the Court in *Talley*

imposed. In that context such solicitation would be quite different from the solicitation involved here. It would be free speech plus conduct akin to the activities which were present, and which it was said the State might regulate").

57 *Id.*

58 357 U.S. 449 (1958) (finding that members had been subjected "to economic reprisal, loss of employment, threat of physical coercion, and other manifestations of public hostility").

59 *Id.* at 462.

60 *Id.* at 463.

61 *Id.* at 462.

62 *Bates v. City of Little Rock*, 361 U.S. 516, 524 (1960).

63 *Id.*

v. California articulated a First Amendment right to anonymity that went beyond freedom of association and applied to individual speech.[64] *Talley* addressed a challenge to a Los Angeles ordinance that required names and addresses to be printed on the cover of handbills. Restricting anonymity, the Court reasoned, interferes with the protected freedom of distribution, and deters discussion by creating a fear of reprisal.[65] Without requiring evidence of actual reprisals, the Court explained that "identification and fear of reprisal might deter perfectly peaceful discussions of public matters of importance."[66] The Court found the ordinance unconstitutional on its face, without requiring any additional evidence.[67] The three dissenting justices disagreed, stating that they would have required both allegations and proof of reprisals or coercion restraining freedom of speech.[68]

The 1960s was a good period for constitutional protections of intellectual freedom, beyond overturning registration and identification requirements. In 1960, the Court decided *Shelton v. Tucker*, holding unconstitutional an Arkansas statute requiring teachers to list every organization to which they belonged within the preceding five years.[69] The Court held that the law violated the teachers' freedom of association, despite the state's interest in discovering the fitness and competence of its teachers. The Court articulated the connection between social freedom and intellectual freedom: "Scholarship cannot flourish in an atmosphere of suspicion and distrust. Teachers and students must always remain free to inquire, to study and to evaluate, to gain new maturity and understanding."[70]

The Court thus connected freedom to teach, freedom of inquiry, and freedom of association with privacy. In *Griswold v. Connecticut* in 1965, the Court made these connections even more explicit, and explained that privacy protection was central to these freedoms. *Griswold* involved a constitutional challenge to Connecticut's Comstock Act, which prohibited the use of contraception. The Court held the restriction breached a constitutional right to privacy found in the "penumbras" of enumerated constitutional protections, including First Amendment protections. The Court explained that the First Amendment includes "peripheral" rights such as "the right to distribute, the right to receive, the right to read and freedom of inquiry, freedom of thought, and freedom to teach."[71] The Court recognized that to protect these necessary peripheral rights, "the First Amendment has a penumbra where privacy is protected from governmental intrusion."[72]

64 *Talley v. California*, 362 U.S. 60, 65 (1960).
65 *Id.*
66 *Id.*
67 *Id.*
68 *Id.* at 69 (Clark, J., dissenting) ("Unlike *NAACP v. Alabama*, 357 U. S. 449 (1958), which is relied upon, there is neither allegation nor proof that Talley or any group sponsoring him would suffer 'economic reprisal, loss of employment, threat of physical coercion [or] other manifestations of public hostility.' *Id.* at 357 U. S. 462. Talley makes no showing whatever to support his contention that a restraint upon his freedom of speech will result from the enforcement of the ordinance. The existence of such a restraint is necessary before we can strike the ordinance down").
69 *Shelton v. Tucker*, 364 U.S. 479, 487 (1960).
70 *Id.* at 487 (quoting *Sweezy v. New Hampshire*, 354 U.S. 234, 250 (1957)).
71 *Griswold v. Connecticut*, 381 U.S. 479 (1965).
72 *Id.* at 483.

That privacy protection includes protection for reading records. Also in 1965, the Court held in *Lamont v. Postmaster General* that requiring addressees to actively request communist literature, rather than passively receive it, violated the First Amendment.[73] This requirement would have "a deterrent effect, especially as respects those who have sensitive positions."[74] The Court feared that the recipients of this literature would be "likely to feel some inhibition in sending for literature which federal officials have condemned."[75]

Perhaps the most famous articulation of the centrality of intellectual freedom to the First Amendment occurs in the 1969 case *Stanley v. Georgia*. In *Stanley*, the Court held that a Georgia law criminalizing the knowing possession of obscenity – that is, illegal material for which "to the average person, applying contemporary community standards, the dominant theme of the material, taken as a whole, appeals to the prurient interest"[76] – violated the First Amendment, because it impinged on the right to receive information in the privacy of one's own home.[77] The Court famously explained that

> if the First Amendment means anything, it means that a State has no business telling a man, sitting alone in his own house, what books he may read or what films he may watch. Our whole constitutional heritage rebels at the thought of giving government the power to control men's minds.[78]

Despite the grandiose language, *Stanley*'s practical effect was more limited. While states could not ban the mere possession of obscenity, they could still regulate its distribution and creation.[79] The Court also later found that banning the mere possession of child pornography was constitutional, because of the strong state interest in preventing harm to children.[80] The Court distinguished between a legitimate state desire to destroy the market for child pornography, thereby preventing physical and psychological harm to children, and a "paternalistic interest in regulating … [a person's] mind."[81]

More recently, the Supreme Court built on its 1960s cases about registration and identification requirements, and explicitly recognized fairly robust First Amendment protections for anonymous speech. In *McIntyre v. Ohio*, in 1995, the Court found that Ohio's statutory prohibition against the distribution of anonymous campaign literature was a law abridging the freedom of speech.[82] The Court touted anonymity as "a shield from the tyranny of the majority," explaining that anonymity protects "unpopular individuals from retaliation – and their ideas from suppression – at the hand of an intolerant society."[83] Citing *Talley*, the Court explicitly recognized the long tradition in the United States of anonymous pamphleteering.[84] In 2002, the Court affirmed its protection for

73 *Lamont v. Postmaster General*, 381 U.S. 301, 307 (1965).
74 *Id.*
75 *Id.*
76 *Roth v. United States*, 354 U.S. 476, 489 (1957).
77 *Stanley v. Georgia*, 394 U.S. 557, 564 (1969).
78 *Id.* at 565.
79 *Miller v. California*, 413 U.S. 15 (1973) (recognizing that obscene material is not protected under the First Amendment); *United States v. Reidel*, 402 U.S. 351 (1971) (finding constitutional a ban on the sale of obscene materials).
80 *Osborne v. Ohio*, 495 U.S. 103 (1990).
81 *Id.* at 109.
82 *McIntyre v. Ohio Elections Comm'n*, 514 U.S. 334, 342 (1995).
83 *Id.* at 357.
84 *Talley v. California*, 362 U.S. 60, 64 (1960); *see also McIntyre v. Ohio*, 514 U.S. 334, 360 (1995).

anonymous speech in *Watchtower Bible v. City of Stratton*, holding unconstitutional registration requirements for door-to-door pamphleteering.[85]

However, the right to anonymous speech is not absolute. The Court suggested in *McIntyre* that a strong enough state interest in a nonspeech harm – for example, in preventing fraud and libel – could "justify a more limited identification requirement."[86] Lyrissa Lidsky, a free speech scholar, has therefore characterized the anonymous speech right as a privilege, where First Amendment interests are weighed against other societal interests and process concerns.[87] This is the approach lower courts have taken when considering how to protect anonymous speech online.[88]

The Supreme Court has thus found First Amendment protection for privacy in the name of protecting freedom of speech, association, and assembly. The Court has pointed to a U.S. tradition of anonymous political speech, and repeatedly noted that fear of reprisals resulting from identification and surveillance of intellectual and social activities can have a chilling effect. The Court has noted that registration requirements and identification requirements, especially where mandated by the state, can deter individuals from expressing or associating with deviant views. It is no coincidence that these concerns track precisely the demonstrated dangers to intellectual and social freedom posed by surveillance.

1 Limits to First Amendment Protection

There are limits, however, to the extent of First Amendment protections. Constitutional protections alone do not guarantee freedom from surveillance in the United States. Given these limitations, the First Amendment scholar Neil Richards has noted that "intellectual privacy" is a First Amendment value, rather than a true right.[89]

There are several potential limitations to using the First Amendment to protect intellectual freedom by regulating surveillance. First, the Supreme Court's case law on First Amendment privacy addresses the legality of affirmative government requirements: that speakers affirmatively identify themselves to the government, or register before speaking or while seeking information. It is not clear that this case law can be applied to general government surveillance, as discussed later. Second, the question of what constitutes a cognizable privacy harm is rife with conflict, as is the case in most of United States privacy law.[90] Despite the fact that the Court appeared to resolve the issue of whether reprisals must be shown in its 1960s cases on registration requirements, the question of whether privacy harm is real harm has become a central issue of the day.

85 *Watchtower Bible v. Vill. of Stratton*, 536 U.S. 150, 165–66 (2002) ("It is offensive … to the very notion of a free society that … a citizen must first inform the government of [his or her] desire to speak to [his or her] neighbors and then obtain a permit").

86 *McIntyre v. Ohio*, 514 U.S. at 353.

87 *See* Lidsky, *Silencing John Doe: Defamation and Discourse in Cyberspace*, *supra* note 1; Lidsky, *Anonymity in Cyberspace: What Can We Learn from John Doe?*, *supra* note 1.

88 *See* Lidsky, *Silencing John Doe: Defamation and Discourse in Cyberspace*, *supra* note 1, at 920.

89 Richards, *Intellectual Privacy*, *supra* note 1; Balkin, *supra* note 50, at 50–52 ("Free speech rights are rights of individuals enforceable by courts. Free speech values are values that we seek to promote through legislative and administrative regulation and through technological design").

90 See e.g. Danielle Citron & Daniel Solove, Risk and Anxiety: A Theory of Data Breach Harms, 96 Texas L. Rev. (forthcoming 2017), available at https://papers.ssrn.com/sol3/papers.cfm?abstract_id=2885638 (discussing how privacy harms are treated in data breach cases in the United States).

In nearly all of the preceding cases in which the Supreme Court addressed privacy and intellectual and social freedom under the First Amendment, the nexus between government action and the chilling of individual speech was relatively clear. The government in the cases discussed affirmatively required individuals to identify themselves, or affirmatively sought records containing identification information from associative groups such as the NAACP. The Court reasoned in those cases that requiring individuals to identify themselves to the government would chill speech and association, and that the same would be true for members of the NAACP.

The Court, however, has been less eager to respond to First Amendment challenges of general government surveillance, differentiating general government investigative activity from affirmative identification requirements that require action on the part of the person being watched. In *Laird v. Tatum* in 1972, the Court upheld an Army surveillance program against a First Amendment challenge.[91] The challenged surveillance program sent Army agents to public meetings, and monitored news articles for information about individuals.[92] It required no action on the part of those being surveilled. The respondents challenged the program as chilling expression and association, but provided no objective evidence of chill and no showing of misuse of the information.[93] The Court found that the plaintiffs could not bring their claim into court, finding no standing to assert a First Amendment challenge where the claim was that individuals were "being chilled by the mere existence … of a government investigative and data-gathering activity."[94]

The majority explicitly distinguished *Laird* from the affirmative obligations in *Lamont*, the case in which individuals had to request communist mail.[95] The Court explained that "[a]llegations of a subjective 'chill' are not an adequate substitute for a claim of specific present objective harm or a threat of specific future harm."[96] As discussed in Section IV, "Recent Developments," *Laird* both presents hurdles to current First Amendment challenges to mass government surveillance and may be distinguishable on its facts. Unlike the Army program challenged in *Laird*, NSA surveillance goes well beyond public meetings and publications to the illicit interception of communications. And unlike the challenge in *Laird*, we have evidence of chilling effects resulting from NSA surveillance.[97]

The question of what harm must be shown also potentially restricts First Amendment protection against surveillance. Although in *Laird* the Court held that the showing of a "subjective chill" was not enough, in *McIntyre*, discussed earlier, the Court required no additional showing of pending harm or retaliation for McIntyre to assert her anonymous speech claim. Merely requiring McIntyre to disclose her identity was enough.

91 *Laird v. Tatum*, 408 U.S. 1 (1972).

92 *Id.* at 6 (characterizing the program as "collection of information about public activities that were thought to have at least some potential for civil disorder.… The information itself was collected by a variety of means, but it is significant that the principal sources of information were the news media and publications in general circulation. Some of the information came from Army Intelligence agents who attended meetings that were open to the public and who wrote field reports describing the meetings, giving such data as the name of the sponsoring organization, the identity of speakers, the approximate number of persons in attendance, and an indication of whether any disorder occurred").

93 *Id.* at 10, 13.

94 *Id.* at 10.

95 *Id.* at 12.

96 *Id.* at 13–14.

97 Penney, *supra* note 11; The FDR Group, *supra* note 39.

More recently in *Doe v. Reed*, the Court once again referenced a need for a showing of retaliation. The Court found that disclosing the signatories of referendum petitions in Washington State did not violate the First Amendment.[98] Writing for the majority, Chief Justice Roberts repeatedly noted, however, that this case was specific to the electoral context.[99]

What harm is necessary to show for a person to assert a First Amendment privacy claim remains unclear. Registration requirements trigger a First Amendment claim, unless they exist in the electoral context, in which case under *Reed* retaliation must be shown for a plaintiff to prevail. For more general surveillance, asserting a "subjective chill" alone is likely not enough under *Laird*. This issue of what constitutes sufficient harm to get into court, let alone win a First Amendment privacy claim, is discussed further in Section IV.

B *The Fourth Amendment*

The Fourth Amendment to the U.S. Constitution protects against unreasonable government searches and seizures. In multiple Fourth Amendment cases, the Supreme Court has recognized that intellectual and social freedoms are at stake when privacy is violated by the government. These cases reference many of the same themes that arise in First Amendment cases: intellectual freedom, social freedom, and privacy.

As early as 1877, the Supreme Court linked Fourth Amendment rights against unreasonable search and seizure to intellectual freedom in *Ex Parte Jackson*, a case about whether the Post Office could open and examine the contents of the mail.[100] The Court held that the government must get a warrant to inspect the contents of an envelope. It explained that opening printed matter would interfere with freedom of the press, reasoning that "liberty of circulating is as essential to [the freedom of the press] as liberty of publishing; indeed, without the circulation, the publication would be of little value."[101] If the government could inspect the contents of the mail without a warrant, then circulation would not be free.

Justice Louis Brandeis's dissent in *Olmstead v. United States* around fifty years later in 1928 was a rallying cry for protecting intellectual freedom through privacy. *Olmstead* addressed police practices of warrantlessly wiretapping telephone conversations between the defendants, who were convicted of conspiracy to violate the National Prohibition Act by possessing and transporting intoxicating liquors. In *Olmstead*, the majority held that the government did not need a warrant to wiretap a phone conversation. Justice Brandeis, dissenting, outlined the strong connection between privacy and intellectual freedom.[102] Justice Brandeis argued that the Fourth Amendment protects telephone conversations because the framers of the Constitution "sought to protect Americans in their beliefs, their thoughts, their emotions and their sensations."[103]

98 561 U.S. 186 (2010).
99 *Id.* at 187 ("That does not mean that the electoral context is irrelevant to the nature of this Court's First Amendment review").
100 *Ex Parte* Jackson, 96 U.S. 727 (1877).
101 *Id.* at 733.
102 *Olmstead v. United States*, 277 U.S. 438 (1928) (Brandeis, J., dissenting).
103 *Id.* at 478.

Justice Brandeis's dissent was influential. Nearly forty years later, the Supreme Court effectively overruled *Olmstead* and found that the Fourth Amendment does require a warrant for wiretapping phone calls in *Katz v. United States*.[104] The Court recognized that the telephone had come to play a "vital role ... in private communication."[105] The *Katz* Court established that rather than protecting individuals merely from physical trespasses by the government, the Fourth Amendment protects a "reasonable expectation of privacy."[106] A person in a public phone booth has a reasonable expectation of privacy in the conversation, and "the Fourth Amendment protects people, not places."[107]

Between *Ex Parte Jackson* and *Katz*, it was clear that courts could use the Fourth Amendment to protect communications systems from surveillance, thus protecting aspects of intellectual and social freedom. In the 1972 case *United States v. United States District Court*, which is often referred to as the *Keith* case, the Court again connected privacy with intellectual freedom.[108] The Court in *Keith* connected privacy with the protection not just of channels of communication, but of dissenting viewpoints. Holding that the government needed prior judicial approval for wiretaps used during investigations involving domestic terrorism, the Court explained that "Fourth Amendment protections become the more necessary when the targets of official surveillance may be those suspected of unorthodoxy in their political beliefs."[109] With untrammeled government surveillance in the name of "domestic security," the Court explained, the "danger to political dissent is acute."[110]

Much more recently, the Court has connected privacy with intellectual and social freedoms when contemplating Big Data and extended surveillance. In *United States v. Jones*, a unanimous Court found that attaching a GPS unit to a car violated the Fourth Amendment. In her concurring opinion, Justice Sonia Sotomayor linked Fourth Amendment protections to intellectual freedom and freedom of association, noting that "awareness that the Government may be watching chills associational and expressive freedoms."[111]

Two years later in *Riley v. California*, Chief Justice John Roberts, writing for an eight-justice majority, cited this passage of Justice Sotomayor's concurrence, thereby signaling broad agreement on the Court for the proposition that the Fourth Amendment is bound up with intellectual and social freedom.[112] The *Riley* Court held that the Fourth Amendment protects against searches of a person's cell phone without a warrant. Chief Justice Roberts noted the extent of potential privacy violations and their connection to intellectual endeavors, explaining that "an Internet search and browsing history ... could reveal an individual's private interests or concerns – perhaps a search for certain symptoms of disease, coupled with frequent visits to WebMD."[113]

104 *Katz v. United States*, 389 U.S. 347 (1967).
105 *Id.* at 352.
106 *Id.* at 360 (Harlan, J., concurring).
107 *Id.* at 351.
108 *United States v. U.S. Dist. Court*, 407 U.S. 297 (1972).
109 *Id.* at 314.
110 *Id.*
111 *United States v. Jones*, 132 S. Ct. 945, 956 (2012) (Sotomayor, J., concurring).
112 *Riley v. California*, 134 S. Ct. 2473, 2490 (2014).
113 *Id.*

1 Limits to Fourth Amendment Protection

There are, however, significant doctrinal limits to Fourth Amendment protections as well. Perhaps the biggest hurdle to invoking Fourth Amendment protection of intellectual and social freedom is a doctrine known as the "third party doctrine." The third party doctrine dictates that when less-sensitive information is shared with a third party, such as a phone company or bank, police do not need to obtain a warrant to access it.[114] The reasoning in one well-known third party doctrine case, *United States v. Miller*, had two prongs.[115] The Court in *Miller*, which again involved illicit alcohol production (the defendant ran an illegal still, allegedly to defraud the government of whiskey tax), evaluated whether the police could obtain copies of checks and other bank records via subpoena, without a warrant. The Court reasoned that the papers at issue were not "private papers," but bank business records.[116] This meant both that they were of lower privacy value than "confidential communications," and that the depositor knew he was taking a risk by revealing information to a third party, the bank.[117]

This two-prong reasoning – that the information at issue was less sensitive than confidential communications like those addressed in *Katz*, and that the information has been voluntarily entrusted to a third party company – formed the basis for the Court's decision in a later case, *Smith v. Maryland*.[118] There, the Court held that the petitioner had no reasonable expectation of privacy in the phone numbers he dialed, and thus no warrant is required to obtain phone number information through a pen register. The Court reasoned both that the petitioner had voluntarily turned over the phone numbers to the phone company "in the ordinary course of business,"[119] and that the phone numbers differed in kind from the contents of communications acquired in *Katz*.[120]

Both prongs of this reasoning behind the third party doctrine have recently come under fire. The purportedly less sensitive category of information into which phone numbers and envelope addresses fall has been referred to as "envelope" information after *Ex Parte Jackson*, or "metadata" when referring to phone calls and emails. Katherine Strandburg has noted that metadata surveillance does reveal highly sensitive information, such as extraordinarily detailed relational information, thereby threatening freedom of association.[121]

The second prong of the third party doctrine, that an individual assumes a risk of exposure any time she entrusts information in a third party, has also been challenged. Nearly everything we do online is shared with a third party. One court of appeals has recognized that there can be an expectation of privacy in email despite the fact that it is shared with

114 *United States v. Miller*, 425 U.S. 435 (1976) (holding that no warrant was required to obtain bank records); *Smith v. Maryland*, 442 U.S. 735 (1979) (holding that no warrant was required to obtain phone numbers dialed from a telephone company).

115 *United States v. Miller*, 425 U.S. 435 (1976).

116 *Id.* at 440.

117 *Id.* at 442–43.

118 *Smith v. Maryland*, 442 U.S. 735 (1979)

119 *Id.* at 744.

120 *Id.* at 741 ("Pen registers do not acquire the contents of communications").

121 Katherine J. Strandburg, *Freedom of Association in a Networked World: First Amendment Regulation of Relational Surveillance*, 49 B.C. L. Rev. 741 (2008); Katherine J. Strandburg, *Membership Lists, Metadata, and Freedom of Association's Specificity Requirement*, 10 I/S: J. L. Pol'y for Info. Soc'y 327 (2014).

online service providers,[122] which is consistent with what Stephen Henderson has articulated as the Court's "limited third party doctrine," excluding from Fourth Amendment protection only information provided for the third party's use.[123] Justice Sotomayor in her *Jones* concurrence explicitly contemplated overturning aspects of the third party doctrine. Justice Sotomayor wrote that "it may be necessary to reconsider the premise that an individual has no reasonable expectation of privacy in information voluntarily disclosed to third parties. This approach is ill suited to the digital age, in which people reveal a great deal of information about themselves to third parties in the course of carrying out mundane tasks."[124]

A second significant limitation to Fourth Amendment protection for intellectual and social freedom is that the Supreme Court has carved out an implicit foreign national security exception to its coverage. While the Court required a warrant for a wiretap in *Katz*, the majority explicitly noted that there might be a national security exception to that requirement.[125] The Court subsequently found in the *Keith* case that domestic national security investigations nonetheless require prior judicial approval.[126] The Court left open in *Keith*, however, the question of whether foreign national security intelligence constituted an exception to the Fourth Amendment's warrant requirement.

Lower courts have recognized a foreign national security exception. In 1974, the Third Circuit found that there was no warrant required for foreign intelligence gathering,[127] and, in 1980, the Fourth Circuit held the same. The Fourth Circuit reasoned that "the needs of the executive are so compelling in the area of foreign intelligence, unlike the area of domestic security, that a uniform warrant requirement would, following *Keith*, 'unduly frustrate' the President in carrying out his foreign affairs responsibilities."[128] To the extent that surveillance is conducted for purposes of foreign intelligence gathering, the Fourth Amendment may therefore provide more limited protection. It is against this backdrop of judicial deference to the executive branch that the U.S. national security surveillance regime has been established and grown.

III Statutory Protection

Although there are significant limitations to both First and Fourth Amendment protections for social and intellectual freedom, legislatures have in some places filled the void by enacting laws. This section provides a brief, nonexhaustive overview of some of the U.S. laws that protect intellectual or social freedom.[129]

After the Supreme Court held in *Smith v. Maryland* that the Fourth Amendment did not require a warrant for the government to obtain phone records, Congress responded by enacting the Pen Register Act.[130] The act, which is part of the Electronic Communications

122 *United States v. Warshak*, 631 F.3d 266 (6th Cir. 2010).

123 Stephen E. Henderson, *A Rose by Any Other Name: Regulating Law Enforcement Bulk Metadata Collection*, 94 Tex. L. Rev. 28, 32–36 (2016).

124 *United States v. Jones*, 565 U.S. ___, ___, 132 S. Ct. 945, 957 (2012) (Sotomayor, J., concurring).

125 *Katz v. United States*, 389 U.S. 347, 359 n.23 (1967) ("[A] situation involving the national security is a question not presented by this case").

126 *United States v. U.S. Dist. Court*, 407 U.S. 297 (1972).

127 *United States v. Butenko*, 494 F.2d 593, 606 (3d Cir. 1974).

128 *United States v. Truong*, 629 F.2d 908, 913 (4th Cir. 1980).

129 For more coverage of these laws, see Richards, Intellectual Privacy, *supra* note 1.

130 Pen Register Act, 18 U.S.C. §§ 3121–1327.

Privacy Act, requires law enforcement to obtain a court order to obtain phone records, despite the lack of a Fourth Amendment backstop. That court order provides less process and less protection than a warrant, but nevertheless shows that Congress was concerned about leaving this area completely unprotected.

Federal wiretap and cable laws can also be understood as protecting intellectual freedom by enabling people to associate freely and to gather information in private.[131] In 2015, largely in response to holes left by the third party doctrine, California enacted the California Electronic Communications Privacy Act (CalECPA), requiring the government to obtain a warrant before accessing emails and other digital information shared with online service providers.[132]

Federal laws protecting intellectual freedom have been enacted in response to public events. When Supreme Court nominee Robert Bork had his video rental history published by journalists, Congress took action, presumably out of fear that their own viewing records might be revealed. Congress enacted the Video Privacy Protection Act (VPPA), which protects against the "wrongful disclosure of video tape rental or sale records."[133] In 2013, after heavy lobbying by Netflix, Congress revised the VPPA to make it easier for companies to get approval for online disclosure of video records.[134]

Some state laws also protect intellectual privacy. Nearly every state has a reader privacy law protecting library information.[135] As discussed earlier, these laws were largely enacted in reaction to the FBI's Library Awareness Program of the 1970s and 1980s. In 2013, Arizona added e-book protection to its library law.[136] California has enacted a reader privacy statute extending to digital media.[137] A wide array of other state privacy laws, such as wiretap laws, can be understood to protect intellectual freedom and social freedom as well.

IV Recent Developments

The central challenge facing constitutional protections of intellectual and social freedom from surveillance is how to articulate privacy harm. In 2013, before the Snowden revelations, the Supreme Court addressed a challenge to a provision of national security surveillance law, Section 702 of the Foreign Intelligence Surveillance Amendments Act (FISAA), in *Clapper v. Amnesty International*.[138] Section 702 on its face loosened the targeting requirements for national security surveillance to a point where civil liberties advocates claimed it allowed the gathering of intelligence about ordinary, innocent Americans.[139] When the Supreme Court decided *Amnesty*, there was no public evidence

131 *See* Electronic Communications Privacy Act, 18 U.S.C. § 2710(b) (2012); Cable Communications Policy Act of 1984, 47 U.S.C. § 551(b)–(c) (2012).

132 S.B. 178, 2015–2016 Leg., Reg. Sess. (Cal. 2015).

133 Video Privacy Protection Act, Pub. L. No. 100–618, 102 Stat. 3195 (codified at 18 U.S.C. § 2710 (1988)).

134 Video Privacy Protection Act Amendments Act of 2012, Pub. L. No. 112–258, 126 Stat. 2414 (2013).

135 *See State Privacy Laws Regarding Library Records*, Am. Library Ass'n, http://www.ala.org/advocacy/privacyconfidentiality/privacy/stateprivacy.

136 Ariz. Rev. Stat. Ann. § 41–151.22 (2014).

137 California Reader Privacy Act, Cal. Civ. Code § 1798.90 (Deering 2013).

138 50 USC § 1881a; 568 U.S. ___, ___, 133 S. Ct. 1138, 1143 (2013).

139 Jennifer Granick, *FISA Amendments Act Is Way Worse for Privacy than Title III*, Ctr. Internet & Soc'y (Nov. 3, 2012), https://cyberlaw.stanford.edu/blog/2012/11/fisa-amendments-act-way-worse-privacy-title-iii ("In sum, innocent Americans are far more likely to be monitored under the FAA than under Title III").

of mass surveillance. Moreover, the lawsuit was filed the day that Section 702 passed, and the Court was asked to address the law as it was written, not consider a particular surveillance program in practice.

The Court in *Amnesty* declined to address both the First and Fourth Amendment challenges to Section 702, reasoning that the plaintiffs could not show that a surveillance program existed, let alone that they were harmed by it. The Court therefore rejected the case for a failure to establish standing to assert a claim. The plaintiffs could not show that their information had been intercepted, and thus could not assert a subjective chilling effect to demonstrate injury in fact. As Justice Breyer pointed out in his dissent, however, actual illegal interception of the content of communications would be a clear privacy harm.[140] The problem in *Amnesty* was that the plaintiffs could not show they had been subjected to such interception.

After the death of Justice Antonin Scalia, an eight-member court again addressed privacy and standing in *Spokeo v. Robins*.[141] The death of Justice Scalia matters for purposes of this discussion because Justice Scalia often railed against using intangible harms to establish standing.[142] Privacy was no different: as a judge on the D.C. Circuit, then-Judge Scalia held that plaintiffs did not have standing to challenge government surveillance under an executive order just by asserting a chilling effect.[143]

After Scalia's death, the remaining members of the Court decided *Spokeo*, a case challenging a plaintiff's standing under the Fair Credit Reporting Act to claim harm purportedly caused by an inaccurate profile. The Court bounced the case back down to the Ninth Circuit, explaining that the court of appeals had failed to consider whether the plaintiff had suffered a concrete injury. The Court did not provide much guidance as to what exactly what might constitute a "concrete injury."[144] Since *Spokeo*, lower courts have split on when to recognize privacy harms.[145] Thus, privacy injury remains an open and difficult legal question.

140 *Amnesty Int'l*, 133 S. Ct. at 1155 (Breyer, J., dissenting) ("No one here denies that the Government's interception of a private telephone or e-mail conversation amounts to an injury that is 'concrete and particularized'").

141 578 U.S. ___, 136 S. Ct. 1540 (2016).

142 Seth F. Kreimer, *Spooky Action at a Distance: Intangible Injury in Fact in the Information Age*, 18 U. Pa. J. Const. L. 745, 751 (2016) ("Justice Scalia and his acolytes take the position that Article III doctrine requires a tough minded, common sense and practical approach. Injuries in fact should be 'tangible' 'direct' 'concrete' 'de facto' realities").

143 *United Presbyterian Church in U.S.A. v. Reagan*, 738 F. 2d 1375, 1378 (D.D.C. 1984) (Scalia, J., majority opinion).

144 Daniel Solove, *When Is a Person Harmed by a Privacy Violation? Thoughts on Spokeo v. Robins*, LinkedIn (May 17, 2016), https://www.linkedin.com/pulse/when-person-harmed-privacy-violation-thoughts-spokeo-v-daniel-solove.

145 Some courts have found no standing to sue. *See* Smith v. Ohio State Univ., No. 15-CV-3030, 2016 WL 3182675, at *4 (S.D. Ohio June 8, 2016). See also Tyus, v. United States Postal Service, No. 15-CV-1467, 2016 WL 6108942, at *6 (E.D. Wis. Oct. 19, 2016) (inclusion of extraneous information on (b)(2) notice is not a "concrete" injury); Nokchan v. Lyft, Inc., No. 15-CV-03008 JCS, 2016 WL 5815287, at *9 (N.D. Cal. Oct. 5, 2016) (holding the same); Fisher v. Enter. Holdings, Inc., No. 4:15-CV-00372 AGF, 2016 WL 4665899, at *1 (E.D. Mo. Sept. 7, 2016) (holding the same). Others have managed to find privacy harms. See But see Perlin v. Time, finding post-Spokeo that a violation of Michigan's video privacy act (VRPA) "is sufficient to satisfy the injury-in-fact requirement" and is "not a bare procedural violation") https://leagle.com/decision/In%20FDCO%2020170215H22/Perlin%20v.%20Time%20Inc. See also Church v. Accretive Health, Inc., No. 15-15708, 2016 WL 3611543, at *3 (11th Cir. July 6, 2016) (applying Spokeo and holding that "through the [federal Fair Debt Collection Practices Act], Congress

The biggest related legislative event since the Snowden revelations is that Congress restricted the government's dragnet phone records surveillance. Congress passed the USA FREEDOM Act in June 2015.[146] The act ended the bulk collection of phone records by the government under Section 215 of the PATRIOT Act, and reformed the Foreign Intelligence Surveillance Court (FISA Court). Although civil liberties organizations criticized the USA FREEDOM Act for not going far enough, it represents a significant change of momentum as the first time in more than thirty years that Congress restricted the NSA's surveillance.[147]

In April 2016, the House of Representatives unanimously passed the Email Privacy Act. (It passed the House again by voice vote in February 2017.[148]) This act would require a probable cause warrant from law enforcement before obtaining documents stored online with companies.[149] The act would need to pass the Senate to become law, but the Email Privacy Act may be a historic indicator of a shift in attitude in Congress. At the same time, however, as noted previously, the FBI is seeking legislation that will give it access to Internet browsing history without a warrant.[150]

V The Future of Intellectual and Social Freedom

As new technologies develop and are deployed, the future of intellectual and social freedom can take many paths. As members of the Supreme Court recognized in *Jones*, the GPS monitoring case, public surveillance implicates individuals' abilities to associate, gather, and gather information freely. Public surveillance technologies such as drones, or unmanned aerial systems, pose similar concerns. Facial recognition technologies also implicate social and intellectual freedom. By making it easier to comb through video and photographs to identify where people are, whom they are with, and what places they seek out – from churches to abortion clinics to Alcoholics Anonymous meetings – facial recognition will make it harder to keep social and intellectual interactions private. The United States currently does not have federal law governing privacy in biometric information,[151] although some states, such as Illinois, have passed laws governing technologies such as facial recognition.[152] Nor are there countrywide drone privacy regulations

has created a new right—the right to receive [certain] required disclosures in communications governed by the [Act]—and a new injury—not receiving such disclosures"); In re Nickelodeon Consumer Privacy Litig., No. 15-1441, 2016 WL 3513782, at *7 (3d Cir. June 27, 2016) (holding that disclosure of information in violation of the federal Video Privacy Protection Act resulted in a concrete harm "in the sense that it involve[d] a clear de facto injury, i.e., the unlawful disclosure of legally protected information").

146 USA Freedom Act, Pub. L. No. 114–23, 129 Stat. 268 (2015).

147 Cindy Cohn & Rainey Reitman, *USA Freedom Act Passes: What We Celebrate, What We Mourn, and Where We Go from Here*, Elec. Frontier Found. (June 2, 2015), https://www.eff.org/deeplinks/2015/05/usa-freedom-act-passes-what-we-celebrate-what-we-mourn-and-where-we-go-here.

148 https://www.congress.gov/bill/115th-congress/house-bill/387

149 Sophia Cope, *House Advances Email Privacy Act, Setting the Stage for Vital Privacy Reform*, Elec. Frontier Found. (Apr. 27, 2016), https://www.eff.org/deeplinks/2016/04/house-advances-email-privacy-act-setting-stage-vital-privacy-reform.

150 Nakashima, *supra* note 29.

151 Laura K. Donohue, *Technological Leap, Statutory Gap, and Constitutional Abyss: Remote Biometric Identification Comes of Age*, 97 Minn. L. Rev. 407 (2012).

152 Andrea Peterson, *The Government's Plan to Regulate Facial Recognition Tech Is Falling Apart*, Wash. Post: Switch (June 16, 2015), https://www.washingtonpost.com/news/the-switch/wp/2015/06/16/the-governments-plan-to-regulate-facial-recognition-tech-is-falling-apart/ (citing Texas and Illinois as having facial recognition laws).

in place. Some states have passed drone privacy laws, but the federal agency tasked with governing airspace, the Federal Aviation Administration, has declined to take up the privacy issues.[153]

Another developing technological practice with clear implications for intellectual freedom is the rise of use of predictive educational software. The Department of Education recommended greater use of these tools.[154] Monitoring educational advancement outside historically traditional assessments such as tests has serious implications for intellectual freedom. Elana Zeide has suggested that this can restrict intellectual play and experimentation, and produce students who are less likely to be innovative.[155]

Although it may seem to be the technology of the far future, the use of neuroscience to determine people's actual thoughts clearly implicates freedom of mind. Numerous scholars have suggested that such a device would implicate another provision of the Constitution, the Fifth Amendment, which protects against self-incrimination.[156] Kiel Brennan-Marquez, however, challenges this conclusion, positing a "modest defense of mind-reading."[157]

Conclusion

Surveillance threatens social and intellectual freedom. U.S. courts have recognized how surveillance implicates the ability of individuals to enjoy fundamental rights. However, constitutional protections have their limitations. Both federal and state governments consequently protect some intellectual freedom beyond the floor of constitutional protection. This chapter is an introduction to a complex and quickly evolving area of law. Newer technologies and social practices on the horizon, such as drones, educational software, and even "mind reading," will raise these questions again in new contexts in the years to come.

153 Margot E. Kaminski, *Enough with the "Sunbathing Teenager" Gambit: Drone Privacy Is about Much More than Protecting Girls in Bikinis*, SLATE (May 17, 2016), http://www.slate.com/articles/technology/future_tense/2016/05/drone_privacy_is_about_much_more_than_sunbathing_teenage_daughters.html.

154 Office of Educ. Tech., *FUTURE READY LEARNING: REIMAGINING THE ROLE OF TECHNOLOGY IN EDUCATION* (2016), http://tech.ed.gov/netp/.

155 Elana Zeide, *The Credentialing Effect: Psychological Implications of Ubiquitous Capture and Constant Assessment* (on file with author).

156 *See, e.g.*, Nina Farahany, *Incriminating Thoughts*, 64 STAN. L. REV. 351, 354 (2012); Michael S. Pardo, *Disentangling the Fourth Amendment and the Self-Incrimination Clause*, 90 IOWA L. REV. 1857, 1879 (2005).

157 Kiel Robert Brennan-Marquez, *A Modest Defense of Mind-Reading*, 15 YALE J. L. & TECH. 214 (2013).

21 The Surveillance Regulation Toolkit: Thinking beyond Probable Cause

Paul Ohm[†]

We are in the midst of a long-standing debate about how to balance the need for government surveillance with the privacy and liberty interests of the targets of surveillance. Too often, we have tried to strike the proper balance using only two tools: justification standards (e.g. probable cause, reasonable suspicion, or mere relevance) and judicial review. With the rapid rate of change in the technology of surveillance, these two regulatory tools alone cannot keep up. To spur us to consider a broader toolkit of surveillance regulation, this chapter identifies sixteen distinct tools of surveillance regulation, grouping them into five categories: justification, meaningful review, limited surveillance, accountability, and transparency. By identifying many neglected approaches beyond justification standards and judicial review, the chapter hopes to spur creative thinking about alternative methods of accountability and control.

Introduction

How best should we balance the need for government surveillance for law enforcement, national security, and intelligence purposes, with the privacy and other civil liberties of individuals and groups? Despite the roiling debate we have been having about this question, many of the solutions we have proposed have been far too constrained to do much good. To date, we have devoted far too much of our energy to two specific tools for striking this balance: justification standards and judicial review. Those wanting to limit surveillance too often do little more than argue for probable cause review by judges where it is not already required. Those wanting to loosen constraints on surveillance argue, in kind, for lower standards, such as mere relevance, and argue it is unnecessary to require a judicial check on some forms of surveillance.

Judicial review and justification standards alone cannot keep up with the evolution of surveillance technology. Some law enforcement tools, such as the use of machine learning to analyze crime patterns in massive databases and make predictions about future crime patterns, do not lend themselves naturally to judicial review or probable cause. For other types of technologies, justification standards and judicial review continue to play an important role, but they are blunt instruments of regulation, which provide an

† Professor of Law, Georgetown University Law Center, and Faculty Director, Center on Privacy and Technology. Thanks to David Gray and Stephen Henderson for their editorial leadership. Thanks finally to Jason Rotstein for research assistance.

essential floor of protection from certain kinds of government overreach and abuse but do not do nearly enough to protect privacy and civil liberties. This is because a justification standard such as probable cause is a gatekeeping standard: once it is satisfied, it tends to say little about the scope, scale, or particularity of surveillance that is allowed. This is a significant shortcoming given the way new technologies generate massive amounts of information about individual communications and habits.

For example, given the enormous quantity of information about our geolocation and communications stored in databases held by third parties, a police officer with probable cause that a crime has been committed can range deeply into the digital past of a suspected target, raising concerns about the need for particularity and the right we ought to enjoy periodically to wipe the slate clean. As another example, the increasing use of malware as a surveillance tool raises the risk that the government has upset the balance of power between surveillance and privacy-enhancing technology too dramatically and too abruptly.

The main goal of this chapter is to broaden the debate over government surveillance to matters beyond justification standards and judicial review. It advances this goal primarily through an act of classification, by collecting other regulatory tools that have been proposed or implemented in various judicial opinions and legislative enactments. Nothing in the resulting taxonomy is original. The chapter reinvents no new wheel, but is premised on the theory that many regulatory approaches have been underutilized and undertheorized in current surveillance debates as a result of relative inattention. The hope is that by building a list of regulatory possibilities, this chapter will spur judges, legislators, advocates, and agencies to think more often beyond probable cause and judicial review.

The chapter proceeds in three parts. Part I presents the argument for looking beyond probable cause and judicial review as we debate government surveillance. Part II offers a kit of sixteen tools we might use to regulate government surveillance, organizing them into five categories. Finally, Part III serves as a "user's manual" for the toolkit, explaining how it can be used in various contexts, and arguing that the toolkit deserves to be developed and extended by law enforcement and intelligence officials, courts, legislatures, and administrative agencies as they explore how to respond to threats to privacy and security from the government's use of new and emerging surveillance technologies.

I Thinking beyond Probable Cause and Judicial Review

The principal tools we have so far devised to regulate government surveillance are the requirements of probable cause (or some lesser justification standard such as reasonable suspicion or mere relevance) and judicial review. Until and unless a police officer, federal agent, or intelligence officer can convince a judge that he or she possesses enough evidence to meet the supposedly stringent probable cause justification requirement, some forms of surveillance are off limits.

These two tools are no longer enough by themselves to limit government surveillance properly. The culprit is the march of technology. Advances in surveillance and in the way ordinary people communicate have meant that probable cause and judicial review alone permit surveillance that is too powerful, too invasive, and too easy to justify.

Fortunately, over the past half-century, courts and legislatures have periodically thought outside the review-and-justification box, providing us with an entire toolkit of other regulatory possibilities.

A *New Surveillance Technologies and Probable Cause*

In a sense, the modern history of both the Fourth Amendment and the various statutes we have enacted to regulate surveillance has been the history of technology, particularly the technology of communications. The telegraph and telephone gave rise to early wiretapping tools, which spurred early wiretapping laws. Today fierce fights surround email, the Web, smartphones, and GPS.

But as the rate of technological change increases, the courts have strained to keep the Fourth Amendment and these statutes relevant. At the very least, Fourth Amendment case law has been chaotic and unpredictable. The Supreme Court alone has worked minor revolutions in recent years in a trio of cases, *Kyllo v. United States*,[1] *United States v. Jones*,[2] and *Riley v. California*,[3] issuing opinions that suggest that further and even more seismic changes may be coming.[4]

But the bigger looming problem is that all of these changes might not be enough. The state and federal courts and legislatures are focused almost single-mindedly on two important but threshold tools for regulation: justification standards and judicial review. A justification standard is the minimum standard an officer or agent must possess on the basis of the evidence gathered before the request for surveillance. The most debated justification standard is probable cause, which is the justification standard required by the Fourth Amendment for search warrants. The probable cause standard has also been imported into numerous surveillance laws. Other laws allow surveillance with lesser justification, such as reasonable suspicion or mere relevance.

First, consider the increasing use of government malware to search computers across the Internet. In 2015, the FBI gained control of a web server hosted on the so-called dark web and used by people interested in illegally transmitting images of child pornography. Rather than take down the site, the FBI instead sought and gained judicial approval for a search warrant based on probable cause allowing it to use "network investigative techniques" (NITs) to plant malware on the computers of suspects visiting the website.

Reasonable minds have differed about what we are to make of the government's increasing embrace of malware as a tool of surveillance. Some might even argue that the government should never be permitted to take this step. But if we are going to permit malware-as-surveillance, we should be attentive to the new and unusual risks it poses. Malware can invade the privacy of the home and worm its way into our most sensitive and protected communications and files. Malware can cross jurisdictional and international boundaries without respecting local laws. When government malware exploits

1 537 U.S. 27 (2001).
2 132 S. Ct. 945 (2012).
3 134 S. Ct. 2473 (2014).
4 *E.g.*, *Jones*, 132 S. Ct. at 957 (Sotomayor, J., concurring) ("It may be necessary to reconsider the premise that an individual has no reasonable expectation of privacy in information voluntarily disclosed to third parties").

software vulnerabilities that are not yet widely known, it raises a significant risk of introducing additional insecurity into an already bleak cybersecurity landscape.

For all of these reasons, probable cause and judicial review seem insufficient to the task of regulating this invasive new practice. Probable cause should be the start of the conversation but certainly not the end. Just as the police should not be allowed to kick down the door of a home without probable cause, so too should they be forbidden to "break in" to a computer using undocumented software vulnerabilities without probable cause. But the application of this standard alone does nothing to address the special concerns about the nature of government malware.

Second, the police increasingly track the location of individuals using so-called cell-site location information. Every cell phone user is tracked by his or her cell phone provider for business purposes. Knowing where each user is on a minute-by-minute basis helps the provider route phone calls, and storing that data can be useful for analyzing past patterns to improve future service. But the existence of this data means the police can retrace any individual's past movements, often dating back years.

A number of judges have weighed in on the rules regarding police access to cell-site location information, again focusing largely on justification standards and judicial review.[5] As with government malware, the debate should not end with probable cause. It is an awesome and new government power to be able to retrace the steps of any individual on an hour-by-hour basis dating back years and extending well before any suspicion of criminal behavior.

Third, consider search warrants for access to devices with massive storage, such as desktop computers, laptops, cloud servers, and smart phones. These warrants are issued by every jurisdiction in the country as a matter of course. In the vast majority of these cases, these warrants permit the police to search everywhere in the storage on these devices. Once again, satisfied by probable cause and judicial review, judges signing these warrants have seen no reason to limit the police to certain parts of a computer's hard drive or to require a preapproved list of search terms.

The problem that some have noted is that, given the enormous capacity of modern storage devices, the diversity of the kind of information typically stored on them, and the long life span of data, warrants to search computers might permit an investigation into a person's entire history. As I have written, "Computer search warrants are the closest things to general warrants we have confronted in the history of the Republic."[6]

Fourth, and finally, consider the rise of big data techniques for fighting crime such as machine learning. Advanced statistical and computational machine learning techniques combine with massive databases that track individual behavior to empower the police in new and potentially worrisome ways. For example, so-called predictive policing methods help some municipal police departments deploy officers to parts of the city where crime is predicted to spike. Because techniques such as these often operate on information in the public domain, and because these techniques are inherently not focused on any particular crime or individual, probable cause and judicial review may be ill suited or completely incompatible as protective techniques. If we are to regulate techniques such as these, we need to find different tools to do so.

5 *United States v. Graham*, No. 12–4659, 2016 WL 3068018 (4th Cir. May 31, 2016); *United States v. Carpenter*, 819 F.3d 880 (6th Cir. 2016).

6 Paul Ohm, *Massive Hard Drives, General Warrants, and the Power of Magistrate Judges*, 97 Va. L. Rev. In Brief 1, 11 (2011).

B *Beyond the Narrow Debate*

For the most part, activists and policy makers tend to focus far too much attention on justification standards and judicial review and far too little on other tools for regulating government surveillance.

Consider the multiyear campaign to reform the Electronic Communications Privacy Act (ECPA) to require search warrants for government access to stored email messages. A broad coalition of civil society advocates and corporations have urged Congress to amend ECPA to require the police to obtain warrants based on probable cause before they can access the content of stored email messages. The House of Representatives unanimously passed a bill that would make this change in 2016, but it made little progress in the Senate.

I think requiring a probable cause search warrant for email is a necessary change, but I think it is just a good start, not an end, to rebalancing the privacy invasions inherent when the police want to read years (maybe even decades) of private correspondence. We need to think far beyond probable cause, but the bills that have been proposed and voted upon focus on very little else.

A similar dynamic plays out in constitutional litigation. Whenever a new and invasive surveillance technology comes to light, the defense bar fights vigorously to have courts recognize the use of the technology as a search, once again with the goal of requiring a warrant based on probable cause. Often, they are led (or at least supported) by the privacy advocacy community, which supplies amici briefs also focused on the "search or no search" question. In contrast, relatively little energy is spent debating other techniques a court might deploy to try to detect and rein in invasive surveillance.

To be fair and clear, in both legislation and scholarship, sometimes other tools in the regulatory toolkit have arisen. After all, the survey of the toolkit in Part II draws heavily from rules embedded in the Wiretap Act and Foreign Intelligence Surveillance Act. But I think that much more attention, energy, and creativity deserve to be focused beyond probable cause. Particularly in the legislative debates leading to the laws I list earlier, I sense that there is little systematic attention to tools aside from probable cause. We occasionally refer to a fairly stagnant list of possibilities, and we pick and choose from this list (or sometimes simply point to the list wholesale). It would be better if we breathed life into each of these elements on the list. I wish some of the energy focused today on the definition of search would go instead to thinking about expanding the necessity requirement, or shoring up minimization, both of which are key features of the regulatory regime enforced by the Wiretap Act.

The bottom line is that probable cause can never do enough alone to keep up with the way technology empowers and expands surveillance and concomitantly invades privacy and shifts the balance of power from the citizenry and to the state. We need to spend much more time looking at the rest of the toolkit, and I hope this chapter – by diagnosing the problem and surveying the landscape – is a good (if modest) first step in that direction.

C *Precedents*

The toolkit developed in the next part has been collected primarily from two sources: the Supreme Court case *Berger v. New York* and federal legislation.

1 Berger v. New York

Berger v. New York[7] was decided six months before *Katz v. United States*[8] and has been overshadowed by its later in time and much more famous successor. In *Berger*, the United States Supreme Court suppressed evidence arising from the use by New York state officials of eavesdropping devices. These devices surreptitiously recorded conversations held inside private offices involving the chairman of the New York State Liquor Authority, a man named Berger, who had been accused of requiring the payment of bribes in order to obtain liquor licenses.

Berger differed from *Katz* in two important respects. First, the court considered the use of the eavesdropping devices to be "a trespassory intrusion into a constitutionally protected area," thereby allowing the court to sidestep the kind of difficult questions involving claims of privacy in public that it would soon face in *Katz*.

Second, in *Berger* unlike in *Katz*, the police had obtained prior, judicial approval to conduct the surveillance pursuant to a New York state eavesdropping statute, Section 813-a of the New York Code of Criminal Procedure. The Supreme Court held that surveillance under this statute was unconstitutional, notwithstanding the statute's requirement for judicial review and without regard to whether the statute required probable cause, which was apparently the subject of some dispute.

"The statute is deficient on its face in other respects," the Court held. *Berger* thus serves as the constitutional lodestar for the argument of this chapter. In its holding, but also its reasoning, it stands for the idea that the judge's role is not completed once he or she finds probable cause for surveillance. Judges can and should impose other procedural safeguards tailored to address special problems with technological surveillance. This is not simply a matter of prudence or the supervisory administration of the court system, *Berger* teaches: it is a matter of constitutional law.

The Court rooted this unusual scrutiny of procedural safeguards beyond probable cause in the requirement in the Fourth Amendment that warrants must "particularly describ[e] the place to be searched, and the persons or things to be seized." Critical in its analysis was that "by its very nature, eavesdropping involves an intrusion on privacy that is broad in scope." Eavesdropping's nature "imposes 'a heavier responsibility on this Court in its supervision of the fairness of procedures.'"

With this analysis as impetus, the Court then scrutinized the procedural safeguards in the New York law, finding many of them constitutionally insufficient. It faulted the statute for, among other things, failing to require the police to express belief that a particular crime had been committed; failing to require the police to specify particular conversations sought; failing to require notice to the target of the surveillance; and allowing periods of surveillance that were too long, were too easy to renew, and did not expire once the conversation sought was seized.

Despite this invitation in *Berger* for creative and capacious thinking about various ways to cabin the potential for surveillance abuses, this form of reasoning has mostly vanished in the subsequent four decades. *Katz* is almost surely to blame. By emphasizing solely the threshold question – has a search occurred? – and by giving rise to a vague new test – the reasonable expectation of privacy – the Court, probably inadvertently, shifted

7 388 U.S. 41 (1967).
8 389 U.S. 347 (1967).

the weight of commentary and litigation away from the kind of analysis it had conducted in *Berger*. Today, we see *Katz* often as the end, not the beginning, of the analysis. Once litigants and privacy advocates establish a surveillance technique as a search requiring judicial review and a probable cause warrant, the community breathes a sigh of relief, assuming the battle has been won, and turning its collective attention to the next fight. The result is that today there are stasis and little energy from the Courts in thinking through additional ways to police surveillance.

2 Congressional Development

Unlike the courts, Congress and many state legislatures have not treated justification standards and judicial review as the end of the analysis. Numerous federal and state statutes governing surveillance implement many additional procedural safeguards. This is unsurprising because legislatures can build protections above the constitutional floor of Fourth Amendment protection, meaning legislatures are free to be more creative and wide-ranging than judges. Legislatures also probably feel more pressure to provide a nearly complete regulatory framework for surveillance, and they are less inclined to be content with a vague standard, such as "reasonable expectation of privacy." Finally, legislatures are aggressively lobbied by law enforcement and privacy advocates alike, and thus might turn to more finely tuned tools than probable cause and judicial review in pursuit of more flexible methods of addressing concerns and hammering out compromises. Unwilling to bend on probable cause, for example, a legislature might see minimization or public reporting as a way to ameliorate the disappointment of one or both sides.

Even though legislatures have implemented more parts of the toolkit, the pace of development has been unacceptably slow. For the most part, Congress has done little else other than implement the direct teachings of *Berger* in a series of federal laws: FISA, the Wiretap Act, the Pen Register Act, and the Stored Communications Act. Debates about how to reform surveillance laws such as ECPA or FISA tend still to center on justification standards and judicial review. Consider the ongoing debates to require search warrants for email under ECPA. Years of debate and energy have been poured into trying to amend ECPA to require search warrants based on probable cause to read email messages stored with email providers. Yet if this change is ever enacted, those email warrants will still be subject to very few of the procedural safeguards from the toolkit. It might be that some of the alternatives would be even more effective at surfacing or deterring abuse and misconduct, meaning it might be better to rechannel some of the energy directed at the fight for probable cause to proposals for some of the other fifteen, relatively neglected, alternatives. We turn to these alternatives next.

II The Toolkit

This part, the heart of the chapter, surveys statutes and cases in an attempt to provide a list of tools in the regulation-of-surveillance toolkit. This is not an exhaustive list, although I have tried to be as complete as possible. I hope that this represents the beginning of an ongoing project, one that I and others will continue to develop, studying the tools I have listed, identifying currently existing tools that I have missed, and creating new tools not yet in use.

I hope that by merely collecting this list in one place and providing a little structure to it, I might help spur a bit more attention to regulatory approaches beyond, or in place of, probable cause and judicial review. Even for those who already think about some of the items in the list – there are many privacy advocates who focus on notice and reporting, for example – this list might spur focus on other possible tools. For every participant in these debates, the discussion of the items in the list suggests how undertheorized some of these tools are, a product of the little attention that has been given to them.

I have organized the sixteen tools that follow into five broader categories. The first category includes tools to require justification, but also poses a related but subtler question, "Probable cause of what?" The second category includes rules to ensure meaningful review by people outside the investigatory team. This includes judicial review, of course, but also requirements of a particular level of detail by the investigators when speaking to a judge (e.g. "specific and articulable facts"). I also include in this category requirements for intraagency review, perhaps by a unit in a different part of the prosecutorial organization chart, or perhaps by a higher-ranking and ostensibly more politically accountable official.

The third category includes tools used to limit the amount, scope, and nature of the surveillance. This category includes six tools: time limits, minimization, expiry conditions, predicate crimes, necessity, and limits on the plain view rule. The fourth category provides tools for increasing the accountability of the police seeking judicial permission to conduct the surveillance. Requiring officers to swear an oath in the application opens the door to sanctions if they are later to have been discovered to have lied, and suppression remedies provide a mechanism for deterring police misconduct and gives those surveilled some incentive to discover and challenge improper surveillance. Finally, the fifth category seeks to ensure the transparency of government surveillance, through notice, limits on gag orders, and public accounting.

A *Justification*

The tools in the first category require the government to justify its reasons in advance for conducting surveillance. The first, justification standards, has been discussed extensively already. This category also includes rules that specify or vary the thing that must be justified by a justification standard, requiring, for example, not only probable cause that the surveillance will uncover evidence of a crime but also probable cause that the alleged criminals are using a particular form of communications technology to communicate.

1 Justification Standards

By far the great bulk of commentary has focused on the level of police suspicion that ought to be required to justify the deployment and use of a particular surveillance technique or technology. Traditionally, recommendations have spanned a spectrum of four categories: probable cause, reasonable suspicion, mere relevance, and no suspicion.

In earlier work, I have argued that, thanks to the spread of intermediated online communications, these four categories are no longer as meaningful as they once were.[9] To

[9] Paul Ohm, *Probably Probable Cause: The Diminishing Importance of Justification Standards*, 94 MINN. L. REV. 1514 (2010).

boil down the argument, an Internet protocol (IP) address or email address is never mildly suspicious. Instead, evidentiary leads on modern networks almost always satisfy the highest standard, probable cause. Investigations on modern networks, thus, see probable cause as little more than a mild speed bump. If this argument is valid, then we waste our time and accomplish little if we focus too much attention on increasing justification standards, for example trying to require probable cause for surveillance traditionally executed with relevance or reasonable suspicion.

2 Probable Cause of What?

Another way to regulate surveillance is by varying the object of analysis for probable cause or reasonable suspicion. Whereas search warrants tend to be justified by probable cause that the searching officers will find evidence of a crime in the specified place to be searched at the time of the search, under federal law, wiretap orders must also independently establish probable cause that the target of surveillance has committed one of the crimes enumerated under the statute (which tend to be relatively serious offenses); particular communications concerning that offense will be intercepted; and the facilities from which the communications are to be intercepted are being used in connection with the offense.[10] Under FISA, orders permitting electronic surveillance must establish probable cause that the target is an agent of a foreign power as well as that the facilities to be placed under surveillance are being used by that person.[11]

Berger discussed this approach, faulting the New York law for requiring the police to specify "no more than identify the person whose constitutionally protected area is to be invaded, rather than 'particularly describing' the communications, conversations, or discussions to be seized."

B *Meaningful Review*

The second category in the toolkit includes tools that require the core investigative team – perhaps a prosecutor and small number of agents – to test its theory of justification through a process of external review. Most importantly, in our system of separated powers government, many of our surveillance laws require a "detached and neutral" judge to review an application for surveillance. This category also includes rules that require the surveillance application to provide the reviewing judge with more than a specified level of detail in such an application. Finally, rules often require intrabranch review, sometimes in lieu of judicial review, but often in addition, by higher-ranking officials or external units within the same agency.

1 Judicial Review

The Supreme Court has long focused on the importance of review by a "neutral and detached magistrate" of police surveillance. The theory is that we should interpose somebody who is not "engaged in the often competitive enterprise of ferreting out crime."[12]

10 18 U.S.C. § 2518.
11 50 U.S.C. § 1805.
12 *United States v. Johnson*, 333 U.S. 10, 14 (1948).

The theory rests ultimately on the constitutional separation of powers, embracing the idea that judicial officers outside the executive branch will detect when the police fail to live up to the other requirements on this list and will possess the power (and institutional incentives and fortitude) to reject requests when the police do not.

I have great faith in these theories and, ultimately, think judicial review is the most important check on police behavior. That said, there are some limits to judicial review. First, surveillance requests are usually *ex parte* affairs. Judges do not have the benefit of briefing by any party but the government, much less the party with the incentive to challenge surveillance most vigorously, the surveilled party himself or herself. Second, judges are often at a significant information disadvantage when conducting this kind of review.

Third, judicial review can only be effective when judges are given leeway to scrutinize facts and reject requests. Some surveillance regimes treat the judge almost as a rubber stamp. Most notably, the Pen Register Trap and Trace statute, which governs real-time surveillance of many forms of metadata on telephone and computer networks, requires judicial review but orders judges to approve requests upon a government attorney's mere "certification" of certain facts,[13] prompting one court to describe this role as merely "ministerial."[14]

2 Level of Detail Requirements

Some surveillance laws require the officer applying for permission to conduct surveillance to state the predicate facts upon which the application depends at a particular level of detail, such as "articulable facts." Level of detail requirements connect with judicial review, because judges benefit from receiving more and better facts, as well as with justification standards, which might require not only "reasonable suspicion," but "reasonable suspicion based on articulable facts." The Fourth Amendment itself provides that "no warrants shall issue … [without] particularly describing the place to be searched, and the persons or things to be seized." Under the Stored Communications Act, a court order that can be used to access some forms of communications and noncontent metadata requires the government to "offer[] specific and articulable facts."[15]

3 Intraagency Review

Many surveillance laws require review within the law enforcement organization itself. Sometimes the law mandates review from higher-level managers. For example, the NSA's Section 215 metadata collection program, which was revealed by Edward Snowden, allowed NSA officials to search the trove of telephone transaction data only after review and approval by designated agency officials. Reports suggest this limited approval authority to about twenty-two NSA employees.

Other rules mandate review by politically appointed officials, probably on the theory that these officials bear more accountability and responsibility than career employees.

[13] 18 U.S.C. § 3123.

[14] *United States v. Fregoso*, 60 F.3d 1314, 1320 (8th Cir. 1995) ("The judicial role in approving use of trap and trace devices is ministerial in nature").

[15] 18 U.S.C. § 2703(d).

For example, before a federal wiretap request can be submitted to a court for judicial review, it must first be approved by a political appointee bearing one of six job titles in the Justice Department.[16] Intraagency review may also be conducted by a staff attorney assigned to a specialized unit external to the prosecuting unit. For example, before being submitted for agency approval, federal wiretap orders are reviewed by an office in the Justice Department known as the Office of Enforcement Operations. FISA orders are reviewed by the Justice Department's Office of Intelligence.

C *Limited Surveillance*

The third category requires a wide variety of rules designed to limit the scope of surveillance. This category includes six specific tools, making it the largest of the categories. These rules limit surveillance to a particular amount of time and require even earlier expiry under some conditions. Other rules limit surveillance to particular types of investigations, for example limiting wiretaps to cases involving crimes appearing on a limited menu of laws. Necessity rules treat some forms of surveillance as a last resort, obligating the investigating team to try other, less invasive forms of surveillance first. The final two tools limit surveillance *ex post* rather than *ex ante*. Minimization rules limit the information that can be obtained, retained, or searched to those related to the reasons justifying the surveillance. Finally, and perhaps most unusually, at least one court has tried to limit the operation of the so-called plain view rule, a kind of minimization with teeth that would not let the government use information falling outside the initial justification.

1 Time Limits

Under federal law, judicial approval to wiretap is good for only thirty days,[17] and approval to install and use a pen register is good for only sixty days.[18] Rules like these prevent perpetual surveillance and ensure that the facts justifying the surveillance have not "gone stale."

This tool can be undermined through renewal provisions. Both the Wiretap Act and the Pen Register Trap and Trace law allow the term of surveillance to be renewed upon application, but only in increments of time shorter than or equal to the initial time limits. Importantly, these extensions are not available as of right, but instead law enforcement must apply for the extensions under substantially the same standards governing an initial request. It seems important, as the *Berger* court pointed out, that a renewal should not rest solely on the initial application but should be refreshed to include evidence gathered since the beginning of surveillance.

16 18 U.S.C. § 2516 (requiring that applications for federal wiretaps be authorized by "the Attorney General, Deputy Attorney General, Associate Attorney General, or any Assistant Attorney General, any acting Assistant Attorney General, or any Deputy Assistant Attorney General or acting Deputy Assistant Attorney General in the Criminal Division or National Security Division specially designated by the Attorney General").

17 *Id.* § 2518.

18 *Id.* § 3123.

2 Minimization

Minimization restricts the scope of what may properly fall within a particular surveillance technique. Surveillance laws often obligate the agency conducting the surveillance to put in place procedures that help filter relevant information from irrelevant information.

In a predigital age, minimization procedures often worked in line with surveillance collection. Police officers with wiretaps would literally hang up the line once they determined a phone call was not relevant to their court authorization.

In the digital age, law enforcement has tended to adopt (with at least tacit and often express approval from judges) an after-the-fact approach to minimization. These procedures allow them to collect everything but require them to use filters and search queries to separate the responsive from unresponsive. These procedures sometimes obligate them to delete old information.

3 Expiry Conditions

Combining the logic behind time limits and minimization, surveillance laws often require surveillance to end once the desired object of the surveillance is obtained. I am referring to these as "expiry conditions." The Wiretap Act, for example, requires that orders specify "the period of time during which such interception is authorized, including a statement as to whether or not the interception shall automatically terminate when the described communication has been first obtained."[19] *Berger* complains that the New York law "places no termination date on the eavesdrop once the conversation sought is seized."[20]

4 Substantive Predicates

Surveillance laws often restrict a particular technique to a particular category of investigation. Roughly speaking, the more invasive the technique, the more limited the types of cases in which it may be used, focusing on the most severe or urgent types of cases. National security surveillance is limited to particular types of targets (e.g. "agents of a foreign power") and certain types of activities (e.g. "international terrorism"). Telephone wiretaps can be used only in cases involving investigations into a prescribed list of crimes, which, admittedly, is long and ever-growing.

The Wiretap Act's list demonstrates the problems with substantive predicates. The list of crimes that may be investigated using a voice wiretap has grown steadily since the law was first enacted in 1968. Today it covers more than fifty crimes, including some relatively minor offenses such as obscenity or bribery in sporting contests.[21] Congress went even further when it expanded the Wiretap Act in 1986 to permit data wiretaps of computer networks, which are authorized in cases involving "any Federal felony."[22]

19 *Id.* § 2518.
20 388 U.S. 41 (1967).
21 18 U.S.C. § 2516(1).
22 *Id.* § 2516(3).

5 Necessity

Under the Wiretap Act, wiretapping must be surveillance of last resort. The federal act requires that "normal investigative procedures have been tried and have failed or reasonably appear to be unlikely to succeed if tried or to be too dangerous,"[23] before a wiretap can be authorized. Law enforcement agencies have interpreted this to mean that investigators must stake out a person's house, interview his neighbors, pull his trash, and subpoena his utility bills, if such approaches are relevant and do not jeopardize the investigation, before applying for a wiretap order.

6 No Plain View

The Ninth Circuit Court of Appeals has proposed a rule that appears to have little precedent: a suspension of the plain view rule, the principle that law enforcement officials may use evidence unrelated to the justification of surveillance, if the criminal nature of the evidence is made immediately apparent, and if the evidence was found in the ordinary course of properly authorized surveillance. This proposal arose in a case involving a search warrant to search through massive hard drives full of data. In an initial opinion, the court suggested that such warrants should not be issued by judges in the Ninth Circuit, unless the government agreed to "waive reliance upon the plain view doctrine" in such cases.[24]

Although this is a single outlier and an unorthodox proposal, it exemplifies well the major theme of this chapter: technology creates significant new privacy problems, and we need to engage in creative thinking about new tools for constraining it.

D *Accountability*

The fourth category consists of measures to ensure that government officials are held accountable when they fail to follow rules governing surveillance. The limited text of the Fourth Amendment requires officers to swear an "oath or affirmation" when applying for a warrant, in order to ensure accountability if they are not truthful. Suppression remedies are designed to deter violations of the rules, by requiring the exclusion of evidence when the rules are not followed.

1 Oath

The Fourth Amendment declares that "no warrants shall issue," except by "oath or affirmation." This can be seen as an accountability enhancing measure. By requiring the attesting officer to present a search warrant application under oath, judges can have greater confidence that the officer is telling the truth, because he or she faces penalties for lying under oath. Similar statutory requirements require the applying officer to sign the request and to attest to the truth of the contents of the request.

[23] *Id.* § 2518.
[24] *United States v. Comprehensive Drug Testing*, 579 F.3d 989 (9th Cir. 2009) (en banc), *amended by* 621 F.3d 1162, 1165 (9th Cir. 2010).

2 Suppression

In Fourth Amendment jurisprudence, the principal remedy when the police violate the right against unreasonable search and seizure is suppression. Evidence obtained in violation of the Fourth Amendment (including the so-called fruit of the poisonous tree, meaning evidence obtained by a chain of events triggered by the violation) is suppressed. The theory is that fear of suppression will deter police misconduct. Suppression also gives defendants an incentive to detect and challenge potential rights violations.

For subconstitutional violations, federal statutory law often does not provide for suppression. In these cases, the deterrent effect disappears, and defendants have far less incentive to challenge potential violations. That said, even in the constitutional context, suppression has its critics.[25] Proposals to create new exclusionary rule regimes are therefore likely to be controversial and vigorously opposed.

E *Transparency*

The fifth and final category of rules require transparency into the usually secretive surveillance practices of the government. These rules regulate notice to the surveilled, set limits on gag orders issued to third parties who assist in surveillance, or require periodic reporting to the public or other branches of government.

1 Notice (and Delayed Notice)

One characteristic that distinguishes modern, technologically abetted surveillance from its physical world antecedents is that physical search often supplies an intrinsic notice to the person under scrutiny. In the physical world, it is difficult to search an individual's home without her knowing.[26] Notice is often part and parcel of the search, and judges and legislatures have required notice as a result.

With technological help, the police can often conduct surveillance without any notice to the target. This is true whether the police are conducting the surveillance directly (e.g. StingRay technology, which masquerades as a cell phone tower) or with the assistance of a third party (e.g. a cell phone provider).

A person who does not realize he has been a target of surveillance cannot take steps to ensure that his rights have been respected. Many surveillance laws thus require notice. These notice requirements are often watered down if not entirely blunted by provisions that allow for delayed notice upon application. Statistics suggest that notice is delayed in a majority of cases. Worse, some have suggested that notice in many cases is not merely "delayed" but in fact never given.

25 *E.g.*, Akhil Reed Amar, *Fourth Amendment First Principles*, 107 Harv. L. Rev. 757 (1994); Christopher Slobogin, *Why Liberals Should Chuck the Exclusionary Rule*, 1999 U. Ill. L. Rev. 363 (1999).

26 Police officers applying for a warrant to search a physical location can request permission to enter the location surreptitiously, delaying the requirement for notice. The USA PATRIOT Act codified the requirement for this kind of warrant, known colloquially as a "sneak-and-peek" warrant.

2 Limiting Gag Orders

In close connection with notice and delayed notice, many surveillance laws directed at obtaining evidence stored with third parties allow the police to apply for a gag order requiring the third party recipient to tell no one, particularly the target of surveillance, about the request. These have been challenged both under the First Amendment and as significant limits on transparency, and many commentators have proposed to roll back or limit the gag order enabling provisions.

3 Public Reporting

Some surveillance reforms target systemic problems rather than individual cases. Along these lines are measures to increase awareness of the scope and scale of surveillance. Many surveillance laws require annual reporting to the legislature or judiciary. These provisions tend to mandate statistics at such an aggregated and vague level, however, that they tend not to do more than reveal broad trends.

The gag orders discussed previously factor into public accounting as well. Increasingly, companies have been issuing "transparency reports," typically quarterly reports summarizing recent law enforcement requests, once again aggregated. The companies who compile these reports often need to navigate broad and perpetual gag orders in the underlying cases, putting them at risk of liability and also limiting the detail with which they can release information.

III Using the Toolkit

How can this list be useful? Who should consult it? How should it be incorporated into our rules and laws? How will this help us balance the need for government surveillance with the civil rights of the potentially surveilled?

A *Legislation*

At the very least, we should add tools from the toolkit to the laws governing surveillance, at both the federal and state levels. The burden to do this rests primarily with those who seek to constrain the police, meaning legislators worried about the scale and type of government surveillance permitted under today's rules as well as nongovernmental organizations who lobby for increased privacy protections through legislation.

Consider one of the examples given in Part I, the increasingly common use by the police of historical cell site location records stored by cell phone companies. Because no single surveillance statute expressly provides for access to these kinds of records, law enforcement has typically requested this information through varying combinations of many different statutory authorities including search warrants, pen register and trap and trace act orders, stored communication act orders, orders under the All Writs Act, subpoenas, and even informal requests. Although some of these orders borrow small bits from the surveillance regulatory toolkit, for the most part, they seem to differ primarily as different levels of justification.

It would be better to enact a new law focused on cell site location information specifically or, even better, government access to location information generally. And in crafting a new location privacy act, Congress should look well beyond justification standards when considering the tools at its disposal. For example, Congress should definitely consider reasonable time limits that both apply to prospective location tracking and, importantly, apply when looking backward in time at a person's historical location record. Such a law might permit, for example, access to only a few days of location information, perhaps increasing that to a week or even a month upon a greater showing.

A location privacy act could also incorporate substantive crime limitations. When the government defends its use of cell site location information, it tends to focus on a small list of highly charged exemplary crimes, such as terrorism, child exploitation, and sex trafficking. Congress could respond directly to these legitimate needs while dealing with concerns about slippery slopes by limiting access to location information to a short list of specifically enumerated predicate crimes.

B *Constitutionalizing the Toolkit*

Because probable cause and judicial review can no longer keep up with changes in surveillance technology, these two tools alone are no longer enough to guarantee protection from "unreasonable searches and seizures" under the Fourth Amendment. The surveillance regulation toolkit thus has constitutional, not merely statutory, applicability. This, of course, was the unmistakable message of *Berger*, but one that was lost when *Katz* was decided the same year, and one that deserves to be revived with the impending fiftieth anniversary of those two decisions. Simply put, following *Berger*, judges can and should create new restrictions on police surveillance from the toolkit (or beyond) as a flexible way to limit unreasonable searches and seizures.[27]

To revisit another earlier example, is the current use by the government of malware constitutional? In every case that has been litigated to date, the government has used a probable cause search warrant before deploying malware. But surely probable cause, a standard devised in physical world searches that differ in many significant, privacy-impacting ways from malware, cannot do all of the work necessary to prevent unreasonable searches.

I would argue that, given the risks of government malware, the Constitution should require finely specified rules that limit the use of this category of tools to exceptional cases. Specifically, government malware seems to be a prime candidate for a revitalization of the necessity requirement. Malware should be a last resort tool, never a tool used early in an investigation or when other investigative avenues have yet to be tried. A judge, following the lead of *Berger* and the Wiretap Act, could require that "normal investigative procedures have been tried and have failed or reasonably appear to be unlikely to succeed if tried or to be too dangerous," before authorizing the use of malware.

[27] For an extended analysis of how this broader toolkit might apply to various contemporary surveillance technologies as a matter of Fourth Amendment law, *see* David Gray, THE FOURTH AMENDMENT IN AN AGE OF SURVEILLANCE (2017).

C A *Dynamic and Evolving Toolkit*

Ultimately, if legislatures and courts (and the advocates who argue before them) embrace the expanded toolkit outlined in this chapter, then they will begin to see that the tools are dynamic and evolving. The toolkit laid out previously may appear to be a static list, which is, I would argue, a reflection of our lack of attention to most of these approaches. Once we shift our focus to the neglected categories in the list, we will also breathe new life into their development, in time discovering nuances within categories and relationships among categories that we cannot see at this time.

For example, consider the work of Susan Freiwald, who has looked beyond review and justification in her work. Freiwald has repeatedly argued that surveillance that is "hidden, continuous, indiscriminate, and intrusive" ought to be governed not only by a warrant requirement but also by the procedural requirements of the Wiretap Act.[28]

I think this chapter bolsters Freiwald's proposal, but also offers an opportunity to expand it. Freiwald advocates a wholesale adoption of all of the Wiretap Act's requirements, following what the lower courts have done with silent video. I think that scholars should tease apart the monolith that is the Wiretap Act's bundle of requirements into its constituent parts. Each entry in the toolkit plays a slightly different role than the others and advances different values and provides different protections.

As we begin to unbundle the toolkit, we will of course learn how the various tools interact with one another. The taxonomy may help with this effort, because bolstering one protection within a taxonomic category may open the door possibly to slacken other protections in that same category. Most importantly, the six menu items within the "limit surveillance" category all go about that particular goal in slightly different ways from the rest of the group. A policy maker, advocate, or scholar might reasonably conclude that a stronger necessity requirement decreases the need for substantive predicates, and vice versa.

Allow me to focus in closing on only one category from among the toolkit that I think holds great promise as a tool for regulatory discipline: necessity. The necessity requirement – seemingly required only for wiretaps and silent video – ensures that certain invasive techniques are rare tools of last resort. If we expand the use of a necessity by, for example, adding a necessity requirement to government use of malware, then we need to face a new question: as between wiretap and malware, which ought to be tried first?

It would not do to place wiretap, silent video, and malware into a single category, allowing any one of these three to occur before any other. Malware will not be the last powerfully invasive surveillance technology the police develop, meaning we are likely to continue to grow the list of tools subject to necessity to include a fourth, fifth, and so on. The longer this list, the more we will water down the "rare tools of last resort" goal of necessity, ending up with just two categories, tools that are so invasive they must be used "after" and the rest of the tools, which may be used "before."

It would be better to let judges or legislatures continue to rank-order exceptional tools. This would be difficult to do with any scientific precision, of course, so we need to aim for approximate approaches. But it might be, for example, that we begin to develop a rich ladder of necessity, placing many surveillance techniques into a rank order. Thus malware might be considered the most privacy- and libertyiinvasive and thus might be

28 *First Principles of Communications Privacy*, 2007 Stan. Tech. L. Rev. 3 (2007).

placed on a higher rung than wiretaps, meaning that wiretaps can occur before malware, and that malware cannot be deployed until wiretaps have been tried or otherwise are shown to be futile.

Over time, this approach will truly begin to resemble a ladder. Cell site location information might be permitted before wiretaps, but only after everything else has been tried. We might judge (again either as a constitutional requirement or through legislative enactment) that searches of DNA databases might take place only after telephone pen registers have been tried or otherwise shown to be futile.

Conclusion

Our legal system has devised at least sixteen ways to limit and regulate government surveillance. Fourteen of these approaches have suffered from the neglect of those worried about what dramatic changes in technology are doing to privacy and other civil liberties. This chapter hopes to spur increased attention and creative thinking by collecting these approaches into a single, organized, and focused list. Probable cause is a very old and well-established tool for limiting surveillance, but the modern age of technology reveals that it is not nearly enough. Judges should see it as their constitutional prerogative to impose new forms of necessity and minimization. Legislators should increase public reporting and limit the widespread use of gag orders. Advocates should push both judges and legislatures to think more often about suppression and time limits. Only by expanding and enriching our regulatory toolkit can we hope to achieve what everybody in this debate claims to be looking for, a proper balance between empowering our government to detect, prevent, and punish crime and other threats to society with the need for privacy, candid discourse, and liberty the members of our society demand.

22 European Human Rights, Criminal Surveillance, and Intelligence Surveillance: Towards "Good Enough" Oversight, Preferably but Not Necessarily by Judges

Gianclaudio Malgieri[†] & Paul De Hert[*]

Article E 8, European Convention on Human Rights – *Right to respect for private and family life*

1. Everyone has the right to respect for his private and family life, his home and his correspondence.
2. There shall be no interference by a public authority with the exercise of this right except such as is in accordance with the law and is necessary in a democratic society in the interests of national security, public safety or the economic wellbeing of the country, for the prevention of disorder or crime, for the protection of health or morals, or for the protection of the rights and freedoms of others.

Article 13, European Convention on Human Rights – *Right to an effective remedy*

1. Everyone whose rights and freedoms as set forth in this Convention are violated shall have an effective remedy before a national authority notwithstanding that the violation has been committed by persons acting in an official capacity.

The two European Courts (the European Court of Human Rights, ECtHR and, to a lesser degree, the European Union Court of Justice, EUCJ) have contributed greatly to the development of a legal framework for surveillance either by law enforcement agencies in the criminal law area or by secret services. Both courts put great emphasis on a system of control *ex ante* and *post hoc* by independent supervisory authorities. A complex and controversial issue remains understanding whether the human rights to privacy, respect of communications, and an effective remedy (enshrined in Article 8 and 13 of the European Convention on Human Rights (ECHR)), require judicial review as a necessary safeguard for secret surveillance or, alternatively, determining under which conditions parallel systems of non-judicial review can be accepted as adequate safeguards against illegitimate interference in citizens' private life.

The European Courts have not yet established a clear doctrine in determining suitable thresholds and parameters. In particular, the ECtHR has a flexible approach in interpreting Article 8 and 13 ECHR, depending on several factors ("vital" interests at stake, political considerations, etc.). In general terms, the Court has shown a preference towards judiciary oversight, but in the European legal order there are several examples of alternative oversight systems assessed positively by the Court, such as the quasi-judiciary

[†] PhD Researcher in Law at Vrije Universiteit Brussel, Brussels.
[*] Law professor at Vrije Universiteit Brussel and Tilburg University.

systems (where the independence of the supervisory body, its wide jurisdiction, its power to access data and its power to effective reactions are confirmed) or the system of oversight set by Data Protection Authorities in the EU member states. However, in recent judgements of the ECtHR and the EUCJ we see an increasing emphasis on declaring the necessity of a "good enough" judicial (*ex ante* or *post hoc*) control over surveillance, meaning not simply a judicial control, but a system of oversight (judicial, quasi-judicial, hybrid) which can provide an effective control over surveillance, supported by empirical checks in the national legal system at issue.

I Introduction: Does Surveillance Require a Judge?

Surveillance raises many questions about human rights acceptability. Be it public or private, what it needs is a framework – organisational, legal, and technological – that allows the protection of the society and maintains a framework of freedoms.[1]

European human rights case law on surveillance is considerable, and this chapter will review the leading opinions from the European Court of Human Rights (hereafter ECtHR or Strasbourg Court), and, to a lesser degree, from the European Union Court of Justice (hereafter EUCJ or Luxembourg Court) – most notably *Schrems v. Data Protection Commissioner* (2015).[2]

An indispensable element in every surveillance framework, at least for surveillance done by public actors, is a system of control *ex ante* and *post hoc* by an independent supervisory authority, which might be a judge or another national authority. A central question in European human rights law on surveillance is whether Article 8 of the European Convention on Human Rights (ECHR)[3] – containing the right to privacy and secrecy of communications and the inviolability of the house – requires judicial review as a necessary safeguard for secret surveillance or, alternatively, what conditions and systems of non-judicial review can be accepted as adequate safeguards against illegitimate interference in citizens' private lives.

So far, the question has not been resolved in a decisive way. In general terms, we can affirm that in the field of surveillance, where "abuse is potentially so easy in individual cases and could have such harmful consequences for democratic society as a whole, *it is in principle desirable to entrust supervisory control to a judge*,"[4] but this is not a hard rule. In fact, the European Court of Human Rights has adopted a flexible approach. We will

1 David Lyon, Surveillance Studies: An Overview (Polity Press, 2007).

2 Under the term "European human rights" law we mean both the "Convention for the Protection of Human Rights and Fundamental Freedoms," better known as the *European Convention on Human Rights*, ECHR (which was opened for signature in Rome on 4 November 1950 and came into force in 1953 and whose application scope includes the forty-seven Member States of the Council) and the EU Charter of Fundamental Rights (proclaimed in Nice in 2000) applicable to the twenty-eight Member States of the European Union. Our text will focus on the ECHR.

3 Article 8 ECHR, Right to respect for private and family life: "1. Everyone has the right to respect for his private and family life, his home and his correspondence. 2. There shall be no interference by a public authority with the exercise of this right except such as is in accordance with the law and is necessary in a democratic society in the interests of national security, public safety or the economic well-being of the country, for the prevention of disorder or crime, for the protection of health or morals, or for the protection of the rights and freedoms of others."

4 *Klass & Others v. Germany*, No. 5029/71, Eur. Ct. H.R. 1, 21 (1978).

highlight when and under which conditions the ECtHR has accepted systems of non-judicial control over surveillance.

In recent judgements of both the ECtHR and the EUCJ we see an increasing emphasis on declaring the necessity of a *good enough* (*ex ante* or *ex post*) control over surveillance: not necessarily a judicial control, but a system of oversight (judicial, quasi-judicial, hybrid) which can provide an effective control over surveillance, supported by empirical checks in the national legal system at issue.

Part II of this chapter will clarify the general content of Article 8 ECHR and the terminology used in the field of surveillance oversight, considering different national criminal procedure legal systems. Part III will address specifically the application of Article 8 ECHR in criminal law surveillance, as crystallised in *Huvig v. France* (1990), one of the first cases of "strict scrutiny" by the Court. Next, Part IV will analyse the different measures of scrutiny in the Court's surveillance case law.

Considering that surveillance can be conducted by different actors for different purposes, a specific focus should be dedicated to secret service surveillance. Part V will analyse how the Court has assessed the necessity of an individual's effective remedy against secret service surveillance, according to Article 13 ECHR combined with Article 8 ECHR.

Typically, member states have provided "non-judiciary" oversight of secret service surveillance. Therefore, Parts VI and VII will highlight how the Court has assessed these "non-judiciary" methods of surveillance control. Particular attention will be dedicated to "quasi-judiciary" systems, as in the case of Data Protection Authorities (Part VIII).

Lastly, Part IX will analyse how the Court is assessing these oversight systems by using empirical means to assess the effectiveness of each system.

II Some Preliminary Clarifications – Oversight and Remedy: Who and When

Before discussing European case law on surveillance, some clarifications are necessary, especially regarding the system of judicial control warranted by European human rights law.

Article 8 ECHR is divided into two paragraphs. In the first paragraph four rights are enumerated: the right to respect for an individual's private life, family life, home, and correspondence. A second paragraph contains three requirements for acceptable privacy limitations: these must have a legal basis (the ""in accordance with the law" requirement), must seek legitimate purposes (the legitimacy requirement), and must be proportional (the "necessary in a democratic society" requirement).

Second, we need to clarify some terms used in this chapter. *Oversight* means supervision, management, or control, while *review* means to view again, survey again, or take a retrospective view of events and activities that have already occurred.[5] Oversight can be *ex ante* and/or *ex post*. *Ex ante* oversight consists of an authorization for surveillance measures given by a supervisory authority, normally a judge. *Ex post* oversight consists of review over surveillance measures already started. This review may be triggered by individuals who suspect they are under surveillance, or it could be automatic (e.g., a random

5 Marina Caparini, Controlling & Overseeing Intelligence Services in Democratic States 8 (Hans Born & Marina Caparini eds., Democratic Control of Intelligence Services, Hampshire 2007).

control by judges or other supervisory authority), also within a criminal trial (i.e., during a judicial proceeding after investigation by surveillance).[6]

It is necessary to remind the non-European reader that in some European states investigatory powers within criminal law investigations are exercised by a *prosecutor*, and a *control judge* must authorize specific surveillance measures. This is the typical *adversarial* system.[7] In other countries, investigative powers are exercised by *investigative judges*, and no other judges control investigation until the trial. This is typical of *inquisitorial* systems.[8]

Unlike the US Constitution (Fourth Amendment), there is no provision in European human rights law stating that in some cases a warrant (by a judge) is needed. Neither the 'who' nor the 'when' of oversight is made concrete. To understand the European approach (or lack of it), one must look at the conjunction between Article 8 ECHR (right to privacy) and Article 13 ECHR (right to an effective remedy): when the right to private life is violated, an "effective remedy by a national authority" is necessary. The Strasbourg Court considers judges an "effective remedy provided by national authorities," but it has never stated that Article 13 ECHR can be satisfied solely by judicial oversight (see more detail in Part IV).

Articles 8 and 13 ECHR both fail to clarify the relation or choice between *ex ante* or *ex post* oversight, but in principle at least a *post hoc* control should be guaranteed. We will address this particular topic during our case law overview.

III Article 8 ECHR and the Huvig Requirements for Criminal Surveillance

The canonical judgements on surveillance mostly relate to interception of telecommunications, in particular telephone lines. Judgements such as *Klass v. Germany* (1978) and *Malone v. UK* (1984), respectively on surveillance of telecommunications by German secret services and by UK police, are classics in this respect. Both centre around Article 8 ECHR and contain clarifications of notions such as 'privacy' and the requirements of legality and proportionality. These judgements contain the first guidelines on surveillance in Europe, that further crystallised in *Huvig v. France* (1990).[9]

In *Huvig*, rendered at a time when most European states had recognized powers to intercept telecommunication, the ECtHR clarified in detail which safeguards are required with regard to telephone surveillance according to Article 8 ECHR (see Table 22.1). In particular, the Court gave a broad characterization of the requirement that privacy-limiting powers need a legal basis. The Court stated that the expression "in accordance with the law," within the meaning of Article 8(2) ECHR, requires 1) that the impugned measure should have *some basis in domestic law*, where "law" is understood in its substantive sense including both enactments of lower rank than statutes and unwritten law;[10] 2) that "law" also refers to the quality of the law in question, requiring that it

6 *See* Eur. Commission For Democracy Through Law (Venice Commission), Report On The Democratic Oversight Of The Security Services § 195 (2007).

7 *See id.* at § 197.

8 *See* P. De Hert, "Het recht op een onderzoeksrechter in Belgisch en Europees perspectief. Grondrechtelijke armoede met een inquisitoriale achtergrond" [The investigating judge in Belgian and European Law], Panopticon. Tijdschrift voor strafrecht, criminologie en forensisch welzijnswerk, 2003, vol. 24/2, 155–98.

9 No. 11105/84 Eur. Ct. H.R. (1990).

10 *Id.* at § 28.

Table 22.1. Minimum Safeguards That Law Should Provide in Order to Avoid Abuse of State Powers (Huvig)

Elements that surveillance law must provide, according to *Huvig*
a) *categories* of people liable to be monitored
b) the *nature of the offenses* subject to surveillance
c) limits on the *duration* of such monitoring
d) *procedure* [for examining, using and storing the data]
e) *precautions* to be taken [in order to communicate the data intact and in their entirety for inspection by judge and by defence]
f) circumstances in which data is *erased* or destroyed
g) *judicial control* (eventual requirement)

should be *accessible* to the person concerned,[11] who must moreover be able to *foresee* its consequences for him; and 3) that the measure must be *compatible with the rule of law*.[12]

In substance, what the law should indicate with reasonable clarity is *the scope and manner* of exercise of the relevant discretion conferred on the public authorities.[13] In particular, the Court insisted on six mandatory clarifications: the categories of people liable to be monitored; the nature of the offenses subject to surveillance; limits on the duration of such monitoring; the procedure to be followed for storing the data; the precautions to be taken when communicating the data; and the circumstances in which data is erased or destroyed.[14]

An optional, seventh requirement concerned the need for a judge authorizing or reviewing surveillance measures: "The Court does not in any way minimise the value of several of the safeguards, *in particular the need for a decision by an investigating judge*, who is an independent judicial authority, the latter's supervision of senior police officers *and the possible supervision of the judge himself by the Indictment Division (chambre d'accusation) of the Court of Appeal, by trial courts and courts of appeal and, if need be, by the Court of Cassation*."[15] This quote shows that the Strasbourg Court – though approving the French system of judicial control over surveillance – is unclear about the importance and the general necessity of this safeguard for any surveillance system. Indeed, its statement "*The Court does not in any way minimise the value of several of the safeguards*" is ambiguous, and the judgement therefore does not answer the question whether *a priori* judicial control is a necessary safeguard for surveillance in European human rights law. The reluctance of the Court can be explained by considering the different structure of criminal procedure in Europe.[16] If we wanted to consider *Huvig* as a

11 *Id*. at § 29.
12 *Id*. at § 26.
13 *Id*. at § 35. Note that these principles on surveillance partly return in *Rotaru v. Romania*, No. 28341/95, Eur. Ct. H.R. (2000), where the Court looks at the law on processing data from surveillance for national security purposes.
14 *Huvig*, No. 11105/84, Eur. Ct. H.R. at § 34; *see*, in this regards, P. De Hert, "Het recht op een onderzoeksrechter in Belgisch en Europees perspectief. Grondrechtelijke armoede met een inquisitoriale achtergrond" [The investigating judge in Belgian and European Law], Panopticon. Tijdschrift voor strafrecht, criminologie en forensisch welzijnswerk, 2003, vol. 24/2, 155–98.
15 *Huvig*, No. 11105/84, Eur. Ct. H.R. at § 33.
16 French criminal procedure is based on the inquisitorial system, where *investigative judges* lead investigations and authorize interceptions and *control judges* supervise investigation measures and review

model for *adversarial* systems, would it be sufficient that prosecutors authorize interceptions, or, instead, would it be preferable that ordinary judges (acting as "control judges") authorize it?[17]

Another open question relates to the scope of *Huvig*: are the six or seven surveillance requirements generally applicable or only needed for individual surveillance measures in the context of criminal law? What about less intrusive measures or more intrusive measures (such as mass surveillance)? What about surveillance led by secret services?

For our purposes here, the intrusiveness of telephone interceptions at issue in *Huvig* may well justify the high degree of detail in safeguards the Court required for surveillance laws.[18]

IV The Inconsistent ECtHR Scrutiny of Article 8(2) ECHR: Strict v. Weak Scrutiny

The seven *Huvig* requirements with regard to the legality requirement in Article 8 ECHR place the bar very high and guarantee strict scrutiny. These requirements have been reiterated in many other cases including *Rotaru v. Romania* (2000),[19] *Kennedy v. United Kingdom* (2010),[20] *Gillian & Quinton v. United Kingdom* (2000),[21] *Zakharov v. Russia* (2015),[22] *Dragojević v. Croatia* (2015),[23] *Szabò and Vissy v. Hungary* (2016).[24]

However, no "robust" scrutiny or strict checking on surveillance safeguards took place in other surveillance cases such as *Uzun v. Germany* (2010)[25] and *Colon v. Netherland*

surveillance *post hoc*. Instead, in adversarial systems, investigations are led by prosecutors and not by investigative judges (thus, for example, there have not been any "investigative judges" in the United Kingdom since the 1970s).

17 The following cases offer interesting stimuli to answer many of the questions mentioned. In particular, while in the next case (*Uzun v. Germany*, No 35623/05, Eur. Ct. H.R. (2010)) the safeguards required are consistently less strict than in *Huvig*, because of less intrusive measures of surveillance at issue (GPS tracking); the ECJ cases analysed *infra* (*Digital Rights Irelands* and *Schrems*) unexpectedly use the *Huvig* safeguards paradigm for mass surveillance, which is generally less intrusive and less delicate than individual surveillance. The reason for this apparent contradiction is the increasing development of technologies which is blurring the difference between more intrusive and less intrusive surveillance measures, on the one hand; and a stricter scrutiny of the European Courts on surveillance after Snowden's revelations (*See* A. Galetta & P. De Hert, *Complementing the Surveillance Law Principles of the ECtHR with its Environmental Law Principles: An Integrated Technology Approach to a Human Rights Framework for Surveillance*, 10 Utrecht L. Rev. 1, 55, 61 (2014); *see also* Nora Loidleain, *Surveillance of Communication Data and Article 8 of the European Convention on Human Rights*, *in* Reloading Data Protection: Multidisciplinary Insights & Contemporary Challenges, 197 (S. Gutwirth et al. eds., 2014). However, these topics will be more fully addressed in the next paragraphs.

18 *Huvig*, No. 11105/84, Eur. Ct. H.R. at § 32 ("Tapping and other forms of interception of telephone conversations represent a serious interference with private life and correspondence and must accordingly be based on a 'law' that is particularly precise. It is essential to have clear, detailed rules on the subject, *especially as the technology available for use is continually becoming more sophisticated*").

19 No. 28341/95, Eur. Ct. H.R. (2000).

20 No. 26839/05, Eur. Ct. H.R. (2010).

21 No. 4158/05, Eur. Ct. H.R. (2000).

22 No. 47143/06, Eur. Ct. H.R. (2015).

23 No. 68955/11, Eur. Ct. H.R. (2015); *see* G. Gonzalez Fuster, *What Prior Judicial Scrutiny of Secret Surveillance Stands For*, 1–6 Eur. Data Protection L. Rev. 3 (2016).

24 No. 37138/14, Eur. Ct. H.R. (2016).

25 No. 35623/05, Eur. Ct. H.R. (2010).

(2012)[26] or in cases concerning workplace surveillance such as *Barbulescu v. Romania* (2016).[27]

Scholars have wondered why the Court sometimes adopts robust scrutiny and in other cases does not. As for surveillance in the workplace (e.g., employers reading employees' emails and messages or installing CCTV cameras), the reason for less strict scrutiny could relate to the fact that there is a conflict between two "individuals' rights" (privacy of employees versus economic rights of employers), and no public interests are at issue.[28] As regards *Uzun v. Germany*, for example, scholars have suggested that the scrutiny of the Court was fainter because of the less intrusive means of interception at issue (geo-position-system instead of the telephone interceptions at issue in *Huvig*).[29]

The choice between strict and weak scrutiny is sometimes overtly political. Both *Gillian* and *Colon* concern not covert surveillance but patent physical surveillance: police "stop and search."[30] Though they are similar cases – we see strict scrutiny in *Gillian* and weak scrutiny in *Colon* – revealing a tendency for increasingly "less robust scrutiny over policing powers" and a "greater reluctance of the Court to exert oversight in relation to counter-terrorist powers of general application than those of individual application."[31]

Most of the foregoing is guesswork, since the Court seldom theorizes its approach. Only sometimes does the ECtHR explicitly adopt strict scrutiny, either declaring it will interpret Article 8(2) ECHR narrowly or affirming a principle of "strict necessity." Such is the case in *Rotaru*[32] and *Kennedy*.[33] In *Szabò and Vissy*,[34] the Court clearly affirms that "*given the particular character of the interference in question and the potential of cutting-edge surveillance technologies to invade citizens' privacy*, the requirement 'necessary in a democratic society' must be interpreted in this context as requiring '*strict necessity*.'"[35]

The EUCJ has also adopted, in its recent judgements, a strict necessity principle. In particular, in *Digital Rights Ireland Ltd.*[36] and then in *Schrems v. Data Protection Commissioner*,[37] the Court applied a "strict necessity" principle. Again, however, we find very little justification in terms of doctrine – little explanation of what this principle

26 No. 49458/06, Eur. Ct. H.R. (2012).
27 No. 61496/08, Eur. Ct. H.R. (2016).
28 *See* Tor-Inge Harbo, *The Function of the Proportionality Principle in EU Law*, 16:2 Eur. L. J. 160 (2010) ("The court took a less coherent approach when applying the suitability and necessity test, applying a *strict test in cases where it believed that the individual interests should prevail and a less strict approach when it believed that public interest should prevail*").
29 *See* Galetta & De Hert, *supra* note 17, at 55–75 (2014); *see also* Loideain, *supra* note 17, at 197.
30 *See* G. Lennon, *Stop and Search Powers in UK Terrorism Investigations: A Limited Judicial Oversight?*, 20 Int'l J. of Hum. Rts. 634–648 (2016).
31 *Id.* at 639.
32 *Rotaru*, No. 28341/95, Eur. Ct. H.R. at 15–16 ("That paragraph [Art. 8(2) ECHR], since it provides for an exception to a right guaranteed by the Convention, *is to be interpreted narrowly*. While the Court recognises that intelligence services may legitimately exist in a democratic society, it reiterates that powers of secret surveillance of citizens are tolerable under the Convention only in so far as *strictly necessary* for safeguarding the democratic institutions").
33 *See Kennedy*, No. 26839/05, Eur. Ct. H.R. at 46 ("The Court recalls that powers to instruct secret surveillance of citizens are only tolerated under Article 8 to the extent that they are *strictly necessary* for safeguarding democratic institutions").
34 *Szabò*, No. 37138/14, Eur. Ct. H.R. at 33 (Article 8(2) "is to be narrowly interpreted."); *see also id.* at 38–39.
35 *Id.* at 38–39.
36 Case C-293/12, 2014 Eur. Ct. Just. §§ 52, 56, 62.
37 Case C-362/14, 2015 Eur. Ct. Just. § 92.

means. Most likely, these statements influenced the ECtHR in judgements after *Digital Ireland* and *Schrems* (e.g., *Szabò and Vissy*).[38]

We should clarify that "strict necessity" refers to the three requirements of Article 8 ECHR, while the general discussion that we have conducted so far refers to the legality requirements of the surveillance framework. If all the six (or seven) requirements from *Huvig* mentioned are applied by the Court, for us that is a case of "strict scrutiny." In general, the Court has never really set a clear doctrine about the strictness of its assessment: there are merely some sporadic suggestions and a multiform (or even ambiguous) use of the term "strict." In order to organise the case law of the ECtHR and to understand better when this Court adopts strict or weak scrutiny, we have identified in Table 22.2 the degree of scrutiny combined with other variables (means of interception, surveillance body, and nature of the investigation).

Table 22.2 allows us to see that the Court adopted robust scrutiny in cases in which a) the claimant was a protester against the government (*Rotaru, Gillian, Zakharov, Szabò*) or b) an "economic crime" was at issue (tax evasion, forgery, drug dealers) (*Malone, Huvig, Dragojevi*). On the other hand, the scrutiny was weak when terrorism (*Uzun*), safety (prevention of murder, *Colon*), or workplace surveillance (*Barbulescu*) was at issue. From these findings, we can infer that the ECtHR does a strict balancing when there is no "vital" security interest at issue (economic crimes, anti-government protesters) or in general when public interests at issue are more political (anti-government) or economic (tax, forgery, drugs trade). The court is less strict when public interests at issue concern the protection of the life of an individual (terrorism, murder).

When surveillance is directed to protect (including indirectly) the safety of individuals, the ECtHR seems to accept a non-strict balancing approach, because life should typically prevail over privacy,[39] whereas where other issues are at stake – economic crimes, anti-government protesters – privacy as a human right of individuals should typically prevail and so the scrutiny is stricter. Additionally, in cases of anti-government protesters, the risks of limiting democracy are high (see later discussion on the empirical check of the rule of law effectiveness).

Again, all this is educated guesswork. What is sure is that the Court uses the flexibility afforded by the wording of Articles 8 and 13 ECHR and so it sometimes adopts a weak scrutiny approach, and sometimes a robust scrutiny approach. The Court never explicitly explains its reasons for the different measures of scrutiny, but the logic inferred here – if confirmed in the future by other studies – could be a useful tool to foresee the degree of scrutiny the Court will apply under Article 8(2) ECHR in different circumstances.

38 *See* Mark D. Cole & Annelies Vandendriessche, *From Digital Rights Ireland and Schrems in Luxembourg to Zakharov and Szabó/Vissy in Strasbourg: What the ECtHR Made of the Deep Pass by the CJEU in the Recent Cases on Mass Surveillance,* 2 Eur. Data Protection L. Rev. 128 (2016).

39 *See, e.g.*, *General Data Protection Regulation* (Regulation (EU) 2016/679 of the European Parliament and of the Council of 27 April 2016 on the protection of natural persons with regard to the processing of personal data and on the free movement of such data, and repealing Directive 95/46/EC), recitals n. 46, 73, 112, where it appears clearly that any restriction to privacy and data protection is tolerated if it is due to the protection of "vital interests, including physical integrity" or to the "the protection of human life especially in response to natural or manmade disasters, the prevention, investigation and prosecution of criminal offences or the execution of criminal penalties, including the safeguarding against and the prevention of threats to public security."

Table 22.2. ECtHR Scrutiny When Applying Article 8(2) ECHR

ECtHR Surveillance Cases	Degree of Scrutiny	How We Can Infer That the Scrutiny Is Strict	Means of Interception	Surveillance Body	What Triggered Surveillance	Conviction
Klass v. Germany	Low		Telephone	Secret service	None declared	No
Malone v. United Kingdom	**Strict**	**Strict requi-rements**[a]	Telephone and metering	Police	**Property crimes**	Yes
Huvig v. France	**Strict**	**Strict requi-rements**[b]	Telephone tapping	Police	**Tax crimes**	Yes
Rotaru v. Romania	**Strict**	**Declared byCourt**[c]	Public articles	Secret services	**Protesters against the government**	Yes
Kennedy v. United Kingdom	**Strict**	**Declared byCourt Strict requirements**[d]	Telephone tapping	Police & secret services	**Protester against the government**	No
Uzun v. Germany	Low		GPS	Police	Terrorism[e]	No
Barbulescu v. Romania	Low		E-mails	Employer	Work	No
Gillian v. United Kingdom	**Strict**	**Strict requi-rements**[f]	Stop and search	Police	**Protesters against the government**	Yes
Colon v. Netherlands	Low		Stop and search	Police	Prevention of crimes against life, e.g. murders	No
Zakharov v. Russia	**Strict**	**Strict parameters used** (same as ***Huvig***)[g]	Telephone tapping	Secret service	**Protesters against the government**	Yes
Dragojević v. Croatia	**Strict**	**Strict parameters (same as *Huvig*)**[h]	Telephone tapping	Police	**Drug crimes**	Yes
Szabò v. Hungary	**Strict**	**Declared byCourt** [i]	Telephone tapping	Police	**Protesters against the government**	Yes

[a] *Malone v. United Kingdom*, No. 8691/79, Eur. Ct. H.R. §§ 67–68, 70.

[b] *Huvig*, No. 11105/84, Eur. Ct. H.R. at § 34.

[c] *Rotaru*, No. 28341/95, Eur. Ct. H.R. at 15–16.

[d] *Kennedy*, No. 26839/05, Eur. Ct. H.R. at 46.

[e] As for the assessment of the Court in terrorism affairs, *see* Lennon, *supra* note 30, at 644.

[f] *Gillian*, No. 4158/05, Eur. Ct. H.R. 34–35.

[g] *Zakharov*, No. 47143/06, Eur. Ct. H.R. 57–58.

[h] *Dragojević*, No. 68955/11, Eur. Ct. H.R. at 23–24.

[i] *Szabò*, No. 37138/14, Eur. Ct. H.R. at 33, 37–38.

V Article 13 ECHR and an Effective Remedy for Secret Service Surveillance

Surveillance is not always conducted by private actors (such as employers) or by law enforcement authorities (such as the police); it is often conducted by secret services, or what in America would be referred to as "national security" services. The supervision of secret service surveillance is a delicate issue, which was first discussed in *Klass* (1978) and later on in judgements such as *Rotaru* (2000) and *Szabò and Vissy* (2016).

For the sake of clarity, we distinguish between "criminal law surveillance or criminal surveillance" and "intelligence surveillance or secret services surveillance." The first is generally led by police for the purpose of crime detection; the latter by secret service agencies for the purpose of national security, public safety, and general national strategic interests.[40] In practice, we see that a system of *judicial overview*, generally based on judicial review, is always used for criminal law surveillance, whereas intelligence surveillance is sometimes (in some countries) controlled via *judicial overview* but more often via alternative systems of safeguards – *non-judicial overview*.

This difference in regulation is due to the different purposes for which the surveillance is conducted: while for criminal law investigations ordinary judges are the most appropriate supervisory authority, intelligence affairs involve a more political evaluation, which is often better assessed by non-judiciary authorities (ministers, national agencies, parliamentary committees, etc.). Also, criminal law surveillance usually leads to prosecution and is therefore usually assessed by judges during ordinary trials, whereas secret service surveillance usually remains secret even after it is finished.

This separation of tasks and oversight mechanisms between police and secret services is typical of the German legal system, but is echoed in several other systems. It is based on the so-called "*Trennungsgebot*,"[41] a German constitutional principle according to which the differences between police and secret service activities in terms of *purposes* (national security vs. crime detection) and *means* (police investigations are usually led by investigative judges or prosecutors within criminal procedure law) impose strictly separate regulations of the national bodies in order to preserve the rule of law.

In other countries, such as the United Kingdom or Russia, this separation is not considered a constitutional safeguard. An example is the UK Regulation of Investigatory Power Act (RIPA) of 2000 (assessed in *Kennedy v. UK* discussed later), which regulates both police and secret service surveillance in the same manner. Another example is the Russian Operational-Search Activities Act (OSAA) of 12 August 1995 (assessed in *Zakharov v. Russia*, discussed later), which is "applicable to the interception of communications both in the framework of criminal proceedings and outside such framework" and does not make a distinction according to the purposes of the surveillance.[42]

40 *See* Hans Born & Marina Caparini, Democratic Control of Intelligence Services, 5–6 (Routledge 2007) (regarding the specific purposes of secret services: counterintelligence and security intelligence).

41 *See, e.g.*, A. Dorn, Das Trennungsgebot in verfassungshistorischer Perspektive: zur Aufnahme inlandsnachrichtendienstlicher Bundeskompetenzen in das Grundgesetz vom 23. Mai 1949 (Verlag Duncker & Humblot, 2004); *see also* J. Singer, Das Trennungsgebot – Teil 1: Politisches Schlagwort oder verfassungsrechtliche Vorgabe?, (Die Kriminalpolizei, 2006).

42 According to OSAA, "the aims of operational-search activities are: (1) the detection, prevention, suppression and investigation of criminal offences and the identification of persons conspiring to commit, committing, or having committed a criminal offence; (2) the tracing of fugitives from justice and missing

This non-separation between police and secret services has been increasing lately. For example, a recent Hungarian law regulates both police and secret services surveillance without a strict separation: the police can act both for the purpose of crime detection and for the purpose of national security, which positions them in the territory traditionally occupied by secret services.[43] This example illustrates a trend in many states to provide police forces with broader and broader powers, especially in areas once reserved to secret services, such as terrorism investigation or national security.[44] Another trend, relevant here, is the increasing reduction of judicial procedural guarantees towards police and prosecutors' activity.[45]

With regard to judicial oversight in secret service surveillance, the ECHR provides in Article 13 that "everyone whose rights and freedoms as set forth in this Convention are violated shall have an *effective remedy* before a national authority," but it does not require judicial redress as the only effective remedy, as already discussed. For the ECtHR, judges are an "effective remedy provided by national authorities," but it has never stated that Article 13 strictly requires judicial review. On the contrary, the Court has often accepted alternative remedies, including for secret services surveillance. In the Court's view, "the authority referred to in Article 13 … may not necessarily in all instances be a judicial authority in the strict sense. Nevertheless, the powers and procedural guarantees an authority possesses are relevant in determining whether the remedy before it is effective."[46]

In the following sections, we will describe how the Court has differently interpreted the flexible wording of Articles 8 and 13 ECHR,[47] especially in the field of secret service surveillance.

VI The "Non-Judicial Oversight" from *Klass* to *Szabò*

Klass (1978) is the first case in which ECtHR accepted non-judicial oversight as adequate in the light of Articles 8 and 13 ECHR.[48] The Court had to assess a new German law

persons; (3) obtaining information about events or activities endangering the national, military, economic or ecological security of the Russian Federation." *Zakharov*, No. 47143/06, Eur. Ct. H.R. 6–7.

43 On 1 January 2011, a specific Anti-Terrorism Task Force was established within the Hungarian *police* force under the control of the Police Act, amended by a reform in 2011, which gave the task force prerogatives *in the field of secret intelligence gathering*, including surveillance with recording and secret house search.

44 Lennon, *supra* note 30, at 634–48.

45 J. Vervaele, *Surveillance and Criminal Investigation: Blurring of Thresholds and Boundaries in the Criminal Justice System?* 115 *in Reloading Data Protection: Multidisciplinary Insight and contemporary challenge*, (S. Gurtwirh, R. Leenes, & P. De Hert eds., 2014).

46 *See Klass*, No. 5029/71, Eur. Ct. H.R. at 25;.*see also* the Golder judgment of 21 February 1975, Series A no. 18, p. 16, para. 33.

47 *See, e.g.*, Fuster, *supra* note 23, 4.

48 The case deals with legislation passed in Germany in 1968 ("G10" Law) amending Article 10.2 of the German Constitution which authorized in certain circumstances secret surveillance without the need to notify the person concerned and excluded legal remedy before the Courts. The applicants claimed that the legislation was contrary to Articles 6.1, 8 and 13 of the ECHR. The conclusion of the Court is that "some compromise between the requirements for defending democratic society and individual rights is inherent in the system of the Convention" and so "a balance must be sought between the exercise by the individual of the right guaranteed to him under paragraph 1 (art. 8–1) and the necessity under paragraph 2 (art. 8–2) to impose secret surveillance for the protection of the democratic society as a whole." *Klass*, No. 5029/71, Eur. Ct. H.R. at 23,.

organising the supervision of surveillance methods (such as interception of telephone conversations and postal letters) via two different, alternative methods: judicial control over criminal law investigations[49] and non-judicial control over secret service surveillance.[50] The starting point in the Court's reasoning is its understanding that the "rule of law implies that an interference by the executive authorities with an individual's rights should be subject to an effective control which should normally be assured by the *judiciary*, at least in the last resort, *judicial control* offering the *best guarantees* of independence, impartiality and a proper procedure."[51] A *fortiori*, in a field where "abuse is potentially so easy in individual cases and could have such harmful consequences for democratic society as a whole, *it is in principle desirable to entrust supervisory control to a judge*."[52]

Nevertheless, "having regard to the nature of the supervisory and other safeguards provided for" by the law,[53] the Court "conclude[d] that the exclusion of judicial control does not exceed the limits of what may be deemed necessary in a democratic society."[54] Therefore, the ECtHR accepts, under certain conditions, a system of non-judicial review over secret surveillance,[55] though it considers judicial review highly preferable.

We saw earlier that control of surveillance, whether judicial or otherwise, can operate either *ex ante* or *ex post*. *Klass* teaches that the number of options is considerable in the light of the acceptance of non-judicial oversight as an alternative or complement to traditional, judicial oversight.

In *Szabò and Vissy* (2016), the Court takes a much more critical view of non-judiciary oversight systems. Without abandoning *Klass* doctrine (accepting a "two tracks" system of supervision), the Court scrutinizes oversight systems – especially those of a more political nature – much more strictly, advancing the requirement that whatever system of oversight is used, it needs to make possible an 'assessment of strict necessity.'[56]

49 Under Article 100 (b) of the Code of Criminal Procedure, surveillance measures "may be ordered only by a court and for a maximum of three months; they may be renewed. In urgent cases, the decision may be taken by the public prosecutor's department but to remain in effect it must be confirmed by a court within three days." *See Klass*, No. 5029/71, Eur. Ct. H.R. at 9.

50 In particular, the German review system over secret service surveillance was based on two parliamentary committees: "a Board consisting of five Members of Parliament, appointed by the Bundestag in proportion to the parliamentary groupings, the opposition being represented on the Board" and a Commission (the "G 10 Commission") consisting of "three members, namely, a Chairman, who must be qualified to hold judicial office, and two assessors." *Klass*, No. 5029/71, Eur. Ct. H.R. at 21. The Commission members are appointed for the current term of the Bundestag by the Board mentioned after consultation with the Government; "they are completely independent in the exercise of their functions and cannot be subject to instructions." *Id.* at 8. The competent Minister must, at least once every six months, report to the Board on the application of the G 10. In addition, "the Minister is bound every month to provide the G 10 Commission with an account of the measures he has ordered (Article 1, § 9). In practice, and except in urgent cases, the Minister seeks the prior consent of the Commission." *Id.* at 19.

51 *Id.* at 20.

52 *Id.*

53 *Id.* ("The Parliamentary Board and the G 10 Commission are independent of the authorities carrying out the surveillance, and are vested with sufficient powers and competence to exercise an effective and continuous control").

54 *Id.*

55 *Id.* at 22–23.

56 See *supra*, Part IV. The Court will also consider and accept hybrid systems of supervision mixing judicial and non-judicial elements, as is the case in *Kennedy*, where a hybrid "quasi-judicial" control was tested.

Szabò and Vissy deals with legal provisions creating new police powers concerning national security, of which some are typical of secret services.[57] The Court notes that the Hungarian law at issue in that case does not offer a proper framework of prior *judicial review* for police investigations acting for the purpose of national security. According to the Court, the supervision created by the Hungarian law, eminently political and carried out by the Minister of Justice, who appears to be formally independent of both the police force and the Minister of Home Affairs –

> is inherently incapable of ensuring the requisite assessment of strict necessity with regard to the aims and the means at stake. In particular, although the security services are required, in their applications to the Minister for warrants, to outline the necessity as such of secret information gathering, this procedure does not guarantee that an assessment of strict necessity is carried out, notably in terms of the range of persons and the premises concerned.[58]

In particular, the Court restated that "it is desirable to entrust supervisory control to a judge,"[59] and, specifically in cases like *Szabò*, "the external, preferably judicial, *a posteriori* control of secret surveillance activities, both in individual cases and as general supervision, gains its true importance."[60]

The departure from *Klass* is evident: the Court explained that it "recalls that in *Klass and Others* a combination of oversight mechanisms, short of formal judicial control, was found acceptable," but that was in particular because of "an initial control effected by an

57 [The] Hungarian Police Act – as amended in 2011 – gave the [police "task force"] prerogatives *in the field of secret intelligence gathering*, including surveillance with recording and secret house search, checking and recording the contents of electronic or computerized communications and opening of letters and parcels, all this without the consent of the persons concerned. The 2011 reform of the Hungarian Police Act allows surveillance activities in two cases: on the one hand, in cases where secret surveillance is linked to the investigation of *certain specific crimes* enumerated in the law, the surveillance is subject to *judicial authorization* (Section 7/E (2) of the 2011 Hungarian Police Act). On the other hand, in cases where secret surveillance takes place *within the framework of intelligence gathering for national security*, the surveillance takes place within the framework of intelligence gathering for national security, the surveillance is authorized by the Minister in charge of justice, in order to prevent terrorist acts or in the interests of Hungary's national security, or in order to rescue Hungarian citizens from capture abroad in war zones, or in the context of terrorist acts (Section 7/E (3) of the 2011 Hungarian Police Act).

In June 2012, the two applicants denounced that the prerogatives presented earlier under Section 7/E (3) breached their right to privacy. They argued that the framework on secret surveillance linked to the investigation of particular crimes provided more safeguards for the protection of the right to privacy than the provision on secret surveillance measures for national security purposes.

58 *Szabò*, No. 37138/14, Eur. Ct. H.R. at 39. Regarding the procedures for redressing any grievances caused by secret surveillance measures, the Court noted that the executive did have to give account of surveillance operations to a parliamentary committee. However, it could not identify any provisions in Hungarian legislation permitting a remedy granted by this procedure to those who are subjected to secret surveillance but, by necessity, are not informed about it during their application. Nor did the twice-yearly general report on the functioning of the secret services presented to this parliamentary committee provide adequate safeguards, as it was apparently unavailable to the public. Moreover, the complaint procedure outlined in the National Security Act also seemed to be of little relevance, since citizens subjected to secret surveillance measures were not informed of the measures applied. Indeed, no notification of secret surveillance measures is foreseen in Hungarian law. The Court reiterated that as soon as notification could be carried out without jeopardising the purpose of the restriction after the termination of the surveillance measure, information should be provided to the persons concerned. *Id.* at 43.

59 *Id.* at 40–41.

60 *Id.* at 41.

official qualified for judicial office,"[61] which is not provided by the Hungarian scheme of authorization.[62]

In other words, it seems that, according to the ECtHR, the general system of non-judicial oversight is appropriate only if it is somehow related to a judicial office.

VII Alternative Tracks: Quasi-Judiciary and Hybrid Systems

Before one concludes on the basis of *Szabò and Vissy* that all oversight needs to involve judges, it is worthwhile to go back to *Kennedy v. UK* (2010), where the Court assessed positively other forms of (non-judicial) surveillance oversight. The Court focused on the specific surveillance framework established by the UK Regulation of Investigatory Powers Act (RIPA) of 2000, which utilizes two supervisory bodies: the Interception of Communications Commissioner and the Investigatory Powers Tribunal (IPT).[63]

The *Kennedy* Court notes that the Commissioner is independent of both the executive and the legislature, and is a person who holds or has held high judicial office. The obligation on intercepting agencies to keep records ensures that the Commissioner has effective access to details of surveillance activities undertaken. Therefore, "the Court considers that the Commissioner's role in ensuring that the provisions of RIPA and the Code are observed and applied correctly is of particular value."[64] As for the Investigatory Powers Tribunal, the Court – though recalling its previous indication that judicial supervisory control is in principle desirable in a field where abuse is potentially so easy in individual cases and having such harmful consequences – "highlights the extensive jurisdiction of the IPT to examine any complaint of unlawful interception and emphasises that "the IPT is an independent and impartial body, which has adopted its own rules of procedure."[65]

In conclusion, the combination of an *ex ante* authorization by an independent Commissioner (who holds judicial office) and a *post hoc* review by a special court (IPT) can well approach the requirement of judicial control.[66] In particular, the important characteristics that a quasi-judicial system of control should have are independence, wide jurisdiction (any person may apply to it), and effective powers to access data and documents and to react appropriately.[67]

61 *Klass*, No. 5029/71, Eur. Ct. H.R. at 21–22.

62 *Szabò*, No. 37138/14, Eur. Ct. H.R. at 43.

63 The first is tasked with overseeing the general functioning of the surveillance regime and the authorization of interception warrants in specific cases. The latter must examine any complaint of unlawful interception by any person who suspects that his communications have been or are being intercepted, who may apply to the IPT. The jurisdiction of the IPT does not, therefore, depend on notification to the interception subject that there has been an interception of his communications.

64 *Kennedy*, No. 26839/05, Eur. Ct. H.R. at 51.

65 *Id.* at 51–52. Note also that "members of the [IPT] tribunal must hold or have held high judicial office or be a qualified lawyer of at least ten years' standing." *Id.* at 19.

66 *See* P. De Hert & F. Boehm, *The Rights of Notification after Surveillance Is Over Ready for Recognition?* Digital Enlightenment Yearbook 2012, 33.

67 *See* A. Deeks, *An International Legal Framework for Surveillance*, 55:2 Va. J. Int'l L., 391–68, 362 (2014); *see also* The Council of Europe Commissioner for Human Rights, *Democratic and effective oversight of national security services*, 13 (2015) ("on the effectiveness of oversight bodies").

A different form of quasi-judicial oversight (which has not been assessed by the ECtHR yet) is by the Belgian Commission on "exceptional methods of surveillance,"[68] an administrative commission composed of three security-cleared magistrates (acting in a non-judicial capacity) appointed by the executive, which gives "binding advice" to the security services when they apply to use "exceptional measures" (including surveillance).[69]

Some might be tempted to label these two examples as 'judicial oversight.' For example, the Council of Europe Commissioner for Human Rights has defined the UK oversight system set by RIPA as "judiciary" oversight.[70] On the other hand, more political oversight, such as the system set by Law G10 in Germany (and addressed in *Klass v. Germany*), is sometimes defined as a "quasi-judicial" supervisory system.[71] In our view, systems like the one in the United Kingdom and Belgium should be understood as "quasi-judicial." We prefer to reserve the term "judicial oversight" for control operated by ordinary courts, while by "quasi-judicial" we mean all special supervisory bodies that are independent and have effective powers of information and reaction (and eventually of auto-regulation).

VIII Reinforced Quasi-Judicial Systems: The Case of Data Protection Authorities

Another well-known example of quasi-judicial oversight are the Data Protection Authorities established in most European states to monitor processing activities by governments, corporations, and private persons. Data Protection Authorities are specific, independent national bodies created by European data protection laws – such as EU Data Protection Directive (1995/46/EC) – in order to enforce personal data protection principles and rules and to provide individuals with a guarantee similar to an Ombudsman. Data Protection Authorities do not replace the role of the courts, because they are administrative bodies.[72] But are they an effective remedy when it comes to answering questions about surveillance raised by concerned citizens.

68 Its full title is "La commission administrative chargée de la surveillance des méthodes spécifiques et exceptionnelles de recueil de données des services de renseignement et de sécurité."

69 Belgium 2010, Articles 18(2)(3)(9)(10),43(1); *see also* The Council of Europe Commissioner for the Human Rights, *supra* note 76, at 56.

70 The Council of Europe Commissioner for the Human Rights, *supra* note 76, at 56.

71 *Id.* at 57.

72 *See* Antonella Galetta & Paul De Hert, *The Proceduralisation of Data Protection Remedies under EU Data Protection Law: Towards a More Effective and Data Subject-Oriented Remedial System?* 8:1 Rev. Eur. Admin. L. (REALaw) 125–51 (2015) (on the three-layer system of remedies built in to European data protection law). The right to remedy data protection breaches is laid down in Directive 95/46/EC (Art. 22), as well as in the Council of Europe Data Protection Convention no. 108 (Art. 8 (d)). As a result of an unlawful processing operation, this right is coupled with the right to obtain compensation for the damage suffered. These rights are implemented in Member States' law with some variations. The right to remedy data protection violations can be exercised in several ways under EU law. The remedial system in place relies on individual initiatives taken by citizens who need to exercise their data protection rights by contacting the data controller or processor first. Secondly, violations can be remedied by Data Protection Authorities (Data Protection Authorities), which assist individuals and enforce data protection law through the exercise of administrative power. Thirdly, all kinds of courts can remedy data protection violations (from civil and commercial courts to criminal courts). Fourthly, European courts can provide remedies for data protection violations.

The role of these new authorities was scrutinized both by the ECtHR in *Segerstedt-Wiberg and others v. Sweden* (2003) and by the EUCJ, in the *Schrems* Case (2015).[73]

Segerstedt-Wiberg and others v. Sweden deals with Article 13 ECHR and the question of Data Protection Authorities' roles, and it affirms that, in view of their competencies, Data Protection Authorities can be considered government authorities that offer an actual possibility of appeal, within the meaning of Article 13 ECHR if it has *effective powers* to block data processing and to have data destroyed.[74]

The *Schrems Case* concerns the transfer of personal data from European Union countries to the United States, regulated by the European Commission Decision 2000/520/EC, which implemented Article 25 of the Data Protection Directive, 95/46/EC.[75] After Edward Snowden's revelations and the consequential scandal regarding the surveillance program PRISM of the US National Security Agency, the applicant considered that the law and practices of the United States offer no real protection against surveillance by the United States and in general offer much lower safeguards than required by the EU data protection paradigm. The EUCJ stated that the existence of a Commission decision declaring 'adequate' certain parts of the American legal system in terms of data protection, cannot eliminate or even reduce the national supervisory authorities' (i.e., the Data Protection Authorities') powers,[76] especially since the contested decision of the Commission – Decision 2000/520[77] – does not contain any redress mechanism for European citizens and does not refer to the existence of effective legal protections against interference of that kind.[78]

In principle, one could consider European data protection law's insistence on a system of Data Protection Authorities to be an alternative to judicial review. The system of requirements provided by data protection law is based on several strict safeguards – the "consent" rule, the principle of necessity, controller's duties, processor's duties, individual rights such as the right to data access, the right to object, the right to information, the right to rectification, etc. – that can be 'easily' checked by these authorities so long as they have sufficient effective powers, such that judicial control is not as necessary as in secret surveillance.[79]

In the *Schrems* Case, the Court[80] affirms that "the very existence of *effective judicial review* designed to ensure compliance with provisions of EU law *is inherent in the*

73 Case C-362/14, *Data Protection Commissioner v. Schrems*, 2015.

74 De Hert, *supra* note 8, at 26.

75 According to that article, the Commission may find that a third country ensures an adequate level of protection and so it can adopt a decision to that effect. Consequently, the transfer of personal data to the third country concerned may take place.

76 Indeed, the access enjoyed by the United States constituted an interference with the right to respect for private life and such interference is contrary to the principle of proportionality. *Schrems*, 2015 Eur. Ct. Just. §§ 66, 71–97.

77 "Commission Decision of 26 July 2000 pursuant to Directive 95/46/EC of the European Parliament and of the Council on the adequacy of the protection provided by the safe harbour privacy principles and related frequently asked questions issued by the US Department of Commerce."

78 *Schrems*, 2015 Eur. Ct. Just. § 90. Moreover the Commission has found that the United States authorities were able to access the personal data transferred from the EU to the United States and process it in a way incompatible with the purposes for which it was transferred. Therefore the Commission's decision allowing data transfers from the EU to the USA was declared invalid. *See* X. Tracol, *"Invalidator" Strikes Back: The Harbour Has Never Been Safe*, 32 Computer L. & Security Rev., 361 (2016).

79 *See* De Hert, *supra* note 26.

80 Following Article 47 of the EU Charter of Fundamental Rights, which echoes Article 13 of ECHR: "Everyone whose rights and freedoms guaranteed by the law of the Union are violated has the

existence of the rule of law."[81] Interestingly, the Court seems to compare "judicial review" to the function of Data Protection Authorities, implicitly comparing traditional judicial powers in reviewing surveillance activities (analysed earlier) and the typical functions of Data Protection Authorities, as provided by Article 28 of the Data Protection Directive.[82] In *Schrems*, the EUCJ does not consider judicial review as a necessary requirement, but it assesses Data Protection Authorities as effective remedies provided by national authorities.

We think it is indeed possible to understand a Data Protection Authority's tasks within the "quasi-judicial control" paradigm settled in *Kennedy v. UK* (see Table 22.3). This authority can indeed act both as an *ex ante* authorization authority (like the UK Interception of Communications Commissioner) and as *post hoc* review authority (like the UK Investigatory Powers Tribunal).

Its functioning as an *ex ante* authorization authority is made possible by Article 18 of the Data Protection Directive: "Member States shall provide that the controller or his representative, if any, *must notify the supervisory authority* referred to in Article 28 before carrying out any wholly or partly automatic processing operation or set of such operations intended to serve a single purpose or several related purposes." Consequently, Data Protection Authorities, "following receipt of a notification from the controller," shall carry out "*prior checks*" over "processing operations likely to present specific risks to the rights and freedoms of data subjects."[83]

A Data Protection Authority's role as a *post hoc* review authority is laid down in Article 28 of the Data Protection Directive, providing rules and powers of Data Protection Authorities, and there we can find interesting parallels to the UK Investigatory Power Tribunal. A Data Protection Authority is "an independent and impartial body,"[84] and a public "authority acting with complete independence."[85]

Moreover, as for the power of "effective access to details of surveillance activities"[86] and to all related "documents and information"[87] which is provided for UK IPT, Data Protection Authorities have "powers of access to data forming the subject-matter of processing operations and powers to collect all the information necessary for the performance of its supervisory duties."[88]

right to an effective remedy before a tribunal in compliance with the conditions laid down in this Article. Everyone is entitled to a fair and public hearing within a reasonable time by an independent and impartial tribunal previously established by law. Everyone shall have the possibility of being advised, defended and represented. Legal aid shall be made available to those who lack sufficient resources in so far as such aid is necessary to ensure effective access to justice."

81 *Schrems*, 2015 Eur. Ct. Just. § 95.

82 *See id.* in conjunction with §§ 99–103.

83 Article 20, DP directive.

84 *Kennedy*, No. 26839/05, Eur. Ct. H.R. at 51–52.

85 Article 28 (1), 95/46/EC; *see also* recital 62: "Whereas the establishment in Member States of supervisory authorities, exercising their functions with complete independence, is an essential component of the protection of individuals with regard to the processing of personal data." About the independence of the Data Protection Authorities, *see also* the *EUCJ in Case C-518/07, Commission v. Germany (2010)*, Case C-614/10, *Commission v. Austria* (2012) and Case C-288/12, *Commission v. Hungary* (2014).

86 *Kennedy*, No. 26839/05, Eur. Ct. H.R. at 20; *see also* The Council of Europe Commissioner for Human Rights, *supra* note 76, at 13.

87 *Kennedy*, No. 26839/05, Eur. Ct. H.R. at 20.

88 Article 28(3)

Table 22.3. Comparison between Quasi-Judicial System Set by Kennedy and Data Protection Authorities Assessed by Schrems and Segerstedt-Wiberg

	Quasi-judiciary (Kennedy)	**Data Protection Authorities (*Schrems* and *Segerstedt-Wiberg*)**
Establishment	Commissioner is "*independent of the executive and the legislature and is a person who holds or has held high judicial office*" (§ 167) *IPT is an independent and impartial body*, which has adopted its own rules of procedure (§ 167)	National "authorities acting with *complete independence*" Article 28(1), 95/46/EC directive
Jurisdiction	*Extensive jurisdiction* of the IPT (Investigatory Powers Tribunal) to examine *any complaint of unlawful interception*. It has jurisdiction to investigate any complaint that a person's communications have been intercepted and, where interception has occurred, to examine the authority for such interception (§ 76)	Data Protection Authorities "shall hear claims lodged by *any person*, or by an association representing that person, concerning the protection of his rights and freedoms in regard to the processing of personal data" Article 28(4), 95/46/EC directive
Powers to access to information	Commissioner has *effective access to details* of surveillance activities undertaken The IPT has the power to require a relevant Commissioner to provide it with all such assistance as it thinks fit. Section 68(6) and (7) require those involved in the authorisation and execution of an interception warrant to disclose or provide to the IPT all documents and information it may require (§78)	Data Protection Authorities have "*powers of access to data* forming the subject-matter of processing operations and powers to collect all the information necessary for the performance of its supervisory duties" Article 28(3), 95/46/EC directive
Powers of intervention	"*In the event that the IPT finds in the applicant's favour, it can, inter alia, quash any interception order, require destruction of intercept material and order compensation to be paid (see paragraph 80 above)*" (§167)	Data Protection Authorities have "*effective* powers of intervention, such as, for example, that of ordering the blocking, *erasure or destruction of data*, of *imposing a temporary or definitive ban on processing*, of warning or admonishing the controller, or that of referring the matter to national parliaments or other political institutions" Article 28(3), 95/46/EC directive

Furthermore, as for the scope of jurisdiction, *Kennedy* refers to the "extensive jurisdiction of the IPT (Investigatory Powers Tribunal) to examine *any complaint* of unlawful interception."[89] Similarly, Article 28(4) states that Data Protection Authorities "shall hear claims lodged by *any person*, or by an association representing that person, concerning the protection of his rights and freedoms in regard to the processing of personal data".[90]

Finally, as for the power of intervention, the UK IPT can "*quash any interception order, require destruction of intercept material and order compensation to be paid.*" Analogously, Data Protection Authorities have "effective *powers of intervention*, such as, for example, that of... *ordering* the *blocking, erasure or destruction of data*, of *imposing* a temporary or definitive *ban on processing*, of warning or admonishing the controller, or that of referring the matter to national parliaments or other political institutions."[91] Moreover, as for the power (of IPT) to "adopt its own rules of procedure," we must acknowledge that in several member States auto-regulation is also a reality for Data Protection Authorities.[92]

In sum, as the EUCJ noted, "National supervisory authorities must be able to examine, with complete independence, any claim concerning the protection of a person's rights and freedoms in regard to the processing of personal data relating to him,"[93] and this too is typical of Data Protection Authorities.[94] It therefore seems clear that Data Protection Authorities guarantee a level of safeguards that is perfectly comparable to the best-developed quasi-judiciary supervisory systems, and it is not just a coincidence that Data Protection Authorities have been defined an "indispensable link in the modern constitutional state."[95]

Interestingly, Data Protection Directive (95/46/EC) also creates an interesting link between Data Protection Authorities and the judicial system: according to Article 28(3), Data Protection Authorities have the "power to engage in legal proceedings where the national provisions adopted pursuant to this Directive have been violated or to bring these violations to the attention of the judicial authorities." This could be interpreted to reveal the non-autonomy of Data Protection Authorities from the judicial power. But it should be interpreted as an interesting safeguard for any non-judicial review system: upon certain conditions (e.g., serious violations of law), non-judicial authorities should engage ordinary judges in the decision because it will enhance the protection of individuals' rights.[96] Furthermore, considering that interceptions are a form of data

89 "It has jurisdiction to investigate *any complaint* that a person's communications have been intercepted and, where interception has occurred, to examine the authority for such interception." *Kennedy*, No. 26839/05, Eur. Ct. H.R. at 20.

90 Article 28(4) (emphasis added).

91 Article 28(3).

92 *See, e.g.*, Dutch Data Protection Authorities, as analysed by De Hert, *supra* note 8, 30 ("A legal framework is needed that provides *discretionary powers that allow the Dutch Data Protection Authorities to decide the enforcement methods* (and also allows it to take no action if desired) and that provides for the organisation of a consultation procedure prior to the current imposition of sanctions. Call it negotiated enforcement or enforced negotiation.") (emphasis added).

93 *Schrems*, 2015 Eur. Ct. Just. § 99.

94 *See also* De Hert, *supra* note 8, 30.

95 *Id.*

96 Compare this double oversight (independent authorities at the first step and judges at the second eventual step): it "could enable close, independent scrutiny providing a robust method of oversight." Lennon, *supra* note 30, at .643; *id.* ("The authorization of oversight powers could be subjected to *judicial confirmation*, whether as an alternative or *in addition to oversight by other bodies*. This could enable close, independent scrutiny providing a robust method of oversight") (emphasis added).

processing, Data Protection Authorities could in principle be invested with the control of any form of surveillance.

In conclusion, *Segerstedt-Wiberg* and *Schrems* have emphasised the role of Data Protection Authorities as a safeguard comparable to the most developed "quasi-judicial control" systems. The only problem for Data Protection Authorities is that in national legal systems they are often excluded entirely from the domain of surveillance in order to prevent an overlap between Data Protection Authorities and other entities specifically committed to surveillance control (e.g., the G10 Commission in Germany).[97] However, there are several opportunities that should be explored in the near future: taking into account the new approval of the GDPR and the new proposal for a directive on the use of personal data for police purposes ("Police directive"),[98] EU Member States may choose to "use" the supervisory authorities of a Data Protection Authority for monitoring compliance with the Police Directive, or to set up "special" supervisory authorities for the purposes of the Police Directive.[99]

IX "Good Enough Judicial Oversight" and Empirical Checks

We can summarize the foregoing as follows: the ECtHR considers that "control by an independent body, normally a judge with special expertise, should be the rule and substitute solutions the exception, warranting close scrutiny,"[100] but neither judicial *ex ante* authorization nor judicial *post hoc* review is an absolute requirement.[101]

Judicial oversight is generally considered the best safeguard for human rights[102] since judges are generally regarded as impartial, independent, and consequently unlikely to be swayed by political considerations surrounding secret service activity (which might for example influence a minister making authorisation decisions). Judges are also regarded as "being better suited to assessing legal criteria such as necessity and proportionality, which is clearly important when the measures sought may have significant human rights implications."[103]

97 *See* The Council of Europe Commissioner for Human Rights, *supra* note 76, at 52.

98 *Proposal for a Directive of the European Parliament and of the Council on the protection of individuals with regard to the processing of personal data by competent authorities for the purposes of prevention, investigation, detection or prosecution of criminal offences or the execution of criminal penalties, and the free movement of such data*, EUR-Lex (2012), http://eur-lex.europa.eu/legal-content/en/ALL/?uri=CELEX:52012PC0010.

99 For example, Belgium already decided to set up a special police and criminal justice data protection authority (DPA).

100 *See Szabò*, No. 37138/14, Eur. Ct. H.R. at 40–41; *see also Klass*, No. 5029/71, Eur. Ct. H.R. at 42, 55.

101 *See, e.g., Szabò*, No. 37138/14, Eur. Ct. H.R. at 40–41 ("The ex ante authorisation of such a measure is not an absolute requirement per se, because where there is extensive post factum judicial oversight, this may counterbalance the shortcomings of the authorisation"); *see also Kennedy*, No. 26839/05, Eur. Ct. H.R. at 51–52.

102 Council of Europe Parliamentary Assembly Recommendation 1402 (1999), *Control of Internal Security Services in Council of Europe Member States*, http://assembly.coe.int/nw/xml/XRef/Xref-XML2HTML-en.asp?fileid=16689&lang=en.

103 The Council of Europe Commissioner for Human Rights, *supra* note 76, at 55. It is interesting to notice that similar reflections can also be found in the late eighteenth-century jurisprudence of the English High Court: judicial control on surveillance is highly preferable to prevent arbitrary powers that can adversely affect rights of individuals. In the late 1700s a number of judgments strictly scrutinized such "general warrants" delivered by the Secretary of State arguing that only a judge can order search and seizure of letters, papers, etc. At the same time, the arbitrary powers of administrative officers (as the

But the foregoing should not be understood as an exclusive preference in law for judicial oversight. For example, the Geneva Academy of International Humanitarian Law and Human Rights has affirmed that an independent judiciary should scrutinize surveillance requests,[104] but it also argues that judicial oversight alone is not enough. Rather, all three branches of government should be engaged because many states have not established effective, independent oversight mechanisms to monitor surveillance practices.[105] Equally careful is the Council of Europe Commissioner for Human Rights and the Venice Commission. Both emphasize that judicial control is not a panacea that guarantees respect for human rights in the authorisation and use of intrusive measures by security services.[106]

Scholars have underlined several potential drawbacks to judicial authorisation or oversight: first, the lack of independence and impartiality in countries where judges are not fully independent, and, second, that expertise is integral to the efficacy of judicial authorisation.[107] Judges with limited experience in security matters may be highly reluctant to second-guess the national security assessments of a security service official applying for a warrant.[108] Even for a specialised judge, the invocation of "national security" is very potent, conveying as it does a need for urgent and decisive action.[109] This is sometimes amplified by the tendency of some judges to be strongly deferential to the government on matters of national security. Third, in many jurisdictions judicial authorisation amounts to "rubber-stamping" decisions taken by security services, with very few requests for warrants being refused.[110] And, fourth, judges cannot normally be held to account for the warrants they issue to security services. In order to preserve judicial independence and the separation of powers, warrant-issuing processes are not usually subject to *ex post* scrutiny by an oversight body.[111] By contrast, a minister or quasi-judicial authorising body is considered more easily controllable by parliament or by an independent oversight body for the decisions it makes.[112]

Secretary of State) for more "political" purposes of investigation (i.e., national interests) were looked at askance. *See Wilkes v. Wood*, 98 Eng. Rep. 489, 489–99 C.P. 1763 in *The Founders' Constitution*, Volume 5, Amendment IV, Document 4, http://presspubs.uchicago.edu/founders/documents/amendIVs4.html; *Entick v. Carrington*, 95 Eng. Rep. 807 K.B. 1765, in *The Founders' Constitution*, Volume 5, Amendment IV, Document 6, http://presspubs.uchicago.edu/founders/documents/amendIVs6.html; *see also* B. White, The Canadian Freeholder: in Three Dialogues between an Englishman and a Frenchman, settled in Canada (Vol. II, London 1779) *distributed by* Internet Archive of the Univ. of Cal.

104 Geneva Academy, *The Right to Privacy in the Digital Age: Meeting Report* 9, http://www.geneva-academy.ch/docs/ResearchActivities/Report_TheRightoPrivacy.pdf.

105 *Id.* at 5; *see also* Lennon, *supra* note 30, at 644.

106 The Council of Europe Commissioner for Human Rights, *supra* note 78, at 55; Venice Commission, Report on the democratic oversight of the security services, CDL-AD (2007)016, §§ 205–06 (2007).

107 Venice Commission, *supra* note 115, §§ 205–06.

108 I. Cameron, *National Security and the European Convention on Human Rights – Trends and Patterns*, Stockholm International Symposium on National Security & the European Convention on Human Rights, 4–5 (Dec. 2008,).

109 Venice Commission, *supra* note 115, at 208.

110 UNHCR, The Right to Privacy in the Digital Age, A/HRC/27/37, UN High Commissioner for Human Rights, (30 June 2014), http://www.ohchr.org/EN/Issues/DigitalAge/Pages/DigitalAgeIndex.aspx §38.

111 I. Cameron, *Parliamentary and Specialised Oversight of Security and Intelligence Agencies in Sweden*, *in* Parliamentary Oversight of Security and Intelligence Agencies in the European Union," European Parliament, (A. Willis & M. Vermeulen eds., Brussels, 2011).

112 J. Borger, *Minister Should Assess UK Surveillance Warrants, Says Philip Hammond*, The Guardian, 23 October 2014.

Therefore, scholars – in order to find a balance between advantages and drawbacks – are increasingly proposing not "judicial oversight" but a "*good enough judicial oversight.*"[113] How should one understand this term? Judging by the case law of the ECtHR it definitely invites consideration of *realpolitik* or, in general, empirical evaluations.[114] Indeed, we believe the Strasbourg Court has never failed to do so. As early as *Klass*, it not only considered independence and effectiveness of surveillance control, but also assessed the national legal framework in its totality and the effectiveness of the rule of law in this field, noting that "various provisions are designed to reduce the effect of surveillance measures to an unavoidable minimum" so that "in the absence of any evidence or indication that the actual practice followed is otherwise, the Court must assume that *in the democratic society of the Federal Republic of Germany*, the relevant authorities are properly applying the legislation in issue."[115]

And recently with *Colon* (2006), *Zakharov* (2015), and *Szabò and Vissy* (2016), this evidence-based approach rises more to the surface and becomes more understandable. Indeed, the Court in these most recent surveillance cases is considering more and more the effectiveness of the rule of law safeguards in the specific member state at stake.

For example, in *Colon*, the Court highlighted the fact that the Dutch government had provided two independent studies attesting to the effectiveness of powers and recommending their continued use.[116] Whereas in *Zakharov*, the Court noted that "the shortcomings in the *legal framework as identified above* appear to have an impact on the actual operation of the system of secret surveillance which exists in Russia. ECtHR is not convinced by the Government's assertion that all interceptions in Russia are performed lawfully on the basis of a proper judicial authorisation."[117] Therefore, "the Court finds that *Russian law does not met the "quality of the law" requirement* and is incapable of keeping the "interference" to what is "necessary in a democratic society"".[118] In addition, the *Zakharov* Court explicitly affirmed the *empirical* nature of its scrutiny; the secret nature of surveillance measures should not stand in the way of an effectiveness review – remedies must be *practical and effective*, rather than *theoretical and illusory*.[119] Also, the Council of Europe Report on the democratic and effective oversight of national security services emphasises the importance of scrutinizing practical effectiveness of safeguards (rather than merely assessing national legal provisions).[120]

In other words, the Court is now more focussed on an *empirical check* or *reality check* on the compatibility of a Member State legal framework with Article 8 ECHR, rather than merely an abstract legal check.[121] This new tendency has led the court to apply stricter rules in the assessment of a specific legal system if the quality of rule of law and the application of democratic rules have proved inadequate with regard to the European Charter of Human Rights.

113 *See* Lennon, *supra* note 30, at 644.
114 *Id.* at 642.
115 *Klass*, No. 5029/71, Eur. Ct. H.R. at 22–23.
116 *See* Lennon, *supra* note 30, at 640.
117 *Zakharov*, No. 47143/06, Eur. Ct. H.R. 79.
118 *Id*, [at 304, italics added]
119 *Id.* at 74; *see also* Cole, *supra* note 38, 128.
120 The Council of Europe Commissioner for Human Rights, *supra* note 78, at 13–14.
121 *See also* Fuster, *supra* note 23, at 4–5.

In sum, the choice between judicial oversight and an alternative model retains relevance for the ECtHR, which still prefers the judicial system (as it made clear in *Szabò)*, but even such a system needs to be assessed through the "test" of reality and so needs to prove its quality and effectiveness in the specific legal order at issue.

Conclusion

In this chapter we addressed how the European human rights framework deals with surveillance, and in particular surveillance oversight. We have not addressed other relevant issues of the European surveillance law, such as the interpretation of the legality principle or the victim's requirement. Our scope has instead been limited to an issue that deserves particular theoretical attention. The two European Courts (the ECtHR and the EUCJ) have not yet established a clear doctrine in determining suitable thresholds and parameters, but recent European jurisprudential trends show relevant developments. There are also interesting similarities with common law cases.[122]

After Part II's general clarification of the ECHR surveillance framework and the terminology used in the field of surveillance oversight (taking into account different national criminal procedure legal systems), in Part III we addressed the application of Article 8 ECHR in criminal law surveillance, as crystallised by the ECtHR in *Huvig v. France* (1990), which established six (or seven) requirements within the legality principle. Although *Huvig* is a fine example of strict scrutiny, one cannot claim that the Court has always used a strict approach when assessing surveillance law. Part IV analysed the Court's different standards of scrutiny in this field, acknowledging that the ECtHR has a flexible approach in interpreting Articles 8 and 13 ECHR,[123] which depends upon several factors: specific facts at issue, "vital" interests at stake, and political considerations.

One interesting variable is the public body conducting surveillance. In particular, secret service surveillance is problematic in terms of oversight. In Part V we analysed how the ECtHR has assessed the respect of individuals' right to a remedy against intelligence surveillance, according to Article 13 ECHR (combined with Article 8 ECHR). The ECtHR has shown a preference towards judiciary oversight, but in the European legal order there are several examples of non-judicial oversight systems. In Parts VI and VII we highlighted how the Court has accepted these alternative methods of surveillance control, where the *independence* of the oversight body, its *wide jurisdiction*, its *power to access data*, and its *power to effective reactions* are proved. An interesting example of such a recognized alternative is the oversight conducted by Data Protection Authorities in the EU Member States because of the eventual involvement of ordinary judges as a second step of oversight according to Article 28(3) of Data Protection Directive (Part VIII).[124]

122 *See Wilkes*, 98 Eng. Rep. at 489–99; *Entick*, 95 Eng. Rep.; *see also* White, *supra* note 112.

123 *See, e.g.*, Fuster *supra* note 23, at 4. The preference for flexibility in surveillance law is also highlighted by Deeks, *supra* note 76, at 366.

124 This eventual double (*non-judicial* and *judicial*) oversight has already been positively welcomed by scholars (*see, e.g.*, Fuster, *supra* note 76, at 4). The preference for flexibility in surveillance law is also highlighted by Deeks, *supra* note 76, at 366) also considering that Data Protection Authorities have constant relationships with national Parliaments; *see* Lennon, *supra* note 30, at 643 ("The authorization of oversight powers could be subjected to *judicial confirmation*, whether as an alternative or *in addition to oversight by other bodies*. This could enable close, independent scrutiny providing a robust method of oversight" (emphasis added)).

After this overview, we acknowledge that although the ECtHR prefers judicial oversight, alternative methods of surveillance control could be considered suitable. However, this assessment is based not merely on the independence and powers of the non-judicial authorities deputed to review surveillance activities, but also on empirical tests proving the effectiveness of the rule of law in the field of secret surveillance in a specific Member State (Part IX).[125]

In conclusion, we noticed an increasing emphasis on requiring a *good enough* judicial (*ex ante* or *ex post*) control over surveillance, meaning not a mere judicial control, but a system of oversight (preferably judicial, but also "quasi-judicial" or "hybrid") which can provide an effective control over surveillance, supported by *empirical checks* in the national legal system at issue.

125 *See* P. De Hert, Human Rights Perspective on Privacy and Data Protection Impact Assessment, in Privacy Impact Assessment, 47 (Springer Netherlands 2012) ("It is less painful to tell a Member State that it has violated the Convention because of a problem with its legal basis that to pass the message that an initiative favoured by Member States or accepted by a Member State is, in fact, not necessary in a democratic society").

23 Lessons from the History of National Security Surveillance

Elizabeth Goitein, Faiza Patel, & Fritz Schwarz[†]

There is a less pessimistic side to the philosopher George Santayana's warning that "those who cannot remember the past are condemned to repeat it."[1] Those who familiarize themselves with the past can learn from it, and they can design policies and institutions that will help avert the mistakes of history.

The Church Committee's 1975–1976 investigation of surveillance abuses embodied this approach. Looking back over three decades, the committee found that intelligence agencies, subject to few substantive legal restrictions and little external oversight, had abused their powers throughout this period. It recommended – and the government implemented – a range of reforms, including laws that required agencies to have individualized, fact-based suspicion before collecting Americans' information, as well as oversight bodies to ensure that agencies did not overstep their new limits. These institutions and policies remained in place for more than thirty years. Since 9/11, however, many of them have been weakened or set aside, with results that would not surprise students of history.

This chapter sets out to elucidate – and learn from – the historical trends in surveillance law and policy. It details the abuses of the early Cold War as revealed by the Church Committee's investigation, and describes the rules and mechanisms created to stem those abuses and to prevent their recurrence. It discusses the unraveling of these limitations in the years since the attacks of 9/11. It explores the known consequences of this unraveling, including the use of surveillance to target dissenting and minority communities and the measurable effect on public discourse. It concludes with recommendations to restore sensible limits on, and robust oversight of, national security surveillance.

[†] Elizabeth Goitein and Faiza Patel codirect the Liberty and National Security Program at the Brennan Center for Justice at NYU School of Law. Fritz Schwarz is the Center's Chief Counsel; he previously served as Chief Counsel to the Church Committee. Material in Parts I.B.1-2, I.C.1, and I.C.3 of this chapter has been taken or adapted from Elizabeth Goitein & Faiza Patel, Brennan Ctr. for Justice, WHAT WENT WRONG WITH THE FISA COURT (2015). Material in Part I.C.5.a is taken from *Oversight and Reauthorization of the FISA Amendments Act: The Balance Between National Security, Privacy and Civil Liberties: Hearing Before the S. Comm. on the Judiciary*, 114th Cong. (2016) (statement of Elizabeth Goitein, Co-Director, Liberty and National Security Program, Brennan Center for Justice at New York University School of Law). The authors would like to thank Brynne O'Neal, Mishal Pahrand, and Patricia Stottlemyer for their research assistance.

1 George Santayana, REASON IN COMMON SENSE 284 (1980).

I History: The Rise and Fall of Limits on National Security Surveillance

A *Early History and the Emergence of the National Security State*

During the colonial era, Americans protested against broad, unchecked surveillance by the British. "General warrants" and "writs of assistance," used by British colonial officers primarily to conduct searches focused on smuggling, prompted particular outrage. These searches were "general" – they lacked specificity or, indeed, any limit.[2] The strongly held antipathy toward these broad searches found expression in the Fourth Amendment to the Constitution, which provides that "the right of the people to be secure in their persons, houses, papers and effects, against unreasonable searches and seizures, shall not be violated; and no Warrants shall issue but upon probable cause, supported by Oath or affirmation, and particularly describing the place to be searched and the persons or things to be seized." Although the word "privacy" is not mentioned in the Fourth Amendment, it is understood today to safeguard "reasonable expectations of privacy" – namely, those subjectively held expectations that society is prepared to accept as reasonable.[3] When the government intrudes on such expectations, it must first obtain a warrant from a neutral magistrate, unless the search falls into one of several long-standing exceptions to the warrant requirement.

Despite the Fourth Amendment's guarantees, there were repeated instances of broad surveillance in the years between the founding of the United States and the emergence of the American national security state around the time of World War II. For example, the Alien and Sedition Act in the late eighteenth century under President John Adams, some of President Abraham Lincoln's actions during the Civil War, Woodrow Wilson's passage of the Espionage Act in 1917, and the Palmer Raids at the end of the Wilson administration were all coupled with increases in surveillance. Notably, however, the surveillance was known to Congress, the courts, and the public. It was therefore subject, in theory if not always in practice, to criticism and challenge.

Expansive surveillance coupled with secrecy is a distinguishing feature of the national security state. President Franklin D. Roosevelt took two important (and secret) steps to pave the way. In 1938, he expanded the authority of the Federal Bureau of Investigation (FBI) to include the investigation, not only of criminal conduct, but also of "subversion" – an amorphous term that neither Roosevelt nor FBI Director J. Edgar Hoover defined. Roosevelt did not consult or even inform Congress about this expansion because Hoover had counseled him that it was "imperative" that the expansion go forward with the "utmost degree of secrecy in order to avoid criticism or objections."[4]

2 *See generally* Michael W. Price, *Rethinking Privacy: Fourth Amendment "Papers" and the Third Party Doctrine*, 8 J. Nat'l Security L. & Pol'y 247, 250–58 (2015). For a critique by colonists, see *The Rights of the Colonists* and A *List of Infringements and Violation of Rights*, drafted in 1772 by, among others, Samuel Adams. Samuel Adams et al., *The Rights of the Colonists, in* 1B Bernard Schwartz et al., The Bill of Rights: A Documentary History 199 (1971); Samuel Adams et al., *A List of Infringements and Violation of Rights, in* Schwartz, *supra* note 2, at 205–06. For other references to colonial concerns about general warrants, see, e.g., *Olmstead v. United States*, 277 U.S. 438, 476 (1928) (Brandeis, J., dissenting) and *United States v. Ehrlichman*, 376 F. Supp. 29, 32 (D.D.C. 1974).

3 *Katz v. United States*, 389 U.S. 347, 360–61 (1967) (Harlan, J., concurring).

4 U.S. S. Select Comm. to Study Governmental Operations with Respect to Intelligence Activities ("Church Committee"), Intelligence Activities and the Rights of Americans, S. Rep. No. 94–755, bk. III at 398 (1976) [hereinafter Church Committee Report] (quoting Hoover memo enclosed with letter from [Attorney General Homer S.] Cummings to the president [FDR]).

Then–Attorney General Homer Cummings similarly urged that the proposal for expanded domestic investigations "be handled in the strictest confidence."[5]

A second action that opened the door to expanded surveillance occurred in 1940, when President Roosevelt secretly overruled then–Attorney General Robert Jackson's order ending FBI warrantless wiretapping (Jackson had read a recent Supreme Court case as implicitly prohibiting it).[6] Roosevelt told the attorney general he was "convinced" the Court did not mean to apply its decision to "grave matters involving the defense of the nation." He ordered government agents to continue their warrantless interceptions of communications of persons "suspected of subversion." Once again, he provided no explanation of what "subversion" meant.[7]

The national security state came into its own in 1947, with the passage of the National Security Act.[8] The act fundamentally restructured the government's military and intelligence agencies, merging the Department of War (renamed the Department of the Army), the Department of the Navy, and a newly created Department of the Air Force into a National Military Establishment. It also established the National Security Council to coordinate national security policy within the executive branch and the Central Intelligence Agency (CIA). The National Security Agency (NSA) was subsequently created within the Department of Defense. While the CIA's charter barred it from spying domestically, there were few legislative constraints on intelligence gathering by any of the agencies conducting such activities.

As the Cold War intensified and fears of the Soviet Union's intentions and nuclear capacities grew, these agencies expanded in power, resources, and reach, until President Eisenhower in 1961 warned of a "military–industrial complex," and the potential for a "disastrous rise of misplaced power" to threaten Americans' liberties and democratic processes.[9] At the same time, some American officials, most notably FBI Director Hoover, also feared political dissent and social justice movements that threatened the existing sociopolitical order. The same powerful tools that could be used to ferret out Soviet spies could be used to track protesters and activists, particularly if a Soviet or communist connection could be posited.

All of these factors led to broad surveillance of law-abiding Americans, which began to come to light in the 1970s. In 1972, the *Washington Post* revealed that President Nixon's White House was spying on and sabotaging political opponents.[10] Two years later, the *New York Times* reported that the CIA, on President Lyndon Johnson's orders, had conducted a massive intelligence operation against critics of the Vietnam War, other domestic dissidents, and journalists whom the administration considered unfriendly.[11]

5 *See id.*

6 Joseph E. Persico, Roosevelt's Secret War: FDR and World War II Espionage 35 (2002); David C. Unger, The Emergency State: America's Pursuit of Absolute Security at All Costs 41 (2013); *Nardone v. United States*, 308 U.S. 338 (1939) (interpreting 47 U.S.C. § 605, *et seq.*).

7 *See* Alexander Charns, Cloak and Gavel: FBI Wiretaps, Bugs, Informers, and the Supreme Court 23 (1992); Darren E. Tromblay, The U.S. Domestic Intelligence Enterprise: History, Development, and Operations 15 (2015).

8 National Security Act of 1947, Pub. L. No. 80–235, 61 Stat. 495 (codified as amended at 50 U.S.C. § 401, *et seq.*).

9 Dwight D. Eisenhower, Military-Industrial Complex Speech (1961), http://coursesa.matrix.msu.edu/~hst306/documents/indust.html.

10 Carl Bernstein & Bob Woodward, *FBI Finds Nixon Aides Sabotaged Democrats*, Wash. Post, Oct. 10, 1972, at A1, http://www.washingtonpost.com/wp-srv/national/longterm/watergate/articles/101072-1.htm.

11 Seymour M. Hersh, *Huge C.I.A. Operation Reported in U.S. against Antiwar Forces, Other Dissidents in Nixon Years*, N.Y. Times, Dec. 22, 1974, at A1, http://s3.documentcloud.org/documents/238963/huge-c-i-a-operation-reported-in-u-s-against.pdf.

These reports triggered congressional investigations, the best known of which was conducted by a specially convened Senate committee popularly known as the Church Committee.[12] Over the course of its two-year-long investigation, the Church Committee cataloged a host of abuses spanning every administration from Franklin Roosevelt through Richard Nixon. It found that the FBI opened more than 500,000 files on Americans, including files on the women's liberation movement, conservative Christian groups, the nonviolent civil rights movement, and a wide variety of university and church groups opposed to the Vietnam War. The CIA investigated at least 200,000 individuals inside the United States opposed to the war. Army intelligence officials opened files on some 100,000 Americans. The NSA obtained copies of millions of telegrams leaving the United States. The Internal Revenue Service opened intelligence files on more than 11,000 Americans on the basis of political rather than tax criteria. The FBI and CIA opened hundreds of thousands of letters, including from the Federation of American Scientists and numerous American peace groups such as the American Friends Service Committee.[13]

Some investigations continued for decades, long after it became clear – if it was not clear from the start – that there was no Soviet connection or criminal activity. For example, the FBI opened an investigation of the National Association for the Advancement of Colored People (NAACP) in 1941 because of protests by fifteen black mess attendants about racial discrimination in the navy. Although bureau reports from the outset made clear that the NAACP's activities were wholly lawful, the investigation lasted for twenty-five years. The FBI also investigated the Socialist Workers Party (SWP) for twenty-six years. Despite officials' admission that they could find no evidence of illegal activity, the FBI's informants continued to report back the SWP's positions on the Vietnam War, on "racial matters," on food prices, and on candidates for political office. And the bureau investigated Bayard Rustin – who introduced Martin Luther King Jr. to the nonviolent teachings of Gandhi and organized the 1963 March on Washington – for several decades. The investigation was instituted on the basis of the allegation that Rustin had Communist ties. After the responsible FBI officials reported that he had no such ties, Hoover ordered the investigation to continue because there was no "substantial evidence that he is anti-Communist."[14]

Many of the activities unearthed by the Church Committee were marked by "mission creep," with the surveillance expanding beyond its initial, more limited purpose. Under Operation SHAMROCK, for instance, the NSA (and its predecessor, the Army Security Agency) received from telegraph companies a copy of every telegram leaving the United States. Initially, the purpose was to review encrypted cables sent from foreign embassies in Washington back to their home countries. But eventually the NSA perused the telegrams of American citizens, particularly anti–Vietnam War protesters and civil rights leaders.[15]

On occasion, intelligence agencies concealed from the president the extent or nature of their surveillance activities. To persuade President John F. Kennedy and Attorney

12 The eleven-member "Select Committee to Study Government Operations with Respect to Intelligence Activities" was referred to as the "Church Committee" after its chairman, Sen. Frank Church (D-ID). David Rudgers, *The Church Committee on Intelligence Activities Investigation, 1975–76*, *in* Congress Investigates: A Critical and Documentary History 932 (Roger A. Burns et al. eds., 2011).

13 *See* Church Committee Report, *supra* note 4, bk. II at 6–7, 165–69.

14 For the NAACP, see *id.* at 8, 179–80; for the SWP, see *id.* at 180; for Rustin, see *id.* at 181–82. The report did not use Rustin's name, but it was later revealed.

15 *See* Church Committee Report, *supra* note 4, bk. III at 733–83.

General Robert Kennedy to allow wiretaps of the phones of Martin Luther King Jr., his close associates, and the Southern Christian Leadership Conference, Hoover claimed that a King adviser was currently a Communist. In fact, as Hoover knew, the adviser's aid to the Communist Party had ended several years earlier.[16] Similarly, when President Nixon withdrew his authorization for intelligence agencies to engage in illegal conduct to garner information from law-abiding Americans, the intelligence agencies continued their activities without informing the president.[17]

In other cases, however, the White House itself was behind the illegal surveillance activities. SHAMROCK's expansion was a result of White House pressure: Presidents Lyndon Johnson and Richard Nixon both believed that the anti–Vietnam War movement must be sponsored by foreign Communists, and they secretly pressed the intelligence agencies – including the NSA and CIA – to conduct surveillance that would produce evidence of this suspected connection.[18] And the Nixon White House ordered the "plumbers" to break into the office of Daniel Ellsberg's psychologist (Ellsberg leaked the Pentagon Papers) to try to discover, and steal, supposedly incriminating or embarrassing reports.[19]

The surveillance activities in question were generally kept secret. But at times, intelligence agencies sought to foster fear that citizens were being watched. For example, Hoover instructed his agents to target American activists and to "enhance the paranoia ... and get the point across that there is an FBI agent behind every mailbox."[20] Hoover also let officials from the White House to the Supreme Court know that he possessed embarrassing personal information concerning them.[21]

B *Congress and the Courts Step In*

In the 1960s and 1970s, the other two branches of government stepped in and began setting limits on the executive branch's surveillance authorities. The Supreme Court clarified that electronic communications surveillance of domestic organizations required a warrant even when conducted for national security purposes. Although it left open the possibility of a more permissive regime for foreign intelligence surveillance, the abuses revealed by the Church Committee led Congress to enact a foreign intelligence surveillance scheme that required case-by-case judicial review. Congress and federal agencies also put in place a number of other mechanisms to ensure proper limits on, and oversight of, intelligence activities.

16 The facts relating to this matter are collected in Frederick A.O. Schwarz, Jr., DEMOCRACY IN THE DARK: THE SEDUCTION OF GOVERNMENT SECRECY 67–70 (2015).

17 *See National Security, Civil Liberties, and The Collection of Intelligence: A Report on the Huston Plan, in* CHURCH COMMITTEE REPORT, *supra* note 4, bk. III at 921–86.

18 James Bamford, BODY OF SECRETS: ANATOMY OF THE ULTRA-SECRET NATIONAL SECURITY AGENCY 428–80 (2001).

19 Richard Reeves, PRESIDENT NIXON: ALONE IN THE WHITE HOUSE 337–53 (2001).

20 *See* Betty Medsger, *Stolen Documents Describe F.B.I. Surveillance Activities*, WASH. POST, Mar. 24, 1971, at A1.

21 Schwarz, *supra* note 16, at 67. Louisiana Congressman Hale Boggs explained that "our apathy in this Congress, our silence in this House, our very fear of speaking out in other forums, has watered the roots and hastened the growth of a vine of tyranny which is ensnaring that Constitution and Bill of Rights which we are each sworn to uphold. Our society can survive many challenges and many threats. It cannot survive on a planned and programmed fear of its own government bureaus and agencies." CHURCH COMMITTEE REPORT, *supra* note 4, bk. II at 240 (quoting 117 Cong. Rec. 11562 (1971) (remarks of Rep. Hale Boggs)).

1 The Courts and the Fourth Amendment

Until the late 1960s, the Supreme Court had not recognized a Fourth Amendment right to privacy in telephone communications because wiretapping required no intrusion into a person's physical property.[22] The Court reversed itself in *Katz v. United States*,[23] ruling that the Fourth Amendment "protects people – and not merely 'areas' – against unreasonable searches and seizures."[24] In a footnote, however, the majority inserted a caveat: "Whether safeguards other than prior authorization by a magistrate would satisfy the Fourth Amendment in a situation involving the national security is a question not presented by this case."[25]

The principal holding of *Katz* was enshrined into law in the 1968 Omnibus Crime Control and Safe Streets Act.[26] Title III of the law authorized surveillance of electronic communications in investigations of specified crimes. Wiretaps had to be authorized by a judge or magistrate who would evaluate whether there was probable cause to believe that one of these crimes had been, was being, or was about to be committed. In keeping with the *Katz* footnote, however, Title III explicitly refrained from regulating national security surveillance.[27]

In the 1972 case *United States v. U.S. District Court* (known as the *Keith* case after the district court judge who wrote the initial decision), the Supreme Court partially addressed the question that *Katz* and Title III avoided: it held that surveillance of domestic organizations for national security purposes did require a warrant.[28] It acknowledged, however, that the standards and procedures surrounding the warrant requirement "may vary according to the governmental interest to be enforced and the nature of citizen rights deserving protection."[29] The Court thus invited Congress to create special rules for domestic security surveillance. Moreover, the Court expressly left open – and has never ruled on – the question of whether a warrant would be required if the government were seeking intelligence about a foreign power or its agent.

Several federal appeals courts took up this question in the following years, and held that no warrant was needed if the president or the president's delegate had certified that the purpose of intercepting individuals' communications was to collect foreign intelligence.[30] The Fourth Circuit's 1980 decision in *United States v. Truong Dinh Hung* distills the reasoning presented in these cases: a warrant requirement would "unduly frustrate" the president's exercise of his foreign affairs responsibilities.[31] The *Truong* court, however, set two important limitations on the president's authority to conduct warrantless surveillance inside the United States: the object of the search must be "a foreign

22 *Olmstead v. United States*, 277 U.S. 438, 466 (1928).
23 *Katz v. United States*, 389 U.S. 347 (1967).
24 *Id.* at 353.
25 *Id.* at 358 n.23.
26 Omnibus Crime Control and Safe Streets Act of 1968, Pub. L. No. 90–351, 82 Stat. 197 (codified as amended in scattered sections of 5, 18, and 42 U.S.C.).
27 *Id.* at § 802 (codified as amended at 18 U.S.C. § 2511(3)).
28 *United States v. U.S. Dist. Court for E. Dist. of Mich. (Keith)*, 407 U.S. 297, 323–24 (1972).
29 *Id.* at 323.
30 *United States v. Truong Dinh Hung*, 629 F.2d 908, 913 (4th Cir. 1980); *United States v. Brown*, 484 F.2d 418, 426 (5th Cir. 1973); *United States v. Butenko*, 494 F.2d 593, 604–05 (3d Cir. 1974) (en banc); *United States v. Buck*, 548 F.2d 871, 875 (9th Cir. 1977).
31 *Truong*, 629 F.2d at 913.

power, its agent or collaborators," and the surveillance must be conducted "primarily" for foreign intelligence reasons.[32] The other courts of appeal applied a similar analysis, and underscored that a departure from the warrant requirement required caution and close judicial review (albeit after the fact) of each particular case in which surveillance was challenged.[33]

During this same period, courts were considering the question of whether the government needed a warrant to obtain sensitive personal information held by business entities. The Supreme Court issued two landmark decisions on this question in the late 1970s: *United States v. Miller*,[34] which involved government access to financial records held by a bank, and *Smith v. Maryland*,[35] which involved government access to telephone records held by a telephone company. Together, these decisions established the rule – known as the "third party doctrine" – that there is no Fourth Amendment interest in information knowingly and voluntarily revealed to private companies, even in the course of an otherwise confidential business relationship.

2 The Foreign Intelligence Surveillance Act

The findings of the Church Committee in 1975–1976, discussed in Part I.A, served as a clarion call for reform. One of the most important changes recommended by the committee and implemented by Congress was the creation of a special court and legal regime to govern electronic surveillance for foreign intelligence purposes.

In enacting the Foreign Intelligence Surveillance Act (FISA), Congress squarely rejected the notion that the executive branch had unilateral authority to collect foreign intelligence in the United States. It also declined the *Keith* Court's invitation to make special rules for warrants seeking to obtain domestic intelligence, leaving in place a regular warrant requirement. And, while it created a special scheme for foreign intelligence surveillance conducted at home, it placed strict limits on such surveillance and required case-by-case judicial oversight to ensure that it would not be used to suppress domestic dissent or to evade the warrant requirement in ordinary criminal cases.

The law created the Foreign Intelligence Surveillance Court (commonly called "the FISA Court"). The FISA Court was designed to accommodate the government's need to obtain surveillance orders secretly and in a hurry. It consists of eleven federal trial judges[36] appointed by the chief justice of the United States for a single seven-year

32 *Id.*

33 *Butenko*, 494 F.2d at 606 ("Since the primary purpose of these searches is to secure foreign intelligence information, a judge, when reviewing a particular search must, above all, be assured that this was in fact its primary purpose and that the accumulation of evidence of criminal activity was incidental. If the court, for example, finds that members of a domestic political organization were the subjects of wiretaps or that the agents were looking for evidence of criminal conduct unrelated to the foreign affairs needs of a President, then he would undoubtedly hold the surveillances to be illegal and take appropriate measures"); *Brown*, 484 F.2d at 427 (Goldberg, J., specially concurring) ("The judiciary must not be astigmatic in the presence of warrantless surveillance; rather judges must microscopically examine the wiretaps in order to determine whether they had their origin in foreign intelligence or were merely camouflaged domestic intrusions. The serious step of recognizing the legality of a warrantless wiretap can be justified only when, as in the case before us, the foreign and sensitive nature of the government surveillance is crystal clear").

34 *United States v. Miller*, 425 U.S. 435 (1976).

35 *Smith v. Maryland*, 442 U.S. 735 (1979).

36 The initial number of FISA Court judges was seven. Foreign Intelligence Surveillance Act of 1978, Pub. L. No. 95–511, § 103, 92 Stat. 1783 (codified at 50 U.S.C. § 1803). This was increased to 11 by the

term.[37] These judges continue serving on their regular courts, but spend one week out of every eleven on the special court in Washington, D.C., ensuring a continuous rotation.[38] Congress also created the Foreign Intelligence Surveillance Court of Review ("FISA Appeals Court"), consisting of three federal trial or appellate judges also selected by the chief justice of the United States, to hear appeals in the event the FISA Court denies the government's application.[39]

The law requires the government to apply to the FISA Court when seeking to conduct "electronic surveillance" for foreign intelligence purposes. The term "electronic surveillance" encompasses, inter alia, any wire communication to or from a person inside the United States that is acquired within the United States, as well as any electronic monitoring within the United States to obtain information other than through a wire or radio communication (e.g., planting bugs). For complex historical reasons, "radio" communications – mainly those traveling by satellite – fell within FISA's scope only if all parties were inside the United States.[40]

To obtain the court's permission to conduct surveillance, the government had to show probable cause that the target of surveillance was – and that the facilities to be surveilled were being used by – a foreign power or its agent. (The law has since been amended, but this requirement still applies when the government seeks to target an American citizen or resident.)[41] The statute defines "foreign power" broadly to include not only foreign governments, but also factions of foreign nations, international terrorist groups, and foreign-based political organizations.[42] For American citizens and residents, however, the term "agent of a foreign power" is defined more narrowly and requires some connection to criminal activity.[43]

The government also was required to certify that the purpose of the surveillance was to obtain "foreign intelligence information." This term is defined to include information relating to various specified external threats, as well as information that "relates to" – and,

PATRIOT Act, which also added a requirement that at least three of the judges reside within twenty miles of the District of Columbia. Uniting and Strengthening America by Providing Appropriate Tools Required to Intercept and Obstruct Terrorism (USA PATRIOT) Act of 2001, Pub. L. No. 107–56, § 208, 115 Stat. 272 (2001) (codified as amended at 50 U.S.C. § 1803) [hereinafter PATRIOT Act].

37 50 U.S.C. §§ 1803(a)(1), 1803(d).

38 David S. Kris & J. Douglas Wilson, National Security Investigations & Prosecutions at § 5.3 n.14 (2d ed. 2012).

39 50 U.S.C. § 1803(b).

40 50 U.S.C. § 1801(f). For a discussion of the history underlying how FISA treats radio communications, see Elizabeth Goitein & Faiza Patel, Brennan Ctr. for Justice, What Went Wrong With the FISA Court 25 (2015), https://www.brennancenter.org/sites/default/files/analysis/What_Went_%20Wrong_With_The_FISA_Court.pdf; *Oversight and Reauthorization of The FISA Amendments Act: The Balance between National Security, Privacy and Civil Liberties: Hearing before the S. Comm. on the Judiciary*, 114th Cong. 15–16 (2016) (statement of Elizabeth Goitein, Co-Director, Liberty and National Security Program, Brennan Center for Justice at New York University School of Law).

41 50 U.S.C. § 1804(a)(3).

42 50 U.S.C. § 1801(a).

43 Specifically, U.S. persons qualify as agents of foreign powers if they (i) knowingly engage in clandestine intelligence gathering for a foreign power, which involve or may involve a violation of U.S. criminal statutes; (ii) knowingly engage in "any other clandestine intelligence activities" at the direction of a foreign intelligence service, if the activities involve or are about to involve a violation of U.S. criminal statutes; (iii) knowingly engage in sabotage or terrorism (or preparatory activities) for a foreign power; or (iv) knowingly aid, abet, or conspire with a person to do any of the above. 50 U.S.C. § 1801(b)(2). A fifth category, "knowingly enter the U.S. using a false identity on behalf of a foreign power" was added to this list in 1999. Intelligence Authorization Act for Fiscal Year 2000, Pub. L. No. 106–120, § 601 (codified as amended at 50 U.S.C. § 1801(b)(2)(D)).

if concerning an American citizen or resident, is "necessary to" – the national defense, security, or the conduct of foreign affairs.[44]

There are differences, to be sure, between this scheme and the process for obtaining wiretaps in criminal investigations, which is governed by Title III.[45] Title III requires the government to show probable cause of criminal activity, whereas traditional FISA requires a connection to criminal activity only if the target is an American citizen or resident – and even then, the connection may be more attenuated in practice.[46] Moreover, FISA orders require less proof that the surveillance activities would yield the information sought.[47]

Another key difference bears mentioning. Like warrant applications under Title III, FISA applications are generally heard on an *ex parte* basis. However, unlike individuals monitored under Title III, those whose communications are intercepted under FISA are highly unlikely to receive notice of the intrusion. Title III requires notice to the target (and, within the discretion of the judge, to other persons whose communications were intercepted) once the surveillance order expires.[48] FISA requires notice only if the government "intends to enter into evidence or otherwise use or disclose" such communications in a trial or other enumerated official proceedings,[49] a rare occurrence in foreign intelligence surveillance investigations. Moreover, recent reports suggest that the government has taken a very narrow view of when and how this notice requirement applies.[50]

Nonetheless, despite these differences, orders issued by the FISA Court share a critical feature with regular Title III warrants: both require prior judicial scrutiny of an application for an order authorizing electronic surveillance in a particular case.

3 The Attorney General Guidelines

The Church Committee also recommended that Congress pass a statutory charter governing the FBI,[51] which would include limitations on its investigative powers.[52] To preempt this outcome, Attorney General Edward Levi in 1976 issued a set of guidelines to

44 50 U.S.C. § 1801(e).

45 *Compare* 50 U.S.C. § 1805 (FISA Court orders), *with* 18 U.S.C. § 2518 (Title III orders).

46 *See* Goitein & Patel, *supra* note 40, at 18.

47 Under Title III, the government must demonstrate probable cause to believe that particular communications concerning specified crimes will be obtained through an interception. 18 U.S.C. § 2518(3)(b). Under FISA, the government instead must show probable cause that the facilities at which the surveillance is directed are used by a foreign power or its agent; it need not show probable cause that collecting on these facilities will yield the desired information. 50 U.S.C. § 1804(a)(3)(B).

48 18 U.S.C. § 2518(8)(d).

49 50 U.S.C. § 1806(c).

50 *See* Patrick Toomey, *Why Aren't Criminal Defendants Getting Notice of Section 702 Surveillance – Again?* Just Sec. (Dec. 11, 2015), https://www.justsecurity.org/28256/arent-criminal-defendants-notice-section-702-surveillance-again/; Charlie Savage, *Door May Open for Challenge to Secret Wiretaps*, N.Y. Times (Oct. 16, 2013), http://www.nytimes.com/2013/10/17/us/politics/us-legal-shift-may-open-door-for-challenge-to-secret-wiretaps.html?pagewanted=all; Adam Liptak, *A Secret Surveillance Program Proves Challengeable in Theory Only*, N.Y. Times (July 15, 2013), http://www.nytimes.com/2013/07/16/us/double-secret-surveillance.html?pagewanted=all. For further discussion of issues relating to notice, see *infra* text accompanying notes 132–38.

51 Office of the Inspector Gen., U.S. Dep't of Justice, The Federal Bureau of Investigation's Compliance with the Attorney General's Investigative Guidelines 35 (2005).

52 *Id.* (quoting *Legislative Charter for the FBI: Hearings Before the Subcomm. on Civil and Constitutional Rights of the H. Comm. on the Judiciary*, 96th Cong. 3 (1980) (statement of Benjamin R. Civiletti, Att'y Gen. of the United States)).

govern the FBI's domestic intelligence activities.[53] The "Levi Guidelines," as they were known, incorporated many of the recommendations of the Church Committee. They focused on a few main themes: "[requiring] progressively higher standards and higher levels of review for more intrusive investigative techniques[, requiring] … that domestic security investigations be tied closely with the detection of crime … [and requiring] safeguards against investigations of activities that are merely troublesome or unpopular."[54]

The guidelines established three investigative phases: preliminary, limited, and full investigations. As summarized by one scholar: "For each successive phase, a higher threshold of suspicion was necessary to proceed; the investigative tools agents were permitted to use were more intrusive; and procedural safeguards, such as supervisory approval before using certain techniques, were more stringent. This basic structure – increasingly intrusive levels of investigation, accompanied by higher suspicion thresholds and greater procedural constraints – has been retained in all subsequent versions of the guidelines, although the entire scheme has grown more permissive with time."[55]

Under the Levi Guidelines, the lowest level of investigation (i.e., "preliminary") had to be based on "allegations or other information that an individual or group may be engaged in activities which involve or will involve the use of force or violence and which involve or will involve the violation of federal law."[56] In a preliminary investigation, agents could review public sources of information, along with federal, state, and local government records; also question existing informants; and conduct physical surveillance, and interview others if their goal was to identify the subject of the investigation.[57] Collecting the information on the outside of a piece of mail (known as "mail covers"), the recruitment and tasking of informants, and electronic surveillance were prohibited.[58] Under the next level of investigation (i.e., "limited"), agents could use the same techniques, and they could also conduct physical surveillance and interviews for a wider range of purposes.[59] When conducting "full" investigations, agents could make use of the full panoply of the FBI's investigative techniques.

Perhaps most important, the Levi Guidelines required a close connection between domestic security investigations and the prevention of criminal activity. Investigations at all phases were thus limited to ascertaining "information on the activities of individuals, or the activities of groups, which involve or will involve the use of violence and which involve or will involve the violation of federal law."[60]

4 Business Records Privacy

In the 1970s and 1980s, Congress took several steps to shore up the privacy of information held by third parties. The first was the enactment in 1970 of the Fair Credit Reporting

53 The guidelines, officially entitled Domestic Security Investigation Guidelines, "were intended, in part, to diminish the perceived need for legislation to regulate and restrict the FBI's use of informants." *United States v. Salemme*, 91 F. Supp. 2d 141, 190–91 (D. Mass. 1999).

54 *FBI Oversight: Hearings before the Subcomm. on Civil and Constitutional Rights of the H. Comm. on the Judiciary*, 94th Cong. 263 (1976) (testimony of Edward Levi, Att'y Gen. of the United States).

55 Emily Berman, Brennan Ctr. for Justice, Domestic Intelligence: New Powers, New Risks 11 (2011), https://www.brennancener.org/sites/default/files/legacy/AGGReportFINALed.pdf.

56 Domestic Security Investigation Guidelines, § I.A (Mar. 10, 1976) [hereinafter Levi Guidelines]

57 *Id.* at § II.E.

58 *Id.* at § II.G.

59 *Id.* at § II.G.

60 *Id.* at § I.A.

Act (FCRA),[61] which was enacted to "protect personal information collected by credit reporting agencies."[62] The act specifies the permissible purposes for which credit reports may be disseminated and used. In 1996, it was amended to allow the FBI and several other government agencies to obtain basic consumer information in foreign intelligence investigations, including names, current and former addresses, and current and former employers.[63] To access this information, the FBI had to supply a certification that the information was "necessary for the conduct of an authorized foreign counterintelligence investigation" and that there were "specific and articulable facts giving reason to believe that the consumer is" a foreign power, a non-American official of a foreign power, or an agent of a foreign power who "is engaging or has engaged in an act of international terrorism or clandestine intelligence activities" that may be criminal.[64]

In 1978, in direct response to the Supreme Court's holding in *United States v. Miller*, Congress enacted the Right to Financial Privacy Act (RFPA).[65] The legislation generally requires that individuals receive advance notice when the federal government is requesting their records and have the opportunity to challenge that access.[66] In 1986, Congress enacted a "National Security Letter" exception to the RFPA, allowing the FBI to bypass the advance notice requirement when records were being requested for foreign counterintelligence cases. To qualify for this exception, the FBI had to certify "specific and articulable facts giving reason to believe that the customer or entity whose records are sought is a foreign power or an agent of a foreign power."[67]

Also in 1986, responding in part to the Supreme Court's ruling in *Smith v. Maryland*, Congress passed the Electronic Communications Privacy Act (ECPA).[68] In addition to extending the Title III warrant requirement to electronic data transmitted by computer, the law afforded varying levels of protection to stored data and communications records. It allowed the FBI to obtain customer information (name, address, and length of service), toll billing records, and certain transactional information only if there were "specific and articulable facts giving reason to believe" that the subject of the request was a "foreign power or an agent of a foreign power."[69] In 1993, Congress broadened the scope of information available via an ECPA National Security Letter to include "the subscriber and toll billing records of additional persons, such as those who were in contact with agents of a foreign power."[70]

61 Fair Credit Reporting Act of 1970, Pub. L. No. 91–508, 84 Stat. 1127 (codified as amended at 15 U.S.C. §§ 1681-1681u).

62 Office of the Inspector Gen., U.S. Dep't of Justice, A Review of the Federal Bureau of Investigation's Use of National Security Letters xiii (2007) [hereinafter National Security Letters Report], https://oig.justice.gov/reports/2014/s1410.pdf.

63 *Id.* (citing to Intelligence Authorization Act for Fiscal Year 1996, Pub. L. No. 104–93, § 601(a), 109 Stat. 961, codified as amended at 15 U.S.C. § 1681u).

64 15 U.S.C § 1681u.

65 Right to Financial Privacy Act of 1978, 12 U.S.C. §§ 3401–3422.

66 National Security Letters Report, *supra* note 62, at xi.

67 12 U.S.C § 3414(a)(5)(A).

68 Electronic Communications Privacy Act of 1986, Pub. L. No. 99–508, 100 Stat. 1848 (codified as amended in scattered sections of 18 U.S.C.); *Smith v. Maryland*, 442 U.S. 735 (1979).

69 18 U.S.C. § 2709(b)(1)(B).

70 National Security Letters Report, *supra* note 62, at 13 (citing Pub. L. No. 103–142, § 2, 107 Stat. 1491 (1993)).

5 The Intelligence Committees

In the period before the Church Committee's revelations, legislative oversight of the executive branch's intelligence activities was sporadic and informal. The armed services and appropriations committees would send letters to the agencies explaining the purposes for which appropriated lump-sum funds should be used, and intelligence officials would occasionally brief members of those committees regarding their activities.[71] The historian Loch Johnson refers to this period as the "Era of Trust"; he recounts an incident in which the then–CIA director, James Schlesinger, mentioned a proposed operation to Senate Armed Services Committee Chairman John Stennis (D-MS), and Stennis responded, "Just go ahead and do it, but I don't want to know!"[72]

Concluding that this regime had been woefully insufficient, the Church Committee recommended that permanent intelligence oversight committees be established in the Senate and House. The Senate created the Select Committee on Intelligence in 1976, and the House created the Permanent Select Committee on Intelligence the following year. Both committees were made responsible for authorizing expenditures for intelligence activities and for conducting necessary oversight.

In 1991, the National Security Act was amended to require the heads of intelligence agencies and components, "to the extent consistent with due regard for the protection from unauthorized disclosure of classified information relating to sensitive intelligence sources and methods or other exceptionally sensitive matters," to keep the intelligence committees "fully and currently informed of all intelligence activities," and to provide them with any information or material they requested in order to carry out their responsibilities.[73] There is an exception for "covert actions," which notably cannot include "activities the primary purpose of which is to acquire intelligence," or traditional counterintelligence, military, diplomatic, or law enforcement efforts.[74] If the president finds that there are "extraordinary circumstances affecting vital interests of the United States," a covert action may be reported only to the so-called Gang of Eight, which comprises the chairmen and ranking minority members of the congressional intelligence committees, the Speaker and minority leader of the House of Representatives, and the majority and minority leaders of the Senate.[75]

6 The Inspector General Act

In addition to shoring up its own oversight capacity, Congress acted to create independent oversight bodies within many agencies through passage of the Inspector General Act of 1978.[76]

71 *See* Dakota Rudesill, *Coming to Terms with Secret Law*, 7 Harv. Nat'l Security J. 241, 258–59 (2016).

72 Loch K. Johnson, Governing in the Absence of Angels: On the Practice of Intelligence Accountability in the United States 13 (2003), https://www.wilsoncenter.org/sites/default/files/johnson.doc.

73 50 U.S.C. § 3092(a).

74 50 U.S.C. § 3092(e).

75 50 U.S.C. § 3092(c).

76 Inspector General Act of 1978, Pub L. No. 95–452, 92 Stat. 1101 (reprinted as amended in 5 U.S.C. App. § 1–13).

In the United States, the position of "inspector general" can be traced as far back as the Continental Congress, which in 1778 passed a resolution confirming George Washington's appointee, Wilhelm Friedrich von Steuben, as an inspector general within the Continental Army. Congress deemed the post "essential to the promotion of discipline in the American Army, and to the reformation of the various abuses which prevail in the different departments."[77] Since then, similar posts have existed within the military branches, eventually leading to the formal administrative creation of Offices of Inspector General.[78]

These nonstatutory inspectors general have been perceived as lacking independence because they report only to their agency heads, not to Congress.[79] The inspector general for the U.S. Department of Agriculture (USDA), for instance – who was the first inspector general at a civilian agency, appointed in 1962 in response to a major criminal fraud scandal[80] – was described as "a strong right arm of the secretary, one of the family, an important source of inside advice and counsel, as tough as the secretary would permit, someone to dig up the dirt but not spread it."[81]

In 1978, following Watergate, the revelations of the Church Committee, and a scandal at the General Services Administration (GSA) involving allegations of fraud, corruption, and mismanagement,[82] Congress passed the Inspector General Act, which established offices of inspectors general (OIG) in many federal agencies. Under the statute, inspectors general were required to report both to their agency heads and to their respective oversight committees in Congress.[83] This dual reporting structure was intended to bolster the independence of the inspector general while ensuring that problems were brought to the attention of the agency head.

The act set forth several purposes that inspectors general are intended to serve: conducting and supervising audits and investigations related to agency programs and operations; providing leadership and coordination, as well as recommending policies for activities designed to promote the economy, efficiency, and effectiveness of the affiliated agencies' programs and operations; providing for the prevention and detection of fraud and abuse in such programs and operations; and keeping the agency head and Congress "fully and currently informed about problems and deficiencies relating to" such programs and the necessity for and "progress of corrective action."[84] To those ends, IGs have broad authority to conduct audits and investigations; access any records or information related to the agency's programs and operations; subpoena information and documents; request assistance from other federal, state, and local government agencies; hire staff and manage their own resources; and receive and respond to complaints from agency employees.[85]

77 Paul C. Light, Monitoring Government: Inspectors General and the Search for Accountability 16 n.6 (1993).
78 Project on Government Oversight, Inspectors General: Many Lack Essential Tools for Independence 8, 9 (2008) [hereinafter POGO Report], http://pogoarchives.org/m/go/ig/report-20080226.pdf.
79 *Id.*
80 *About OIG Investigative Division*, Office of Inspector Gen., U.S. Dep't of Agriculture (Oct. 1, 2014), https://www.usda.gov/oig/invest.htm.
81 Light, *supra* note 77, at 28.
82 POGO Report, *supra* note 78, at 9.
83 5 U.S.C. App. § 5(a).
84 5 U.S.C. App. § 2.
85 5 U.S.C. App. §§ 6(a), 6(e), and 7.

Nonetheless, until 2010, nonstatutory inspectors general remained the norm in agencies that were housed within the Department of Defense, including the National Security Agency, the Defense Intelligence Agency, and the National Reconnaissance Office[86] (although the Department of Defense itself had a statutory inspector general, as did the CIA and ODNI).[87] In 2010, however, Congress created an inspector general of the Intelligence Community (IC) with express cross-agency authority; it also created IG posts in the DIA, NSA, NRO, and the National Geospatial-Intelligence Agency.[88]

C *9/11 and the Unraveling of Surveillance Limits*

For several decades, the legal regime established in response to the Church Committee's findings governed national security surveillance and oversight. Then came the attacks of 9/11. With the fear of an overreaching government having long receded, and the fear of another terrorist attack front and center in Americans' minds, lawmakers and the public were willing to grant the executive branch expansive new surveillance authorities – sometimes supplying the legal authority for activities the executive branch had already undertaken illegally. The carefully crafted legal limits on surveillance began to unravel. Across a range of laws and policies, the requirement of individualized suspicion in order to conduct surveillance was weakened or jettisoned.

1 The PATRIOT Act

The first volley was the USA PATRIOT Act. Representative Sensenbrenner introduced the legislation on October 23, 2001. The bill was 341 pages long and made sweeping changes to multiple volumes of the U.S. Code. Nonetheless, the House voted on it the next day, passing it by a vote of 357–66. The Senate passed the bill the following day with a vote of 98–1, and on October 26, 2001, it became law.

Civil liberties advocates voiced concern with many of the PATRIOT Act's provisions, but in the area of national security surveillance, three of them were particularly consequential. *First*, Congress expanded the government's authority to obtain business records in foreign intelligence investigations. Previously, the FBI could obtain an order from the FISA Court to require transport companies, hotels and motels, car and truck rental agencies, and storage rental facilities to turn over records of transactions with their customers. The government had to certify that the records were sought for a foreign intelligence or international terrorism investigation being conducted by the FBI. Further, it had to present "specific and articulable facts giving reason to believe" that the subject of the records was a foreign power or agent of a foreign power[89] – a status that, in the case of an American, necessarily entailed involvement in criminal activity.[90]

86 POGO Report, *supra* note 78, at 8.

87 *Id.* at 8 n.13.

88 Wendy Ginsberg & Michael Greene, Cong. Research Serv., R43814, Federal Inspectors General: History, Characteristics, and Recent Congressional Actions 2 n.10 (2014), https://www.fas.org/sgp/crs/misc/R43814.pdf.

89 Intelligence Authorization Act for 1999, Pub. L. No. 105–272, § 602, 112 Stat. 2411 (codified as amended at 50 U.S.C. § 1852).

90 FISA's definition of "agent of a foreign power," as applied to U.S. persons, encompasses a range of criminal activities such as espionage. *See* 50 U.S.C. § 1801(b)(2).

Section 215 removed the limitation on the types of records the government could obtain, granting authority to obtain "any tangible thing." It also removed the requirement that the government show a connection to a foreign power or its agent. The government need only provide a statement of facts showing that "there are reasonable grounds to believe that the tangible things sought are relevant to an authorized investigation ... to obtain foreign intelligence information not concerning a United States person or to protect against international terrorism or clandestine intelligence activities."[91] The actual subject of the record need not be suspected of any wrongdoing or associations with a foreign power.

Section 215 thus lowered the level of suspicion required, and shifted it from the person who was the subject of the records to the records themselves. Moreover, while the need to show "relevance" appeared to provide some limitation on collection, this proved illusory. In 2013, Edward Snowden revealed that the FISA Court had issued orders allowing the NSA to collect Americans' telephone records in bulk.[92] The records in question, known as "metadata," included the numbers dialed, the numbers of those who called, and the times and lengths of calls – information that could be used to create a detailed picture of a person's associations and activities.

The FISA Court authorized the collection on the theory that vast amounts of irrelevant records could be deemed "relevant" if there were relevant records buried within them.[93] While the court required the government to have "reasonable articulable suspicion" of a terrorist link in order to search the records, the level of suspicion (or even relevance) required to collect them in the first instance was effectively zero.

Second, the PATRIOT Act made a key two-word change to FISA. Previously, FISA allowed the government to obtain electronic surveillance orders if it certified that "the purpose" of surveillance was the acquisition of foreign intelligence. Under the PATRIOT Act, however, the government need only certify that acquiring foreign intelligence is "a significant purpose" of the surveillance.[94]

A complex history underlies this deceptively simple change. Before FISA's enactment, several courts had recognized a so-called foreign intelligence exception to the Fourth Amendment's warrant requirement, allowing the government to obtain Americans' communications in foreign intelligence investigations without obtaining a warrant. As discussed in Section I.B.1, however, they insisted that acquiring foreign intelligence be the primary purpose of the surveillance, in order to justify the exception and prevent it from swallowing the rule. Indeed, in the Fourth Circuit's seminal decision, the court refused to apply the exception because the Department of Justice prosecutors appeared to be directing the surveillance, suggesting that the primary purpose was to bolster a criminal prosecution.[95]

91 50 U.S.C. § 1861(b)(2)(A). In addition, if directed at a U.S. person, the investigation could not be based solely on that person's First Amendment activities. 50 U.S.C. § 1861(a)(1).

92 Glenn Greenwald, *NSA Collecting Phone Records of Millions of Verizon Customers Daily*, GUARDIAN (June 6, 2013, 6:05 AM), http://www.theguardian.com/world/2013/jun/06/nsa-phone-records-verizon-court-order.

93 *In re* Application of the Fed. Bureau of Investigation for an Order Requiring the Production of Tangible Things from [REDACTED], No. BR 13–109, slip op. at 18 (FISA Ct. Aug. 29, 2013), https://www.aclu.org/files/assets/br13-09-primary-order.pdf.

94 PATRIOT Act, *supra* note 36, at § 218 (codified as amended at 50 U.S.C §§ 1804(a)(6)(B), 1823(a)(6)(B)).

95 *United States v. Truong Dinh Hung*, 629 F.2d 908, 914 (4th Cir. 1980).

The Department of Justice responded to this ruling by voluntarily adopting a set of practices designed to facilitate the sharing of information between intelligence and law enforcement components, while avoiding any appearance that prosecutors were directing the intelligence investigations. The FISA Court later described these procedures as permitting "broad information sharing," as well as "substantial consultation and coordination."[96] Nonetheless, there was a strong perception within the government that the procedures erected a "wall" between intelligence and law enforcement that inhibited robust cooperation.[97]

After 9/11, the "wall" was blamed for impeding cooperation that conceivably could have averted the attacks. Indeed, the report of the 9/11 Commission documents a tragic lack of coordination, but the culprit appears to lie elsewhere: as reflected in the report, the CIA failed to share vital information with the FBI because of a combination of poor judgment on the part of a small number of individual employees and a turf battle between the two organizations.[98] In any event, the Department of Justice dismantled its procedures, and to discourage any renewed or additional limits on coordination, Congress enacted the "significant purpose" test.

By specifying that acquiring foreign intelligence need not be the "primary purpose" of surveillance, the PATRIOT Act enabled the government to bypass the typical warrant requirement, and instead obtain an order from the FISA Court, even where the government's primary purpose was to obtain evidence for ordinary criminal prosecutions against Americans. This change became even more significant after FISA was amended in 2007 and 2008, as discussed later in this chapter, to permit the collection of phone calls and e-mails between foreign targets and Americans without any individualized court order.

Third, the PATRIOT Act lowered the standard required to issue National Security Letters (NSLs). NSLs are the administrative equivalent of Section 215 orders to produce business records; they are subpoenas that the FBI can serve on companies and other third parties without judicial approval. NSLs originated as exceptions to laws protecting the privacy of business records. The types of records the FBI can obtain using NSLs are more limited than under Section 215. They include financial information from banks, credit unions, and the like; records of purchases at travel agencies or real estate agencies;

[96] *In re* All Matters Submitted to the Foreign Intelligence Surveillance Court, 218 F. Supp.2d 611, 619 (FISA Ct. 2002), *rev'd*, *In re* Sealed Case, 310 F.3d 717 (FISA Ct. Rev. 2002).

[97] There is certainly some evidence that officials were interpreting these procedures in a very conservative way, and erring on the side of not sharing information even when the procedures arguably would have allowed sharing. Nat'l Comm'n on Terrorist Attacks upon the U.S., The 9/11 Commission Report 79 (2004) [hereinafter 9/11 Commission Report] (noting that the use of the term "the wall" to describe the Justice Department's procedures is "misleading," and that lack of coordination occurred because these procedures "were almost immediately misunderstood and misapplied"); David S. Kris & J. Douglas Wilson, National Security Investigations & Prosecutions 2d § 10.8 (2012) (describing the development of Department of Justice FISA coordination procedures in 1995 and how interpretations of these procedures limited coordination).

[98] *See* 9/11 Commission Report, *supra* note 97, at 266–72. On the few occasions in which an analyst believed "the wall" prevented her from sharing information, the 9/11 Commission concluded that "she appears to have misunderstood the complex rules that could apply to this situation," and that no such actual barrier existed. *Id.* at 271. *See also* James Bamford, The Shadow Factory 18–20 (2008) (describing one instance in which the CIA failed to share critical information about the 9/11 hijackers with the FBI because of a turf battle between the two organizations).

credit history and consumer credit reports; and records from communications providers, including basic account information and billing records.

Before the PATRIOT Act, as set forth previously in Part I.B.3, the FBI could issue an NSL if the records sought were relevant to a foreign intelligence investigation *and* there were "specific and articulable facts" that the person or entity to whom the records pertained was a foreign power or its agent. The PATRIOT Act removed the latter requirement. Today, almost all NSLs may be issued upon a certification that the information is "relevant to," "necessary for," or "sought for" a counterterrorism or foreign intelligence investigation.[99]

The change Congress made to NSLs was thus similar to the change it made to Section 215 orders. The level of suspicion required to issue both NSLs and Section 215 orders was lowered, and was transferred from the person who was the subject of the records to the records themselves. The FBI can now obtain certain types of sensitive business records pertaining to individuals not suspected of any offense, and can do so without judicial review.

2 Revised Attorney General's Guidelines for Domestic Investigations

As discussed previously, the first set of Attorney General's Guidelines governing the FBI's domestic activities was implemented in 1976 to address concerns over abuse of the FBI's domestic intelligence role. The guidelines attempted to tether the FBI's intelligence-gathering activities to the detection and prevention of specific crimes, requiring a higher level of evidence of possible criminal activity (past or future) in order to use more intrusive investigative techniques. Over time, however, their restrictions eroded, and the bureau once again expanded its intelligence-collection activities.

The expansion was slow at first, but in the wake of the attacks of 9/11, it accelerated markedly, as the balance between the FBI's focus on solving crimes and its focus on preventing them was wholly reconceived. The FBI's "central mission" became "preventing the commission of terrorist acts against the United States and its people."[100] The guidelines issued by Attorney General Ashcroft in 2002 were intended to reflect this new mission, along with a new approach to intelligence gathering. To that end, the Ashcroft Guidelines "affirmatively authorize[d] agents to 'scour public sources for information on future terrorist threat' even in the absence of 'specific investigative predicates.'"[101]

One of the 2002 guidelines' most significant changes related to the FBI's ability to infiltrate political and religious gatherings. Although agents generally may attend events that are open to the public, there was previously a special rule for political or religious events, given their sensitive nature and the potential for the presence of law enforcement to chill the exercise of First Amendment rights. Agents thus were required to have some factual basis to suspect possible criminal or terrorist activity before attending such gatherings. The Ashcroft Guidelines removed that rule, allowing FBI agents to attend religious

99 PATRIOT Act, *supra* note 36, at § 505, 18 U.S.C. § 2709(b)(1)-(2), 12 U.S.C. § 3414(a)(5)(A), 15 U.S.C. § 1681u(a)-(b) (U.S. Code citations are to relevant parts only); 15 U.S.C. § 1681v.

100 Memorandum from Charles Doyle, Senior Specialist, American Law Division, CRS, to Senate Select Committee on Intelligence 16 (Sept. 22, 2008) (on file with the Brennan Center) (citing Ashcroft Guidelines § VI).

101 Robert M. Chesney, *Civil Liberties and the Terrorism Prevention Paradigm: The Guilt by Association Critique*, 101 Mich. L. Rev. 1408, 1425 (2003) (quoting Attorney General Ashcroft).

services or political meetings undercover, and even to record surreptitiously what takes place there, without any suspicion of wrongdoing.[102]

Another critical change was brought about by Attorney General Mukasey's 2008 revisions to the guidelines. The most notable feature of the Mukasey Guidelines was their authorization of "assessments" – an investigative stage prior to a preliminary investigation – without "factual predicates." Assessments require only an "authorized purpose" and can take place even if there is no factual basis to suspect criminal or terrorist activity.[103] The Mukasey Guidelines authorize FBI agents to use highly intrusive investigative techniques when conducting assessments, such as "(1) recruiting and tasking informants to attend meetings or events surreptitiously; (2) questioning people or engaging them in conversation while misrepresenting the agent's true identity (so-called 'pretext interviews'); and (3) engaging in indefinite physical surveillance" of individuals, including following them throughout the day and monitoring the outside of their homes or offices.[104] As with the FBI's infiltration of religious and political gatherings, these techniques were previously reserved for investigations in which there was fact-based suspicion of unlawful conduct.

3 Protect America Act and FISA Amendments Act

In 2005, the *New York Times* broke the story that the administration of President George W. Bush was engaged in warrantless surveillance of communications between suspected terrorists abroad and Americans.[105] This activity violated FISA, which at the time required the government to obtain an order from the FISA Court if it wished to obtain wire communications involving Americans. After the illegal surveillance was revealed, the administration sought the FISA Court's approval for the program; one of the court's judges agreed to grant approval, but when the administration sought reauthorization, another judge balked.[106] Accordingly, the administration pressed Congress to amend FISA in order to legalize the warrantless surveillance.

In response to the administration's push, Congress passed two statutes: the Protect America Act (PAA) of 2007,[107] which expired the following year, and the FISA

102 John Ashcroft, U.S. Dep't of Justice, The Attorney General's Guidelines on General Crimes, Racketeering Enterprise and Terrorism Enterprise Investigations § VI.A-B (2002), http://www.fas.org/irp/agency/doj/fbi/generalcrimes2.pdf.

103 Michael B. Mukasey, U.S. Dep't of Justice, The Attorney General's Guidelines For Domestic FBI Operations § II (2008) [hereinafter Mukasey Guidelines], http://www.justice.gov/ag/readingroom/guidelines.pdf.

104 Berman, *supra* note 55, at 22; *see also* Muskasey Guidelines, *supra* note 103, at § II.A.4.e, f, h.

105 Eric Lichtblau & James Risen, *Bush Lets U.S. Spy on Callers without Courts*, N.Y. Times (Dec. 16, 2005), http://www.nytimes.com/2005/12/16/politics/16program.html?pagewanted=all&_r=1&.

106 *In re* Various Known and Unknown Agents of [REDACTED] Presumed United States Persons, No. [REDACTED] (FISA Ct. Jan. 10, 2007), https://www.dni.gov/files/documents/1212/FISC%20Order%2001%2010%2007%20-%2012-11%20-%20Redacted.pdf (order authorizing collection of Internet and telephony content of United States Persons for foreign intelligence purposes); *In re* [Redacted], No. [REDACTED] (FISA Ct. Jan. 10, 2007), https://www.dni.gov/files/documents/1212/FISCOrder01100712-11–Redacted.pdf (order authorizing collection of Internet and telephony content of foreign targets for foreign intelligence purposes); *In re* [REDACTED], No. [REDACTED] (FISA Ct. Apr. 3, 2007), https://www.dni.gov/files/documents/1212/CERTIFIED COPY – Order and Memorandum Opinion 04 03 07 12-11 Redacted.pdf (finding that an email address is a "facility" under FISA and that probable cause findings must be made by the Court, not the NSA).

107 Protect America Act of 2007, Pub. L. No. 110–55, 121 Stat. 552 (expired 2008).

Amendments Act (FAA),[108] which replaced it. While the FAA walked back a handful of the PAA's most significant changes, the two statutes were fundamentally similar in that they both authorized a regime of "programmatic surveillance."

The FAA, which is still in place today, eliminated the requirement of an individual court order for any acquisition, within the United States, of communications between foreign targets and Americans. Instead, under a new section of FISA (Section 702) created by the FAA, the government may collect foreign intelligence on persons or entities reasonably believed to be non-U.S. persons overseas – and may acquire the targets' communications with Americans in the United States – without any individualized judicial approval.[109] Section 702 also eliminated the requirement that the target be a foreign power or an agent of a foreign power.

There are three primary limitations on this authority. First, the government must certify that obtaining foreign intelligence information is a "significant purpose" of the collection. It need not be the only purpose or even the main purpose, as discussed previously. Second, the government must have in place targeting and minimization procedures that are approved by the FISA Court. The targeting procedures must ensure that the program's targets are indeed "reasonably believed" to be foreigners overseas, while the minimization procedures must be "reasonably designed" to minimize the collection and retention – and prohibit the sharing – of Americans' information, consistent with the need to obtain and use foreign intelligence.[110] Third, the law prohibits the practice of "reverse targeting" – i.e., collecting the international communications of a foreigner abroad when the government's true motive is to target "a particular, known person reasonably believed to be in the United States."[111]

These limitations, taken together, suggest that Section 702 should not be used to obtain evidence against Americans in domestic criminal cases. Nonetheless, the Privacy and Civil Liberties Oversight Board – an independent board charged with overseeing the civil liberties implications of counterterrorism policies – reported in 2014 that the FBI routinely searches databases that contain communications obtained under Section 702 for Americans' calls and e-mails, in ordinary criminal investigations as well as national security cases.[112] Any resulting "hits" may be used as evidence in prosecutions that involve serious crimes.[113] The practice of searching Section 702 data for Americans' communications to use in domestic criminal cases, after certifying to the FISA Court that the government has a foreign intelligence purpose and is targeting only foreigners, was dubbed the "backdoor search loophole" by Senator Ron Wyden.[114]

108 Foreign Intelligence Surveillance Act of 1978 Amendments Act (FAA) of 2008, Pub. L. No. 110–261, 122 Stat. 2435.

109 *Id.* at § 101(a)(2) (codified as amended at 50 U.S.C. § 1881a) (creating Section 702 of FISA).

110 50 U.S.C. § 1881a(d)(1)(A), (e)(1).

111 50 U.S.C. § 1881a(b)(2).

112 Privacy & Civil Liberties Oversight Bd., Report on the Surveillance Program Operated Pursuant to Section 702 of the Foreign Intelligence Surveillance Act (2014) [hereinafter PCLOB 702 Report], https://www.pclob.gov/library/702-Report.pdf.

113 Robert S. Litt, Gen. Counsel, Office of the Dir. of Nat'l Intelligence, Remarks on Signals Intelligence Reform at the Brookings Institution (Feb. 10, 2015), https://www.dni.gov/index.php/newsroom/speeches-and-interviews/208-speeches-interviews-2015/1171-odni-general-counsel-robert-litt%E2%80%99s-as-prepared-remarks-on-signals-intelligence-reform-at-the-brookings-institute.

114 Senator Ron Wyden, Remarks on the FISA "Backdoor Search" Loophole (Dec. 27, 2012), http://www.c-span.org/video/?c4279361/wyden-fisa-backdoor-search-loophole.

Regardless of how the data is used, the changes wrought by the PAA and the FAA meant that the collection of communications between foreign targets and Americans in foreign intelligence investigations no longer requires individualized suspicion, or even generalized suspicion, of any connection to a foreign power or its agent. A case-by-case showing of suspicion has been replaced by suspicionless "programmatic" surveillance.

4 The Role of Technology and Surveillance under Executive Order 12333

During the same period that legal limits on surveillance were being eroded, advances in communications technology were occurring at a dizzying pace. There is now a broad range of digital devices that can be used to communicate, and an even broader range of communication services, such as texting, popular "apps" such as SnapChat or Instagram, and VOIP services such as Skype or FaceTime. The cost of long-distance communications has plummeted, in some cases to zero. The amount of data stored by third parties has also skyrocketed, with Americans storing much of their most sensitive information in the cloud, and Internet service or mobile application providers amassing enormous amounts of transactional data based on their customers' usage.[115]

Technology also has affected the government's ability to keep and use data. Practical limitations on storage capacity and/or the cost of such storage once served to limit the amount of information the government could collect. The need for human analysis also weighed against mass collection of potentially irrelevant information. Today, the government can store petabytes of data at an ever-diminishing cost, and sophisticated computer algorithms exist to tease patterns and relationships out of the morass.

These developments greatly amplify the effect of the loosening of legal limitations on surveillance. They also play a significant role even where legal limits have remained the same, or even – as in the case of Executive Order 12333 – tightened somewhat.

Executive Order 12333, a directive issued by President Ronald Reagan in 1981, governs surveillance activities conducted overseas.[116] These operations are largely unregulated by Congress and not subject to judicial review, and they constitute the majority of the NSA's surveillance activities. The government may not deliberately target particular American citizens or residents when conducting surveillance overseas. However, the government need not target particular foreigners, either. It may (and does) engage in bulk collection of communications: for instance, under one program code named "SOMALGET," the government collects the content of all phone calls transiting in and out of the Bahamas and Afghanistan and keeps them for thirty days.[117]

Technological advances have fundamentally changed the nature of Executive Order 12333 surveillance. Bulk collection programs such as SOMALGET would have been impossible in the past, because the government lacked both the capacity to store all the data and the technological ability to process and analyze it. Moreover, because digital

115 *See* Goitein & Patel, *supra* note 40, at 19–21 (discussing changes in communications technology).

116 *See generally* Amos Toh, Faiza Patel & Elizabeth Goitein, Brennan Ctr. for Justice, Overseas Surveillance in an Interconnected World (2016), https://www.brennancenter.org/sites/default/files/publications/Overseas_Surveillance_in_an_Interconnected_World.pdf.

117 Barton Gellman & Ashkan Soltani, *NSA Surveillance Program Reaches 'Into the Past' to Retrieve, Replay Phone Calls*, Wash. Post (Mar. 18, 2014), http://www.washingtonpost.com/world/national-security/nsa-surveillance-program-reaches-into-the-pastto-retrieve-replay-phone-calls/2014/03/18/226d2646-ade9-11e3-a49e-76adc9210f19_story.html.

communications today – even wholly domestic ones – are routinely transmitted or stored overseas, large-scale collection that takes place in other countries will inevitably sweep in large amounts of Americans' information, not to mention the information of law-abiding private citizens of other countries. Although, as discussed later, President Obama imposed some new limits on how the collected data may be used,[118] they do not offset the seismic changes in the amount of data being collected.

5 Diminished External Oversight

As legal and technological changes vastly expanded the government's ability to collect and exploit sensitive information without suspicion of wrongdoing, one might have expected to see a commensurate strengthening of external oversight of surveillance activities. In fact, for the most part, the opposite has occurred.

a *Judicial Review*

Both the bulk collection of Americans' telephone records under Section 215 of the PATRIOT Act and surveillance under Section 702 of FISA represented a shift from case-by-case judicial approval to judicial approval of the broad contours of programs. To some extent, the external oversight provided by the FISA Court in individual cases was replaced by internal oversight by officials within the intelligence establishment as well as other internal compliance measures, such as training requirements, requirements for supervisory approval, and audits by the Department of Justice's National Security Division.

Executive officials have emphasized the layers of internal oversight in defending the expansions of surveillance authority. However, FISA Court opinions released in response to Snowden's disclosures show that the NSA and FBI frequently failed to comply with the court's orders setting the parameters for programmatic surveillance. These failures occurred across all of the major post-9/11 collection programs – including the bulk collection of Americans' Internet metadata,[119] the bulk collection of Americans' telephone records,[120] and the collection of phone calls and e-mails under Section 702 of FISA[121] – and resulted in overcollection, improper access and sharing, and improper retention of data.

The executive branch described the violations as inadvertent, and there is no evidence to the contrary. Nonetheless, some of the most serious violations continued for years, during which time Department of Justice officials repeatedly furnished inaccurate information to the court.[122] The pattern of noncompliance with court orders and inaccurate representations calls into question the efficacy of replacing case-by-case judicial oversight with internal agency review.

At the same time, judicial review by regular Article III courts was undermined by a sweeping new interpretation of the "state secrets privilege" advanced by Presidents

118 *See infra* text accompanying notes 166–67.

119 [REDACTED], No. PR/TT [REDACTED] (FISA Ct. [REDACTED]) [hereinafter Bates PR/TT Opinion], https://www.dni.gov/files/documents/1118/CLEANEDPRTT%202.pdf.

120 *In re* Production of Tangible Things from [REDACTED], No. BR 08-13 (FISA Ct. Mar. 2, 2009) [hereinafter Walton Mar. 2009 Order], https://www.dni.gov/files/documents/section/pub_March%202%20 2009%20Order%20from%20FISC.pdf.

121 [REDACTED], 2011 WL 10945618 (FISA Ct. Oct. 3, 2011) [hereinafter Bates 2011 Opinion].

122 *Id.* at 77.

George W. Bush and Obama. The Supreme Court first explicitly recognized the privilege in the 1953 case of *United States v. Reynolds*,[123] describing it as an evidentiary privilege that may be used to prevent the use of particular evidence in litigation if its disclosure would harm national security. After 9/11, the Bush administration began asserting the privilege to shut down entire cases at the pleadings stage, i.e., before the evidence was even identified. It thus transformed from a narrow evidentiary privilege into a jurisdictional bar – a transformation that the courts largely accepted. The Obama administration pledged a different approach, but in fact continued to use the privilege in the same way. The invocation of state secrets played a role in shutting down many of the legal challenges to the government's most controversial post-9/11 practices, including "extraordinary rendition" (the practice of apprehending individuals and sending them to other countries to be tortured), warrantless wiretapping, and (at the time of writing) FBI surveillance of mosques.[124]

Another barrier to civil lawsuits has been the Supreme Court's recent jurisprudence on standing and the sufficiency of pleadings. The Constitution confers on the courts jurisdiction over "cases and controversies"; to show that a case or controversy exists, plaintiffs' initial pleadings must allege facts showing that they have been injured by the defendants' actions. Plaintiffs need not prove their case at the pleadings stage, however – pleadings are simply meant to put the other party on notice of the claims being brought – and courts historically have not required extensive detail about the alleged misconduct or a high probability that it occurred when assessing a plaintiff's standing to bring suit.

Within the past decade, however, two key Supreme Court cases tightened pleading standards. In *Bell Atlantic Corp. v. Twombly*, the Court held that in order to go forward, plaintiffs' claims should be "plausible," not just "conceivable."[125] As it elaborated in *Ashcroft v. Iqbal*, an "unadorned, the-defendant-unlawfully harmed-me accusation" or "threadbare recitals of the elements of a cause of action" could be disregarded as mere "legal conclusions."[126] The enhanced pleading requirements set out in these cases have been criticized by many legal scholars as a departure from the tradition of notice pleading in U.S. courts. They have been viewed as preventing the pursuit of civil rights claims where evidence of malfeasance lies mostly with the government and requires discovery through the judicial process.[127]

More stringent pleading standards have also been a barrier to judicial review of surveillance. In multiple cases, plaintiffs plausibly alleged that their communications were highly likely or even certainly subject to surveillance, either because of the nature of those communications (e.g., communications between attorneys representing Guantánamo detainees and the detainees' family members overseas)[128] or because of the broad sweep

123 345 U.S. 1 (1953).

124 Josh Gerstein, *Court Mulls FBI Mosque Surveillance*, Politico (Dec. 8, 2015), http://www.politico.com/blogs/under-the-radar/2015/12/court-mulls-fbi-mosque-surveillance-216529.

125 *Bell Atlantic Corp. v. Twombly*, 550 U.S. 554, 570 (2007).

126 *Ashcroft v. Iqbal*, 556 U.S. 662, 678 (2009).

127 Roger M. Michalski, *Assessing Iqbal*, Harv. L. & Pol'y Rev. Online (Dec. 8, 2010), http://harvardlpr.com/online-articles/assessing-iqbal/; Jonathan D. Frankel, *May We Plead the Court? Twombly, Iqbal, and the "New" Practice of Pleading*, 38 Hofstra L. Rev. 1191 (2010); Jonah B. Gelbach, *Locking the Doors to Discovery? Assessing the Effects of Twombly and Iqbal on Access to Discovery*, 121 Yale L.J. 2270 (2012).

128 *See Amnesty Int'l USA v. Clapper*, 638 F.3d 120 (2nd Cir. 2011), *rev'd*, 133 U.S. 1140 (2013).

of surveillance programs being challenged (e.g., the bulk collection of Americans' phone records[129] or the so-called upstream collection program described later in this chapter).[130] They also alleged that they suffered harm as a result, because they were forced to take costly and burdensome measures to try to avoid the surveillance. The courts found that the plaintiffs' pleadings were insufficient because they did not establish that the plaintiffs were in fact subject to surveillance. Rather than allowing plaintiffs to draw reasonable and natural inferences from the public record, the courts seemed to require that the government concede that a program of the type alleged existed in order to allow plaintiffs to move forward with their case.[131]

Of course, civil litigation is not the only way in which surveillance programs are brought before courts. Criminal cases in which evidence is derived from surveillance provide an alternative mechanism for ensuring judicial review. Such challenges, however, can only be mounted if the defendant knows about the underlying surveillance.

The FAA requires the government to notify defendants when using evidence "obtained or derived from" FAA surveillance. Before 2013, however, the government interpreted "obtained or derived from" so narrowly that it notified no one. In the the four years since the government's approach reportedly changed,[132] the government has provided notification in only seven cases, even though the PCLOB reports that the FBI searches Section 702 data every time it conducts a national security investigation[133] and there have been several hundred terrorism and national security convictions during this time.[134] Some observers have expressed concern that the government is avoiding its notification requirements by engaging in "parallel construction" – i.e., recreating the Section 702 evidence using less controversial means.[135]

Moreover, the government still does not provide notification of other types of surveillance. For example, the government has taken the position that it is not required to provide notice when it relies on evidence derived from the NSA's bulk collection of phone records.[136] Thus far, the only criminal case in which a defendant has been able to challenge this program came about because the government acknowledged its use as part of its efforts to defend the program publicly after the Snowden disclosures.[137] And

129 *Klayman v. Obama*, 957 F. Supp. 2d 1, 43 (D.D.C. 2013), *vacated*, 800 F.3d 559 (D.C. Cir. 2015).

130 Complaint for Declaratory and Injunctive Relief, *Wikimedia v. Nat'l Sec. Agency*, 143 F. Supp. 3d 344 (D. Md. 2015) (No. 1:15-CV-662).

131 At time of writing, one of these cases is currently pending on appeal before the Fourth Circuit. *See Wikimedia v. Nat'l Sec. Agency*, 143 F. Supp. 3d 344, 356 (D. Md. 2015), *appeal docketed*, No. 15–2560 (4th Cir. Dec. 18, 2015). In another case, the court of appeals remanded to allow the district court to determine "whether limited discovery to explore jurisdictional facts is appropriate." *Obama v. Klayman*, 800 F.3d 559, 564 (D.C. Cir. 2015).

132 For more background, see Toomey, *supra* note 50.

133 PCLOB 702 Report, *supra* note 112, at 59.

134 Dep't of Justice, United States Attorneys' Annual Statistical Report Fiscal Year 2015 at 14; Dep't of Justice, United States Attorneys' Annual Statistical Report Fiscal Year 2014 at 12; Dep't of Justice, United States Attorneys' Annual Statistical Report Fiscal Year 2013 at 60.

135 *See* Toomey, *supra* note 50; John Shiffman and Kristina Cooke, *Exclusive: U.S. Directs Agents to Cover Up Program Used to Investigate Americans*, Reuters (Aug. 5, 2013, 3:25 PM), http://www.reuters.com/article/us-dea-sod-idUSBRE97409R20130805#X7BeCQSb0GrEDTJX.97.

136 Letter from S. Amanda Marshall, U.S. Attorney, & Charles F. Gorder, to The Hon. Michael W. Mosman, U.S. Dist. Ct. J. (Oct. 15, 2014), https://www.aclu.org/files/assets/KhanNoticeResponseEXBGovtLetter11052014.pdf.

137 *United States v. Moalin*, No. 10CR4246, 2013 WL 6079518 (S.D. Cal. Nov. 18, 2013).

there is no known case of the government's providing notice to criminal defendants that evidence was derived from overseas surveillance programs under Executive Order 12333. As reported in the *New York Times*, "officials contend that defendants have no right to know if 12333 intercepts provided a tip from which investigators derived other evidence."[138]

b *Legislative Oversight*

There were no significant legal restrictions added to the congressional oversight scheme after 9/11. There is anecdotal evidence, however, that the National Security Act's requirement to keep the congressional intelligence committees fully informed of intelligence activities was diluted by heavy reliance on both the "Gang of Eight" and "Gang of Four" mechanisms. The Gang of Eight provision, discussed in Section I.B.5, is reserved for "covert actions," which the statute defines to exclude traditional military activities or activities designed primarily to gather intelligence. Yet it has been used for highly sensitive operations regardless of whether they meet the statutory definition of a "covert activity."[139] Moreover, although there is no statutory basis for this practice, the executive branch on occasion restricts notification of particularly sensitive noncovert operations to a group of four members: the chairs and ranking members of the intelligence committees.[140]

The National Security Act states that "each of the congressional intelligence committees shall promptly call to the attention of its respective House, or to any appropriate committee or committees of its respective House, any matter relating to intelligence activities requiring the attention of such House or such committee or committees."[141] The executive branch nonetheless takes the position that it may prohibit members of the smaller "gangs" from disclosing information to others, and the members have agreed to this restriction. Unfortunately, individual members can do little on their own; meaningful action generally requires the full committees and often (where legislation is involved) the full Congress. Reliance on the Gang of Eight or Four, as occurred when the executive provided notification of major post-9/11 national security programs, thus dramatically undercuts the effectiveness of legislative oversight.

In addition, at least one intelligence agency has gone to extreme and possibly unprecedented lengths to resist legitimate committee oversight. In March 2014, the then-chair of the Senate intelligence committee, Dianne Feinstein, gave a speech on the Senate floor in which she accused CIA officials of monitoring the computers used by intelligence committee staffers in the course of their investigation into the CIA's torture program.[142]

138 Charlie Savage, *Reagan-Era Order on Surveillance Violates Rights, Says Departing Aide*, N.Y. Times (Aug. 13, 2014), http://www.nytimes.com/2014/08/14/us/politics/reagan-era-order-on-surveillance-violates-rights-says-departing-aide.html?_r=1.

139 For this reason, the former director of national intelligence Dennis Blair and former CIA director Leon Panetta both criticized the use of the "Gang of Eight" mechanism in connection with the NSA's warrantless wiretapping program and the CIA's detention and interrogation activities. *See* Alfred Cumming, Sensitive Covert Action Notifications: Options for Congress 7 (2009), http://fpc.state.gov/documents/organization/126834.pdf.

140 Marshall Curtis Erwin, "Gang of Four" Congressional Intelligence Notifications (2013).

141 50 U.S.C. § 3091(d).

142 160 Cong. Rec. S1487-91 (daily ed. Mar. 11, 2014) (statement of Sen. Feinstein).

The CIA director flatly denied the claim,[143] but the CIA's inspector general subsequently found that agency officials improperly accessed the computers, filed an unsupported "crimes report" with the Justice Department accusing committee staffers of acting unlawfully, and gave untruthful answers when interviewed by the inspector general's office.[144]

c *Oversight within the Executive Branch*

As noted previously, statutory inspectors general operate with relative independence and have substantial investigative authority. Although their effectiveness has varied significantly from office to office, they have in many instances been instrumental in uncovering misconduct and prompting reforms. In recent years, however, they have encountered barriers to obtaining information that have prevented them from doing their jobs.

Pursuant to Section 6(a) of the IG act, federal Inspectors general are "to have access to all records, reports, audits, reviews, documents, papers, recommendations, or other material available to the applicable establishment which relate to programs and operations with respect to which that Inspector General has responsibilities under this Act." Despite this provision, in 2014, forty-seven inspectors general sent a letter to Congress complaining that three particular federal agencies – the Peace Corps, the Chemical Safety and Hazard Investigation Board, and the Department of Justice – were resisting requests for records.[145]

Congress responded by enacting a statutory provision specifying that agencies could not block inspector generals' access to records "unless in accordance with an express limitation of section 6(a) of the Inspector General Act, as amended, consistent with the plain language of the Inspector General Act, as amended."[146] The inspector general for the Department of Justice subsequently reported that the legislation improved his ability to obtain records from all Department of Justice components except the FBI. Since 2010, the bureau has taken the position that the inspector general is not legally entitled to review grand jury, electronic surveillance, or Fair Credit Reporting Act information without the attorney general's approval.[147] In July 2015, the Department of Justice's Office of Legal Counsel issued an opinion backing the FBI's interpretation.[148] Later that year, the *New York Times* reported that "at least 20 investigations across the government that have been slowed, stymied or sometimes closed because of a long-simmering dispute between

143 Interview by Andrea Mitchell with John O. Brennan, Dir., CIA, at the Council on Foreign Relations (Mar. 11, 2014), http://www.cfr.org/intelligence/cia-director-brennan-denies-hacking-allegations/p32563.

144 Mark Mazzetti & Carl Hulse, *Inquiry by C.I.A. Affirms It Spied on Senate Panel*, N.Y. TIMES (July 31, 2014), http://www.nytimes.com/2014/08/01/world/senate-intelligence-commitee-cia-interrogation-report.html.

145 Josh Hicks, *Dozens of Inspectors General Say Federal Agencies Hindering Oversight*, WASH. POST (Aug. 6, 2014), https://www.washingtonpost.com/news/federal-eye/wp/2014/08/06/dozens-of-inspectors-general-say-federal-agencies-hindering-oversight/.

146 Consolidated and Further Continuing Appropriations Act, 2015, Pub. L. No. 113–235, § 218, 128 Stat. 2130, 2200 (2015).

147 Office of the Inspector Gen., Dep't of Justice, 180 DAY REPORT TO CONGRESS ON THE IMPACT OF SECTION 218 OF THE DEPARTMENT OF JUSTICE APPROPRIATIONS ACT FOR FISCAL YEAR 2015 at i-ii (2015), https://oig.justice.gov/press/2015/2015-06-16.pdf.

148 The Department of Justice Inspector General's Access to Information Protected by the Federal Wiretap Act, Rule 6(e) of the Federal Rules of Criminal Procedure, and Section 626 of the Fair Credit Reporting Act, 39 Op. O.L.C. (2015), https://www.justice.gov/sites/default/files/olc/opinions/attachments/2015/07/23/2015-07-20-doj-oig-access.pdf.

the Obama administration and its own watchdogs over the shrinking access of inspectors general to confidential records, according to records and interviews."[149]

In the waning days of the Obama administration, Congress passed legislation to remove this obstacle and to clarify that inspectors general must have access to all information relating to their spheres of oversight, absent an explicit legislative exception.[150] In theory, this change should serve to restore the level of access Congress originally intended inspectors general to have, although it is too early to assess its actual impact.

A notable exception to the pattern of reduced oversight was the establishment of the PCLOB. The board is composed of five members – only three of whom may be from the same political party – appointed by the president; its mission is to ensure that counterterrorism policies take into account privacy and civil liberties considerations.[151] Although the PCLOB is located inside the executive branch and is therefore not truly "external," it is, in its current iteration, an independent body and thus can serve some of the same function.

PCLOB had an inauspicious start. An earlier version was established by legislation in 2004 in response to a recommendation of the 9/11 Commission.[152] The members were not appointed until 2006, however, and the board ceased operations the following year after the chairperson resigned, claiming improper interference from the White House. Congress responded by reconstituting the board as an independent agency, but the board then sat vacant and inoperative for the subsequent six years.

Despite this history, PCLOB made significant contributions after it resumed operations in 2013. It held several public hearings and issued two major reports: one on the bulk collection of Americans' phone records under Section 215 of the PATRIOT Act[153] and one on surveillance under Section 702 of FISA.[154] In the process of issuing these reports, the PCLOB secured the declassification of a substantial amount of information about both programs.

Nonetheless, the board's resources are limited – as of 2016, it had a staff of twenty-seven and an operating budget of $10 million[155] – and its work cannot be expected to compensate fully for diminished oversight by the judicial and legislative branches. Even more concerning, following the resignation of the board's chairman in mid-2016 and the expiration of three other members' terms in early 2017, the board now has only one member and lacks a quorum to proceed with its work. There is no indication of when or

149 Eric Lichtblau, *Tighter Lid on Records Threatens to Weaken Government Watchdogs*, N.Y. TIMES (Nov. 27, 2015), http://www.nytimes.com/2015/11/28/us/politics/tighter-lid-on-records-threatens-to-defang-government-watchdogs.html.

150 Inspector General Empowerment Act of 2016 §5, Pub. L. No. 114-317, 130 Stat. 1595 (to be codified at 5 U.S.C. App. 3 §§ 1 to 13 (2016)).

151 42 U.S.C. § 2000ee.

152 For a brief description of the board's history, see Rachel Weiner, *Never Heard of the Privacy and Civil Liberties Oversight Board? You Should*, WASH. POST (June 10, 2013), https://www.washingtonpost.com/news/the-fix/wp/2013/06/10/never-heard-of-the-privacy-and-civil-liberties-oversight-board-you-should/.

153 Privacy & Civil Liberties Oversight Bd., REPORT ON THE TELEPHONE RECORDS PROGRAM CONDUCTED UNDER SECTION 215 OF THE USA PATRIOT ACT AND ON THE OPERATIONS OF THE FOREIGN INTELLIGENCE SURVEILLANCE COURT (2014), https://www.pclob.gov/library/215-Report_on_the_Telephone_Records_Program.pdf.

154 PCLOB 702 REPORT, *supra* note 112.

155 Baird Webel, Cong. Research Serv., R44701, FINANCIAL SERVICES AND GENERAL GOVERNMENT (FSGG) FY2017 APPROPRIATIONS: INDEPENDENT AGENCIES AND GENERAL PROVISIONS 23 (2016); Privacy and Civil Liberties Oversight Board, FISCAL YEAR 2017 BUDGET JUSTIFICATION 16 (2016).

if new appointments will be made, and so the PCLOB is at risk of lapsing into dormancy yet again.

D *Snowden and the post-Snowden Era*

On June 6, 2013, the *Guardian* and the *Washington Post* published the first in a series of articles that relied on disclosures by a former NSA contractor, Edward Snowden. The initial revelation that the NSA was collecting Americans' telephone records set in motion a remarkable progression of events, leading to the first major legislative intelligence reform in decades and an attempt by the intelligence establishment to remake its image through greater engagement with the public. Terrorist attacks in late 2015 and 2016, however, led some lawmakers to call for changes in the other direction.

1 Increased Transparency on the Part of the Intelligence Establishment

In the immediate aftermath of the Snowden disclosures, the director of national intelligence was essentially forced to declassify and release a large volume of documents about the programs at issue. The strong public reaction to Snowden's revelations required a response, and the administration could not provide that response without declassifying aspects of the programs. The administration also found itself beset with Freedom of Information Act (FOIA) requests for records relating to the subject matter of the disclosures, and once the information itself had been declassified, there was no basis to resist these requests. The result was the public release of an unprecedented amount of information about some of the U.S. government's intelligence activities.

Beyond these factors, the administration seemed to realize that, in order to win back the trust of the American public, the intelligence establishment had to address the perception that it was excessively secretive. The Office of the Director of National Intelligence (ODNI) created a public-facing Web site on which it regularly posted documents that it declassified, either on its own initiative or in response to FOIA requests.[156] Representatives of ODNI and the NSA began to meet regularly with civil society organizations. ODNI established an Intelligence Transparency Working Group and issued a set of "Principles of Intelligence Transparency for the Intelligence Community,"[157] along with an implementation plan that called for structural changes to help institutionalize a focus on transparency.[158] The FISA Court created an online public docket, where members of the public could find any unclassified or declassified filings.[159]

Open government advocates have acknowledged the importance of these steps. They have cautioned, however, that they lack the information necessary to determine the extent and nature of the information that remains secret, which is necessary to measure the progress made toward transparency. Moreover, on some issues – such as surveillance

156 IC on the Record, https://icontherecord.tumblr.com/.

157 Office of the Dir. of Nat'l Intelligence, Principles of Intelligence Transparency for the Intelligence Community (2015), https://www.dni.gov/index.php/intelligence-community/intelligence-transparency-principles.

158 Office of the Dir. of Nat'l Intelligence, Principles of Intelligence Transparency Implementation Plan (2015), https://icontherecord.tumblr.com/transparency/implementation-plan-2015.

159 *Public Filings – U.S. Foreign Intelligence Surveillance Court*, U.S. Foreign Intelligence Surveillance Court, http://www.fisc.uscourts.gov/public-filings.

that takes place overseas under the auspices of Executive Order 12333 – there is still very little public information. And the public still learns of many important developments (for instance, proposed new rules on interagency sharing of data collected under Executive Order 12333)[160] through leaks to reporters rather than voluntary disclosures by the government. Despite notable improvements, the record of transparency after Snowden thus remains mixed.

2 Presidential Policy Directive 28

The Snowden disclosures prompted an international backlash as well as a domestic one. In response, President Obama issued Presidential Policy Directive 28 (or PPD-28), which applies primarily to overseas surveillance activities conducted under Executive Order 12333. The directive acknowledges for the first time that non-U.S. citizens overseas are entitled to some measure of privacy, stating, "All persons have legitimate privacy interests in the handling of their personal information"[161] – an admission of high symbolic importance. The impact of the procedural changes it orders, however, is difficult to assess.

PPD-28 establishes four general principles to govern collection. First, any collection activities must be authorized under a statute or presidential directive.[162] Second, privacy and civil liberties must be "integral considerations," and surveillance must be conducted for "foreign intelligence or counterintelligence purpose[s]," not "for the purpose of suppressing or burdening criticism or dissent, or for disadvantaging persons based on their ethnicity, race, gender, sexual orientation, or religion."[163] Third, the government may collect "foreign private commercial information or trade secrets" only to protect the national security (broadly defined) of the United States, its partners, or its allies.[164] Fourth, the directive requires intelligence gathering to be as "tailored as feasible."[165] Given their generality and non-self-enforcing nature, further information on specific steps taken to implement and enforce these principles will be needed to determine their significance.

More concretely, PPD-28 provides that data gathered in bulk may be used only to detect and counter (1) threats of espionage and other activities directed by foreign powers against the United States, (2) terrorist threats to the United States, (3) threats to the United States posed by weapons of mass destruction, (4) cybersecurity threats, (5) threats to U.S. or allied armed forces and (6) transnational criminal threats.[166] However, these limits do not apply to data that is collected in bulk and held for a temporary (but

160 Charlie Savage, *Obama Administration Set to Expand Sharing of Data That N.S.A. Intercepts*, N.Y. Times (Feb. 26, 2016), http://www.nytimes.com/2016/02/26/us/politics/obama-administration-set-to-expand-sharing-of-data-that-nsa-intercepts.html?_r=0.

161 Exec. Office of the President, Presidential Policy Directive/PPD-28 1 (2014) [hereinafter PPD-28], https://www.whitehouse.gov/the-press-office/2014/01/17/presidential-policy-directive-signals-intelligence-activities.

162 Id. at § 1(a).

163 Id. at § 1(b).

164 Id. at § 1(c).

165 Id. at § 1(d).

166 Id. at § 2; Nat'l Sec. Agency, PPD-28 Section 4 Procedures § 5.2 (2015) [hereinafter NSA PPD Procedures], https://fas.org/irp/nsa/nsa-ppd-28.pdf.

unspecified) period in order to facilitate "targeted" surveillance,[167] so it is unclear how broad their application is in practice. Specific information regarding implementation is needed here, as well.

One of PPD-28's most notable changes was its requirement that the rules for retaining and sharing information about non-U.S. persons must be the same as those for "comparable" information about U.S. persons, if consistent with national security.[168] This could in theory be a significant change, but much depends on how strictly the requirement of "comparability" is applied, and on how broadly the national security exception is construed. Moreover, it should be noted that the limits on keeping and sharing Americans' information are subject to multiple loopholes. For instance, these limits do not apply to information that constitutes "foreign intelligence" (which is defined extremely broadly under Executive Order 12333 to include almost any information about foreigners), information that may be evidence of a crime, or information that is encrypted or has "secret meaning."[169]

3 USA FREEDOM Act: Historic Surveillance Rollback

In response to the public outcry that followed the Snowden disclosures, Senators Patrick Leahy and Mike Lee introduced the USA FREEDOM Act in October 2013. In its original iteration, the bill would have made sweeping changes to a range of surveillance authorities, including Section 215 of the PATRIOT Act, Section 702 of FISA, and National Security Letters. In order to obtain broader support for the bill – and, in particular, to gain the administration's support and endorsement – the bill's sponsors negotiated and introduced a less far-reaching bill the following year. This version focused primarily on ending the NSA's Section 215 bulk collection program, although it contained other elements.

With provisions of the PATRIOT Act set to expire at the end of May 2015, many lawmakers took the position that they would not vote to reauthorize that legislation without reform of Section 215. For a short period, there were insufficient votes in the Senate either to break a Republican filibuster of the USA Freedom Act (which reauthorized the PATRIOT Act, but with reforms) or to pass a straight reauthorization, and provisions of the PATRIOT Act lapsed. Faced with intense pressure to revive it, many Republicans dropped their opposition to the USA Freedom Act, and the bill became law on June 2, 2015.[170]

The legislation was controversial, with some civil liberties advocates hailing its provisions and others claiming it did not go far enough. It is incontrovertible, however, that the USA Freedom Act was the first major legislative restriction of foreign intelligence surveillance authorities since the enactment of FISA in 1978.

The law requires any collection of business records – under Section 215 or certain other foreign intelligence collection authorities – to be based on a "specific selection term," such as a name or account, that limits the scope of collection "to the greatest extent practicable."[171] The bill includes a nonexhaustive list of selection terms that are deemed too broad,

167 PPD-28, *supra* note 159, at § 2 n.5.
168 *Id.* at § 4(a)(i)(9).
169 Exec. Order No. 12333, 3 C.F.R. § 200 (1981); NSA PPD PROCEDURES, *supra* note 164, at § 6.1(a).
170 USA FREEDOM Act of 2015, Pub. L. No. 114–23, 129 Stat. 268.
171 *Id.* at § 402(a).

including area codes, zip codes, and names of telecommunications companies.[172] These provisions were designed to end the NSA's bulk collection of telephone records and to preclude any analogous program for Internet, financial, or credit records.

In addition, the law contains provisions intended to enhance transparency. It requires the director of national intelligence to make public either a redacted version or a summary of any opinion by the FISA Court containing a novel or significant legal interpretation. It also requires somewhat more detailed statistical reporting on the use of surveillance authorities. And it establishes a panel of paid attorneys who can appear in significant FISA court proceedings as amici curiae ("friends of the court") to present a perspective other than the government's, if the FISA Court agrees to their participation.[173]

Despite these reforms, some privacy advocates have expressed concern about the imprecision in the law's definition of "specific selection term." Although Congress clearly intended to rein in the NSA's practices, the absence of a bright-line restriction could enable collection that is far broader than necessary, even if it falls short of "bulk" collection. Moreover, the bill addresses only collection that takes place under foreign intelligence authorities. Even as the USA Freedom Act was being debated, *USA Today* revealed that the Drug Enforcement Administration had for decades relied on an administrative subpoena authority to engage in the bulk collection of records of calls between Americans and people in certain other countries.[174] Nor does the law affect surveillance activities under Section 702 of FISA or Executive Order 12333, which constitute the overwhelming bulk of the NSA's surveillance.

4 Post-post-Snowden: Terrorist Attacks and Their Fallout

On November 13, 2015, a series of coordinated terrorist attacks took place in Paris and Saint-Denis in France. The attacks killed 130 people and injured 368. The incident was described as the deadliest on French soil since World War II. Less than three weeks later, a married couple shot and killed 14 people and wounded 22 at a mental health facility in San Bernardino, California. President Obama described the shooting as an act of terrorism, and FBI Director James Comey stated that the perpetrators were "homegrown violent extremists."[175] Then, on June 12, 2016, a twenty-nine-year-old American security guard shot and killed 49 people and wounded 53 inside a gay nightclub in Orlando. Although the motive for the shooting remains unclear, the shooter swore allegiance to the leader of the Islamic State of Iraq and the Levant (ISIL) during a 911 call that he placed shortly after the attack began.

The legislative response to these attacks was swift. It included the introduction of several nonsurveillance measures, such as bills to revoke the citizenship of people suspected of supporting terrorism or to prohibit the purchase of firearms by people who appear on certain government "watch lists." It also included bills intended to enhance surveillance authorities. For instance, after the Paris attacks, Senator Tom Cotton introduced a bill that would have

172 *Id.* at § 107 (4)(a)(ii)(II).

173 *Id.* at §§ 103, 402(a)-(c), 603.

174 Brad Heath, *U.S. Secretly Tracked Billions of Calls for Decades*, USA Today (Apr. 8, 2015), http://www.usatoday.com/story/news/2015/04/07/dea-bulk-telephone-surveillance-operation/70808616/.

175 Halimah Abdullah & Pete Williams, *FBI: San Bernardino Shooters Radicalized before They Met*, NBC News (Dec. 9, 2015), http://www.nbcnews.com/storyline/san-bernardino-shooting/fbi-san-bernardino-shooters-radicalized-they-met-n476971.

delayed the November 29, 2015, implementation date for the USA Freedom Act and would have made permanent certain PATRIOT Act authorities. On the day of the San Bernardino shooting, he introduced another version of the bill that also would have expanded the reach of National Security Letters and made Section 702 of FISA permanent.[176]

These measures did not move forward in Congress. It is likely, however, that the attacks smoothed the passage of the Cybersecurity Information Sharing Act, which was signed into law on December 18, 2015.[177] Although both chambers of Congress had passed versions of the legislation when the Paris attacks occurred, it was unclear what the final product would look like, with several provisions undergoing intense public debate. After the Paris and San Bernardino attacks, lawmakers negotiated a version of the legislation (which then became law) that significantly rolled back privacy protections. It overrode all existing laws that restricted companies' sharing of their customers' personal data with the government, and allowed companies that perceived a cyber threat (broadly defined) to share data, generally without stripping personally identifiable information. It also allowed the government to use that data for purposes unrelated to cybersecurity.

The fallout continues. Shortly after the shooting in Orlando, the House voted on an amendment that would have prohibited "backdoor searches" of Americans' calls and e-mails collected under FISA Section 702. It also would have prohibited the government from weakening encryption standards or requiring technology companies to alter their products to weaken security features. The same amendment easily passed the House in 2014 and 2015, but failed in 2016 after its opponents invoked Orlando.[178] Lawmakers also have introduced legislation that would expand the types of records the FBI can obtain using National Security Letters to include a range of information about Internet transactions.[179]

Finally, there is a drive within Congress to enact legislation that would essentially prohibit U.S. companies from offering strong encryption to their customers, based on a perception that encrypted communications could stymie counterterrorism efforts. There are different legislative approaches; many would require companies to retain a "key" that would enable decryption of their customers' communications and/or to write software that could override their products' security features.[180] Technologists point out, however, that these measures would make it easier for actors other than the U.S. government to access the data.[181] Ordinary citizens would thus become more vulnerable to hacking, and those with a special need for strong data protection – including journalists, lawyers, human rights activists, or people communicating trade secrets – would be at particular risk. Terrorists, on the other hand, would likely respond by developing their own encryption services or obtaining them from non-U.S. companies.[182]

176 Liberty through Strength Act II, S. 2344, 114th Cong. §§ 5(a)-(b), 6 (2015).
177 Cybersecurity Information Sharing Act, S. 754, 114th Cong. (2015).
178 Department of Defense Appropriations Act, H. Amend. 1204 to H.R. 5293, 114th Cong. (2016).
179 Commerce, Justice, Science, and Related Agencies Appropriations Act, S. Amend. 4787 to S. Amend. 4685, 144th Cong. (2016).
180 *The Next Encryption Battleground: Congress*, NPR (Apr. 15, 2016), http://www.npr.org/sections/alltechconsidered/2016/04/14/474113249/the-next-encryption-battleground-congress; Andy Greenberg, *The Senate's Draft Encryption Bill Is 'Ludicrous, Dangerous, Technically Illiterate,'* Wired (Apr. 8, 2016), https://www.wired.com/2016/04/senates-draft-encryption-bill-privacy-nightmare/.
181 Harold Abelson et al., Keys under Doormats: Mandating Insecurity by Requiring Government Access to All Data and Communications (2015), https://www.schneier.com/academic/paperfiles/paper-keys-under-doormats-CSAIL.pdf.
182 *Encryption Technology and Possible U.S. Policy Responses: Hearing before the H. Subcomm. on Info. Tech. of the Comm. on Oversight and Gov't Reform*, 114th Cong. 7 (2015) (statement of Kevin S. Bankston, policy

II Where We Are in 2016: The Effects of post-9/11 Changes

The changed legal and technological landscape detailed in Section I.C puts at risk the constitutional rights to privacy; to freedom of speech, association, and religion; and against discrimination. As indicated, in the 1970s, the Church Committee revealed that government surveillance programs had targeted the civil rights movement, war protesters, and others whose politics were considered threatening.[183] In the post-9/11 years, we are beginning to see echoes of these activities, as federal, state, and local law enforcement agencies have established government surveillance programs targeting Muslim Americans without suspicion of wrongdoing and have monitored political activity and protests in the name of counterterrorism.

A *Targets of Surveillance: Muslim Americans, Ethnic and Racial Minorities, and Dissenters*

The Church Committee's investigation and report sharply revealed the ways in which broad surveillance authorities can be used to suppress unpopular viewpoints and disrupt political movements.[184] The post-9/11 weakening of restrictions on surveillance has unsurprisingly led to the targeting of individuals, groups, and communities who are considered threatening because of their political views or religious beliefs.

Muslim Americans have borne the brunt of post-9/11 domestic counterterrorism laws and policies, particularly surveillance. As discussed previously, under the Mukasey Guidelines, the FBI may gather "information needed for broader analytic and intelligence purposes" even if it has no reason to suspect criminal activity.[185] According to its former director, this entails "understand[ing] every inch of a given community – its geography, its populations, its economy, and its vulnerabilities."[186] The FBI interprets this authority as allowing it to collect information about "concentrated ethnic communities."[187]

Over the years, information has emerged that demonstrates that the FBI has made use of its new and expanded powers to undertake non-threat-based intelligence gathering programs in Muslim communities around the country, including Arab-American communities in Dearborn, Michigan; other Middle Eastern and Muslim communities in Michigan; and Iranian communities in San Francisco.[188] Documents also show that the FBI kept tabs on

director of New America's Open Technology Institute & co-director of New America's Cybersecurity Initiative), http://oversight.house.gov/wp-content/uploads/2015/04/4-29-2015-IT-Subcommittee-Hearing-on-Encryption-Bankston.pdf; *see also* Human Rights Watch & Am. Civil Liberties Union, WITH LIBERTY TO MONITOR ALL: HOW LARGE-SCALE US SURVEILLANCE IS HARMING JOURNALISM, LAW, AND AMERICAN DEMOCRACY (2014), https://www.hrw.org/sites/default/files/reports/usnsa0714_ForUPload_0.pdf.

183 *See supra* text accompanying notes 12–21.

184 *See id.*

185 *See* MUKASEY GUIDELINES, *supra* note 103, at 16.

186 Robert S. Mueller, III, Dir., Fed. Bureau of Investigation, Address to Int'l Ass'n of Chiefs of Police: Using Intelligence to Protect Our Communities (Nov. 10, 2008), https://archives.fbi.gov/archives/news/speeches/using-intelligence-to-protect-our-communities.

187 Charlie Savage, *Loosening of F.B.I. Rules Stirs Privacy Concerns*, N.Y. TIMES (Oct. 29, 2009), http://www.nytimes.com/2009/10/29/us/29manual.html?_r=1&hpw.

188 Scott Shane & Lowell Bergman, *F.B.I. Struggling to Reinvent Itself to Fight Terror*, N.Y. TIMES (Oct. 10, 2006), http://www.nytimes.com/2006/10/10/us/10fbi.html.

Muslim Americans' speech and religious observance, including the subject and tenor of sermons at mosques and charitable donations.[189]

The broad authorities granted to the FBI have also been used to infiltrate mosques and Muslim community groups and spaces with informants and undercover agents. This tactic was aided by another change to the Mukasey Guidelines: the elimination of the rule that the bureau may collect information on the political or religious activities of Americans only when investigating a specific crime.[190] The FBI claims that it "generally" only investigates mosques "if there is evidence or information as to individual or individuals undertaking illegal activities in religious institutions."[191] However, information disclosed in prosecutions and civil lawsuits and in response to FOIA requests suggests that the bureau has recruited paid informants and Muslim community members to monitor speech and activity in mosques generally. For example, the FBI informant in the so-called Newburgh Four case testified that he was sent to three separate mosques in upstate New York and instructed to report to the FBI if "somebody was expressing radical views or extreme views."[192] Another FBI informant, this time in California, claimed in a civil case against the bureau that he was sent to infiltrate several mosques in Islamic centers in Orange, Los Angeles, and San Bernardino Counties with a similar mandate.[193]

The FBI also reportedly obtained authorization from the FISA Court to monitor prominent Muslim leaders in the United States. According to a 2014 report based on documents provided by Snowden, five American Muslims were subjected to surveillance: Nihad Awad, the executive director of the Council on American–Islamic Relations, the largest Muslim civil rights organization in the country; Hooshang Amirahmadi, an Iranian-American professor of international relations at Rutgers University; Asim Ghafoor, a leading attorney who represented clients in terrorism-related cases; Faisal

189 Am. Civil Liberties Union, EYE ON THE FBI ALERT: MOSQUE OUTREACH FOR INTELLIGENCE GATHERING (2012), https://www.aclu.org/aclu-eye-fbi-alert-mosque-outreach-intelligence-gathering. Also, in 2009, the Council of Islamic Organizations of Michigan, an umbrella group of nineteen mosques and community groups, filed an official complaint with Attorney General Holder because American Muslims had reported being asked to monitor people at mosques and to report on their charitable donations. Letter from the Council of Islamic Organizations of Michigan to Hon. Eric Holder, Attorney Gen. (Apr. 15, 2009) (on file with the Brennan Center).

190 *See* ASHCROFT GUIDELINES, *supra* note 102, at § VI.A & B.

191 *Oversight of the Federal Bureau of Investigation: Hearing before the S. Comm. on the Judiciary*, 111th Cong. 20 (2009) (question and answer session with Robert S. Mueller, III, Dir., Fed. Bureau of Investigation), http://frwebgate.access.gpo.gov/cgi-bin/getdoc.cgi?dbname=111_senate_ hearings&docid=f:52800.pdf; *see also FBI Chief Defends Use of Informants in Mosques*, AP (June 8, 2009), http://www.msnbc.msn.com/id/31177049.

192 Transcript of Record at 674, 2452, *United States v. Cromitie*, No. 09-558 (S.D.N.Y. Oct. 18, 2010).

193 Second Amended Complaint at 24–25, *Monteilh v. FBI*, No. 8:2010-cv-00102 (C.D. Cal. Sept. 2, 2010). For a description of Monteilh's claims, see Scott Glover, *Suit by Alleged Informant Says FBI Endangered His Life*, L.A. TIMES (Jan. 23, 2010), http://articles.latimes.com/2010/jan/23/local/la-me-informant23-2010jan23, and Teresa Watanabe & Scott Glover, *Man Says He Was Informant for FBI in Orange County*, L.A. TIMES (Feb. 26, 2009), http://articles.latimes.com/2009/feb/26/local/me-informant26. *See also FBI Director Questioned about Muslim Relations, Southern California*, INFOCUS NEWS (Mar. 31, 2009), http://pluralism.org/news/fbi-director-questioned-about-muslim-relations/; Thomas Cincotta, *From Movements to Mosques, Informants Endanger Democracy*, PUBLIC EYE MAGAZINE (Summer 2009), http://www.publiceye.org/magazine/v24n2/movements-to-mosques.html.

Gill, a longtime Republican Party operative who served in the Department of Homeland Security under President George W. Bush; and Agha Saeed, a former political science professor at California State University who champions Muslim civil liberties and Palestinian rights.[194]

To varying degrees, state and local police departments have also undertaken surveillance programs targeted at Muslim Americans.[195] The most extensive and intrusive program was developed by the New York City Police Department under the leadership of Commissioner Ray Kelly. The program, which was revealed by an Associated Press investigation, included many of the same elements as the FBI's activities. The police Demographics Unit was charged with mapping Muslim communities in New York City and beyond; keeping lists of bookshops, kebab houses, hookah bars, and food stores frequented by Muslims; and visiting these locales in order to take notes on the mundane conversations overheard there. The NYPD also monitored, and in some cases infiltrated, student groups at college campuses across the Northeast, providing information about their activities in regular reports to the police commissioner.[196]

Like the FBI, the NYPD sent informants into mosques to eavesdrop on sermons and conversations among worshippers. Documents show that it wanted to gauge reactions to world and local events, such as the 2006 protests in parts of the Arab world about Danish cartoons depicting the Muslim prophet Muhammad[197] and the small plane that accidentally crashed into a Manhattan building the same year.[198] In an affidavit filed in litigation challenging the NYPD's surveillance program, a young man who was an informant for the police said that he was encouraged to use a tactic called "create and capture," which involved creating conversations about jihad or terrorism, then capturing the responses and sending them to the NYPD.[199]

The NYPD's Demographics Unit was dismantled by the new police commissioner, William Bratton, who took over the department in 2013.[200] Concerns about the surveillance program, as well as the department's controversial "stop-and-frisk" policy, spurred the New York City Council to establish an inspector general to provide independent oversight of the NYPD.[201] In August 2016, the inspector general reported signficant

194 Glenn Greenwald & Murtaza Hussain, *Meet the Muslim-American Leaders the FBI and NSA Have Been Spying On*, INTERCEPT (July 9, 2014), https://theintercept.com/2014/07/09/under-surveillance/.

195 *See* Michael Price, Brennan Ctr for Justice, NATIONAL SECURITY AND LOCAL POLICE (2013), https://www.brennancenter.org/sites/default/files/publications/NationalSecurity_LocalPolice_web.pdf (discussing intelligence collection by 16 police departments).

196 Chris Hawley, *NYPD Monitored Students All Over Northeast*, AP (Feb. 12, 2012), http://www.ap.org/Content/AP-In-The-News/2012/NYPD-monitored-Muslim-students-all-over-Northeast.

197 NYPD Intelligence Division Central Analysis Research Unit, INTELLIGENCE NOTE: NYC MOSQUE STATEMENTS ON DANISH CARTOON CONTROVERSY (2006), http://hosted.ap.org/specials/interactives/documents/nypd/nypd_cartoons.pdf.

198 NYPD Intelligence Division Central Analysis Research Unit, INTELLIGENCE NOTE: DD5S REFERENCING 10/11/06 PLANE CRASH INTO BUILDING AT 524 E. 72ND STREET (2006), http://hosted.ap.org/specials/interactives/documents/nypd/nypd_planecrash.pdf.

199 Declaration of Shamiur Rahman at 2, *Handschu v. Special Services Division*, No. 71 Civ. 2203 (CSH), 2014 WL 407103 (S.D.N.Y. Oct. 28, 2012), http://www.brennancenter.org/sites/default/files/analysis/Declaration_of_Shamiur_Rahman.pdf.

200 Matt Apuzzo & Joseph Goldstein, *New York Drops Unit That Spied on Muslims*, N.Y. TIMES (Apr. 16, 2014), http://www.nytimes.com/2014/04/16/nyregion/police-unit-that-spied-on-muslims-is-disbanded.html.

201 NEW YORK CITY, N.Y., Local Law No. 70, Int. No. 1079 (Aug. 22, 2013).

problems with the department's surveillance programs.[202] The police also settled two lawsuits challenging the Muslim surveillance program, agreeing to tighten the standards for initiating and continuing investigations and to add civilian oversight to the process of selecting surveillance targets.[203]

Other minority communities, as well as political protest groups, have also been targeted for surveillance. FBI documents disclosed through FOIA litigation show that the bureau's field offices relied on stereotypes about the propensity of certain races and ethnicities to commit certain types of crimes to map entire racial and ethnic communities, including African Americans in Georgia, Arab Americans in Michigan, Chinese and Russian Americans in California, and broad swaths of Latino American communities in multiple states.[204] A 2005 report revealed that the FBI had targeted environmental and animal rights advocacy groups, claiming that the "eco-terrorism, animal-rights movement" had become the number one domestic threat.[205] A 2010 report by the Justice Department's inspector general found that the FBI had inappropriately tracked the activities of left-leaning groups, including People for the Ethical Treatment of Animals (PETA), Greenpeace, and the Catholic Worker.[206] Documents obtained through FOIA showed that the FBI closely monitored the Occupy Wall Street movement.[207] Most recently, the Black Lives Matter movement, which coalesced in the wake of high-profile cases of police brutality directed at African Americans, has been monitored by the Department of Homeland Security and the Oregon Department of Justice.[208]

202 New York City Dep't of Investigation, Office of the Inspector Gen. for the NYPD, An Investigation of NYPD's Compliance with Rules Governing Investigations of Political Activity (Aug. 23, 2016), http://www1.nyc.gov/assets/oignypd/downloads/pdf/oig_intel_report_823_final_for_release.pdf.

203 Stipulation of Settlement and Order, *Raza v. City of* N.Y., No. 13-CV-3448 (E.D.N.Y. 2016), https://www.aclu.org/legal-document/raza-v-city-new-york-settlement-stipulation-and-order; *Handschu v. Special Services Division*, 288 F.Supp.2d 411 (S.D.N.Y. 2003). Citing to the NYPD inspector general's report, the reviewing court declined to approve the initial version of the settlement. Ruling on Proposed Settlement Agreement, *Handschu v. Police Dep't of the City of* N.Y., No. 71 Civ. 2203 (CSH) (S.D.N.Y. 2016), http://nlgnyc.org/wp-content/uploads/2016/10/handschu-final-oct28-16.pdf. The parties negotiated further safeguards and the settlement was eventually approved in March 2017. Ruling and Order on Proposed Revised Settlement Agreement, *Handschu v. Police Dep't of the City of* N.Y., No. 71 Civ. 2203 (CSH) (S.D.N.Y. 2017), https://www.aclu.org/legal-document/raza-v-city-new-york-exhibit-b-order-approving-stipulation-settlement-handschu-court. A third lawsuit in New Jersey federal court is still ongoing. *Hassan v. City of* N.Y., No. 12-CV-3401 (D. N.J. 2016).

204 Am. Civil Liberties Union, *supra* note 187.

205 Henry Schuster, *Domestic Terror: Who's Most Dangerous?*, CNN (Aug. 24, 2005), http://www.cnn.com/2005/US/08/24/schuster.column/; *FBI: Eco-Terrorism Remains No. 1 Domestic Terror Threat*, FOX News (Mar. 31, 2008), http://www.foxnews.com/story/2008/03/31/fbi-eco-terrorism-remains-no-1-domestic-terror-threat.html.

206 Office of the Inspector Gen., U.S. Dep't of Justice, A Review of the FBI's Investigations of Certain Domestic Advocacy Groups (2010), https://oig.justice.gov/special/s1009r.pdf.

207 Michael S. Schmidt & Colin Moynihan, *F.B.I. Counterterrorism Agents Monitored Occupy Movement, Records Show*, N.Y. Times (Dec. 24, 2012), http://www.nytimes.com/2012/12/25/nyregion/occupy-movement-was-investigated-by-fbi-counterterrorism-agents-records-show.html; Jason Cherkis & Zach Carter, *FBI Surveillance of Occupy Wall Street Detailed*, Huffington Post (Jan. 23, 2014), http://www.huffingtonpost.com/2013/01/05/fbi-occupy-wall-street_n_2410783.html.

208 George Joseph, *Exclusive: Feds Regularly Monitored Black Lives Matter Since Ferguson*, Intercept (July 24, 2015), https://theintercept.com/2015/07/24/documents-show-department-homeland-security-monitoring-black-lives-matter-since-ferguson/.

B *Impact of Surveillance on Freedom of Speech, Association, and Religion*

Lawyers and judges often talk about how surveillance can chill speech, association, and the practice of religion. In the golden age of surveillance, these effects have been documented. A report prepared by the City University of New York and the Muslim American Civil Liberties Coalition captured Muslim American reactions to the NYPD's surveillance program.[209] Interviewees reported avoiding prayers and social activities at mosques, political discussions, activism, and participation in Muslim student organizations. They were suspicious of anyone new or vocal about politics in a Muslim space. Many were even reluctant to call the police when they were victims of a crime.

Snowden's disclosures about the NSA's mass surveillance programs also triggered self-censorship, as well as attempts to avoid government monitoring. Just months after the disclosures, PEN America surveyed 528 U.S. writers. Fully 85 percent were worried about government surveillance, with 28 percent curtailing their use of social media, 24 percent avoiding certain topics by phone or e-mail, 16 percent choosing not to write or speak on a certain topic, and 13 percent taking extra steps to cover up Internet activity.[210] A 2014 Human Rights Watch and ACLU study showed that many journalists and lawyers changed the way they work when they learned about the NSA's surveillance programs.[211] To protect sources and clients, both groups avoided e-mail in sensitive situations and used encryption programs.

Americans at large have had similar reactions. An analysis of Google Trends showed a significant 5 percent drop in United States-based searches for government-sensitive terms (such as "dirty bomb" or "CIA") after the Snowden stories first broke.[212] And, according to a 2015 Pew survey, 30 percent of American adults had taken at least one step to hide their information from the government, such as changing privacy settings, avoiding social media, not using certain words online, or communicating off-line instead.[213]

The type of self-censorship suggested by these surveys undermines the health of a democratic and pluralistic society. Freedom of speech, association, and religion, as well as privacy, are not only rights in and of themselves; they are the pillars on which robust civic participation and informed self-government are built. If citizens cannot speak their minds or join together without fear that the government is watching, they will become less willing to do so. This is particularly true of groups who occupy minority or non-mainstream positions

209 Muslim Am. Civil Liberties Coalition et al., Mapping Muslims: NYPD Spying and its impact on American Muslims (Ramzi Kassem et al. eds. 2013), http://www.law.cuny.edu/academics/clinics/immigration/clear/Mapping-Muslims.pdf.

210 PEN Am. Ctr, Chilling Effects: NSA Surveillance Drives U.S. Writers to Self-Censor 6 (2013), https://pen.org/sites/default/files/Chilling%20Effects_PEN%20American.pdf.

211 Am. Civil Liberties Union, *supra* note 180, at 23, 60.

212 Alex Marthews & Catherine Tucker, Government Surveillance and Internet Search Behavior (2015), http://papers.ssrn.com/sol3/papers.cfm?abstract_id=2412564&download=yes. A control list of popular search terms did not show the same change; nor did personally sensitive terms (e.g. "abortion" or "herpes").

213 Lee Rainiee & Mary Madden, *Americans' Privacy Strategies Post-Snowden*, Pew Research Ctr (Mar. 16, 2015), http://www.pewinternet.org/2015/03/16/americans-privacy-strategies-post-snowden/. People who say they have heard a lot about NSA surveillance are more likely to try to avoid it. And a failure to take such steps does not necessarily suggest a lack of concern: 54 percent of those surveyed believe such efforts would be futile, opining that it would be "somewhat" or "very" difficult to find tools or strategies to protect their privacy.

within society, whether in terms of race, religion, ethnicity, or belief. Overbroad surveillance thus has the potential to undermine the open societies whose security it is meant to protect.

C *Risk of Abuse or Mishandling of Data*

Any time the government has the authority to amass large amounts of personal, sensitive information about private citizens, there is the potential for abuse. As discussed in detail in Section II.A, law enforcement and intelligence agencies have used their expanded authorities to target Muslim Americans, a range of racial and ethnic minorities, and political activists. In addition, there is evidence that officials have committed abuses of a more petty nature, accessing and using data for improper personal reasons. According to an NSA inspector general report, agency employees reported that they had spied on love interests in twelve instances.[214] The number of employees who misused databases in a similar manner but did not self-report their misconduct is undoubtedly much greater.

Intentional misconduct is not the only concern. Documents released since Snowden's disclosures show that the NSA has on several occasions violated the conditions laid down by the FISA Court for its programs. Under the program to collect Americans' Internet metadata in bulk, which operated until 2011, the FISA Court issued orders establishing limits on the types of data the NSA could acquire and the circumstances under which it could be shared with other agencies. The NSA repeatedly violated these limits, systematically acquiring information it was barred from collecting and sharing data without the necessary authorization, while misrepresenting its activities to the court. Although the NSA insisted that the transgressions were unintentional, the FISA Court's Judge Bates expressed alarm over "the NSA's long-standing and pervasive violations of the prior orders in this matter," as well as the agency's "history of material misstatements" in its court submissions.[215] Similarly, in operating the program to collect Americans' phone records in bulk, the NSA for years failed to ensure that reasonable articulable suspicion of a terrorist link was present before querying the data. According to the FISA Court's Judge Reggie Walton, this was a serious violation of the conditions for the operation of the program. Judge Walton took little comfort from the NSA's claims that the violation was inadvertent. In a 2009 opinion, he wrote, "The minimization procedures proposed by the government in each successive application and approved and adopted as binding by the orders of the court have been so frequently and systematically violated that it can fairly be said that this critical element of the overall [bulk collection] program has never functioned effectively."[216]

Another significant case of noncompliance is related to the Section 702 program, which is supposed to target only foreigners who are located overseas.[217] In May 2011, three years after the FISA Court approved collection under Section 702, the NSA

214 *See* Letter from Dr. George Ellard, Inspector Gen., Nat'l Sec. Agency, to Sen. Charles E. Grassley (Sept. 11, 2013), http://www.privacylives.com/wp-content/uploads/2013/09/09262013-NSA-Surveillance-09-11-13-response-from-IG-to-intentional-misuse-of-NSA-authority.pdf (detailing twelve instances of intentional abuse of NSA bulk surveillance data, most involving employees searching for information on their romantic partners).

215 [Redacted], No. PR/TT [Redacted], slip op. at 77, 115 (FISA Ct. [Redacted]), https://www.dni.gov/files/documents/1118/CLEANEDPRTT%202.pdf.

216 Walton Mar. 2009 Order, *supra* note 120, at 10–11.

217 *See supra* text accompanying notes 110–11.

informed the court that the process was not functioning in the way the government had previously represented, and that the NSA was in fact employing a technique known as "upstream collection" that routinely swept in tens of thousands of wholly domestic communications. The court's presiding judge ordered the NSA to shut down the upstream program until it could find a technical solution to segregate transactions most likely to contain Americans' communications and implement new rules for handling the data.[218] He wrote, "By expanding its Section 702 acquisitions to include the acquisition of Internet transactions through its upstream collection, NSA has, as a practical matter, circumvented the spirit of [the law]."[219] He added, "The Court is troubled that the government's revelations regarding NSA's acquisition of Internet transactions mark the third instance in less than three years in which the government has disclosed a substantial misrepresentation regarding the scope of a major collection program."[220]

Five years later, the *New York Times* reported – and the NSA confirmed – that the agency had repeatedly failed to comply with the special rules that had been developed for data collected "upstream."[221] With the program at risk of being shut down once again, the NSA was forced to stop collecting the type of communications that were most problematic: those that are neither to nor from a target, but include certain information about the target. It is not yet known when, or if, the NSA will attempt to resume this type of collection.

Another risk of mass surveillance is the potential that the NSA's vast databases, which include sensitive information about people not suspected of any wrongdoing, will be compromised. The whistle-blowers Edward Snowden and Chelsea Manning were able to remove large quantities of information from the government's most secret systems: those of the NSA and the U.S. military.[222] While Snowden and Manning were insiders who removed documents in order to bring government malfeasance to the attention of the public, hackers with other motives may also be interested in the information stored by the NSA. Two recent attacks demonstrate the vulnerability of government databases. In 2015, hackers (believed to be working for the Chinese government) stole the personal data of more than 21 million current and former federal employees from an Office of Personnel Management database.[223] In early 2016, hackers published

218 [REDACTED], No. [REDACTED], 2011 WL 10945618 (FISA Ct. Oct. 3, 2011).

219 *Id.* at *16.

220 *Id.* at *5 n.14.

221 Charlie Savage, *N.S.A. Halts Collection of Americans' Emails About Foreign Targets*, N.Y. TIMES (Apr. 28, 2017), https://nyti.ms/2qfmHmb; Press Release, National Security Agency, NSA Stops Certain Foreign Intelligence Collection Activities Under Section 702 (Apr. 28, 2017), *available at* https://www.nsa.gov/news-features/press-room/press-releases/2017/nsa-stops-certain-702-activites.shtml; Statement, National Security Agency, NSA Stops Certain Section 702 "Upstream" Activities (Apr. 28, 2017), *available at* https://www.nsa.gov/news-features/press-room/statements/2017-04-28-702-statement.shtml.

222 Manning provided some 700,000 documents and video files to WikiLeaks. Peter Walker, *Bradley Manning Trial: What We Know from the Leaked WikiLeaks Documents*, GUARDIAN (July 30, 2013), https://www.theguardian.com/world/2013/jul/30/bradley-manning-wikileaks-revelations. The total number of documents that Snowden removed from the NSA is not known, but government officials have estimated that it could be in the millions. *Snowden Obtained Nearly 2 Million Classified Files in NSA Leak – Pentagon Report*, RT (Jan. 9, 2014), https://www.rt.com/usa/snowden-downloaded-millions-documents-389/.

223 Kaveh Waddell & Dustin Volz, *OPM Announces More than 21 Million Victims Affected by Second Data Breach*, ATLANTIC (July 9, 2015), http://www.theatlantic.com/politics/archive/2015/07/opm-announces-more-than-21-million-affected-by-second-data-breach/458475/.

contact information for twenty thousand FBI employees and ten thousand Department of Homeland Security employees that they may have obtained from a Department of Justice database.[224]

III Charting a Course Correction

The historical pattern is clear: surveillance authorities are prone to abuse if not adequately constrained. Moreover, even absent abuse, perceptions of excessive surveillance can chill democratic participation and the exercise of rights. In the authors' view, several measures are necessary to restore appropriate limits on national security surveillance. Each could occupy its own chapter; they will be discussed briefly here.

A *Reinstate the Requirement of Individualized, Fact-Based Suspicion*

The post-9/11 legal changes discussed in Part I.C have one common thread. They all discard the requirement that the government have individualized, fact-based suspicion before conducting surveillance of Americans. This requirement in the past was a critical bulwark, not only against deliberate abuse, but against subconscious prejudice. It also limited the total scope of surveillance, putting fewer innocent individuals' data at risk of security breaches and avoiding the perception of "Big Brother" surveillance that is leading more and more Americans to refrain from speaking their minds in public or private. As discussed, the elimination of this protection already is having a range of deleterious effects.

Restoring the requirement of individualized, fact-based suspicion is both the simplest and most important step that should be taken now. That does not mean the government needs to show probable cause of criminal activity and obtain a warrant from a magistrate judge every time it collects information. For collection activities that do not trigger the Fourth Amendment, the degree of suspicion required and the process that must be followed to initiate collection will depend on the intrusiveness of the surveillance activity. But there should be no situation in which law enforcement or intelligence officials are permitted to collect, store, and analyze the personal information of private citizens without any facts present to suggest possible criminal or terrorist activity.

Moreover, the courts and Congress alike should update their understanding of what the Fourth Amendment *does* cover. It is a common observation that the law fails to keep pace with technology. The "third party doctrine" is a prime example: whatever logic there may once have been to the notion that people have no reasonable expectation of privacy in the information they convey to telephone companies and banks, we now live in a world in which it is impossible to go twenty-four hours without disclosing highly personal information to Internet service providers, text messaging services, cell phone service providers, and others. Sophisticated computer algorithms allow the government to tease out a wealth of information about our associations, activities, and even beliefs from these digital bread crumbs. This is exactly the kind of information the Fourth Amendment was designed to protect.

224 Mary Kay Mallonnee, *Hackers Publish Contact Info of 20,000 FBI Employees*, CNN (Feb. 8, 2016), http://www.cnn.com/2016/02/08/politics/hackers-fbi-employee-info/.

B *Reinvigorate Oversight in All Three Branches*

1 Judicial Oversight

It is often difficult to challenge surveillance programs in court because information about how the programs operate and about those impacted is kept secret. Reforming some of the restrictive doctrines and rules applied by courts and the executive branch has the potential to reinvigorate judicial oversight over surveillance significantly.

As noted previously, the government has relied on broad assertions of state secrets to prevent adjudication of challenges to various counterterrorism programs, including extraordinary rendition and torture.[225] The overuse of state secrets in the Bush administration led to the introduction of legislation that would restore it to its role as an evidentiary privilege. The State Secrets Protection Act, which has been introduced on several occasions in Congress, provides a useful path forward that resets the balance between executive branch claims of secrecy and plaintiffs' claims for justice.[226] It directs courts to evaluate claims of state secrets after privately reviewing the information or evidence at issue. If a court determines that the government's claim is valid, it could require the government to provide nonprivileged substitutes such as summaries, redacted versions, or lists of relevant facts that would allow the case to go forward. Where these mechanisms are not workable, plaintiffs must be afforded the opportunity to prove their case without privileged information. And, finally, where secret information is vital to the decision of a legal issue, the court would rule on the matter "in the interest of justice," taking the privileged information into account.

In addition, several bills have been introduced in Congress to reform pleading standards to make it easier to bring cases.[227] To address the specific problems faced in litigating surveillance programs, Senators Rand Paul, Wyden, and Udall submitted an amendment to the 2014 appropriations bill that would have amended Section 702 of the FAA to provide that an injury in fact occurred when an individual had a "reasonable basis" to believe that her communication "will be acquired" and had taken "objectively reasonable steps to avoid surveillance."[228] A "reasonable basis" would be presumed if "the profession of the person requires the person regularly to communicate foreign intelligence information" to non-U.S. persons located outside the United States.[229] Measures such as these would increase the likelihood of judicial oversight of secret surveillance.

The law also should be amended to ensure that criminal defendants and parties to other legal proceedings have the opportunity to challenge evidence derived from surveillance. If a particular form of surveillance plays any role whatsoever in developing the

225 *See supra* text accompanying notes 123–24.

226 The law was initially introduced by Senators Kennedy, Leahy, and Specter in 2008 and has subsequently been introduced in every Congress, but has never had a vote. S. 2533, 110th Cong. (2007–2008); H.R. 984, 111th Cong. (2009); H.R. 5956, 112th Cong. (2012); H.R. 3332, 113th Cong. (2013); H.R. 4767, 114th Cong. (2016).

227 *See, e.g.*, Notice Pleading Restoration Act of 2009, S. 1504, 111th Cong. (2009); Open Access to Courts Act of 2009, H.R. 4115, 111th Cong. (2009).

228 S. Amend. 2223, National Defense Authorization Act for Fiscal Year 2014, S. 1197, 113th Cong. (2013), 159 Cong. Rec. S8230 (daily ed. Nov. 19, 2013).

229 *Id.*

government's evidence – even if it simply provides the tip that prompts the government to employ other investigatory methods – its use should be disclosed. Moreover, Congress should prohibit the practice of recreating evidence through other means to avoid disclosure of particular surveillance authorities or practices. Finally, for foreign intelligence surveillance programs, Congress should consider requiring notice to people who are not themselves targets of surveillance but whose communications were "incidentally" collected. Such notice does not have to be contemporaneous, but could be delayed using the model used for notice of wiretaps under Title III.[230]

2 Legislative Oversight

Legislative oversight has not done its job in the post-9/11 era. The most obvious and irrefutable proof of this point is that two plainly illegal programs, the torture of detainees and warrantless wiretapping in violation of FISA, were briefed to a handful of members of Congress – and were allowed to continue.

In 2015, the Brennan Center for Justice issued a report, *Strengthening Intelligence Oversight*, that was endorsed by eighteen former Church Committee staff members as well as two members of the committee itself, the Hon. Walter F. Mondale and the Hon. Gary Hart. The report discusses what has and has not changed since the Church Committee conducted its review, and where the oversight mechanisms put in place as a result of the committee's recommendations have fallen short. It recommends a new investigative committee within Congress to conduct "a comprehensive examination of intelligence, law enforcement, homeland security, and national defense activities" in order to "determine where gaps have developed and how Congress might more effectively exercise its constitutional mandate."[231] As the report points out, it has been forty years since Congress last conducted a holistic examination of intelligence authorities, activities, and institutions; given the enormous changes in law and technology that have taken place since then, we are overdue for another such reckoning.

One critical limitation on the effectiveness of legislative oversight has been restrictions on the flow of executive branch information to, within, and (where necessary) from Congress. The Gang of Eight provision of the National Security Act has not served its function, in part because it is too often ignored or bypassed in favor of the smaller Gang of Four, and in part because members of these gangs too willingly accept constraints on their ability to share information with colleagues. Moreover, even when classified information is made available to the full Congress, most members cannot take full advantage of it because they lack staff with the necessary clearances. And Congress has never exercised its authority to disclose classified information to the public in cases of overriding public interest.[232]

Congress should enact legislation prohibiting Gang of Four briefings, unambiguously requiring notification of *all* intelligence activities to at least the Gang of Eight, clarifying

230 18 U.S.C. § 2518(8)(d).

231 Michael German, Brennan Ctr for Justice, STRENGTHENING INTELLIGENCE OVERSIGHT 16 (2015), https://www.brennancenter.org/sites/default/files/publications/Church_Committee_Web_REVISED.pdf.

232 *See* S. Res. 400 § 8, 94th Cong. (1976) (unenacted).

that members of these gangs have the authority and responsibility to keep other members of Congress appropriately informed even where classified information is involved, and ensuring that all members can obtain the assistance of cleared staff. It also should use the authority it granted itself in 1976 to disclose classified information publicly where the public interest would outweigh any risk of national security harm.

Of course, none of these tools matters if members of Congress lack the will to exert robust oversight. Members are responsive to voters and donors; when those constituencies are unaware of the members' activities (because they relate to classified matters), the incentive to pick difficult fights with intelligence agencies is much diminished.[233] Moreover, any regulatory body runs the risk of "capture" by the entity it regulates; publicity usually serves to hold this dynamic at least somewhat in check. Intelligence committees are particularly prone to capture given the insular nature of the national security establishment – when "read into" a classified program, members become part of an elite club – and there is no publicity to discourage this phenomenon. There is no easy answer on how to counteract these dynamics, and the issues they present merit much more in-depth study.

3 Internal Oversight

As discussed previously, one of the most important forms of internal executive branch oversight is reviews by inspectors general. However, the ability of these offices to serve as a check on surveillance authority has been undermined by the executive branch's position that agencies are not required to provide them with certain types of information.[234]

While Congress has taken action in response to complaints about the withholding of information, further legislation is needed to ensure inspector generals' independence and bolster their authority. Congress should amend the Inspector General Act to include a "removal for cause" provision, clarifying the grounds on which an inspector general may be removed from office (certain recent dismissals having raised questions about whether inspectors general were removed for being too critical of the agencies). In addition, to increase the chances that inspector general reviews will lead to meaningful reforms, the offices should be required to publish all completed audits or reports, with only those redactions necessary to protect classified information or personal privacy.

C *Ensure Adequate Transparency*

Ultimately, the best check against abuse or unwarranted expansion of surveillance authorities is public awareness of how those authorities are being interpreted and used. There are necessary limits to this awareness, as the details of specific intelligence operations often must remain secret. However, it is widely recognized that the government

233 *See* Jack Goldsmith, Power and Constraint 91–92 (1st ed. 2012).

234 *See supra* text accompanying notes 145–149. *See also* Josh Hicks, *Dozens of Inspectors General Say Federal Agencies Hindering Oversight*, Wash. Post (Aug. 6, 2014), https://www.washingtonpost.com/news/federal-eye/wp/2014/08/06/dozens-of-inspectors-general-say-federal-agencies-hindering-oversight/.

classifies far too much information. Former national security officials have estimated that anywhere from 50 to 90 percent of classified documents could safely be released.[235] With 53 million decisions to classify information in fiscal year 2015 alone,[236] this adds up to a massive amount of unnecessary secrecy.

A problem this significant requires a fundamental change in the underlying system. In 2009, President Obama ordered the Public Interest Declassification Board (PIDB) – an independent committee that advises the president on classification and declassification policy – to develop recommendations for just such a fundamental change. However, open government advocates argued that the board's ultimate recommendations (issued in 2012) were not sufficiently far-reaching, and the vast majority of them have not been implemented, in any event.[237]

The PIDB should go back to the drawing board. This time, any recommendations should include concrete measures to ensure accountability for overclassification, and the White House should move quickly to implement any recommendations that hold promise.

In addition, Congress should enact legislation that expressly prohibits secret law.[238] This would include not only legislation that incorporates provisions of classified committee reports by reference, but also agency rules or regulations (including those issued by intelligence agencies) and binding legal interpretations issued by courts or the executive branch. There is no justification for concealing general rules or regulations, which do not include specific operational details such as times, locations, targets, or human sources of intelligence. Moreover, while legal opinions issued by courts and agencies today often commingle legal analysis and sensitive facts, a general rule requiring publication would prompt the opinions' authors to write them in a manner that facilitates redaction and release.

Conclusion

The history of surveillance regulation and oversight reveals patterns that are rich with lessons and guidance for the future. Through decades and across administrations, weak limits on surveillance and timid oversight led to surveillance abuses, the brunt of which was borne by minorities and political dissenters. The legislative and regulatory scheme that governed surveillance in the decades after the Church Committee's investigation served as a critical check on such misconduct. Since 9/11, however, this scheme has unraveled. At the same time that advances in technology are enabling surveillance of unprecedented scope and intrusiveness, the laws and policies that limit surveillance are being systematically eroded. Already we are seeing the impacts: intelligence-gathering programs targeted at Muslims, racial minorities, and political protest movements, and a measurable drop in Americans' willingness to speak their minds openly. The 2016

235 *Espionage Act and the Legal and Constitutional Implications of Wikileaks: Hearing Before the H. Comm. on the Judiciary*, 111th Cong. 74 (2010) (statement of Thomas Blanton, Dir., Nat'l Sec. Archive).

236 Info. Sec. Oversight Office, 2015 Report to the President 7 (2016), http://www.archives.gov/isoo/reports/2014-annual-report.pdf.

237 Public Interest Declassification Board, Transforming the Security Classification System (2012), https://www.archives.gov/declassification/pidb/recommendations/transforming-classification.pdf.

238 *See generally* Elizabeth Goitein, Brennan Ctr. for Justice, The New Era of Secret Law (2016), http://www.brennancenter.org/sites/default/files/publications/The_New_Era_of_Secret_Law_0.pdf.

election of Donald J. Trump,[239] who holds a sweeping view of executive power and has called for more surveillance of Muslim Americans, is likely to accelerate and intensify these trends. Against this backdrop, the small steps taken to rein in the NSA's collection activities after the Snowden disclosures will not suffice. If the United States is to avoid repeating the mistakes of history, we must shore up intelligence oversight and restore sensible limits on surveillance.

239 The 2016 election took place after this chapter was written. In a few necessary instances, the authors have updated information to reflect post-election events. They have not attempted to address the potential impact of the election results on the surveillance landscape more generally, however, as that topic could merit its own chapter.

Part IV

Regulation of Surveillance

24 Regulating Surveillance through Litigation: Some Thoughts from the Trenches

Mark Rumold[†]

This chapter discusses the substantial obstacles to, and the promise of, using litigation as a tool for regulating government surveillance. In particular, the chapter will explore the relative advantages and disadvantages of criminal and civil litigation as a check on government surveillance powers. In the civil context, obstacles to obtaining a final merits judgment are myriad – especially at the outset of the case. Pleading standards, Article III standing requirements, and limitations on the availability of relief against the government severely limit the ability of civil plaintiffs to regulate surveillance through litigation. Criminal litigation, the time-tested method of regulating government surveillance, suffers from fewer threshold or procedural obstacles than civil litigation, yet the practical limitations of criminal litigation work to distort surveillance law in the government's favor. Finally, the chapter will conclude with thoughts on the future of surveillance litigation and the role corporations play in shaping surveillance norms.

Introduction

This was it – *the* defining legal battle over surveillance. According to experts, this case would shape the law and the contours of privacy and security for generations to come. Ultimately, these pundits agreed, the case was headed all the way to the Supreme Court. That is, until it was not.

This description applies to an untold number of surveillance cases.[1] But Apple's 2016 battle with the FBI provides, perhaps, the best known example.[2] In the wake of a terrorist attack in San Bernardino, California, a battle was brewing in a federal courthouse nearby. The FBI had the attacker's iPhone, but the security software on the phone prevented the FBI's full access to its contents.[3] The FBI sought, and obtained, a warrant to search the

† Senior Staff Attorney, Electronic Frontier Foundation.

1 To give just one example, a case involving a secure email provider, Lavabit, received similar breathless headlines, but ultimately fizzled out in the Fourth Circuit. *See, e.g.*, Jennifer Granick, *Fourth Circuit Upholds Contempt against Lavabit, Doesn't Decide Gov't Access to Encryption Keys*, JustSecurity (April 16, 2014), https://www.justsecurity.org/9417/fourth-circuit-upholds-contempt-lavabit-doesnt-decide-govt-access-encryption-keys/.

2 *See, e.g.*, Jordan Orlando, *The Case of the Century*, Slate (February 25, 2016), http://www.slate.com/articles/news_and_politics/jurisprudence/2016/02/the_fbi_s_fight_with_apple_will_be_the_case_of_the_century.html.

3 It should be noted that the FBI's need for *full* access to the phone was likely greatly exaggerated. With third party applications (such as Facebook or Twitter) and communication service providers (such as AT&T or T-Mobile), most information about the data, calls, texts, or usage is not stored exclusively on an individual's

phone. After discovering the phone was encrypted, the FBI sought an order under the All Writs Act compelling Apple to circumvent security features on the device. Apple moved to unseal, and later to vacate, the order, and the battle lines were drawn: Apple versus the FBI, the world's most valuable company – attempting to defend privacy in the digital age – pitted against America's leading law enforcement agency, seeking to advance the needs of law enforcement. Media attention was intense, and amicus briefs poured in on both sides.[4]

Then, just a day before the hearing, the FBI asked for more time. Over the weekend, according to the FBI, an "outside party" had demonstrated a method of accessing the phone that would not require Apple's compelled assistance.[5] A week later, the government announced it had accessed the phone and would no longer seek to enforce the controversial order it had obtained. The case was finished without even leaving the federal magistrate judge's courtroom.

For those of us who regularly litigate surveillance cases against the government, this case's last-minute collapse was no surprise. Indeed, this is the profound reality – and limitation – of using litigation to regulate surveillance. The government controls almost all the cards, and the deck is stacked in their favor.

In Apple's battle with the FBI, perhaps it is not immediately clear who walked away the winner. Apple did not have to comply with the order, but it also did not win in court, and it had the (dis)pleasure of having the FBI announce to the world that Apple's products were not so secure after all. The FBI, on the other hand, did not win in court, but it certainly did not lose either: it is free to try again, with a different judge and, perhaps, a less combative company, to obtain an order requiring access to encrypted materials. If the world's most valuable corporation cannot secure a clear win in federal courts against government surveillance, then that leaves less hope for positively shaping surveillance law through litigation for the rest of us.

This difficulty has been borne out in other contexts and cases. Even where a surveillance program is publicly known, ongoing, and effectively encompassing *everyone* in the United States, the federal government has managed to avoid broad decisions that would tend to curtail its practices significantly – as was the case with the National Security Agency's program of mass surveillance of Americans' call records under Section 215 of the USA PATRIOT Act. Indeed, in some cases, *even where the government hands over evidence of its illegal surveillance*, it has still managed to avoid merits decisions that would affect its practices.[6]

device. Thus, the sliver of data stored exclusively on most phones is likely quite slim. This fact led many (perhaps rightly) to conclude that the San Bernardino case was, for the FBI, an attractive vehicle for precedent rather than a necessary investigative step. *See, e.g.*, *The Encryption Meltdown*, Wall St. J., March 22, 2016, http://www.wsj.com/articles/the-encryption-meltdown-1458690131.

4 Twenty-one amicus briefs or letters were filed on behalf of Apple; four on behalf of the government. *See A Reader's Guide to the Apple All Writs Act* Cases, JustSecurity (Mar. 1, 2016), https://www.justsecurity.org/29634/readers-guide-magistrate-judge-writs-act-cases/.

5 Government's Ex Parte Application for a Continuance at 3, In the Matter of the Search of an Apple iPhone Seized during the Execution of a Search Warrant on a Black Lexus IS300, California License Plate #5KGD203 (2016) (ED No. CM 16–10 (SP)), https://cdn1.vox-cdn.com/uploads/chorus_asset/file/6225845/motion-to-vacate.0.pdf.

6 *See, e.g.*, Jon Eisenberg, *Suing George W. Bush: A Bizarre and Troubling Tale*, Salon (July 9, 2008), https://www.salon.com/2008/07/09/alharamain_lawsuit/. The Al-Haramain case was eventually dismissed on sovereign immunity grounds.

Which is all to say: litigation as a regulatory tool for surveillance has limits. Hard ones. Nevertheless, some of the most substantial limitations on government surveillance over the past decade have come about through court victories. *United States v. Jones* moved GPS tracking within the Fourth Amendment.[7] *Riley v. California* recognized the significant privacy intrusions worked by warrantless searches of electronic devices, requiring law enforcement to get a warrant prior to searching the contents of a cell phone.[8] And *United States v. Warshak* recognized, for the first time, that the Fourth Amendment protects emails stored with a third-party provider.[9]

Indeed, as *Warshak* shows, litigation is often more effective and more nimble than legislation. Despite 315 cosponsors and a unanimous vote in the House, the "Email Privacy Act" – a simple attempt to update the Stored Communications Act, 18 U.S.C. §§ 2701–2712, to require a warrant for emails stored more than 180 days (effectively, a codification of the *Warshak* decision) – once again stalled in Congress in 2016.[10] While Congress dragged its heels on updating the law, the nation's major email providers all required law enforcement to obtain a warrant to access email – relying on the Sixth Circuit's decision in *Warshak*, not federal legislative protections.[11]

Thus, despite significant obstacles and limitations, regulating surveillance through litigation can be a useful tool for shaping privacy protections. And that is the purpose of this chapter: to sketch, in broad strokes, the nature of surveillance litigation – both its challenges and its benefits – with some thoughts from the courtroom and recent cases, and to give a picture of the utility of using judicial decisions as a tool for regulating surveillance.

This chapter's scope is limited, however. Principally, it will only cover regulating surveillance carried out by the government – with a primary emphasis on the federal government, although many of the same principles apply to state governments as well. Surveillance or encroachments on privacy carried out by nonstate actors, or by foreign governments, all raise a host of their own separate issues – some thornier for a litigant seeking to challenge them, some less so. But, in any event, it is beyond the scope of this chapter.

This chapter also only focuses on the creation of legal precedent as a way of regulating surveillance. There are, of course, other ways in which litigation – even in the absence of a merits decision – can positively shape surveillance norms. For example, litigation can generate publicity about new government surveillance techniques, leading to popular or political opposition. Another possibility is that litigation challenging new or otherwise untested techniques can raise legal issues that the government's counsel fails to consider internally. It also can serve as a check on further expansion of

7 *United States v. Jones*, 132 S. Ct. 945 (2012).

8 *Riley v. California*, 134 S. Ct. 2473 (2014).

9 *United States v. Warshak*, 631 F.3d 266 (2010).

10 Right now, under the SCA, a warrant is required for emails stored *less* than 180 days, but is not required for emails stored beyond that. *See* 18 U.S.C. § 2703(a) (2012). This discrepancy is the result of the state of the art in the 1980s, when the Electronic Communications Privacy Act was passed. *See, e.g.*, *ECPA Reform: Why Now?* Digital Due Process, http://www.digitaldueprocess.org/ (last updated 2010).

11 *See Who Has Your Back? Protecting Your Data from Government Requests*, Electronic Frontier Foundation (June 17, 2015), https://www.eff.org/files/2015/06/18/who_has_your_back_2015_protecting_your_data_from_government_requests_20150618.pdf (noting that all major providers listed required a "warrant for user content").

surveillance techniques; specifically, lawsuits put the government on notice that legal, popular, or political resistance may be more likely, or more likely to succeed, if the surveillance is expanded.

With those caveats, it is my hope that the chapter will provide some insight into the difficulties, and the promise, of using litigation as a tool to regulate surveillance. First, I will discuss civil litigation as a tool for regulation and its (somewhat imposing) challenges, including pleading standards, Article III standing, and the difficulties associated with relief. Second, I will discuss some of the practical and structural challenges that arise in the criminal context, and the relative successes and limitations of these types of challenges. Finally, I will offer some parting thoughts: on corporate litigation challenging government surveillance practices and the future (and necessity) of civil litigation as a regulatory tool for surveillance.

I Civil Cases

In 2005, a whistle-blower walked into the offices of the Electronic Frontier Foundation (where I work) with documents showing that AT&T was diverting Internet traffic passing through its San Francisco facility to surveillance devices controlled by the National Security Agency.[12] We filed suit against AT&T, *Hepting v. AT&T*, in 2006.[13] And, two years later, we filed a separate suit against the NSA and other government officials.[14]

In 2008, Congress passed a law, the FISA Amendments Act, that gave AT&T full immunity for any participation it had in the national security surveillance. That grant of retrospective immunity killed our case against AT&T. Our suit against the NSA, *Jewel v. NSA*, proceeded: but, as of September 2016, after two trips to the Ninth Circuit, and nearly a decade of litigation, the government had yet to file an answer to our complaint.[15]

Although national security litigation may be an especially tough species of surveillance litigation, as EFF's experience with *Hepting* and *Jewel* demonstrates, litigating civil challenges to government surveillance programs can be a slog, littered with government-specific privileges and standards that seem to arise (or apply) only (or especially rigorously) in challenges to government surveillance programs. Substantial obstacles to civil challenges arise at the outset of the case. In particular, a litigant faces the three-headed gatekeeping Cerberus of Supreme Court precedent: *Ashcroft v. Iqbal*, *Clapper v. Amnesty International*, and *City of Los Angeles v. Lyons*. The three cases – dealing with pleading standards, Article III's standing requirements, and the relief available in civil suits – create a high bar for any civil plaintiff seeking to challenge a government surveillance program.

12 Declaration of *Mark Klein*, *Hepting v. AT&T*, 06-cv-0672 (N.D. Cal. 2006), https://www.eff.org/document/public-unredacted-klein-declaration.

13 *EFF's Case against AT&T*, Electronic Frontier Foundation, https://www.eff.org/nsa/hepting (last visited Sept. 9, 2016).

14 NSA *Spying on Americans: Jewel v.* NSA, Electronic Frontier Foundation, https://www.eff.org/cases/jewel (last visited Sept. 9, 2016).

15 Although they have not answered, the plaintiffs were allowed to open discovery just this year – eight years after the litigation began. *See* David Greene, *Big Victory: Judge Pushes* Jewel v. NSA *Forward*, Electronic Frontier Foundation (February 19, 2016), https://www.eff.org/deeplinks/2016/02/big-victory-judge-pushes-jewel-v-nsa-forward.

A *The First Hurdle:* Iqbal

There is little doubt that the Supreme Court's 2009 decision in *Ashcroft v. Iqbal* was a landmark ruling, fundamentally altering the pleading standards for all federal litigation.[16] Surveillance cases are no exception.

The case was brought by a Pakistani immigrant who challenged the basis for his arrest, treatment, and detention by federal authorities. Iqbal alleged he was verbally and physically abused while in federal detention after being swept up in immigration raids following the September 11 attacks. He sued thirty-four current and former federal officials, including high-level federal officials such as the attorney general and the director of the FBI, alleging that they bore ultimate responsibility for the pattern of racial and religious discrimination that led to his detention conditions. It was the claims against these high-level officials that the Supreme Court reviewed. Expounding upon its recent decision in *Twombly*, the Supreme Court articulated the following standard for federal pleadings:

> [A] complaint must contain sufficient factual matter, accepted as true, to "state a claim to relief that is plausible on its face." A claim has facial plausibility when the plaintiff pleads factual content that allows the court to draw the reasonable inference that the defendant is liable for the misconduct alleged. The plausibility standard is not akin to a "probability requirement," but it asks for more than a sheer possibility that a defendant has acted unlawfully. Where a complaint pleads facts that are "merely consistent with" a defendant's liability, it "stops short of the line between possibility and plausibility of 'entitlement to relief.'"

Iqbal unquestionably raised the pleading standard for cases in federal court – especially for individuals challenging illegal government action.[17]

But what does this mean for surveillance cases? As one commentator has recognized, *Iqbal* "rewards access to information."[18] And *knowing* surveillance has occurred, necessary to satisfy *Iqbal*'s requirement of "judicial experience and common sense," can be a daunting task – especially with a government defendant arguing *Iqbal* has not been satisfied.[19] Indeed, the covert nature of surveillance is both its great virtue (to the government) and vice (to those surveilled): at once, surveillance offers "broad and unsuspected governmental incursions into conversational privacy"[20] and yet it "proceeds surreptitiously, [thus] evad[ing] the ordinary checks that constrain abusive law enforcement practices," including resource constraints or public hostility.[21] This informational asymmetry works to keep surveillance plaintiffs out of court.

In some circumstances, *Iqbal* is an efficient and appropriate gatekeeper. A plaintiff suffering delusions about government surveillance is required to do more than allege that the FBI has implanted a chip in his brain. But the line between tinfoil hats, and, say,

16 Adam Liptak, *Supreme Court Ruling Altered Civil Suits, to Detriment of Individuals*, N.Y. Times, May 18, 2015, http://www.nytimes.com/2015/05/19/us/9-11-ruling-by-supreme-court-has-transformed-civil-lawsuits.html.

17 *See* Alexander A. Reinert, *Measuring the Impact of Plausibility Pleading*, 101 Va. L. Rev. 2117 (2015).

18 Liptak, *supra* note16.

19 It is important to note that a government argument that *Iqbal* has not been satisfied is quite different from the government arguing the claims are false or otherwise unsupported. Yet that distinction may blur in the minds of many judges (or their clerks).

20 *United States v. United States District Court* (*Keith Case*), 407 U.S. 297 (1972).

21 Jones, 132 S. Ct. at 955 (Sotomayor, J., concurring).

the claims of EFF in 2006 – that the government had installed surveillance devices on the Internet's fiber-optic backbone and was subjecting the entire nation to surveillance – can be difficult to delineate to a court's satisfaction. Although the disclosures of the past decade have vindicated our position nicely, in 2006, it was not so clear that we were not wearing tinfoil hats.

But the bind for a victim of surveillance *is* clear: how can I prove I have been subjected to government surveillance, sufficient to satisfy *Iqbal*? Of late, one particularly productive vein has been whistle-blowers. Mark Klein provided evidence for EFF (and a host of others) to file suit challenging AT&T's cooperation with the NSA. So, too, with Edward Snowden: his leaks, especially those concerning the NSA's bulk collection of Americans' call records, provided the foundation for a number of suits challenging the program. At other times litigants get lucky, and the government just hands the evidence to them. Inadvertently disclosed documents formed the basis for the charity al-Haramain's lawsuit against the U.S. government: the charity claimed to have received Top Secret documents proving the government had illegally surveilled them.[22] But, generally speaking, plaintiffs need some set of fortunate (or unfortunate) events to occur before they can plausibly allege they have been subject to surveillance.

Today, with the wealth of publicly available information about the scope and nature of government surveillance, *Iqbal* may not be the obstacle it once was. Satisfying a "plausibility" standard about government surveillance in this, the "golden age of surveillance," is likely less difficult than it was a decade ago. However, *Iqbal* remains a bar, especially when considered in conjunction with the Supreme Court's decision in *Clapper v. Amnesty International*.[23]

B *The Second (and Related) Hurdle:* Amnesty

While *Iqbal* worked a sea change in federal pleading requirements, the change to the law of Article III standing by the Supreme Court's decision in *Clapper v. Amnesty International* was far more modest. Indeed, in the term following its decision in *Amnesty*, the Supreme Court appeared to walk back the reach of the case in *Susan B. Anthony List v. Driehaus*.[24] Nevertheless, for surveillance cases, *Amnesty* – itself a surveillance challenge – remains the leading case on the allegations necessary to satisfy Article III standing.

In *Amnesty*, the plaintiffs, a group of nonprofits, criminal defense attorneys, and journalists, initiated a facial challenge to Section 702 of the Foreign Intelligence Surveillance Act, 50 U.S.C. § 1881a, filed the day the law went into effect.[25] The suit was filed before the government *even began* surveillance under the law. Thus, the plaintiffs could only allege "an objectively reasonable likelihood" that, "at some point in the future," "their communications will be acquired under § 1881a." Little was known about the surveillance the government would implement under its new authority, save the generalities that could be gleaned from the face of the statute.

22 Even this, however, was not enough to produce a merits judgment in al-Haramain's favor. The case was ultimately dismissed on the basis of qualified immunity. *Al Haramain Islamic Foundation, Inc. v. Obama*, 690 F. 3d 1089 (9th Cir. 2012).

23 133 S. Ct. 1138 (2013).

24 *Susan B. Anthony v. Driehaus*, 134 S. Ct. 2334 (2014).

25 *Clapper*, 133 S. Ct. at 1146.

In a 5–4 decision, the Supreme Court tailored its standing analysis to injury based on the anticipated future conduct. The Court thus took issue with the plaintiffs' failure to allege an injury that was "certainly impending" as it was only "based on potential future surveillance."[26] The Court laid out what it believed to be a "speculative chain of possibilities" on which the plaintiff's claims were based: (1) whether the government would target communications to which they were parties; (2) whether the government would rely on Section 702 to target those communications; (3) whether the Foreign Intelligence Surveillance Court would authorize surveillance targeting communications of which the plaintiffs were a party; and (4) whether the government would *actually succeed* in intercepting plaintiff's communications.

The plaintiffs' inability to allege that communications had actually been intercepted was critical to the Supreme Court's decision in *Amnesty*. As the Court noted, "Respondents fail to offer any evidence that their communications have been monitored under § 1881a, a failure that substantially undermines their standing theory."[27] Indeed, the *Amnesty* plaintiffs *could not* provide that evidence (or even make those allegations): the lawsuit was filed before government surveillance under Section 702 began. At best, the *Amnesty* plaintiffs could only argue that something might happen in the future.

Amnesty thus requires, at a minimum, allegations that plaintiffs themselves have been subjected to the surveillance they are challenging. Taken in combination with *Iqbal*'s heightened pleading requirements, the two cases can erect a formidable bar to challenging surveillance programs.

Wikimedia v. NSA perfectly illustrates the toxic combination that *Iqbal* and *Amnesty* pose for plaintiffs challenging surveillance programs. In *Wikimedia*, a group of plaintiffs, including Wikimedia (the parent organization of Wikipedia, one of the most visited Web sites in the world), brought a challenge to the NSA's "upstream" surveillance – the interception of content as at flows through the nation's fiber-optic backbone – under Section 702 of the Foreign Intelligence Surveillance Act (FISA). Wikimedia alleged that its communications had *actually* been subject to surveillance by the NSA, on the basis of (1) evidence that the NSA was intercepting massive quantities of communications directly from the fiber-optic cables; (2) the fact that Wikipedia was responsible for a vast quantity of Internet communications around the world. Thus, as a result of those two facts – the NSA's interception of massive quantities of communications and Wikimedia's production of massive quantities of communications – there was almost a statistical certainty that *at least one* of Wikimedia's communications would have been intercepted through the program. Plaintiffs were also able to point to internal NSA slides, leaked by Edward Snowden, that bore Wikipedia's name and described why the NSA was "interested in HTTP" traffic.[28]

The plaintiffs' claims were undeniably *plausible*. And they alleged their communications had *actually* been subjected to surveillance, a fact the *Amnesty* Court found conspicuously absent. Nevertheless, the district court dismissed the case. The court viewed its task, in assessing whether standing and pleading requirements had been satisfied, as follows: "[A] complaint alleges facts that plausibly establish standing only if the

26 *Id.* at 1155.
27 *Id.* at 1148 (emphasis added).
28 *Why Are We Interested in HTTP?* ACLU, https://www.aclu.org/files/natsec/nsa/20140722/Why%20Are%20We%20Interested%20in%20HTTP.pdf.

'well-pleaded allegations' allow for a 'reasonable inference,' rather than a 'sheer possibility,' that the plaintiff has satisfied" the elements of standing.[29] The court then parsed every allegation in the complaint, weighing facts and evidence to conclude that *every* allegation amounted to speculation and that *none* was entitled to the "reasonable inference" available at the motion to dismiss stage.

The court described plaintiffs' allegations – based on government documents – as dependent on "suppositions and speculation, with no basis in fact, about how the NSA implements upstream surveillance."[30] In effect, the court required the plaintiffs to prove their case – to know precisely how the NSA implements its upstream surveillance and that plaintiffs' communications were intercepted – at the pleading stage.

Were this standard imposed on all litigation, it would eliminate much of the federal docket. Discovery and trials would be unnecessary; all cases could simply be disposed of through dispositive motions at the outset of the case. But, obviously, this is not how federal litigation operates. Some amount of uncertainty – of proof, of damages, or otherwise – at the pleading stage is unavoidable, yet the standard imposed by the *Wikimedia* court in applying *Iqbal* and *Amnesty* – that an individual must not only know she was surveilled but also know precisely how the surveillance operated – would essentially render most civil surveillance challenges a dead letter.

The Ninth Circuit's decision in *Jewel* – decided after *Iqbal* but before the Supreme Court's decision in *Amnesty*[31] – stands in contrast to the district court's treatment of *Wikimedia*. In *Jewel*, the district court had dismissed the case *sua sponte* for lack of standing, finding that Jewel's complaint alleging mass surveillance of AT&T customers by the NSA amounted to a "generalized grievance" suitable for resolution in the political branches of government, not the courts. Reviewing that decision, the Ninth Circuit accepted as true all well-pleaded allegations in the complaint and drew all reasonable inferences in the plaintiff's favor, as courts normally do at the motion to dismiss stage. On that basis, the court then reversed, finding that Jewel had adequately alleged facts sufficient to establish her standing.

Conspicuously, the court never cited *Iqbal*. But *Jewel* should have survived, regardless: the plaintiffs had documentary evidence and eyewitness descriptions of the surveillance configurations in use, and, as AT&T customers themselves, could plausibly allege that their communications had passed through those configurations. And that is all that is required.

Nevertheless, as *Wikimedia* shows, the obstacles for surveillance challenges at the outset can be substantial. *Iqbal* and *Clapper* work together to create a formidable bar for plaintiffs seeking to challenge surveillance programs.

C *The Third Hurdle:* Lyons, *Equitable Relief, and Damages*

Even if a civil plaintiff manages to navigate through *Amnesty* and *Iqbal*, a final problem remains: seeking appropriate relief. There are two ways the government can prevent a

29 *Wikimedia v.* NSA, 143 F. Supp. 3d 344, 351 (D. Md. 2015) (citing *Ashcroft v. Iqbal*, 556 U.S. 662 (2009)).
30 *Id.* at 356.
31 In fact, the Ninth Circuit distinguished *Jewel* from *Amnesty*, then at the Second Circuit. The Court concluded: "Jewel has much stronger allegations of concrete and particularized injury than did the plaintiffs in *Amnesty International*." *Jewel v.* NSA, 673 F.3d 902, 910–11 (9th Cir. 2011).

decision on the merits through the relief requested: first, through the limited availability of equitable relief and, second, through qualified and sovereign immunity.

Equitable relief in surveillance cases presents a particular difficulty because of the Supreme Court's decision in *City of Los Angeles v. Lyons*. In *Lyons*, the plaintiff had been choked by Los Angeles police during a traffic stop, and he sought damages as well as declaratory and injunctive relief enjoining the police department from using choke holds in the future. In a 5–4 decision, the Court determined that, despite already having been subjected to the choke hold, Lyons lacked standing to obtain injunctive and declaratory relief because he had not, and in the Court's view could not, adequately alleged a fear or risk of being subject to a choke hold again *in the future*. For the Court, it was not enough that Lyons had already been placed in a choke hold, causing damage to his larynx; that African Americans, such as Lyons, were routinely subject to choke holds; and that some had died as a result. Instead, the Court wrote:

> In order to establish an actual controversy in this case, Lyons would have had not only to allege that he would have another encounter with the police but also to make the incredible assertion either, (1) that all police officers in Los Angeles always choke any citizen with whom they happen to have an encounter, whether for the purpose of arrest, issuing a citation or for questioning or, (2) that the City ordered or authorized police officers to act in such manner. Although Count V alleged that the City authorized the use of the control holds in situations where deadly force was not threatened, it did not indicate why Lyons might be realistically threatened by police officers who acted within the strictures of the City's policy.[32]

Plainly, the Court set a high bar for civil plaintiffs seeking to obtain injunctive and declaratory relief. And this high bar, in the surveillance context, can be difficult to overcome: it requires plaintiffs both to know that illegal surveillance was conducted against them and to know that it will happen again in the future. As described previously, it can be difficult, if not impossible, to be certain that one was subject to surveillance; that difficulty is only magnified when a plaintiff must show that the surveillance is likely to be ongoing or occur again. In other words, to obtain injunctive relief against the government, two circumstances are required: (1) a plaintiff must know the surveillance has occurred and is ongoing and (2) the government must also want to continue that surveillance. That is a rare combination.

Somewhat reassuringly (and strangely), perhaps, equitable relief is most likely available when the surveillance program being challenged is extraordinarily broad. Once evidence emerges of a sufficiently broad surveillance program – such as the NSA's bulk collection of Americans' phone records – there is a sound basis to believe that the surveillance will later sweep in a plaintiff's communications. Indeed, two challenges to the NSA's call record program serve as a useful example of the principle, as well as demonstrating the importance of including a claim for monetary damages.

In *ACLU v. Clapper*, the ACLU sought only injunctive and declaratory relief – cessation of the program and the destruction of the phone records. In contrast, in *First Unitarian Church of Los Angeles v. NSA*, another case brought by EFF on behalf of a coalition of advocacy groups, the plaintiffs sought both the same injunctive and declaratory relief – cessation of the program and destruction of records – *and* damages for

[32] *City of Los Angeles v. Lyons*, 461 U.S. 95, 105–06 (1983).

violations of the Stored Communications Act. The *ACLU* plaintiffs obtained an important victory from the Second Circuit when that court determined the program exceeded its statutory authorization, but the Court refused to enjoin the program pending congressional review. Ultimately, Congress amended the law and ended the program. With nothing left to enjoin, the ACLU's case reached its productive end.[33] However, the only precedent from the case is a decision concerning a statute that is no longer on the books. In contrast, the damages claims in *First Unitarian* live on and at least offer a possibility (however slim) of a merits decision with possible enduring value – i.e., a decision that the program, as operated, violated the Stored Communications Act.

Indeed, in *Lyons*, the Supreme Court took solace in the fact that the plaintiff still had damages claims against the City of Los Angeles, and that those damages claims would inevitably invite a decision about the legality of the police choke holds. But whatever the likelihood of damages claims in choke hold cases, surveillance cases present unusual and at times impossible obstacles. This is so for two reasons: qualified immunity and sovereign immunity.

First, in suits brought under Section 1983 alleging violations of constitutional rights,[34] qualified immunity blocks damages claims for all but the most clear-cut violations of established constitutional law. Under *Harlow v. Fitzgerald*, civil damages are unavailable for violations of the law unless the surveillance "violate[s] clearly established statutory or constitutional rights of which a reasonable person would have known."[35] This opens up government officials to liability – but only for surveillance techniques or practices that have already been "clearly" adjudicated to violate the law. For new surveillance techniques or surveillance programs that have remained untested in the courts, qualified immunity offers yet another opportunity for government argument: damages are unavailable because the program had not been "clearly established" to be illegal, either because the program or technique was new and uncertain or because it was kept sufficiently secret that its illegality could not have been previously established.[36] An example may be helpful: imagine, before the Supreme Court's decision in *Kyllo* – which held that warrantless use of thermal imaging technology to monitor a marijuana greenhouse inside a home violated the Fourth Amendment – that an innocent bystander had been wrongly subjected to warrantless FBI surveillance of the heat signatures of her house. Without an apparent statutory restriction on the use of the technology (and an accompanying waiver of sovereign immunity), the person could only resort to a § 1983 suit to vindicate the encroachment on her constitutional rights. However, without *Kyllo*, a

33 I do not mean to suggest the ACLU's case was not substantial in shaping positive surveillance reform. In fact, the Second Circuit's decision forced Congress's hand either to approve the program explicitly, to alter it substantially, or to end it – a move that, absent the Second Circuit's decision, may not have happened.

34 42 U.S.C. § 1983 (2012).

35 *Harlow v. Fitzgerald*, 457 U.S. 800, 818 (1982).

36 *See Pearson v. Callahan*, 555 U.S. 223 (2009) (rolling back the requirement, established in *Saucier v. Katz*, that courts should first determine whether allegations that a violation of a constitutional right occurred). Before *Pearson*, courts were to employ a rigid two-step analysis in addressing qualified immunity cases: step one required an assessment of the constitutionality of the action. Step two required determining whether the constitutional right that was infringed was "clearly established." *Pearson* eliminated that mandatory framework, allowing courts to apply the analysis in any order they choose. As a general matter, constitutional avoidance would generally require a federal court to look first to the second factor, especially in cases involving novel or otherwise untested surveillance techniques.

plaintiff would have an almost insurmountable obstacle in establishing that such surveillance violated "clearly established" Fourth Amendment law. Indeed, the likelihood that a court would even reach the merits of the surveillance is low: deciding that the technique had not been clearly adjudicated to be illegal is all a court would need to grant a dismissal.

With qualified immunity blocking damages claims for all but the most flagrant (and clearly established) constitutional violations, the primary remaining possibility for damages against the federal government arises via explicit waivers of sovereign immunity. Fortunately, federal law provides one. Section 2712 of Title 18 of the United States Code offers a broad waiver of sovereign immunity for any "willful violation" of certain significant federal surveillance statutes – the Wiretap Act, the Stored Communications Act, and some parts of the Foreign Intelligence Surveillance Act.[37] However, despite this broad waiver, since Section 2712's passage in 2001 as part of the PATRIOT Act, I am not aware of any court's holding the government liable for such damages. I will leave it for the reader to decide whether that is a testament to the unflinching legality of government surveillance, or to the obstacles to reaching merits decisions that I have described.

II Criminal Cases

Criminal cases provide the tried and true method of regulating surveillance through litigation – particularly suppression motions tied to violations of the Fourth Amendment. Almost without exception, every significant Supreme Court decision imposing Fourth Amendment limitations on surveillance has arisen in the context of a criminal case. *Katz v. United States* and *Berger v. New York*, two landmark 1967 Supreme Court decisions on wiretapping and the Fourth Amendment, and more recently *Jones* and *Riley*, to name just a few – all were criminal prosecutions, and all arose from attempts to suppress the fruits of the government's surveillance. Many of the obstacles to challenging government surveillance that exist in the civil context – for example, standing – are generally less prominent in the criminal context;[38] some obstacles – for example, knowing that the surveillance occurred – are diminished but still exist; and some obstacles – such as the government's power to shape the law through selective appeals – are even more pronounced. Overall, and despite its obstacles, litigation in criminal cases provides a relatively robust method for regulating government surveillance.

[37] 18 U.S.C. § 2712 (2012).

[38] This, of course, is not to say that the standing concerns never exist. Standing may still be an obstacle for Fourth Amendment purposes in some cases, *see United States v. Payner*, 447 U.S. 727 (1980), although how such an issue might manifest in a surveillance case is unclear. And, as with civil cases, there are ways for courts to avoid reaching difficult constitutional issues: the "good faith" exception, harmless error, or other numerous exceptions to the exclusionary rule all allow courts to avoid addressing the legality of the challenged surveillance. However, for a variety of reasons, courts are more likely to address the constitutional questions in criminal cases. For one, courts may believe criminal cases have a more prominent role to play in law enforcement norm shaping than civil cases. Second, because these exceptions are often contingent on a finding of illegality in the first place, courts may still be required to address the legality of the surveillance, even if the evidence obtained from the surveillance is ultimately not suppressed. Finally, perhaps in light of the actual liberty interests at stake, courts may be less inclined to dodge difficult questions than in the civil context.

A *Bad Facts, Bad Law, and the DOJ's Strategic Appeal Process*

One limitation to using litigation in criminal cases to shape surveillance regulation positively is a common concern for all attorneys: bad facts making bad law. And, compared with civil cases challenging surveillance – where plaintiffs are often relatively sympathetic, civic-minded individuals attempting to vindicate their rights in court[39] – criminal cases are full of bad facts. Those bad facts, invariably, test judges' willingness to apply the protections guaranteed by the Constitution and other laws.

To give just one example, in early 2016, hundreds of federal prosecutions were brought across the country, all stemming from the FBI's investigation of a website hosting child pornography.[40] To investigate the site, the FBI delivered malware to search hundreds, if not thousands, of computers located around the world. This investigation easily accounted for the largest deployment of malware by a U.S. domestic law enforcement agency in the country's history. And all those searches, of thousands of computers located throughout the world, were based on a single warrant, issued from the Eastern District of Virginia.

Plainly, such a vast quantity of novel searches raises constitutional questions. Executing those searches on the basis of a single warrant raises even graver questions. And yet, the decisions on the motions to suppress have managed to reconcile those searches with the Fourth Amendment, in some cases bending current Fourth Amendment law to accommodate the FBI's actions. For example, one judge went so far as to conclude that the defendant lacked a reasonable expectation of privacy in his *personal computer*, located *inside his home*.[41] Although almost assuredly incorrect as a matter of law (it is difficult to understand how that conclusion could be squared with *Riley*, which requires a warrant to search a cell phone),[42] the decision is illustrative: judges, in an entirely human reaction to gruesome facts,[43] are loath to interpret the Constitution in a manner that allows (alleged) criminals to escape punishment. That, in turn, puts a thumb on the scale for the government in the development of surveillance-related case law.

A secondary consideration is the government's ability to take appeals selectively, versus a defendant's near-universal interest in appealing and preserving appealable issues. A few bad district court decisions, here and there, are generally of little consequence to the federal government. If a relatively low-level offender has evidence suppressed on the basis of illegal surveillance, the government might well decide that an appeal, given the particular facts of the case, carries greater risk to law enforcement by broadly limiting the ability to use the technique in question.[44]

39 *See, e.g.*, Second Amended Complaint for Constitutional and Statutory Violations, Seeking declaratory and Injunctive Relief, *First Unitarian Church of Los Angeles v. NSA* (N.D. Ca. Aug. 20, 2014) (No. 4:13-cv-03287), 2014 WL 4693046.

40 *See, e.g.*, Joseph Cox, *The FBI's 'Unprecedented' Hacking Campaign Targeted over a Thousand Computers*, Vice (Jan. 5, 2016), https://motherboard.vice.com/read/the-fbis-unprecedented-hacking-campaign-targeted-over-a-thousand-computers.

41 *United States v. Matish*, No. 4:16cr16, 2016 WL 3129203 (E.D. Va Jun. 2, 2016).

42 *Riley v. California*, 134 S. Ct. 2473 (2014)

43 And the facts were, indeed, gruesome. The defendant was alleged to have downloaded and received child pornography involving bestiality.

44 The decisions of states to appeal suppression decisions can also affect the development of federal surveillance law. They also throw an element of uncertainty into DOJ's ability to control outcomes. *See Riley v. California*, 134 S. Ct. 2473 (2014).

Take, for example, a case from the Eastern District of Washington: there, the government subjected the target of its investigation to warrantless video surveillance from a camera installed on a utility pole across from the suspect's rural home.[45] The camera ran twenty-four hours a day for more than a month and ultimately captured the suspect and his friends taking target practice, shooting at an empty beer bottle in the front yard. On the basis of that video and the government's suspicion that the suspect was residing in the United States illegally, agents obtained a warrant to search for evidence of the crime of being an alien in possession of a firearm. The search of the home uncovered a few guns (presumably, a not-uncommon occurrence for a rural area) as well as a small quantity of methamphetamine. Ultimately, in later suppression motions, the district court found that twenty-four-hour, warrantless video surveillance for six weeks violated the Fourth Amendment and suppressed the evidence forming the basis for the initial search warrant. And that, in turn, required dismissal.

At this point, the government had a choice: it could appeal the suppression order, receive a positive ruling from the Ninth Circuit, and reinitiate its prosecution. But such an appeal has a downside risk: presented with a relatively innocuous crime and relatively egregious warrantless surveillance, the Ninth Circuit could affirm the district court's order, thereby severely curtailing the government's use of warrantless video surveillance throughout the Ninth Circuit. Or, the government could let a relatively-low level offender evade prosecution and go about its business of warrantless pole-camera surveillance. It should be no surprise that, in this case, the government chose the latter.[46] And the federal government does this with regularity: picking its surveillance battles carefully, with an eye toward preserving its capabilities and avoiding judicial review of its techniques.[47] The government has dropped prosecutions entirely or offered favorable plea deals to avoid merits decisions concerning surveillance.[48]

To be sure, the government's ability to take appeals selectively is also present in the civil context. However, because civil litigants usually seek an end to surveillance programs or techniques as their relief, the government is often *compelled* to appeal an adverse ruling – solely to preserve their ability to use the program or technique.

On the other hand, in criminal cases, convicted defendants appeal. And they appeal without regard to the facts – both of the crime and the surveillance. This is not to say defendants should not appeal; of course, attorneys have ethical obligations to raise meritorious issues on appeal, and defendants are rightfully interested in contesting their convictions. But the defense bar's inability to take strategic appeals, in contrast to the

45 *United States v. Vargas*, 13-cr-6025 (E.D. Wa. Dec. 15, 2014) (ECF No. 106).

46 The consequences for the government were especially low in *Vargas*: the defendant remained in custody, and immigration proceedings that would ultimately lead to his deportation were initiated.

47 Indeed, as described previously, *supra* note 3, in light of the relative paucity of information likely available to the FBI on the San Bernardino shooter's iPhone, many observers believe it was a carefully selected test case – the FBI's equivalent of impact litigation. And, when public opinion and scrutiny seemed to turn against them (or, at least, not overwhelmingly for them), the FBI withdrew its case. Notably, it did the same in a similar case, pending in Brooklyn, with far less fanfare. *See* Kevin McCoy & Jon Swartz, *Feds Gain Access to iPhone in N.Y. Drug Case, Drop Apple Pressure*, USA Today, Apr. 23, 2016, http://www.usatoday.com/story/money/2016/04/22/feds-gain-access-iphone-drug-case-drop-apple-pressure/83397224/.

48 Law enforcement use of Stingrays – a type of cell-site simulator – offer another high-profile example of government prosecutors' offering favorable plea deals or opting to dismiss charges altogether rather than disclose information about the technique. This practice is discussed in more detail later.

government, tends to distort results and, thus, the efficacy of regulating surveillance through criminal litigation.

Somewhat perversely, the best hope for positively shaping surveillance law through criminal litigation requires (1) relatively egregious surveillance coupled with a relatively innocuous crime, (2) a district court denial of a motion to suppress, (3) a conviction, and (4) an appellate reversal. At that point, the government is presented with a stark choice: can it live with the bad decision at the appellate level, or should it petition for the Supreme Court's review and roll the dice with the highest court? In *Warshak*, the government opted against seeking Supreme Court review, choosing to fight the battle over Fourth Amendment protections in email and other records stored with third parties in another – and future – case.[49] In *Jones*, it gambled, and as a result it has lost the ability to place GPS trackers on cars without a warrant.

B *Discovering the Use of Surveillance and Government Attempts to Protect Its "Sources"*

Although criminal defendants are far better positioned than civil litigants to receive information about government surveillance techniques that lead to their arrests, defendants are by no means assured of receiving that notice. In many instances, the government takes affirmative steps to conceal new surveillance techniques or programs from judges and defendants. Thus, even when a defendant was subject to surveillance and would have standing to challenge that surveillance, government efforts to obscure the technique work to shield it from legal review.

In the domestic law enforcement context, one recent, illustrative example involves law enforcement's use of "StingRays" to locate and track suspects. StingRays are a common name[50] given to "cell-site simulators" or "IMSI catchers" – essentially, devices that serve as a kind of "mock" cell tower, tricking cell phones in a given area to connect to them, and thereby allowing police to locate and track cell phones – and, by extension, users – nearby.

Law enforcement agencies across the country – at both the state and federal levels – initially took great pains to avoid disclosing their use of StingRays. And for good reason: StingRays are blunt instruments of surveillance. StingRays trick *all* cell phones in a given location into connecting to the device. Thus, law enforcement is vacuuming up location information about a great number of nonsuspects in its attempt to locate an individual. The use (and especially the warrantless use) of StingRays is thus susceptible to Fourth Amendment challenge.

To avoid those challenges, federal and local law enforcement agencies entered into nondisclosure agreements (NDAs) as a condition of the purchase of their device – either when purchasing the devices from the FBI or from the manufacturer itself. One such NDA contained this language:

[49] It also preserved its right to obtain emails without a warrant outside the Sixth Circuit. As noted earlier, however, that ability is now largely illusory: relying on *Warshak*, most major providers now require a warrant for law enforcement access to email.

[50] Stingray is actually a brand name, used by the Harris Corporation, for the device. However, it has become a shorthand for the device itself.

> To ensure that [] wireless collection equipment/technology continues to be available for use by the law enforcement community, the equipment/technology and any information related to its functions, operation, and use shall be protected from potential compromise by precluding disclosure of this information to the public in any manner including b[ut] not limited to: in press release, in court documents, during judicial hearings, or during other public forums or proceedings.[51]

The NDAs thus were intended to preclude public disclosure, to "ensure that [] wireless collection equipment/technology continues to be available for use by the law enforcement community." The collateral effect, of course, is that the use of cell-site simulators in criminal cases has been unchallenged in many cases.

Law enforcement sometimes uses a process known as "parallel construction" to obscure the source of its information and, thus, insulate surveillance techniques, such as StingRays, from judicial review. Parallel construction works as follows: agents "recreate" or manufacture "an investigative trail to effectively cover up where the information originated."[52] As one former federal agent described the DEA's process of laundering information obtained from surveillance programs: "You'd be told only, 'Be at a certain truck stop at a certain time and look for a certain vehicle.' And so we'd alert the state police to find an excuse to stop that vehicle, and then have [a] drug dog search it."[53] Obviously, it is impossible for a defendant to challenge surveillance he does not know about.

Challenging surveillance in criminal cases thus not only requires scrupulous adherence by prosecutors to their duty to disclose relevant and material evidence; in many cases, it depends on affirmative investigation by prosecutors to understand and uncover the techniques used to identify and surveil a defendant. This is a problem former–Solicitor General Donald Verrilli learned about firsthand. In his defense of the government's standing position in *Amnesty*, discussed eaqrlier, Verrilli argued the Supreme Court need not worry about insulating Section 702 of FISA from judicial review, because criminal defendants would have standing to challenge the law.[54] As Verrilli noted, the government was required to give notice of its intent to use information "obtained or derived from" surveillance under the FISA Amendments Act. The Supreme Court, in its opinion, took comfort in that requirement and in Verrilli's assertion that it would be honored. Yet, in 2013 – five years after the law was passed – no criminal defendant had ever received notice of surveillance.[55]

In the fallout after the Snowden revelations, it became apparent that the government had interpreted its disclosure obligations in an insupportably crabbed way – effectively rendering Section 702 surveillance unchallengeable, despite the fact that millions, if not billions, of communications were being collected under the law annually. Ultimately, the government reexamined its policies and provided notice to a handful of defendants

[51] *Maryland v. Andrews*, 134 A.3d 324, 338 (Md. Ct. Spec. App. 2016)

[52] Jon Schiffman & Kristina Cooke, *Exclusive: U.S. Directs Agents to Cover Up Program Used to Investigate Americans*, REUTERS (Aug. 5, 2013) http://www.reuters.com/article/us-dea-sod-idUSBRE97409R20130805.

[53] *Id.*

[54] Adam Liptak, *A Secret Surveillance Program Proves Challengeable in Theory Only*, N.Y. TIMES, July 15, 2013, http://www.nytimes.com/2013/07/16/us/double-secret-surveillance.html.

[55] Charlie Savage, *Federal Prosecutors, in a Policy Shift, Cite Warrantless Wiretaps as Evidence*, N.Y. TIMES, Oct. 26, 2013, http://www.nytimes.com/2013/10/27/us/federal-prosecutors-in-a-policy-shift-cite-warrantless-wiretaps-as-evidence.html.

across the country – opening the door to a constitutional challenge to the law.[56] To this day, however, it is not clear what prompted the about-face, or particularly how the DOJ interprets its disclosure obligations in the 702 context.[57]

Even receiving "notice" that Section 702 surveillance was used in a criminal case has its limits. Thus far, it has only offered the opportunity to bring a general constitutional challenge to the law, divorced from any specific facts, such as how the surveillance was carried out, whose communications were "targeted," or the content of the particular intercepted communications. The government has never provided access to any information obtained through the surveillance, nor information about the circumstances of the surveillance or the particular techniques used. Indeed, in the first and only instance in FISA's four-decade history when a court ordered information disclosed to a defendant, the order was reversed on appeal.[58]

Despite the vagaries of criminal litigation and the obstacles to discovering surveillance undertaken during the criminal investigation, criminal cases offer strong opportunities to shape surveillance law. The questions of standing, mootness, and immunity that plague civil litigation are either absent entirely or less prominent in the criminal context, offering a time-tested method of shaping surveillance policy through litigation.

The Future of Surveillance Litigation

Regulating surveillance through civil suits is a litigation minefield, littered with well-intentioned plaintiffs suffering concrete harms, but rarely resulting in positive judicial outcomes. Challenging surveillance through suppression motions in criminal cases, the time tested method of checking surveillance, more frequently results in important victories, but suffers from the downside risk of generating bad law from bad facts – a problem only exacerbated by the government's ability to take appeals selectively.

But there is a third way. And, coincidentally, it is where this article began: with companies challenging government surveillance practices. In the digital age, when billions of users around the world entrust our most sensitive information and communications with third parties, this type of surveillance litigation – a type of hybrid between criminal and civil challenges – is invariably the future of positively shaping surveillance norms through litigation.

I describe these types of corporate challenges as "hybrids" because, while still squarely civil legal challenges, they often arise in the context of an ongoing national security or criminal investigation, and thus share some similarities with litigation in criminal cases. Because the government relies on these companies to accomplish their surveillance, many of the threshold obstacles present in civil challenges – pleading standards, standing,[59] and relief – typically pose no obstacle: the company has already received an order or a request from the government to conduct the surveillance and a company challenging the order is

[56] Patrick Toomey, *Why Aren't Criminal Defendants Getting Notice in Section 702 Surveillance – Again?* JustSecurity (Dec. 11, 2015), https://www.justsecurity.org/28256/arent-criminal-defendants-notice-section-702-surveillance-again.

[57] *Id.*

[58] *See United States v. Daoud*, 755 F.3d 479 (7th Cir. 2014).

[59] Standing, of course, can still present an obstacle in hybrid challenges. Even in a case when a company moves to quash legal process targeting one of its users, a company may not be able to assert every legal basis for resisting the process. In particular, raising Fourth Amendment claims on behalf of a user may

seeking to avoid that compliance. Thus, in many respects, these kinds of corporate challenges are more akin to criminal cases: indeed, these types of challenges frequently arise in the course of ongoing criminal investigations. And while hybrid challenges inherently have the concreteness typical of criminal challenges, they generally lack (or at least mitigate) the ugly facts present in typical criminal cases. Instead of suspected (or convicted) drug dealers, child pornographers, and terrorists challenging the surveillance, these hybrid challenges see some of America's largest and most respected companies (and their expensive lawyers) raising legal concerns. For all these reasons, hybrid challenges may offer some of the best opportunities for positively shaping surveillance law going forward.

The history of corporate challenges to government surveillance is not an illustrious one.[60] In fact, for many telecommunications companies, cooperation – not principled opposition – has served as the defining characteristic of their approach to government surveillance.[61] Indeed, for many companies, facilitating government surveillance serves as just another revenue stream.[62]

But the Internet, expanding global markets and customer bases, and – especially – the revelations in 2013 concerning the NSA's almost limitless reach into global online communications, all have shifted companies' approaches to government surveillance. Today, guaranteeing customer privacy is a bottom line issue for American tech giants. Their capacity to build global customer bases hinges on their ability to convince users around the world that the United States government does not have unfettered access to their customers' communications. And, to protect that bottom line, companies have increasingly relied on litigation to protect their users.

Recent examples abound, including companies challenging the constitutionality of the Protect America Act in litigation before the Foreign Intelligence Surveillance Court (FISC) and its court of review,[63] companies challenging the constitutionality of gag orders associated with National Security Letters[64] and other forms of national security[65] and domestic surveillance process,[66] and numerous others.[67]

prove vexing. Some courts have allowed companies to bring Fourth Amendment claims on their users' behalf. *See* In re Directives, 551 F.3d 1004 (FISCR 2008); *United States v. Golden Valley Elec. Assn.*, 689 F.3d 1108, 1116 (9th Cir. 2012); In re Verizon Internet Services, 257 F. Supp. 2d 244, 248 (D.D.C. 2003), *rev'd on other grounds*, 351 F.3d 1229 (D.C. Cir. 2003) ("The relationship between an Internet service provider and its subscribers is the type of relationship courts have found will ensure that issues will be 'concrete and sharply presented'"). Under any circumstances, courts *should* allow companies to stand in the shoes of their users: these companies easily fit within the recognized exception for third party standing. *See Powers v. Ohio*, 499 U.S. 400, 411 (1991).

60 There are some examples from the past of telephone companies standing up for customers. *See United States v. New York Telephone Co.*, 434 U.S. 159 (1977); *see also* Brief in Support of Petitioners' Contention, *Olmstead v. United States*, 277 U.S. 438 (1927) (No. 493, 532, and 533), https://www.washingtonpost.com/news/volokh-conspiracy/wp-content/uploads/sites/14/2016/07/Olmstead-v.-U.S._Amici-Brief_Telephone-Companies.pdf?tid=a_inl.

61 Julia Angwin, Charlie Savage, Jeff Larson, Henrik Moltke, Laura Poitras, & James Risen, *AT&T Helped U.S. Spy on Internet on a Vast Scale*, N.Y. Times, Aug. 15, 2015, http://www.nytimes.com/2015/08/16/us/politics/att-helped-nsa-spy-on-an-array-of-internet-traffic.html.

62 *Id.*

63 In re Directives, 551 F.3d 1004 (FISCR 2008).

64 In re National Security Letter, 930 F.Supp.2d 1064 (N.D. Cal. 2013).

65 *Twitter v. Holder*, 14-cv-04480, 2016 WL 1729999 (N.D. Cal. May 2, 2015).

66 Steve Lohr, *Microsoft Sues Justice Department to Protest Electronic Gag Orders*, N.Y. Times, Apr. 14, 2016, http://www.nytimes.com/2016/04/15/technology/microsoft-sues-us-over-orders-barring-it-from-revealing-surveillance.html.

67 *United States v. Microsoft*, No. 14–2985 2016 WL 3770056 (2nd Cir. Jul. 14, 2014).

Nevertheless, these hybrid challenges are unlikely to serve as a complete substitute for other challenges. For evidence, one need look no further than the surveillance challenges to the NSA's upstream surveillance. *Ex parte* judicial review of the program in the Foreign Intelligence Surveillance Court has failed to yield an exacting review, no criminal defendant has ever been informed that his communications were intercepted through such surveillance, and the telecommunications companies facilitating the NSA's surveillance – AT&T and Verizon, for example – have shown no interest in challenging its legality. Yet, upstream surveillance – with its electronic sorting and sifting of billions of Americans' international communications – represents one of the most sweeping surveillance programs ever instituted domestically. It invariably has touched almost every American's communication, yet, to date, no court has ever adjudicated its legality. Challenges to upstream surveillance, such as *Jewel* and *Wikimedia*, remain critical.

Despite the difficulties described here, both civil and criminal litigation function as an imperfect check on overzealous government surveillance. Courts should be cautious about pushing any of these kinds of challenges outside the reach of judicial review.

25 Legislative Regulation of Government Surveillance

Christopher Slobogin*

Most of the law governing surveillance is found in legislation. This is so even in the United States (the focus of this chapter),[1] where the usual source of regulation for traditional police investigative techniques is not statutory but rather judicial interpretation of the Fourth Amendment's prohibition on unreasonable searches and seizures. As other chapters in this book describe in detail, the U.S. Supreme Court has decided that neither nontrespassory surveillance of public activities nor efforts to obtain information about an individual from third parties implicates the Fourth Amendment. Legislatures have stepped in to fill this vacuum. Furthermore, even when the Fourth Amendment does apply to surveillance – as is the case with nonconsensual interception of private communications via phone or computer – Congress's tendency to devise rules that are more protective than anything the Fourth Amendment requires has meant that legislation is the dominant regulatory mechanism in those settings as well.[2]

This chapter first outlines the most important federal surveillance statutes in the United States and a sampling of representative state legislation, organized under three categories: interception of communications, physical surveillance, and accessing of surveillance records. It then discusses the advantages and disadvantages of regulating surveillance through legislation rather than judicial decision, and through state or local laws rather than through federal legislation. Finally, it contends that, if legislation is to be the principal means of regulating the government's surveillance activities, law enforcement agencies should also have to adhere to administrative law principles in implementing that legislation.

I Significant Surveillance Legislation

The first major surveillance statutes focused on interception of phone communications. These statutes were amended as other forms of communication developed. Legislation has also authorized government surveillance of physical movements, usually limited to those that occur in spaces open to the public. Finally, statutes have authorized access to

* Milton Underwood Professor of Law, Vanderbilt University Law School.

1 In the absence of strong traditions of judicial review, other countries have relied on statutory law as a means of regulating surveillance to an even greater extent than the United States, although recent decisions by the European Court of Human Rights have significantly changed the dynamic in Europe. *See, e.g.*, *Secretary of State for the Home Department v. Watson and Others*, C-698/15, Court of Justice of the European Union, Dec. 21, 2016 (holding unlawful under the European Convention on Human Rights warrantless bulk collection of data).

2 *See* Part I.A.

records held by third parties that contain data about communications, physical movements, or other activities; although this type of investigation does not monitor citizens in real time, it is another method of covert information gathering about the population, and thus has sometimes been called "transaction surveillance."[3] There follows a brief description of legislation governing these three types of surveillance.

A *Interception of Communications*

Long before the Supreme Court had anything to say about surveillance, state legislatures were prohibiting tapping of telegraph lines and telephones, and the Justice Department also banned the practice.[4] While the U.S. Supreme Court's first case involving electronic surveillance, decided in 1928, refused to apply the Fourth Amendment unless the surveillance was effected through a physical trespass,[5] Congress later passed the Federal Communications Act of 1934, which prohibited all nonconsensual interception of communications.[6] Under the act even a warrant was insufficient authorization; unless one of the parties to the communication consented, eavesdropping was illegal. Although throughout the 1940s, 1950s, and 1960s the FBI and the Treasury Department continued to conduct nonconsensual wiretaps,[7] the act, as interpreted by the Court, required exclusion of evidence thereby obtained in any federal case.[8] Some state courts also followed this practice, while others accepted such evidence, under authority of statutes allowing interception of communications under certain circumstances.[9]

All of these practices underwent substantial change in the late 1960s, beginning with the Supreme Court's decision in *Katz v. United States*.[10] That case focused Fourth Amendment analysis on privacy rather than trespass, in the course of holding that warrantless bugging of a phone booth was unconstitutional. Within the same year the Court decided *Berger v. New York*,[11] which found New York's electronic surveillance statute deficient because, inter alia, it did not require probable cause that a particular offense had been committed, did not require a particularized description of the types of conversations to be seized, and did not place limits on the length of the surveillance.

In response to uncertainty about the scope of the Communications Act and to *Katz* and *Berger*, Congress enacted Title III of the Omnibus Crime Control and Safe Streets Act of 1968 (Title III).[12] Title III prohibits the "interception" of wire and oral communications

3 *See* Christopher Slobogin, Privacy at Risk: The New Government Surveillance and the Fourth Amendment 3 (2007).
4 *See Berger v. New York*, 388 U.S. 41, 45 (1967) (state laws); Walter F. Murphy, Wiretapping on Trial: A Case Study in the Judicial Process 13 (1965) (DOJ ban).
5 *Olmstead v. United States*, 277 U.S. 438. 464 (1928) ("There was no entry of the houses or offices of the defendants.").
6 47 U.S.C. § 605 (1934).
7 Wayne R. LaFave et al., Criminal Procedure 464 (3d ed. 2009).
8 *Nardone v. United States*, 302 U.S. 379, 384 (1937).
9 *Berger*, 388 U.S. at 46. In those states that prohibited such evidence, state officers frequently handed over the intercepted information to federal authorities, who could use it in federal trials without fear of exclusion since *they* had not violated the law. *See* Jonathan Turley, United States v. McNulty: *Title III and the Admissibility in Federal Court of Illegally Gathered State Evidence*, 80 Nw. U. L. Rev. 1714, 1717 (1986).
10 389 U.S. 347 (1967).
11 *Berger*, 388 U.S. at 41.
12 Pub. L. No. 90–351, tit. III, 82 Stat. 197, 211–25 (codified as amended at 18 U.S.C. §§ 1510–1520 (2012)).

unless authorized by the statute or unless one party to the conversation consents. In contrast to the Communications Act, the 1968 statute permits nonconsensual communications surveillance pursuant to a warrant; at the same time a Title III warrant is harder to obtain than a typical Fourth Amendment warrant. Consistent with *Berger*, a Title III warrant must be based on probable cause to believe that the communications intercepted will concern a specified offense and that the facility or person named in the warrant is connected with the offense. But Title III also imposes requirements beyond the Fourth Amendment minimum, including a finding that "normal investigative procedures have been tried and failed or reasonably appear to be unlikely to succeed if tried or to be too dangerous," a direction that the interception "be conducted in such a way as to minimize the interception of communications not otherwise subject to interception," and specific durational limitations (a maximum of thirty days before a new warrant must be obtained).[13] Further, upper level executive officials must approve the surveillance,[14] only district court judges (not magistrates) or the state equivalent may issue the warrants,[15] and surveillance is permitted only in felony cases.[16]

The statute also calls for recording of all surveillance, sealing of the recordings, and notice of the surveillance to the subjects of the recordings within ninety days unless delaying notice would serve the "interests of justice."[17] Finally, Title III establishes criminal sanctions against those who "intentionally" violate its provisions, and creates a civil cause of action for any person whose communications are intercepted, disclosed, or used in violation of the act.[18] It also provides for a suppression remedy,[19] although the Supreme Court has limited that sanction to violations of provisions that play a "central role" under the statute (so that, for instance, violation of the minimization requirement may not call for exclusion).[20]

In 1986, Congress enacted the Electronic Communications Privacy Act (ECPA), which extended Title III to encompass "electronic communications," including communications by computer and texting.[21] While the ECPA applied the same warrant requirement to interception of electronic communications that Title III had applied to wire and oral communications, it did not include the supervisory approval requirement found in Title III;[22] nor did it provide for a suppression remedy, meaning that exclusion only occurs in an electronic communication case if the Fourth Amendment is implicated.[23] The ECPA also introduced other forms of authorization for situations that do not involve real-time interception of the content of communications, discussed in Part I.C of this chapter.

Title III/ECPA defines interception as "the aural or other acquisition of the contents of any wire, electronic, or oral communication."[24] The focus on content led the Supreme

13 *Id.* § 2518(1)–(5).
14 *Id.* § 2516(1).
15 *Id.* § 2516(2).
16 *Id.* §2516(3) (indicating the surveillance may be for "any Federal felony").
17 *Id.* § 2518(8) & (9).
18 *Id.* § 2511 (criminal penalties); § 2520 (civil cause of action).
19 *Id.* § 2518(10)(a).
20 *United States v. Giordano*, 416 U.S. 505, 528 (1974).
21 Pub. L. No. 99–508, 100 Stat. 1848 (codified as amended at 18 U.S.C. § 2511(2)(a)(ii) (2008)).
22 *Id.* § 2516(3).
23 *See* 1986 U.S.C.C.A.N. 3577.
24 18 U.S.C. § 2510(4).

Court to hold in 1977 that Title III warrants are not required before law enforcement uses devices that ascertain only the phone numbers involved in a communication;[25] two years later the Court held that, as far as the Fourth Amendment is concerned, not even a traditional warrant is required to obtain such information, on the theory that one knows or should know phone companies maintain that information and assumes the risk it will be revealed to the government.[26] The same reasoning presumably applies to "envelope" or "metadata" information associated with emails, texting, and the like.[27] While the ECPA requires a court order for such data, law enforcement can obtain it simply by asserting that the information is "relevant" to an ongoing investigation; the court's sole function is to certify the completeness of the police application, not examine the basis of the assertion.[28]

Congress has also set up a separate regulatory framework for surveillance aimed at foreign and domestic threats to national security, which has gone through several changes. As with Title III, this framework was presaged by a Supreme Court decision. In 1972, the Court stated that, while Title III generally governs surveillance relevant to "internal security matters" not linked to foreign powers, its dictates could perhaps be relaxed when domestic activities implicate national security.[29] Congress took the hint and in 1978 passed the Foreign Intelligence Surveillance Act (FISA), which for the first time directly regulated surveillance carried out by the intelligence services,[30] but also made clear that this regulation would not be as restrictive as Title III. The act created a Foreign Intelligence Surveillance Court (FISC) authorized to issue interception warrants *in camera* upon a simple finding of probable cause to believe the surveillance targeted a foreign power or the agent of a foreign power; probable cause to believe criminal activity would be discovered was not required, and authorized surveillance periods were significantly longer than permitted under Title III.[31] Further, while the act stated that obtaining national security intelligence must be the "purpose" of the surveillance,[32] subsequent judicial decisions declared that national security need merely be the "*primary* purpose" of the surveillance.[33]

The USA PATRIOT Act of 2001 loosened the latter standard even further, to permit a FISA warrant when intelligence gathering was a "significant purpose" of the surveillance,[34] and the 2007 Protect America Act went further still, eliminating judicial review entirely if the director of national intelligence and the attorney general certified that such a purpose existed and that they had a "reasonable belief" the target was a person

25 *United States v. New York Telephone Co.*, 434 U.S. 159 (1977).
26 *Smith v. Maryland*, 442 U.S. 735 (1979).
27 *See, e.g., United States v. Forrester*, 495 F.3d 1041 (9th Cir. 2007).
28 18 U.S.C. § 3121 *et seq*.
29 *United States v. United States District Court*, 407 U.S. 297 (1972).
30 The Foreign Intelligence Surveillance Act marked the culmination of an extensive investigation by the Senate Select Committee to Study Governmental Operations with Respect to Intelligence Activities, which is referred to colloquially as the Church Committee after its chairman, Senator Frank Church.
31 Pub. L. No. 95–511, 92 Stat. 1783 (codified at 50 U.S.C. § 1801 *et seq*. (1978)).
32 *Id.* § 1804(a)(7)(B).
33 The leading case in this regard is usually said to be *United States v. Truong*, 629 F.2d 908, 913–17 (4th Cir. 1980).
34 50 U.S.C. § 1801 (2001). This provision was upheld in In re Sealed Case, 310 F.3d 717, 744 (Foreign Intelligence Surveillance Ct. Rev. 2002). One court subsequently indicated, to the contrary, that the "primary purpose" test is constitutionally required. *Mayfield v. United States*, 504 F. Supp. 2d 1023 (D. Or. 2007).

located outside the United States.[35] One year later the act was amended again, to reinstate the FISA warrant requirement for surveillance of a U.S. person outside the country or for surveillance of a non-U.S. person reasonably believed to be inside the country, but the "significant purpose" language was retained and probable cause to believe any non-U.S. person who is subject to interception is an agent of foreign power is no longer required.[36] Under current law, the FISC approves the procedures for selecting targets and minimizing access to American citizens, but does not approve the targets themselves,[37] thus potentially permitting interception of communications of a wide array of individuals.[38] According to news reports, under authority of the act the government is monitoring virtually all Internet communications flowing in or out of the United States and subsequently accessing the content of many of these messages, a significant proportion of which are from U.S. citizens.[39]

Most states have their own statutes authorizing interception of communications.[40] Title III allows such statutes so long as they provide equal or greater limitations on surveillance.[41] Some states provide greater protection. For instance, a number of states require special procedures before law enforcement may rely on an informant as the consenting party to a communication interception,[42] and some states also require exclusion where the federal statute does not.[43] However, most lower federal courts have held that evidence suppressible under state law need not be excluded from federal court adjudications absent a violation of a "central" aspect of Title III or the Fourth Amendment.[44] In the wake of *Virginia v. Moore*,[45] which held that evidence obtained from an arrest that violates state law but not the Fourth Amendment is admissible as far as the Fourth Amendment is concerned, the Supreme Court is likely to agree with those holdings.

B *Physical Surveillance*

The three most prominent types of technologically assisted physical surveillance are closed circuit camera surveillance (CCTV); Unmanned Aerial Systems (UAS), or drone, surveillance; and tracking using GPS or some other form of electronic device. In contrast

35 Pub. L. No. 110–55, 121 Stat. 552 (codified as amended 50 U.S.C. § 1804 (2010)).

36 *Id.* § 1881a.

37 50 U.S.C. § 1881a(i)(1)(A).

38 50 U.S.C. § 1881a(g)(2)(A)(v); 50 U.S.C. § 1801(e)(2)(B).

39 Charlie Savage, *N.S.A. Said to Search Content of Messages to and from U.S.*, New York Times (Aug. 8, 2013), http://www.nytimes.com/2013/08/08/us/broader-sifting-of-data-abroad-is-seen-by-nsa.html; Barton Gellman et al., *In NSA-intercepted Data, Those Not Targeted Far Outnumber the Foreigners Who Are*, Washington Post (July 5, 2014), https://www.washingtonpost.com/world/national-security/in-nsa-intercepted-data-those-not-targeted-far-outnumber-theforeigners-who-are/2014/07/05/8139adf8-045a-11e4-8572-4b1b969b6322_story.html.

40 *See, e.g.*, Ariz. Rev. Stat. §§ 13–3004 to 13–3017 (2012); W.Va. Code §§ 62-1D-1 to 62-1D-16 (2007); Haw. Rev. Stat. §§ 803–41 to 803–48 (2016).

41 18 U.S.C. § 2516(2) (2015).

42 *See, e.g.*, 18 Pa. Cons. Stat. § 5704(2)(ii) (2014) (requiring prosecutorial or judicial findings of probable cause before eavesdropping based on informant consent is permitted); Ga. Code Ann. § 16-11-66(b) (2000) (requiring judicial approval where consentor is a minor child).

43 *See, e.g.*, 18 Pa. Cons. Stat. § 5721.1 (1998).

44 *See* Clifford Fishman & Anne McKenna, Wiretapping and Eavesdropping § 34:30.20 (2015) ("[A] defense attorney seeking federal suppression on the basis of state court suppression is unlikely to succeed, but arguments exist, despite prevailing case law to the contrary").

45 553 U.S. 164 (2008).

to interception of communications, physical surveillance of public activities is governed largely by state and local statutes. The federal government has provided funding mechanisms and a regulatory infrastructure for some types of physical surveillance, but has left regulation of their use by law enforcement to other entities.

For instance, the federal government has allocated significant sums of money to states and localities for establishing CCTV systems.[46] Yet the few laws regulating local camera surveillance are found solely at the municipal level.[47] These ordinances tend to address issues such as the purpose of the camera system, how to notify people that cameras are recording them, how to train system operators, and how long to retain video footage.[48] The assumption of these laws, consistent with Supreme Court case law,[49] is that surveillance of public activities does not require cause, although some of these ordinances prohibit use of zoom and audio capacity under certain circumstances.[50]

Similarly, while the federal government has imposed rules for private drone use,[51] the principal limitations on law enforcement deployment of UAS come from the states.[52] Many of these states require a warrant as a general matter, but allow warrantless use under "recognized" exceptions to the warrant requirement, which apparently include the doctrine that warrants are not required to monitor activities in public spaces associated with low expectations of privacy.[53] Other state statutes are more restrictive. For instance, Florida law limits UAS use to situations that pose a significant risk of a terrorist attack, or where law enforcement officers are reasonably certain that the use of a drone is necessary to prevent imminent physical harm or the imminent escape of a suspect.[54] Thus in Florida even a warrant will not immunize law enforcement UAS use in other situations. A compromise is illustrated by a proposed statute in Connecticut, which would permit warrantless UAS surveillance for up to thirty minutes, surveillance for up to twenty-four hours within a thirty-day period if there is reasonable suspicion, and surveillance of longer duration based on probable cause and a warrant.[55]

Law enforcement tracking of individuals or cars through GPS or other technology[56] is also governed largely through state and local law. Several federal statutes govern the maintenance and security of GPS satellite systems, but none of this legislation regulates

46 Somini Sengupta, *Privacy Fears Grow as Cities Increase Surveillance*, N.Y. Times, Oct. 13, 2013 (describing how federal funding in Oakland, New York City, and elsewhere has enabled creation of surveillance systems).

47 Jeremy Brown, *Pan, Tilt, Zoom: Regulating the Use of Video Surveillance of Public Places*, 23 Berkeley Tech. L.J. 755, 760 (2008) (noting that "there is no federal or state legislation governing police video surveillance of public places" and that even many municipalities do not have such policies).

48 *See CCTV – Policies and Procedures* D.C. Metropolitan Police Dep't., http://mpdc.dc.gov/node/214522 (last visited June 6, 2016).

49 *See United States v. Knotts*, 460 U.S. 276 (1983) (holding that surveillance of public travels is not a search).

50 D.C. Metropolitan Police Dep't, *supra* note 48.

51 Fed. Aviation Admin., *Overview of Small UAS Notice of Proposed Rulemaking* (Feb. 15, 2015), http://www.faa.gov/uas/nprm/.

52 Michael L. Smith, *Regulating Law Enforcement's Use of Drones*, 52 Harv. J. Legis. 423, 427–32 (2015) (cataloguing state drone statutes).

53 *Id.* at 472.

54 Fla. Stat. § 934.50 (2014).

55 Conn. Gen. Assembly Legislative Program Review & Investigations Comm., Staff Findings & Proposed Recommendations: Drone Use Regulation (2014).

56 Several states have proposed or passed statutes regulating use of Radio Frequency Identification Devices to identify or track individuals, but to date these laws have not addressed law enforcement use of RFIDs;

the use of GPS by law enforcement.[57] Thus, Federal Rule of Criminal Procedure 41, which applies only in federal cases, governs the issuance of warrants when police use "an electronic or mechanical device which permits the tracking of the movement of a person or object," and requires both a particular description of the person or thing to be tracked and a durational limit of forty-five days.[58] But ultimately Rule 41 is designed to permit judges to authorize tracking outside the judge's jurisdiction, not set the substantive standards for tracking; accordingly, GPS use on less than probable cause and without a warrant would not violate the rule.[59] States that have enacted statutes regulating tracking have tended to follow the same route, with some requiring the court to find that the tracking procedure will produce evidence "relevant" to an ongoing investigation and others requiring the court to find "probable cause" to believe the tracking will produce relevant information.[60]

C *Transaction Surveillance*

Another form of "surveillance" involves obtaining records pertaining to past transactions, whether they involve communication, travel, or some other type of activity. In this setting, Congress has been active in regulating government access as it relates to communications, whereas the states have taken the lead in regulating government collection and access of travel records. Statutory restrictions on accessing other types of records, ranging from medical records to logs of video rentals, are found in a wide array of federal and state laws that are described more fully in other chapters and are covered only very briefly here.

The ECPA distinguishes between real-time interception of electronic communications and access to "stored" communications. If the government is seeking the content of a communication, interception requires a Title III warrant; in contrast, as of this writing,[61] access to that same content held in an account requires only a regular warrant for communications that are stored on a server for less than 180 days, and only a subpoena based on a relevance showing for communications that sit on a server longer than that period.[62] Further, under the USA PATRIOT Act, the government only needs an *ex parte* subpoena (that is, one that is not challengeable by the subject of the records) if the goal is to obtain noncontent information. If the government seeks "subscriber

in any event, RFID tracking can only occur short-range. *See generally*, Kyle Sommer, *Riding the Wave*, 35 J. LEGIS. 48 (2009).

57 Jennifer Ann Urban, *Has GPS Made the Adequate Enforcement of Privacy Laws in the U.S. a Luxury of the Past?* 16 WAKE FOREST J. BUS. & INTELL. PROP. L. 400, 413 (2016) (noting that federal legislation does not explain "how courts should address privacy issues that arise due to GPS, the government's operation of GPS or the government's use of GPS for criminal suspect surveillance").

58 FED. R. CRIM. P. 41(e)(2)(C). *See also* 18 U.S.C. § 3117 (1986).

59 Kimberly Smith, *Hiding in Plain Sight: Protection from GPS Technology Requires Congressional Action, Not a Stretch of the Fourth Amendment*, 62 MERCER L. REV. 1243, 1266 (2010).

60 Jordan Miller, *New Age Tracking Technologies in the Post-United States Jones Environment: The Need for Model Legislation*, 48 CREIGHTON L. REV. 553, 592 n. 244 (2015).

61 At the time of this writing, Congress was considering passage of H.R. 699, which would require a warrant to obtain all content information, whether stored or not, a practice already followed by the Department of Justice. Serrin Turner, *Are Changes in Store for the Stored Communications Act?* GLOBAL PRIVACY & SECURITY COMPLIANCE LAW BLOG (April 22, 2106), http://www.globalprivacyblog.com/privacy/are-changes-in-store-for-the-stored-communications-act/.

62 18 U.S.C. § 2703 (1986).

information" – e.g., name, address, sessions times and durations, means and source of payment (including credit card numbers) and the identity of Internet users who employ a pseudonym – an ordinary showing of relevance is sufficient,[63] whereas if it seeks account logs and email addresses of other individuals whom the account holder has contacted, it must show "reasonable and articulable facts" providing "reasonable grounds to believe that . . . the records or other information sought are relevant and material to an ongoing criminal investigation."[64]

In the national security context, the PATRIOT Act, as amended in 2006, expanded on this concept when the surveillance is "relevant to an authorized investigation [designed] to protect against international terrorism or clandestine intelligence activities."[65] Assuming that the Foreign Intelligence Surveillance Court finds that this standard is met and that the attorney general has authorized the investigation, Section 215 of the act allows the government to obtain "any tangible thing."[66] While that phrase covers a wide range of information, it is relevant here because it was the authority relied upon by the National Security Agency to collect the metadata or envelope information associated with millions of communications between 2006 and 2015.[67] Partly as a result of Edward Snowden's revelations, in the latter year Congress passed the USA FREEDOM Act, which prohibits the NSA from storing these data.[68] However, the NSA may still access metadata from common carriers that is relevant to the investigation of a national security threat; further, Section 215 may still permit government collection of many other types of communications and Internet material.[69]

Law enforcement also often seeks historical locational information, either to track a particular person or to determine the identity of people near a particular place at a particular time. The federal government has yet to pass a statute regulating police access to this type of information. Nor, outside the use of police body cam recordings,[70] have state and local governments yet focused on government access to legitimately obtained camera and drone recordings; at most, some jurisdictions require destruction of stored camera data within a given period if no crime is reported for the relevant place and time.[71]

63 *Id.* § 2703(c)(2).
64 18 U.S.C. § 2703(c).
65 50 U.S.C. § 1861(b)(2)(B).
66 *Id.* § (a)(1).
67 *See* David S. Kris, *On the Bulk Collection of Tangible Things*, 7 J. Nat'l Sec. L. & Pol'y 209, 210 (2014).
68 Pub. L. No. 114–23, 129 Stat. 268. *See* Sabrina Siddiqui, *Congress Passes NSA Surveillance Bill in Vindication of Snowden*, The Guardian (June 3, 2015), http://www.theguardian.com/us-news/2015/jun/02/congress-surveillance-reform-edward-snowden/.
69 Zack Whittaker, *Freedom Act Will Kill Only One of NSA's Programs (and Not Even One of Its Worst)*, Zero Day (May 4, 2014), http://www.zdnet.com/article/freedom-act-metadata-phone-records-prism/#!; Faiza Patel, *Bulk Collection under Section 215 Has Ended . . . What's Next?* Brennan Center for Justice (Nov. 30, 2015), www.Brennacenter.org/print/14777.
70 Regulation of body cams has been voluminous. *See* Karson Kampfe, *Police-Worn Body Cameras: Balancing Privacy and Accountability through State and Police Department Action*, 76 Ohio St. L.J. 1153, 1184–91 & accompanying notes (2015) (noting state and departmental provisions governing police-worn body cameras).
71 *See, e.g.*, Remarks of Stephen McMahon (Central District Commander for Baltimore City), *Int'l Assoc. Chiefs of Police Meeting, Apr. 17, 2002* at 39 (requiring destruction of video recordings within ninety-six hours unless relevant to an investigation). Several states prohibit warrantless use of drones to record, *see, e.g.*, Idaho Code § 21–213(2) (2013), but such statutes do not address subsequent accessing of

However, a handful of state statutes do require a warrant, subpoena, or court order to obtain historical cell site data.[72]

Although this chapter will not address in detail statutes that regulate access to records unrelated to communications or public movements, worth noting for comparison purposes is that many of these other laws provide more protection of records than the ECPA and the PATRIOT Act. For instance, the Privacy Protection Act requires, at a minimum, probable cause to obtain certain types of information from the press,[73] the Video Privacy Protection Act also requires probable cause,[74] the Cable Communications Privacy Act requires more than probable cause ("clear and convincing evidence"),[75] and the IRS Code mandates that, for non-tax-related investigations, government demonstrate "reasonable cause" and an inability to obtain the information from another source.[76] The statutes that regulate law enforcement access to bank and educational records, while requiring only a subpoena based on a relevance showing, nonetheless require that the subject of the records be notified of the subpoena and given a chance to challenge it unless that notice would compromise the investigation.[77]

II An Assessment of Legislation as the Primary Source of Surveillance Regulation

Legislation provides the basis for much of the regulatory regime governing surveillance. The courts have also been involved in regulating surveillance, but not nearly to the same extent. Thus, as already mentioned, the Supreme Court has held that interception of communication content requires a warrant, but that interception of metadata is not governed by the Fourth Amendment. It has held that physical surveillance that involves a trespass is a Fourth Amendment search, but to date has resisted holding that nontrespassory physical surveillance raises a constitutional issue. Many commentators have bemoaned the minimalist approach of the Court toward the Fourth Amendment as it applies to surveillance, while others believe that its move toward privacy protection in *Katz* improperly expanded the scope of the amendment.

Rather than address this debate over substance, which is well covered elsewhere in this book, this section describes the parallel debate about the extent to which courts, as opposed to legislatures, should be involved in creating surveillance law. Of course, controversy over the proper trade-off between legislative and judicial rule making permeates constitutional jurisprudence. The following discussion lays out the opposing positions solely as they apply in the surveillance context. It then addresses the advantages and disadvantages of federal as opposed to more local surveillance legislation, an equally

any records produced through warrant-based drone use. *See generally*, Gregory S. McNeal, *Government-Operated Drones and Data Retention*, 72 Wash. & Lee L. Rev. 1139, 1149–51 (2015).

72 Lauren E. Babst, *No More Shortcuts: Protect Cell Site Locations with a Warrant*, 21 Mich. Telecomm. & Tech. L. Rev. 363, 383 (2015) (canvassing statutes). At the time of this writing, the Supreme Court was considering this issue in *Carpenter v. United States*, 2017 WL 2497484.

73 42 U.S.C. §2000aa(a)(1) (1996).

74 18 U.S. C. § 2710(b)(3) (2013). The act permits access pursuant to either a warrant or a court order based on "probable cause." The distinction between the two is not made clear.

75 47 U.S.C. § 551(h)(1) (2001).

76 I.R.C. § 6103(h) (2015).

77 *See, e.g.*, Right to Financial Privacy Act, 12 U.S.C. §§ 3405(2), 3406(b), 3407(2) (1978); Family Educational Rights and Privacy Act, 20 U.S.C. § 1232g(b)(2) (1994).

important issue in determining the source of law governing surveillance. Finally, Part III discusses a third regulatory mechanism: rules developed by administrative – as opposed to judicial or legislative – bodies.

A *Legislatures v. Courts*

Much has been written about the relative worth of legislative and judicial regulation of surveillance. Before one can tackle this issue, the goals of surveillance regulation need to be identified. Orin Kerr has suggested that two such goals are "a workable and sensible balance between law enforcement needs and privacy interests" and "rule clarity."[78] A third goal, in some tension with the second, is a set of rules that is flexible enough to cover unforeseen developments, and a fourth, closely related to the third, is a facility for changing the rules if developments have made them obsolete. A fifth goal is a sound means for ensuring accountability and compliance. A final goal, more relevant to the next subsection than this one, is ensuring respect for federalism principles. With the exception of the first, all of these goals are common to any regulatory effort. But they may point in a different direction in the surveillance context than in other contexts. The views of scholars who have addressed these types of issues are worth considering.

Kerr argues that legislation should be the primary means of regulating surveillance. He first points out that the Supreme Court has not been particularly protective of privacy.[79] Even though the Court purports to be implementing a reasonable expectation of privacy test, its cases have for the most part simply tracked pre-*Katz* trespass doctrine; thus, "existing Fourth Amendment rules are not necessarily the rules that sensible legislators might enact and reasonable citizens might desire."[80] Kerr also notes, as the discussion in Part I indicated, that on the whole legislation has been more protective of privacy interests in the surveillance context, and has also addressed postinterception issues (such as sealing of records) that Fourth Amendment case law does not address.[81]

Kerr then moves from substantive points to process concerns. He argues that, while the institutional competence of legislatures over courts may be ambiguous in some situations, in the Fourth Amendment context, and when technology is "in flux," legislative rule making is clearly superior.[82] He asserts that, while legislation can be created at will, judicial rule making depends upon a case and controversy and a prolonged appellate process, and thus Fourth Amendment rules have tended to lag behind analogous legislative rules governing surveillance "by a least a decade"; as a result, judicial decisions are more likely to be based on outdated facts about technology and of limited precedential value.[83] Kerr notes that Congress passed laws regulating wiretapping, use of pen registers, access to stored email, and interception of emails long before the courts addressed these issues.[84]

78 Orin S. Kerr, *The Fourth Amendment and New Technologies: Constitutional Myths and the Case for Caution*, 102 Mich. L. Rev. 801, 861 (2004).

79 *Id.* at 838 ("Most existing Fourth Amendment rules in new technologies are based heavily on property law concepts, and as a result offer only relatively modest privacy protection in new technologies").

80 *Id.*

81 *Id.* at 857 ("Since the 1960s Congress rather than the courts has shown the most serious interest in protecting privacy from new technologies").

82 *Id.* at 859.

83 *Id.* at 868.

84 *Id.* at 869–70.

Kerr also points out that, while courts are limited by stare decisis interpreting the Constitution, Congress can and has amended surveillance statutes frequently.[85] Further, these statutory changes often enact creative responses to legal problems that judges would have difficulty replicating. For instance, the ECPA regulates private as well as government monitoring of emails by prohibiting common carriers from handing over data to the government on their own initiative, something courts could not pull off under the Fourth Amendment, given the state action requirement.[86] Congress also created the "specific and articulable facts" court order described earlier, a hybrid between a warrant and the relevance standard that courts would be very reticent about inventing on their own.[87] Even when courts do decide to create a rule that anticipates technological change, Kerr asserts, their tendency is to opt for a vague, open-ended mandate that is subject to misinterpretation.[88] Finally, Kerr notes that, compared to courts, legislatures have access to a wide range of information sources – hearings, legislative staffing, reports, and the like – a difference that is particularly useful in technological surveillance cases given the rapidity and complicated nature of new developments.[89]

Kerr anticipates two criticisms of legislative rule making. First, some have argued that, when relevant facts are in a state of flux, as they are in the surveillance setting, the type of "interstitial" rule making that flows from the common law method is often preferable to legislative action because the parties, abetted by the courts, can negotiate results on a case-by-case basis until clear solutions develop.[90] But Kerr notes that, while this reasoning may make sense in civil cases, prosecutors and defense attorneys do not palaver over the rules police should follow, and in any event the criminal justice system cannot afford to wait for clear rules to develop through the relatively slow common law method, given the power that government wields in the surveillance setting.[91] The second criticism of legislative solutions that Kerr anticipates, a common one, is that deficits in collective action may lead legislatures to devise unbalanced rules, which courts can avoid, given their relatively nonpolitical status.[92] But Kerr asserts that "rent-seeking" is rare in the criminal justice context, because "law enforcement does not 'profit' more or less based on how restricted its investigative powers may be, and does not have a clear economic incentive to lobby Congress for less privacy-protecting rules."[93]

Daniel Solove takes issue with virtually all of Kerr's points.[94] Although he concedes that statutes have occupied the field in the surveillance context,[95] he believes that situation is due to the Supreme Court's abdication of its proper role, not the inevitable superiority

85 *Id.* at 871.
86 *Id.* at 872.
87 *Id.*
88 *Id.* at 873.
89 *Id.* at 875 ("The information environment of judicial rulemaking is usually poor"); *id.* at 881–82 (describing legislative rule-making process).
90 *Id.* at 882 (citing, inter alia, Neil K. Komesar, Imperfect Alternatives: Choosing Institutions in Law, Economics, and Public Policy, 53–97, 123–52 (1994)).
91 *Id.* at 883–84.
92 *Id.* at 884 (citing, inter alia, Jonathan R. Macey, *Public Choice: The Theory of the Firm and the Theory of Market Exchange*, 74 Cornell L. Rev. 43 (1988)).
93 *Id.* at 885.
94 Daniel J. Solove, *Fourth Amendment Codification and Professor Kerr's Misguided Call for Judicial Deference*, 74 Fordham L. Rev. 747 (2005).
95 *Id.* at 760.

of legislation. He asserts that the many exceptions to the warrant requirement illustrate that Fourth Amendment jurisprudence can be flexible, and thus that courts should not be reticent about expanding the scope of the amendment.[96] At the same time, he points to the many types of surveillance Congress has failed to regulate (e.g., silent video surveillance, tracking, and sensory enhancement technologies such as thermal imagers); regulated in only a minimal fashion (by requiring only a subpoena rather than a warrant for many types of transaction surveillance); regulated in an inconsistent fashion (e.g., by protecting financial information only when possessed by certain entities); or exempted from the exclusionary rule, which Solove regards as the most effective sanction.[97]

Solove also notes that statutes can be at least as confusing and vague as Fourth Amendment standards, as Kerr himself has argued with respect to the ECPA.[98] He further points out that, as Part I noted, some statutes (Title III and the Foreign Intelligence Surveillance Act) were not passed until the Supreme Court gave Congress a nudge, others (such as the PATRIOT Act) only exist because of a dramatic event, and still others (such as the ECPA) remain outdated despite the ability to amend.[99] Finally, he questions the ability of legislators to understand technology any better than judges, especially given the availability to judges of amicus briefs and other readily accessible information about technology.[100] In light of these views, Solove believes that courts should defer to legislation regulating surveillance only if it conforms to fundamental Fourth Amendment principles, which he describes as "minimization" (prevention of dragnets), "particularization" (of suspicion), and "control" (meaningful oversight).[101]

Peter Swire mostly sides with Solove in this debate.[102] What he adds to Solove's comments is a riposte to Kerr's assertion that rent seeking at the legislative level is relatively uncommon in the surveillance context. He argues that, just like any other regulated industry, the Department of Justice and state law enforcement agencies will try to reduce regulation, and that public choice theory suggests that their concentrated power can often easily trump that of privacy advocates, especially after events such as 9/11 (which Swire says explains much of the PATRIOT Act's significant expansion of law enforcement surveillance powers).[103] Like Solove, Swire notes that congressional acts have usually departed from the Fourth Amendment's warrant norm, and that to the extent they have not it has usually been because courts have forced their hand.[104] But he goes further than Solove in pointing out that even those congressional statutes that merely require a subpoena or some other lesser protection may well have been motivated by the courts – because of their *failure* to apply the Fourth Amendment.[105] Thus, for instance, he notes

96 *Id.* at 762.
97 *Id.* at 763–65.
98 *Id.* at 767 (citing, inter alia, Orin S. Kerr, *Lifting the "Fog" of Internet Surveillance: How a Suppression Remedy Would Change Computer Crime Law,* 54 Hastings L.J. 805 (2003), and Orin S. Kerr, *A User's Guide to the Stored Communications Act, and a Legislator's Guide to Amending It,* 72 Geo. Wash. L. Rev. 1208 (2004)).
99 *Id.* at 770–71.
100 *Id.* at 771–72.
101 *Id.* at 775.
102 Peter P. Swire, *Katz Is Dead, Long Live Katz,* 102 Mich. L. Rev. 904 (2004).
103 *Id.* at 914 ("The regulated industry of law enforcement has a concentrated interest in reducing regulation – pushing for fewer warrants, less onerous reporting requirements, and so on"); *id.* at 915 (describing genesis of the Patriot Act).
104 *Id.* at 915–16.
105 *Id.* at 916–17.

that the ECPA was in part a response to the Court's holding in *Smith v. Maryland* making the Fourth Amendment inapplicable to pen register information,[106] and that the Financial Privacy Act requiring a subpoena to obtain bank records was a response to the Court's decision in *United States v. Miller*, permitting warrantless access to such records.[107] He then argues that because these types of decisions are less likely now, responsive legislation is also less likely to be enacted.[108]

Thus Swire contends, like Solove, that the courts need a more aggressive approach to the Fourth Amendment, in particular an expansion of its scope. But rather than propose specific substantive guidelines, he argues for a "procedural approach" to defining reasonableness, borrowing from the work of Anthony Amsterdam and others who advocated legislative or police rules that set forth with some specificity the types of searches allowed and that limit discretion.[109] Although Amsterdam believed this approach should apply to all police investigative techniques, Swire finds it particularly apt in connection with "emerging technologies, new types of surveillance, and complex record-keeping systems."[110] It is here that law enforcement is most likely to have expertise that judges lack, that achieving optimal substantive rules is likely to be most difficult, and that the Fourth Amendment warrant and probable cause requirements are least likely to make sense.

Erin Murphy agrees with Swire's procedural approach and in fact coauthored an article with him, subsequent to the work of Swire's just described, which expanded upon that notion.[111] But she also wrote independently about the interaction of the Fourth Amendment and statutory enactments in an article that closely examines all of the federal statutes mentioned in Part I that impinge upon privacy.[112] Among her findings are that statutes are more likely to protect the privacy of the "economic mainstream" than that of the poor and that they tend to favor subpoenas over other protective mechanisms.[113] At the same time, she concludes that

> although statutes at first blush appear to lower the standard for law enforcement access to covered materials by infrequently imposing a warrant or probable cause requirement, in significant respects they offer greater protection from intrusion in that they may raise proof thresholds, require advance notice of disclosure [that allows the target or third party to challenge disclosure], restrict subsequent transfer or use, and mandate destruction of records.[114]

She also notes that statutes tend to impose, sometimes through conditionally withholding funding,[115] transparency, reporting, and record keeping requirements that courts

106 *Id.* at 916 (discussing *Smith v. Maryland*, 442 U.S. 735 (1979)).

107 *Id.* (discussing *United States v. Miller*, 425 U.S. 435 (1976)).

108 *Id.* at 917–18.

109 *Id.* at 925–26 (discussing, inter alia, Anthony G. Amsterdam, *Perspectives on the Fourth Amendment*, 58 Minn. L. Rev. 349 (1974).

110 *Id.* at 925.

111 Erin Murphy & Peter P. Swire, *How to Address Standardless Discretion After Jones*, (Ohio St. Pu. L., Working Paper No. 177), http://ssrn.com/ abstract=2122941.

112 Erin Murphy, *The Politics of Privacy in the Criminal Justice System: Information Disclosure, the Fourth Amendment, and Statutory Law Enforcement Exemptions*, 111 Mich. L. Rev. 485 (2013).

113 *Id.* at 507.

114 *Id.* at 521.

115 *Id.* at 526 n. 202 (noting such a condition in connection with medical and educational record statutes).

rarely if ever address under the Fourth Amendment, whose language appears to focus on acquisition of information, not its maintenance.[116]

That is not to say that Murphy signs on to Kerr's optimistic assessment of legislative regulation, however. She not only joins Swire in expressing concern about the ability of legislatures to resist law enforcement lobbying (noting that such lobbying is "a clear and constant voice in the political process") but also notes the political power of the private sector, which might push for expansive use of profit-making technologies such as GPS tracking devices and drones and for "legal safe harbors" and gag orders that minimize any public relations damage from consumer outrage over their use.[117] Thus, the aforementioned article coauthored with Swire expands on the idea that courts should require legislative- or executive-branch policies that cabin police activity and provide "mechanisms for transparency and accountability."[118] At the same time, Swire's and Murphy's procedural approach is willing to countenance protections short of the warrant and probable cause requirements, as well as accountability mechanisms other than exclusion, such as record keeping requirements, periodic audits, or public disclosure.[119] The hope is that these more relaxed constraints would encourage courts to declare more types of investigative activities searches under the Fourth Amendment and encourage legislatures to be creative in establishing *ex ante* rules governing surveillance practices that might even be superior to variable *ex post* judicial rulings based on single fact situations.

A close look at the arguments of these various commentators indicates that they are not all that far apart. While Solove, Swire, and Murphy may not trust the competence or neutrality of legislatures as much as Kerr, they all concede that legislative regulation has advantages in terms of comprehensiveness of treatment and flexible solutions. They are all willing to abandon traditional Fourth Amendment requirements in the surveillance setting, if adequate legislative or administrative substitutes for constraining law enforcement are in place.

Although not focusing on surveillance per se, John Rappaport adds a reason to move in that direction: greater compliance with the law. He argues that legislation and its implementing regulations are more likely than judicial decisions to produce precise mandates rather than standards, to be preventive rather than reactive, to require continuous monitoring of the police, to facilitate structural reforms (of the type Murphy describes), and to give officers "an opportunity to participate in their own self-governance" and thus feel less imposed upon by unempathetic entities, all of which should enhance allegiance to whatever rules are created.[120] This increased compliance, Rappaport argues, might also offset any reduced protection that legislative regulation produces: "We should not regret the loss of paper-tiger rights if they are replaced with rules that, because better obeyed, will actually improve net social realities."[121]

116 *Id.* at 526–27.

117 *Id.* at 536 ("Contrary to the notion that there are few rent-seeking actors in criminal justice, in fact there are strongly motivated and highly organized interest groups to lobby for rules that promote the purchase and use of their products").

118 Murphy & Swire, *supra* note 111, at 3.

119 *Id.* at 1 (noting that "the warrant requirement … is too blunt an instrument to address the challenges from new surveillance technologies" and proposing instead a reasonableness test that would examine "the adequacy of and compliance with procedural safeguards").

120 John Rappaport, *Second-Order Regulation of Law Enforcement*, 103 Cal. L. Rev. 205, 237–43 (2015).

121 *Id.* at 255.

Thus surveillance scholarship, while diverging on the role of the courts, suggests a consensus that legislative regulation has substantial benefits. But the distinction between legislative and judicial rule making is not the only relevant factor in determining how surveillance might best be governed. Differences between federal and local legislation, as well as the role of administrative rules, should also be considered.

B *Federal v. Local Legislation*

As Part I indicated, surveillance legislation has been enacted by Congress, most state legislatures, and a number of municipalities. The existence of these multiple sources of legislative power raises two questions. First, to the extent federal legislation is not meant to apply solely to federal law enforcement efforts, to what extent does it impose nationwide requirements? Second, assuming federal legislation does not automatically preempt the field, to what extent should it override local laws? These questions are particularly important because most policing is not federal, but state and local. They focus attention on whether a predominately federal approach to surveillance regulation is optimal, or whether instead decentralized regulation might be preferable in some circumstances.

A few federal privacy statutes purport to impose a federal standard on the entire country.[122] But most of these statutes only set a regulatory floor, meaning that states may provide more, but not less, privacy protection. For instance, Title III adopts the latter position, as do most federal statutes providing for transaction surveillance.[123] The ECPA probably does as well, although some have argued that states may depart from its requirement in either direction.[124] One might argue that, in the absence of Fourth Amendment prohibitions, Congress does not have the authority to impose a floor on surveillance by local and state police. But given Congress's commerce and spending clause powers, such an argument is unlikely to be successful. For instance, in *Reno v. Condon*[125] the Supreme Court rejected a claim that the privacy provisions of the Driver's Privacy Protection Act, which apply nationwide, violate the commerce power and the Tenth Amendment (which reserves power not given to the federal government to the states).[126]

Thus, the primary question has not been whether Congress has the authority to regulate surveillance but whether it should do so. The debate here has mirrored the debate over whether legislation or case law is the better mechanism for dealing with surveillance issues. Just as Kerr argues that courts should exercise "caution" before co-opting legislative efforts to regulate surveillance, Paul Schwartz argues for "regulatory parsimony," by which he means that Congress should avoid preemptive statutes that inhibit statutory creativity at the state level and should avoid omnibus statutes that treat all surveillance situations similarly.[127] In contrast, just as Solove and Swire argued for more aggressive

122 *See* Murphy, *supra* note 112, at 528–29 (noting that while some statutes, such as the Privacy Act, only apply to federal agencies, others, including those that regulate educational records and driver's licenses, "cover issues typically entrusted entirely to states or localities").

123 *Id.* at 530 (using Title III and other federal statutes to support the proposition that "federal statutory privacy tends to lay floors rather than raise ceilings").

124 *Id.* n. 235 (citing Leonard Deutchman & Sean Morgan, *The ECPA, ISPs & Obtaining E-mail: A Primer for Local Prosecutors*, AM. PROSECUTORS RES. INST. 6 (2005).

125 528 U.S. 141, 150–51 (2000).

126 *See also Gonzales v. Raich*, 545 U.S. 1, 26 (2005) (suggesting that even intrastate information markets can have an impact on interstate commerce).

127 Paul M. Schwartz, *Preemption and Privacy*, 118 YALE L.J. 902, 913 (2009).

Supreme Court interpretation of the Fourth Amendment's scope, Patricia Bellia sees significant benefits in federal preemption, although she agrees that omnibus federal legislation would be a bad idea.[128]

Schwartz notes that, at least in the information privacy setting, state legislatures have often beaten the federal government to the punch.[129] He is also concerned that preemptive federal regulation would stymie experimentation by states and lead to ossified regulatory structures, given the low likelihood of amendment at the federal level.[130] Bellia counters that most state legislation in the privacy field has mimicked federal precedent rather than motivated it,[131] and suggests that, in any event, it is precisely when state law precedes federal law that federal preemption might be most easily justified, on the ground that Congress is picking the "best" solution of those tried out by the states.[132] Although she prefers "floor-preemption" she argues that even strong preemption might be justified when conflicting state rules are leading to confusion and inability to predict behavior, or when state law has become the de facto national standard without input from the national political process.[133]

Other than brief mention of Title III, neither Schwartz nor Bellia focuses on those aspects of privacy law that govern law enforcement. Given that interception of communications, tracking, camera surveillance, and records access are usually carried out by state and local police in the course of investigating or trying to deter state and local criminal law, one might argue, consistent with Rappaport's observations noted previously, that nonconstitutional rules might best originate from state and local government. Consistent with this view, others have argued that, as a general matter, the fractionalized nature of policing does not lend itself to national mandates.[134] In the area of privacy regulation, however, Bellia discounts the relevance of both the presumption of "decentralization" – the notion that regulation should occur at the state level unless a compelling basis for federal regulation exists – and the principle of "subsidiarity" – the idea, based on self-determination values, that regulation "should occur at the lowest level of government capable of appropriately addressing a particular problem."[135] She notes that privacy harms can cross state borders, and that "inconsistent regulations generat[e] compliance burdens."[136]

While those concerns are seldom salient in traditional search and seizure settings, they might easily apply to regulation of certain types of surveillance. The typical physical

128 Patricia L. Bellia, *Federalization in Information Privacy Law*, 118 Yale L.J. 868, 900 (2009) ("Strong preemption is unproblematic if the resulting regulation strikes the right privacy balance; the real concern is that federal law will be broadly preemptive and will underregulate").

129 Schwartz, *supra* note 127, at 916–18.

130 *Id.* at 927–28.

131 Bellia, *supra* note 128, at 881 (pointing to state statutes following Title III and the federal pen register and trap and trace legislation).

132 *Id.* at 889.

133 *Id.* at 899 ("Even where a federal statute responds to constitutional underdevelopment or fills a perceived gap before substantial state regulation can occur, preemption may be justified to prevent such conflicts or to displace a law that has national consequences but that has not been subject to the national political process").

134 *See* Alexander M. Bickel, The Supreme Court and the Idea of Progress 91 (1970). *See also* C. Boyden Gray, *Regulation and Federalism*, 1 Yale J. on Reg. 93, 93 (1983) (describing the presumption of decentralization as a "basic precept" of the Reagan Administration's approach to regulation).

135 Bellia, *supra* note 128, at 891–92.

136 *Id.* at 894.

search and seizure – a search of a home or a stop and frisk – is usually carried out by a single law enforcement agency within a particular jurisdiction. The same is not true for virtual searches involving surveillance: so-called fusion centers obtain transactional information about large numbers of people in different jurisdictions;[137] police may track an individual from one state to the next; interception of communications often transcends not just national but international borders. The problem is exacerbated by modern surveillance techniques that no longer always target a particular person but rather are data focused. As Kerr has pointed out, "The identity of who sent data or where that person is located will often be unknown or unknowable,"[138] with the result that law enforcement may not have any clue as to the target's location or the source of the data. To the extent these activities are not protected by the Fourth Amendment, nationwide standards dealing with the necessary authorization and providing for the same type of accountability mechanisms (exclusion, administrative penalties, and so on) would prevent conflicting mandates. At the least, floor preemption would provide police with a default position in cases of uncertainty.

At the same time, state and local police have long had to deal with inter-jurisdictional enforcement. Further, most surveillance, even of the type just discussed, will take place within a single state, and some surveillance – in particular CCTV – will be solely local. Thus, Schwartz's caution against precipitous nationalization of standards should not be ignored. As the Supreme Court has said:

> The federalist structure of joint sovereigns preserves to the people numerous advantages. It assures a decentralized government that will be more sensitive to the diverse needs of a heterogeneous society; it increases opportunity for citizen involvement in democratic processes; it allows for more innovation and experimentation in government; and it makes government more responsive by putting the States in competition for a mobile citizenry.[139]

Federal legislation is most obviously preferable when dealing with surveillance on a national scale, as with national security investigations. Surveillance that impinges solely on a particular locale, such as citywide cameras systems, is probably best handled through municipal ordnances. In other situations, floor preemption by Congress might often be the best approach, assuming that sufficient state experimentation occurs before Congress weighs in.

C *The Case for Surveillance Legislation*

Legislation is not only a viable means of regulating surveillance but often a preferable one, at least if the courts stand ready to monitor its constitutionality. Indeed, some have argued that under certain conditions courts should affirmatively encourage legislative regulation of criminal procedure, even in matters that are considered within the constitutional domain, a position that has found some support on the Supreme Court.[140]

137 *See* The Constitution Project, Recommendations for Fusion Centers: Preserving Privacy and Civil Liberties While Protecting Against Crime and Terrorism 4 (2012).

138 Orin S. Kerr, *Updating the Foreign Intelligence Surveillance Act*, 75 U. Chi. L. Rev. 225, 226 (2008).

139 *Gregory v. Ashcroft*, 501 U.S. 452, 458 (1991).

140 *United States v. Jones*, 132 U.S. 945, 964 (2012) (Alito, J., concurring, with Ginsburg, J., Breyer, J., and Kagan, J., concurring) ("In circumstances involving dramatic technological change, the best solution to

Rappaport has proposed five principles that could govern the decision as to when legislative rather than judicial rulemaking might be preferred:

> (1) when "political policy makers' institutional advantages" are superior; (2) "when little expert consensus exists about optimal constitutional safeguards or when different safeguards are likely to be optimal in different places;" (3) when certain political policy makers are perceived to be "better agents" than others, as might sometimes be true of federal, as opposed to local, entities; (4) when judicial remedies such as exclusion or damages are "inadequate or problematic," and "structural reform" that courts are unwilling to impose directly would work better; and (5) when the issue is one that "is currently receiving democratic attention," as opposed to one where "democracy functions especially poorly," as might be the case where the majority is very likely to ignore the valid claims of the minority.[141]

Applied to the surveillance setting, all of these factors will often push in the direction of legislation. Rappaport himself uses "privacy regulation of new and emerging technologies" as an illustration of his first, institutional-advantage factor, thus agreeing with Kerr.[142] As to the next three factors, previous discussion has made clear that proposed approaches to regulating surveillance are often in conflict, may differ significantly depending upon the locale, and will often include structural aspects dealing with security, retention, and accountability. Finally, surveillance by the government continues to be a highly publicized and topical matter to which Congress and state and local governments have often responded quickly. Perhaps most relevant with respect to this final factor is that many types of surveillance – metadata collection, drones, camera and tracking systems – tend to affect everyone rather than only politically powerless groups.[143]

Simply because these conditions are met, however, does not mean that courts will encourage or that legislatures will enact surveillance statutes, or that the statutes will be adequate. As Part I indicated, while legislatures have generally been active, they have avoided regulation in a number of areas touching on surveillance. The Supreme Court has demonstrated little inclination to follow Swire and Murphy's suggestion that the Fourth Amendment be used as leverage to force legislatures into acting, and on those few occasions when it has held that legislative or executive policies can fulfill the Fourth Amendment's reasonableness requirement, it has indicated that virtually any policy will do.[144] Furthermore, the Fourth Amendment is useless as leverage even in this weak sense in situations that do not infringe reasonable expectations of privacy; unfortunately, those

privacy concerns may be legislative. A legislative body is well situated to gauge changing public attitudes, to draw detailed lines, and to balance privacy and public safety in a comprehensive way").

141 Rappaport, *supra* note 120, at 263–65.

142 *Id.* at 263.

143 *See* Christopher Slobogin, *Panvasive Surveillance, Political Process Theory, and the Nondelegation Doctrine*, 102 Geo. L.J. 1721, 1738 (2014) ("[T]he political process is often well situated to deal with panvasive searches and seizures because these searches and seizures affect wide swaths of the population that can have access to the legislature").

144 *Florida v. Wells*, 495 U.S.1 (1990) (holding that, while inventories are only valid if conducted pursuant to a policy, "policies of opening all containers or of opening no containers are unquestionably permissible [as are policies that] allow the opening of close containers whose contents officers determine they are unable to ascertain from examining the containers' exteriors"); *Marshall v. Barlow's, Inc.*, 436 U.S. 307, 323 (1978) (holding, without elaboration, that where the government proceeds without a warrant, it "must ensure that there are reasonable legislative or administrative standards for conducting an inspection with respect to a particular establishment").

situations include police use of many of the surveillance and data mining techniques that most commentators would like to see regulated. Added to this concern is the worry, evidenced in particular by Swire, that legislatures will often cater to law enforcement interests, if only because law enforcement entities are better organized and their needs more salient to legislatures than the groups that are most directly affected by the police. Finally, while courts may not always be the best institution for developing detailed, structural prescriptions, legislatures might not be either; while legislators can hold hearings and consult experts, they may be as likely to be befuddled by new technologies and nuanced privacy intrusions as judges.

All of these concerns suggest that a third source of law, beyond legislation and case decisions, might also be a useful means of regulating surveillance. Part III examines the potential for administrative law as a means of developing standards for regulating surveillance.

III Administrative Regulation

Administrative law principles can accomplish a number of aims.[145] They can provide a vehicle for forcing a rule-making process to take place (something the Supreme Court has been unwilling to do). They can encourage public participation in that process. Finally, they can require law enforcement to justify the rules that are created and provide grounds for judicial review of the rules to ensure that they have a rational basis and are not implemented in a biased manner.

These points are developed here in turn, using for illustrative purposes, New York City's Domain Awareness program and the transaction surveillance program known as the "fusion center." The Domain Awareness program, in operation since 2012, endeavors to collate and provide officers in the field information gleaned from thousands of surveillance cameras, geospatial data that reveals crime "hot spots," feeds from license recognition systems, and GPS signals that permit real-time and historical tracking of cars.[146] As such, the program is representative of numerous types of physical monitoring systems, including the recent surge in wide-ranging drone surveillance.[147] Fusion centers exist in virtually every state, and use computers to collect financial, rental, utility, vehicle, and communications data from federal, state, and local public databases, law enforcement files, and private companies in an effort to identify suspicious individuals or provide information on already-identified suspects.[148] Fusion centers are, in essence, junior versions of the NSA-metadata program and similar federal record-collection efforts.[149]

145 The following section is taken largely from Christopher Slobogin, *Policing as Administration*, 165 U. Pa. L. Rev. 91 (2016).

146 *See* Colleen Long, *NYPD, Microsoft Create Crime-Fighting "Domain Awareness" Tech System*, Huffington Post, Feb. 25, 2013. *See also Privacy Security Guidelines* (Guidelines), New York City (Feb. 2009) (describing the program), www.nyc.gov/html/nypd/downloads/pdf/crimeprevention/public.

147 On the increase in drone surveillance and attempts to regulate it, *see* Marc Jonathan Blitz, James Grimsley, Stephen E. Henderson & Joseph Thai, *Regulating Drones under the First and Fourth Amendments*, 57 Wm. & Mary L. Rev. 49 (2015).

148 *See* The Constitution Project, *supra* note 137, at 4 (describing the establishment of 77 fusion centers nationwide); Tom Nolan, Chapter 6, this volume.

149 The Constitution Project, *supra* note 137, at 7.

A *Why Law Enforcement Entities Must Develop Rules*

Most federal agencies and state agencies are governed by administrative procedure acts (APAs). Some municipalities also have enacted such statutes, applicable to their agencies.[150] These acts control how government agencies make decisions and promulgate rules. Of most relevance here, the federal APA, which in this respect is the model for most other APAs, provides that an agency must follow certain procedures whenever it develops a policy that is a "statement of general or particular applicability and future effect"[151] and that affects "the rights and obligations" of the citizenry.[152] These procedures include providing notice to the public of any proposed policy and an opportunity for interested parties to comment on the rule. As explained in more detail below, case law has also established that such policies must be justified in writing, must be implemented even-handedly, and must stay within the bounds of the relevant legislative authorization.

Even though police departments are administrative agencies and most APAs do not specifically exempt them from their provisions, they have typically not had to follow these types of rule-making procedures.[153] One possible reason is that, as noted, much policing is local. But to the extent municipal police departments that are not governed by a municipal APA are enforcing state or federal criminal laws, they should be covered by state and federal APAs. A second reason for the de facto exemption is the notion that any search and seizure rules the police develop are merely interpreting the criminal law or the Fourth Amendment, and thus are not subject to the process agencies must follow when they promulgate statutelike rules on their own. While that reason may exempt rules that tell police when to conduct a stop, arrest, or search, rules governing surveillance programs are different. The policies that establish programs such as Domain Awareness and fusion centers are not interpreting a law defining crime or a judicial decision about search or seizure, but rather originate with the police themselves and, in effect, operate as statutes. As is true with the rules of other agencies that must abide by rule-making procedures, these policies have "general and future effect" on the "rights" of citizens because they require concededly innocent citizens to modify their legitimate behavior if they want to avoid police intrusion. Further, in such cases it is the police agency's surveillance policy, not the law of crimes or the Fourth Amendment, that determines who is affected by the police action.

If that is so, then the APA's rule-making process applies. Because it requires public participation, written reasons, even-handed implementation, and legislative authorization, this process helps address concerns about inadequate or biased rules. It also must be followed regardless of whether the Fourth Amendment applies to the surveillance.

[150] Furthermore, in at least nine states, municipalities are considered agencies of the state. Eugene Mcquillin, The Law of Municipal Corporations 2.8.10 (3d ed. 1999).

[151] 5 U.S.C. § 551(4) (2011) (defining "rule" in this manner).

[152] *See, e.g.*, *Long Island Care at Home, Inc. v. Coke*, 551 U.S. 158, 172–73 (2007).

[153] Kenneth Culp Davis & Richard J. Pierce, Jr., Administrative Law Treatise 1 (3d ed. 1994) ("Administrative law includes the entire range of action by government with respect to the citizen or by the citizen with respect to the government, except for those matters dealt with by the criminal law").

B *Notice and Comment*

Under the federal APA, if an agency engages in informal rule making it must issue a generally available notice of "either the terms or substance of the proposed rule or a description of the subjects and issues involved."[154] The goal is to permit public comment on the proposed rule or rule change, and thereby improve the agency's decision-making process and enhance political legitimacy. Case law establishes that if the agency fails to pinpoint critical issues covered by the proposed rule, any regulation that results can be challenged in court and nullified.[155]

Application of the APA would have a dramatic impact on the usual cloistered police policy making process. For instance, despite numerous news stories about Domain Awareness and fusion centers, the public still does not know the extent to which New York City is keeping tabs on its citizens, or the precise types of records (bank accounts, medical documents, communication logs?) that fusion centers are compiling.[156] Requiring some sort of notice-and-comment period would mandate transparency about these types of issues and provide at least a patina of democratic participation in the decision-making process.

A perennial concern of the police, and one reason their policy making is so secretive, is that knowledge of their tactics will undermine crime detection efforts. But the federal APA and most state APAs accommodate this concern by providing that police need not disclose "techniques and procedures for law enforcement investigations or prosecutions, or … guidelines for law enforcement investigations or prosecutions if such disclosure could reasonably be expected to risk circumvention of the law."[157] In any event, fear that public notification will tip off the criminal element is highly exaggerated. First, of course, the primary aim of surveillance involving technology such as cameras is often deterrence, which publicity can only enhance. Second, matters of specific implementation need not be revealed to the public. For instance, if camera surveillance is meant to be covert, the fact of such surveillance should be disclosed, but camera locations obviously need not be; if the police have a method of obtaining metadata that is not widely known, it need not be revealed. Third, and most importantly, police should have to accept the fact that they function in a democracy.[158] Democratic accountability – a key value sought to be implemented by administrative law – requires that the public be told not only what surveillance capacities police have but how those capacities will be used.

C *Explanation of the Rule*

A much discussed issue in administrative law circles is the extent to which an agency must take public comments into consideration and, when it does not follow the route suggested by a comment, explain why it failed to do so. The APA does not require a response to every comment; demanding that an agency answer all submissions it receives,

[154] 5 U.S.C. § 553(b)(3) (1966).

[155] *See, e.g.*, *AFL-CIO v. Donovan*, 757 F.2d 330 (D.C. Cir. 1985).

[156] *See, e.g.*, Torin Monahan & Neal A. Palmer, *The Emerging Politics of DHS Fusion Centers*, 40 Sec. Dialogue 617, 630 (2009) (quoting fusion center trainer saying, "If people knew what we were looking at, they'd throw a fit").

[157] 5 U.S.C. § 552(b)(7)(E) (2009).

[158] David Alan Sklansky, Democracy and the Police 157–58 (2008) (defending the idea that policing practices and fundamental aspects of democracy are irretrievably linked).

regardless of coherence or number, would be inefficient and unproductive.[159] At the same time, the APA does state that agency rules and their underlying findings may not be "arbitrary and capricious."[160]

The Supreme Court's solution to this dilemma has been to require a written rationale for rules that are promulgated,[161] and require as well that the rationale link the agency's evidence, policies, and actions in a cogent way.[162] Thus, courts are entitled to ensure that agencies have taken a "hard look" at the rules they generate. As Kevin Stack states:

> Under the leading formulation of [the hard look] doctrine, "the agency must examine the relevant data and articulate a satisfactory explanation for its action including a 'rational connection between the facts found and the choices made.'' The court "consider[s] whether the decision was based on a consideration of the relevant factors and whether there has been a clear error of judgment." In addition, the agency may not "entirely fail[] to consider an important aspect of the problem," may not "offer[] an explanation for its decision that runs counter to the evidence before the agency," nor offer an explanation that is "so implausible that it could not be ascribed to a difference in view or the product of agency expertise." The agency must also relate the factual findings and expected effects of the Regulation to the purposes or goals the agency must consider under the statute as well as respond to salient criticisms of the agency's reasoning.[163]

Application of hard look doctrine to Domain Awareness and fusion centers would require the relevant agencies to produce written rules. Further, courts would be empowered to assess the proffered rationales for those rules. Given the fact that the rules originate in an administrative agency rather than a democratically elected legislature, that assessment would apply a standard somewhere between the "strict scrutiny" and "rational basis" tests used in cases involving judicial review of legislation.[164]

Even under this heightened standard, the two programs at issue would probably pass, at least initially. Domain Awareness is touted as a more efficient way of facilitating communication of crime-relevant information to police in real time, and as a means of enhancing police safety by alerting officers to the location and history of suspects.[165] Fusion center repositories likewise make information access and collation more efficient.[166]

159 The APA requires that the rules incorporate "a concise general statement of [their] basis and purpose," *Tri-State Generation and Transmission Ass'n., Inc. v. Environmental Quality Council*, 590 P.2d 1324, 1330 (Wyo. 1979), but the agency need not discuss "every item or factor or opinion in the submissions made to it." Bernard Schwartz, Administrative Law 200–01 (1991).

160 5 U.S.C. § 706(2)(A) (1966) (authorizing reviewing courts to "set aside agency action, findings, and conclusions found to be ... arbitrary, capricious, and abuse of discretion, or otherwise not in accordance with law.").

161 *SEC v. Chenery Corp.*, 332 U.S. 194, 196 (1947).

162 *Motor Vehicle Mfrs. Ass'n of U.S., Inc. v. State Farm Mut. Auto. Ins. Co.*, 463 U.S. 29, 41–42 (1983) (indicating that agency rationales that do not meet this test risk judicial invalidation on "arbitrary and capricious" grounds).

163 Kevin Stack, *Interpreting Regulations*, 111 Mich. L. Rev. 355, 379 (2012).

164 *Id.* at 379 ("Hard-look review further distinguishes regulations from legislation; it has long been understood as requiring a higher standard of rationality than the minimum rational basis standard of constitutional review").

165 Chris Francescani, *NYPD Expands Surveillance Net to Fight Crime as Well as Terrorism*, Reuters (June 31, 2013), www.reuters.com/article/usa-ny-surveillance-idUSL2N0EV0D220130621 (recounting how the system collects together data from multiple technological sources and makes it available to the individual police officer).

166 *See* Dep't Homeland Security, *Fusion Center Success Stories*, http://www.dhs.gov/fusion-center-success-stories (last updated July 23, 2015). *But see* Danielle Keats Citron & Frank Pasquale, *Network*

However, the judicial hard look would not end with such abstract assessments of program rationales. Just as important is an evaluation of whether the program, as implemented, is rationally aimed at achieving its objectives. If, for instance, domain awareness and fusion center policies do not specify how the information collected will be kept secure, screened for accuracy, and accessed, they fail, quoting from the preceding excerpt, "to consider an important aspect of the problem."

Agency deployment of a surveillance program must be rational as well. For instance, some applications of Domain Awareness are meant to focus police presence in "hot zones" that are thought to be particularly prone to crime but that also may tend to be heavily populated by people of color.[167] Fusion centers might be focused on collecting records of people belonging to disfavored groups. In such situations, hard look review leads to a third inquiry, discussed below, which can help uncover biased, capricious, or pretextual programs.

D *Implementation of the Rule*

Once a rule is promulgated, the federal APA says nothing about how it should be carried out, apparently because implementation is considered a form of informal adjudication, for which the APA has not developed standards. Here, however, the logic of administrative law, consistent with Fourth Amendment jurisprudence, dictates that regulations be implemented in a "regularized" fashion; as formulated by one commentary, "It is firmly established that an agency's unjustified discriminatory treatment of similarly situated parties constitutes arbitrary and capricious agency action."[168] Thus, courts have held that, unless the rationale for the rule signals a different result, all potential targets of a program should be treated in the same manner.[169] This would meant that cameras and fusion centers should collect the same type of information from everyone affected.

The even-handedness requirement goes well beyond ensuring that a particular implementation of a surveillance program is carried out in a nondiscriminatory fashion, however. Agencies must also ensure that the program as a whole does not irrationally fixate on a particular area or group but rather, to use Stack's formulation, "relate[s] the factual findings and expected effects of the Regulation to the purposes or goals the agency must

Accountability, 64 Hastings L.J. 1141, 1444 (2001) ("Years after they were initiated, advocates of fusion centers have failed to give more than a cursory account of the benefits they provide").

167 National Institute of Justice, *How to Identify Hot Spots*, http://nij.gov/topics/law-enforcement/strategies/hot-spot-policing/pages/identifying.aspx (last updated May 25, 2010) (describing the use of Geographic Information Systems "to more accurately pinpoint hot spots to confirm trouble areas, identify the specific nature of the activity occurring within the hot spot and then develop strategies to respond").

168 Joseph T. Small Jr. & Robert A. Burgoyne, *Criminal Prosecutions Initiated by Administrative Agencies: The FDA, the Accardi Doctrine, and the Requirement of Consistent Agency Treatment*, 78 J. Crim. L. & Criminology 87, 103–04 (1987).

169 *See, e.g.*, *Green County Mobilephone, Inc. v. FCC*, 765 F.2d 235, 237 (D.C. Cir. 1985) ("We reverse the Commission not because the strict rule it applied is inherently invalid, but rather because the Commission has invoked the rule inconsistently. We find that the Commissioner has not treated similar cases similarly"); *Distrigas of Mass. Corp. v. Fed. Power Comm'n*, 517 F.2d 761, 765 (1st Cir. 1975) ("[An administrative agency] has a duty to define and apply its policies in a minimally responsible and even-handed way"); *Crestline Memorial Hosp. Ass'n, Inc. v. NLRB*, 668 F.2d 243, 245 (6th Cir. 1982) (stating that the NLRB cannot "treat similar situations in dissimilar ways"); *Contractors Transport Corp. v. United States*, 537 F.2d 1160, 1162 (4th Cir. 1976) ("Patently inconsistent application of agency standards to similar situations lacks rationality" and is prohibited under the APA's arbitrary and capricious standard).

consider." In effect, this aspect of hard look analysis mimics disparate treatment doctrine, but without requiring the usual predicate of race or religion. If it turns out that a hot zone is not really hot, or that groups whose records are accessed by fusion centers are not more crime prone, the administrative policy begins to look irrational. To avoid the potential for rejection under the hard look standard, the differences in crime rates in these various scenarios should be noticeable. Otherwise the agency would be well advised to apply the program either across the board to all similarly situated zones or groups or on some other neutral basis (as the Supreme Court has required, for instance, with checkpoints[170]).

In short, hard look doctrine requires that, when carrying out surveillance, police agencies provide a rationale for any distinctions they make between places or groups of people. This requirement would force recognition of the fact that policing is redistributive. Police do not execute surveillance in a vacuum; they choose where, when, and how they will carry out their investigations and, as a result, affect some localities and types of people more than others. Today, these choices occur with little or no oversight. The result, some allege, is that some communities unfairly bear the brunt of police activity.[171] Administrative law principles give the courts the authority to make sure that is not the case.

E *Legislative Authorization*

A predicate to administrative rule making is that legislation must authorize the agency action about which rules are being made.[172] Sometimes the legislation directly mandates the action. Most of the time, however, the statute sets out a general directive that the agency must interpret and attempt to implement through its own policies. If an agency generates a rule, it must be consistent with its statutory delegation. Any agency rule that is *ultra vires* is void.

This principle could have significant implications for surveillance programs, because many such programs are not explicitly authorized by legislation. For instance, New York's Domain Awareness is, at best, grounded on omnibus statutory delegation of law enforcement powers.[173] Similarly, fusion centers often operate without any explicit statutory

170 *See Delaware v. Prouse*, 440 U.S. 648, 663 (1979).

171 Nirej S. Sekhon, *Redistributive Policing*, 101 J. Crim. L. & Criminology 1171, 1211 (2011) ("In proactive policing, police departments have considerable discretion to ration arrests as they see fit. These departmental choices generate winners and losers, with significant distributive consequences").

172 Schwartz, *supra* note 159, at 171 ("The statute is the source of agency authority as well as of its limits. If an agency act is within the statutory limits (or vires), its action is valid; if it is outside them (or ultra vires), it is invalid").

173 The New York City Domain Awareness Program was based on the authority of Chapter 18, 435(a) of the New York City Charter, which states that police shall "preserve the public peace, prevent crime, detect and arrest offenders, suppress riots, mobs and insurrections, disperse unlawful or dangerous assemblages … protect the rights of persons and property, guard the public health, preserve order… regulate, direct, control and restrict the movement of vehicular and pedestrian traffic for the facilitation of traffic and convenience of the public as well as the proper protection of human life and health … inspect and observe all places of public amusement, all places of business … enforce and prevent the violation of all laws and ordinances in force in the city; and for these purposes to arrest all persons guilty of violating any law or ordinance for the suppression or punishment of crimes or offenses." *Privacy Security Guidelines* (Guidelines) New York City 1 (Feb. 2009) (describing the statute), www.nyc.gov/html/nypd/downloads/pdf/ crime prevention/public).

authority;[174] thus, there is no legislative directive as to the types of information they can collect, the length of time they may maintain the information, or the types of wrongdoing they can attempt to detect. In an administrative paradigm, courts might well conclude that a more specific legislative mandate is required when government action is so significant in scope and involves such sensitive information.[175]

At the federal level, the Supreme Court has indicated that, at most, legislation need only set out a vague "intelligible principle" to guide agencies.[176] But if the only relevant legislative pronouncement is "to enforce the criminal law," even that vacuous mandate might not be met. It is also worth noting that the nondelegation doctrine – which is the genesis of the intelligible principle requirement – is much more robust in the states than it is at the federal level.[177] Thus, for instance, one state court has held that the nondelegation doctrine "requires that the legislature, in delegating its authority, provide sufficient identification of the following: (1) the *persons* and *activities* potentially subject to regulation; (2) the *harm* sought to be prevented; and (3) the general *means* intended to be available to the administrator to prevent the identified harm."[178]

As this language suggests, taken seriously the nondelegation doctrine would force the relevant legislature to be specific in authorizing surveillance programs. Enforced stringently, this language would require the legislating body to endorse in a statute the use of cameras and license plate recognition systems necessary to carry out the Domain Awareness program and the collection of information from financial and communications entities that occurs with fusion centers. Mandating that these issues be debated at the highest policy level ensures democratic accountability.

Just as importantly, the specific legislative directive requirement of the "persons or activities" sought to be regulated, the "harm" to be prevented, and the "means" of prevention would provide crucial guidance for law enforcement agencies implementing the types of "panvasive" surveillance at issue here,[179] especially with respect to the first category: persons and activities to be affected. If, for instance, a municipal legislature authorized camera surveillance for purposes of detecting and deterring violent crime, the principle of even-handed application would require cameras to be established in all areas of the city or, in the alternative, randomly selected areas of the city or areas of the city that are demonstrably more likely to be involved in violent criminal activity. The legislative provision would define the group to be subjected to the surveillance, which

174 *See* Constitution Project, *supra* note 137, at 6 (stating that fusion centers "derive their authority from general statutes creating state police agencies or memoranda of understanding among partner agencies"); *see also* Citron & Pasquale, *supra* note 166, at 1453–55 (discussing "confusing lines of authority" with respect to fusion centers).

175 *See* Barry Friedman & Maria Ponomarenko, *Democratic Policing*, 90 N.Y.U. L. Rev. 1827, 1843 (2015) ("As compared with the regulation of almost any other aspect of society that fundamentally affects the rights and liberties of the people, rules adopted by democratic bodies to govern policing tend to be few and far between").

176 *See Whiteman v. Am Trucking Ass'ns, Inc.*, 531 U.S. 457, 472 (2001) (quoting *J. W. Hampton, Jr. & Co. v. United States*, 276 U.S. 394, 409 (1928).

177 Jim Rossi, *Institutional Design and the Lingering Legacy of Antifederalist Separation of Powers Ideals in the States*, 52 Vand. L. Rev. 1167, 1172 (1999).

178 *Stofer v. Motor Vehicle Casualty Co.*, 369 N.E.2d 875, 879 (1977) (emphasis in original).

179 I coined the term "panvasive" to refer to police actions that are "pervasive, invasive and affect large numbers of people, most of whom police know are innocent of wrongdoing." Slobogin, *supra* note 145, at 3 n.3.

would force both the legislature and the law enforcement agency to be clear about the stakes involved and cabin the agency's discretion. Administrative law principles thus fit comfortably within a regulatory regime founded on legislation.

Conclusion

Integrating these observations about administrative law's role with other points made in this chapter suggests the following general outline of the how courts, legislatures, and agencies might interact in the surveillance context. Courts interpreting the Fourth Amendment establish the constitutional framework, which sets the minimum requirements and lays out the values that should inform regulation. Legislatures – at the federal level when interstate coordination is important or consensus has developed, at the state or local level in most other situations – then fill in the framework with more comprehensive, detailed, and up-to-date statutes. At that point, police agencies devise policies, consistent with both the Fourth Amendment and authorizing legislation, that reflect public input and the principle of even-handed application.

26 California's Electronic Communications Privacy Act (CalECPA): A Case Study in Legislative Regulation of Surveillance

Susan Freiwald†

This chapter looks in depth at a state surveillance law passed in 2016, the California Electronic Communications Privacy Act (CalECPA). CalECPA provides a good case study for how legislation may regulate surveillance given its unprecedented scope, high procedural hurdles, and strong remedies, and because of the ways it promotes transparency and limits the overcollection of private data. In addition to comparing CalECPA's provisions to its federal counterparts, this chapter describes the process by which CalECPA became law. Finally, it discusses some of its most significant innovations and the limits of its achievements.

Introduction

Most discussions of electronic surveillance law concern constitutional provisions such as the Fourth Amendment or federal statutes such as the 1968 Wiretap Act[1] and the 1986 Electronic Communications Privacy Act (ECPA).[2] This chapter focuses on state statutory law. The Wiretap Act sets the procedures by which law enforcement agents may acquire, in real time, the contents of phone calls or other private conversations. ECPA is divided into three titles, all of which regulate different investigative techniques. ECPA's first title updates the Wiretap Act so that its rules also apply when law enforcement agents acquire the contents of our electronic communications, such as our emails, as they are transmitted. ECPA's second title, the Stored Communications Act (SCA), sets the rules by which agents may acquire the electronic communications information that service providers store, such as users' emails and the records associated with users' communications.[3] The third title, known as the Pen Register Act because it regulates tools known as pen registers, regulates law enforcement's interception of communications addressing.[4]

† Associate Dean and Professor, USF School of Law. The author thanks Chi Vu and Arlette Noujaim for their research assistance and Chris Conley, Nicole Ozer, Everett Monroe, Brian Owsley, and Lee Tien for their helpful editing suggestions and discussions about CalECPA.

1 18 U.S.C. §§ 2510–2522. Others refer to the Wiretap Act as Title III because it was Title III of the Omnibus Crime Control and Safe Streets Act of 1968, P.L. 90–351, 801, 82 Stat. 197, 212.

2 The Electronic Communications Privacy Act of 1986, Pub. L. No. 99–508, 100 Stat. 1848 (1986) (codified as amended in scattered sections of 18 U.S.C.). Some surveillance discussions look at both the constitutional and statutory regulation of foreign intelligence surveillance, but this chapter will not.

3 18 U.S.C. §§ 2701–2712.

4 18 U.S.C. §§ 3121 et seq. Pen registers and related trap and trace devices, which collect incoming rather than outgoing information, are investigative methods for acquiring information as it is produced rather than out of electronic storage. This chapter will use "pen registers" as shorthand for pen registers and trap and trace devices.

Such data includes the telephone numbers dialed when a call is made and email header information. As this chapter will show, ECPA's use of categories, subcategories, and a host of defined terms makes study of its provisions difficult. It also yields weak privacy protection for users of new communications technologies.

This chapter looks in depth at a state surveillance law passed in 2015, the California Electronic Communications Privacy Act (CalECPA).[5] CalECPA's comprehensive surveillance regulation covers more investigative practices than ECPA. It provides rules for when agents obtain information directly from electronic devices that federal law does not. Unlike ECPA, CalECPA imposes the same rules when agents obtain information from electronic storage as when they intercept information in real time. Also unlike ECPA, CalECPA fully protects the full range of metadata, which is information associated with a communication but not the contents of the communication.[6] Besides its unprecedented scope and the higher level of its privacy protections, CalECPA provides more transparency and stronger remedies and does more to limit overcollection of data than ECPA.

Before turning to CalECPA's specific provisions, consider why statutory regulation of surveillance by a state merits study. First, states have room to regulate in the surveillance area, unlike in other areas, where federal law occupies, or preempts, the field. To have practical effect, state electronic surveillance statutes must be more restrictive than applicable federal law, which means that state statutory law may regulate law enforcement practices if it protects privacy above the floor that ECPA establishes.[7] So, for example, if federal law requires that law enforcement agents obtain a relevance-based court order before they may compel a provider to disclose stored communication records, a state's surveillance statute may require a more privacy-protective procedural hurdle. The state statute, could, for example, require that agents obtain a probable cause-based court order, or a warrant, because warrants involve more judicial oversight and are harder to obtain. But a state statute permitting agents to compel disclosure using only a subpoena would effectively be trumped by the stricter federal law, because subpoenas may issue without a judge's prior approval and are considered a weaker procedural hurdle.

Second, state statutes have significant effect in the surveillance arena, albeit regulating only the activities of state actors, such as state and local law enforcement agents and other state entities, because those agents currently conduct a significant amount of surveillance. According to a recent Wiretap Report, for example, state agents installed 2,313 wiretaps in 2015, as compared to 440 at the federal level.[8] In addition, state agents request a large amount of transactional data from companies.[9]

5 Pen. Code § 1546 et seq. *See infra* notes 104, 108 for information about the author's involvement with the passage of CalECPA.

6 CalECPA does not protect subscriber information, which is arguably not metadata because it is not associated with any particular communications. *See infra* text associated with notes 59–62.

7 *See* Memorandum from California L. Rev. Commission 2014–33, "State and Local Agency Access to Customer Information from Communication Service Providers: Electronic Communications Privacy Act of 1986" (Aug. 21, 2014) at 38–51, http://www.clrc.ca.gov/pub/2014/MM14-33.pdf (conducting preemption analysis and concluding that federal law likely "leaves room" for a statute like CalECPA).

8 *See* Wiretap Report 2015: Authorized Intercepts Grants, United States Courts (Dec.31, 2015), http://www.uscourts.gov/file/20055/download. The vast majority of wiretaps were authorized to be installed on portable devices.

9 *See, e.g.*, Google Transparency Report, https://www.google.com/transparencyreport/userdatarequests/US/; AT&T Transparency Report, http://about.att.com/content/csr/home/frequently-requested-info/governance/transparencyreport.html.

Because different states may pass surveillance statutes that have different practical consequences, the question becomes, When should one focus on a particular state's surveillance statute?[10] A case study of CalECPA make sense because it is a landmark achievement. While some state statutes passed prior to CalECPA are more privacy-protective than ECPA, none matches CalECPA's breadth and depth.[11] Although CalECPA does not achieve everything privacy advocates could ask for, its provisions furnish a sort of benchmark by which to measure other surveillance statutes.[12] In fact, immediately after its passage, commentators called CalECPA "the best digital privacy law in the nation"[13] and urged other states to follow the CalECPA example.[14]

This chapter provides that case study, and proceeds as follows. Part I describes CalECPA by contrasting it with ECPA. Parts II and III details the process by which the landmark legislation was able to make it through the legislative process in California. And Part IV provides a brief assessment of CalECPA's positive innovations and the limits of its achievements.

I CalECPA's Provisions Compared to Federal Law

The following sections view the law in California after passage of CalECPA through the lens of federal law – namely, ECPA.[15] Part A explains that CalECPA protects both those who store information with third party service providers and those whose information is stored on their own electronic devices, while ECPA protects only the first group. Part B covers the procedural hurdles that each statute imposes on law enforcement investigations.[16] It starts by detailing the broad array of information subject to CalECPA's warrant requirement, and then contrasts that with the much narrower set of information protected with ECPA's warrant requirement. It goes on to outline the various lesser protections that ECPA provides for all of the information that it does not subject to a warrant requirement. Part C covers the other privacy provisions found in CalECPA, such as the way it requires notice in all cases, limits overcollection of data, and furnishes strong

10 There have been useful surveys of all or most states' surveillance statutes. *See, e.g.*, Charles H. Kennedy & Peter P. Swire, *State Wiretaps and Electronic Surveillance After September 11*, 54 Hastings L.J. 971 (2003).

11 *See, e.g.*, Utah, HB 128 (2014) (enacted in Utah Code 77-23c-101 et. seq.) (requiring a warrant when government entities obtain "the location data, stored data or transmitted data of an electronic device"); Texas Code of Crim. Proc. 18.21 § 4 (requiring a warrant for access to "electronic customer data" other than records that reveal a customer's identity or his use of the applicable service); Maine, SP 157 (2013) (requiring a warrant for law enforcement access to stored location data).

12 *See infra* Part IV.B for a discussion of some limits of CalECPA's achievements.

13 Kim Zetter, *California Now Has the Nation's Best Digital Privacy Law*, Wired (Oct. 8, 2015, 9:58 PM), https://www.wired.com/2015/10/california-now-nations-best-digital-privacy-law/; *see also In Landmark Victory for Digital Privacy, Gov. Brown Signs California Electronic Communications Privacy Act into Law*, ACLU (Oct. 8, 2015), https://www.aclunc.org/news/landmark-victory-digital-privacy-gov-brown-signs-california-electronic-communications-privacy.

14 *See, e.g.*, Chris Conley, *California Leads on Electronic Privacy: Other States Must Follow*, ACLU (Oct. 13, 2015), https://www.aclunc.org/blog/california-leads-electronic-privacy-other-states-must-follow.

15 ECPA also governs state investigations to the extent that the applicable state statute does not override ECPA with more privacy-protective rules for that state's agents.

16 Both CalECPA and ECPA cover the actions of government entities generally, but this chapter will refer to law enforcement investigations. CalECPA does not impose a warrant when government entities compel disclosure of information for purposes other than "investigating or prosecuting a criminal offense." Pen. Code § 1546.1(b)(4) (permitted such compelled disclosures pursuant to otherwise authorized subpoenas).

remedies. CalECPA's additional privacy provisions are all the more remarkable when considered alongside ECPA's comparatively weaker provisions.

A *Statutory Scope*

ECPA protects the privacy of people who use third party service providers to store and transmit information. Its Title II, the Stored Communications Act (SCA), sets out complicated rules for when law enforcement agents may compel service providers to disclose stored electronic communications. ECPA's first title and the Pen Register Act provide rules for when agents intercept information in real time, often with the assistance of providers such as telephone companies and Internet service providers. As discussed previously, ECPA's first title amended the Wiretap Act to cover the interception of the contents of electronic communications.[17] ECPA separates out wire communications (telephone calls) from electronic communications (emails), but because CalECPA considers telephone calls, emails, and other Internet communications all to be electronic communications, this chapter will use that convention.[18] The Pen Register Act covers the interception of dialing, routing, addressing and signaling information.[19]

CalECPA's scheme is broader in scope and simpler in design. Because CalECPA regulates "the *production of* or *access to* electronic communication information" together, it treats real-time interception and acquisition of stored data identically.[20] In other words, CalECPA sets the terms by which a California law enforcement agent can demand that Google disclose a user's stored emails and metadata. But the same CalECPA provision also governs when an agent demands that Google assist the agent in obtaining access to that user's real-time email contents and addressing information.[21]

Unlike ECPA, CalECPA also protects those whose information is obtained directly from their electronic devices, such as their laptops and cell phones. CalECPA is designed to be technology-neutral; it defines devices by their function – to store, generate, or transmit information – rather than by listing the devices it covers.[22] As people use new technologies to accomplish the same functions, those devices will fall under CalECPA's protection. Again, although there are Fourth Amendment restrictions, federal law currently provides no statutory regulation for device-acquired data.

California law enforcement agents must follow CalECPA when they obtain information from an electronic device, for example by taking a person's smart phone or computer and typing commands into it to extract information.[23] They must also abide by CalECPA when they use an electronic communication to obtain information from

17 Unlike the SCA and the Pen Register Act, and confusingly, there is no short title for Title I of ECPA. Commentators refer to the first Title of ECPA as just ECPA, or the Wiretap Act, Title III, or even Title III/ECPA.

18 Pen. Code § 1546(c).

19 18 U.S.C. § 3121(c).

20 Pen. Code §§1546.1(b) (emphasis added). Technically, CalECPA retains separate provisions for traditional wiretap orders in Pen. Code §1546.1(b)(2), as it must to comply with federal law. It also uses slightly different orders for pen register investigations that still require probable cause. Pen. Code § 1546.1(b)(5) (added by 2016 amendment and cross-referencing to Pen. Code § 638.52(b)).

21 *See id.*

22 Pen. Code §§ 1546.1(a)(2), (3); 1546(f) (defining electronic device as "a device that stores, generates, or transmits information in electronic form").

23 Pen. Code §§ 1546.1(a)(2), (3).

an electronic device. Law enforcement agents have used cell-site simulators, or IMSI (International Mobile Subscriber Identity) catchers, to obtain electronic device information via electronic communications.[24] Sometimes known by product names such as StingRay, TriggerFish, or Hailstorm, cell-site simulators may learn the location of a cell phone and other information through electronic interactions with it.[25] The FBI has also used network investigative techniques (NITs) to gain remote access to targeted computers. In one case, the government surreptitiously launched a software program from a server it secretly controlled onto the target's computer when the target signed onto the server dedicated to child pornography. After installing itself on the target's computer, the government's software reported back enough information for the government to identify the target and locate his home for further investigation.[26] Had California law enforcement agents used an NIT to gain access to a target's computer, CalECPA would have governed and required those agents to obtain a warrant.[27] Because the FBI conducted the investigation, ECPA governed and imposed no restrictions.

B *Procedural Hurdles Imposed on Access to Information*

It is also important to assess the procedural hurdles a surveillance statute imposes on the agents who want to use the investigative methods that fall within its scope. ECPA uses many categories and several different types of procedural hurdles, while CalECPA generally groups all the information it covers into one category and relies on one procedural hurdle: a warrant based on probable cause.

Commentators consider the warrant requirement to be the second highest procedural hurdle available, with the highest being that found in the Wiretap Act. The Supreme Court has specified that wiretapping and related techniques such as electronic bugging must be subject to the highest level of judicial oversight because of their extremely intrusive nature.[28] Professor Orin Kerr has called the procedural hurdle for wiretap orders a super search warrant because it requires additional requirements besides probable cause.[29] There is no meaningful difference between the way federal law and CalECPA treat wiretaps, in that they both require super warrants.[30] Because this chapter focuses on more modern investigative methods and on the differences between ECPA and

24 *See, e.g.*, *Maryland v. Andrews*, 227 Md. App. 350 (Md. 2016).

25 *See* Brian L. Owsley, *Triggerfish, Stingrays, and Fourth Amendment Fishing Expeditions*, 66 HASTINGS L.J. 183 (2014); Stephanie K. Pell & Christopher Soghoian, *A Lot More than a Pen Register, and Less than a Wiretap: What the StingRay Teaches Us about How Congress Should Approach the Reform of Law Enforcement Surveillance Authorities*, 16 YALE J. L. & TECH. 134 (2013–14).

26 Although the government obtained a search warrant to search the target's home, the court held in dicta that no warrant was needed to launch the NIT. *United States v. Matish*, 2016 WL 3545776 (E.D. Va. 2016).

27 The target's laptop is clearly an electronic device and the government would have been using an electronic communication to access electronic device information under PEN. CODE § 1546.1(c).

28 *Berger v. New York*, 388 U.S. 41, 69 (1967); Susan Freiwald, *Online Surveillance: Remembering the Lessons of the Wiretap Act*, 56 ALA. L. REV. 9 (2004).

29 Orin Kerr, *Internet Surveillance Law after the USA Patriot Act: The Big Brother That Isn't*, 97 U. L. REV. 607, 620 (2003) (describing the hurdle for a wiretap order as a "super" search warrant).

30 California's Wiretap Law, PEN. CODE, § 629.50 et seq., is patterned on the federal model. *See* Memorandum from California L. Rev. Commission 2014–50, at 8–17, "State and Local Agency Access to Customer Information from Communication Service Providers: California Wiretap Statute and Related Law," Oct. 1, 2014 [hereinafter CLRC Memo 2014–50], http://www.clrc.ca.gov/pub/2014/MM14-50.pdf.

CalECPA, the following discussion will exclude discussion of wiretap orders and discuss traditional warrants and other procedural hurdles that are easier to surmount than the warrant requirement.

To obtain a standard warrant, agents must demonstrate probable cause, which means reason to believe that the investigation will yield evidence of a crime.[31] Judges review the facts submitted to ensure that probable cause has been established before issuing a warrant. That review is more searching than the review for a relevance-based court order. A warrant based on probable cause is a higher hurdle to overcome than the subpoena standard; subpoenas can issue without any judicial oversight and the basis for challenging subpoenas is limited. As this section will show, federal investigators obtain little of the information that ECPA protects subject to the probable cause warrant requirement. CalECPA, by contrast, imposes the warrant requirement on almost everything.

1 Subject to a Warrant Requirement

As a first cut, federal law subjects only investigations that acquire the contents of communications to a warrant requirement. That means that agents may conduct investigations under the Pen Register Act and many of those subject to the SCA without first obtaining warrants because those investigations obtain only noncontent information. As Section I.B.2 describes, federal statutory law permits law enforcement agents to compel the disclosure of noncontent data and to intercept metadata after first obtaining court orders that are easier to obtain than by establishing probable cause. Federal law also permits law enforcement agents to use subpoenas to obtain a significant amount of both content and non-content information.[32]

Although the SCA requires law enforcement agents to obtain a warrant when they compel the disclosure of the contents of electronic communications, only a subset of electronic communications contents are subject to this warrant requirement.[33] The SCA's provisions require a warrant to compel the disclosure of the contents of electronic communications when, and only when, those communications have been in electronic storage for 180 days or less on an electronic communications service.[34] The defined terms "electronic storage" and "electronic communications service" further limit the scope of the SCA's warrant protection.[35] For example, courts interpreting the SCA have held that electronic communications posted to a Web site are not subject to a warrant requirement because they are not in "electronic storage" according to the statutory definition.[36]

31 For CalECPA warrant requirements, *see* Pen. Code §§ 1546.1(b)(1); 1546.1(c)(1); 1546.1(d); Cal. Penal Code 1525 (containing also a particular description requirement). For federal warrant requirements *see* Fed. Rule. Crim. Pro. 41.

32 *See, e.g.*, 18 U.S.C. § 2703(b)(1)(B).

33 *See* 18 U.S.C. § 2510 (defining "contents" as "any information concerning the substance, purport, or meaning of that communication").

34 18 U.S.C. § 2703(a).

35 The SCA's use of defined terms like electronic communication service (ECS) and remote computing service (RCS) limit warrant protection. *See* U.S. Department of Justice Computer Crime & Intellectual Property Section Manual, "Searching and Seizing Computers and Obtaining Electronic Evidence in Criminal Investigations," Third Edition, (2009) [hereinafter DOJ Search Manual], https://www.justice.gov/sites/default/files/criminal-ccips/legacy/2015/01/14/ssmanual2009.pdf. Since 2013, however, it has been the Department of Justice Policy to use a warrant for access to all email contents. H. Rep. No. 114–528, at 9 (2014).

36 *See* DOJ Search Manual, *supra* note 35, at 124–26.

By contrast, CalECPA imposes its warrant requirement on access to both communications contents and associated noncontents, without distinction.[37] In addition, the broad application of CalECPA's warrant requirement across myriad investigations greatly simplifies its structure. CalECPA imposes a warrant requirement whether agents compel the disclosure of information by third party service providers or obtain information directly from electronic devices.[38] Access to information on electronic devices may occur through direct physical access or by electronic access. The warrant requirement applies whether agents obtain electronic information out of electronic storage or intercept it as it is generated in real time.

CalECPA's definitions broaden rather than narrow the scope of its warrant requirement. For example, CalECPA expansively defines electronic communication information, which is protected by the warrant requirement, to include "any information about an electronic communication or the use of an electronic communication service."[39] Electronic communication services are also broadly defined. They include services "that provide[] to its subscribers or users the ability to send or receive electronic communications, including any service that acts as an intermediary in the transmission of electronic communications, or stores electronic communication information."[40] By including as service providers those who merely store electronic communication information, CalECPA's definition includes cloud storage services such as DropBox, and social media sites such as Facebook, as well as traditional email providers such as Google (Gmail). That means that law enforcement agents in California must obtain a warrant before compelling the disclosure of electronic communication information about the use of social media sites and cloud storage services, which is a less certain result under federal law.

CalECPA also specifically lists information that agents need a warrant to obtain. The statute broadly defines "electronic communication information" as "including, but not limited to, the contents, sender, recipients, format, or location of the sender or recipients at any point during the communication, the time or date the communication was created, sent, or received, or any information pertaining to any individual or device participating in the communication, including, but not limited to, an IP address."[41] That expansive list goes beyond other law of its kind in protecting metadata, and particularly Internet protocol addressing information.[42]

Unlike ECPA, CalECPA subjects a second type of information to its warrant requirement: electronic device information.[43] Like electronic communication information, electronic device information may be stored or generated in real time. It may be stored

[37] CalECPA excludes subscriber information from its warrant requirement. *See infra* text accompanying notes 59–62.

[38] Pen. Code § 1546.1.

[39] CalECPA defines an electronic communication as "the transfer of signs, signals, writings, images, sounds, data, or intelligence of any nature in whole or in part by a wire, radio, electromagnetic, photoelectric, or photo-optical system." Pen. Code § 1546(c). This definition closely follows the federal version. 18 U.S.C. § 2510(12).

[40] Pen. Code § 1546(j).

[41] Pen. Code § 1546(d).

[42] The broad scope of California's statute is largely attributable to California's constitutional privacy provisions, which the California Supreme Court interpreted, in the 1970s, as extending enhanced protection to metadata such as telephone numbers. *See infra* text associated with notes 98–101.

[43] Pen. Code § 1546(g).

with a third party service provider or on the electronic device itself. But electronic device information does not have to be associated with a particular electronic communication to be protected by CalECPA's warrant requirement; it just has to be "information stored on or generated through the operation of an electronic device, including the current and prior locations of the device."[44] Individual photos, videos, directories, and other information may not be associated with a particular electronic communication but could still be electronic device information. Similarly, information that a cell phone generates about its location does not have to be associated with a particular communication to be protected.[45] Device identification numbers would also be included as electronic device information. For example, if a California government entity compelled a device manufacturer not acting as a service provider to divulge a device's unique device ID (not electronic communication information) in order to facilitate cracking its encryption, CalECPA would require a warrant.[46]

To review, ECPA requires a warrant only when law enforcement agents acquire the contents of some electronic communications stored with some service providers, subject to a time limit and other restrictions.[47] CalECPA requires a warrant when law enforcement agents obtain any electronic contents, most noncontent information, and electronic device data, which together is known as electronic information.[48] CalECPA imposes the warrant requirement on a wide range of law enforcement investigative techniques: the compelled disclosure of electronic information by electronic communication providers and access to electronic information on devices themselves.

2 Available without a Warrant

The procedural hurdles law enforcement agents face under the SCA when they compel a service provider to disclose stored electronic communications depend on the type of information sought. When agents seek the disclosure of electronic communication contents that are stored for more than 180 days, they may generally use a court order subject to an intermediate standard between mere relevance and probable cause. The order is called a D Order because of the SCA provision that authorizes it;[49] courts grant them when agents establish "specific and articulable facts" showing the information they seek is "relevant and material to an ongoing criminal investigation."[50]

When agents seek information that is not the contents of an electronic communication, ECPA imposes different procedural hurdles for information sought in real time as

44 Pen. Code § 1546(g).

45 *See also* Abby Liebeskind, 8 *Things to Know about CalECPA*, ZwillGen Blog (Dec. 4, 2015) (suggesting that electronic device information includes information obtained from an IMSI catcher, or a cell site simulator device such as a StingRay).

46 *See* In the Matter of the Search of an Apple IPhone Seized during the Execution of a Search Warrant, 2016 WL 618401 (C.D. Ca. Feb. 16, 2016).

47 In 2016 there was considerable support in Congress to simplify the SCA by requiring a warrant for all stored contents, independent of the length of storage. A bill that achieved unanimous support in the House of Representatives failed to progress in the Senate. *See* Email Privacy Act, H.R. 699, 114th Cong.

48 Pen. Code § 1546(h).

49 18 U.S.C. §§ 2703(b), (d). The D Order is also available for contents that do not otherwise require a warrant. *See id.*; *but see supra* note 35 (noting DOJ policy to require obtain a warrant for all email contents since 2013).

50 18 U.S.C. § 2703(d).

opposed to information sought out of electronic storage. Agents may obtain dialing, routing, addressing, and signaling (DRAS) information in real time if they first obtain a court order based on a lower hurdle than a D Order; the Pen Register Act requires only that agents certify that the information they seek is "relevant to a law enforcement inquiry."[51] Judges are to grant such orders when applications are complete, without conducting an independent review of the facts.[52] CalECPA, by contrast, requires law enforcement agents to obtain a warrant before agents may use pen registers because the devices obtain electronic information.[53]

Under the SCA, agents may obtain a D Order to compel service providers to disclose a "record or other information pertaining to a subscriber to or customer of an electronic communication service."[54] But agents do not need to obtain a D Order for *all* "records pertaining"; they may obtain some records using only a subpoena, including data that CalECPA protects with a warrant requirement. In particular, the SCA permits government entities to obtain call data records and subscriber numbers or identities with a subpoena, while CalECPA requires a warrant for access to that information, including IP addresses.[55] In addition, because records have to "pertain to a subscriber to or customer of an electronic communication service" to be protected, the SCA seems to exclude electronic device data that is not associated with electronic communications. CalECPA protects that information with its warrant requirement.

The SCA provides unclear coverage for location data, while CalECPA clearly protects it with its warrant requirement.[56] The SCA leaves opaque whether "records pertaining" includes data collected by cell phone service providers that indicate which cell towers cell phones use when they make and receive calls. Some judicial opinions have characterized cell tower data as tracking data that is not covered by the SCA.[57] If such data is included in the records pertaining category, then the SCA requires a D Order when government agents compel service providers to disclose it. If not, then it lacks statutory protection and its protection depends on whether the Fourth Amendment considers its acquisition a search, which is an unsettled question.[58]

Unlike ECPA, CalECPA does not provide for any intermediate or weaker court orders. It does, however, explicitly exclude one category of information from its warrant requirement.[59] CalECPA does not apply its warrant requirement to the compelled disclosure

51 18 U.S.C. §§ 3121, 3123.

52 S.Res. No. 99–541, 99th Cong. (2d Sess. 47 (1986)), *reprinted in* 1986 U.S.C.C.A.N. 3601.

53 Pen. Code § 1546.1(b)(5) (added by 2016 amendment and cross-referencing Pen. Code § 638.52(b), which requires a court order based on both relevance and probable cause).

54 18 U.S.C. § 2703(c).

55 *Compare* 18 U.S.C. § 2703(c)(2) *with* Pen. Code § 1546(d); *see also* Abby Liebeskind, *supra* note 45 (noting that CalECPA requires a warrant for payment information, call detail records and IP address information versus subpoena access under the SCA).

56 *See* Pen. Code § 1546(d) (definition of electronic communication information includes sender's/recipient's location); Liebeskind, *supra* note 45 (device data includes location data).

57 *See* Susan Freiwald, *Light in the Darkness: How the LEATPR Standards Guide Legislators in Regulating Law Enforcement Access to Cell Site Location Records*, 66 Okla. L. Rev. 875, 883–86 (2014).

58 *See infra* note 111.

59 As passed, CalECPA narrowly excluded some investigations, such as access to devices in some correctional facilities. Pen. Code § 1546.1(c)(7). Amendments to CalECPA in 2016 excluded a few more investigatory methods from the law's coverage, such as access to probationers' and parolees' devices. Pen. Code §§ 1546.1(c)(9), (10) (added by S. 1121 (Leno) (approved by the Governor on September 23, 2016)).

of subscriber information from service providers.[60] CalECPA defines subscriber information as "the name, street address, telephone number, email address, or similar contact information provided by the subscriber to the provider to establish or maintain an account or a communication channel, a subscriber or account number or identifier, the length of service, and the types of services used by a user of or subscriber to a service provider."[61] CalECPA explicitly preserves California government entities' existing authority to use administrative, grand jury, trial, or civil discovery subpoenas to obtain subscriber information.[62]

C *Other Provisions*

As the following discussion explains, CalECPA provides for more notice to targets of surveillance than ECPA. Without notice, subjects of surveillance may have no means to determine whether applicable rules were followed. CalECPA also provides for the destruction and sealing of irrelevant information and requires that warrants issued pursuant to its terms be tailored to their purpose. Finally, those who are subject to surveillance investigations that fail to adhere to CalECPA's terms may choose from a set of remedies that CalECPA provides. ECPA's remedies are far more limited.

1 Notice

Under ECPA, it is more the exception than the rule for notice to be provided to targets of surveillance. The Pen Register Act fails to require that notice be provided to targets. More than that, its rules provide that pen register orders are to be automatically sealed and that gag orders are to be imposed on providers who assist the government in installing pen registers.[63] The SCA explicitly requires notice to the target in only one context: when government entities use D Orders or subpoenas rather than warrants to access electronic communications contents held in electronic storage.[64] For all other methods that the SCA regulates, the statute dispenses with notice.[65]

By contrast, CalECPA requires that government entities furnish notice to the targets of all of their investigations.[66] Notice shall be furnished contemporaneously with the

[60] Pen. Code §§ 1546(d); 1546.1(a)(1); 1546.1(i)(3). In my view, CalECPA's exclusion of subscriber information from its warrant requirement reflects that such information does not change as much over time as do other types of electronic communication information. Patricia L. Bellia & Susan Freiwald, *Fourth Amendment Protection for Stored E-mail*, 2008 U. Chi. L. Forum 121, at 163–64 (describing subscriber information as "static information").

[61] Pen. Code § 1546(l).

[62] Pen. Code § 1546.1(i)(3).

[63] 18 U.S.C. § 3123(d).

[64] 18 U.S.C. § 2703(b)(1)(B). Note that notice can be delayed under the SCA for similar reasons as under CalECPA. 18 U.S.C. § 2705.

[65] 18 U.S.C. § 2703(b)(1)(A) (no notice required when a warrant is used to obtain contents); 18 U.S.C. § 2703(b)(1)(A) (no notice needed for records). Note that 18 U.S.C. § 2703(a), which requires a warrant, does not explicitly dispense with notice, but the government views notice as unnecessary when a warrant is used. *See* DOJ Search Manual, *supra* note 35, at 133–34.

[66] Pen. Code § 1546.2(a). Notice may be delayed in similar circumstances under CalECPA and ECPA. Pen. Code 1546.2(b)(1); 18 U.S.C. § 2705. CalECPA requires that extensive information be furnished to the target when notice is delayed, including the reason for the delay and the information, or a summary of it, that was collected in the investigation. § 1546.2(b)(3). ECPA has no such requirement.

warrant's execution, or, in the case of an emergency orders, within three days of receiving the information. CalECPA requires notice to include a copy of the warrant and to inform the target of the nature of the information about her that has been compelled or requested.[67]

As an interesting innovation that federal law lacks, CalECPA requires that investigating agents furnish information to the California Department of Justice (CalDOJ), in lieu of notice to the target, in cases when the target is not identified.[68] The CalDOJ must publish reports it derives from such information on its Web site within ninety days of receiving the information.[69] This mechanism will provide transparency to interested parties in investigations such as cell tower dumps and others that involve the collection of information from unspecified groups rather than a specific target.[70]

2 Tailoring

CalECPA further limits the scope of information gathered pursuant to its authority to reduce the risk of unjustified collection. While background California and Fourth Amendment law requires that a warrant particularly describe what is to be searched, CalECPA further requires that warrants issued pursuant to its terms specify "as appropriate and reasonable, the time periods covered, the target individuals or accounts, the applications or services covered, and the types of information sought."[71]

By contrast, even for those investigations for which the SCA requires a warrant, the federal statute includes no tailoring to limit the use of broad warrants. Service providers responding to SCA warrants may be compelled to disclose everything they have about a target. In one famous case, the service provider disclosed tens of thousands of emails from the target's account, spanning the nine years that he held his account with that provider.[72]

In addition to tailored warrants, CalECPA further mandates that any information obtained pursuant to its warrants that is "unrelated to the objective of the warrant" be sealed and made unavailable without a further court order. A court shall issue such an order, under CalECPA, only when federal or state law requires it or on a finding of probable cause to believe the information is relevant to an active investigation.[73] Limiting the use of nonpertinent information after its collection is consistent with data privacy principles. Judges who issue CalECPA warrants may, in their discretion, take other steps to reduce overcollection such as by appointing special experts to oversee the investigation[74]

67 Notice must also state the government investigation under which the information is sought with reasonable specificity. For emergency disclosures not involving warrants, the government entity must include a written statement that describes the facts that gave rise to the emergency.

68 Pen. Code §1546.2(c).

69 *Id.* It may redact names, of police officers presumably, and other personal identifying information from the reports.

70 *See* Brian Owsley, *The Fourth Amendment Implications of the Government's Use of Cell Tower Dumps in Its Electronic Surveillance*, 16 U. Pa. J. Const. L. 1, 3 (2013).

71 Pen. Code § 1546.1(d)(1) (as amended). Special masters are already provided for in Pen. Code § 1524(d), to which CalECPA refers.

72 *See* Bellia and Freiwald, *supra* note 59, at 130. (discussing the federal case against Warshak).

73 Pen. Code § 1546.1(d)(2).

74 Pen. Code § 1546.1(e)(1); *see* Liebeskind, *supra* note 45 (noting that law enforcement sometimes refers to the special master as part of a "taint team"). The judge may decide to appoint a special master on her own or in response to a petition brought by the target or recipient of the order. Pen. Code § 1546.1(e).

and by requiring the destruction of any information that investigators turn up that is "unrelated to the objective of the warrant."[75]

None of ECPA's provisions pertains to the segregation or deletion of irrelevant data.[76]

3 Sanctions and Remedies

Unlike federal law, CalECPA provides a statutory suppression remedy. Under its terms, "any person in a trial, hearing or proceeding may move to suppress any electronic information obtained in violation of the Fourth Amendment of the United States Constitution or [CalECPA]."[77] CalECPA also provides a broad data destruction provision that permits individuals, service providers, and others involved in investigations to petition the issuing court to "order the destruction of any information obtained in violation of [CalECPA], the California Constitution, or the United States Constitution."[78] Alternatively or in addition, petitioners may ask the court to void or modify a warrant, order, or other legal process that violates CalECPA.[79] Finally, the attorney general can bring a civil action to compel any government entity to comply with CalECPA.[80]

The SCA does not provide a suppression remedy, for the modification of an order granted under its terms, or for the attorney general to bring a civil action. Respected commentators have viewed the SCA's lack of a suppression remedy as its most significant failing, largely because without the possibility of having evidence against them excluded, criminal defendants lack an incentive to challenge law enforcement practices.[81] Without those challenges, the law fails to develop, in addition to the government's benefiting from improperly obtained evidence. The SCA does permit victims of unlawful acquisition to bring a damages action against a service provider that discloses their communications data in violation of the act, so long as the provider did not act in good faith.[82] CalECPA lacks that civil remedy.

While ECPA provides no remedies for improper pen register installations, there is the theoretical possibility of a criminal prosecution against an agent who conducts an improper pen register investigation.[83] The full range of CalECPA's remedies are available to victims of pen register–type investigations.

75 PEN. CODE § 1546(e)(2). To avoid the destruction of exculpatory information, the destruction obligation does not kick in until the government entity has terminated the current investigation and related investigations.

76 Consistent with the rest of Part I, the text discussion is not referring to the rules governing wiretaps, which are subject to special restrictions.

77 PEN. CODE § 1546.4 (a). CalECPA incorporates the procedures already in place under California law for handling suppression motions. PEN. CODE § 1546.4 (a) (referring to the procedures in California Penal Code §§ 1538.5(b) to (q)).

78 PEN. CODE § 1546.4(c).

79 PEN. CODE § 1546.4(c).

80 PEN. CODE § 1546.4(b).

81 *See, e.g.*, Orin S. Kerr, *Lifting the "Fog" of Internet Surveillance: How a Suppression Remedy Would Change Computer Crime Law*, 54 HASTINGS L. J. 805, 824 (2003).

82 18 U.S.C. § 2707 (providing for administrative discipline).

83 18 U.S.C. § 3121(d) (imposing criminal liability for the knowingly improper installation or use of a pen register).

II The Hurdles to CalECPA's Passage

State Senators Mark Leno and Joel Anderson introduced Senate Bill (SB) 178, which became CalECPA, in early 2015, but the push to reform California's electronic surveillance laws started years before. Senator Leno had previously sponsored other bills designed to give greater protection to modern users of electronic communications; those bills made it through the legislative process only to be vetoed by Jerry Brown, California's long-standing governor. One such bill, introduced in 2012, would have required a warrant for government access to location information but would not have covered other metadata or access to devices.[84] Another, introduced the next year, would have required a warrant and notice to the target when government entities compelled the disclosure of communications contents from service providers. That bill did not cover location data, metadata, or device-accessed data, and it did not include a suppression remedy.[85]

That Governor Brown had a practice of vetoing bills of significantly more modest scope than CalECPA led many observers to be skeptical of CalECPA's prospects. As discussed earlier, SB 178 goes far beyond federal law. What made its proponents think that the governor would sign a bill that accomplishes so much more than the others that he had previously vetoed? What made them think he would sign this bill when, in a prior veto message, Governor Brown had complained about notice provisions that went beyond federal law requirements?[86] Because of his veto messages and his former service as attorney general of California, which is California's top law enforcement official, many viewed Governor Brown as the most significant hurdle to passage of CalECPA.

But getting past the governor's desk would not be the only significant challenge. SB 178's statutory suppression remedy increased the number of votes needed to get it through the California legislature. A provision in the California constitution, created by voter initiative in 1984, abolished the ability of courts in California to exclude evidence from criminal proceedings unless pursuant to federal law or to a state statute that specifically provided for the suppression of evidence that had passed by two-thirds or more of the state legislature.[87]

The lack of comparable reform at the federal level acted as both a strong motivator for SB 178's proponents and a daunting example of the difficulty of obtaining privacy-enhancing reform of electronic surveillance statutes. Congress had passed ECPA in 1986 when the cell phone industry was in its infancy, nearly a decade before the World Wide Web became popular, and almost two decades before social networking and cloud computing had taken off. In the three decades since, Congress maintained ECPA's structure and terminology, and its weak protection of electronic communications.[88] The only

84 S. 1434 (Leno) (vetoed Sept. 9, 2012). The bill provided for a limited suppression remedy to exclude improperly gathered evidence from civil and administrative, but not criminal, proceedings.

85 S. 467 (vetoed Oct. 12, 2013) (providing for a civil action of $1,000). *See also* S. 914 (Leno) (vetoed Oct. 9, 2011) (requiring a warrant for access to electronic devices during a search incident to arrest, overturning a California Supreme Court decision preceding the Supreme Court's decision).

86 S. 467 (Leno). In vetoing S. 1434, which required a warrant for location data, Governor Brown remained unconvinced that the bill "struck the right balance between the operational needs of law enforcement and individual expectations of privacy."

87 Right to Truth-in-Evidence, Cal. Const. art. I, § 28(f)(2).

88 *See supra* Part I.

reforms to ECPA have not been substantially privacy-protective.[89] Privacy-enhancing bills of much more modest scope than CalECPA had failed to achieve passage in recent years.[90]

The prospects for reform looked daunting indeed for SB 178. Part III discusses how such an ambitious bill nonetheless made it through the legislative process into law.

III CalECPA's Passage

A *California Legal Backdrop*

Despite the hurdles, aspects of its legal landscape made California a promising state for statutory surveillance reform. California had passed significant privacy-protective legislation in the commercial context. It was an early adopter of aggressive antispam legislation[91] and the first to pass a data breach notification law to protect consumers' data security.[92] California's requirement that online providers post their privacy policies in a conspicuous position had set the nationwide standard.[93] In a 2016 book on California data privacy law, the attorney Lothar Determann urged privacy compliance officers to update their compliance policies regularly because "the California legislature constantly enacts new laws."[94]

California has an exceptionally privacy-protective state constitution, which imposes restrictions on both private parties and state actors. California's constitution expressly protects privacy in Article 1, Section 1, which states: "All people are by nature free and independent and have inalienable rights. Among these are enjoying and defending life and liberty, acquiring and possessing, and protecting property, and pursuing and obtaining safety, happiness, and privacy."[95]

Most pertinent to CalECPA, the California Supreme Court had flatly rejected the Supreme Court's third party doctrine.[96] That doctrine provides no constitutional protection to information people share with third parties, such as the bank records people store with their banks and the telephone numbers they dial that are accessible to their phone companies. In two decisions from the 1970s, the Supreme Court held that because people assume the risk that third parties will disclose that information to the government,

89 *See, e.g.*, Susan Freiwald, *Uncertain Privacy: Communication Attributes After the Digital Telephony Act*, 69 S. Cal. L. Rev. 949 (1996) (recounting the background and passage of CALEA); Beryl A Howell, *Seven Weeks: The Making of the USA PATRIOT Act*, 72 Geo. Wash. L. Rev. 1145 (2004).

90 *See, e.g.*, Email Privacy Act, H.R. 699 (114th Cong.) (expanding application of the warrant requirement to all of stored contents data but not to metadata and not providing a suppression remedy).

91 *See* David E. Sorkin, *Technical and Legal Approaches to Unsolicited Electronic Mail*, 35 U.S.L. Rev. 325 (2001); David T. Bartels, *Canning Spam: California Bans Unsolicited Commercial Email*, 30 McGeorge L. Rev. 420 (1999) (describing 1998 Act).

92 Cal. Civ. Code § 1798.82(a). *See* InfoLawGroup LLP, *10 Years after SB 1386, California Attorney General Issues First Ever Report and Recommendations on Data Breaches*, Information Law Group (July 1, 2013), http://www.infolawgroup.com/2013/07/articles/breach-notice/10-years-after-sb-1386-california-attorney-general-issues-first-ever-report-and-recommendations-on-data-breaches/.

93 California Online Privacy Protection Act, Cal. Bus. & Prof. Code § 22575(a) (effective Jan. 1, 2014).

94 Lothar Determann, *California Privacy Law: Practical Guide and Commentary*, 3–12 at 290 (2016).

95 Cal. Const. art. 1, § 1.

96 Academics have criticized the third party doctrine. *See, e.g.*, Stephen E. Henderson, *The Timely Demise of the Fourth Amendment Third Party Doctrine*, 96 Iowa L. Rev. Bull. 39 (2011); Erin Murphy, *The Case against the Case for the Third-Party Doctrine: A Response to Epstein & Kerr*, 24 Berkeley Tech. L. J. 1239 (2009); Susan Freiwald, *First Principles of Communications Privacy*, 2007 Stan. Tech. L. Rev. 3.

people lack a reasonable expectation of privacy in it and Fourth Amendment fails to protect it.[97] For that reason, at the federal level, legal protection for bank records, telephone numbers dialed, and analogous information is provided only by statutes and not by the Constitution. The lack of a constitutional backdrop helps explain federal law's weak regulation of pen registers, which obtain telephone numbers dialed, and its weak oversight of records acquisition under the SCA.

Just as the United States Supreme Court was establishing the third party doctrine, the California Supreme Court rejected that approach under the California constitution. Instead, California's highest court determined that information sufficient to form a "virtual current biography" is subject to a reasonable expectation of privacy and California constitutional protection.[98] The California Supreme Court found that a list of telephone numbers, an early form of metadata, could create such a virtual current biography.[99] Applying that reasoning, California's attorney general subsequently determined that California law enforcement agents would not be able to use pen registers under the federal standard because California requires prior judicial review.[100] Until CalECPA, however, no pen register rule was codified.[101]

California's constitutional protection for third party data fueled proponents' arguments that California could and should do more than federal law. Further, before CalECPA, California statutory law was odd and incomplete when it came to the procedures by which California government entities could obtain electronic communication information. Besides California's Wiretap Act, which paralleled the federal law, and the Reader Privacy Act, which requires a warrantlike court order before government agents may obtain customer records of book services, California's statutory scheme left much uncovered.[102] Regarding in-state law enforcement demands for information from in-state companies, California statutes required a warrant only for some information associated with a small subset of crimes in a narrow set of contexts.[103] For much of the information SB 178 would cover, Californians were left with a constitutional privacy right but no effective enforcement remedy.

B *Coalition*

A small group of privacy activists in the American Civil Liberties Union (ACLU) of Northern California and the Electronic Frontier Foundation (EFF) advised the bill's

97 *Smith v. Maryland*, 442 U.S. 735, 744–46 (1979); *United States v. Miller*, 425 U.S. 435, 443 (1976).

98 *Burrows v. Superior Court*, 529 P.2d 590, 593 (Cal. 1974) (finding a reasonable expectation of privacy in bank records); *People v. Blair*, 602 P.2d 738, 746 (Cal 1979) (en banc) (finding a reasonable expectation of privacy in telephone numbers dialed).

99 *Blair*, 602 P.2d at 746–48; *see also In re*: Application for Telephone Information Needed for a Criminal Investigation, 119 F. Supp. 3d 1011, 1025 (N.D. Ca. 2015) (relying in part on Blair to require a warrant for access to historical location data).

100 86 Ops. Cal. Atty. Gen. 198 (2003).

101 CLRC Memo 2014–50, *supra* note 35, at 19.

102 CLRC Memo 2014–50, *supra* note 35, at 18 (describing California's "fragmented statutory approach to government access to stored communications" and noting it "has produced some odd inconsistencies.").

103 See CLRC Memo 2014–50, supra note 35, at 18 (discussing an identity theft statute requiring warrants to request some information associated with some misdemeanor property crimes and some crimes involving fraud or embezzlement but noting that "staff could not find any California statute governing a search warrant issued by a California court for service on a California corporation").

sponsors, Senators Leno and Anderson.[104] They assisted in drafting and amending SB 178, preparing supporting documents, testifying before legislative committees, and coordinating the communications and lobbying efforts.

Throughout the more than year-long process to achieve passage of SB 178, the sponsors and their advisers received substantial support from a broad coalition of private and public enterprises. Technology companies in the coalition complained that current law was insufficiently privacy protective and was not supplying enough consistency or certainty to build customer trust, particularly for cloud users.[105] A large number of civil society and civil rights organizations applauded the way SB 178 would, if passed, enhance privacy, increase government transparency, and reduce the excessive surveillance that had chilled First Amendment–protected activities.[106] Criminal defense organizations also supported the bill's enhanced protections, as did consumer groups and groups supporting online civil liberties.[107]

I drafted, and a group of thirty-nine academic experts submitted, a letter in support of SB 178.[108] That letter emphasized California's special constitutional recognition of privacy in third party records, in contrast to the position taken by the federal courts. The letter also emphasized that the Supreme Court and lower federal courts had increasingly recognized the need to protect citizens' privacy in new communications technologies against excessive intrusion by government investigators. The Supreme Court had recently found enhanced privacy interests in cell phones and required a warrant (or exigent circumstances) for the search of a cell phone incident to an arrest.[109] In that decision, as in one the court had issued a few years earlier, the Court had held that cases decided before the advent of powerful new communications technologies were not adequate precedents and that new approaches were needed.[110] Those decisions supported the need for specially tailored legislation such as SB 178.

104 The ACLU of Northern California, the California Newspaper Publishers Association, and the EFF were official cosponsors of SB 178. Staff members from the Center for Democracy and Technology also advised the bill's sponsors, as did the author of this chapter, who served on the language and policy teams and testified before the California legislature as an issue expert.

105 *See, e.g.*, Adobe S. 178 Support Letter, https://www.eff.org/document/adobe-sb-178-support-letter. Companies submitting letters of support also included Apple, Facebook, Foursquare, Google, LinkedIn, Mozilla, Namecheap, and Twitter, with many others on the record in support. Business organizations such as Engine, the Internet Association, and Small Business California also supported S. 178. *See* California's Electronic Communications Privacy Act (CalECPA) S. 178, https://www.eff.org/cases/californias-electronic-communications-privacy-act-calecpa (posting all support letters) [Hereinafter Support Letters].

106 Organizations such as Asian Law Caucus, Council on American–Islamic Relations, and the National Center for Lesbian Rights submitted support letters for SB 178. *See* Support Letters, *supra* note 105.

107 The California Attorneys for Criminal Justice and the California Public Defenders Association submitted support letters, as did the Consumer Federation of California and Consumer Action. Restore the Fourth, the Privacy Rights Clearinghouse, Tech Freedom, the New America: Open Technology Institute and the Internet Archive also submitted letters in support of SB 178. *See* Support Letters, *supra* note 105.

108 *See* Scholar's Support Letter, Sept. 12, 2015, https://www.usfca.edu/sites/default/files/law/sb178scholarssupportletterforgovernorbrownseptember12.pdf.

109 *California v. Riley*, 134 S. Ct. 2473 (2014); *see also id.* at 2490 (recognizing an interested in location data by noting that "historic location information is a standard feature on many smart phones and can reconstruct someone's specific movements down to the minute, not only around town but also within a particular building").

110 *See Riley*, 134 S. Ct. at 2488–92; *United States v. Jones*, 132 S. Ct. 945 (2012) (protecting a privacy interest in the movements of a car over time); *see also United States v. Cooper*, 2015 WL 881578, *6 (N.D.

At the same time, the federal courts' privacy decisions were limited. The doctrine of exigent circumstances, under which agents may access cell phones incident to arrest, is more expansive than the comparable provisions of SB 178. The federal appellate courts had remained split on whether to require a warrant for location information stored with service providers, with the trend rejecting protection under the third party doctrine.[111] The federal courts had withheld protection entirely from other types of metadata, following the same interpretation of the third party doctrine that had led them to withhold protection from location data.[112]

C Scattered Opposition

Law enforcement groups initially opposed SB 178. Prosecutors complained that the bill's new procedures would undermine efforts to stop child exploitation and sheriffs complained about the burden of new reporting requirements, which were lost to later amendments.[113] The police raised concerns about whether the proposed limits on the use of electronic communications to access electronic device data would inhibit online investigations of child predators, stalkers, cyber bullies, and Internet fraudsters.[114]

The coalition engaged in intensive negotiations with law enforcement representatives and the bill was amended to reduce opposition. In addition to dropping the reporting requirements because of cost concerns, the bill's sponsors facilitated online undercover investigations by refining the notion of specific consent. By the time the bill was presented to the floors of the state assembly and the state senate, the following influential groups had removed their opposition to the bill: the California District Attorneys Association, the California State Sheriffs' Association, and the California Police Chiefs Association.[115] The California Police Chiefs Association letter announcing its neutrality indicated that "in its current form, SB 178 strengthens community relationships and increases transparency without impeding on law enforcement's ability to serve the needs of their communities."[116]

Truly heated opposition to the bill nonetheless arose on the floor of the assembly. Protect.org, an advocacy group dedicated to protecting children, opposed the bill on the ground that it would inhibit online investigations of child predators. The group marshaled considerable late-breaking opposition to the bill from lawmakers, which

Ca. 2015) (citing *Riley* for the proposition that courts should not rely on old precedents for determining how to regulate new surveillance methods).

111 *See United States v. Davis*, 785 F.3d 498 (11th Cir. 2015) (en banc) (finding no reasonable expectation of privacy in cell site location records); *In re* Application of the United States for Historical Cell Site Data, 724 F.3d 600 (5th Cir. 2013) (same); *but see United States v. Graham*, 796 F.3d 332 (4th Cir. 2015) (finding an expectation of privacy in cell site location records), *reh'g en banc granted*, 624 Fed. Appx. 75 (2015).

112 See, e.g., *United States v. Forrester*, 521 F.3d 500, 509 (9th Cir. 2007).

113 CA B. An., S.B. 178 Sen., March 24, 2015, http://www.leginfo.ca.gov/pub/15–16/bill/sen/sb_0151-0200/sb_178_cfa_20150323_154657_sen_comm.html.

114 CA B. An., S.B. 178 Assem., June 23, 2015 (summarizing the concerns of the California Police Chiefs Association), http://leginfo.ca.gov/pub/15–16/bill/sen/sb_0151-0200/sb_178_cfa_20150619_152455_asm_comm.html.

115 *See* Support Letters, *supra* note 105.

116 California Police Chiefs Notice of Neutrality on 178 dated Aug. 24, 2015, Support Letters, *supra* note 105. The San Diego Police Chiefs Association came out in support of the bill. *See* Support Letters, *supra* note 105.

jeopardized getting the two-thirds votes needed. Protect.org objected that the bill's emergency provisions did not apply in child pornography investigations not raising the risk of death or serious injury.[117] But the group merely opposed the bill rather than offering workable alternative language. Faced with overwhelming support for the bill, their blanket opposition did not carry the day.

SB 178's proponents ultimately prevailed in the legislature. One month later, the governor signed the bill into law.[118] But of course the full story has yet to be told. In September of 2016, Governor Brown signed an amendment to CalECPA that made minor changes and excluded some more investigative categories from the statute' reach.[119] A controversial amendment that would have entirely excluded school's from CalECPA's coverage was proposed in early 2017.[120]

IV CalECPA's Positive Innovations and Limits on Its Effectiveness

A *Positive Innovations*

CalECPA's comprehensive and uniform approach represents one of its greatest features. The new law avoids many of the line-drawing problems ECPA raises when it uses different procedural hurdles and protections based on categories of information.[121] CalECPA protects metadata, location data, electronic communications contents, and electronic device data with the same warrant requirement. That dispenses with the need to determine where a piece of data resides, how long it has resided there, and the nature of the provider that stores it. It also obviates the need to distinguish between contents and noncontents, a task that has befuddled courts and commentators.[122] CalECPA's clear approach not only enhances privacy protections, but inhibits efforts to end-run those protections by fitting an investigation into a category subject to less oversight.[123]

CalECPA does not distinguish between access to information in real time and access to the same information in record form because it does not subscribe to the third party doctrine.[124] CalECPA codifies the opposite of the third party doctrine because its drafters recognized that a service provider's access to or retention of a person's emails or metadata is no reason to withhold privacy protection from that information. CalECPA reflects the principle that modern users of online intermediaries and electronic devices should not forfeit the right to have surveillance take place only subject to judicial supervision.

CalECPA's efforts to limit the overcollection of data also represent an important innovation. As we store more and more information on our devices and in the cloud, it is crucial that authorization to access some information not be leveraged to see the entirety of a person's life.

117 *See Protect Analysis of S.B. 178*, Protect (Sept. 9, 2015), http://protect.org/178.

118 SB 178 passed the Senate 34 to 4, with 2 abstentions and the Assembly 57 to 13 with 10 abstentions.

119 SB 1121 (Leno) (2016). *See supra* note 59.

120 AB 165 (Cooper) (2017).

121 *See* Susan Freiwald & Sylvain Métille, *Reforming Surveillance Law: The Swiss Model*, 28 Berkeley Tech. L.J. 1261 (recommending a recently passed Swiss statute as a model for surveillance legislation).

122 *See, e.g.*, Steven M. Bellovin, et al., *It's Too Complicated: How the Internet Upends* Katz, Smith, *and Electronic Surveillance Law*, 30 Harv. J. L. & Tech . *1* (2016).

123 *See, e.g.*, Freiwald, *supra* note 57, at 894–97 (describing how agents used requests that providers momentarily store cell site location records and then deliver them, on an ongoing basis, in an apparent attempt to avoid higher procedural hurdles on real-time access).

124 *See supra* text accompanying notes 96–102.

It is difficult to implement workable restrictions on access and use given legitimate concerns that targets will hide data and that destruction of data risks destroying exculpatory information as well as inculpatory. But CalECPA's tailored warrant and its other provisions designed to limit the information collected and stored to only that which is relevant to an investigation resulted from engaged negotiations and attempt to balance all interests.

B *Limits on CalECPA's Effectiveness*

Perhaps the most significant limit of CalECPA is that it did not achieve as much as it might have in terms of transparency. The first versions of CalECPA included detailed reporting requirements that would have significantly aided in assessing how much surveillance is conducted under its terms and the efficacy of those surveillance efforts. Those requirements had to be dropped from the bill to get past the State Senate Appropriations Committee, as a result of concerns about the costs of record keeping.[125] Without the reporting requirements, it will be much harder to assess both the impact of CalECPA and the need for any further reform.

If one considers CalECPA's goal to be reining in excessive law enforcement practices, then one might complain about the fact that its remedies are limited to the suppression remedy. CalECPA does not provide any fines or other damage awards to victims of unlawful investigations. It also does not authorize suits against private entities. Instead, CalECPA provides that no corporations or their agents shall be subject to any cause of action for complying with any process issued pursuant to the chapter.[126] Monetary damages against improperly acting agents or improperly acting providers would have increased the deterrence potential of CalECPA. At the same time, it would have been difficult to obtain the strong support of private companies in the CalECPA coalition without the provision of this type of civil immunity.

Conclusion

We will only know how anomalous CalECPA is when we see whether and to what extent its reforms are replicated by other states and even at the federal level. Significant reform from Congress will likely have to await more movement from the federal courts.[127] Limiting or getting rid of the third party doctrine would open the way for federal surveillance reform, as it has in some states.[128] In any case, time will tell whether new statutes, including CalECPA, effect meaningful change in police practices and in the privacy of our electronic communications. With its heightened procedural hurdles, expansive scope, strong remedies, and other privacy-protective provisions, CalECPA is likely to enhance people's privacy in their new communications technologies significantly.

125 *See Senate Committee on Appropriation SB 178 Analysis*, Electronic Frontier Foundation (2015), https://www.eff.org/document/senate-appropriations-committee-sb-178-analysis.

126 Pen. Code § 1546.4(d).

127 Note that the introduction of H.R. 699, The Email Privacy Act, was spurred by the decision in *United States v. Warshak*, 631 F.3d 266 (6th Cir. 2010), which found stored email contents protected by the Fourth Amendment's warrant requirement. *See* H. Rep. No. 114–528, at 9 (2014).

128 *See* Stephen E. Henderson, *Learning from All Fifty States: How to Apply the Fourth Amendment and its State Analogs to Protect Third-Party Information from Unreasonable Search*, 55 Cath. U. L. Rev. 373 (2006) (discussing states that have rejected the third party doctrine by constitution and by statute).

27 Surveillance in the European Union

Cristina Blasi Casagran*

This chapter provides an overview of the major regulations and case-law governing surveillance in the European Union (EU) over the last several years. It examines the EU instruments that collect and process data for security purposes, and it identifies the new legal basis included in the Treaty of Lisbon with regard to security measures. As for EU bodies involved in surveillance activities, this chapter focuses on the role of Europol as the main EU agency that provides support to the member states in the prevention, combat, and prosecution of crimes. In addition, it examines the tasks of the EU centre "IntCen," in an attempt to determine whether the EU has legal authority to regulate surveillance practices conducted by intelligence services in the member states.

Introduction

The number of victims of terrorist attacks in Europe has tremendously increased in the last few years. Whereas in 2014 only four people were killed in terror-related assaults, the number grew to 267 in 2015, and there have been other 181 killings in terror attacks until April 2017.[1] To the same extent, surveillance measures consisting of the collection and processing of personal data have lately expanded in Europe.

Yet, the use of surveillance measures by police and intelligence forces is not a new practice. In the aftermath of the terrorist attacks of September 11, 2001, and especially after the attacks that occurred in Madrid in 2004, the EU adopted numerous surveillance laws and instruments. These regulate such aspects as Internet surveillance, wiretapping or telephone surveillance, camera or video surveillance, and biometric surveillance, and they all have in common that they consist of the collection and processing of huge volumes of personal data.

In 2013, the former analyst of the National Security Agency (NSA) Edward Snowden, disclosed more than 1.7 million documents on global surveillance programmes and other controversial activities conducted by the NSA. These revelations sparked a heated debate about the NSA as well as about the activity of EU law enforcement and intelligence agencies. Although the NSA is located on US soil, the United States is not the only

* Postdoctoral researcher, Autonomous University of Barcelona, email: cristina.blasi@uab.es.

1 Sarah Dean, *Continent of Fear: Terrifying Map Shows How 443 Victims Were Killed in 18 Deadly Terror Attacks in the Last Two Years in Europe*, Daily Mail (July 27, 2016), https://www.thereligionofpeace.com/attacks/europe-attacks.aspx.

country that carries out massive surveillance activities. Most countries in the world are engaging in similar surveillance practices.

In the EU, as in the US, a significant part of the information exchanged for the prevention and combat of serious crimes is collected by law enforcement and intelligence agencies. According to Snowden's documents, many studies have concluded that Internet surveillance programmes in the European Union are equivalent to those of the NSA.[2] Thus, after the Snowden revelations, one of the biggest debates around the EU security measures has been the potential violation of individual rights to privacy and data protection.

This chapter will provide an overview of the major regulations and case-law governing surveillance in the EU over the last several years. In order to do that, it will firstly examine EU legislation adopted in the aftermath of 9/11. Secondly, it will look at the Treaty of Lisbon and particularly at the new legal bases that allow the collection and processing of data for the prevention, combat, and prosecution of crimes. Thirdly, it will assess the potential clash between EU surveillance activities based on the processing of data and the EU right to privacy. After that, it will discuss the blurry concept of 'national security' and the limits that the EU has in regulating surveillance measures adopted for national security purposes. Finally, this chapter will offer some insights on future issues and challenges related to the regulation of surveillance measures within the EU.

I Post-9/11 EU Surveillance Measures

EU member states originally had exclusive authority to legislate security measures in the field of criminal law. National governments had wide discretion for passing security measures, which led to significant differences between member states' criminal justice systems.[3] The same diversity existed for the particular surveillance rules on the collection and processing of data in the prevention, detection, investigation, and prosecution of crimes. The main problem resulting from this disparity was the lack of cross-border police cooperation in the exchange of relevant information during a criminal investigation.

In 2001, the 9/11 attacks led to the reinforcement of these surveillance policies. Supranational organizations such as the United Nations (UN), the North Atlantic Treaty Organization (NATO), and the European Union (EU) adopted new strategies as a reaction to the global war on terror.

In an effort to contribute to global security, the Security Council of the United Nations (UNSC) announced a number of resolutions for the prevention and combat of crimes. These resolutions had to be implemented by the UN contracting parties, which included all EU member states. However, since UNSC resolutions are not self-executing, EU measures implementing UN resolutions were needed before these were incorporated as national laws of the member states. The Common Position on counter-terrorism[4] implemented by UNSC Resolution 1373 is an example of such a measure.

2 Stefan Heumann & Ben Scott, *Law and Policy in Internet Surveillance Programs: United States, Great Britain and Germany*, 25 Impulse: Stiftung Neue Verantwortung, 1–17 (2013); Kai Biermann, *German intelligence service is as bad as the NSA*, The Guardian (Oct. 4, 2013), https://www.theguardian.com/commentisfree/2013/oct/04/german-intelligency-service-nsa-internet-laws.

3 Michael Luchtman, *Choice of Forum in An Area of Freedom, Security and Justice*, 7 Utrecht L. Rev. 74, 74–101.

4 2001 O.J. (L 344) 90–92.

Likewise, the EU adopted several new legislative acts after the attacks in order to prevent and combat terrorism and other serious crimes, many of which were based on surveillance activities. Also, the EU reinforced its cooperation with the United States in the field of law enforcement. In support of these efforts, the EU institutions and US agencies established international relations departments that would deal with external security matters.

The EU released its first action plan on terrorism on 16 October 2001. In it, intelligence services were encouraged to increase their cooperation as well as to exchange more information.[5] Moreover, the EU established the so-called Counter-terrorism Group (CTG) and the CP 931 Working Party[6] right after the attacks. All these measures were complemented by the adoption of the European Security Strategy two years later.[7]

Three years after 9/11, new atrocities took place, this time on European soil. On 11 March 2004 two bombs were detonated on a commuter train in Madrid and, on 7 July 2005 three underground trains and a bus were bombed in London . The attacks in Madrid and London led to the proposal of new security measures by the EU institutions. For instance, the Council of the EU released declarations in 2004[8] and 2005[9] underlining the need to adopt an instrument for the retention of telecommunications. As a response, the commission issued five communications[10] proposing mechanisms to reinforce coordination among law enforcement authorities within the EU. In 2005, the EU adopted a Council Decision on the exchange of information and cooperation concerning terrorist offences[11] and the Hague Programme.[12] This programme included several clear recommendations for intensifying police cooperation among EU member states and creating new systems for exchanging information with a cross-border dimension.

More specifically, the EU has adopted four fundamental instruments in order to accelerate, simplify, and intensify cooperation among member states in the exchange of crime-related information. The first instrument was Council Framework Decision 2006/960/JHA[13] (also known as the Swedish initiative), which ensures that a member state requesting information from another member state does not get stricter conditions than those imposed on its national law enforcement authorities for a purely internal case. The Swedish initiative was later complemented by the Prüm procedures, which provide data-exchange mechanisms for DNA, fingerprints, and vehicle registration data within the EU.[14] Along with the Swedish initiative and the Prüm mechanisms, a further instrument was launched in 2004[15] and amended in 2008:[16] the European Criminal Records

5 European Commission Press Release 12800/01, *Note from the Presidency. Co-Ordination of Implementation of the Plan of Action to Combat Terrorism* (Oct. 16, 2001).

6 2001 O.J. (L 344) 93–96.

7 European Commission Press Release, *A Secure Europe in a Better World* (Dec. 12, 2003).

8 European Commission Press Release, *Declaration on combating terrorism* (Mar. 25, 2004).

9 European Commission Press Release, *Declaration on Condemning the Terrorist Attacks on London* (July 13, 2005).

10 COM (2004) 376 final (May 18, 2004); COM (2004) 429 final (June 16, 2004); COM (2004) 698 final, COM (2004) 702 final, COM (2004) 701 final, and COM (2004) 700 final (Oct. 2004).

11 2005 O.J. (L 253) 22–24.

12 2005 O.J. (C 53) 1–14.

13 2006 O.J. (L 386) 89–100.

14 2008 O.J. (L 210) 1–11; 2008 O.J. (L 210) 12–72.

15 COM (2010) 385 final, (July 20, 2010,) at 12.

16 2008 O.J. (L 220) 32–34.

Information System (ECRIS). It sought to exchange information on convictions among member states, allowing police and judicial authorities to obtain information about any previous criminal record registered in other member states. The last of the EU data-sharing instruments is the European Investigation Order (EIO).[17] It allows exchanging evidence in cross-border cases by integrating all previously existing criminal evidence-exchange systems into a single, efficient, and flexible instrument for obtaining evidence.

Before 2009, the EU competence to adopt surveillance acts was rather limited. Therefore, all the instruments mentioned gave broad discretion to EU member states for their implementation and enforcement. Many of these limitations disappeared in December 2009 with the adoption of the Treaty of Lisbon.

II New Legal Bases in the Treaty of Lisbon

The Treaty of Lisbon is the core piece of legislation in the EU today. It establishes legal bases for every policy sector that falls within the EU mandate, and it defines the particular legislative procedures that EU institutions need to follow to adopt legislation on each of these matters. In particular, provisions on EU security measures are expanded with the Treaty of Lisbon.

It was not a surprise that on 30 November 2009, exactly one day before the Treaty of Lisbon took force, a number of security instruments were adopted in the EU.[18] By adopting them before the new treaty, the council skipped having to negotiate all of those measures in co-decision with the European Parliament (EP). In contrast, since 1 December 2009 any act adopted under the scope of the so-called Area of Freedom, Security, and Justice (AFSJ) is decided through the ordinary legislative procedure, in which both the EP and the council have equal legislative powers. Before the Treaty of Lisbon, the EP did not have any legislative role to play in the formulation of security laws. It was consulted, but its opinion was not always taken into account in the negotiations of an international agreement. Since the Treaty of Lisbon, the EP participates in the ordinary legislative procedure and, therefore, it now has the right to veto EU international agreements.

When the Treaty of Lisbon took force, the legal regime regarding EU surveillance laws changed. One of the main amendments was the establishment of shared competences between the EU and its member states on the AFSJ,[19] including data-sharing security measures.[20] The Treaty of Lisbon also includes an explicit legal basis for the approximation of national criminal laws in Article 83 of the Treaty on the Functioning of the European Union (TFEU). According to this provision, the EU can establish "minimum rules concerning the definition of criminal offences and sanctions in the areas of particularly serious crime with a cross-border dimension resulting from the nature or impact of

17 2014 O.J. (L 130) 1–36.

18 These EU measures are Framework Decision 2009/902 setting up a European Crime Prevention Network (EUCPN) and repealing Decision 2001/427; Decision 2009/917 on the use of information technology for customs purposes; Decision 2009/934 adopting the implementing rules governing Europol's relations with partners, including the exchange of personal data and classified information; Decision 2009/936 adopting the implementing rules for Europol analysis work files; Decision 2009/968 adopting the rules on the confidentiality of Europol information.

19 Consolidated Version of the Treaty on the Functioning of the European Union art. 3(2) [hereinafter TFEU] and TFEU art. 4(2)(j).

20 TFEU art. 82(1), 87(2)(a).

such offences or from a special need to combat them on a common basis." This clause has been used by the EU to expand the definition of terrorism and establish a common list of terrorist groups. Such EU common rules complement national criminal laws but they do not fully replace them.

One of the most controversial surveillance instruments adopted under the Treaty of Lisbon, particularly under Articles 82(1)(d) and 87(2)(a) of the TFEU, is the EU Passenger Name Record Directive (hereinafter, the EU PNR Directive). After five years of negotiations among the commission, the council, and the EP,[21] the EU adopted that directive with the aim to "harmonise Member States' provisions on obligations for air carriers operating flights to or from the territory of at least one Member State regarding the transmission of PNR data to the competent authorities for the purpose of preventing and fighting terrorist offences and organised crime."[22]

The EU PNR Directive authorises the collection of up to nineteen categories of data from both EU and non-EU citizens by airline companies at the moment of the ticket purchase. This information will be sent to specific Passenger Information Units (PIUs) in the member state prior to flight departures. The main reason why the proposal for this directive generated so much debate is because of the potential clashes it had with the EU data protection legislation.[23] As analysed in Section III, the EU has one of the most robust data protection and privacy regimes in the world. Although the EU scheme has been taken as a reference to draft similar legislation in third countries, it has also caused new obstacles to law enforcement agencies when executing some of their surveillance measures.

It is also worth mentioning that one of the amendments of the Treaty of Lisbon is that the EU Charter of Fundamental Rights is now a binding instrument and has the same value as EU treaties. Pursuant to Article 6 of the Treaty on European Union (TEU), the charter becomes positive law, and it is not just an interpretative element. It grants legal certainty for all European citizens too.[24] Because of that new nature of the EU charter, the Court of Justice of the European Union (CJEU) was able to annul the Data Retention Directive in April 2014.

In the Madrid bombings of 2004 terrorists used pre-paid SIM cards to detonate the bombs. Consequently, the EU adopted the Data Retention Directive in order to give police authorities access to telecommunication data for the prevention, detection, investigation, and prosecution of crimes. The directive established that member states could adopt domestic laws that obliged telecommunication service provider (TSPs) to retain data for a period of no less than six months and no more than two years. The categories of data retained in a communication were a) the source; b) the destination; c) the time, date, and duration: d) the type; e) the equipment; and f) the location.[25] This directive was annulled by the CJEU because the Court found that data retained failed to comply with the necessity and proportionality tests. Law enforcement authorities were able to

21 For an in-depth study of the pros and cons of this instruments, *see* Cristina Blasi Casagran, *The Future EU PNR system: Will Passenger Data Be Protected?* 23 Eur. J. of Crime, Crim. L. & Crim. Just., no. 3, 241–57.

22 COM (2007) 654 final, (Nov. 6, 2007) at. 6.

23 *See* Cristina Blasi Casagran, Global Data Protection in the Field of Law Enforcement: An EU Perspective, (Taylor & Francis Group, Oxfordshire, UK, 2016).

24 Cristina Blasi Casagran *The Reinforcement of Fundamental Rights in the Lisbon Treaty*, in The European Union after Lisbon, 79–80 (Søren Dosenrode ed., Ashgate Pub. Ltd. 2012).

25 Council Directive 24/2006, art. 5, (EC).

access all EU citizens' communications even if there was no link to or evidence of any threat. No exceptions or distinctions depending on the categories of data were provided. Therefore, the Court determined that the nature of that measure was abusive. The case is especially relevant since it was the first time that the CJEU annulled an entire directive because of its incompatibility with the provisions of the EU charter.

III Surveillance vs. EU Privacy Law

One of the main debates in the EU with regard to the current surveillance programmes has to do with the potential conflict between those security measures and the individual right to data protection and privacy.

The EU data protection legal framework has its origins in the 1980s, and it was directly influenced by two international instruments: the Recommendation of the Council Concerning Guidelines Governing the Protection of Privacy and Transborder Flows of Personal Data (OECD Privacy Guidelines)[26] in September 1980, and the 108 Convention of the Council of Europe for the Protection of Individuals with Regard to the Automatic Processing of Personal Data (the 108 CoE Data Protection Convention).[27]

At first, the European Union's competence to legislate on data protection matters was closely linked to the creation of an internal market within the EU. The establishment of a common market had created the free movement of goods, people, services, and capital, and with it, a free flow of personal data from one member state to the other. Thus, the objective of EU data protection laws was to systematise the substantial increase in the cross-border movement of personal data because of the intensification of social and economic activities within the EU. Within that context, Directive 95/46/EC[28] was the first and main EU legislative act that regulated the protection of personal data within the EU. The scope of that directive was limited in that Article 3(2) expressly refrained from addressing those activities concerning public security, defence, or state security. Hence, member states retained sole authority to legislate on data processed by judicial and police authorities.

That changed in 2008 when the EU adopted a framework decision on data protection aspects falling within the scope of police and judicial matters. Framework Decision 2008/977/JHA (hereinafter, FD 2008/977)[29] aimed at ensuring that data made available among member states had a high level of data protection while guaranteeing public safety.[30] Thus, law enforcement authorities would need to comply every time data was transferred to another member state for the "prevention, investigation, detection or prosecution of criminal offences or the execution of criminal penalties."[31]

Although the adoption of FD 2008/977 established some progress with respect to the protection applicable to data processed within the field of criminal law, that instrument had several shortcomings. For instance, FD 2008/977 did not apply to purely internal

26 *Recommendation of the Council Concerning Guidelines Governing the Protection of Privacy and Transborder Flows of Personal Data*, OECD (Sept. 23, 1980).

27 Convention for the Protection of Individuals with Regard to Automatic Processing of Personal Data, Council of Europe, Jan. 28, 1981.

28 1995 O.J. (L 281) 31–50.

29 2008 O.J. (L 350) 60–71.

30 Framework Decision 2008/977/JHA, 2008 O.J. (L 350) 60, art. 1(1).

31 Framework Decision 2008/977/JHA, 2008 O.J. (L 350) 60, recital 6.

situations in which information was collected and used for one single member state. Moreover, data protection principles of FD 2008/977 were not fully equivalent to those included in Directive 95/46/EC.[32] But the major disappointment as regards the content of FD 2008/977 was the exclusion of several sector-specific EU legislative instruments from its scope.[33] Thus, data processed by Europol, Eurojust, under Prüm, under international agreements with third countries, and under any other existing EU act on data exchanges (e.g., the Swedish initiative) did not have to comply with the provisions of FD 2008/977. Therefore, the need for a new EU legislative act on data protection for police and judicial matters was clear, especially after the Treaty of Lisbon came into force.[34]

The Treaty of Lisbon significantly changed the European framework with regard to the protection of personal data. The EU and its member states for the first time share responsibility for legislation on data processed for criminal matters. Also, Articles 16 of the TFEU and 39 of the TEU were introduced as new legal bases for the right to data protection.

Article 16 of the TFEU replaces former Article 286 of the TEC. According to this new provision, the right to data protection is now applicable to all EU sectors. This right is EU law and therefore prevails over any international agreement that might be in conflict. Likewise, Article 16(2) of the TFEU expands the scope of the provision by providing that rules on data protection bind not only EU institutions, bodies, agencies, and offices, but also "Member States when carrying out activities which fall within the scope of Union law." Hence, EU data protection legislation is today not only applicable to activities related to the EU internal market, but also to data processing activities in the field of law enforcement.

The relationship between Article 16 of the TFEU and Article 39 of the TEU is today still unclear, since it is unknown in which situations Article 39 of the TEU will be applicable. It is presumed that Article 39 of the TEU, together with Declarations 20 and 21 of the Lisbon Treaty,[35] was introduced with the expectation that there will be situations in

32 For a discussion on the disappointments of FD 2008/977 in comparison to the provisions of Directive 95/46/EC, *see* Paul De Hert & Vagelis Papakonstantinou, *The PNR Agreement and Transatlantic Anti-Terrorism Co-Operation: No Firm Human Rights Framework on Either Side of the Atlantic*, 46 Common Market L. Rev.885–919 (2009); Paul De Hert & Vagelis Papakonstantinou, *Data Protection in the Area of Freedom, Security and Justice: A System Still to Be Fully Developed?* European Parliament, Directorate General Internal Policies of the Union, Policy Department C, Citizens' Rights & Constitutional Affairs, PE 410.692, 6–7; Franziska Boehm, Information Sharing and Data Protection in the Area of Freedom, Security & Justice Towards Harmonised Data Protection Principles for Information Exchange at EU-level, 138–44 (Springer, Berlin 2012); Hielke Hijmans & Alfonso Scirocco, *Shortcomings in EU Data Protection in the Third and the Second Pillars: Can the Lisbon Treaty Be Expected to Help?* 46 Common Market L. Rev., no. 5, 1494 (2009); Michele Nino, *The Protection of Personal Data in the Fight against Terrorism: New Perspectives of PNR European Union Instruments in the Light of the Treaty of Lisbon*, 6 Utrecht L. Rev no. 1, 67–69 (2010).

33 Framework Decision 2008/977/JHA, 2008 O.J. (L 350) 60, recital 39. This restriction regarding the scope was not foreseen in the original proposal by the commission in 2005, but it was added afterwards because of the political interest of some member states. Hijmans, *supra* note 33, at 1497.

34 FD 2008/977 did not fulfil the criteria of Article 16 TFEU because it does not apply to domestic data processing activities and it excludes the participation of the EP.

35 Declaration 20 recalls that this legal framework includes specific derogations when rules on the protection of personal data have direct implications for national security; and Declaration 21 acknowledges that data protection in the fields of judicial cooperation in criminal matters and police cooperation may require provisions specific to this area.

which general EU data protection laws might clash with third countries' security rules. In such situations, new standards will be adopted.

After four years of negotiations, Directive (EU) 2016/680 was adopted under the legal basis of Article 16 of the TFEU in April 2016.[36] This directive derogates FD 2008/977, and it enhances the scope of application of its former framework decision. Thus, it does not only apply to cross-border data exchanges within the EU, but also to the processing of personal data at the purely national level. Also, it includes small improvements for the protection of individual rights, such as the obligation to notify data subjects about the processing of their data.[37]

Yet, the fact that the new act has not been adopted in the form of a regulation has drawn criticism from various EU data protection watchdogs. Particularly, the European Data Protection Supervisor (EDPS),[38] the Article 29 Working Party,[39] and the European Parliament[40] expressed their disappointment about this issue. They highlighted the inadequate level of protection in the new directive as being greatly inferior to the standards in the General Data Protection Regulation.[41] Furthermore, Article 2(3) of Directive (EU) 2016/680 explicitly excludes from the scope of application the processing of data by EU institutions, bodies, and agencies.[42] It means that, for instance, data processed by Europol will not be covered by the directive. However, Europol has its own data protection regime, as seen in Section IV.

IV Europol and IntCen

Until relatively recently, European transnational governmental organizations did not have authority to pass laws to prevent, combat, and prosecute crimes. Instead, member states retained exclusive powers to legislate in these areas. However, the terrorist attacks which occurred during the 1972 Olympic Games in Munich led to the creation of the first transnational forum on counter-terrorism issues within the European Communities: The Terrorism, Radicalism, Extremism, and Political Violence (TREVI) Group.

The TREVI Group was created in 1976. It consisted of an intergovernmental forum of national officials from ministries of justice and ministries of interior who would meet periodically to coordinate effective counter-terrorism responses among European governments. One of the projects of the TREVI Group was the development of Europol, first called Europol Drugs Unit (EDU).

EDU started functioning in 1994 as a body in charge of drug-trafficking and money-laundering cases. At first, it had no competence to process personal data. One year

36 Directive (EU) 2016/680 of the European Parliament and of the Council of April 27, 2016 on the protection of natural persons with regard to the processing of personal data by competent authorities for the purposes of the prevention, investigation, detection, or prosecution of criminal offences or the execution of criminal penalties, and on the free movement of such data, and repealing Council Framework Decision 2008/977/JHA, May 4, 2016.

37 Proposed Directive (EU) 2016/680, art. 11.

38 EDPS Opinion on the data protection reform package, Mar. 7, 2012, at iv.

39 WP 191, Mar. 23, 2012, at 26.

40 Eur. Par. Resol. on the European Union's Internal Security Strategy ((2010)2308 (INI)), point 26 (May 22, 2012).

41 2016 O.J. (L 119) 1–88.

42 This has been criticised by the Committee of the Regions, *see* 2012 O.J. (C 391); and by Belgium, Germany, Spain, Finland, Latvia, Portugal, Romania and Sweden.

after its creation, in 1995, EDU was replaced by the European Police Office (Europol), which had expanded authority covering counter-terrorism investigations. The Europol Convention was ratified by all member states in 1999, and from that moment Europol became the European law enforcement organisation in charge of assisting member states and third countries in the prevention and combatting of crime.

Europol has continued increasing its powers in the last several years. For instance, after the 9/11 attacks, a new unit called Counterterrorism Task Force (CTTF) was established at Europol's headquarters seeking to reinforce cooperation between police agents and intelligence analysts from the member states. However, the main changes occurred in 2010 and 2016. In 2010, the Europol Convention was replaced by a council decision (hereinafter, the ECD)[43] and Europol turned into a full EU agency. This change was possible because the Treaty of Lisbon provided an explicit legal basis in Article 88 TFEU. Moreover, in May 2016, a new Europol Regulation entered into force[44] and derogated the previous ECD. As a consequence, Europol's competences in collecting, processing, and storing crime-related information have been significantly enhanced.

Large amounts of personal data are currently stored in Europol's files, usually sent by member states. This information is analysed by the Europol's staff and exchanged among its units, member states, and even third parties. A problem that Europol often experienced within the terms of the former ECD is that member states had no clear obligation to provide information to Europol and the agency had no formal access to member states' national law enforcement databases. Hence, while some member states were convinced of the added value of the agency and sent information to Europol, other member states did not provide Europol with sufficient information during cross-border criminal investigations. The reason for that was basically a lack of trust among some member states about the value of the agency for them. The new Europol Regulation has addressed these limitations, and now the agency is able to retrieve information from member states' databases. It can also initiate or conduct cross-border criminal investigations when necessary.

Surveillance activities carried out by Europol are usually in cooperation with member states through Joint Investigation Teams (JITs). Europol is allowed to participate in JITs under three requirements: a) if the involvement is expressly requested by a member state; b) if the JIT includes at least two member states; and c) if the offence investigated falls under the Europol's mandate.[45] If all these conditions are met, Europol can be part of an investigation team for a fixed period. Again, on this matter, Europol has gained recent new powers with the adoption of the Europol Regulation:

> Where Europol has reason to believe that setting up a joint investigation team would add value to an investigation, it may propose this to the Member States concerned and take measures to assist them in setting up the joint investigation team.[46]

[43] 2009 O.J. (L 121) 37–65.
[44] 2016 O.J. (L 135) 53–114. For a detailed study of the Europol Regulation, Cristina Blasi Casagran, *El Reglamento Europeo de Europol: Un nuevo marco jurídico para el intercambio de datos policiales en la UE*, Revista General de Derecho Europeo, no. 40 (Oct. 2016).
[45] Bart de Buck, *Joint Investigation Teams: The Participation of Europol Officials*, 8 ERA Forum 257 (June 2007).
[46] Europol Regulation, 2016 O.J. (L 135) 53, art. 5(5).

As for data protection safeguards applied by Europol, it has been mentioned that it falls outside the scope of Directive (EU) 2016/680. Nevertheless, the agency claims to have one of the strongest data protection regimes in the world,[47] offering higher standards than those found in the majority of member states. One of the reasons is that Europol has its own communication tool, called the Secure Information Exchange Network (SIENA). SIENA consists of a tailor-made messaging system that complies with the privacy-by-design principle and carries less risk of interception as a result of its secure and user-friendly design.[48] Moreover, individuals who want to access data about them stored by Europol can contact the competent national authority – normally the national data protection authority (DPA) or a special police department – and file a formal request. It is also worth mentioning that Europol has a supervisory scheme composed of two bodies, the Europol Data Protection Officer (DPO) and European Data Protection Supervisor (EDPS), providing the agency with an exemplary external oversight mechanism.

Europol has enhanced both its powers and its data protection safeguards over the last two decades. It is the main law enforcement agency of the EU, but not the only body that uses surveillance programmes for the prevention and combatting of crime. Besides law enforcement agencies, intelligence services in Europe have plenty of software and programmes that monitor people for security purposes. Yet, any information collected by intelligence services in the national level is not within the control of Europol.

At the EU level, the only body today that coordinates information collected by intelligence services of the member states is the Intelligence Analysis Centre (IntCen). It is composed of representatives of intelligence services in the member states and it is the evolution of the former Joint Situation Centre (SitCen). SitCen was created one year before the 9/11 attacks and, as with Europol, its authority increased considerably over the years. After 9/11, SitCen enhanced its scope in order to examine internal and external threats related to terrorism and other serious crimes.[49] There were other attempts to improve SitCen capabilities after the attacks in Madrid (2004), London (2005), and Oslo (2011).[50] For instance, in 2005 the Analysis Unit established links with the CTG, which started to influence EU decisions on internal security matters.[51] SitCen also recruited seconded analysts from member states and internal security services[52] and started to provide strategic reports to the Council of the EU and to member states. Yet, the tasks and information stored in IntCen are rather limited,[53] mainly because the regulation

47 Publications Office of the European Union, Data Protection at Europol 4, 11 (2012).

48 Emma Disley, Barrie Irving, William Hughes & Bhanu Patruni, Evaluation of the implementation of the Europol Council Decision and of Europol's activities, 78 (RandEurope 2012).

49 John D. Occhipinti, *Availability by Stealth? EU Information-Sharing in Transatlantic Perspective*, Eur. Security, Terrorism & Intelligence 160 (Christian Kaunert & Sarah Leonard, eds., Palgrave Macmillan, 2013).

50 On July 22, 2011, Anders Behring Breivik detonated a bomb in Oslo and subsequently killed seventy-seven (mostly young) people on the island of Utoya.

51 Aidan Mills, Vermeulen, Hans Born, Martin Scheinin, Micha Wiebusch & Ashley Thornton, *Parliamentary Oversight of Security and Intelligence Agencies in the European Union*, European Parliament- Directorate General for Internal Policies, Policy Department c: Citizens' rights and Constitutional Affairs, 54–55 (Brussels 2011).

52 Madalina Busuioc & Martijn Groenleer, *Beyond Design: The Evolution of Europol and Eurojust*, 14 Perspectives on European Politics & Society 294 (2013).

53 In fact, the 80 percent of the intelligence stored by IntCen is from only four EU countries. *See* Nikola Nielsen, *No New Mandate for EU Intelligence Centre*, EUobserver, (Feb. 6, 2015), https://euobserver.com/justice/127532.

of intelligence services still falls within the exclusive competence of the member states. IntCen mainly provides information on crisis management situations. It does not have information collection powers or any operational role, and it only shares assessed intelligence among member states or other EU institutions and bodies.[54]

Unlike Europol, IntCen and the national intelligence services of the member states do not need to comply with the EU data protection laws. In this sense, the Snowden revelations of June 2013 proved that intelligence services in the EU had maintained a close collaboration with the NSA in the United States and that they were also using massive surveillance programmes, even if the information was not sent to the US. These programmes violated the EU right to data protection,[55] but because of their secrecy, it has not been easy to get information about their actual functions and scope.

IntCen and Europol exchange crime-related information, especially after the high number of terrorist attacks in Europe in the last few years. Although IntCen and Europol have no cooperation agreement in force, *de facto* both EU bodies maintain close collaboration. For example, they collaborate with each other in the preparation of annual threat assessments that will later be sent to the council and to the Standing Committee on Operational Cooperation on Internal Security (COSI). Yet, as seen in Section V, on matters regarding national security, both Europol and IntCen have very limited powers to act.

V The Blurry Concept of National Security and Its Implications

There is today no single accepted definition in European and international treaties on what 'national security' covers.[56] Some countries provide their own legal definitions, but these only apply within that specific territory. For example, the Hungarian Security Services Act defines national security as the interest of ensuring sovereignty and safeguarding of the constitutional order.[57] Also, several bilateral agreements include clauses that limit compliance with international obligations for national security purposes.[58]

Numerous scholars and politicians have also offered definitions.[59] Most of them agree that the term describes certain actions that society entrusts to governments to prevent adversaries from inflicting harm. These definitions have, however, no legal support.

The concept of national security has often been connected to surveillance activities carried out by intelligence services and closely linked to the collection and processing

54 Mills, *supra* note 51, at 55–56.

55 *See* Case C-362/14, Judgment of the Court (Grand Chamber) of October 6, 2015 (request for a preliminary ruling from the High Court (Ireland)) – *Maximilian Schrems v. Data Protection Commissioner.*

56 Gozalvo Navarro, *Una Definición Jurídica Válida*, 4; Art. 29 Working Party, WP 228, 5 Dec. 5, 2014.

57 Act CXXV of 1995, Section 74.

58 For instance, *see* art. XXI.1.e) of Treaty of Friendship, Commerce and Navigation between the United States of America and the Republic of Nicaragua, Jan. 21, 1956, 367 U.N.T.S. 3.

59 Charles S. Maier, *Peace and Security for the 1990s*, unpublished paper for the MacArthur-Social Science Research Council Fellowship Program in International Peace and Security Studies, prepared for the SSRC, 1990. Distributed internally only. An updated report was commissioned by the Foundation and written in July 1992; Peter Mangold, NATIONAL SECURITY AND INTERNATIONAL RELATIONS, 1–14 (Routledge, New York 1990); Prabhakaran Paleri, NATIONAL SECURITY: IMPERATIVES AND CHALLENGES 521 (Tata McGraw-Hill, Delhi, 2008); Sam C. Sarkesian, John Allen Williams & Stephen J. Cimbala, NATIONAL SECURITY: POLICYMAKERS, PROCESSES AND POLITICS, 4 (Lynne Rienner, Boulder, CO 2008); David Omand, SECURING THE STATE (INTELLIGENCE AND SECURITY), 9 (Oxford University Press, Oxford 2010).

of data. The first problem encountered in these practices is that it is not always easy to determine whether the data has been processed for law enforcement purposes or as part of intelligence services' activities. Although there are notorious legal differences between data processed by intelligence services and data processed by law enforcement authorities, in practice, the line dividing the tasks of these two bodies is difficult to draw.

In the past, law enforcement authorities' methodology was clearly to "see and strike," whereas intelligence services' functions were to "wait and watch."[60] For example, Germany still has a law of separation (*Trennungsgebot*) that divides the roles between intelligence and police forces.[61] Also, before 9/11, US intelligence investigations differed from US criminal investigations because of the existence of a so-called "FISA wall." There was a sharp division between intelligence and law enforcement. The relevant agencies had limited collaboration in information sharing. According to this division, collection of evidence for criminal investigations required search warrants while evidence for foreign intelligence collections had its own procedure through the Foreign Intelligence Surveillance Act (FISA).

The division between law enforcement and intelligence has become more and more blurred over the years. In fact, the "wall" that separated law enforcement agencies from intelligence services disappeared after 9/11.[62] A few days after the 9/11 attacks, the US Congress passed the PATRIOT Act.[63] This act lowered barriers imposed by the "FISA wall," which previously had minimised interaction between law enforcement and intelligence agencies. Hence, federal intelligence and law enforcement agencies started to develop lasting relationships. Currently, police officers and intelligence analysts maintain regular contact in most countries. In some EU member states such as Spain there is even a department assigned to police agents within the intelligence services' headquarters so that both entities can easily share information. Hence, every time intelligence services in Spain gather relevant information on an imminent crime, this is directly transferred to police authorities, who can initiate an investigation.

As stated previously, the EU has no legal authority to regulate intelligence service activities, which remain within the exclusive competence of the member states. Yet, today there is a blurred line between intelligence services and law enforcement activities. Therefore, Section V.A. examines whether there is any legal basis in EU treaties for adopting surveillance laws among intelligence agencies of the member states. It also analyses whether the CJEU has any margin on defining the scope of national security issues by examining relevant case-law on matters related to intelligence services activities.

A *EU Laws and the National Security Exemption*

Article 4(2) of the TEU and Article 72 of the TFEU state that any processing of data carried out for national security purposes falls out of the scope of the EU treaties. Also,

60 Adam D. M. Svenden, *On a 'Continuum with Expansion'? Intelligence Cooperation in Europe in the Early 21st Century*, 7 J. of Contemporary Europ. Research 523.

61 Claudia Hillebrand, Networks in the European Union. Maintaining democratic legitimacy after 9/11, 94 (Oxford University Press, Oxford 2012).

62 Els de Busser, *EU Data Protection in Transatlantic Cooperation in Criminal Matters Will the EU Be Serving Its Citizens an American Meal?* 6 Utrecht L. Rev. 98.

63 The name stands for Uniting and Strengthening America by Providing Appropriate Tools Required to Intercept and Obstruct Terrorism Act of 2001. The PATRIOT Act, Pub. L. No. 56.

Article 73 of the TFEU establishes that it is the responsibility of the member states to cooperate and coordinate among themselves for the safeguarding of national security. These provisions were introduced in the Treaty of Lisbon after the UK insisted that intelligence matters should not be part of the EU competences.[64] The clause expressly states that national security matters remain within the sole authority of the member states. Such exclusion is likewise found in specific data protection laws including Directive 95/46/EC and the Council of Europe's Convention for the Protection of Individuals with Regard to the Automatic Processing of Personal Data (108 CoE Data Protection Convention). Yet, none of these laws includes a definition of the term "national security."

Surveillance activities in the member states of the EU are conducted by three main bodies: law enforcement authorities, intelligence agencies, and the military. A number of the security activities conducted by these groups consist of collecting and processing information for the prevention, combatting, and prosecution of crimes. Although security actions are often carried out by member states, the EU has been cooperating with national authorities in these data-sharing activities through the EU agency Europol, as well as by the adoption of several laws within the scope of the Area of Freedom, Security, and Justice (AFSJ), which are a collection of norms and policies designed to secure human rights and freedom of movement within the EU.[65] These laws refer, for the most part, to data processed by law enforcement agencies, rather than by intelligence and military agencies. Yet, as mentioned earlier, the division of roles between law enforcement and intelligence services is not fully clear.

Although the regulation of national security issues falls under the exclusive competence of member states, EU involvement can be found in some national security measures. This is because the term "national security" is often linked to the concepts of "EU internal security" and "EU external security."[66] Pursuant to the Lisbon Treaty, provisions on EU internal security matters belong to a different policy than EU external security measures. In particular, internal security issues belong to the Area of Freedom, Security, and Justice (AFSJ),[67] whereas external security issues are part of the Common Foreign and Security Policy (CFSP).[68] Furthermore, the EU can coordinate a few "national security" measures that are operational in the member states. For instance, regarding the coordination of the Schengen Information System,[69] Article 93 of Schengen Agreement Application Convention states:

> The purpose of the Schengen Information System shall be in accordance with this Convention to maintain public policy and public security, including **national security**, in the territories of the Contracting Parties and to apply the provisions of this Convention

64 Rik Coolsaet, *EU Counterterrorism Strategy: Value Added or Chimera?* 86 Int'l Affairs 865 (2010).

65 For instance, the recently annulled Data Retention Directive or the EU–US Passenger Name Records agreements.

66 *Draft Report on the US NSA Surveillance Programme, Surveillance Bodies in Various Member States and Their Impact on EU Citizens' Fundamental Rights and on Transatlantic Cooperation in Justice and Home Affairs*, Research Paper 2013/2188(INI) at 9 (2013); Opinion of the Advocate General Bot on the case C-658/11, Jan. 30, 2014, para. 113.

67 TFEU art. 67–89.

68 TFEU art. 21–46.

69 Regulation (EC) No 1987/2006 of the European Parliament and of the Council of Dec. 20, 2006 on the establishment, operation and use of the second generation Schengen Information System (SIS II), 2006 O.J. (L 381) 4–23.

relating to the movement of persons in those territories, using information communicated via this system. [emphasis added]

The same EU involvement in national security matters is seen in the tasks carried out by the European Cybercrime Centre (EC3) and IntCen. Although the intelligence services of the member states are the main bodies in charge of national security activities, these two EU bodies also collect and process a considerable amount of intelligence. The EC3, which was established in 2013, mainly collects and processes cyber intelligence. IntCen is part of the European External Action Service (EEAS) and its functions include the exchange of intelligence and the drafting of terrorism reports.[70]

Therefore, it can be concluded that the EU has *de facto* certain competences in the regulation of intelligence services' activities, despite the general national security exception of Articles 4(2) of the TEU and Articles 72–73 of the TFEU.

B *The Leading Role of the CJEU*

As we have seen, according to Article 4(2) of the TEU, national security issues fall outside the scope of EU competences. Consequently, these matters cannot be reviewed by the Court of Justice of the European Union (CJEU).[71] In keeping with these constraints, Article 276 of the TFEU states:

> The Court of Justice of the European Union shall have no jurisdiction to review the validity or proportionality of operations carried out by the police or other law-enforcement services of a Member State or the exercise of the responsibilities incumbent upon Member States with regard to the maintenance of law and order and the safeguarding of internal security.

This provision confirms that the CJEU, unlike other supranational courts,[72] lacks jurisdiction to examine preliminary rulings that refer to activities adopted in the member states for national security purposes.[73] The only questions that can be addressed by the Court in the field of internal security are the compatibility between security activities of the member states and EU laws. In that sense, the CJEU has already concluded that even if member states retain competence on certain measures in the area of security, the Court has jurisdiction to review whether they conform to the EU treaties.[74]

Unfortunately, the Court has not yet clarified the concept of "national security" or what exactly national security activities cover. As was suggested in 2014 by the German

70 Javier Argomaniz, A *Rhetorical Spillover? Exploring the Link between the European Union Common Security and Defence Policy (CSDF) and the External Dimension in the EU Counterterrorism*, 17 *European Foreign Affairs* 50 (2012).

71 Douwe Korff, *Expert Opinion Prepared for the Committee of Inquiry of the Bundestag into the '5EYES' Global Surveillance Systems Revealed by Edward Snowden, Committee Hearing*, Paul-Löbe-Haus, Berlin, 35.

72 For instance, the European Court of Human Rights has numerous cases referring to the compatibility of the right to privacy with specific intelligence service activities. In this sense, see the cases of *Roman Zakharov v. Russia*, Application no. 47143, (Dec. 4, 2015); and *Szabó and Vissy v. Hungary*, Application no. 37138, (Jan. 12, 2016).

73 For a criticism on this provision, *see* Alicia Hinarejos, *Law and Order and Internal Security*, 270–71.

74 *See* the CJEU Case C-265/95 *Commission v. France* ('Spanish Strawberries'), 1997 ECR I-6959, para. 33–35, 56–57; and Case C-124/95 The Queen, ex parte Centro-Com Srlv. HM Treasury and Bank of England, 1997 ECRI-81, para. 25.

delegation, a clear definition of internal security is necessary "in order to avoid overlapping with tasks assigned to intelligence services in order to protect the security of the State from internal threats."[75] Ideally, a clear-cut list with concrete national security activities should be released. That would help determine whether there is a full coincidence between national security actions and intelligence services' operations.[76] If it were concluded that there are intelligence service activities that tackle issues unrelated to national security, EU principles would still apply for these matters.[77]

On the topic of intelligence services, the CJEU recently decided a landmark case. After the Snowden disclosures on PRISM, an Austrian student named Max Schrems started legal action before the Irish High Court because the Irish Data Protection Authority (DPA) had not stopped data transfers between Facebook Ireland and Facebook Inc. The Irish DPA claimed that Facebook complied with the now-void Safe Harbor principles, and, therefore, there was no reason to suspend its data transfers.[78] The Irish High Court referred the matter to the CJEU for a preliminary ruling, questioning whether the Irish DPA had an obligation to examine the complaint regarding Facebook data transfers.[79] On 6 October 2015, the CJEU annulled the Safe Harbor agreement because it did not comply with the adequacy criteria for international data transfer in the terms of Article 25 of Directive 95/46/EC, as well as Articles 7, 8, and 47 of the EU Charter of Fundamental Rights.[80] The Court emphasised the importance that EU and US legal orders be "essentially equivalent" in the field of privacy. It also pointed out that the system was inadequate because it was based on self-certification and self-assessment by private companies themselves, but it did not cover interferences conducted by public agencies such as the NSA. Yet, the decision did not address the issue of surveillance for national security, and it only indirectly tackled the alleged incompatibility of programs such as PRISM with Article 8 of the charter, Directive 95/46/EC, and the 2000 Safe Harbor Decision.

In contrast, the opinion that Advocate General (AG) Bot released in that case[81] referred to the concept of "national security" in several places. In fact, national security was one of the reasons why he argued that Safe Harbor principles could be derogated according to Annex 1 of Decision 2000/520. The AG addressed this problem in paragraph 164:

> The problem arises essentially from the United States authorities' use of the derogations provided for in that provision. Because their wording is too general, the implementation of those derogations by the United States authorities is not limited to what is strictly necessary.

Advocate General Bot stated that the wording of the derogations (i.e., national security, public interest, and law enforcement requirements) was too broad and imprecise, and he questioned the compatibility of these derogations with EU law.[82] Likewise, he reminded the Court that it had already decided that the processing of data for security purposes had some legal limitations.[83] For example, the annulment of the EU Data

75 Parl. Eur. Doc., 15659/1/14 REV 1 (2014).
76 Korff, *supra* note 71, at 41.
77 *Id.*
78 Case C-362/14, *Maximilian Schrems v. Data Protection Commissioner*, 2014 IEHC 310.
79 Reference for a preliminary ruling from High Court of Ireland (Ireland) made on July 25, 2014 – *id.*
80 *Id.*
81 Case C-362/14, Opinion of the AG Bot, 2015.
82 *Id.*, para. 168 & 183.
83 *Id.*, para. 46 & 189.

Retention Directive in April 2014 implied that any data processing for law enforcement purposes had to comply with the proportionality principle. But in the *Schrems case* the situation was different: As examined earlier, if the data access is carried out for 'national security' purposes, then the EU has no competence at all.

Paragraph 170 of the AG opinion was particularly interesting in this sense:

> The access enjoyed by the United States intelligence services to the transferred data therefore also constitutes an interference with the fundamental right to protection of personal data guaranteed in Article 8 of the Charter, since such access constitutes a processing of that data.

According to this, the AG seemed to imply that not all intelligence service activities are by default falling within the general exclusion of "national security," because some were subject to the principles of the EU charter, which means that such activities are not part of the general national security exemption.[84]

In conclusion, the CJEU has taken a role in intelligence services' matters. However, it has not yet clarified the term "national security" or what it includes. Also, no case has been referred to the CJEU to date on IntCen activities. IntCen falls within the scope of the EU Common Foreign and Security Policy (CFSP). Although the CJEU has no jurisdiction over CFSP matters,[85] Article 24 TEU foresees an exception of this general rule when the decision concerns the delimitation between areas:

> The Court of Justice of the European Union shall not have jurisdiction with respect to these provisions, with the exception of its jurisdiction to monitor compliance with Article 40 of this Treaty and to review the legality of certain decisions as provided for by the second paragraph of Article 275 of the Treaty on the Functioning of the European Union.

In light of this exception, the CJEU could eventually decide whether IntCen falls completely under the scope of the CFSP or if only certain activities do. If there are actions that are not part of the scope of the CFSP, then the CJEU could issue judicial decisions regarding these aspects.

Future Challenges

This chapter has offered an examination of the main current surveillance laws and instruments in the EU. Much of the analysis has focused on making sense of the distribution of competences between the EU member states and the EU itself, emphasising the progressive acquisition of powers by EU institutions for the adoption of cross-border security measures.

In the wake of terrorist attacks like the one occurred in Madrid in 2004 or the bombings in London in 2005, there has been an imperative to implement new EU measures in the field of security. The Treaty of Lisbon has provided some of this necessary legal basis since 2009. In the aftermath of the terrorist attacks that took place in Europe during 2015–2016, the EU has adopted new security laws through the EU Internal Security

84 *Id.*, para. 170, 177 & 200.
85 TFEU art. 275(1).

Strategy 2015–2020,[86] such as the 2015 Additional Protocol to the Convention on the Prevention of Terrorism.[87]

A landmark case has been recently decided by the CJEU and will have crucial consequences for the adoption of new EU surveillance laws. In the *Tele2 case*,[88] the CJEU determined that Swedish telecommunications companies that are storing traffic data and providing it to the Swedish police under the now-void Data Retention Directive are violating the EU charter. Another important future decision will refer to the compatibility of the proposed EU–Canada PNR Agreement with the EU Treaties and the EU Charter of Fundamental Rights. On this topic, Advocate General Paolo Mengozzi of the CJEU issued a 2016 opinion concluding that "the agreement envisaged is incompatible with Articles 7 and 8 and Article 52(1) of the Charter of Fundamental Rights of the European Union."[89] The decision will have a direct impact on the EU PNR Directive, which entered into force in 2016.

It remains to be seen whether the CJEU decides whether these two instruments are infringing the EU laws. In any event, they show one of the complexities analysed throughout this chapter: the establishment of the right balance between the collective need for security – by the adoption of surveillance measures – and the individual right to data protection and data privacy.

Another issue that needs to be addressed in the EU is the clarification of the concept of "national security." As seen in this chapter, the EU has competence to adopt surveillance laws that are part of the EU internal security policy or the EU external security policy. Nevertheless, if that surveillance measure is considered as necessary for national security purposes, then it will be excluded from the EU competences and only member states will have authority to approve such law. As a result, a divergence of surveillance measures for national security reasons remains within the European territory. For such measures, there is no obligation to comply with the EU data protection principles, and there is a risk of abuses and excessive intrusions on EU citizens' basic rights. It is uncertain which activities carried out by intelligence services in the member states are under the scope of national security and which are not. If all intelligence activities were considered part of the national security exclusion, it would mean that no EU data protection laws are applicable for these agencies. What is the purpose of protecting individuals' data collected by law enforcement authorities if intelligence services can still freely break into their computers or intercept their calls?

In conclusion, the notions of privacy and data protection should not oppose the objective of surveillance, but rather complement it. This is precisely the primary challenge for the adoption of new surveillance laws within the EU.

86 European Commission Press Release. Doc. 9798/15, *Draft Council Conclusions on the Renewed European Union Internal Security Strategy 2015–2020* (June. 10, 2015).

87 Council Decision (EU) 2015/1914 of 18 Sept.18, 2015 on the signing, on behalf of the European Union, of the Additional Protocol to the Council of Europe Convention on the Prevention of Terrorism (CETS No. 196), 2015 O.J. (L 280) 24–25.

88 Joined Cases C-203/15 and C-698/15, Tele2 Sverige AB v Post- och telestyrelsen and Secretary of State for the Home Department v Tom Watson and Others, 21 December 2016.

89 Opinion 1/15 of Advocate General Mengozzi, Sept. 8, 2016.

28 Mutual Legal Assistance in the Digital Age

Andrew Keane Woods†

Fifty years ago, a law enforcement agent in India or England or Brazil could effectively do his job – investigating crimes such as murder and theft – without ever leaving his country's territorial borders. A theft in New Delhi would typically involve evidence collection in New Delhi. There were exceptions, of course, but for the most part, local crimes produced local evidence. This is no longer true. Today, an Indian law enforcement officer investigating an entirely local crime – one with a local suspect, local victim, in violation of local law – will typically involve a great deal of digital evidence, much of which is controlled by a foreign Internet company and is therefore difficult for local law enforcement to obtain.[1] Very often, a local official will need to request mutual legal assistance (MLA) from the country with jurisdiction over the data. Typically, this is done in accordance with a mutual legal assistance treaty (MLAT) – whereby one country will provide legal assistance to another country, pursuant to whatever treaty the two countries have negotiated. This process worked well enough for physical evidence, extradition requests, and other forms of twentieth-century cross-border legal assistance, but today it is buckling under the weight of demands for digital evidence produced by the global Internet.

This chapter provides an overview of the sudden importance of mutual legal assistance in an age when an increasing amount of criminal evidence is both digital and held by offshore firms. The chapter begins with a description of the current – regrettable – state of affairs. Part II describes some of the easiest ways to improve the existing MLA regime, reforms that may require money or manpower, but will not require legal change. These are critical reforms, but even a streamlined and well-oiled MLA regime will never be able to satisfy the needs of local law enforcement demands for digital evidence. Part III therefore looks to alternative avenues for obtaining digital evidence controlled by a foreign service provider. Regardless of which of these procedural paths reformers take, each will require substantive guidelines for determining the conditions under which a law enforcement agent in Country A can lawfully gain access to digital evidence controlled by a firm in Country B. Part IV suggests substantive requirements for delimiting that access.

† Assistant Professor of Law, University of Kentucky College of Law. Much of this chapter builds on my earlier research. *See, e.g.*, Andrew Keane Woods, *Against Data Exceptionalism*, 68 Stan. L. Rev. 729 (2016); Andrew K. Woods, Data Beyond Borders (2015), https://globalnetworkinitiative.org/sites/default/files/GNI%20MLAT%20Report.pdf.

1 This evidence includes both noncontent data (location information, log-in times, etc.) as well as content data (emails, photos, etc.).

It is worth noting that the stakes are especially high in this arena. This special concern is not caused by a risk that law enforcement will gain too much or too little access to crucial evidence – this is important, but all regulatory regimes are under- or overinclusive in one way or another. Rather, the stakes are especially high because the countries that must typically request MLA – meaning the countries with populations who use primarily foreign Internet services, and therefore the countries without the ability to access criminal evidence in a fair and timely way – are beginning to lash out in ways that threaten the Internet as we know it. The MLA debate, in other words, is not just about striking the right balance between how much evidence one police officer ought to be able to collect, or how much privacy a user reasonably ought to expect, but about what kind of Internet we want to have.

I The Problem

In order to understand the inadequacies of the current regime for cross-border data requests, it helps to grasp the underlying trends that force law enforcement agents to request MLA for routine cases. There are three relevant trends: 1) an increasing amount of criminal evidence is digital; 2) much of that digital evidence is controlled by foreign service providers; and 3) very often, that service provider cannot or will not respond directly to local law enforcement requests for data. Let us examine each trend in turn.

A *The Digitization of Criminal Evidence*

Twenty or even ten years ago, a law enforcement agent investigating a physical crime such as theft would rarely need access to evidence stored in another jurisdiction. Phone records were maintained by local phone companies, fingerprints were taken from the crime scene, and suspects' assets and papers could be found in their apartment or house. Today, however, much of the most valuable evidence is digital. For example, rather than relying on a local telephone network, a criminal suspect may use WhatsApp to communicate with conspirators. Moreover, that same person might communicate by email, using a cloud-based service such as Gmail, which is accessed remotely. Digital evidence is found in nearly every criminal case today, regardless of whether the crime was perpetrated using digital services. For example, in a drunk driving accident, police will not just rely on skid marks or blood-alcohol samples taken from the scene, but also the digital data about the vehicle's course taken from the car's computer, possibly from the car's cloud services provider, and from the phones of the driver and any passengers, not to mention texts, emails, and other digital records from the driver's phone.

To get a sense of just how much evidence we are talking about, consider Table 28.1. This tabulates the self-reported values provided by just six Internet service providers in the United Kingdom. The United Kingdom constitutes just 2 percent of the world's Internet traffic,[2] yet in one year, law enforcement officials sought nearly fifty-four thousand pieces of digital evidence from just six Internet firms. Even if law enforcement critics are right that the police are overly aggressive in seeking digital evidence, these are

2 *See Internet Users in the World by Regions*, INTERNET WORLD STATS (June 30, 2016), http://www.internetworldstats.com/stats.htm.

Table 28.1. 2014 UK Government Requests for Internet Data from Major U.S. Service Providers

Internet Service Provider	Number of Requests for Data	Number of Users or Devices Affected	Percentage of Time Some Data Revealed
Apple (Jan–Jun)	1180	19,057	51
Apple (Jul–Dec)	1052	4171	54
Facebook (Jan–Jun)	2110	2619	72
Facebook (Jul–Dec)	2366	2890	75
Google (Jan–Jun)	1535	1991	72
Google (Jul–Dec)	2080	2755	75
Microsoft (Jan–Jun)	4090	7562	78
Microsoft (Jul–Dec)	4518	8034	75
Twitter (Jan–Jun)	78	220	46
Twitter (Jul–Dec)	116	371	34
Yahoo! (Jan-Jun)	1408	2037	47
Yahoo! (Jul–Dec)	1570	2240	30
TOTAL	22,103	53,947	59

large numbers – the kind of volume that requires a well-designed system for processing requests.

These numbers – from a relatively small country – suggest that the global demand for electronic criminal evidence is large and poised to become even larger. The demand is great enough that global Internet firms now have compliance teams to manage law enforcement requests from around the world. They also have web portals for screening and validating law enforcement requests for user data, even providing training to law enforcement about how to make a request. If an Internet firm collects data about its customers, it is collecting evidence that might be used in a criminal trial – potentially in many jurisdictions. Evidence, in other words, has become both digital and global.

B *American Internet Dominance*

The Internet is dominated by American firms. For example, eight of the top ten most popular Web sites in India are United States–based services.[3] And India is not an anomaly in this regard. United States firms run seven of the ten most popular Web sites in Brazil, nine of ten in the United Kingdom, and seven of ten in Germany.[4] The fact is that the vast majority of the world's Internet users are outside the United States, but they are using services headquartered in the United States. The result is that digital criminal evidence – evidence that would historically have been physically located in the same jurisdiction as the crime – is now very often stored in the cloud, and often with a service provider that is foreign.

3 The ranking is as follows: 1. Google.co.in; 2. Google.com; 3. Youtube.com; 4. Facebook.com; 5. Amazon.in; 6. Yahoo.com; 7. Flipkart.com; 8. Wikipedia.org; 9. Linkedin.com; 10. Indiatimes.com.

4 *See Top 500 Sites on the Web*, ALEXA, http://www.alexa.com/topsites/ (last visited Apr. 4, 2016).

This is partly a function of the cloud's structure. The services referred to as "cloud" services typically share two key features: (1) the data is stored on remote servers, and (2) those servers are connected to the Internet. Since many cloud services are operated by global Internet companies – which design their networks so as to optimize storage cost, energy cost, latency times, and such – this means that customer data is inevitably spread around multiple jurisdictions. If a customer in Italy signs up for an American company's Internet services, his or her data may be stored in Italy, Ireland, and the United States, all without the customer ever leaving Italy.

Of course, one of the greatest features of the Internet is that it spans national boundaries. Indeed, this is partly why it is such a huge draw for companies. The cost of accessing new markets is essentially zero. Put your Web site online, and it is available wherever the Internet is available and open. Yet these same features are what frustrate law enforcement. A company can establish a huge presence in a country without being responsive to local law enforcement demands.

Why is this such a problem for local law enforcement? The fact that evidence is digital and controlled by foreign firms may, on its own, make life marginally more difficult for local law enforcement officers, who may not have an easy way of communicating with the Internet firm to request the data they seek as evidence. But this is not an insurmountable problem – if law enforcement officers reach the compliance team at Google or Facebook, they could, in theory, ask for and receive cooperation in obtaining the evidence sought. The problem, however, is that American service providers are often barred, by law, from providing that cooperation. Privacy laws in many countries, including the United States, make it extremely difficult for firms to comply with foreign law enforcement requests for data – even when those requests are legitimate, justified, and fully consistent with both local law and international standards.

C *Blocking Statutes*

The most significant legal barrier to the world's largest Internet companies complying with local law enforcement around the world is the Electronic Communications Privacy Act (ECPA).[5] ECPA draws an important distinction between content data and metadata. "Content" refers to the contents of emails, photographs, and other uploaded files, while "metadata" refers to basic subscriber information such as user identification, as well as location and time data (known as communications data in the United Kingdom). ECPA prohibits American firms from producing most customer content – such as emails sent in the last 180 days – except in response to a warrant issued by a U.S. judge based on her finding of probable cause.[6]

The effects of ECPA's blocking features are profound for law enforcement agents around the world. Recall our example of an Indian law enforcement officer investigating a routine crime such as theft. Suppose that the police know their suspect uses a phone that is running the Android operating system – the world's most popular phone operating system – made by Google. This person's location information, call records, and communications – all crucial evidence related to a crime – will be controlled by Google, a firm

5 18 U.S.C. § 2703.

6 *See* Orin S. Kerr, *The Next Generation Communications Privacy Act*, 162 U. Pa. L. Rev. 373, 378–85 (2014).

based in California, with servers storing customer information located in dozens of countries around the world.[7] The Indian law enforcement official can ask Google directly for data, and Google, at its own discretion and consistent with its terms of service, may hand over some basic subscriber information and location data.[8] But in order to obtain emails or photos or other digital content associated with a criminal investigation, the Indian police officer will need to get a warrant from a U.S. court in order to compel Google to produce those emails. This means, essentially, that the Indian officer will need to ask for mutual legal assistance from the United States.

Blocking statutes such as ECPA – and confusion about how they apply outside the United States – have also allowed American Internet firms coyly to resist law enforcement demands even when there is no clear legal barrier to their cooperation. For example, ECPA does allow American firms to produce metadata in response to non-U.S. law enforcement demands. Yet those firms are often unwilling to hand over metadata on the grounds that doing so is inconsistent with their terms of service or would otherwise anger civil liberties groups or threaten customer privacy. Metadata requests constitute a significant number of overall cross-border data requests, and companies could take significant strides to clarify under exactly what circumstances they are willing to provide metadata to non-American law enforcement. Hiding behind blocking statutes – which often do not apply – does not help an overburdened system.

These three trends – digitization of criminal evidence, dominance of American firms, and American law that prevents those firms from responding to local law enforcement – conspire to create a world in which law enforcement officers must request mutual legal assistance from the U.S. Department of Justice's Office of International Affairs.[9]

II Improving Mutual Legal Assistance

In order to compel Google to produce a suspect's emails that reside on a server located in America, a non-American law enforcement agent must take the following steps. First, law enforcement personnel must ask their central national law enforcement authority, which is likely in the country's capital, for a letter requesting mutual legal assistance from the United States. In the United States, that central authority is the Department of Justice (DOJ) in Washington, D.C. If the central authority approves, then it will typically pass the request through diplomatic channels – often through its ambassador to the United States – to ensure that the request reaches the DOJ's Office of International Affairs (OIA). OIA agents will then review the request and, if they deem it valid and actionable, then they will forward it to the relevant regional U.S. Attorney's Office – which is typically the United States Attorney for the Northern District of California,

7 The data may be managed by Google's India subsidiary, Google India Private Limited, but Google will nonetheless assert that the data is hard to locate and is not under the control of the local subsidiary. *See*, Exhibit 21.01: List of Subsidiaries of Registrant Google Inc., Sec. & Exch. Comm'n, http://www.sec.gov/Archives/edgar/data/1288776/000119312507044494/dex2101.htm.

8 *See* Greg Nojeim, *MLAT Reform Proposal: Protecting Metadata*, Lawfare (Dec. 10, 2015, 2:43 PM), https://www.lawfareblog.com/mlat-reform-proposal-protecting-metadata.

9 Other countries' laws matter as well, of course. EU privacy laws have a significant impact on a company's ability to transfer customer data out across the Atlantic for processing or storage. But since most of the world's criminal evidence is managed by U.S. firms, U.S. law is, for the moment, paramount.

which covers Silicon Valley, or, increasingly, the United States Attorney for the District of Columbia.[10] The local U.S. attorney will then produce either a subpoena or a court order asking the technology firm for the relevant data. If the court grants the order, the company will review it and comply, producing the relevant evidence, which will then be passed back to the Department of Justice (with the FBI playing a screening roll) before being passed back to the foreign law enforcement agents who originally requested it. This process takes on average ten months, and in many cases much, much longer.[11]

There are a number of problems with the existing mutual legal assistance regime, including staffing, training, digitization, and sovereignty concerns. What follows is a brief overview of these shortcomings. Note that these are shortcomings only for the countries that have an MLAT with the United States (or other country they are asking for assistance). The United States has MLA agreements with many of its larger international partners, including the United Kingdom and India, but there are also significant gaps in coverage, such as Chile, Vietnam, and China.[12] (Outside the MLA regime, legal assistance is either provided in an ad hoc manner – typically via letters rogatory from courts in one country to courts in another, an entirely voluntary and painfully slow process – or not at all.)

A *OIA Capacity*

As Part I made clear, the number of cross-border requests for data is already enormous and is poised to increase. Of the fifty-four thousand requests that the British government makes annually to American technology firms, many of those requests are for content, and that means that many requests will be routed through the MLAT process. The final number is somewhat depressed by the fact that foreign law enforcement are painfully aware of how slow the process is, so many potential requests are never made – that is a problem unto itself. But we know that the numbers are large and growing larger.

In the year 2000, the OIA received 1,716 requests for mutual legal assistance, 84 of which were for computer records.[13] In 2015, the OIA received 3,352 requests for MLA, 2,183 of which were for computer records. In just fifteen years, the percentage of all MLA requests for computer records increased from around 4 percent to around 65 percent. This trend is toward greater and greater numbers of digital records – in both relative and absolute terms – and as Tables 28.2, Figure 28.1, and Table 28.3 show, that trend appears to be getting worse.

While these numbers have gone up, the OIA's funding has hardly changed.[14] (Some additional funding was finally granted in 2016.) If these dual trends continue – increases in MLA requests for computer evidence combined with a stagnant OIA budget – not only will MLA continue to be inefficient, but it will likely worsen to a considerable

[10] As of 2015, the Department of Justice was testing a pilot project to route all mutual legal assistance requests to a single U.S. Attorney's Office in Washington, D.C., rather than whatever U.S. Attorney's office might otherwise have handled the request – typically the one with jurisdiction over the company holding the requested data.

[11] *See* President's Review Grp. on Intelligence & Commc'ns Techs., Liberty and Security in a Changing World: Report and Recommendations 227 (2013), http://www.whitehouse.gov/sites/default/files/docs/2013-12-12_rg_final_report.pdf.

[12] *See* Bureau of Int'l Narcotics & Law Enf't, *2012 International Narcotics Control Strategy Report (INCSR)*, U.S. Dep't of State (Mar. 7, 2012), http://www.state.gov/j/inl/rls/nrcrpt/2012/vol2/184110.htm.

[13] *See* Andrew Keane Woods, *Against Data Exceptionalism*, 68 Stan. L. Rev. 729, 749–51 (2016).

[14] *FY 2015 Budget Request: Mutual Legal Assistance Treaty Process Reform*, U.S. Dep't of Justice, http://www.justice.gov/sites/default/files/jmd/legacy/2014/07/13/mut-legal -assist.pdf.

Table 28.2. MLA Requests for Computer Records by Year

Year	Foreign MLA for Computer Records
2000	84
2001	97
2002	125
2003	167
2004	272
2005	312
2006	359
2007	426
2008	529
2009	580
2010	718
2011	859
2012	945
2013	1095
2014	1160
2015	2183

Table 28.3. MLAT Requests by Year

Year	Foreign MLAT Requests	U.S. MLAT Requests
2000	1716	603
2001	1634	622
2002	1722	729
2003	2137	662
2004	2082	786
2005	2138	676
2006	2270	598
2007	2480	658
2008	2707	667
2009	2633	827
2010	2947	751
2011	2847	966
2012	3044	987
2013	3282	1099
2014	3270	1042
2015	3352	1173

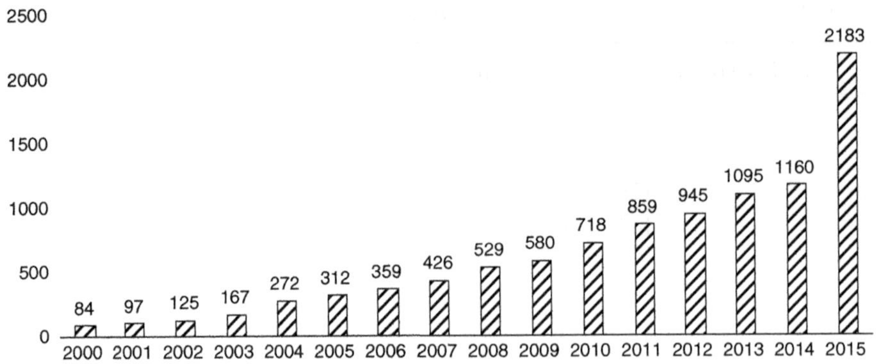

Figure 28.1. Foreign MLA requests for computer records.

degree in terms of responsiveness, further hampering legitimate law enforcement efforts. In terms of existing data, the growth curve for incoming requests for MLA regarding electronic evidence is logarithmic, whereas OIA budget increases are incremental.

B *Foreign Officer Training*

Although the OIA is undertaking a number of important reforms to improve its handling of foreign requests for MLA regarding computer records, the OIA is only one-half of the story. Many requests arrive at the Department of Justice badly formatted, in a foreign language, or with insufficient evidence to meet the probable cause standard that is required for a U.S. judge to grant a warrant, which is what ECPA requires for the production of digital content.[15] The problem, very often, is a lack of training of requesting law enforcement officials.

To draft an expeditious and successful request for MLA, our Indian law enforcement agents should know a few key things. First, they should know English, or how to have their request translated into English. This is not always a huge problem – the OIA regularly uses translators – but if the request is not in English, the process is slowed down considerably. Second, they should know the relevant legal standard in the receiving country – which in the case of the United States, where a warrant is required for stored communications, means the Fourth Amendment's probable cause standard. Too often, requests arrive without any articulable due process standard, or the standard articulated is the *requesting* country standard rather than the *receiving* country standard (i.e., probable cause in the United States). The Department of Justice hardly cares whether a request meets local law in the requesting country; what it is trying to determine is whether the request contains sufficient evidence to pass muster before a U.S. judge. This relates to the third requirement – the requester must provide enough evidence to satisfy that legal standard. Too often, requests are written on the basis of sketchy assertions without any evidence. A request for the emails of a suspect based on the assertion that the person "is a suspect" or "there are reasons to suspect" this individual will not suffice to establish probable cause; the requester must both articulate the reason and support it with some evidentiary showing. Finally, and often critically, the requesting law enforcement agent must know whom to contact in their country in order to have the MLA request

15 Andrew K. Woods, Data beyond Borders (2015), https://globalnetworkinitiative.org/sites/default/files/GNI%20MLAT%20Report.pdf.

forwarded on to the appropriate officials in the responding country. One reason many MLA requests languish for months is the fact that they are sent to the wrong person and bounce around in bureaucratic purgatory before reaching the appropriate destination.

The solution to each of these challenges, of course, is better training. Just as law enforcement officials in the twenty-first century must contend with novel forms of digital evidence, they must contend with novel interjurisdictional processes to obtain that digital evidence. Crossing borders to collect digital evidence for largely local crimes is likely to be a reality for many law enforcement officials going forward. Training about every step of the process will go a long way to ensuring a swift, efficient, and just MLA regime. Also helpful would be better internal and external processes for handling mutual legal assistance.

C *Better MLA Processes*

One way to ensure that MLA requests are formatted properly – in the right language, with reference to the appropriate legal standard, supported by evidence, and so on – is to create intake and outtake processes for MLA requests that meet three key criteria. Well-designed MLA processes will be 1) centralized, 2) form-based, and 3) digital. Importantly, these reforms should be developed both within countries seeking MLA (requesting countries) and by countries responding to MLA requests (responding countries). Let us consider each of these key elements in turn.

1 Centralization

If too many authorities are in charge of the MLA process – or if no one is in charge – investigators will not know whom to approach about initiating a cross-border request. The result will be needless delay in the handling of MLA requests, which may become lost as they bounce around from office to office. Centralization is especially important in the MLA process because requests for legal assistance are rarely one-way transmissions. Rather, when the request finally reaches its destination, the receiving country will often have questions about the request: questions about the crime in question, questions about evidence to support the claims made in the request, and more. If the request is routed through several offices on its way to the receiving country, how is the receiving country to know whom to contact? Just as countries have centralized offices for handling incoming MLA requests – like the OIA at the Department of Justice – they should establish centralized offices with highly trained officials for coordinating outgoing MLA requests.

2 Form-Based Requests

The second reform that would drastically improve the existing MLA regime – as much as or more than better training for law enforcement officials – is the use of standardized forms. Such forms could include standard fields for items such as "evidence requested," "crime under investigation," "person under investigation," "law violated," and so on. These fields are important not only because they promise to provide some uniformity to MLA requests, but also because they effectively train officers about the MLA process. They can make clear, for example, what questions must be answered before a receiving country will agree to provide legal assistance. They can also explain – in simple terms, in a local language – how to satisfy the legal standards of the receiving country. Rather than simply ask, "Do you have probable cause to request these emails?" – a question that likely will not have much significance for investigators and lawyers outside the United States – the form would ask, "What makes you think the data being requested is evidence of a crime?" This is much more likely to yield an answer that allows the receiving country to evaluate the likelihood of success of a request for a warrant.

3 Digitized Request Portals

Too many MLA requests today are made on paper and transmitted through the requesting country's diplomatic pouch. A better process would be electronic. Of course, this is not a small undertaking, and it likely can only be implemented in countries where the MLA process is centralized and the requests are made according to a form. Importantly, countries must develop two portals for MLA: internal (or outgoing requests) and external (for incoming requests). The internal portal should make clear to any law enforcement officer what standards are required, what fields must be completed, who the central authority is, and so on. The external portal should do two things: guide the requester through all necessary steps to request evidence successfully and allow him to track the progress of his request. At the moment, a customer of FedEx or UPS has a much better sense of where his package is at any given moment than a law enforcement official may about her request for critical evidence.

Digitizing the MLA process is not a panacea – each request for MLA must still be screened by lawyers, and this is time-consuming work. But even if the offices handling MLA are well-trained and well-staffed, time is wasted when requests are made through analog channels. One of the easiest ways to accelerate the existing process is to digitize it as much as possible. This will not be easy: because we are talking about evidence, portals will need to be secure, the same way that diplomatic channels of communications are – relatively speaking – secure.

III Alternatives to MLA

No matter how much the current MLA process improves, it will be unable to handle the entire burden of law enforcement requests for digital evidence. First, there is the simple matter of capacity. Requesting countries' demands for MLA are likely to outstrip receiving countries' capacities for quite a long time. If almost every crime around the world produces digital evidence, and that evidence often continues to reside in a foreign jurisdiction necessitating the use of MLA, the demands on the MLA regime will be enormous. But even if MLA capacity were magically able to match demand, there is a deeper reason that cross-border data requests cannot be entirely handled by existing MLA procedures: politics. Law enforcement agents, and more importantly political leaders, resent the idea that they must request legal assistance from another country in order to access evidence that relates to a crime that occurs on their soil. This is an entirely understandable reaction. Why, national leaders ask, should we have to ask the United States for legal assistance when the company in charge of the evidence is operating on our soil, making money on our citizens? In a world where 90 percent of global Internet users are outside the United States, yet Internet services are dominated by American firms, international politics matter a great deal.

A *Three Dangerous Alternatives to MLA*

So what options does a jealous sovereign have, if it wants to enforce its laws faithfully, and the evidence necessary to prosecute crimes such as murder and theft is held by American technology firms? If domestic law enforcement cannot conveniently access criminal evidence held by American Internet companies, it might 1) demand that data be held on local servers, where it can more easily be accessed (and surveilled); 2) deploy covert surveillance efforts to access the data (and perhaps demand a way around the service provider's encryption); and/or 3) assert extraterritorial jurisdiction over the foreign-held data, throwing Internet companies into an unfortunate conflict of laws. Each of these problematic policies has resulted from states' frustrations with the existing regulatory and technological framework.

1 Data Localization

First, a foreign state could demand that all data be stored within the country – a process known as forced data localization. This is problematic for a number of reasons. It imposes huge costs on Internet firms, which must now store duplicate copies of data in every country in which they operate. Imagine a customer who flies around the world accessing his Gmail account. Google would have to store all of that customer's multigigabyte email in every single country that has data localization laws. This would be a huge cost on Google, and effectively destroys the scaling benefits of a global Internet. Moreover, even if Google could absorb this huge cost, imagine what it does to the small technology startup with limited resources. The effect of forced data localization on global entrepreneurship would likely be enormous. Just as troubling, if not more so, data localization makes it much easier for states to surveil their citizens. Without naming names, we can imagine a state where due process and privacy are neither respected nor protected. In such a state it would be relatively difficult for the government to pore over online data stored securely offshore. Not so with data stored locally.[16]

2 Weaken Encryption

A second option the state has is to demand a backdoor on all encrypted services, such that even if foreign Internet firms cannot hand over evidence because of a blocking statute like ECPA, the data can be intercepted and read in plain text as it passes through local telecommunications networks. It is beyond the scope of this short chapter to evaluate the potential harms of government-mandated weaker forms of encryption, but the overwhelming consensus of the computer security community is that such policies are extremely bad for privacy and stability on the Web. This is true not just for protecting personal privacy, such as safeguarding one's emails and photos, but also for protecting banking and health records, which are crucial in a modern economy.

3 Strain Foreign Firms

A third option would be to enforce draconian state law when the foreign Internet company does not comply with local law. For example, Brazil could seize Google's assets,

[16] *See* Anupam Chander & Uyên P. Lê, *Data Nationalism*, 64 Emory L.J. 677, 713 (2015).

arrest Microsoft's employees, and shut down Facebook and Twitter because the company refuses to comply with a production order from a Brazilian court outside the existing MLA regime. As Brazil's arrest of Facebook employees in 2016 shows, this is a problematic, if increasingly common, reaction to frustration over companies' refusals to comply with local demands for criminal evidence in deference to laws, such as ECPA, that govern them in their places of business or where the relevant data is stored.[17]

B *Better Alternatives to MLA*

Fortunately, these are not the only options for states seeking an alternative to the traditional MLA regime – whether in its current form or in a more efficient and fair MLA process. Before resorting to data localization, antiencryption, and anticompetitive practices, states have a number of options. Some of these – such as striking new multilateral treaties – will take some time to implement. But others, such as lifting domestic blocking statutes like ECPA, can be done relatively quickly. Given the difficulty in achieving these reforms, reformers may want to pursue several different avenues simultaneously.

1 New Multilateral Treaty

A number of people have argued that we need a new multilateral treaty delimiting government access to data. Microsoft President and General Counsel Brad Smith has repeatedly made the case for a global treaty.[18] David Kris has also advocated this kind of international regime.[19] This makes sense. A good multilateral treaty signed by all relevant parties would be ideal. But in practice, it has at least one of two problems: if it is good, it will not be signed by all relevant parties, and if it is signed by all relevant parties, it will not be good.

Anyone having even a passing familiarity with Internet governance debates knows that the topic is highly politicized and that achieving agreement between the major powers is extremely difficult. Even the relatively benign Budapest Convention on Cybercrime, discussed later, found nonuniversal adherence among like-minded Western countries and no accessions by major non-Western countries. Add to this the questions of sovereignty, due process, and privacy rights that are inherent in MLAs and you have a recipe for deep divisions among many of the most important countries. For example, it is unlikely that the United States and China will agree to the same set of due process provisions regarding cross-border law enforcement access to cloud data. An international agreement that satisfied India, China, Brazil, Russia, and the United States would likely be so watered down, it would have little utility; in fact, there is a serious risk that the resulting agreement would lead to an erosion of privacy rights, not an enhancement,

[17] Will Connors, *Facebook Executive Arrested in Brazil*, WALL ST. J. (Mar. 1, 2016), http://www.wsj.com/articles/facebook-executive-arrested-in-brazil-1456851506?mg=id-wsj.

[18] Adam Segal, *Do Local Laws Belong in a Global Cloud?: Q&A with Brad Smith of Microsoft (Part One)*, COUNCIL ON FOREIGN RELATIONS (Aug. 26, 2015), http://blogs.cfr.org/cyber/2015/08/26/do-local-laws-belong-in-a-global-cloud-qa-with-brad-smith-of-microsoft-part-one/; *Time for an International Convention on Government Access to Data*, MICROSOFT (Jan. 20, 2014), http://blogs.microsoft.com/on-the-issues/2014/01/20/time-for-an-international-convention-on-government-access-to-data/.

[19] David Kris, *Preliminary Thoughts on Cross-Border Data Requests*, LAWFARE (Sept. 28, 2015, 9:00 AM), https://www.lawfareblog.com/preliminary-thoughts-cross-border-data-requests.

while also unduly hampering legitimate law enforcement investigations – the worst of both worlds.

It is for precisely this reason that treaty advocates have suggested starting small with a handful of like-minded states. The United States, the United Kingdom, and France might relatively easily be able to forge an international agreement with high due process standards and privacy protections – an agreement that produces a cross-border process that is much more streamlined than the existing mutual legal assistance process. But how much does this agreement accomplish? If you ask people at the Office of International Affairs which international partners they have the most problems with, they will likely not list the United Kingdom, France, or any other country with whom we might easily forge a new international agreement. Missing from such an agreement would be Brazil, India, and China, all of whom rejected the cybercrime convention. These are the countries putting enormous pressure on American tech firms, and if they are not part of a new treaty regime for cross-border data requests, this pressure will not ease.

2 ECPA Reform

The reason foreign law enforcement must ask the U.S. government for MLA in the first place is ECPA's requirement that U.S. data holders only release stored digital content in response to a warrant from a U.S. judge. That is, ECPA acts as a blocking statute, preventing U.S. data holders from complying with foreign law enforcement requests for data. If this blocking feature were removed, American tech firms could comply directly with foreign law enforcement requests for data and the "cross-border" nature of cross-border data requests would essentially go away. The upshot is that reforming one bill in Congress is likely easier than forging a new global treaty or revising dozens of bilateral agreements. However, the problem with this proposal is that it requires congressional action. Congress has not been terribly productive lately. And besides Congress, it is not clear that civil society, companies, and government agencies can agree on how to reform ECPA effectively. (The Senate's hearings on this matter in June of 2016 suggested that different agencies within the government feel very differently about ECPA reform.)[20] There are other substantive reasons that auger for and against ECPA reform, of course, but from a procedural standpoint, ECPA reform is the simplest and most direct route to solving the bulk of cross-border data requests.

3 Budapest Convention on Cybercrime Amendment

The Budapest Convention on Cybercrime foreshadowed this cross-border data request problem, but it did not resolve it. Article 32b of the convention governs "Trans-Border Access to Stored Computer Data," and it weakly provides that in most cases, countries should seek that data by requesting mutual legal assistance from the country with the authority to compel it. The drafters of the convention discussed the idea of allowing signatories the ability to request data directly from foreign data holders operating in their jurisdiction, but the provision was deemed too controversial. Rather than negotiate a

[20] *Reforming the Electronic Communications Privacy Act*, U.S. Senate Comm. On the Judiciary, http://www.judiciary.senate.gov/meetings/reforming-the-electronic-communications-privacy-act.

new treaty on government access to data, then, countries could simply revise the agreement already in place.

While the Budapest Convention is primarily concerned with cybercrime, many commentators overlook the fact that the convention's provisions explicitly apply to all crimes for which there is digital evidence. This makes it a prime candidate for reforming the cross-border data request problem. The problem, however, is that the treaty has political baggage. The convention has been signed by some fifty states, but implementation has been spotty and a number of key states, such as Russia and China, have expressed their opposition to the treaty on the grounds that they were not part of the original negotiations. Reforming the treaty therefore carries some of the same limitations as forging a new global treaty on cross-border data requests.

4 Bilateral Agreement(s)

MLAT agreements cover much more than data – they are omnibus agreements between states regarding the cross-border requests for criminal evidence and other law enforcement matters. They worked reasonably well, in some cases for decades, before the explosion in digital evidence. Revising each agreement simply because ECPA (and other blocking statutes) requires foreign law enforcement to seek U.S. government assistance to compel the data would be onerous and ultimately counterproductive. It would require the United States to renegotiate dozens of treaties, a costly and unpredictable process that could ultimately lead to weaker agreements than the ones currently in place; it could also take years to complete. A better approach would be to fix ECPA so as to allow new bilateral agreements to be struck.

The United States and the United Kingdom are currently negotiating a treaty on cross-border requests for data.[21] If such an agreement comes to fruition, and it is inconsistent with ECPA (and self-executing and properly worded), it could supersede the statute at least with regard to UK government requests for data. While such an agreement would presumably mitigate the cross-border data problem vis-à-vis the United Kingdom, it would do nothing for other countries and may in fact anger them by leaving them outside the agreement. While such an agreement would not resolve what to do about Brazilian or French government requests for data, companies might look at the U.S.–UK agreement as a firm commitment of the U.S. government position on cross-border data requests. This would not be unlike company policies in the wake of *United States v. Warshak*, the Sixth Circuit's ruling that the U.S. government can only compel emails with a warrant, a view that many Internet companies immediately treated as national law, despite the court's limited jurisdiction over the Sixth Circuit.

5 Executive Agreements

Finally, rather than forge entirely new treaties, the U.S. president could sign executive agreements with other countries. This would have the advantage of being much simpler

[21] Ellen Nakashima and Andrea Peters, *The British Want to Come to America – With Wiretap Orders and Search Warrants*, Wash. Post Feb. 4, 2016, available at: https://www.washingtonpost.com/world/national-security/the-british-want-to-come-to-america--with-wiretap-orders-and-search-warrants/2016/02/04/b351ce9e-ca86-11e5-a7b2-5a2f824b02c9_story.html?hpid=hp_hp-more-top-stories_uk-wiretap-725pm%3Ahomepage%25&utm_term=.56c52edde1b3.

politically because it would not require consent by the Senate. However, assuming that it falls within the president's authority to conclude such an executive agreement, it would have one significant drawback: without Senate consent (or Congress's consent via congressional–executive agreement) such an agreement would almost certainly not supersede ECPA. This could put companies in a difficult position if, for example, the data sharing agreement encouraged or required them to comply with a foreign government's request, while ECPA bars the very same thing. Indeed, this fact alone explains why the president would likely not enter into such agreements at all.

IV Key Principles for Cross-Border Data Access

Whatever procedural form they take, it seems that the best avenue for reform is for states to strike principled agreements that resolve the current forcing of nearly all requests through the MLA regime. The aim of such an agreement ought to be maximizing sovereignty of a state over its own affairs while protecting basic privacy and rule of law principles. This includes a few key features: 1) allowing states to request data directly from foreign Internet firms, regardless of where the data is stored 2) as long as the crime in question implicates the state's domestic interests, defined in a way that is consistent with long-standing notions of territorial sovereignty and 3) requiring basic due process protections.

A *Direct Access to Data*

The underlying goal of these reforms is to allow states to request crucial evidence directly from Internet service providers, rather than having to route those requests through the government of whatever state has jurisdiction over the service provider (as we have seen, typically the United States). This means that a local government can approach a foreign Internet service provider to request evidence, just as it would request physical evidence in the custody of the service provider. It also means that the service provider must be free to comply without violating its own state's laws (for American service providers, this means revising ECPA, as discussed).

This is a key component of the proposed U.S.–UK agreement. The British government is fed up with having to choose between two unsavory options. As an analysis by the British parliament reveals, foreign governments have two main channels for accessing data stored on corporate servers held in the United States: (1) MLA and (2) what the British call "goodwill."[22] That is, foreign governments can (1) pull their hair out while they wait for the MLA process to work its slow, slow magic, or (2) ask for the information directly from the company and potentially get what they want immediately. As one can imagine, governments much prefer the latter approach. As a result, they put enormous pressure on companies to give them what they want outside the MLA process.

That is why American companies, such as Microsoft, have been pushing for a way around the current MLA regime. On the one hand, consumers are increasingly worried about how Internet companies handle government requests for user information – so much so that Microsoft has taken pains to reassure consumers who are worried about

[22] *Jurisdictional Issues*, PARLIAMENT (Dec. 11, 2012), http://www.publications.parliament.uk/pa/jt201213/jtselect/jtdraftcomuni/79/7909.htm.

their data falling into government hands. Given this climate of concern, you might think that Microsoft would welcome the chance to drag its feet through a convoluted bureaucratic procedure like the current MLA regime. But, instead, Microsoft wants to reform the MLA process, making it easier to give foreign police access to the data deemed appropriate. This is the only sensible alternative to a world in which states take increasingly aggressive measures to ensure their sovereignty.

Direct access will require that firms evaluate the legitimacy of the requests they receive, a process that in some cases will mean increasing their capacity for managing compliance. But this is not so different from the role they play now when they receive requests from law enforcement for nondigital evidence. Essentially, this reform would mean that when police in Brazil show up at Google's offices to request a piece of evidence, Google would respond the same way whether the evidence in question were a piece of paper in the offices in Rio or a megabyte of data stored on servers (perhaps many of them) around the world.

B *Domestic Crimes*

Of course, the Brazilian government does not have a legitimate interest in access to all of a Google's customer data – it only has a legitimate interest in accessing customer data regarding crimes that affect Brazil. There must be, in other words, some sort of jurisdictional hook for determining when direct access ought to be allowed. The traditional bases for asserting jurisdiction can be lumped into five general categories. A state can generally prescribe law with regard to (1) conduct that takes place within its territory, (2) persons or things within its territory, (3) extraterritorial conduct that has or is intended to have substantial effects within its territory, (4) the activities of its own nationals regardless of location, and (5) conduct outside the state that is directed against the security of the state or its interests.[23] There are limits on a state's enforcement jurisdiction, but a treaty might reasonably clarify that a foreign Internet firm should cooperate with local law enforcement, subject to local due process constraints, where a law is consistent with any of these five grounds for asserting prescriptive jurisdiction.[24]

Another way to think about this is to consider each possible jurisdictional hook as further proof that the state has a compelling interest in the case in question. So the easiest cases are those we might call "wholly local" – where the crime is British, the suspect and victim are British, and every other aspect of the case is British but for the domicile of the company that controls the digital evidence in question. It seems least controversial to say that in these cases, the British government can ask Google or Microsoft to hand over digital evidence in their possession if it meets whatever due process standards apply locally for relevance. In other words, digital data would be no different from physical data in these cases. The case for asserting a state interest – and therefore for justifying direct access to data – is incrementally more controversial as you remove each jurisdictional hook. So it is more controversial to allow the United Kingdom to request evidence from

23 Restatement (Third) of the Foreign Relations Law of the United States § 402 (Am. Law Inst. 1987).

24 Local courts would seem to be the most logical place to resolve any disputes about whether a state's claims are overbroad. While it might seem unlikely that a state's own judges would rule that the state does not have the authority to compel an Internet firm to produce evidence in compliance with local law, it is not uncommon.

a foreign service provider where the crime occurs in London but the victim and suspect are thought not to be British. There are still compelling reasons grounded in conflicts of laws principles for allowing a state to assert its jurisdiction over any event that occurs within its territory, regardless of the citizenships involved, but this is nonetheless more complicated because now the states of the victim and suspect also have an interest in the handling of the case.

C *Minimum Due Process Protections*

One of the most significant hurdles to achieving this direct access regime is overcoming the concerns of privacy groups. Critics of this proposal suggest that it will, in many cases, mean a reduction in privacy because governments will have more direct access to more data. Why, they ask, should we make it easier for governments to get personal data in a time when governments have too much access? There is a logic to this argument, but it is ultimately myopic. States are increasingly jealous of their territory regarding access to digital evidence. Either that evidence will prove not to be as important as it appears, or states will find another way to get it – via such means as data localization, forced decryption, and so on.

Still, the politics of cross-border data reform require compromise. In order for serious reform to occur – in order for the United States and the United Kingdom to pass a treaty, for example – states will need to amend their blocking statues, like ECPA. And that will trigger a political push by privacy groups in the United States, who will insist on imposing due process protections in whatever agreement is struck. It may not be the United States' place to say what due process protections apply to criminal cases in the United Kingdom (or anywhere else) – indeed, at some level dictating these terms will smack of legal imperialism – but the United States will likely ultimately have significant say in any case as a matter of political necessity.

What due process protections are these? At a minimum, considerations such as particularity (that the request for data not be overly broad), notice (that the person whose data is being requested receive notice, even if after the fact, that his or her data is being released), transparency reporting (that governments regularly inform their citizens what sorts of data are being collected and in what sorts of cases); independent authorization (that requests be authorized by someone outside the line of command of the law enforcement agency seeking the evidence – ideally by a judicial official or an independent data commissioner); cause (that the state has a strong factual basis to believe that a crime has been committed and that the evidence is necessary to solving that crime), and more.

Conclusion

The regime through which law enforcement agents gain access to data across borders is broken. Since privacy laws like ECPA prevent companies from responding to non-U.S. law enforcement requests for content, they effectively force those requests to be routed through the mutual legal assistance regime. Therefore, reforms ought to be aimed at improving the efficiency and fairness of the MLA regime. But they should also aim to revise blocking statutes where possible and replace them with well-crafted agreements that seek to minimize conflicts of laws. This chapter describes important reforms to the existing cross-border data requests regime, many of which are either under way or being discussed with select partners (as in the case of the U.S.–UK agreement). There are some deep, intractable issues about which states are not likely to agree –the contents of their criminal laws, for example – but that should not be a barrier to resolving what is essentially a jurisdictional question. In particular, this jurisdictional question can be resolved by reference to long-standing principles of prescriptive and enforcement jurisdiction. If states are not able to work out these jurisdictional differences, the Internet will likely continue to splinter to suit state needs, which is to say that the Internet will look less like a global space and more like a national one, and companies will have to take greater steps to accommodate all of the governments of the world, where before an entrepreneur could effectively launch a global business from her garage.

29 The Privacy and Civil Liberties Oversight Board

David Medine & Esteban Morin†

The Privacy and Civil Liberties Oversight Board (PCLOB or Board) is an independent bipartisan agency that first convened in 2012. Congress created the PCLOB to review counterterrorism efforts taken by the executive branch to ensure that the need for such efforts is balanced with the need to protect individual's privacy and civil liberties. The agency was also tasked with ensuring that liberty concerns are appropriately considered in the development and implementation of counterterrorism laws, regulations, and policies. Since the Board's formation, it has engaged in oversight of two large-scale surveillance programs operated by the National Security Agency (NSA) and has released detailed reports describing the operations of these programs and analyzing their legal foundation, policy implications, and effectiveness. In both reports the Board offered recommendations that have, to some extent, been adopted by all three branches of the federal government. Congress adopted legislation in 2015 implementing two of the Board's key recommendations, which was effectuated and supported by the executive branch, and a federal appellate court has relied on the legal analysis in a PCLOB report declaring aspects of the NSA's domestic surveillance program illegal.

The PCLOB's impact on national policy in its first few years has been significant, and is attributable to the agency's unique structure, mission, and position within the federal government. In order to explain these characteristics, and foster a greater understanding of the PCLOB more generally, this chapter proceeds in five sections. First, it examines the state of American surveillance and oversight leading to the PCLOB's creation. Second, it looks at the agency's purpose and how it serves a novel role in American government. Third, it describes the findings and impact of the agency's first report on

† David Medine is the former Chairman of the Privacy and Civil Liberties Oversight Board. Previously, Mr. Medine was an Attorney Fellow for the Securities and Exchange Commission and a Special Counsel at the Consumer Financial Protection Bureau. He has also served as a partner at the law firm WilmerHale, a Senior Advisor to the White House National Economic Council, and the Associate Director for Financial Practices at the Federal Trade Commission. Mr. Medine has taught at the Indiana University (Bloomington) School of Law and the George Washington University School of Law. Mr. Medine earned his B.A. from Hampshire College and his J.D. from the University of Chicago Law School.

Esteban Morin was Counselor to Chairman Medine, and is currently an Attorney Advisor at the PCLOB. Prior to joining the Board, Mr. Morin was an associate in the Washington office of Jenner & Block LLP and a D.C. Bar Associate Fellow in the Appellate Division of the D.C. Public Defender Service. He also served as a law clerk to Judge Carlos Lucero of the U.S. Court of Appeals for the Tenth Circuit. Mr. Morin earned his B.A. from Yale University and his J.D. from Stanford Law School.

The views expressed in this article are those of Mr. Medine and Mr. Morin, and do not represent the views of the Privacy and Civil Liberties Oversight Board or those of any of its Board members.

the NSA's telephone records surveillance program conducted under Section 215 of the USA PATRIOT Act. Finally, the chapter concludes with a discussion of the PCLOB's role going forward.

I Surveillance and Oversight before the PCLOB

Throughout the nation's history, executive agencies have been quick to adopt new technologies to aid them in protecting the American public and fighting crime. In response, both courts and Congress have worked to protect the privacy rights of citizens through constitutional interpretation, statutes, and internal oversight. This back-and-forth dynamic between new surveillance techniques and privacy safeguards has persisted for decades, and has helped balance the government's interest in domestic security and individuals' civil liberties. However, the rapid growth of digital technology and the rise of global terrorism altered the calculus underlying this balance. Starting in the 1990s, it became possible for the government to operate surveillance programs at scales that were previously unimaginable, and to keep virtually all details about its programs (including their very existence) completely secret outside the confines of the Intelligence Community (IC).[1] This new technology and insulation, coupled with the heightened need for intelligence following the terrorist attacks of September 11, 2001, led to the creation of a number of unprecedented surveillance programs. Congress created the PCLOB to provide advice about and oversight of these new programs.

A *Preexisting Privacy Safeguards*

Before discussing the origins of the PCLOB, it is necessary to examine briefly the safeguards and oversight mechanisms in place at the time of its creation. Looking at these mechanisms reveals their inherent limitations, and demonstrates the growing oversight gap that took shape in the modern age of governmental surveillance and bulk data collection.

1 The Constitution

In the United States, the oldest and most foundational privacy rights are enshrined in the Constitution. Starting in 1789, the Constitution incorporated the Fourth Amendment, which prohibits unreasonable searches and, in some cases, requires that authorities obtain judicial warrants before engaging in searches.[2] As technology evolved, the Supreme Court interpreted the Fourth Amendment to extend protections to conversations over wireline

[1] The IC is composed of seventeen separate federal entities that engage in intelligence activities considered necessary for the conduct of foreign relations and national security of the United States. The IC member entities are Air Force Intelligence Army Intelligence Central Intelligence Agency Coast Guard Intelligence Defense Intelligence Agency Department of Energy Department of Homeland Security Department of State Department of the Treasury Drug Enforcement Administration Federal Bureau of Investigation Marine Corps Intelligence National Geospatial-Intelligence Agency National Reconnaissance Office National Security Agency Navy Intelligence and Office of the Director of National Intelligence. *See Members of the IC*, Off. of the Dir. Of Nat'l Intelligence, www.dni.gov/index.php/intelligence-community/members-of-the-ic.

[2] U.S. Const. amend. IV.

telephones,[3] digital information stored on mobile devices,[4] and many other aspects of modern life. Through these decisions, the Court demonstrated its understanding of the "power of technology to shrink the realm of guaranteed privacy,"[5] and established that a substantial amount of information can be gathered from seemingly minimal intrusions by law enforcement.[6]

The First Amendment protects the rights of individuals to speak freely, to associate, and to keep their associations private. More than fifty years ago, the Supreme Court explained the "rights of free speech and association ... are protected not only against heavy-handed frontal attack, but also from being stifled by more subtle governmental interference."[7] Building on this notion, the Court declared that the government could not compel individuals to disclose their affiliation with people, groups, or movements because the First Amendment "encompasses protection of privacy of association in organizations."[8] Since that time, the right to privacy of association has become enshrined in case law, premised on the notion that forced disclosure could have a chilling effect on choices about those with whom people affiliate and what they say.[9] Advances in culture and technology have not changed the simple fact that individuals who support controversial causes may be subject to harassment or intimidation if their connections with organizations promoting such causes are disclosed.

Although the rights guaranteed under the First and Fourth Amendments remain in force, several factors can make it difficult for individuals to invoke them to challenge government surveillance. Foremost, the text of these amendments speaks of rights and protections in an abstract manner. This has posed a challenge for the judiciary, which has been responsible for determining how established rights map onto novel factual scenarios involving emerging technologies. The judiciary has also had to grapple with new and existing exceptions to certain rights, which further complicate the question of how to extend long-standing constitutional doctrine in the modern era. For example, in the Fourth Amendment context, the Supreme Court has permitted officials to collect information without a warrant when an individual has no reasonable expectation of privacy in that information.[10] Building on this reasoning, the Court created the "third party doctrine," which holds that individuals have no reasonable expectation of privacy in information they voluntarily convey to third parties – including the numbers that they dial from their telephones.[11] Just as the scope of the Fourth Amendment has expanded with the advent of modern technology, the third party doctrine has taken on new meaning in an era when Americans relay their home Internet activity through Internet Service

[3] *Katz v. United States*, 389 U.S. 347 (1967).

[4] *Riley v. California*, 134 S. Ct. 2473 (2014).

[5] *Kyllo v. United States*, 533 U.S. 27, 34 (2001).

[6] *Cf. United States v. Jones*, 132 S. Ct. 945 (2012). *Jones* involved authorities putting a GPS tracking device on an individual's vehicle. The Court held that placing the tracking device on the vehicle was enough of an intrusion to constitute a search under the Fourth Amendment.

[7] *Gibson v. Fla. Legislative Investigation Comm.*, 372 U.S. 539, 544 (1963); *see also NAACP v. Alabama*, 357 U.S. 449 (1958).

[8] *Gibson*, 372 U.S at 544.

[9] *See, e.g., Brown v. Gardner*, 513 U.S. 115, 88 (1994); *Baird v. State Bar of Ariz.*, 401 U.S. 1 (1971); *Gibson*, 372 U.S. at 558.

[10] *See Jones*, 132 S. Ct. at 948.

[11] *Smith v. Maryland*, 442 U.S. 159 (1977).

Providers ("ISPs") and carry devices that constantly transmit their locations, calls, and other personal details to their cell phone carriers.

The challenges associated with expanding constitutional protections to new technologies have led many judges to take a cautious approach, and, in turn, case law has developed at a gradual pace. As a result, litigants have limited bases for establishing what rights they may invoke when challenging government surveillance practices. Adding to this difficulty, the details of surveillance programs are largely shrouded in secrecy, as are the court proceedings authorizing them and analyzing their legality.[12] Individuals thus have virtually no way of knowing whether they are being targeted by the U.S. government and to what extent their privacy rights might be jeopardized. The dearth of information about surveillance can create standing problems, as evidenced by the seminal case *Clapper v. Amnesty Int'l USA*.[13] In *Clapper*, the Supreme Court dismissed a challenge to the FISA Amendments Act empowering the Foreign Intelligence Surveillance Court (FISC) to authorize surveillance without a showing of probable cause. The Court held that the claims that the plaintiffs were likely subject to such surveillance were based too much on speculation and on a predicted chain of events that might never occur, so they could not satisfy the constitutional requirement under Article III for a "case or controversy," which is a prerequisite for being allowed to challenge a practice in federal court.[14] This precedent continues to pose challenges to potential plaintiffs.

2 Statutes and Executive Orders

In addition to the Constitution, which protects individuals from government action by guaranteeing certain rights, federal statutes and executive orders provide some restraints on government surveillance. Looking first to statutes, Congress has passed several laws that include procedural safeguards against intercepting electronic communications. For example, the Federal Communications Act of 1934 dictates that "no person not being authorized by the sender shall intercept any radio communication and divulge or publish the existence, contents, substance, purport, effect, or meaning of such intercepted communications to any person."[15] Title III of the Omnibus Crime Control and Safe Streets Act of 1968, often referred to as the Wiretap Act, complements this prohibition by requiring that "each application for an order authorizing or approving the interception of a wire, oral, or electronic communication ... be made in writing upon oath or affirmation to a judge of competent jurisdiction."[16] The Electronic Communications Privacy Act (ECPA) of 1986, which amends the Wiretap Act of 1968, creates additional restraints on surveillance by dictating that, except under special enumerated circumstances, a telephone company "shall not knowingly divulge a record or other information pertaining

[12] The Foreign Intelligence Surveillance Court, which is referred to often as the FISC, also conducts its proceedings behind closed doors. Many scholars have commented on the FISC's lack of transparency and the issues it creates. *See, e.g.*, Richard A. Clarke et al., *Liberty & Security in a Changing World: Report and Recommendations of the President's Review Group on Intelligence & Communications Technologies*, 207 (Dec. 12, 2013), www.whitehouse.gov/sites/default/files/docs/2013-12-12_rg_final_report.pdf; Alan Butler, *Standing Up to Clapper: How to Increase Transparency & Oversight of FISA Surveillance*, 48 New Eng. L. Rev. 55, 75 (2013).

[13] 133 S. Ct. 1138 (2013).

[14] *Id.* at 1154–55; *see also ACLU v. NSA*, 493 F.3d 644 (6th Cir. 2007).

[15] 47 U.S.C. § 605(a) (2012).

[16] 18 U.S.C. § 2518 (2012).

to a subscriber to or customer of such service … to any governmental entity."[17] These statutes are only a few examples of the evolving congressional awareness of government information collection practices that seek to provide some legal safeguards against government surveillance.

Executive orders supplement statutory limits on government surveillance. Drawing on the president's inherent executive power under the Constitution, it is not uncommon for such orders to authorize broad surveillance and simultaneously espouse the importance of privacy rights. This is seen in Executive Order 12333, which is a key authority enabling many of the information collection activities conducted within the Intelligence Community. E.O. 12333 announces several principles that "are intended to achieve the proper balance between the acquisition of essential information and protection of individual interests,"[18] but ultimately establishes few meaningful protections or limitations in its text. For example, while the order requires IC elements to receive attorney general approval before implementing certain guidelines, it creates no mechanism for ensuring that the guidelines are properly interpreted, enforced, and updated in accordance with changes in the law.[19] Similarly, E.O. 12333 tasks the National Security Council (NSC) with conducting "a periodic review of ongoing covert action activities, including … consistency with applicable legal requirements," but does not state how regularly such reviews should take place or how to address problems if they are discovered.[20]

More recent executive orders and policies have imposed more concrete limits on activities conducted by the Intelligence Community. Notably, Presidential Policy Directive (PPD) 28, issued in January 2014, dictates that "privacy and civil liberties shall be integral considerations in the planning of U.S. signals intelligence activities" and declares that "signals intelligence activities shall be as tailored as feasible."[21] The long-term impact of PPD 28 remains to be seen, but IC elements have already acknowledged that it will have a nontrivial impact on their collection activities. Specifically, in January of 2015, the NSA publicly released new supplemental procedures for implementing PPD 28 titled USSID SP0018,[22] and several months later, the director of national intelligence (DNI) announced that "all Intelligence Community elements have reviewed and updated their existing policies and procedures, or have issued new policies or procedures, to provide safeguards for personal information collected through SIGINT."[23]

Statutes and executive orders are the basis for many executive branch surveillance activities, and, accordingly, serve as natural platforms for imposing meaningful limitations on such activities. At present, however, the restrictions that these authorities impose are limited. They largely espouse general principles and rarely include external oversight and accountability mechanisms. Looking once more to E.O. 12333, the order offers no clear path for an individual to question whether the NSA is abiding by the broad

[17] 18 U.S.C. § 2702(a)(3) (2012).

[18] Exec. Order No. 12333, § 2.2, 3 C.F.R. 200 (1981).

[19] *Id.* § 2.3.

[20] *Id.* § 1.2(b). The order also mandates that IC elements "cooperate with the Congress in the conduct of its responsibilities for oversight of intelligence activities shall be" implemented in accordance with applicable law. *Id.* § 3.1.

[21] *Presidential Policy Directive 28: Signals Intelligence Activities*, The White House Off. of the Press Secretary, §§ 1(b), 1(d) (Jan. 17, 2014), https://fas.org/irp/offdocs/ppd/ppd-28.pdf.

[22] Nat'l Sec. Agency, PPD-28 Section 4 Procedures (2015), www.dni.gov/files/documents/ppd-28/NSA.pdf.

[23] *Signals Intelligence Reform 2015 Anniversary Report*, Off. of the Dir. of Nat'l Intelligence: IC on the Record, http://icontherecord.tumblr.com/ppd-28/2015/privacy-civil-liberties.

principles that are included in its text.[24] And to the extent that statutes and orders create more concrete safeguards, they are often very limited in scope or are difficult to apply to secret programs authorized by other authorities.[25]

3 Intragovernment Oversight

The final form of surveillance safeguards that preceded the PCLOB is oversight by federal entities. Whereas the Constitution, statutes, and executive orders impose limits on how surveillance is conducted and create protections that individuals can invoke in court, intragovernment oversight is focused on detecting and preventing problematic conduct. Intragovernment oversight of the Intelligence Community involves numerous entities from at least two branches of government, each with jurisdiction over particular agencies and activities. This tapestry of oversight is vital to the functioning of the Intelligence Community, but is not necessarily comprehensive.

a *Congressional Oversight*

Both the Senate and House have permanent committees that play a role in intelligence oversight. The Senate Select Committee on Intelligence (SSCI) comprises fifteen senators who serve a maximum of eight-year terms.[26] In addition to authorizing appropriations for intelligence activities annually, SSCI conducts oversight investigations and inquiries. According to the committee, one of its core activities is "track[ing] the regular collection and analysis activities of the Intelligence Community, enabling the Committee to engage with the Intelligence Community early on if it becomes aware of an issue."[27] There is also the House Permanent Select Committee on Intelligence (HPSCI). HPSCI membership is currently set at twenty members, each of whom may be appointed for a term of up to eight years.[28] As its Senate counterpart does, HPSCI conducts oversight investigations and inquiries in addition to processing the annual authorization of appropriations for intelligence. These responsibilities are divided among four subcommittees: the CIA Subcommittee, the Department of Defense Intelligence and Overhead Architecture Subcommittee, the Emerging Threats Subcommittee, and the NSA and Cybersecurity Subcommittee.[29]

The National Security Act dictates that Congress must receive written notification of significant anticipated intelligence activities and significant intelligence failures.[30] Under

[24] *See ACLU v. Clapper*, 959 F. Supp. 2d 724, 742 (S.D.N.Y. 2013) ("Congress did not intend that targets of section 215 orders would ever learn of them. And the statutory scheme also makes clear that Congress intended to preclude suits by targets even if they discovered section 215 orders implicating them").

[25] Similar to constitutional claims, it is difficult for individuals to establish standing to challenge the governmental surveillance regime under ECPA (or any other statute). As such, application of ECPA to surveillance programs was only conducted by the FISC. *See* Section 215 Report at 91–93.

[26] *ODNI FAQ*, Off. of the Dir. of Nat'l Intelligence Leading Intelligence Integration, www.dni.gov/index.php/about/faq?start=1 ("ODNI FAQ"); *The CIA and Congress: The Creation of HPSCI*, Cent. Intelligence Agency, www.cia.gov/news-information/featured-story-archive/2011-featured-story-archive/cia-and-congress-hpsci.html ("Creation of HPSCI").

[27] *About the Committee*, U.S. Senate Select Committee on Intelligence, www.intelligence.senate.gov/about ("About SSCI").

[28] ODNI FAQ; Creation of HPSCI.

[29] *House Intelligence Committee Subcommittee Members*, U.S. House of Representatives Permanent Select Committee on Intelligence, http://intelligence.house.gov/subcommittees.

[30] 50 U.S.C. § 3091(a)–(b).

the statute, "intelligence activities" expressly include covert actions, and the Intelligence Community may not withhold information merely because disclosure would constitute an unauthorized disclosure of classified information or information relating to intelligence sources and methods.[31] These requirements are reinforced by Executive Order 12333, which mandates that the heads of IC elements "cooperate with the Congress in the conduct of its responsibilities for oversight of intelligence activities."[32] Other statutes require that specific offices and officers within the Intelligence Community issue reports to Congress. For example, civil liberties and privacy officers are required to provide regular reports to numerous committees, including SSCI and HPSCI, summarizing the work of their offices.[33]

Congressional oversight has historically been one of the most important catalysts for reform within the Intelligence Community. Both SSCI and HPSCI have the jurisdiction to examine the activities of any IC element, and can introduce bills that fundamentally reshape the authority wielded by such elements. But given the other responsibilities of SSCI and HPSCI members and their staffs, there are practical limitations to the committees' work. These limitations are made worse by the secrecy constraints inherent in intelligence oversight. Committee members can only review classified materials in secure rooms, and in some cases are unable to discuss matters with some of their trusted advisers or other colleagues in Congress freely.[34] Accounting for these realities, the oversight committees cannot realistically look at more than a handful of policies, programs, and activities at any given time.

b *Executive Oversight*

Numerous offices within the executive branch provide some form of oversight to the agencies that engage in surveillance activities. At a high level, entities such as the Office of the Director of National Intelligence (ODNI) and the President's Intelligence Advisory Board (PIAB) are responsible for overseeing activities across multiple IC elements. ODNI was formed in 2005 under the Intelligence Reform and Terrorism Prevention Act of 2004, and represented various reforms contemplated by the 9/11 Commission Report.[35] At its core, the agency facilitates the work of the ODNI, who serves as the head of the Intelligence Community and acts as the principal adviser to the president, the NSC, and the Homeland Security Council for intelligence matters related to the national security.[36] The ODNI also dedicates substantial resources to ensuring the Intelligence Community is respecting legal boundaries through its Civil Liberties Protection Office, General Counsel's Office, and Mission Integration Division.

31 *Id.* § 3091(a)–(b).

32 Exec. Order No. 12333, § 3.1, 3 C.F.R. 200 (1981).

33 42 U.S.C. § 2000ee-1(f)(2) (2012).

34 L. Elaine Halchin & Frederick M. Kaiser, Cong. Research Serv., RL32525, Congressional Oversight of Intelligence: Current Structure and Alternatives 34–35 (2012). The 9/11 Commission was a bipartisan panel established to "make a full and complete accounting of the circumstances surrounding" the September 11, 2001, terrorist attacks, and to provide "recommendations for corrective measures that can be taken to prevent acts of terrorism." Intelligence Authorization Act for Fiscal Year 2003, Pub. L. No. 107–306, §§ 602(4)-(5), 116 Stat. 2383, 2408 (2002).

35 Nat'l Commission on Terrorist Attacks upon the United States, Final Report of the National Commission on Terrorist Attacks upon the United States 399–428 (W. W. Norton ed., 2004) ("The 9/11 Commission Report").

36 ODNI FAQ.

Members of the PIAB are likewise responsible for advising the president and engaging in some direct oversight. The PIAB is a "nonpartisan body, independent of the [IC], free from day-to-day management or operational responsibilities, and with full access to the complete range of intelligence-related information."[37] It exists primarily to advise the president on the quality and adequacy of intelligence collection, of analysis and estimates, of counterintelligence, and of other intelligence activities. Additionally, up to five members of the PIAB can serve on the Intelligence Oversight Board (IOB), which engages in reviews and investigations of activities within the Intelligence Community and receives regular reports from ODNI and other IC elements.[38] On the basis of its oversight, the IOB provides additional advice to the president on intelligence activities that it believes may be unlawful, contrary to an executive order, or not otherwise properly being addressed.[39]

Entities such as ODNI and PIAB are responsible for overseeing policies and activities across multiple IC elements, a position that may give them a perspective that individual agencies lack. However, given their size and specialized mandates, they are not capable of monitoring even a fraction of the intelligence activities that may raise privacy and civil liberties concerns. It thus falls on offices within IC elements to oversee most day-to-day intelligence activities. Most IC elements disperse oversight and civil liberties responsibilities across multiple internal offices. The NSA, for example, relies on its director of compliance, general counsel, inspector general, and civil liberties and privacy officer.[40] Others have closely examined and described the roles of each of these oversight offices,[41] but for the purposes of this chapter, it is enough to say that hundreds of skilled men and women assist in regulating the activities of the agencies that operate surveillance programs.

The oversight provided by the executive branch, while vitally important, arises from a structured, institutional perspective. Internal oversight offices are, by definition, located within the very entities and programs they are tasked with regulating. Although proximity allows these offices to develop a deep and informed understanding of their respective agencies, it can also mean that they are consistently exposed to their agencies' culture, perspectives, and priorities. Some scholars have speculated that this exposure raises questions about the objectivity of internal oversight offices,[42] especially when tasked with evaluating programs that affect the rights of constituencies to which they are not directly accountable.[43] Whether this is true or not, relying almost exclusively on internal entities

37 *About the PIAB*, The White House: President's Intelligence Advisory Bd. & Intelligence Oversight Bd., www.whitehouse.gov/administration/eop/piab/about ("About the PIAB").

38 *See* Exec. Order No. 13,462, §§ 5(b), 7, 8, 73 Fed. Reg. 11,805 (2008).

39 About the PIAB.

40 Rebecca J. Richards, NSA Dir. of Civil Liberties & Privacy Off. Report, NSA's Civil Liberties & Protections for Targeted SIGINT Activities under Executive Order 12333, at 6–7 (Oct. 7, 2014), https://fas.org/irp/nsa/clpo-12333.pdf ("NSA CLPO Report").

41 Margo Schlanger, *Intelligence Legalism & the Nat'l Security Agency's Civil Liberties Gap*, 6 Harv. Nat'l Sec. J. 112 (2015).

42 As one scholar opined, "Agency lawyers are unlikely to lie down on the railroad tracks to stop an agency train; they are far more inclined by training, career incentives, and professional norms, to construct arguments to justify the train's forward motion." *Id.* at 148.

43 Far from being accountable to the individual citizens implicated by mass surveillance programs, agency attorneys have worked for superiors willing to push against the edges of legal and constitutional boundaries. This is exemplified by former NSA Director Michael Hayden, who explained: "Give me the box you will allow me to operate in. I'm going to play to the very edges of that box; I'm going to be very

to determine the propriety and civil liberties implications of an agency's practices raises some questions, especially given the complexity and importance of legal issues involved.

c *The FISC*

Beyond the numerous offices within the executive branch that provide internal oversight, the Foreign Intelligence Surveillance Court (FISC) and Foreign Intelligence Surveillance Court of Review play special roles in the system of checks and balances that our nation has created around the exercise of national security powers. The FISC is a specialized court[44] that was established in 1978[45] and currently consists of judges appointed by the chief justice of the United States from among sitting U.S. district court judges. Although the FISC was originally only delegated authority to review applications for "electronic surveillance," Congress has subsequently expanded its jurisdiction and function. Statutes enacted in 1994 and 1998 provided the FISC with authority to issue orders allowing physical searches, pen registers, and trap and trace devices.[46] The 1998 amendments also included an expansive "business records" provision, which authorizes the FISC, at the government's request, to order a common carrier to release records in its possession pertaining to a foreign power or agent of a foreign power.[47] Under this provision, which was expanded by the 2001 USA PATRIOT Act (PATRIOT Act),[48] the FISC both arbitrates and authorizes many of the government's most controversial surveillance programs. The modern FISC thus not only approves searches and surveillance related to foreign intelligence, but also has the authority to modify and oversee such activities.[49]

B *The Surveillance Status Quo before September 11*

Domestic government surveillance has been an issue of contention since the founding of the United States, as evidenced by the Constitution's prohibition on general warrants.[50] As Chief Justice John Roberts has explained, "The Fourth Amendment was the founding generation's response to the reviled 'general warrants' ... which allowed British officers to rummage through homes in an unrestrained search for evidence of criminal activity.

aggressive.... I'll get chalk-dust on my cleats, I'll be so close to the out-of-bounds markers." Interview with former NSA Director General Michael Hayden by Charlie Rose (July 29, 2013), http://perma.cc/Q83V-422B.

44 The Congressional Research Service identifies the FISC as a "specialized Article III Court." Andrew Nolan & Richard M. Thompson II, Cong. Research Serv., R43362, Reform of the Foreign Intelligence Surveillance Cts.: Proc. & Operational Changes (2014). However, given that the court is structured and operates in a distinct manner, some scholars have questioned whether it is consistent with Article III. *See, e.g.*, Steve Vladeck, *The FISA Court and Article III: A Surreply to Orin*, Lawfare (Aug. 5, 2014, 9:31 AM), www.lawfareblog.com/fisa-court-and-article-iii-surreply-orin.

45 FISA, which is discussed in more detail throughout this article, also created the FISC.

46 *See* Pub. L. No. 103–359, § 807, 108 Stat. 3423, 3443 (1994) (codified at 50 U.S.C. §§ 1821–29); Pub. L. No. 105–272, § 601, 112 Stat. 2396, 2404 (1998) (codified at 50 U.S.C. §§ 1841–46). *See generally* Edward C. Liu, Cong. Research Serv., R40138, Amendments to the Foreign Intelligence Surveillance Act (FISA) Extended Until June 1, 2015 (2011).

47 Pub. L. No. 105–272, § 602, 112 Stat. 2396, 2410 (1998) (codified at 50 U.S.C. §§ 1861–63).

48 *See* Pub. L. No. 107–56, § 215, 115 Stat. 272, 287 (2001).

49 50 U.S.C. §§ 1801–64.

50 Thomas Y. Davies, *Recovering the Original Fourth Amendment*, 98 Mich. L. Rev. 547, 556 (1999) ("The larger purpose for which the Framers adopted the [Fourth Amendment] to curb the exercise of discretionary authority by officers").

Opposition to such searches was … one of the driving forces behind the Revolution itself."[51] Yet the era of modern communications surveillance only dates back to the dawn of the twentieth century. In earlier times, surveillance was limited to intercepting postal letters and overhearing conversations through physical proximity. This changed with the advent of the telephone as a common household item, which ushered in a new age of convenient,[52] instantaneous communications among Americans and presented new opportunities for the government. For the first time, federal agents could gather information on suspected wrongdoers and matters of national security without having an agent nearby.[53]

Supreme Court decisions during the twentieth century tracked trends in surveillance technology and techniques. For example, in the 1928 case *Olmstead v. United States* the Supreme Court held that wiretapping an individual's line without a warrant did not violate the Constitution because "those who intercepted the projected voices were not in the house of either party to the conversation."[54] The Court adopted a similarly cabined view of the Fourth Amendment slightly more than a decade later in *Goldman v. United States*, which involved government agents using a large microphone to overhear a target's conversation from an adjoining room.[55] Although these decisions gave way to a more expansive view of privacy rights and the reasonable expectation of privacy standard in *Katz*, they highlight a key facet of twentieth-century surveillance: namely, that before the advent of computers, surveillance required that agents review individual wire, letter, or oral communications. The manpower that this type of investigation required was itself a limit on the scope of government surveillance. Only in times of war or national crisis did intelligence agencies have the increased funding and authority to engage in surveillance over large segments of the American population.[56]

Even though the Intelligence Community's surveillance practices in previous decades were technologically primitive by today's standards, they still aroused ire and distrust among the American people at various points throughout the past century. For example, the public's realization in the 1920s that the War Department was conducting surveillance of so-called radicals within the United States caused political backlash, and ultimately the abolition of the General Intelligence Division of the Bureau of Investigation, a precursor to the FBI.[57] Similar revelations in the 1970s concerning the CIA programs involving assassination attempts and United States–led efforts to overthrow foreign governments[58] spurred Congress to launch several investigations that exposed the breadth

51 *Riley*, 134 S. Ct. at 2494.

52 Between 1900 and 1910, the number of telephone lines climbed from 600,000 to 5.8 million. This expansion was further hastened by the nationalization of telephone and telegraph lines between 1918 and 1919. *See Imagining the Internet: A History and Forecast*, Elon Univ. Sch. of Comm., http://www.elon.edu/e-web/predictions/150/1870.xhtml.

53 *See generally* Charlie Savage, Power Wars: Inside Obama's Post 9/11 Presidency 170–71 (Little, Brown & Co. 2015).

54 277 U.S. 438, 466 (1928).

55 316 U.S. 129, 131 (1942).

56 Seth F. Kreimer, *Watching the Watchers: Surveillance, Transparency, and Political Freedom in the War on Terror*, 7 U. Pa. J. Const. L. 133, 139 (2004).

57 David M. Crane, *Divided We Stand: Counterintelligence Coordination Within the Intelligence Community of the United States*, 1995 Army L. 26, 31.

58 The 9/11 Commission Report at 90. *See also* Savage, *supra* note 53, at 171–72; Richard. A. Best, Cong. Research Serv., RL32500, Proposals for Intelligence Reorganization 1949–2004, 21–25 (2004).

of domestic intelligence programs.[59] The reports from the committees revealed that the FBI gathered information about many important public figures, including the Reverend Martin Luther King Jr., and in some cases, sought to discredit these individuals.[60] This information shocked the public, as evidenced by opinion polls showing that the percentage of Americans holding a "highly favorable" view of the FBI dropped from 84 percent to 37 percent.[61] The FBI's Domestic Intelligence Division was subsequently dissolved,[62] but this did not result in a long-term decline in domestic surveillance. Over the next few decades, federal agencies continued to monitor potentially dangerous individuals both at home and abroad[63] and were provided with additional authority through statutes such as Foreign Intelligence Surveillance Act (FISA).[64]

FISA represented a kind of grand legislative bargain in the wake of the congressional investigations and the Supreme Court's expanding view of Fourth Amendment protections in the 1970s. Although *Katz*'s holding did not address the national security context,[65] it did not take long for the Court to take up the issue in *United States v. United States District Court* (better known as the *Keith* case).[66] In *Keith*, the Supreme Court declared that, in the case of intelligence gathering involving domestic security surveillance, prior judicial approval was required to satisfy the Fourth Amendment.[67] This new judicial requirement, coupled with the revelations of the broad and often unchecked discretion under which the Intelligence Community was operating, called for legislative intervention. FISA was the result, which represented an attempt to "reach some kind of fair balance that will protect the security of the United States without infringing on our citizens' human liberties and rights."[68] To attain this balance, the statute authorized surveillance activities while seeking to subject such activities to oversight and keeping them in accord with the Constitution.

The ideals of balance underlying FISA represented an important step in how Congress conceived of its role and authority relative to the Intelligence Community and executive branch more generally. In a number of ways, the passage of FISA also represented a very contemporary understanding of the relationship between civil liberties and national security. But as the findings of the Church Committee and its House contemporary, the Pike Committee, faded from memory and the Cold War intensified, the balance was gradually altered. The Intelligence Community grew, technology advanced, and

59 The two most notable investigations were by the Church and Pike Committees. The Church Committee refers to the Senate Select Committee to Study Governmental Operations with Respect to Intelligence Activities. The Pike Committee refers to the 1975–1976 investigation of the United States Intelligence Community by the House Select Committee on Intelligence.

60 The 9/11 Commission Report at 75.

61 *Id.*

62 David M. Alpern, Anthony Marro, & Stephan Lesher, *This Is Your New FBI*, NEWSWEEK, Jan. 5, 1976, at 14.

63 The 9/11 Commission Report at 75–77.

64 50 U.S.C. § 1801 *et seq.*

65 389 U.S. at 353.

66 407 U.S. 297 (1972).

67 *Id.* at 323–24. *See also* Elizabeth B. Bazan, CONG. RESEARCH SERV., RL30465, THE FOREIGN INTELLIGENCE SURVEILLANCE ACT: AN OVERVIEW OF THE STATUTORY FRAMEWORK OF THE U.S. FOREIGN INTELLIGENCE SURVEILLANCE COURT AND U.S. FOREIGN INTELLIGENCE SURVEILLANCE COURT OF REVIEW DECISIONS, 3–6 (2007).

68 REPORT OF THE SENATE COMMITTEE ON THE JUDICIARY TO ACCOMPANY S. 1566, S. REP. NO. 95–604, Part I (1977), *reprinted in* 1978 U.S.C.C.A.N. 3904, 3910.

sporadic amendments to FISA provided the executive branch with increased discretionary authority to engage in electronic surveillance.[69] Within a few decades, the oversight structure and accountability contemplated in the original FISA were outpaced.

C *September 11 and the New Frontier of Surveillance*

The September 11, 2001, terrorist attacks in New York set in motion changes within the federal government that would lead to unprecedented mass surveillance and bulk data collection.[70] Prior to the attacks, technology had advanced to the point where executive agencies, telephone companies, ISPs, and other private sector entities could acquire and analyze vast amounts of information from individuals around the world. In the wake of the September 11 attacks there was a flurry of congressional legislation and executive orders supporting a newly invigorated fight against terrorism. Agencies including the NSA, CIA, and FBI launched ambitious new surveillance initiatives.[71] As time progressed, these initiatives evolved and expanded, in turn making it more difficult for anyone outside the Intelligence Community to understand fully the scope of government activity that was taking place on a daily basis. Looking briefly at the NSA's bulk telephone metadata collection, which was the subject of the PCLOB's first public report, demonstrates this evolution.[72]

In October 2001, only weeks after the attacks on the World Trade Center and Pentagon, President George W. Bush expressly authorized the NSA (1) to collect the contents of certain international communications, a program that was later referred to as the Terrorist Surveillance Program (TSP) and (2) to collect in bulk noncontent information, or "metadata," about domestic telephone and Internet communications.[73] Embracing its new authority, the NSA began collecting telephone metadata – consisting of information about the participating telephone numbers and the date, time, and duration of calls[74] – from telephone companies on a regular basis. This collection included information about millions of calls between and including U.S. citizens, and was compiled in a NSA database that could be searched by analysts under certain circumstances. The president renewed authorization for the NSA's collection activities in November 2001 and repeatedly thereafter until 2006, when the USA PATRIOT Improvement and Reauthorization Act became law.[75]

Section 215 of the PATRIOT Act empowered the FBI to seek a FISC order requiring production of any tangible things in aid of an authorized investigation against

69 *See* Bazan, *supra* note 67, at 11–68.

70 The following section borrows from the PCLOB's Section 215 Report. *See* Privacy & Civil Liberties Oversight Bd., Report on the Telephone Records Program Conducted under Section 215 of the USA PATRIOT Act and on the Operations of the Foreign Intelligence Surveillance Court 37–56 (2014), www.pclob.gov/library/215-Report_on_the_Telephone_Records_Program.pdf ("Section 215 Report").

71 *See generally* Savage, *supra* note 53, at 177–83.

72 The history of the Board's Section 215 report, and the report's findings and impact are discussed at length in Section II.

73 *See DNI Announces the Declassification of the Existence of Collection Activities Authorized by President George W. Bush Shortly after the Attacks of September 11, 2001*, Off. of the Dir. of Nat'l Intelligence: IC on the Record (May 5, 2016), http://icontherecord.tumblr.com/; Section 215 report 37.

74 Section 215 Report at 37, n.105.

75 *See* Pub. L. No. 109–177, 120 Stat. 192 (2006).

international terrorism.[76] The 2006 amendments to the PATRIOT Act made these requirements more stringent by requiring FISC judges to determine that the records being sought were likely "relevant" to an FBI investigation before approving collection activities. Specifically, the law now demanded that each application contain "a statement of facts showing that there are reasonable grounds to believe that the tangible things sought are relevant to an authorized investigation (other than a threat assessment)."[77] In light of these rules, the government requested that the FISC issue an order directing certain U.S. telephone companies to provide the NSA with call detail records created by those companies. The requested order sought to put the companies under a continuing obligation, for a period of ninety days, to provide the NSA with all of their newly created calling records on a daily basis. If approved, the NSA would be authorized to collect and analyze the records and disseminate intelligence from those records to "the FBI, CIA, or other appropriate U.S. Government and foreign government agencies."[78]

In May 2006, the FISC approved the government's request and issued an order permitting the ongoing collection of telephone metadata.[79] Although the FISC order imposed some rules on the NSA's use and storage of collected metadata and expired approximately ninety days from the time it was issued, it permitted the NSA to engage in the same records collection that had previously been authorized by the president. There was no break in collection caused by the increased involvement of the FISC; and going forward, the FISC continued to reauthorize the collection every ninety days. As a 2009 report by the inspectors general of several defense and intelligence agencies observed, "the program became less a temporary response to the September 11 terrorist attacks and more a permanent surveillance tool."[80]

The Bush administration also authorized the collection of Internet metadata directly from "backbones" of the Internet.[81] This metadata included, among other things, addressing information that helps route a message to the proper destination, such as the "to" and "from" lines attached to an email.[82] Similar to the telephone metadata collection, the administration transitioned authority to approve the bulk collection of Internet metadata from the president to the FISC in 2004. After that transition, the administration argued to the FISC that it should approve the collection because it fell within FISA's pen/trap provisions, under which the court could authorize the use of devices known as pen registers and "trap and trace" devices.[83] The FISC granted the

76 *See* 50 U.S.C. §§ 1861(a)(1)-(2) (2002); Section 215 report 40–41.

77 50 U.S.C. § 1861(b)(2)(A); *see id.* § 1861(c)(1) (requiring FISA court judge to find that an application meets this requirement before entering an order).

78 Memorandum of Law in Support of Application for Certain Tangible Things for Investigations to Protect Against International Terrorism, at 15, In re Application of the Federal Bureau of Investigation for an Order Requiring the Production of Tangible Things, No. BR 06 05 (FISA Ct. May 23, 2006).

79 *See* Order at 10, In re Application of the Federal Bureau of Investigation for an Order Requiring the Production of Tangible Things, No. BR 06 05 (FISA Ct. May 24, 2006).

80 *See* Unclassified Report on the President's Surveillance Program, Inspectors Gen. of the Dep't of Def., Dep't of Justice, Cent. Intelligence Agency, Nat'l Sec. Agency, & Off. of the Dir. of Nat'l Intelligence 31 (2009).

81 An Internet backbone is one of the principal data routes between large, strategically interconnected networks and core routers on the Internet. Virtually all Internet traffic involving servers within the United States or traveling through the United States passes through domestic backbones.

82 Section 215 report at 37, n.105.

83 Such devices are used to gather information of particular phones or telephone lines.

government's application in July 2004. The court's order permitted Internet metadata to be acquired only if it traveled through certain designated communications channels that were relatively likely to contain messages of counterterrorism interest, "in order to build a meta data archive that will be, in relative terms, richly populated" with terrorism-related communications.[84] NSA employees were permitted to access this collected data by running queries targeting particular Internet accounts and addresses upon showing that there was a "reasonable articulable suspicion" that the account or address was "associated with" a target.[85] However, after several years, the NSA terminated its bulk collection of Internet metadata, concluding that the program's value was limited.[86]

In sum, the NSA's bulk telephone and Internet metadata collection programs demonstrate the new realities of government surveillance after September 11. The programs were devised, authorized, operated, and overseen by entities with little public accountability. These programs operated for years, in secret, and relied on multiple shifting sources for authorization. This added complexity, combined with the fact that information about millions of Americans was being compiled into databases without suspicion, desperately needed some form of accountability. But unfortunately, as discussed previously, the existing government protections and oversight were not designed to address this scale of surveillance, which posed vastly different questions than the traditional targeted investigations undertaken by the intelligence community. Acknowledging this problem, Congress endeavored to create an organization to fill the oversight gap.[87]

II The Creation, Structure, and Importance of the PCLOB

Efforts to create a new federal oversight body percolated for years before the PCLOB coalesced in its current structure. During this time, several other oversight bodies were formed and disbanded, each offering important insights about how to engage and analyze the Intelligence Community's counterterrorism activities effectively. The enabling statute for the current PCLOB appears to reflect these insights, creating an agency that is the first of its kind in the United States and has few, if any, parallels in other countries. The Board was crafted to fill an oversight gap that has only emerged in recent years and is statutorily entitled to access and review extremely sensitive information held by other agencies. This access, coupled with the Board's independence, distinguishes it from existing accountability mechanisms.

A *The Creation of the PCLOB*

The first push for a new federal entity that would provide oversight and advice about counterterrorism activities was from the National Commission on Terrorist Attacks on the United States (known as the "9/11 Commission"). In July 2004, the commission recommended that "there should be a board within the executive branch to oversee adherence to the guidelines we recommend and the commitment the government makes to

84 Section 215 report at 39.
85 *Id.*
86 Section 215 report at 40.
87 This acknowledgment is seen in the "Findings" section of the PCLOB enabling statute, 42 U.S.C. § 2000ee(b), and its earlier iterations discussed in the next section.

defend our civil liberties."[88] In August 2004, President George W. Bush responded by creating the President's Board on Safeguarding Americans' Civil Liberties (President's Board) by executive order.[89] In accordance with the 9/11 Commission's recommendation, the order establishing the President's Board recognized that "the United States Government has a solemn obligation … to protect the legal rights of all Americans, including freedoms, civil liberties, and information privacy guaranteed by Federal law, in the effective performance of national security and homeland security functions."[90]

The President's Board was chaired by the deputy attorney general and consisted of twenty-two representatives from the Departments of State, Defense, Justice, Treasury, Health and Human Services, and Homeland Security; the Office of Management and Budget; and the Intelligence Community. Although this Board only convened a total of six times, it was scrutinized by outside observers. Critics were quick to point out that the President's Board was composed of individuals from the very agencies that engage in surveillance, and that it was limited to an advisory role with no obligation to provide information to the public.[91] These issues raised further questions about the Board's independence and usefulness in serving as a legitimate check on the new surveillance and other counterterrorism programs authorized after September 11.

Upon the enactment of the Intelligence Reform and Terrorism Prevention Act of 2004,[92] the President's Board ceased to meet. The act created a new Privacy and Civil Liberties Oversight Board within the Executive Office of the President, composed of two Board members appointed by the president, with the advice and consent of the Senate, and three additional Board members appointed by the president.[93] However, it was not until mid-2005 that President Bush nominated members, who were not confirmed by the Senate until early 2006.[94] Once formed, this iteration of the PCLOB received criticism from myriad sources (including one of its members) for not being sufficiently independent. Of particular concern was the fact that the president had the authority to fire Board members at will.[95]

In 2007, the Implementing Recommendations of the 9/11 Commission Act reconstituted the Board as an independent agency within the executive branch, which is its current form.[96] The act explains that the "shift of power and authority to the Government calls for an enhanced system of checks and balances to protect the precious liberties that are vital to our way of life and to ensure that the Government uses its powers for the purposes for which the powers were given."[97] It lays out a structure for the new PCLOB that is distinct from its predecessors. The act requires that all five Board members be appointed by the president, with the advice and consent of the Senate, for staggered six-year terms. The act further requires that the Board be bipartisan in composition.[98] No

88 The 9/11 Commission Report at 395.
89 *See* Exec. Order No. 13,353, 69 Fed. Reg. 53,585 (2004).
90 *Id.* § 1.
91 *See* Richard Ben-Veniste & Lance Cole, *How to Watch the Watchers*, N.Y. Times, Sept. 7, 2004, at A23.
92 *See* Pub. L. No. 108–458, § 1061(b), 118 Stat. 3638, 3684 (2004).
93 *Id.* § 1061(e)(1).
94 *See* Garrett Hatch, Cong. Research Serv., RL34385, Privacy & Civil Liberties Oversight Bd.: New Independent Agency Status 2 (2009).
95 *Id.* at 2–4; Ellen Nakashima, *Civil Libertarians Protest Privacy Policy; New Guidelines Do Little to Protect Established Rights, White House Bd. Told*, Wash. Post, Dec. 6, 2006, at A11.
96 *See* Pub. L. No. 110–53, § 801(a), 121 Stat. 266, 352–58 (2007).
97 42 U.S.C. § 2000ee(b) (2012).
98 *Id.* § 2000ee(h).

more than three of the five members may be from the same political party, and before appointing members who are not from the president's political party, the President must consult the leadership of the opposing party.[99] With the reconstitution of the Board, the terms of the individuals then serving as Board members within the Executive Office of the President were terminated effective January 30, 2008.[100]

Over the next four and one-half years, the PCLOB did not exist, as none of the positions on the Board was filled. It was not until 2010 that the president nominated James Dempsey and Elisabeth Collins as Board members to the new PCLOB, though their nominations expired at the end of the 111th Congress.[101] In 2011 the president submitted Mr. Dempsey's and Ms. Collins's names to the Senate, and later in the year nominated me (David Medine) as chairman and Rachel Brand and Patricia Wald as Board members.[102] The four Board members were subsequently confirmed by the Senate in August 2012, providing the reconstituted Board with the necessary quorum to begin operations.[103] I was confirmed as chairman[104] on May 7, 2013, and sworn in on May 29. Less than one week later, news stories based upon the leaks by the NSA contractor Edward Snowden began to appear in the media.

B *The PCLOB's Functions and Jurisdiction*

Congress resolved many of the criticisms leveled at earlier versions of the PCLOB in crafting the current Board's enabling statute. As a general matter, the statute provides the PCLOB with a focused mandate and limited jurisdiction centering on the relationship between individual civil liberties and federal counterterrorism efforts. But beyond these subject matter limitations, the current version of the Board possesses far more independence than its previous iterations. The Board's enabling statute establishes it as an independent agency within the executive branch and invests it with four distinct functions. Looking at each of four statutory functions in turn demonstrates the breadth of the Board's authority.

Oversight One of the PCLOB's primary functions is to oversee and evaluate counterterrorism programs operating within the executive branch. This oversight role was the basis for the Board's first two public reports analyzing aspects of the NSA's collection and use of

99 *Id.*

100 121 Stat. 355.

101 *President Obama Announces More Key Administration Posts*, The White House: Off. of the Press Secretary (Dec. 16, 2010), https://www.whitehouse.gov/the-press-office/2010/12/16/president-obama-announces-more-key-administration-posts-121610.

102 Board Members Collins and Dempsey were nominated on January 5, 2011. Chairman Medine and Board Members Brand and Wald were nominated on December 15, 2011. *See Presidential Nominations Sent to the Senate*, The White House: Off. of the Press Secretary (Jan. 5, 2011), www.whitehouse.gov/the-press-office/2011/01/05/presidential-nominations-sent-senate; *President Obama Announces More Key Administration Posts*, The White House: Off. of the Press Secretary (Dec. 15, 2011), www.whitehouse.gov/the-press-office/2011/12/15/president-obama-announces-more-key-administration-posts.

103 The Board's original four part-time members were confirmed by the Senate on August 2, 2012, and were appointed by the president and sworn into office later that month. They are Rachel L. Brand, Elisebeth Collins, James X. Dempsey, and Patricia M. Wald. The Board's first chairman and only full-time member was David Medine.

104 The chairman is the only member of the PCLOB who is required by statute to work for the Board on a full-time basis.

communications information and its examination of Executive Order 12333. According to the PCLOB's enabling statute, the agency is tasked with continually reviewing (1) the implementation and substance of regulations[105] of executive branch elements[106] relating to counterterrorism to ensure that privacy and civil liberties are protected and (2) the information sharing practices of executive branch elements relating to counterterrorism to determine whether they appropriately protect privacy and civil liberties.[107] The statute further states that the PCLOB shall review "other actions by the executive branch relating to efforts to protect the Nation from terrorism" to determine whether they (1) protect privacy and civil liberties and (2) are consistent with other laws and regulations regarding privacy and civil liberties.[108] In essence, the PCLOB can use its oversight authority to review existing programs and regulations, provide independent analysis to the relevant agency, and provide Congress with a greater understanding of how agencies are exercising their authority.

Advice The advice function provides the Board with similar discretion and is composed of three enumerated responsibilities.[109] The enabling statute establishes that the Board shall (1) review proposed legislation, regulations, and policies related to counterterrorism; (2) review the implementation of new and existing legislation and regulations related to counterterrorism; and (3) advise the president, agencies, and other executive branch elements to ensure that privacy and civil liberties are appropriately considered in the development and implementation of such legislation, regulations, and guidelines.[110] Underlying these functions is the mandate that, when advising another governmental entity about whether it should retain or enhance a particular governmental power, the PCLOB must consider whether the entity has established that (1) the need for the power is balanced with the need to protect privacy and civil liberties, (2) there is adequate supervision of the power to ensure protection of privacy and civil liberties, and (3) there are adequate guidelines and oversight to confine its use properly.[111]

Although the advice function also allows the PCLOB to analyze and provide feedback to agencies about a range of programs and policies, it differs from the oversight function in some significant ways. Exercising its advice function, the Board can provide its views about programs that are less developed or still being conceived, and is not obligated to engage in continual review. This allows executive branch elements to approach the PCLOB for advice about timely challenges and discrete topics without concern that they are immediately subjecting themselves to long-term, ongoing oversight. Although the Board is entitled to engage in oversight of programs for which it has previously provided advice, it is less likely to find issues if an IC element addresses any concerns raised as part of the advice process. Requesting advice thus allows IC elements to identify and address issues before they become routine, while also reducing the likelihood that future

105 "Regulations" in this context refers broadly to regulations, policies, and procedures.

106 "Executive branch elements" refers broadly to agencies, departments, and other organizations within the executive branch.

107 42 U.S.C. § 2000ee (2012).

108 42 U.S.C. § 2000ee(d)(2)(A)–(B) (2012).

109 *Id.* §§ 2000ee(d)(2)(C)(i)–(ii).

110 *Id.* §§ 2000ee(d)(1)(A)–(C).

111 *Id.* §§ 2000ee(d)(1)(D)(i)–(iii).

oversight will reveal problems. The PCLOB is statutorily required to alert Congress if an executive branch element implements a program or policy after the Board has advised against doing so, but outside unusual circumstances,[112] the Board is able to provide confidential advice without triggering this requirement.

Testimony In addition to the PCLOB's oversight and advice functions, the enabling statute mandates that "the members of the Board shall appear and testify before Congress upon request."[113]

CLPO Relations Finally, the Board is directed to work with civil liberties and privacy officers (CLPOs) from agencies within the Intelligence Community. CLPOs are appointed to provide advice on privacy and civil liberties issues to their respective agencies.[114] A companion statute to the PCLOB's enabling statute requires several executive branch elements to appoint CLPOs and requires that these officers interact with the PCLOB on a regular basis.[115] The companion statute also allows the Board to require that executive branch elements not enumerated in the statute appoint CLPOs, and requires that CLPOs send their reports to the Board (among other recipients).[116] Complementing this arrangement, one of the enumerated duties in the PCLOB's enabling statute is to receive and review reports from CLPOs and, when appropriate, make recommendations to and coordinate activities with CLPOs.[117]

The PCLOB's four defined functions – and particularly its authority to provide oversight and advice – impose relatively few restrictions on the Board's activities. Under the enabling statute, the Board is permitted to review virtually any activity conducted by an executive branch element with a counterterrorism nexus, and analyze the privacy and civil liberties implications of that activity. Although the Board is entitled to keep these reviews private when necessary to protect classified information, it is institutionally inclined to make its reports available to the public and Congress to the greatest extent possible. The enabling statute requires that the PCLOB provide semiannual reports to Congress and the president about its activities, and provide information to Congress under several other circumstances.[118] Additionally, the PCLOB is required to make its reports public when possible and to hold public hearings.[119] Taken together, the reporting provisions build transparency and public accountability into the PCLOB's DNA, which lend even greater significance to the Board's core functions.

C *The PCLOB's Unique Role*

The PCLOB was structured to operate within the current statutory and executive branch frameworks while also retaining its independence. This sets it apart from preexisting

112 *Id.* § 2000ee(e).
113 *Id.* § 2000ee(d)(4).
114 42 U.S.C. 2000ee-1(a) (2012).
115 *Id.*
116 *Id.* § 2000ee-1(f)(1)(A)(iii). These are sometimes referred to as "Section 803" reports, in reference to Section 803 of the Implementing Recommendations of the 9/11 Commission Act of 2007.
117 42 U.S.C. §§ 2000ee(d)(3)(A)–(C) (2012).
118 *Id.* § 2000ee(e).
119 *Id.* § 2000ee(f).

oversight mechanisms that were formed before the significant paradigm shift in the United States' counterterrorism efforts following the September 11 attacks. At a high level, the PCLOB's dedicated focus on the overlap between counterterrorism and individual rights speaks to both a need for additional oversight and the value in having oversight that spans the full spectrum of the Intelligence Community. The fact that the PCLOB can compare how different agencies utilize similar authorities and cooperate with each other provides it with a perspective not available to other oversight bodies within the executive branch. Moreover, unlike citizen activists, the Board is entitled to access classified information, and is able to bypass the difficulties of requesting documents through the Freedom of Information Act (FOIA) and wrestling with standing issues in court. In fact, the PCLOB's enabling statute provides a detailed section requiring that other executive branch elements cooperate with the Board and provide it with access to information.[120]

The existence of civil liberties and privacy officers and their statutorily defined relationship with the PCLOB further reflects the modern thinking that shaped the Board's structure. Instead of relying on diverse oversight mechanisms scattered throughout the myriad entities that work on counterterrorism issues, the PCLOB has access to CLPOs located in key executive branch elements. CLPOs are responsible for advising their respective agencies about privacy and civil liberties issues and issuing periodic reports to Congress and the PCLOB. These periodic CLPO reports are capable of providing the PCLOB with insight into emerging issues that fall within its jurisdiction, and allow the Board to understand whether, how, and to what extent agencies are utilizing their CLPOs. The Board thus benefits from having direct access to personnel within many of the agencies it oversees, and is uniquely situated to observe whether those personnel are being effectively utilized.[121] This structure reflects an understanding of the complexity and diversity within the modern executive branch, and provides remedies to some of the inherent difficulties in overseeing it.

In addition to statutory access to classified information and dedicated CLPOs in other agencies, the PCLOB benefits from a diversity of views inherent in its bipartisan makeup. Although only a majority is needed for the PCLOB to take action,[122] members of at least two political parties will have the opportunity to weigh in on any issue being considered by the Board, an arrangement that promotes thoughtful decision making and deters institutional entrenchment. Unlike internal oversight mechanisms, the PCLOB is designed to prevent sharing a mission or being subject to the culture of any administration, agency head, or interest group. As such, even if a majority of the Board consistently takes a certain position, the public can be assured that other perspectives were considered and that Board members in the minority had the opportunity to express their views in separate concurring or dissenting statements.

120 *Id.* §§ 2000ee(g)(1), (4).

121 The PCLOB is required to review CLPO reports, which must include information about the type of advice they provide to their agencies, and how their agencies respond to this advice. 42 U.S.C. § 2000ee-1(f)(2)(B) (2012).

122 The statute provides that three members shall constitute a quorum, 42 U.S.C. §§ 2000ee(h)(5), and only permits the Board to request a subpoena from the Attorney General "at the direction of a majority of ... members." *Id.* § 2000ee(g)(1)(D).

III The Section 215 Report: A Case Study

In its first few years of operation, the PCLOB issued reports that have been relied upon by all three branches of government and informed substantive legal changes to government surveillance programs.[123]

A close examination of the first such report, which focused on the NSA's Section 215 Program, is representative of both the type and the impact of the work undertaken by the Board. Although not all of the Board's reports will analyze issues as publicly charged as the NSA's telephone metadata program, the Section 215 Report exemplifies the Board's careful process and potential to impact national policy debates.

A *Origins of the Section 215 Report*

On June 5, 2013, the British newspaper *The Guardian* published the first of several articles containing information derived from unauthorized disclosures of classified documents by Edward Snowden, a contractor for the NSA.[124] The article described an NSA program to collect millions of telephone records, including records about purely domestic calls, under Section 215 of the PATRIOT Act. Several articles in the following weeks provided further details about this program, as well as another NSA program referred to in leaked documents as "PRISM." After the publication of this leaked information, policy makers and pundits began to question the scope and nature of the NSA programs. Central among the issues raised was the degree to which the programs included appropriate safeguards for privacy and civil liberties.

One week after the first news article appeared, a bipartisan group of thirteen U.S. senators asked the PCLOB – which had only been fully reconstituted in its current form with all five members as of the previous month – to investigate the two NSA programs. The senators specifically asked the Board to provide an unclassified report "so that the public and the Congress can have a long overdue debate" about the privacy issues raised.[125] On June 21, 2013, the Board met with President Obama and his senior staff at the White House, and the president asked the Board to review "where our counterterrorism efforts and our values come into tension."[126] A July 11, 2013, letter from House Minority Leader Nancy Pelosi further requested that the Board consider the operations of the FISC, which approved the two programs.

The Board immediately set to work, and soon determined that it would first complete its review of the Section 215 Program. Pursuant to the PCLOB's statutory duty to advise the president, the Board provided senior White House staff with its tentative views on December 5, 2013.[127] Over the following month, the Board provided near-final drafts of

123 Note: This section summarizes and borrows heavily from the Section 215 report.

124 *See* Glenn Greenwald, *NSA Collecting Phone Records of Millions of Verizon Customers Daily*, The Guardian June 6, 2013, 6:05 PM, www.theguardian.com/world/2013/jun/06/nsa-phone-records-verizon-court-order.

125 Letter from Senator Tom Udall *et al.* to the Privacy & Civil Liberties Oversight Bd. (June 12, 2013), www.pclob.gov/library/Letter-Senate_letter_to_PCLOB-Jun2013.pdf.

126 *See* Letter from Democratic Leader Nancy Pelosi to Chairman David Medine (July 11, 2013), www.pclob.gov/library/Letter-Pelosi.pdf; *Remarks by the President in a Press Conference at the White House*, The White House: Off. of the Press Secretary (Aug. 9, 2013, 3:09 PM), www.whitehouse.gov/the-press-office/2013/08/09/remarks-president-press-conference.

127 Section 215 report at 6.

several sections of the report to the White House, and on January 8, 2014, the full Board met with the president, the vice president. and senior officials to present the Board's conclusions and the views of individual Board members.[128] Subsequently, on January 23, the PCLOB issued its full report on the NSA's Section 215 Program.

B *Substance and Recommendations of the 215 Report*

The Section 215 Report provides a detailed explanation and analysis of an NSA surveillance program that involved the collection, storage, and querying of the metadata associated with millions of domestic telephone records. The report serves three distinct functions. First, it provides a detailed description of the creation, evolution, and operation of the Section 215 program. Second, it analyzes the legal, constitutional, and policy implications of the program. Third, it offers recommendations. Although these functions logically build on each other, each represents a noteworthy aspect of the Board's unique oversight role. It is thus valuable to examine each aspect.

1 Description

At the outset, the Section 215 Report contains a description of the history and processes behind one of the NSA's far-reaching, large-scale surveillance programs. Much of the information in the report had not previously been compiled and released from an official source, and the report provided the public with its first comprehensive view of the NSA's collection and use of telephone metadata. As discussed previously, the emergence and evolution of the Section 215 Program track the rise of the Intelligence Community following September 11 and was authorized (in at least some sense) by Congress, the president, and the FISC.[129] The narrative including this information alone provided insight into the legal uncertainty underlying modern surveillance programs, and the process by which such programs were adapted over the years.

In addition to the history of the Section 215 program, the report detailed the program's operation and purpose. At its most basic level, the program was intended to enable the government to identify communications among known and unknown terrorism suspects, particularly those located inside the United States. Pursuant to a FISC order first issued in 2006 that was renewed approximately every ninety days thereafter, the NSA collected call detail records generated by certain telephone companies in the United States and handled them according to detailed rules for the use and retention of these records.[130] Call detail records typically included much of the information that appeared on a customer's telephone bill: the date and time of a call, its duration, and the participating telephone numbers, but not the contents of the call. This metadata[131] was then stored and compiled in a large centralized database.[132]

128 *Id.*
129 *See supra* Section I.C.
130 Section 215 report at 22–23.
131 The call detail records were limited to metadata and did not reflect the content of telephone conversations, which the NSA did not collect under the 215 program. *Id.* at 8, 22.
132 *Id.* at 22–24.

Initially, NSA analysts were permitted to access the Section 215 calling records only through "queries" of the database.[133] Before any specific number could be used as the search target or "seed" for a query, one of twenty-two designated NSA officials was required to determine that there was a reasonable, articulable suspicion (RAS) that the number was associated with terrorism.[134] Once the seed had been RAS-approved, NSA analysts were permitted to run queries that could return the calling records for that seed, and permit "contact chaining" to develop a fuller picture of the seed's contacts. Contact chaining enabled analysts to retrieve not only the numbers directly in contact with the seed number (the "first hop"), but also numbers in contact with all first hop numbers (the "second hop"), as well as all numbers in contact with all second hop numbers (the "third hop").[135] An analyst's query, therefore, could provide access to a massive number of calling records, most of which could be domestic and not reasonably suspected of being associated with terrorism.[136] When the NSA identified communications that may be associated with terrorism through this process, it issued intelligence reports to other federal agencies, such as the FBI, that work to prevent terrorist attacks or apprehend terrorists.[137]

By publicizing all of these details, the report conferred transparency on the program that initially sparked public concern. Previously, the public could only speculate about the Section 215 program on the basis of (1) information the NSA decided to release and (2) leaked documents. The report changed this situation by providing a detailed narrative from a credible, independent source with access to classified information and the ranking officials within the IC operating the Section 215 program. In doing so, the Board helped dispel misunderstanding about the NSA's practices and provided a basis for an informed national discussion about the propriety and value of the program.

2 Analysis and Conclusions

Having laid out the details of the Section 215 program, the report proceeded to analyze whether the program operated within the bounds of federal law and the Constitution, and whether it was an effective tool for combating terrorism. The analysis section provided the perspective of the Board[138] and was supplemented by dissenting statements by two Board members who drew different conclusions about the legality and efficacy of the Section 215 program. Although the report provided details that allow anyone to scrutinize the NSA's program, the analysis section was distinctly valuable because it provided a diversity of perspectives from individuals who both were very familiar with the underlying facts and had devoted time to thinking through their legal implications.

133 A query is a search for a specific number or other selection term within the database. *Id.* at 25–26.

134 *Id.* at 26–28.

135 *Id.*

136 For example, if a seed number had 75 direct contacts, and all of these first-hop contacts had 75 new contacts of their own, then each query provided the government with the complete calling records of 5,625 telephone numbers. And if all of those second-hop numbers had 75 new contacts of their own, a single query would result in a batch of calling records involving more than 420,000 telephone numbers. *See id.* at 29.

137 *Id.* at 31–32.

138 The Board agreed to certain analysis and conclusions by a split vote.

a *Statutory Analysis*

In its analysis, the Board focused on Section 215's requirement that the government provide a statement of facts showing reasonable grounds to believe that records collected by the government are "relevant to an authorized [FBI] investigation" to obtain foreign intelligence information or to protect against international terrorism.[139] Interpreting this requirement, and other aspects of the statute, the Board reached four conclusions: *First*, the telephone records acquired under the NSA's Program had no connection to any specific FBI investigation at the time of their collection.[140] *Second*, the records were collected in bulk, and therefore could not be regarded as "relevant" to any FBI investigation as required by the statute.[141] *Third*, the NSA's approach of putting telephone companies under an obligation to furnish new calling records on a daily basis lacked foundation in the statute.[142] *Fourth*, the statute permits only the FBI to obtain items for use in its investigations; it does not authorize the NSA to collect anything.[143]

The Board provided detailed analyses for each of these conclusions, including citations to court opinions and legal doctrines. For example, to justify the conclusion that the government was stretching words beyond their normal definitions in attempting to justify the Section 215 program, the Board examined the meaning of "relevance" and "necessity" in a variety of other contexts.[144] The Board also determined that the "reenactment doctrine," under which Congress is presumed to have adopted settled administrative or judicial interpretations of a statute, could not override the plain meaning of a law or justify any administrative or judicial interpretation that contradicts the statute itself.[145] These determinations, along with the numerous other legal issues that the Board addressed, represented the first fact-based, in-depth public analysis of the relationship between Section 215 and the NSA's collection of bulk information.

b *Constitutional Analysis*

Turning next to the constitutional implications of the Section 215 program, the Board concluded that the NSA's conduct raised serious concerns under both the First and Fourth Amendments. At the outset, the Board acknowledged that existing Supreme Court doctrine does not provide a clear answer because the scope and duration of the Section 215 program are beyond anything ever before confronted by the judiciary.[146] This is in large part because the NSA's bulk collection utilizes new technologies that enable the government to collect, store, and analyze data in manners inconceivable when existing constitutional doctrines were developed.[147] As such, it was difficult to determine how (and whether) concepts, such

139 50 U.S.C. § 1861(b)(2)(A) (2012) ("Each application under this section ... shall include ... a statement of facts showing that there are reasonable grounds to believe that the tangible things sought are relevant to an authorized investigation (other than a threat assessment) conducted in accordance with subsection (a)(2) to obtain foreign intelligence information not concerning a United States person or to protect against international terrorism or clandestine intelligence activities[.]").

140 Section 215 report at 58–60.

141 *Id.* at 79–81.

142 *Id.* at 81–87.

143 *Id.* at 87–91.

144 *See generally id.* at 61–80.

145 *Id.* at 95–102.

146 *Id.* at 103–105.

147 *Id.* at 103.

as the third party doctrine, under which information is considered to have lost its Fourth Amendment protection if an individual voluntarily provides that information to a third party, should be applied.[148]

Working through these challenges, the Board began by examining how the Section 215 program interacted with existing precedent. Regarding the Fourth Amendment, the Board noted that the "Section 215 program . . . is dramatically broader than the practice[s] approved by the Supreme Court" in previous cases, which involved surveillance directed at single criminal suspects and only collected the numbers they dialed during a limited period.[149] Building on this observation, the report summarized critiques of the third party doctrine – which has failed to evolve with modern technology – and elaborated on the disconcerting implications of this failure for Americans' privacy rights.[150] The Fourth Amendment analysis then concluded with a section aptly titled "Just Because We Can Do Something Doesn't Mean We Necessarily Should."[151]

In its First Amendment analysis, the Board focused on how the Section 215 program could undermine the rights of individuals to communicate privately with each other, by chilling free speech and association. Although the NSA's surveillance presented a scenario unlike past civil liberties cases in which the government mandated that individuals disclose their affiliations with certain organizations, the report nevertheless concludes that the Section 215 program "results in the compulsory disclosure of information about individuals' associations to the government."[152] This disclosure included information about relationships established among individuals and groups for political, religious, and other expressive purposes, which in turn "can have a chilling effect on the exercise of First Amendment rights."[153]

c *Efficacy Analysis*

The Board's third major analysis considered whether the Section 215 program was an effective tool, and whether there was justification for the program's disconcerting civil liberties implications.[154] In order to understand the effectiveness of the NSA's methods, the Board examined twelve cases compiled by the Intelligence Community in which telephone records collected under Section 215 "contributed to a success story" in a counterterrorism investigation.[155] Each of the twelve cases was analyzed and assigned to one (or more) of several categories devised to illustrate the different forms of value that a counterterrorism program could provide. The seven categories were (1) Enabling Negative Reporting,[156] (2) Adding/Confirming Details, (3) Triaging, (4) Identifying

148 *Id.* at 110–119. *See also Katz*, 389 U.S. at 357; *Smith*, 442 U.S. at 742.

149 Section 215 report at 116.

150 *Id.* at 116–125.

151 *Id.* at 127–128 (quoting *Press Conference by the* President, THE WHITE HOUSE: OFF. OF THE PRESS SECRETARY (Dec. 20, 2013, 2:18 PM), http://www.whitehouse.gov/the-press-office/2013/12/20/press-conference-president).

152 Section 215 report at 132.

153 *Id.* at 135.

154 *Id.* at 143–155.

155 *Id.* at 145–147.

156 Information enables negative reporting when it establishes that a known terrorism suspect overseas has not been in telephone contact with anyone in the United States, suggesting that a known terrorist or terrorist plot in a foreign country does not have a U.S. nexus.

Counterterrorism Suspects, (5) Discovering U.S. Presence of Unknown Terrorism Suspects, (6) Identifying Terrorist Plots, and (7) Disrupting Terrorist plots.[157]

Providing a detailed description of four of the cases, the report noted that telephone metadata was only utilized in counterterrorism investigations for two primary purposes. First, it helped investigators confirm suspicions about the target of an inquiry or about persons in contact with that target. Second, it demonstrated that known foreign terrorism suspects do not have U.S. contacts or that known terrorist plots do not have a U.S. nexus.[158] This meant that information obtained under Section 215, while of some value, was not decisive in any of the four terrorism investigations. Although the Board chose not to provide extensive details, it confirmed the same was true in the remaining eight cases and concluded that it could not identify "a single instance involving a threat to the United States in which the telephone records program made a concrete difference in the outcome of a counterterrorism investigation."[159] In fact, the Board could not identify a situation in which Section 215 surveillance directly contributed to the discovery of a previously unknown terrorist plot or the disruption of a terrorist attack.[160]

3 Recommendations

The report concludes with recommendations based on the Board's investigation and analysis of the Section 215 program. Balancing the program's civil liberties implications against its limited role in counterterrorism investigations, the Board asserted that the government should end the program. To justify this recommendation, the Board explained that the NSA's collection of bulk metadata "lacks a viable legal foundation under Section 215, implicates constitutional concerns under the First and Fourth Amendments, raises serious threats to privacy and civil liberties as a policy matter, and has shown only limited value."[161] Recognizing that it would take time to shutter the Section 215 program, the Board further recommended that the NSA immediately implement certain privacy safeguards that would put the program on sounder footing. These safeguards included a more limited retention period for bulk telephone records, reduction in the number of "hops" used in contact chaining, and more stringent requirements for querying the relevant databases.[162]

The report also included several recommendations concerning the operation of the FISC. The Board specifically urged Congress to empower the FISC to hear independent views when considering novel or technologically complicated issues, and to make it easier to appeal FISC decisions to other courts.[163] While these recommendations may have garnered less media attention, they arose from the same concerns that animated the recommendations about Section 215: transparency and accountability. By seeking to provide the FISC with access to outside views and expertise, the Board hoped to bolster public confidence in the Court's decisions and improve the Court's decision-making

157 *Id.* at 146–148.
158 *Id.* at 146.
159 *Id.*
160 *Id.*
161 *Id.* at 168–169.
162 *Id.* at 170.
163 *Id.* at 183–189.

process, especially in regard to controversial programs that may come before it in the future.[164]

C *Impact of Section 215 Report*

As the first comprehensive description and analysis of the NSA's telephone metadata program, the Section 215 report received a great deal of publicity upon being released. Academics, policy wonks, and politicians did not hesitate in offering their thoughts on the report, and more generally, the role of government surveillance in the twenty-first century. Some individuals, such as Senator Patrick Leahy, immediately praised the report as lending transparency to a problematic program,[165] while other commentators criticized both the Board's approach and its conclusions.[166] In any event, the report supplanted much of the speculative (and in some cases, incorrect) analysis of information leaked by Edward Snowden, and helped promote a more informed national conversation about surveillance. This conversation would evolve in the coming months, and ultimately, have a significant impact on policy decisions made by all three branches of the federal government.

1 Impact on Congress

Congress was not insulated from the national conversation about surveillance that was initially sparked by the Snowden leaks and reinvigorated by the PCLOB report. Over the course of nearly two years of debate, legislators discussed how much authority to provide the Intelligence Community, and argued over how best to balance national security with the protection of privacy and civil liberties. In the course of this debate, several members of Congress cited the report as adding to the "growing momentum behind genuine, legislative reform,"[167] and "underscore[ing] the need to rein in the government's overbroad interpretation of Section 215 and to provide for greater transparency."[168] These deliberations continued until June 1, 2015, when large sections of the PATRIOT Act – including Section 215 – expired. The following day, the Senate passed a replacement, the USA Freedom Act,[169] which President Obama quickly signed into law.

The USA Freedom Act implements many of the PCLOB report's most significant recommendations. For example, it restricts Section 215, the provision that the NSA relied on to query bulk telephone records metadata, and affirmatively limits the scope of future

164 *Id.* at 182.

165 Patrick Leahy, *Comment of Senator Patrick Leahy (D-Vt.), Chairman, Senate Committee on the Judiciary, on the Report of the Privacy & Civil Liberties Oversight Bd.*, U.S. Senator Patrick Leahy of Vermont (Jan. 23, 2014), www.leahy.senate.gov/press/senator-patrick-leahy-comment-on-pclob-report.

166 Stewart Baker, *The PCLOB's Willful Blindness on Section 215*, Wash. Post, Jan. 23, 2014, www.washingtonpost.com/news/volokh-conspiracy/wp/2014/01/23/the-pclobs-willful-blindness-on-section-215/.

167 Jim Sensenbrenner, *Sensenbrenner Responds to PCLOB Report*, Congressman Jim Sensenbrenner (Jan. 23, 2014), sensenbrenner.house.gov/news/documentsingle.aspx?DocumentID=367530.

168 Patrick Leahy, *Statement of Senator Patrick Leahy (D-Vt.), Chairman, Senate Judiciary Committee, Hearing on the Report of the Privacy & Civil Liberties Oversight Bd. on Reforms to the Section 215 Telephone Records Program and the Foreign Intelligence Surveillance Court*, U.S. Senator Patrick Leahy of Vermont (Feb. 12, 2014), www.judiciary.senate.gov/imo/media/doc/02-12-14LeahyStatement.pdf.

169 The House had previously passed the USA Freedom Act on May 13, 2015. *See* H.R. 2048, 114th Cong. (2015), www.congress.gov/bill/114th-congress/house-bill/2048/text.

collections "to the greatest extent reasonably practicable."[170] In place of the old system, under which the NSA collected bulk metadata and queried the collected data itself, the act requires phone companies to run queries of their call records in response to a FISC order procured by the government. For its part, the government can only obtain a FISC order if it has "reasonable articulable suspicion" that the requested query will yield information about international terrorism and is limited to only two "hops" worth of information.[171]

The USA Freedom Act also provides private companies with the opportunity to report how many requests for information they receive pursuant to FISA, facilitates the declassification of FISC opinions, and creates a system by which the FISC can obtain perspectives from outside advocates when deciding important issues.

Although no compromise is universally praised, the USA Freedom Act received broad support from national security experts and civil liberties advocates alike. Staunch opponents of the Section 215 program, such as the Electronic Frontier Foundation and the Center for Democracy and Technology, referred to the act as a step in the right direction,[172] while FBI Director James B. Comey testified that "in theory, [the new program] should work as well or better than what we used to have."[173] Many of the new provisions only took effect in late 2015, and it may be years before information about their impact is known. Nonetheless, the act represents the realization of several recommendations made by the PCLOB, and has real implications for the other branches of government and the U.S. population at large.

2 Impact on the Judiciary

The detailed description of the Section 215 program contained in the PCLOB report was relied upon by litigants and courts wrestling with the legality of the NSA's actions. Before the report was issued, the ACLU filed a lawsuit against several officials alleging that the NSA was collecting records from United States citizens in a manner that violated FISA and the First and Fourth Amendments. In its early filings, the ACLU was only able to rely on an assortment of documents leaked by Snowden and others, while its opponents maintained that there was no standing and that the NSA's program was

170 Pub. L. No. 114–23, § 201(b)(A)(ii), 129 Stat. 274. For an overview of the key reforms included in the USA Freedom Act *see* House of Representatives Judiciary Committee, USA FREEDOM ACT, http://judiciary.house.gov/index.cfm/usa-freedom-act.

171 In contrast, the Section 215 program allowed the NSA to look at three "hops" worth of information. Thus, where the government could see information about a friend of a friend of a friend of a suspect, they could now only see information about a friend of a friend of a suspect.

172 Rainey Reitman, *The New USA Freedom Act: A Step in the Right Direction, but More Must Be Done*, Elec. Frontier Found., Apr. 30, 2015, www.eff.org/deeplinks/2015/04/new-usa-freedom-act-step-right-direction-more-must-be-done; *Victory: Passage of USA FREEDOM Act Reins in NSA Surveillance*, Ctr. for Democracy & Tech. (June 2, 2015), https://cdt.org/press/victory-passage-of-usa-freedom-act-reins-in-nsa-surveillance/.

173 Editorial Bd., *After San Bernardino: Terror and Intel*, Chi. Tribune (Dec, 9, 2015, 4:16 PM), www.chicagotribune.com/news/opinion/editorials/ct-san-bernardino-rubio-patriot-act-surveillance-edit-jm-20151209-story.html. The Office of the Director of National Intelligence likewise acknowledged that "the overall volume of call detail records subject to query pursuant to court order is greater under USA FREEDOM Act." *Fact Sheet: Implementation of the USA FREEDOM Act of 2015*, Off. of the Dir. of Nat'l Intelligence: IC on the Record (Nov. 27, 2015), http://icontherecord.tumblr.com/post/134069709168/fact-sheet-implementation-of-the-usa-freedom-act.

statutorily authorized.[174] Unsurprisingly, a New York federal court dismissed the claim in late 2013, finding that the ACLU could not bring a statutory challenge against FISA, and that the NSA's program did not violate the Constitution.[175] The ACLU appealed the decision, and with the aid of the newly released Section 215 report, was able to provide the appellate court with a much more detailed explanation of its claims and reasoning.[176]

More than a year later, in May 2015, the Second Circuit reversed a portion of the district court's ruling, and declared that the NSA's program exceeded the authority granted to the agency under FISA.[177] In its analysis, the court repeatedly cited to the PCLOB Section 215 report, and specifically agreed with key aspects of the Board's analysis.[178] On the basis of information provided by the PCLOB, as well as other sources such as the 9/11 Commission Report, the court held that "the text of § 215 cannot bear the weight the government asks us to assign to it, and that it does not authorize the telephone metadata program."[179] It reached this conclusion "comfortably in the full understanding that if Congress chooses to authorize such a far-reaching and unprecedented program, it has every opportunity to do so, and to do so unambiguously."[180] This was a momentous occasion, and marked the first time that the PCLOB helped enable the judiciary to scrutinize a program that had previously evaded judicial review by virtue of its secrecy.

Shortly after the Second Circuit issued its opinion, Congress passed the USA Freedom Act, which replaced the Section 215 program, and thus obviated the NSA's need to act on the court's decision. In response to the new law, the Second Circuit stayed the mandate it had previously issued and requested more briefing.[181] In October 2015, the court lifted its stay, but held that the NSA could continue collecting telephone metadata through the 180-day transition period authorized by Congress. The court explained that "Congress has balanced privacy and national security by providing for a 180-day transition period, a decision that it is uniquely suited to make. Congress's decision to do so should be respected."[182] Thus, the first appellate decision to rely on the PCLOB report required no action by the NSA because a statute was passed that itself recognized and implemented many of the Board's recommendations.

3 Impact on the Executive Branch

In several ways, the executive branch sits at the beginning, center, and end of the PCLOB's examination of Section 215. The president was one of the first to request that the PCLOB examine the NSA's bulk telephone metadata collection program and

174 Defs.' Memorandum of Law in Opp. to Pls.' Mot. for a Preliminary Injunction, *ACLU v. Clapper*, No. 13 Civ. 3994 (WHP) (S.D.N.Y. Oct. 1, 2013), www.aclu.org/files/assets/2013.10.01_govt_oppn_to_pi_motion.pdf.

175 *Clapper*, 959 F. Supp. 2d 724 (S.D.N.Y. 2013).

176 Br. for Pls.-Apps., *ACLU v. Clapper*, No. 14–42 (2d. Cir. Mar. 3, 2014), www.aclu.org/sites/default/files/assets/corrected_brief_of_plaintiffs-appellants__final_stamped_03_07_2014.pdf.

177 *ACLU v. Clapper*, 785 F.3d 787 (2d. Cir. 2015).

178 *Id.* at 817.

179 *Id.* at 821.

180 *Id.*

181 *ACLU v. Clapper*, No. 14–42, 2015 WL 4196833, at *1 (2d Cir. June 9, 2015).

182 *ACLU v. Clapper*, 804 F.3d 617, 626 (2d. Cir. 2015).

identify "where our values come into tension."[183] Acting on the president's request, the Board spent months working with numerous executive branch officials to understand the NSA's practices and analyze their legal and policy implications. This effort resulted in the Section 215 report, which discussed the scope of executive authority and recommended shutting down a program that the president had defended.[184] Furthermore, by providing the first independent analysis of the NSA program from an agency within the executive branch, the Board helped to guide the ongoing national discussion on the role of the government's ability to balance the fight against terrorist threats and the need to safeguard civil liberties properly.

President Obama announced in January 2014 that he was ordering a transition to end the bulk communications metadata program as it then existed, which was reiterated by the White House two months later.[185] In the following two years, the president would be vocal in his support of congressional efforts in drafting the USA Freedom Act,[186] and issued praise for the bill when he signed it into law.[187] Other executive branch officials also openly praised the act, including some individuals from within the Intelligence Community, who believe that the new program could be more effective at combating terrorism.[188] Looking past these statements to the present, when the USA Freedom Act is law, the executive branch is in a very different position than it was at the start of 2013. The Section 215 program investigated by the Board is no more, the NSA's authority has been curtailed by Congress, and a federal court has declared a secret surveillance program illegal. While it is impossible and inaccurate to say that all of these changes are a direct result of the PCLOB report, there is no question that the Board's description, analysis, and recommendations made practical contributions to executive branch decision making about reforms and played some role in establishing the new status quo.

IV The PCLOB and Independent Oversight Going Forward

The Section 215 report stands as a testament to the important work that the PCLOB can accomplish, and only marks the beginning of the Board's tenure as an oversight entity. Since the Section 215 report was released, the Board has issued a second report on

183 *Remarks by the President in a Press Conference at the White House*, The White House: Off. of the Press Secretary (Aug. 9, 2013, 3:09 PM), www.whitehouse.gov/the-press-office/2013/08/09/remarks-president-press-conference.

184 Zeke J. Miller, *President Obama Defends NSA Surveillance Programs as "Right Balance,"* Time (Jan. 7, 2013), http://swampland.time.com/2013/06/07/president-obama-defends-nsa-surveillance-programs-as-right-balance/.

185 *Statement by the President on the Section 215 Bulk Metadata Program*, The White House: Off. of the Press Secretary (Mar. 27, 2014), www.whitehouse.gov/the-press-office/2014/03/27/statement-president-section-215-bulk-metadata-program; Barack Obama, *Speech on NSA Reforms*, Wash. Post, Jan. 17, 2014, www.washingtonpost.com/politics/full-text-of-president-obamas-jan-17-speech-on-nsa-reforms/2014/01/17/fa33590a-7f8c-11e3-9556-4a4bf7bcbd84_story.html. However, this declaration was not acted on expediently – it was not until the USA Freedom Act was passed that Section 215 was truly overhauled.

186 Julian Hattem, *White House 'Strongly Supports' NSA Reform bill*, The Hill, May 12, 2015, 12:29 PM, http://thehill.com/policy/national-security/241740-white-house-strongly-supports-nsa-reform-bill.

187 *Statement by the President on the USA FREEDOM Act*, The White House: Off. of the Press Secretary (Jan. 2, 2015), www.whitehouse.gov/the-press-office/2015/06/02/statement-president-usa-freedom-act.

188 For example, in 2015 FBI Director James B. Comey testified that "in theory, [the USA Freedom Act framework] should work as well or better than what we used to have." Testimony of James B. Comey,

Section 702 of the Foreign Intelligence Surveillance Amendments Act.[189] Section 702 permits the attorney general and the DNI jointly to authorize surveillance targeting non-U.S. persons who are reasonably believed to be located outside the United States in order to acquire foreign intelligence information. This surveillance is undertaken with the compelled assistance of electronic communication service providers in one of two ways. Under PRISM collection, ISPs and other providers begin acquiring information based on specific "selectors" approved by the government and provide results based on these selectors. In contrast, upstream collection involves compelling providers that control the telecommunications "backbone" over which telephone and Internet communications transit to facilitate NSA access to the backbone.

Approaching Section 702 in a similar manner to Section 215, the Board issued a detailed public report in July 2014 that described the program, analyzed its legal and policy implications, and made several recommendations. The Board concluded that "the core Section 702 program is clearly authorized by Congress, reasonable under the Fourth Amendment, and an extremely valuable and effective intelligence tool,"[190] but noted that "the applicable rules potentially allow a great deal of private information about U.S. persons to be acquired by the government."[191] In order to "ensure that the program remains tied to its constitutionally legitimate core," the Board outlined a set of ten policy proposals aimed at increasing accountability, transparency, and efficacy of the surveillance program.[192]

Following up on the Section 702 report, the Board has engaged with the Intelligence Community on an ongoing basis about implementation of its recommendations, almost all of which have been accepted by the IC.[193] The fact that all ten of the PCLOB's 702 recommendations have been implemented (at least in part) or are in the process of being implemented[194] is significant; it shows the Board can effect change through productive, sustained relationships with the agencies it oversees. Going forward, maintaining this dynamic will be essential to the Board's work. Although Board Member Wald and I wrote separately to state our belief that certain recommendations should go further, there was consensus that the Section 702 program was reasonable and valuable but nevertheless could be improved.

In 2014, the PCLOB announced that it would investigate counterterrorism activities conducted under Executive Order 12333, and in 2015, described its plans to issue a public report on that subject.[195] The president also invited the Board to assess the implementation of PPD 28, which provides new protections for non-U.S. persons and requires

Director, Federal Bureau of Investigation before the Senate Judiciary Committee, Dec. 9, 2015, http://www.c-span.org/video/?401606-1/fbi-director-james-comey-oversight-hearing-testimony&start=8304.

189 Privacy & Civil Liberties Oversight Bd., Report on the Surveillance Program Operated Pursuant Section 702 of the Foreign Intelligence Surveillance Act (2014), www.pclob.gov/library/702-Report.pdf ("Section 702 Report").

190 Section 702 report at 15.

191 Section 702 report at 11.

192 Section 702 report at 9, 134–48.

193 Privacy & Civil Liberties Oversight Bd., PCLOB Recommendations Assessment Report (2016), www.pclob.gov/library/Recommendations_Assessment_Report_20160205.pdf.

194 *Id.*

195 *PCLOB Examination of E.O. 12333 Activities in 2015*, Privacy & Civil Liberties Oversight Bd., www.pclob.gov/library/20150408-EO12333_Project_Description.pdf.

further tailoring of certain surveillance activities.[196] These projects continue the tradition of the Board's thorough investigation and analysis, yet represent only a fraction of the Board's work. In addition to public reports, the Board provides advice to the individual agencies about programs and issues within the PCLOB's jurisdiction. As the Board's staff grows in size and expertise, it is likely that the advice function will be utilized even more, and the PCLOB can establish itself as both an effective oversight entity and a consistent independent sounding board for the Intelligence Community.

Ultimately, the PCLOB is an innovative experiment in oversight. No other entity is tasked with independently examining the government's counterterrorism efforts from within and providing transparency into the operations of the most secretive agencies. If the Board continues to carry out its mission successfully in the coming years, it will prove that there is value in independent oversight, and that new entities can supplement rather than duplicate the efforts of congressional committees and inspectors general. The Board's ongoing success may also have an impact on the perceived tension between security and liberty. As an agency dedicated to balancing interests, the Board is always open to reforms that simultaneously enhance civil liberty protections and increase the effectiveness of the government's counterterrorism efforts.[197] If the PCLOB can encourage national security experts and civil liberties advocates to embrace more mutually beneficial solutions, it can do much to ensure that the U.S. government, privacy advocates, and the private sector find large zones of common ground. Taking such an approach can also preserve institutional energy for the areas in which the tension between security and liberty seems most stark. If the PCLOB can contribute in this way, it also may serve as a model that can be adapted and applied to other levels of the government, as well as in some international contexts.

196 *See Privacy & Civil Liberties Oversight Bd. Comments on the Intelligence Community's Signals Intelligence Reform Anniversary Report*, Privacy & Civil Liberties Oversight Bd. (Feb. 3, 2015), www.pclob.gov/newsroom/20150203.html.

197 One example of this is the USA Freedom Act, which required the NSA to conduct searches in a more targeted manner while also allowing the NSA to access more records than it could under Section 215, albeit in a less direct manner.

30 FTC Regulation of Cybersecurity and Surveillance

Chris Jay Hoofnagle[†]

The Federal Trade Commission (FTC) is the United States' chief consumer protection agency. Through its mandate to prevent unfair and deceptive trade practices, it both regulates surveillance and creates cybersecurity law. This chapter details how the FTC regulates private-sector surveillance and elucidates several emergent properties of the agency's activities. First, private-sector surveillance shapes individuals' reasonable expectations of privacy, and thus regulation of the private-sector has effects on the government as surveillant. The FTC's activities not only serve dignity interests in preventing commercial inference in one's life, they also affect citizens' civil liberties posture with the state. Second, surveillance can make companies directly liable (for intrusive web monitoring, for tracking people off-line, and for installing malware) or indirectly liable (for creating insecure systems, for using deception to investigate, and for mediating the surveillance of others) under the FTC Act. Third, the FTC's actions substitute for private actions, because the class action is burdened in novel ways. Fourth, the FTC's actions increase the quality of consent necessary to engage in surveillance, and in so doing, the FTC has made some kinds of surveillance practically impossible to implement legally. Finally, the FTC's actions make companies more responsible for their surveillance technologies in several ways – by making software vendors liable for users' activities, by imposing substantive security duties, and by narrowing Internet intermediary immunity.

Introduction

Surveillance evokes notions of big brother – of law enforcement and national security agencies using tools to rein in the bad guys. So, why should the Federal Trade Commission (FTC), our nation's main consumer protection agency, occupy a chapter in this volume? The answer is that if the National Security Agency is the ultimate surveillant on Earth, the penultimate one may be American businesses.

This chapter builds on other works in this volume, particularly those focusing on the Internet of things, big data, computer networks, communications, and privacy. This chapter details commercial surveillance techniques, discusses the incentives for these monitoring programs, and explains how commercial surveillance technology may make consumers vulnerable. The analysis section also situates the FTC's actions among different approaches to surveillance regulation, such as class action litigation and statutory prohibitions.

† Adjunct Full Professor, University of California, Berkeley School of Information & School of Law.

Marketers and advertisers have assembled a fantastic surveillance system to watch how people act online and off. My research shows that Google alone has tracking infrastructure on 92 percent of the top 1,000 most popular Web sites.[1] One cannot even open a web browser window without its pinging Google's servers. The desire to track consumers in their activities and communications is so strong that it causes reputable companies to behave as computer attackers.[2] This chapter will detail several FTC cases when mainstream companies have used their technical might to reverse user choices about tracking online so that users can be surveilled.[3]

Moreover, private-sector tracking empowers the government, because both law enforcement and national security agencies use private actors to monitor individuals. In fact, Google's online tracking is so ubiquitous that the NSA has been shown to rely upon it.[4] Private-sector tracking also can reduce individuals' expectations of privacy, thereby affecting the application of the Fourth Amendment.

This chapter discusses how the FTC regulates private companies that surveil people. FTC activities shield individuals from some invasive monitoring, and have knock-on effects on law enforcement and national security surveillance, because of the government's piggybacking on private-sector monitoring.

It also discusses the FTC's role in cybersecurity. The FTC has interpreted its organic statute to require all companies to have reasonable security protections. This security mandate can help reduce the risk of unwanted disclosure of personal information and surveillance.

This chapter proceeds from an assumption that should be made explicit. The contours of the FTC's powers, embodied in the Federal Trade Commission Act (FTC Act), are not clear, because Congress gave the FTC a broad but vague mandate, and because few companies challenge the FTC in court. In the style of a common law court, the FTC brings matters against companies, and in the process, continually evolves the meaning of the prohibition on unfair or deceptive acts or practices. Thus, this chapter discusses uncontested matters that are settled by companies, and treats these matters as a form of case law that elucidates the FTC's interpretation of the FTC Act.[5] Companies choose to settle these matters because the FTC is conservative in its case selection, and because FTC investigations typically unearth more wrongdoing than is initially suspected.

1 Ibrahim Altaweel, Nathaniel Good & Chris Jay Hoofnagle, *Web Privacy Census*, TECHNOLOGY SCIENCE (Dec. 15, 2015), http://techscience.org/a/2015121502.

2 In 2015, Lenovo was discovered to have implemented a man-in-the-middle attack on SSL in its low-end computers in order to place advertising selected by Lenovo on Web sites that the consumer visited. Annalee Newitz, *Lenovo Joins the Malevolent Side of the Online Advertising Industry*, Gizmodo (Feb. 20, 2015), http://gizmodo.com/lenovo-joins-the-malevolent-side-of-the-online-advertis-1686922941.

3 Several other examples of aggressive marketing-driven erosions of privacy and security are not covered because the FTC has not yet taken cases to address them. Professor Lorrie Cranor's team at Carnegie Mellon University has documented that thousands of Web sites were using code to trick the Microsoft Internet Explorer browser, which by default rejects most advertising cookies, to accept advertising tracking. Pedro Giovanni Leon et al., *Token Attempt: The Misrepresentation of Website Privacy Policies through the Misuse of P3P Compact Policy Tokens*, Workshop on Privacy in the Electronic Society (2010).

4 Ashkan Soltani, Andrea Peterson & Barton Gellman, *NSA Uses Google Cookies to Pinpoint Targets for Hacking*, THE WASHINGTON POST, Dec. 10, 2013.

5 Daniel J. Solove & Woodrow Hartzog, *The FTC and the New Common Law of Privacy*, 144 COLUM. L. REV. 583 (2014).

Finally, this chapter focuses only on the direct monitoring of individuals, rather than "dataveillance," the monitoring of data about people.[6] Thus, discussions of consumer reporting, debt monitoring, and data broker activities are omitted.[7]

This chapter begins by explaining the FTC's statutory basis for consumer protection that is used in privacy cases. It then proceeds to discuss enforcement actions and policy positions taken by the FTC to protect consumers from surveillance. It concludes with an analysis of the FTC's interventions, and explains how the FTC cases shape surveillance.

I The FTC's Statutory Basis for Protecting Consumers

The FTC is responsible for more than seventy laws concerning consumer protection. But its principal power derives from the responsibility to prevent "unfair or deceptive acts or practices in commerce."[8] Deceptive practices involve a representation, omission, or practice that is likely to mislead a reasonable consumer to her detriment. Deception proves to be a fruitful legal theory in regulating surveillance, as many companies make claims that turn out to be misleading about the security protections and other features of their products.

Unfair practices are those that cause substantial consumer injury. Such injury must not be outweighed by countervailing benefits to competition or consumers produced by the practice, and it must be an injury that the consumer could not have reasonably avoided. Starting in 2003, the FTC began using its unfairness authority to police insecure products and services, and to address particularly aggressive information practices. This body of cases is one of our nation's most important regulations of cybersecurity. As explained in section II, the FTC interprets the FTC Act to require all companies to employ reasonable information security precautions.

The unfairness authority is more controversial politically because it suggests no role for disclosure or other curative means to allow a given business practice. That is, it sets a normative standard against the practice in question. Indeed, in recent years, the Chamber of Commerce and conservative legal activists have tried to prune back the unfairness power, but they have been unsuccessful. Instead, they have created a new generation of case law that reaffirms broad powers of the FTC.[9]

The legal theory of unfairness is powerful because it can address companies that impose externalities on others, even where there is no relationship between the company and the consumer. Thus, unfairness would seem to be a viable legal theory to address many problems in the consumer product space where a privacy invasion is present but there is no privity between the privacy invader and consumer. To address situations where a

6 Roger Clarke, *Information Technology and Dataveillance*, 31(5) Comm. ACM 498 (May 1988).

7 These topics receive fuller treatment in my book on the FTC. *See* Chris Jay Hoofnagle, Federal Trade Commission Privacy Law and Policy (Cambridge University Press 2016).

8 15 U.S.C. §45(a)(2)(2016).

9 For three recent examples, *see FTC v. Amazon.com, Inc.*, No. 2:14-cv-01038-JCC (D.D.C. 2016)(transaction costs associated with obtaining refunds for software ordered by children could be a "substantial injury"); *POM Wonderful, LLC v. FTC*, 777 F.3d 478 (D.C. Cir. 2015) (FTC can require maker of sugary fluid to engage in a random controlled trial before making claims about its health benefits); *FTC v. Wyndham Worldwide Corp.*, 799 F.3d 236 (3d Cir. 2015) (company's failure to take reasonable security measures could be charged as "unfair" practice).

company aids or abets a privacy invasion, the FTC sometimes argues that providing the "means and instrumentalities" of unfairness violates the FTC Act.

It is important to note what deception and unfairness do not require. First, they do not require intent to deceive.[10] This is because companies can deceive or act unfairly by mistake, and because companies sometimes subjectively believe their own false advertising claims.[11] The omission of intent was deliberate in order to lower the hurdles imposed by the common law in fraud cases. At the turn of the century, even advertisers endorsed legal approaches that eliminated intent as a requirement.[12]

Second, neither deception nor unfairness requires economic injury. However, unfairness does require the showing of "substantial injury," which can include aggregated, noneconomic harms to many individuals. For instance, the inconvenience of obtaining refunds[13] or addressing fraudulent charges can form a substantial injury.[14]

Third, deception has an "I know it when I see it" quality. Technically, the FTC must establish that an act has a "tendency or capacity" to deceive a substantial minority of consumers. In practice, however, if the FTC claims that an act is deceptive, the courts generally defer to the agency's determination. The FTC need not present survey research, copy tests, or even meet a reasonable person standard of proof.

Finally, these factors taken together show the FTC Act was a radical rejection of common law approaches to consumer protection. In addition to freeing the FTC from showing intent and harm, the common law elements of causation and reliance were not included in the FTC Act. Thus, the FTC need not show that consumers relied on a specific misrepresentation, or tie the misrepresentation to a specific loss. The FTC is charged with the prevention of unfairness and deception[15] and therefore can act before injury has occurred.[16] Furthermore, the FTC can pursue a company for a single act of wrongdoing – the practice complained of need not be official policy or even a routine procedure.

To balance these powers with due process rights, Congress limited the FTC's ability to levy civil penalties. Generally speaking, the FTC cannot levy a fine unless a promulgated rule is violated. Because there is no privacy or general security rule, civil penalties are usually only available when a company already under consent decree violates an agreement with the FTC by having further privacy and security lapses. Still, FTC actions are

10 *FTC v. Freecom Commc'ns, Inc.*, 401 F.3d 1192 (10th Cir. 2005); *United States v. Johnson*, 541 F.2d 710, 712 (8th Cir.1976), *cert. denied*, 429 US 1093, 97 S.Ct. 1106 (1977); *FTC v. Balme*, 23 F.2d 615 (2d Cir. 1928); *Indiana Quartered Oak Co. v. FTC*, 26 F.2d 340, 342 (2d Cir. 1928).

11 Lowell Mason, The Language of Dissent 162 (1959) ("many of those who get into trouble over false and misleading claims for their good do so from sheer industrial conceit. They truly think their merchandise is not only good, it's the best").

12 *See* the "Printers' Ink" model statute, John Irving Romer, *Legal Repression of Dishonest Advertising*, 77(8) Printers' Ink 66, 68 (Nov. 23, 1911).

13 *FTC v. Amazon.com, Inc.*, No. 2:14-cv-01038-JCC (D.D.C. 2016).

14 *FTC v. Neovi, Inc.*, 604 F.3d 1150 (9th Cir. 2010)

15 *FTC v. Sperry & Hutchinson*, 405 U.S. 233 (1972).

16 *Spiegel, Inc. v. FTC*, 494 F.2d 59 (7th Cir. 1974), *cert. denied*, 419 US 896 (1974); *Bear Mill Mfg. Co. v. FTC*, 98 F.2d 67 (2d Cir. 1938) ("We think that the Commission is authorized to guard the public against such dangers. Indeed, it exists to promote fair rules of trade and in so doing to curb practices that involve a likelihood of injury to the public, even if in a particular case the acts complained of are, as here, innocent in purpose and may thus far have done little harm").

costly and embarrassing for companies. The reputational damage and costs of compliance with an FTC action are often sufficient punishment.

With its broad mandate, the FTC can do much to prevent surveillance by establishing good security practices, and by setting limits on the private sector's instinct to monitor people.

II The FTC's Regulation of Surveillance

The FTC's regulation of surveillance falls into five categories, encompassing both direct and indirect invasions of privacy. Direct liability can be present 1) for invasive tracking online, through Web sites or apps; 2) for tracking people in person, such as in stores or in their daily travels; and 3) through using spyware to generate or to obtain information from individuals' devices. Indirect liability can inure 1) where there is poor product design or insecure services that result in customer vulnerability to surveillance, and 2) for facilitating invasions of privacy, such as stalking, by selling data about individuals' communications and activities. The FTC's role in cybersecurity is most pronounced in these areas of indirect liability, which form a general duty to secure personal information.

After discussing the cases, this section turns to how the FTC signals the scope of acceptable surveillance through policy statements.

A *The FTC's Antisurveillance Case Efforts*

1 Invasive Web Tracking

The FTC has brought a series of cases concerning tracking performed online through the web browser or through consumer applications. On the most basic level, affirmative misrepresentations about tracking are deceptive, and such deceptions make easy cases for the FTC. For instance, in Compete, a company marketed a web browser "toolbar" to consumers. Toolbars presumably offer the consumer some benefit, such as quick access to a service or comparative offers on products, but the privacy price is high: the toolbar provider can monitor all browser traffic. Compete disclosed its monitoring, but tried to allay privacy concerns by stating that personal information was stripped from the data stream before it even left the user's computer. In reality, the technology was not up to the task, and consumers' browsing information was transferred in a personally identifiable format. This was a deception, according to the FTC.[17]

Affirmative misrepresentations clearly violate the FTC Act. Omissions and ambiguous or incomplete disclosures violate the FTC Act as well, but are more difficult to evaluate. The FTC has taken a "surprise" approach: that is, if an information collection or use violates consumer expectations, it needs to be disclosed, sometimes prominently. This approach is important because many if not most deceptions today probably are in the form of implied claims or material omissions.[18]

[17] In the Matter of Compete, Inc., FTC File No. 102 3155 (2013). *See* also In the Matter of Upromise, Inc., FTC File No. 1023116 (2012).

[18] Guang-Xin Xie & David M. Boush, *How Susceptible Are Consumers to Deceptive Advertising Claims? A Retrospective Look at the Experimental Research Literature*, 11 The Marketing Rev. 293, (2011) ("Many alleged deceptive claims nowadays are implicitly manipulative rather than outright false").

Some omissions, particularly when the omission masks disproportionate data collection, are deceptive.[19] The most controversial example of this doctrine comes from the department store company Sears. In order to understand better how people shop online, Sears offered some customers the opportunity to be paid ten dollars in exchange for installing software that functioned much as spyware does. Selling one's privacy for cash would seem to be an acceptable transaction in the United States. However, the FTC found it deceptive, because the extent of tracking that Sears' application enabled was not sufficiently disclosed. While Sears did present the consumer with the basic details of the transaction – money in exchange for "confidential" tracking of online browsing – the complete details of this tracking, which included monitoring of secure sessions (such as Internet purchasing and banking), only appeared in a lengthy end-user license agreement.[20] A consumer would be surprised, unpleasantly, by this data surveillance.

Similarly, in Goldenshores Technology, a company marketed a popular free application for phones that turned the device into a flashlight. The company disclosed that the application collected information for its own purposes, but not well enough for a consumer to understand its full range of data uses. Although the application simply adjusted the screen to its brightest setting, it also collected a unique device identification number from the phone and the phone's precise GPS coordinates, and then handed this information off to advertisers. The FTC thought this deceptive because the omission was important enough to cause consumers to choose a different application. Enabling surveillance by advertisers was both counterintuitive and unnecessary for the functioning of the application.

Some consumers have taken efforts to avoid web tracking of various sorts. Efforts to undo consumer avoidance of this form of surveillance can violate the FTC Act. One frequent area of tension is tracking through cookies. Many consumers report that they delete their cookies, and, in fact,[21] marketers have complained that cookie deletion is impairing targeting efforts.[22] To address this problem, some marketing companies have used technologies to reinstate tracking that the user has disabled. This behavior could be seen as a computer intrusion, and it is included here because such behavior is a form of communications surveillance.

Flash Cookies, one of a series of unfortunate technologies created by the Adobe Corporation, can be used to undo consumer self-help. Flash cookies enable providers of "Flash" content to store information persistently about users. By embedding a tiny movie – even an invisible one – Web site operators used Flash to enumerate users, and this tracking was difficult to detect and could not be blocked in web browsers until recently. Advertisers also learned that Flash Cookies could "back up" ordinary cookies, so if a user deleted cookies in order to avoid tracking, Flash could undo that deletion. In so doing, the use of Flash Cookies resembles a computer intrusion, because Flash Cookies interfere with the confidentiality and integrity of users' computers.

19 *United States v. Path, Inc.*, No. C-13–0448 (N.D. Cal. Jan. 31, 2013) (company automatically collected data from users' contact/address books; a reasonable consumer would have assumed that such data were only transferred when the user clicked a feature to "add friends").

20 *In re* Sears Holdings Management Corporation, FTC File No. 082 3099 (2009).

21 Chris Jay Hoofnagle & Jennifer M. Urban, *Alan Westin's Privacy Homo Economicus*, 49 Wake Forest L. Rev. 261 (2014).

22 Mickey Alam Khan, *Rising Cookie Rejection Bites into Metrics*, Direct Marketing News, Jul. 11, 2005.

In one case, a company made representations that users could control tracking by blocking or deleting regular cookies. However, this was only partially true, because the company also used Flash cookies for tracking. It thus engaged in a deceptive trade practice.[23] This case suggests that the FTC believes that a company cannot give privacy advice and then work actively to undermine proprivacy efforts using some unfamiliar technology.

Various forms of scripting allow Web sites to commandeer users' browsers and cause the browser to take actions in tension with user intent. For instance, Apple's Safari browser blocks third party cookies by default, thereby giving its users a form of technical privacy protection that some competing products lack. Google, perhaps in order to make its services work better on the Safari browser, implemented a method to undo this blocking. The method used by Google was particularly brazen. It opened a web page invisible to the user and used a program to simulate the user's clicking on it.[24] It was as if a Google engineer grabbed the user's mouse and clicked on a "track me" button while the user was not watching. Because Google had promised in its privacy policy that users relying on Safari's embedded controls would not be tracked, the FTC found that Google's actions were deceptive. The FTC sued Google because the company was already under a consent order for other privacy wrongdoing, and the company agreed to pay a $22.5 million civil penalty.[25] At the time, this was the largest civil penalty that the FTC had ever obtained in privacy matters.

"History sniffing" is another example of web surveillance, one that can be unfair under FTC norms. The technique can subtly determine the Web sites that a user has visited. In one case, a company used scripts that presented the user's web browser with many different URLs. The script could determine whether the URLs were rendered in a blue or in a purple font. Presumably, a URL rendered in purple was marked so because the user had visited it. The company could test whether a user visited more than fifty-four thousand different sites with this trick, and when it found a match, it used the information to bucket the user in various profiles.

The FTC found the company's behavior deceptive because it did not disclose the history sniffing, and because the company's privacy policy said it only collected information on Web sites in its affiliate network. According to the FTC, because a reasonable consumer would find the history sniffing material, it should have been disclosed. Furthermore, a reasonable consumer would only expect the company to obtain information on Web sites with which it had a relationship. Thus, being able to infer visits to the fifty-four thousand other sites would be a surprising and unbargained-for result of a visit to the company's Web site.[26]

2 Tracking in Physical Space

Off-line retail businesses – the standard brick and mortar stores we visit – have started to adopt the tracking and identification schemes of their online cousins. Just a few years ago, purchases made in a retail store were essentially anonymous, even when paying

[23] In the Matter of ScanScout, Inc., FTC File No. 102 3185 (2011).
[24] Julia Angwin & Jennifer Valentino DeVries, *Google's iPhone Tracking*, WALL ST. J., Feb. 17, 2012.
[25] *United States v. Google*, No. 512-cv-04177-HRL (N.D.Cal. 2012).
[26] In the Matter of Epic Marketplace, Inc., and Epic Media Group, LLC, FTC File No. 112 3182 (2013).

with plastic because card network rules[27] and technological barriers made it difficult for retailers to link individuals to their purchases. State laws also limited credit card number reverse appends, the process of matching a credit card number to other personal information, such as home address and email. To overcome these legal and technical restrictions, retailers started using data brokers to identify individuals[28] and to link consumers' unrelated activity with their behavior at the register.

But what about shoppers who merely browse and do not make a purchase? In the online world, nonpurchasers are surveilled perfectly. How could off-line retailers leave the bodies of consumers untracked? Nomi Technologies began to fill this gap by offering a service that passively detected the MAC addresses that are emitted by all phones with Wi-Fi capability. These MAC addresses are unique identifiers that enable wireless networks to link to phones, laptops, and other computing devices. Presumably, similar tracking could be accomplished through "ISMI catchers" to monitor non-smart phones, and through Bluetooth, because it too broadcasts a MAC address. One can block this tracking only by turning off Wi-Fi (in Nomi's case) or by turning off the phone if a retailer is using IMSI tracking.

Nomi partnered with retail stores to deploy the tracking technology. However, Nomi's privacy policy promised that shoppers would be provided with in-store notices and the ability to opt out from Nomi's tracking service. But it failed to ensure that notices were posted, and there was no mechanism to opt out at the stores. The FTC found this to be deceptive.[29]

Although it is very likely that other companies are engaging in similar tracking of individuals, Nomi is the single case brought so far by the FTC. Additionally, if Nomi had no privacy policy (there was no legal mandate for it to have one), the FTC's only hook would have been unfairness, a theory unlikely to be successful because of the burden of proving "substantial injury."

3 Malware

Modern web tracking occurs "in the cloud," on the servers owned by publishers, advertisers, and others. When this same tracking is effectuated on the user's machine, it is called "malware." "Malware" is a term that encompasses spyware, ransomware, adware, and other software that operates maliciously. Of course, there is some disagreement about what software constitutes malware.[30]

27 The American Express agreement for accepting credit cards specifies that retailers cannot use card data for any purpose except to process the transaction and expressly bars marketing use of the data: "You shall not use any Cardmember Information or lists of partial or complete cardmember names for the purpose of providing or selling this information to third parties or other internal uses (e.g., marketing)." American Express, Merchant Regulations – U.S. (Apr. 2011).

28 After California prohibited retailers from asking customers their home addresses during credit card transactions, data brokers created tools that allowed retailers to infer this same information by merely asking for a telephone number. When requesting the phone number was prohibited, data brokers encouraged retailers to collect the ZIP code, which also could be used to identify the customer's home address. In the words of one data broker, the system was designed to avoid "losing customers who feel that you're invading their privacy." *See generally Pineda v. Williams-Sonoma Stores, Inc.*, 246 P.3d 612 (Sup. Ct. Cal. 2011).

29 In the Matter of Nomi Technologies, Inc. FTC File No. 132 3251 (2015).

30 Nathaniel Good, Jens Grossklags, David Thaw, Aaron Perzanowski, Deirdre K. Mulligan & Joseph Konstan, *User Choices and Regret: Understanding Users' Decision Process about Consensually Acquired Spyware*, 2(2) I/S: A J. L. Pol'y Info. Soc. 283 (2006). A broad consumer–industry coalition, the

The FTC thought that CyberSpy, software that logged users' keystrokes, was spyware. But this determination had much to do with how the software maker marketed CyberSpy. The company allegedly instructed buyers of the software how to deploy it secretly, even providing a configuration wizard and tutorial to disguise the program as an innocuous e-mail attachment. It also advertised the software as "100% undetectable." The FTC argued that CyberSpy's selling of the spyware was unfair, that it was unfair for CyberSpy to collect information from victims of the spyware, and that CyberSpy provided others the means and instrumentalities both to install software and to engage in deception.[31]

The commission obtained a temporary restraining order against CyberSpy, and, almost two years later, CyberSpy signed an order to settle the case. In the settlement, CyberSpy agreed to remedies that set out the FTC's stance on highly intrusive software. The settlement crafted an imperfect compromise that allows users to surveil their own computers, while creating some protections for others. The company must cause the software to initiate a pop-up at installation, warning the user of the software; and it must display a "tray icon" to indicate that the software is running. However, users who have full administrative privileges on the computer can install the software so that the notice and tray do not display. The company also has to warn users that it is illegal to install the software on others' computers, and it must monitor licensure of the product to prevent the software from being installed on multiple computers.

Owning a computer can give one authority to install spyware on it – that is why CyberSpy was able to continue to operate. But just as a landlord cannot place a listening device in a tenant's apartment, FTC actions make it difficult to install monitoring software on leased or rented computers. One articulation of these efforts concerned "rent-to-own" businesses. In these cases, "rent-to-own" is actually a lease.

In one matter, the commission brought an administrative action against both the rental company and a software company for installing a program to monitor lessors. DesignerWare, LLC, marketed and supported "PC Rental Agent," a program that enabled companies to track the physical location of leased computers.[32]

DesignerWare recommended, but did not require, that rental companies disclose the presence of the software. It was generally undetectable, and the user could not delete it. The software also supported a "Detective Mode" to respond to the commercial problem of those who did not pay, as well as the problem of stolen and lost computers. It enabled keylogging and screen captures and could take pictures with the webcam. As in CyberSpy, the FTC noted DesignerWare's licensing practices, pointing out that it did not monitor how the software was used, and that this could lead to abuse by licensees. The FTC alleged that it was unfair to install software and monitor users, and that DesignerWare provided the means and instrumentalities for rental companies to engage in unfairness. Crucial to DesignerWare's liability were its failure to monitor licensees of

Anti-Spyware Working Group, defines spyware as "technologies deployed without appropriate user consent and/or implemented in ways that impair user control over: Material changes that affect their user experience, privacy, or system security; Use of their system resources, including what programs are installed on their computers; and/or Collection, use, and distribution of their personal or other sensitive information." ANTI-SPYWARE WORKING GROUP, ANTI-SPYWARE COALITION DEFINITIONS DOCUMENT, Nov. 12, 2007.

31 *FTC v. Cyberspy Software, LLC*, 6:08-CV-1872-ORL-316JK (M.D. Fla. 2008).

32 In the Matter of DesignerWare, LLC, 155 F.T.C. 421 (2013); In the Matter of Aaron's, Inc., FTC File No. 122 3256 (2013).

the technology and its coaching of rental companies on how they should give notice of the monitoring. It also directly collected information on its own servers and generated a fake registration page to fool users into disclosing their credit card data.

DesignerWare and the rental company agreed to an order prohibiting direct monitoring and licensing software to monitor users. The FTC allowed DesignerWare to create systems that locate user computers, so long as there was prominent notice of and consent to the tracking at rental, and notice each time the location beacon was activated. Companies continue to be free to condition rental on the user's giving consent.

In these malware cases, the FTC was creating greater protections for communications privacy than provided for by federal statute. After all, even under the wiretapping laws, users can consent to having their computers comprehensively monitored, if the consent is actual consent or fairly implied from the circumstances.[33] Here, however, the FTC created a flat ban on content surveillance, allowing only an exception for GPS tracking after prominent notice is given to the user.

In physical spaces, companies are legally prohibited from some antifraud efforts, such as installing cameras in changing rooms and bathrooms to catch shoplifters. The FTC's efforts draw similar lines with respect to computing, much of which is personal, and much of which occurs in the home. Arguably, the FTC is extending the long-established principle that antifraud efforts have to be reasonable into the new realm of personal computing.

4 Insecure and Poorly Designed Services

Software programs and Internet-connected devices can be reprogrammed or configured to monitor the consumer. When those products are poorly designed or suffer from basic security flaws, the FTC may consider the manufacturer of the product or creator of the service liable under the FTC Act. In this determination, the FTC has created both a general duty of cybersecurity and indirect liability for surveillance. The FTC even declares that some companies have acted unfairly by providing the "means and instrumentalities" to monitor others. The FTC's enforcement actions in information security more broadly make it a key player in cybersecurity. In essence, the FTC's decisions require all companies to have reasonable protections for information security.[34] This section discusses cases when insecure products and services exposed consumers to surveillance.

TRENDnet illustrates bad security that arises to what the FTC considers unfair. TRENDnet manufactured Internet-connected cameras. Hundreds of its cameras were discovered to be broadcasting on the Internet without any password protection. A clever Internet user discovered this and created a simple system that allowed anyone to discover these broadcasts. Soon, more than seven hundred such broadcasts were linked online, leading to the camera users being watched in their homes by anyone who visited the broadcast links. In an administrative action, the FTC accused TRENDnet of engaging in deceptive trade practices for labeling the cameras "secure," and unfair trade practices because the company failed to provide "reasonable security" for the products.[35]

33 18 U.S. Code § 2511 (2016). In re Pharmatrak, Inc., 329 F.3d 9 (1st Cir. 2003) (Constructive consent (e.g. "consent" because one clicked on a license agreement where wiretapping was mentioned somewhere) does not satisfy the wiretapping laws).

34 *FTC v. Wyndham Worldwide Corp.*, 799 F.3d 236 (3d Cir. 2015).

35 In the Matter of TRENDnet, FTC File No. 122 3090 (Feb. 7, 2014).

A growing number of cases are similar to TRENDnet, in that the FTC finds that a practice is unfair because it presents an unreasonable risk of privacy invasion to consumers. The first such case involved Sony BMG Music Entertainment in 2007.[36] The company, concerned that its music would be copied by computer users, deployed two different content protection programs, XCP and MediaMax. These programs were installed on users' computers when they tried to play Sony music CDs. XCP introduced a "rootkit," a computer process that masks itself from the user's operating system. Rootkits can be used to mask malicious activity on a computer and make it possible for others to take over the computer. MediaMax created a folder on users' computers that could be commandeered by others and used for malicious purposes. Upon discovery of these problems, Sony stumbled, releasing poorly designed patches that intensified the insecurity. The FTC investigated Sony, finding that it engaged in both deception and unfair practices. The FTC found it unfair for Sony to install such an invasive program without more prominent notice. It also found that consumers suffered unjustified injury because it was difficult to find the programs and to uninstall them.[37]

More recently, in Compete, the browser toolbar case discussed previously, the FTC found the company unfairly put consumers at risk because it transmitted sensitive information from secure web pages in clear, readable text. In effect, Compete's toolbar decrypted secure sessions that no reasonable consumer would allow to be transmitted in plaintext online.[38]

The FTC's most important cybersecurity case concerned HTC America, a major manufacturer of wireless phones. Because it involved a device manufacturer instead of a service provider, the case has captured the attention of many in the consumer product space. In essence, the HTC case creates responsibilities for how products interact with software. The HTC case thus erodes the longtime immunity software developers have enjoyed from product liability.

In the case, the FTC found that HTC's inclusion of "bundled software" profoundly reduced the privacy and security measures built into the Android operating system, the software that runs on many cheap wireless phone models. HTC's bundled software circumvented privacy and security controls in Android, which, by default, restricted third party applications from accessing a phone's microphone, functions (such as sending text messages), and diagnostic logging information. HTC's software allowed any third party application to gain access to the phone's core functions, potentially making the device a form of mobile spyware. This creation of systemic insecurity was both unfair and deceptive to consumers.[39]

Similarly, design prompts that cause consumers to set up a device such that it can be monitored by others can trigger FTC Act liability. For instance, in one case a manufacturer of routers presented users with a dialogue box to set up FTP access to the users' files. Selecting "Enable FTP" enabled public access to all the user's files. The user had to take an additional, confusing step to limit the access to certain folders.[40]

36 In the Matter of Sony BMG Music Entm't, FTC File No. 062 3019 (2007).

37 Deidre K. Mulligan & Aaron K. Perzanowski, *The Magnificence of the Disaster: Reconstructing the Sony BMG Rootkit Incident*, 22 Berk. Tech. L. J. 1157 (2007).

38 In the Matter of Compete, Inc., FTC File No. 102 3155 (2013). *See also* In the Matter of Upromise, Inc., FTC File No. 1023116 (2012).

39 In the Matter of HTC America, Inc., FTC File No. 1223049 (2013).

40 In the Matter of ASUSTeK Computer, Inc., FTC File No. 142 3156 (Feb. 23, 2016).

Finally, a failure to disclose a serious risk of insecurity can form the basis of a FTC action. For instance, in 2016 the FTC settled an administrative action against Oracle for the way the company handled updates to Java. The company promised the upgrading would make users' computers more secure; however, there was inadequate disclosure that older, vulnerable versions of Java would remain on the computer. These older versions of Java would make users vulnerable to surveillance, because merely visiting a Web site could trigger a Java-based installation of malware.[41]

5 The Use of Deception in Order to Engage in Surveillance

The FTC has long regulated the use of deception for the purpose of obtaining personal information. In the 1951 Gen-O-Pak matter, the FTC brought an administrative proceeding against a company that helped creditors locate debtors by sending debtors postcards promising a free gift in exchange for their personal information. One card read, "Dear Friend: We have on hand a package, which we will send to you if you will completely fill out the return card, giving sufficient identification to warrant our sending this package to you.... There are no charges whatsoever and the package will be sent to you all charges prepaid. Yours very truly, The Gen-O-Pak Co." The cards and surveys sent by the company solicited extensive personal information. The FTC found this practice both unfair and deceptive.[42]

In 1971, the FTC filed a complaint invoking both unfairness and deception against a company for generating direct mail lists from consumer questionnaires. The company wrote to consumers promising that they would have a chance to win prizes, and that there was "nothing to buy" and "no salesman will call on you."[43] The FTC found the collection of this information under false pretenses for the generation of mailing lists to be unfair.

In more recent years, the FTC pursued private investigators who used deception to obtain personal information about people, presumably so that the private investigator's clients could surveil others. In the FTC's 1999 case against Touch Tone Information, Inc., the agency argued that "pretexting" was both deceptive and unfair.[44] Pretexting is the practice of using various false pretenses in order to cause another business to disclose information about a customer. Touch Tone allegedly did this for clients in order to provide financial and contact information of individuals. Following the 1999 case, the FTC conducted a sweep against private investigators who used pretexting to obtain phone records.[45] As part of this sweep, the Tenth Circuit upheld an FTC unfairness claim against Abika.com, a Web site that connected consumers with investigators who would obtain others' information through pretexting.[46]

Many Web sites are used to pursue illegal ends, such as the solicitation of prostitution, the sale of counterfeit or copyright-infringing goods, or the sale of illicit drugs. The

41 In the Matter of Oracle Corp., FTC File No. 132 3115 (Mar. 29, 2016).
42 Lester Rothschild, Trading as Gen-O-Pak Co., 49 F.T.C. 1673 (1952); *Rothschild v. FTC*, 200 F.2d 39 (7th Cir. 1952).
43 In the Matter of Metromedia, Inc., 78 F.T.C. 331 (1971).
44 *FTC v. Rapp d/b/a Touch Tone Information, Inc.*, No. 99-WM-783 (D. Colo. 1999).
45 *See, e.g., FTC v. 77 Investigations, Inc., and Reginald Kimbro*, No. EDCV06-0439 VAP (C.D. Cal. 2006).
46 *FTC v. Accusearch Inc.*, 570 F.3d 1187 (10th Cir. 2009).

Communications Decency Act (CDA)[47] is frequently used to argue that Internet services should not be held responsible for illegal activities of users.[48] This is because Section 230 of the CDA broadly immunizes online services from defamation and other torts for the content posted by third parties. For instance, under the CDA, a Web site that allows user comments would not be liable if a user defamed another person. The law's provisions are so exceptional that few manage to beat a CDA defense.

The CDA has become the refuge of many online scoundrels. Recall that in the case against Abika.com, the FTC sued a Web site operator that connected third party private investigators with consumers interested in buying confidential phone records of others. The respondent claimed that it was entitled to immunity under the CDA because it "merely provided 'a forum in which people advertise and request' telephone records." However, the Tenth Circuit disagreed, holding that the Web site was involved in the creation of content:

> Accusearch solicited requests for confidential information protected by law, paid researchers to find it, knew that the researchers were likely to use improper methods, and charged customers who wished the information to be disclosed. Accusearch's actions were not 'neutral' with respect to generating offensive content; on the contrary, its actions were intended to generate such content. Accusearch is not entitled to immunity under the CDA.[49]

The FTC has thus been able to pursue companies that claim merely to be intermediaries for surveillance.

B *FTC Remedies for Privacy Invasions*

Almost all FTC privacy matters are settled. The FTC uses a standard form when resolving matters with respondents, and a familiar set of remedies are agreed to in privacy proceedings. All orders require the respondent company to refrain from similar misrepresentations as alleged in the complaint. Typically, these consent orders last twenty years. Violation of the orders can trigger civil penalties, which are currently set at forty thousand dollars a day per violation.

The commission tailors other remedies, many of which constitute "fencing-in" relief that may go beyond the underlying violations of the FTC Act. In some privacy matters, the commission has required respondents to establish a comprehensive privacy program. These require risk assessments, ongoing assessment of services, care in selecting service providers, review of design processes, and measures of accountability. Such programs entail great expense for companies, because they require significant staff resources devoted to identifying and remedying privacy risks across the enterprise. In some matters, companies have to self-report compliance with the order; in others the FTC imposes a duty for a third party assessment of compliance.

In other matters, the FTC has ordered respondents to delete data. The FTC has also obtained agreements for companies to change the technical design of their services. For example, in the Frostwire case, a company disseminated an application that caused users

47 47 U.S.C. § 230 (2016).
48 *FTC v. LeanSpa, LLC*, 920 F. Supp. 2d 270 (D. Conn. 2013).
49 *FTC v. Accusearch, Inc.*, 570 F.3d 1187 (10th Cir. 2009).

to place their files, unwittingly, on peer-to-peer sharing networks. The agency obtained an agreement that the company would only share files if the user affirmatively selected the file to be placed on the network.[50] In the Sony matter, in which the company installed software that endangered the security of users' computers, the FTC obtained remedies requiring the company to provide a tool to remove the software. Sony also agreed to buy keyword advertising so that people searching for how to remove the offending software would be directed to Sony's tool.[51]

C *The FTC's Antisurveillance Policy Efforts*

The FTC also attempts to limit consumer tracking through policy guidance. This section details two examples of such guidance. The two initiatives are so new that their implications and effects are not yet known.

1 Audio Beacon Technology

Wireless phones form the largest network of distributed sensors. A wireless phone includes a microphone, computational power, and the ability to transmit data it collects to others. Recognizing this capability, some companies have tried to use wireless phones as sensors for a commercial purpose. For instance, Silverpush is a software used to detect signals embedded in television broadcasts. Through detection of such signals, the software could report on ratings or whether a wireless phone user was within earshot of a certain commercial.

In March 2016, the FTC identified mobile application developers on the Google Play platform that were likely using Silverpush and sent them a letter warning that the technology may violate the FTC Act. The technology can "listen" through the microphone, and, in testing, the FTC found that such monitoring was possible without a user notice or dialogue warning of the risks of such monitoring.[52] The FTC is likely to require prominent, affirmative consent to Silverpush monitoring because it resembles intrusive wiretapping technology.

2 Strong Encryption

One FTC commissioner, Terrell McSweeny, has staked out policy positions on encryption. As more consumers have devices that include strong encryption by default, such as Apple's iPhone, law enforcement agencies have encountered greater difficulty in performing forensic investigations of devices. Some have called for encryption systems that have technical and legal procedures to give law enforcement access to these devices. Others, such as McSweeny, have opposed such access provisions, arguing that they will undermine communications privacy and make surveillance easier.[53]

50 *FTC v. Frostwire*, No. 111-CV-23643 (S.D.F.L. Oct. 11, 2011).

51 In the Matter of Sony BMG Music Enm't, FTC File No. 062 3019 (2007).

52 Letter from Maneesha Mithal, Associate Director, Division of Privacy and Identity Protection, FTC to unnamed application developers, Mar. 17, 2016.

53 Jimmy H. Koo, *FTC's McSweeny Defends Encryption*, 15 BNA PRIVACY LAW & SECURITY REPORT 241, Jan. 25, 2016; *see also* Harold Abelson et al., *Keys Under Doormats: Mandating insecurity by*

III Analysis

Several high-level observations can be made about the FTC's policing of surveillance. First, the FTC is free of some of the pathologies of our civil litigation system. Thus, it can bring cases that likely would have failed, even if pursued by earnest, credible plaintiffs. In this, the FTC is filling in for class action attorneys and other private litigants who might otherwise bring suits to prevent surveillance. Second, the FTC's cases have developed stronger norms about the quality of consent required for people to agree to surveillance. In requiring prominent and explicit notices and consent dialogues, the FTC in effect bans some kinds of surveillance. This is because most companies either cannot technically or would prefer not to tell people so directly about how they will be monitored. Finally, the FTC has eroded immunities for technology providers and imposed general cybersecurity duties. This has the potential to open the door to more consumer litigation against Internet services that facilitate fraud and surveillance.

A *The FTC Is Filling the Plaintiff Litigation Void*

Information privacy litigation is extremely difficult to mount. Victims of privacy invasions often do not realize that a problem is afoot, and rectifying it through litigation often requires a new invasion of privacy – putting the allegations and embarrassment into a publicly available legal complaint. There are also basic economic disincentives to suing, such as the cost of suit, and the collective action problems that arise from small privacy invasions that are distributed among many different people. Finally, defendant web services might decide to publicize information collected about the plaintiff in order to embarrass or extort her. Just imagine suing Google or FaceBook—years of search strings and posts, even deleted ones that the service retains but does not erase, might be invoked in depositions in order to argue that the plaintiff was promiscuous with data and does not genuinely care about privacy.

But even those willing to sue face high hurdles, as antipathy to consumer litigation has increased. Federal Rule of Civil Procedure Rule 23, now five decades old, was intended to ease the problem of mounting collective actions. In recent decades, however, courts have imposed requirements that essentially stop class litigation before discovery even begins.

Aside from procedural hurdles, substantive barriers to suit have also increased. The U.S. Supreme Court has held that selling personal information for marketing purposes is protected by the First Amendment.[54] One appellate court even held that opt-in restrictions on the sale of telephone calling records violate the First Amendment.[55] Furthermore, the conservative legal movement has made it more difficult to sue by increasing standing requirements. In a 2016 Supreme Court case, several information-intensive companies argued that they should not be subject to suit unless the consumer

requiring government access to all data and communications, Computer Science and Artificial Intelligence Laboratory, Technical Report (Jul. 2015).

54 *Sorrell v. IMS Health et al.*, 131 S.Ct. 2653 (2011).

55 *United States West v. FCC*, 182 F.3d 1224 (10th Cir. 1999); *but see Nat'l Cable & Telecommunications Ass'n v. FCC*, 555 F.3d 996 (D.C. Cir. 2009).

suffers financial injury – even if the company violates a privacy law intentionally.[56] Their legal theory would mean that activities such as wiretapping, long considered a harm – even a crime punishable by prison time – could not be enforced by the average person unless a financial injury could be shown. Fortunately, the Supreme Court did not embrace that extreme position.

The FTC enjoys deference in its determinations that an unfair or deceptive practice has occurred, and it has a relaxed standing requirement to get into court. Because the FTC is not subject to the skepticism that class action litigation attracts, it has been successful in policing wrongs that the private bar has failed to rectify. As a result, the FTC is in essence filling in for the privacy activities of an active plaintiff bar.

B *The FTC's Actions Bolster Consent Requirements for Surveillance*

Individuals in America are free to alienate their privacy rights and be wiretapped by companies and others. However, quality of consent to surveillance is a key, overlooked issue. A full consideration of whether consent occurred would include whether the user had the competence to consent, whether there was adequate information about the bargain and its risks, whether consent was voluntary, and the terms of withdrawal of consent. Furthermore, federal wiretapping law requires consent to be actual or implied. But in many transactions, consent is simply constructive – critical terms are buried in a lengthy privacy policy or end-user license agreement that no one actually reads, and is given on a take-it-or leave-it basis. The previous section explains that the FTC's actions have established a floor for these disclosures: if they cause unwanted surprise in consumers, they are deceptive. This requires companies' consent experiences to move from constructive forms to methods where consent is implied under the circumstances or is actual.

As the FTC imposes higher-quality consent experiences, surveillance becomes more difficult to implement. Sometimes it is impossible. Recall the Sears matter, when a company paid consumers in order to monitor their Internet use. The FTC found the arrangement deceptive because Sears was monitoring all Internet use – even secure sessions such as online banking. The Sears consent order required the company to obtain affirmative consent for tracking in the future, and this consent had to contain a clear and prominent disclosure, separate from the privacy policy, of the types of data monitored, the scope of the monitoring, whether data would be shared with third parties, whether secure sessions might be monitored, and how data would be used. The description of Sears' notice and consent obligation takes up nine lines in the settlement.

In making the notice requirements so detailed, the FTC may in effect prohibit some kinds of spying on the basis of consent exceptions. Under the FTC's order, Sears had to disclose so many terms, in such a prominent manner, that it became clear that gaining consent was practically impossible. A mobile screen would never accommodate the warning adequately. Even a desktop screen would be completely occupied with warnings. Companies fear telling the consumer so directly and so much about surveillance activities. Thus, the FTC mandate in effect stops some kinds of data collection through

56 *See* Amicus Curie Brief of eBay, Inc., et al., for Petitioner, *Spokeo v. Robins*, 136 S. Ct. 1540 (2016), No. 13–1339.

surveillance, because companies find it distasteful and/or practically impossible to implement the notice requirements.

C *The FTC Is Making Companies More Responsible for Their Technologies*

The FTC's regulation of surveillance pins more responsibility on technology creators. Three responsibility-related trends can be observed from the cases: First, the FTC is imposing more duties upon vendors to address the privacy-invasive activities of users. Second, the security duties imposed by the FTC are eroding companies' immunities for providing insecure products and services. Third, the FTC's cases have pierced overbroad intermediary immunity provided by statute and represent an important reconsideration of how intermediaries should be responsible for the wrongs they encourage.

1 Vendors Are Sometimes Responsible for Privacy Invasions of Users

Several FTC matters focus on software vendor–licensee relationships, and the opportunity for vendors to control licensee misbehavior. Recall that in the matters against CyberSpy and the laptop rental companies, the FTC was concerned about how companies were actively involved in helping end users deploy secretive surveillance tools. The DesignerWare complaint repeatedly recounts how the company was in touch with licensees and helped them monitor renters of laptops. That involvement in the spying made DesignerWare partially responsible for it. In the CyberSpy case, the FTC went so far as to require the respondents to oversee carefully how the software was licensed. CyberSpy settled and agreed to monitor situations when the software is deployed on multiple computers, and even to obtain explanations for multiple installations in writing. Presumably, this is to prevent individuals from installing the spy software on many other users' computers.

As a result of these cases, creators of surveillance tools now have the potential to be liable when they know customers are invading the privacy of others. For better or worse, this approach leaves a void for tools with no technological tether to the creator. The surveillance Frankensteins – the technologies that are set free for anyone to use – presumably will not attract FTC attention. However, this void is probably narrowing. Businesses have a taste for subscription models for services, and that subscription model is likely to keep the vendor in touch with users. The continuous nature of the user relationship in subscription models will carry with some obligation for user misbehavior.

2 Software Vendors Can Be Liable for Insecurity

Second, the FTC is expanding software vendor liability for security defects. Software vendors have enjoyed an extended period of immunity from suit and limitations on damages for badly designed software through contract. The FTC's imposition of reasonable security mandates through the agency's unfairness theory narrows this immunity. For instance, the HTC case concerned how the device maker installed software that undermined the security posture of its customers. The HTC case and others that find services are unfairly insecure is a form of software liability. Although most consumer-initiated suits for security breaches have failed – usually for lack of standing – the FTC's activities have established that companies have a general duty to have reasonable cybersecurity measures.

3 FTC Actions Erode Internet Intermediary Immunity

Finally, the FTC's actions are helping courts understand when intermediaries should be liable for facilitating noxious behavior. The CDA provides an important and potent set of immunities for intermediaries online. But in its potency, the CDA has given refuge to practices that were never tolerated in the off-line world.

The FTC has been able to overcome the broadest readings of the CDA immunities. For instance, in the Abika people search case (discussed earlier), the respondent argued that it merely connected investigators with consumers, and had no involvement in the illegal activity in which the investigators and consumers engaged. The Tenth Circuit rejected that rationale, as it saw the Web site as intricately connected to the privacy invasions afoot.

A similar CDA defense may have been available to Craig Brittain, a man who ran a "revenge pornography" site.[57] Brittain used a series of tactics to obtain nude images of people (primarily women), which he annotated with personal information. The FTC found Brittain's business model unfair, because he did not obtain permission from the women to post their photographs; nor would the women have expected their nude bodies to be commercialized. In pursuing this case, the FTC could remedy a gross wrong against these women. In so doing, the FTC avoided the blame-the-victim dynamics present when individual women accuse a person of some sexually related wrongdoing.

With these actions, the FTC may be able to provide a pressure release valve for the CDA, providing some justice for people who are wronged by those hiding under the skirt of intermediary immunity.

Conclusion

At first, the FTC might seem to be an unlikely topic for the regulation of surveillance. Upon closer inspection, we see that the FTC's role is important. The FTC polices minimum standards of information security for most of the economy. These security protections, if followed, presumably give the United States a better cybersecurity posture, and protect users individually from surveillance. The FTC's efforts to prevent consumer deception require companies to be more candid with their surveillance. The FTC's standards for what constitutes adequate consent also make it more burdensome for services to induce consumers to consent to surveillance.

FTC privacy and security actions have three metaeffects on surveillance policy. First, creators of surveillance tools that facilitate invasions of privacy by users of the tools can be liable for the surveillance. The FTC's interventions require surveillance toolmakers that license their software to monitor end-user behavior more carefully. Second, the FTC's cybersecurity mandate is narrowing immunities for software vendors and providers of consumer services. All companies now must have reasonable security precautions. Third, the FTC's actions have made some intermediaries responsible for the surveillance that they aided and abetted. Intermediary immunity law threatens to create

57 In the Matter of Craig Brittain, FTC File No. 132 3120 (2016).

a zero-responsibility space for gross misconduct, yet the FTC has been successful in curbing its worst abuses.

The FTC's activities profoundly affect one's role as a citizen. As the FTC limits private-sector surveillance, it has knock-on effects on the government as surveillant. The FTC's role complements procedural and substantive criminal procedure, and strengthens individuals' civil liberties posture against government surveillance.

31 The Federal Communications Commission as Privacy Regulator

Travis LeBlanc[†] & Lindsay DeFrancesco[‡]

Twenty-first-century surveillance technologies provide commercial, government, and individual actors with the ability to monitor citizens' communications, day-to-day activities, and personal information. These capabilities make citizens uneasy, and rightly so. By tracking everything we do, these technologies have the capacity to infringe on not only our privacy, but also our livelihood, affecting employment, housing, education, and professional opportunities. Nevertheless, such modern technologies also provide great benefits and conveniences, many of which citizens have become accustomed to using on a daily basis. As a result, government actors must take measures to balance these benefits while ensuring citizens' privacy. In the past, the Federal Communications Commission (FCC) has taken an active role advancing the public good as a privacy regulator, promulgating and enforcing rules in an effort to maintain and protect citizens' privacy. This chapter describes the FCC's role as a privacy regulator, providing a description of the commission's history, rule making process, pertinent regulatory authority, and enforcement actions.

The twenty-first century has ushered in an age of privacy. New technologies, many of which are detailed in this volume, provide individual, commercial, and government actors with unprecedented abilities to monitor voice and written communications whether they are in transit or stored on a device. While gathering and analyzing this data would have consumed innumerable resources and person-hours in years past, it is now possible to gather, store, and, in real time, analyze vast amounts of information relating to online and off-line activities of consumers, with or without the consumers' awareness. This level of surveillance has consequences for our quietude and sense of personal well-being. After all, most of us assume that, so long as we are minding our own business, nobody is, needs to be, or should be monitoring everything we do and everywhere we go. It is also quite unsettling for many people to think that they might be subjected to constant surveillance. Both the threat and reality of widespread surveillance could very well change our behaviors and even shape our characters in ways both subtle and profound. As other contributors to this volume show, modern surveillance can also affect us in practical ways that materially impact our lives, including our abilities to secure

† Partner, Boies Schiller Flexner LLP; Former Chief of Enforcement, Federal Communications Commission; Affiliated Scholar, University of California Hastings College of the Law. This chapter has been written in my personal capacity. The opinions expressed in the chapter are my own and do not reflect the views of the Federal Communications Commission, any commissioner thereof, or the federal government.

‡ Associate, Reed Smith LLP; University of Maryland, Francis King Carey School of Law.

employment, establish credit, pursue an education, obtain housing, speak freely, and maintain personal, political, and professional associations.

Faced with these realities, it is natural to wonder whether there is any way to stem the tide. Many contend that this is an impossible dream. Privacy, they argue, is dead in all but name, and there is no way to reconstitute traditional notions of privacy short of turning back the clock by turning off the technologies. We reject this view. Consumers across the world have consistently embraced the connected world, and they have accepted the concept of sharing personal information through and across digital platforms. The truth of the matter is that these connected technologies provide great benefits to consumers in terms of convenience, efficiency, and security, among others. At the same time, however, it is also apparent that consumers want to have control over what personal information they share, and when they do share personal information, they do not want to relinquish ownership of that information. Many now find themselves seemingly conflicted between protecting their privacy, on the one hand, and the necessity of being connected to the Internet in the twenty-first century. The societal task that individual, commercial, and government actors now confront is to balance protection of privacy with real and substantial benefits afforded in a connected world, both real and virtual.

The project of setting rules and regulations designed to advance the public interest by balancing potential benefits and harms is a critical function of administrative agencies in the United States. Often considered the fourth branch of government, regulatory agencies operate at the nexus of legislation, executive enforcement, and judicial review. Generally speaking, administrative agencies interpret laws passed by Congress and distill them into regulatory rules that carry the force of law. They investigate and prosecute violations of legislative code and regulatory rules. They also may have the power to adjudicate controversies and to impose injunctive relief and monetary penalties. Although all actions by administrative agencies ultimately are subject to constraints imposed by the constitutional branches, administrative agencies often operate with substantial autonomy. It is therefore not much of a surprise that several administrative agencies (the Federal Trade Commission prime among them) have a decorated history addressing issues such as privacy and security.

In this chapter, we discuss the role of the Federal Communications Commission (FCC) as a privacy regulator. The FCC is particularly well suited to promulgate and enforce regulations designed to balance the competing interests at stake in the deployment and use of digital communications, and yet little has been written to compile the privacy authorities and activities of the FCC. As we shall see in this chapter, the FCC was created in 1934 to protect the public interests at stake in the use of communications technologies. At that time, the two primary communications technologies regulated by the FCC were telephones and radio. In the intervening decades, we have seen an explosion in communications technologies. The FCC's role and mandate have attempted to keep pace with that growth. The FCC therefore finds itself with an important role to play in regulating many of the means and methods of protecting privacy that impact communications from cable television to cellular telephones and broadband Internet.

In this chapter, we aim to describe the FCC's role as a privacy regulator, recognizing, of course, that within the confines of this one chapter, we are limited to describing this role at fairly general levels. We start in Part I by providing a brief history of the FCC and an overview of its structure. In Part II, we describe the FCC's rulemaking process and its mandate to protect the public interest. Part III focuses in more detail on the FCC's core areas of regulatory responsibility, including telephone communications, broadcast technologies, and broadband Internet. Part IV considers some major recent privacy and data security enforcement actions.

I History and Structure of the FCC

In 1933, President Franklin D. Roosevelt ordered Secretary of Commerce Daniel Roper to lead a committee examining federal coordination of oversight for radio, telephones, cable, and the telegraph.[1] At the time, several different government agencies regulated components of the communications industry, including the Radio Commission and the Interstate Commerce Commission. After an extensive and contested investigation, the Roper Committee concluded in its primary report that the federal agencies then governing the communications industry were "not working in accordance with any national plan," and, as a result, their regulatory procedures were scattered and inefficient.[2] To unify this disjointed system, the committee recommended consolidating control of all communications within a single federal communications commission.[3] Observing that a divided regulatory scheme was inefficient and incoherent, President Roosevelt adopted the committee's recommendation and sent a special message to Congress proposing the creation of a single federal communications regulatory body:

> I have long felt that for the sake of clarity and effectiveness the relationship of the Federal Government to certain services known as utilities should be divided into three fields: Transportation, power, and communications.... In the field of communications, however, there is today no single Government agency charged with broad authority.... I recommend that the Congress create a new agency to be known as the Federal Communications Commission, ... the services affected to be all of those which rely on wires, cables, or radio as a means of transmission.[4]

Congress promptly considered the president's recommendation and passed the Communications Act of 1934, which established the Federal Communications Commission as the federal regulator of interstate and international communications by radio, television, wire, cable, and satellite.[5]

1 Glen O. Robinson, *The Federal Communications Act: An Essay on Origins and Regulatory Purpose, in* A Legislative History of the Communications Act of 1934, at 3–4 (Max. D. Paglin, ed., Oxford University Press 1989).

2 Staff of Sec'y of Commerce, Study of Communications by an Interdepartmental Committee 108 (Comm. Print 1934), *reprinted in* A Legislative History of the Communications Act of 1934, at 105–18 (Max. D. Paglin, ed., Oxford University Press 1989).

3 *Id.* at 112.

4 President Franklin D. Roosevelt, Message from the President of the United States, S. Doc. No. 144 (1934), *reprinted in* A Legislative History of the Communications Act of 1934, at 99 (Max. D. Paglin, ed., Oxford University Press 1989).

5 Communications Act of 1934, Pub. L. No. 73–416 (1934) (codified in sections of 47 U.S.C. §§ 151–621); *A Bill to Provide for the Regulation of Interstate and Foreign Communications by Wire or Radio, and for Other Purposes: Hearing on S. 2910 before the Committee on Interstate Commerce*, 73d Cong. 2d Sess. (1934), *reprinted in* A Legislative History of the Communications Act of 1934, at 119–279 (Max. D. Paglin, ed., Oxford University Press 1989).

A *The Federal Communications Act*

In its original form, the Communications Act of 1934 (act) borrowed significantly from the Interstate Commerce Act of 1887, which was designed to regulate railroads,[6] and the Radio Act of 1927.[7] Since then, the act and the FCC's scope of authority have expanded to keep pace with evolutions in communications technologies. Among the most notable amendments to the Communications Act are the Cable Communications Act of 1984, which officially positioned cable broadcasts within the ambit of FCC regulation; the Cable Television Consumer Protection and Competition Act of 1992, which required cable television providers to carry local broadcasts; and, most significantly, the Telecommunications Act of 1996,[8] which effected broad changes in telecommunications markets by "eliminating economic barriers to entry in local telecommunications markets, eliminating regulatory barriers to entry in all telecommunications markets, and [effecting] universal service reform."[9] The Telecommunications Act also shifted much power from state and local governments to the federal government by asserting federal preemption.[10] The year 1996 also saw passage of the Communications Decency Act, which sought to prevent the transmission of obscene material and granted the FCC broad authority to enforce that mandate through both the promulgation of rules and enforcement actions.[11]

As amended, the modern Communications Act comprises seven subchapters. Title I, "General Provisions," outlines the basic principles by which the Federal Communications Commission operates.[12] According to Title I, the commission's primary purpose is "regulating interstate and foreign commerce in communication by wire and radio so as to make available … to all people of the United States … a rapid, efficient, Nation-wide, and world-wide wire and radio communication service."[13]

Title II articulates the commission's scope of authority as it relates to regulating common carriers, which are defined under 47 U.S.C. § 153(11) as "any person engaged as a common carrier for hire, in interstate or foreign communication by wire or radio

6 Kenneth A. Cox & William J. Byrnes, *The Common Carrier Provisions – a Product of Evolutionary Development*, *in* A Legislative History of the Communications Act of 1934, at 25–26 (Max. D. Paglin, ed., Oxford University Press 1989). The framers of the 1934 act adopted this regulatory structure because it had been developed over the course of fifty years; thus, it was considered refined and "adaptable to a variety of economic conditions." *Id.* at 60.

7 J. Roger Wollenberg, *The FCC as Arbiter of "The Public Interest, Convenience, and Necessity," in* A Legislative History of the Communications Act of 1934, at 61 (Max. D. Paglin, ed., Oxford University Press 1989).

8 Fed. Comm. Comm'n, https://transition.fcc.gov/telecom.html (last updated May 14, 2015) (noting that the Telecommunications Act of 1996 was "the first major overhaul of telecommunications law in almost 62 years"). The Telecommunications Act is divided into seven titles: Title I – Telecommunication Services, Title II – Broadcast Services, Title III – Cable Services, Title IV – Regulatory Reform, Title V – Obscenity and Violence, Title VI – Effect on Other Laws, and Title VII – Miscellaneous Provisions. *See generally* Telecommunications Act of 1996, Pub. L. No. 104–104, 110 Stat. 56 (1996) (codified as amended in sections of 47 U.S.C.); *see also* H.R. Rep No. 104–458 (1996) (Conf. Rep.).

9 Jonathan E. Nuechterlein & Philip J. Weiser, Digital Crossroads: Telecommunications Law and Policy in the Internet Age 52 (2d ed. 2013).

10 *See e.g.*, 47 U.S.C. § 276(c) (2012); 47 U.S.C. § 252(e)(5) (2012); 47 U.S.C. § 253(d) (2012).

11 47 U.S.C. § 230 (1996).

12 47 U.S.C. §§ 151–162 (2012).

13 47 U.S.C. § 151 (2012).

or interstate or foreign radio transmission of energy."[14] Title II also addresses the goal of developing competitive markets for communications and broadcasting and contains special provisions governing the various Bell entities and AT&T, which commanded much of the FCC's attention in the twentieth century. Most recently, the commission has relied upon Title II as the basis for its authority to regulate broadband Internet access services (BIAS).[15] Of particular import to this article, Title II contains specific provisions that regulate the privacy practices of common carriers, including provisions that impose a duty to protect the confidentiality of the proprietary information of customers and Customer Proprietary Network Information (CPNI).[16]

Title III, "Special Provisions Relating to Radio," outlines how the FCC may regulate "the dissemination of radio communications intended to be received by the public, directly or by the intermediary of relay stations."[17] When Congress passed the Communications Act, the commission had the authority to regulate common carriers and broadcasting, meaning that Title II and Title III essentially outlined the scope of the Federal Communications Commission's substantive regulatory authority. With great advances in wireless communications technologies relying upon radio frequencies, Congress expanded the commission's authority to encompass several other facets of communication, including over-the-air radio frequency transmissions[18] and satellite television,[19] which fall under Title III.

Title IV enumerates the act's procedural and administrative provisions, which describe the processes by which the commission may make new rules, have its rules reviewed, enforce its rules, and investigate new areas of communication.[20] We will discuss this rule making process in some detail later in Part II of this chapter.

Title V contains the act's penal provisions and forfeiture rules. It describes procedural rules governing enforcement actions, what must be shown in order to establish a violation, and the range of penalties that can be imposed.[21] As we shall see in Part IV, FCC enforcement plays a significant role in the FCC's regulatory efforts and is likely to continue to play an important role in its ongoing efforts to guarantee the public interest in the face of risks to privacy and security posed by evolving communications technologies.

Title VI was not a part of the original Communications Act of 1934, but was added by the Cable Communications Act of 1984. Title VI grants the FCC authority to regulate cable communications[22] in order to "promote competition in cable communications"

14 47 U.S.C. § 153(11) (2012). In other words, a common carrier is a "compan[y] that provide[s] telephone service indiscriminately to the public at large." Jonathan E. Nuechterlein & Phillip J. Weiser, Digital crossroads: Telecommunications Law and Policy in the Internet Age 17 (2d ed. 2013).

15 Report and Order on Remand, Declaratory Ruling, and Order, *Protecting and Promoting the Open Internet*, 30 FCC Rcd 5601 (2015) ("Open Internet Order"). While the FCC's Title II reclassification of Broadband Internet Access Services has been controversial, the FCC's reclassification in the 2015 Open Internet Order has been upheld by a federal appellate court. *United States Telecom Assoc. v. FCC*, 825 F.3d 674, 689 (D.C. Cir. 2016) (denying petitions for review of the Open Internet Order), *reh'g en banc denied*, No. 15-1063, 2017 WL 1541517 (D.C. Cir. May 1, 2017) (per curiam).

16 47 U.S.C. § 222 (2012).

17 47 U.S.C. § 153(7) (2012).

18 *See e.g.*, 47 U.S.C. § 307 (2012); 47 U.S.C. § 322 (2012).

19 47 U.S.C. § 338 (2012).

20 47 U.S.C. §§ 401–416 (2012).

21 47 U.S.C. §§ 501–510 (2012).

22 47 U.S.C. §§ 521–573 (2012).

and "assure that cable communications provide and are encouraged to provide the widest possible diversity of information sources" to the public.[23] In order to facilitate these goals, Title VI gives the FCC authority to write and enforce rules governing licensing, content, and fees associated with cable broadcasts.[24] Title VI also describes privacy laws governing the protection and security of the personal information of cable subscribers.[25]

Title VII contains a number of miscellaneous provisions, including provisions regulating the interception or publication of communications and provisions governing the encryption of Public Broadcasting Service programming.[26] Title VII also grants emergency powers to the president in times of war or national emergency[27] and sets forth guidelines governing accessibility for disabled customers, including telephone services for the hearing impaired and closed captioning for some television and cable broadcasts.[28]

B *The Commission's Organizational Structure*

The Federal Communications Commission is an independent regulatory agency headed by five commissioners, one of whom serves as chairman.[29] Each commissioner is nominated by the president and confirmed by the Senate.[30] The commissioners serve five-year terms, which are staggered so that no two expire in the same year.[31] In addition, no more than three of the five commissioners may be from the same political party.[32] Historically, the commissioners have had legal training or experience in the broadcasting field or have held government office prior to appointment.[33] The commissioners are required to meet together once a month, and these meetings are regularly open to the public. During the monthly open meetings, the commissioners make decisions on the business items that the chairman has placed before the commission, but they also regularly make decisions outside open meetings by registering their votes on circulated matters without actually getting together in person as a group.

Many of the commission's functions are delegated to one of its seven bureaus: the Consumer and Governmental Affairs Bureau, the Enforcement Bureau, the International Bureau, the Media Bureau, the Public Safety and Homeland Security Bureau, the Wireless Telecommunications Bureau, and the Wireline Competition Bureau.[34] Each of these bureaus is staffed by specialists who both advise the commissioners and effectuate rules and policies promulgated by the commission.

23 47 U.S.C. §§ 521(1)-(6) (2012).
24 *See e.g.*, 47 U.S.C. § 542 (2012); 47 U.S.C. § 543 (2012); 47 U.S.C. § 533 (2012); 47 U.S.C. § 559 (2012).
25 47 U.S.C. § 551 (2012).
26 Ronald A. Cass, *Review, Enforcement, and Power under the Communications Act of 1934: Choice and Chance in Institutional Design*, *in* A Legislative History of the Communications Act of 1934, at 79 (Max. D. Paglin, ed., Oxford University Press 1989); 47 U.S.C. §§ 601–621 (2012); *see also* 47 U.S.C. § 605 (2012).
27 47 U.S.C. § 606 (2012).
28 *See e.g.*, 47 U.S.C. § 617 (2012); 47 U.S.C. § 611 (2012); 47 U.S.C. § 610 (2012).
29 47 U.S.C. § 154 (a) (2012).
30 47 U.S.C. § 154 (a).
31 47 U.S.C. § 154(c).
32 47 U.S.C. § 154(b)(5).
33 Erwin G. Krasnow & Lawrence D. Longley, The Politics of Broadcast Regulation 27 (1973). For instance, Tom Wheeler worked for the National Cable Television Association from 1976 to 1984 and was the CEO of numerous technical companies prior to his appointment by President Obama. Fed. Comm. Comm'n, https://www.fcc.gov/about/leadership/tom-wheeler?qt-leadership_tabs=0#qt-leadership_tabs.
34 Fed. Comm. Comm'n, https://www.fcc.gov/offices-bureaus.

II The FCC's Rule Making and Enforcement Processes

The Federal Communications Commission operates under the "public interest standard."[35] This standard charges the commission to exercise regulatory authority whenever it is in the "public interest, convenience, and [or] necessity"[36] through both *ex ante* prescriptive rules and *ex post* adjudicatory proceedings.

A *Rule Making Process*

The Administrative Procedure Act of 1946 (APA), which controls how all federal agencies make both formal and informal rules, governs the commission's legislative rule making process.[37] Rule making is the "agency process for formulating, amending, or repealing a rule."[38] Rules promulgated by the FCC fall into three general categories: legislative rules, nonlegislative rules, and organizational and procedural rules.[39] Legislative rules "create legally binding rights and obligations for the agency and the public." Nonlegislative rules "interpret the meaning of statutes or legislative rules that the Commission administers" or "tell the public how the agency plans to exercise some discretionary power that is has."[40] Organizational and procedural rules "describe the agency's structure and the way in which its determinations are made."[41]

The FCC's substantive legislative rules are promulgated pursuant to congressionally delegated authority, which may be specific or provide the commission with broad discretionary authority. The agency typically follows the APA's "notice and comment process" to issue legislative rules.[42] This process does not apply to nonlegislative rule makings or organizational and procedural rule makings, which generally do not require notice and comment to the public.[43] The "notice and comment" process generally begins with a Notice of Proposed Rulemaking (NPRM), a publicly available document that provides citizens with adequate notice that the commission is contemplating a new rule or a change to an existing rule. The NPRM also initiates a period of meaningful public comment.[44] Citizens and other organizations generally have at least thirty-days to comment, after which time the commission will review the comments, make its decision,

35 Erwin G. Krasnow & Jack N. Goodman, *The "Public Interest" Standard: The Search for the Holy Grail*, 50 Fed. Comm. L.J. 605, 606 (1997); Harry P. Warner, *The Administrative Process of the Federal Communications Commission*, 19 S. Cal. L. Rev. 191, 191 (1946).

36 *See supra* note 1, at 14–15; *see also Mid-Texas Commc'n Systems, Inc. v. Am. Tel. & Tel. Co.*, 615 F.2d 1372, 1379 (5th Cir. 1980); *Nat'l Broad. Co. v. United States*, 319 U.S. 190, 216–17 (1943).

37 Vanessa K. Burrows & Todd Garvey, A Brief Overview of Rulemaking and Judicial Review 1 (Cong. Research Serv. 2011), http://www.wise-intern.org/orientation/documents/crsrulemakingcb.pdf; The Administrative Procedure Act, Pub. L. No. 79–404, 60 Stat. 237 (1946) (codified at 5 U.S.C. §§ 551–559).

38 5 U.S.C. § 551(5) (2012).

39 Fed. Comm. Comm'n: Rulemaking Process, https://www.fcc.gov/about-fcc/rulemaking-process.

40 *Id.*

41 *Id.*

42 5 U.S.C. § 553 (2012).

43 Fed. Comm. Comm'n: Rulemaking Process, https://www.fcc.gov/about-fcc/rulemaking-process.

44 *Id.* Citizens of the public can make comments through an electronic online filing system on the FCC's Web site at Fed. Comm. Comm'n, http://apps.fcc.gov/ecfs/;ECFSSESSION=2sGtWPghvQjYnGmpC1pnXhgHJnTpy8GWqRJQGyNZh3pdnQZQLWZv!1951721665!-1566059965.

and publish a report and order detailing that decision. The APA permits an interested party to challenge the agency's final rules and actions in federal court.[45]

It is worth noting that the APA's requirements set the floor for the commission's legislative rule making process. Thus, the FCC may supplement the "notice-and-comment" period with additional rule making procedures when it deems further steps are necessary. For example, in some instances, the FCC will publish a Notice of Inquiry (NOI), requesting public commentary about a broad topic prior to issuing an NPRM in an effort to secure early input from experts and interested parties. The commission may also issue a Further Notice of Proposed Rulemaking (FNPRM) after an NPRM is released, seeking additional public comment about an issue or proposed rule.[46] The Commission can also seek advice and feedback by holding public or *ex parte* proceedings and by allowing the submission of oral and written testimony. In keeping with its overall goal of regulating in the public interest, the FCC regularly makes use of these additional pathways for seeking and receiving advice and public comment with the goal of increasing public participation and facilitating better decision making.

B *Enforcement Process*

It is well established that a federal agency may set policy through *ex ante* rule makings as well as adjudicatory proceedings,[47] such as *ex post* case-by-case enforcement actions.[48] The Communications Act empowers the Commission to enforce the provisions of the act and the commission's rules and orders.[49] The commission has designated the Enforcement Bureau to "serve as the primary Commission entity responsible for enforcement of the Communications Act and other communications statutes, the Commission's rules, Commission orders and Commission authorizations."[50] The bureau exercises this delegated authority in two primary ways: "(1) by initiating investigations, and taking appropriate action if violations are found; and (2) by resolving disputes between industry participants either through mediation and settlement, or adjudication of formal complaints."[51] As in all federal agencies, any enforcement action taken by the bureau or commission must also comply with the APA.[52]

While FCC enforcement actions can take several different forms and processes, typically they begin after the Enforcement Bureau learns of a potential violation, for example, through a consumer or competitor complaint, referral from another FCC

45 5 U.S.C. § 706 (2012).

46 Fed. Comm. Comm'n, https://www.fcc.gov/general/rulemaking-fcc.

47 The FCC's enforcement process is complex and unique and can have several different forms and processes. A full discussion of all the enforcement processes could easily take up the entire chapter. For the sake of brevity and providing of sufficient information to contextualize the specific enforcement actions discussed in the chapter, we have focused our description of the enforcement process on the major components, with a full recognition, of course, that there are several additional nuances and processes that also may apply.

48 5 U.S.C. §§ 553–554 (2012); *see e.g.*, *FCC v. Fox Television Stations Inc.*, 556 U.S. 502, 514–17 (2009); *Encino Motorcars, LLC v. Navarro*, 136 S. Ct. 2117 (2016) (noting that "agencies are free to change their existing policies").

49 47 U.S.C. § 151 (2012). See also 47 U.S.C. §§ 501–510 for a list of several enforcement provisions.

50 47 C.F.R. § 0.111 (2012).

51 Fed. Comm. Comm'n: Enforcement Primer, https://www.fcc.gov/general/enforcement-primer.

52 5 U.S.C. § 554 (2012).

component, referral from another government agency or official, or even a news media source. Once a potential violation has been identified, the Enforcement Bureau implements several investigative tools to collect necessary "fact-specific information."[53] The bureau may, for example, issue Letters of Inquiry (LOI) or subpoenas demanding the production of relevant documents or other evidence, interview witnesses and victims, and visit the site of alleged violations.[54] Once such information has been collected, the Enforcement Bureau analyzes the information to determine whether an apparent violation has indeed occurred. If an investigation produces evidence of an apparent violation, then the Enforcement Bureau has several different options for taking action. For example, it may issue a Notice of Apparent Liability for Forfeiture (NAL) proposing a fine for the alleged violation;[55] a Notice of Violation (NOV), a Notice of Unauthorized Operation (NOUO), or a Citation[56] directing parties to cease and desist violating FCC rules; or it may refer the matter to an administrative law judge or other agency official to adjudicate the potential violation issue an admonishment finding a violation without imposing a forfeiture, or engage the investigation target in settlement negotiations.

In many cases, enforcement matters are resolved by negotiated consent decrees in which targets may admit liability, pay a civil penalty, and submit to a compliance plan. If the Enforcement Bureau is unable to settle with the investigation target, it routinely proceeds to issue an NAL. An NAL is the FCC's version of a complaint. It sets forth the nature of the alleged violation, describes the legal and factual grounds supporting the FCC's alleged violation, and proposes the maximum potential forfeiture. When calculating a proposed forfeiture, the Enforcement Bureau takes into consideration the "nature, circumstances, extent, and gravity of the violation and, with respect to the violator, the degree of culpability, any history of prior offenses, ability to pay, and such other matters as justice may require."[57] It also abides by the commission's forfeiture guidelines, first published in 1997.[58]

The NAL directs the target to pay the proposed forfeiture or file a written response, usually within thirty days. Alternatively, the target may choose to settle the matter through a consent decree with the Enforcement Bureau. If a settlement is not reached, the target does not pay the proposed forfeiture, and the Enforcement Bureau concludes that there is a violation after reviewing the NAL response and the full record, the bureau may issue a formal Forfeiture Order imposing a fine or make a recommendation to the commission to issue such an order upon the majority vote of the commission.[59] The Forfeiture Order

[53] Letters from Tom Wheeler, Chairman, Federal Communications Commission, to Senators Johnson, Moran, Blunt, Heller, and Daines, https://apps.fcc.gov/edocs_public/attachmatch/DOC-337281A1.pdf.

[54] *Id.*

[55] 47 C.F.R. § 0.311 (2014) provides that the chief of the Enforcement Bureau is "delegated authority to perform all functions of the Bureau, described in § 0.111, provided that" certain matters are "referred to the Commission en banc for disposition." Such matters include "forfeiture notices and forfeiture orders if the amount is more than $100,000 in the case of common carriers or more than $25,000 in the case of all other persons or entities." 47 C.F.R. § 0.311 (2014).

[56] Notably, citations are typically issued to entities that are not licensed or otherwise authorized by the commisison.

[57] Travis LeBlanc, *Enforcement Fines: The Collection Process*, Fed. Comm. Comm'n (Nov. 25, 2015, 1:17 PM), https://www.fcc.gov/news-events/blog/2015/11/25/enforcement-fines-collection-process.

[58] Letters from Tom Wheeler, Chairman, Federal Communications Commission, to Senators Johnson, Moran, Blunt, Heller, and Daines, https://apps.fcc.gov/edocs_public/attachmatch/DOC-337281A1.pdf.

[59] *Id.*

adjudicates the violation and imposes a forfeiture penalty that must typically be paid within thirty days. Parties subject to these orders may seek reconsideration or review by the bureau or commission by filing a timely Petition for Reconsideration or Application for Review. These petitions or applications are resolved by published orders.

The target of an enforcement action may, of course, pay a proposed or imposed fine at any time. If, however, a party does not pay an imposed forfeiture, the commission refers the matter to the Department of Justice, which is authorized to file an action in federal district court to collect the forfeiture. Because most of the parties subjected to an enforcement action are FCC regulates who regularly interact with the commission, most enforcement actions are resolved through settlement or payment of the forfeiture before the Department of Justice prosecutes the violation. Thus, the resolution of virtually all enforcement actions takes the form of FCC administrative written notices and orders, which are published and available on the FCC's Web site.[60] This body of actions and precedental orders could be seen as a sort of common law of the FCC, providing an invaluable complement to the Communications Act and FCC regulations.

III The Federal Communications Commission's Privacy Authority

The commission has a long history of safeguarding citizens' privacy interests in their communications and personal information.[61] Authority for these efforts derives from the Communications Act and the commission's rules. In this section, we review the major sources of this authority.[62]

A *Section 222 of the Communications Act*

Over twenty years ago, Congress enacted Section 222 of the Communications Act as part of the Telecommunications Act of 1996.[63] Section 222 establishes that "every telecommunications carrier has a duty to protect the confidentiality of proprietary information of, and relating to, other telecommunication carriers, equipment manufacturers, and customers."[64] Section 222 also protects CPNI, which the act defines as "information that relates to the quantity, technical configuration, type, destination, location, and amount of use of a telecommunications service subscribed to by any customer … and information contained in the bills pertaining to telephone exchange service or telephone toll

60 For example, adjudicatory orders and consent decrees are available at http://transition.fcc.gov/eb/Orders/. NOVs and NOUOs are available at http://transition.fcc.gov/eb/FieldNotices/.

61 Report and Order, *Application of Open Network Architecture and Nondiscrimination Safeguards to GTE Corp.*, 9 FCC Rcd 4922, 4944–45 (1994); Memorandum Opinion and Order, *Application of Open Network Architectures and Nondiscrimination Safeguards to GTE Corp.*, 11 FCC Rcd 1388, 1419–25 (1995); Report and Order, *Furnishing of Customer Premises Equipment by Bell Operating Telephone Companies and the Independent Telephone Companies*, 2 FCC Rcd 143 (1987), *recon. on other grounds*, 3 FCC Rcd 22 (1987), *aff'd*, Ill. *Bell Tel. Co. v. FCC*, 883 F.2d 104 (D.C. Cir. 1989).

62 This section focuses on the principal privacy authorities available to the commission. It does not purport to discuss every authority that the commission has or could use to protect consumer privacy.

63 *See generally* Telecommunications Act of 1996, Pub. L. No. 104–104, 110 Stat. 56 (1996) (codified as amended in sections of 47 U.S.C.).

64 47 U.S.C. § 222(a) (2012). Section 222(b) provides more detail regarding how carriers may use proprietary information: "[a] telecommunications carrier that receives or obtains proprietary information from another carrier for purposes of providing any telecommunications service shall use such information only for such purpose, and shall not use such information for its own marketing efforts."

service."[65] Specifically, except as required by law or with customer approval,[66] Section 222 prohibits telecommunications carriers, also known as common carriers, "from us[ing], disclos[ing], or permitt[ing] access to individually identifiable customer proprietary network information in its provision of (A) the telecommunications service from which such information is derived, or (B) services necessary to, or used in, the provision of such telecommunications service, including the publishing of directories."[67] Unless otherwise authorized by the customer or required by law, carriers may not use CPNI for other purposes or disclose CPNI to third parties.

The Commission has promulgated regulations implementing Section 222.[68] These regulations apply to all common carriers as well as providers of interconnected Voice over Internet Protocol (VoIP) services.[69] Generally speaking, these rules apply to voice services and elaborate on the obligations of common carriers and interconnected VoIP providers to obtain customer approval through opt-in or opt-out processes,[70] notify customers of their privacy rights,[71] safeguard CPNI,[72] and notify the Federal Bureau of Investigation and United States Secret Service of CPNI breaches.[73] In addition, these common carriers are required to file[74] annual certifications with the commission documenting their efforts to protect CPNI, which "includes some of the most sensitive personal information that carriers have about their customers as a result of their business relationship[s]."[75]

Section 222's limits on the use and disclosure of CPNI have important implications for customer privacy. Information about whom a customer calls, when, and from where can be revealing in itself. For example, a call to an abortion clinic or suicide hotline may reveal very intimate details about a consumer's life and circumstances. Aggregated and combined with other consumer data, CPNI could paint a detailed picture of consumers and their lives, often revealing habits, events, and even thoughts.

65 47 U.S.C. § 222(h)(1).

66 Section 222(f) places some qualifications on what constitutes customer approval for the use, disclosure, or access to certain CPNI.

67 47 U.S.C. § 222(c)(1). Sections 222(c)(2)–(3) and (d) enumerate certain instances wherein common carriers may use, disclose, or permit access to CPNI.

68 *See* Second Report and Order and FNPRM, *Implementation of the Telecommunications Act of 1996*, 13 FCC Rcd 8061, 8066–67 (1998); *see also e.g.*, 47 C.F.R. §§ 64.2008–64.2011.

69 Notice of Proposed Rulemaking, *Protecting the Privacy of Customers of Broadband and Other Telecommunications Services*, 31 FCC Rcd 2500, 2511 n.44 (2016) ("Broadband Privacy NPRM"); Report and Order and Further Notice of Proposed Rulemaking, *Implementation of the Telecommunications Act of 1996: Telecommunications Carriers' Use of Customer Proprietary Network Information and Other Customer Information*, 22 FCC Rcd 6927 (2007).

70 47 C.F.R. § 64.2007.

71 47 C.F.R. § 64.2008.

72 47 C.F.R. §§ 64.2009–10.

73 47 C.F.R. § 64.2001.

74 The commission has since reconsidered the requirement that common carriers must file annual certifications documenting their efforts to protect CPNI. Broadband Privacy NPRM at 2552. "Should we require BIAS providers to file an annual compliance certification with the Commission, as is required under the current Section 222 rules? Are there alternative approaches to safeguard customers' proprietary information and boost customer confidence in the privacy of their customer PI that we should consider?" *Id.*

75 FCC Enforcement Advisory, *Annual CPNI Certifications Due March 1, 2014*, No. 2014-2 (Feb. 5, 2014). The commission typically issues annual Enforcement Advisories reminding regulated entities of their obligations to file timely certifications detailing their policies and practices with respect to CPNI.

When Congress originally enacted Section 222, the provision's language "reflect[ed] voice services,"[76] and the regulations the commission promulgated in 1998 and 2007 implementing Section 222 were tailored to voice services. But, on February 26, 2015, the commission's Open Internet Order reclassified providers of broadband Internet access services, also known as Internet Service Providers (ISPs), as common carriers subject to jurisdiction under Title II of the Communications Act.[77] In the Open Internet Order, the commission applied the statutory provisions of Section 222 to ISPs, but declined at that time to apply the FCC's regulations implementing Section 222.[78] Instead, the commission determined that it would pursue a separate rule making to determine what, if any, privacy rules should apply to ISPs.[79]

On April 1, 2016, the commission issued an extensive NPRM seeking comment on the application of the Communications Act's traditional privacy requirements to ISPs and other telecommunications services.[80] In that NPRM, the commission noted that "Internet Service Providers (ISPs) would benefit from additional, concrete guidance explaining the privacy responsibilities created by the Communications Act."[81] The concern was that "ISPs are 'in a position to develop highly detailed and comprehensive profiles of their customers – and to do so in a manner that may be completely invisible.' … they have control of a great deal of data that must be protected against data breaches."[82] In addition to considering the applicability of the FCC's Title II privacy regulations to ISPs, the FCC proposed specifically to define Customer Proprietary Information (CPI) within the meaning of Section 222(a). The commission proposed that CPI would include "both CPNI as established by Section 222(h); and personally identifiable information (PII)," that is, any information "linked or linkable to an individual."[83] In doing so, the commission proposed to "expand the … existing definition [of protected information] to encompass all customer PI (rather than limiting it to CPNI)."[84] The NPRM also set forth several proposals concerning transparency, choice, and security. In particular, the commission sought comment on when ISPs should be required to obtain opt-in versus opt-out approval from customers, the security requirements that ISPs should meet, and under what circumstances data breach notifications should be made, if at all.[85] Importantly, the commission's proposed rules apply to ISPs only, not to general Web sites or "edge providers" such as Facebook and Twitter, or to the non-BIAS services that may be offered by an ISP (e.g., Pay-TV satellite or cable services).

76 FCC Proposes to Give Broadband Consumers Increased Choice, Transparency and Security for Their Personal Data, 2016 WL 1312848, at *6 (2016).
77 Open Internet Order at 5618.
78 *Id.*
79 *Id.*
80 Broadband Privacy NPRM at 2501–02.
81 *Id.* at 2501.
82 *Id.* (internal citation omitted); *see also* Chairman Wheeler's Proposal to Give Broadband Consumers Increased Choice, Transparency & Security with Respect to Their Data, 2016 WL 1221999 (2016) (discussing how "consumers should have effective control over how their personal information is used and shared").
83 Broadband Privacy NPRM at 2507, 2519.
84 *Id.* at 2524.
85 *Id.* at 2508–09, 2557–58.

On October 27, 2016, the FCC officially adopted the proposed privacy regulations implementing Section 222 and ruled that they were indeed applicable to ISPs.[86] The commission's Broadband Privacy Report and Order grouped these regulations into three categories: (1) rules to ensure that telecommunications carriers remain transparent with their customers about how they intend to collect and use customers' personal information, (2) rules to protect consumers' ability to choose how their personal information is used, and (3) rules to secure such personal information from data breaches.[87]

In order to ensure transparency, the commission mandated that telecommunications carriers distribute "privacy notices . . . at the point of sale" that are consistently available to customers on whatever forum the carrier uses for its operations.[88] The commission further required that these notices "clearly and accurately inform customers about" the carrier's privacy policies; namely, "what confidential information the carriers collect, how they use it, under what circumstances they share it, and the categories of entities with which they will share it."[89]

The commission also adopted three rules to ensure that customers have the ability to choose how, if at all, carriers use their personal information: an "Opt-in Approval" provision, an "Opt-out Approval" provision, and an "Exceptions to Customer Approval Requirements" provision.[90] The "Opt-in Approval" provision mandated that ISPs "obtain affirmative 'opt-in' consent from consumers to use and share [their] *sensitive information*."[91] The "Opt-out Approval" provision allowed ISPs to use and distribute "*non-sensitive* information unless a customer 'opts-out.'"[92] The "Exceptions to Customer Approval Requirements" provision allowed ISPs to distribute and utilize consumer information "in order to provide broadband services."[93]

Lastly, the commission implemented the "Data Security and Breach Notification" rules to ensure that consumers' personal information remained secure from data breaches. These rules required that BIAS providers and other carriers (1) "take reasonable measures to secure customer PI"[94] and (2) "notify affected customers, the Commission,

86 Report and Order, *Protecting the Privacy of Customers Broadband and Other Telecommunications Services*, 2016 WL 6538282 (Oct. 27, 2016) ("Broadband Privacy Report and Order"); *see also* FCC Adopts Privacy Rules to Give Broadband Consumers Increased Choice, Transparency and Security for their Personal Data, 2016 WL 6300085, at *1–2 (Oct. 27, 2016).

87 Broadband Privacy Report and Order at 4–6.

88 *Id.* at 4. Examples of such forums include phone applications, websites, or other mediums.

89 *Id.* The FCC further mandated that customers must receive notice of any "material changes" to such privacy policies.

90 *Id.* at 4–5.

91 FCC Adopts Privacy Rules to Give Broadband Consumers Increased Choice, Transparency and Security for their Personal Data, 2016 WL 6300085, at *1 (Oct. 27, 2016) (emphasis added). There are several categories of information that constitute "sensitive information": "precise geo-location, financial information, health information, children's information, social security numbers, web browsing history, app usage history and the content of communications."

92 *Id.* (emphasis added). "Non-sensitive" information includes "all other individually identifiable customer information" that is not considered "sensitive information," including "email address or service tier information."

93 Broadband Privacy Report and Order at 5. For instance, this provision gives ISPs the ability to utilize and distribute consumer information in order to make sure that a communication meant for a certain individual "reaches that destination."

94 *Id.* The FCC did not specifically state how BIAS providers must secure customer PI, but noted "a carrier must adopt security practices appropriately calibrated to the nature and scope of its activities, the sensitivity of the underlying data, the size of the provider, and technical feasibility."

and the FBI and Secret Service" of data breaches unless the provider can "reasonably determine" that the breach does not pose a risk to the affected customers.[95]

Not only did the commission adopt these transparency, choice, and security regulations implementing Section 222, but they also clarified the type of information protected under Section 222. In its Broadband Privacy Report and Order, the FCC stated clearly that Section 222 would protect customer proprietary information, as opposed to just CPNI.[96] The commission went on to note that customer proprietary information included "three types of information collected by telecommunications carriers . . . that are not mutually exclusive: (i) individually identifiable Customer Proprietary Network Information (CPNI) as defined in Section 222(h); (ii) personally identifiable information (PII); and (iii) content of communications."[97]

Approximately five months after the broadband privacy rules were released, however, a newly-elected Congress began efforts to overrule them pursuant to its authority under the Congressional Review Act, which "allows lawmakers to overturn any regulation imposed during the final six months of the previous administration, with a simple majority vote in each chamber of Congress."[98] On March 7, 2017, Senator Jeff Flake introduced a resolution to overrule the Broadband Privacy Report and Order, which states, in its entirety:

> *Resolved by the Senate and House of Representatives of the United States of America in Congress assembled*, That Congress disapproves the rule submitted by the Federal Communications Commission relating to 'Protecting the Privacy of Customers of Broadband and Other Telecommunications Services' (81 Fed. Reg. 87274 (December 2, 2016)), and such rule shall have no force or effect.[99]

After a 50-48 vote in the Senate and a 215-205 vote in the House, Congress succeeded in overruling the new regulations and passed Senator Flake's resolution, which was subsequently signed into law by President Donald J. Trump.[100] FCC Chairman Ajit Pai

95 *Id.* The timeframe within which notice must be given varies depending on how many customers are affected by the breach.

96 *Id.* at 3.

97 Id.

98 Brian Naylor, *Republicans Are Using An Obscure Law to Repeal Some Obama-Era Regulations*, NPR (Apr. 9, 2017, 7:00 AM), http://www.npr.org/2017/04/09/523064408/republicans-are-using-an-obscure-law-to-repeal-some-obama-era-regulations. Prior to President Trump's term, the Congressional Review Act had only been used once before to overturn an ergonomics regulation instituted during the Clinton administration. As of April 2017, however, the Trump-Era Congress has used the Congressional Review Act to overturn 11 different regulations instituted during the Obama administration. *Id.*; *see also* Cecilia Kang, *Congress Moves to Overturn Obama-Era Online Privacy Rules*, N.Y. TIMES (Mar. 28, 2017), https://www.nytimes.com/2017/03/28/technology/congress-votes-to-overturn-obama-era-online-privacy-rules.html.

99 S.J. Res. 34, 115 Cong. (2017), https://www.congress.gov/115/bills/sjres34/BILLS-115sjres34enr.pdf. For more information on the resolution, go to https://www.congress.gov/bill/115th-congress/senate-joint-resolution/34.

100 Cecilia Kang, *Congress Moves to Strike Internet Privacy Rules From Obama Era*, N.Y. TIMES (Mar. 23, 2017), https://www.nytimes.com/2017/03/23/technology/congress-moves-to-strike-internet-privacy-rules-from-obama-era.html; *see also* Cecilia Kang, *Congress Moves to Overturn Obama-Era Online Privacy Rules*, N.Y. TIMES (Mar. 28, 2017), https://www.nytimes.com/2017/03/28/technology/congress-votes-to-overturn-obama-era-online-privacy-rules.html. President Donald Trump officially signed off on Congress's decision to overrule the broadband privacy rules on April 3, 2017. Rob McLean and Seth Fiegerman, *President Trump Just Signed off on Killing Your Internet Privacy Protections*, CNN (Apr. 3, 2017, 10:14 PM), http://money.cnn.com/2017/04/03/technology/internet-privacy-law-trump/.

praised the decision, stating that "President Trump and Congress have appropriately invalidated one part of the Obama-era plan for regulating the Internet. . . . Those flawed privacy rules . . . were designed to benefit one group of favored companies, not online consumers."[101] Nevertheless, Pai has noted that the FCC will still retain its statutory authority under Section 222 of the Communications Act.[102]

Congress may have overruled the broadband privacy rules at the federal level, but several states have begun the process of passing legislation to implement their own state-level broadband privacy protections. For instance, Minnesota, Maryland, and Montana, among others, have drafted, introduced, and or already adopted bills with provisions that mirror the FCC's overruled regulations.[103] Minnesota, in fact, recently passed legislation that requires telecommunications carriers to obtain affirmative consent from customers prior to collecting their personal information.[104] It is unclear how many states will follow suit, but in light of Congress's actions state-level legislation may be the most likely avenue for such protections at this juncture. Several senators introduced a new bill in April 2017 to restore the overruled privacy regulations, but at the time this chapter was written there had been no movement on the bill.[105]

B *Unjust and Unreasonable Privacy Practices*

Section 201(b) of the Communications Act prohibits common carriers from engaging in unjust or unreasonable acts or practices. This provision applies to all "charges, practices, classifications, and regulators for and in connection with" a common carrier service. In the past, the commission has analogized its Section 201(b) authority to the Federal Trade Commission's Section 5 authority, which prohibits unfair and deceptive acts and practices.[106] Thus, the commission has found that deceptive acts and practices, for example, are unjust and unreasonable in violation of Section 201(b).[107] Just as the Federal

101 Rob McLean and Seth Fiegerman, *supra* note 100. Notably, Chairman Pai has also stated that stripping the FTC of its original jurisdiction over the Internet two years ago was a mistake, as the FCC has "no real experience in the field." So, now that the broadband privacy rules have been overruled, the FCC can work with the FTC to "restore the FTC's authority" and create a "comprehensive framework that will protect [consumer] privacy." Ajit Pai and Maureen Ohlhausen, *No, Republicans Didn't Just Strip Away Your Internet Privacy Rights*, WASH. POST (Apr. 4, 2017).

102 Amir Nasr, *Pai: FCC Required to Ensure Internet Privacy Even Without Agency Rules*, MORNING CONSULT (Mar. 8, 2017), https://morningconsult.com/2017/03/08/pai-fcc-required-ensure-internet-privacy-even-without-agency-rules/.

103 Tony Romm, *At least Three States Are Trying to Replace the Online Rules Nixed by Trump*, RECODE (Apr. 6, 2017, 2:47 PM), https://www.recode.net/2017/4/6/15208800/states-fix-law-online-privacy-congress-trump-white-house-fcc; *see also* Michael Dresser, *Maryland Republicans Head Off Democrats' Effort to Introduce Internet Privacy Bill*, BALT. SUN (Apr. 3, 2017, 4:35 PM), http://www.baltimoresun.com/news/maryland/politics/bs-md-internet-privacy-20170403-story.html.

104 S.F. 1937, 2017 Leg., 90 Sess. (Minn. 2017) ("No telecommunications or internet service provider . . . may collect personal information from a customer resulting from the customer's use of the telecommunications or internet service provider without express written approval from the customer."). For more information on the Minnesota bill, go to https://www.revisor.mn.gov/bills/bill.php?b=senate&f=SF1937&ssn=0&y=2017.

105 VAN HOLLEN, https://www.vanhollen.senate.gov/content/van-hollen-introduces-legislation-fully-restore-broadband-privacy-protections (last visited May 4, 2017).

106 15 U.S.C. § 45.

107 *See* Notice of Apparent Liability for Forfeiture, *STI Telecom Inc.*, 26 FCC Rcd 12808 (2011); Notice of Apparent Liability for Forfeiture, *Locus Telecommunications, Inc.*, 26 FCC Rcd 12818 (2011).

Trade Commission has, the FCC has used Section 201(b) to enforce measures against deceptive, unfair, or unreasonable privacy practices such as a common carrier's failure to comply with the representations contained in its privacy policy or having unreasonable security practices.[108]

C *The Telephone Consumer Protection Act and the Telephone Broadcast Rule*

As early as 1945, the FCC actively protected citizens' privacy in their telephone conversations by regulating the use of telephone recording devices. During World War II, the Navy, Army, and other government entities used recording devices, and in the years following World War II, civilians and various business organizations also began to operate recording devices. In response, six telephone companies created tariff regulations that appeared to prohibit the use of recording devices altogether.[109]

In 1945, the FCC initiated an investigation into the use of telephone recording devices to determine whether the tariff regulations were appropriate and who should have the authority to use the devices.[110] The FCC's subsequent investigation revealed few objections to the use of recording devices in the abstract. Rather, the main concerns went to whether and how parties should be *notified* that their conversations were being recorded.[111] The commission ultimately decided in 1947 that, although recording could not be forbidden entirely, the devices should be used only when parties were given proper notice by way of an automatic beep-tone warning.[112]

The FCC's rules governing the recording of telephone conversations remained controversial for decades. In 1978, the commission issued a Notice of Proposed Rulemaking wherein it stated that it was "keenly appreciative of the importance and desirability of privacy in telephone conversations," but nonetheless believed that the beep-tone notice requirement was "unenforceable in its present form."[113] Thus, the commission shifted its focus from notice to consent among the parties being recorded.[114] But this did not settle the matter, and the commission's rules remained in flux until they were ultimately abandoned. Currently, the commission "has no rules regarding recording of telephone conversations by individuals,"[115] but it maintains a role in ensuring that citizens' wireless

[108] See infra Part IV for a more detailed discussion of the bureau's enforcement actions.

[109] Report, *Use of Recording Devices in Connection with Telephone Service*, 11 F.C.C. 1033, 1033, 1038–39 (1947).

[110] *Id.* at 1039–43.

[111] *Id.* at 1042–43. The telephone companies argued that notice was necessary to protect user privacy. The recording device manufacturers, however, argued that the notice function was superfluous because telephone "users could be generally advised … that the recorders may be used," and that would ultimately put them on notice. *Id.* at 1050.

[112] *Id.* at 1054.

[113] Notice of Proposed Rulemaking, *Use of Recording Devices in Connection with Telephone Service*, 67 F.C.C.2d 1392, 1398 (1978) (internal citation omitted).

[114] *Id.* at 1399–1400. The commission ruled that consensual recordings did not require beep-tone notice; that users making emergency calls, such as those made to fire and police departments, constructively consented to recording; and that persons making phone calls for unlawful purposes waive their right to notice and consent. *Id.*

[115] Fed. Comm. Comm'n, Consumer Guide: Recording Telephone Conversations (2015), http://transition.fcc.gov/cgb/consumerfacts/recordcalls.pdf. There are, however, a host of federal and state laws governing both government and private recording of land telephone lines, which the FCC regards as sufficient to preserve the public interests at stake without additional regulatory intervention.

telephone conversations remain private by implementing and interpreting several provisions: Section 705 of the Communications Act, the Telephone Consumer Protection Act, and 47 C.F.R. § 73.1206.

Section 705 governs the interception of cellular and wireless telephone signals.[116] It prohibits the interception of cellular and wireless telephone signals for personal or commercial gain and bars the use, manufacture, or sale of devices capable of intercepting and decoding cellular or wireless telephone signals.[117] Though not related to preventing wireless interception, the Telephone Consumer Protection Act (TCPA) also serves as a major source of telephone privacy authority. Enacted by Congress in 1991, and codified at 47 U.S.C. § 227, the TCPA protects customers' privacy rights by prohibiting unlawful telephone solicitation. In particular, the TCPA generally prohibits nonconsensual robocalls, which are calls "using any automatic telephone dialing system or an artificial or prerecorded voice" for the purposes of advertising and other solicitation.[118]

The TCPA requires that the commission "prescribe regulations to implement the methods and procedures for protecting [subscriber] privacy rights."[119] Acting on this authority, the commission has promulgated a number of important rules relating to telephone privacy. Take, for example, 47 C.F.R. § 64.1200. Like Section 227, Section 64.1200 prohibits unlawful telemarketing solicitation over phone, fax, and computer,[120] mandates that companies allow users to unsubscribe from or "opt-out" of unwanted solicitation,[121] and prohibits companies to call persons who are on national or company-specific "do-not-call" registries.[122]

The commission also relies on 47 C.F.R. § 73.1206 to protect the privacy of consumer telephone conversations. Section 73.1206 requires that persons intending to "recor[d] a telephone conversation for broadcast, or broadcas[t] such a conversation simultaneously with its occurrence, ... shall inform any party to the call of the ... intention to broadcast the conversation, except where such party is aware, or may be presumed to be aware from the circumstances of the conversation, that it is being or likely will be broadcast."[123]

Regulations such as Section 705, the TCPA, 47 C.F.R. § 64.1200, and 47 C.F.R. § 73.1206 advance the public interest by protecting consumers' privacy interests in their telephone communications. Moreover, the commission has broad authority under the TCPA to prescribe additional rules necessary to ensure that privacy going forward. In light of that authority, there is no doubt that the commission will continue to play a significant role in securing telephone privacy in the future.

116 47 U.S.C § 605 (2012).

117 For a discussion in more depth of Section 705 see infra notes 129–32.

118 47 U.S.C. § 227(b)(1)(a) (2012).

119 47 U.S.C. § 227(c)(2) (2012).

120 47 C.F.R. § 64.1200(a)(4) (2012).

121 47 C.F.R. § 64.1200(a)(4)(iii)(C).

122 47 C.F.R. § 64.1200(c)(2).

123 47 C.F.R. § 73.1206 (2012). "Such awareness is presumed to exist only when the other party to the call is associated with the station (such as employee or part-time reporter), or where the other party originates the call and it is obvious that it is in connection with a program in which the station customarily broadcasts telephone conversations." *Id.*

D *Privacy for Paid Television Services*

The commission relies on Sections 631 and 338 of the Communications Act to protect the privacy of consumers of cable and satellite television. Congress enacted Section 631, codified at 47 U.S.C. § 551, as part of the Cable Communications Act of 1984.[124] Section 631 mandates that cable operators inform cable subscribers of the nature of any PII they collect.[125] Section 631 also prohibits cable operators from collecting PII or disclosing PII without prior subscriber consent[126] and requires that operators "take such actions as are necessary" to store and protect any PII they collect from unauthorized access.[127] For PII that cable operators do collect, Section 631 places an affirmative obligation on the operators to "destroy" PII "if the information is no longer necessary for the purpose for which it was collected."[128]

In addition to the subscriber notice requirements, Section 631 provides cable subscribers with several important privacy rights. Cable subscribers have a right to request access to all PII about the subscriber that is collected and maintained by the cable operator.[129] The section also contains a private right of action permitting "any person aggrieved by an act of a cable operator in violation of [Section 631]" to file a civil action in federal court for actual and punitive damages as well as reasonable attorneys fees, "in addition to any other lawful remedy available to a cable subscriber."[130] Sections 338(i)(1)–(8) of the Communications Act similarly prohibit the unlawful use, collection, and disclosure of PII in the context of satellite television.

Unlike Section 222, which refers to the broader concept of customer proprietary information of which PII is a component, Section 631 expressly applies to PII only. In its Broadband Privacy NPRM, issued in 2016, the commission proposed to define PII to include not only information that identifies a specific individual, but also information that is "linked or linkable to an individual."[131] The commission also sought comment on the implications of this definition for common carriers, cable providers, and satellite providers.[132] In essence, the commission considered whether consumer privacy protections

124 The commission had previously promulgated several rules citing its general authority to regulate cable television, which were upheld by the Supreme Court in 1968 in *United States v. Southwestern Cable Co.*, 392 U.S. 157 (1968). But it was not until 1984 that Congress ultimately ratified those rules through the Cable Communications Act.

125 47 U.S.C. § 551(a)(1)(A) (2012).

126 47 U.S.C. § 551(b)(1).

127 47 U.S.C. § 551(c)(1). "[A] cable operator … shall take such actions as are necessary to prevent unauthorized access to [PII] by a person other than the subscriber or cable operator." *Id.* This provision, however, does have exceptions. For example, under 47 U.S.C. § 555(h) a cable operator may pursuant to court order disclose PII to government officials investigating criminal cases as long as the subject of the information is permitted to contest the request in court. Notably, there is not a provision permitting governmental entities to obtain this information in noncriminal proceedings Furthermore, under 47 U.S.C. § 555(c)(2)(a) "[a] cable operator may disclose such information if the disclosure is – necessary to render, or conduct a legitimate business activity related to, a cable service."

128 47 U.S.C. § 551(e). There are two exceptions limiting this destruction requirement when a subscriber request for PII is pending or pursuant to a court order. *See id.*

129 47 U.S.C. § 551(d).

130 47 U.S.C. § 551(f).

131 Broadband Privacy NPRM at 2519.

132 *Id.* at 2513 ("To the extent we adopt rules that harmonize the privacy requirements under Section 222 with the requirements for cable and satellite providers under Sections 631 and 338, should we understand

should differ on the basis of communications service provided or whether the protections should be consistent across the various technologies regulated by the FCC.

In the 2016 Broadband Privacy Report and Order, the commission adopted a new definition of customer proprietary information, including "any information that is linked or reasonably linkable to an individual or device."[133] It also "extend[ed] this definition to all Section 222 contexts,"[134] which include the conduct of "all telecommuncations carriers providing telecommunciations services subject to Title II, including broadband Internet access service (BIAS)," and interconnected VoIP services.[135] As previously noted, however, Congress overruled the Broadband Privacy Report and Order rules in March of 2017. In overruling these regulations, one may presume that Congress also overruled the new definition of personally identifiable information. However, the effect of Congress's conduct on parts of the Broadband Privacy Report and Order other than the transparency, choice, and security rules truly remains to be seen.[136]

E *Wireless, Wi-Fi, and GPS Jamming and Interception*

The Communications Act and the commission's rules contain several provisions protecting wireless communications from unauthorized interception or access. Sections 301 and 333 of the Communications Act generally prohibit the unlawful transmission and interception of wireless communications. These provisions serve as sources of authority for the commission to protect consumer privacy in the context of radio transmissions. Section 301 prohibits the use or operation of "any apparatus for the transmission of energy or communications or signals by radio … when interference is caused by such use or operation with the transmission of such energy, communications, or signals from within said State to any place beyond its borders," unless such use is licensed and authorized.[137] Section 333 further prohibits persons from "maliciously interfer[ing] with or caus[ing] interference to any radio communications of any station licensed or authorized by or under this Act or operated by the United States Government."[138] Together, these two provisions work to proscribe the unauthorized interception or blocking of wireless transmissions.

Traditional radio transmissions are not the only kinds of transmissions that Sections 301 and 333 protect. Wireless transmissions also include any kind of communications

the term 'subscriber' in those provisions of the Act to be coextensive with the term 'customer' we propose here?").

133 Broadband Privacy Report and Order at 26. "Information is linked or reasonably linkable to an individual or device if it can reasonably be used on its own, in context, or in combination to identify an individual or device, or to logically associate with other information about a specific individual or device." *Id.*

134 *Id.* at 29.

135 *Id.* at 12–13.

136 Up until now, the commentary regarding Congress's overruling of the Broadband Privacy Report and Order has been focused on how the transparency, choice, and security regulations were overturned. There has been no mention, however, that we could find, as to whether other aspects of the Report and Order, like the new definitions of PII, CPNI, and customer PI, were overruled as well. That, in conjunction with the brevity and vagueness of Senator Franks' resolution, see supra note 99, makes it truly unclear whether Congress intended to overrule the Report and Order in its *entirety*, or *just* the transparency, choice, and security regulations.

137 47 U.S.C. § 301 (2012).

138 47 U.S.C. § 333 (2012).

that use portions of the radio spectrum (licensed or unlicensed). For instance, Wi-Fi and Bluetooth transmissions as well as global positioning system (GPS) signals rely on radio frequency for transmission. Thus, Sections 301 and 333 also prohibit interference with Wi-Fi, Bluetooth, and GPS signals. In this context, "jammers" have become the topic of much discussion. Jammers, "which are commonly called signal blockers … are illegal radio frequency transmitters that are designed to block, jam, or otherwise interfere with authorized radio communications."[139] Among other disruptions, these devices can prevent cell phones from receiving calls and text, prevent Wi-Fi enabled devices from connecting to the Internet, and prevent GPS devices from receiving correct location information.

Specifically, the commission has relied on Section 333 to protect consumer access to Wi-Fi from being blocked or jammed by third parties. Wi-Fi blocking occurs when a company or person inhibits another individual from using his or her own personal Wi-Fi hotspots. The FCC's Enforcement Bureau has issued multiple advisories explaining that Wi-Fi blocking is prohibited[140] and both an FCC chairman and FCC commissioner have publicly criticized the practice.[141]

F *Intercepting Cellular Phone Communications*

Though not traditional "jammers," international mobile subscriber identity (IMSI) catchers, also called cell site simulators, could be regulated under Sections 301 and 333. Much has already been written about the use of these devices by law enforcement, but the prohibitions of Sections 301 and 333 apply to all nonfederal users as well, including private individuals and corporations.[142] Cell site simulators have several varieties; in general they can be used to gather device identification numbers, location information, call metadata, and, in some cases, content from cellular phones.[143] These devices obtain this information by imitating cellular base towers linked to legitimate cellular networks.[144] By impersonating cell towers, cell site simulators effectively "trick" cellular devices within their areas of operation into registering with them instead of an authorized cell tower. This allows the cell site simulator to gather the same location and device identifying

139 Fed. Comm. Comm'n, GPS, Wi-Fi, and Cell Phone Jammers: Frequently Asked Questions, https://transition.fcc.gov/eb/jammerenforcement/jamfaq.pdf.

140 FCC Enforcement Advisory, *Jammer Use is Prohibited: Prohibition Applies to Use by the Public and State and Local Government Agencies, Including State and Local Law Enforcement Agencies*, No. 2014–05 (Dec. 8, 2014); FCC Enforcement Advisory, *Wi-Fi Blocking is Prohibited: Persons or Businesses Causing Intentional Interference to Wi-Fi Hot Spots Are Subject to Enforcement Action*, No. 2015–01 (Jan. 27, 2015).

141 Tom Wheeler, Chairman, Statement on Protecting Consumers from Hotel Wi-Fi Blocking (Jan. 2015), https://apps.fcc.gov/edocs_public/attachmatch/DOC-331706A1.pdf.

142 Our discussion here is limited to the implications of cell site simulators on radio frequencies. Any implications from law enforcement use of cell site simulators on criminal procedure, civil liberties, or constitutional rights (for example) are beyond the scope of this chapter.

143 Stephanie K. Pell & Christopher Soghoian, *A Lot More than a Pen Register, and Less than a Wiretap: What the StingRay Teaches Us about How Congress Should Approach the Reform of Law Enforcement Surveillance Authorities*, 16 Yale J.L. & Tech. 134, 142 (2014).

144 *Id.* at 144–46. Cell phones are in constant communication with local cellular base towers. This allows cellular service providers to know where to direct calls and other communications. In order to operate, cellular base towers must therefore gather location and other identifying information from every cellular device within their areas of operation.

information (and possibly other information) routinely shared with authorized network base towers.[145]

Although there are several kinds of cell site simulators, StingRays, a model sold by Harris Corporation, have been the topic of much debate. It is believed that some local law enforcement officials have been using StingRays for years,[146] but the deployment and use of commercially sold cell site simulators have been strictly limited to law enforcement agencies that have signed nondisclosure agreements.

In the wake of revelations about the use of cell site simulators by law enforcement and others, the FCC was asked to determine whether the deployment and use of these devices infringe upon citizens' "reasonable expectation of privacy in their communications."[147] Then-Chairman Wheeler responded that, under Title III of the Communications Act, "the FCC has the statutory authority to address the threat posed by illicit IMSI catchers and to work closely with industry on mechanisms to secure our nation's wireless networks and to ensure the privacy of consumers' conversations."[148] The chairman also organized an internal FCC task force to examine the issue. At the time of publication, it is unclear whether current FCC Chairman Ajit Pai has retained the internal FCC task force or whether he intends to take any actions with regard to the use of unlawful IMSI catchers.

G *Section 705 and the Wiretap Act*

Additional sources of authority allowing the commission to protect the privacy of citizen communications from interception are provided by Section 705 of the Communications Act of 1934 and the Wiretap Act of 1968. Section 705, codified as 47 U.S.C. § 605, prohibits the unauthorized publication and interception of communications except as allowed under certain conditions articulated in the Wiretap Act.[149] Similarly, the Wiretap Act prohibits persons from "intentionally intercept[ing] ... any wire, oral, or electronic communication," but also articulates several exceptions to this general rule.[150] Originally, the Wiretap Act prohibited only interception of wire and oral communications, but in 1986, the Electronic Communications Privacy Act amended the 1968 Wiretap Act to add prohibitions on the interception of electronic communications, including electronic mail.[151]

145 *Id.* at 146. Depending upon the encryption protocol used by a target device, IMSI catchers can also collect the content of telephone calls, web pages visited, numbers dialed, and text messages.

146 For example, the ACLU has identified sixty-one agencies in twenty-three states and the District of Columbia in addition to more than a dozen federal agencies that commonly use these devices. Am. Civil Liberties Union, *Stingray Tracking Devices: Who's Got Them?* https://www.aclu.org/map/stingray-tracking-devices-whos-got-them.

147 Letter from Alan M. Grayson to Chairman Wheeler, 2014 WL 4197876, at *3 (Aug. 1, 2014); Letter From Bill Nelson to Chairman Wheeler, 2015 WL 1939748 (Apr. 13, 2015).

148 Grayson Letter at *1.

149 Carla Voigt, *Wi-Fi Security: Shaping Data Privacy Rules*, 66 Fed. Comm. L.J. 537, 545–46 (2014); *see also* Notice of Apparent Liability for Forfeiture, *Google Inc.*, 27 FCC Rcd 4012 (2012) (noting that Section 605 makes specific reference to chapter 119, Title 18, which is the Wiretap Act).

150 18 U.S.C. § 2511(1)(a) (2012). To review a list of exceptions to the general prohibition against communications interception, see 18 U.S.C. § 2511(2)(b)-(i). For instance, Section 2511(2)(b) allows employees and agents of the commission to intercept communications in the normal course of their employment. *Id.* § 2511(2)(b).

151 Carla Voigt, *Wi-Fi Security: Shaping Data Privacy Rules*, 66 Fed. Comm. L.J. 537, 545–46 (2014).

The commission reevaluated the scope of these privacy regulations to determine whether they apply to communications transmitted across broadband Internet connections. As previously mentioned, the commission issued a Notice of Proposed Rulemaking in April 2016. One issue on which it sought comment was whether Section 705 could be interpreted as barring the interception of broadband Internet communications.[152] Despite comment on the matter, the subsequent Broadband Privacy Reoprt and Order did not elaborate on whether or not Section 705 could indeed prohibit the interception of broadband Internet communications. And, given that Congress recently overruled the Report and Order, it is unclear how this issue will be treated in the future, or whether it will be broached at all.

H *Communications Assistance for Law Enforcement Act*

Congress enacted the Communications Assistance for Law Enforcement Act (CALEA) in 1994 in order to "preserve the ability of law enforcement officials to conduct electronic surveillance effectively and efficiently in the face of rapid advances in telecommunications technology."[153] CALEA outlines the extent and limit of law enforcement authority to intercept various electronic communications such as telephone communications, voice over Internet protocol communications (VoIP), and communications that take place across broadband Internet connections. CALEA requires that telecommunications carriers provide law enforcement officials with call-identifying information and generally facilitate their investigatory process.

In support of CALEA, Section 229 of the Communications Act grants the FCC authority to "prescribe such rules as are necessary to implement the requirements of the Communications Assistance for Law Enforcement Act."[154] For example, the FCC has interpreted CALEA as allowing law enforcement officials access to the location of "subject's cell site location at the beginning and termination of a call" because this location information falls under the act's definition of "call-identifying information," which, as previously noted, carriers are required to provide.[155] Opponents of these rules argue that allowing law enforcement access to this information infringes upon citizens' expectations of privacy. When the commission considered the privacy implications of CALEA, it noted that individual "tracking capabil[ities] … could undermine individual privacy … [but] a more generalized capability that will identify only the location of a cell site, and only at the beginning and end of a call … is adequate" for purposes of CALEA without unreasonably infringing upon privacy interests.[156] In *United States Telecom Association v. FCC*, the United States Court of Appeals for the District of Columbia Circuit upheld the commission's compromise position.[157]

152 Broadband Privacy NPRM at 2597.

153 Report & Order, *Communications Assistance for Law Enforcement Act*, 14 FCC Rcd 4151, 4152 (1999); *see generally* The Communications Assistance for Law Enforcement Act, Pub. L. No. 103–414, 108 Stat. 4279 (1994) (codified at 47 U.S.C. §§ 1001–1010).

154 47 U.S.C. § 229 (2012).

155 Report & Order and Further Notice of Proposed Rulemaking, *Revision of the Commission's Rules to Ensure Compatibility with Enhanced 911 Emergency Calling Systems*, 14 FCC Rcd 16794, 16815 (1999).

156 *Id.* at 16816.

157 227 F.3d 450, 463–64 (D.C. Cir 2000).

The commission has also issued interpretations of 47 U.S.C. §§ 229(a)–(d), which not only grant the commission authority to prescribe rules related to CALEA's implementation, but also articulate standards that telecommunications carriers must meet to remain in compliance with the CALEA. Section 229(b) requires that telecommunications carriers "establish appropriate policies and procedures for the supervision and control of its officers" and "maintain secure and accurate records of any interception or access with or without such authorization."[158] In 1999, several telecommunications companies sought relief from these provisions as they had been interpreted by the Department of Justice, arguing that they were overly burdensome.[159] In response, the Federal Bureau of Investigation argued that all common carriers must comply with Section 229(b) to ensure that they do not "compromise the security of surveillance activities."[160] Ultimately, the commission established a regulatory scheme that prescribed the minimum standards that carriers had to meet in order to be in compliance with Section 229(b), but otherwise allowed carriers to set their own policies in order to maintain systems security.

The FCC occupies a unique position at the nexus of law enforcement, industry, and the public that provides it with unique authority and opportunities to protect consumer privacy, secure communications networks, and regulate both the public and private uses of communications technologies. The commission has used this authority to promulgate rules designed to protect communications technologies and consumer privacy. Rule making is not the commission's only means of protecting communications, however. It also protects the public interests at stake in communications networks by pursuing enforcement actions. We discuss some contributions made by these enforcement actions in Section IV.

IV Protecting Consumer Privacy: The Enforcement Bureau

The Enforcement Bureau of the Federal Communications Commission is charged with enforcing the Communications Act as well as rules and regulations issued by the commission. As we discussed earlier, the bureau fulfills this mandate by issuing advisory notices, conducting investigations, and prosecuting violations.

The Enforcement Bureau's work represents a critical component of the FCC's overall efforts to advance the public interest in protecting citizen privacy. The bureau's work also ensures that the regulations that the commission promulgates are actually complied with by the industry. Further, the bureau's work complements rule making by interpreting and applying the rules to specific factual circumstances. Last, it is worth noting that enforcement actions, because they are adjudicatory in nature, also effectively constitute a body of common law, providing important guidance for Regulatees and the public. While this authority may be developed in the enforcement context, it is very important to note that the same commissioners who vote on rule makings also vote on the enforcement of those rules. This process ensures the rules are applied as the commission deems appropriate.

158 47 U.S.C. § 229 (2012).

159 Report & Order, *Communications Assistance for Law Enforcement Act*, 14 FCC Rcd 4151, 4157 (1999).

160 *Id.* at 4159.

The Enforcement Bureau has brought, settled, and prosecuted several significant actions in recent years as part of its efforts to protect consumer privacy. These actions deserve special attention because they demonstrate the important role of the enforcement process as a means of identifying opportunities to advance the privacy interests at stake in the deployment and use of contemporary technologies.

A *Protecting Consumer Privacy*

The Enforcement Bureau is in a unique position to protect the privacy and civil liberties of customers by policing the security of CPNI. Enforcement actions also provide unique opportunities for exposing and exploring the shifting balance among the various interests at stake in gathering, aggregating, storing, analyzing, and using CPNI and similar consumer data. In this regard, FCC enforcement actions under Section 222 offer important forums for elaborating rules through a common law process and for signaling needs when new legislative or regulatory interventions would be more appropriate.

Through its enforcement actions, the bureau has enforced requirements for companies to take reasonable precautions to protect customers' CPNI.[161] For example, the commission entered into a consent decree with AT&T in 2015 in response to breaches at several of the company's vendor-operated call centers located in Mexico, Colombia, and the Philippines.[162] The call centers' employees facilitated access to account-related CPNI and other sensitive personal information, including partial Social Security numbers, belonging to almost 280,000 customers. This information was then used by third parties on AT&T's Web site to obtain codes to unlock handsets. As part of this settlement, AT&T paid a civil penalty of $25 million and agreed to implement strict compliance protocols. This settlement is important as evidence of not only the commission's critical role in protecting consumers' private information, but also its transnational reach when FCC regulatees transmit proprietary information abroad. And, of course, the amount of the settlement served as notice to others that they must take seriously their responsibilities under Section 222.

In addition to bringing actions for failures to protect CPNI and customer proprietary information, the Enforcement Bureau has targeted companies' misuse of CPNI. For example, in January 2013 Verizon notified the Enforcement Bureau that it had failed to adhere to commission rules regarding the gathering and use of customer information, including "how many calls a customer makes, what services the customer subscribes to, the destination or numbers called, and the customer's location at the time of the call."[163] Since at least 2006, Verizon had apparently gathered CPNI from more than 2 million customers and had then used that information for marketing purposes without giving customers prior notice and an opportunity to opt out, as required by the commission's

161 47 U.S.C. § 222(a) imposes a general duty on common carriers to "protect the confidentiality of proprietary information of, and relating to … customers." *See* Report and Order and Further Notice of Proposed Rulemaking, *Implementation of the Telecommunications Act of 1996: Telecommunications Carriers' Use of Customer Proprietary Network Information and Other Customer Information*, 22 FCC Rcd 6927, 6945–46 (2007).

162 Order, *AT&T Services, Inc.*, 30 FCC Rcd 2808 (2015).

163 Adopting Order, *Verizon Compliance with the Commission's Rules and Regulations Governing Customer Proprietary Network Information*, 29 FCC Rcd 10303 (2014), https://www.fcc.gov/document/verizon-pay-74m-settle-privacy-investigation.

regulations.[164] The Enforcement Bureau conducted a thorough investigation of Verizon's conduct and internal policies. At the end of that investigation, the bureau entered into a consent decree with Verizon under which the company agreed to pay a fine of $7.4 million and to abide by the terms of a detailed compliance plan.

More recently, the Enforcement Bureau entered into a consent decree with Verizon Wireless for failing to disclose to its customers that the company inserted Unique Identifier Headers (UIDH) in its customers' http Internet traffic for the purpose of delivering targeted advertising. Further, for more than two years, consumers were not given the option to opt out. Unlike traditional tracking cookies that can be deleted by the user, UIDH was implemented at the network level and therefore could not be deleted by the user. Thus, the UIDH has sometimes been referred to as a "supercookie," potentially capable of tracking all of the consumers' Internet activities.[165] Verizon and its partners could then use this data to target advertisements to customers. To resolve the bureau's investigation, Verizon entered into a consent decree under which it paid a fine of $1.35 million and agreed to the terms of a compliance plan to ensure appropriate disclosure of the UIDH program to consumers and, most importantly, the requirement that Verizon obtain a customer's opt-in consent before sharing that customer's UIDH with a third party for the purpose of targeted advertising. For sharing the UIDH within Verizon, the company agreed to obtain either opt-in or opt-out approval from the consumer.

In addition to protecting CPNI, the Enforcement Bureau has used Section 222 to protect consumers' privacy interests in their propriety information, such as their Social Security number or other personally identifiable information. The commission's actions against TerraCom, Inc., and YourTel America, Inc., in 2014 were predicated largely on Section 222(a)'s duty of common carriers to protect the confidentiality of their customer's proprietary information.[166] Both companies specialized in marketing wireless telephone services to low-income customers. In the course of their businesses, the companies gathered names, addresses, Social Security numbers, drivers' license numbers, and other personal information from hundreds of thousands of low-income customers in Texas, Oklahoma, Puerto Rico, and the United States Virgin Islands. Both companies also stored that sensitive information on unprotected servers that could be accessed directly from the Internet without need of a password or other authentication.

Despite the serious privacy concerns implicated by leaving unprotected this kind of very personal information, the data was not, strictly speaking, CPNI. The commission brought action against both companies under Section 222(a) for their failures to secure their customers' proprietary information properly, with the commission proposing to fine the two companies $10 million, although the case ultimately settled for $3.5 million and a detailed compliance plan.

[164] 47 C.F.R. § 64.2007.

[165] Order, *Cellco Partnership, d/b/a Verizon Wireless*, 31 FCC Rcd 1843 (2016), https://www.fcc.gov/document/fcc-settles-verizon-supercookie-probe; 47 U.S.C. § 222(b) ("A telecommunications carrier that receives or obtains proprietary information from another carrier for purposes of providing any telecommunications service shall use such information only for such purpose, and shall not use such information for its own marketing efforts").

[166] Terracom and Yourtel to Pay $3.5 Million to Resolve Consumer Privacy & Lifeline Investigations, 2015 WL 4159271 (July 9, 2015); Notice of Apparent Liability for Forfeiture, *Terracom, Inc. and Youtel America, Inc.*, 29 FCC Rcd 13325 (2014).

B *Protecting Telephone Conversations*

In an effort to protect consumer privacy from threats of unwanted calls and texts, the commission has adopted rules pursuant to Section 227 of the Communications Act, allowing consumers to put their contact numbers on national and company-specific "Do Not Call Lists" and barring companies from calling numbers on those lists without express permission. The Enforcement Bureau has steadfastly enforced these rules, imposing substantial financial penalties in cases when regulated companies fail to honor consumers' privacy requests. Among these is the largest penalty that was issued against Sprint Communications in a 2014 consent decree.[167]

The bureau first investigated Sprint's violations of Do Not Call rules in 2009. That investigation ultimately revealed that Sprint had subjected consumers on Do Not Call lists to sales calls. Sprint admitted its mistakes, which were due largely to technology failures, and committed to resolve the problems. In 2012, Sprint disclosed that it had continued to call consumers on Do Not Call lists. These calls could be traced to both human and technical malfunctions. After that disclosure, Sprint ceased its sales call operations and submitted to a complete overhaul of its systems. It also agreed to pay a civil penalty of $7.5 million.

As discussed, the Telephone Consumer Protection Act prohibits unsolicited "robocalls" to consumers' cellular phones except in cases of emergency.[168] When passing the TCPA, Congress recognized that

> automated telephone calls that deliver an artificial or prerecorded voice message are more of a nuisance and a greater invasion of privacy than calls placed by "live" persons. These automated calls cannot interact with the customer except in preprogrammed ways, do not allow the caller to feel the frustration of the called party, fill an answering machine tape or voice recording service, and do not disconnect the line even after the customer hangs up the telephone.[169]

On the basis of that finding, Congress determined that "it is legitimate and consistent with the Constitution to impose greater restrictions on automated calls than on calls placed by 'live' persons."[170]

In keeping with this congressional mandate, the Enforcement Bureau issues regular advisory notices regarding robocalls.[171] It has also been active in pursuing TCPA violators.[172] For example, in 2012 the bureau issued a Letter of Inquiry to Dialing Services,

167 Order, *Spring Corporation f/k/a Sprint Nextel Corp.*, 29 FCC Rcd 4759 (2014).

168 *See* 47 U.S.C. § 227 (2012).

169 S. Rep. No. 102–178, 102d Cong., 1st Sess. (1991) at 2.

170 *Id.*

171 *See, e.g.*, FCC Enforcement Advisory, *Biennial Reminder for Political Campaigns about Robocall and Text Abuse*, No. 2016–3 (Mar. 14, 2016).

172 *See, e.g.*, Citation and Order, *Lyft, Inc.*, 30 FCC Rcd 9858 (2015) (citing violations of the TCPA and warning against future violations); Citation and Order, *First National Bank, Corp.*, 30 FCC Rcd 9851 (2015) (same); Forfeiture Order, *Travel Club Marketing, Inc. DBA Diamond Vacations DBA Great Vacations*, 30 FCC Rcd 8861 (2015) (issuing a Forfeiture Order in the amount of $2,960,000 for 185 unsolicited robocalls); Citation Order, *M.J. Ross Group, Inc., d/b/a Politicalrobocalls.com*, 30 FCC Rcd 4548 (2015) (citing a violations of the TCPA and issuing a warning against future violations); Citation and Order, *Ifonoclast, Inc. d/b/a Phonevite*, 30 FCC Rcd 4541(2015) (same); Citation and Order, *Call-Em-All, LLC*, 30 FCC Rcd 4532 (2015) (same); Citation Failure to Comply with an FCC Order, *Calling Post Communications, Inc.*, 30 FCC Rcd 1026 (2015) (fining Calling Post Communications for failing

LLC, which advertised its ability to reach hundreds of thousands of consumers by using robocalls.[173] The bureau's investigation revealed that Dialing Services made more than 4.7 million unsolicited, nonemergency robocalls to consumers' cellular phones during a three-month period. After providing a notice of violation and an opportunity for Dialing Services to correct its practices, the bureau again reviewed the company's call records and found a continuing pattern of violations.[174] Dialing Services attempted to avoid liability by arguing that it merely acted as a conduit for its customers, who were solely responsible for initiating the unlawful calls. The commission rejected that argument in a Notice of Apparent Liability and proposed a forfeiture penalty against Dialing Services in the amount of $2,944,000.

The Enforcement Bureau has been similarly aggressive in pursuing companies that send unsolicited telephone facsimiles. In ways similar to unsolicited robocalls, unsolicited fax transmissions invade customer privacy and impose unwanted costs. In order to protect consumers from these invasions, the bureau has investigated and fined a number of violators in recent years. For example, it issued a Forfeiture Order against Worldwide Industrial Enterprises in 2015 after the company ignored repeated warnings and continued to send unsolicited fax advertisements, resulting in an $87,500 fine.[175]

Pursuant to 47 C.F.R § 73.1206, broadcasters and their agents are prohibited from recording telephone conversations for subsequent broadcast without the express permission of the recorded parties.[176] Failures to abide by these rules "invad[e] consumers' rightful expectation[s] of privacy when they answer the telephone."[177] The Enforcement Bureau has also recently prosecuted violations of 47 C.F.R § 73.1206.[178] For example, the operator of KTVX in Salt Lake City, Utah, agreed to a pay a civil penalty of $35,000 for twice broadcasting a recorded conversation during news broadcasts.[179] WSKQ in New York, New York, paid a $16,000 fine when one of their broadcasters made a "prank" call to an unsuspecting woman, represented himself as a hospital employee, reported that her husband had been killed in a traffic accident, and then broadcast her cries of despair over the air.[180] In another action, Spanish Broadcasting System Holding paid $25,000 for two such prank call broadcasts.[181]

to respond to lawful request for information relating to alleged robocalling issued by the Enforcement Bureau); Forfeiture Order, *Message Communications, Inc.*, 30 FCC Rcd 1039 (2015) (fining Message Communications, Inc., $25,000 for "willful, repeated, and continuing violation of Section 503(b)(1) of the Communications Act").

173 Notice of Apparent Liability for Forfeiture, *Dialing Services, LLC*, 29 FCC Rcd 5537, 5539–40 (2014).

174 *Id.*

175 Forfeiture Order, *Worldwide Industrial Enterprises, Inc.*, 30 FCC Rcd 845 (2015).

176 Order, *Newport Television, LLC for Former Licensee of Station KTVX(DT), Salt Lake City, Utah*, 29 FCC Rcd 14293 (2014) ("The Commission prohibits television and radio broadcasters from invading consumers' rightful expectation of privacy when they answer the telephone. Specifically, the Commission's rules prohibit broadcast licensees from broadcasting telephone conversations with consumers without first informing the consumer that the conversation is being broadcast or recorded for later broadcast"), https://transition.fcc.gov/eb/Orders/2014/DA-14-1676A1.html.

177 *Id.*

178 *See, e.g.*, Forfeiture Order, *Nassau Broadcasting III, LLC, Debtor-In-Possession*, 27 FCC Rcd 5273 (2012), https://transition.fcc.gov/eb/Orders/2012/DA-12-778A1.html.

179 *Id.*

180 Forfeiture Order, *WSKQ Licensing, Inc.*, 27 FCC Rcd 10108 (2012), https://transition.fcc.gov/eb/Orders/2012/DA-12-1370A1.html.

181 Forfeiture Order, *Spanish Broadcasting System Holding, Inc.*, 27 FCC Rcd 10107 (2012), https://transition.fcc.gov/eb/Orders/2012/DA-12-1369A1.html.

Although decidedly low-tech, these kinds of broadcasts represent persistent threats to consumer privacy. Those concerns go beyond the incidents themselves. As the Supreme Court held in 1967, we all expect that our telephone conversations are private.[182] That expectation is not only reasonable, but critical to the broad adoption of technology and its role in society. These enforcement actions therefore represent important efforts by the commission to protect our communications infrastructure from privacy threats whether low-tech or high-.

C *Protecting Privacy in Cable Communications*

Just as the commission relies on Title II when investigating data breaches by common carriers, it relies on Section 631 as its source of authority when investigating breaches involving PII by cable television providers. As discussed earlier, Section 631 imposes several important privacy requirements on cable operators, such as requirements to notify subscribers of the PII they collect, to take necessary steps to protect that information, and to permit subscribers to learn what PII the cable operator has about them.

In 2015, the commission entered into a consent decree with Cox Communications, Inc. (Cox) after hackers used "a common social engineering ploy known as pretexting" to gain access to customers' private information.[183] In short, these intruders phoned Cox customer service representatives and asked those representatives to input their log-in information into what appeared to be a Cox Web site. Once these intruders had the log-in information, they had the same access that the Cox customer service representative would have had to Cox's customer records. Although Cox kept that information in a secure server, the company did not require multifactor authentication or other sufficiently robust safeguards that could have prevented these unauthorized persons from obtaining access to Cox's systems. Cox ultimately paid a relatively modest fine – $595,000 – and acceded to a compliance plan involving the implementation of stricter security measures.

The Enforcement Bureau's aggressive enforcement of rules governing the storage and protection of personal data marks what is sure to be a critical area of regulatory action going forward. Enforcement actions have played and likely will continue to play a particularly important role in elaborating and clarifying companies' obligations under the Communications Act and commission regulations.

D *Protecting RF Communications*

Section 333 of the Communications Act bars unlawful interference with broadcasts. Although this prohibition traditionally applies to radio broadcasts,[184] the commission has extended its protections to Wi-Fi and GPS broadcasts as well.[185] For example, in

[182] *Katz v. United States*, 389 U.S. 347 (1967).

[183] Order, *Cox Communications, Inc.*, 30 FCC Rcd 12302 (2015), https://apps.fcc.gov/edocs_public/attachmatch/DA-15-1241A1.pdf.

[184] FCC Enforcement Advisory, *Jammer Use Is Prohibited: Prohibition Applies to Use by the Public and State and Local Government Agencies, Including State and Local Law Enforcement Agencies*, No. 2014–05 (Dec. 8, 2014).

[185] FCC Enforcement Advisory, *Wi-Fi Blocking Is Prohibited: Persons or Businesses Causing Intentional Interference to Wi-Fi Hot Spots Are Subject to Enforcement Action*, No. 2015–01 (Jan. 27, 2015).

2015 the Enforcement Bureau identified a "disturbing trend in which hotels and other commercial establishments block wireless consumers from using their own personal Wi-Fi hot spots on the commercial establishment premises."[186] In order to ensure the security of Wi-Fi communications, the bureau issued an enforcement advisory representing that it would be "aggressively investigating and acting against such unlawful interference."[187]

As promised, the bureau has fined hotel chains and convention centers found liable for Wi-Fi blocking in violation of Section 333.[188] For instance, in 2014 the commission received a complaint from an individual staying at the Gaylord Opryland, alleging that the hotel was "jamming personal hotspots so that you could not use them in the convention space."[189] Marriott, which managed the Gaylord Opryland, admitted to blocking the signals and entered into a consent decree with the FCC wherein the commission fined the company $600,000. Section 333 also prohibits the operation of GPS jammers. The bureau has initiated numerous additional enforcement actions to penalize companies and citizens for engaging in jamming activities in violation of the act.[190]

E *Protecting Broadcast Privacy*

Section 705, codified at 47 U.S.C. § 605, prohibits the unauthorized publication and interception of communications except as allowed under certain conditions articulated in the Wiretap Act.[191] These rules obviously apply to traditional means of communication such as telephones, but the Enforcement Bureau has also explored whether this authority applies to the interception of Wi-Fi signals. The most famous example is the commission's investigation of Google in 2012.

While assembling images and location information for the Street View function of Google Maps, Google incidentally collected payload data from scores of private, unencrypted Wi-Fi networks.[192] This payload data often included private information, including the identities of operators and search activity. The Enforcement Bureau initiated an investigation of Google on suspicion that these interceptions violated the Wiretap Act and the Communications Act. Although the commission ultimately determined that there was no clear prior precedent at the time demonstrating that incidental collection of unencrypted Wi-Fi data was unlawful, the commission's interest and investigation served notice going forward that it takes seriously the privacy interests at stake in Wi-Fi broadcasts.

186 Fed. Comm. Comm'n: enforcement Bureau, https://apps.fcc.gov/edocs_public/attachmatch/DA-15-113A1.pdf.

187 *Id.*

188 *See* Christopher Elliot, *The FCC Is Cracking Down on Hotels' Wi-Fi Blocking*, Fortune (Nov. 4, 2015, 6:05 AM), http://fortune.com/2015/11/04/fcc-hotels-wifi-blocking.

189 Order, *Marriot International, Inc.*, 29 FCC Rcd 11760 (2014).

190 For a list of recent enforcement actions see Fed. Comm. Comm'n, *Cell Phone and GPS Jamming*, https://www.fcc.gov/general/cell-phone-and-gps-jamming.

191 Carla Voigt, *Wi-Fi Security: Shaping Data Privacy Rules*, 66 Fed. Comm. L.J. 537, 545–46 (2014); *see also* Notice of Apparent Liability for Forfeiture, *Google Inc.*, 27 FCC Rcd 4012 (2012) (noting that Section 605 makes specific reference to chapter 119, Title 18, which is the Wiretap Act).

192 Notice of Apparent Liability for Forfeiture, *In the Matter of Google, Inc.*, 27 FCC Rcd 4012 (2012), https://transition.fcc.gov/DA-12-592A1.pdf.

Conclusion

Although only a sampling of recent enforcement actions, the cases discussed here make clear the central role of the Enforcement Bureau in the commission's ongoing efforts to protect privacy and secure the backbone of our modern communications networks. By steadfastly enforcing the Communications Act and the commission's regulatory rules, enforcement actions deter violations and encourage compliance. The fact that the bureau regularly seeks and secures large civil penalties in its cases encourages regulated entities to be proactive in guaranteeing their compliance. Enforcement actions also allow the commission to be nimble and responsive in the face of new and emerging threats to consumer privacy. In some cases, this means applying existing privacy authorities to new circumstances. In others, it means signaling the need for new regulations or authorities. In either event, enforcement actions provide important forward momentum, guaranteeing that communications networks will continue to work in the public interest even as times, and technologies, change.

Index